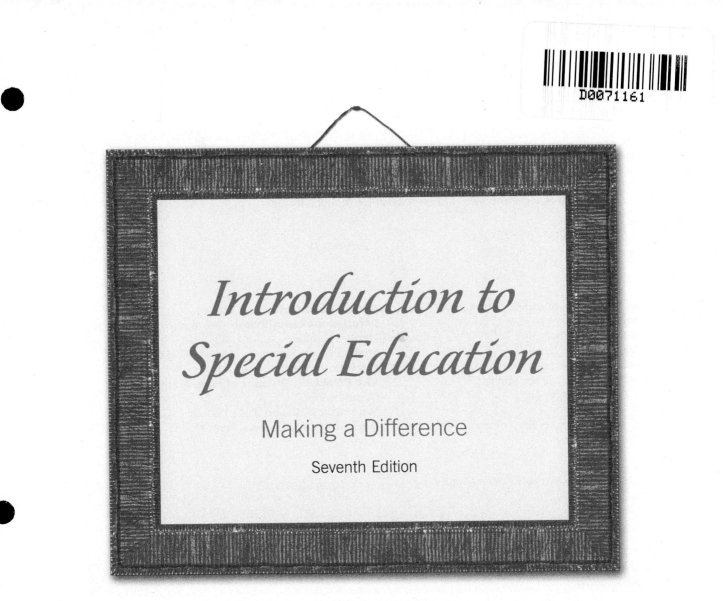

Introduction to Special Education

Making a Difference

Seventh Edition

Deborah Deutsch Smith
Claremont Graduate University

Naomi Chowdhuri Tyler
Peabody College, Vanderbilt University

Merrill
Upper Saddle River, New Jersey
Columbus, Ohio

Library of Congress Cataloging-in-Publication Data

Smith, Deborah Deutsch.
  Introduction to special education: making a difference/Deborah Deutsch Smith, Naomi Chowdhuri Tyler.
--7th ed.
  p. cm.
  Includes bibliographical references and index.
  ISBN-13: 978-0-205-60056-4
  ISBN-10: 0-205-60056-5
1. Special education--United States--Textbooks. I. Tyler, Naomi Chowdhuri. II. Title.
LC3981.S56 2010
371.90973--dc22

2008047441

Vice President and Editor in Chief: Jeffery W. Johnston
Executive Editor: Ann Castel Davis
Development Editor: Alicia Reilly
Editorial Assistant: Penny Burleson
Senior Managing Editor: Pamela D. Bennett
Production Editor: Sheryl Glicker Langner
Art Director: Candace Rowley
Cover Design: Kristi Holmes
Cover Image: Digital image courtesy of the Getty's Open Content Program

Photo Coordinator: Lori Whitley
Permissions Coordinator: Rebecca Savage
Media Producer: Autumn Benson
Media Project Manager: Rebecca Norsic
Operations Specialist: Laura Messerly
Vice President, Director of Sales & Marketing: Quinn Perkson
Marketing Manager: Erica DeLuca
Marketing Coordinator: Brian Mounts

This book was set in Garamond by Nesbitt Graphics, Inc. It was printed and bound by LSC Communications.

Photo Credits: photo credits are on pages xxvii and xxviii.

Pearson Education Ltd., London
Pearson Education Singapore Pte. Ltd.
Pearson Education Canada, Inc.
Pearson Education–Japan
Pearson Education Australia PTY, Limited

Pearson Education North Asia, Ltd., Hong Kong
Pearson Educación de Mexico, S.A. de C.V.
Pearson Education Malaysia Pte. Ltd.
Pearson Education Upper Saddle River, New Jersey

Merrill
is an imprint of

www.pearsonhighered.com

ISBN-13: 978-0-205-60056-4
ISBN-10:   0-205-60056-5

Dedication

To the individuals with disabilities and their family members who have touched our lives and remind us that social justice is not yet achieved,

each term's college students who help us better understand what delivering a responsible and responsive education truly means, and

our graduates who seek opportunities to make a difference in the lives of others.

Preface

There is no doubt that the lives of individuals with disabilities have improved over the last 50 years. Many years of social activism have had positive effects on the lives of these individuals and their families. Normalized participation for people with disabilities—a dream only a few decades ago—is today more of a part of American life than ever before. Changes are reflected in every aspect of society: in day-to-day life, in literature, in the media, and in the pop culture. They reflect improvements in societal attitudes toward individuals with differences and their participation in society. We believe that in many ways these changes are due to successes accomplished at schools where students with disabilities are taught the skills needed to assume their rightful places in the community, and where students without disabilities learn to recognize that their participation is just, "normal," and what should be expected in day-to-day life.

This edition reflects our vision of what all schools should provide to students with special needs: schooling and services that are truly responsive to the needs of each individual. Opportunities to make a difference abound, and such possibilities occur everywhere—at schools, in the community, and through advocacy. Even the smallest action can make a difference, whether it is being certain that a child can see the board, hear the teacher, can join schoolmates on a fieldtrip, or has instruction individualized. We believe that it is everyone's responsibility to be knowledgeable about proven and effective practices, socially responsible, and also sensitive to unique situations. We are confident that when all falls into place, each of us will seize opportunities and make a difference in the lives of individuals with special needs and their families.

Our goals are for individuals with disabilities and for gifted and talented individuals to achieve to their potential because schools met their unique learning needs. Our best wishes to you for a productive and engaging semester, where notions about social justice, responsive educational system, and individualized special services become more than just ideas about "what can be." They become a description of "what *is*."

Text Organization and Special Emphases

A consistent and standard outline for each categorical chapter was followed so broad and important concepts are consistently addressed and easily located. We want to call your attention to some concepts that are given new and special attention in this revision. They include:

- The *Assessment* sections of each chapters 3–14 highlight *early identification, prereferral, identification,* and academic *evaluation* with particular emphasis on current procedures for high stakes testing, alternate assessments, and progress monitoring.

- Multitiered instruction that addresses the needs of all struggling learners, including those with disabilities, receives considerable attention. In particular, Chapter 5 reflects current innovations being made in the field of learning disabilities and includes up-to-date information about *early intervening, response to intervention (RTI) services,* and new ways to identify students with learning disabilities.

- Throughout the text, increased attention is given to data-based practices, particularly those proven effective across years of implementation and solid research. Easy to follow tips and steps to follow are given about how to use already proven strategies and interventions. Discussions are also provided about being excellent consumers of research findings, so as new knowledge is generated educators can determine how and when these practices should be incorporated into students' instructional programs.

- In recognition of the importance of collaboration among members of multidisciplinary teams delivering individualized programs through related and specialized education services, the *Collaboration* sections are totally revamped. Each one features a specific educational professional or related service provider, along with a description of a collaborative practice that is particularly relevant to the category discussed in the chapter.

Through our work developing The IRIS Center for Training Enhancements, we have learned a lot about schools, students with disabilities, and adult learners. Those lessons have informed this edition. The resources created for distribution through the center's Web site (see http://iris.peabody.vanderbilt.edu) are used in professional development activities and in colleges and universities across the nation. Their intent is to better prepare the next generation of educators to work in inclusive educational settings, upgrade the skills of current practicing professionals, and in turn improve the results of students with disabilities. When educators use proven and best practices, the end-result will be an accountable and responsive education system where every student succeeds. Thus you'll find many references to IRIS materials woven into the content of this text, most often providing opportunities to extend and apply the concepts and strategies discussed.

myeducationlab Go to the Building Teaching Skills and Dispositions section in Chapter 2 of MyEducationLab and complete the activities in the IRIS Module "Accessing the General Educational Curriculum: Inclusion Considerations for Students with Disabilities." This module highlights classroom considerations that promote access to the general educational curriculum for students with disabilities.

MyEducationLab

Throughout the chapters we include margin notes that help link content with a practical focus—MyEducationLab. This new online learning tool offers Self-Assessment to test mastery of chapter objectives; Review, Remediation and Enrichment Exercises to deepen understanding. Activities and Application exercises to foster comprehension of chapter concepts, and Building Teaching Skills activities to provide interactive practice applying the core principles and concepts of special education. MyEducationLab provides readers with convenient entry to IRIS modules related to specific content. The IRIS modules and case studies provide a wealth of information about data-based, effective practices; much of which we also present in this text. When topics discussed in the text are also presented through interactive technology in IRIS modules or in IRIS problem-based case studies, we include a MyEducationLab link to those IRIS resources.

Lessons from the Past . . .
Optimism About
the Future . . .
A Spirit of Advocacy

The presence of people with disabilities is becoming an expectation of normal daily life, yet these achievements offer only a glimmer of what's on the horizon. So that particularly deplorable situations of the past will never repeated in the future, in each chapter we take the opportunity to include a brief history focusing on how individuals with special needs were treated across time.

- *Where We've Been . . . What's on the Horizon?* This section provides historical context and perspective to better understand how far we have come and hints at what the future could hold for people with disabilities.

- *Imagine a World*—an advance organizer for the heart—provides at the beginning of each chapter a photo and inspiring words for readers to take with them into the content of each chapter.

- *Making a Difference* sections appear near the beginning of each chapter, each profiling individuals and organizations that exemplify social responsibility and advocacy that inspire us all. Examples include:

  - Southern Poverty Law Center

  - Operation Smile

  - Best Buddies

  - Hole in the Wall Camps

  - Bookshare.org

  - Autism Speaks

  - 100 Black Men of America, Inc.

Making a Difference

Best Buddies

Across America, the dream of families and of their sons, daughters, brothers, and sisters with intellectual disabilities is to be a part of everyday communities. Unfortunately, successful integration in schools, workplaces, and mainstream society remains elusive for many. Sufficient opportunities for socialization and job coaching are not available for people with intellectual disabilities to become independent and to be fully included in their communities. The necessary supports are not yet in place for an inclusive America to be a reality.

Probably because of his family's long history of advocacy and volunteerism on behalf of people with intellectual disabilities, Anthony Shriver (shown at

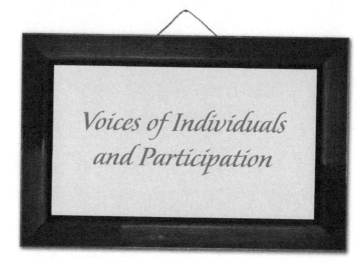

Voices of Individuals and Participation

Although there is considerable room for improvement, the broader culture has become more and more accustomed to the community presence and participation of individuals with disabilities. Television, film, advertising, and literature reflect changes that people with disabilities experience and expect today. We bring you the voices of people with disabilities, their family members, and those who have devoted their careers to them through the following special features.

- *Chapter Opening Art*: Artistic masterpieces created by well-known and established artists (such as Van Gogh, Toulouse-Lautrec) who have first-hand experience with the special need discussed in the chapter. Their creations enable us to see the world from the perspective of artists with special needs and show us how it is important to never make assumptions about people and their talents and skills.

- *Spotlighting . . . A Day in the Life:* This new feature presents stories told by people with disabilities, by their family members, and their teachers. They talk about the challenges they have faced, the solutions they have discovered, people who have made a difference in their lives, and their hopes and dreams for the future.

Spotlighting *Lizzy:* A Day in the Life

Sarah Elizabeth Solomon, or Lizzy, is a high school student with spastic quadriplegic cerebral palsy. Her mother expands on Lizzy's story in Chapter 14's Spotlighting feature.

Hi! My name is Sara Elizabeth Solomon, but everyone calls me Lizzy. I am in the tenth grade at Hillsboro High School in Nashville, Tennessee. I am not really sure there is a typical day in my life. They are all busy and full of school, work, and, of course, play.

I have spastic quadriplegic cerebral palsy, which makes doing some of the routine things in life a little more difficult. Having cerebral palsy makes it hard to move my muscles; therefore, it takes me twice as long or sometimes even longer to do the things I need to do (e.g., dressing, doing homework). In the morning, I start my day with getting dressed. Recently, my mom went out of town and left my 17-year-old sister Skye in charge. I was worried that my sister would oversleep and we would not have enough time to get dressed and ready for school. So I got up at 2 o'clock in the morning and was completely dressed by 7 when we had to leave. That morning I used my dressing stick and my reacher as aids to get myself dressed. My dressing stick helps me with getting my shoes and socks on and off. My reacher helps me pick up things when I drop them or get them when they are out of my arm's reach.
My [persist]ence and [deter]mination k[ept me go]ing! Even tho[ugh it took me] 5 hou[rs to dress], [I was proud] of my[self].

nity. He carries things for me if we go shopping. Not only is he a big help, but he is a constant friend and companion.

Because of my physical needs and the demands of my schedule, I have an assistant at school, Mrs. Worthy. Mrs. Worthy helps me with things like toileting and getting to and from class. I take mostly honors classes and some AP classes, so I have a very busy schedule and LOTS of homework. I leave my classes a few minutes early so I have time to get from class to class without getting run over by the other students. Really, they are probably more worried that I will run over them, as I'm a pretty fast walker!

After I get home from school, I usually spend 3 to 4 hours on homework. It probably takes me twice as long on homework because of my motor skills. Once I am done with homework, I take a bath or a shower. If it is a night when I don't have too much homework, I spend more time trying to get undressed and shower. I can almost shower independently, but it does take me a while. Otherwise, my mom helps me take a bath and get ready for bed.

Aside from my schoolwork, I am busy with other extracurricular activities, both in and out of school. My favorite thing to do is to go to my Young Life Christian group. We do lots of fun things together like swimming, playing games, having dances, and making photo albums. I am active in Girl Scouts and am a member of the school's marching band. Several days a week I practice my piano, and I have a piano lesson every [week to]day. Much [of my] time is spent on the bus[. I have log]ged 4 [hours on the bu]s [each day... Blue Li]nes

- *On the Screen:* Expanded to almost every chapter because of popular demand, this feature highlights popular films in which characters with a disability have major roles. In some cases the character portrayal is appropriate, but in other cases the portrayal is insensitive or even cruel. We hope the content presented here draws attention to the impact the media has on reinforcing or reducing stereotypes. We believe it is particularly significant that individuals with disabilities now more often appear as "regular characters" in films and television shows, wherein a charac-

On the Screen: *If the Shoe Fits*

Carmen Diaz, nominated for a Golden Globe award in 2005, brings to life the challenges and frustrations faced by many individuals who have reading/learning disabilities. In the charming film *In Her Shoes*, we experience complex family relationships, the stigma of disabilities, sibling rivalry and jealousy, and feelings of triumph when challenges presented by reading problems are overcome. Maggie, through manipulation and deceit, has hidden the fact that she cannot read from almost everyone she meets. She uses her beauty and wit to get whatever she wants—that is, until she gets tripped up by a patient at the hospital where she works. The patient is a blind man who wants Maggie to read to him every day, a task she cannot do. When he realizes she has learning disabilities, he confronts her, forces her to face her challenges, and during months of painstaking efforts teaches her to read. From that point on, we watch Maggie develop feelings of self-reliance and self-worth, and we come to understand how family relationships change and grow when challenges presented by disabilities are not kept as secrets, but rather shared and met by all.

—By Steven Smith

ter's disability is not a focus of the story and their inclusion in the plot is not portrayed as remarkable or out of the ordinary.

- *Considering Culture:* The increasing diversity of America's school children presents both challenges and opportunities to those responsible for their education. "Minority" students represent a majority in more and more school districts across the nation, and the number of students who are not native speakers of English increases annually. This feature provides mini-cases to help educators gain insight into special considerations that arise in the instruction of these culturally diverse students.

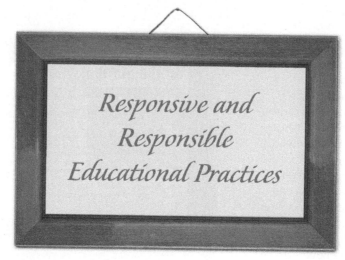

Responsive and Responsible Educational Practices

We describe effective practices in some detail, in part so you will know what to look for when you visit or work in schools and what to seek out when being responsive to the individual needs of each student. Emphasis is placed on methods and instructional procedures, along with examples of how these are implemented though practical classroom applications.

A Closer Look at Data-Based Practices:

Peer-Assisted Learning Strategies (PALS)

What Is PALS?

Peer-Assisted Learning Strategies (PALS) uses classmates as tutors who exchange the roles of coaches and players. PALS is used across a wide range of grade levels—from kindergarten through high school—to teach students many different skills. For example, kindergarteners have helped each other learn the core or foundations skills of reading (e.g., sound–symbol relationships, sight words). English language learners (ELLs) with learning disabilities have improved their reading comprehension, and middle school students have improved their number skills to chart and graph data.

Why PALS Is Beneficial

The PALS instructional approach multiplies the opportunities for individualized instruction and the implementation of validated instructional tactics across entire classes of students. Using classmates as teachers frees the teacher to provide more intensive supports to students who need them the most. The procedures also actively involve students in learning. When students are trained in how to tutor and taught the instructional tactic they are applying, peer tutoring has proven to be consistently effective, causing great gains in learning. Also, students report that they enjoy tutoring each other, adding a motivating element to the classroom routine.

Implementing PALS

PALS is designed to supplement, not replace, standard instructional routines or elements of the standards-based curriculum. Before classmates work together, the teacher instructs the class about the application of the tactic, the roles of each pair, when to take turns, and how to provide corrective feedback. The teacher practices the instructional routines with the entire class until they demonstrate understanding of their roles and responsibilities. Student pairs work together on a specific academic task (e.g., letter–sound recognition in reading, sight-word vocabulary, math facts, story comprehension) for 4 weeks and then switch partners. Here's a general example of how PALS is applied:

Frequency

- PALS is usually scheduled three or four times per week.
- Sessions last 20 to 35 minutes.
- Each session is divided into 10-minute segments so each peer has a turn as coach and player.

- Sessions may be divided in half so more than one skill can be the target of instruction.
- Sessions continue for a semester or half of the school year.

Partners

- Rank-order students in a class from the strongest to the weakest on the targeted skill.
- Divide the class in half.
- Pair the top-ranked student from the high-performing group with the top-ranked student in the low-performing group.
- Continue the process until every student has a partner.
- Each member of the pair, during every session, takes a turn at being the "coach" or tutor and the "player" (the student being tutored).
- Student pairs work together for about a month and then are assigned new partners.

Roles

- The coach asks the player to do the task (e.g., read a passage, compute subtraction problems).
- The player performs the task (e.g., reads out loud, solves the problems).
- The coach listens or watches and provides corrective feedback.
- Pairs change roles every 10 minutes.

  A sample worksheet used by a pair of kindergarteners learning sight words is shown in this box. Special worksheets or materials do not have to be prepared to implement peer tutoring. Texts and workbooks used for standard instruction can be utilized for PALS lessons.

"What Word?" Activity

and	on	was	is	What word?
the	and	is	was	😊😊😊😊

myeducationlab Go to the Building Teaching Skills and Dispositions section in Chapter 3 of MyEducationLab and complete the activities in the IRIS MODULES; several activities allow you to become familiar with the use of PALS strategies for students at various grade levels.

- *A Close-up on Data-Based Practices:* The most recent passages of IDEA and NCLB stress the importance of educators implementing instructional methods and classroom practices that have been "proven" through rigorous research. Reflecting this expectation of teachers and schools, the feature re-conceptualized for this edition, provides step-by-step guidelines for implementation of teaching practices that are validated, individually determined, explicit, strategic, sequential, and accountable. Some of the strategies detailed include:
  - Peer Assisted Learning Strategies
  - Collaborative Strategic Reading (CSR)
  - Curriculum-Based Measurement (CBM)
  - Functional Assessment-Based Measures
  - Self-determination
  - Picture Exchange Communication System (PECS)

- *Accommodations for Inclusive Environments*: These features provide ideas for adjusting the instruction, the curriculum, or learning environment with the goal of enhancing the students' success. Particular emphasis is placed on steps needed for effective inclusion of students with disabilities as they access the general education curriculum.

- *Tips for Classroom Management* and *Tips for Effective Teaching*. These short features list simple, practical procedures to apply in specific teaching and management situations.

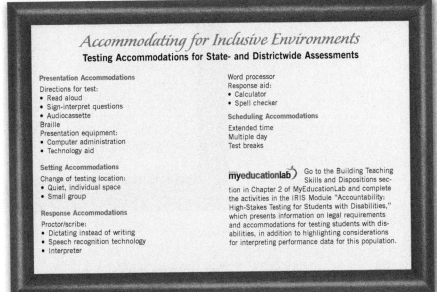

Accommodating for Inclusive Environments

Testing Accommodations for State- and Districtwide Assessments

Presentation Accommodations

Directions for test:
- Read aloud
- Sign-interpret questions
- Audiocassette

Braille

Presentation equipment:
- Computer administration
- Technology aid

Setting Accommodations

Change of testing location:
- Quiet, individual space
- Small group

Response Accommodations

Proctor/scribe:
- Dictating instead of writing
- Speech recognition technology
- Interpreter

Word processor

Response aid:
- Calculator
- Spell checker

Scheduling Accommodations

Extended time

Multiple day

Test breaks

myeducationlab Go to the Building Teaching Skills and Dispositions section in Chapter 2 of MyEducationLab and complete the activities in the IRIS Module "Accountability: High-Stakes Testing for Students with Disabilities," which presents information on legal requirements and accommodations for testing students with disabilities, in addition to highlighting considerations for interpreting performance data for this population.

- *Addressing Professional Standards:* Each chapter concludes with a list of the *CEC Common Core Knowledge and Skill Standards for all Entry Level Special Education Teachers* relevant to the content covered in the chapters. In addition, two appendices provide valuable resources for important standards information: *Appendix A* provides a listing of the *CEC Common Core Knowledge and Skill Standards for all Entry Level Special Education Teachers of Students in Individualized General Education Curriculums.* Appendix B provides a list of the *CEC Common Core Knowledge and Skill Standards for all Entry Level Special Education Teachers of Students in Associated Subcategories*

Supplements

The seventh edition of *Introduction to Special Education, Making a Difference* is accompanied by the a comprehensive and integrated collection of supplements designed to assist students and professors alike to maximize learning and instruction. The text is central to the course, and its supplements were created to support the text with an outstanding array of learning activities for the entire term.

myeducationlab

Teacher educators who are developing pedagogies for the analysis of teaching and learning contend that analyzing teaching artifacts has three advantages: it enables new teachers time for reflection while still using the real materials of practice; it provides new teachers with experience thinking about and approaching the complexity of the classroom; and in some cases, it can help new teachers and teacher educators develop a shared understanding and common language about teaching. . . . [1]

As Linda Darling-Hammond and her colleagues point out, grounding teacher education in real classrooms—among real teachers and students and among actual examples of students' and teachers' work—is an important, and perhaps even an essential, part of training teachers for the complexities of teaching today's students in today's classrooms. We have created a website that provides you and your students with the context of real classrooms and artifacts that research on teacher education tells us is so important. Through authentic in-class video footage, interactive skill-building exercises and more, MyEducationLab offers you and your students a uniquely valuable teacher education tool.

MyEducationLab is easy to use! Look for the MyEducationLab logo and directive at the beginning and end of each chapter, in the margins, and at the end of several of the boxed features. Follow the directive and the simple navigation instructions to access the multimedia ***Individualized Study Plan, Activities and Application*** exercises, and ***Building Teaching Skills and Dispositions*** assignments in MyEducationLab that correspond with the chapter content.

- **Individualized Study Plan:** Students have the opportunity to take self-assessment quizzes after reading each chapter of the text. Each self-assessment question is tied to a chapter objective, so the students are assessed on their knowledge and comprehension of all of the concepts presented in each chapter. The quiz results automatically generate a personalized study plan for each student, identifying areas of the chapter that still need some

[1] Darling-Hammond, l., & Bransford, J., Eds. (2005). *Preparing Teachers for a Changing World*. San Francisco: John Wiley & Sons

additional study time. In this study plan, students are presented with Review and Enrichments exercises to help ensure learning and to deepen understanding of chapter concepts—when just re-reading and studying chapter content is not enough. The study plan is designed to help each student perform well on exams and to promote deep understanding of chapter content.

- **Activities and Applications:** These exercises offer opportunities to understand content more deeply and are explicitly connected to chapter content. These exercises present thought-provoking questions that probe the students' understanding of the concept or strategy that is presented in the text through classroom video footage, simulations or teacher and student artifacts.
- **Building Teaching Skills and Dispositions:** These application assignments help students practice and strengthen skills that are essential to quality teaching. Students watch authentic classroom video footage or interact with thought-provoking interactive learning modules and critically analyze how they can learn these skills and strategies and then hopefully incorporate them into their teaching repertoire or portfolio.

The rich, authentic, and interactive elements that support the Individualized Study Plan, the Activities and Applications and the Building Teaching Skills you will encounter throughout MyEducationLab include:

- **Video:** The authentic classroom videos in MyEducationLab show how real teachers handle actual classroom situations. Viewing videos and discussing and analyzing them not only deepens understanding of concepts presented in the book, but also builds skills in observing and analyzing children and classrooms.
- **Learning Modules:** Created by the IRIS Center at Vanderbilt University, these interactive modules give you hands-on practice at adapting instruction for a full spectrum of learners.
- **Student & Teacher Artifacts:** Authentic preK–12 student and teacher classroom artifacts are tied to course topics and offer you practice in working with the different materials you will encounter daily as teachers.
- **Case Studies:** A diverse set of robust cases illustrate the realities of teaching and offer valuable perspectives on common issues and challenges in education.
- **Lesson & Portfolio Builders:** With this effective and easy-to-use tool, you can create, update, and share standards-based lesson plans and portfolios.

Visit www.myeducationlab.com for a demonstration of this exciting new online teaching resource.

For the Professor

All of the instructor supplements are available at the Instructor Resource Center. To access the manual, the PowerPoint lecture presentation, and the test bank and TestGen software (see below) go to the Instructor Resource Center at www.pearsonhighered .com and click on the "Educators" link. Here you will be able to login or complete a one-time registration for a user name and password.

Online Instructor's Manual with Test Items

The Instructor's Manual helps to synthesize all of the resources available for each chapter, but also helps to sift through the materials to match the delivery method (e.g., semester, quarter) and areas of emphasis for the course. These materials can be used for traditional courses as well as online or online supported courses. The Instructor's Manual is fully integrated with the MyEducaitonLab that accompanies this text.

Online Test Bank and TestGen Software

That is why we have developed a bank of over 50 test questions per chapter in a variety of formats (including multiple choice, short answer, and essay) that match the issues, questions, and activities that we set out in each chapter. The Test Bank is available online at the Instructor Resource Center for ease of use. Questions have been updated and cross-referenced to match the content of this new edition.

Online PowerPoint Slides

These visual aids display, summarize, and help explain core information presented in each chapter. They can be downloaded from our Instructor's Resource Center. All PowerPoint slides have been updated for consistency and to reflect current content in this new edition.

Acknowledgments

We want to take this opportunity to thank some very important people who made this edition a special one to us. First to our families, who once again saw the midnight lights burning or were awakened by the early morning sounds of the printer churning pieces of paper through its rollers. To Jim and Ken, thank you for your patience and support, helping with all those little things you shouldn't have to do. We want to acknowledge our children. Steve, thank you for being so thoughtful, caring, and perceptive; you are a role model to so many. Kyra and Kailyn, thank you for your patience and understanding that life would return to normal and time for some special attention was not just a promise. And to our parents, the Meyers and Chowdhuris be proud, it's the best book we know how to do.

We also want to thank the staff of IRIS-Central and IRIS-West who covered for us here and there, made sure all was running smoothly at the office, and understood our collective and independent distractibility and crankyness. The IRIS-Central team at Peabody College of Vanderbilt University make it possible for both of us to keep so many plates spinning in the air: Janice Brown, Janet Church, Pam Dismuke, Erik Dunton, John Harwood, Jason Miller, Kim Skow, Amy Harris-Solomon, and Zina Yzquierdo. The IRIS-West team at Claremont Graduate University also made this revision possible in so many ways. In particular, we want to thank Sue Robb, Roxanne Watson, Chris Castaneda, Mary Brennan, Jackie Lewis, and Heather Halk.

We also want to extend our very special thanks to two treasured colleagues. Kathleen Lane of Peabody College of Vanderbilt University revised the chapter about students with emotional or behavioral disorders, doing an outstanding job of explaining current knowledge about data-based practices that make a difference in the results of these students. Matt Tincani of Temple University revised the chapter about Autism Spectrum Disorders, bringing the absolutely latest knowledge about the baffling disability to this edition.

We wish to thank our friends, colleagues, and folks we've never met who shared their stories in the on-going feature, *Spotlighting: A Day in the Life*. These vignettes bring to you the very special nature of some everyday folks who make a different in all of our lives: Kelly Barnhart, Ann Bielert, Sara Ezell, Christopher Hartman, Paul K. Longmore, Norma Lopez-Reyna, Karisa Lopez-Reyna, Michael Naranjo, Christy Neria, Geri A. Nicholas, Alaine OCampo, Belinda Pandey, Amy Harris Solomon, Sara Elizabeth Solomon, and Susan Storey. We thank and acknowledge Steve Smith, who found the films that feature special needs characters and who wrote the *On the Screen* features found in this edition. We also thank Ellie Lynch and Marci Hansen who wrote many of the *Considering Culture* cases.

We are also very grateful to the reviewers whose thoughtful and intelligent comments on the sixth edition informed what we hope are our thoughtful and intelligent updates in this edition: Alfredo Artiles (Arizona State University); Richard

Baum (Buffalo State College); Linda Duncan (Anderson University); Phyllis Genareo (Grove City College); Karen Hager (Boise State University); Thomas P. Hebert (University of Georgia); Florence Shaunee Higgins (Champlain College); Jack Hourcade (Boise State University); Brenda Naimy (California State University – Los Angeles); Zandile Nkabinde (New Jersey City University); Julie Norflus-Good (Felician College); Layne Pethick (Our Lady of the Lake University); Kay Reeves (University of Memphis); Jacques Singleton (University of Memphis); Rick Van Sant (Ferris State University); Glenda Windfield (Jackson State University)

Our gratitude is extended to Virginia Lanigan who was the editor for the previous three editions of this text, saw the beginning of this revision, and who represented Pearson Publishing in its partnership with The IRIS Center. She is a friend, editor, and colleague. This edition would not have seen the ink of the printer if it had not been for Ann Davis, who inherited us and adopted us like no other doting parent would, and her team at Merrill, Sheryl Langner, Lori Whitley, and Penny Burleson, as we all learned that there is no one way to get a book through production as we showed them our ignorance about the "way it should be done." We thank them for helping us work through all those unpredicted glitches. And, certainly not least, we could not have done this revision without the continual help and support of our development editor, Alicia Reilly, who lives east, but became a midwesterner for us who are from the south and the west!

D. D. S. & N. C. T
12/08

Brief Contents

Contents

Note: Every effort has been made to provide accurate and current Internet information in this book. However, the Internet and information posted on it are constantly changing and it is inevitable that some of the Internet addressed listed in this textbook will change.

Selected Features

Tips for Classroom Management

Tips for Effective Instruction

What IDEA '04 Says About . . .

What NCLB Says About . . .

Photo Credits

Chapter 1

ZUMA Press, Inc./Alamy, p. 2; Digital image courtesy of the Getty's Open Content Program, p. 3 (top); Jupiterimages/Thinkstock, p. 3 (bottom); Photos 12/Alamy, p. 9 (top); AF Archive/Alamy, p. 9 (bottom); Merrill Education, p. 10; Comstock/Getty Images, p. 15; Q/Fotolia, p. 17; Merrill, p. 18; Moviestore Collection Ltd/Alamy, p. 22; Tyler Hicks/Redux Pictures, p. 24; David Mager/Pearson Learning Photo Studio, p. 26.

Chapter 2

iofoto/Fotolia, p. 32; Digital image courtesy of the Getty's Open Content Program, p. 33 (top); Pictorial Press Ltd/ Alamy, p. 33 (bottom); David Grossman/Alamy, p. 36; Anthony Magnacca/Merrill Educationl, p. 40; MERRILL, p. 46; Lori Whitley/Merrill Education, p. 52; Dan Race/ Fotolia, p. 57; JupiterImages/Thinkstock, p. 59; Tyler Hicks/Redux Pictures, p. 69

Chapter 3

Zurijeta/Shutterstock, p. 72; Peter Horree/Alamy, p. 73; MERRILL, pp. 76, 77, 112; AF Archive/Alamy, p. 82; David Grossman/Alamy, p. 83; MBI/Alamy, p. 86; sparkmom/ Fotolia, p. 91; Blend Images/Alamy, p. 92; Hope Madden/ Merrill Educationl, p. 94; Lisa F. Young/Fotolia, p. 97; Carlos Santa Maria/Fotolia, p. 101; Kimberly Cossairt/ Fotolia, p. 102 (left); Arch White/Alamy, p. 102 (right); Corbis, p. 109; Stockbyte/Getty Images, p. 111.

Chapter 4

Joggie Botman/Fotolia, p. 114; MERRILL, p. 115 (top); Deborah Smith, p. 115 (bottom); librakv/Fotolia, p. 117; Pictorial Press Ltd/Alamy, p. 118; MERRILL, p. 119; Marc Asher / Operation Smile/Deborah Smith, p. 119 (in box); Shmel/Fotolia, p. 120; sonya etchison/Fotolia, p. 127; (clockwise from top left) crestajohnson/Fotolia, Margot Petrowski/Fotolia, auremar/Fotolia, SUDIO 1ONE/Fotolia, robhainer/Fotolia, maska82/Fotolia, Wavebreakmedia-Micro/Fotolia, juiceteam2013/Fotolia, marchibas/Fotolia, nami66/Fotolia, sakkmesterke/Shutterstock, Kadmy/ Fotolia, p. 133; Image Source, p. 134 (Figure 4.5); Getty Images, p. 137; matka_Wariatka/Fotolia, p. 141; courtesy of the Saltillo Corporati/MERRILL, p. 147; MERRILL, p. 150; BSIP SA/Alamy, p. 151; Julian Rovagnati/Fotolia, p. 152.

Chapter 5

atikinka/Shutterstock, p. 154; MERRILL, pp. 155 (top and-bottom), 164, 188; SparkTop name, logo, and content: TM & (c) Professor Garfield Foundation All Rights Reserved/ MERRILL, p. 158 (top); Jim Sully/Deborah Smith, p. 158 (bottom); AF Archive/Alamy, p. 161; Anthony Magnacca/ Merrill Education, pp. 169, 185; Katelyn Metzger/Merrill Education, p. 174; ZUMA Press, Inc./Alamy, p. 177; RichardBakerFarnborough/Alamy, p. 186.

Chapter 6

mr.markin/Fotolia, p. 194; MERRILL, p. 195 (top and center) ;www.theknittingmachine.com/MERRILL, p. 195 (bottom); Marmaduke St. John/Alamy, p. 199 (top of page); MERRILL, p. 199 (top of box); Courtesy of Deborah Smith, p. 199 (bottom of box); Tetra Images/Getty Images., p. 202; PCN Photography/Alamy, p. 206; SW Productions/ Getty Images., p. 212; Getty Images, p. 218; Blend Images/Alamy., p. 221.

Chapter 7

Denis Tabler/Fotolia, p. 224; National Portrait Gallery, Smithsonian Institution/Art Resource NY (top); Library of Congress Prints and Photographs Division[LC-USZ62-124138], p. 225 (bottom); MERRILL, pp. 228, 257; Moviestore collection Ltd/Alamy, p. 229; www .chicagoy-outhcenters.org, p. 230; Getty Images, p. 237; Monkey Business Images/Shutterstock, p. 243; Merrill Education, p. 247; Lisa F. Young/Fotolia, p. 259.

Chapter 8

Peter Casolino/Alamy, p. 262; Gottfried Mindt/Getty Images, p. 263; Moviestore Collection Ltd/Alamy, p. 265; Deborah Smith, p. 267 (top of page); Everett Collection Inc/Alamy, p. 267 (in box at bottom of page); Deborah Smith, p. 268 (top); INTERFOTO/Alamy, p. 268 (bottom); MERRILL, 273; ZUMA Press, Inc./Alamy, p. 280 (right); Deborah Smith, p. 280 (left); Provided by Downi Creations, p. 283; karelnoppe/Fotolia, p. 288.

Chapter 9

yanlev/Fotolia, p. 296; "Christina's World", 1948. Tempera ©Andrew Wyeth. Digital Image ©The Museum of Modern Art/Licensed by SCALA/Art Resource, NY,NY, p. 297 (top); Peter Ralston/MERRILL, p. 297 (bottom); United Archives GmbH/Alamy, p. 299; Lydia Gans/World Institute on Disability, p. 300; Bob Child/AP Images, p. 301; Matthew Cavanaugh/EPA/Newscom, p. 306 (Figure 9-2); MERRILL, pp. 310, 328; Digitalpress/Fotolia, p. 318; Fotosearch/SuperStock, p. 324; Courtesy of Helping Hands: Monkey Helpers for the Disabled, Inc./MERRILL, p. 325.

Chapter 10

Vladimir Mucibabic/Fotolia, p. 330; The Owings Gallery, Santa Fe, New Mexico, p. 331; Thomas Hart Benton, "The Lord is my Shepherd", tempura on canvas. Collection of the Whitney Museum of American Art, New York, p. 333; Caleb Jones/AP Images; p. 335 (right, top); Gallaudet University, p. 335 (right, bottom); Mattel/Getty Images, p. 352;Mattel/Getty Images, p. 352; United Archives GmbH/Alamy, p. 354; Deborah Smith, p. 360; MERRILL, p. 362.

Chapter 11

Pavel Svoboda/Fotolia, p. 366; MERRILL, p. 367 (top); Naranjo Studio/Deborah Smith, p. 367 (bottom); AF Archive/Alamy, p. 369; Deborah Smith, p. 370; MERRILL, p. 371 (left); Michael Collopy/Courtesy of Skoll Foundation/MERRILL, p. 371 (right); Courtesy of the IRIS Center/MERRILL, pp. 374; Karen Hildebrand Lau/Shutterstock, p. 379; Huntstock/Getty Images, p. 381; Deborah Smith, p. 384, 385 (top right); Copyright (c) 2008 By Earl Dotter and AFB. All Rights Reserved./MERRILL, p. 385 (bottom, left); courtesy of 1-World Globes & Maps/MERRILL, p. 393; Courtesy of the IRIS Center/MERRILL, pp. 394, 395; Michael Naranjo/MERRILL, p. 397.

Chapter 12

SuperStock, p. 402; MERRILL, pp. 403 (top and bottom), 429; Everett Collection Inc/Alamy, p. 405; Pauline Cutler/Alamy, p. 410; Photos 12/Alamy, p. 411; MICHAEL NARANJO/MERRILL, p. 414; Matt Tincani/MERRILL, p. 424 (left and right).

Chapter 13

DURIS Guillaume/Fotolia, p. 432; *MERRILL* p. 433 (top and bottom); Photo courtesy of New England Historic Genealogical Society, Boston, MA/MERRILL, p. 436; MERRILL, p. 437 (top of page); Sprout Film Festival www.gosprout.org/MERRILL, p. 437 (bottom); MERRILL , pp. 438, 440, 456; Moviestore Collection Ltd/Alamy, p. 444; Getty Images, p. 445; Fotosearch/Superstock, p. 453; Bill Freeman/Alamy, p. 454; Jupiterimages/Getty Images, p. 455.

Chapter 14

ZouZou/Shutterstock, p. 460; Andrew Howe/Getty Images, p. 461 (top); Georgios Kollidas/Fotolia, p. 461 (bottom); dotshock/Shutterstock, p. 463; Monkey Business/Fotolia, p. 466 (top); Lebrecht Music and Arts Photo Library/Alamy, p. 466 (bottom); Getty Images, p. 470; MICHAEL NARANJO/MERRILL, p. 473; William Campbell/Corbis, p. 478 (left); © Corbis All Rights Reserved, p. 478 (right); malija/Fotolia, p. 479; Vacclav/Fotolia, p. 485 (in box); ZUMA Press, Inc/Alamy, p. 486; AF Archive/Alamy, p. 487; SuperStock, p. 488.

CHAPTER 1

Disabilities and Special Education

Making a Difference

Imagine a World . . .

free from discrimination and barriers. . .

Chapter Objectives

After studying this chapter, you will be able to

1. Explain the different perspective of "disabilities."

2. Explain how the civil rights of people with disabilities are protected.

3. Discuss why Congress passed IDEA in 1975 and its ensuing reauthorizations.

4. Discuss the key features of "people first" language.

5. List the defining features of effective special education programs.

 *Vincent Van Gogh,* better known as an artistic genius long after his death, was troubled throughout his life. Although it is unclear what the roots of his disability might actually have been, he spent a considerable portion of his life alone and troubled, spending considerable time in hospitals for what at the time was thought to be melancholy and mental illness. Perhaps because he was so conflicted, his art broke with all traditions of the time. Painting in the late 1800s, as shown in this painting of *Irises,* his work includes a powerful use of color and dramatic and bold brushstrokes.

These are exciting times for people with disabilities, their families, their teachers, and the field of special education in general. We can now say with confidence today's educational practices along with supports available in the community can and do make real differences in the lives and futures of individuals with disabilities! We are so positive because this is a time of convergence—a convergence of knowledge, activism, and innovation. This is a time of transition for special education services, a time when education's response to students who struggle is making a difference in their lives and in their outcomes (Fuchs & Young, 2006; Severson et al., 2007).

Today, life for individuals with disabilities, whether they are adults or children, is remarkably different from what it was only a few years ago. And, we know tomorrow holds the promise of even greater community presence, more opportunities for accomplishment, fewer barriers and challenges caused by disabilities, and more of these members of our society leading happy and productive lives. Evidence now tells us for certain that well-prepared teachers make a difference in the results of their students (Darling-Hammond, 2005, 2006a, 2006b; Futernick, 2007; Hammond & Ingalls, 2003). So that you, too, will be well prepared to assume the responsibilities for children's education, across this academic term, we will introduce you to instructional innovations and practices, proven through practice and research that will help you contribute to improved results of every student you work with, whether they be gifted and talented individuals, typical learners, those who struggle, or those with disabilities. Our hope is that you will join the ranks of new teachers and other professionals who are dedicated to students with disabilities and are happy with their career choices (Gehrke & Murri, 2006).

Why in a time of worldwide turmoil would we be so positive about improved circumstances for people who have been marginalized throughout history? Adults with disabilities are taking their places in the community and no longer are absent from the routines of the day. Their improved community presence is a result of many factors, but important reasons are years of activism, changed attitudes, and barriers restricting access being reduced. Because they are better prepared and more opportunities are available, people with disabilities work in the community, instead of sheltered and segregated workplaces. Very few are relegated to isolated institutions; most live independently in houses and apartments, and those who need supports receive them. However, as you learn in this chapter and in the Where We've Been sections of chapters throughout this text, we must be always vigilant and help ensure that the history of discrimination and bias is never repeated.

To better understand what role you can take to make a difference, it is important to understand the complexities of disability and know the history of people with disabilities, the events that have brought us to this period of hope and optimism that is renewed today. So, let's start this exciting journey of learning about making a difference in the lives of students with disabilities and their families by thinking about disabilities and how we, as individuals and as a society, respond to the situations that disabilities present.

Disability and Social Justice

Social justice is an illusive concept, hard to define, but one we all support. At its core are sets of values about equality, human rights, entitlements, and fairness. One judge of every society is how it treats its citizens, all of them, despite being viewed as different on some perceived dimension. Across history, individuals with disabilities have experienced injustice, received unfair and even cruel treatment, and been denied rights provided to others. For example, although not enforced today, a section of the New Jersey Constitution written in 1844 prohibits "idiots" from voting in elections; such laws remain in statutes across the country (Peters, 2007). In many places in the world today, the rights of individuals with disabilities still are denied and abuses abound. In response, world leaders, advocates, and individuals with disabilities themselves are raising everyone's awareness about uniform application of principles of social justice (United Nations [UN] General Assembly, 2007). Martha Nussbaum helps us understand why it is an issue we must all embrace. She says that people with disabilities "have not as yet been included, in existing societies, as citizens on a basis of equality with other citizens. The problem of extending education, health care, political rights and liberties, and equal citizenship more generally to such people seems to be a problem of justice, and an urgent one" (2006, p. 2).

One contributing factor to unequal treatment experienced by many of these individuals is the way we define or think about disabilities (Institute of Medicine [IOM], 2007). These perceptions and attitudes, then, influence how we respond to individuals with disabilities. So, to help understand the idea of disability, answer this seemingly simple yet very complex question: "What is a disability?" Your response might reflect the notion that **disability** is an absolute, something an individual has or doesn't have. Or, your answer might include an explanation of the complexity of disability, that there are many different perspectives about what it is and what it means to each individual, each family, and each culture involved. You might talk about the intensity of a disability as the result of different conditions or experiences. And, you might include some mention of how society's and education's response to a disability should depend on each individual's unique needs. Such answers reflect the idea that individualized accommodations and assistance can reduce the impact of a challenge presented by a disability.

disability Result of conditions or impairments

The way we think about what it means to have a disability affects how we interact with people who have a disability. In turn, those interactions become events that influence individuals' outcomes (Branson & Miller, 2002; Winzer, 2007). For example, the beliefs of teachers and other professionals who work with students are important to understand because different perspectives result in different responses to a disability; some responses—like low or unreasonably high expectations—can have long-term negative results (Artiles & Bal, 2008; Harry et al., 2008). Responses to disability impact on whether or how the principles of social justice are applied. So, let's think together about various ways to conceptualize "disability" and then how resulting attitudes make a difference in the lives of these individuals.

Differing Perspectives About Disabilities

Different disciplines, cultures, and individuals do not agree about the concept of "disabilities," what disabilities are, or how to explain them (Bacon et al., 2007; Lynch & Hanson, 2004; Obiakor & Utley, 2007). Typically in such conversations, characteristics are used to help describe or define a condition or a disability and are compared with some idea of what is "normal," "typical," or "average." So, educators often hear descriptions of students that use comparisons of their skills and behaviors. However, perspectives or orientations about individuals also guide people's thinking. These perspectives or orientations can provide a framework to understand various actions and reactions to disabilities and special needs. Let's turn our attention to three different orientations that guide people's thinking about disabilities:

- Deficit perspective
- Cultural perspective
- Sociological perspective

The Deficit Perspective of Disabilities The *deficit perspective* follows the idea that human behavior and characteristics shared by people are distributed along a continuum. For example, many psychologists, education professionals, and medical professionals describe children and youth by various characteristics, such as intelligence, visual acuity, academic achievement, or behavior. Actually, scores or measurements received by people tend to create a distribution where the majority of people fall in the middle of the distribution, and that's why they are called

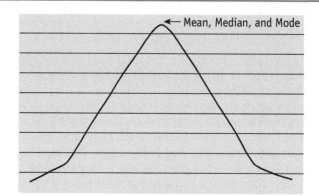

"average." For example, people are of different heights. Some people are short, some tall, but most people's height falls somewhere in the middle; the average of everyone's height is at the center of the distribution. The scores from most human characteristics create such patterns or form what is called a **normal curve**, like the one shown in Figure 1.1. Because of the way the distribution tends to fall, with the highest number of scores in the middle and proportionally fewer as the distance from the average score increases, the distribution is also referred to as the **bell-shaped curve**.

The expectation, according to this idea, is for the academic achievement of all third graders to also create such a distribution. The number of students obtaining each score would be plotted on the graph. Few students would obtain low scores on the achievement test, and their scores would be plotted at the left side of the graph. The number of students receiving higher scores increases until the average or mean score is reached. So, using this scheme, somewhere in the middle of the distribution are **typical learners**, those whose behaviors and characteristics represent the average or majority of students. Then, progressively, fewer students obtain higher and higher scores on the test completing the right-side of the distribution or curve. The number of characteristics that could be counted in this way is endless, and each individual student probably provides different patterns as to where he or she falls on each dimension measured. The tall student has slightly below-average visual acuity and has average scores on the distance he or she can kick a ball. So, you should be able to see that the hypothetical average student, or typical learner, probably does not actually exist, or exists very rarely because the possible combinations of human characteristics are almost endless.

Regardless, in mainstream America quantifying human performance is the most common method used to describe individuals. Unfortunately, this way of thinking about people puts half of everyone "below average" and forces individuals to be considered in terms of how different they are from the average. For students with disabilities, this approach contributes to the tendency to think about them as deficient or being somehow less than their classmates without disabilities.

The Cultural Perspective of Disabilities A second way to think about disabilities and the people who might be affected does not use a quantitative approach; rather, it reflects a *cultural perspective*. Alfredo Artiles of Arizona State University aptly points out that America today includes many different cultures, and some have values and hold to concepts that differ greatly from mainstream ideas. Nonmajority cultures often hold different perspectives about the concept of disabilities, and many do not think about disabilities in terms of deficits or quantitative judgments about individuals (Artiles & Bal, 2008; Harry, 2007). We believe that this is a very important point for teachers to understand. First, education professionals and the families

normal or bell-shaped curve Theoretical construct of the typical distribution of human traits such as intelligence

typical learners Students and individuals without disabilities

with whom they work might not share the same understanding of disability. Second, they might not have a common belief about what causes disabilities. Third, family members might not agree with educators' ideas about appropriate responses to a student's disability.

Knowing that not all cultures share the same concept of disability helps us understand why families approach education professionals differently when told that their child has a disability. Because disability does not have a single orientation or fixed definition, it is not thought about uniformly or universally (Harry & Klingner, 2007; Lynch & Hanson, 2004). Families with whom teachers work are likely to have different understandings about their child from those of school professionals. Also, not all cultures respond the same to individuals identified as having a disability. In other words, the same individual might be considered "different" or as having a disability in one culture but not in another (Jim Green, April 2008, personal communication). Or, the degree of difference might not be considered uniformly.

The Sociological Perspective of Disabilities   The *sociological perspective* or orientation presents yet another way to help us think about individuals with disabilities. Instead of focusing on people's strengths or deficits, differences across people's skills and traits are thought of as being socially constructed (Longmore, 2003; Riddell, 2007). In this perspective, how a society treats individuals is what makes people different from each other, not a condition or set of traits that are part of the individual's characteristics. Here, the thought is that if people's attitudes and the way society treats groups of individuals change, the result and impact of being a member of a group also change. In other words, according to this perspective, what makes a disability is how we treat individuals we think of as different. Some scholars and advocates hold a radical view, suggesting that disabilities are a necessity of American society, its structure, and values. Some scholars, like Herb Grossman, believe that when societies are stratified, variables such as disability, race, and ethnicity become economic and political imperatives (Grossman, 1998). They are necessities to maintain class structure. Classifications result in restricted opportunities that then force some groups of people to fall to the bottom (Erevelles, 1996; Grossman, 1998). The logic continues that *all* people have strengths and weaknesses. So, if supporting services were available to help *every* individual when problems occur, then no individual would not be negatively treated and would be viewed successful. In other words, if individuals with significant differences are just treated like everyone else, problems associated with disabilities will disappear. Clearly, debate about this rationale or explanation for disabilities is controversial. One danger of the sociological perspective of disabilities is that it minimizes disabilities and could lead to a reduction of services (Kauffman, 1997; Kauffman & Hallahan, 2005).

The way we think about groups of people does make a difference in how they are treated, the opportunities they have, and the accomplishments they achieve. Let's turn our attention to these issues now.

Perceptions Make a Difference

Throughout history, there are many examples of how perceptions and attitudes are related to the way people are treated (Deutsch, 2005). Unfortunately, too often in human history the way people with disabilities were treated demonstrates stigma and discrimination. Because we must never lose sight of such travesties, in each chapter's Where We've Been section, we share such stories in hopes that history will never repeat itself. For example, in Chapter 4 we tell the story about Balbus Balaesus the Stutterer, who was the amusement of ancient Romans who would take outings to the Appian Way and throw coins in his cage if he would talk to them. In Chapter 8 we make sure that you know about made-up families, the Jukes and Kallikaks, who were said to be the source of crime and poverty because of their

myeducationlab)   Go to the Building Teaching Skills and Dispositions section in Chapter 1 of MyEducationLab and complete the IRIS Activity: What Do You See? Perceptions of Disability. This activity encourages you to explore your own attitudes and beliefs about people with disabilities.

intellectual disabilities. Those stories were meant to put fear into the hearts and minds of Americans. The results were that people with mental retardation or intellectual disabilities were shunned, forced to live in isolated institutions, and sterilized so that society would be protected from such dangerous people (Smith & Lazaroff, 2006). But, there were also times in history when people with disabilities were not discriminated against or stigmatized.

Possibly in the history of the United States, there is no better illustration that perceptions and attitudes make a difference than the fascinating story of the settlers of Martha's Vineyard. The 17th-century settlers of Martha's Vineyard came from Kent, England. You will learn more about these pioneers and the founders of America's Deaf culture movement in Chapter 10. For this discussion, it is important to know that apparently these settlers carried with them both a recessive gene for deafness and the ability to use sign language (Van Cleve, 2007). The hearing people living on the island were bilingual, developing their oral and sign language skills simultaneously early in life. Generation after generation, well over 25% of the islanders could not hear. Probably because deafness occurred at such a high rate and in almost everyone's family, these deaf people were treated differently from those who lived on the mainland. Those living on Martha's Vineyard had a real community presence and were included in all aspects of work, play, and church life. Unlike their counterparts on the mainland, they were free to marry whomever they wished. According to tax records, they generally earned average or above-average incomes, with some becoming quite wealthy. Many were real leaders in their communities. Deaf individuals did have some advantages over their hearing neighbors and family members. They were literate and better educated than the general population because they received tuition assistance to attend the school for the deaf in Connecticut. There are numerous accounts about hearing people asking their Deaf neighbors to read something to them or write a letter for them. For more than 200 years, life in this relatively restricted and confined environment was much the same for those who had this disability and those who did not. Groce (1985) provides an important observation:

> The most striking fact about these deaf men and women is that they were not handicapped, because no one perceived their deafness as a handicap. As one woman said to me, "You know we didn't think anything special about them. They were just like anyone else. When you think about it, the Island was an awfully nice place to live." Indeed it was. (p. 110)

Of this there should no longer be doubt: People are treated as a reflection of how they are perceived. So, one way to measure and evaluate how any group of people is perceived by a society is to analyze how that group is portrayed in literature and on the screen in both film and television (Longmore, 2003; Prater, 2003). Films tend to mirror reality, reflecting beliefs and attitudes of society at the time they were made. Although they can perpetuate stereotypes, they also have the potential to influence the way people think and interact with others (Safran, 1998, 2000). Films produced at the beginning of the last century rarely depicted people with disabilities in a positive light. Most characters were villainous or evil, often punished through their disabilities by God for some sin of theirs or a family member. Many of those characters were bitter and self-pitying. In this regard, we have the opportunity literally to see how beliefs, bias, actions, and stereotypes about people with disabilities have changed across time by analyzing how people with disabilities have been portrayed in cinema. For one such example, see On the Screen, which uses the original and remakes of the movie *The Hunchback of Notre Dame* to illustrate how perceptions have changed over time.

Certainly, not all portrayals of people with disabilities across time are negative or unfair in their use of characters with disabilities (e.g., *Shine*, 1996; *Ray*, 2004). Many films made worthy efforts—like *My Left Foot* (1989), which tells the story of Christy Brown, an artist, writer, and disability advocate—and give accurate representations of what life is like for many people with disabilities. More commonly, however, characters with disabilities were developed along these common themes:

On the Screen: *Disability Across a Century*

Victor Hugo's classic 1831 novel, *Notre Dame of Paris,* has been translated often into films typically titled *The Hunchback of Notre Dame.* These movies reveal societal attitudes about people with disabilities at the time each film was made. For example, in the 1923 silent film rendition, Lon Chaney creates Quasimodo, who lives in the bell tower of the Paris cathedral of Notre Dame, as frightening and grotesque. This moving and tragic hero saves the beautiful gypsy, Esmaralda, from the evil judge, but he is brutally killed at the end. In the 1939 version, Charles Laughton's portrayal is the centerpiece of a shocking horror film. Although in this version Quasimodo and Esmaralda survive, at the end Quasimodo speaks to a stone gargoyle on the church and asks, "Why was I not made of stone?" Much more recently, the story was both animated and made into a musical by Disney. In this version, although a cruel crowd rejects and torments Quasimodo, he battles heroically to save the people and city he loves. The film makes the point that people should be seen for who they are, not for how they appear.

—By Steven Smith

monsters who have grotesque physical appearances portrayed shallowly to scare and horrify, "crippled" criminals, pitiful war veterans, and amusing cartoon characters that stutter (e.g., Porky Pig), have speech impairments (e.g., Elmer Fudd), have visual disabilities (e.g., Mr. Magoo), or have cognitive problems (e.g., Dopey). Sometimes characters with disabilities were included to elicit pity, as in the tragic victim with mental retardation, Lenny, in the story *Of Mice and Men.* Paul Longmore, a disability scholar and founder of the Disabilities Studies Program at San Francisco State University, insists that disabilities, particularly physical disabilities, are used as a melodramatic device to signal evil or to separate and isolate the key character (Longmore, 2003). Along with many other characters, he makes his case by highlighting such characters as Captain Ahab, the peg leg tyrant in *Moby Dick,* Captain Hook in *Peter Pan,* and Darth Vader from the classic trilogy about good and evil, *Star Wars.* According to Longmore, another frequent message embedded in the stories that have included characters with disabilities is that social integration is impossible and the "final and only possible solution is often death. In most cases, it is fitting and just punishment. For sympathetic 'monsters,' death is the tragic but inevitable, necessary, and merciful outcome" (Longmore, 2003, p. 135). Look again at On the Screen to see how movies can reflect attitudes of the time in which the films were made and how such representations change across time. Also, meet Paul

Spotlighting *Paul K. Longmore:* A Day in the Life

Paul K. Longmore is a professor of history at the San Francisco State University, founder of that university's Disability Studies program, respected scholar, leader in the disability advocacy movement, and coeditor of The New Disability History: American Perspectives.

At the end of my first year of doctoral studies, I applied for a fellowship. Both members of the history department's Fellowships Committee knew my scholarly capabilities. I had done well in their seminars. Nonetheless, they rejected my application. I thought I knew why, but I wanted them to tell me in person. I guess I thought that putting them on the spot might make them reconsider or at least feel a little guilty. So one afternoon I met with them. They obviously didn't feel guilty, and they certainly weren't going to reconsider their decision. They bluntly said that no college or university would ever hire me. They meant, of course, that no one was going to hire me because of my disability. In other words, they didn't want to waste the department's money on me. They recommended that I think about becoming an archivist. I pointed out that archival work is quite physical. "Besides," I said, I want to teach, "and I am going to become a college teacher whether you help me or not." They said that they felt sure I would succeed, because "we really admire your courage." I've always wished that I had told them I didn't need their admiration. I needed their money.

The prejudice my professors expressed was hardly something new to me. As early as the seventh grade, I had realized that people were discounting me and my talents because of my disability. At the ages of 12 and 13, I didn't yet have the world *prejudice* to describe what I was up against, but I knew what it was. And within a couple of years, watching TV news coverage of the African American civil rights movement, I realized that the word *prejudice* explained what I was facing as a young man with a physical disability. So I decided that the best way to counter that bias was to work hard at everything I did and especially to develop my intellectual and verbal skills.

Despite my efforts, I was repeatedly stung by wounding words of prejudice and sometimes set back by overt acts of discrimination. In college, one of my teachers, learning that I planned to become a college history professor like him, said that no one would ever hire me. Maybe he thought he was toughening me up to face the hard facts of life. But he just confirmed for me that I was butting up against social prejudices. What he said brought to mind a passage I had read in *The Autobiography of Malcolm X*. As a high school student, Malcolm wanted to go to college and then law school. But bright and eager though he was, one of his teachers told him his dream was unrealistic. I felt that both Malcolm's teacher and mine were discounting our abilities and urging us to give in to discrimination.

Despite my professor's discouragement, I pursued an M.A. in history. One day as I was finishing up that degree, the history department's chair told me he believed I could do well in a history Ph.D. program, because, he said, "You're not bitter like most cripples." But he also stated matter-of-factly that because of my disability, no college would ever hire me. Fortunately, a number of other teachers supported and encouraged me because they believed in my talents. Partly because of their encouragement, I eventually became a university history professor.

One last point: My professors' discriminatory denial of a fellowship was not illegal at the time. No law prohibited disability-based discrimination. I needed that legal protection as much as I needed my teachers to believe in me.

Longmore in this chapter's Spotlighting feature, and think about how his perceptions can help you make a difference in the lives of people with disabilities.

Perceptions held by society in general matter, but so, too, do the attitudes of individual teachers. Unfortunately, after some 40 years of routinely including students in the educational system, many educators still do not welcome these students in their inclusive classrooms (Cook, Cameron, & Tankersley, 2007; Gehrke & Murri, 2007). The result can be indifference about school success and even teacher rejection of students with disabilities. In this regard, principals, collaborative teachers, special educators, and classmates make a difference in the acceptance, supports, and accommodations provided to all students (Siperstein et al., 2007). This is true whether the demands of the general education classroom and curriculum are either too challenging or boring. When principals and school leaders encourage success, hold students accountable, and provide a supportive environment for teachers, everyone benefits (DiPaola & Walther-Thomas, 2003; IRIS Center, 2008).

Language Makes a Difference: People First

The way we talk communicates attitudes and perceptions. And, the language used to refer to people with disabilities sends many messages, some intended and many not intended. Careless language can be offensive, disrespectful, and demeaning, so people with disabilities express some strong feelings about the words and phrases used to describe them. Language is a very sensitive issue with many individuals with disabilities and their advocates.

Language evolves to reflect changing concepts and beliefs, and what people say that might be socially acceptable at one point in history can be offensive at another (Prabhala, 2007). As you will learn in Chapter 8, many believe that changing terms used to refer to people, at least temporarily, shakes off the stigma that has become associated with the term. For example, at the beginning of the 20th century, such terms as *imbecile, moron,* and *mental retardate* were commonly used, and at the time they were *not* offensive but later took on negative connotations. This is a reason that in 2007, one professional organization and several of its publications no longer use the term *mental retardation* in their titles and instead use the term *intellectual and developmental disabilities.*

The language preferred by people with disabilities can be confusing because different groups and individuals have very different preferences. Although there are some exceptions (especially for the Deaf[1]), here are some basic guidelines to follow (Easter Seals, 2008):

1. Put people first.
2. Do not make the person equal or be the disability.
3. *Disabled* is *not* a noun.
4. People with disabilities are neither victims nor wheelchair bound.

The concept of "**people first language**" is applied in this way: students with intellectual disabilities, individuals who have learning disabilities, toddlers with cerebral palsy, adults with speech impairments. Of course, as with almost everything in life, exceptions to these basic rules about the language of disabilities exist. One group who tends to prefer a different language style is individuals with profound vision problems. Most seem to use the term *blind individuals* instead of *people with visual loss.* The second exception comes with those individuals with profound hearing loss, who use American Sign Language (ASL) for communication, consider themselves members of the Deaf community, and participate in the heritage and culture of the Deaf (learn more about Deaf culture in Chapter 10). So, even though most people with disabilities would be offended if a non–people first language approach were used to talk about them, for blind and deaf people the people first rule often does not apply. Remember, however, that not all members of any group agree unanimously on every issue; some people with disabilities might not agree with the rules of language described here. And the rules will certainly change over time. Remember that it is everyone's responsibility to remain sensitive to these issues.

people first language Appropriate way to refer to most groups of people with disabilities

Disability as a Minority

Paul Longmore, whom you met in this chapter's Spotlighting feature, is a founder of the disabilities studies movement. He is the director of the Disability Studies Department at San Francisco State and also a person with disabilities and maintains that like other minority groups, individuals with disabilities receive negative treatment because of discrimination (Longmore, 2002, 2003). The idea continues that the ways people are treated by society and other individuals are what present real barriers that influence people's outcomes. Many individuals with disabilities believe that their disabilities (e.g., conditions and impairments) then **handicap** them (e.g., present challenges

handicaps Challenges and barriers imposed by others

---

[1] Using a capital *D* in the word *deaf* and placing the word before the person's referent signals association with Deaf culture, which you will learn about in Chapter 10. The lowercase *d* is used to refer to profound hearing loss and an individual who is not part of the Deaf culture movement.

and barriers). This belief leads many people to think about people with disabilities as belonging to a minority group, much like race and ethnicity has resulted in African Americans, Hispanics, Native Americans, and Asian/Pacific Islanders[2] being considered as part of historically underrepresented groups. Difficult situations occur not because of a condition or disability but rather because people with disabilities are denied full participation in society because of their minority status (Wizner, 2007). In fact, the Individuals with Disabilities Education Act (IDEA)—the special education law that guarantees children with disabilities a right to a public education—is often referred to as a civil rights law. IDEA is thought of as belonging to the same category of laws as the Voting Rights Act of 1965, which put an end to discriminatory practices that denied some Americans from exercising their right to vote in state and national elections.

Protections for Civil Rights and Education

civil rights Rights that all citizens of a society are supposed to have to ensure social justice

As we learned from the **civil rights** movement, sometimes, positive attitudes are not enough to ensure social justice. Often, it takes legal actions—intercession from the courts and protections of laws—to guarantee that each of us is treated fairly and not presented with barriers that hinder our achieving our potential, attaining community presence, or exercising civil rights. Such has been the case of individuals with disabilities, for both adults and children.

Litigation   Nationally, the courts stepped in to protect the rights of children before laws were put into place. After years and years of segregation and exclusion from schooling, the courts made it clear that education was a right of all children in America. Court rulings are the foundation for the national special education law that was passed later. Table 1.1 summarizes these important court cases.

In the case of IDEA, it is the responsibility of the U.S. Department of Education to implement the law and the role of the courts to clarify it. Although Congress thought it was clear in its intentions about the educational guarantees it believed were necessary for children with disabilities and their families, no legal language is perfect. Since 1975, when PL 94-142 (IDEA) initially became law, a very small percentage of all the children who have been served have been involved in formal disputes, and the number of Supreme Court case decisions is few. Those disputes concern the identification of students with disabilities, evaluations, educational placements, and the provision of a free appropriate public education. Most disputes are resolved in noncourt proceedings or **due process hearings**. Some disputes, however, must be settled in courts of law—a few even in the U.S. Supreme Court. Major examples of court cases that clarify IDEA also are found in Table 1.1.

due process hearing Noncourt proceeding before an impartial hearing officer used if parents and school personnel disagree on a special education issue

Legislation   The nation's policymakers reacted to injustices revealed in court case after court case at the state and national levels by passing laws to protect the civil rights of individuals with disabilities (Florian, 2007). In the 1950s, the courts ruled in *Brown v. the Board of Education* that schools separating children by race were not equal and mandated that students be integrated and attend school side by side. Using *Brown* as part of its rationale, Congress passed a national law to guarantee students with disabilities and their families the right to a free public education. At about the same time, issues of injustices were coming to light about adults with disabilities and the discrimination and bias they face in the community and workplace. The 1970s saw great activity. Across the nation, laws were being passed to halt injustice and ensure basic civil rights to people with disabilities. One of the excellent Web sites that offers explanations of these laws is www.wrightslaw.com. Some of the major laws are summarized in Table 1.2. In the next paragraphs, we tell the stories about why these laws were passed, so we can all be vigilant to ensure that the spirit of these laws is never dampened.

---

[2] Although regional and personal preferences about specific terms used to reflect how ethnic and racial groups vary, these terms are the ones used by the federal government. Throughout this text, we use a variety of terms in an attempt to achieve balance.

Table 1.1 • Landmark Court Cases (Litigation) Affecting Students with Disabilities

Case	Date	Issue	Finding/Importance
Landmark Court Cases Setting the Stage for IDEA			
Brown v. Board of Education	1954	Ended White "separate but equal" schools	Basis for future rulings that children with disabilities cannot be excluded from school
Pennsylvania Association for Retarded Children (PARC) v. Commonwealth of Pennsylvania	1972	Guaranteed special education to children with intellectual disabilities (mental retardation)	Court case that signaled a new era for special education and set the stage for the national special education law
Mills v. Board of Education of the District of Columbia	1972	Extended the right to special education to all children with disabilities	Reinforced the right of all children with disabilities to a free public education
Landmark U.S. Supreme Court Cases Defining IDEA			
Rowley v. Hendrick Hudson School District	1984	FAPE	School districts must provide those services that permit a student with disabilities to benefit from instruction.
Irving Independent School District v. Tatro	1984	Defining related services	Clean intermittent catheterization (CIC) is a related service when necessary to allow a student to stay in school.
Smith v. Robinson	1984	Attorney's fees	Parents are reimbursed legal fees when they win a case resulting from special education litigation.
Burlington School Committee v. Department of Education	1984	Private school placement	In some cases, public schools may be required to pay for private school placements when the district does not provide an appropriate education.
Honig v. Doe	1988	Exclusion from school	Students whose misbehavior is related to their disability cannot be denied education.
Timothy W. v. Rochester New Hampshire School District	1989	FAPE	Regardless of the existence or severity of a student's disability, a public education is the right of every child.
Zobrest v. Catalina Foothills School District	1993	Paid interpreter at parochial high school	Paying for a sign language interpreter does not violate the constitutional separation of church and state.
Carter v. Florence County School District 4	1993	Reimbursement for private school	A court may order reimbursement to parents who withdraw their children from a public school that provides inappropriate education, even though the private placement does not meet all IDEA requirements.
Doe v. Withers	1993	FAPE	Teachers are responsible for the implementation of accommodations specified in individual students' IEPs.
Cedar Rapids School District v. Garrett F.	1999	Related services	Health attendants are a related service and a district's expense if the service is necessary to maintain them in educational programs.
Schaffer v. Weast	2005	Appropriate education	In legal decisions, parents, not schools, must prove their children are not receiving an appropriate education.

Table 1.2 • Landmark Laws (Litigation) Affecting Children and Adults with Disabilities

Number of Law or Section	Date	Name of Law	Key Provisions
Section 504	1973	Rehabilitation Act of 1973, Section 504	• Guarantees basic civil rights to all people with disabilities • Requires the provision of accommodations
PL 94-142	1975	Education for All Handicapped Children Act (EHA)	• Guarantees FAPE in the LRE • Requires each student to have an IEP
PL 99-457	1986	EHA (reauthorized)	• Adds provision of services to infants and toddlers • Requires IFSPs
PL 101-476	1990	Individuals with Disabilities Education Act (IDEA)	• Changed name of the law retroactively • Adds transition plans • Adds autism as a special education category • Added traumatic brain injury as a category
PL 101-336	1990	Americans with Disabilities Act (ADA)	• Bars discrimination in employment, transportation, public accommodations, and telecommunications • Implements principles of normalization • Requires phased-in accessibility of school buildings • Insists on the removal of barriers inhibiting access and participation in society
PL 105-17	1997	IDEA '97 (reauthorized)	• Adds ADHD to the "other health impairments" category • Adds functional behavioral assessments and behavior intervention plans • Altered transition plans to become an IEP component
PL 107-110	2001	NCLB (reauthorization of the Elementary and Secondary Education Act [ESEA])	• Implemented a high-stakes accountability system based on student achievement • Requires use of data-based practices and instruction • Insists on highly qualified teachers
PL 108-364	2004	Assistive Technology Act of 2004 (ATA) (reauthorized)	• Supports school-to-work transition projects • Continues a national Web site on assistive technology • Assists states in creating and supporting device loan programs, financial loans
PL 108-446	2004	IDEA '04 (reauthorized)	• Requires special education teachers to be highly qualified • Requires that all students with disabilities participate annually in either state and district testing with accommodations or in alternative assessments • Eliminates IEP short-term objectives and benchmarks, except for those who use alternative assessments • Changes identification procedures for learning disabilities • Allows any student to be placed in an interim alternative educational setting for weapons, drugs, or violence
PL 110-235	2008	Americans with Disabilities Amendments Act of 2000	• Broadens definition of disability • Provides that impairments or conditions that could limit a major life activity but are in remission still be considered disabilities

Rehabilitation Act of 1973, Section 504 First law to outline the basic civil rights of people with disabilities

accommodations Supports to compensate for disabilities, adjustments to assignments or tests

Section 504 of the Rehabilitation Act was passed by Congress in 1973. This law requires **accommodations**, such as access to public buildings, for people with disabilities. Section 504 provides all individuals with disabilities—both adults and children—civil rights and necessary accommodations needed to access society. It is this provision that requires schools to provide accommodations to students whose disabilities or conditions require some special attention, but not special education services. This law set the stage for both the special education law, IDEA, and the Americans with Disabilities Act (ADA), because it included some protection of the rights of students with disabilities to public education and many

Unlike children born in the 1970s and before, this young child and his mom are filled with excitement as they are welcomed on the first day of class at their neighborhood school.

provisions for adults with disabilities and their participation in society and the workplace.

The Individuals with Disabilities Education Act (IDEA) was written and passed by Congress after it had investigated how students with disabilities and their families were welcomed into the education system. Congress found widespread patterns of exclusion, denial of services, and discrimination. Although positive attitudes about the benefits of educating students with disabilities emerged centuries ago, the delivery of programs in the United States remained inconsistent for almost 200 years. In 1948, only 12% of all children with disabilities received special education services (Ballard, Ramirez, & Weintraub, 1982). As late as 1962, only 16 states had laws that included students with even mild cognitive problems under mandatory school attendance requirements (Roos, 1970). In most states, even those children with the mildest levels of disabilities were not allowed to attend school. Children with more severe disabilities were routinely excluded. When Congress studied the problem in the early 1970s, here's what it found (20 USC Section 1400 [b]):

Education for All Handicapped Children Act (EHA) or Public law, 94-142; Individuals with Disabilities Education Act (IDEA) Originally passed in 1975 to guarantee a free appropriate public education for all students with disabilities; the special education law

- One million of the children with disabilities in the United States were excluded entirely from the public school system.
- More than half of the eight million children with disabilities in the United States were not receiving appropriate educational services.
- The special educational needs of these children were not being fully met because they were not receiving necessary related services.
- Services within the public school system were inadequate and forced families to find services outside the public school system, often at great distance from their residence and at their own expense.
- If given appropriate funding, state and local educational agencies could provide effective special education and related services to meet the needs of children with disabilities.

Collectively, these findings resulted in Congress taking action, and in 1975, the first national special education law was passed, making a real difference in the lives of these children and their families.

Public Law (PL) 94-142, Education for All Handicapped Children Act (EHA) was the first version of the special education law. (The first set of numbers refers to the session of Congress in which the law was passed, the second set to the number of the law. Thus, EHA was the 142nd law passed in the 94th session of Congress.) Congress gave the states 2 years to get ready to implement this new special education law, so it was actually initiated in 1977. From the inception of IDEA, two important and overriding principles have been key to the services extended to students with disabilities and their families: free appropriate education (FAPE) and least restrictive environment (LRE).

Educational services for students with disabilities are to be available to parents at no additional cost to them. These students—despite the complexity of their educational needs, the accommodations or additional services they require, or the cost to a school district—are entitled to a **free appropriate public education (FAPE)**. FAPE must be individually determined because what is appropriate for one student with a disability might not be appropriate for another. Students with disabilities are to receive their education in the **least restrictive environment (LRE)**. In other words, special education services are not automatically delivered in any particular place and should provide as much access to the general education curriculum and the general education classroom as possible. LRE, and its balance with FAPE, can be confusing. LRE is often misinterpreted as meaning that students with disabilities are to receive all or most of their education in general education classes. Such is not the mandate of IDEA '04; rather, the goal is to ensure that students receive an individualized education with the least amount of segregation or isolation from peers without disabilities. To quickly compare these two concepts, see What IDEA '04 Says About FAPE and What IDEA '04 Says About LRE.

While FAPE and LRE have remained consistent components of IDEA across time, new elements were added each time the law was reauthorized. Table 1.2 also highlights each of these major additions. For example, note that in 1986 it extended services to all children with disabilities, including infants and toddlers. The 1990 version retroactively changed the name of the law to the Individuals with Disabilities Education Act (IDEA). When the law was passed again in 2004, many changes were made in how students with learning disabilities can be identified and services can be delivered early to all students who struggle to learn basic skills, such as reading, through high-quality general education instruction (U.S. Department of Education, 2006).

The **Americans with Disabilities Act (ADA)** was passed to bar discrimination in employment, transportation, public accommodations, and telecommunications. Its intent is to guarantee access to people with disabilities and implement the concept of **normalization** across all aspects of American life. Remember, Congress first considered civil rights issues related to people with disabilities when it passed Section 504 of the Rehabilitation Act of 1973. However, after almost 20 years of implementation and convinced by advocates, many of whom were themselves adults with disabilities, Congress felt that Section 504 was not sufficient. It did not end discrimination for adults with disabilities. The first president Bush signed the ADA, on July 26, 1990. The impact of ADA has been great, with accommodations and greater access not part of

---

free appropriate public education (FAPE) Ensures that students with disabilities receive necessary education and services without cost to the family

least restrictive environment (LRE) Educational placement with the most inclusion and integration with typical learners as possible and appropriate

Americans with Disabilities Act (ADA) Antidiscrimination legislation guaranteeing basic civil rights to people with disabilities

normalization Making available ordinary patterns of life and conditions of everyday living

---

What IDEA '04 Says About . . .

Free Appropriate Public Education (FAPE)

Special education and related services

- Will be provided without charge, although parents of infants and toddlers with disabilities may be charged for some services based on a sliding fee scale.
- Must meet state standards and curriculum requirements.
- Include appropriate preschool, elementary, or secondary school education in that state.
- Must be consistent with the student's Individualized Educational Program (IEP).

American life (Steinmetz, 2006). Senator Tom Harkin (D-IA), the chief sponsor of the original act, spoke of this law as the "emancipation proclamation" for people with disabilities (West, 1994). Both Section 504 and ADA are considered civil rights and antidiscrimination laws and seek to provide adults with disabilities greater access to employment and participation in everyday activities that adults without disabilities enjoy. ADA requires new public transportation (buses, trains, subways) and new or remodeled public accommodations (hotels, stores, restaurants, banks, theaters) to be accessible to persons with disabilities. It requires telephone companies to provide relay services so that deaf individuals and people with speech impairments can talk to people who use ordinary telephones. ADA reinforces and applies the principles of **universal design**, which help everyone access the environment more easily because physical barriers, such as steps and stairways, are removed or an alternative means of access, such as a ramp or elevator, are made available. ADA has had broad impact on American society and the community presence of individuals with disabilities. To learn more about citizens with disabilities, go to www.census.gov.

Both Section 504 and ADA affect the education system, but there are some important differences between them and IDEA. Section 504 and ADA have a wider authority and broader definition of disabilities than does IDEA. These laws extend beyond school age. For example, it is under the authority of ADA that college students with special needs are entitled to special testing situations (untimed tests, someone to read the questions to the test taker, braille versions). It is because of Section 504 that students with attention deficit/hyperactivity disorder (ADHD) who do not qualify for special education services receive special accommodations at school. It is important to remember that everyone benefits

What IDEA '04 Says About . . .

Least Restrictive Environment (LRE)

- Provides that to the maximum extent possible, children with disabilities are to be educated with nondisabled peers
- Ensures a continuum of alternative placements
- Provides for supplementary services (resource room or itinerant instruction) in conjunction with general education
- Is individually determined and is based on evaluations of the student
- Is evaluated at least annually
- Is based on the child's IEP
- Is as close to the child's home as possible, and whenever possible is at that child's neighborhood school

universal design Barrier-free architectural and building designs that meet the needs of everyone, including people with physical challenges

myeducationlab Go to the Activities and Applications section in Chapter 1 of MyEducationLab and complete Activity 1. As you watch the video and answer the accompanying questions, consider the value of assistive technology and universal design in helping students with disabilities achieve success in the classroom.

Although designed for people with disabilities, everyone moves more freely because of ADA accommodations like curb cuts.

from innovations developed for people with disabilities (Chamberlain, 2007). For example, TV open captioning lets us read what a newscaster is saying when at a busy and noisy airport. Curb cuts and ramps make it easier for everyone to roll carts, drag luggage, push strollers, and use skateboards and even roller skates when crossing streets.

No Child Left Behind Act (NCLB) Reauthorization of the Elementary and Secondary Education Act mandating higher standards for both students and teachers, including an accountability system

No Child Left Behind Act (NCLB) is the name given to the Elementary and Secondary Education Act when it was reauthorized in 2001. Unlike earlier versions, NCLB includes many provisions that speak to the needs and education of students with disabilities. You will learn in many of the Assessment sections of this text that NCLB requires students with disabilities to participate in states' and districts' accountability systems. Here are a few of the main features of NCLB as they relate to students with disabilities (Browder & Cooper-Duffy, 2003; National Center for Learning Disabilities, 2004):

- Use of scientifically based (i.e., data-based) programs and interventions
- Access to the general education curriculum
- Insistence on highly qualified teachers
- Evaluation of students' performance with appropriate accommodations or modifications

Assistive Technology Act (ATA) Law that facilitates increased accessibility through technology

assistive technology (AT) Equipment (devices) or services to help compensate for an individual's disabilities

The **Assistive Technology Act** (ATA or Tech Act) is of growing importance to people with disabilities because increased accessibility in their future rests, in part, with technology. The Tech Act applies to both the educational system and community access. **Assistive technology (AT)** is critical to the participation of people with disabilities in the workplace, in the community, and at school; it removes barriers that restrict people's lives. For example, AT allows for people with hearing problems to go to their neighborhood theaters and hear the movie's dialogue through assistive listening devices or read it via captions. The potential of AT is limited only by our lack of creativity and innovation. However, AT is expensive and far outside many people's budgets, particularly those who are under- or unemployed. For both students and adults, the Tech Act offers, through the states' loan programs, training activities, demonstrations of new devices, and other direct services. This law allows students to test equipment and other AT devices both at school and at home before actually purchasing them. Access to information technology is important and unfettering to all of us, and restrictions to its access result in barriers with considerable consequences. For these reasons, you will find more about AT in Chapter 2 and in separate Technology sections in Chapters 3–14.

myeducationlab Go to the Activities and Applications section in Chapter 1 of MyEducationLab, and complete Activity 2 in order to learn more about students receiving and using related services and assistive technology.

Now everyone can hear. FM transmission devices have been used for many years to help students with hearing impairments hear the teacher. Because of the advantages for everyone, now some school districts are equipping all of their classrooms with them. The benefits are many when everyone can clearly hear the teacher's instructions, can focus better on learning, and doesn't have to strain to hear over a loud heating system or other background noise that interferes with their learning.

Disabilities and Students

Classification systems are used in part to allocate resources; to ensure that additional resources are reserved so equal opportunities can be provided to specific groups of people (Florian et al., 2007). Such is the case for English learners, those who are poor, and students with disabilities. For schoolchildren, the federal government, through IDEA, defines and classifies disabilities and insists that special education services are delivered only to those who are eligible. These services are restricted to those who qualify because these services provide intensive supports, individualized instruction, **related services** offered through **multidisciplinary teams** of experts that are expensive in both person-power and costs. Costs, of course, vary by intensity of services required, but the National Center on Special Education Finance estimates that it costs over twice as much to educate students with a disability than their general education classmates (Chambers, Parrish, & Harr, 2004). So, the delivery of these services needs to happen judiciously. Nationally, over 11% of students between the ages of 6 and 17 are identified as having disabilities and are provided special education services (Office of Special Education Programs [OSEP], 2008).

Through IDEA '04 and its regulations that are developed by the U.S. Department of Education, the federal government describes 14 **special education categories** that can be used to qualify infants, toddlers, preschoolers, and students as eligible to receive special education services (U.S. Department of Education, 2006). Within these categories are many different conditions, such as stuttering included as a speech impairment, or ADHD included under the other health impairment category, or Tourette syndrome within its emotional disturbance category. In an attempt to avoid incorrectly labeling young children as either having a disability when they do not or identifying them with the "wrong" disability, the developmental delay category is general (non-disability-specific group) and can be used for children under the age of 8 (Müller & Markowitz, 2004; U.S. Department of Education, 2006). Here are the 14 special education categories called out by the federal government:

Autism	Orthopedic impairment
Deaf-blindness	Other health impairment
Deafness	Specific learning disability
Emotional disturbance	Speech or language impairment
Hearing impairment	Traumatic brain injury
Mental retardation	Visual impairment including blindness
Multiple disabilities	Developmental delay

Across the country, the names used for each of these categories is not exactly the same. Some states in their rules and guidelines use slightly different terms. And, the terminology used by the federal government is not always preferred by parent and professional groups or the individuals with disabilities themselves. An overview of the disabilities and the different ways they are referred to in school settings is shown on Table 1.3. Sometimes, these categories are combined or blended. Deafness and hearing impairment are separate special education categories in IDEA '04 but are usually thought of together.

Special education categories can also be ordered and divided by **prevalence** or the size of the category: **high-incidence disabilities** (disabilities that occur in greater numbers) and **low-incidence disabilities** (disabilities that occur less often). Regardless of the specific names for the categories or organization system, states are required to report the number of students who qualify for special education by the 14 categories called out in IDEA '04. Notice that the special education categories found on Table 1.3 are ordered by prevalence or the number of individuals served through each category. Figure 1.2 helps us visualize prevalence of each disability, clearly showing how students with learning disabilities, for

related services Special education services from a wide range of disciplines and professions

multidisciplinary teams Individually determined groups of professionals with different expertise

special education categories System used in IDEA '04 to classify disabilities for students

prevalence Total number of cases at a given time

high-incidence disabilities Special education categories with the most students

low-incidence disabilities Special education categories with few students

Table 1.3 • IDEA '04: High- and Low-Incidence Disabilities

IDEA Term	Other Terms	Comments
High-Incidence Disabilities		
Specific learning disabilities	Learning disabilities (LD)	Includes reading/learning disabilities, mathematics/learning disabilities, overall and unexpected underachievement
Speech or language impairments	Speech disorders or language disorders; communication disorders	Divides speech impairments (articulation, fluency problems or stuttering, and voice problems) from language impairments
Mental retardation	Intellectual and developmental disabilities, cognitive disabilities	Ranges from mild to severe, but often occurs with other low-incidence disabilities
Emotional disturbance	Emotional and behavioral disorders (EBD)	Does not include conduct disorders as a reason for special education services
Low-Incidence Disabilities		
Multiple disabilities	Multiple-severe disabilities; developmental disabilities	Does not include all students with more than one disability, varies by state's criterion
Deafness; hearing Impairment	Hard of hearing and deaf	Includes full range of hearing losses; *Deaf* is used to signify those who consider themselves part of the Deaf community
Orthopedic impairments	Physical impairments (PI); physical disabilities	Category often combined with health impairments because of many overlapping conditions
Other health impairments	Health impairments; special health care needs	IDEA '04 includes attention deficit/hyperactivity disorder (ADHD) in this category causing overall prevalence to reflect high incidence
Visual impairments	Visual disabilities; low vision and blind	Includes full range of visual loss
Autism	Autism spectrum disorders (ASD)	*ASD* is more inclusive; autism considered as one of three ASD conditions; actual national prevalence numbers place this group of learners in the low-incidence category although many consider it more frequent.
Deaf-blindness	Deafblind	Does not necessarily mean both deaf and blind
Traumatic brain injury (TBI)		Must be acquired after birth
Developmental delay		Allows for noncategorical identification between the ages of 3 to 9

myeducationlab Go to the Activities and Applications section in Chapter 1 of MyEducationLab and complete Activity 3. This IRIS Activity asks you to calculate changes in prevalence across different federal categories of exceptionality and to speculate as to why some have changed so dramatically.

example, far outnumber those students with other types of problems. Study the chart carefully, for it might not match what you think about the prevalence of occurrence of certain disabilities. For example, the public and even some states' officials refer to autism as a high-incidence disability, despite the comparative data that would place it in the low-incidence group (Jan Jones-Wadsworth, personal communication, 2006). While still a low-incidence disability, its diagnosis is increasing for many reasons: broader definitions and criteria, reclassification of some children, better diagnostic procedures, and more cases (Science Daily, 2008). To check these data out yourself, go to www.ideadata.org and compare the prevalence of specific disabilities for your state with the nation. The important lesson here is for each of us to be careful consumers of research and use data to inform our work and thinking.

One last point on this topic: Some people tend to think that prevalence relates to severity or significance of the disability. In other words, high-incidence disabilities are less severe than low-incidence disabilities. Drawing this conclusion is a terrible mistake. All disabilities are serious, and mild to severe cases occur within each disability type.

Figure 1.2 • Prevalence of High- and Low-Incidence Disabilities

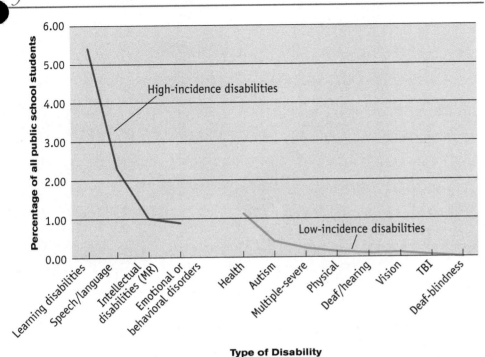

Type of Disability

Source: Office of Special Education Programs (OSEP), "Percentage (Based on 2006–2007 School Year, as Percentage of Population Served), Children Ages 6–17 Served Under IDEA, Part B by Disability," Data Tables, www.ideadata.org, 2008.

Making a Difference Through Special Education

Special education principles and services continually evolve, responding to research findings, data, and proven practices regarding its services and educational programs.

Origins of Special Education

Although many people believe that special education began in the United States in 1975 with the passage of IDEA, special education actually began over 200 years ago with an amazing story in southern France. In 1799, farmers in southern France found a young boy in the woods and brought that "wild child" to a doctor in Paris. The child was named Victor. Jean-Marc-Gaspard Itard, the doctor who now is recognized as the "father of special education," used many of the principles and procedures of explicit instruction implemented today to teach the boy, who most probably had mental retardation or intellectual disabilities. If you want to learn more about this amazing time in the history of special education, see the movie that is featured in Chapter 8's *On the Screen* feature.

In the early 1800s, Edouard Seguin, one of Itard's students, came to the United States and began efforts in this country to educate students with disabilities. In fact, these early efforts were taking root across Europe as well. For example, in Italy, Maria Montessori worked first with children with cognitive disabilities and showed that children could learn at young ages through concrete experiences offered in environments rich in manipulative materials. Meanwhile, Thomas Hopkins Gallaudet began to develop deaf education, and Samuel Gridley Howe founded the New England Asylum for the Blind (later the Perkins Institute). Elizabeth Farrell initiated public school classes for students with disabilities in 1898.

Although special education and the idea of educating students with disabilities had emerged centuries ago, its delivery was inconsistent with relatively few receiving the services they needed. Once Congress stepped in and passed IDEA, special

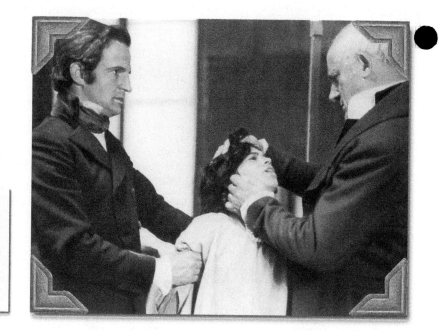

Victor, the Wild Child, is credited as being the first special education student. In 1799, he was found and captured in the woods by farmers in southern France and brought to Jean-Marc-Gaspard Itard in Paris.

special education services Individualized education and services for students with disabilities and sometimes includes gifted and talented students

education services became consistently available across the United States. These services are now guided by many rules and regulations, all with the intent of protecting students with disabilities and their right to education. Special education is meant for infants, preschoolers, elementary through high school students with disabilities, and in some cases individuals with disabilities up through the age of 21. **Special education services** are specially designed to meet each individual's unique learning needs. Instruction might be delivered in many different types of settings, such as hospitals, separate facilities, and homes, but most commonly at the student's local school in the general education class with neighborhood friends. It also might not reflect the same instructional targets: braille for blind students, manual communication systems for deaf students, social skills training for students with emotional or behavioral disorders, and so on.

Although general education and special education must work together, these two educational approaches are *not* the same. They differ along some very important dimensions. First and foremost, special education and general education are not designed for students with the same learning styles or needs. Second, some differences are based in law—what is stated in IDEA and its regulations—and result in key components of what is special education. For example, the role of parents is called out in IDEA and extends far beyond expectations for involvement of parents and their children without disabilities. Third, general education tends to focus on groups of learners, while the special education approach focuses on individuals.

As you read and study this academic term, you will learn more about how the IDEA law translates into services and an appropriate, individualized education for each student with a disability. For now, we want to highlight and introduce some key features, emerging trends, and innovative practices that make *special education special* for these students and their families and hold the promise of making a difference for students with disabilities long into the future.

Responsive Education

Across this academic term, you will learn that students with disabilities require an education that is responsive and individualized to meet each student's unique learning needs. There is no single answer for the appropriate response to disabilities. Perhaps meeting these students' diverse needs and knowing that "getting it right" makes such a difference in their lives is one reason that so many educators enjoy working with students with disabilities.

Students with disabilities can receive their education in a variety of settings, from traditional classrooms to the community. In fact, most—almost 80% of all students with disabilities, including those with moderate to severe disabilities—receive at least 60% of their education at local public schools in general education classes (OSEP, 2008). The participation rates for students with disabilities in general education classes has increased consistently over the past 15 years, with the percentage of those students with disabilities attending separate schools or facilities at about 4% today, down from 20% in 1993 (U.S. Department of Education, 1995).

Despite the trend to include more and more students with disabilities in general education settings, accessing the general education is *not* the goal for every student with a disability. A high school student with severe disabilities might not seek access to the standard high school curriculum leading to a diploma (e.g., including science and foreign language requirements) but rather learn important skills to become an independent adult through a proven practice called ***community-based instruction***, where on-the-job training, independent transportation, and home management are taught in real-life settings. A Deaf middle school student who uses American Sign Language (ASL) might attend a special school where everyone uses sign language for communication and instruction. Why might this be so? In cases when the student is the only one who can sign at a school, educational opportunities are missed and feelings of exclusion surmount. In such cases, a special school, where everyone knows how to sign, can allow for more chances to participate in sports, extracurricular activities, and even class discussions. Here are some important points to remember about making education responsive to the individual needs of the student:

community-based instruction
Functional and vocational skills are taught in real life situations

- Identification procedures must be systematic and cautious.
- Decisions about special education services must be individually determined and tailor-made to match the needs of each student with disabilities.
- No single answer to service or program decisions are possible for all students with disabilities.
- An array of services must be available.
- The intensity and duration varies according to the needs of each student.

Increased Accessibility

People with disabilities are experiencing in-creased accessibility to society and to education. Quite likely, improved access to education results in improvements in daily life, where and how one lives and works, and community presence in general. So being accessible to an appropriate education that prepares individuals to achieve to their potential is important. However, while access to American society is a goal for all individuals with disabilities, and receiving a free appropriate education is a right of all students with disabilities, exclusive participation in the general education curriculum may not be an appropriate goal for every student with a disability. Clearly, however, it is for the vast majority. One reason is that success in the general education curriculum is the path to high school graduation and attaining a standard high school diploma. It can be a ticket to better jobs, higher earnings, and college attendance.

Because NCLB requires higher standards for high school graduation, many states now offer students with disabilities many diploma options, making it almost impossible to determine how well students with disabilities are faring along this dimension (Burdette, 2007). It is safe to assume, however, that more of them are graduating from high school. Here is why this is probably a safe conclusion: College participation is clearly on the rise, with some 11% of college students reporting a disability (National Center for Education Statistics, 2008). Therefore, consensus exists among parents, policymakers, and advocates that more students with disabilities should leave school with a standard diploma (U.S. Department of Education, 2006). To do so, more of them must access the general education curriculum and be part of the accountability measures (e.g., state- and districtwide tests) that monitor all students' progress. What IDEA '04 Says About Access to the General Education Curriculum highlights some key points about such participation.

For a relative few students with disabilities, to achieve the goals of community presence and access to society requires intensive instruction in targets that are not part of the general education curriculum. Remember, IDEA insists on a balance of FAPE and LRE. In some cases, FAPE means that the general education curriculum is not appropriate. Some students with disabilities require an alternative curriculum, intensive treatment, or supplemental instruction on topics not available or suitable for instruction in the general education classroom. Here are a few examples of such individualized programs that might require removal from the general education setting and reduced access to its curriculum: orientation and mobility training for blind students, learning job skills in community placements, learning how to use public transportation, physical therapy for a student with cerebral palsy, speech therapy for a student with a stuttering problem, and so on. Remember, placement issues, LRE, access to the general education curriculum, and alternative curricular options are not mutually exclusive. Each can be in effect for part of the school day, school week, or the school year. So, in some countries, like Italy, inclusion only in the general education curriculum is considered "the right thing to do," even though research findings support the practice of having other curricular options available (Begeny & Martens, 2007).

Data-Based Practices

evidence- or data-based practices Thoroughly researched, validated, proven effective through evidence or years of clinical practice

With the passage of NCLB in 2001 and IDEA in 2004, emphasis has been placed on teachers applying **evidence- or data-based practices** (sometimes referred to as scientifically based practices). These interventions or teaching tactics have been proven effective through systematic and rigorous research. Special education can be defined, in part, by its practices. In some ways, these practices distinguish special education from general education. When a student with disabilities needs intensive intervention on a particular topic or skill, that is the time to put a validated practice into action. Although any teacher (general educator, special educator, or paraprofessional) can successfully implement such interventions, many of these methods differ in various ways (such as focusing on the individual instead of the group or targeting mastery of skills rather than understanding process) from the methods generally used with typical learners. Special education methods are more intensive and supportive than those used for students without learning problems. What you will notice is that many of these proven interventions share six common features (Deshler, 2003; Torgeson, 1996). That is, effective special education can be thought of as

- *validated:* uses practices proved effective through research;
- *individually determined:* matches teaching procedures to individuals;
- *explicit:* applies interventions directly to content and skills;
- *strategic:* helps students apply methods to guide their learning;
- *sequential:* builds upon previous mastery; and
- *accountable:* monitors effectiveness of instruction by evaluating students' progress frequently and systematically.

In recent years, there has been a call for teachers and administrators to use evidenced-based practices (a) with students with exceptionalities who are currently receiving special education services and (b) within the context of a multitiered model of preventions (e.g., response to intervention [RTI] models and positive behavior supports [PBS] models) to determine which students in fact need special education services. (You will learn more about these innovative approaches across the text.) Therefore, it is very important that teachers have training in how to identify which practices are actually "evidence or data based" and then how to implement these practices in their classrooms (Lane, 2007).

A variety of criteria are now available to help teachers evaluate practices to determine if they meet the rigorous criteria set forth by the research community (e.g., Gersten et al., 2005; Horner et al., 2005). In addition, Web sites such as the What Works Clearinghouse, http://ies.ed.gov/ncee/wwc, lists practices the group has determined have been proven through scientifically sound research, and it therefore supports the use of these practices.

Once teachers select evidence-based practices to implement, the next step is to use these practices at the school site in such a way that a balance is achieved between scientific rigor and feasibility (Lane, 2007). For example, it is important that the intervention is put in place as planned (with treatment integrity) and data be collected to monitor student progress. Yet, at the same time, it is important that the teacher or other interventionist receive support with the initial implementation and that the data collection procedures are reasonable in light of the multiple task demands.

Frequent Monitoring of Progress

As just mentioned, special educators must be accountable for the effectiveness of the services and instruction they deliver. The unique learning needs of students with disabilities often mean that the results of even the most proven practices might not produce the gains in learning or changes in behavior that are desired. In other words, even though practices and instruction implemented are proven through rigorous and systematic research, they are not uniformly effective. Therefore, teachers must be continually informed about the effectiveness of their instruction. For this reason, teachers use **progress monitoring**—a set of evaluation procedures that assess the effectiveness of instruction on skills while they are being taught. The four key features of this approach are that students' educational progress is measured

- directly on skills of concern,
- systematically,
- consistently, and
- frequently.

progress monitoring
Systematically and frequently assessing students' improvement directly on the skills being taught

Although all effective teachers know how well their instructional procedures are working and how well their students are responding to the challenges of the curriculum, one hallmark of special education may well be the continuous monitoring of student progress. Some of these students participate in progress monitoring every day at school on almost every subject that they are learning. For these reasons, we introduce you to various forms of progress monitoring in several chapters of this text and feature one version, curriculum-based measurement, in the Closer Look at Data-Based Practice feature found in Chapter 5. You can also learn more about progress monitoring by visiting www.studentprogress.org.

When teachers frequently monitor students' progress in learning academic tasks, they can immediately differentiate their instruction to improve their instruction and their students' results.

collaboration Professionals working in partnerships to provide educational services

co-teaching Team teaching; special education and general education teachers working in partnership in the general education classroom

Collaborative Teams

Special education is truly special when its key features are put into place. **Collaboration** is one of those key features. It is a necessary ingredient when multidisciplinary teams of professionals work together to respond to the unique learning needs of students with disabilities. No education professional should work in isolation, particularly those working with the greatest academic gifts and talents or who are sometimes thought of as the most "difficult to teach," those who need the most intensive instruction and assistance (Friend & Bursuck, 2006). In all cases, general and special educators come together to design and implement response education programs. Collaboration is essential for success.

For students who receive special education services, teams of professionals, including those from related services, come together to form a truly special education for each student with a disability. For example, one student might receive speech therapy services from a speech/language pathologist (SLP), physical therapy from a physical therapist, and follow-through assistance from a paraprofessional. These professionals work together on behalf of this student. Another team with different expertise might form a different team for another student. Every chapter addresses collaboration. Because of the important role of related service providers, the services they provide and the teamwork they inspire are also featured in every chapter. For now, we are just reminding you that the collaboration of multidisciplinary teams of professionals is often necessary to meet the special needs of students with disabilities and their families.

One outgrowth of collaboration of general and special education teachers who work in inclusive settings is a concept called *co-teaching*. The idea is that teachers, working together in the same classroom, form partnerships to provide greater expertise and supports to all students (Scruggs, Mastropieri, & McDuffie, 2007). The practice is gaining in popularity because of national credentialing standards for special education high school teachers, requiring them to be highly qualified in every subject area in which they teach (Rice et al., 2007). However, there are some cautions about co-teaching, and education professionals working together should be alert to potential pitfalls. Too often, roles are not equal, and the special education teacher is relegated to an assistant (Harbort et al., 2007). The result is loss of talent and knowledge that students with and without disabilities would find beneficial.

For now, a final commentary about the practice of co-teaching: Some groups of students would rather receive special education services outside the general education classroom (Leafstedt et al., 2007). Students with learning disabilities often report that the teaching styles of special education teachers match their learning styles better and provide more appropriate accommodations than general educators. These students also are concerned about how their peers perceive their special needs.

Astute educators can address and respond to concerns about co-teaching, and when it is applied, it is done so where everyone benefits.

Another key person in the collaborative effort at every school is the school principal (DiPaola & Walther-Thomas, 2003; Rodríguez, Gentilucci, & Sims, 2005). Because principals often coordinate management efforts at their site, they can be most helpful in developing and ensuring the delivery of accommodations and adaptions (particularly for large-scale assessments), in monitoring the variety of services indicated on a student's IEP, and in coordinating services throughout the school and across the district. They bring the expertise at their school together; allowing time for collaboration and ensuring that every student receives instruction necessary to meet their learning needs.

Emerging Trends: Differentiating for All

The entire educational system is shifting the way it delivers instruction to all students—whether they have disabilities; struggle to learn; are typical learners; or are gifted, talented, and creative. The idea is that by **differentiating instruction** for all students, when any student requires more intensive instruction, it is readily in place to be put into action. Also, not all students—those with or without disabilities as well as those with or without special gifts and talents—learn in the same way. Different approaches to learning should be available so that differences in learning styles, culture, and need for supports are available. Figure 1.3 illustrates how almost all students at school can benefit from an instructional model that differentiates instruction along a continuum by using less intensive supports and instruction for most students and more intensive services for the few who need them most. When the instructional needs of a group of learners are met early, they struggle less and across time require less specialized instruction.

Many of the latest innovations in education build upon the concepts and fundamental principles of differentiation—adjusting curriculum, services, and instruction to meet the needs of learners. For most students, these adjustments or adaptations are minor. Not only students with disabilities are supported, but all students who struggle or whose learning needs are not met through high-quality general education instruction. For example, gifted students who do not need basic instruction on a particular topic are allowed and encouraged to study in more depth, while students with disabilities may study content that has been adapted or modified. Next, we present two broad areas—technology integration and multitiered intervention—as examples of innovations that apply the trend to support all learners by making supports universally available.

differentiating instruction
Adjusting instruction to meet the needs and learning styles of individuals or groups of learners

Figure 1.3 • A Differentiating Instruction Continuum

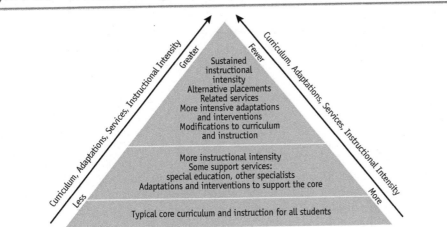

Source: From *Teaching Students with Special Needs in Inclusive Settings,* by D. P. Bryant, D. D. Smith, & B. Bryant, 2008, (p. 203.), Boston: Allyn & Bacon. Reprinted with permission.

Technology Integration

Technology advancements are allowing more and more students to access the general education curriculum and society. More students with disabilities receive all or most of their education in the general education classroom, accessing the general education curriculum (OSEP, 2008). Technology can help "level the playing field" for students with special needs, those with and those without disabilities.

Earlier in this chapter, you learned about ADA and how one major concept embedded in that law seeks to remove barriers that restrict participation in daily life. Taken from the concepts of universal design, **universal design for learning (UDL)** adapts the curriculum so that more students can access it (Hitchcock & Stahl, 2003; Peters & Bill, 2004). While ADA requires that the physical environment be made more accessible by removing barriers that inhibit people with disabilities from participating in events and activities of daily life, UDL seeks to remove barriers in the curriculum through technology (Center for Applied Special Technology [CAST], 2006; for more about UDL, visit www.cast.org). Here's an example: IDEA '04 requires every state to adopt the **National Instructional Materials Accessibility Standard (NIMAS)** so that electronic versions of texts are readily available, allowing for those who need print to be enlarged, a braille version, or voice outputs to be immediately produced through commonly available computers (OSEP, 2006).

IDEA '04 requires that technology be considered during the development of individualized programs for each student with a disability. Congress acknowledged that assistive technology services and equipment can be a critical component of daily life for many students when it passed the Assistive Technology Act you learned about earlier in this chapter (Sopko, 2008). Remember, assistive technology (AT) has a range of services and equipment, some simple and some complex. AT includes wheelchairs, devices to help turn pages in a book, as well as computers. For these reasons, we discuss assistive technology again in Chapter 2 and have devoted a section in each of the following chapters to technology and how it makes a difference in the lives of students with disabilities. Now let's turn our attention to a trend that is sweeping the nation: multitiered instruction.

Multitiered Instruction

Described as a "sea change," **multitiered instruction** is a landmark shift in philosophy about how struggling students should be supported (Fuchs & Young, 2006). Multitiered instruction and intervention is changing how educators think about some kinds of disabilities. It is also redefining educators' roles in prevention and in reducing the impact of a disability by intervening early, long before many students are formally identified as having a disability. The concept also is being applied to help students learn social skills (Fairbanks et al., 2007). And, it is helping all students struggling to learn the core skills of reading and mathematics (Fuchs, Fuchs, & Vaughn, 2008).

Multitiered intervention provides tiers of increasingly intensive supports to students with and without disabilities and is grounded in the principles of differentiated instruction (Sandomierski, Kincaid, & Algozzine, 2008). For behavior, **positive behavior support (PBS)** seeks to prevent inappropriate behavior by helping *all* students learn and use expected classroom behaviors with three levels of increasingly intensive supports of instruction and reinforcement (Center on Positive Behavioral Interventions and Supports, 2007; Severson et al., 2007). Chapter 7 provides more information about PBS. **Response to intervention (RTI)** uses a conceptually comparable system to help students learn basic academic skills (Fuchs & Deshler, 2007; Fuchs et al., 2008). One purpose of RTI is to provide help to those who struggle as soon as possible (California Teachers Association, 2007). Chapter 5 provides more information about RTI and academic instruction.

One very important idea at the core of multitiered instruction is that when students receive assistance *early,* problems can be either corrected or minimized (Division for Learning Disabilities, 2007). In some cases, disabilities can even be prevented,

universal design for learning (UDL) Typically by using technology increases access to the curriculum and instruction for all students

National Instructional Materials Accessibility Standard (NIMAS) Assists states in providing accessible or e-versions of textbooks to students with disabilities; called out in IDEA '04

multitiered instruction Differentiating instruction for behavior, social skills, or academic areas to intervene early, prevent disabilities, and support struggling learners with and without disabilities

positive behavior support A three-tiered model of support with progressively more intensive levels of intervention

response to intervention (RTI) A multitiered prereferral method of increasingly intensive interventions; used to identify "nonresponders" or students with learning disabilities

or the need for special education services can be avoided. Whether for students with challenging behaviors or struggling to learn basic academic skills, high-quality instruction is the foundation for *all* learners, and progressively intensive instruction and help is brought to the students whose performance in the classroom so indicates. Figure 1.4 illustrates the idea that many students, some 80%, from time to time may need some extra help to meet classroom behavioral expectations or to master core academic skills. And, fewer and fewer students need additional intensive services to meet their learning needs. Students at the top of the triangle require individualized and sustained supports and interventions—those available through special education.

Although many support the idea that PBS and RTI have three tiers or levels, some schools have increased the number of levels so that students receive more help before actual referral to special education occurs. Regardless of the number of tiers, here's the basic idea of these early intervention, prevention approaches:

- *Universal screening:* All students are assessed.
- *Tier 1:* All students receive high-quality instruction on either basic or core academic skills or social skills all students are expected to use.
- *Tier 2:* Groups of students whose performance in Tier 1, as documented through data collected on the behaviors and skills of concern, indicate need for additional supports and instruction receive additional help through general education; their progress is carefully monitored, and data-based practices are implemented in an attempt to resolve students' problems.
- *Tier 3:* Individual students, whose direct classroom performance so indicates insufficient progress, receive more intensive and individualized intervention, usually through the auspices of special education.

To learn more about PBS, explore the wealth of information at the federally supported technical assistance center www.pbis.org housed at the University of Oregon. For more information about response to intervention, the government supports a center at the American Institute for Research in Washington, DC. Information is available at www.rti4success.org. These new innovative approaches are improving the results of all students, including those with disabilities. Our hope is that you will join the ranks of new education professionals, whether in general education, in special education or its related services, and use the tools we describe in this text to make a difference in the lives of students with disabilities and their families.

Figure 1.4 • Multitiered Prevention and Early Intervening Services

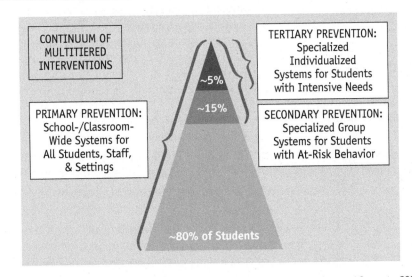

Source: Adapted from *What Is School-Wide PBS?* Center on Positive Behavioral Interventions and Supports, 2007, University of Oregon, www.pbs.org/schoolwide.htm. Used by permission.

Summary

After centuries of neglect, exclusion, inconsistent treatment, and restrictions to their participation at school and in the community, people with disabilities are taking their places alongside classmates, coworkers, teammates, and neighborhood friends. Adults with disabilities are seeing physical and social barriers being reduced, so they have better chances of having successful careers, choosing from a wide selection of leisure-time activities, and living independently. Today's students with disabilities have access to an array of services, instructional techniques, and curricula that support each and every individual so that all will achieve their potential.

Answering the Chapter Objectives

1. What are the different perspectives that are often applied to "disabilities"?

   - *Deficit perspective:* People are distributed along a continuum; the majority fall in the middle of any distribution (i.e., normal or bell-shaped curve); they are called "average"; those below average are somehow deficient or less than their classmates.
   - *Cultural perspective:* Various cultures often hold many different values and concepts that differ greatly from mainstream ideas; not all cultures think about disabilities in terms of deficits or make quantitative judgments about individuals; no single orientation or fixed definition of disability exists; an individual may be thought of as having a disability in one culture but not in another.
   - *Sociological perspective:* Differences across people's skills and traits are thought to be socially constructed, people's attitudes and the way society treats groups of individuals create disabilities; *all* people have strengths and weaknesses; *all* people should get the supports they need without judgments.

2. How are the civil rights of people with disabilities protected?

   - Attitudes and public opinion are encouraged that do not tolerate injustices or cruel and inhumane treatment of others.
   - Legislation (national and state laws) provides individuals with disabilities, both students and adults, with legal protections.
   - Litigation and court decisions clarify the laws that protect individuals' rights (e.g., free appropriate education, barrier-free environments, no discrimination in the workplace, right to vote).

3. Why did Congress pass IDEA in 1975 and its ensuing reauthorizations?

   - To correct injustices that occurred before the original passage of IDEA

     - Only 12% of children with disabilities received special education services (1948).
     - Only 16 states had mandatory education laws (1962).
     - One million U.S. children with disabilities were excluded entirely from the public school system.
     - Over four million students with disabilities were receiving inappropriate educational services.
     - Needs of children and their families were not being met.
     - Effective special education and related services guaranteeing FAPE in the LRE possible can meet these children's needs.
   - To add needed services
     - For infants and toddlers
     - For the successful transition to adult life
   - To qualify conditions as eligible for special services or to change conditions from one category to another
     - Added traumatic brain injury (TBI) as a separate special education category (changed from "other health impairments")
     - Added autism as a separate special education category (changed from "other health impairments")
     - Added ADHD to "other health impairments"
   - To permit, encourage, or require delivery of specific services
     - Behavior intervention plans
     - Functional behavioral assessments
     - Multitiered intervention and instruction (i.e., positive behavior supports, response to intervention)

4. What are the key features of "people first" language?

   - Put people first.
   - Do not make the person equal or be the disability.
   - *Disabled* is *not* a noun.
   - People with disabilities are neither victims nor wheelchair bound.

5. What are the defining features of effective special education programs?

- Special education is
  - *validated:* uses practices proved effective through research;
  - *individually determined:* matches teaching procedures to individuals;
  - *explicit:* applies interventions directly to content and skills;
  - *strategic:* helps students apply methods to guide their learning;
  - *sequential:* builds upon previous mastery;
  - *accountable:* monitors effectiveness of instruction by evaluating students' progress frequently and systematically.

Special education services make a difference when they are

- *responsive:* meet each student's unique and individual learning needs;
- *accessible:* make society and appropriate education available in the least restrictive environment possible;
- *data based:* use proven practices and instruction;
- *monitored frequently:* assess directly student growth and learning on a continuous basis (e.g., daily, weekly, monthly);
- *collaborative:* build upon partnerships of educators and multidisciplinary team members.

myeducationlab Now go to MyEducationLab at www.myeducationlab.com and take the Self-Assessment to gauge your initial comprehension of chapter content. Once you have taken the Self-Assessment, use your individualized Study Plan for Chapter 1 to enhance your understanding of the concepts discussed in the chapter.

Council for Exceptional Children **ADDRESSING THE PROFESSIONAL STANDARDS**

Council for Exceptional Children (CEC) knowledge standards addressed in this chapter:

CC1K8, CC1K5, CC1056, CC1K1, CC1K4, CC1K2, CC7S1

Appendix A: CEC Knowledge and Skill Standards Common Core has a full listing of the standards listed here.

Appendix B: CEC Knowledge and Skill Common Core Standards and Associated Subcategories are broken down by chapter.

CHAPTER 2

Individualized Special Education Programs

Planning and Delivering Services

Imagine a World . . .

where all children receive an
appropriate education . . .

Chapter Objectives

After studying this chapter, you will be able to

1. Explain how six specific, yet general, approaches support students' improved performance in the general education curriculum.

2. Discuss each special education service delivery option.

3. Describe special education's related services and how multidisciplinary teams are formed.

4. Explain each step in the IEP process.

5. Describe each type of individualized education plan and its purpose.

 *Henri de Toulouse-Lautrec,* born into a noble French family, was closely related to the royal families of France and England. His childhood was privileged but also tragic. Probably due to a hereditary condition, he had a speech impairment and was frail. He was highly intelligent but missed months of school. His bones were weak, and he used a wheelchair for many long periods during his childhood. Early on, Lautrec retreated to painting and became highly productive and successful. However, because of his disabilities, his adult life was often in turmoil and plagued by alcoholism.

myeducationlab After reading this chapter, complete the Self-Assessment for Chapter 2 on MyEducationLab to gauge your initial understanding of chapter content.

Individuals with disabilities require a very specialized education if they are to achieve to their potential and reach their dreams of happy and productive lives. For some, this specialized education is truly unique, including instructional targets that teach personal independence and community presence. For most, it means accessing the general education curriculum with whatever supports and accommodations necessary for them to master the content and develop skills along with their classmates without disabilities. Special education is individualized. It may include one-on-one instruction, but most often individualized merely means that the skills and abilities of each learner with a disability are considered, as instruction is tailor-made for each individual.

Individualized education is what can make the real difference in the long-term results of people with disabilities. Goals that reflect high yet realistic expectations lead to real community presence and participation, meaningful careers, independence, and maximal achievement. How are these goals, tailored to each student's abilities and needs, determined and attained? The paths taken by educators, individual students with disabilities, and their families are planned and charted through the individualized special education process. Individualized programs are the heart of the process, guaranteeing every infant, toddler, and student with a disability and their families services and supports essential to successful school experiences. The cornerstones that guarantee an appropriate education in the least restrictive environment (LRE) to each student with a disability are

- *individualized family service plans* (IFSPs) for infants and toddlers,
- *individual education programs* (IEPs) for schoolchildren,
- *statements of transitional services* for adolescents, and
- *behavioral intervention plans* for those whose disabilities present challenging behaviors.

All education professionals must know the key components or essential features of special education because the responsibility for these individuals' education belongs to all of us. So, let's first think about ways to help students with disabilities participate successfully in general education; then turn our attention to special education's services, settings, and personnel; and finally learn about the plans that put special education's services and supports into action.

Access to the General Education Curriculum

Special education is part of a system that begins with effective and high-quality general education and provides a series of safety nets that support students with disabilities who struggle learning the standard curriculum. Today, many approaches are available to support students, those with and without disabilities, as they access and learn the content of the general education curriculum. New principles and practices can and do make real differences, such as intervening early when students begin to struggle learning the skills and content presented in the general education class. They also assist in the prevention of disabilities, with their early identification, and in providing needed special education services to those in need. Figure 2.1 shows how some concepts like universal design for learning help all students, while other supports such as assistive technology are designed for only a few. Systematic application of increasingly intensive supports can result in more individuals accessing the general education curriculum successfully and thus achieving their individualized goals. Let's first consider ways educators can help all students better access the general education curriculum by first laying the foundation with a high-quality education.

High-Quality General Education

myeducationlab Go to the Building Teaching Skills and Dispositions section in Chapter 2 of MyEducationLab and complete the activities in the IRIS Module "Accessing the General Educational Curriculum: Inclusion Considerations for Students with Disabilities." This module highlights classroom considerations that promote access to the general educational curriculum for students with disabilities.

An effective general education program is the foundation for positive special education services, when they are needed, because it

- uses data-based instructional procedures,
- supports students who struggle,

- prevents unnecessary referrals,
- welcomes students with disabilities,
- provides access to the general education curriculum, and
- follows through with individualized plans and interventions.

Knowledge about proven educational practices for both typical learners and those with disabilities is mounting. As you will learn throughout this text, research findings and information about data-based practices should inform instruction because they prevent school failure and reduce the number of referrals to special education (McMaster et al., 2005).

Universal Design for Learning

As you learned in Chapter 1, universal design provides people with disabilities greater access to the community and the workplace by removing or reducing barriers found in the environment. These principles, first outlined in the Americans with Disabilities Act (ADA), require that the physical environment be made more accessible. Removing barriers is necessary for people with disabilities to participate more fully in events and activities of daily life, but it provides universal benefits as well. For example, curb cuts and ramps allow people who use wheelchairs to use sidewalks, cross streets, and move independently as they shop or get from a parking lot to a restaurant to meet friends. But, curb cuts also help mothers with strollers walk through neighborhoods, people with shopping carts get from the grocery store to their cars, and skateboarders roll easily from sidewalks to cross streets. Universal design has countless benefits for everyone, not just people who face challenges from the physical environment. Doors are easier to open when handles push down instead of turning. Think of other ways life is easier for everyone because of the ADA law.

Now, the concept of universal design is being applied to instruction and access to the general education curriculum (Samuels, 2007). In the broadest sense, applying principles of universal design to instruction seeks to remove barriers any individual might face when participating in instructional activities (Center for Applied Special Technology [CAST], 2007). This extension and application of the principles of universal design is called **universal design for learning (UDL)**. It is a way to help *all* students, not just those with disabilities, approach

universal design for learning (UDL) Increases access to the curriculum and instruction for all students

Figure 2.1 • Supporting All Students' Access to the General Education Curriculum

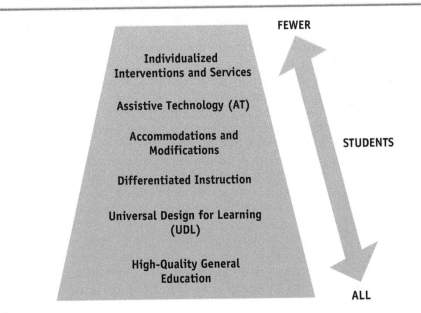

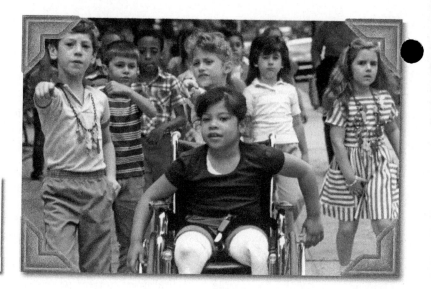

In Chapter 1, you saw a photo of how curb cuts help everyone move around more easily. Here you see how removing barriers makes it possible for those who use wheelchairs to cross streets with their classmates.

the curriculum in nonstandard ways. What IDEA '04 Says About Universal Design for Learning highlights how these principles are applied to students' education. Although there are many applications, most often, UDL has technology at the core of its solution to finding increased ways for students to approach and participate in instruction (CAST, 2007; Whitbread, 2004). Here are some key features of UDL:

- It creates alternatives open to all students.
- It is part of the standard delivery of instruction, not added to instruction.
- It provides multiple and flexible options for presentation, expression, and engagement.

One goal of UDL is for more students to be able to access the content of instruction, thereby reducing the number of students who need special accommodations and supports. This goal is accomplished by creating multiple pathways for students to access the curriculum and the learning environment (CAST, 2007). Here's a common application of UDL. Current technology allows publishers to produce **e-books**, electronic or digital versions of traditionally printed books, easily and inexpensively. Because of these electronic (digital) versions, print does not have to be the only way to access content presented in books. For students with visual impairments or print disabilities, the computer can be used to immediately enlarge the size of the print, convert to braille, or to change its mode of access from seeing to listening. Students no longer have to wait for a manually produced braille version to come from some centralized resource center. The benefits are great for many. A science text might be "heard" instead of "read" by those (e.g., students with learning disabilities, English learners) who find the reading level too challenging to comprehend the content. Also, because the burden of supplying digital versions of textbooks is no longer substantial, IDEA '04 requires publishers to make digital versions of their textbooks available to school districts whose states sign up with the National Instructional Materials Access Center (Müller & Burdette, 2007; NIMAS Development and Technical Assistance Center, 2007). Use your imagination and see how many applications of UDL you can create to solve challenges associated with access to the curriculum, extra curricular activities, environment, and

e-books Electronic versions of textbooks allowing for the application of universal design for learning

What IDEA '04 Says About . . .

Universal Design for Learning

Products or services developed under the concept of universal design may be used

- by people with the widest possible range of functional capabilities;
- with or without assistive technologies;
- when developing and administering student assessments;
- to maximize access to the general education curriculum.

community. Each new idea can make a world of difference for many more students who struggle, including those with disabilities!

Differentiated Instruction

Even when the instruction is of high quality and UDL features are applied, many students, those with and without disabilities, struggle when learning the general education curriculum when standard methods are used. General education teachers use **differentiated instruction** to help all struggling students. With this approach, students are all learning the same content, but different instructional methods are applied that better match their different learning needs, preferences, and styles. In other words, instruction is adjusted in response to individuals' readiness, interests, strengths, and struggles (Haager & Klingner, 2005; Hoover & Patton, 2004; Tomlinson et al., 2003). Differentiation can be accomplished in four general ways (Bryant, Smith, & Bryant, 2008), through variations in the following:

differentiated instruction
Providing an individualized array of instructional interventions

- *Instructional activity:* Different types of instruction are provided to small groups of students who continue to struggle when high-quality instruction was not effective.
- *Instructional content:* A portion or chunks of the lesson's content is taught and mastered by initially focusing on a small amounts of information (e.g., the "times 5" multiplication facts are taught separately and first, then combined with the "times 6" facts).
- *Instructional delivery:* Flexible grouping practices that include either same-ability groups or mixed-ability groups allow the pace of instruction to differ and students to complement each other's strengths as they solve problems or complete assignments.
- *Instructional materials:* Different types of materials or adjustments to current materials are made (e.g., fewer practice items; content formatted to emphasize key points; technology or learning aides such as manipulatives and graphics added to support instruction).

Instructional Accommodations and Modifications

Most students with disabilities require some **accommodations**, as they complete the same assignments or tests. Whether they qualify for special education or for extra assistance through Section 504 (see Chapter 1 for a review), these students because of their disabilities require more adjustments to standard instructional routines than differentiating instruction can provide. So that their disabilities do not mask their learning, some of these students require many supports; others only a few. Most require only simple changes in elements such as timing, formatting, setting, scheduling, response, or presentations. But it is very important for all educators to remember: Do not make assumptions about individuals or groups of students with disabilities; they differ on the types and extent of adjustments they need (Soukup et al., 2007). Here are a few examples of accommodations:

accommodations Supports to compensate for disabilities; adjustments to assignments or tests

myeducationlab Go to the Activities and Applications section in Chapter 2 of MyEducationLab and complete Activity 1. As you watch the video and answer the accompanying questions, think about how the testing modifications discussed could be implemented in the classroom.

- Enlarged text
- Sign language interpreter
- Audio versions of books
- Braille
- Removing extraneous details from worksheets
- Word processors

For some students with disabilities, accommodations are not sufficient. They require more adjustments or **modifications**, where assignments or tests are reduced or altered. In these situations, students may be required to master fewer objectives or may be asked to provide only specific parts of answers. In some cases, they may be given alternative assignments (e.g., posters or photo essays instead of written reports).

modifications Adjustments to assignments or tests, reducing the requirements

Assistive Technology

An assistive technology device

- is an object, piece of equipment, or product system;
- can be purchased commercially, modified, or customized;
- is used to improve, increase, or maintain the skills of a child with a disability;
- does not include any surgically implanted medical device or its replacement.

Assistive technology services include the provision of

- a functional evaluation of student needs in the school setting;
- the assistive technology device for the child;
- support for the use of the device (e.g., selection, fitting, repair, replacement);
- coordination of other necessary services and use of the assistive technology device;
- training on the device for the child, family members, and education professionals, as appropriate.

assistive technology (AT) Equipment (devices) or services to help compensate for an individual's disabilities

low-tech devices Simple assistive technology devices such as communication boards, homemade cushions, or a classroom railing

high-tech devices Complex assistive technology devices that use computers or computer chips

Assistive Technology

For many students with disabilities, universal design features, differentiated instruction, together with accommodations and modifications, still are not sufficient for success. Advancements in a variety of technologies range from simple to complex and help compensate for disabilities. As you can see from the information found in What IDEA '04 Says About Assistive Technology, **assistive technology (AT)** is *both* equipment and a special education–related service, which is guaranteed through IDEA '04. We often associate technology with something that is complex or for students with multiple-severe disabilities. Such, however, is not the case, particularly for AT (Bryant & Bryant, 2003; Marino, Marino, & Shaw, 2006). AT equipment can be **low tech**, being as simple as a rubber band wrapped around a pencil so a student can more easily use it to write or stands designed for those without the necessary strength to hold books. AT can also be **high tech**, being technically complex to allow those who cannot speak to participate in conversations with friends and join in question-and-answer sessions in class through electronic speech devices. Table 2.1 gives some examples of how instructional areas can be supported with low-tech and high-tech AT options (Demchak & Greenfield, 2003; King-Sears & Evmenova, 2007). When a student's IEP indicates a student needs a specific type of equipment to benefit from instruction, that device becomes one of the accommodations to the learning situation the student must receive. However, not every device you can think of is considered as assistive technology by IDEA '04. For example, IDEA '04 clarified for school districts and families that costs for the follow-up and maintenance of surgically implanted medical devices, such as cochlear implants, are not the responsibility of the schools (Kravetz, 2005).

Individualized Data-Based Interventions and Services

One can think about assistance to students who struggle, those with and those without disabilities, as a series of increasingly intensive interventions and supports. Some of these interventions and services, however, are exclusively for students with disabilities who have qualified for special education services. Here's how the logic or sequence works:

- High-quality general education, universal design for learning techniques, and differentiated instruction help *all* students profit from the general education curriculum and its content.

Table 2.1 • Examples of Low- and High-Tech Assistive Technology

Instructional Area	Low-Tech Example	High-Tech Example
Communication	Picture (communication) board	Voice output device
Writing	Pencil with rubber band grip	Spell checker software
Mathematics	Clocks with large numbers	Calculator
Reading	Book holder	E-text
Study skills	Color-coded files	Electronic graphic organizers

- Accommodations and modifications help students with disabilities, those who qualify for special education services or have their special needs met through Section 504.
- AT and other related services are offered through special education.
- Individualized, tailor-made instructional programs offer data-based interventions and services.

At this last step, highly qualified special education teachers design, implement, coordinate, and monitor each student's progress in tailor-made programs. In Chapter 1, you learned about the importance of being a good consumer of research, critical in your acceptance and use of instructional practices. Throughout the rest of this text, you will learn about instructional methods and interventions that have been developed for or validated specifically with students with disabilities. Special education can be and is special for students whose needs can be great. However, this is only true when data-based practices that have the highest probability of success are implemented. For too long, many parents and professionals have believed that assignment to special education too often includes low expectations, locking students into a curriculum that prohibits them from achieving their real potential (Obiakor & Ford, 2002). When special education services are needed, and when general educators and school leaders (e.g., principals) support those services, the results for students with disabilities are remarkable (Sataline, 2005)! We have just considered the foundation for special education; now let's think about what it is.

Settings, Services, and Personnel

Special education is an evolving concept: Its services and interventions continue to develop. Special education includes support and guidance for general educators, direct classroom instruction, as well as related services. Together, these services are meant to be flexible and responsive so that the unique needs of each student are met and all achieve their potential. Support varies in type, intensity, location, personnel, and duration. One way to think about special education and its related services is to envision a support system that contains a rich array of services consisting of components that are individually determined and applied. The term **array of services** means students do not have to travel, step by step, up and down a ladder of services and settings but rather have many selections available to them. For example, in some cases, with support from a consulting teacher or specialist (e.g., an SLP), the general education classroom can meet the needs of the student. In other cases, students require more intensive services from many different specialists. Intensive services might be required for a short period of time, or they may be needed across an entire educational experience. The models and approaches for providing an appropriate education to each and every infant, toddler, preschooler, and student with a disability are many. Let's consider the major approaches now.

array of services Constellation of special education services, personnel, and educational placements

Models for Inclusive Special Education

Remember, the word *inclusion* has many different meanings. To most people, inclusion means being able to attend a neighborhood school and participate as much as possible in the general education curriculum and in other activities alongside classmates without disabilities. To some, however, it means being provided a free appropriate education (FAPE) in a setting that guarantees opportunities for full participation. To a student who is Deaf and uses American Sign Language (ASL), the most inclusive setting may well be a residential school for the Deaf where everyone uses American Sign Language to communicate, rather than a general education class where no one is proficient signing. However, it is important to understand that some parents and educators believe that inclusive education must be delivered totally in the general education classroom.

General and special education teachers work side by side in the pull-in service delivery model.

continuum of services Describes each level of special education services as being more restrictive and coming in a lock-stepped sequence

pull-in programming Special education or related services delivering exclusively in the general education classroom

co-teaching General and special education teachers team teaching

consulting teacher Special education teachers serving as a resource to general education teachers

collaboration Professionals working in partnerships to provide educational services

Inclusive education (see Chapter 1 again for the introduction to this concept and its rationale) and the full inclusion model gained momentum toward the end of the last century. Regardless, IDEA '04 reinforces the idea of a **continuum of services**—services of increasing intensity and duration. This continuum includes a variety of alternatives and ways to deliver special education services. For example, **pull-in programming** is when special education and its related services are brought to the student exclusively in the general education classroom. In this model, speech services are delivered in the student's general education classroom rather than in another room. **Co-teaching**, another full inclusion model, is where general education and special education teachers team-teach (Friend & Cook, 2007; Magiera et al., 2005). They blend their expertise and work side by side to modify the curriculum, implement a variety of teaching strategies, and help students work with instructional materials.

When participating in the general education curriculum, most students, even those with mild disabilities, require some accommodations (e.g., extended time on the weekly math test) and possibly additional assistance from a classmate (e.g., peer tutoring). In such instances, the special education teacher often works as a **consulting teacher** who helps design services and supports that are implemented by the general educator. Typically, these two educators work as partners in close **collaboration**. Together, they might plan how the student with disabilities would have some help with note taking from a classmate. Whether attending the general education classroom setting all day long or for a substantial part of the school day, the hope for all is maximal integration and participation in typical school activities.

Intensive and Sustained Services and Supports

Remember, all disabilities are serious, requiring unique responses. While some students need special education services to succeed in only one area of the curriculum (e.g., reading), most require intensive special education services across many parts of the curriculum (e.g., math, reading, social studies, and science). And, some individuals require services beyond what one specialist or profession can provide. In such cases, a multidisciplinary team must be formed to address all of the students' needs. Some students' needs bring together many different disciplines (e.g., SLPs, audiologists, interpreters for the deaf, school counselors), while others have many different special education teachers (e.g., orientation and mobility teachers, vision experts who teach braille).

Special education is often a balance of intensive services that are followed up with sustained supports. So, first, a problem area is resolved through **explicit**

explicit instruction Directly instructing on the topic of concern

instruction, where the skills of concern are directly taught. Then, some accommodations or instructional supports (e.g., prompts to use a newly mastered strategy, corrective feedback regarding appropriate behavior) are arranged to ensure that continued progress is made and program continuity is achieved. Therefore, IDEA '04 requires that students' progress must be carefully monitored frequently, sometimes even daily, to ensure they continue learning at a sufficient pace. It is very common for students with disabilities to perform sporadically, needing additional intensive services, more accommodations, or new supports from time to time.

Setting and Grouping Options

As we just discussed, IDEA '04 insists that a continuum of increasingly intensive services be available to students with disabilities. Remember, there is no single answer to what comprises an appropriate education for students with disabilities. Although not always true, as the intensity of services increases, the setting for their delivery changes, and most believe those are more restrictive. Table 2.2 describes

Table 2.2 • Service Delivery Options			
Type	**Description**	**Government Category**	**Government Criterion**
Pull-in programming (full inclusion)	All special education and related services are brought to the student in the general education classroom setting.	Regular (general education) class	No separate government category exists. Although all services are delivered in the general education classroom, placement data are reflected in the "less than 21%" category.
Co-teaching	General education and special education teachers teach together in the same classroom for the entire school day. Students may be "pulled out" for related services.	Regular (general education) class	No separate government category exists. Although all services are delivered in the general education classroom, placement data are reflected in the "less than 21%" category.
Consultation/ collaborative teaching	General education and special education teachers work together to meet the needs of students with special needs. Students are seldom removed from the general education class.	Regular (general education) class	Students receive special education and related services outside the general education class for less than 21% of the school day.
Itinerant or consultative services	The teacher and/or student receives assistance from a specialist who may serve many students at many schools.	Regular (general education) class	Students receive special education and related services outside the general education class for less than 21% of the school day.
Resource room (pullout programming)	Student attends a regular class most of the day but goes to a special education class several hours per day or for blocks of time each week.	Resource room	Includes students who receive special education and related services for at least 21% and not more than 60% of their school day.
Special education class (partially self-contained)	Student attends a special class but is integrated into regular education classes for a considerable amount of time each day.	Separate class	Students receive special education for more than 60% of their day, outside of the general education classroom.
Special education class (self-contained)	Student attends a special class most of the school day and is included in regular education activities minimally.	Separate class	Students receive special education for more than 60% of their day, outside of the general education classroom.
Special education schools (center schools)	Center schools—some private, others supported by the state—typically serve only students with a specific category of disability. Some offer residential services; others do not.	Public separate school facility; private separate school facility; public residential facility; private residential facility	Includes students who receive their education (a) in a separate day school, (b) in a public or private residential facility at public expense, (c) in a hospital setting, or (d) at home.

Figure 2.2 • The Challenge of Balancing FAPE and LRE

Achieving a balance between free appropriate public education and least restrictive environment can be difficult.

the placement options or settings typically used for the delivery of special education services.

LRE and FAPE are complex concepts. While some parents and professionals believe that LRE equals the general education classroom, others feel that LRE is to be balanced with FAPE (see Figure 2.2). Therefore, debate will continue about where students with disabilities should receive all or part of their education, and what are the best models for delivery of services. Regardless, it is important to recognize that few advocate only for fully inclusive settings or for fully segregated settings for any group of students. The guiding principle for placement decisions should be how a student can best access the general education curriculum, master academic targets, and develop life skills needed to succeed as independent adults. So, now let's think about what factors must be considered to balance LRE and FAPE.

Setting Options Almost *all* students with disabilities attend general education classes for a significant part of their school day, but most receive at least some of their special education services outside the general education setting. Let's look at some facts about where these students are educated. In the 2006–2007 school year, 95% of all students with disabilities—those with mild to moderate disabilities as well as those with severe disabilities—attended neighborhood schools (Office of Special Education Programs [OSEP], 2007). The participation rates for students with disabilities in general education classes have increased consistently over the years. Today, over half of all students with disabilities spend over 80% of their school day learning in the general education classroom. Compare today's data with those of years past, and think about how they reveal important trends about the inclusion of these students (National Center for Education Statistics [NCES], 2002; OSEP 2007; U.S. Department of Education, 2002):

- 1984–1985: Only about 25% of all students with disabilities attended general education classes for more than 80% of the school day.
- 1988–1989: This statistic increased to 31%.

- 1998–1999: It rose to 47%.
- 2006–2007: It then increased to 54%.

In addition to these statistics, it is important to know that participation rates, how much time students spend in any particular type of setting, vary greatly across states. In Vermont, for example, 71% of students with disabilities spend over 80% of their school day learning in the general education classroom, while in New Jersey that percentage is 41. Obviously, there is no single answer to the question "Which setting is most appropriate for the education of students with disabilities?" Clearly, it is not only students' characteristics that determine where they receive their special education. Beliefs and stereotypes must also play a role in placement decisions.

When students with disabilities are not receiving their education in the general education classroom, they use other settings, usually on the school site they are attending. **Pull-out programs** offer special education services and include resource rooms, partially self-contained special classes, and special therapy settings. The most common is the resource room where they receive intensive instruction, supports, tutoring, and assistance.

pull-out programs Providing special services outside the general education classroom

One type of setting should not be associated with a specific type of disability. For example, when you think of a student with intellectual disabilities, you should not connect that student with a self-contained classroom setting. Also, more restrictive settings (e.g., special schools) should not necessarily be associated with more severe situations. The assumption that a student with a severe disability is most appropriately served in a full-day special education classroom is just as inaccurate as concluding that another student with a moderate disability will profit maximally in the general education classroom. Make no assumptions about what is "right." For example, a student with a reading disability may need intensive and individualized reading instruction, available through special education services, in addition to the reading instruction delivered in the general education classroom—that is, until basic reading skills are mastered.

Students' age is often a factor considered when making placement decisions, with more younger students attending fully inclusive preschools than high school students attending fully inclusive secondary schools (OSEP, 2007). For example, many children with severe disabilities attend inclusive preschools, with parents universally positive about those experiences. However, as these students get older and their educational goals become more and more different from those of their peers without disabilities (e.g., life and vocational skills vs. preparation for college), specialized and more restrictive programs often become the preferred choice. Smaller classes, more specialized therapies and services, community-based learning opportunities, peer acceptance, and specialized teaching skills are available outside the general education setting.

Grouping Options Very rarely are students with disabilities grouped together exclusively by their disability label. Although students receiving special education services who are over the age of 9 must be identified as having at least one of the disabilities listed by IDEA '04, most states and school districts do not deliver educational services grouped by these special education categories. Instead, services are designed for students who share similar types of problems regardless of their disability. Such mixing of students with different types of disabilities is called **noncategorical** or **cross-categorical** special education. For example, students, regardless of their disability, who need to master learning strategies that help them study and remember academic content gleaned from high school science texts may be grouped. Or, students who need specific instruction on beginning reading skills might be grouped together. Considerable support exists for such grouping arrangements (Bryant et al., 2008; Fisher, Frey, & Thousand, 2003).

noncategorical or cross-categorical special education Special education services delivered by students' needs, not by their identified disability

Therefore, it is unusual today to find public school programs offered exclusively to students with one particular type of disability, such as classes for solely for students with intellectual disabilities.

Related Services and Providers

related services Special education services from a wide range of disciplines and professions

Related services are definitely a unique feature of special education, offering a wide range of services and expertise to students and their families. Many students with disabilities need help beyond that given through the partnership of general and special education. As you learned in Chapter 1, related services bring an important multidisciplinary component to special education services (Etzel-Wise & Mears, 2004; Neal, Bigby, & Nicolson, 2004). The three most commonly used related services are speech therapy, physical therapy, and assistive technology. IDEA '04 does not provide a precise list of related services, because its authors did not want to be too prescriptive; these services are to be determined by the exact needs of the individual. As Table 2.3 shows, related service

Table 2.3 • Examples of Related Service and Providers

Related Service	Explanation	Provider
Adaptive physical education (therapeutic recreation)	Assesses leisure function, provides therapeutic recreation and leisure education	Recreational therapist
Assistive technology	Assists with the selection, acquisition, or use of any item, piece of equipment, or product system used to enhance functional capabilities (assistive technology device)	Assistive technologist
Audiology services	Identifies and diagnoses hearing loss; determines proper amplification and fitting of hearing aids and other listening devices	Audiologist
Counseling services/ rehabilitative counseling	Provides psychological and guidance services, including career development and parent counseling, develops positive behavior intervention strategies	School counselor, social worker, psychologist, guidance counselor, vocational rehabilitation counselor
Diagnostic and evaluation services	Identifies disabilities	School psychologist, diagnostician, psychometrician
Occupational therapy	Improves, develops, or restores the ability to perform tasks or function independently	Occupational therapist (OT)
Orientation and mobility training	Enables students who are blind or have low vision to move safely and independently at school and in the community	Orientation specialist, mobility specialist
Physical therapy	Works to improve individual's motor functioning, movement, and fitness	Physical therapist (PT)
School health services	Provides health services designed to enable a student with a disability to participate in FAPE	School nurse
Social work	Mobilizes school and community resources and works in partnership with family members to resolve problems in a child's living situation that affect school adjustment	Social worker
Speech/language therapy	Provides services for the prevention and treatment of communicative disorders	Speech/language pathologist (SLP)
Transportation	Assists with travel to, from, between, and within school buildings, typically using specialized equipment (e.g., special or adapted buses, lifts, ramps).	Transportation specialist

Sources: Adapted from the U.S. Department of Education Final Regulation for IDEA '04 U.S. Department of Education (2006), pp. 1257–1258, 1264–1294.

professionals may include those who provide assistive technology, audiology, occupational therapy, physical therapy, school health services, speech/language therapy, or other services needed by the student. It is important for all teachers to understand that students, regardless of their disabilities, are guaranteed needed related services by IDEA '04.

With exceptions for very young children in some states, related services are provided *at no cost* to the student's family. However, in some cases, costs for related services are paid for by agencies other than schools (e.g., Medicare or private insurance companies). Some medical services are considered related services. Here's a guideline as to whether a medical service is also a related service: If a school nurse can provide the medical services the student needs, they are likely to be related services. If, however, the services need to be performed by a physician, they are not (Bigby, 2004; National Association of School Nurses [NASN], 2006).

Highly Qualified Special Educators

A special educator might be a resource specialist, a consultant, an itinerant teacher, a special education classroom teacher, a job coach, a home or hospital teacher, or an administrator. He or she might also be an orientation and mobility expert who teaches students with severe vision problems how to find their way independently at school and in the community. Special educators could be teachers of the Deaf who help students become proficient in using ASL or oral communication. Special educators' jobs are important and complex. Without these highly skilled professionals, special education can never be special. It is the special education teacher who is often at the heart of these intensive and rewarding educational experiences. The Spotlighting feature tells about Kelly Barnhart, one special education teacher who successfully uses data-based decision making to help determine what will comprise an appropriate education for one student with a disability.

The skills needed by special educators are many. They must have in-depth knowledge about making accommodations, differentiating instruction, implementing practices validated through rigorous research or documented to be best practices, monitoring students' progress, and ensuring that every student with a disability receives an appropriate education and achieves to the greatest degree possible. As you can see from the What NCLB Says About Highly Qualified Teachers feature, NCLB requires all general education teachers to be "highly qualified." NCLB expects teachers to hold a credential, have a degree, or demonstrate competency in every content area in which they teach. When IDEA was reauthorized in 2004, language was included affirming that special education teachers also must be highly qualified. What IDEA '04 Says About Highly Qualified Teachers summarizes requirements for special education teachers. These requirements are more complex than initially thought (Hyatt, 2007). In particular, because of the requirements for middle and secondary special education teachers to be highly qualified in every core academic subject they teach (e.g., math, science, history, English), co-teaching is gaining in popularity. Blending expertise of general education professionals and special educators through co-teaching arrangements can make the education students with disabilities receive truly special (Magiera et al., 2005).

Clearly, high-quality special educators are important ingredients to ensuring an effective education for every student with a disability. But the recipe for success also includes the expertise of professionals who come from different disciplines. It is the IEP process that brings together experts who have unique skills to meet the individual needs of students with disabilities. Now let's think about the process and plans that guide everyone's actions to make highly successful programs a reality.

Spotlighting *Kelly Barnhart:* A Day in the Life

Kelly Barnhart is a special education teacher of students with autism spectrum disorders.

The summer before my freshman year in college, my life changed forever. After spending the summer tutoring students with ASD, I decided to major in special education. Now in my fifth year of teaching elementary school students with ASD, I couldn't be happier with my career choice. The work is challenging, but it's worth it. I make a difference, and I see it every day in how far my students have come.

My philosophy of teaching centers on my view that every student can be taught. By using good methods with a lot of consistency and a good team, all students can come very far and reach their highest potential. My philosophy is reflected in my classroom routine, which is highly structured. When my students arrive in the morning, each begins to follow an activity schedule. Activity schedules help students with ASD understand routines, anticipate changes, and transition between activities. My teaching assistant and I both follow through on everything we do. We create a great deal of structure, but we incorporate enough change to help students generalize their skills.

Another critical aspect of my approach is the use of rewards. All of my students participate in an individualized reward system. Reward systems help students with ASD stay on task, complete assignments, and learn the daily routine.

In addition, I have discovered the benefits of teaching my students to use augmentative and alternative communication (AAC) systems, such as the Picture Exchange Communication System (PECS). I have found that AAC systems like PECS help students with ASD learn to communicate functionally. Specifically, PECS helps my students request preferred items and activities, request breaks, and express their frustrations in acceptable ways (see the Chapter 12 box on data-based practices).

I am proud of the remarkable gains my students have made, and I'm gratified that their parents recognize them. One of my most memorable moments was when, during an end-of-the-year classroom party, one of my student's parents exclaimed, "I've never found a more caring or more hard-working team." That kind of feedback makes the job worth it.

What NCLB Says About . . .

Highly Qualified Teachers

NCLB considers teachers to be highly qualified if they

- hold at least a bachelor's degree;

- are appropriately licensed or certified according to state licensing and certification requirements;

- have not had certification or licensure requirements waived on an emergency, temporary, or provisional basis;

- can demonstrate adequate knowledge in the core academic subjects (English, reading or language arts, mathematics, science, foreign languages, civics and government, economics, arts, history, and geography) that they currently teach by passing a state academic subject test; completing coursework equivalent to an academic major, degree, certification or credentialing; pass a "high objective uniform state standard of evaluation" (HOUSSE).

The IEP Process

IDEA '04 mandates that an individualized program be delivered to every infant, toddler, and student who is identified as having a disability and is in need of special education. The purposes of these individualized programs are to ensure that each of these individuals

- receives FAPE,
- is provided an education in the LRE,
- receives an education specific to the student, and
- is provided services with the expectation of outstanding results.

Students' IEPs are the plans or road maps created to guide instruction and the delivery of services that are the foundation for an appropriate education with access to the state's standards and adopted curriculum (Holbrook, 2007). Although some students with special needs receive accommodations for their special conditions through Section 504, only those with disabilities defined by IDEA '04 are required to have IEPs. Thus, some students with a disability that does not require special education services (e.g., a limb deficiency that does not affect educational performance) do not have an IEP. Conversely, sometimes students without disabilities do have an IEP. For example, in some states, students who are gifted or talented are included in special education. Although education of the gifted is not included in the federal special education law, those states often take their lead from IDEA '04, and IEPs are developed for these students.

IEPs focus on students' strengths and on their individual needs. Parents and school districts' education professionals must agree on these plans for the delivery of special services. IDEA '04 is very specific about the basic requirements of IEPs and the process to be used in their development and implementation (U.S. Department of Education, 2006). States, however, often impose further requirements in addition to those that are outlined in IDEA '04 and monitored by the federal government. It is quite likely that your state requires more steps or features. Here, we present what the national law requires and do not address specific regulations that various states expect school districts and teachers to follow. Let's study the general IEP process next.

Steps in the IEP Process

As we said, the national law spells out the minimum process or steps that are to be used when developing individualized programs offered under the auspices of special education. The formation of an individualized program can be organized into seven steps, shown in Figure 2.3, that begin with prereferral and end with evaluation of a student's program. Let's look at these seven steps in more detail to get a better understanding of what each means and how they form the IEP process.

Step 1: Prereferral The IEP process begins in the general education classroom. Students who are struggling with the general education curriculum—despite receiving high-quality education that includes evidence-based practices, UDL, and differentiated instruction—are targets of concern. More and more schools are using new and innovative **multitiered approaches** (e.g., response to intervention for reading that you will learn about in the chapter about learning disabilities, positive behavior support for behavioral interventions that you will read about in the chapter about emotional or behavioral disorders) during the early stages of the referral process (Brown-Chidsey, 2007). Here, students not learning at a sufficient rate or not able to meet the expected behavioral norms of the classroom setting begin receiving additional assistance in their general education program through what is often referred to as Tier 1. For schools using the more traditional approach, when individual students continue to struggle, the formal IEP process is initiated through what is usually called **prereferral**. Whether the process includes a multitiered approach or prereferral of an individual, the special education identification process has begun. Of course, not all students will eventually qualify for services.

At this first step, the general education teacher and the school's support team ensure that the target student has received high-quality instruction and additional instructional assistance if necessary. During this step, the school's support team must become confident that neither "poor teaching" (the application of practices that are not data-based) nor a need to learn the English language explains the student's inadequate performance. The major purposes of this step of the IEP process are to

- document and explain how and when the student is struggling,
- determine the effectiveness of classroom adaptations and additional assistance, and

What IDEA '04 Says About . . .

Highly Qualified Teachers

IDEA '04 considers teachers to be highly qualified if they

- meet all the standards for highly qualified teachers required for NCLB,
- hold state certification or licensure as a special education teacher, and
- demonstrate competency in every core academic area (e.g., math, science, social studies) in which they teach.

A special education resource room teacher who only consults with general education teachers does not have to demonstrate competency in core academic subjects, but must hold a special education credential.

Highly qualified standards do not apply to private school teachers.

States must establish highly qualified standards for related services personnel and paraprofessionals.

multitiered approaches
Approaches that provide levels of more and more intensive services to prevent or intervene early

prereferral First step in the IEP process that begins to determine a student's eligibility for special education services

Figure 2.3 • Steps in the IEP Process

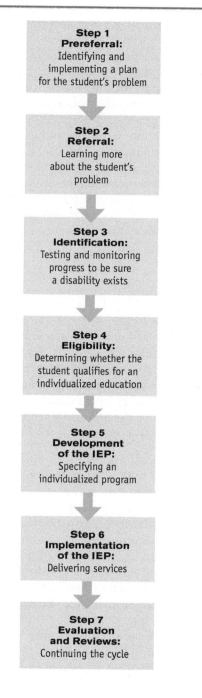

• monitor the student's progress during the application of high-quality instruction.

Prereferral activities include screening students for learning or behavioral difficulties, implementing data-based practices, and documenting student responses to these practices. In general, before any formal referral for special education services is made, teachers, school-based education professionals, the school's support team, and family members work together to determine whether the general education teacher alone can resolve a student's educational or behavioral difficulties. The assessments used during this step of the IEP process are intervention based and conducted in the student's general education class using direct measures of performance (Burdette, 2007). Teachers implement different validated teaching approaches and use assessment measures to document how students respond to this instruction.

Prereferral activities are intended to address individual student's learning or behavioral needs through the use of effective practices to prevent unnecessary referrals to special education, which are costly in time, money, and resources for formal assessments. Students whose learning remains challenged—those who continue to struggle—are referred to special education and the next step of the IEP process.

Step 2: Referral Some students come to school already identified as having a disability and needing special education. Some of these students have already received special education services for many years. Why is this so? For infants, toddlers, and preschoolers, IDEA '04 stresses the importance of an activity called **child find**, wherein those with disabilities are actively sought (U.S. Department of Education, 2006). In these cases, referrals can come from parents, a social service agency, public health nurses, day care professionals, or a doctor (Küpper, 2007). Young children who are at risk of having disabilities because of improper prenatal care, low birthweight, family history, accident or trauma during infancy, or child abuse are referred for special services. Also, those with visible indications of a disability (e.g., a missing arm or leg or facial differences resulting from Down syndrome), diagnosis through infant screenings (e.g., universal screenings for deafness), or signals of significant developmental delay (e.g., an infant not responding to sounds, an 18-month-old child not walking independently, a toddler who tantrums excessively, a 3-year-old not talking) are usually referred and identified early. They receive early intervention services during infancy or their preschool years. Typically, the referral process begins sooner for children with multiple-severe disabilities than it does for students with learning disabilities, because their disabilities are obvious at birth or during infancy. Such children and their families usually come to school expecting an individualized education because they have received multidisciplinary services during the preschool years.

child find A requirement of IDEA '04 to help refer and identify children and youth with disabilities

Students identified as having disabilities during the elementary or secondary school years present different reasons for referral. For example, students whose academic performance is significantly behind that of their classmates are prime candidates for special education referrals. Also, those students who continually misbehave and disrupt the learning environment often draw the attention of their teachers and are targeted for intervention and often eventually are referred for special education services.

Step 3: Identification Assessment is one foundation of the identification process. The purpose of this step in the IEP process is to determine whether a student has a disability, whether special education services are required, and what types of services are needed. The professional who actually coordinates the identification process varies by state and district. In some states, the assessment team leader is a school psychologist, an educational diagnostician, or a psychometrician. In other states, a teacher from the student's school leads the team's efforts.

Evaluations are conducted by multidisciplinary teams consisting of professionals who have expertise in each area of concern. Each member helps evaluate the student's unique strengths and struggles. For example, if a student is suspected of having a language impairment, a speech/language pathologist (SLP) is a member of the team. If there may be a hearing problem, an audiologist participates, and so on. For students who are 16 years old or older, evaluation includes assessments related to the need for transition services for moving either from school to work or from secondary to postsecondary education (Madaus & Shaw, 2006). The student's parents, family members, and individuals from the community are also wonderful sources of information, and their input should also be part of the identification process.

At this step, many different types of data are used to inform the team about the student's abilities. Medical history, information about social interactions at school and at home, adaptive behavior in the community, direct measures of educational performance, and other relevant factors are considered. Evaluations include an array of assessment instruments and procedures. Information should be collected from the student, family members, and school personnel who know the student. Formal tests—tests of intelligence, of academic achievement, and of acuity (vision and hearing)—are usually part of the information used to make decisions about students and their potential special education status.

Less formal assessments—assistive technology evaluations, school observations of classroom and social behavior, examples of academic assignments, direct measurements of academic performance, curriculum-based measurements (CBM) of reading and mathematics skills being taught, and portfolio samples of classroom performance—also provide important pieces of evidence used in this step of the IEP process. Together, these data are used to develop a profile of the student. One result of the evaluation step of the IEP process can be a determination that the individual does not have a disability. In these instances the IEP process is discontinued. For those individuals who do have disabilities, this phase of the process results in a baseline of performance data to guide the development of the individualized education program and, later, help judge the program's effectiveness.

Step 4: Eligibility   Information from the assessment step is used to identify students who actually have a disability and qualify for special education services. Determining eligibility usually includes a "battery of tests" (more than one test or type of assessment) and is conducted by evaluation experts (e.g., school psychologists, diagnosticians, audiologists, ophthalmologists). Such evaluations typically include standardized tests that were normed with large groups of people. (Intelligence and achievement tests are examples of standardized instruments.) However, the use of standardized tests concerns many educators; one reason is that such tests can contribute to the overrepresentation of culturally and linguistically diverse students in special education (see Chapter 3). In an attempt to resolve or at least monitor this problem, the authors of IDEA '04 require states to collect data and change practices that may be discriminatory. Bias and unfair treatment is one reason why at every step along the way, professionals must ensure that culturally and linguistically diverse students who go through the disability identification process

- have received high-quality, typically effective instruction prior to referral, and
- have been thoroughly reviewed to rule out limited English proficiency or diversity as the reason for the learning or behavior problem.

Remember, all evaluation instruments or procedures selected should reflect the purpose or intended outcomes of the evaluation process. The education of those students who do not meet the eligibility requirements remains the sole responsibility of general educators; the education of those students with disabilities who are eligible for special education services becomes the *shared* responsibility of general education teachers and administrators, special education teachers and administrators, and the appropriate related service professionals. For those students, the IEP Team then determines what components of the full range of special education and related services are needed so that an appropriate education can be planned and ultimately delivered.

Step 5: Development of the IEP   After thorough completion of the prereferral, referral, identification, and eligibility steps of the IEP process, it is time to develop the actual plan for the student's individualized education—an IFSP for infants and toddlers, an IEP for preschoolers and schoolchildren, and a transition component of the IEP for those students with disabilities who are 16 years old or older. If behavior is a concern, a behavior intervention plan will be written for the individual student as well. We discuss the development of the IEP in more detail later in this chapter, but for now, it is important for you to know that parents and the education professionals who are all part of the student's IEP Team now make important decisions about services that constitute an appropriate education and where those services will be delivered. The assessment results are used to help make these decisions. It is at this point that the IEP Team begins its work to outline the individualized education needed by the student. Collectively, the team members, who include parents and the student (if appropriate), now use the knowledge they have gained to identify resources needed for that student to access the general education curriculum, determine the appropriate goals for improvement, and then craft a good education program for the student. Of course, goals must include greater success with the general education curriculum or independence and a community presence later in life. It is at this point that the services and supports that become part of the student's appropriate education are specified.

Step 6: Implementation of the IEP   Once the IEP is developed, the student's services and individualized program begin. The IEP has laid out what constitutes an appropriate education for the student, the extent to which the student participates in the general education curriculum, the accommodations the student receives both for instruction and for assessment, and the array of multidisciplinary services from related service providers that support the student's educational program. For students who are participating in a different curriculum or whose goals differ from those of the general education curriculum, the IEP has specified alternate assessment procedures as well.

Minor adjustments in students' goals or in the benchmarks that indicate attainment of those goals do not signal a need for a new IEP or another IEP meeting. Services continue. However, major changes in goals, services, or placement do require parents to be notified in writing. Some changes, particularly if they involve a more restrictive placement, may necessitate a meeting of the IEP Team and the parent or guardian. Most often, this situation arises when issues surrounding discipline are the reason for the change in placement or services. Later in this chapter, you will learn more about behavior intervention plans, which must be developed as part of students' IEPs when serious behavioral infractions (e.g., bringing guns or drugs to school, fighting, or being out of control) occur.

Step 7: Evaluation and Reviews   IDEA '04 requires accountability for each IEP developed. In most states, students' IEPs are reviewed annually. Under an IDEA '04 pilot program, which is attempting to reduce paperwork and administrative burdens on educators, 15 states conduct these reviews every 3 years. The purpose of the IEP review meetings is to ensure that students are meeting their goals and making educational progress. Because accountability measures determine whether the student is making progress, educators are careful to describe expectations for tasks and skills the student needs to learn in terms that can be evaluated. Whether the IEP process is for an infant or toddler (an IFSP) or for a schoolchild (an IEP and possibly a transition component), the expectation is that frequent assessments of the individual's performance will occur, even if major IEP reviews occur once a year or only every 3 years.

All students with disabilities participate in annual state- or districtwide testing or in alternate assessments. You will learn more about these assessments later in this chapter and also in each of the following chapters. You will learn which students participate in which type of evaluation effort and what types of accommodations and supports they can receive so their disabilities do not mask their yearly achievement gains. For now, remember that participation in these assessments is important because they help retain high standards and expectations for all students. Remember, in addition to annual assessments, students with disabilities have their progress monitored frequently on the information and skills they are learning in the classroom. Sometimes these assessments are made weekly or even daily. The purpose of such measurements of progress is to guide instruction and to ensure that scheduled interventions are effective.

The IEP Team: Collaborative Multidisciplinary Partnerships

At the heart of special education are the professionals who join with families to collaborate and provide multidisciplinary services and supports to students with disabilities. **IEP Teams** are unique because they are individually determined and their membership reflects the individual needs of the student. These multidisciplinary teams of experts not only deliver critical services to students with disabilities and their families but also are valuable resources to teachers as they strive to meet the needs of each student. IDEA '04 is very specific about the people who must comprise IEP Teams (U.S. Department of Education, 2007b). The law states that membership is not fixed but must include

- at least one general education teacher (if the student is participating in general education);
- at least one special education or (when appropriate) related service provider(s);
- a representative of the school district who is knowledgeable about the general education curriculum, available school resources, and who can provide or supervise the provision of uniquely designed instruction to meet the student's needs;
- someone to interpret the instructional implications of the assessment results;
- the parent(s);
- the student (if appropriate); and
- other people whom the school or parents invite.

Many others also contribute to the appropriate education of students with disabilities. Advocates and lawyers are examples. Teachers should always remember that related services professionals are available to help them as well as students. Related service professionals are important members of these teams, and every student who faces challenges because of disabilities should have access to them, when

IEP Teams Multidisciplinary teams that guide individualized special education services for each student with a disability

myeducationlab Go to the Activities and Applications section in Chapter 2 of MyEducationLab and complete Activity 2. As you watch the video and answer the accompanying questions, consider the benefits of co-teaching and collaboration in the development of an IEP—for both teachers and students.

When parents, teachers, and students share the results from IEP Team meetings, everyone understands goals, expectations, and the purpose of education.

appropriate. Unfortunately, particularly for students with high-incidence disabilities (such as learning disabilities), IEP Teams often fail to fully consider students' needs or related services (Mitch Yell, as quoted in Earles-Vollrath, 2004).

When everyone works together, multidisciplinary teams ensure more than the protection of basic rights guaranteed by IDEA '04: They orchestrate the best education possible! When each individually arranged team develop partnerships, so that students' programs are coordinated, the results are remarkable, allowing individuals to overcome many challenges caused by disabilities. Each person working together to provide not only an appropriate education but the best education possible has important roles to fulfill. Some of those roles and responsibilities are highlighted next.

Roles of Education Professionals

All education professionals working at every school are crucial to positive experiences for students with disabilities. As we mentioned at the beginning of Chapter 1, it is surprising to us that after some 30 years of including more and more students with disabilities in general education classes, many teachers, principals, and other education professionals still report that they feel ill prepared to accept responsibilities associated with the education of these students (Futernick, 2007; Hammond & Ingalls, 2003). Those who harbor such attitudes (particularly if they are uneasy with, or even reject, students with disabilities) can negatively influence outcomes for these students (Cook et al., 2007). Such negative attitudes are often subtly expressed in the ways in which inadequately prepared educators talk about students with disabilities and the adaptations they need for successful participation in the general education curriculum (Smith, Salend, & Ryan, 2001). We also know that well-prepared educators can and do make a real difference in the lives and the educational achievements of their students (Darling-Hammond, 2005, 2006a, 2006b; Futernick 2007). So, one responsibility of every educator is to be well prepared to meet the needs of these students.

The school principal is a key person in the collaborative effort at every school (Brown-Chidsey, 2007; IRIS Center, 2007). Because principals often coordinate management efforts at their site, they can be most helpful in developing and ensuring the delivery of special education services (particularly for large-scale assessments), in monitoring the array of services indicated on every student's IEP, and in ensuring the coordination of services throughout the school and across the district. Effective principals also set the tone for positive attitudes crucial to all students' success. They welcome and facilitate the efforts of the many different professionals who are **itinerant**, coming to their school to work with individual students. Sometimes, the coordination and scheduling of these professionals' services can be challenging to principals. Some students with disabilities have many members of their multidisciplinary teams. For example, one child may receive services from SLPs, physical therapists, experts in assistive technology, and occupational therapists—all of whom are itinerant. They are not permanent or full-time members of the school's staff. Their schedules are complicated and often hard to coordinate because each of them travels from school to school, sometimes long distances, to work with individual students and their teachers who need their services. Also, these professionals often find themselves in crowded schools where they do not have sufficient space or appropriate places to work with individual students or to store their equipment. Principals can lead their school's staff to solve complex coordination issues that itinerant multidisciplinary team members often present, smoothing the way for efficient delivery of related services.

Neither IDEA '04, individual states' regulations, nor school districts' guidelines have established definitive roles for each profession's IEP Team member. Teams must determine each member's role and responsibility when they collaborate as members of IEP Teams and work together to plan for the delivery of an effective and appropriate education for each student with a disability. In part, this lack of uniformity exists because no single or uniform action can reflect what special

itinerant Working in different locations

education services any particular student needs. Also, government officials do not want to dictate how groups of professionals elect to work together. For example, at one school, the principal and IEP Teams might assign duties differently than the principal and team members at another school (Praisner, 2003). At one school, the school counselor coordinates the entire schedule; at another, a special education teacher schedules related services for all students with disabilities, and the principal's assistant develops the other teachers' and students' schedules. In short, the way in which these professionals collaborate is partially determined by how they are organized at each school.

Roles of Families

Families are an important part of every person's life, but for students with disabilities, their roles in their child's education is greater than it is for typical learners. IDEA '04 stresses the importance of involving families of students with disabilities in the IEP process and as members of their child's IEP Team (U.S. Department of Education, 2006). The IEP process can help develop partnerships among parents and extended family members, schools, and professionals (Sopko, 2003). This purpose should be actively fostered, for the importance of these partnerships cannot be overestimated.

When parent involvement is high, student alienation is lower and student achievement is increased (Brown, Paulsen, & Higgins, 2003; Dworetzky, 2004). Educators need to recognize, however, that many parents believe schools control the special education process. As a result, many families feel disenfranchised or confused about rules, regulations, and the purpose of special education (Zarate, 2007). Most parents do want to participate in their children's education, but sometimes they do not understand the educational system. Read Considering Culture to learn how one teacher took some extra steps to build meaning connections with such a family.

Often, families need help to participate effectively in IEP meetings and in the resulting individualized programs (Tornatzky, Pachon, & Torres, 2003). Here are some tips that teachers can give parents to help them better prepare to participate in IEP meetings (Buehler, 2004):

- Outline points to make about your child's strengths.
- Bring records regarding your child's needs.
- Ask for clarification.
- Be assertive and proactive, but not aggressive or reactive.
- Listen and compromise.
- Remain involved with the professionals on the IEP Team.
- Know about placement and service options, and explore each with the Team.

For families who do not speak English well enough to understand the complicated language used to talk about special education issues, participation may seem impossible (Hughes, Valle-Riestra, & Arguelles, 2002). In such instances, schools must welcome family members and people from the community who are fluent in the family's native language and culture. They must also be knowledgeable about the special education process and procedural safeguards guaranteed them through IDEA '04 (for a summary of those safeguards, see What IDEA '04 Says About Procedural Safeguards). The law encourages the family's maximal participation, so it requires schools to find interpreters to the extent possible. Remember, it is the obligation of educators to actively seek out, include, and inform parents and students about the efforts that will be made on their behalf (Hyatt, 2007; Küpper, 2007).

What IDEA '04 Says About . . .

Procedural Safeguards

Parents of each student with a disability have the right to

- receive a written explanation of the procedural safeguards afforded by law (in their native language unless it is feasibly impossible to do so);
- be invited to all meetings held about their child's educational program;
- give permission for their child to be evaluated and to obtain independent evaluations;
- have access to their child's educational records;
- understand requirements for their child's placement in interim alternate educational settings, private schools, and during due process proceedings;
- resolve complaints through the use of mediation, due process hearings, state-level appeals, and civil actions, within specified time periods and with opportunities for the agency to resolve the complaints;
- collect attorneys' fees if they prevail in court.

Considering Culture: *Parents, Involvement, and the IEP Process*

Individualized Special Education Programs

Janelle, the Special Education Resource Teacher at Hurston Elementary School, is concerned that so few parents of students she serves participate in their son's or daughter's IEP. She believes that parental input is extremely valuable, and she is a little irritated that so many parents "just don't seem to care." When Janelle expressed her frustration to the school principal, the principal suggested that she get better acquainted with the families whose children are on her caseload by making home visits or meeting parents at a location convenient for them. So Janelle began contacting families. Many agreed to meet with her, and she visited with them at a variety of places, including homes, fast-food restaurants, and malls. Janelle then shared what she had learned with the principal.

"Nhan's mother met me in a small apartment that she, her husband, their three children, two cousins, their wives, and their six children share. Her role in the family is to take care of the children—nine in all—while the other family members are at work. As recent immigrants from Vietnam, they are all adjusting to a new language and to a world with different ways of living, rearing children, and doing business. Each family member works long hours, and Nhan's mother can't leave the children she is watching. Even if she could, she doesn't know how to drive. It was clear that she loves and cares about Nhan and the whole family, but special education is completely new to her. I can certainly see that it can't be her highest priority."

"I thought that I was never going to get to meet Martha's family. Both parents had all kinds of excuses for putting off our meeting. Martha's mother finally agreed to meet me at the park where she takes her toddler to play. When I said that I would like to learn more about her family and their goals for Martha, she became very nervous, so I switched the topic of conversation to her toddler, the park, all kinds of things. She relaxed and seemed more comfortable. I asked again if there was anything that she could tell me that might help me develop a better school program for Martha. She said that Martha is shy and embarrassed that she doesn't do well in school. We talked about ways to help her learn at school and at home, and Martha's mother seemed relieved. When I asked if there was anything else that she would like to tell me, she hesitated then said, 'My husband and I don't have the right documents. I was afraid that you were going to take Martha out of school and turn us in. I am so glad that you are going to teach her instead.' Of course she and her husband don't want to come to a school. They're afraid."

"There were many reasons why parents weren't involved in the IEP process. I was wrong in thinking they didn't care. Every parent I met cared about their child, their family, and me as their child's teacher. They just can't show it in the ways I expected them to. The best part is that each parent and I worked out a way to communicate, share information, and involve them in their child's IEP. This has been one of the best experiences I've ever had."

Questions to Consider

1. How do you define parental involvement? Compare your responses with those of others in the class.

2. What are some strategies you might use with the parents that Janelle talked with?

—By Eleanor Lynch, San Diego State University and Marci Hanson, San Francisco State University

Roles of Students

You just learned that IDEA '04 calls out students, when appropriate, as members of their own IEP Teams. This participation is particularly important for adolescents who are about to transition out of high school. The law stresses student involvement, because special education experts found many years ago, and teachers confirm today, that students with disabilities are too often unfamiliar with their IEPs and do not know the goals established for them (Lovitt & Cushing, 1994). One result is a lack of "ownership" in the school program especially designed for them. Another reason may be that these students need explicit instruction about IEPs and how to participate in IEP meetings (Konrad & Trela, 2007). Involving students has many benefits (Test et al., 2004). Particularly if students are active participants, they can learn important skills needed in life. Here are two examples. **Self-determination** is the ability to identify and achieve goals for oneself. **Self-advocacy** consists of the skills necessary to stand up and advocate for what one needs to achieve those goals. These two skills are interrelated and can be fostered during the IEP process when students are involved (Wood et al., 2004). Here are some ways in which older students can contribute to their IEP meetings:

- Describe personal strengths, weaknesses, and needs.
- Evaluate personal progress toward accomplishing their goals.
- Bring a list of adaptations and explain how each is helpful.
- Communicate their preferences and interests.
- Articulate their long-term goals and desires for life, work, and postsecondary schooling.

Now, let's turn our attention to the documents that serve as road maps to each student's appropriate education and the special education services that comprise each individualized program.

Tools for Individualized Programs

Four tools, or plans for individualized programs, serve to coordinate and document what constitutes the appropriate education for each infant, toddler, and student with disabilities. The tools that guarantee an appropriate education to those with disabilities are

- the *individualized family service plan* (IFSP)—for infants and toddlers;
- the *individualized education program* (IEP)—for preschoolers through high school students;
- an additional *statement of transitional services*—initiated at age 16 to help those students who require special education services to make successful transitions to independence, community living, and work; and
- a *behavior intervention plan*—for those students with disabilities who commit serious behavioral infractions.

Let's examine each of these plans in turn.

Individualized Family Service Plans (IFSPs)

Infants or toddlers (birth through age 2) who have disabilities or who are at great risk for disabilities were originally guaranteed the right to early intervention programs through PL 99-457, which was passed in 1986. That right continues today through IDEA '04 (U.S. Department of Education, 2006, 2007b). (For a review of IDEA legislation, see Chapter 1 and Table 1.2.) **Individualized family service plans (IFSPs)** are written documents that ensure that special services are delivered to these young children and their families. The IFSP is the management tool that guides professionals as they design and deliver these children's special education programs. **Service managers** are the professionals who provide oversight and coordination of the services outlined in IFSPs. The key components of these early education management plans are as follows:

- The child's current functioning levels in all relevant areas (physical development, cognitive development, language and speech development, psychosocial development, and self-help skills)
- The family's strengths and needs in regard to the development of their child
- The major outcomes expected, expressed in terms of procedures, evaluation criteria, and a time line

self-determination Behaviors that includes making decisions, choosing preferences, and practicing self-advocacy needed for independent living

self-advocacy Expressing one's rights and needs

individualized family service plan (IFSP) Identifies and organizes services and resources for infants and toddlers (birth to 3) and their families

service manager Case manager or coordinator who oversees the implementation and evaluation of IFSPs

cial development, and self-help skills)

- The family's strengths and needs in regard to the development of their child
- The major outcomes expected, expressed in terms of procedures, evaluation criteria, and a time line
- The services necessary and a schedule for their delivery
- Projected dates for initiation of services
- The name of the service coordinator
- A biannual (every 6 months) review, with the child's family, of progress made and of any need for modifications in the IFSP
- Indication of methods for transitioning the child to services available for children ages 3 to 5

Young children with disabilities get a "good start" when they receive services from related service providers, like this physical therapist, in natural settings and as early as possible.

To many service coordinators and early childhood specialists, the IFSP is a working document for an ongoing process in which parents and specialists work together, continually modifying, expanding, and developing a child's educational program. Children and families who participate in early intervention programs often find these years to be an intense period, with many professionals offering advice, training, guidance, and personalized services, as well as care and concern. Also, the transition to preschool at the age of 3 can be particularly difficult and frightening. One reason is that services that were delivered primarily at the family's home now will be delivered at a preschool. Therefore, IFSPs include plans for these youngsters and their families to transition from very intensive and individually delivered interventions to more traditional classrooms (U.S. Department of Education, 2007b). IDEA '04 allows states to give families the option of delaying entrance into school-based preschool programs by keeping their child in an early intervention program, but making this decision sometimes results in the family having to pay for some or all of the services (U.S. Department of Education, 2006).

individualized education program (IEP) Management tool to identify and organize needed services

Individualized Education Programs (IEPs)

Individualized education programs (IEPs) are the documents that describe the special education and related services appropriate to the needs of students with dis-

Table 2.4 • Differences Between IFSPs and IEPs

Feature	IFSP	IEP
Target of services	Infants and toddlers with disabilities (birth to two) Families of these children	Preschoolers with disabilities Students with disabilities (ages 3 to 21)
Place for services	Natural environment Homes Day Care Clinics	Schools Homes or hospitals
Costs to families	Costs for some services may be charged to families (on a sliding scale according to income)	No cost to families (unless they elect other options) (FAPE)
Lead agency	State designates (considerable variation)	State education agency (schools)

delineated what the IEP must contain at the very least, and it is important that every educator know these key components:

- *Current performance:* the student's present levels of academic achievement and information about how the student's disability influences participation and progress in the general education curriculum
- *Goals:* statement of measurable goals related to participation in the general education curriculum or to meeting other educational needs resulting from the disability
- *Special education and related services:* specific educational services to be provided, including accommodations, program modifications, or supports that allow participation in the general education curriculum and in extracurricular activities
- *Participation with students without disabilities:* explanation about the extent to which the student will not participate in general education classes and in extracurricular activities alongside peers without disabilities
- *Participation in state- and districtwide testing:* description of assessment adaptations needed for these assessments, or, if the student will not be participating, a statement listing reasons for nonparticipation and explaining how the student will be alternately assessed
- *Dates and places:* projected dates for initiation of services, where services will be delivered, and the expected duration of those services
- *Transition service needs:* beginning at age 16, for those students whose goals are related to community presence and independence, a transition component to identify postschool goals and to describe transitional assessments and service needs
- *Age of majority:* beginning at least 1 year before the student reaches the age of majority, explanation of those rights that transfer to the student
- *Measuring progress:* statement of how the student's progress toward achieving IEP goals will be measured and how parents will be informed about this progress

To stress the importance of including all of these components in each student's IEP, the federal government provided a template for school districts to use as a model (U.S. Department of Education, 2007b). We used this template in Figure 2.4 and show statements from four different students' IEP objectives, which are meant to illustrate the range of individualized statements, objectives, and benchmarks possible. Because of the importance and complexity of IEPs, most state departments of education have sample IEPs for districts to follow. Also, the National Association for State Directors of Special Education (NASDSE) has developed examples (see www.nasdse.org) that show how to relate IEP objectives and benchmarks to state standards and the general education curriculum (Holbrook, 2007).

In part because of the excessive time teachers and IEP Teams often spend developing IEPs, many districts are using technology to reduce the burden. Many templates and software programs are now available (Serfass & Peterson, 2007). Of course, such technology presents many risks. For example, when objectives and benchmarks are available from a databank, the result can be that IEPs are not truly individually determined for each student. Also, concerns have been raised about confidentiality, where and how documents are stored, and how to control access to them. Regardless, technology-facilitated IEPs have many benefits, such as ease of transferring information from one school or district to another when a student moves, reduction of time and effort for members of the IEP Team, sharing of data among education professionals, and creation of reports efficiently and in a timely fashion.

IEPs must be written for each student with a disability, so each IEP should be different from the next, each reflecting a unique array of services, accommodations,

Individualized Education Program

The individualized education program (IEP) is a written document developed for each eligible child with a disability. The IDEA '04 regulations specify the procedures that school districts must follow to develop, review, and revise the IEP for each child. The document here sets out the IEP content that those regulations require.

A statement of the child's present levels of academic achievement and functional performance, including

- how the child's disability affects the child's involvement and progress in the general education curriculum (i.e., the same curriculum as for students without disabilities) **or**, *for preschool children*, as appropriate, how the disability affects the child's participation in appropriate activities.

> *Miguel* will participate in the general education curriculum and be evaluated with modified achievement standards. His learning will be provided with accommodations that support his English language learning (e.g., read-aloud accommodations, extended time) and modifications (e.g., abbreviated assignments that require written responses).

A statement of measurable annual goals, including academic and functional goals designed to

- meet the child's needs that result from the child's disability to enable the child to be involved in and make progress in the general education curriculum;
- meet each of the child's other educational needs that result from the child's disability.

> *Susie* will participate in the general education reading program in both Tiers 1 and 2 and also receive Tier 3 reading instruction in special education. She will increase her correct reading fluency rate to the aim score of 120 words per minute and improve the trend of maze comprehension scores by 2 times.

For children with disabilities who take alternate assessments aligned to alternate achievement standards (in addition to the annual goals), a description of benchmarks or short-term objectives.

> *John* will master individualized transportation objectives and job skills through the assistance of a job coach and community mentor. He will be placed, initially, in a job at a local grocery store, stocking and sacking, for 3 hours per day, and meet expectations of coworkers and grocery store managers. His annual goals will also include mastery of 150 additional survival sight words, 20 new objectives in the district's survival math skill areas.

A description of the following:

- how the child's progress toward meeting the annual goals will be measured.
- Periodic reports on the progress the child is making toward meeting the annual goals will be provided, such as through the use of quarterly or other periodic reports, concurrent with the issuance of report cards.

(continued)

Figure 2.4 • Continued

> *John's* annual goals and objectives will be measured through authentic assessments, including portfolios of progress in mastering job skills, curriculum-based measurements, and progress monitoring of sight words and math skill areas.

A statement of the *special education and related services* and *supplementary aids and services*, based on peer-reviewed research to the extent practical, to be provided to the child, or on behalf of the child, and *a statement of the program modifications or supports* for school personnel that will be provided to enable the child

- to advance appropriately toward attaining the annual goals;
- to be involved in and make progress in the general education curriculum and to participate in extracurricular and other nonacademic activities;
- to be educated and participate with other children with disabilities and nondisabled children in extracurricular and other nonacademic activities.

> *John* will receive services from a multidisciplinary team, including
>   an assistive technology staff person: computerized calendar
>   a job coach: community job placement
>   a speech/language pathologist: articulation and language therapy
> *John* will participate in leisure-time activities with the high school bowling club and the intermural baseball team.

An explanation of the extent, if any, to which the child will not participate with nondisabled children in the regular classroom and in extracurricular and other nonacademic activities.

> *Susie* will participate in all general education instructional and extracurricular activities with students without disabilities.

A statement of any individual appropriate accommodations that are necessary to measure the academic achievement and functional performance of the child on state- and districtwide assessments.

> *Miguel* will be provided with accommodations that support his English language learning (e.g., read-aloud accommodations, extended time) and modifications (e.g., abbreviated assignments that require written responses). These accommodations and modifications, along with others that teachers document as effective in the instructional setting, will also be used in assessment and other testing situations.

If the IEP Team determines that the child must take an alternate assessment instead of a particular regular state- or districtwide assessment of student achievement, a statement explaining

- why the child cannot participate in the regular assessment;
- the particular alternate assessment selected.

(continued)

> *John* will not participate in annual districtwide assessments, rather, his goals and objectives relating to community presence, independent transportation abilities, job skills, and life skills will be assessed monthly, and a comprehensive portfolio will be submitted to parents and the IEP Team in April.

The projected date for the beginning of the services and modifications and the anticipated frequency, location, and duration of *special education and related services* and *modifications and supports*.

Service, Aid, or Modification	Frequency	Location	Beginning Date	Duration
Job coaching	Afternoon each day	Local grocery store	9/15	One semester; placement change 1/1
SLP	Twice a week	MLK School	9/10	All year

Transition Services

Beginning not later than the first IEP to be in effect *when the child turns 16, or younger if determined appropriate by the IEP Team*, and updated annually thereafter, the IEP must include

- appropriate measurable postsecondary goals based on age-appropriate transition assessments related to training, education, employment, and where appropriate, independent living skills.

> *John* will demonstrate mastery of grocery job tasks as evaluated by the manager and coworkers at the store, he will travel independently from home to school to job to home daily, he will participate in leisure-time activities of bowling and basketball, and he will achieve survival reading and math skills by the end of the school year.

- the transition services (including courses of study) needed to assist the child in reaching those goals.

Transition Services (Including Courses of Study)
John will participate in full life skills and job placement curriculum.

Rights That Transfer at Age of Majority

- Beginning not later than 1 year before the child reaches the age of majority under state law, the IEP must include a statement that the child has been informed of the child's rights under and consistent with IDEA '04, if any, that will transfer to the child on reaching the age of majority.

Source: Adapted From U.S. Department of Education, Office of Special Education Programs, *Model Form: Individualized Education Program*, 2006, IDEA.ed.gov. Modified to eliminate code references.

related services providers, and objectives. Services indicated on the IEP *must be* provided. Here are some important rules of thumb about such services:

- They cannot be traded for other services, such as more time in the general education classroom.
- Availability is *not* a legitimate reason for omitting services from the student's plan.
- Cost is *not* to factor into the decision about whether to include a service or, in the case of AT, provide a device.
- All of the components of the service must be put into place (e.g., software for voice output capabilities, a computer, headphones, e-text versions of adopted textbooks, help to learn use of devices).

In addition, any changes in placement, related services specified in the IEP, or annual goals necessitate another IEP meeting and mutual approval by the family and the school district.

The contents of a student's IEP must be available to all educators who work with the student (U.S. Department of Education, 2006, 2007b). IEPs are meant to be a communication tool. Surprisingly, it is common for teachers to be unaware of the goals, objectives, and services required by their students' IEPs. This situation leads one to ask how an appropriate education can be delivered when the educators who interact with students with disabilities do not understand what the students' education should comprise! The answer is obvious: An appropriate education cannot be delivered under these circumstances.

Transition Components of IEPs

When IDEA was reauthorized in 1997, plans to help students transition from school to postsecondary experiences became a special education requirement. At that time, such a plan was a separate document—a mini-IEP of its own—for students aged 14 and older and was called an individualized transition plan (ITP). Since the 1997 reauthorization of IDEA, these plans for assessments and services to prepare for postschool life, or **statements of transitional services**, are a part of the students' IEPs; they are not stand-alone documents. What IDEA '04 Says About Transition Services summarizes the law's current requirements. One very important change that educators need to know is that IDEA '04 increased to 16 the age for initiation of the transition component of students' IEPs (U.S. Department of Education, 2007b). Transitional planning is very important for high school students with disabilities, because these individuals' results have much room for improvement.

Concerns about the graduation rates abound (Hall, 2007). These rates for all of America's students have vast room for improvement, particularly those for students from diverse backgrounds, those who live in inner cities, and those with disabilities (OSEP 2007). Substantially more students with disabilities graduate from high school with a standard diploma than did some 15 years ago. Actually, national figures indicate a 17% increase (National Center for Education Statistics [NCES, 2007a]. However, with some 28% of students with disabilities leaving high school with no diploma or certificate of completion, it is clear that too many still drop out of school (Wagner et al., 2006). Graduation matters. The results of students who have high school diplomas are better than those who do not, and each year of postsecondary education opens the doors for better and more job opportunities and higher income, and jobs with health insurance and other important benefits.

statement of transitional services Component of IEPs for students older than age 16 to assist students moving to adulthood

---

What IDEA '04 Says About . . .

Transition Services

The IEP in effect when a child turns 16 must

- include postsecondary goals that are appropriate, measurable, and based on the results of transition evaluations in the areas of training, education, employment, and independent living skills (when appropriate);
- list transition services and coursework required to help the student meet those goals;
- include (at least 1 year prior to the student's reaching the age of majority) a statement that the student has been informed about his or her rights as an adult;
- include (upon the student's exiting high school) a summary of transition needs and accomplishments;
- be reviewed and updated annually thereafter.

Probably related to the increases in high school graduation rates, more individuals with disabilities are attending college (NCES, 2007b). As they create transition statements, it is important for IEP Teams to carefully consider postsecondary options for each student with a disability. Such plans are often not made for individuals with disabilities because of bias and unfortunate misconceptions about disabilities.

It is also important for teachers who participate in transition planning to understand that adults with disabilities tend to engage in active leisure activities less than individuals without disabilities. They participate in organized community groups at a rate much lower than would be expected, and they also get in trouble with the law more often than their typical peers (Wagner et al., 2006). Helping students set goals for themselves, gain work experience, and develop skills needed for independent living can be critical to the life satisfaction experienced by adults with disabilities (Neubert, 2003). Because more students with disabilities are now attending college, educators must also help them develop skills, beyond academics, that are needed for success (Hong et al., 2007). All these issues need to be considered, as the transition component of the IEP is developed.

Behavioral Intervention Plans

When any student with a disability commits serious behavioral infractions, IDEA '04 requires that a **behavioral intervention plan**, which is like an IEP but addresses the behavioral infraction, be developed (U.S. Department of Education, 2006). Inappropriate behavior is so often at the root of special education referrals, of teachers' dissatisfaction with working with students who have disabilities, and of lifelong challenges, you will find a Tips for Classroom Management box in each of the following chapters. Also, in the chapter about emotional or behavioral disorders, you will learn about effective interventions that help resolve behavior issues that affect both the individual and his or her classmates when rules are violated; many of these procedures are effective with many students who need to resolve challenging behaviors. IDEA '04 has some definite requirements about students who have an IEP and also engage in seriously disruptive or violent behavior. Those are highlighted in What IDEA '04 Says about Behavioral Intervention Plans.

Why did such plans become part of IEPs for those students who have major behavioral issues? One reason reflects concerns of Congress and the public about violence, discipline, and special education students. Students without disabilities are expelled for breaking school rules such as bringing guns to school or engaging in serious fighting. However, some students with disabilities cannot be expelled. These students can, however, be removed from their current placement and receive their education away from their assigned classroom(s) in what is called an **interim alternative educational setting (IAES)** for up to 45 school days. Continued progress toward the attainment of IEP goals must be one intention of the IAES placement. Students who cannot be expelled are those whose disruptive behavior was caused by their disability. Under the older versions of IDEA, this protection was called the **stay-put provision**. Through a process called **manifestation determination**, educators figure out whether the disability caused the infraction. All students with disabilities who are violent or "out of control" must have behavior intervention plans developed for them. These plans focus not only on the control or elimination of future serious behavioral infractions but also on the development of positive social skills.

behavioral intervention plan Includes a functional assessment and procedures to prevent and intervene for behavioral infractions

interim alternative educational setting (IAES) Special education placement to ensure progress toward IEP goals, assigned when a serious behavioral infraction requires removal from current placement

stay-put provision Prohibits students with disabilities from being expelled because of behavior associated with their disabilities

manifestation determination Determines whether a student's disciplinary problems are due to the disability

What IDEA '04 Says About . . .

Behavioral Intervention Plans
When considering a situation where student behavior

- *Interferes with learning*, the IEP team should consider the use of positive behavioral interventions and supports, and other strategies.

- *Violates the student conduct code*, a functional behavioral assessment may be administered and behavioral intervention services and modifications (which include a behavioral intervention plan) may be implemented if appropriate.

- *Is determined to be the result of manifestation determination*, the IEP team must

  - Conduct a functional behavioral assessment and implement a behavioral intervention plan, or

  - for students with a current behavioral intervention plan in place, review previous functional behavioral assessments and modify the existing plan, if necessary.

Because educators must learn how to develop behavior intervention plans and use a process called **functional behavioral assessment (FBA)**, we discuss these procedures in A Closer Look at Data-Based Practices in Chapter 7. We included the more detailed discussion of FBAs there, even though they are used with any student with a disability who engages in serious behavioral infractions. For now, it is important to know that FBAs help clarify the offending student's preferences for specific academic tasks and determines when the undesirable behavior is likely to occur. The FBA process leads teachers directly to effective interventions with socially validated outcomes (Barnhill, 2005; Ryan, Halsey, & Matthews, 2003). However, they often miss behaviors that occur rarely, and this is a real problem because many low-frequency infractions (e.g., hitting a teacher, setting a fire, breaking a window) are the most dangerous and serious. Regardless, FBAs are important tools that help educators understand the reasons for some behavior problems and therefore resolve them quickly.

Evaluating Progress and Revising Programs

Assessments of students' performance have many different purposes. They are used to measure the yearly academic growth of individuals as well as groups of students. In turn, those results are used to assess the effectiveness of schools and their teachers. Assessments for students with disabilities serve additional purposes. They are an important component of the process used to identify and qualify students for special education services. They are also used to monitor the results of individualized educational programs and then they help to determine whether special education services can be discontinued, modified, or remain in place.

Eligibility

Review again the general explanation presented earlier of how students are identified as being eligible for special education services in Step 4 of the IEP process. Remember, special education services are only for students with disabilities that affect their education and learning. Another very important point is that eligibility is not a permanent situation. For this reason, students' eligibility, or identification as having a disability that requires special services, is reconsidered every year, or every 3 years if the child's state is part of the pilot project mentioned in Step 7 of the IEP process.

Standardized tests are typically part of the assessment package used to determine whether a student has a disability and qualifies for special education. They are used again when students are reevaluated to determine whether special education services are still necessary. In addition, direct measures of the student's academic and behavioral performance are part of the eligibility determination. Because specific identification methods vary somewhat by disability, a section in each chapter about specific disabilities is devoted to tests used for identification purposes.

State- and Districtwide Assessments

For improved school accountability, NCLB and IDEA '04 require *all* students to participate in their school district's accountability system. Almost all (some 95%) of those with disabilities take the same state- or districtwide assessments as their classmates without disabilities (U.S. Department of Education, 2007a). For a summary of what these two laws say about students' participation in these assessments, see What NCLB Says and What IDEA '04 Says About High-Stakes Testing. We talk about those few students who are excused from these tests and whose yearly growth is

evaluated through different means in the next section. Here, we discuss large-scale assessments and how participation of students with disabilities can be supported through accommodations.

Because the overall results from individual schools—their adequate yearly progress—are used to "grade" a school's effectiveness, affect student promotion, and sometimes impact the school's funding, these yearly assessments are often referred to as **high-stakes testing**. The ultimate expectation is that all students will achieve proficiency in reading and math, along with mastery of the content presented through the general education curriculum. If students' test scores indicate that they do not reach those levels, the schools they attend experience significant disincentives (penalties). Herein lies the source of pressure and controversy surrounding these high-stakes tests and the inclusion of the scores of students with disabilities. While some say that participation increases expectations, others say the tests are not fair (Bowie, 2007). Reports are increasing that attribute increases in the dropout rate to the stress these tests create, with students with disabilities just giving up and then dropping out of school (J. Williams, 2007). And, evidently the stakes are so high that many suspect that incidents of "teacher-assisted cheating" are on the rise as well (J-J. Williams, 2007).

All 50 states have guidelines or policies in place about the use of testing accommodations; however, they differ widely from state to state (Thurlow, 2007). The National Center on Educational Outcomes (NCEO) studies the participation of students with disabilities in large-scale assessments, the accommodations they are allowed to use, and their effectiveness. (For more about high-stakes testing and related issues, see www.education .umn.edu/nceo.) This group found that many different accommodations are used across the states to help students with disabilities demonstrate how well they have learned (NCEO, 2007). Some states allow a specific accommodation (e.g., read the tests directions aloud) that is banned by others (Crawford, 2007). Research findings about the effectiveness of testing accommodations are just coming in, but most studies so far have focused on students with learning disabilities and the influence of extended time to take the test (Zenisky & Sireci, 2007). In most cases, extended time produced positive results. "Read aloud" is also showing to have benefits, particularly for students who have low reading skills when taking mathematics tests (Ketterlin-Geller, Yovanoff, & Tindal, 2007). Another commonly applied and successful accommodation is called *proctor/scribe* (Cox et al., 2006). Here the student can use a computer, possibly through the voice recognition option, or have someone else record the answer to a question.

Accommodations are referred to by different names across the nation, limiting the information about which are most effective or most widely used. Also, no standard grouping system exists for testing accommodations. Four general categories do seem to be emerging (Crawford, 2007):

- Presentation
- Response
- Setting
- Scheduling

What NCLB Says About . . .

High-Stakes Testing

NCLB requires schools to make *adequate yearly progress* (AYP) according to three conditions:

- At least 95% of students in every subgroup (e.g., students with disabilities, students who are English language learners) must participate in state assessments.
  - Students with disabilities may participate with or without accommodations.
  - Students with significant cognitive disabilities may take an alternate assessment.
- Students (including each subgroup) must meet or exceed the state's AYP objectives for students scoring at or above the proficient level.
  - If one subgroup fails to make the required progress, the school can still make AYP if that subgroup's "not proficient" percentage has declined by 10% and made progress on other indicators.
- Progress must be made on one additional academic indicator.
  - Graduation rate is the high school indicator.
  - States can determine their own elementary and middle level indicators.

Schools that fail to make their goals are subject to improvement, corrective action, or restructuring measures. Schools that meet or exceed their goals are eligible for awards.

high-stakes testing State- and districtwide assessments to ensure all students' progress in the curriculum

High-Stakes Testing

IDEA '04

- allows funding to be used for technical assistance and direct services to schools identified for improvement under NCLB based on scores of students with disabilities;

- requires all children with disabilities to participate in assessments with the appropriate accommodations, modifications, or in alternate assessments as delineated in their IEPs;

- stipulates that alternate assessments must be aligned with the state's challenging academic content and student achievement standards or measure student achievement against alternate academic standards, if applicable;

- requires states to report the numbers of students taking assessments with and without accommodations, and the numbers of those taking alternate assessments.

We used this scheme in Accommodating for Inclusive Environments: Testing Accommodations for State- and Districtwide Assessments, which should help you understand the wide range of accommodations that are available.

Alternate Assessments

One purpose of including students with disabilities in states' and districts' accountability systems is to ensure that the expectations for these students' achievement is high (National Association of State Directors of Special Education [NASDSE], 2007). However, there is now general agreement that for some students such expectations are too high or unreasonable because they cannot achieve proficiency on regular content standards. When IDEA was passed in 2004, only about 1% of students could be excused from large-scale assessments and be evaluated through **alternate assessments**. These students are those not participating in the general education curriculum, usually because of severe cognitive disabilities. The law as written in 2004 also excused students just learning English as their second language (U.S. Department of Education, 2006).

As these rules were put into place, many came to believe that more students should be excused from these high-stakes tests (NASDSE, 2007). Parents and education professionals felt that it was unfair to more students with disabilities, their schools, and their teachers than the 1% initially excused. They believed that some 2% to 3% of all students, or approximately 10% to 30% of students with disabilities should be evaluated differently and not subjected to unreasonable curricular standards and impossible tests.

In 2007, the U.S. Department of Education released new regulations for both NCLB and IDEA '04 that increased the percentage of students who could demonstrate their annual learning through alternate means. What NCLB and IDEA '04 Say About Modified Achievement Standards provides a summary of these changes in the national regulations. When the federal government changed its rules, it basically created three groups:

- Students who demonstrate grade-level proficiency by taking large-scale assessments (without accommodation because they do not need them or with the accommodations called out in their IEPs) along with their classmates without disabilities
- Students with disabilities who participate in the general education, but whose achievement standards have been significantly modified (about 2% of all schoolchildren)
- Students with disabilities who do not participate in the general education curriculum but participate in alternate assessment that reflect their IEP objectives (about 1% of all schoolchildren)

Earlier we talked about the first group of students who participate in the state- or districtwide assessments. They usually use accommodations that allow them to show what and how well they have learned without their disabilities masking their achievements. The second, new group of students with disabilities are responsible to demonstrate attainment of **modified achievement standards**. These students are learning the general education curriculum but do so at a slower pace than their typical peers. They are now allowed to take assessments that are modified and that reflect reasonable benchmarks with grade-level content (Morrier, 2007).

alternate assessments Means of measuring the progress of students who do not participate in the general education curriculum

modified achievement standards Goals and benchmarks from the general education curriculum but modified by reducing the number of objectives or their complexity

Accommodating for Inclusive Environments
Testing Accommodations for State- and Districtwide Assessments

Presentation Accommodations

Directions for test:
- Read aloud
- Sign-interpret questions
- Audiocassette

Braille
Presentation equipment:
- Computer administration
- Technology aid

Setting Accommodations

Change of testing location:
- Quiet, individual space
- Small group

Response Accommodations

Proctor/scribe:
- Dictating instead of writing
- Speech recognition technology
- Interpreter

Word processor
Response aid:
- Calculator
- Spell checker

Scheduling Accommodations

Extended time
Multiple day
Test breaks

myeducationlab Go to the Building Teaching Skills and Dispositions section in Chapter 2 of MyEducationLab and complete the activities in the IRIS Module "Accountability: High-Stakes Testing for Students with Disabilities," which presents information on legal requirements and accommodations for testing students with disabilities, in addition to highlighting considerations for interpreting performance data for this population.

The third group of students participates in a curriculum that targets life skills and community presence. They most often participate in alternate assessments, which evaluate students' progress toward meeting benchmarks for targeted achievement of skills that are not part of the general education curriculum (Thompson et al., 2004; U.S. Department of Education, 2007a). Remember, only 1% of all students, or about 10% of all students with disabilities, can use alternate assessments to demonstrate their achievements (U.S. Department of Education, 2006).

Monitoring Progress

As you learned in the sections about state- and districtwide assessments or high-stakes testing, monitoring every school's overall improvement in academic achievement is important because such evaluations encourage all school personnel to attend to how well its students are mastering the general education curriculum's goals, objectives, and benchmarks of achievement. However, yearly large-scale assessments do not provide teachers with enough information about the progress of individual students to guide instruction. Other types of assessments are better suited for that purpose. Careful and consistent **progress monitoring** is important to avoid wasting instructional time by using a tactic that is ineffective. Teachers need to document these students' improvement in academic achievement, behavior, or attainment of life skills. Teachers often collect more authentic assessments for students with disabilities than they do for their students without disabilities (Fuchs et al., 2001).

progress monitoring Assessing student's learning through direct and frequent assessments directly on the target of concern

What NCLB and IDEA '04 Say About...

Modified Achievement Standards

Additional flexibility is given to states to develop modified achievement standards to more appropriately measure the achievement of those students with disabilities who

- participate in the general education curriculum;
- have IEP goals based on grade-level content standards;
- find the mastery of grade-level content within the same time frames as their classmates without disabilities too challenging;
- have alternate curriculum goals that are either not appropriate or not sufficiently challenging.

States may develop modified achievement standards

- to give parents and teachers that better informs instruction
- to attain a more appropriate measure of students' achievement of grade-level content

States may develop alternate assessments based on modified achievement standards:

- Proficient and advanced scores may be included when measuring adequate yearly progress (AYP).
- The number of scores included does not exceed 2%.
- Students from solely one disability do not comprise this group of students.

authentic assessments
Performance measures that use work generated by the student

portfolio assessment Authentic assessments where students select their work for evaluation

curriculum-based measurement (CBM) Evaluating students' performance by collecting data frequently and directly on academic tasks

All students experience assessments of their classroom performance. Weekly spelling tests, math tests, exams after the completion of social studies units, and history papers are all examples of students' classroom work that is graded. Such evaluations of students' work are **authentic assessments**, because they use the work that students generate in classroom settings as the evaluation measurements (Layton & Lock, 2007). Results on students' class assignments, anecdotal records, writing samples, and observational data on behavior are examples of authentic assessments. In other words, evaluation is made directly from the curriculum and the students' work.

Authentic assessments can be comprehensive and include ongoing, systematic evaluations of students' performance. **Portfolio assessment** is one example of an authentic assessment. Here, actual samples of a student's work, over a period of time are kept together to demonstrate improvement (Layton & Lock, 2007). This evaluation process involves students in both instruction and assessment because they select the exhibits of their work to include (Curran & Harris, 1996; Hébert, 2001). A portfolio may include prizes, certificates of award, pictures, dictated work, photographs, lists of books read, and selections from work done with others. It may also include reports, written by the teacher or by others who work with the child, about challenging situations or patterns of behavior that should be a focus of concern.

Another authentic assessment or progress monitoring method is one typically used in multitiered systems for early intervening to assist students who are struggling in reading or math (i.e, response to intervention [RTI] that you will learn more about in the chapter about learning disabilities). **Curriculum-based measurement (CBM)** also includes direct measurements of individual student's performance in the subjects and skills being taught, but this system is more structured, consistent, and frequently applied than others. It is a detailed data collection system that frequently measures how well a student is learning specific instructional targets. CBM provides instant information about a student's performance and progress toward achieving important benchmarks. For these reasons, CBM data are often part of the documentation teachers include during the prereferral stage of the IEP process (Bradley, Danielson, & Hallahan, 2002; Fuchs, Fuchs, & Powell, 2004). Teachers quickly know how well their students are learning and whether the chosen instructional methods are efficient and effective (Capizzi & Fuchs, 2005; Safer & Fleishman, 2005). For example, a teacher instructing a student in math keeps a record of the number of different types of arithmetic problems correctly solved within consistent time samples (Foegen, Jiban, & Deno, 2007). Depending on the instructional content, the teacher may use 1-, 3-, or 5-minute timings. A teacher concerned about a student's progress in writing might take frequent measurements on the students' learning and correct use of upper- and lowercase letters, writing letters from the dictation of the sounds letters make, and spelling of three-letter words, such as *cat* and *top*, letter sequences, or written words (McMaster & Espin, 2007; Ritchey, 2006). These data are recorded and graphed perhaps daily or weekly to monitor a student's learning across time. For example, using this system, teachers track gains in reading fluency and comprehension, and mastery of different types of mathematics problems (Compton et al., 2006; Fuchs et al., 2007). Progress in virtually every academic area can be monitored through CBM techniques.

In addition to being an evaluation system, CBM is also a data-based intervention that causes improvement in students' learning (Stecker, Fuchs, & Fuchs, 2005). In other words, CBM has multiple benefits:

- It tracks student's progress in the curriculum.
- It informs teachers of the power of their instructional techniques.
- It is an effective instructional intervention.

Details about why CBM is considered an effective data-based procedure and how it is put into practice are found in the chapter about learning disabilities.

Change in Services or Supports

Remember, IDEA '04 guarantees students with disabilities and their families a continuum of services. However, the intention is not for these services to be offered in a fixed sequence. Rather, they are to be a flexible constellation, invoked when supports need to be increased because a student's progress has slowed, or phased down when they are no longer necessary. In other words, the needs of individual students are not fixed but, rather, change across time. A student with a reading disability might, for some period of time, need intensive instruction outside the general education classroom for some portion of the school day. There, intensive instruction is delivered either to a small group of learners, all struggling with the same reading skill, or to an individual student who needs one-on-one instruction. However, once the reading difficulty is resolved, the student sees intensive instruction reduced or removed and progress monitored to ensure reading performance maintains at the desired level.

When changes in placement, either more or less restrictive, are considered, the IEP Team—including the family and in some cases the student—must be in communication (U.S. Department of Education, 2006). In some cases, the whole IEP Team, which includes the parents, holds a meeting. In other cases, only selected members of the team who have expertise related to a particular portion of the student's individualized program need to meet. IDEA '04 requires schools to notify parents in writing about changes being made to the student's program (U.S. Department of Education, 2007b). Regardless, for correct decisions to be made about whether a student's services need to be more or less intensive, information must be current and precise. Typically, authentic assessments, including CBM, are used for such decisions.

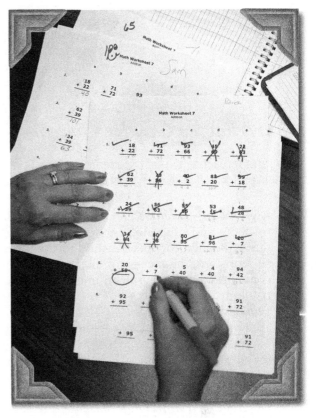

CBM math worksheets that include problems of different types are used to measure students' progress mastering arithmetic across a semester or school year.

Summary

A cornerstone of the federal laws ensuring all infants, toddlers, preschoolers, and students with disabilities a free appropriate education in the least restrictive environment is the individualized education created through the special education process. IDEA '04 guarantees these individuals and their families a tailor-made education program that is guided by uniquely created planning documents: the individualized family service plan (IFSP) and the individualized education program (IEP). The IEP is further supported, when necessary, by behavioral intervention plans and the statements of transitional services. These plans bring together multidisciplinary teams of general educators, special educators, and related service provides for the purpose of assisting each young child and student with a disability reach their full potential and achieve community presence and independence as adults.

Answering the Chapter Objectives

1. What approaches support students as they improve their performance in the general education curriculum?

   - *High-quality general education:* using data-based practices and supporting students who struggle, the foundation for special education services and supports and the means for all students to master content and skills presented in the general curriculum
   - *Universal design for learning (UDL):* extended application of the principles of universal design outlined in the ADA law, to provide multiple paths for all students to approach the curriculum in non standard ways and benefit from current technology (e.g., e-books)
   - *Differentiated instruction:* teaching the same content to all students but using different instructional methods and various grouping practices to match students' interests, preferences, and styles
   - *Instructional accommodations and modifications:* individualized supports or adjustments to assignments provided to students with disabilities that help compensate for disabilities
   - *Assistive technology:* both a related service and equipment that may be low tech (e.g., stands to hold books) or high tech (e.g., electronic speech devices) provided through special education
   - *Individualized data-based interventions and services:* a wide range of instructional methods and interventions, validated through research or clinical practice, that comprise the tailor-made special education program that produce high results and provided through IDEA '04

2. How is each placement option used to deliver special education to students with disabilities?

   - *Pull-in programming:* all services provided in the general education classroom
   - *Co-teaching:* general and special education teachers team-teaching

   - *Consultation/collaborative teaching:* general education and special education teachers working together, but with some services offered outside the general education classroom
   - *Itinerant/consultative services:* the special education teacher consulting with the general educator, who delivers most of the specialized services
   - *Resource room:* special education delivered outside the general education classroom for at least 21%, but not more than 60% of the school day
   - *Self-contained special education class:* special education delivered for more than 60% of the school day in a separate class
   - *Special education (center) schools:* separate day or residential facilities
   - *Home or hospital:* special education services delivered to the students home or to a hospital setting

3. What are special education–related services, and how are multidisciplinary teams formed?

   - Specialized services that support special education
   - Delivered by specialized professionals from different disciplines (e.g., SLPs, PTs, assistive technologists, school nurses)
   - Individually determined by the specific needs of the individual with disabilities

4. What is the IEP process?

   - Prereferral
   - Referral
   - Identification
   - Eligibility
   - Development of the IEP
   - Implementation of the IEP
   - Evaluation and reviews

5. What are the different individualized education plans used for individuals with disabilities (birth through 21)?

   - Individualized family service plans (IFSPs)
   - Individualized education programs (IEPs)
     - Statement of transitional services
     - Behavioral intervention plan

myeducationlab Now go to MyEducationLab at www.myeducationlab.com and take the Self-Assessment to gauge your initial comprehension of chapter content. Once you have taken the Self-Assessment, use your individualized Study Plan for Chapter 2 to enhance your understanding of the concepts discussed in the chapter.

ADDRESSING THE PROFESSIONAL STANDARDS

Council for Exceptional Children (CEC) knowledge standards addressed in this chapter:

GC4K1, GC1K5, GC8K2, GC8K3, GC8S3

Appendix A: CEC Knowledge and Skill Standards Common Core has a full listing of the standards listed here.

Appendix B: CEC Knowledge and Skill Common Core Standards and Associated Subcategories are broken down by chapter.

CHAPTER 3

Cultural and Linguistic Diversity

Naomi Chowdhuri Tyler

Imagine a World . . .

where everyone has a fair start and an equal chance for success . . .

Chapter Objectives

After studying this chapter, you will be able to

1. Explain what is meant by the term *diverse*.

2. Discuss the interplay between poverty and other systemic factors that puts many culturally and linguistically diverse students at risk for low educational results and placement in special education.

3. Describe key features of multicultural education.

4. Discuss how schools can be more responsive to students learning English.

5. Describe additional considerations that diverse students with disabilities and their families require.

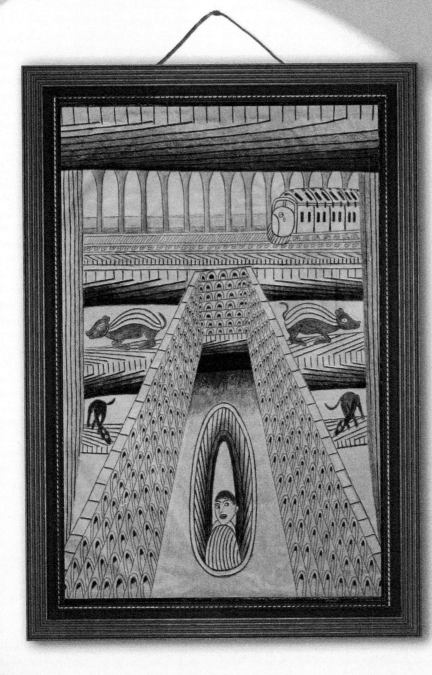

Martín Ramírez was a self-taught master artist of the 20th century. For the last 15 years of his life, he painted from within the confines of DeWitt State Hospital in California. Ramirez came to the United States from Mexico in 1925 in hopes of finding work to support his wife and children, whom he had left in their hometown of Jalisco. During the Great Depression of 1929, he became homeless and unemployed, living on the streets of northern California. Confused and unable to speak English, Ramirez was picked up by the police and taken to a mental hospital. He spent 32 years living in one mental institution after another, rarely speaking to anyone but creating a remarkable series of drawings.

Students who are considered historically underrepresented in the United States are those students who fall into one of these federal categories: African American (Black), Hispanic (Latino/a), Asian/Pacific Islander, American Indian/Alaska Native (Native American).[1] Whether in the majority or not, they are often referred to as *minorities*. Other terms used to refer to this group of students include *culturally and linguistically diverse* (CLD) and *students of color*. Cultural or linguistic diversity is not a disability. However, it can put children and their families at risk for discrimination, bias, reduced opportunities, and challenging life situations. Concerns about CLD students' educational outcomes and high rates of identification as having disabilities are widespread. In addition, because a disproportionate number of students from diverse backgrounds are poor, they are exposed to the ravages of limited access to health care, being homeless, and attending low-quality schools, all of which create further inequities within these students' lives. Government officials are very concerned about special challenges faced by diverse students with disabilities and their families. Therefore, these students' situations are addressed in the IDEA '04 laws, its regulations, and the annual data about the implementation of IDEA (see www.ideadata.org; U.S. Department of Education, 2006). Schools must address and pay attention to the specific learning characteristics and needs of CLD students. When disability is compounded by diversity, it is everyone's responsibility to ensure that the educational system's response is truly special.

Where We've Been . . .What's on the Horizon?

America is a nation founded in diversity, and it remains a country whose populace reflects great and increasing differences (Goode, 2002). Since the nation's beginning, the face of the United States has been one of perpetual change, and so it remains today. America's schoolchildren are diverse in so many different ways. The languages, beliefs, and traditions they bring to school represent cultures from all over the world. Their heterogeneity is marked along multiple dimensions: language, values, religion, perspectives, priorities, and culture. All schools and teachers face the challenge of creating appropriate educational opportunities where instruction is effective for every student. The United States is clearly a multicultural country, so we must judge ourselves in terms of what we do with our diversity, how we treat each other, how we understand each other's similarities and differences, and how we learn from one another. By using this diversity to our advantage, we can make the educational environment richer, and all children will flourish.

Historical Context

Education in the United States has faced issues of bilingualism and multiculturalism throughout the country's history (see Banks, 2006, for a thorough description). In the late 1800s and early 1900s, families often lived in communities where everyone had the same background, and children attended schools where they were taught in their home language (e.g., Swedish, German). Toward the end of the 19th century, immigrants from southern, central, and eastern Europe, who were mainly Catholic, began arriving in the United States. Americans, many of whom at that time had immigrated from northern and western Europe and

myeducationlab After reading this chapter, complete the Self-Assessment for Chapter 3 on MyEducationLab to gauge your initial understanding of chapter content.

---

[1] Many different terms are used to refer to different groups of people in the United States. The federal government uses one set (American Indian/Alaska Native, Asian/Pacific Islander, Black, Hispanic, White); people from specific locales use other specific referents (Anglo, African American, Latino/Latina, Chicano/Chicana); and for broad inclusion, other terms are used (Native American for all Native peoples). The terms used in this text reflect a balance of national and local preferences.

who were predominantly Protestant, felt threatened by the newcomers. The new immigrants became victims of **nativism**, a movement to further the interests of those who considered themselves to be native inhabitants of the country (even though many were immigrants themselves!) and to protect the American culture. Foreign language instruction was prohibited in many schools, and new immigrants were treated with great suspicion and distrust. Then, during the time of World War I, Americans looked inward and came to foster "Americanization," the idea that the United States should become a "**melting pot**"—a country where individuals were assimilated and abandoned their home languages and cultures as soon as possible. The anticipated result was a new, homogenized American experience. But the melting pot model seemed to fail. Instead of creating a harmonious new culture, it led to racism, segregation, poverty, and aggression toward each new immigrant group. The nation also lost the richness that results when a country welcomes and celebrates its many cultures and languages. By the 1960s, however, a new model emerged. **Cultural pluralism** is the idea that people should not abandon their home culture but rather maintain their various ethnic languages, cultures, and institutions, while still participating in society as a whole.

Despite what was thought to be a more accepting climate for diversity, the harsh reality was that racial, cultural, and language differences resulted in some students being inappropriately labeled as having mental retardation or intellectual disabilities. Important court cases involving diverse students and their schooling discovered major examples of discrimination. In 1970, the case of *Diana v. State Board of Education* found that using IQ tests to identify Hispanic students as having mental retardation was discriminatory. In 1971, the case of *Larry P. v. Riles* brought to the attention of the courts and schools the overrepresentation of African American children in classes for students with intellectual disabilities and possible discrimination through biased testing. In 1974, the U.S. Supreme Court ruled, in *Lau v. Nichols* (a case brought on behalf of students whose native language was Chinese), that schools must offer services to help students overcome language barriers. Since the Supreme Court's decision in *Lau*, education laws passed by Congress—including IDEA '04—require schools to help students whose home language is not English access the curriculum and participate in instruction at school.

Periodically, the right of diverse children to an education comes into question. In 1982, the Supreme Court decided a Texas case about whether children of Mexican nationals residing in Texas without proper documentation had a right to a free public school education (*Phyler v. Doe*). The Supreme Court ruled that such children do have this right. Despite the highest court's decision, California voters in 1994 passed Proposition 187, prohibiting undocumented immigrants from receiving public benefits, including education. (This action was later ruled illegal by the federal government.) In many states (e.g., Arizona, California, and Massachusetts), bilingual education has come under attack as opponents attempt to end the provision of these services. Some of the recent focus on illegal immigrants and undocumented workers is, unfortunately, reminiscent of the nativism movement that occurred at the beginning of the last century.

In part because of the 1960s civil rights movement, the attention from court cases, and the continuing challenges faced by CLD students, education

nativism A strong opposition to immigration, which is seen as a threat to maintaining a country's dominant culture

melting pot The concept of a homogenized United States in which cultural traditions and home languages are abandoned for the new American culture

cultural pluralism The concept that all cultural groups are valued components of the society with each group's language and traditions maintained

Source: www.CartoonStock.com

professionals and policymakers are focusing special attention on this group of learners. Because too many of them fail or underachieve, advocacy agencies (e.g., Children's Defense Fund [CDF]), policy institutes (e.g., Tomás Rivera Policy Center [TRPC], Pew Hispanic Center), information clearinghouses (e.g., National Clearinghouse for English Language Acquisition and Language Instruction Educational Programs [NCELA]), federal agencies (e.g., U.S. Department of Education), and research centers (e.g., National Center for Culturally Responsive Educational Systems) are diligently working to understand why these students' education is so precarious and how educators can make a difference.

Challenges That Diversity Presents

Culturally and linguistically diverse children are more likely to find themselves challenged by a multitude of factors that put them at risk for unnecessarily unsatisfactory outcomes. Disproportionately, these students have a greater chance of

- being poor,
- having limited access to health care,
- being homeless,
- living migrant lives,
- attending inferior schools,
- having learning styles and experiences at variance with schools,
- experiencing school failure,
- being identified as having a disability,
- struggling with English language acquisition, and
- dropping out of school.

Each subsequent chapter in this text has a brief section that discusses challenges faced by a particular group of students, like those in the preceding paragraph. What is important to remember is that each group of students also comes with its own unique sets of strengths. In this chapter, you will learn that most CLD students do not have disabilities, but many do have special needs attributable to their diversity. You will learn about the risk factors listed here, but most importantly, you will see that when their strengths are utilized and their special needs are attended to correctly, the outcomes for these children can be outstanding. Quality education can and does make a difference.

Making a Difference
Southern Poverty Law Center and Teaching Tolerance

SPLC co-founders Morris Dees (left) and Joe Levin

Morris Dees and Joe Levin, two Alabama lawyers committed to racial equality, founded the Southern Poverty Law Center (SPLC) in 1971 to address civil rights issues. Their initial legal battles challenged segregation and fought for fair African American representation in the Alabama state legislature and in the state trooper force. Over the years, their work has grown to include several landmark cases in which millions of dollars in damages were awarded to victims of hate groups (e.g., Ku Klux Klan), forcing several of the organizations to declare bankruptcy. Dees's ongoing struggle to fight extremist groups was portrayed in a 1991 TV movie *Line of Fire: The Morris Dees Story.*

Obviously, hate crimes represent one extreme end of human prejudice. Other forms of bias can be subtle and less easily recognized. Interpersonal conflicts in the school setting, often based on students' lack of knowledge or understanding of each others' backgrounds or cultures, can create uncomfortable learning environments. As we'll discuss shortly, teachers' misinformation about the home lives and customs of children from poor or culturally and linguistically diverse backgrounds can contribute to lowered expectations for those students (Harry & Klingner, 2006). When children are specifically taught to understand and respect the differences in their peers, they are far less likely to engage in discriminatory behavior as adults. Teaching Tolerance, a division of the SPLC, strives to increase the cultural knowledge of teachers and students in order to reduce conflicts and improve learning and educational opportunities. Its free antibias education offerings include

- a Web site that provides curricula to address issues such as social justice, gender bullying, classroom activities for teachers, practical resources for parents; games for young children that are both instructional and fun;
- the *Teaching Tolerance* magazine, a semiannual publication available free to educators, that provides articles, activities, and recommended readings to increase awareness and respect for others;
- grants to teachers for the development and implementation of projects aimed at reducing prejudice, improving relations in schools, or supporting professional development activities for educators.

The organization's Web sites provide more information on both the SPLC (**http://www.splcenter.org/index.jsp**) and *Teaching Tolerance* (**http://www.splcenter.org/center/tt/teach.jsp**).

Cultural and Linguistic Diversity Defined

Generally, three groups of students are thought of as diverse: culturally diverse students, linguistically diverse, and culturally and linguistically diverse students with disabilities. Let's look at each of these groups more closely.

Cultural Diversity

Students who come from backgrounds different from American mainstream society, which predominantly adheres to Western European cultural traditions, are thought of as **culturally diverse**. The number of different cultures represented by America's students has not been determined, but it could be over a thousand. Being from a culture different from the dominant American culture does not directly cause disabilities or poor academic performance. However, because of misunderstandings of culturally accepted and expected behaviors and norms of conduct, being culturally diverse can put students at risk of being inaccurately identified as having a disability (Baca & Cervantes, 2004; Gollnick & Chinn, 2006; Voltz, 2005).

culturally diverse Being from a cultural group that is not Eurocentric or of mainstream America

Linguistic Diversity

Individuals whose home language or native language is other than English are referred to as **linguistically diverse**. Many culturally diverse students are also linguistically diverse. Most education professionals use the term *English language learners* (ELLs) or just *English learners* (ELs) to describe these students. The older term, *limited English proficient* (LEP), is the one used in IDEA '04. (See Table 3.1 for the IDEA '04 definition.)

linguistically diverse Having a home or native language other than English

English language learners (ELLs), English learners (ELs) or limited English proficient (LEP) Students learning English as their second language

Diversity and Disability

CLD students with disabilities comprise the third subgroup of diverse learners. The focus of this text is on students with disabilities. Thus, in the remaining chapters you will learn about students with particular disabilities (e.g., learning disabilities,

Table 3.1 • Definitions of Diverse Learners

Term	Definition

Limited English proficient (LEP)
 	
English language learner (ELL)
 	
English learner (EL)
	1. An individual, aged 3–21, enrolled or preparing to enroll in an elementary or secondary school,
	  a. who wasn't born in the United States or whose native language isn't English
	  b. who is a Native American or Alaska Native, or native resident of the outlying areas and comes from an environment where a language other than English has significantly impacted level of English language proficiency, or
	  c. who is migratory, with native language other than English, from an environment where a language other than English is dominant; and
	2. whose difficulties in speaking, reading, writing, or understanding English may be sufficient to deny the child
	  a. ability to meet proficient level of achievement on State assessments;
	  b. ability to successfully achieve in class where instruction is in English; or
	  c. opportunity to participate fully in society

Culturally diverse	Students who come from backgrounds different from American mainstream society; may or may not be of immigrant status
Linguistically diverse	Students whose home, primary, or native language is one other than English; are considered LEP or ELL; require language supports in classroom settings
Diverse students with disabilities	Culturally and/or linguistically diverse students who also have at least one of the 13 disabilities identified in IDEA '04.

Sources: Elementary and Secondary Education Act, Section 9101(25) Authority: 20 USC 1401(18); U.S. Department of Education (2006).

deafness, special health care needs). You will learn about specific causes, characteristics, and ways education can make a real difference for students who have disabilities. Diverse students, like all others, can and do have disabilities, and their cultural backgrounds can affect the way their disability is conceptualized by both the family and the community (Potter, 2002).

Characteristics

CLD students are distinctive in many ways. Many of their unique qualities are not the result of personality or behavioral traits but rather are attributes that are reflective of a language or culture that is different from that of America's mainstream. These students are often confusing to educators, who sometimes mistakenly misinterpret a difference as a disability or a problem. Instead, teachers should understand that a difference can be considered a strength and might best be addressed through a change in teaching approach or an accommodation. Let's look at three areas that teachers should be particularly knowledgeable about:

- Understanding differences between language differences and language disorders
- Preventing clashes between home and school cultures
- Distinguishing between behavioral differences, behavioral disorders, and attention deficit hyperactivity disorders

Language

Both culturally diverse and linguistically diverse children exhibit language and communication differences that often raise educational questions but should not always result in special education (Cheng, 1999). It is not always easy to tell a speech or language impairment from a language difference. Let's first look at characteristics exhibited by many linguistically diverse students and then turn our attention to the language skills of culturally diverse students.

Some children may speak forms of a language that vary from its literate or standard form (Cheng, 1999). For example, the spoken Spanish used in southern Texas generally varies from the spoken Spanish used in New Mexico, both of which may differ from the standard form of Spanish. These variations are dialects and should not automatically be considered language deficiencies. Some languages do not include certain sounds or grammatical structures found in English. For example, the /f/, /r/, /th/, /v/, and /z/ sounds do not exist in Korean. Many English consonant sounds do not exist in Chinese, so a Chinese-speaking child's difficulty with some English sounds may reflect the child's inexperience with the sounds, rather than speech impairments (see Chapter 4). Although many of these children are referred for speech therapy for an articulation problem, their distinctive speech is simply an accent, and therapy probably is not necessary.

Detecting the differences among language impairments, learning disabilities, and language differences can be difficult, even for well-trained professionals (Salend & Salinas, 2003). Sometimes children are wrongly identified and find themselves placed in special education even though they have no language impairment or learning disability (Ruiz, 1995). At other times, children's disabilities are masked by the language difference, and they wait years for the special services they need. One general guideline for determining whether a bilingual student has a language impairment is to discover whether the impairment occurs in both English and the child's dominant language. For example, a Spanish-speaking child who converses perfectly in Spanish with his brothers on the playground but who has limited ability to use conversational English has a problem, but it is not a language impairment. Actually, it is due to an inadequately developed second language. Figure 3.1 provides a visual representation to help teachers understand

Figure 3.1 • Language Differences Versus Language Disorders

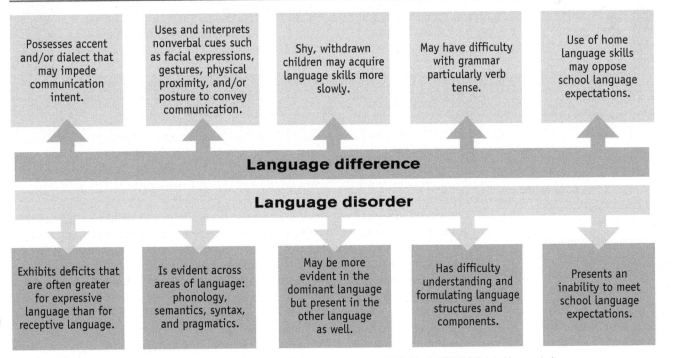

Source: Courtesy of and thanks to Zina Yzquierdo, Department of Special Education, Vanderbilt University, 2005. Reprinted by permission.

Considering Culture: *New World, New Language: Multicultural and Bilingual Special Education*

Maria Perea is a cute, petite first grader who shyly plays near, but rarely with, her peers. The Perea family recently emigrated from Mexico, and this is Maria's first school experience. The first grade teacher, Patty, enjoys having Maria in her classroom, and she wants Maria to be successful. Maria likes to help the teacher care for the classroom's pet guinea pig, and she often sits on the teacher's lap for story time and songs. Patty, however, is worried that Maria never makes a peep! She doesn't talk, join in songs or rhymes, or play much with the other children—and they seem to exclude her from their play. Patty wonders if Maria is exhibiting signs of a language delay, but she first decides to consult with Sonia, Maria's ESL teacher down the hall.

Sonia visits Patty's class and observes, then gently engages Maria in play while speaking with her in Spanish. Patty notices that Maria actually speaks to Sonia! Patty explains that Maria's lack of verbalization is probably due to the fact that she is learning English; however, she agrees to monitor Maria's language development carefully, to make sure they are not overlooking a possible disability.

Patty and Sonia meet with Mr. and Mrs. Perea to keep them informed and to let them know that they will be carefully monitoring Maria's language development in both English and Spanish. Mr. and Mrs. Perea indicate that they want Maria to learn English, but they also are afraid that she will forget her native Spanish. The team, including Maria's parents, agree to continue her current ESL services but also look into ways that they can support her bilingual development in her first-grade classroom.

Questions to Consider

1. Imagine that you move to another country where you do not speak the language. What do you think your experiences would be? How would you feel? Even in your daily life here at home, are you ever frustrated that you can't make your opinions or needs clearly understood? Are others ever exasperated or impatient with your inability to communicate effectively? Can you imagine being treated as though you were a child or were too inept to understand? What would it be like to be ignored because you can't speak adequately with others?

2. If you know teachers who have linguistically diverse students in their class, ask them these questions: What curricular goals do they have for these students? How do the diverse students differ from those students who are not bilingual? What communication challenges do they face as teachers? What communication challenges do their ELL students face?

—By Eleanor Lynch, San Diego State University, and Marci Hanson, San Francisco State University

---

code switching Using two languages in the same conversation; a sign of developing dual language proficiency

dialects Words and pronunciation from a geographical region or ethnic group, different from those of standard language

Ebonics A learned and rule-governed dialect of nonstandard English, spoken by some African Americans

these differences, and the scenario described in Considering Culture reinforces these points.

Many students use both English and their home language within the same communication, referred to as **code switching** (Brice & Rosa-Lujo, 2000). Code switching is not a disorder but rather a way for people to achieve mastery of two languages, and it is often a sign that dual language proficiency is developing.

There are other issues surrounding language, even for those who speak English at home. Many African American children, for example, come to school speaking a **dialect** or variation of standard English often referred to as **Ebonics**. The issue of using Ebonics in schools has come to the attention of educators, Congress, and the public (Seymour, Abdulkarim, & Johnson, 1999). What is the concern? Most schools and mainstream American institutions do not approve of this form of English, and many leaders in the Black community believe its use in educational settings causes teachers to perceive students negatively. They believe strongly that schools must "teach standard English to all of our nation's children yet celebrate their diversity and their ability to communicate effectively in a variety of settings" (Taylor, 1997, p. 3). Interestingly, although some consider this form of American English to be substandard, it is used to generate millions of dollars in advertisements, music, television, and film.

Our nation's diverse population ensures that teachers will have students in their classrooms who are learning English as well as those who speak various English dialects. Educators must continually find effective ways to teach students who may encounter academic difficulties as a result of language differences. The majority of academic learning is language based; students who struggle linguistically face exceptional disadvantages in the classroom.

Cultural Comprehension

Children come to school with a good understanding of the norms and expectations of their homes, which is typically developed by the time they are five years old (Lynch & Hanson, 2004). They understand proper behavior when interacting with adults, and they know what is appropriate when playing with each other. What children do not know, particularly if kindergarten is their first school experience, is that the rules of home might not match the rules or conventions of school. Diverse children and their families may not understand that they have a new culture—that of American schools—to learn.

It is important that teachers understand the roles that culture and language play in the learning process (Yates, Hill, & Hill, 2002). Some students' cultural characteristics, behaviors, and actions can be at odds with the classroom culture or teachers' expectations. A mismatch of home and school cultures (sometimes referred to as **cross-cultural dissonance**) may explain why many diverse students seem to be constantly in trouble and why traditional classroom instruction is often ineffective (Harry, 2008). A good example of this dissonance occurs in the seemingly innocent use of competition, common in American classrooms (Lynch & Hanson, 2004). Spelling bees, behavior games, even earning stars of different colors for excellent performance are forms of competition that some diverse students find peculiar. In many Native, Latino, and Asian cultures, cooperation, not competition, is valued. Hence, children who come from cultures that do not value individual competition are often uncomfortable when encouraged to be better than everyone else, and they may even feel torn between feelings of pride and guilt if they win in competitive situations. At school, their lack of competitiveness might be interpreted as a lack of motivation. Yet, if they show their newly developed competitiveness at home, a sudden lack of cooperation might be interpreted by their family and friends as a behavioral problem. Such students might learn more readily in school settings when assigned to cooperative learning groups to work together on academic assignments (Fletcher, Bos, & Johnson, 1999). This chapter's On the Screen selection shows how different families and students think about academic competitions and differing viewpoints on the concept of school success.

"Caught between two cultures" is a phrase frequently used to describe the experience of many Native students who do not attend a tribal school. Native children's communication at home tends to be symbolic and filled with nonverbal nuances. To these children, adults at school talk too much, are overly blunt, seek disturbingly direct eye contact, and ask questions that are inappropriately personal (Garrett et al., 2003). The result can be disengagement, incorrect referrals to special education, misidentification as having a disability, and eventual dropout (Artiles, 2003). When home and school cultures clash, children can become terribly confused and poorly educated (Obiakor, 1994).

Teachers who are **culturally competent** can prevent cross-cultural dissonance in their classrooms. They know the backgrounds, heritages, and traditions

cross-cultural dissonance When the home and school cultures are in conflict

culturally competent Knowing and understanding the cultural standards from diverse communities

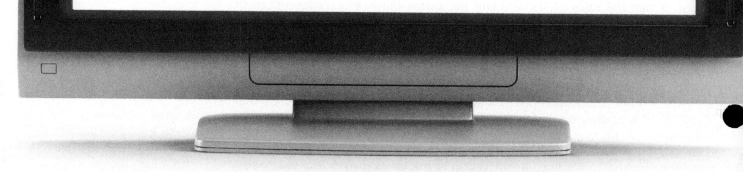

On the Screen: *All Eyes on the Bee*

In the delightful and uplifting movie *Akeelah and the Bee,* the hard work and dedication of an 11-year-old African American girl, Akeelah, reveals that success is possible, even when the odds are not equal. The film reveals much about the diversity among families as students enter into fierce competition for the prestigious title of Scripps National Spelling Bee Champion, and it brings to light the challenges faced by teachers and students in South Los Angeles. Akeelah has to overcome many obstacles, including her own reluctance to compete at first and the initial lack of support from her friends who do not understand the importance she places on achieving her goal. She is one of the few diverse students who participates in the regional and the final competitions; most of the other students she competes against are from public schools in affluent districts or elite private schools. In the end, the strength of her family and community support her victory, and the audience celebrates her triumph in a heart-warming story of well-earned success.

—Steven Smith

of their students, and they adjust their teaching and make accommodations accordingly. A culturally competent teacher

- understands culture and its role in education;
- engages in self-reflective examination of his or her own cultural attitudes and assumptions and their subsequent impact on classroom instruction and activities;
- takes responsibility for learning about students' culture and community;
- uses student culture as a basis for learning; and
- creates learning environments that are **culturally responsive**, where the curriculum includes multiple perspectives and examples (Ladson-Billings, 2001; Gay & Kirkland, 2003; Kozleski, Sobel, & Taylor, 2003).

culturally responsive Curriculum that includes multiple perspectives

Behavior

It is important to keep in mind that behavioral issues can arise when behavior appropriate in one environment, such as the home, is considered inappropriate in another, such as the school (Harry, 2002; Voltz, 2005). Much of behavior is based in culture, so children from nondominant backgrounds are more likely to be at variance with the norms of school (Cartledge & Loe, 2001). A silent child might be behaving in a desirable way according to standards of his home culture but be characterized at school as withdrawn or anxious. Having fun with a group of friends, "messing around," engaging in verbal sparring, and physically kidding around might bring positive attention and make the child popular after school but be perceived as disruptive in school. Table 3.2 provides examples of potential areas in which cul-

Table 3.2 • Examples of Cross-Cultural Dissonance in the Classroom

Action	Possible Misinterpretation
A teacher gives a thumbs-up sign to indicate that a student answered a question correctly.	Students from some Middle Eastern countries, Nigeria, and Australia believe this is an obscene gesture, equivalent to the American middle-finger sign.
A teacher employs a passive communication style with her students, using phrases such as "Let's all think quietly" or "Jada, would you like to sit down?"	Many African American students are used to a more straightforward communication style. Without a clear directive (i.e., "Jada, sit down"), they may not understand that the teacher is actually giving them a command. The teacher, in turn, thinks the students are being defiant when they do not comply with her requests.
A student looks down at the floor while a teacher is speaking to him, which is a sign of respect in many Asian, Latin American, and Caribbean cultures.	The teacher believes the child is not listening to her or is disinterested in the conversation.
A student from Southeast Asia smiles when being scolded by a teacher as a sign that she admits her misbehavior and holds no hard feelings.	The teacher interprets the smile as a smirk and a sign that the child thinks the situation is funny or is not taking her seriously.

Sources: Dresser (1996); Weinstein et al. (2004).

turally appropriate behavior (for both teachers and students) could be misinterpreted in the classroom. When the cultures of school and home collide, students usually suffer the negative consequences (Bryant, Smith, & Bryant, 2008).

Teachers are more likely to refer boys whom they feel act out, do not comply with expectations at school, and demonstrate aggressive behavior. Black males who display these behaviors, which are acceptable and even expected in some neighborhoods, are more often identified as having emotional or behavioral disorders than would be expected (Hosp & Reschly, 2002, 2003) and screen positively for ADHD (see Chapter 6), particularly when referred and tested by White educators (Reid et al., 2001). Neal and colleagues (2003) found that this inaccurate interpretation of African American boys' behavior is often based on their nonverbal behaviors and their movement styles, such as assuming an assertive or defiant posture, swinging one's arms, and walking with a swagger or stroll.

myeducationlab Go to the Activities and Applications section in Chapter 3 of MyEducationLab, and complete Activity 1, IRIS Activity, "Understanding BICS and CALP," to gain a better understanding of the difference between basic interpersonal communication skills (BICS) and cognitive academic language proficiency (CALP), and to understand how language differences affect classroom learning.

Using behavior and dress that are cool among friends, but not acceptable by teachers, can send messages to educators that result in significant negative consequences.

mutual accommodation Acceptance and use of students' language and culture within the classroom, while also teaching them the expectations and culture of the school

It is difficult for children (and their teachers) to understand that a particular behavior is acceptable in one setting but not another. Most children learn to sort out different behavioral expectations across a variety of settings and situations, but some do not and therefore need help to learn. Educators can prevent many teacher–student conflicts by being knowledgeable and understanding of different cultural expectations, and by helping students "walk in two worlds." When **mutual accommodation** occurs in a classroom, teachers can specifically explain what is expected in the classroom, while acknowledging the appropriateness of the behaviors outside the school setting (Nieto & Bode, 2008).

Classroom management exerts a powerful influence on student achievement (Weinstein, Tomlinson-Clarke, & Curran, 2004). While cultural differences do not explain all behavioral infractions that teachers have to deal with in classroom settings, understanding the basis for some of the problems can lead to more effective solutions. When genuine misbehavior does occur, teachers who are "warm responders" and deal with students in a consistent, caring, yet firm manner while still maintaining high student expectations have better classroom control (Bondy et al., 2007). Furthermore, a positive environment, coupled with explicitly expressed commitment to helping all students achieve, can prevent the psychological disengagement that can occur when students sense lowered expectations or inequitable treatment (Cartledge & Kourea, 2008). In culturally responsive classrooms, "discipline becomes something that students possess rather than something imposed on them (Cartledge & Kourea, 2008, p. 362). This chapter's Tips for Classroom Management suggest some simple guidelines when addressing classroom management issues with diverse students.

Prevalence

demographics Characteristics of a human population

Of this there is no question: The **demographics** of America's students are changing, particularly because they reflect growing numbers of different immigrant groups. At the turn of the 20th century, Irish, English, Italians, Germans, and Swedes were all thought of as belonging to different and unique immigrant groups. At the turn of the 21st century, however, descendants from all those groups were typically thought of as one group representing "mainstream" America, while Hmongs, Vietnamese, East Indians, Mexicans, and hundreds of others from many different countries are viewed as the "new face" of America. Before considering groups of students and then the number or percentage of them with disabilities, it is important to understand how easy it is to misinterpret national data, particularly when they reflect people's race, ethnicity, and culture.

National data about diversity and students must be interpreted carefully for several reasons. First, the federal government uses only five categories to describe all Americans along the dimensions of race and ethnicity: White (Caucasian), Black (African American), Hispanic (Latino/a), Asian/Pacific Islander, and American Indian/Alaska Native (Native American). Most Americans do not fit discretely into these five categories. For example, when asked about their backgrounds, many people (e.g., the golfer Tiger Woods) think of themselves as best belonging to a group that might be called "multiracial," but the government does not have such a category. At the same time, many of these categories are too inclusive. Consider tribal communities, all with very different values and traditions. Even though these communities speak as many as 187 different languages (Krause, 1992), they are all grouped together as American Indian/Alaska Natives.

Another problem with this classification system is that it makes assumptions that immigrants, first-generation Americans, and multigenerational Americans who are from the same ethnic group are similar. Take, for example, two Asian/Pacific Islanders or, even more specifically, two Chinese American students. One student, Peter Chin, is a fifth-generation American whose family has lived in the United States for 150 years. Peter's family does not follow Chinese traditions, and they all

TIPS for Classroom Management

BEING CULTURALLY RESPONSIVE

Teachers who engage in culturally responsive classroom management do the following:

1. Recognize their own cultural beliefs and assumptions.
   - Acknowledge that their personal beliefs and assumptions are not universally accepted.
   - Understand how their personal beliefs influence teacher behavior and expectations in the classroom.
   - Identify potential sources of cross-cultural conflict.
   - Monitor whether they exhibit equitable treatment of students.

2. Develop genuinely respectful, caring relationships with their students.
   - Share information about themselves with their students.
   - Show an authentic interest in their students' lives, within and outside the classroom.
   - Communicate in a calm and respectful manner.

3. Actively learn about their students' cultural backgrounds, and use that knowledge in the classroom.
   - Understand how factors like family background and structure, relationship styles, discipline, perceptions of time, and interpersonal space impact student behavior and are perceived by students and their families.
   - Use verbal and nonverbal communication styles that are familiar to the students (e.g., terms of endearment and humor, familiar words and expressions, call-and-response interaction pattern, straightforward directives).

4. Use culturally appropriate classroom management strategies.
   - Clearly define classroom expectations (e.g., rules, procedures, consequences), particularly if these differ from those to which students are accustomed.
   - Hold students accountable for meeting classroom expectations.
   - Focus on positive behavior.
   - Deal with inappropriate behavior immediately, consistently, and fairly.

5. Build caring classroom communities.
   - Help students learn about one another.
   - Stress the importance of respecting and being kind to each other.
   - Set clear, high expectations for all students.
   - Nurture personal development.

Sources: Bondy et al. (2007); Cartledge & Kourea, (2008); Weinstein et al. (2004).

myeducationlab Go to the Activities and Applications section in Chapter 3 of MyEducationLab and complete Activity 4. As you watch the video, think about the techniques used by the teacher to facilitate instruction.

speak only English. The other student, Ping Mao, was born in the United States and is a first-generation American. Her family adheres to Chinese traditions and speaks a dialect of Chinese at home. Although the federal government's classification system places these two students in the same category, they bring to school very different backgrounds. Many people who find themselves counted in one of these categories feel no personal connection with it. Common assumptions about the backgrounds of diverse individuals and where they live may well be wrong because population demographics are not static (Suro, 2002; Suro & Singer, 2002). Generalizing about individuals who belong to a group can lead to some terrible mistakes.

One final problem with using national data is that regional, state, or even local school district data may vary widely. Patterns of immigration, numbers of ELLs, and other relevant information may be masked by the large national data sets. It is important for educators to also identify data from their local areas. Let's now turn our attention back to the racial and ethnic composition, or diversity, of today's students.

Diverse Students

According to the National Center for Educational Statistics (2007a), 48.6 million students were enrolled in public elementary and secondary schools in the 2005–2006 school year. The federal government reports that 1.2% of these students were American Indian/Alaska Native, 4.6% were Asian/Pacific Islander, 19.8% were Hispanic, and 17.2% were Black. The remaining 57.1% were reported in the White category. Interestingly, students who are not included in the count of White students are often considered "minority" students, even if they constitute the majority of the school population. For example, in ten states (Arizona, California, Georgia, Hawaii, Maryland, Louisiana, Nevada, Mississippi, New Mexico, and Texas) and the District of Columbia, White students made up less than half of the student population. In New Mexico, over half of the students attending public school were Hispanic, and in Hawaii, Asian/Pacific Islanders represent 72.8% of the student population. African Americans, Latinos, Native Americans, and Asian Americans are still often referred to as minority students, even when they make up between 66% and 92% of the overall student population in cities like Nashville and Chicago (Chicago Public Schools, 2008; Metropolitan Nashville Public Schools, 2008). The risk of using only national data is that they mask variations seen in specific locales. In many states and cities, the "minority" is the majority.

As mentioned earlier, students whose native or home language is other than English are considered linguistically diverse. Around 10% of the current school population has limited proficiency in English, an increase of 57% in the last 10 years (NCELA, 2008). In many school districts, including Chicago, Los Angeles, and Fairfax

Culture is reflected in many ways, and the diversity it presents enriches all of us.

County, Virginia, students and families use over 100 different languages; nearly 170 different languages are spoken in New York City schools (Stiefel, Schwartz, & Conger, 2003). Native Americans speak over 187 different languages (Krause, 1992), and people from Southeast Asia and the Pacific speak hundreds of different languages and dialects (Cheng & Chang, 1995). Asian Americans currently represent the most rapidly growing segment of the population, yet the majority of ELLs speak Spanish, with Latino/a children under the age of 5 comprising 22% of the entire U.S. population (Diaz et al., 2008; NCELA, 2003; Pew Hispanic Center, 2008).

Diverse Students with Disabilities

Although students who are diverse bring special challenges to schools, remember that neither cultural nor linguistic diversity results in a need for special education services. Not all White students have disabilities or learning problems, and neither do all diverse students. Likewise, giftedness should not be thought of as belonging to one group more than to another. The federal government requires the states to report data about the race/ethnicity of all students with disabilities. (Because IDEA '04 does not include gifted students, comprehensive data are not available about diverse students' representation in these programs.) Collectively across all categories, 58% of those students provided with special education services are White, 21% are Black, 17% are Hispanic, 2% are Asian/Pacific Islanders, and 2% are American Indian/Alaska Native (Office of Special Education Programs [OSEP], 2008).

Over- and Underrepresentation of Diverse Students

A consistent, worldwide pattern has emerged showing that the lowest achievers in many countries are from groups who have typically experienced exclusion and discrimination within a particular society (Artiles & Bal, 2008; Harry, 2007). Many of these students end up receiving special education services (Dyson & Gallannaugh, 2008; Harry et al., 2008; Kalyanpur, 2008; Werning, Loser, & Urban, 2008). You just learned about the prevalence, or representation, of students grouped by race or ethnicity who attend public schools in the United States. You also learned about their prevalence in special education. Let's look more closely at these two sets of data to see why education professionals, policymakers, and parents are concerned about some groups' participation in special education (Coutinho & Oswald, 2006).

One simple way to use the data is to compare the percentage of a group of students in the general population to their percentage in special education—referred to as the **composition index** (National Center for Culturally Responsive Educational Systems) [NCCRESt], 2006; Skiba et al., 2008). If a group's percentage in special education is higher than its percentage in the general school population, the situation reflects **overrepresentation** of that group. The reverse situation is called **underrepresentation**: A group's percentage in special education or gifted education is lower than it is in the general population. Any variance between a group's representation in the general population and in one of these subgroups is called **disproportionate representation**.

The bottom row of Table 3.3 shows the percentages of public school enrollment by race/ethnicity (OSEP, 2008). Note that the overall percentages for each racial/ethnic category are similar to the percentages for students with disabilities in the row above, except for Asian/Pacific Islanders, whose representation in special education is approximately half that of their overall enrollment. This situation could reflect an underrepresentation of students from this group. Let's take a closer look, however, at some of the disability categories. Notice that while Black students represent only 19.8% of the overall enrollment, they represent 28.8% of the students in the emotional disturbance category and 32.8% of the students in the IDEA mental retardation (intellectual disabilities) category. These percentages could indicate a case of overrepresentation. Remember also that these data reflect only national averages; state and local data often reflect very different patterns of disproportionality.

composition index A tool for measuring disproportionate representation in which the percentage of students from a particular racial group receiving special education services is compared with their percentage in the overall school population

overrepresentation Too many students from a diverse group participating in a special education category, beyond the level expected from their proportion of students

underrepresentation Insufficient presence of individuals from a diverse group in a special education category; smaller numbers than would be predicted by their proportion of students

disproportionate representation Unequal proportion of group membership; over- or underrepresentation

Table 3.3 • Percentage of Students Ages 6–21 Served, by Disability and Race/Ethnicity, 2005–2006

Disability	American Indian/ Alaska Native	Asian/ Pacific Islander	Black (non-Hispanic)	Hispanic	White (non-Hispanic)
Specific learning disabilities	1.7	1.7	20.5	21.2	54.8
Speech or language impairments	1.4	3.2	15.4	17.5	62.5
Intellectual disabilities (MR)	1.3	2.1	32.8	14.1	49.8
Emotional disturbance	1. 6	1.1	28.8	11.1	57.4
Multiple disabilities	1.4	2.7	20.9	13.2	61.8
Hearing impairments	1.3	5.0	16.3	22.7	54.8
Orthopedic impairments	1.0	3.5	14.8	20.9	59.8
Other health impairments	1.3	1.5	17.4	9.9	70.0
Visual impairments	1.4	4.2	17.2	18.0	59.2
Autism	0.7	5.4	14.4	11.6	68.0
Deafblindness	1.9	4.1	13.9	18.6	61.5
Traumatic brain injury	1.6	2.5	16.5	13.2	66.2
Developmental delay	3.7	2.7	22.4	9.8	61.4
All disabilities	1.5	2.2	20.6	17.3	58.4
Total public school enrollment	1.2	4.6	19.8	17.2	57.1

Note: Due to rounding, rows may not sum up to 100%. Data based on Fall 2006 count

Source: OSEP (2008).

risk index A tool for measuring disproportionate representation, representing the percentage of students from a particular racial group who receive special education services

risk ratio A tool for measuring disproportionate representation where the risk index for one group is divided by the risk index for another group. A risk ratio of 1.0 indicates proportionate representation. Risk ratios above or below 1.0 represent over- and underrepresentation, respectively

Another way to assess disproportionality is to calculate a group's representation in special education as compared to that of other groups (de Valenzuela et al., 2006; Skiba et al., 2008). For example, a school district discovers that 2.4% of all African American students are identified as having emotional disturbance (referred to as the **risk index**). The risk index alone tells us very little unless it is compared to the risk index for another group. The district discovers that only 1.2% of all White students are identified as having the same disability. In this case, the **risk ratio**, which is calculated by dividing the risk index for African Americans (2.4) by the risk index for White students (1.2), shows that African Americans are twice as likely to be identified as having emotional

Table 3.4 • Risk Ratios for all Disability Categories and Racial/Ethnic Categories from the 26th Annual Report to Congress

Disability	American Indian/ Alaska Native	Asian/ Pacific Islander	Black (not Hispanic)	Hispanic	White (not Hispanic)
Specific learning disabilities	1.53	0.39	1.34	1.10	0.86
Speech/language impairments	1.18	0.67	1.06	0.86	1.11
Intellectual disabilities (MR)	1.10	0.45	3.04	0.60	0.61
Serious emotional disturbance	1.30	0.28	2.25	0.52	0.86
Multiple disabilities	1.34	0.59	1.42	0.75	0.99
Hearing impairments	1.21	1.20	1.11	1.20	0.81
Orthopedic impairments	0.87	0.71	0.94	0.92	1.15
Other health impairments	1.08	0.35	1.05	0.44	1.63
Visual impairments	1.16	0.99	1.21	0.92	0.94
Autism	0.63	1.24	1.11	0.53	1.26
Deaf-blindness	1.93	0.94	0.84	1.04	1.03
Traumatic brain injury	1.29	0.59	1.22	0.62	1.21
Developmental delay	2.89	0.68	1.59	0.43	1.06
All disabilities	1.35	0.48	1.46	0.87	0.92

Note: Drawn from U.S. Department of Education, Office of Special Education and Rehabilitative Services (2006), *26th Annual Report to Congress on the Implementation of the Individuals with Disabilities Education Act, 2004.* Washington, DC: Westat. Risk ratios were calculated by dividing the (prerounded) risk index for the racial/ethnic group by the risk index for all other racial/ethnic groups combined for students age 6 through 21 with disabilities, by race/ethnicity and disability category.

Source: From p. 269 of Skiba, R. J., Simmins, A. B., Ritter, S., Givv., A. C., Rausch, M. K., Cuadrado, J., & Chung, C. (2008). Achieving equity in special education: History, status, and current challenges. *Exceptional Children, 74*(3), 264-288. Used courtesy of the Council for Exceptional Children.

disturbance—a risk ratio of 2.0. Similarly, if 0.2% of American Indian students are identified for gifted programs, compared to 2% of all other groups, then it would appear that American Indians are underrepresented at ten times that of the rest of the school population, with a risk ratio of 0.1. A risk ratio of 1.0 indicates exact proportionality, risk ratios above 1.0 indicate overrepresentation, and ratios below 1.0 indicate underrepresentation. The two cases here show examples of over- and underrepresentation, respectively. Table 3.4 shows the national risk ratios for all disability categories and racial/ethnic groups (Skiba et al., 2008). Notice the wide variation in several of the disability and race categories. For example, African Americans are three times more likely than any other group to be identified as having intellectual disabilities, a disability in which Asian/Pacific Islanders are significantly underrepresented.

As we have noted, IDEA does not include gifted education, and states are not required to report data about these students. Regardless, reports from researchers who study these issues overwhelmingly indicate that African American, Hispanic, and Native American students are underrepresented in programs for the gifted, particularly males (Bernal, 2000; Ford, 2000; Ford, Grantham, & Whiting, 2008). Here again, because of these students' lower proportion in the general population, their situation is masked when you look at national data. When you look at state or district data, disparities become more obvious. With the exception of Native Hawaiian students, for whom overrepresentation in special education is of concern, students from an Asian background are far less likely than other diverse students to be identified as having a disability (Kishi, 2004; OSEP, 2008). They are more likely to be included in gifted education, but the reverse is true for their Black, Latino/a, and American Indian peers.

Another disproportionality concern that has arisen recently focuses on special education placement settings. Researchers are finding that students from diverse backgrounds have a greater probability of being placed in more restrictive or segregated educational settings than are their peers from the majority culture (de Valenzuela et al, 2006; Skiba et al., 2008). As you learned in Chapter 2, students in more restrictive educational settings often have less access to the general education curriculum. This fact, coupled with the potential for lowered expectations, can have deleterious effects on the long-term educational outcomes for these students.

All of the previous discussion leads up to one overarching question: Why is disproportionality in special education problematic? The simple answer is that it is wrong to place students who have no disabilities in special education. One substantial concern is that placement in special education often means that the student is removed from the general education setting and, in the case of CLD students, is too often placed in a more restrictive curriculum. IDEA '04 stresses the importance of students' access to the general education curriculum. Special education placement can reduce this opportunity and increase the potential for lowered expectations for student achievement. Second, inaccurate disability identification indicates potentially inappropriate instructional and behavioral practices in the general education classroom. Teachers may truly believe that special education services will help a child whose skills are below grade level or who need a little extra help to catch up. However, placing children who do not have true disabilities into special education places an unnecessary burden on that system, when the students' needs could and should be met in the general classroom. Third, a societal stigma is associated with the concept of disability (Harry, 2007). Students who are incorrectly placed in special education are needlessly exposed to the negative perceptions, actions, and comments of peers and others who do not fully understand disabilities or the needs of those who have them. Finally, some researchers argue that special education is too often imposed on students, rather than being freely chosen by parents as a source of support for their children (Harry, 2007). This makes the process more suspect to many families from diverse backgrounds, who have historically experienced inequitable and discriminatory practices.

Causes and Prevention

As you continue through this text, you will learn that there are many known causes of disabilities—and there are also many disorders for which no known cause has been identified. When the education of diverse students is examined, particularly with an eye toward disproportionate representation in special education, there is no single explanation for the situation. Rather, it appears that there are a number of factors whose interactions result in the disparate provision of special education services (Skiba et al., 2008). Causes of clearly identified disabilities and potential causes of misidentification both need to be examined.

Causes

Regardless of our background, we are all susceptible to thousands of individual causes of disabilities. Some, such as those stemming from genetics and heredity, are biological causes and are at the root of many disabilities. For example, Down syndrome and fragile X syndrome are genetic causes. Muscular dystrophy is an inherited condition passed on through families. Not all health conditions are inherited, and certainly not all are serious enough to cause a disability or special education services. A virus can also be considered a biological cause, such as in the case of a virally induced hearing loss. In addition to biological reasons for disabilities or special needs, other causes are environmentally based. For example, toxins abound in our environment. All kinds of hazardous wastes are hidden in neighborhoods and communities. Anyone can get sick—and even have a resulting disability—from exposure to environmental toxins. This type of exposure can happen anywhere, including the United States, where old dump sites hide dangerous wastes out of sight but not so far away that neighbors are safe from harm.

Some causes of disabilities, however, are unusually common among children and youth who come from diverse backgrounds. Some of these causes are biological, but most are environmental. Sickle cell anemia (discussed in Chapter 9 under special health care needs) is hereditary and is disproportionately present in African Americans. Lead is one environmental toxin that causes intellectual disabilities and learning disabilities. Corroded lead pipes, solder, and brass fixtures are all sources of lead in household and schools' drinking water. Most of us do not think of lead poisoning as much of a concern in America today, because its two major sources—lead-based paint and exhaust fumes from leaded gasoline—have been largely eliminated. Leaded gas and lead-based paint are no longer sold in this country. Unfortunately, the lead has remained in dirt that children play in, and lead-based paint remains on the walls of older apartments and houses, where children breathe the lead directly from the air and household dust, or put their fingers in their mouths after touching walls or window sills. The Children's Defense Fund (CDF) reports that some 16% of low-income children have lead poisoning, compared with 4% of all children in the United States (CDF, 2006). Lead is not the only source of environmental toxins that government officials worry about; other concerns include mercury found in fish, pesticides, and industrial pollution from chemical waste (Schettler et al., 2000).

The major source of lead exposure among U.S. children is lead-based paint and lead-contaminated dust, which should be professionally removed

Social and economic inequities have a significant impact on our nation's children (CDF, 2006; Kozol, 1991, 1995). Many situations can put children at risk for disabilities or conditions that result in special needs. Let's look at two that are of critical concern: unequal educational opportunities and poverty.

Unequal Educational Opportunities Russell Skiba and his colleagues (2008) wrote, "One of the most consistent findings in educational research is that students achieve in direct proportion to their opportunity to learn" (p. 274). This simple statement underscores a key factor in the poor educational achievement of many students from diverse backgrounds: Too often, students of color receive an inadequate public education. Despite the Supreme Court decision over 50 years ago in *Brown v. Board of Education* (Topeka, Kansas) that separate schools are not equal, White students and students of color still remain apart today (Rothstein, 2004). Students of color too frequently attend inferior schools, often located in lower-income neighborhoods, and in both inner city and rural areas. These schools tend to be larger, have higher student–teacher ratios, and have fewer human and financial resources, as reflected in their low budgets, few materials, and poor course and service offerings (Fry, 2005). They tend not to offer **advanced placement (AP) courses** or college-prep classes and have fewer or no after-school enrichment activities.

advanced placement (AP) courses High school courses that carry college credit

Troubled schools, particularly those in low-income neighborhoods, also have great difficulty attracting and retaining highly qualified teachers (Harry & Klingner, 2006; Skiba et al., 2008). As a result, these schools have more than their fair share of the least prepared, inexperienced, and uncertified teachers. Because of their lack of preparation, these teachers have great difficulty providing motivating, culturally responsive, high-quality instruction. Charles Greenwood and his colleagues (1994, as reported in Skiba et al., 2008) reported that weak instruction in poor schools resulted in their students receiving the equivalent of 57 weeks less instruction by sixth grade than their counterparts in higher–socioeconomic status schools, which resulted in an achievement gap of 3.5 grade levels by sixth grade! Ineffective teachers also lack the necessary behavior management skills to

Students who are engaged in learning, and whose teachers have high expectations for them, flourish in the learning environment.

maintain classroom order, further decreasing the amount of quality instruction provided to students. Because of their frustrations in the classroom, these teachers frequently have the highest turnover rates, resulting in situations where students receive inconsistent instruction from an ever-changing roster of inexperienced teachers (Ingersoll, 2001). All of these factors put many diverse learners at even greater disadvantage and reduce the probability for positive educational outcomes.

Compounding the effects of poor schools and inexperienced teachers is the fact that too few teachers maintain high expectations for CLD students (Cartledge & Kourea, 2008). In fact, low expectations and negative attitudes are prominent, frequently based on inaccurate, stereotypical perceptions of the students' families. Beth Harry and Janette Klingner (2006) found that the source for these perceptions was often a single piece of information (e.g., the father is in jail, the mother uses illegal drugs), which teachers had failed to verify. Students for whom teachers have high expectations are given many opportunities to respond in class, are given sufficient time to respond to questions, are given positive feedback on correct responses, and, when they answer incorrectly, are guided by the teacher through the reasoning necessary to obtain a correct answer. In contrast, when teachers have lower expectations, they ask students fewer questions, give less "wait time" for responses, provide little feedback on student responses, and simply call on someone else when a student gives an incorrect answer. Student performance is impacted by teachers' actions, as they internalize the negative perceptions and become disengaged, resulting in poor academic performance or disruptive behavior (Good & Nichols, 2001).

Poverty Race, ethnicity, and poverty are intertwined (Lee & Burkam, 2002; U.S. Department of Education, 2002). When we look at overall data, the largest numbers of people living in poverty are White. However, when considering percentages, 25% of African Americans and 22% of Hispanics are poor, compared to only 11% of Whites. Far more poor students than one would expect from their representation in the general population arrive at kindergarten already identified as having a disability (D'Anguilli et al., 2004). The CDF (2006) gives us some additional and alarming facts to consider when we think about the relationship between the conditions under which children live and the incidence of disabilities in children. Each day in America,

- 390 babies are born to mothers who received late or no prenatal care,
- 720 babies are born at low birthweight,
- 1,153 babies are born to teen mothers,

- 1,879 babies are born without health insurance,
- 2,411 babies are born into poverty, and
- 77 babies die before their first birthday.

There is no denying the lifelong impact of poor nutrition, limited or no access to health care (being uninsured), and not receiving immunizations on time during childhood (CDF, 2006). During the school years, the effects can be seen in learning and behavior problems. Across a life span, the effects can be seen in employment and life satisfaction outcomes.

Not all poor children are homeless, but the relationship between homelessness and poverty is obvious. **Homeless** children and those of immigrants and migrant workers often experience disruption and dislocation—circumstances that can adversely affect their physical, mental, and academic abilities (Markowitz, 1999). Children who live in shelters experience daily humiliation at school when peers learn that they have no home. These students often change schools every few months, breaking the continuity of their education and leaving gaps in their knowledge that result in reduced academic achievement. Educators must understand that their low academic performance occurs because of many factors, including fragmented education, absenteeism, and high risk for health problems. Being homeless in rural areas is also challenging because of the lack of social services and shelters (Van Kuren, 2003). Because of the high percentage of homeless children who also have disabilities, IDEA '04 pays special attention to them and their unique needs (see What IDEA '04 Says about Homeless Students).

Although not necessarily considered homeless, migrant workers' children are also at risk for poor school performance. Over 80% of migrant and seasonal farm workers are U.S. citizens or legal immigrants (Henning-Stout, 1996). These workers earn incomes below the federal poverty level. Most migrant families live in Florida, Texas, or California between November and April and move to find agricultural work the rest of the year. Approximately half a million migrant students live in the United States, and about 75% of them are Hispanic.

Poverty's impact on students can be significant. Yet, a growing body of research indicates that poverty alone does not account for the academic difficulties exhibited by many students, and instead it is teachers' perceptions of students who live in poverty that has an undue influence (Harry & Klingner, 2006; Skiba et al., 2005). To quote Skiba and his colleagues (2008) again, "Where poverty made any contribution above and beyond race in predicting disability identification, its primary effect was to magnify existing racial disparity" (p. 273). In other words, students from diverse backgrounds are still overrepresented in special education, even when the poverty factor is removed. Educators must be vigilant to maintain high expectations for low-SES students.

Prevention

How can disabilities in diverse children be prevented or avoided? According to CDF (2006), the most effective and efficient way to reduce the number of children who actually have disabilities, and thus to make an enormous difference in the outcomes of children, is to remove the risk variables discussed earlier by

- improving access to health care,
- guaranteeing universal vaccinations against disease, and
- ensuring safe living environments.

What IDEA '04 Says About . . .

Homeless Students

IDEA '04 defines *homeless children* as children who do not have a regular or adequate nighttime residence. They might be living in a motel, hotel, trailer park, campground, or emergency or transitional shelter. They might have been abandoned in a hospital or might be awaiting foster care placement. They could be living in cars, public spaces, abandoned buildings, substandard housing, train depots or bus stations. They could also be mobile, living for a while in any of the above-mentioned situations. Those homeless children with disabilities must

- receive the special education services specified in their IEPs,
- have those services monitored and evaluated, and
- have their IEPs follow them if they move from one school to another or from one district to another.

homeless Not having a permanent home

When students master the foundation skills of learning early, they are more likely to succeed at school and less likely to drop out.

Of course, affecting such sweeping social changes is beyond individuals' capabilities, but there are actions that alert educators can take to make a real difference in the lives of children. For example, even without universal health care or guarantees that all workers will be insured, many free services are available to the poor and to people who live in urban areas. Unfortunately, available community health care services are often not accessed because families are afraid or unaware of them (Tornatzky et al., 2003). Being knowledgeable about resources in your community and then helping increase awareness of their availability could help poor parents gain access to medical services that would prevent disabilities from occurring.

Overcoming Challenges

Earlier in this chapter, we listed some challenges that students from diverse backgrounds face such as inferior schools, cross-cultural dissonance, English-language acquisition, and school dropout. Fortunately, many positive and effective actions are available to diminish these challenges and improve learning outcomes for diverse students.

Education is one of those important responses. Research findings are beginning to reveal why many diverse students fare poorly and what we can do to improve results for these students. We have already discussed one related issue—that of inferior schools. Let's look at two other areas of needed improvement:

- Little or no access to high-quality preschool experiences
- Disengagement, alienation, and dropping out of school

Children from low-SES backgrounds experience disadvantages from the start (Thurston & Navarrete, 2003). They come to kindergarten and first grade the least prepared for schooling, with fewer readiness skills than more affluent peers, and one and a half times more likely already to have been identified as having a disability and to have had an IEP developed (D'Angiulli et al., 2004). These children's achievement is not on a par with others' when they begin elementary school (Lee & Burkam, 2002). Why might this be so? One reason is that fewer diverse children have had a school experience before first grade: 55% of White 3- and 4-year-olds attend preschool, whereas only 35% of Latinos/as do (Pew Hispanic Center, 2002). African Americans attend preschool at rates commensurate with their White peers, in part due to programs like Head Start, which were specifically designed for low-income children (Sadowski, 2006). However, researchers are now distinguishing differences in school outcomes between children who attend preschool and those who attend prekindergarten (pre-K) programs (Waldfogel, as cited in Sadowski, 2006). Pre-K programs are generally designed to provide a bridge to school, incorporate a more stringent curriculum, and often tie their goals and expectations to those of a school system. In contrast, preschool programs are less structured, with less focus on the development of school readiness skills. In order to combat this early educational inequity, experts at the Tomás Rivera Policy Center at the University of Southern California suggest that all poor children, along with those of working parents living at the margins of poverty, should have access to free, high-quality early learning experiences (Tornatzky et al., 2003). With appropriate early supports, diverse students can catch up. New research findings show that with intensive and sustained education, even those learners who come to school far behind can match the achievement of their more affluent classmates (D'Anguilli et al., 2004). This intensive education must focus on phonics, reading, and literacy (National Reading Panel, 2000). It must be rich in reading experiences and multitiered so that those who gain skills quickly can move on, while those who progress more slowly receive additional, intensive instruction (see discussion of response to intervention [RTI] in Chapter 5). When this education is sustained, the dismal path that so many diverse students find themselves moving along can be altered.

Second, diverse students are often disengaged from the learning process, feel alienated, and as a result drop out at a higher rate than their White peers. The message sent by inferior schools and low expectations is clear, so it is not surprising that diverse students often feel alienated from the educational system (Brown et al., 2003). Perceived injustices fuel this alienation, such as when African American students are suspended for not buttoning their overall straps but White students receive no disciplinary actions when they wear jeans with large holes and tears in the legs (Cartledge & Kourea, 2008). In fact, a strong predictor of psychological disengagement from school for African American and Hispanic students is the degree to which they sense injustice within the school setting (Cartledge & Kourea, 2008). And when students see little value in schooling, they are more likely to have a high absentee rate and eventually to drop out; indeed, the dropout rate for poor Latinos/as is as high as 30% to 40% (Tornatzky et al., 2003). Look at Figure 3.2 to see the dramatic differences in dropout rates for Black and Hispanic students. The graph shows us that although all students are less likely to leave school before graduating than they were some 10 years ago, the differences among racial and ethnic groups remain a problem (NCES, 2007a). Fortunately, these statistics can be turned around. Schools that are smaller, offer more

Figure 3.2 • Dropout Rates by Race and Ethnicity

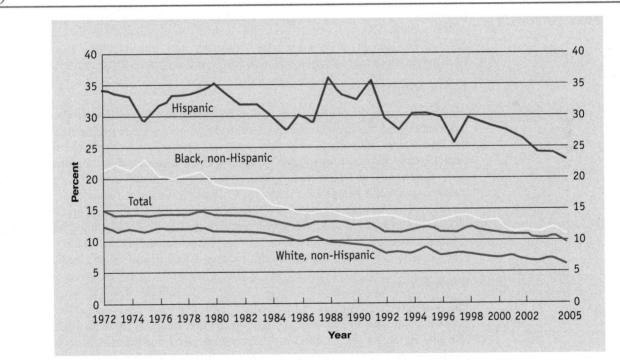

Note: The status dropout rate indicates the percentage of 16-through 24-year-olds who are not enrolled in high school and who lack a high school diploma or equivalent credential such as a General Educational Development (GED). Beginning in 2003, respondents were able to identify themselves as being more than one race. The 2003 through 2005 categories for White, non-Hispanic and Black, non-Hispanic contain only respondents who indicated just one race. The Hispanic category includes Hispanics of all races and racial combinations. Because of small sample size for some or all of the years shown in the figure, American Indians/Alaska Natives and Asian/Pacific Islanders are included in the totals but not shown separately. The "more than one race" category is also included in the total in 2003 and 2004 but not shown separately because of small sample size. The variable nature of the Hispanic status rates reflects, in part, the small sample size of Hispanics in the CPS. Estimates beginning with 1987 reflect new editing procedures for cases with missing data on school enrollment items. Estimates beginning with 1992 reflect new wording of the educational attainment item. Estimates beginning with 1994 reflect changes due to newly instituted computer-assisted interviewing.

Source: National Center for Educational Statistics, (2007a).

personalized instruction, and demand higher performance have better retention rates (Furger, 2004). How can we make a difference? Here are a few ideas (D'Anguilli et al., 2004; Tornatzky et al., 2003):

- Provide diverse students with high-quality early education experiences.
- Give them intensive and sustained instruction during their school years.
- Make education relevant to them.
- Anchor instructional content and activities to students' culture and backgrounds.

Assessment

Evaluating students' performance, abilities, and achievement has many different purposes. One purpose is to evaluate students' general academic performance. This type of assessment is undertaken to answer this question: How well are students mastering all of the curriculum targets that are part of the state's standards? This question is usually answered by administering an achievement test to a group of learners once a year. A second purpose of assessment is to get an indication of how well a student is learning skills or knowledge being taught. These assessments are taken more frequently than yearly achievement tests and come in many different forms (e.g., weekly spelling tests, a test on a history unit, a portfolio of a semester's writing assignments, curriculum-based measurements on oral reading, or summary data taken on a student's classroom behavior). These evaluations of students' performance are more direct because they use students' actual schoolwork or measurements of classroom behavior to answer these questions: How well is the student doing with his or her school work? How effective are the teaching procedures being implemented? A third purpose of assessment is to determine whether a student has a disability and whether that disability seriously affects his or her educational performance. This assessment process is conducted to answer this question: Does a student qualify for special education services? We will briefly consider each of these purposes as they affect culturally and linguistically diverse learners with disabilities, but first let's turn our attention to students identified as having disabilities before they start kindergarten.

Early Identification

Whether they are diverse learners or not, children identified as having disabilities during infancy and the preschool years tend to have very serious problems that come to the attention of physicians, day care workers, preschool teachers, and family members. Discussions about the signals of each specific disability that are apparent during early childhood are found in the respective chapters of this text (e.g., physical disabilities or special health care needs in Chapter 9, and low vision and blindness in Chapter 11). What is important to remember is that more culturally and linguistically diverse children come to kindergarten and first grade already identified as having disabilities and already having had an IEP developed for them (D'Angiulli et al., 2004). One possible explanation is the limited access to health care (CDF, 2006).

Prereferral

The prereferral process has many benefits, including early intervention for diverse students who are struggling and are having trouble keeping up with their classmates (Grupp, 2004). As you learned in Chapter 2, general and special educators are very much involved in the identification process, and they work together long before formal testing begins. For school-age children, general education teachers are the usual source of referrals to special education. They, along with special educators, typically work together to gather information about a student of concern before a formal referral is made. Remember, the prereferral phase is the step in the process that is intended to reduce the number of unnecessary and inappropriate assessments. The hope is that this step will also help avoid misidentifying diverse students as having disabilities (Baca & Cervantes, 2004; Donovan & Cross, 2002). The National Alliance of Black

School Educators (NABSE) and the Council for Exceptional Children's ILIAD Project (2002) suggest that administrators (e.g., principals) create prereferral teams at every school. These teams of experts work together to design and test interventions and modify instruction to be certain that students who are actually referred to special education have first had many opportunities to learn and improve their performance. Members of these teams should collectively have expertise that includes knowledge and experience in educating diverse learners, individualizing instruction, taking part in the special education identification process, and working collaboratively. Additionally, prereferral team members need to ensure that

- the child's parents or other relevant extended family members are involved in this process;
- interpreters are provided, if necessary, to ensure family participation;
- the child's academic problems are not the result of ineffective classroom instruction or a lack of proficiency in English;
- a classroom observation occurs to determine whether cross-cultural dissonance may be causing any behavior problems;
- the classroom teacher understands the importance of recommended prereferral strategies and implements them with **fidelity**;
- recommended interventions not only address skill remediation but also encourage higher-order thinking processes;
- documentation of the students' progress should be comprehensive (Ortiz et al., 2006).

fidelity Instruction or intervention is implemented effectively and is consistent with the methods outlined by the program's instructions

Identification

Students from ethnic and racial groups that are not part of the dominant American culture are often at a disadvantage when taking standardized tests. Also, students who have not yet fully mastered English cannot demonstrate their abilities in such testing situations (Thurlow & Liu, 2001; Yzquierdo & Blalock, 2004). Differences in culture and in language contribute to some students being misidentified as having a disability or to their being excluded from education of the gifted (Ochoa et al., 1999). For other students, test results present an incorrect and depressed picture of their abilities. Despite all of the negative attention and charges of discrimination leveled at IQ tests and other standardized tests, and despite court rulings that bias plagues these testing procedures, educators still rely on what appears to be the simplest and most clear-cut form of student evaluation: the standardized test (Ford et al., 2008).

How can discrimination in the assessment process occur? There are many reasons for bias, but some of the major ones are worthy of attention and thought. First, opportunities for unfair evaluations are created when an individual untrained in multicultural

Educators must ensure that tests are nondiscriminatory and accurately reflect a student's knowledge.

nondiscriminatory testing Assessment that accounts for cultural and linguistic diversity

multiple intelligences Multidimensional approach to intelligence; allowing those exceptional in any one of eight areas to be identified as gifted

and bilingual techniques conducts the evaluation. Second, the content of the test items often assumes specific knowledge of mainstream U.S. culture (Joseph & Ford, 2006). A third concern is that diverse groups are not always represented in the standardization population. The following provides an example that addresses these concerns. A test contains a simple question about what one would need to make a sandwich. The majority of students in the test's standardized population consisted of White, middle-income students who are used to eating sandwiches. As a result, the test developers expect one of the answers to be "bread." However, a Hispanic student who has a great deal of knowledge about tortillas but little experience with bread would be at a disadvantage with the cultural knowledge expected and possibly with the linguistical requirements if the word *sandwich* is not in his English vocabulary. Since Hispanics were not a large portion of the standardizing population, the test developers wouldn't realize that answers pertaining to tortillas might also be correct, and the testing key would indicate this answer as wrong. If the person conducting the evaluation does not recognize the problem with the test items, understand the need to select an assessment that is less discriminatory, or acknowledge the necessity of creating a less biased testing situation, then the student may be unnecessarily qualified to receive special education services (Joseph & Ford, 2006). To stress the importance of nonbiased evaluations, IDEA requires that **nondiscriminatory testing** be established in each state. Take a look at What IDEA '04 Says About Nondiscriminatory Testing to see how the law and regulations address this important issue.

How might bias be removed? One way might be to rethink and broaden the narrow view of intelligence reflected in standardized tests. A restricted concept of aptitude—that it reflects only students' abilities to achieve academically—may be one reason why disproportionate numbers of students from CLD groups continue to be unidentified when they need special education, to be misidentified as needing special education, and to be underrepresented in education of the gifted (Ford et al., 2008). Although this theory is invoked more often when considering gifted children, educators of diverse children have taken a growing interest in Howard Gardner's (1983) theory of **multiple intelligences**. In this model, intelligence consists of many different intelligences: verbal linguistic, logical/mathematical, visual/spatial, musical/rhythmic, bodily/kinesthetic, naturalistic, interpersonal, and intrapersonal (Kornhaber, Fierros, & Veenema, 2004). To be considered gifted, individuals need to demonstrate talent in only one area. June Maker and her colleagues (Maker, Nielson, & Rogers, 1994) originally applied Gardner's theory to children from diverse backgrounds, believing that a multiple approach better reflects talent fostered across cultures. They point out that one's culture may influence how ability is expressed. They give as an example the fact that oral storytelling may be a common form of linguistic giftedness in one culture, whereas writing a novel may be a predominant form in another. Students identified as gifted through this process often made gains equal to or greater than those of other gifted students identified through the standard IQ testing process. Applying such innovative concepts to the identification process may well help reduce the underrepresentation of diverse students in programs for gifted students.

Another means of solving the problem may rest with the use of different assessment procedures. Performance-based diagnostic procedures, such as authentic and portfolio assessments, have particular merit for students at risk for over- or underrepresentation in special education (Hébert & Beardsley, 2001; Joseph & Ford, 2008). Curriculum-based measurement has also been suggested as a means of more fairly evaluating students' abilities, because assessment is based on classroom performance (Cartledge & Kourea, 2008; Donovan & Cross, 2002; Reschly, 2002). Yet another solution may be to incorporate flexible and sensitive identification systems that change depending on the individual's situation: stage of English language acquisition, family, culture, length of time in the United States, economic status, and region (Cuccaro, 1996; Yzquierdo & Blalock, 2004). The identification process could include input from multiple sources, such as parents, extended family members, church and community leaders, and service clubs (Patton & Baytops, 1995; Rogers-Dulan, 1998). Experts agree on one thing: Even minor changes in current practice can make a difference (Ortiz, 1997; Ortiz & Yates, 2001). Here are some of their recommendations:

- Provide early prereferral intervention.
- Develop assessment portfolios.
- Conduct assessments in the student's dominant language.
- Use qualified personnel competent in their own and the student's language and familiar with the student's culture.
- Use interpreters, if necessary, who are proficient in the child's native language and familiar with the special education system and the assessment process.

Evaluation: High-Stakes Testing

NCLB and IDEA '04 require that all students participate in state and district assessments. However, special arrangements can and should be provided for students who have special needs or circumstances. For example, ELLs who have been in the United States less than 1 year are exempted from taking the tests. ELLs, particularly those with disabilities, are entitled to either alternate assessments or accommodations (see Accommodating for Inclusive Environments for some examples). The National Center for Educational Outcomes (NCEO) stresses that the purpose of these accommodations is to give students an opportunity to demonstrate their knowledge and skills, rather than emphasizing their disabilities or lack of English fluency (NCEO, 2005a). How do educators decide which accommodations ELLs with disabilities should be provided in testing situations? One guideline is that the accommodations made for instruction should also be provided during testing (Baca & Cervantes, 2004; Thurlow & Liu, 2001). Thus, if a student is allowed extra time to complete assignments, then allowing extra time would be a proper accommodation during an assessment. How many ELLs with disabilities might warrant special accommodations? Martha Thurlow and Kristin Liu (2001) estimate that the number approaches half a million students.

Accommodating for Inclusive Environments

English Language Learners with Disabilities Participating in High-Stakes Testing

Native Language Accommodations

- Have text passage in both English and native language
- Provide questions in both languages
- Accept answers in either language
- Translate directions

English Language Accommodations

- Read questions orally in English
- Explain the directions
- Simplify the test's language

Nonlinguistic Accommodations

- Give extra time to take the test
- Administer the test either individually or in a small group
- Allow for short breaks

Alternate Assessments

- Monitor growth in language proficiency
- Use portfolio assessment documentation

What are some of the benefits of including diverse students with disabilities in high stakes testing and other reform agenda items? Although both the testing movement and the inclusion of these youngsters is new, some positive outcomes have already been noted (McLaughlin, Pullin, & Artiles, 2001; NCEO, 2005b):

- High-stakes accountability has put pressure on schools to get their ELLs to learn English faster and earlier.
- Accountability measures have now brought diverse students' educational needs to the attention of school district administrators, which in turn will bring additional resources and help to these students and their teachers.
- Learning problems are addressed early and intensively.
- An atmosphere of high expectations is created.

Early Intervention

The early childhood years represent a critical period for cognitive, social, and emotional development. It is during these early years that children develop a readiness for school and for life. The basic building blocks for language, learning, and literacy are formed before children head off to kindergarten and first grade. Children from low-SES backgrounds and those with poor health tend not to have the same readiness skills as their more affluent peers (Lee & Burkam, 2002). High-quality preschool and pre-K experiences include exposure to oral language, reading, and storytelling and to models of standard English, how to work in groups, and how to follow instructions. It is at preschool that many children learn the rules and conventions of the school culture. These skills are the fundamentals to a "good start" on the path toward school success (Tornatzky et al., 2003).

Although it is not universally available, many poor children benefit greatly from the federal Head Start program, begun in 1964 as part of the federal initiative called the War on Poverty. Head Start is for children from low-income families. In 1994, the program was expanded to include children from birth to age 3 through the Early Head Start program. Head Start services include a physical examination and full health assessments (immunization status; assessment of growth, vision, hearing, and speech; and screening for anemia, sickle cell anemia, lead poisoning, tuberculosis, and infections). Remember, access to health care is an important factor in preventing disabilities. Results from early intervention programs are outstanding, reflected by long-term positive changes for children and families (Malveaux, 2002). Participating preschoolers end up with better academic outcomes when they enter school, have fewer referrals to special education, and show lower high school dropout rates. All of this results in saving school districts over $11,000 per child, proving that early prevention now is a much better option for everyone than remediation later!

Correctly including preschoolers with disabilities, particularly those from diverse backgrounds, in early intervention programs is not always an easy task. The process involves considerable planning and thought, but long-term results clearly justify the effort. Here are a few ideas about how to accomplish good integration in preschool settings (Kraft, 2001):

- Incorporate pictures of diverse children with disabilities into the classroom decor along with pictures of typically developing youngsters.
- Monitor the accessibility of the physical environment to be sure all children can move around freely and safely.
- Communicate with families consistently and frequently (not just when there is a problem).
- Teach typical peers how to play and interact with their peers who have disabilities.

Direct efforts focused on developing language and literacy skills should begin during the preschool years. Teachers can anchor instruction by developing literacy through the culture and history of preschoolers' diverse communities (Harry &

Young children often use toys and dolls to practice and expand language and learn social conventions. They also learn they are valued when dolls reflect their own appearances. Notice the adaptive devices that accompany these toys.

Klingner, 2006). Accordingly, rather than a unit about each cultural group being presented during a designated week, the history, customs, art, literature, music, and famous people from all cultures should be woven into every curriculum topic presented across the school year. The curriculum can be enhanced to reflect more culturally appropriate components. For example, it can include activities involving creative arts from different cultures—music, artwork, and drama from students' diverse backgrounds and home experiences (Santos et al., 2000). The curriculum can also incorporate stories from a wide variety of cultural and ethnic traditions. As the next section explains, all students benefit from the exposure to broader experiences when a multicultural curriculum is implemented.

Teaching Diverse Students with Disabilities

When culturally and linguistically diverse students have disabilities, the response to their education needs to be truly special. Three critical components should be present. Their education must

- be steeped in the practices of multicultural education,
- include intensive support for language development, and
- incorporate the most current evidence-based practices to address each student's particular disabilities.

Access to the General Education Curriculum: Multicultural Education

Multicultural education incorporates students' cultural backgrounds to help all students find relevance in the general education curriculum, thereby improving their access to academic content. Multicultural education "supports and extends the concepts of culture, diversity, equality, social justice, and democracy in the school setting" (Gollnick & Chinn, 2006, p. 5). Who exactly is multicultural education for? Everyone! All students profit from learning more about classmates and their home communities, and the advantages continue far into students' futures (Banks, 2006). The benefits of multicultural education extend to promote success for adults in a global marketplace. According to Artiles and Bal (2008, p. 11), "a key feature of globalization is the compression of time and space due in part to the advent of sophisticated (and relatively inexpensive) communication technologies." Improvements in transportation and technology have enabled the movement of people and

multicultural education Incorporates the cultures of all students into instruction

When students can share their talents and achievements, the entire school is enriched.

information across large geographic areas in relatively short amounts of time, creating an interdependency among regions, countries, and continents. Students who are not culturally competent risk being unprepared to participate in this century's global economy, which requires that professionals are culturally competent, cross-cultural communicators. The benefits for students from diverse backgrounds are especially great. Technology such as e-mail and the Internet allow new immigrants to maintain better contact with family members in their home countries than in previous generations. When their home cultures are understood, valued, and respected at school, they do not feel marginalized, rejected, or isolated. Teachers who use key features of multicultural education (Gollnick & Chinn, 2006; Lynch & Hanson, 2004; Tiedt & Tiedt, 2005)

- connect instruction to students' experiences and background by incorporating examples that celebrate diversity;
- understand differences between home and school cultures;
- avoid clashes resulting from differences between the traditions, values, expectations, and view of appropriate behavior typical of the home and those typical of the school; and
- provide reading assignments that come from many different sources, where the central characters reflect the ethnic and racial diversity of students in the class and at the school.

contextualized instruction
Embeds students' cultures, interests, and backgrounds into instruction

Professionals must work hard to become better prepared to work with children from many different backgrounds, as teachers are increasingly White, middle-income females and do not reflect the diversity of their students (Tyler, Lopez-Reyna, & Yzquierdo, 2004). Of course, no one teacher can reflect all of the diversity seen in America's students. By developing culturally responsive schools and classrooms, teachers demonstrate respect for children's home cultures. **Contextualized instruction** with relevant and interesting content motivates students to do their best (Montgomery, 2001). Teachers can provide contextualized instruction by teaching with examples from many American experiences (Castellano & Díaz, 2002; Kea & Utley, 1998). It is important not to become "cultural tourists" by only celebrating holidays or traditions of other countries (Rueda, Lim, & Velasco, 2008). Instead, cultures can be meaningfully linked to instruction and the classroom experience (Artiles et al., 2002). Some teachers post pictures of neighborhood events and have community leaders lead discussions and lessons on relevant topics. Teachers can use magazines such as *Essence, Ebony, Canales, Latina, Pamir,* or *Indian Country Today* for supplemental reading activities to pique students' interest and provide them with excellent role models (Christina Amanapour, the journalist;

nalist; Venus Williams, the tennis star; Zubin Mehta, the musician) (Jairrels, Brazil, & Patton, 1999; Sileo & Prater, 1998). Schools can also recognize and value different cultures by supporting their clubs and groups (ESL clubs, Movimiento Estudiantil Chicano de Aztlan [MEChA] clubs, chapters of African American sororities and fraternities; and arts, music, dance, and crafts clubs).

It is important not to stereotype groups of individuals or make assumptions that people from the same culture hold similar beliefs and traditions (Rueda et al., 2008). For example, to assume that an American-born child of Japanese heritage maintains the same cultural belief system as a recent Japanese immigrant is just as erroneous as assuming that a child of Cherokee heritage who lives in Denver is completely assimilated into the dominant U.S. culture. These beliefs can be influenced not only by the cultural background of students but also by such factors as the length of time their families have been in America; the geographic region of the country in which they live; the age, gender, and birthplace of each child; the language spoken at home; the religion practiced by the family; the proximity to other extended family members; and the socioeconomic level of the family (Gollnick & Chinn, 2006).

Instructional Accommodations

It is imperative that teachers make accommodations for students who are not on a par with classmates in their English language competence. It is impossible to access learning, profit from instruction, or participate in a learning community if you do not understand the language being spoken or read. Learning to speak English and developing enough proficiency to profit from academic instruction in English is slow and complex; it is not an automatic or natural process for many children (Baca & Cervantes, 2004). ELLs' language acquisition can often be confusing to educators, to their families, and even to themselves. Over 20 years ago, Jim Cummins (1984) helped us appreciate what mastery of a language means for students, and his theory holds true today. Achieving basic interpersonal conversation skills (BICS) or **conversational English** allows children to communicate well on the playground and interact in English with friends and teachers. However, conversing at this level is different from having the language skills necessary for cognitive academic language proficiency (CALP) or **classroom English**. Table 3.5 provides some examples of these types of language. Conversational skills in a second language can be acquired within 2 to 3 years, but the more complex language abilities needed for academic work require 5 to 7 years of meaningful exposure and practice (Zelasko & Antunez, 2000). These two abilities do not develop sequentially, nor do they develop independently. Sometimes educators hear children engaged in conversational English in school hallways, lunchrooms, and playgrounds, and they incorrectly assume that their English skills are well developed. Then, when these same students struggle with classroom English, teachers do not realize that they are still developing their academic vocabulary and mistakenly refer them for special education services. Teachers also need to understand that the ability to translate one language into another is not sufficient (Cheng, 1996). Mastery of a language also requires appreciation and understanding of idioms and of nuances that express feelings, anecdotes, and nonverbal messages.

For linguistically diverse students to profit from instruction, they must master English. The goal of **bilingual education** is for students to master both their home language and English. Many experts point out that across the world, mastering more than one language is the norm and that it has many social, economic, and personal benefits (Antunez & Zelasko, 2001). However, debate about the use of bilingual education has raged in many states, and three (California, Arizona, and Massachusetts) have stopped or curtailed such programs. Yet, without appropriate supports, ELLs may be more likely to receive referrals to special education. Why is there such controversy? One explanation is that becoming truly bilingual is a very slow process, and it takes time away from learning content in the standard curriculum. Thus, many

conversational English Being able to use English in general communications but not necessarily for academic learning

classroom English English skills required to access the general education curriculum and profit from instruction

bilingual education Teaching in and seeking mastery of students' native language and English

Table 3.5 • Examples of Different English Skill Levels

Conversational English	Classroom English
Do you want to go to the movies on Saturday?	Read pages 67 to 184 for homework tonight, and use the glossary to define all of the vocabulary words in the chapter summary.
Look at the beautiful flowers.	Plants generate their own food using sunlight, carbon dioxide, and water through a process called photosynthesis.
The video game costs $29.99 plus tax.	Write a fraction with a denominator of 10 that equals ½. Now write that fraction as a decimal. Finally, write the number as a percent.

English as a second language (ESL) Instructing students in English until English proficiency is achieved; does not provide support in the student's native or primary language

sheltered English instruction Restating concepts and instructions, using visuals and concrete examples, to provide language support to ELLs

experts advocate using methods that help students learn English as quickly as possible (Tornatzky et al., 2003). One approach that has rapid mastery of English as its goal is **English as a Second Language (ESL)**. Schools across the country have adopted different ways to help students master English and thereby be able to access the general education curriculum, often combining ESL and bilingual education. Table 3.6 summarizes these methods. One validated method, **sheltered English instruction**, helps students master the elements of the English language that are necessary for success when learning specific academic content (Rossell, 2004/2005; Short & Echevarria, 2004/2005). Teachers help students by explicitly teaching the vocabulary and concepts used in the curriculum after identifying the language demands of the subject to be taught. They also relate these new language skills to students' background knowledge, give them many opportunities for practice, and provide them with feedback to help with comprehension. Students' success increases when teachers use sheltered English, because language learning and content instruction are integrated.

Although the federal government does not mandate that states and districts use any specific accommodation or method, it does have some clear requirements about ELLs and their schooling (Antunez, 2001). The Office of Civil Rights and the U.S. Department of Education mandate that schools provide equal educational opportunities to ELLs, and they must include remediation of deficiencies in using the English language. They also make it clear that federal law is violated if

- students cannot participate in instruction or access the curriculum because they do not speak or understand English,
- they are assigned to special education because of their lack of English skills,
- their educational programs do not teach them English as quickly as possible,
- educational programs are "dead end tracks," or
- parents receive notifications and communications from schools in a language they do not understand.

Data-Based Practices

As you learned in Chapters 1 and 2, the special education knowledge base is already rich in effective practices that enhance the learning and performance of students with disabilities. Although many proven interventions and instructional strategies are designed to help students with a particular problem (e.g., positive behavior supports for students with behavioral issues, intensive reading instruction for those with learning disabilities), others are more generic (e.g., learning strategies, differentiating and individualizing instruction). In each subsequent chapter of this book, at least one validated, or data-based, practice is featured for each specific disability. Practices such as positive behavior intervention supports (PBIS), progress monitoring, peer-mediated instruction, and response to intervention (RTI) have demonstrated effectiveness

Table 3.6 • Language Approaches Used with English Language Learners

Language(s) of Instruction	Typical Program Names	Native Language of LEP Students	Language of Content Instruction	Language Arts Instruction	Linguistic Goal of Program
English and the native language	• Two-way bilingual education, • Bilingual immersion, or • Dual language immersion	Ideally, class consists of 50% English-speaking and 50% LEP students sharing same native language.	Both English and the native language	English and the native language	Bilingualism
	• Late-exit or • Development bilingual education	All students speak the same native language.	Both; at first, mostly the native language is used. Instruction through English increases as students gain proficiency.	English and the native language	Bilingualism
	• Early-exit or • Transitional bilingual education	All students speak the same native language.	Both at the beginning, with quick progression to all or most instruction through English.	English; native language skills developed only to assist transition to English	English acquisition; rapid transfer into English-only classroom
English	• Sheltered English, • Structured immersion, or • Content-based ESL	Students can share the same native language or be from different language backgrounds.	English adapted to the students' proficiency level and supplemented by gestures and visual aids.	English	English acquisition
	• Pull-out ESL	Students can share the same native language or be from different language backgrounds; students may be grouped with all ages and grade levels.	English adapted to the students' proficiency level and supplemented by gestures and visual aids.	English; students leave their English-only classroom to spend part of their day receiving ESL instruction	English acquisition

Source: From "If Your Child Learns in Two Languages" by N. Zelasko and B. Antunez, 2008, pp. 20–22, askncbe@ncbe.gwu.org. National Clearinghouse for Bilingual Education, George Washington University. Public domain.

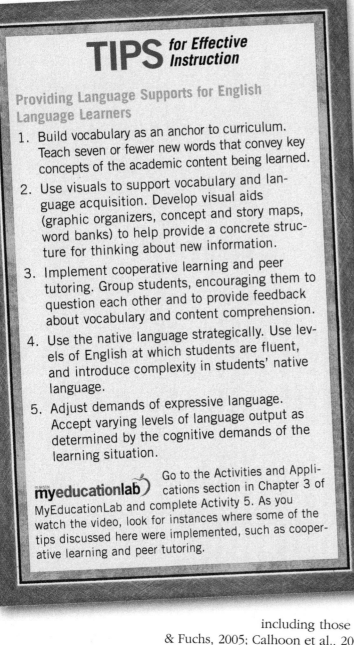

TIPS for Effective Instruction

Providing Language Supports for English Language Learners

1. Build vocabulary as an anchor to curriculum. Teach seven or fewer new words that convey key concepts of the academic content being learned.

2. Use visuals to support vocabulary and language acquisition. Develop visual aids (graphic organizers, concept and story maps, word banks) to help provide a concrete structure for thinking about new information.

3. Implement cooperative learning and peer tutoring. Group students, encouraging them to question each other and to provide feedback about vocabulary and content comprehension.

4. Use the native language strategically. Use levels of English at which students are fluent, and introduce complexity in students' native language.

5. Adjust demands of expressive language. Accept varying levels of language output as determined by the cognitive demands of the learning situation.

myeducationlab Go to the Activities and Applications section in Chapter 3 of MyEducationLab and complete Activity 5. As you watch the video, look for instances where some of the tips discussed here were implemented, such as cooperative learning and peer tutoring.

cooperative learning Small groups of students working together to learn to same material

peer tutoring Classmates helping each other

Peer-Assisted Learning Strategies (PALS) A validated method in which students coach each other to improve academic learning; peer tutoring for reading and mathematics

with CLD students (Cartledge & Kourea, 2008; Linan-Thompson et al., 2006). Diverse students with disabilities need a dually special program that includes interventions that are appropriate for their particular disability *and* address their needs as CLD learners.

ELLs with disabilities must have educational programs that support their development of full English competence and also include key instructional components (see Tips for Effective Instruction) that address their specific disability (Gersten & Baker, 2000; Müller & Markowitz, 2004). Two strategies in particular are very useful to teachers of ELLs: cooperative learning and peer tutoring. Both approaches have students work together on academic tasks; for **cooperative learning** they work in small groups, and for **peer tutoring** they work in pairs (Fletcher et al., 1999). These approaches are thought to be powerful in several different ways. Students who come from cultures that do not value individual competition are more comfortable, and peers can help each other learn academic tasks. Of course, merely assigning students to small groups and telling them to help each other does not guarantee academic improvement. Although classmates can be very helpful to each other, students also need structure and guidance from the teacher. **Peer-Assisted Learning Strategies (PALS)** combine aspects of cooperative learning and peer tutoring with instruction that is rich with demonstration, careful instruction, and feedback (see A Closer Look at Data-Based Practices for an example) (Fuchs et al., 1997, 2001). Furthermore, PALS has been shown to be effective with a wide range of students, including those whose first language is not English (Saenz, Fuchs, & Fuchs, 2005; Calhoon et al., 2006). Additional information supporting PALS' effectiveness can be found on the U.S. Department of Education's What Works Clearinghouse Web site (http://ies.ed.gov/ncee/wwc/).

The importance of providing the support of multicultural education to all diverse students with disabilities cannot be understated. It is critical that teachers be sensitive to their students' home cultures and backgrounds and use differences to their advantage as they enrich the curriculum and their teaching routines. As a reminder, when multicultural education is infused into special education, some key features set it apart (Baca & Cervantes, 2004; Gollnick & Chinn, 2006):

- Sensitivity to students' backgrounds and home cultures
- High expectations and opportunities for success
- Family and community involvement
- Respect for nonmajority values and attitudes
- Support and inclusion
- Accommodations
- Individualized instruction
- Documented results

A Closer Look at Data-Based Practices:

Peer-Assisted Learning Strategies (PALS)

What Is PALS?

Peer-Assisted Learning Strategies (PALS) uses classmates as tutors who exchange the roles of coaches and players. PALS is used across a wide range of grade levels—from kindergarten through high school—to teach students many different skills. For example, kindergarteners have helped each other learn the core or foundations skills of reading (e.g., sound–symbol relationships, sight words). English language learners (ELLs) with learning disabilities have improved their reading comprehension, and middle school students have improved their number skills to chart and graph data.

Why PALS Is Beneficial

The PALS instructional approach multiplies the opportunities for individualized instruction and the implementation of validated instructional tactics across entire classes of students. Using classmates as teachers frees the teacher to provide more intensive supports to students who need them the most. The procedures also actively involve students in learning. When students are trained in how to tutor and taught the instructional tactic they are applying, peer tutoring has proven to be consistently effective, causing great gains in learning. Also, students report that they enjoy tutoring each other, adding a motivating element to the classroom routine.

Implementing PALS

PALS is designed to supplement, not replace, standard instructional routines or elements of the standards-based curriculum. Before classmates work together, the teacher instructs the class about the application of the tactic, the roles of each pair, when to take turns, and how to provide corrective feedback. The teacher practices the instructional routines with the entire class until they demonstrate understanding of their roles and responsibilities. Student pairs work together on a specific academic task (e.g., letter–sound recognition in reading, sight-word vocabulary, math facts, story comprehension) for 4 weeks and then switch partners. Here's a general example of how PALS is applied:

Frequency

- PALS is usually scheduled three or four times per week.
- Sessions last 20 to 35 minutes.
- Each session is divided into 10-minute segments so each peer has a turn as coach and player.

- Sessions may be divided in half so more than one skill can be the target of instruction.
- Sessions continue for a semester or half of the school year.

Partners

- Rank-order students in a class from the strongest to the weakest on the targeted skill.
- Divide the class in half.
- Pair the top-ranked student from the high-performing group with the top-ranked student in the low-performing group.
- Continue the process until every student has a partner.
- Each member of the pair, during every session, takes a turn at being the "coach" or tutor and the "player" (the student being tutored).
- Student pairs work together for about a month and then are assigned new partners.

Roles

- The coach asks the player to do the task (e.g., read a passage, compute subtraction problems).
- The player performs the task (e.g., reads out loud, solves the problems).
- The coach listens or watches and provides corrective feedback.
- Pairs change roles every 10 minutes.

A sample worksheet used by a pair of kindergarteners learning sight words is shown in this box. Special worksheets or materials do not have to be prepared to implement peer tutoring. Texts and workbooks used for standard instruction can be utilized for PALS lessons.

"What Word?" Activity

and	on	was	is	What word?
the	and	is	was	
			☺ ☺ ☺ ☺	

Go to the Building Teaching Skills and Dispositions section in Chapter 3 of MyEducationLab and complete the activities in the IRIS MODULES; several activities allow you to become familiar with the use of PALS strategies for students at various grade levels.

myeducationlab Go to
the Activities and Applications
section in Chapter 3 of MyEducationLab and complete Activity
2. As you watch the video and
answer the accompanying questions, consider the roles of the
teachers and students, how peer
tutoring was individualized, and
the advantages and concerns
with peer tutoring.

digital divide Unequal availability
of technology due to socioeconomic status

Technology

Technology has changed all of our lives. And technology will certainly continue to affect the lives of those with disabilities and their families. It seems the possibilities are endless. Technology can be used as a tool to help teachers enrich the curriculum, facilitating opportunities to make instructional activities and learning more relevant to diverse students. It can also become a tool for accommodations in assessment and instruction. However, it is important for educators to understand that some diverse families' access to technology may be restricted. Children in low-income families are less likely to have access to a computer. What is often called the **digital divide** could well become one more challenge for diverse students and their families to overcome, separating them from others who have home Internet access and the availability of Web sites in their home languages (Tornatzky et al., 2003). Thus, teachers must be cautious about assigning homework where computer and Internet access is either required or very useful. One helpful option in such cases is for teachers to schedule time in the school's computer lab so these students can develop important computer literacy skills and also enrich their learning of content presented in the general education curriculum.

One recurrent theme of this chapter centers on anchoring instruction to students' culture, thereby making instruction more relevant to diverse learners. The Internet can help greatly in this regard (Haynes, 2005). Materials and information are even organized into thematic units that enable students to explore and learn about topics of special interest to them. For example, through the Internet, teachers are sharing units they have developed for others to use and adapt for their own instruction (e.g., see http://www.everythingESL.net for activities about Martin Luther King Jr., Teaching About America). Students can also be given the option of searching out specific topics of their own choice (e.g., historical figures from different countries, or cultures from a specific period of time) for reports or independent study.

Technology is becoming an important accommodation for ELL students. For example, **computerized language translators** (see photo) are able to translate words and phrases into many languages. Translators can help students expand their vocabularies. Seiko, among many other companies, produces not only inexpensive bidirectional dictionaries but also translators that can handle complicated verb conjugations. Such devices may have a significant impact for ELL special education students. For instance, they may be able to use computers to write assignments in their primary language, check the spelling and punctuation, and then press a button to translate their work into English! Such devices can also save time for the bilingual teacher or volunteer, who can use them for immediate translations of specific words or explanations of phrases and idioms. They are being used as accommodations in both instructional and assessment situations. And teachers can use language translators to improve communications (both written and oral) between home and school, regardless of the language used at home.

computerized language translators
Computers that provide translations of written text from one language to another

Transition

The relationships among education, wages, and life outcomes are clear: High school graduates are more likely to be employed and earn more than high school dropouts, and people with college degrees have higher earnings than people without. High school graduation is one criterion for entrance into a community college, a college, or a university. Unfortunately, data indicate that diverse students are underrepresented in postsecondary education and also have a high rate of not completing college (Slater, 2004; TRPI, 2005). Why might this be so? Remember, CLD students more often attend poor schools where a rich curriculum is not offered, textbooks are outdated, and teachers are less experienced. At many inner-city schools, advanced placement courses are not even available. Also, teachers are less likely to refer students from diverse backgrounds for advanced classes or gifted programs, even when they show exceptional promise (Ford et al., 2008). Sometimes, diverse students are not advised to take the core

Technology, like this computerized translator, can help children transition more independently as they learn a second language.

subjects required for admission to college (and hence do not get enough science, math, and foreign language courses), and these students' parents are less likely to know which high school courses are necessary for college admission and which courses are not.

When disability compounds diversity, the challenges can be even greater. Diverse students with disabilities graduate from high school with a standard diploma at a much lower rate than their White peers with disabilities. Whereas Whites with disabilities have a 59% high school graduation rate, diverse students' rates are 64% for Asian/Pacific Islanders with disabilities, 44% for Hispanics, 43% for American Indian/Alaska Natives, and 36% for Blacks (OSEP, 2008). Although these rates are dismal, they are showing some improvement. Possibly, now, with increased attention to the challenges that diverse students with disabilities face, outcomes will improve even more.

Collaboration

In this chapter and each of the following ones, we highlight different collaborative efforts of professionals—teachers and related service providers—who come together to provide an appropriate education to students with disabilities. Here, we emphasize the unique needs and special partnerships that can be formed to benefit linguistically diverse students with disabilities. For them, **collaboration**—school personnel with different areas of expertise working together—often means forming partnerships in nontraditional ways. For diverse students, collaboration might mean seeking expertise from a range of experts who can form a unique multidisciplinary team. Such a team might consist of many special education colleagues, migrant education teachers, teachers who are themselves bilingual and fluent in the language of a particular student with disabilities, SLPs, and ESL teachers (Salend & Salinas, 2003). Bilingual and ESL teachers can provide ideas to the classroom teacher on how to adapt their teaching so that ELLs can learn the material, and can also help with adapting instructional materials.

collaboration School personnel with different expertise working in partnerships

Collaborating with Related Services Providers: Bilingual Paraprofessionals

Sometimes, teachers are provided with the assistance of paraprofessionals who are bilingual and speak students' native language. **Bilingual paraprofessionals** are assistants who help students learn the English required to profit from classroom instruction. They might provide needed testing accommodations (e.g., explaining directions for a test in both English and Spanish) or help these students access the curriculum by explaining, in both the child's native language and in English, concepts being taught or vocabulary that is unfamiliar. Teachers need to work closely

bilingual paraprofessionals Classroom assistants fluent in at least two languages

myeducationlab Go to the Activities and Applications section in Chapter 3 of MyEducationLab and complete Activity 3 in the IRIS Module, "Cultural and Linguistic Differences: What Teachers Should Know" This module examines curricular considerations, teacher bias, and the roles of general education teachers in the education of culturally diverse students.

with bilingual paraprofessionals, however, to be sure that they know the language accommodation that is supposed to be provided and that they understand their role in helping students learn English as their second language.

Collaborative Practices: Interpreters

For family members who speak a language other than English, interpreters are an important part of the special education process. Members of the community are frequently used to interpret at parent conferences and IEP meetings. At the same time, educators should be sensitive to issues regarding interpreters from the family's community during times when confidential student information will be discussed. Some parents may feel uncomfortable discussing aspects of their child's education using a community interpreter, especially if academic or behavioral troubles are involved. Interpreters must be fully cognizant of their role and the confidentiality that prohibits them from sharing information from the meeting with neighbors, friends, or other members of the community. All of these issues contribute to the trust that educators must develop with the home. IDEA '04 and the Office of Civil Rights (OCR) provide guidance about communicating with and involving families of students with disabilities whose first language is not English (see What IDEA '04 Says About Native Language and Families).

When communicating with families, teachers must avoid using language and special education jargon that parents do not understand. Even those who speak English may not be proficient enough in this second language to understand and communicate with educators using technical language or jargon (Holman, 1997). To them, the word *disability* may mean only a physical or sensory disability or only a severe disability—an interpretation very different from educators' views of disability (Thorp, 1997). Teachers should work to ensure that their communications are jargon-free and clearly explain their observations about the student's school performance so that parents understand any concerns that the school has.

Partnerships with Families and Communities

The strength of families and their involvement in school can make a real difference in the lives of children (Garcia, 2001). However, school personnel often express disappointment with the participation of parents of diverse students with disabilities (Shapiro et al., 2004). In fact, what appears to be lack of interest may instead be unfamiliarity with the process. Recognize, though, that some cultures ascribe a very high status to school personnel. In these cases, parents who seem disengaged could in fact be deferring to the teacher's authority, which is considered irrefutable in their home country. In other words, they might consider it rude to make a request or suggestion!

In other cases, perceived parental apathy could be a result of educators' actions (Davis et al., 2002). In many home–school relationships, cross-cultural dissonance (acute misunderstanding of fundamental issues and values about education, disability, and home–school interaction) may undermine special education for students with disabilities (Harry, 2002, 2008). Many culturally and linguistically diverse families come to the school situation themselves burdened with alienation, feelings of distrust, and lack of information (Brown et al., 2003). Some Latina and African American mothers say they have received negative treatment and have been subjected to condescending attitudes and disapproving judgments from school and social service personnel (Harry, 2002, 2008; Shapiro et al., 2004). They also report poor and inefficient ways in which educators communicate

(Davis et al., 2002). Native parents also object to indifference, inaccurate understanding of their culture and traditions, and inappropriate communication styles (Banks, 2004).

Parents should be considered full, participating members of the team, rather than limited to the role of "consent giver" and "educational planner" (Harry, 2002). Instead of just encouraging parents to be loyal supporters and passive recipients of information, educators should seek parents' input about how they would like to be involved in their child's educational program and how they would like information provided to them (Thorp, 1997). In fact, families report they are more satisfied with the school when they receive frequent communications (Hughes, Valle-Riestra, & Arguelles, 2002).

Parents' needs should also be determined and respected. Norma Lopez-Reyna, professor of special education and a director of an important federal project that serves minority colleges and universities across the nation, provides touching insights about also being a parent of a child with a disability in this chapter's Spotlighting feature.

An overwhelming majority of Hispanic families report that they want their children to go to college, but they do not understand that a few simple choices, such as enrolling in the right courses and signing up correctly for the SAT, will make that option more probable (TRPI, 2005). Knowledgeable school personnel should share the necessary information with them. School personnel should be aware of parents' literacy levels in English and not give them assignments they are unable to complete. For example, many parents who are not proficient in English are embarrassed that they cannot help their children with homework (Milian, 1999). To avoid humiliation, they might agree to help their children with schoolwork but then be unable to follow through.

Educators tend to assume that "working with parents" means "working with Mom and Dad." In many cultures, the family is a large constellation that may include people who are not actually related. Often, extended family members play a crucial role in the life of the individual with disabilities. For some African American families, church and community leaders lend support and resources to the student with disabilities (Rogers-Dulan, 1998). For that child, the concept of extended family may well include key members of the community. For Native American children, these may be tribal elders whose exclusion would be considered an offense (Vraniak, 1998). Before making any decisions about treatments or educational strategies, it may be necessary to consult with these tribal elders and allow time for their response. Without understanding the cultural demands and expectations of the child's family, educators can inadvertently create unfortunate and unnecessary obstacles to the development of real partnerships.

In part, a child's success in school depends on respect between the school and the family. Children must feel confident that their teachers and schools value diverse cultural heritages and languages. To encourage confidence and cooperation, a teacher can bring the strengths, contributions, culture, and language of the family directly into the school experience. For example, a grandmother who creates pottery following ancient techniques might demonstrate her art. A church leader could explain a religious holiday or event. And a tribal leader might be asked to officiate at a school awards ceremony. Any such family participation in school events helps foster home–school partnerships and promote children's suc-

The diversity of schoolchildren in the United States is increasing dramatically. Teachers have wonderful opportunities to enrich their instruction with interesting information, stories, and learning opportunities from many different cultures and heritages.

Spotlighting *Karisa:* A Day in the Life

This story is written by Karisa's mother, Norma A. Lopez-Reyna, Ph.D., an associate professor of special education at the University of Illinois at Chicago. She is also the director of the Monarch Center, which is a federally funded technical assistance project serving the nation's minority colleges' and universities' special education programs.

Karisa will be 16 years old in a few days: a lifetime ahead of her, a lifetime behind her. In the quiet of my thoughts, I let my memories skim across my mind. I think of all the long hours I have spent e-mailing and meeting with school personnel, all the hours spent helping with homework, reading texts and creating visual supports. And then all of the hours spent reading about language disorders, executive functioning, attention deficit/hyperactivity disorder; seeking the meaning of their interaction in my child . . . of all the times I have cried alone in sadness and anger—not because of something Karisa did or what she couldn't do, but because of the inability or unwillingness of so many educators to think; to imagine that this quirky child might be a real person with real feelings, thoughts, ideas, and aspirations and not just one more diverse kid with a disability label.

Mostly, though, I have enjoyed watching her laugh and kid around with her family and those who accept her, listening to her make connections among events across years and settings, and laughing aloud as she exchanges text messages with a friend or with her dad. Having two other children before her

who were labeled "gifted," it's taken so long to convince the same school personnel that Karisa is also gifted. Not as a reader, or artist, or musician, or mathematician . . . though she is a reader, is artistic and creative, sings with the choir, and uses math in daily living. Rather, she is gifted with tolerance for others, with caring for animals, with concern for those who may be sad or homeless, with courage in the face of her awareness of not always being able to communicate what she knows and feels. Her kindergarten teacher one day said, as we stood together watching Karisa in the playground, "She is the bravest child I have ever seen. Can you imagine not being able to communicate? Can you imagine how frustrating that must be? But she keeps smiling, and she keeps trying!" I still think these are the two best and true characterizations of Karisa, even today.

Each time we are in the library, I am reminded of the range of people Karisa will experience across her life, as she does today. For example, one checkout girl stares at Karisa every single time we are in the store, watching her affect as she struggles to assert herself while trying to collect those items she reserved online. I want to say, "Why are you staring?" But then, there is another girl, who talks and interacts with Karisa as if she were just like any other teenager coming through her checkout area. She probably has no idea the load she lifts from my heart each time she smiles and converses with Karisa. It is these small moments that make me realize that Karisa will be OK, that there will be many who will take the time to know her, understand her, and be her friend.

cess at school. Here are a few tips about how to foster meaningful partnerships with diverse families (Brown et al., 2003; Kraft, 2001; Milian, 1999; Parette & Petch-Hogan, 2000; Thorp, 1997):

- Develop an atmosphere of trust and respect.
- Make families and communities feel welcome at school.
- Select community leaders to serve as representatives of both school and home, and involve them regularly.
- Identify families' preferred means of communication and use it effectively.
- Communicate on a regular, ongoing basis (not just when there is a problem).
- Use interpreters who are knowledgeable about schools, special education, and its programs.
- Incorporate materials and activities that reflect the diversity of the community.
- Seek meaningful ways (e.g., actively sharing culture, art, music, and recreational activities) to involve families and communities (as they feel comfortable).
- Hold meetings with families at times and places that are manageable for them.

Summary

Education should reflect the rich diversity of culture and language found in communities across this country, and special education should capitalize on each student's background as an appropriate individualized education program is created. Many exceptional children are bilingual, and many more come from diverse cultural backgrounds. The combinations of disability, giftedness, cultural diversity, and linguistic differences present many challenges to these children, their families, and educators as schools attempt to ensure that special education services are delivered to children who need and are entitled to them.

Answering the Chapter Objectives

1. What is meant by the term *diverse*?
   - Being from one of these groups: African American (Black), Hispanic (Latino/a), Asian/Pacific Islander, American Indian/Alaska Native
   - Being from a culture different from "mainstream America"
   - Speaking a language at home other than English
   - Whether accurate or not, being considered a minority

2. How does the interplay between poverty and other systemic factors put many CLD students at risk for low educational results and having disabilities?
   - Poverty results in reduced access to health care.
   - Diverse young children are less likely to attend preschool.
   - Poor children are more likely to be homeless or to live a mobile or migrant life.
   - Fewer poor children have computers at home (the digital divide).
   - Schools attended by poor students have low expectations, few resources, unqualified teachers, and a less demanding curriculum.

3. What are the key features of multicultural education?
   - Students' cultural backgrounds and traditions are integrated into the curriculum.
   - Students' home cultures are respected and understood.
   - Relevant and meaningful examples anchor instruction.
   - Clashes between home and school cultures are minimized.
   - Culturally diverse family members and communities feel included and welcome.
   - All educators are culturally competent.

4. How can schools and teachers be more responsive to students learning English?
   - Be sensitive to the different patterns and rates of language acquisition.
   - Understand the differences between conversational and classroom English.
   - Encourage quick mastery of English through ESL, bilingual, and sheltered English instruction.
   - Ensure meaningful communications and partnerships with families and communities.
   - Provide bilingual paraprofessionals and volunteers.
   - Use language accommodations.

5. What additional considerations do diverse students with disabilities and their families require?
   - All the components of multicultural education
   - Intensive assistance in learning English
   - Explicit instruction
   - Intensive efforts for family involvement
   - Application of validated practices

myeducationlab Now go to MyEducationLab at www.myeducationlab.com and take the Self-Assessment to gauge your initial comprehension of chapter content. Once you have taken the Self-Assessment, use your individualized Study Plan for Chapter 3 to enhance your understanding of the concepts discussed in the chapter.

Council for Exceptional Children ADDRESSING THE PROFESSIONAL STANDARDS

Council for Exceptional Children (CEC) knowledge standards addressed in this chapter:
CC5K9, CC1K5, CC6K2, CC8K3, CC8S2, CC3K5, CC5S1, CC10K4, CC10S10

Appendix A: CEC Knowledge and Skill Standards Common Core has a full listing of the standards listed here.

Appendix B: CEC Knowledge and Skill Common Core Standards and Associated Subcategories are broken down by chapter.

CHAPTER 4

Speech or Language Impairments

Naomi Chowdhuri Tyler

Imagine a World . . .

where communication has no boundaries . . .

Chapter Objectives

After studying this chapter, you will be able to

1. Describe characteristics of speech impairments and language impairments.

2. Discuss the prevalence of speech or language impairments, and indicate how the prevalence of this type of disability is related to that of learning disabilities.

3. Describe the differences among language delays, language differences, and language impairments.

4. Discuss how classroom teachers can make a difference in the development of children's language.

5. Describe key resources for students with speech or language impairments.

Judy Stermer Taylor majored in speech therapy at the University of New Mexico, in part to resolve her own stuttering problem. As a child, she was convinced that she could not draw or paint (or compete with her highly successful and talented sister, who was painting murals by the age of 7) because she was left-handed, had dyslexia, and had learning disabilities. She discovered her artistic talents when working with a patient at a nursing home who needed help communicating with others. The woman's stroke had left her unable to read printed words. When Taylor could not find suitable pictures to use to help the woman communicate her needs, she sketched images to represent items and actions. Judy Taylor is now an award-winning artist, whose work is collected worldwide.

myeducationlab *After reading this chapter, complete the Self-Assessment for Chapter 4 on MyEducationLab to gauge your initial understanding of chapter content.*

Language is the foundation for learning. We use it to clarify what we observe, engage others, express our needs, and interact with friends and family. For most of us, learning to communicate effectively comes naturally. We don't even remember learning our first language. For some of us, however, speaking or acquiring the fundamentals of language and mastering its nuances are challenging. For those individuals, teachers can play an instrumental role in providing the foundation for one of the most important skills of a successful life: knowing how to communicate effectively with others.

Our society places a high value on oral communication, and for most of us, it is the primary method of interacting with others. We talk with each other to share knowledge, information, and feelings. Most of us, in fact, prefer talking to other forms of communication. Note the intensity of conversations in college dining halls, in hallways at schools, and on cell phones. Clearly, communication with others is a crucial part of life, a fundamental aspect of the human condition.

In this chapter, you will learn about students who have speech or language impairments. These problems are common for many students with disabilities; in fact, the majority of students with learning disabilities and those with emotional or behavioral disorders also have co-occurring language impairments (Sunderland, 2004). Many of these students show similar developmental traits: As preschoolers, their language development is delayed. By third grade, their difficulties learning to read have signaled learning disabilities to their teachers; and throughout their schooling, they struggle with most academic subjects that require mastery of skills related to the applications of language: reading, writing, and oral communication. As you will learn in this chapter (and in the next, on learning disabilities), language is the foundation for almost everything we do. Difficulties with language impede success at school and in life. You will also learn that many proven ways to help individuals with speech or language impairments are now available; it is our job to know when and how to help.

Where We've Been . . . What's on the Horizon?

speech/language pathologist (SLP) The professional who diagnoses and treats speech or language impairments; a related services provider

Long before the first passage of IDEA in 1975, **speech/language pathologists (SLPs)**—the professionals who help students maximize their communication skills—worked in schools and provided support services to teachers and direct services to students and their families (American Speech-Hearing-Language Association [ASHA], 2002). After World War II and until the 1970s, the majority of their time was spent with students who had trouble correctly producing speech sounds. After 1975, special education became more developed, and the roles of SLPs changed. More students with complex speech and language problems attended public schools. Because most teachers had little preparation in the area of language development, SLPs assumed a greater role in providing an appropriate education to students with significant language problems. They provide unique expertise to these students and their families, and the high quality of their services makes a real difference in the results for these individuals.

Enhancing the work of SLPs are advances in technology. Today, technology allows individuals to speak who do not have the motoric abilities to make speech sounds on their own. These students can participate in class discussions, chat with their friends, and participate in community activities with the assistance of communication devices. We can only imagine how future technological developments will provide even more benefits to individuals with speech or language impairments, their teachers, and their families.

Historical Context

Records dating before 1000 B.C. reveal that many individuals with disabilities were historically considered fools, buffoons, and sources of entertainment, often because of their speech or language problems. For example, as we noted in

Chapter 1, in the time of the Roman Empire, people with disabilities were exhibited in cages along the Appian Way—the main road into and out of Rome—for the amusement of those passing by. People even planned special family outings to see Balbus Balaesus the Stutterer, who would attempt to talk whenever a coin was thrown into his cage (Van Riper & Erickson, 1996).

Speech or language impairments have been documented throughout the centuries, as have their treatment programs. The foundation for services for students with these disabilities was laid at the beginning of the last century. At that time, what was called speech correction was offered in clinics, not at schools. The first school-based programs were offered in 1910 when the Chicago public schools hired an itinerant teacher to help children who stammered (Moore & Kester, 1953). In 1913, the superintendent of the New York City schools began a program of speech training for children with speech impairments. A year later, Smiley Blanton opened the first university speech clinic at the University of Wisconsin. In 1925, a small group of professionals created the American Academy for Speech Correction (later called the American Speech and Hearing Association, now called the American Speech-Language-Hearing Association but typically referred to as ASHA) to share their ideas and research. By 2004, ASHA had grown to over 130,000 speech, language, and hearing professional members (ASHA, 2008b).

Technology designed for everyone can have unique benefits for individuals with disabilities. Texting allows for communications that might otherwise be impossible. We can only imagine what's on the horizon.

During the late 1950s and 1960s, SLPs—then called speech therapists or speech clinicians (notice the emphasis on the word *speech*)—each worked with more than 200 children per week primarily in small groups and for as little as 30 minutes a day. Most of these children could not produce speech sounds correctly; nearly all had articulation problems. Students with significant language and cognitive problems typically did not receive services from SLPs because the general belief of that day was that they were not developmentally able to profit from therapy. All of that changed in 1975 with the passage of IDEA. SLPs began providing more and more individual services to a broader range, but fewer, students with disabilities; accordingly, ASHA coined the term *speech/language pathologist* (SLP) to reflect the wider range of the services these specialists now provide to students with many more types of conditions and disabilities.

Challenges That Speech or Language Impairments Present

Speech impairments can affect how a person interacts with others in all kinds of settings and can influence an individual's success in school, social situations, and employment. Stuttering, for example, can create stress when listeners react to nonfluent speech with embarrassment, guilt, frustration, or anger (Conture, 2001; Ramig & Shames, 2006). The long-term effects can be quite serious. Some individuals respond by acting overly aggressive, denying their disability, and projecting their own negative reactions onto their listeners. Others withdraw socially, seeking to avoid all situations in which they have to talk, and ultimately they become isolates. Some spend considerable effort avoiding words that contain sounds that are difficult for them.

Many individuals with disabilities deal with multiple problems, and this sometimes leads people to draw inaccurate conclusions about the individuals involved. For example, Christy Brown, whose life story was both a book and a movie, *My Left Foot*, had a condition called cerebral palsy (CP). CP, which usually results from brain damage that occurred at or before birth, affects individuals' abilities to control their muscles. (You will learn more about CP in Chapter 9.) CP can hinder a person's ability to control muscles for walking, writing, or forming speech sounds.

On the Screen: *A Hero Arrives on the Scene*

People with disabilities do need heroes, not uncomplaining overcomers, but real disabled heroes who fight bias and battle for control of their lives and insist that they will make their mark in the world. Christy Brown, difficult and dangerous as he is, is such a hero —Paul Longmore (2003, p. 130)

Sometimes, a film becomes a landmark portrayal representing an issue larger than the film itself. To many people with disabilities, the film *My Left Foot,* depicting the life of Christy Brown, is such a movie. The movie and its expression of rage—not due to his disabilities, but rather to the way he is treated because of them—combined with humor made Christy Brown a "hero" or symbol of the disability movement.

Christy Brown, a man born with cerebral palsy to a poor Irish family, was able to develop control of only his left foot, which he used as his means of communication because his speech was difficult to understand. His mother's strength and love, along with individual attention from a qualified instructor, helped Christy find his voice both literally and creatively, becoming an acclaimed artist, poet, and author. This documentary-like film offers insight into the emotional psyche of someone with disabilities. We empathize with him not just because of his physical limitations or difficulty communicating, but also because of those universal problems that everyone experiences, such as heartache and grief. Also portrayed is the importance of integrating people with disabilities into mainstream society and receiving special and individualized instruction. Oscars for Best Actor and Best Supporting Actress, respectively, rewarded Daniel Day-Lewis and Brenda Fricker for their performances in this film, which presented the lives of real people with dignity and respect.

—By Steven Smith

But because the condition sometimes causes labored and slow speech, some people wrongly assume that other signs of CP go hand in hand with reduced mental abilities. The result, as clearly depicted in the movie about Brown's life (see On the Screen), is often discrimination and bias (Longmore, 2003). Like Christy Brown, Lizzy Solomon has CP (she is featured in the Spotlighting boxes in the physical or health disabilities *and* the giftedness and talent development chapters), and both of them are proof that we should never make hasty assumptions about people's possibilities!

Using and understanding language is the foundation for school success. Problems with acquiring and developing language during early childhood are strong predictors of problems not only in communicating with others but also in learning to read, write, and succeed in most academic areas (Ely, 2005). Language impairments can be even more serious than speech impairments because they can affect all aspects of a student's classroom experiences (Wetherby, 2002). Students with language impairments may struggle to follow a teacher's instructions, understand a class lecture, or interpret their peers' nonverbal behavior.

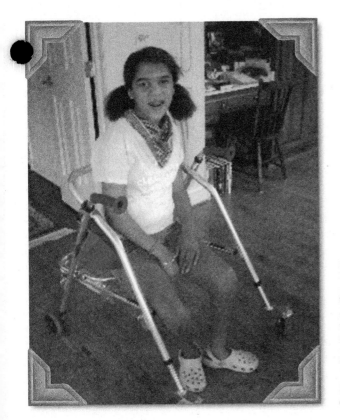

Lizzy Solomon has just completed her freshman year in high school, where she participated in marching band, excelled in the International Baccalaureate program, was active in Girl Scouts, and oversaw her greeting card company, Lizzy's Lines. For more about Lizzy, read the Spotlighting features in Chapters 9 and 14.

Making a Difference

Operation Smile

Children with facial deformities usually experience rejection and ridicule. Around the world, people's reaction to these individuals is harsh, as they are shunned and denied personal interactions. In recent years, techniques in reconstructive surgery have improved greatly, making it possible for surgeons to change people's appearance and repair cleft lips so that the birth defect is almost unnoticeable. The repair of cleft palates makes intelligible speech a reality. However, the costs of such procedures put surgery out of the reach of most families, making the possible impossible for many children around the world.

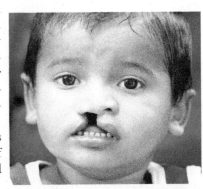

In 1982, Dr. William Magee, a plastic surgeon, and Kathleen Magee, Dr. Magee's wife, a nurse and clinical social worker, traveled to the Philippines with a group of medical volunteers. The purpose of their trip was to repair children's cleft lips and cleft palates. They had no idea how many children were in need, but there were far more than those volunteers could help on their first trip. The Magees saw a need, and so Operation Smile was founded to provide free reconstructive surgery to children and young adults.

Today, thousands of volunteers join together to serve tens of thousands of children. They offer medical training and continuing education to health care professionals who assist children and their families in their home communities, provide surgery in over 20 countries, and bring sponsored patients with the most complicated and intensive needs to the United States. Today, according to *Forbes* magazine's annual survey of U.S. charities, Operation Smile is one of the 200 largest in the United States. To learn more about Operation Smile, go to the organization's Web site: **www.operationsmile.org**.

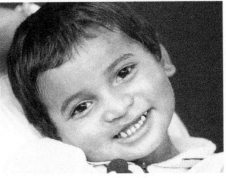

Speech or Language Impairments Defined

To understand speech or language impairments, you must first understand the communication process used to interact with others. At least two people are needed: a sender and a receiver. The process also requires a message. The sender translates the message into a code that the receiver can understand. Communication occurs only when the receiver understands the message as the sender intended it. There are three ways in which speech or language impairments can cause a communication breakdown: first, when the sender incorrectly produces sounds, so that the receiver does not understand what they are saying; second, when the sender's message is unclear because of difficulties using language; and third, when the receiver has difficulty understanding the message because of his or her own language impairment. Speech impairments are the root of the first communication breakdown, and language impairments cause the second and third communication problems. Before thinking about these two overarching communication problems, let's take a closer look at the communication process.

The Communication Process

The process of transferring one's thoughts into symbols or signals, or coding, is an important part of communication. **Communication symbols**—such as speech sounds, written words, or hand gestures (e.g., waving hello or pointing a finger)—relay messages. Communication symbols are used in combination with each other (e.g., speaking the words "Come here, please" while beckoning with a hand movement) and are governed by rules that allow language to have meaning. They can refer to something: a past, present, or future event; a person or object; an action; a concept or emotion. They are needed to exchange knowledge and information. **Communication signals** are nonverbal expressions of a social formality or convention and usually announce some immediate event, person, action, or emotion. For example, the U.S. Marine Band playing "Hail to the Chief" signals the appearance of the president of the United States. A teacher rapping on a desk announces the need to pay attention or to be quieter.

communication symbols Voice, letters of the alphabet, or gestures used to send communication messages

communication signals A variety of nonverbal cues that announce some immediate event, person, action, or emotion

Children with speech or language impairments need many opportunities to practice their newly acquired skills with their friends.

Figure 4.1 • The communication process was effective in the first scenario, as the receiver interpreted the message just as the sender intended it. While technically accurate, the sender in the second scenario did not provide the necessary information for the receiver to interpret the message correctly. What could the sender have said instead?

Once a thought is coded into a symbol or signal, the sender must select from a number of mechanisms for delivering the message: speaking, sign language, gestures, writing. The delivery system must be useful to the receiver. For example, selecting to talk via telephone to transmit a message to a deaf person is useless (unless that person has a voice-decoding telephone device). Sending a written message to someone who cannot read also results in ineffective communication.

Communication requires the receiver to use eyes, ears, or even touch (as do those who use braille) to convey the message to the brain where it is understood. Receivers must understand the code the sender uses and must be able to interpret the code so that it has meaning. Communication is unsuccessful if the sender or receiver cannot use the signals or symbols adequately. And if either person has a defective mechanism for sending or receiving the information, the communication process is ineffective. Figure 4.1 illustrates two examples of the communication process—one where the message is conveyed successfully, and one where it is not.

At this point, it might be helpful to distinguish among three important and related terms: speech, language, and communication.

- **Speech** is the vocal production of language (e.g., the speaker says the word *ball*).
- **Language** is a rule-based method of communication involving the comprehension and use of the signs and symbols by which ideas are represented (e.g., the word *ball* represents the actual object).
- **Communication** is the process of exchanging knowledge, ideas, opinions, and feelings through the use of verbal or nonverbal language (e.g., the speaker uses the word for a purpose: "Give me the red ball").

Understanding how our bodies work to produce speech and language is helpful in understanding what happens when a breakdown in the system results in speech or language impairments. Refer to the diagram of the head and chest cavity shown in Figure 4.2 as you read the following description of the process of generating speech. When we want to speak, the brain sends messages that activate other mechanisms. The **respiratory system** is the group of muscles and organs (diaphragm, chest muscles, lungs, throat) that take in oxygen and expel gases from our bodies. Its secondary function is to provide the air and pressure

myeducationlab Go to the Activities and Applications section in Chapter 4 of MyEducationLab and complete Activity 1. As you watch the video and answer the accompanying questions, consider how learning sign language might benefit students with and without communication disorders.

speech Vocal production of language
language Rule-based method used for communication

communication Transfer of knowledge, ideas, opinions, and feelings

respiratory system The system of organs whose primary function is to take in oxygen and expel gases

Figure 4.2 • The Body's Systems for Generating Voice and Speech

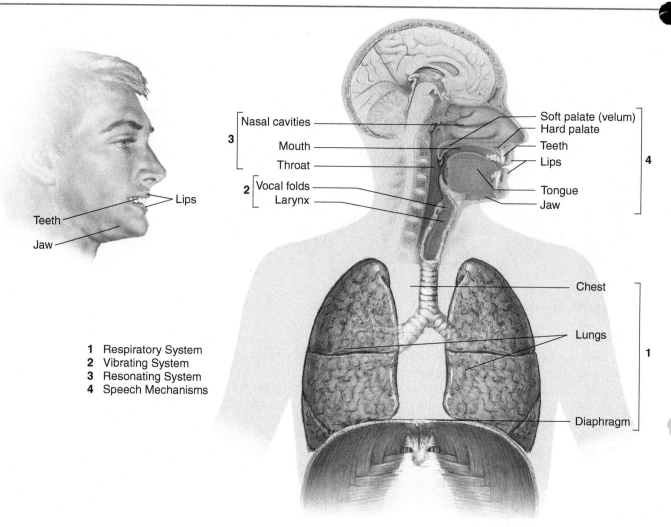

1 Respiratory System
2 Vibrating System
3 Resonating System
4 Speech Mechanisms

vibrating system The orderly function of the larynx and vocal folds to vibrate and produce sounds and pitch

resonating system Oral and nasal cavities where speech sounds are formed

speech mechanisms Includes the various parts of the body—tongue, lips, teeth, mandible, and palate—required for oral speech

communication disorders Disorders in speech, language, or hearing that impair communications

necessary to produce speech sounds. The **vibrating system** includes the larynx and the vocal folds, and together they produce the voice. The larynx sits on top of the trachea, which houses the vocal folds. As air is expelled from the lungs, the flow of air causes the vocal folds to vibrate and produce sounds; the vocal folds lengthen or shorten to cause changes in pitch. As the sounds travel through the throat, mouth, and nasal cavities—the **resonating system**—the voice is shaped into speech sounds by the **speech mechanisms**, sometimes called the *articulation mechanisms*, which include the tongue, soft and hard palates, teeth, lips, and jaw.

Next, let's turn our attention to impairments in communication. When an individual has a problem producing speech or using language to the extent that communication is impaired, the individual has a disability. **Communication disorders** is a broad, umbrella term often used by speech and language professionals to include all disabilities that result in difficulties with speech, language, and hearing. IDEA '04, however, considers speech or language impairments as one disability and hearing impairments (hard of hearing and deafness) as two others. And, while IDEA '04 considers speech impairments and language impairments to be one special education category, you will learn that they are truly distinct. Table 4.1 provides official definitions of this disability. Note the differences in terminology; IDEA has used the term *impairments* for years, while ASHA has used the term *disorders*. The terms will be used interchangeably in this chapter as you will probably encounter

Table 4.1 • Definitions of Speech or Language Impairments

Source	Definition
Federal government	Speech or language impairment: *a communication disorder, such as:* • *stuttering,* • *impaired articulation,* • *a language impairment,* • *or a voice impairment,* *that adversely affects a child's educational performance.* **U.S. Department of Education, 2006, Section 300.8 (a)(11) p. 46757**
American Speech-Language-Hearing Association	Speech and language disorder: *A speech and language disorder may be present when a person's speech or language is different from that of others of the same age, sex, or ethnic group; when a person's speech and/or language is hard to understand; when a person is overly concerned about his or her speech; or when a person often avoids communicating with others.* **American Speech-Language-Hearing Association Ad Hoc Committee on Service Delivery in the Schools, 1993 pp. 40–41**

Sources: From 34 CFR Parts 300 and 303, Assistance to States for the Education of Children with Disabilities and the Early Intervention Program for Infants and Toddlers with Disabilities; Final Regulations, Section 300.8 (a)(11), U.S. Department of Education, 2006, p. 46757; and "Definitions of Communication Disorders and Variations" by American Speech-Language-Hearing Association Ad Hoc Committee on Service Delivery in the Schools, 1993, *ASHA, 35* (Suppl. 10), pp. 40–41. Rockville, MD: ASHA. Reprinted with permission.

both during your career in education. Let's look at each type to better understand how each area associated with these disabilities influences the effective communication.

Speech Impairments

The receiver of communication must understand the sounds of the words spoken to understand the full message. If speech sounds are incorrectly produced, one sound might be confused with another (e.g., "thought" becomes "fought"), either changing the meaning of the message or yielding no meaning. When speech is abnormal, it can be unintelligible, unpleasant, or interfere with communication (Bernthal & Bankson, 2004; Hall, Oyer, & Haas, 2001). **Speech impairments** include three major types of difficulties: articulation, fluency, and voice. Problems with any one of these speech impairments are distracting to the listener and can negatively affect or interrupt the communication process.

speech impairments Abnormal speech that is unintelligible, is unpleasant, or interferes with communication

Articulation Disorders The most common, **articulation disorder**, exists when the process of producing speech sounds is flawed, and the resulting speech sounds are incorrect. Some individuals have no physiological reason for their articulation difficulties. Others correctly articulate a sound when it occurs in one position in words but not in other positions. For example, a young child might have difficulty pronouncing the /l/ sound at the beginning of a word ("*Yet's* go!" instead of "*Let's* go!") but have no problem pronouncing it at the end of the word ("That's my ba*ll*"). The four kinds of articulation errors described in Table 4.2 can be remembered using the acronym SODA (substitution, omission, distortion, addition) (Plante & Beeson, 2008). Remember that articulation is related to the speaker's age, culture, and environment. For example, a young child's errors may be developmentally correct, whereas the same speech product made by an older child could reflect an articulation problem. The difference could also be due to regional speech patterns, foreign

articulation disorder Abnormal production of speech sounds

Table 4.2 • Four Kinds of Articulation Errors

Error Type	Definition	Example
Substitution	A common misarticulation among small children; one sound is used for another.	Intended: *I see the rabbit.* Substitution: *I tee the wabbit.*
Omission	A sound or group of sounds is left out of a word. Small children often leave off the ending of a word (sounds in the final position).	Intended: *I want a banana.* Omission: *I wanna nana.*
Distortion	A variation of the intended sound is produced in an unfamiliar manner.	Intended: *Give the pencil to Sally.* Distortion: *Give the pencil to Sally* (the /p/ is nasalized).
Addition	An extra sound is inserted or added to one already correctly produced.	Intended: *I miss her.* Addition: *I missid her.*

language accents, or cultural speech preferences, but none of these differences reflects a speech disorder. Regional speech differences (dialects) do not need attention from an SLP.

Fluency Problems When the rate and flow pattern of a person's speech is of concern, the individual most likely has difficulty with fluency. Fluency problems, or **dysfluencies**, usually involve hesitations or repetitions of parts of words that interrupt the flow of speech (Conture, 2001). Some young children (ages 3 to 5) demonstrate dysfluencies in the course of normal speech development, and these are not usually in need of therapy. **Stuttering** is one type of fluency problem where sounds or parts of words are repeated. With older individuals, the repetition of words or phrases (e.g., "The boy went to . . . went to the show") is typically *not* a sign of stuttering, but frequently repeating sounds or parts of words (e.g., "the b-b-boy w-w-went to the sh-sh-show") is a signal of this speech impairment (Plante & Beeson, 2008; Ratner, 2009).

Voice Problems The third type of speech disorder, a **voice problem**, is not very common in students, but if a child's voice is unusual given the age and sex of the individual (e.g., too husky for a young girl or too high for an older teenage boy), immediate attention from a professional should be arranged. Two qualities of voice are important. **Pitch** is the perceived high or low quality of voice. **Loudness** is the other main aspect of voice.

Age is a critical variable for all three types of speech impairments (Bernthal & Bankson, 2004). Correct production does not develop at the same time for all speech sounds (Small, 2005). Thus, articulation behavior that is developmentally normal at one age is not acceptable at another. The chart in Figure 4.3 gives examples of the ages when various speech sounds develop (Sander, 1972). By age 8½, most children have mastered the last sound (/z/, as in *was*) at 90% accuracy. In the case of stuttering, age is also important; it is normal for very young children (between the ages of 3 and 5) to be dysfluent—their speech includes many hesitations and repetitions—as they master oral communication and language. Young children (below age 6) often exhibit high rates of dysfluencies and may even fit a definition of stuttering. Dysfluencies are likely to occur in exciting, stressful, or uncommon situations (Conture, 2001; Gregory et al., 2003). However, more than half of those preschoolers who stutter recover by the age of 7 (Ratner, 2009). Pitch changes during puberty, particularly for boys. Of course, this pitch change is a normal part of development and disappears as the boy's body grows and voice pitch becomes stabilized. It is important that adults avoid unnecessary alarm and consider a child's age when determining whether a child may have a speech disorder.

dysfluencies Hesitations or repetitions of sounds or words that interrupt a person's flow of speech—stuttering, for example; a speech disorder

stuttering The lack of fluency in an individual's speech pattern, often characterized by hesitations or repetitions of sounds or words

voice problem An abnormal spoken language production, characterized by unusual pitch, loudness, or quality of sounds

pitch An aspect of voice; its perceived high or low sound quality

loudness An aspect of voice, referring to the intensity of the sound produced while speaking

Figure 4.3 • Sander's Chart, Indicating When 90% of All Children Typically Produce a Specific Sound Correctly

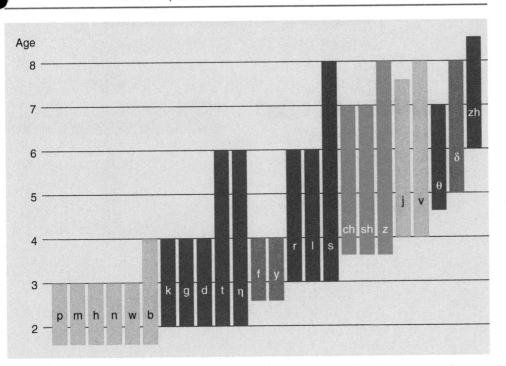

Notes: Average-age estimates and upper-age limits of customary consonant production. The solid bar corresponding to each sound starts at the median age of customary articulation; it stops at the age level at which 90% of all children are customarily producing the sound.
The θ symbol stands for the breathed "th" sound, as in the word *bathroom*. The δ symbol stands for the voiced "th" sound, as in the word *feather*. The η symbol stands for the "ing" sound, as in the word *singing*. The zh symbol indicates the sound of the medial consonant in *measure* or *vision*.

Source: "When Are Speech Sounds Learned?" by E. K. Sander, 1972, *Journal of Speech and Hearing Disorders, 37*, p. 62. © American Speech-Language-Hearing Association. Reprinted by permission.

Language Impairments

Language is the complex system we use to communicate our thoughts to others. Oral language is expressed through the use of speech sounds that are combined to produce words and sentences. The use of sounds, letters (symbols), and words is governed by the rules of language. What we know about speech sounds, letters, words (or vocabulary), and rules of language influences the way we speak, read, write, and spell. Not all language systems use speech sounds (consider manual communication or sign language), but they all follow rules that guide communication and conversations. When an individual has a language impairment or **language disorder**, there is a breakdown in one of the three aspects of language, and effective communication is hindered. It is helpful to understand how these components come together in order to recognize when a language malfunction is present. As you read this section, follow along using the language scheme depicted in Figure 4.4. Now, let's think about the three aspects of language:

- Form
- Content
- Use

The rule system used in all language (oral, written, and sign) is the **form** of language. Oral language uses sounds or sound combinations; written language uses letters and letter combinations to produce the words and word combinations (sentences) of language; manual communication uses hand and finger movements. In oral language, form has three components: phonology, morphology, and syntax.

language disorder Difficulty or inability to master the various systems of rules in language, which then interferes with communication

form The rule system of language; includes phonology, morphology, and syntax

Figure 4.4 • Scheme of Language

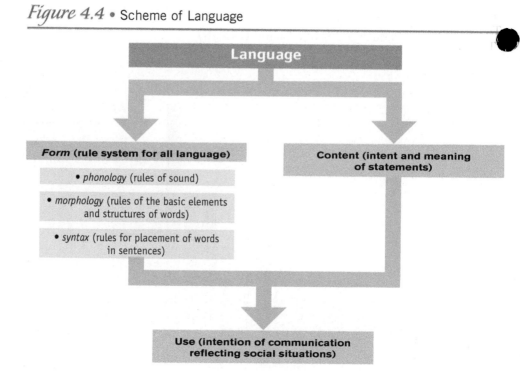

The sound system of language, **phonology**, includes rules that govern various sound combinations (Small, 2005). Phonology varies depending on the language being spoken. For example, the speech sounds of Hawaiian are different from those of English. The English language uses 45 different speech sound combinations; the Hawaiian language uses only half that number. Swahili and some Native American languages use "clicking" sounds not found in European languages. Rules in each language govern how vowels, consonants, their combinations, and words are used. Awareness of the relationship between sounds in words and sound symbols is called **phonological awareness**. These skills develop during the preschool years and appear to be a prerequisite for reading (Jenkins & O'Connor, 2002; Norris & Hoffman, 2002; Vaughn & Linan-Thompson, 2004). Phonological awareness and the development of reading are discussed in the Early Intervention sections of this chapter and the next ("Learning Disabilities"). For now, remember that the foundation for language is also the foundation for reading and that phonological awareness is one key element of this foundation.

Morphology consists of the rules that govern the parts of words that form the basic elements of their meanings and structures. For example, prefixes and suffixes change the meanings of the roots of specific words: The suffix *-ed* changes the tense to past; the prefix *un-* signals negation, while *re-* usually means that something is done again. Note the difference in the meanings of the following words: *cover, covered, uncover, recover, uncovered, recovered, discovered, discovering, discover,* and *discovery.* The rules governing the structure of words enable us to understand the words' meanings.

Words are placed in sentences in accordance with the rules of **syntax**. Like phonology rules, syntax rules vary in different languages. Compare how a sentence is made into a question in the English language ("I want to eat"; "Do you want to eat?") to the way statements and questions are formed in Spanish ("Quiero comer"; "¿Quiere comer?"). Note that in English, the placement of the verb and the subject change when the question is formed. But in Spanish they do not; rather, the person's intonation indicates that a question is being asked. The rules within a language determine the meaning of the communication. In English, nouns and pronouns generally precede verbs in a sentence, and when they do

phonology The rules within a language used to govern the combination of speech sounds to form words and sentences

phonological awareness Understanding, identifying, and applying sound–symbol relationships (letter sounds, rhyming)

morphology Rules that govern the structure and form of words and comprise the basic meaning of words

syntax Rules that govern word endings and order of words in phrases and sentences

not, the construction might be a question: "It is one o'clock"; "Is it one o'clock?" The placement of the words in sentences can change their meaning. For example, "The car hit the boy" has a meaning very different from "The boy hit the car." Rules also structure our placement of adverbs and other parts of speech. Knowing the difference between "I hardly studied this chapter" and "I studied this chapter hard" requires an understanding of how the elements of the English language are put together. For some youngsters these subtleties can be difficult to master.

The second aspect of language, **content**, reflects the intent and meaning of spoken or written statements. The rules and form of language are important, but for communication to be effective, words must be meaningful. **Semantics** is the system where the intent and meanings of words and sentences make up the content of the communication. The key words in a statement, the direct (e.g., "Antonella chased the dog into the street") and implied referents (e.g., "She chased it over there") to these words, and the order of the words used all affect the meaning of the message. When senders of messages use indirect or implied referents without providing sufficient background information, the receiver may not understand the message that is intended. When a child comes home and tells his mother, "I left that thing at school," she might be unclear about what the child left at school, unless he is answering a direct question such as "Where is your jacket?

Being able to produce speech and language correctly is only one part of effective communication; their appropriate use across a variety of settings is also necessary (Gleason, 2009). The application of language in various communications according to the social context of the situation is called **pragmatics**. For example, an individual may make a request, give an order, or supply some information through a communication; the communication is different depending on the individual's intent or purpose, and on the intended recipient. **Communicative competence** also requires that one knows when and how to communicate appropriately in a variety of situations. Learners need to develop an understanding about what may be said and what should not be said in different settings, and to use language correctly in a social context. Social competence and communicative competence are related (Olswang, Coggins, & Timler, 2001). Social conventions or rules are used to initiate conversations and to communicate with others. Children who have problems with pragmatics and communicative competence may not know how to join in a ball game at recess, so instead they barge in, disrupt the game, and alienate their peers in the process. Other students may have difficulties understanding how to transition from one subject to another during a conversation. As a result, an individual could appear to make random comments that do not pertain to the topic at hand, as when a group is discussing something that happened in the news and a student makes a comment about his top score on a video game. Students who have not developed communicative competence also face challenges when interacting with adults and people in authority. For example, the student might know that it's fine to say, "Hey, dude!" or "Like, duh" to a peer but not understand that using such expressions with the principal (instead of "Good morning, Mrs. Rodgers" or "Yes, ma'am") may lead to trouble. Teachers can help by providing many opportunities for students to practice using language correctly and appropriately every school day.

content An aspect of language that governs the intent and meaning of the message delivered in a communication

semantics The system within a language that governs content, intent, and meanings of spoken and written language

pragmatics The appropriate use of language in social contexts

communicative competence Proficiency in all aspects of communication in social and learning situations

Characteristics

Children with speech or language impairments are a large and diverse group of learners. Some have speech disorders, many have language disorders, some have both speech and language disorders, and still others have coexisting disabilities (e.g., learning disabilities and language disorders). In this chapter, we focus on speech and language disorders. In later chapters, we will concentrate on other primary disabilities.

These children are engaged in the communication process by taking turns sending and receiving messages.

Table 4.3 • Signs or Characteristics of Speech or Language Impairments

Speech

- Makes consistent and age-inappropriate articulation errors
- Exhibits dysfluencies (repetitions, prolongations, interruptions) in the flow or rhythm of speech
- Has poor voice quality, such as distracting pitch
- Is excessively loud or soft

Language

- Is unable to follow oral directions
- Is unable to match letters with sounds
- Cannot create rhymes
- Cannot break words into syllables
- Has an inadequate vocabulary
- Demonstrates poor concept formation
- Does not understand nuances, nonverbal messages, or humor
- Struggles to understand or convey messages
- Shows difficulties when conversing with others
- Has difficulty expressing personal needs

Individuals with different speech disorders have different characteristics and learning needs (see Table 4.3). For example, a child with a voice problem needs a different remediation program than a child who has articulation difficulties. As would be expected, students with speech disorders have entirely different characteristics and remediation programs than those with language difficulties.

Speech

Some children fail to exhibit normal speech patterns at expected ages or levels of development. Many parents understand their babies' or toddlers' babbling or attempts at speech. Intelligibility, or the ability of those outside the immediate family to understand the child's speech, is an indicator of potential speech problems (Menn & Stoel-Gammon, 2009). As you learned earlier, there are key milestones on which young children's speech can be compared (refer again to Figure 4.3). Children with speech impairments lag behind these milestones.

Most students whose primary disability is a speech disorder (articulation, fluency, or voice) attend general education classes and function well academically with their peers. Usually their disability does not influence their academic learning. If their speech disorder is severe and sustained, however, they may have difficulties with peers in social interactions. Depending on how the peer group reacts to an individual's disability, many people with severe speech impairments have long-term difficulties with self-concept and independence (Anderson & Shames, 2006).

Social difficulties are particularly common for those who stutter (Ramig & Shames, 2006). Stuttering can negatively affect a person's sense of adequacy and confidence. Many people who stutter avoid situations in which they have to talk. Consequently, their disability can influence the types of jobs they seek, the friends they make, their relationships with others, and their overall quality of life. Think about how you react to people with severe speech impairments. Do you look away from them? Do you try to be helpful to the stutterer by finishing his or her sentence? Do you try to avoid the person? Now think about how young children treat their peers who use different speech sounds, who stutter, or who have a different voice quality. Facing these reactions is an everyday reality for individuals with speech disorders. It is understandable that some would like to withdraw from a society that treats them as different. Teachers and peers can be helpful; their actions can make a real difference in the way students with speech disorders feel about themselves and others (Gregory et al., 2003; Salend, 2005). For example, teachers can make a difference by

- creating classroom environments where all peers are supportive of each other,
- maintaining eye contact with the student with speech or language impairments throughout the duration of every conversation, and
- not finishing sentences or filling in words for individuals who stutter.

Classmates' reaction to students with speech or language impairments can be insensitive and, in some cases, even worsen the individual's problems. When reactions are intense, the result can be disruptions to the learning environment or even conflicts during recess or after school. Teachers can turn such situations around by involving peers in positive ways, such as teaching them how to respond constructively and encouraging them not to laugh or tease their classmate. Tips for Classroom Management gives more ideas about how peers can become positive elements in the lives of individuals who face challenges caused by speech or language disorders.

Language

Young children with language impairments develop language late. While their peers without disabilities are talking by the age of 3, they are not. And problems continue to mount as they progress through school. As their classmates without disabilities

TIPS for Classroom Management
DEVELOPING SENSITIVITY

Focus on the Classmates

1. Help classmates understand how they can help a peer with speech or language impairments, such as giving simple instructions about how to play a game or showing how to complete the last steps in a long set of directions.
2. Have class discussions about how feelings, attitudes, and reactions matter.
3. Hold classmates responsible for any teasing and laughing when they hear speech impairments.
4. Instruct classmates not to avoid eye contact when a person with speech or language impairments is having a problem communicating.
5. Teach classmates not to fill in remaining parts of words or sentences for a person who is stuttering.

Focus on the Individual

1. Think with the student with the speech or language problem about constructive and positive ways to deal with awkward or confronting situations.
2. Practice ways to seek assistance from classmates.
3. Create opportunities to practice new speech and language skills in a "safe" environment before practicing these skills with the entire class.

A teacher needs to be a good role model!

are beginning to read independently by third grade, they are not. As they continue through school their problems with reading inhibit their achievement in all academic areas where speaking and writing are the foundations. In addition, like their peers with speech impairments, many of these individuals have problems making friends and developing positive social relationships (ASHA, 2002). Let's think a little more about these issues.

Language Differences, Delays, and Disorders In the previous chapter about culturally and linguistically diverse students, you learned that many students attending U.S. public schools are at great risk for being incorrectly identified as having disabilities. You learned that students' differences in language are often the root of their misidentification as having a disability, particularly a speech or language disorder. In fact, considerable confusion surrounds these students, and it often takes an expert in normal language development—such as an SLP—to sort out those students with from those without disabilities. Some of the issues and situations that contribute to this confusion include language differences, acquisition of a second language, and language delays.

Many times, **language differences**—regional speech patterns, foreign accents, or second language acquisition—are confused with language disorders (Salend, 2005). Language differences, which result from historical, social, regional, and cultural influences—and are sometimes perceived by educators as inferior or nonstandard—may take the form of **dialects** (Payne & Taylor, 2006). Children from diverse backgrounds who use dialects, whether they are from Appalachia or from a predominantly Black inner-city community, are often misidentified as having language disorders. Another type of language difference occurs when individuals are learning English and have not yet fully mastered their second language (Salend & Salinas, 2003). Professionals who are able to discriminate between language differences and language disorders are proficient in the rules of the particular student's dialect, in those of the individual's first language, and also in nondiscriminatory testing procedures. It is important that identification procedures be applied to diverse groups of learners carefully.

English language learners (ELLs) may or may not have language disorders. Again, as you learned in Chapter 3, truly mastering a second language takes a long time. It is not easy to determine if a struggling student who is not a native English speaker is displaying characteristics of learning a new language or if that child has a language disorder (Baca & Cervantes, 2004; Ortiz et al., 2006; Salend, 2005). ELLs may appear to be fluent in English because they converse with their classmates on the playground and express their basic needs in the classroom, but even so, they may not yet have developed sufficient fluency in their second language to participate fully in academic instruction. These abilities, however, are only some of the language skills acquired on the way to communicative competence. Cultural differences and family values also influence how individual children learn language skills, and it is important to understand that different interaction styles result in different paths to communicative competence. Educators need to be aware of two concerns regarding language disorders and diverse students and be careful about (a) possibly misdiagnosing a student who is learning English as having a language disorder and (b) postponing possible intervention for an ELL student because of a mistaken belief that his or her struggles are due to language differences. In other words, be cautious about both over- and underidentifying English learners as having language disorders! Someone proficient in the student's native language can be most helpful. That person can assist in determining whether mastery of English is not yet complete or whether, because the student has similar problems in both languages, she or he may have a language disorder that requires intervention.

Delays in development—be they delays in physical development, motor coordination, or language development—are often signs that a young child may have disabilities. **Language delays**, usually evident when the child has not developed language skills at the same age as most children do, are a common indication of

language differences Emerging second language acquisition or nonstandard English

dialects Words and pronunciation from a geographical region or ethnic group, different from those of standard language

language delays Slowed development of language skills; may or may not result in language impairments disabilities in very young children. But language delays are not a characteristic of disabilities for every child; some children are just slower to develop language than other children, often referred to as "late talkers." Late talkers are usually children between 1½ and 2½ years of age whose language skills are far below the majority of their same-age peers. For example, late talkers

- are slow to acquire their first 50 words and combine words into phrases,
- seem to understand fewer words than their peers,
- have poor comprehension skills, and
- display few gestures when communicating (Plante & Beeson, 2008).

Because late talkers are at a significantly higher risk for having language impairments, all children with delayed language acquisition should be referred for screening to determine if language therapy is needed. However, they do not have to be identified as having a specific disability. IDEA '04 specifically addresses the issues of developmental delays, allowing children younger than age 8 to qualify for special education services without being labeled—or mislabeled—with a specific disability. What IDEA '04 Says About Developmental Delays explains more about what the law requires.

Children with typical language development gain skills in an orderly fashion, in roughly the same sequence across the first 18 months of life (Owens, 2006). Look first at the profile of the normally developing child; the typical ages when a child achieves major language milestones are shown in the left column of Table 4.4. Note that most children after age 3 (40 months) use some fairly sophisticated language, but the 3-year-old with language problems is only beginning to use two-word combinations. The gaps between these two children widen quickly. For many individuals with intellectual disabilities, delays continue. They develop language in the correct sequence but never complete the acquisition of complex language; their language development remains below that of their peers without

What IDEA '04 Says About . . .

Developmental Delays

In addition to the specific disability categories listed in IDEA '04, a child within the ages of 3 to 9 may be considered as having a disability if

- he or she meets their state's definition of having a developmental delay;
- the developmental delay was identified through the use of appropriate diagnostic instruments and procedures;
- the child shows delays in any one or more of five specified areas (physical development, cognitive development, communication development, social or emotional development, adaptive development); or
- the delay is significant enough to warrant special education and related services.

Table 4.4 • Comparison of Language Acquisition Skills

Age in Months		Attainment	Examples
Typical	Delayed		
13	17	First words	Mamma; Here; Doggie; Bye-bye; This
17	38	50-word Vocabulary	
18	40	First 2-word combinations	More juice; Here ball; Here, kitty
22	48	Later 2-word combinations	Mommy purse; Cup floor; Keys chair
24	52	Mean sentence length of 2 words	Andy sleeping
27	55	First appearance of -ing	
30	63	Mean sentence length of 3.1 words	
30	66	First appearance of is	My car's gone!
37	73	Mean sentence length of 4.1 words	
38	76	Mean sentence length of 4.5 words	
40	79	First appearance of indirect requests	Can I get the ball?

disabilities (Wetherby, 2002). For many students with language disorders, however, it is not just at what rate (how slowly) a child develops language but also how it develops differently, that signals a problem. Often, both lateness and an uncharacteristic pattern of language development signal language disorders. Children with this disorder make language mistakes at an age when their peers don't. They might omit the verb, put the wrong ending on a word, or have incomplete vocabulary development for their age (Plante & Beeson, 2008). So, the kindergartener with language impairments might say, "I go, too" (instead of "I want to go with you") or "This clay green" (omitting *is*) or "The paint guy [instead of *the painter*] get [instead of *gets*] more big one [instead of *bigger* brushes]."

receptive language Understanding information that is received, either through seeing, hearing, or touching

Receptive and Expressive Language   Being able to understand communication well is important to all interactions, including those in the classroom. Students must comprehend instructions for completing their assignments, following classroom and school rules, and understanding lectures. Students with language disorders often exhibit problems with **receptive language**, which can create negative academic and social outcomes. For example, the student who has trouble understanding oral directions might experience confusion or embarrassment. When the teacher says to the class, "Put away your pencils and workbooks, get your coats, and line up at the door for recess," a student with receptive language difficulties might process only the last thing she heard. Thus, she might line up at the door without having either put her work away or put her coat on. The teacher may think that the individual is defiant, rather than experiencing problems with receptive language. To help, the teacher could restate the three-part instructions slowly and simply or have a peer help the student who continually has such difficulties.

expressive language The ability to convey thoughts, feelings, or information

Many people find that their receptive language skills are better than their **expressive language** skills. For example, people who studied a second language in high school or college often find that they can better understand what they read or hear in that language compared to what they are able to write or speak. Similarly, many children with language disorders find it difficult to express their thoughts or feelings, or to write them down on paper. A student may know the answer to a teacher's question but may have difficulty formulating their thoughts into a spoken sentence. Students with language impairments often have difficulty with word retrieval, such as the 11-year-old who couldn't recall the word *rectangle* to describe the shape of a log cabin seen on a field trip. She worked around her retrieval problem by describing it "like a square but with longer sides on the top and bottom." A teacher can provide extended wait time after asking a question or use prompts to help the student express him- or herself in these instances.

Social Competence   Language plays a key role in developing and maintaining social relationships; social communication requires linguistic and communicative competence (Olswang et al., 2001). Being able to understand messages and to communicate well is important in interactions with peers and adults. Here are a few reasons why this is so: Effective communication is required to resolve conflicts and disagreements, solve problems, negotiate solutions, share, and develop friendships. Being able to apply complex language skills is a key to understanding others' points of view and to clearly presenting one's feelings. Being adept in the pragmatics of language contributes to successful conflict resolution, comprehension of social situations, and understanding of communications that are ambiguous (Salend, 2005). Students with language impairments are at a higher risk of having difficulties developing positive peer relationships (Ratner, 2009). Some areas where students with language disorders have difficulty include these:

- Initiating and maintaining conversations
- Interpreting body language and facial expressions
- Exhibiting sensitivity to the listener's need for more information or clarification

Can you identify the feelings being expressed by the people in these photos? Most people can. However, students with language disorders often have difficulty interpreting facial expressions and body language. These skills need to be taught directly.

- Engaging in common social customs (e.g., greetings, saying good-bye)
- Producing appropriate requests or responses to the requests of others

It can be difficult to recognize the characteristics of students who need help developing effective communication skills. Consider the situation described in Figure 4.5, "Brandon's Stuck at School." Brandon's language disorder caused a great deal of confusion for everyone involved. Teachers and family members who do not recognize the signs of a language impairment may experience frustration due to the inaccurate or incomplete information provided during an interaction. In classroom settings, perceptive teachers can recognize the characteristics of language impairments and implement effective interventions to alleviate many of the problems this disorder can create (Anderson & Shames, 2006).

Reading and Academic Performance Mounting research evidence shows that children identified with language impairments during the preschool years are very likely to be identified as having learning disabilities by third or fourth grade (Ely, 2005; Falk-Ross, 2002; Fuchs & Fuchs, 2005). Preschoolers with language impairments who later have problems learning to read have great difficulty identifying or understanding the relationships between the sounds in words and the symbols that represent those sounds in print (Fletcher et al., 2002). In other words, what initially is a problem with oral language later manifests itself in challenges with what is seen and read on the printed page. The co-occurrence of language disorders with learning disabilities is high. Federal data about the prevalence of these two disabilities support the strong connection between language disorders diagnosed in preschoolers and a diagnosis of learning disabilities during the school years. Because reading skills lead to literacy and are the basis of nearly every academic assignment given in high school, students with language disorders are vulnerable to school failure. But early intervention—teaching preschoolers the skills of phonemic awareness and the sounds that letters of the alphabet represent—can reduce the number of elementary students who have problems learning how to read (Jenkins & O'Connor, 2002; Lyon et al., 2001).

Figure 4.5 • Brandon's Stuck at School

Twelve-year-old Brandon appears in Ms. Sastray's classroom, 45 minutes after school has let out. When she questions why he is still at school, he tells her that no one has come to pick him up. Upon further questioning, Ms. Sastray learns that Brandon's dad was supposed to pick him up but has not shown up and that Brandon cannot reach his mother, father, or stepfather by cell phone. He had, however, left messages on all three phones, stating that he was stuck at school with no way to get home. Ms. Sastray also tries unsuccessfully to reach all of Brandon's caregivers, and she tells him he can stay in her classroom until someone comes to get him.

Brandon's father arrives at 5:00 and is surprised to find Brandon in Ms. Sastray's classroom. At the same time, Brandon's mother calls the school, frantic to locate him after receiving his numerous messages on her cell phone. At this point, Ms. Sastray learns that Brandon was supposed to be at soccer practice until 5:00, at which time he would go home with his father. Brandon then explains that he forgot his soccer clothes at home, so he decided to skip practice. While it was unusual for all three caregivers to be unavailable by cell phone (his father's phone battery was dead, his stepfather was on an airplane, and his mother—a counselor—had her phone turned off while meeting with a client), Brandon's language impairment contributed significantly to the situation in several ways.

- *Impaired problem-solving skills:* Brandon could have worn his PE clothes to soccer practice, or he could have sat on the sidelines and watched his teammates. He was unable to problem-solve effectively to brainstorm possible options.

- *Inability to determine Ms. Sastray's level of knowledge:* It did not occur to Brandon that Ms. Sastray might not know he was supposed to be at soccer practice or that his father would arrive at 5:00, both of which were key facts.

- *Inability to identify and convey the critical elements of his situation:* He was unable to determine that a communication breakdown had occurred (i.e., soccer practice, father arriving at 5:00), nor did he think it important to convey those very important bits of information.

Prevalence

Official reports show that learning disabilities (see Chapter 5) make up the largest single category of exceptional learners and that speech or language impairments make up the second-largest category, containing 19% of all students with disabilities (Office of Special Education Programs, [OSEP], 2008). However, more students actually have speech or language impairments than have learning disabilities. How could this be? Well, the federal government "counts" students in only one category, the category reflecting the student's primary disability. However, many students have more than one disability. When both primary and secondary disabilities are considered, speech or language impairments emerge as the largest special education category

(ASHA, 2002). Parents of all students with disabilities confirm this fact (Blackorby et al., 2002). They report students in every special education category as having difficulties communicating. Although the majority of these students can speak clearly enough to be understood, the remainder experience considerable difficulties speaking, conversing, or understanding others' communications.

Data from the federal government confirm the relationship between early identification of speech or language impairments and later identification of learning disabilities (OSEP, 2008). Figure 4.6 shows the number of individuals diagnosed with speech or language impairments across age groups, compared to those identified with learning disabilities. Note that many more young children are found to have speech or language impairments, but as they get older their diagnosis changes to learning disabilities, most often because language difficulties impact their ability to stay on a par with others academically, particularly in subjects that require reading mastery. For example, at age 3—when children who are not developing oral language are first identified—the speech or language impairments category is almost nine times larger than the learning disabilities category. However, at third grade (age 8)—when reading problems become clearly apparent—the learning disabilities category becomes almost the same size as the speech or language impairments category. From that point on, as reading becomes a more integral part of all schoolwork, the number of students assigned to the learning disabilities category grows dramatically, while those assigned to the speech or language impairments category decreases. These data certainly support the premise that as the expectations and demands of the curriculum increase, the impact of language impairments becomes more and more apparent.

Causes and Prevention

Researchers work hard to find factors that cause specific disabilities because the cause often provides clues to effective prevention. Unfortunately, as with so many disability areas, the causes for most cases of speech or language impairments are unknown.

Figure 4.6 • Number of Individuals Served Through IDEA '04 by Age
The number of students identified as having learning disabilities begins to increase substantially as the demands of school (and independent reading) intensify, particularly in grades 2 and 3. In contrast, the number of students identified as having speech or language impairments decreases about the same time, indicating that many of these students' disabilities may be reclassified, from speech or language impairments to LD.

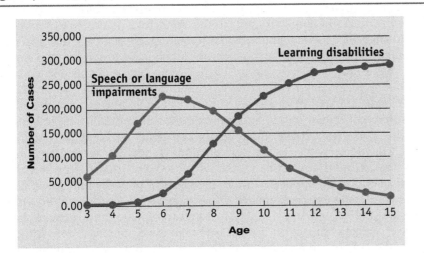

Source: OSEP (2008), Table 1-7.

Consequently, ways to prevent them from occurring in the first place have not yet been identified. The causes of certain conditions, however, are well known. For some of those conditions, impairments are preventable or can be treated to reduce or eliminate the challenges they present. The known causes of speech impairments tend to differ from the known causes of language impairments. We will first consider speech impairments and then turn our attention to language impairments.

Causes

Speech impairments can result from many different conditions, including brain damage, malfunction of the respiratory or speech mechanisms, and malformation of the articulators. Some children make articulation errors because they do not use the right physical movements to form sounds correctly. They make errors because of the way they use the speech mechanisms—tongue, lips, teeth, mandible (jaw), and/or palate—to form the speech sounds. For others, the cause may be a physical or organic problem, such as a **cleft palate**, where an opening exists in the roof of the mouth, or a **cleft lip**, where the upper lip isn't connected, resulting in an inability to form some speech sounds.

Approximately 1 of every 700 children is born with a cleft lip or palate, which is more than 5,000 in the United States alone (ASHA, 2008a). The proportions of cleft lips and palates tend to be consistent; about 25% involve only the lip, 50% involve the lip and the palate, and the remaining 25% involve the palate alone. Between 50% and 75% of these students will require the services of an SLP. Most cleft lips can be repaired through plastic surgery and do not have a long-term effect on articulation. A cleft palate, however, can present continual problems because the opening of the palate (the roof of the mouth) allows excessive air and sound waves to flow through the nasal cavities. The result is a very nasal-sounding voice and difficulty in producing some speech sounds, such as /s/ and /z/. A cleft palate is one physical cause of a speech impairment that requires the intensive work of many specialists. Plastic surgeons (such as the specialists highlighted in the Making a Difference section earlier), orthodontists, and SLPs often join forces to help individuals overcome the speech disability that results from cleft lips and palates.

Although professionals can describe stuttering, they are unable to pinpoint or agree on a single cause for the problem (Ratner, 2009). Experts do believe, however, that stuttering episodes are related to stress, particularly when the conversational situation is very complex or unpredictable (Hall et al., 2001). Dysfluencies are more likely to occur and reoccur when the situation is challenging or confusing.

Voice problems, which are less common in schoolchildren, can be symptomatic of a medical problem. For example, conditions that interfere with muscular activity, such as juvenile arthritis, can result in a vocal disturbance. Voice problems also can be caused by the way the voice is used. Undue abuse of the voice by screaming, shouting, and straining can damage the vocal folds and result in a voice disorder. Rock singers frequently strain their voices so much that they develop nodules (calluses) on the vocal folds, become chronically hoarse, and must stop singing or have the nodules removed surgically. Teachers who notice changes in children's voices that are not associated with puberty should refer the student to an SLP.

Language impairments have many causes, including genetic conditions, hearing impairments, illness, injury, and the existence of coexisting disabilities like autism (Plante & Beeson, 2008). Brain injury can result in conditions such as aphasia, which interferes with language production. Genetically caused language disorders may impact brain development and its subsequent capacity for language development, and they are implicated when members of both the immediate family and the extended family exhibit language impairments (Owens et al., 2006). Impaired hearing, and the subsequent inability to listen to, imitate, and replicate language, can have a dramatic impact on normal language development. The environment, especially the lack of experiences that stimulate language development, is also a major factor contributing to language impairments.

cleft palate An opening in the roof of the mouth causing too much air to pass through the nasal cavity, resulting in a speech impairment

cleft lip A congenital condition where the upper lip is not formed or connected correctly to allow for correct articulation of sounds, resulting in a speech impairment

Caregivers who engage in discussions with their young children can enhance their language development and help prevent language delays.

The quality and quantity of early language input have a definite effect on vocabulary development and language development (Harwood, Warren, & Yoder, 2002). An inability to benefit from language models can also contribute to inefficient or delayed language acquisition. For example, chronic **otitis media**, or middle ear infection, reduces opportunities for toddlers to hear and imitate others' language during key developmental periods and may result in difficulties with language development (Roberts & Zeisel, 2002). Poor language development can be caused by environmental factors, including lack of stimulation and of the proper experiences for cognitive development and learning language. Some children do not develop language because they have no appropriate role models. Others are left alone too often or are not spoken to frequently. Some are punished for speaking or are ignored when they try to communicate. Many of these children have no reason to speak; they have nothing to talk about and few experiences to share. Such youngsters are definitely at risk for developing significant language impairments.

otitis media Middle ear infection that can interrupt normal language development

Prevention

Many measures can be taken to prevent speech or language impairments. Many preventive measures have a medical basis and are implemented prior to the birth of a baby. For example, polio and rubella can have devastating effects on an unborn baby; proper immunization protects adults and children from these and other diseases. A nutritional supplement of folic acid during pregnancy can reduce the risk of cleft palates and lips by 25% to 50% (Maugh, 1995). Proper prenatal care is important to the health of babies. Good nutrition influences the strength and early development of very young children.

Children who live in poverty are less likely to have access to information and medical programs, which puts them at risk for diseases that result in disabilities (Utley & Obiakor, 2001). The availability of proper medical care before and after birth is crucial. Access to health care during childhood is important so that diseases in early childhood, such as measles, can be avoided or treated early. Better public education programs available to the entire population inform people of the necessity of good prenatal care, nutrition, and medical care. Innovative information dissemination on the importance of protecting children from disease can make real differences in reducing the numbers of individuals who have language problems because they did not receive immunizations or early treatment for illness. For example, TV or radio advertisements may reach some families; different approaches might be more effective when informing other families. Health fairs sponsored by churches, sororities, fraternities, and other community organizations may prove to be more effective than traditional means in communicating important informatio to the African American community (Children's Defense Fund [CDF], 2005).

Overcoming Challenges

Not all disabilities and conditions are permanent. In many cases therapy, effective instruction, and lots of hard work can restore effective speech or language functioning (ASHA, 2002). In others, individuals can learn to compensate for the problems presented by disabilities. It is critical that intervention is provided early enough to reduce or prevent the residual problems created by the disability or condition.

Assessment

It is important to bring services to a student with a speech or language impairment as soon as it is clear that a problem exists. The sooner intervention can begin, the bigger the long-term results. But before treatment can begin, the problem must be diagnosed.

Early Identification

About 40% of children who show delayed language development at age 2 continue to demonstrate significant language problems as they get older (Ratner, 2009). These youngsters are often identified by their significantly deficient vocabulary (Plante & Beeson, 2008). Even for preschoolers, parents and educators can request that the local school district help arrange a speech or language evaluation for those who are not developing skills on par with their peers. As you saw in Figure 4.6, the relationship between early identification of language problems and later identification of learning disabilities is clear (Ratner, 2009). The importance of identifying these children as soon as possible is also now universally recognized, because the association between language impairments and learning disabilities is so strong (Bakken & Whedon, 2002). Review Table 4.4 and use it as a guide to when preschoolers should be referred for a speech and language evaluation. The story in Considering Culture demonstrates how vigilant preschool teachers can help get services to students and their families as quickly as possible. Remember, early identification and treatment make a real difference in students' long-term results.

Prereferral

As you are learning, the prereferral stage in the special education identification process is important to ensure that students are not incorrectly identified as having a disability they do not have. Prereferral activities are conducted primarily by the general education classroom teacher, with the help and consultation of special educators and related service providers. When the speech or language abilities of a student present concerns, SLPs play a vital role in helping teachers schedule different interventions and instructional procedures to determine whether alterations to the learning environment result in improved performance or whether intensive special education services are required (ASHA, 2002).

Remember discussions in the previous chapter about the dangers of misidentifying culturally and linguistically diverse students as having disabilities. Remember also the dangers of not identifying those students who *do* have language impairments quickly enough to avoid those problems compounding. Neither general nor special education teachers typically have the expertise to make these distinctions. That is the specialty of SLPs (ASHA, 2002). During this prereferral assessment phase, SLPs

- analyze the student's school records,
- conduct evaluations in the classroom,
- suggest alternative instructional procedures and evaluate their effectiveness,
- collaborate with the student's family, and
- consult with the school-based team and help determine whether the IEP process needs to continue.

Considering Culture: *Speech Disorders or Linguistic Differences?*

Twins Amazu and Jaja seem to enjoy their Head Start class. They actively play with the other children on the playground, sit and listen during story time, and love playing in the blocks area. Trina, the twin's teacher, is pleased that the boys have made such a good transition to preschool after moving with their family from Nigeria. Many children in her class are English language learners, and Trina tries especially hard to support their learning English as quickly as possible. However, she has noticed that Amazu is not learning English as rapidly as his brother, Jaja. In fact, he does not appear to use speech when communicating with his brother or others, and Trina worries that he might have developmental difficulties. Furthermore, the program's screening tests revealed that he is not functioning at age level in his language development.

Trina approached the boys' parents, Mr. and Mrs. Madubuike, and suggested that Amazu be referred for further testing. Although the parents were not particularly worried about their son, they agreed. Indeed, subsequent testing revealed that Amazu shows marked delays in speech and language skills. Thus, both an early childhood special educator and a speech/language pathologist who work with the Head Start program were asked to assist in developing appropriate learning strategies for Amazu. Like Amazu's teacher, these professionals are uncertain about the reasons for the boy's delays in speech and language skills. They might be a result of a developmental disorder or might be attributed to his family speaking a primary language other than English. After all, exposure to the English language at preschool is a new experience. On the one hand, they want to ensure that Amazu receives early support, but on the other hand, they don't want to jump to conclusions that may be inaccurate.

Everyone meets and shares their observations honestly. Trina, Amazu's parents, the early childhood special educator, and the SLP agree on a strategy. The specialists will consult with Trina and Amazu's parents, suggesting activities to encourage Amazu to use speech—in either his native language or English. They will help Trina develop language enrichment experiences at school that can also be used at home. All agree to monitor Amazu's development and meet again in a few months to review their findings.

Questions to Consider

1. If possible, observe a teacher or speech/language pathologist (SLP) working with English language learners (ELLs) in a classroom or assessment situation. Can you sort out which behaviors result from cultural or language differences and which might be the result of language impairments?

2. What are your experiences working with children whose language is different from your own? What resources will you seek out when you have concerns about a linguistically diverse student in your classroom?

—By Eleanor Lynch, San Diego State University, and Marci Hanson, San Francisco State University

Identification

For those individuals whose performance improves with teacher-implemented instruction or whose speech or language problems do not reflect disabilities (i.e., they are attributable to dialects or typical second language acquisition), the assessment/identification process is discontinued. In those cases where multiple classroom interventions have been unsuccessful, the next step usually involves a variety of instruments and procedures, such as

- checklists of developmental milestones,
- informal hearing assessments,
- standardized interview protocols,
- questionnaires for family members, or
- formal observations in natural settings.

All of this information helps determine which professionals need to be involved for more formal assessment procedures.

In most states and school districts, when the problem is suspected to be based in either speech or language skills, the SLP is a member of the assessment team and often coordinates the entire assessment and identification process. The SLP brings together a multidisciplinary team of experts that reflects the initial understanding of the individual student's abilities, as well as her or his needs. Team membership reflects information that was gathered during earlier steps in the IEP process. Thus, if a hearing problem is suspected, an audiologist is a member of the team. This specialist conducts formal hearing assessments and also interprets the results to the individual's family and teachers. If the student's primary or native language is not English, an expert in second language acquisition is brought into the assessment effort to determine whether problems are rooted in the process of learning a new language or are compounded by language impairments.

When language impairments are suspected, much valuable information is gathered that not only can be used in the identification process but also can help teachers as they plan instruction. It is important for educators to know what facts are available—even if gathered for another purpose—to guide instruction. Let's take a look at what constitutes a balanced assessment, often coordinated by the SLP.

Evaluation: Diagnosis of Language Impairments

Determining whether a student has language impairments, identifying the exact nature of the problem, making specific intervention plans for both direct services and follow-through activities, and developing accountability systems to ensure progress is being made—it all adds up to no simple task. SLPs use multiple methods, combined in such a way as to provide balanced assessments. Typically, these evaluations include standardized tests and descriptive assessment methods. Because data are collected to provide information about the individual's functional communication abilities, testing often occurs both in the clinic and in the student's natural environments (home, classroom, playground) and situations (with teachers, family members, friends). Balanced assessments may include some or all of the following evaluation measures (ASHA, 2002).

- *Parent/staff/student interviews:* People who interact frequently with the individual of concern have considerable insight and information to contribute during the assessment process. Particularly for students with severe disabilities, relatives know how well the individuals can express their needs and desires, how well they understand others' communications, and the extent of their ability to play and socialize with others.

- *Student history:* Creating a comprehensive record of the student's medical, family, and school history is most helpful in complicated situations. Gathering information from all possible sources can reveal much about the causes of the difficulties, the nature of the problems, and what interventions might be most effective.

- *Checklists and developmental scales:* Collecting information that is organized or categorized to indicate where individuals are having difficulties and where they are not having problems is important for several reasons. First, it provides profiles and patterns that help direct the SLP toward potentially effective methods, and second, it begins the process of creating a baseline of performance to use when evaluating the effectiveness of the treatment program.

- *Progress monitoring:* By using direct measurements of students' performance on academic and other classroom activities, SLPs determine where and how language impairments manifest themselves in students' educational performance. Learning that an individual's language impairments are the root of a learning problem not only helps the SLP determine where to target therapy but also helps the teacher schedule appropriate instructional remediation.

n *Dynamic assessment:* The evaluation process used to "test out" different language interventions is referred to by SLPs as **dynamic assessment**. The purpose is to guide instruction to determine the student's potential for learning. Experts in learning disabilities use a similar process to determine whether the student is **resistant to treatment** and, therefore, in need of more intensive and sustained explicit instruction. Through this process of multilevel intervention, successively more (and more intensive) procedures are used until the severity of the individual's problem is clear.

n *Portfolio assessment:* As described in Chapter 2, creating a collection of the student's work is called portfolio assessment. For the purpose of language evaluations, the following items might be included:

- Samples of written assignments
- Video and/or recordings of communications with the SLP, family members, teachers, and classmates
- Transcriptions of oral communications

n *Observational and anecdotal records:* Notes about how well students communicate in a variety of natural settings helps the SLP develop a descriptive record of their abilities and challenges.

n *Standardized tests:* Finally, as one would expect, SLPs administer nationally normed tests and interpret those results as they plan treatment programs and later evaluate the effectiveness of these programs.

dynamic assessment Assessment process used by SLPs to determine potential effectiveness of different language interventions

resistant to treatment Describes students who do not learn through validated methods typically applied in general education settings

Early Intervention

For most very young children identified as having disabilities, it is their late language development patterns that set them apart from their normally developing peers. Yet, young children with early language delays are less likely to receive early intervention services than toddlers and preschoolers with speech disorders (Ratner, 2009). So when young children do not develop language at the expected rate, intervention both at home and at preschool (or day care) is needed. In every community, early intervention programs are available to provide therapy and instruction to children and to assist parents in helping their children develop language skills. With training and guidance from SLPs, parents can be excellent language teachers for their children with language impairments. In fact, when home-based intervention is provided by parents, children's language scores improve more than when only clinic-based instruction is provided by professionals (Cleminshaw et al., 1996; Hall et al., 2001).

What tactics are included in effective preschool programs? First, the preschool experiences should be in "language-rich" environments where young children have opportunities to explore, exchange ideas, interact with familiar and novel toys and objects, and engage in interesting activities that motivate children to talk (Justice, 2004). Second, language development should be integrated into every lesson throughout the day, not allocated to a specific unit or time of the day. Some of those procedures are found in Tips for Effective Instruction.

The language development of preschool children can be fostered through exciting activities that provide many opportunities to share, explore, play, and learn.

TIPS for Effective Instruction

Promoting Preschoolers' Language

1. Encourage literacy by connecting oral, written, and print language experiences through telling, reading, enacting, and creating stories, and through trips to the library.

2. Arrange classrooms with interesting materials and provide high-interest activities.

3. Provide reasons for oral communication by placing materials within view of the children but out of their reach.

4. Arrange the environment to encourage more communication from children, such as by providing insufficient materials (e.g., paper, paints, or crayons), thus requiring them to request more.

5. Create situations in which children do not have all the materials they need to perform an activity (e.g., painting without brushes, using sandbox pails but no shovels) so that they have to make verbal requests for the supplies they need.

6. Make children make choices and request their preferred activity or the materials they want.

7. Develop situations in which children are likely to need help and must communicate their needs to each other or an adult.

8. Create absurd and surprising situations (e.g., giving them clay instead of crackers at snack time).

9. Allow children to talk frequently and develop elaborative vocabulary using make-believe situations that they generate.

Also, two specific areas for instruction should be included in the preschool curriculum:

- Pragmatics
- Phonological awareness

Professionals first recognized the importance of pragmatics over a quarter of a century ago (Blank, Rose, & Berlin, 1978). Young children must develop a rich and deep vocabulary early in life so that they have the words to communicate with others. But for vocabulary to be useful, the child must understand the *function* of the object the word represents. That is, children must know what an object is before they can label it meaningfully, describe it, or refer to it when communicating. For example, a child must know what a cup is—an object that holds liquid, is picked up, and is used to drink from—before that child can develop a concept about cups or use the word meaningfully in conversation. Teachers and family members can help children expand their abilities in the area of language use and pragmatics by including explanations about the purpose or function of specific objects during the natural course of events across the day. As a child is getting ready to draw a picture, the adult might say, "Let's find the *green* crayon, so you can draw a picture of the grass. Where is the *yellow* crayon so you can draw the sun? What *color* will the flowers be? Find those crayons so you can color the flowers those colors."

As you have learned (and will learn more about in Chapter 5), phonological awareness skills impact later reading ability (Compton, 2002). Skills that are part of phonological awareness include being able to

- detect sound segments,
- match beginning sounds,
- identify sound segments in words and phrases, and
- rhyme.

Children who do not develop these skills appear to be at great risk for reading failure during the elementary years. Fortunately, research findings also show that this situation can be corrected for many individuals (Jenkins & O'Connor, 2002; Lyon et al., 2001). These findings explain why the federal government strongly encourages the early teaching of phonics, sound segmentation, sound–symbol relationships, and the use of books that incorporate rhymes (e.g., *Cat in the Hat* and other Dr. Seuss books). In this regard, SLPs can be most helpful to teachers who may not feel proficient with these complex language models and related remediation strategies.

Teaching Students with Speech or Language Impairments

Look again at Figure 4.6. Notice that at ages 5, 6, and 7—kindergarten, first, and second grade—the students identified as having speech or language impairments far outnumber those identified as having learning disabilities. But as children reach third grade, the picture changes, with dramatic increases in the number of students with learning disabilities. As you have learned, the phenomenon occurs because as the demands of the curriculum increase, being able to read well and independently becomes a necessity. How can more students be helped so that fewer face these difficulties? Let's see if we can figure out some ways.

Access to the General Education Curriculum

The ways to enrich classroom environments and help all students develop better language skills are many. Let's focus on three general methods that benefit all students now, and then we'll turn our attention to methods that are of even greater benefit to those with language impairments. We will first consider

- instructional supports,
- explicit language instruction, and
- language-sensitive environments.

Source: www.CartoonStock.com

One way in which teachers can help students develop language skills is to modify their standard instructional procedures by adding instructional supports that foster a language-rich instructional environment and help more students profit from typical instruction. Here are a few key elements that effective teachers consider when creating such supportive classrooms (Culatta & Wiig, 2006; McCormick, 2003; Wetherby, 2002).

- Match language with the comprehension abilities of the students.
- Be responsive to students' language needs by adjusting, modifying, and supplementing instruction.
- Supply examples relevant to students' experiences and cultures.
- Provide multiple examples to illustrate a point or explain a concept.
- Use specific referents (e.g., instead of "Open your book," say, "Open your geography book to page 105").
- Avoid indirect expressions (e.g., instead of "Do you get it?" say, "Do you understand how to complete your homework assignment?").

A second way to help all students is to give **explicit instruction**—that is, to teach the specific skills desired, whether the instructional targets are oral language or reading. Language development should be part of the curriculum. The benefits of direct language instruction are many for students both with and without disabilities. Just as time is devoted to teaching mathematics, reading, spelling, and social studies, time should be allocated to teaching the language skills that underlie these subjects. During these sessions, students should be encouraged to listen, expand their vocabularies, and extend their communication skills. All students can profit from explicit instruction in particular language areas. For example, using and understanding metaphors and analogies is challenging for most students, even the most able (Pan, 2005). Figures of speech are difficult for many students to comprehend, for they are not literal or direct translations of the words used in such phrases: "That man is a real couch potato." "The eyes are windows to the soul." "He's between a rock and a hard place." "My heart goes out to you." "Time flies." Students whose abstract thinking skills are not well developed, and those who are learning English as a second language, frequently find it difficult to grasp the meaning of common metaphors and analogies used in texts and in oral presentations. Teachers should not assume that children understand nonliteral language and should help their students develop the flexible thinking skills needed to solve the problems that such language use presents. Mere exposure to analogies and metaphors is not enough.

explicit instruction Directly teaching the instructional target

Teachers need to include direct instruction about the use of figurative language; when they do, students' facility with language expands into a new dimension. As with most language skills, instruction about these conceptually difficult aspects of language use should be integrated into content lessons.

Instructional Accommodations

Even slight modifications in teaching style and instructional activities can be most helpful and can have great benefits for all students, particularly those who are struggling with the foundational language skills needed for academic success (McCormick, 2003). Providing opportunities for language use and for expanding comprehension of receptive language, and incorporating these opportunities into standard classroom routines, is just the support that many students with language impairments, as well as linguistically diverse students, urgently need. Making such adjustments or accommodations is not difficult. The first step in making a difference for these students is being aware that they have some special needs (Salend, 2005). The second step is recognizing that many of these students benefit greatly even when some simple methods—creating more opportunities for students to talk about academic content, reviewing difficult vocabulary before and after each day's lesson, restating instructions for class and homework assignments—are implemented. And the final step is creating **language-sensitive environments**, classrooms where language development is fostered and all students' language needs are supported. Some easy and helpful suggestions about how to create classrooms where all students' language development is enriched can be found in Accommodating for Inclusive Environments.

language-sensitive environments Classrooms that encourage, foster, and support language development

Data-Based Practices

As you have learned in this chapter, students with language impairments struggle with many aspects of academic learning, because so much of what occurs in the classroom is language based. Reading class textbooks can be especially daunting for several reasons. First, many students with language impairments have poor reading skills. Second, the writing style in many texts uses a more complex sentence structure, which can be confusing to students. Finally, textbook passages are filled with higher-level vocabulary, and students with language impairments are less able to determine unknown word meaning using other syntactical features of the text (Ratner, 2009). Let's look at the following text passage—about the Trail of Tears and the removal of the Cherokee people from their ancestral lands—to get a better understanding of where problems with comprehension may occur.

> Federal troops and state militias began to move the Cherokees into stockades. In spite of warnings to troops to treat them kindly, the roundup proved harrowing. A missionary described what he found at one of the collection camps in June:
>
> The Cherokees are nearly all prisoners. They have been dragged from their houses, and encamped at the forts and military posts, all over the nation. In Georgia, especially, multitudes were allowed no time to take any thing with them except the clothes they had on. Well-furnished houses were left prey to plunderers, who, like hungry wolves, follow in the trail of the captors. These wretches rifle the houses and strip the helpless, unoffending owners of all they have on earth. (U.S. National Park Service, 2008)

For most people, this passage is relatively straightforward and easy to understand. But, even though the writing style is fairly simple (no long or convoluted sentence structures), a student with a language impairment may have difficulties in several areas. She may have trouble decoding (reading) words like *militia, missionary, multitudes,* and *wretches.* She may not know the meanings of many of the highlighted words in the text. There could also be confusion about the comparison of the plunderers to hungry wolves or the reference to "rifle the houses." Many students with language disorders may incorrectly interpret these phrases to mean

Accommodating for Inclusive Environments
Creating Language-Sensitive Classrooms

For Expressive Language

- Ask for clarification when a student uses nonspecific vocabulary. Explain why the initial verbalization was unclear.
- Create opportunities for students to use new vocabulary and talk about concepts being learned.
- Give students reasons to talk.
- Encourage students to use new vocabulary words learned in class in other situations.
- When a student uses incorrect grammar or vocabulary, model the correct language.
- Provide extended wait time for students who may be experiencing word retrieval difficulties.

For Receptive Language

- Rephrase directions (if student appears unresponsive) and instruction (if student appears confused).
- Repeat instructions, if necessary.
- Start with one-step instructions and gradually build to multistep instructions.
- Provide physical cues when giving instructions (e.g., holding up the book they should be opening, pointing to the line-up area).

- Rather than ask students if they understand something (to which a yes response is usually given), ask them to
  - repeat the instructions back to you,
  - restate content in their own words,
  - show you what they are supposed to be doing, or
  - work one or two problems and then check with you to be sure they are doing them correctly.
- Have students partner to provide support and enhance comprehension during activities
- Teach students to recognize when they do not understand something and how to verbalize that.
- Allow students to ask questions if they are confused.

For Pragmatics

- Teach and practice how to interpret facial expressions and body language.
- Teach scripted responses for certain social conventions.
- Teach the importance of different communication styles expected by different people (peers or siblings vs. adults in authority) and when and how to use them.
- Avoid using sarcasm, which can be interpreted literally.

---

that real wolves followed the captives or that rifles were used to shoot at the houses. They may also not understand that the last paragraph was a quote from a missionary and instead think it was just part of the regular text. When you consider that this is only one small passage of a much larger assignment, it is understandable how students can get overwhelmed when completing activities requiring a lot of independent reading.

Classroom teachers can use Collaborative Strategic Reading (CSR) to improve the reading comprehension skills of their students. Validated by years of research (Bremer et al., 2002; Klingner et al., 1998a, 1998b; Vaughn, Klingner, & Bryant, 2001), CSR uses four very specific comprehension strategies while building upon the advantages of using peers as instructional supports. Furthermore, and in line with the concepts of universal design for learning (UDL), because many students (not just those with disabilities) struggle with textbook passage comprehension, this is a strategy that can be used with *all* students in a class.

A Closer Look at Data-Based Practices provides an overview about how to implement CSR in classroom settings, along with the simple steps to follow. An interactive, online module provided by the IRIS Center, at http://iris.peabody.vanderbilt.edu provides more detailed information.

A Closer Look at Data-Based Practices

Collaborative Strategic Reading (CSR)

Collaborative Strategic Reading (CSR) combines reciprocal teaching and cooperative learning to improve students' vocabulary and reading comprehension skills, particularly for expository text, such as that found in textbooks. CSR incorporates four strategies that students use before, during, and after reading a passage:

- Preview
- Click and clunk
- Get the gist
- Wrap up

Steps to Follow

Before reading a passage

1. *Preview:* Students write down everything they know about the topic and share their responses with a partner or small group. They then skim the text, write down their predictions about what they think they will learn, and share these with their peers.

During the passage reading

2. *Click and clunk:* Students read the text, noting any passages that made sense (clicks) or were difficult to understand (clunks). When a clunk is encountered, students may use several fix-up strategies to determine the meaning.

   - Reread the passage and try to find a synonym for the clunk.
   - Reread the passage using clues from the sentences before and after to make sense of the clunk.
   - Use prefixes or suffixes to help determine the clunk's meaning.
   - Break the clunk into smaller words.

3. *Get the gist:* Identify the main idea of the passage. Students determine whether the passage was about a person, place, or thing, and then specify the person, place, or thing that was discussed. Students then identify what was written about that particular person, place, or thing, and then restate the general idea of the passage (the gist).

After reading the passage

4. *Wrap up:* Students generate a list of questions where correct responses would demonstrate passage comprehension, and then determine the answers to those questions. They summarize what they learned in writing.

Example of a CSR Worksheet

Worksheets such as this can guide students through the four strategies, structure the activity, and provide a concrete record of what they learned.

 Go to the Building Teaching Skills and Dispositions section in Chapter 4 of MyEducationLab, and complete the activities in the IRIS Module, "CSR: A Reading Comprehension Strategy," to gain a more thorough and practical understanding of the strategies you've just learned: In CSR, students work together in small groups to apply comprehension strategies as they read text from a content area, such as social studies or science.

CSR Learning Log

Topic: **Ecosystems**			Date: **03/10/XX**

BEFORE READING — Preview	**1. What I already know about the topic:** *An ecosystem is the environment.* **2. What I think I will learn:** *I will learn something about deserts and rain forests.*		

DURING READING — Clunks and Gists	**First Section**	**Second Section**	**Third Section**
	Clunks: <u>harmony</u> – in peace with each other Gists: *The parts of an ecosystem rely on each other.*	Clunks: <u>interdependence</u> – relying on each other Gists: *An ecosystem can be broken.*	Clunks: Gists:

AFTER READING — Wrap Up	**Questions about the important ideas in the passage:** *What is an ecosystem?* *What happens if a part of an ecosystem is damaged?* **What I learned:** *The ecosystems need to be taken care of.*		

Worksheet courtesy of the IRIS Center for Training Enhancements, http://iris.peabody.vanderbilt.edu

Figure 4.7 • Communication Board A communication board shows pictures of frequently needed or requested items or actions. The user points to pictures to communicate needs or wants. See if you figure out which pictures indicate "I want to listen to music," "I want lunch," "I want a snack," "Please stop," or "I need to use the restroom." Can you figure out what the other pictures represent?

Now let's turn our attention to applications of technology that support individuals with speech or language impairments.

Technology

Applications of medicine and technology can help many individuals with speech or language impairments communicate more effectively so they can participate fully at school and in the community. Some medical breakthroughs can correct speech mechanisms that are faulty or damaged. For example, many children have their cleft palates repaired through surgery by the time they are 18 months old (Bauman-Waengler, 2008). An **obturator** forms a closure between the oral and nasal cavities when the soft palate is missing or has been damaged by a congenital cleft. When vocal folds have become paralyzed or have been removed because of a disease, an artificial larynx can be implanted in cases. Advances in technology have made a tremendous difference in the lives of individuals with speech or language impairments, and no doubt the future holds unimaginable breakthroughs that will change their lives even further.

Other technologically advanced equipment is designed specifically for those with communication challenges. **Augmentative and alternative communication (AAC)** devices provide different means for individuals with speech or language impairments to interact and communicate with others (Kangas & Lloyd, 2006). AAC includes both **low-tech devices** (e.g., **communication boards**; See Figure 4.7) and **high-tech devices** (e.g., **speech synthesizers**; see the photo). You will learn more about AAC devices in Chapter 9 ("Physical or Health Disabilities").

Students with language disorders need extra supports to help them organize, study, and understand information. **Content enhancement strategies** are designed to help them organize their learning and remember complex content presented either in lectures or in textbooks. Content enhancement strategies come in many different forms. They are designed to help students see relationships among

obturator A device that creates a closure between the oral and nasal cavities when the soft palate is missing or damaged; helps compensate for a cleft palate.

alternative and augmentative communication (AAC) Assistive technology that helps individuals communicate, including devices that actually produce speech

low-tech devices Simple assistive technology devices such as communication boards

communication boards Low-tech assistive technology devices that display pictures or words that the individual can point to in order to communicate

Technology, like this simple-to-use speech synthesizer, can allow individuals to communicate their needs and engage in conversations with others.

high-tech devices Complex assistive technology devices that use computers

speech synthesizers Assistive technology devices that create voice

content enhancement strategies Methods to help students organize and remember important concepts

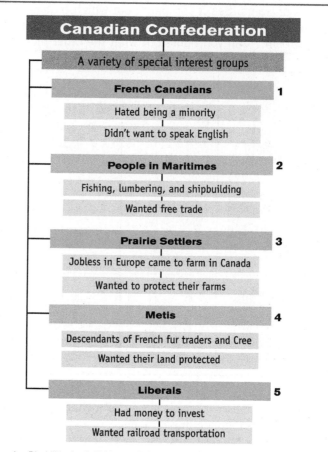

Source: *Journal of Learning Disabilities* by S. V. Horton, T. C. Lovitt, and D. Bergerud. Copyright 1990 by Sage Publication Inc. Journals. Reproduced with permission of Sage Publications Inc. Journals in the formats Textbook and Other book via Copyright Clearance Center.

graphic organizers Visual aids used to assist students organize, understand, and remember academic content

concepts and vocabulary (Rock, 2004; Vaughn, Bos, & Schumm, 2007). One type of these strategies is **graphic organizers**, which help students structure their learning, visualize the way information is presented in lectures and organized in texts, map out stories to improve comprehension, and see the relationships among vocabulary and concepts (Boulineau et al., 2004; Ives & Hoy, 2003). Graphic organizers come in many different forms; see Figure 4.8 for an example.

There is a close relationship between oral language ability, vocabulary skills, and writing (Dockrell et al., 2008). For this reason, writing assignments can be a challenge for students with language disorders. Software like Kidspiration (for young children in kindergarten through fifth grade) and Inspiration (for students in grades 6 through 12), can be helpful to these students. Programs like these can assist students with the creation of graphic organizers, such as attribute webs. The software can also transform the content of the web into an outline to help students study for tests or write reports. In Figure 4.9, Inspiration was used to organize and visualize Shakespeare's play *Macbeth*. Students using programs such as these can better organize their writing assignment, and the end product enhances their ability to remember information. First, the programs provide structure for learning concepts; they impose organization on what might initially appear to the students to be overwhelming and confusing. Second, they give learners a strategy for approaching the writing task and addressing its elements sequentially. Third, students can paraphrase content using simpler vocabulary or make connections with their own experiences. Finally, they allow students to visualize content being learned, which helps many students remember key points and concepts.

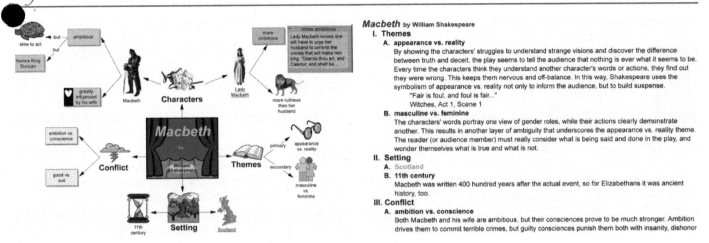

Macbeth by William Shakespeare

I. Themes

  A. appearance vs. reality

  By showing the characters' struggles to understand strange visions and discover the difference between truth and deceit, the play seems to tell the audience that nothing is ever what it seems to be. Every time the characters think they understand another character's words or actions, they find out they were wrong. This keeps them nervous and off-balance. In this way, Shakespeare uses the symbolism of appearance vs. reality not only to inform the audience, but to build suspense.

    "Fair is foul, and foul is fair..."
    Witches, Act 1, Scene 1

  B. masculine vs. feminine

  The characters' words portray one view of gender roles, while their actions clearly demonstrate another. This results in another layer of ambiguity that underscores the appearance vs. reality theme. The reader (or audience member) must really consider what is being said and done in the play, and wonder themselves what is true and what is not.

II. Setting

  A. Scotland

  B. 11th century

  Macbeth was written 400 hundred years after the actual event, so for Elizabethans it was ancient history, too.

III. Conflict

  A. ambition vs. conscience

  Both Macbeth and his wife are ambitious, but their consciences prove to be much stronger. Ambition drives them to commit terrible crimes, but guilty consciences punish them both with insanity, dishonor

Source: © 2005 Inspiration Software®, Inc. Diagram created in Inspiration® by Inspiration Software®, Inc. Used with permission.

Transition

Adults with speech or language impairments comprise several different subgroups. Some have only speech impairments, others have only language impairments, and some have both impairments. Despite having great difficulties as children, the vast majority of these individuals, when adults, experience a lifetime of using normal communication (Owens et al., 2006). Typically, the problems experienced by adults who were not identified as having speech or language disorders when they were children are caused by disease, accidents, or aging. Those who had some kind of speech or language impairment during childhood represent a small percentage of this adult group. Relatively little is known about how these children fare when they are adults.

In one of the few, completed comprehensive follow-up studies of youth with disabilities, students with speech and language impairments appeared to have better outcomes than most other youth with disabilities (Wagner et al., 2005). They are among the most likely to show signs of early independence such as having a driver's license, checking account, or credit card, and they are among the least likely to have experience in the criminal justice system (i.e., being arrested, spending time in jail). After high school, this group is the most likely to be employed *and* attending some sort of postsecondary educational program (community or 4-year college).

Their long-term prospects, however, may not be as good. Only 68% of students with speech or language impairments graduate with a diploma (OSEP, 2008), raising serious concerns about their success as adults. Twenty-three percent drop out of school. Changing this situation will require offering more services while these students are in high school and expanding the roles of SLPs to provide assistance with the development of literacy by linking therapy to the high school curriculum (AHSA, 2002). Also, to remain in academic content courses, these students may require more access to tutoring, more services from guidance counselors, more accommodations and special services, and increased instruction in language skills.

Collaboration

SLPs are an important resource to general and special education teachers. Almost every school in the United States has an SLP working there at least once a week, usually more often. At some schools, an SLP is a permanent faculty member. In most cases, however, SLPs' time is shared across several schools. SLPs are typically itinerant related services providers who travel from one school to another providing services to students and to teachers. Some SLPs conduct therapy outside the general education classroom, and others—like Alaine Ocampo, who is featured in

Spotlighting *Alaine Ocampo:* A Day in the Life

Alaine Ocampo is a speech language pathologist.

The phrase "thinking out of the box" has much more meaning to me these days as a speech-language pathologist working in the public school setting. I think differently now as I continue to enjoy working with students within their general education classrooms. During my early years as a speech-language pathologist, I was quite comfortable with the traditional way of providing services. That is, I would "pull out" the students from their classrooms to provide the speech and language therapy they needed during designated times and days of the week. Although the term *collaboration* seemed to be the buzzword during that time, I didn't have experience with co-teaching lessons and felt intimidated by the concept of having to be in front of another professional.

José, a third-grade student, was instrumental in changing my view about collaboration and helped me think differently about my role as a speech-language pathologist. One afternoon as I walked past the cafeteria line, I was taken aback by José's assertiveness to approach me. In his usual soft-spoken manner, he asked, "Mrs. Ocampo, can you read the story *Big Al* again?" I stopped and immediately replied, "Sure" (thinking that a review of the story grammar lesson would be beneficial). Believing that our interaction was over, I proceeded to say good-bye and con-

tinued walking. José turned and said, "No, not in the speech room . . . in my classroom." With hesitation, I agreed and clarified that I would have to arrange it with his teacher first. I knew this was important for José because he was typically very quiet during the language therapy sessions and would require continuous verbal encouragement and prompting to participate. José's request motivated me to overcome my barrier of initiating a collaborative lesson with a general education teacher. Moreover, his request allowed me to realize that the lessons and interactions that were taking place inside the speech room could be just as motivating in the context of his classroom setting while alongside his peers.

Appearing confident with the familiarity of the story, José practiced his expressive language abilities and began to verbally retell the story in front of his peers. The pride and happiness on his face were contagious as his peers anxiously waited for their turn to retell the story with the same animation and excitement that he demonstrated (eye contact; formulating questions.)

I learned the benefits of being able to facilitate José's language needs in the context of his classroom. Not only was it more meaningful for him to practice in front of his peers, but it also provided me with real-time "moments" of how to collaborate with his teacher to better address his needs in both comprehension and expression.

this chapter's Spotlighting box—provide services in inclusive classes. SLPs are experts in the areas of speech, language, and communication. Whenever teachers have concerns or questions about these abilities in their students, they should seek out the advice of their school's speech/language professional. Remember, "early screening, assessment, and treatment of an impairment—typically considered special education or related services—may actually prevent further disability or handicapping conditions" (ASHA, 2002, pp. III–260). There is so much to be gained! Teachers should not hesitate in seeking help from SLPs when they think that a student has a communication problem.

Collaboration with Support Personnel: SLPs

Most SLPs are members of ASHA, the professional organization representing most professionals working in the areas of speech, language, and hearing (audiologists). This organization helps us understand the many responsibilities assumed and duties performed by SLPs as they work with teachers to serve students (ASHA, 2002). Here are a few examples of the major areas where these professionals apply their knowledge and skills:

- *Prereferral:* assisting teachers with the selection and application of intervention strategies, accommodations, or supports that might address a student's learning needs and eliminate the need for special education services
- *Screening:* using commercially available or informal procedures (e.g., checklists, classroom observations, interviews) to distinguish students with

language differences and delays from those needing formal evaluation for suspected language impairments

- *Referral:* requesting implementation of the full, formal assessment process
- *Identification:* conducting assessments to determine special education eligibility for speech or language impairments
- *IEP Team:* working with other professionals to identify student's abilities and need for special education services and develop the individualized plan (the IFSP or IEP)
- *Therapy:* delivering direct services to treat speech or language impairments
- *Consultation:* providing advice and assistance to teachers to guide classroom-based instruction and follow-through activities.
- *Evaluation:* contributing to judgments about the effectiveness of the interventions and programs implemented

Collaborative Practices: SLP Services in the General Education Setting

SLPs provide direct therapy and instructional services. They do so for students whose speech or language impairments are their primary disabilities, as well as for those students whose primary challenges stem from other disabilities, such as intellectual and developmental disabilities or autism. They also consult and collaborate with teachers and families about many students who have problems with their speech or language development.

Approximately 84% of students with speech or language impairments receive their education almost exclusively in general education classrooms (OSEP, 2008). And for most of these students, the services they receive from SLPs are indirect. In other words, SLPs guide classroom teachers in the selection and application of interventions through a consulting model (Sunderland, 2004). They can help teachers with all language-based academic instruction (e.g., reading, spelling, writing). They perform these duties across age groups—from the preschool years through high school—and use many different methods to determine which students have speech or language impairments.

In addition to collaborating with teachers, SLPs often work in collaboration with families, particularly with families of those with disabilities. We conclude this chapter by examining how families make a difference in the speech and language development of students with disabilities.

SLPs make a real difference because therapy can reduce or correct speech and language impairments.

myeducationlab Go to the Activities and Applications section in Chapter 4 of MyEducationLab, and complete Activity 2. As you watch the video and answer the accompanying questions, notice how the speech language professional works with a young student with speech problems and mild cognitive disabilities.

Partnerships with Families and Communities

The quality of their home's language environment has significant and long-term effects on young children and their future literacy instruction (Melzi & Ely, 2009; Robinson, 2003). However, children (and adults) spend less time at home with family than ever before (12 million children under the age of 6 receive some sort of child care, through babysitters, day care centers, or preschool classrooms; CDF, 2005), so enhancing parent–child linguistic interactions can be challenging. Because the home environment has such an important impact, most preschool programs include a strong family component, where professionals assist parents in implementing language-learning lessons at home and in helping their children transfer (or generalize) their learning from school to home. Those whose home environment is rich in language—where parents talk to their children, where children are given the opportunity to explore the use of language, and where experiences are broad—usually develop fine speech and language skills. When children do not have appropriate language models—when they do not hear language

Audio versions of books can support difficult reading assignments, allowing students to work independently and access the same content as their peers who do not struggle with reading.

used often, when they do not have experiences to share or a reason to talk—it is not uncommon for their language to be delayed or impaired, putting them at a disadvantage in school (Melzi & Eli, 2009; Robinson, 2003).

What kinds of strategies can parents use at home to improve their child's language skills? Specialists suggest that family members specifically label or name objects in the home (Gleason, 2009). They also suggest that simple words be used more often to describe the objects the child is playing with: "This ball is red. It is round. It is soft." They can encourage repetitions of correct productions of sounds and can repeat the child's error to help the child make a comparison. They can play a game of fill-in-the-blank sentences or ask questions that require expanded answers. The family should include the child in activities outside the home, too, such as visits to the zoo, the market, or a shopping center, so that the child has more to talk about. Practicing good language skills can be incorporated into everyday events. Family members should model language and have the child imitate good language models. Parents can encourage children to engage in storytelling. Through these stories, children should describe, explain, and interpret their experiences or the stories they have read. Children need a reason to talk, and the home environment can foster children's oral expression by providing many rich and diverse experiences for children to talk about and good language models for children to imitate.

As children get older, parents and caregivers need to maintain a language-rich home environment. Older students should be encouraged to read, as the exposure to written language and vocabulary remains closely linked to academic success. Struggling readers can be supported in their reading activities in several ways. Adults can continue to read to their children far into the elementary years; children and teenagers can make use of the growing popularity of audiobooks, many of which can be downloaded to an iPod and listened to at leisure. The quality of adolescent literature has never been better, with classic authors like Laura Ingalls Wilder and S. E. Hinton sharing popularity with newer contributors such as Rick Riordan, J. K. Rowling, and Christopher Paolini (see Chapter 14, "Giftedness and Talents," for more on Christopher).

Summary

Communication requires at least two parties and a message. Communication is impaired when either the sender or the receiver of the message cannot use the signs, symbols, or rules of language effectively. Communication occurs only when the receiver understands the message as it was intended by the sender. The sender may have an idea or thought to share with someone else, but the sender's idea needs to be translated from thought into some code that the other person can understand—that is, into some form of language. For most of us, oral language is the primary mode of socializing, learning, and performing on the job. Therefore, communicative competence—what speakers need to know about language to express their thoughts—is the most important goal for students with speech or language impairments. Because oral communication (or sign language for those who are deaf) occurs in a social context, this ability directly affects an individual's social competence as well.

Answering the Chapter Objectives

1. What are speech impairments and language impairments?

- Speech impairments are present when the sender's speech impairs the communication. They include problems with articulation, fluency, and voice (pitch or loudness).
- Language impairments exist when the sender of the message cannot effectively employ the signs, symbols, or rules that govern the form, content, or use (pragmatics) of language.
- The child's age and the stressfulness of the situation must be considered when determining whether a child should be referred to an SLP for assessment.

2. What is the prevalence of speech or language impairments? How is the prevalence of this type of disability related to that of learning disabilities?

- Speech or language impairments category
  - is second largest (when only primary disability is counted);
  - is largest (when both primary and secondary disabilities are counted);
  - includes 19% of all students with disabilities.
- Speech or language impairments
  - can coexist with every disability and
  - coexist with the majority of cases of learning disabilities.
- The prevalence of language impairments is related to age and to increased demands of the curriculum as students get older.
  - More preschoolers are identified as having language impairments.
  - More students above third grade are identified as having learning disabilities.

3. How do language delays, language differences, and language impairments differ?

- In *language delays,* language acquisition follows the normal developmental sequence but proceeds more slowly than in the typical learner; they may be a signal of disabilities.
- In *language differences,* English is being learned as a second language, or a regional dialect is involved.
- In *language impairments,* language is acquired in an abnormal or atypical developmental sequence; this hinders communication and the transfer of knowledge and information.

4. How can teachers enhance language development and help remediate language impairments?

- *Instructional supports:* Match language to students'; adjust, modify, and supplement instruction; relate instruction to students' experiences and culture; use specific (concrete) referents; give multiple examples.
- *Explicit instruction:* Directly teach language skills, and include language development as a curricular target.
  - *Content enhancements:* Graphic organizers, such as attribute webs, visually impose structure on content and assist with learning and remembering.
  - *Specific instructional strategies:* (CSR and others) help students understand the content of class readings.
  - *Language-sensitive classrooms:* Provide opportunities to use language, motivation and reasons to talk, multiple language experiences, support for different levels of language skills; includes evaluation.

5. Who can be consulted as a key resource for students with speech or language impairments?

- Teachers collaborate with SLPs about all students whose language or communication abilities are of concern and provide classroom follow-through on targets mastered in therapy.

myeducationlab) Now go to MyEducationLab at www.myeducationlab.com and take the Self-Assessment to gauge your initial comprehension of chapter content. Once you have taken the Self-Assessment, use your individualized Study Plan for Chapter 4 to enhance your understanding of the concepts discussed in the chapter.

Council for Exceptional Children **ADDRESSING THE PROFESSIONAL STANDARDS**

Council for Exceptional Children (CEC) knowledge standards addressed in this chapter:

CC1K8, CC1K5, CC6K2, CC6K1, CC8K4, CC6K4, CC7S14, CC10S9, CC10K3

Appendix A: CEC Knowledge and Skill Standards Common Core has a full listing of the standards listed here.

Appendix B: CEC Knowledge and Skill Common Core Standards and Associated Subcategories are broken down by chapter.

CHAPTER 5
Learning Disabilities

Chapter Objectives

After studying this chapter, you will be able to

1. List the key features of the IDEA '04 definition of learning disabilities.

2. Discuss the different types of learning disabilities.

3. Explain how an individual's response to intervention (RTI) is assessed.

4. Explain what is meant by the practice of "early intervening," and explain why it holds great promise.

5. Describe two data-based practices that make a difference in the learning outcomes of students with disabilities.

P. Buckley Moss, often referred to as "The People's Artist," is a highly successful contemporary painter who faced a childhood filled with school failure and challenge. As role model to individuals with learning disabilities, she openly tells her story in her autobiography, sharing the challenges of growing up with reading problems. She remembers that she knew that she was not stupid; and when the diagnosis of learning disabilities was made, she felt relief. She continues her work and charitable activities near her home in Waynesboro, Virginia.

learning disability (LD) A disability of unexpected underachievement typically involving reading that is resistant to treatment

PEARSON
myeducationlab After reading this chapter, complete the Self-Assessment for Chapter 5 on MyEducationLab to gauge your initial understanding of chapter content.

A learning disability (LD) is a condition that can cause significant problems both at school and in life. Unfortunately, people often think of learning disabilities as a mild condition and, therefore, assume that these students only need minimal help to overcome the challenges this disability presents. As you will learn, such assumptions are unfounded and can be harmful if they result in withholding or delaying needed assistance. What you will also learn in this chapter is that educators can and do make real differences in the lives of these students and their families.

Since the concept of this disability was formed some 50 years ago, the field of learning disabilities has been the focus of considerable controversy, debate, as well as innovation (Bradley, Danielson, & Hallahan, 2002; Hammill, 1990; Kirk, 1977). Some experts and policymakers have questioned whether learning disabilities is truly a disability, proposing that the condition is merely an extension of low achievement (Bradley et al., 2002; Fletcher et al., 2002). Regardless of these doubts, we believe that the evidence is clear: Learning disabilities can be severe, pervasive, chronic, and life-long, a condition that requires sustained and intensive intervention (Bender, 2008; National Institutes of Health, 2007; Shaw, 2007). Evidence shows that these students learn differently from their classmates without disabilities, other students with disabilities (such as those with intellectual disabilities), and each other, and their reading achievement is unlike that of low achievers (Caffrey & Fuchs, 2007).

Although the concept of learning disabilities began in the United States, it is now recognized worldwide (Sideridis, 2007). The term *learning disabilities* was first coined in the 1960s by Sam Kirk at a meeting in Chicago of an association that is now called Learning Disability Association of America (LDA), an organization of American parents concerned about their children's learning problems. Internationally, it is defined, as it is here in the United States, as a disability that typically affects one's ability to read and write, which contributes to overall school failure as the demands of the curriculum increase across the grades (Lloyd, Keller, & Hung, 2007). Mike Gerber of the University of California at Santa Barbara argues that such widespread attention to learning disabilities reflects the high social and economic costs of underachievement and an understanding that it is almost impossible "to provide universally effective schooling in the face of human differences" (Gerber, 2007, p. 216). Research focusing on these students' challenges has spawned remarkable instructional strategies that inform us about how to improve these students' outcomes and also is influencing the way all struggling learners are instructed.

Where We've Been . . . What's on the Horizon?

Today is a period of transition, a sea change, for the field of learning disabilities and for the individuals and families who confront this disability (Fuchs & Young, 2006). New findings about effective instruction and intervening early hold promise for many students who struggle to learn at the same pace as their classmates without disabilities. In particular for those with learning disabilities, these new and innovative practices halt the negative sequence of language problems during the preschool years, reading problems by third grade, writing problems by middle school, pervasive academic problems as the demands of the curriculum increase through middle school and high school, a high probability of dropping out of school, and not attending or finishing college. If not interrupted during the early school years, this sequence can be irreversible. Throughout this chapter, you will be introduced to these exciting procedures, but first let's learn about how this field developed.

Historical Context

The study of learning disabilities put down roots long before April 6, 1963 when Professor Sam Kirk and others coined the term *learning disabilities* at that landmark meeting of parents and professionals in Chicago (Hammill, 1990; Wiederholt, 1974). During the 1920s and 1930s, Samuel Orton, a specialist in neurology, developed theories and remedial reading techniques for children with severe reading problems, whom he called "dyslexic" and believed to be brain damaged. In the 1930s, Helen Davidson studied letter "reversals"—writing some letters (e.g., *b, d, q,* and *g*) backward—a problem consistently observed in many students with learning disabilities (Davidson, 1934, 1935). In the 1930s and 40s, Sam Kirk, who worked at the Wayne County School (you will learn more about this school in Chapter 6), helped develop a set of word drills and other teaching procedures he referred to throughout his career. In 1961, he and his colleagues published the *Illinois Test of Psycholinguistic Abilities* (ITPA), which sought to identify individuals' strengths, weaknesses, learning styles, and learning preferences (whether they learned better by seeing or by hearing information presented). This test was used for many years to identify students with learning disabilities. Also in the 1960s, Marianne Frostig developed materials designed to improve students' visual perception, which is the ability to understand information that is seen. Her notion was that if visual perceptual skills were enhanced, reading abilities would also show improvement (Frostig, 1978)—a theory that in later years rigorous research could *not* validate.

The 1970s saw the field of learning disabilities embroiled in heated debate, and at the heart of the controversy was what approach for treatment of learning disabilities was most effective. In what was called the **process/product debate,** one group promoted instruction directed at improving students' perceptual abilities to improve their academic performance (e.g., reading). The other group argued that directly teaching academic skills (e.g., explicitly teaching students to read) is the best approach. The dispute was resolved when Don Hammill and Steve Larsen's research analysis showed that perceptual approaches were seldom effective in teaching academic skills but that direct instruction, or explicitly teaching academic skills, makes a difference in learning outcomes (Hammill & Larsen, 1974). Once the debate was put to rest, Tom Lovitt at the University of Washington and Stan Deno at the University of Minnesota conducted research that is the foundation for much of the work done today using explicit instruction to teach academic skills while monitoring the progress of students with learning disabilities through frequent and direct assessments of their academic work (Deno & Mirkin, 1974; Eaton & Lovitt, 1972). These pioneers did so by extending the evaluation methods of applied behavior analysis.

process/product debate The argument about whether perceptual training or direct (explicit) instruction is more effective to teach reading

As with autism spectrum disorders today, fads and invalidated practices were promoted, often through the press, with the promise of "curing" children's learning disability. For example, one fad suggested having students with learning disabilities, regardless of their ages, use crawling exercises to "repattern" or retrain their brains. Others have claimed that special diets or plants on students' desks improve academic and behavioral performances. Still others blamed fluorescent lighting for learning disabilities. Most of these claims were backed up by very little scientific evidence of effectiveness (Keogh, 1974). Such promotion of invalidated practices is one major reason for today's emphasis in both IDEA '04 and NCLB on the use of scientifically validated or evidence-based practices that are thoroughly tested through rigorous research before being used with children at school.

Challenges That Learning Disabilities Present

We have all had the occasional experience: No matter how hard we try, we have trouble understanding the information presented. In school we may sit through lectures and not understand the messages the instructor is trying to deliver. We may not understand the reading material for a particular class. We find it impossible to organize our thoughts to write a coherent essay or report. Sometimes we stumble over words and are unable to convey our thoughts, feelings, or knowledge. And occasionally we are uneasy and uncomfortable with other people. For most of us, these situations are infrequent. For people with learning disabilities, however, one or more of these situations are commonplace.

Achieving reading fluency (being able to read quickly and correctly) and developing reading proficiency (reading efficiently with understanding) are particularly difficult for these individuals (Therrien & Kubina, 2006). Problems learning to read compound as students progress through school and independent reading becomes not just an academic goal but also an expectation of the curriculum. As we have said, once this cycle is established, all aspects of academic performance are affected, and then school failure contributes to feelings of inadequacy and lack of self-confidence. All of this underscores the importance of intervening early by implementing new ways to identify and bring services to those individuals in need as quickly as possible.

Making a Difference

Charles Schwab

Most highly successful businessmen don't reveal what might be construed as vulnerability. Clearly, it just isn't considered good business sense. In highly competitive marketplaces, any sign of weakness could be a signal for a takeover or a "hostile action." At the same time, most Americans are not comfortable openly talking about disabilities, particularly their own. Learning disabilities are not readily "visible"—not immediately signaled by a cane, wheelchair, glasses, or hearing aid. Such disabilities are not even understood by many of the individuals affected or by their families. The result is that too often, individuals with learning disabilities have to struggle on their own and figure it out by themselves, with little opportunity to profit from the guidance of people who have successfully compensated for or overcome the effects of their learning disabilities.

Charles Schwab, the highly successful businessman and founder of the discount stock brokerage house, decided to break with tradition and speak out about the challenges he faced in school (Greatschools.org, 2008). He not only serves as a role model for individuals with learning disabilities but also has provided considerable assistance to parents, teachers, and children with learning disabilities through his personal efforts and the work of his charitable foundations. His academic strengths were math and science, but he struggled with reading and all of its related subjects. Schwab demonstrated his resilience and innovative thinking from a young age when he discovered that classic comic books, such as *Moby Dick,* provided an easier way to read "novels" assigned in English classes. Despite his reading problems, Schwab persevered through college and graduate school, earning a BS and an MBA from Stanford University by focusing on his strengths—subjects related to numbers, such as economics. Two years after graduating from Stanford, he started an investment advisory newsletter, and a few years later, he founded his own brokerage house in San Francisco. Because he thought that the stock market should be accessible to everyone, he initiated the concept of the discount brokerage firm (Jones, 2003).

After discovering that his son had a learning disability, Schwab and his wife, Helen, decided to help other families who struggled with this invisible disability.

They started Schwab Learning, which operated two Web sites—one for parents (www.SchwabLearning.org) and one for kids (www.SparkTop.org). In 2007, the Schwabs decided that their foundation should focus on charitable activities and awarding grants to community service agencies. They felt that it was time for their information Web sites to be passed on to groups that could continue and expand the important work they had established. SchwabLearning.org, under the leadership of Great Schools, gives parents the answers to the million and one questions they have when their child has learning disabilities. The site addresses a parent's practical needs with information about IEPs, behavior issues, and the like; it also provides emotional support so parents know they are not alone in this journey. SparkTop.org was transferred to the Professor Garfield Foundation, a nonprofit organization founded by Jim Davis who is the creator of the cartoon character, Garfield. SparkTop.org is an engaging Web site where kids with learning disabilities can learn about how their brains work, feel good about themselves, get answers to their questions, play wonderful learning games, and connect with other kids just like them. The site reassures kids with learning disabilities that they're just as smart as other kids. They may struggle with reading or writing or math, but there are lots of things they're good at.

Charles Schwab took an invisible disability and made it OK to be visible. To see how these two Web sites make a difference in the lives of teenagers with learning disabilities and parents of children with learning disabilities of all ages, check out **www.schwablearning.org** and **www.sparktop.org**.

Learning Disabilities Defined

Professionals and parents use the term *learning disabilities* to describe a condition of **unexpected underachievement**—academic performance significantly below what would be predicted from the individual's talents and potential shown in other areas. In the 2006 school year, this category included some 4% to 5% of all students and comprises the largest group of students with disabilities served through special education (Office of Special Education Programs [OSEP], 2008). Although in this text we use the term *learning disabilities,* as do most parents, the official name of this special education category, the one used by the federal government and almost every state, is *specific learning disabilities*. The definitions used across the nation are very similar to the ones found in Table 5.1 (Müller & Markowitz, 2004).

Regardless of the definition used, there always seems to be dissatisfaction (Elksnin et al., 2001; Kirk, 1977). Although some of the disagreement is due to

unexpected underachievement A defining characteristic of learning disabilities; when poor school performance cannot be explained by other abilities or potential

myeducationlab Go to the Activities and Application section in Chapter 5 of MyEducationLab, and complete Activity 1. As you watch the video and answer the accompanying questions, think about how Bridget, a student diagnosed with dyslexia, deals with others' perceptions of her and shares her concerns about her future in higher education and employment.

Table 5.1 • Definitions of Learning Disabilities

Source	Definition
Federal government	Specific learning disability means a disorder in one or more of the basic psychological processes involved in understanding or in using language, spoken or written, that may manifest itself in an imperfect ability to listen, think, speak, read, write, spell, or to do mathematical calculations, including such conditions as perceptual disabilities, brain injury, minimal brain dysfunction, dyslexia, and developmental aphasia. The term does not include learning problems that are primarily the result of visual, hearing, or motor disabilities, mental retardation, emotional disturbance, or environmental, cultural, or economic disadvantages. **U.S. Department of Education (2006, p. 1264)**
National Institutes of Health (NIH), National Institute of Neurological Disorders and Stroke (NINDS)	Learning disabilities are disorders that affect the ability to understand or use spoken or written language, do mathematical calculations, coordinate movements, or direct attention. Although learning disabilities occur in very young children, the disorders are usually not recognized until the child reaches school age. **National Institutes of Health, National Institute of Neurological Disorders and Stroke (2007)**

Sources: From 34 *CFR* Parts 300 and 303, Assistance to States for the Education of Children with Disabilities and the Early Intervention Program for Infants and Toddlers with Disabilities; Final Regulations (p. 1264), U.S. Department of Education, 2006, *Federal Register,* Washington, DC, and *"What Are Learning Disabilities?"* NINDS Learning Disabilities Information Page by National Institutes of Health, National Institute of Neurological Disorders and Stroke, 2007, retrieved from www.ninds.nih.gov

differing philosophies and theories about the nature of the condition, most concerns stem from more practical problems:

- Delay in delivering needed services to students
- Overreliance on the use of tests of intelligence (IQ)
- Overwhelming number of students identified with learning disabilities
- Inconsistency of characteristics observed in those identified

Before turning our attention to types of learning disabilities, let's briefly consider these concerns. First, before the passage of IDEA '04, nearly all states insisted that students identified as having learning disabilities demonstrate an **IQ/achievement discrepancy**. This means they show a difference between their potential (score on an intelligence test) and their performance (academic achievement) and that this discrepancy is significant (at least 2 years behind their expected grade level).

Parents and educators have concerns about the IQ/achievement discrepancy criterion used for the diagnosis of learning disabilities. First, students have to wait—sometimes for years—to get help, even though their teachers know they have a problem and that problem will only compound and create more challenges as time goes on. The IQ/achievement discrepancy requirement is a main reason why so many students are identified in third grade: By then scores on achievement tests indicating first-grade performance demonstrate their struggles with schoolwork. A second concern is the reliance on the use of tests of intelligence (IQ). Over the years, growing consensus among practitioners and a more developed knowledge base have caused dissatisfaction about the use of IQ scores to predict poor readers (Fuchs & Young, 2006). A third concern stems from the size of this special education category. While the learning disabilities category recently has seen a reduction in its size, it is still the largest. Consistently, for more than a decade (between 1995 and 2005), almost half of all students receiving special education services, some 6% of the overall school population, were identified as having learning disabilities (OSEP, 2005; U.S. Department of Education, 1995).

The fourth concern comes from these students' unique, individual learning patterns. In other words, this disability does not have the same or consistent outcomes for the individuals who have it. Some have problems in every academic area, some have problems only in reading or in math, and some have additional problems with social skills. In other words, this disability represents a **heterogeneous** group of learners who exhibit a wide range of strengths and abilities, approach learning in a variety of ways, and respond to interventions inconsistently. Their heterogeneity presents challenges to professionals because no single treatment, explanation, or accommodation is uniformly effective.

Although as a group students with learning disabilities present considerable diversity or heterogeneity, some common characteristics can be described. To better understand the condition, let's examine some common profiles of learning disabilities:

- Unexpected underachievement
- Reading disabilities
- Mathematics disabilities
- Resistance to treatment

Unexpected Underachievement

Unlike other groups of students with disabilities, the low academic performance of students with learning disabilities is not expected or predicted from their innate abilities or intelligence. In other words, despite having normal intelligence, students with learning disabilities do not achieve academically like their classmates without disabilities. Some of these students face challenges in almost every academic area. Most experts are certain that cognitive problems, poor motivation, along with an insufficient instructional response to instruction, are key features

IQ/achievement discrepancy The old criterion required for learning disabilities identification; 2-year difference between potential or expected performance (based on a score on a test of intelligence [IQ]) and a score from an achievement test

heterogeneity Variation among members in a group

"May I be excused? The pressure is getting to me."

Source: www.CartoonStock.com

of learning disabilities (Bender, 2008; Hallahan et al., 2005; McNamara, 2007). Experts think that learning disabilities reflect deficits in the ability to process information or remember it (Torgensen, 2002).

Reading/Learning Disabilities

Reading difficulty is the most common reason for these students' referrals to special education. Their reading abilities are much lower than all other students (Fuchs et al., 2002). The term **reading/learning disabilities** is used when the student's reading abilities are significantly below those of classmates without disabilities and significantly below what is expected on the basis of the student's other abilities. Because reading and writing are intimately related, most of these students also have problems with written communication (Graham & Olinghouse, 2008; Harris et al., 2008). Obviously, reading and writing are important skills; in school, students must be able to read information from a variety of texts and write using varying formats. As the complexity of academic tasks increases, students who are not proficient in reading and writing cannot keep pace with the increasing academic expectations of school settings.

So, reading/learning disabilities (sometimes called dyslexia) often begin with problems comprehending language and accessing background language (Jenkins & O'Connor, 2002). Even in the very early years, these students are unable to decode words and gain information from the printed page (Welsch, 2007). Their rates of reading fluency are far from those of their classmates. As these students progress through school, their reading problems compound, making it almost impossible to perform well on other academic tasks. The result is overall underachievement. And, as you can learn from the movie featured in this chapter's On the Screen, reading/

reading/learning disabilities
A condition where a student's learning disability is most significant in reading

On the Screen: *If the Shoe Fits*

Cameron Diaz, nominated for a Golden Globe award in 2005, brings to life the challenges and frustrations faced by many individuals who have reading/learning disabilities. In the charming film *In Her Shoes,* we experience complex family relationships, the stigma of disabilities, sibling rivalry and jealousy, and feelings of triumph when challenges presented by reading problems are overcome. Maggie, through manipulation and deceit, has hidden the fact that she cannot read from almost everyone she meets. She uses her beauty and wit to get whatever she wants—that is, until she gets tripped up by a patient at the hospital where she works. The patient is a blind man who wants Maggie to read to him every day, a task she cannot do. When he realizes she has learning disabilities, he confronts her, forces her to face her challenges, and during months of painstaking efforts teaches her to read. From that point on, we watch Maggie develop feelings of self-reliance and self-worth, and we come to understand how family relationships change and grow when challenges presented by disabilities are not kept as secrets, but rather shared and met by all.

—By Steven Smith

learning disabilities can affect not only individuals on through their adulthood but also their family members and friends. For those of you who want more information about effective interventions for reading and mathematics for struggling learners, and how to evaluate those methods with individual students, go to the Progress Monitoring Center's Web site: www.theprogressmonitoringcenter.org.

Mathematics/Learning Disabilities

mathematics/learning disabilities A condition where a student's learning disability is most significant in areas of mathematics

Some experts estimate that some 5% to 8% of all students have **mathematics/learning disabilities** (Kunsch, Jitendra, & Sood, 2003). These students' performance in mathematics is substantially below what is expected on the basis of the students' other abilities. Relatively few students identified as having learning disabilities have only mathematics disabilities, but many students who have reading disabilities also struggle with mathematics. Today, we are learning that mathematics disabilities have similarities to reading disabilities: Both have their roots in an inability to master core, foundation skills during the preschool years (Chard et al., 2008; Mazzocco & Thompson, 2008). During the school years, these students struggle learning how to correctly solve multistep problems, such as borrowing in subtraction, computing long division, and solving word problems (Bryant & Bryant, 2008). We are also learning that, as with reading, many students who struggle in first, second, and third grade profit greatly from early intervention through a multitiered process of providing high-quality instruction in basic arithmetic skills (Fuchs, Fuchs, & Hollenbeck, 2007). Because math problem solving places demands on both reading and information-processing skills, this area of the mathematics curriculum can be challenging for both teachers and students.

myeducationlab Go to the Activities and Applications section in Chapter 5 of MyEducationLab, and complete Activity 2. As you watch the video and answer the accompanying questions, think about ways in which fluency problems could affect mathematics learning.

Resistant to Treatment

resistant to treatment A defining characteristic of learning disabilities; when validated methods typically applied in general education settings are not effective to cause sufficient learning

dual discrepancy A condition where both rate of learning and performance are below that of classmates

Consensus is growing about some important differences among individuals with and without learning disabilities: Those with learning disabilities are **resistant to treatment**, referred to by some as "nonresponders" (Fuchs & Deshler, 2007). This group does not profit from the instruction typically used in general education classes. It is estimated that no matter what prevention procedures are in place, students with learning disabilities will always comprise some 2% to 6% of the school population. Evidence is mounting that students with learning disabilities, unlike their general education classmates, present a **dual discrepancy** in their learning patterns: Their academic performance is lower than their classmates and their rate of learning is also slower (Fuchs, Fuchs, & Vaughn, 2008; Kovaleski & Prasse, 2008). Clearly, they require intensive, individualized instruction. You will learn in the Assessment section of this chapter that the concept of "resistance to treatment" is incorporated into the identification procedures for learning disabilities outlined by IDEA '04.

Characteristics

Unexpected underachievement and being resistant to treatment are now thought to be defining characteristics of learning disabilities (Kavale & Forness, 1996; Vaughn & Fuchs, 2003). Despite their remarkable individuality or heterogeneity, many specific characteristics are commonly seen with learning disabilities; these are listed in Table 5.2. Some general characteristics seem to be at the root of the problems these individuals face. Understanding these general problem areas can help improve these students' results. So, let's explore each of these commonly observed characteristics:

- Holding negative attributions
- Being nonstrategic
- Being unable to generalize or transfer learning
- Processing information inefficiently or incorrectly
- Possessing poor social skills

Table 5.2 • Characteristics of Learning Disabilities

Academic	Social	Behavioral Style
Unexpected underachievement	Immature	Inattentive
Resistant to treatment	Socially unacceptable	Distractible
Difficult to teach	Misinterprets social and nonverbal cues	Hyperactive
Inability to solve problems	Makes poor decisions	Impulsive
Uneven academic abilities	Victimized	Poorly coordinated
Inactive learning style	Unable to predict social consequences	Disorganized
Poor basic language skills	Unable to follow social conventions (manners)	Unmotivated
Poor basic reading and decoding skills	Rejected	Dependent
Inefficient information processing abilities	Naïve	
Inability to generalize	Shy, withdrawn, insecure	
	Dependent	

Negative Attributions

Motivation and attribution are related. Motivation is the inner drive that causes individuals to be energized and directed in their behavior. **Motivation** can be explained as a trait (a need to succeed, a need not to fail, a sustained interest in a topic) or as a temporary state of mind (preoccupation with a test or class presentation tomorrow, a passing interest in a topic). **Attributions** are self-explanations about the reasons for one's success or failure. Differences in motivation and attributions may account for differences in the way people understand the relationship between effort and accomplishment (Reid & Lienemann, 2006).

By contrast, year after year of frustration and failure at school can negatively affect students' motivation and convince them that there is nothing they can do to be successful. Students can develop a negative attitude and come to believe that their failure is a result of lack of ability, rather than a signal to work harder or ask for help. This cycle can even lead students to believe that external factors—luck, extra help, the teacher giving them a break, or a classmate doing them a favor—are the reasons for whatever successes they do have (Carlson et al., 2002). It was proven long ago that when people expect to fail, they become too dependent on others and give up too easily (Pearl, 1982; Switzky & Schultz, 1988). This situation is called **learned helplessness** and gives the appearance of being passive and not involved in learning. Students with learned helplessness do not ask questions, seek help, or read related material to learn more. They seem to be overwhelmed and complain that school work is too difficult. They come to believe that it is useless to ask for assistance, spend time in the library, read extra materials, or proofread their work. Teachers can help students overcome these problems by involving them in the learning process, using explicit instruction, responding positively, praising them, promoting mastery, and creating a challenging and stimulating instructional environment (Harris et al., 2008; Lienemann et al., 2006). It is important for them to point out the relationship between effort and accomplishment and thereby change students' negative attributions into positive ones that lead to success.

motivation Need to succeed, drive not to fail

attributions Explanations individuals give themselves for their successes or failures

learned helplessness Usually a result of repeated failure or excessive control by others; individuals become less willing to attempt tasks or understand their actions result in success

Nonstrategic Approaches to Learning

Being organized leads to efficient and effective learning. Not paying attention to important features of a learning task or not structuring one's learning is a problem observed among many students with learning disabilities (Deshler, 2005). Applying strategies for organizing information like graphic organizers and content enhancements, described in A Closer Look at Data-Based Practices found in Chapters 4 and 6, can help them remember content and study more efficiently (Ives, 2007). Another way that most of us remember things better is by organizing our thinking. Being proficient in the use of thinking skills—classifying, associating, and sequencing—also helps students become more strategic

Books can play an important role in helping young girls see how they are not so different from everyone. The innovative book series Beacon Street Girls, published by B*tween Productions, targets girls between the ages of 9 and 13 and focuses on the adventures of five teenage girls. Maeve, a main character, has reading/learning disabilities. She and her friends provide great role models to their readers with and without disabilities.

classifying A thinking skill; the ability to categorize items or grouping concepts by their common characteristics

learners. Table 5.3 provides some examples of how **classifying** items enables the learner to categorize and group items together in terms of the characteristics they have in common. With instruction and practice, these thinking skills can be learned and developed into useful tools for learning that help students approach learning tasks more purposefully.

Inability to Generalize

generalize To transfer learning from particular instances to other environments, people, times, or events

Most students with learning disabilities are unable to **generalize**—that is, to transfer their learning to novel situations or extend their learning of one skill to similar skills (D. Byrant, Smith, & Bryant, 2008). For example, they might apply a newly learned study skill in history class but not in English class. Or a child

Table 5.3 • Thinking Skills: Classifying, Categorizing, and Grouping Items

Type of Thinking Skill	Action	Examples
Chunking	Organizing information by groups	If you forget your grocery list and are already at the store, remember items by groups: • Vegetables—potatoes and corn • Frozen foods—ice cream, pizza, and TV dinners
Associating	Connecting items by using relationships among and between facts, ideas, or different knowledge bases	If you need to remember lists of items, sort them by their "common denominators": • Firmness—soft or hard • Style of painting—modern, Renaissance, Impressionism
Sequencing	Sorting or sequencing units of information along a dimension	When you need to remember facts, events, or ideas for social studies or science, have them organize information by their features or by time: • Physical characteristics: size, weight, or volume. • Facts, events, and ideas: time, importance, or complexity

might master borrowing in subtraction but not apply that rule when there is a zero in the tens column. One way to encourage generalization is explicitly to make connections between familiar problems and those that are new or novel (Fuchs et al., 2002). And when teachers carefully broaden the categories—either the skill or the situation—and point out similar features, students extend their learning more readily. Thus, if a student knows how to solve subtraction problems that require borrowing without zeros in the numerator, teachers should carefully point out the similarities between problems that include zeros (500−354 = ?) and those that do not (467−189 = ?).

Faulty Information Processing

Many people with learning disabilities have difficulty learning to read and write, understanding things they are told, and even expressing themselves through oral communication. Many years ago, Janet Lerner helped us think about information processing by comparing the human brain to a computer (Lerner, 1993). Think about the flow of information as input when it is entered into a computer, processing as the human brain acts on that information (makes associations, stores information, calls it up, acts on it), as the computer's hardware and software do, and output as the computer or person generates responses from the stored or received information. Some individuals with learning disabilities either have difficulty with the input, processing, and output cycle or just do it differently than typical learners. Teachers can take some simple actions that make a difference in how well students understand the task and can thereby improve their academic performance. Tips for Effective Instruction provides some examples of how teachers can adjust their instructions and activities to help students with LD focus and process information better.

Poor Social Skills

Over 30 years ago, Tanis Bryan brought to the nation's attention the challenges that many students with learning disabilities face with social skills and expanded our understanding of this disability beyond its effects on academic skills (Bryan, 1974). Deficits in social skills are now considered a common and defining characteristic of learning disabilities (Kavale & Mostert, 2004). Though not all individuals with learning disabilities have problems with social skills, the great majority do (Gresham, Sugai, & Horner, 2001; Vaughn, Elbaum, & Boardman, 2001). Specifically, about a quarter of them are average or above average in social skills and social competence. For the other 75% of these individuals, problems with social skills negatively influence their self-concept, their ability to make friends, their interactions with others, and even the way they approach schoolwork

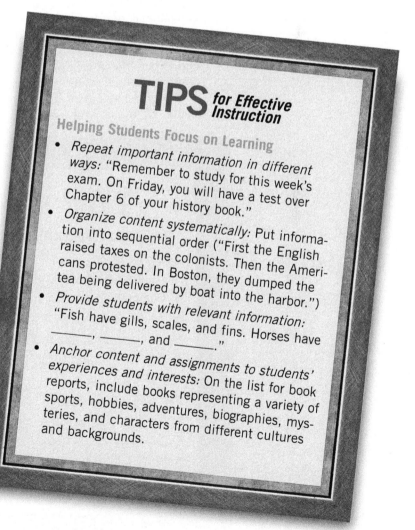

TIPS for Effective Instruction

Helping Students Focus on Learning

- *Repeat important information in different ways:* "Remember to study for this week's exam. On Friday, you will have a test over Chapter 6 of your history book."
- *Organize content systematically:* Put information into sequential order ("First the English raised taxes on the colonists. Then the Americans protested. In Boston, they dumped the tea being delivered by boat into the harbor.")
- *Provide students with relevant information:* "Fish have gills, scales, and fins. Horses have ____, ____, and ____."
- *Anchor content and assignments to students' experiences and interests:* On the list for book reports, include books representing a variety of sports, hobbies, adventures, biographies, mysteries, and characters from different cultures and backgrounds.

(Bryan, Burstein, & Ergul, 2004). Two general reasons account for these students' difficulties developing social competence:

- Relationships among learning disabilities, language impairments, pragmatics, and social competence
- The downward spiral of academic failure to positive peer relationships

For some students, impairment in social skills is part of their learning disability (Wiener, 2004). Those students whose language impairment during the preschool years hindered their developing pragmatics (for a review, see Chapter 4) often have difficulty understanding others' nonverbal behavior and using language effectively in social situations (Olswang, Coggins, & Timler, 2001). These students cannot understand nonverbal behaviors, such as facial expressions, and therefore do not comprehend other people's emotional messages (Teglasi, Cohn, & Meshbesher, 2004). Remember, the relationship between social competence and language impairments is clear. Poor language skills impair the ability to communicate, and communicative competence is necessary for social interaction (Elksnin & Elksnin, 2004). **Social competence** is the ability to perceive and interpret social situations, generate appropriate social responses, and interact with others. Social competence is related, in one way or another, to almost every action and skill that people perform. Thus, the very nature of learning disabilities explains, in part, why many students with learning disabilities have problems developing satisfactory social skills.

The second reason is directly related to these students' academic failure. Poor educational performance lowers self-esteem and self-confidence, which in turn undermines the ability to make friends with classmates who are high achievers. And so it continues: Poor social skills contribute to poor academic performance, and experiencing school failure compounds the social issues the individual must confront (Elliott, Malecki, & Demaray, 2001). Difficulty with social skills, coupled with low achievement and distracting classroom behavior, influences the social status of those with learning disabilities. Their peers see them as overly

social competence Being able to understand and respond appropriately in social situations

TIPS for Classroom Management

TEACHERS HELPING STUDENTS WITH LEARNING DISABILITIES MAKE FRIENDS

Explicitly Teach

- Rules of playground games
- Comprehension of nonverbal expressions
- Social conventions
- When to terminate a conversation
- How to ask permission to join an ongoing game
- Sharing skills

Pair with a Class-Buddy

- Match students with similar interests.
- Create opportunities.
- Reward both members of the pair for working and playing together.
- Change pairs once a month.

dependent, less cooperative, and less socially adept (Kuhne & Wiener, 2000). They are rejected by fellow students and are not included in games on the playground or in groups in the classroom (Le Mare & de la Ronde, 2000; Norwicki, 2003). During adolescence, these students do not seek the support of peers or friends as do their classmates without disabilities, so feelings of loneliness, rejection, and isolation persist (Bryan et al., 2004; Le Mare & de La Ronde, 2000). Of even more concern is their tendency to be victimized—threatened, physically assaulted, or subjected to theft of their belongings—more than their peers. It is not surprising that some students with learning disabilities prefer pull-out programs and do not like inclusive classroom situations (Vaughn et al., 2001). Teachers can make a real difference and help students with learning disabilities who also experience social problems. Some ideas about how to take direct action are listed in Tips for Classroom Management.

Teachers can and do make a difference by teaching these students the importance of self-control and meeting classroom expectations (Lane, Wehby, & Cooley, 2006). Teachers can model, coach, provide specific feedback, and have the student practice a missing social skill. Peer tutoring, reinforcement, and contingencies that reward the entire class (those with and those without disabilities) can help extend or generalize initial learning of important social skills. Teachers can play an instrumental role in reducing peer rejection by pairing classmates in areas of mutual interest. For example, teachers might plan activities so that students with and without learning disabilities who share common interests (sports, music, hobbies) are assigned to work together on an academic task such as a social studies report.

Prevalence

Across the nation, policymakers and parents express great concern about the number of children identified by school personnel as having a learning disability (Finn, Rotherham, & Hokanson, 2001; Vaughn & Fuchs, 2003). Three major issues are the basis for concerns about the prevalence of learning disabilities.

- *Size:* Learning disabilities remains the largest special education category.
- *Cost:* Special education costs almost twice as much as general education.
- *Misidentification:* Diverse learners are disproportionately represented in special education.

Although beginning to reduce in size, this special education category remains the largest, including some 5% of all students and more than double the size of the next-largest group, those with speech or language impairments (OSEP, 2008). When IDEA was first passed and was being implemented in 1976–1977, only about one-quarter of all students with disabilities were served through the learning disabilities category. In the 10-year period from the 1990–1991 to the 1999–2000 school year, the learning disabilities category grew by 34% (U.S. Department of Education, 2002). Because so many individuals are involved, states and the federal government monitor the size of this special education category very closely. To monitor changes in these data yourself, go to www.ideadata.org.

Related to the size of the learning disabilities category is cost: The more students receiving services, the higher the overall costs. Although variation exists across the nation and even district by district, every student with a disability costs more to educate than their classmates without disabilities (Chambers, Shkolknik, & Pérez, 2003). On average, school districts spend 1.6 times more to educate a student with learning disabilities than they spend on the education of a general education student. Because the federal government does not fully cover these costs, the public and the media make the case that students with disabilities are being educated at the expense of their classmates without disabilities. This situation has caused many to believe that the special education rolls should be reduced, and partly because of its size, the learning disabilities category is the one they target (Finn et al., 2001; Lyon et al., 2001). For information about special education costs and financing, go to http://csef.air.org.

The third concern is whether students are being correctly identified. Some experts have called the category of learning disabilities a "dumping ground" where any student unsuccessful in the general education curriculum can be placed easily (Reschly, 2002). Thus, it is possible that some of these students do not have a disability but simply are failing in the general education curriculum and were given the label so they could get extra attention and special assistance. As you will learn, educators and researchers believe that new services that focus on intervening early to prevent academic difficulties will change the path of many students that are certainly heading toward school failure (Fuchs et al., 2008; U.S. Department of Education, 2006). The expectation, and hope, is that the number of students requiring special education services for learning disabilities will decline.

Causes and Prevention

As we have said, many experts are convinced that academic failure and the resulting need for special education services can be prevented for many individuals. However, it is important to remember that learning disabilities can result in significant and life-long challenges.

Causes

In the past, and still somewhat today, students who do not learn core academic skills for reading and mathematics or who struggle learning to read in the early grades are prime candidates for the eventual identification of having learning disabilities. Without intervention, students wait for years before they can receive intensive services, and by then many are doomed to face overwhelming challenges throughout their school careers (Fuchs & Fuchs, 2005). In other words, these students' learning disabilities identification could have been prevented.

Many disabilities carry a stigma, and educators are reluctant to connect the individual with that label. Learning disabilities tends not to stigmatize individuals. For example, many school psychologists prefer to make a student eligible for special education through the learning disabilities category than through, let's say, the IDEA '04 emotional disturbance category. Also, because of concerns about the overrepresentation of diverse students in some disability programs, such as intellectual disabilities, the learning disability label is used to bring services to students in need.

For those who actually have a learning disability, the cause is most often unknown (Bender, 2008). One assumption embedded in definitions of learning disabilities is that the origin of many of these individuals' problems is neurological—that there may be brain damage. For the vast majority of students with disabilities, there is no documentation of neurological impairment, but for those who do have brain damage, many specific causes are possible. For example, lack of oxygen before, during, or after birth can result in neurological difficulties that affect the individual's ability to learn.

As with other disabilities, a genetic link for some cases of learning disabilities is becoming better understood (Hallahan et al., 2005). Many individuals with learning disabilities report they have relatives who have similar problems, but a genetic link to learning disabilities can be difficult to document. However, modern scientific techniques help researchers pinpoint specific genetic causes such as Turner syndrome, which has a definite link to mathematics disabilities in girls (Rovet, 2004).

Prevention

Without knowing specific causes of learning disabilities, it is impossible to develop a set of preventive procedures or strategies. But, when we do know a cause of a disability, we should take action. For example, environmental toxins can cause neurological damage, which in turn can result in a learning disability. Clearly, society

Many students with learning disabilities experience considerable challenges keeping up with their classmates. With explicit and sustained intervention, the results for these students can be outstanding.

at large and local communities should do everything they can to eliminate toxins from children's lives (Children's Defense Fund, 2007). We can all make a difference in the lives of all children by not tolerating situations that place America's children at risk for such harm.

Overcoming Challenges

One theme of this text is that education makes a difference. If poor teaching can cause school failure, then effective instruction can prevent school failure and can also help students compensate for their learning challenges (Menzies, Mahdavi, & Lewis, 2005; Santangelo, Harris, & Graham, 2008). Obviously, poor teaching should be eliminated as a reason for school failure! When educators target the right skills, set goals and expectations high, use validated instructional procedures, and support students as they stretch to meet their goals, reading and related academic challenges can be avoided (Compton, 2002). This knowledge has caused educators to modify the ways in which students with learning disabilities are identified, by merging assessment with instruction. Let's now turn our attention to these new systems.

Assessment

Each Assessment section of this text highlights different features of the evaluation process. Each begins by discussing identification during the preschool years, continues through the prereferral and identification stages, and concludes with at least one aspect of evaluating students' progress. Although IDEA '04 does not require states to change the way they identify students with learning disabilities, it does allow them to adopt a new method (see What IDEA '04 Says About Eligibility for Learning Disabilities). This new approach, now called response to intervention, gives general education teachers more responsibility and also sets the stage for drastic changes in the identification process for students with learning disabilities. Next, we talk about the preschool years, then focus on features of a way to provide all struggling learners the help they need, and finally how students with learning disabilities can receive intensive services in a timely fashion so they do not have to "wait to fail" (IRIS Center, 2008c).

Early Identification

Preschoolers typically are not identified as having learning disabilities. Look again at Figure 4.6 in the previous chapter. During the preschool years, more youngsters are identified with language impairments, but then, in third grade, learning disabilities becomes the prevailing label.

With the importance of early intervention so well understood, why have individuals with learning disabilities not been identified earlier? One reason rests with the IQ/achievement discrepancy criterion we discussed earlier, which has been used since the field's inception in 1977 (Hollenbeck, 2007). Remember, it requires a discrepancy of at least 2 years between ability and academic performance. When children are very young, such discrepancies are impossible to detect. Another reason is that professionals have been reluctant to identify or label children as having a learning or reading disability in the preschool years, or even by first grade, for fear of making a diagnostic mistake. Young children do not develop at exactly the same rate. Some children who do not develop as quickly as their peers do not have a disability; they will catch up. Still others are the youngest in their class and are thus not, and should not be, developmentally equal to their classmates.

Because of the importance of intervening early, when children show signs or indicators of possibly developing future problems, educators are finding ways to provide help to students in need, whether they actually are identified as having a disability or not. Preschoolers who display early warning signs are those who are not developing the precursors to reading, such as phonemic awareness (sound–symbol relationships) and knowing the letters and sounds of the alphabet (Bursuck et al., 2004). Researchers are now confident that these precursors are reliable predictors of reading success; that is, those preschoolers who possess these skills become good readers (Bishop, 2003; Speece et al., 2003; Torgesen & Wagner, 1998). In the Early Intervention section later in this chapter, you will learn more about delivery of services to preschoolers who might be at risk for later learning disabilities. But now let's turn our attention to the new prereferral and identification process being implemented in schools across the country.

Prereferral: Response to Intervention (RTI)

Prereferral is typically one step in the process of identifying and qualifying any student during the school years for special education services. However, for students with learning disabilities, the entire process is experiencing a sea change that includes a series of steps or tiers in the prereferral and formal identification process (Fuchs & Young, 2006; U.S. Department of Education, 2006). These tiers provide successively more intensive instruction to struggling students and incorporate frequent assessments to guide instructional decision making. This process is called **response to intervention (RTI)**. Although only a few years ago most educators had not heard about this innovative approach that helps struggling students, today hardly a classroom teacher or administrator is unaware of RTI or its purpose.

RTI is a response to the growing dissatisfaction with tests of intelligence and their use in identifying students with learning disabilities (Fuchs & Young, 2006). Until the reauthorization of IDEA in 2004, the only process available to identify students with learning disabilities included a prereferral phase when information about classroom performance and instruction was collected. The teacher then referred the student, the diagnostician tested the individual, and the identification process proceeded. IDEA '04 now allows states and school districts to use the prereferral step in the IEP process to provide most of the information needed for the identification of students with learning disabilities. One purpose of RTI is to find those students who are "resistant to treatment" by "filtering" children through many stages of learning opportunities (Fuchs, Fuchs, & Compton, 2004). The system does this evaluation by systematically providing students with more and more intensive instruction (Fuchs et al., 2008). While most of the research about RTI focuses on early reading and multitiered prevention and intervention, efforts are now underway to extend

response to intervention (RTI) A multitiered prereferral method of increasingly intensive interventions; used to identify "non-responders" or students with learning disabilities

myeducationlab Go to the Activities and Applications section in Chapter 5 of MyEducationLab, and complete Activity 3, included in the IRIS Module, "RTI (Part 1): An Overview." This module outlines the differences between the IQ-achievement discrepancy model and the response-to-intervention (RTI) model. It also offers a brief overview of each tier in the RTI model and explains its benefits.

these principles and practices to help students who are struggling learning mathematics as well (Fuchs, Fuchs, Compton, et al., 2007).

How does this prereferral process work? Although RTI can be applied to any academic area, it is receiving most attention for its application to reading—the most common problem among students with learning disabilities. Lynn and Doug Fuchs and Sharon Vaughn are some of the innovators who have researched this concept and developed one approach to its implementation. Here's what they suggest should happen in the general education setting (Fuchs et al., 2008):

1. To ensure that all struggling students are found as quickly as possible, *all* students in kindergarten or in first, second, third, or fourth grade experience **universal screening** and are tested at least once in the fall. (Some schools also conduct universal screenings two additional times, in the middle and at the end of the school year.)

2. Students demonstrating skills that put them at risk for reading failure are identified for intervention. (Estimates are that some 25% of all first and second graders initially fall into the group that then receives Tier 1 instruction.)

3. Data-based procedures (e.g., explicit instruction on reading skills such as sight word vocabulary, phonics, fluency) and curriculum-based measurements (e.g., direct and frequent assessments of student's mastery of curriculum targets being taught) are implemented, and students' progress is monitored frequently.

4. Those students who do not meet expectations receive increasingly intensive instruction. (Tier 2 instruction is typically delivered in small groups and is at least 12 weeks in length. Some schools provide additional tiers of instruction in the general education class to students who continue to show inadequate improvement.)

5. Students who do not make sufficient progress or do not meet their benchmark goal or whose learning trend is too slow have now demonstrated that they need sustained and more intensive instruction. Depending on the district's rules for identification, they are now either identified as having learning disabilities or sent on for further assessments by a multidisciplinary team.

universal screening Testing all students to identify those in need of assistance or more intensive instruction

Figure 5.1 helps us visualize how this process is often implemented. During Step 1, Screening, each first grader in a class read a list of words aloud, and the number of correctly read words in a 1-minute sample was recorded. The data from each student scoring below criterion (Emily, Marco, and Josh) were graphed. These three first graders remained in the general education class but moved on to Step 2, Tier 1 Instruction and Assessment. Their performance on the word identification task was assessed each week to determine whether peer tutoring, extra attention, and modified textbooks resolved their reading problems. Marco, clearly at risk for reading failure, as indicated by the score he received on the initial screening assessment, responded satisfactorily to intervention at this level and returned to the general education program. Emily's and Josh's progress was insufficient, however, so they moved on to Step 3, Tier 2 Instruction and Assessment. They both remained in the general education program but received more intensive instruction from a paraprofessional under the supervision of a reading specialist who carefully matched the types of instruction chosen for them (e.g., active responding, cues, prompts, and/or direct instruction on phonics) to their skill levels. As you can see from Emily's chart in Figure 5.1, she responded to this level of instruction, and this additional instruction was discontinued. Josh's performance, however, indicated that he is "resistant to treatment," and he entered Step 4, Disability Classification/Special Education Placement.

What skills for reading are being tested through the RTI system? Different abilities are assessed in different grades (Fuchs, 2003; Fuchs & Fuchs, 2005).

- *Kindergarten:* letter–sound fluency; saying the sound represented by a letter
- *Grade 1:* word identification fluency; word recognition on a timed test
- *Grades 2–3:* passage reading; reading a paragraph aloud
- *Grade 4:* maze fluency; filling in missing words when reading a passage

Figure 5.1 • The Comparison of CBM Data of Three Students

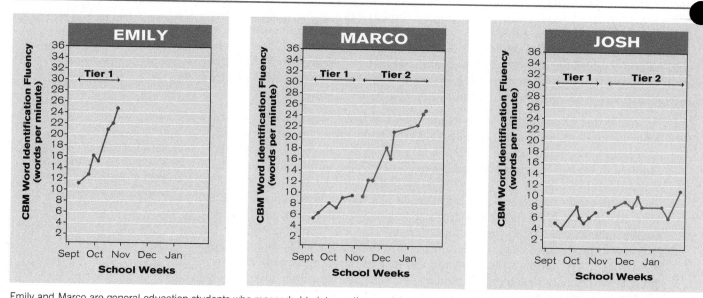

Emily and Marco are general education students who responded to intervention, and Josh is resistant to treatment and needs sustained, intensive, explicit instruction and special education services.

Source: Adapted by permission of Lynn and Doug Fuchs.

Examples of targets for kindergarten through fourth grade are shown in Figure 5.2. There you find segments of the Fuchs' assessments. Now review the three sample graphs shown in Figure 5.1. Compare the performances of Emily, Marco, and Josh to see how students can respond differently to intensive interventions. Such assessments tell teachers which students need sustained and intensive intervention to overcome their challenges mastering reading. What are the benefits of RTI? Proponents of this approach are confident that RTI resolves the problems with the traditional IQ/achievement discrepancy model (Speece, Case, & Molloy, 2003; McNamara & Hollinger, 2003). Here are some of the advantages that RTI is usually described as offering:

- *No delay in receiving intervention.* More intensive instruction is delivered promptly, eliminating a long waiting period of continued failure before help is received.
- *Reduces inappropriate referrals.* RTI provides teachers with better guidance in determining which students are in need of special education.
- *Poor teaching not a reason.* Inefficient instruction is eliminated as a reason for learning disabilities.
- *Assessment leads to intervention.* RTI combines assessment with intervention.
- *No stigma associated with the identification process.* All students enter the process.
- *Low achievement is distinguished from learning disabilities.* Low performance improves, but growth remains insufficient, thereby separating these two groups of students.

The support for RTI and multitiered intervention is growing. In fact, it is being referred to as a "sea change" in learning disabilities (Fuchs & Young, 2006). What will it take to make the RTI system work in schools across the country? Clearly, changing to this new system requires considerably more support for general education teachers who are adding assessment to their instructional duties (Denton, Vaughn, & Fletcher, 2003). General and special education teachers need to collaborate more than ever before by helping each other tie assessment to intervention. And, all educators need to be knowledgeable about data-based practices and how to implement multitiered, increasingly intensive instruction.

Figure 5.2 • Response to Intervention Assessment Samples: Kindergarten through Fourth Grade

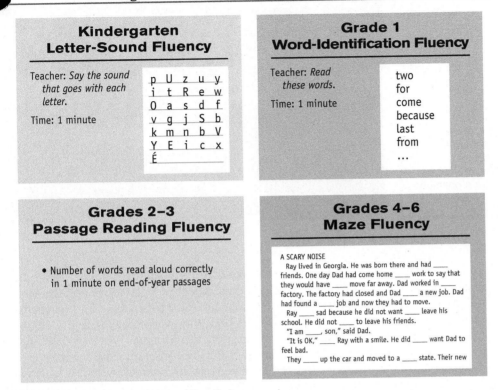

Source: Adapted by permission of Lynn and Doug Fuchs.

Identification

As more and more states adopt RTI and its multitiered prereferral process, traditional assessment procedures may be replaced entirely (Kathy Strunk, personal communication, 2008). However, in most states, traditional diagnostic procedures continue to follow the prereferral stage or first tiers of the RTI process. Some states and districts still use, and will continue to do so, the learning disabilities identification process that has been employed since the field began in the early 1970s. It is important to know and understand this system, for it is still used in many states and school districts either as the primary method of identification or as the verifying method for students who have been through the entire RTI process and have shown their need for intensive special education services.

The standard procedure, used for years to identify students with learning disabilities, relies on **discrepancy formulas** to determine whether the gap between a student's achievement and her or his potential is significant and accounts for that student's learning failures. Two test results are needed to apply every discrepancy formula: an IQ score and the score from a standardized achievement test. As we mentioned, considerable dissatisfaction with discrepancy formulas exists (Bradley et al., 2002). Here is a review of a few criticisms:

discrepancy formulas
Calculations used to determine the gap between achievement and intelligence (potential); used to identify students with learning disabilities

- IQ tests are not reliable and are unfair to many groups of children.
- Results have little utility in planning a student's educational program.
- The process does not help determine which interventions might be successful.
- Outcomes are not related to performance in the classroom, in the general education curriculum, or on state- or districtwide assessments.
- Children must fail before they can qualify for needed services. Thus, early intervention is delayed until the gap becomes great enough for children to meet this criterion.

When all students are screened during prereferral assessments, intervention happens before academic problems become insurmountable, and the probability increases for everyone's success.

With such concerns, why were discrepancy formulas used for so long? One important reason is that they give the identification process some appearance of objectivity. Another reason is that the results are easy for parents and teachers to understand (Ahearn, 2003). Diagnosticians or school psychologists give a child an IQ test and an achievement test and then apply the formula. Whether the child is included in the learning disabilities category thus becomes a cut-and-dried, yes-or-no answer. Another reason is that the achievement/discrepancy system is fairly easy to apply. Support for RTI is growing rapidly. A large proportion of school psychologists, some 75%, endorse RTI; however, over 60% of the group also thinks that information collected during the RTI process should support the traditional achievement/discrepancy approach (Machek & Nelson, 2007).

Whether educators use RTI—its multitiered prevention approach to instruction and its progress monitoring system—alone, achievement/discrepancy alone, or some combination, more information is needed before a final determination that the individual has learning disabilities can be made. In all cases, the possibility that another disability, and not a learning disability, is causing the individual's struggles at school must be eliminated. Therefore, standardized tests of intelligence, achievement, hearing, and vision are part of the battery of tests used by the multidisciplinary team for final determination of the presence of a learning disability.

Evaluation: Progress Monitoring

mastery measurement A system of progress monitoring; evaluates learning of discrete skills frequently, often daily

As you learned in Chapter 2, progress monitoring is an important component of an effective education for students with disabilities. Although somewhat similar, particularly because they both use direct measures of classroom performance, mastery measurement and curriculum-based measurement (CBM) differ in some important ways. **Mastery measurement** was developed and has been used extensively by special education teachers and researchers for many years (Haring, 1978; Lindsley, 1990; Lovett & Hansen, 1978). It uses analysis of behavior to evaluate individual student performance. Still used by many teachers and researchers today, this system of classroom assessment measures student performance and progress on a very frequent basis, often daily (Welsch, 2007). Each skill in an instructional sequence is taught and assessed until mastery is achieved. Then the next skill is taught, using data-based interventions, and assessed. If student learning is insufficient, another intervention is implemented. Once benchmarks or goals are achieved, the next discrete skill in the instructional sequence is introduced.

Curriculum-based measurement (CBM) is also a technique that measures student progress directly from the curriculum, but in this system all skills (i.e., every type of arithmetic problem to be learned) to be mastered are assessed in every probe. (Samples of CBM probes for reading have been shown in Figure 5.2 and for arithmetic in A Closer Look at Data-Based Practices). Since we feature CBM techniques in the Data-Based Practices section of this chapter, we only introduce it here. It is important to remember that in both systems, skill acquisition and mastery are in alignment with the curriculum; students' skills are measured frequently; assessment results influence the selection of instructional methods; immediate information about students' performance and success in the curriculum is available.

Early Intervention

All children deserve a good start. In Chapter 4, you learned of the importance of developing strong language skills during the preschool years. Early childhood is a critical period, in which many developmental milestones—the basis for school achievement and life success—occur. Most youngsters learn these basic skills naturally. Those who are not competitive with their preschool peers, either because they are the youngest in the class or because they are developmentally delayed, often experience **retention**, which is sometimes called academic redshirting (Frey, 2005). It is important for educators to know that consistently little evidence supports holding students back and that retaining students is correlated highly with later school dropout. Instead, as the RTI agenda is beginning to demonstrate, students who struggle benefit from increasingly intensive direct or explicit instruction.

Although very few preschoolers are identified as having learning disabilities, those who do have such disabilities, along with some peers without disabilities, begin their struggles learning to read during these early years. We now know that the skills that make the learning to read easier are also forming during these early years (Compton, 2002). And now, it is becoming clear that the foundation skills for mathematics are also developed early (Chard et al., 2008). The work in early mathematics instruction is just beginning, so we will briefly highlight some of these findings first and then turn our attention to early reading, where researchers have been focusing attention longer.

Core Skills of Mathematics

Some young children show difficulties learning those basic skills needed for later understanding of mathematical concepts (Chard et al., 2008). Fortunately, we are now learning that preschool teachers can divert these children's path away from school failure toward success by explicitly helping those youngsters who show signs of difficulty learning or understanding basic skills, including basic mathematics skills. In recent years, the foundational skills for reading success later in school have been identified (Compton, 2002; Simmons et al., 2008). Comparable information for mathematics is just becoming available as researchers are beginning to concentrate their attention to early mathematics skills and discovering multitiered interventions (Bryant & Bryant, 2008; Mazzocco & Thompson, 2008). The core foundational skills of mathematics that preschool and kindergarten teachers should address include

- counting objects,
- reading one-digit numerals,
- adding one-digit numbers when using manipulatives, and
- comparing two one-digit numbers when using number lines.

While most preschoolers learn such skills without much effort, those who struggle with early mathematical concepts profit and learn when explicitly taught (B. Bryant et al., 2008; Chard et al., 2008).

curriculum-based measurement (CBM) A system of progress monitoring; evaluates performance frequently (e.g., weekly, monthly) by collecting data directly on academic subjects being taught drawn from probes selected from across a curriculum

 Go to the Activities and Applications section in Chapter 5 of MyEducationLab and complete Activity 4. As you watch the video and complete the activities think about ways in which technology enhances this curriculum-based measure.

retention Repeating a school year or delaying entrance into kindergarten or first grade

Core Skills of Reading

Reading is crucial to school success, and it is a skill that is difficult for most students with learning disabilities to master. Researchers are now confident that the essential, foundation, or core skills that make for good readers are developed much earlier than was originally thought (Compton, 2002; Jenkins & O'Connor, 2002). In particular, three core skills begin to develop during the preschool years and are important for later success with reading:

- Phonological awareness
- Rapid naming of alphabetic sounds and letters
- Beginning phonics

phonological awareness
Identifying, separating, or manipulating sound units of spoken language

Mastering language is a prerequisite for reading. As you learned in the previous chapter, poor language development explains why so many preschoolers identified with language impairments during their preschool years are identified later with learning disabilities during their school years. One important set of skills both for language development and for later reading success is **phonological awareness**—identifying, separating, and manipulating the sound units of spoken language (Vaughn & Linan-Thompson, 2004). Indicators of phonological awareness include hearing and identifying sounds in words, breaking or segmenting words and phrases into their smallest units, and rhyming. Although some experts believe that skills such as actual letter and word identification and decoding are superior to phonological awareness as predictors of which students will later have trouble mastering reading, it is clear that these core skills develop early (Ehri et al., 2001; Hammill, 2004; Nelson, Benner, & Gonzalez, 2003). A second skill that seems to predict later success with reading is **letter fluency**, which is indicated by calling out quickly the letters of the alphabet upon seeing them in any order (Speece et al., 2003). A third set of skills that begins to develop during these early years is **phonics**—the ability to decipher printed words or identify the sounds that are represented by individual letters and groups of letters. A good start on learning phonics and on learning how to decode printed words seems to be an indication that the individual will become a good reader (Bursuck et al., 2004). So, phonological awareness, letter fluency, and phonics, along with vocabulary and sight word development, form the early foundations for reading mastery. Fortunately, these skills can be taught. Students with reading/learning disabilities, however, often need intensive instruction to put those and other core skills together to become proficient readers (Hammill, 2004; Simmons et al., 2007).

letter fluency Quickly reading and naming letters of the alphabet

phonics The sounds represented by letters and letter groups

Early Reading Instruction

The origins of literacy take shape during early childhood, long before children actually begin to read (Simmons et al., 2007). Helping students master the core skills of reading is not a simple task (Coyne, Zipoli, & Ruby, 2006). Doing so can be daunting, but it is important to think about all the factors that need to be considered: what to teach, how to teach effectively, and when to teach critical skills.

Early instruction in phonological awareness (e.g., *cat* has three sounds, *fall* and *wall* rhyme), letter naming, and decoding is helpful for all preschoolers (Pullen & Justice, 2003). Whether they are English language learners with or without learning disabilities or native English speakers, for preschoolers and kindergarteners who do not learn these precursors to reading on their own, instruction in these very important skills can avoid later reading problems (Kamps et al., 2007). For some, explicit instruction in the general preschool or general education setting is sufficient; for others, intensive intervention is necessary. Although the problems and struggles of all students are not resolved through RTI, the referral rates to special education have decreased by about one-third across the early school years (Hollenbeck, 2007). As RTI and early intervening become better

Learning and practicing the core skills of basic reading can be fun by using popular books like those of the Dr. Seuss series that incorporate phonics and rhyming in the story.

understood and more widely adopted, the promise is that even fewer students will require special education services.

In addition to explicit instruction on skills that form the foundation for reading, preschool and kindergarten teachers should not lose sight of the importance of developing language- and literacy-rich environments (Simmons et al., 2007). Literacy is not just decoding or even comprehending the printed word; it is a reflection of a greater set of skills and abilities that include reflective thinking. Children need to develop a love of reading, to gain skills and attitudes that favor future literacy, and to recognize both that reading is important to them and that it is fun. Through their retelling and reenacting of their favorite stories, the important concept that print has meaning is understood early and becomes a basis for future instruction.

Teaching Students with Learning Disabilities

As a reminder, the importance of preschoolers and students in the elementary grades developing the foundation skills for reading cannot be overstressed. In the early grades, reading is an academic target for instruction, but quickly it becomes a skill needed for overall academic success. Reading is one important way in which students access the content presented in the basic general education curriculum. Whether students are at risk for school failure, are diverse learners facing the challenges of learning English as a second language, or are on the way to being identified as having learning disabilities, it is critical that they receive extra help so their struggles learning to read are minimized. Without intervention, these students' low achievement separates them more each school year from their classmates without disabilities (Deshler, 2005). Figure 5.3 helps us understand why intervening early is so important.

Access to the General Education Curriculum: Early Intervening

Explicit instruction in the fundamental skill areas of reading makes a genuine difference and can turn many struggling readers into confident readers who are able to access the general education curriculum (Bishop, 2003; Bursuck et al., 2004). You just learned about the basic or core reading skills that begin to develop

myeducationlab Go to the Activities and Applications section in Chapter 5 of MyEducationLab and complete Activity 5, IRIS Activity: He's Just a Goofy Guy. Jake is an energetic third grader who has a learning disability. Should he be included in a general education class?

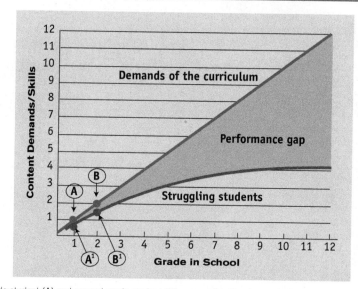

Figure 5.3 • The Widening Performance Gap Between Students with and Without Learning Disabilities Across the Grades

Note: First-grade student (A) and second-grade student (B) are meeting the demands of the curriculum, showing grade-level achievement. Struggling first-grade student (A[1]) and second-grade student (B[1]) begin the path of underachievement.

Source: From "A Closer Look: Closing the Performance Gap," by D. D. Deshler, January 2005, *StrateNotes, 13,* p. 1. Reprinted by permission.

during the preschool years; in Table 5.4, those are reviewed, as are the other important areas that need to be formed during the school years. The power and importance of providing explicit instruction as soon as students show signs of struggling, particularly in reading, is supported by these key findings (Dion et al., 2004; Ehri et al., 2001; Fuchs et al., 2004):

- Students who fail to acquire the core skills of early reading soon after entering school become poor readers.
- Students who complete first grade without having mastered phonological awareness tend to be poor readers in fourth grade.
- Readers who are struggling at third grade tend to be poor readers at ninth grade.
- Struggling readers do not catch up on their own.
- Intensive and explicit instruction on the core skills of reading (such as sound–symbol relationships), delivered early, often helps such students become better readers.

Armed with the knowledge that intervening early can be critical to the success of so many students, federal, state, and school district officials have been trying to figure out how to get additional services to *all* students who need them. Of course, students with reading/learning disabilities qualify for special education. For them, intensive and explicit instruction is part of their IEPs and their guarantee for an appropriate education. However, for those who do not have disabilities (or have not yet qualified for special education), the challenge is to get services to them quickly. IDEA '04 allows restricted funding for a new process to deliver prevention services to struggling learners. **Early intervening** brings intensive instruction to all struggling learners in the hope of preventing learning problems that will only compound as time passes.

early intervening Providing explicit and intensive instruction to all struggling students to prevent compounding learning problems

178   Chapter 5

To provide early intervening services, a local educational agency (e.g., school district) may

- use a specified portion (not more than 15%) of IDEA funds for students in kindergarten through grade 12 who need additional academic and behavioral support to succeed in the general education classroom but have not yet been identified as needing special education or related services, and
- emphasize services for students in kindergarten through grade 3. The services and activities provided may include
- professional development for teachers and other school staff that will enable them to deliver scientifically based academic instruction and behavioral interventions,
- instruction for teachers and school staff on the use of adaptive and instructional software; and
- educational and behavioral evaluations, services, and supports (which may include scientifically based literacy instruction).

As you have learned, early intervening is delivered in tiers. In the prevention phase, high-quality general education instruction is assured. In the early intervening phases, the student has not been identified for special education but is receiving more intensive instruction than do classmates who are not struggling. Whether in reading, writing, or mathematics, students who cannot keep up with their peers or the demands of the general education curriculum are taught with successively more intensive supports and instruction (Troia, 2008). Evidence is clear: Explicitly teaching students how to plan and draft a story, even as early as second grade, can improve the long-term academic results of struggling learners (Lienemann et al., 2006). Setting specific goals for improvement in reading fluency typically result in students reading faster and with better comprehension (Morgan & Sideridis, 2006). In other words, setting a goal for a student reading at 40 words a minute to aim at reading 60 words a minute helps improve reading fluency in students with reading/learning disabilities.

Instructional Accommodations

Universal design for learning (UDL), which we discussed in Chapter 2, provides multiple ways for all students to access the general education curriculum. You may recall that UDL uses the computer to provide greater access to printed material for those

Table 5.4 • Fundamental Reading Skills

Skill Area	Explanation	Example
Phonological awareness	Is able to identify the smallest units of sound, segment words (breaking words into sound units), and manipulate sounds in words	Knowing: *cat* has three sound units, *c-a-t* Saying: each sound (phoneme) in the word *cat* Rhyming: *cat* and *mat*
Letter–sound correspondence	Is able to identify and say the sound of each letter or basic letter combinations	Identifies the names and sounds of letters presented in random order
Phonics	Sound–symbol relationships used for reading and spelling	Knows the two sounds made by the letter s:/s/ in saw and /z/ in was
Word identification	Reads individual words quickly	Reads words from grade-level word lists accurately and at a satisfactory rate
Fluency	Reads passages orally correctly and quickly	Reads sentences and paragraphs accurately and at a satisfactory rate
Comprehension	Understands reading passages	Answers comprehension questions or retells the content of a paragraph

students who profit more by listening to print-to-speech translations of texts or by being able to refer to definitions or examples of difficult words and concepts. Clearly, classroom computers can be used to make excellent accommodations. Also, teachers who adjust the content and presentation of their instruction improve outcomes of students with disabilities. Some techniques are useful for students with many different disabilities but are critically important to the success of students with learning disabilities. For example, as you learned in Chapter 4, the link between learning disabilities and language impairments is now clear. Therefore, teachers who adjust their language to the level of listening comprehension of their students or break learning tasks into smaller segments help many students with many different types of learning needs. Accommodating for Inclusive Environments provides several ideas about adjusting content and providing instructional supports to students.

Data-Based Practices

As we discussed in the Where We've Been section of this chapter, the history of learning disabilities is fraught with the application of unproven practices. Parents and individuals with learning disabilities have wasted time and money in hopes that some new idea would resolve the challenges this disability presents. We now know for certain that merely placing plants on students' desks or having school-age children learn again to crawl does not improve reading skills. Researchers are also

---

Accommodating for Inclusive Environments
Adjusting Content and Providing Instructional Supports

Provide Structure and a Standard Set of Expectations

- Help students develop organizational skills.
- Establish sets of rules for academic and social activities and tasks.
- Adhere to a well-planned schedule.
- Match your language to the comprehension level of the student.
- Be consistent.

Adjust Instructional Materials and Activities

- Individualize instruction; be sure the reading level is appropriate.
- Break tasks down into smaller pieces (or chunks).
- Begin lessons with advance organizers.
- Supplement oral and written assignments with learning aids (computers).
- Assign a peer tutor.
- Modify tests, allowing the student to take more time or complete the test in a different way (listen to a tape of the test).

- Evaluate the effectiveness of your instructional interventions, and when they are not effective, change them.

Give Students Feedback and Reinforcement for Success

- Tell students when they are behaving properly.
- Reward students for improvement.
- Praise students when they have done well or accomplished a goal.
- Inform students when they are not meeting expectations.
- Encourage students to develop partnerships among themselves, and reinforce those who do so.

Make Tasks Interesting

- Develop attention by making assignments interesting and novel.
- Vary the format of instruction and activities.
- Use high-interest curriculum materials.
- Encourage students to work together during extracurricular activities.

helping teachers know which instructional methods are most likely to be effective with many of these students. Remember, however, that students with learning disabilities have great individual differences, and there is no guarantee that a tactic that is useful with one student will be so with the next. It is imperative that teachers assess the progress of individual students consistently and frequently to be sure that a method chosen is producing the desired results. Before turning our attention to a procedure that both monitors students' progress and is also a data-based practice, we wanted to highlight a proven approach that helps middle and high school students meet the demands of the ever-increasing challenges of the core curriculum.

To help middle and high school students with learning disabilities become strategic learners, Don Deshler, Jean Schumaker, and their colleagues at the University of Kansas Center for Research on Learning (CRL) began developing the learning strategies approach some 25 years ago. Their work has grown from one strategy into a powerful and effective curriculum (Swanson & Deshler, 2003). For an amazing look at the high-quality information and resources available about effective instruction and these students, see www.kucrl.org. The purpose of the **Strategic Instruction Model**™ **(SIM)** is to give these students a plan and methods for success. It comprises many strategies that help students learn and remember information more efficiently, improve their test performance and completion of assignments in content classes, and succeed in the general education curriculum (Bui, Schumaker, & Deshler, 2006; Deshler & Roth, 2002). Some strategies help students write multiparagraph themes, personal narratives, reports, letters, and even essays (Isaacson, 2004; Schumaker & Deshler, 2003). The SIM section of the CRL Web site provides descriptions of the almost 50 strategies that have been developed under rigorous standards.

Most of the highly effective SIM strategies incorporate key features that all teachers can apply to help struggling students. One of these features is to begin units of instruction with an **advance organizer** that explains to students why to learn and apply a strategy (e.g., "This strategy will help you remember history better"), why the content is important (e.g., "This information will be on the state's achievement test"), and on what features of the content to focus their attention (e.g., "Notice that the American soldiers in the Revolutionary War used nonconventional fighting tactics, while the British soldiers lined up in rows, shooting their rifles in the traditional way across a field"). Another common feature is the use of **mnemonics**, which are memory aids that help people remember items that go together. So, many of the SIM strategies are named with a mnemonic (e.g., RAP: "*R*ead the paragraph; *a*sk yourself the main idea and details in the paragraph; *p*ut the main idea and details in your own words"). Some mnemonics are simple "word tricks" like the one shown in Figure 5.4, which helps us remember the names of the Great Lakes (Huron, Ontario, Michigan, Erie, and Superior) by thinking of the word *HOMES*.

Now let's turn our attention to a practice that we introduced in the Assessment section and is validated through years of research and practice. CBM has three important, overarching benefits. It is first and foremost a measurement tool that allows for the monitoring of student progress using indicators and benchmarks directly from the curriculum being taught. Second, it is used to guide instruction, informing teachers about which instructional tactics are effective, which are not, and which might have been for a while but are no longer producing sufficient gains in performance to merit their continued use. Tools and procedures have been developed for most academic areas, including reading, writing, and mathematics (Foegen, Jiban, & Deno, 2007; McMaster & Espin, 2007; Wallace et al., 2007; Wayman et al., 2007). And, the last reason for CBM's widespread use is that it is also a proven practice—a practice that causes improvement in students' academic performance even without additional measures such as reinforcement systems. These benefits speak clearly: All teachers, particularly special educators, should be proficient in the use and application of CBM techniques. For more about curriculum-based measurement and monitoring student progress, see this Web site: www.studentprogress.org.

Strategic Instruction Model™ (SIM) Instructional methods to help students read, comprehend, and study better by helping them organize and collect information strategically; a supplemental high school curriculum designed for students with learning disabilities; developed at the University of Kansas Center for Research on Learning (CRL)

advance organizer A tactic that previews lectures and provides organizing structures to acquaint students with the content, its organization, and importance before the lesson

mnemonics A learning strategy that promotes remembering information by associating the first letters of items in a list with a word, sentence, or picture (e.g., HOMES for the Great Lakes)

Figure 5.4 • The Great Lakes Mnemonic: HOMES

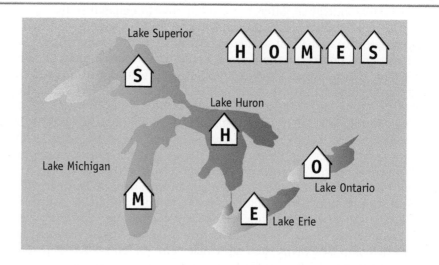

CBM is an integral part of RTI used for screening, prereferral, and identification of students with learning disabilities. Teachers who use CBM find that it facilitates communication with parents and students because it focuses everyone's attention on instructional targets and the student's performance. It helps teachers plan more effective instruction, helps students see that they are responsible for their learning and resulting performance, and reflects progress on learning the curriculum content. To see students' performance that is documented through the CBM approach, look again at the graphs shown in Figure 5.1.

For an overview about how CBM is implemented in classroom settings, this chapter's A Closer Look at Data-Based Practices provides some simple steps to follow. For more detailed instruction about CBM, the two interactive, online modules provided by the IRIS Center, at http://iris.peabody.vanderbilt.edu, will get you off to a great start.

Technology

Much of the technology that benefits everyone is particularly useful to students with learning disabilities by helping them become more efficient and effective learners (Boone & Higgins, 2007; Bryant & Bryant, 2003). Table 5.5 highlights some of these benefits and suggests how assistive technology can reduce the barriers to success that these individuals face at home, at school, and in daily life. The benefits to students with learning disabilities are many; technology can

- augment an individual's strengths,
- compensate for the effects of disabilities,
- provide alternative modes of performing tasks,
- help students with learning disabilities participate more fully in the general education curriculum,
- create active learning environments, and
- teach them how to search for and access information from the Internet.

Here are some examples of applications of technology that have such benefits. Special text reading software using synthetic speech to read words that are highlighted on the computer screen can help students become more independent as they read and study difficult history or science textbooks (Hasselbring & Bausch, 2005/2006). Graphic organizers, like Kidspiration and Inspiration that were described in Chapter 4, have application across academic subjects and ages and are especially useful to organize the content being studied for social studies or science. (See again A Closer Look at Data-Based Practices in Chapter 4.) Using such technology to create visual displays has also

A Closer Look at Data-Based Practices

Curriculum-Based Measurement (CBM)

CBM is a form of progress monitoring that uses direct and frequent measurements of students' actual performance, such as oral reading rate or the percentage of correct answers to mathematics problems. CBM enables elementary, middle school, and high school teachers to evaluate individual students' overall progress across the school year to assess the effectiveness of the instructional methods they are using and to see how well each student of concern is mastering the curriculum.

Steps to Follow

1. Create or select appropriate tests (probes) that reflect skills from the curriculum that the student should master across the school year or semester. Probes are matched to the student's grade, the state's standards, and national benchmarks that indicate mastery. These tests or probes sample skills to be mastered across the school year. Thus, as time progresses, students should get more items correct.
2. Administer and score probes frequently (e.g., weekly or monthly) to ensure that students' data are valid (reflect performance of the same skills being taught) and reliable (consistently represent the students' abilities on the targeted skills).
3. Graph the scores to create visual representations of each student's performance. The student can then see progress being made in the curriculum, and teachers can revisit their instructional decisions based on student performance (see Figure 5.3 again for some sample charts).
4. Set goals, which are targets or benchmarks, that help students and teachers understand how much growth is expected or required.
5. Make instructional decisions for each individual student, based on actual performance on the skills being taught. This important evaluation step helps teachers decide to retain effective strategies and discontinue ineffective ones.
6. Communicate progress to parents, other teachers, and the student by using the CBM data and graphs.

Example of a CBM Chart and Worksheet

This CBM chart was developed to display a student's progress mastering core arithmetic skills presented on similar worksheets across the school year.

 myeducationlab Go to the Building Teaching Skills and Dispositions section in Chapter 5 of MyEducationLab, and complete the IRIS Modules:

"Classroom Assessment (Part 1): An Introduction to Monitoring Academic Achievement in the Classroom"

This module discusses how progress monitoring can affect the academic outcomes of students, and it demonstrates how to implement curriculum-based measurement with a classroom of students.

"Classroom Assessment (Part 2): Evaluating Reading Progress"

This module explores in detail the assessment procedures integral to RTI. It also outlines how to use progress monitoring data to determine if a student is meeting the established performance criteria or if more intensive intervention is needed.

CBM Probe 25
Computation

Name: _____   Date: _____

a	b	c	d	e
9)24̅	52852 +64708	9 × 0	4)72̅	8285 4304 + 90
f	**g**	**h**	**i**	**j**
6)30̅	35 × 74	4 × 5	7 × 9	598 × 45
k	**l**	**m**	**n**	**o**
32 × 23	8 × 6	5)65̅	6)30̅	35 × 57
p	**q**	**r**	**s**	**t**
107 × 3	2)9̅	416 − 44	456 × 27	6 × 2
u	**v**	**w**	**x**	**y**
33 − 2	1504 −1441	9)81̅	130 × 7	5)10̅

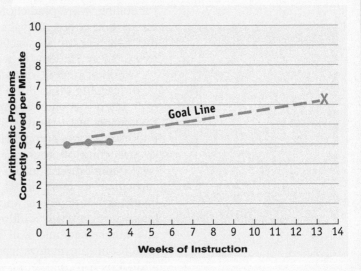

Source: Courtesy of the IRIS Center, Vanderbilt University.

Table 5.5 • Assistive Technology Solutions for Learning Disabilities

Barrier	Challenge Area	Technology Solution
Print	Reading	Print-to-voice output Graphic organizing software E-texts with hyperlinks
	Writing	Word processing software with track tools, outline features, thesaurus Word prediction software
	Spelling	Spellcheckers Voice-to-print input
Communication	Organization	Graphic and design software Presentation software Graphic organizing software
Solving problems	Calculating	Calculators Spreadsheets
Being organized	Daily life	PDAs E-calendars
Study skills	Research	Internet databases Internet search engines Reference organizers
	Remembering	Graphic organizing software Sticky notes Outline software (main ideas/details)

helped students with mathematics/learning disabilities learn algebra—one subject that is a "gatekeeper" to a standard high school diploma (Ives, 2007).

An obvious way technology helps all of us be better writers is through word processing software. For students, it can be essential, allowing them to compensate for their learning disabilities (Harris et al., 2008; Santangelo et al., 2001). Print on a computer screen is easier to see and read than print on paper. The spellchecker, thesaurus, and grammar correction functions help those who struggle get a term paper written. The product is more attractive than one turned in with poor handwriting. Many features of word processing programs (e.g., table features, tracking for editing, word predictions) help students improve both the quality and the quantity of their writing (Bryant & Bryant, 2003). As shown in the accompanying photo, the computer can also facilitate collaboration between students, making it easier for two or more students to work together on a writing task.

Another benefit of technology addresses a common outcome or characteristic of learning disabilities: poor motivation. Students described as "inactive learners" often become engaged when activities are interesting and interactive. Enhancing instruction with technology can make instruction and learning more interesting for everyone! Here are some examples. History units can be enhanced by collecting photographs, music, video, and other artifacts from the period of time being studied in the general education curriculum. In the process, a class can create its own virtual museum and exhibit about a particular time or place in history. Individuals and groups of students can work at their own levels as instruction is easily differentiated with assignments reflecting students' reading and other academic skill levels (Okolo et al., 2007). WebQuests have students search out information from the Internet. They are given a topic, Web site URLs, and steps for completing the assignment (Skylar, Higgins, & Boone, 2007). Perhaps, however, the most important aspect of integrating technology into instruction is that it often provides intrinsic motivation to expand knowledge and develop outstanding research skills.

These students are working together collecting information, artwork, and photos from the Internet about the Long Walk Trail of the Navajos for a social studies paper and report.

Transition

Transition activities are important to high school students with learning disabilities, just as it is for those with other disabilities. Educators must not make assumptions about the needs of any group of individuals. It is a mistake to think that students with learning disabilities cannot succeed in **postsecondary education**. Such notions not only are untrue but also can seriously limit an individual's potential. These students should not be denied the opportunity, but for success to occur planning must begin early; the right courses need to be taken, basic skills mastered, and an understanding of one's own strengths and weaknesses achieved. Unfortunately, transition services, particularly for those who should attend postsecondary schools, are fragmented and inconsistent (Hong et al., 2007).

As you learned in Chapter 2, all students with disabilities should have their transition needs discussed, and, if appropriate, a statement of transition must be included with their IEPs once they have reached the age of 16. This includes students with learning disabilities, whether they are on the path for employment immediately after high school or for postsecondary education (Johnson, Mellard, & Lancaster, 2007; Madaus & Shaw, 2006). In either case, transition education makes a real difference in the success these individuals experience in adulthood. Because many hold the goal of attending and graduating from college, educators who make the wrong assumptions about individuals' potential outcomes dash such dreams.

The high school graduation and college attendance rates have increased for individuals with learning disabilities over the last 30 years. In 1988, only 16% of all college freshmen with disabilities had a learning disability; in 2003, they represented some 40% of those with disabilities who attended college, and the percentage is rising (Madaus, 2006; McBride, Scatton, & Copley, 2007; Ward, 2007). College education does make a difference. More and more adults with learning disabilities are college graduates, earn the same wages as their coworkers without disabilities, and report high satisfaction with their jobs (Madaus, 2006). However, college students with learning disabilities have different profiles as compared to their peers without disabilities (Ward, 2007). Here are some interesting comparisons:

- High school grades are much lower for those with learning disabilities—averaging in the B to C range—than for students with other disabilities—averaging in the A to A– range.
- A much higher percentage attending college graduated from private high schools than other students with or without disabilities, and they also attend a private college.
- Parents of college students with learning disabilities are well educated (often holding graduate degrees) and are more affluent than parents of other college students.

postsecondary education
Educational opportunities beyond high school; 2-year or 4-year colleges and universities

When people successful in business and some of the wealthiest people in the world, like Richard Branson, share publicly about the challenges they met because of reading/learning disabilities, it helps all those affected know that success is not out of reach. Branson is the British entrepreneur whose first business was a mail-order record sales company, whose second business was Virgin Music (a highly successful recording studio), and whose third venture is Virgin Atlantic Air, the discount airline.

These profiles tell us a lot about these individuals and their opportunities, leaving many questions about social justice and students with learning disabilities who do not come from affluent homes. It is clear that this group of students with learning disabilities do not access college at the levels they should. Carefully orchestrated and well-planned transition programs can help change these patterns by assisting these individuals be better prepared to succeed at college. College visits, particularly those with intensive orientation programs, can help students and their families decide which college is the right match or fit for them (Kato et al., 2006).

College students with learning disabilities often need supports to succeed in college. According to the National Center for Educational Statistics (NCES), well over half of all college students with disabilities who asked for accommodations were students with learning disabilities (NCES, 2003). Although not a legal requirement, more colleges and universities offer accommodations to those students with documented disabilities who request them (McBride et al., 2007). More and more postsecondary schools have a separate admissions route for students with disabilities (Madaus, 2005). They also have offices of disability services that provide a wide range of services (e.g., tutoring, study groups, instruction about time management, coordination of testing accommodations). Because the supports available vary widely, transition programs need to help students identify those colleges that offer the supports they need and help document those needs and a summary of performance to the accepting college and its staff of the office of disability services (Gartland & Strosnider, 2007).

The supports and accommodations available to assist students during their college experience have increased greatly in recent years (McBride et al., 2007; Ofiesh, Hughes, & Scott, 2004). Some of the more common ones are listed next:

- Alternative exam formats
- Extra time
- E-textbooks
- Tutors
- Readers, classroom notetakers, or scribes
- Registration assistance, priority class registration, or course substitutions
- Adaptive equipment and technology (calculators, phonetic spellcheckers, handheld organizers)

Some college graduates with learning disabilities make additional recommendations to help others succeed (Mooney & Cole, 2000). One important tip is to get organized: Every notebook should have a return address, backpacks and notebooks need a consistent "home" or place to be stored, notes and notebooks should be reorganized weekly, and mental checklists should be completed at the end of every class ("Do I have all of my stuff?" "Did I leave anything under the seat?"). Middle school and high school teachers can help students master these self-management skills long before they enter college.

Because attending college is an increasingly popular choice of these students and their families and because the process is often a family decision, we continue the conversation about students with learning disabilities and postsecondary experiences in the next two sections: Collaboration and Partnerships with Families and Communities.

Collaboration

Increasingly, students with learning disabilities attend general education classes, access the general education curriculum, and learn alongside their peers without disabilities. While data about just high school students are not available, school-age students with learning disabilities, ages 6 to 21, attend their neighborhood schools. Over 85% of them participate in general education classes over 40% of the school day, and some 54% of them spend over 80% of their school day learning in the general education classes (OSEP, 2008). One benefit of this participation rate is that students with learning disabilities often share the hopes and dreams of their classmates and have set a goal for themselves of continuing their education at either a community college or a 4-year college or university. So, in recent years, school counselors have assumed new roles in helping students with learning disabilities set goals for postsecondary education on the transition component of these students' IEPs. Excellent information about the emerging roles of school counselors and students with disabilities is available through the professional organization that represents these professionals: www.schoolcounselor.org.

Collaboration with Related Services Providers: School Counselors

Of course, school counselors do not work alone when helping adolescents with disabilities set their personalized transition goals. They work as part of a multidisciplinary team, collaborating with families and with each other. They also must involve the student in decisions about future planning (Dollarhide & Saginak, 2008). Remember, students who are at the age of majority, which varies from state to state, have the right to make their own decisions, even if their parents do not agree. So, let's say that a student is over the age of 18 and wants to attend college. The counselor must help that student articulate the goal and make progress toward achieving it. Therefore, counselors must be certain that they know and be aware of each student's age.

Collaborative Practices: Personalized Goal Setting

Person-centered transition planning considers three important transition domains: education/training, employment, and independent living (U.S. Department of Education, 2006). For some students, one area is prioritized over the other two. However, it is during the goal-setting process where balance and consideration of three areas should occur. Specific activities that help the individual achieve the transition goals are developed. Here is how the process typically plays out:

1. Students develop statements describing their future goals.
2. Students meet with the counselor and other school personnel to review and refine these statements.
3. Together, they assess what services and classes are needed in the student's high school program to achieve the stated goals.
4. They determine which postsecondary options have the best probability for success.

During this process, the school counselor takes a leadership role among the student's multidisciplinary team, guiding the process, counseling the student, and helping everyone consider all aspects of choosing the right postsecondary school. For example, if a student decides that a 4-year college program is the right match with his or her goals, then many other issues need to be considered and complex decisions made. Different sets of issues need to be resolved if the decision is that

Spotlighting *Sara Ezell:* A Day in the Life

Sara Ezell, herself a person with a disability, is the program coordinator of Vanderbilt University's Project Opportunity, which provides educational, developmental, and employment opportunities to individuals with disabilities within the Vanderbilt Medical Center.

In my experience, though there are numerous factors to consider in facilitating successful transitions, three main ones can positively or negatively impact the success of that transition for almost all individuals with disabilities, including those with severe learning disabilities. These are strictly anecdotal from my experience at Project Opportunity, but they are probably similar in other programs like ours. The key is to identify these factors so that each can be addressed by families, advocates, and employers, in collaboration, to create smooth transitions.

1. *Family needs.* I was under the assumption (which is clearly wrong, as I now see!) that when I worked with young adults with disabilities, the family would not play as large of a role as it does in young childhood. What I was forgetting was the importance of the family and/or support systems during the life span, not just childhood, for individuals with disabilities. Thus, as job placements were identified, we needed to consider how the job would impact the family and the system of supports currently in place for the student. And since the goal is to place an individual in an *existing* job (i.e., not job carving or job creation), how can we make this work? The answer is careful planning and a team approach. Just like a team plans the educational supports needed for a child, so must a team plan the employment supports for a young adult.

2. *Student versus employee role.* When transitioning from school to work, the expectations of the individual change drastically. This is not to mean that as employees, we are all expected to be perfect, thank goodness. But there is an expectation that a business need will be filled by the employee and that this affects not just the individual employee but the entire work site. For example, if a *student* does not complete an assignment accurately or in a timely manner, the consequences affect the student. If an *employee* does not perform to the supervisor's expectation, the consequences affect not only the employee but coworkers as well. This is a key shift for students with disabilities. Often, I have discovered that family and teachers placed few, or lower, expectations on an individual when he or she was in special education. Thus, part of the transition process is raising expectations gradually to prepare that individual for the workplace. It has been my experience that as these expectations increase, employee performance and self-esteem always rise to meet the challenge.

3. *Perception of others.* The final factor that affects successful transition is the perception of coworkers, supervisors, and employers with respect to working with a person with a disability. As a person with a disability myself, I am continually surprised at how far we have come in this area but equally surprised about how much farther we have to go. At Project Opportunity, we welcome open dialogues with departments about their fears or concerns, and we conduct training for departments who will be hiring our interns. The best way to address misperceptions, in my opinion, is to increase the opportunities for interaction between individuals with and without disabilities. Supervisors who have had experience with individuals with disabilities are likely to influence others' perceptions; thus, programs like ours that provide such experience will positively influence future transitions as well.

Overall, it is clear that "transition" is a much more complicated notion than I had first thought. But the outcome of progressing from one place to another is vital for all of us, those with and without disabilities. By planning appropriately and keeping all of these factors in consideration, we can help ensure that transitions, big or small, will be successful.

---

a community college is a more appropriate selection at this time. The counselor leads the team as transition assessment helps guide everyone in gathering information about the student's strengths, needs, preferences, and interests (IRIS Center, 2008b). Students assess their own needs for accommodations and determine which specific college or university offers the right supports. In this regard, a careful evaluation of services offered through the school's office of disability programs is important. Just as counselors help students without disabilities select good postsecondary options, they are now providing this important service to those with learning disabilities. Clearly, the result will be more students electing to attend college, and with the right choice made, graduation rates will improve as well.

While some high school seniors have reached the age of majority and can make decisions about their education and career goals without their family's input, others have not. Regardless, when possible, students' families should be integrally involved in their children's transition activities—as Sara Ezell points out in this chapter's Spotlighting feature. So, let's turn our attention to partnerships with families and how they help ensure that their child's goals are reasonable, realistic, and even lofty.

Partnerships with Families and Communities

So many issues are important to families of individuals with disabilities. Throughout this text, we highlight many concerns unique to these parents and families. In this chapter, we briefly discuss two issues that on the surface do not seem to be uniquely pertinent to individuals with learning disabilities, but recently they have taken on greater importance to such students. As you have just learned, more and more students with learning disabilities are continuing their educational careers on through the postsecondary years. College selection decisions are a major event for most of us, but if you have learning disabilities, picking the right college is often the key to becoming a graduate. Also, with the ever-increasing inclusion of students with disabilities in general education programs, and with more and more expectations for students with learning disabilities to access the general education curriculum, homework has taken on greater meaning for these students. We will examine both of these issues, first turning our attention to homework and then to selecting the "right" college.

Homework

Homework is a time-honored component of the general education program. It is intended to help students become independent learners, and for those students who are college bound, it could be considered a survival skill that is critical to future success. Homework serves as one communication tool to keep parents informed both about the work being done at school and about their child's progress in the curriculum (Lovitt, 2007). However, the word *homework* can strike terror into parents of students with learning disabilities—and probably into the children as well. The mere mention of the word may revive memories of long, unpleasant nights spent cajoling a student with learning disabilities into completing unfinished assignments. Such nights often end in shouting matches between parent and child, sometimes with one or both in tears.

Homework is a reality of school life, and teachers can make homework a more positive experience by making certain that students know how to do the assignment. Here are some guidelines that teachers can follow to get more benefits from assigning homework and even use it to forge an improved partnership with families (Warger, 2008)

- Make sure the assignment, its due date, and how it is to be graded is clear and understood.
- Assign appropriate topics that the student can complete.
- Coordinate with other teachers to avoid homework overload.
- Allow the use of accommodations and alternative formats (audiotaping rather than written assignments) or the use of learning tools (calculators, word processing, diagrams, and charts).
- Assign a peer to assist and be available for questions.

Although many students and their parents would like to see homework "just go away," it is unlikely that homework will be discontinued. General education teachers place great importance on homework. They consider homework to be a serious part of the instructional program and also to provide opportunities for home–school communication (Warger, 2008). How might communication between teachers and parents about homework improve? Here are a few ideas:

- Parents and teachers need to communicate more about homework, with both parties feeling free to initiate the conversation.
- Parents need to tell teachers about homework difficulties.
- Teachers need to tell parents about the quality and completion of homework assignments.
- Parents need to implement consequences when homework is not completed or is unsatisfactory.
- Parents need to know whom to contact at school about homework issues.
- Teachers need to find ways to communicate with parents who do not speak English.
- Teachers need to determine alternative ways for children to get assistance with homework assignments that their parents do not know how to help them complete.

College Selection

Leaving high school can be a troubling time for both the individual with learning disabilities and her or his family (Madaus, 2005). In high school, students have IEPs to guide the delivery of their educational programs and supportive services. There is no IEP for college. In high school, students' teachers often seek them out; such is not the case in the typical college experience. Flexibility and freedom of choice can be almost overwhelming, and as you will read in Considering Culture, they can be significant issues for many families of these students.

For all students, picking the right college is one key to a successful outcome. College can be a more positive experience for students with learning disabilities if they plan ahead while in high school and choose a college carefully (Shaw, 2005). Many students with learning disabilities elect to attend community colleges close to their homes, where they can continue to receive support from their families, test out their success with college coursework, attend smaller classes, and shift to either a technical program or a bachelor's degree program later (Brinckerhoff, 2005).

Any individual who wants to enter a 4-year college as a first-year student should visit different college campuses, investigate what support services are offered, and meet with college staff. Attending special summer programs or taking a college class can help sharpen study skills and time management skills—a problem that plagues most first-year students, not just those with learning disabilities. Issues related to selecting the "right" college are not the exclusive concern of those with learning disabilities, but such individuals do have more factors to weigh (Lissner, 2005).

Like everyone thinking about attending college, these questions must be considered:

- Does the school have the right academic programs?
- Where is the school located?
- What are its admissions standards?
- How big is the overall student body, and how large are the typical introductory courses?
- Does the school have extracurricular programs? The right ones?
- How much are tuition and fees, along with other costs?

For students with learning disabilities, these additional questions should be considered:

- How comprehensive is the school's office of disability services?
- What types of supports and services are offered?
- What supports and services does the student need for success?

Considering Culture: *Service Challenges in College Learning Disabilities*

All eyes in the family are on Alan. He is to be the first member of the family to go to college. His parents have worked hard all of their lives for this moment, and they are so proud that Alan was admitted to the *premier* university in the state. Their words of advice as he trundled off to his new experience were to "always work hard and make your family proud!" But his first semester at college has been a learning experience in more ways than one! Alan has alternately been thrilled to be in college, and totally disheartened and determined to drop out of college and get a job. He often laments, "Why does this have to be so hard! Why is it happening to me now? How can I face my family? I can't tell them that I need 'special help' in *college*!"

Alan reflects on the support he had in high school. There his teachers did so much to help him, because he was identified as having learning disabilities and he had an IEP. He typically was allowed more time on tests, his teachers reviewed notes with him and worked with him individually, and at times they gave him optional assignments. He also received individualized coaching on study skills. His grades were excellent. In fact, in his senior year when he told a friend that he had learning disabilities, she exclaimed, "How can that be? You're so smart!"

But college was a whole different ballgame. No one seemed to care. He was truly on his own. At the advice of classmates in his dorm, he signed up for a linguistics class that freshmen often took. He floundered. Learning the phonetic alphabet was not his cup of tea! His academic world seemed to be falling apart. But then his life turned around when one of his professors suggested that he work with the campus Office for Students with Disabilities. What a difference that made! The staff there helped him find notetakers for classes, encouraged him to use computers in class as needed, and helped him get approval to have more time for tests. They even worked with him to find an alternative to fulfill the university's foreign language requirement. He also learned to screen classes and then select those that best suited his learning style.

Questions to Consider

1. Think about your family's expectations for your development and your future. What cultural values, beliefs, and events in your family's history have you internalized and have probably played a role in your goal setting? (Some of these may be so subtle that they are difficult to identify.)

2. We often think that cultural issues apply only to people who speak a language other than English or who were not born in this country. What are some primary values inherent in the majority culture? How are these enacted in our educational systems?

—By Eleanor Lynch, San Diego State University, and Marci Hanson, San Francisco State University

Many variables need to be considered, but one thing is clear: Preparation to go to college must begin early in students' academic careers. In elementary school they learn the fundamentals on which future learning will be based. In middle school they begin being independent learners, and in high school they learn the basic content and skills they will need to succeed when they experience the freedom and challenges of college and the transition to adulthood.

Summary

Individuals with learning disabilities do not learn in the same way or at the same pace as their classmates without disabilities. These students are now thought of as resistant to treatment or not sufficiently responsive to high-quality instruction. They often do not learn along with their classmates through validated instructional practices used in general education classes. They require sustained, intensive, and explicit instruction to succeed. Students with learning disabilities can be characterized as having unexpected underachievement because their academic performance does not match their potential or what their other abilities would lead one to expect. Reading/learning disabilities are the most common type of this disability. These students are very different from each other in characteristics, learning preferences, and the accommodations they require to access the general education curriculum and to acquire basic skills needed for content instruction. New methods for prereferral assessments combined with multitiered interventions are now being used in schools across the country to intervene early with those who are struggling to learn in the general education classes. The aim is to prevent school failure but also to identify those with learning disabilities earlier so they can receive the intensive instruction they need as soon as possible.

Answering the Chapter Objectives

1. What are the key features of the current federal definition of learning disabilities?

   - Involves one or more of the psychological processes needed to understand or use spoken or written language
   - May result from central nervous system dysfunctions
   - Can result in problems listening, thinking, speaking, reading, writing, spelling, or computing
   - Excludes students whose primary problems are due to visual disabilities, hearing impairments, physical disabilities, mental retardation (intellectual disabilities), behavioral or emotional disorders, cultural or linguistic diversity, or poverty

2. What are the different types of learning disabilities?

   - *General unexpected underachievement:* overall low academic performance, general school failure
   - *Reading/learning disabilities:* reading performance both below that of classmates and below what is expected on the basis of the student's other abilities; most common type of learning disabilities
   - *Mathematics/learning disabilities:* mathematics performance both below that of classmates and below what is expected on the basis of the student's other abilities; most often co-occurs with reading/learning disabilities

   - *Resistant to treatment:* insufficiently responsive to standard instruction in the general education classroom; requiring sustained, intensive, explicit instruction that is monitored for adequate progress frequently

3. How is an individual's response to intervention (RTI) assessed?

   Through the prereferral process, four general steps are followed:

   - *Universal screening:* While some schools screen more often, all students experience direct assessment of their academic performance at least once at the beginning of every school year.
   - *Primary prevention and early intervening services:* Struggling students or those exhibiting skill levels that put them at risk for school failure receive additional instruction. (This additional instruction is typically called Tier 1.)
   - *Multitiered instructional services:* General educators, peer tutors, or paraprofessionals deliver increasing levels of intensive and individualized instruction to those students who continue to perform unsatisfactorily. (While some schools offer several additional tiers of increasingly intensive instruction to students who show insufficient progress, many offer just one, called Tier 2, before

referral for final assessment and identification as having a learning disability.)

- *Assessment for or identification of learning disabilities:* Students who do not learn sufficiently after experiencing at least multitiered intervention are either referred for special education assessment or identified as having learning disabilities. (The federal government and each state's regulations determine which assessment process is to be used.)

4. What is the practice of "early intervening," and why does it hold great promise?

Early intervening
- is allowed by IDEA '04, and some can be supported with special education funding; and
- provides more intensive instruction to all students who are not profiting from instruction being provided in the general education classroom, whether they have disabilities, are at risk, or are struggling learners

Benefits of early intervening and RTI:
- No delay in receiving intervention
- Reduced inappropriate referrals to special education
- Eliminates poor teaching as a reason for disabilities
- Assessment that directly leads to instruction

- No stigma in being referred to special education because all students are universally screened
- Low achievement distinguished by learning disabilities

5. What are two data-based practices that are effective with the academic performance of students with learning disabilities?

- The Kansas University Center for Research on Learning's (CRL) Strategic Instruction Model™ (SIM): Key features
  - Developed for middle school and high school students with disabilities
  - Goes beyond crisis teaching
  - Helps students become strategic learners
  - Incorporates mnemonics, advance organizers, and structured materials with measures for monitoring progress
- Curriculum-based measurement (CBM): key features
  - Measurement and evaluation system that assesses items taken from the curriculum
  - Applied frequently (e.g., weekly, monthly)
  - Guides and informs instruction
  - Is a data-based practice that causes improvement in students' learning

 **myeducationlab** Now go to MyEducationLab at www.myeducationlab.com and take the Self-Assessment to gauge your initial comprehension of chapter content. Once you have taken the Self-Assessment, use your individualized Study Plan for Chapter 5 to enhance your understanding of the concepts discussed in the chapter.

Council for Exceptional Children ADDRESSING THE PROFESSIONAL STANDARDS

Council for Exceptional Children (CEC) knowledge standards addressed in this chapter:

LD1K1, LD1K5, LD2K1, LD8S1, LD4S9, LD4S9, LD5S1, LD10K1, LD10K2

Appendix A: CEC Knowledge and Skill Standards Common Core has a full listing of the standards listed here.

Appendix B: CSE Knowledge and Skill Common Core Standards and Associated Subcategories are broken down by chapter.

CHAPTER 6

Attention Deficit Hyperactivity Disorder

Naomi Chowdhuri Tyler

Imagine a World . . .

where all human energy is channeled to success and accomplishment

Chapter Objectives

As you read this chapter, ponder these students' needs, the supports they require, and the outcomes they should achieve. After studying this chapter, you will be able to

1. Recognize the characteristics of students with ADHD.

2. Understand the relationship of ADHD to other, coexisting disabilities.

3. Understand medical treatment of ADHD.

4. Identify specific accommodations and classroom interventions used with students with ADHD.

5. Discuss the importance of collaborating and developing partnerships with families and with other professionals.

Dave Cole is a sculptor whose work has been highlighted in such diverse places as the Judi Rotenberg Gallery in Boston, the Haifa Museum of Art in Israel, and the National Gallery of Art in Norway. Dave's artwork has always been an important part of his life, in some respects providing a wonderful escape from the struggles he faced in school because of his ADHD. In college, he and Jonathan Mooney (see the Making a Difference section later in this chapter) partnered to write *Learning Outside the Lines* and founded Project Eye-to-Eye, both of which provide support to students with learning disabilities and ADHD.

Look at the inset picture to better see that Dave constructed the flag by using toy soldiers.

attention deficit hyperactivity disorder (ADHD) A condition of hyperactivity, impulsivity, inattention; included in other health impairments

In recent years, educators, parents, and policymakers have expressed concerns about a large group of today's students. Teachers report that many of their students have great difficulty paying attention. Parents are confused by some of their children's behavior, reporting that these children are disorganized, distracted, or even defiant. Teachers and parents describe this group of students as in "constant motion." A good portion of them has difficulty meeting the expectations of the general education curriculum; their educational performance is negatively influenced. In response, Congress called out the condition, **attention deficit hyperactivity disorder (ADHD)**, in its 1997 reauthorization of the IDEA law.

IDEA '04 does not list ADHD as a separate disability category but instead includes it under the category of "other health impairments." However, teachers and parents consistently note that it is a condition frequently seen among students in America's schools. They report that these students are substantially different from their peers and cause concern because of their inability to focus their attention or control their behavior. Although ADHD is not a distinct IDEA '04 disability category, most teachers are likely to encounter many students who exhibit these characteristics; thus, an entire chapter of this book is devoted to ADHD.

Where We've Been ... What's on the Horizon?

Considerable controversy has surrounded ADHD for decades. There is scientific evidence for the existence of the disorder, and effective treatment options exist for children with ADHD characteristics. However, the validity of the diagnoses and the increasing rates of medical treatment for what some consider typical, energetic behaviors of childhood have received a great deal of public attention (Barkley, 2002, 2005; Kendall et al., 2003). Before the 1997 reauthorization of IDEA, ADHD was considered a symptom of other conditions (e.g., learning disabilities, traumatic brain injury, or emotional or behavioral disorders), and officials were confident that students with ADHD who required special education services were receiving them through the various IDEA disability categories (U.S. Department of Education, 2006). Subsequently, during the 1997 IDEA reauthorization, ADHD was included within the category of "other health impairments" but was not identified as a distinct category of its own. (See What IDEA '04 Says About ADHD for more information about this condition and the law.) Thus, although ADHD might be one of the "newest" conditions recognized by IDEA, it is neither newly discovered nor only recently studied.

Historical Context

In the 1840s, Dr. Heinrich Hoffmann of Germany published a children's book of playful poems and stories filled with characters such as Slovenly Peter, Proud Phoebe Ann, and Idle Fritz, meant to teach young children about the pitfalls of improper behaviors (Hoffman, 1999). "The Story of Fidgety Philip," one of the more famous poems from the book (see the accompanying excerpt), describes a child who clearly has many of the characteristics of ADHD (Barkley, 2006). However, Dr. George Still, a British physician, is generally considered to have been the first to officially document the characteristics that we now associate with ADHD (Barkley, 2006; Gephart, 2003). In his classic 1902 article "Some Abnormal Psychical Conditions in Children," he described children who had problems with inattention and impulsivity, which he attributed to a "defect of moral control" (Still, 1902). Similar to current findings, Still noted the greater prevalence among boys than girls and that most cases were apparent in early childhood.

What Idea '04 Says About ...

Attention Deficit Hyperactivity Disorder (ADHD)

Children with ADHD are not automatically protected by IDEA. Specifically, students with ADHD

- are not guaranteed eligibility for special education or related services, even with medical diagnoses and medication prescriptions;

- are specifically called out under the "other health impairments" category, which does not list every disability and condition;

- may also be eligible for services under other categories, such as learning disabilities and emotional and behavioral disorders;

- may receive special education services if the condition adversely affects educational performance.

Interest in ADHD characteristics was heightened after a 1917–1918 encephalitis epidemic, when doctors noticed distinct behavioral and cognitive issues in children who had survived the brain infection, including problems with attention, activity regulation, and impulsivity (Barkley, 2006). Subsequent researchers in the 1930s and 1940s posited a theory of brain injury (Strauss & Lehtinen, 1947), which was eventually modified to include milder terminology such as "minimal brain dysfunction" when no clear evidence of actual brain injury could be found (Barkley, 2006). Educational practices at that time included instructional environments that were completely distraction-free, where even wearing jewelry was discouraged to avoid distractions for the students (despite the lack of evidence verifying the effectiveness of these practices). Research in the 1960s focused primarily on hyperactivity, while the 1970s saw increased awareness of the problems associated with poor attention span and impulse control. Although studies during this time period became more rigorous with regard to medical treatment for these characteristics (i.e., stimulant use), non-validated treatments that focused on the reduction of sugar and food additives in a child's diet became popular, as did the unfounded belief that hyperactivity could be attributed to poor child-rearing practices. Luckily, studies in the 1980s continued to show the effectiveness of stimulant medication and showed that some of the more negative and controlling parenting behaviors observed by researchers—and initially thought to have caused the child's behavior—were in fact developed in response to their children's inability to effectively control their own actions. Neuroimaging studies conducted during the last 15 years have further verified a biological basis for this disorder, with clear indications of reduced activity in regions of the brain that control attention and inhibition. More recently, identifying characteristics of the disorder have become more refined, and three main subtypes are now distinguished: Predominantly Inattentive, Hyperactive-Impulsive, or Combined Type (in which children display inattentiveness as well as hyperactivity and impulsiveness). Cognitive-behavioral therapy, which trains children to use self-regulation techniques such as self-evaluation, self-correction, and self-talk (discussed in more detail later in this chapter), has been shown to be an effective addition to medical treatment, with a specific focus on improvement of academic skills. Despite the fact that ADHD is the most heavily researched childhood disorder, its history is replete with practices that were not research validated but instead based on popular public opinion. Unfortunately, the often-sensationalized media coverage of ADHD still results in many public misperceptions of this disorder (Barkley, 2006; Children and Adults with Attention-Deficit/Hyperactivity Disorder [CHADD], 2007).

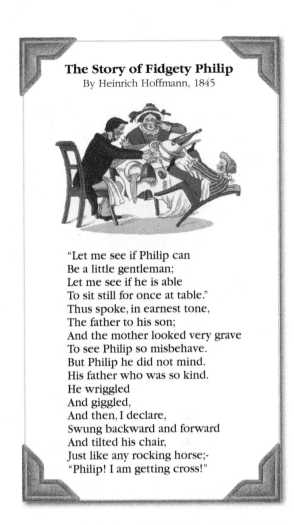

The Story of Fidgety Philip
By Heinrich Hoffmann, 1845

"Let me see if Philip can
Be a little gentleman;
Let me see if he is able
To sit still for once at table."
Thus spoke, in earnest tone,
The father to his son;
And the mother looked very grave
To see Philip so misbehave.
But Philip he did not mind.
His father who was so kind.
He wriggled
And giggled,
And then, I declare,
Swung backward and forward
And tilted his chair,
Just like any rocking horse;-
"Philip! I am getting cross!"

This excerpt and drawing are from the famous poem about Fidgety Philip, who exhibited many of the characteristics we typically associate with ADHD.

Source: From Virginia Commonwealth University, http://www.fln.vcu.edu/struwwel/philipp_e.html

Challenges That ADHD Presents

Many students, not just those diagnosed with ADHD, experience inattentiveness, hyperactivity, or impulsivity. However, students and adults diagnosed with ADHD exhibit these symptoms to such a marked degree that they interfere with many daily activities. In addition, individuals with ADHD face many related challenges in their lives. For example, these students are particularly at risk for failing in school, being suspended, abusing substances, dropping out of school, and having a very high rate of conflicts with their families over doing chores and their homework assignments (Salend & Rohena, 2003). Parents of these students often express frustration and stress (Barkley, 2005), while their children believe that they can never meet their parents' expectations. ADHD can also negatively influence these students' relationships with others. Because of their hyperactivity and poor social skills, many students with ADHD can be rejected by their peers and disliked by their teachers (Bryan, 1997; Olmeda, Thomas, & Davis, 2003), leaving them friendless and lonely.

THE STORY OF JOEY PIGZA

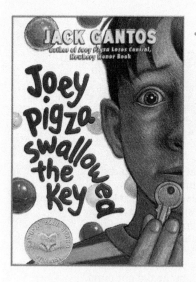

Joey Pigza Swallowed the Key is the story of a young boy's experiences with ADHD. Hysterically funny at some points, heart-wrenchingly painful at others, this wonderful book gives readers an inside look into the mind of a child with ADHD.

At school they say I'm wired bad, or wired mad, or wired sad, or wired glad, depending on my mood and what teacher has ended up with me. But there is no doubt about it, I'm wired.

This year was no different. When I started out, all the days there looked about the same. In the morning I'd be okay and follow along in class. But after lunch, when my meds had worn down, it was nothing but trouble for me.

One day, we were doing math drills in class and every time Mrs. Maxy asked a question, like "What's nine times nine?" I'd raise my hand because I'm really quick at math. But each time she called on me, even though I knew the answer, I'd just blurt out, "Can I get back to you on that?" Then I'd nearly fall out of my chair from laughing. And she'd give me that whitelipped look which meant, "Settle down." But I didn't and kept raising my hand each time she asked a question until finally no other kid would raise their hand because they knew what was coming between me and Mrs. Maxy.

"Okay, Joey," she'd say, calling on me and staring hard at my face as if her eyes were long fingers that could grip me by the chin. I'd stare right back and hesitate a second as if I was planning to answer the question and then I'd holler out really loud, "Can I get back to you on that?" Finally, after a bunch of times of me doing that in a row, she jerked her thumb toward the door. "Out in the hall," she said. And the class cracked up.

So I went and stood in the hall for about a second until I remembered the mini-Superball in my pocket and started to bounce it off the lockers and ceiling and after Mrs. Deebs in the next class stuck her head out her door and yelled, "Hey, cut the racket," like she was yelling at a stray cat, I remembered something I wanted to try. I had seen the Tasmanian Devil on TV whirling around like a top so I unbuckled my belt and pulled on the end really hard, as if I was trying to start a lawn mower. But that didn't get me spinning very fast. So I took out my high-top shoelaces and tied them together and then to the belt and wrapped it all around my waist. Then I grabbed one end and yanked on it and sort of got myself spinning. I kept doing it until I got better and better and before long I was bouncing off the lockers because I was dizzy too. Then I gave myself one more really good pull on the belt and because I was already dizzy I got going really fast and began to snort and grunt like the Tasmanian Devil until Mrs. Maxy came out and clamped her hands down on my shoulders. She stopped me so fast I spun right out of my shoes and they went shooting up the hall.

"You glue your feet to the floor for five whole minutes or you can just spin yourself down to the principal's office," she said. "Now, what is your choice going to be?"

"Can I get back to you on that?" I asked.

Source: From *Joey Pigza Swallowed the Key* (pp. 3–6) by Jack Gantos, 1998, New York: Farrar, Straus, & Giroux. Cover photo used by permission of HarperCollins Publishers.

"The Story of Joey Pigza" provides a humorous portrait of one child with ADHD and the effect of his behavior on his classroom.

Although professionals once believed that children and youth with ADHD would "grow out of their problems," we now know that for most individuals, the symptoms continue throughout their lives (Barkley, 2005, 2006; Weyandt et al., 2003). The characteristics associated with ADHD can affect adult life in many ways. For example, Kessler and colleagues (2005) found that ADHD was associated with an average of 35 lost days of work per year, totaling more than $19 billion in wasted human capital nationally. Adults with ADHD can have very successful lives, but they often require accurate identification and effective services (CHADD, 2007).

Several of these students may have ADHD; the exact numbers are difficult to determine.

Making a Difference

Project Eye-to-Eye

ADHD symptoms of inattention and hyperactivity-impulsivity are self-reported among many college students, including those who have not been diagnosed with the disorder, but professionals estimate that 2% to 4% of college students may have ADHD (DuPaul et al., 2001). These students often struggle without support or knowing others with similar experiences.

Three young men with firsthand knowledge about these frustrations decided to help others and give young students the assistance that they themselves didn't have. Jonathan Mooney and David Cole, two graduates of Brown University, wrote *Learning Outside the Lines,* a handbook for college students with LD/ADHD. They then founded Project Eye-to-Eye, a mentoring program in which college students with LD/ADHD work with public school students with LD/ADHD. David Flink, another Brown alum with a learning disability, helped found the national Project Eye-to-Eye organization and is managing director of the program, currently based in New York City.

The project's mission is to develop a nationwide coalition of partnerships with local community organizations to provide mentors for students with LD/ADHD. The overriding principle is that of empowerment through building self-esteem. The program seeks to facilitate academic achievement through self-advocacy, the development of metacognitive skills, and the use of learning strategies and academic accommodations. Art is a key component of the project, through which students are encouraged to express themselves, empowered to develop strengths, and validated as having unique gifts. An additional project goal is that of parental networking, which connects parents to information and support and enables them to advocate better for their children. Finally, the project provides its members with opportunities for professional development.

Project Eye-to-Eye currently has 24 chapters nationwide, with each site serving mentor–student pairs, parents, and university/school professionals. The mentors spend at least 2 hours per week with their mentees, 1 hour engaged in artistic endeavors and 1 hour outside the art classroom. The project also uses a cohort of speakers, Mouth-to-Mouth, who (along with Mooney, the executive director), talk to thousands of people per year, increasing information dissemination.

For more information on this project, contact Project Eye-to-Eye; 180 West End Ave., #16E, New York, NY 10023; (917) 755-8865; **info@projecteyetoeye.org.**

The cofounders of Project Eye-to-Eye are Jonathan Mooney (above), David Cole (the artist featured at the beginning of this chapter), and David Flink (below).

Attention Deficit Hyperactivity Disorder Defined

Although many people refer to ADHD as attention deficit disorder (ADD), the medically correct term is *attention deficit hyperactivity disorder* (Fowler, 2004). Possibly because ADHD is not a separate disability category under IDEA '04, the condition is not uniformly understood. The federal government provides little guidance to states and school districts about the definition to use when identifying students with this condition and qualifying them as eligible for special education services under the "other health impairment" category. In the United States, the most widely accepted and used definition of ADHD is the one developed by the American Psychiatric Association (APA) in its *Diagnostic and Statistical Manual of Mental Disorders* (DSM-IV-TR) which has a stronger medical theme for diagnosis than the federal criteria. Table 6.1 provides both the IDEA and the DSM-IV-TR definitions. It is important to note that the DSM-IV-TR further breaks down ADHD into three subcategories: Predominantly Inattentive, Predominantly Hyperactive-Impulsive, and Combined.

While nearly everyone, both children and adults, can exhibit inattention, excessive activity, or impulsivity (DuPaul et al., 2001), the DSM-IV-TR further explains ADHD by stating that it "is a persistent pattern of inattention and/or hyperactivity-impulsivity that is more frequent and severe than is typically observed in individuals at a comparable level of development" (APA, 2000, p. 85). Furthermore, these characteristics signal ADHD only when they become excessive and cause "significant impairment in social, academic, or occupational functioning" (APA, 2000, p. 93). Symptoms of the condition must have been present before age 7, endured for at least 6 months, and occur in more than one setting.

General Education Students with ADHD

Like some students with other health impairments whose conditions do not affect their educational performance (see Chapter 9), not all students with ADHD qualify for special education services. If the condition does not cause school failure, students may receive accommodations (such as extended time on tests or assignments) through Section 504 of the Rehabilitation Act, instead of direct special education services to address their unique learning needs. Unfortunately, many professionals feel that Section 504 accommodations are insufficient for students with ADHD (Denckla, 2007).

Special Education Students with ADHD

To qualify for special education services through the IDEA '04 "other health impairments" category because of ADHD, individuals must "experience heightened alertness to environmental stimuli, which results in limited alertness to their educational environment," which adversely affects educational performance (U.S. Department of Education, 2006). In other words, a student with ADHD could be so focused on extraneous classroom events, such as another student's pencil tapping, that he or she is unable to focus on the priority at hand, such as the teacher's lesson.

Coexisting Disabilities

comorbidity Coexisting disabilities

For most students, ADHD coexists with another disability (Pierce, 2003), a situation commonly referred to as **comorbidity**. Because the characteristics of ADHD overlap with other disabilities (e.g., learning disabilities or emotional or behavioral disorders), students with ADHD are often served under these categories.

Comorbidity with Learning Disabilities While estimates vary greatly, research findings indicate that approximately one-third of all students with ADHD have coexisting learning disabilities (DuPaul & Stoner, 2003). Many students with ADHD do score higher on tests of intelligence than other students, including those individuals with learning disabilities and significant reading problems (Kaplan et al., 2000). However, they do tend to score lower on standardized achievement tests than their classmates without disabilities (Barkley, 2006). Studies on whether these students are more likely to have

Table 6.1 • Definitions of ADHD

Source	Definition
Federal government	Defined as one condition included under the "Other Health Impairments" category *having limited strength, vitality or alertness, including heightened alertness to environmental stimuli, that results in limited alertness with respect to the educational environment . . . .* *adversely affects a child's educational performance* **IDEA '97 Final Regulations, 1999, p. 12422**
DSM-IV-TR	**A.** Either (1) or (2) **(1)** six (or more) of the following symptoms of **inattention** have persisted for at least 6 months to a degree that is maladaptive and inconsistent with developmental level: *Inattention* a. often fails to give close attention to details or makes careless mistakes in schoolwork, work, or other activities b. often has difficulty sustaining attention in tasks or play activities c. often does not seem to listen when spoken to directly d. often does not follow through on instructions and fails to finish schoolwork, chores, or duties in the workplace (not due to oppositional behavior or failure to understand instructions) e. often has difficulty organizing tasks and activities f. often avoids dislikes, or is reluctant to engage in tasks that require sustained mental effort (such as schoolwork or homework) g. often loses things necessary for tasks or activities (e.g., toys, school assignments, pencils, books, or tools) h. is often easily distracted by extraneous stimuli i. is often forgetful in daily activities **(2)** six (or more) of the following symptoms of **hyperactivity-impulsivity** have persisted for at least 6 months to a degree that is maladaptive and inconsistent with developmental level: *Hyperactivity* a. often fidgets with hands or feet or squirms in seat b. often leaves seat in classroom or in other situations in which remaining seat is expected c. often runs about or climbs excessively in situations in which it is inappropriate (in adolescents or adults, may be limited to subjective feelings of restlessness) d. often has difficulty playing or engaging in leisure activities quietly e. is often "on the go" or often acts as if "driven by a motor" f. often talks excessively *Impulsivity* g. often blurts out answers before questions have been completed h. often has difficulty awaiting turn i. often interrupts or intrudes on others (e.g., butts into conversations or games) **B.** Some hyperactive-impulsive or inattentive symptoms that caused impairment were present before age 7 years. **C.** Some impairment from the symptoms is present in two or more settings (e.g., at school, work, or home). **D.** There must be clear evidence of clinically significant impairment in social, academic or occupational functioning. **E.** The symptoms do not occur exclusively during the course of a Pervasive Developmental Disorder, Schizophrenia, or other Psychotic Disorder and are not better accounted for by another mental disorder (e.g., Mood Disorder, Anxiety Disorder, Dissociative Disorder, or a Personality Disorder). Code based on type: **Attention-Deficit/Hyperactivity Disorder, Combined Type:** if both Criteria A1 and A2 are met for the past 6 months. **Attention-Deficit/Hyperactivity Disorder, Predominantly Inattentive Type:** If Criterion A1 is met but Criterion A2 is not met for the past 6 months. **Attention-Deficit/Hyperactivity Disorder, Predominantly Hyperactive-Impulsive Type:** If Criterion A2 is met but Criterion A1 is not met for the past 6 months. **APA (2003, pp. 92–93)**

Sources: From 34 *CFR* Parts 300 and 303, Assistance to States for the Education of Children with Disabilities and the Early Intervention Program for Infants and Toddlers with Disabilities; Final Regulations (p. 12422), U.S. Department of Education, 1999, *Federal Register,* Washington, DC; and Reprinted with permission from the *Diagnostic and Statistical Manual of Mental Disorders, Text Revision, Fourth Edition,* (Copyright 2003). American Psychiatric Association.

problems with written communication, reading, math, or spelling have yielded conflicting results (Mayes, Calhoun, & Crowell, 2000; Willcutt & Pennington, 2000). Some experts believe that these students fall into separate cognitive, biological, and behavioral subgroups (Bonafina et al., 2000). Whether subgrouping has any usefulness to teachers at the moment is unclear. What each of these students requires is an individualized educational program to meet his or her specific learning needs.

Comorbidity with Emotional or Behavioral Disorders Students with ADHD often have coexisting emotional or behavioral disorders (Pierce, 2003). In one study, approximately 58% of students receiving special education services under the emotional or behavioral disorders category also had ADHD (Schnoes et al., 2007). Boys exhibit more aggressive and antisocial behavior, resulting in higher referral rates for this category. Many studies show very small samples of girls, who exhibit equal levels of impulsiveness but are referred for the EBD category less often due to lower levels of hyperactivity, aggression, defiance, and conduct problems (Barkley, 2006).

Characteristics

Students with ADHD often exhibit characteristics that undermine success in school (Carlson et al., 2002). They rely, more than others, on external factors to explain their accomplishments, and therefore they are less persistent, expend less effort, prefer easier work, and take less enjoyment in learning.

Behavioral Characteristics

At the root of many academic problems experienced by students with ADHD is at least one of these three behavioral characteristics:

- Inattention
- Hyperactivity
- Impulsivity

These characteristics explain why the students seem to daydream, miss the little (but important) details about assignments, and submit perpetually incomplete schoolwork (Salend, Elhoweris, & van Garderen, 2003). Look again at Table 6.1 and the DSM-IV-TR types of ADHD. The key characteristics are discussed in more detail next.

inattention Inability to pay attention or focus

Inattention **Inattention** is a characteristic commonly observed by parents, teachers, and researchers, particularly when sustained effort is required (Fowler, 2002, 2004; Montague & Dietz, 2006). For example, students with ADHD may miss many problems on a math sheet, even when it is clear that they have the skills needed to

Inattention—a characteristic of ADHD—is often misunderstood as daydreaming or simply not paying attention to the important task of the moment such as studying.

complete them accurately, because they get distracted and do not focus for the seemingly short time span required to complete each individual problem. Students who cannot focus on the smaller details of a task or who pay attention to the wrong features of the task are also said to be inattentive. Carelessness, distractibility, and forgetfulness are all associated with inattention. Problems with attention make it challenging for students to approach learning in an organized or efficient fashion and to shift from one task to another, making transitions from one activity to another difficult.

Hyperactivity Hyperactivity is another defining symptom of ADHD. **Hyperactivity**, while implying an excessive level of activity (Montague & Dietz, 2006), is often difficult to define because the judgment about whether a certain level of a specific activity is too much is subjective. If, for example, the activity is admired, the child might be described as energetic or enthusiastic rather than hyperactive. If the activity is annoying, teachers often describe the individual as "fidgety," "squirming in the chair," or "continually off task" (Fowler, 2002). The DSM-IV-TR also gives some good examples about which there is considerable consensus (APA, 2003). Look again at Table 6.1, reread the DSM-IV-TR description of hyperactivity, and think of individuals you know who display these characteristics.

hyperactivity Impaired ability to sit or concentrate for long periods of time

Some research indicates that hyperactivity diminishes with age (Biederman, Mick, & Garaone, 2000), as students learn to better control their behavior. However, when compared to their same-age peers, adolescents still show significantly greater levels of restlessness and activity (DuPaul & Stoner, 2003). Furthermore, adolescents and adults with ADHD may have continued trouble with distractions due to daydreaming or an ongoing stream of thoughts and ideas flowing through their minds at times when concentration is necessary, such as during a college course or business meeting (Shaw & Giambra, 1993). Still others report that although excessive activity is reduced, it is replaced with feelings of internal restlessness (Weyandt et al., 2003).

Impulsivity The third characteristic, **impulsivity**, is commonly observed among students with ADHD (APA, 2003). Montague and Dietz (2006) describe impulsivity as "an inability to control one's responses to the environment" (p. 1). These students tend to blurt out a quick response before thinking the question through (remember Joey Pigza?). They tend to redirect the topic of class discussion, talk out of turn, or "butt into conversations" (APA, 2003; Fowler, 2002, 2004). These actions add up to fewer positive responses from their classmates and decreased social acceptance (Merrell & Boelter, 2001).

Impulsivity Impaired ability to control one's own behavior

myeducationlab Go to the Activities and Application section in Chapter 6 of MyEducationLab, and complete Activity 1. As you watch the video and answer the questions see if Eric's behavior reflects any of the characteristics discussed here.

Academic Performance

Many students with ADHD experience considerable difficulty with academic performance. Because of their distractibility and inability to focus, they spend less time engaging in academic tasks than their classmates without ADHD (Duhaney, 2003). The result is often lower grades and increased risk for school failure. These students have trouble studying for long periods of time. They tend to be disorganized and forgetful. These are the students who can't find their homework, forgot when an assignment was due, or meant to get the permission form for the field trip signed by a parent . . . but didn't. Many teachers comment that these students' handwriting is messy, their work is sloppy and careless, their assignments are often incomplete, and the work they turn in is not logical or presented in an organized way (Fowler, 2002).

These students, more than others, need structure to support their learning and social performance (Salend et al., 2003). Teachers can help in many ways. First—and this benefits *all* students in class—they should make assignments interesting, individualized when possible, and relevant to students' backgrounds and interests. Content enhancements and the use of learning strategies are also of great benefit. Graphic organizers (see A Closer Look at Data-Based Practices in Chapter 4 for an example) and study guides help students organize their thinking and their work.

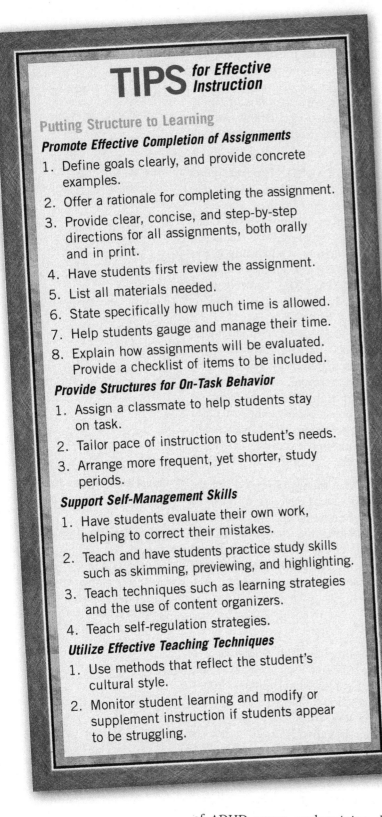

TIPS for Effective Instruction

Putting Structure to Learning

Promote Effective Completion of Assignments

1. Define goals clearly, and provide concrete examples.
2. Offer a rationale for completing the assignment.
3. Provide clear, concise, and step-by-step directions for all assignments, both orally and in print.
4. Have students first review the assignment.
5. List all materials needed.
6. State specifically how much time is allowed.
7. Help students gauge and manage their time.
8. Explain how assignments will be evaluated. Provide a checklist of items to be included.

Provide Structures for On-Task Behavior

1. Assign a classmate to help students stay on task.
2. Tailor pace of instruction to student's needs.
3. Arrange more frequent, yet shorter, study periods.

Support Self-Management Skills

1. Have students evaluate their own work, helping to correct their mistakes.
2. Teach and have students practice study skills such as skimming, previewing, and highlighting.
3. Teach techniques such as learning strategies and the use of content organizers.
4. Teach self-regulation strategies.

Utilize Effective Teaching Techniques

1. Use methods that reflect the student's cultural style.
2. Monitor student learning and modify or supplement instruction if students appear to be struggling.

Such aids, as well as those tactics listed in Tips for Effective Instruction, provide ways to help students with ADHD approach tasks and complete their work. General behavioral supports—that are also helpful for *all* students—can include clear and concise directions, advance notice about upcoming changes in activities, prompts for students who appear to be slipping off task, and consistent, predictable schedules.

Social Behavior

As ADHD characteristics (inattention, hyperactivity, impulsivity) intensify, positive social interactions decrease and antisocial behaviors increase (Merrell & Boelter, 2001). Surprisingly, students with ADHD also describe themselves as having more internalizing behaviors and are more introspective about their problems (Volpe et al., 1999). Because of the rejection discussed earlier, they often judge themselves as social failures and engage in more solitary activities (playing computer games, watching television), contributing to a cycle of increasing alienation and withdrawal. Fortunately, teachers can help students engage in more socially appropriate behavior (turn taking in conversations, asking to join a game rather than barging in and grabbing equipment) by

- providing explicit instruction on how to interact with others and behave in a more socially appropriate manner,
- using functional behavioral assessment data (discussed in Chapter 7) to reduce or eliminate inappropriate behaviors, and
- teaching self-management strategies (discussed later in this chapter) that include rewards for conforming to classroom rules (Reid & Lienemen, 2006; Reid, Trout, & Schartz, 2005).

For students with ADHD who do not qualify for special education services, general educators must make accommodations to the learning environment so that instruction meets their individual needs and academic performance is not forfeited.

Remember, it is the excessive degree to which the specific distracting behaviors of ADHD occur, undermining daily functioning, that is crucial for identification. Most visitors to a classroom can pick out the students with ADHD. They are the students who need to sharpen their pencils more often than their classmates, look for something on the bookshelf several times during quiet time, or play with objects on the desk during the teacher's lecture (Duhaney, 2003). Although these students are seemingly always in trouble, most of their infractions are relatively minor. But when totaled up for an entire school day, the excessiveness of the disturbances becomes readily apparent. Teachers can help these students manage their disruptive and distracting behaviors by planning ahead and implementing some simple procedures, such as those listed in Tips for Classroom Management (Carbone, 2001; Duhaney, 2003).

Although parents and teachers may tend to focus on the negative aspects of ADHD, there are positive characteristics as well. For example, intense creativity, intuitiveness, emotional awareness, and exuberance (see the accompanying photo of Olympic medalist Michael Phelps) are all positive traits associated with ADHD (Honos-Webb, 2005). Individuals with ADHD may take an unusual or nonstandard approach to problem solving, look at situations from a different perspective, and exhibit an ability to "think outside the box" (Hallowell & Ratey, 2005). JetBlue's CEO David Neeleman, for example, attributes his success as an entrepreneur to these positive ADHD traits.

TIPS for Classroom Management
PUTTING STRUCTURE TO BEHAVIOR

Managing the Physical Environment

1. Keep loud noise and distractions to a minimum.
2. Arrange desks for efficient traffic flow.
3. Dismiss students in small groups.

Preventing Problem Behaviors

1. Have a comprehensive behavior management plan.
2. Remind students of classroom rules.
3. Provide frequent feedback.
4. Deliver positive consequences immediately and frequently.
5. Introduce new activities and schedules incrementally.

Supporting Student Independence

1. Teach and support time management skills.
2. Teach students self-regulation strategies.
3. Warn students of approaching transitions (e.g., time for a new activity).

Intervening for Problem Behaviors

1. Stand close to the student (proximity control).
2. Avoid drawing attention to the student's behavior.
3. Conceal your frustration and redirect behavior.
4. Explain clearly why the behavior is inappropriate.
5. Provide alternatives (e.g., teach students to count to 5 before raising their hand).

myeducationlab) Go to the Activities and Applications section in Chapter 6 of MyEducationLab and complete Activity 3. View the IRIS Case Study, "Effective Room Arrangements," and complete the assignments to develop your understanding of how effective room arrangements promote student suc-

Going for the gold! Michael Phelps, who openly discusses his having ADHD, set world record after world record, claiming eight gold medals in swimming at the 2008 Olympics in Beijing.

Prevalence

No national registry or required reporting system exists for ADHD, so exact numbers of children with ADHD are unavailable. However, there is general consensus that 3% to 7% of schoolchildren have ADHD (Barkley, 2006; CHADD, 2008; DuPaul & Stoner, 2003; NIMH, 2006). While boys are generally identified at significantly higher rates, some studies (e.g., Dietz & Montague, 2006) have shown that girls are under-identified, possibly due to a lack of awareness of how their behavioral needs differ from those of boys.

There is also no answer to the question "How many students receive special education services?" You are probably thinking that even though the number of students in America with ADHD is unknown, the government must know how many students with ADHD receive special education services. But it's just not that simple. As you have learned in previous chapters, IDEA '04 requires states to report each year the number of students with disabilities, by disability category (e.g., learning disabilities, intellectual disabilities), that they serve. However, states report the number of students served only by their *primary* disability. Because ADHD is only one condition of many included in the "other health impairments" category, these students are reported as falling in that category and so cannot be counted separately as having ADHD. Further complicating the problem is the fact that ADHD coexists with many other disabilities. Thus, many students with ADHD are counted in the learning disabilities category, others in the emotional or behavioral disorders category, some in the mental retardation or intellectual disabilities category, and a few with their peers who have traumatic brain injury. This is why the number of students with ADHD who receive special education services is unknown, as is the overall number of these students attending public school.

Is ADHD increasing? This is another question with no clear answer. Because (for the reasons just listed) a historical record of the prevalence of ADHD does not exist, it is impossible to know with any confidence whether the number of students with ADHD is increasing more rapidly than the student population in general. While some speculate that we are overidentifying students with ADHD, others counter that less than half of all children with ADHD are receiving the proper diagnosis and treatment (Barkley, 2005).

Are more schoolchildren identified with ADHD in the United States than in other countries? Here we can give you a definitive answer: No. Remember that U.S. prevalence estimates indicate between 3% and 7% of all schoolchildren have ADHD. In comparison, the prevalence rates in Japan (up to 7%), China (6% to 8%), and New Zealand (up to 7%) are quite similar to those in the United States, while countries such as Germany (18%) and Ukraine (20%) showed much higher prevalence rates (Barkley, 2006). Here is an interesting prevalence study: Only slightly more than 2% of Australian schoolchildren were identified as having ADHD because researchers required that parent and teacher behavior ratings had to agree. While parents identified 10% of all schoolchildren and teachers identified 9%, by and large they were different children. When the child had to be identified by both parents and teachers, only 2% of all students were noted as having ADHD (Gomez et al., 1999, as cited in Barkley, 2006). As illustrated in the Australian example, researchers' choices of diagnostic tools or decisions about how to interpret findings can cause significant differences in their results. Even switching from one edition of the APA's diagnostic manual to the next (e.g., the DSM-III to the DSM-IV or to the DSM-IV-TR) can impact prevalence data.

In the United States, experts are beginning to understand the danger of misinterpreting the behaviors of students from diverse cultures as signaling a dis-

Considering Culture: *High Energy, Low Performance*

Derek's transition from elementary school to middle school has been a disaster so far. He is late to classes because he has trouble remembering where the next room is. His homework is usually late, if it is turned in at all, and it always looks as if it has been retrieved from a garbage can. When teachers call on him in class, he doesn't know what they have been talking about or where they are in the lesson. In gym class and on the school campus, he seems to have boundless energy, but he never applies it to accomplish what needs to be done. Concerned about Derek's performance, his teacher, Mr. Neumann, calls Derek's home. Derek's grandmother answers and says, "I'm glad you called. I don't know what to do with that boy. His mother is gone, his father works two jobs, and I'm in charge. Trouble is, I'm 77 and not doing so well myself. I know that Derek wants to do well in school, but he just can't seem to get himself together, and you know how hard it is for African American kids growing up. I'm afraid that if he's not successful at school, he may fall in with the wrong crowd."

Mr. Neumann gets Derek's father's permission for some assessments and permission to talk with his former teachers and the special education resource teacher at the middle school. Mrs. McDonald, his fifth-grade teacher, says, "Derek's always had trouble staying organized, but he's smart and a really cool kid. I helped him find ways to stay organized with different-colored pocket folders, notebooks, and labels. We also developed a quiet signal in class to help Derek pay attention. Of course, middle school presents more challenges, but I'm sure he'll do well with some help."

The assessment results showed that Derek is smart; in some areas, he even scored above grade level. But the results also showed that he has difficulty staying on task, following through with assignments and activities, and focusing on solving problems. When the information was shared with the IEP team, they decided that Derek does have ADHD but that he should remain in Mr. Neumann's class, with consultation from the special education teacher. Now Derek has a special place to keep his school books, notebooks, and papers at home and at school. His notebooks include sections for assignments, homework, and notes from each class. He has a list of things to do each day and when to do them. He also has a group of friends who walk with him from class to class. To help Derek direct some of his boundless energy, Mr. Neumann has arranged for him to try out for some after-school sports teams, where he is an enthusiastic and developing player. The after-school sports have even given Derek's grandmother support in the form of adult supervision, and the grade requirement for athletes has motivated Derek to do well in school. Now that he is doing so much better in school, his father and grandmother worry much less about his future.

Questions to Consider

1. What do you think your first response might be to a student who doesn't pay attention in class, is very active, and is completely disorganized?

2. What do you think might have happened in Derek's life if his teachers, his grandmother, his father, and other members of the IEP team had simply seen him as a "difficult" student?

—By Eleanor Lynch, San Diego State University, and Marci Hanson, San Francisco State University

ability, rather than a mismatch between the culture of the school and teachers and that of the student (Gay, 2002). Experts tend to agree that culture may be an important factor to consider, not only in understanding behavior patterns that don't match those of classmates, but also in selecting the best interventions to help students improve. Considering Culture describes a scenario in which school personnel and family members work together to improve the educational outcomes for a student with ADHD.

Causes and Prevention

Scientists are working diligently to identify the causes of ADHD, for without understanding the direct causes of any disability, it is nearly impossible to figure out how to prevent or correct the problem. New information is changing the ways in which investigators are interpreting ADHD and its origins (Office of Special Education Programs [OSEP], 2003). For example, the problem was once thought to be associated mainly with difficulties related to attention, but today more emphasis is being placed on behavioral inhibition—specifically, an impairment in the ability to inhibit or control one's behavior or an impairment in delayed responding (Barkley, 2006; Dillon & Osborne, 2006).

Causes

The exact causes of ADHD are not known, but researchers believe the condition arises from many different sources that could include some sort of brain injury (from either trauma or infection), genetic contributions, and risk factors such as the prenatal use of alcohol and tobacco (Dillon & Osborne, 2006; DuPaul & Stoner, 2003). A biological predisposition places some individuals more at risk for developing ADHD. Most experts believe the condition is due to inherent differences in the way the brains of individuals with ADHD function (Barkley, 2002, 2006; Fowler, 2002), which supports the growing consensus that ADHD has a neurological basis (Salend & Rohena, 2003). A body of research is now focused on the **executive functions** of children with ADHD (Barkley, 2006)—the cognitive abilities that enable us to plan, self-regulate, inhibit inappropriate behaviors, and engage in goal-directed activities (Bernstein & Waber, 2007; Meltzer, 2007; Meltzer & Krishnan, 2007; Moran & Gardner, 2007). These executive functions, though associated primarily with the frontal lobes and prefrontal cortex of the brain, involve detailed connections between various other brain regions as well. It also appears that genetics may contribute to ADHD; the condition is often observed in many members of the same family (Barkley, 2002, 2006; National Institute of Mental Health [NIMH], 2006). Of course, one must never discount the interplay between biology and the environment. For example, a parent with ADHD may be less likely to follow consistent routines or provide clear and concise expectations or directions. As a result, her child's ADHD characteristics, such as disorganization, may be intensified because of the lack of structure in the home. Many studies have attempted to pinpoint precise neurological conditions related to ADHD (Austin, 2003; Barkley, 2002, 2006; Weyandt, 2007). The results of these studies have found that subjects with ADHD show

executive functions Higher-order cognitive functions that influence the ability to plan, self-regulate, and engage in goal-directed behavior

- decreased blood flow and electrical activity in the frontal lobes of the brain (areas that are responsible for executive functions);
- anatomical differences, in various regions of the brains, from their peers without ADHD;
- differences in neurotransmitter levels (chemicals responsible for the transfer of messages from one part of the brain to another); and
- differences in abilities to track objects visually (e.g., trouble staying on one line of printed text when reading).

These studies indicate clear physiological differences between individuals with and without ADHD, but they provide no definitive answer to the question of the source of these differences. In other words, it is not known whether the structural differences identified are responsible for the ADHD characteristics; whether they result in learning disabilities and emotional or behavioral disorders, which manifest themselves in characteristics shared with ADHD; or whether the physiological attributes are completely unrelated to the ADHD. Further research is needed in this area (Weyandt, 2007).

Prevention

Until more is understood about the exact causes of ADHD and the factors that contribute to it, the development of effective ways to prevent the condition will continue to elude researchers. If indeed there is a biological predisposition to ADHD, there are many ways to lessen its impact on both the individual involved and the family. The behavioral accommodations and interventions discussed later in this chapter can reduce or eliminate the periods when ADHD characteristics tend to manifest themselves (e.g., transition times), thus lessening the effects of the condition and preventing problems at home and in the classroom. Similarly, the instructional techniques and suggestions provided can help students continue to make academic gains, thus avoiding many of the negative school outcomes associated with this disorder.

Overcoming Challenges

Behavioral techniques, direct and systematic instruction that is evaluated on a frequent basis, and highly motivating instructional materials have proved successful with many children currently identified as having ADHD. However, before students even have the opportunity to engage in classroom activities, many of these students need additional help in the form of medication. The American Academy of Pediatrics (AAP) explains it this way: Just as some students need glasses to see better, some students need medication to help them pay better attention and control their behavior (AAP, 2005). Possibly more than any other group of students with disabilities, students with ADHD are prescribed medication to assist them with their school-related problems. In fact, over 2 million students with ADHD take prescriptions such as Ritalin, Concerta, Adderall, or Dexadrine to help them control their behavior (Austin, 2003). These stimulant medications increase the arousal level of the central nervous system, enhancing blood flow to the frontal lobes or increasing electrical activity in the brain and subsequently improving functions such as working memory, attention, planning, and self-regulation attributed to these sections (DuPaul, Barkley, & Connor, 1998). Another possibility is that these stimulants (but not others, such as caffeine in coffee) increase the levels of certain neurotransmitters that enhance brain functioning (Ward & Guyer, 2000). Many different medications are used to treat the symptoms of ADHD. Some are prescribed to younger children than others; and, as shown in Table 6.2, some have longer-lasting effects (Connor, 2007; DuPaul & Stoner, 2003; NIMH, 2006).

Many physicians prescribe stimulants to help children with ADHD focus their attention on assigned tasks, and the medication is effective for most (Forness & Kavale, 2001). However, controversy surrounds the medical treatment for such large numbers of schoolchildren and whether educators should recommend such treatment to parents (Gotsch, 2002). One concern is the rapid increase in prescriptions for these drugs. Other concerns stem from the side effects (e.g, reduction in appetite, problems sleeping, jitteriness, dizziness) experienced by many youngsters and the need to monitor these students' health and performance carefully (AAP, 2005; NIMH, 2006).

When students use such medication, educators need to work with the family closely for several reasons:

- These medications are not uniformly effective. Some drugs work better with particular individuals than with others.
- It may take several adjustments to get the appropriate dosage for optimum performance; teachers need to communicate with families regarding their classroom observations after a dosage change.
- These drugs can have negative side effects (AAP, 2005). Because educators are in contact with students for a large portion of the day, parents depend on them to communicate their observations on the effects of these medications.

A school nurse can be an important part of the IEP team for students who use medication and can assist with both monitoring and parental communications.

In general, while medical treatment can alleviate the symptoms of ADHD, it does not directly improve academic functioning (Miranda, Jarque, & Tarraga, 2006).

Table 6.2 • Common Medications Used to Treat ADHD Symptoms

Type of Medication	Brand Name	Additional Options[1]	Effect Duration for One Dose	Approved Age
Stimulants				
Methylphenidate	Ritalin		3–6 hours	6 and older
		Ritalin SR	4–8 hours	6 and older
		Ritalin LA	6–8 hours	6 and older
	Concerta		12 hours	6 and older
	Metadate		3–6 hours	
		Metadate ER	4–8 hours	6 and older
		Metadate CD	6–8 hours	6 and older
Dextroamphetamine (d-amphetamine)	Dexedrine		4–6 hours	3 and older
		Dexedrine spansule	6–8 hours	
	Dextrostat		4–6 hours	3 and older
Dexmethylphenidate	Focalin		4 hours	6 and older
		Focalin XR		
Mixed amphetamine salts (*d-* and *l-*amphetamine combo)	Adderall		4–6 hours	3 and older
		Adderall XR	10–12	
Nonstimulant				
Atomoxetine	Strattera		6–8 hours	
Other				
Clonidine		Clonidine or Catapres	3–6 hours	

[1] Several of these medications come with intermediate- or extended-release options, allowing for fewer doses per day.

The National Institutes of Health (NIH) indicate that these medications are more effective than behavior therapy alone in controlling the underlying characteristics of ADHD (NIH Consensus Development Conference Statement, 2000). However, they do not have a positive effect on academic performance when used alone. To gain improvement in both academics and behavior requires a combination of behavioral and medical interventions (Jensen, 2000; Pappadopulos & Jensen, 2001).

Assessment

As we have seen in previous chapters, the assessment of students with disabilities occurs across several settings. In some cases, a disorder is suspected early in a child's life, and appropriate evaluations are conducted before a child starts school. In other cases, classroom teachers suspect the existence of a disorder and initiate procedures necessary to determine eligibility for services. Although many experts in ADHD advocate for comprehensive psychological and even medical evaluations, IDEA '04 does not require such costly medical or psychiatric diagnoses for these individuals (U.S. Department of Education, 2006). Also, unless otherwise noted in an IEP, all students must participate in state- and districtwide standardized testing; in these cases, assessment accommodations may be warranted for a child with a disability. All of these situations, and applications for students with ADHD, are discussed next.

Early Identification

The federal government requires that for students to receive special education services for ADHD, the symptoms must have been present before the age of 7 (OSEP, 2003). However, identification in early childhood is less common than during the school years. As their child's primary caregivers, parents may see signs of hyperactivity, impulsivity, or inattention in their toddler and wonder whether they are observing signs of ADHD. Many of these characteristics are common in young children, so a professional's opinion is warranted to determine whether the observed behavior is typical or excessive for the child's age (NIMH, 2006). Many behaviors exhibited by young children with ADHD become noticeable when compared to their peers, so day care and preschool teachers may be the first to notice these differences and express concerns to the child's parents. Often, a pediatrician is the first professional point of contact. Child psychologists or psychiatrists may also be consulted at this point, often making the initial ADHD diagnosis and providing additional services, such as behavioral training for parents or social skills training for the child.

"And this one is my Ritalin patch."

Source: www.CartoonStock.com

Prereferral

The primary purpose of prereferral is to avoid unnecessary referrals to special education by implementing research-validated practices in the general education classroom. If the implemented practices work—that is, if the behaviors of concern decrease significantly or disappear—then a referral is not needed. For students who may have ADHD, the prereferral process should contain multiple steps, and the efficacy of each attempt should be documented.

In the prereferral phase for students with ADHD, a teacher's actions should focus on preventing problem behaviors. For children with a predisposition toward inattention or hyperactivity, the physical and instructional structure of the classroom must be considered. Students with self-regulation difficulties do better in structured settings, so teachers need to have a well-planned behavior management system in place, complete with rules, procedures, and consistently delivered consequences. Maintenance of a regular classroom routine is very important, as are clearly articulated instructions and expectations for academic and social tasks. Well-planned transition times can decrease the opportunities for problem behaviors.

Other colleagues, such as teachers or a school nurse, can be helpful resources. At an initial level, a **school nurse** can be consulted to rule out other conditions (e.g., hearing loss) through general screening procedures. If other conditions might be the source of behavioral problems, then the evaluation process involves professionals with expertise in those areas of concern (e.g., an audiologist). When the school nurse suspects the presence of ADHD, the direction of the evaluation efforts is adjusted accordingly. Other teachers can conduct classroom observations to help the general educator find additional ways to improve the classroom structure and educational environment. Parents and family members are a critical resource at this stage, both to offer feedback regarding interventions that have been successful in the past and to maintain consistency between the home and school environments. If a variety of methods have been employed to increase attention or reduce hyperactivity, with little or no success, then a formal referral to special education is warranted.

school nurse A related service professional providing medical services at school

Identification

Experts strongly suggest that the identification process for ADHD include multidimensional evaluations (Barkley & Edwards, 2007; Weyandt, 2007). Such comprehensive assessments would include many different types of procedures such as

- diagnostic interviews,
- medical examinations,
- behavior rating scales,
- standardized tests, and/or

Parents and school personnel should work together for behavioral and medical management of ADHD.

Because prescription medicines are widely used to assist in the management of hyperactivity, the medical profession often is involved in these students' diagnosis, even though only a few states require diagnosis by either a physician or a mental health professional as part of the eligibility determination for ADHD (Müller & Markowitz, 2004).

Even if the student's pediatrician or family doctor makes a diagnosis of ADHD, school personnel must also make a determination about whether the student qualifies for accommodations though Section 504 or for special education services. They use a multilevel approach to gather all the information they need to understand the nature of the individual's problems and the types of supports and services needed (Merrell & Boelter, 2001; Salend & Rohena, 2003). These education professionals collect data about the student's academic performance, behavioral patterns, social interactions, and medical history. They compare this information with the DSM-IV-TR definition of ADHD to determine both needs and eligibility. The subjectivity of some of the assessment procedures (e.g., a parent's perception of hyperactivity compared to a teacher's) requires that caution be exercised. Cooperation among the many people involved in this process is vital. Remember that for a student to receive special education services, the characteristics of ADHD must be significant, must be observed across several settings, must be documented (even if retrospectively) as having existed before the age of 7, and must seriously affect educational performance.

Once a child is identified as having ADHD, the school's multidisciplinary team goes into high gear to develop the student's IEP and determine what accommodations and services are required. A broad array of professionals from a wide variety of disciplines, including a school nurse and a physician, should work with that student's parents throughout the IEP development and implementation process (Austin, 2003). Each professional uses a variety of assessment tools and techniques to monitor the student's academic and behavioral progress. For those students who are receiving medication, it is important that teachers work closely with the family and health professionals to monitor the effectiveness of the medications and ensure that the student doesn't experience negative side effects (AAP, 2005; OSEP, 2003).

Evaluation: Testing Accommodations

Just as for students with other disabilities, many types of accommodations are available to students with ADHD; however, one accommodation seems to be the most commonly offered. Whether the students' special needs are addressed through IDEA '04 or through Section 504, the most common accommodation to testing situations for students with ADHD is extended time (Elliott & Marquart, 2004). When offered this accommodation, students with disabilities typically take only 8 or 12 minutes longer to answer test items. Surprisingly, extended time does not significantly improve students' scores. What is interesting, however, is that students who are offered extended time feel better about the testing situation, claim they were more motivated to complete the test, felt less frustrated, and thought they performed better (Elliott & Marquart, 2004).

Another accommodation that can be beneficial to students with ADHD is testing in an alternate setting. Allowing students to take an exam in another location where distractions may be minimized may be helpful. Furthermore, not being able to compare their own test-taking completion to those of their peers can relieve some of the internal pressure that students place on themselves (e.g., "Other students are starting to turn their papers in, so I'd better hurry up and finish, too").

Early Intervention

While the majority of ADHD studies have been conducted on school-age children, the few studies conducted with younger children have consistent findings. Preschoolers who exhibit ADHD characteristics have significantly poorer social skills, are more demanding and noisy during peer interactions, display higher levels of verbal and physical aggression, and require more frequent medical attention (probably due to impulsivity) than their non-ADHD peers (DuPaul & Stoner, 2003). In conjunction with medical intervention, parent behavior training has been shown to produce positive results, including a reduction in conflict-ridden parent–child interactions commonly experienced by families of children with ADHD. Classroom-based behavioral interventions, including the use of positive reinforcement, response cost, daily rewards, and additional strategies that you will learn more about in Chapter 7 (i.e., functional assessments and assessment-based interventions), have also shown promise. Community-based interventions that combine medical treatment, parent training, and classroom-based behavioral interventions can reduce the negative characteristics of ADHD and improve social skills and peer interactions, particularly in classroom settings. However, the results are usually short-term and do not produce associated improvements in academic performance (DuPaul & Stoner, 2003). There is a compelling need for further research with this age group.

Teaching Students with ADHD

Because identification of ADHD does not guarantee that a student will qualify for special education services, most students with this disorder—both those with and those without IEPs—are educated in the general education classroom. A variety of instructional accommodations and interventions have proved useful for enhancing instruction and the long-term academic success of these students.

Access to the General Education Curriculum

ADHD has been referred to as an "educational performance problem" (Fowler, 2002, 2004). Over time, the cumulative effects of students' unmet instructional and behavioral needs result in poor academic achievement. To the extent that students with ADHD miss blocks of information and experience interruptions in the learning process, their access to the general education curriculum is inconsistent. Table 6.3 highlights some performance problem areas and how they might be addressed (Fowler, 2002, 2004; OSEP, 2003). Being able to pinpoint where individual students' problems occur increases the likelihood of selecting effective accommodations and interventions sooner. Because ADHD encompasses a range of characteristics, identifying specific challenges (e.g., inattention or impulsivity) and developing strategies to address each area of need can produce positive results for students with varying characteristics.

Table 6.3 • Possible Solutions to Educational Performance Problems

Educational Performance Problems	Potential Solutions
Initiating work	• Gain student's attention. • Use clear, one-step instructions. • Provide directions orally and in writing.
Remaining on task	• Seat student away from distractions (e.g., door, window, computer stations). • Use hands-on activities. • Assign highly motivating activities. • Alternate instructional activities frequently. • Prompt student (verbally, with hand signals) if starting to lose focus.
Making transitions from one activity to another	• Give a 5-minute warning before changing from one activity to another. • Use a standard, predictable schedule. • Remind student about requirements for shift (e.g., clear desk, keep pen and paper on top of desk, line up in small groups).
Completing assignments	• Break assignments down into smaller tasks. • Set a standard for acceptable work. • Provide a rationale for completion. • Assign a peer assistant.

Instructional Accommodations

Accommodations to the classroom's physical environment can help students with ADHD by reducing distracting stimuli. For example, a desk or work area in a quiet, relatively distraction-free area of the classroom is more conducive to concentration than a desk next to high-traffic areas, such as those near the pencil sharpener, hallway door, or trash can. Placing the student near the teacher allows for easier monitoring and reinforcement, and seating next to a peer who models consistent on task behavior can positively influence a student's behavior. Other physical accommodations can include pointers or bookmarks to help a student track words visually during reading exercises, timers to remind students how much time is left before an assignment must be finished, visual cues as prompts to change behavior (e.g., turning the classroom lights off to indicate that the noise level is too high).

Aspects of the learning environment can also be structured to enhance educational outcomes for students with ADHD. As you can see from the suggestions here, many of these accommodations reflect the concepts of universal design. In other words, these accommodations provide benefits for *all* students but are particularly helpful for students with ADHD. Many students learn better when more difficult subjects such as reading and math are taught early in the day; when instruction is exciting, engaging, and culturally relevant to the student; and when the pace of the presentation varies. Students show improved academic results when teachers carefully monitor their understanding of key concepts and adjust the lesson accordingly. Such adjustments can be accomplished easily through teacher questioning and the use of physical responses by the students (e.g., the students each hold up one finger to indicate that the answer to a teacher's question is 'yes' or two fingers to indicate a 'no' response). Furthermore, all classrooms run more smoothly when directions are clear, concise, and thorough (even better when they are presented both visually and orally) so that students understand what they are supposed to be doing (Salend et al., 2003). Because students with ADHD often have difficulty with delayed gratification (which is tied to impulsivity), providing immediate feedback has been shown to be more effective than providing feedback after a prolonged time period (DuPaul & Stoner, 2003). For example, a student whose teacher praises her for correctly completing the first five questions on a science worksheet is more likely to stay on task than the student whose teacher waits until she has finished

Accommodating for Inclusive Environments
Instructional and Testing Accommodations

Instructional Accommodations

- Allow extended time for completion of assignments.
- Break instructional sequences or academic tasks into smaller segments to help maintain attention.
- Arrange more frequent, yet shorter, study periods.
- Set timers for specific tasks to help students stay focused.
- Teach and practice organizational skills (e.g., give guided practice, designate places where students are expected to store instructional materials, and reinforce their doing so).
- Read directions to students to help them refocus.
- Use computer word processing programs to assist with writing activities.

- Allow the use of pointers and tracking devices (e.g., a ruler) to help students track text on a page.

Testing Accommodations

- Testing accommodations should match instructional accommodations whenever possible.
- Select evaluation measures that match the students' preferences.
- Make sure the utility of evaluation measures is not undermined by the impact of ADHD characteristics (e.g., inability to complete lengthy tests due to inattention or impulsivity).
- Allow extended time for test taking.

the entire worksheet before providing reinforcement. In fact, without some sort of positive feedback or prompting, the student in the second scenario might not even finish her worksheet! Similarly, a teacher who decides to wait until the end of class to address the out-of-seat behavior of a student with ADHD, rather than addressing it as soon as it occurs, may find that the student's time out of his or her seat increases as the class period progresses. See Accommodating for Inclusive Environments for additional accommodations to use with students with ADHD.

Data-Based Practices

How does a teacher help the student with ADHD? As for their counterparts who have emotional or behavioral disorders, functional behavioral assessments (FBAs) are useful in determining the reasons why students with ADHD engage in certain behaviors. (We first introduced FBAs in Chapter 2, and you'll learn more about their application for students with emotional or behavioral disorders in Chapter 7.) For example, if FBA results indicate that a student engages in acting-out behaviors to avoid seatwork, the teacher may analyze the work to see whether it is too difficult for the student or implement behavioral techniques to reinforce the student's work completion.

Like their counterparts who have only learning disabilities, students with ADHD respond well to highly structured learning environments where topics are taught directly. Many students with ADHD struggle with motivation and lack the persistence to make the extra effort to learn when it is difficult for them (Carlson et al., 2002). Professionals suggest that carefully planned educational procedures, such as letting students choose their academic assignments from a group of alternatives selected by the teacher, shortening the task, giving clear and precise instructions, and giving rewards can lead to academic improvement (Powell & Nelson, 1997). Peer tutoring has proved to be very effective for students with ADHD, as well as for those with learning disabilities (DuPaul et al., 1998; Fuchs & Fuchs, 1998). Over 50% improvement in academic tasks has been achieved by involving peers in the instructional program. Although it is important for teachers and parents to pay attention to these students' academic problems, it is also imperative to help them develop social skills that are acceptable to their peers.

Self-management tactics (see A Closer Look at Data-Based Practices for one example) help students learn to control their own behavior and be responsible for many aspects of their school programs (Graham, Harris, & Olinghouse, 2006; Harris et al., 2005; Lucangeli & Cabzele, 2006). Typically, experts group **self-management strategies**, also referred to as **self-regulation strategies**, into four categories (Reid & Lienemen, 2006):

- Self-monitoring
- Self-instructions
- Self-reinforcement
- Goal setting

Here's one way that self-management (self-regulation) works. Hayden is unable to stay on task, and she frequently daydreams instead of completing independent work. The teacher and Hayden meet. The teacher explains to Hayden that she is now going to be responsible for monitoring her own behavior. By using **self-monitoring**, Hayden keeps track of her performance (being on task) by collecting data. Each time she hears a beep on the CD that her teacher prerecorded, she asks herself, "Was I paying attention? Was I doing what the teacher asked us to do?" Through this process, Hayden learns to evaluate her own behavior by determining whether it is appropriate (on task) or not (off task). She records this information by marking either a smiley face or a sad face on a chart. Students can also benefit from **self-instruction**, or **self-talk**, in which they use self-induced statements to guide their actions. Hayden reminds herself, "Double-check my answers. Did I answer all of the questions? Just a little bit longer. Stay focused and I can finish this whole worksheet." **Goal setting** is helpful to both teachers and students as they determine the level of expected performance for a task. Hayden and her teacher decide that her goal is to maintain on-task behavior for an entire 30-minute period. **Self-reinforcement** is a powerful self-regulation strategy that allows students to earn rewards for accomplishments. Thus, Hayden earns a sticker for every 10 smiley faces on her chart.

Self-monitoring is particularly helpful both to teachers and to students with ADHD because it does not take much teacher time to implement, and it helps students focus on controlling their own behaviors (Daly & Ranalli, 2003). "Countoons" are one fun interpretation of the techniques discussed here; an example is shown in Figure 6.1. This technique provides a clear picture—a visual—of the target behavior and its occurrence; provides immediate feedback; is an active way to involve students; and facilitates communication among the student, the teacher, and the family.

For students with ADHD, organizers to help them focus their learning can be very beneficial (Salend et al., 2003). Graphic organizers, discussed in Chapter 4, can

self-management or self-regulation strategies Includes many techniques, used individually or in combinations by the individual, to modify behavior or academic performance

self-monitoring Keeping a record (data) of one's own performance

self-instruction or self-talk Self-induced statements to assist in self-regulation

goal setting Determining desired behavior and its criterion

self-reinforcement Awarding self-selected reinforcers or rewards to oneself contingent on achieving criterion

Figure 6.1 • Examples of a Countoon for Self-Recording of Wandering Around

What I do			My count	What happens
Read my book	Wander around	Read my book	1 2 3 4 5 6 7 8 9 10 11 12	I get to play
F1	F2	F3	F4	F5

From *Teaching Exceptional Children* by P. M. Daly and P. Ranali in TEC, 35, 2003. Copyright 2003 by Council for Exceptional Children (VA). Reproduced with permission of Council for Exceptional Children (VA) in the formats Textbook and Other book via Copyright Clearance Center.

A Closer Look at Data-Based Practices

Self-Management

What Is Self-Management?

Self-management techniques are a systematic process used to teach students with severe disabilities to manage their own behavior. The four types of self-management are self-monitoring, self-instruction, self-evaluation and self-reinforcement. When teaching self-management skills to students, teachers first model the process of self-management and then provide students with ample opportunities to learn and practice the strategy on their own. Many students require positive and corrective feedback during the learning process in order to master the technique.

Why Self-Management Is Beneficial

It is important for students to take responsibility for their learning and actions. Students who are able to control their behavior become independent and are able to generalize this ability to other aspects of their lives. In addition, when students are able to use self-management techniques, you will be able to spend more time teaching instead of managing student behavior.

Implementing Self-Management

A brief description of some self-management procedures follows, and Figure A shows an example of a data collection system for a student to use.

Figure A • Sample Self-Monitoring Form for On-Task Behavior

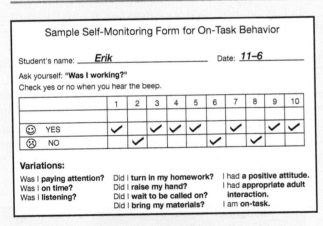

Select the Behavior for Self-Management

Identify and define the behavior.

- Select behaviors you can easily describe, define, count, and evaluate.
- Identify functional behaviors with social value important to the student (e.g., staying on task, completing homework).
- Select behaviors the student has ample opportunities to use.
- Select behaviors manageable for the student to perform and record.

Measure current performance levels.

- Conduct four or five observations to determine the student's current level.

Determine mastery criteria.

- Consider the student's current level of task performance (e.g., on task 50% of the time).
- Compare that level of performance with that of peers to set goals and criteria (e.g., on task 90% of the time).

Choose self-management component.

- Self-monitoring (e.g., "Am I on task?")
- Self-evaluation (e.g., "Did I reach my goal today?")
- Self-reinforcement (e.g., "I did a good job today")

Develop the Self-Management Component

- Finalize and describe behaviors.
- Be sure others can consistently observe those behaviors.
- Determine when and how data will be collected.
- Develop a simple data-recording system.

Teach Students to Use Self-Management

Introduce the procedure.

- State the behavior and provide both examples of effective use of the procedure and examples of its ineffective use.
- Explain the importance of the behavior.
- Provide ample opportunities for supervised practice using the recording system.
- Discuss criteria for mastery.
- Teach self-recording procedure.

Provide practice and assess mastery.

- Provide guided practice and role playing.
- Assess mastery during role playing.
- Discuss when self-management will be implemented.
- Provide independent practice.
- Assess mastery and independence.

Evaluate the Student's Performance

- Assess performance against criteria.
- Assess maintenance.
- Assess generalization.

Source: From *Teaching Self-Management to Elementary Students with Developmental Disabilities* by M. E. King-Sears. Copyright 1997 by American Association on Intellectual Developmental Disabilities. Reproduced with permission of American Association on Intellectual Developmental Disabilities in the formats Textbook and Other book via Copyright Clearance Center.

 myeducationlab Go to the Building Teaching Skills and Dispositions section in Chapter 6 of MyEducationLab, and complete the activities provided in IRIS Module "SOS: Helping Students Become Independent Learners." This module describes how teachers can help students stay on task by learning to regulate their behavior. The four strategies discussed are self-monitoring, self-instruction, goal-setting, and self-reinforcement.

help students identify the important elements of the material being learned. For students whose inattentiveness and distractibility interfere with their ability to see a writing task through to completion, graphic organizers help them break a writing assignment into smaller components. An example is shown in Chapter 4's A Closer Look at Data-Based Practices.

Technology

Advances in technology have improved all of our lives, and for individuals with disabilities, particularly those with ADHD, technology offers many possibilities. Because both those with and those without disabilities use many of these helpful technological devices, they do not call attention to the individual with the problem. Also, because of the increase in the number of devices and software, the increasingly low costs, and the fact that their use is commonly accepted, the distinction between instructional and assistive technologies is becoming blurred (Van Kuren, 2003). Computers help everyone turn in more readable papers. For those students who cannot write legibly or produce a neat report, word processing makes the individual's disability less visible and is one avenue to better grades. Electronic personal organizers and personal digital assistants (PDAs; see accompanying photo) are very "in." Everyone seems to have or want such a device to help manage time, remember appointments, and give reminders of important due dates. For many students with ADHD, personal organizers provide the structure necessary to reduce the number of incomplete homework assignments or skipped meetings with a tutor. Even the new Apple iPods have a calendar (with an alarm/reminder function), notes option ("Don't forget to bring science book home to study"), and other applications that can help students organize their lives.

Some software programs provide special benefits to individuals whose thinking skills seem disorganized. For example, *Report Writer Interactive*® provides the user with structure during the writing process. This software, like other, similar programs, help students organize their thoughts, place them in a logical sequence, and then produce a written document that is formatted and pleasing in appearance. As we noted in Chapter 4, other programs, such as *Kidspiration*® and *Inspiration*®, help students by facilitating their creation of graphic organizers for studying and writing reports.

Some aspects of technologically based learning activities appear to be particularly suited to students with ADHD. Web pages that provide interesting text and stimulating pictures combined with movies or audio clips allow students to change activities frequently, rather than being engaged in a reading activity for a prolonged period of time. Similarly, the ability to click on hyperlinks to access more information or engage in interactive learning activities provides further opportunities to shift attention frequently.

Devices designed for sale to the general public offer unique and wonderful benefits to individuals with disabilities. PDAs are great examples of technology that help everyone be better organized, and for individuals with ADHD, they may well be the perfect solution to avoid missing appointments and being otherwise poor managers of time.

Computer usage does not always equate to the ability to obtain information. When teachers include technology in instruction, they do need to be sure that it is accessible (Hoffman, Hartley, & Broome, 2005). For example, some software programs are not intuitive to students, who cannot figure out how to open files or access or retrieve information. Similarly, not all online learning activities are equally accessible. Determining how useful any type of technology might be should be done carefully, perhaps with help from a specialist in assistive technology.

Transition

Few youngsters "grow out of" their disabilities. For most, disabilities last a lifetime. Of course, with effective education, positive experiences, and a great deal of hard work, people with disabilities are able to compensate for their problems and to participate fully in the community and the workplace. In this respect, individuals with ADHD share experiences with their counterparts who have other disabilities. A combination of medical intervention and counseling—including individual, family/marriage, and/or vocational counseling—can be effective in promoting positive outcomes for adults with ADHD.

As you learned in Chapters 1 and 2, more and more students with disabilities are attending postsecondary schools, but these individuals' success rates are disappointing (NCES, 2007). The transition to college can be difficult for many students, and for those with disabilities, the move away from family and the loss of supports from a school-based IEP team can be devastating. Many colleges and universities have centers on campus designed to help students with disabilities cope with the increased demands of college courses. Some centers offer intensive supports, and evidence now indicates that they make a real difference in the outcomes of college students with ADHD (Getzel, McManus, & Briel, 2004). The supports offered at Virginia Commonwealth University provide a model for the types of services that should be available if the dream of college graduation is to become a reality for more students with ADHD (and learning disabilities). Here are some of the important components of such effective programs:

- Each student has an Individualized Academic Support Plan (similar to an IEP but used for postsecondary students).
- Individual students have frequent communications (through e-mail, telephone, or in-person meetings) with the academic specialist.
- The center provides help and instruction about study skills (e.g., writing strategies, test-taking strategies, time management, organizers).
- Students learn what accommodations are effective for them and advocate for the use of these accommodations in all relevant courses.
- Assistance is provided to help students understand their disabilities and manage stress associated with the challenges the disability brings.
- Career development activities (e.g., internships, résumé development, practice with interviewing) are provided.

Collaboration

Students with ADHD receive a wide variety of educational supports. Some students may spend their entire school day in the general education classroom with only Section 504 accommodations for support. Others may receive resource room services to address educational needs arising from coexisting learning disabilities. Still others may spend a greater portion of their school day in special education classrooms, receiving additional supports due to coexisting emotional or behavioral disabilities. As a result, collaboration among families, teachers, and related services personnel is important, particularly to communicate strategies and supports that are successful, and to note any changes in the student when medication dosages are modified.

Collaborating with Related Service Providers: School Nurses

When medical treatment of ADHD symptoms is used, the school nurse is frequently the individual responsible for dispensing medication at school. Prescription drugs are considered controlled substances, so school nurses must deal with issues related to safe administration of medications, adherence to state guidelines regarding the administration of controlled substances, monitoring the impact of the medication on student performance (including potential side effects), and maintenance of proper documentation (National Association of School Nurses [NASN], 2005). The school nurse is also an important part of the IEP team for students who take stimulant medications, and he or she acts as a liaison among members of the school, home, and medical communities (NASN, 2006). Even if a school nurse is not assigned specifically to an individual school, one should be available through the district office.

Collaborative Practices: Information Sharing

Students on any medication program should be monitored closely to maximize benefits as well as spot any potentially harmful side effects. The teacher is often the adult who spends the most time with a child during the school day and, accordingly, has the potential to provide the most information regarding the impact of the medication. According to Ward and Guyer (2000), a teacher has the opportunity to

- observe the child in a typical academic setting and note responses to the environment,
- observe the child once medication has been prescribed to note the effect on the child,
- note the effects of dosage changes,
- observe the length of time that positive effects from medication last,
- identify possible side effects, and
- note changes in behavior and academic performance.

Collaboration with the school nurse is important to ensure that medically related information is shared with the appropriate partners. As a medical liaison, the school nurse can communicate with the doctor who prescribed the drugs and give feedback that will help determine the appropriate dosage levels for a student. Furthermore, the school nurse may be able to answer questions from both teachers and parents regarding drug-related issues, such as long-term impact and potential side effects.

Partnerships with Families and Communities

The challenges faced by families of students with ADHD are great. Students with this condition receive considerable negative feedback, and they often bring this hostility home (Fowler, 2002). Reports about arguments regarding chores, following families' rules, disobeying, and being "impossible to count on" are common (Barkley, 2005). In addition to these problems, many families struggle with challenges related to cost. Even with insurance, the monthly costs of medication and other supports (e.g., behavioral and social skills training) can be prohibitive. Many families have no health insurance at all; these families, often with the greatest need for supports, must either pay for medication and treatment themselves or forego these services.

Having information empowers all of us. This fact is particularly true for parents of children who have different learning styles, are not typical learners, or behave erratically. Children with ADHD bring many challenges to their families, and their inconsistent behaviors often result in confusion: Maybe Juan isn't trying hard enough, Evan is just forgetful and scattered, Connor doesn't seem to care, or Lyra has an attitude problem. Teachers can help parents of students with ADHD better understand the issues and challenges this condition presents and, as a by-product,

 **myeducationlab** Go the Activities and Applications section in Chapter 6 of MyEducationLab, and complete Activity 2, IRIS Activity, "He Just Needs a Little Discipline." When he was in second grade, Matt was diagnosed with ADHD. Think about issues related to communication with parents and behavior management.

The student, the family, and teacher are all helped by providing organizational supports.

help themselves and their other students as well (Mathur & Smith, 2003). How can teachers help? One way is to assist parents in finding accurate information about this condition through the Internet and community agencies. Teachers can help parents assess the accuracy of the information they find, and they can help families determine the effectiveness of some of the strategies suggested. Another way to help is to put families in touch with professionals or with other parents who have formed support groups.

Teachers can help families as they design ways to organize and structure schoolwork. Through effective home and school communications, teachers can share what they find helps students organize their work and manage their time at school. For families with Internet technology available at home, educators can capitalize on this means of quick and easy communication either through e-mail or via the Web (Salend et al., 2004). Teachers can also assist families in home implementation of those techniques that have proved effective at school (Mathur & Smith 2003; OSEP, 2003). Here are a few examples of ways to help these students at both school and home:

- Post a schedule for the week (*school:* on the corner of the student's desk; *home:* on the refrigerator).
- Set a time to discard out-of-date materials (*school:* clean out desk and locker every Friday afternoon; *home:* sort out the contents of the backpack every Saturday morning).
- Put things in the same place (*school:* worksheets to be completed in a stacking tray; *home:* homework and assignments in progress in a bin by the kitchen door).
- Use specific rewards and consequences for both appropriate and inappropriate behaviors (*school:* reward improved academic performance; lose points or privileges for breaking classroom rules; *home:* movie night for a good week at school; suspension of television privileges for an evening for skipped chores).

Summary

When the U. S. government called out ADHD as a separate condition, it was confident that this designation would cause very few additional students to be included in special education. The government came to this conclusion because it believed that most students with ADHD who qualified for special education services were already being served through existing special education categories. The characteristics that define ADHD—inattention, hyperactivity, and impulsivity—tend to overlap with other disabilities. ADHD is still not a separate special education category; rather, it is a condition specifically addressed in the special education category IDEA '04 calls "other health impairments." Students with ADHD receive special education services only if the disorder significantly affects their school performance. A variety of accommodations and academic interventions are available to enhance the school success of students with ADHD, many of which have been proved effective for students with learning disabilities and emotional or behavioral disorders. Because of the prevalence of medical intervention for students with ADHD, collaboration with the school nurse is important. Finally, outcomes for students with ADHD are improved when there is strong collaboration and consistency between the home and school environments.

Answering the Chapter Objectives

1. What are the common characteristics of students with ADHD?

   - Inattention
   - Hyperactivity
   - Impulsivity
   - Academic difficulties
   - Social difficulties

2. What is the relationship of ADHD to other, coexisting disabilities?

   - ADHD often coexists with other disabilities with which it shares various characteristics.
   - Seventy percent of children with ADHD also have a learning disability.
   - Forty-two percent of children with ADHD also have emotional or behavioral disorders.

3. How is ADHD treated medically?

   - Stimulant medications, such as Ritalin, Dexadrine, and Concerta, are typically prescribed to increase attention and reduce hyperactivity.
   - Medical therapy has proved more effective than behavior therapy alone.
   - Concerns exist about
     - The rapid increase in prescriptions for these drugs (35% over a recent 5-year period)
     - Side effects (e.g, reduction in appetite, problems sleeping, jitteriness, dizziness)

4. What are various accommodations and classroom interventions used for students with ADHD?

   - Reduce distractions.
   - Give preferential seating near the teacher.
   - Use pointers to help with visual tracking.
   - Allow extended time on assignments and tests.
   - Use timers to support time management.
   - Provide visual cues and prompts when student is getting off task.
   - Break activities and assignments into smaller segments.
   - Provide shorter, yet more frequent, study periods.
   - Maintain a highly structured setting.
   - Teach organizational skills.
   - Use peer tutoring.
   - Teach self-regulation strategies.
   - Use learning strategies.
   - Use content organizers.
   - Provide frequent and specific feedback on behavior.

5. Why are collaboration and partnerships with families and other professionals important?

   - Collaboration with the school nurse provides
     - medical liaison between family and medical community,
     - professional knowledge regarding medications, and
     - collaboration with families.
   - Provides teachers with key information about the student
   - Provides families with professional information from teachers
   - Allows for consistency between behavioral interventions at home and at school.

PEARSON
myeducationlab) Now go to MyEducationLab at www.myeducationlab.com and take the Self-Assessment to gauge your initial comprehension of chapter content. Once you have taken the Self-Assessment, use your individualized Study Plan for Chapter 6 to enhance your understanding of the concepts discussed in the chapter.

Council for Exceptional Children **ADDRESSING THE PROFESSIONAL STANDARDS**

Council for Exceptional Children (CEC) knowledge standards addressed in this chapter:

GC1K3, GC1K1, GC2K4, GC2K1, GC8S1, GC4S3, GC7K2, GC10S2, GC10K1

Appendix A: CEC Knowledge and Skill Standards Common Core has a full listing of the standards listed here.

Appendix B: CEC Knowledge and Skill Common Core Standards and Associated Subcategories are broken down by chapter.

CHAPTER 7

Emotional or Behavioral Disorders

Kathleen Lane

Imagine a World . . .

where clear skies are always in view . . .

Chapter Objectives

After studying this chapter, you will be able to

1. Explain how ambiguous definitions can influence how we identify and support students with emotional or behavioral disorders.

2. Identify academic and social characteristics of these students.

3. Describe the causes of emotional or behavioral disorders.

4. Identify strategies for improving academic, behavioral, and social outcomes for these students.

5. List strategies for improving postsecondary outcomes for these students.

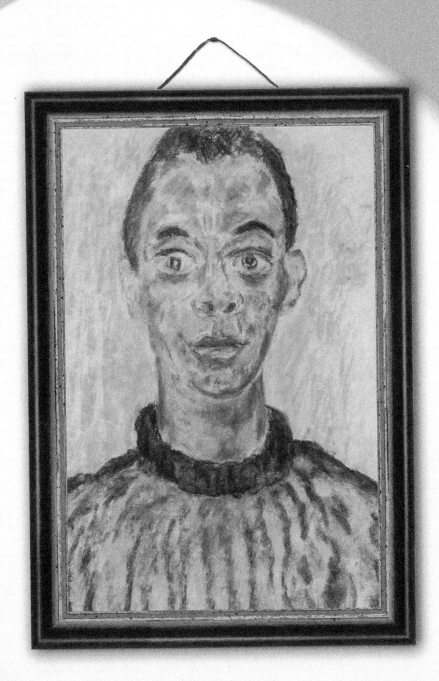

 *Beauford Delaney,* the gifted and talented son of a minister and one of ten children, was born in Knoxville, Tennessee in 1901. In 1924, he moved to Boston to study art. In 1929, he moved to the Harlem section of New York City. During this time in New York, he developed his style using radical colors and became a well-known artist in Greenwich Village art circles. In 1953, like many African Americans of his time, he became an expatriate living in Paris and southern France. He died in 1979 after four difficult years in St. Anne Hospital for the Insane in Paris. James Baldwin, his closest friend, said of Delaney, "He has been starving and working all of his life—in Tennessee, in Boston, in New York, and now in Paris. He has been menaced more than any other man I know by his social circumstances and also by all the emotional and psychological stratagems he has been forced to use and survive; and, more than any other man I know, he has transcended both the inner and outer darkness" (Powell, 2002, p. 7).

Where We've Been . . . What's on the Horizon?

Throughout history, people have recognized emotional or behavioral disorders, most often in adults. Yet, ideas about how to identify and support youth and adults with emotional or behavioral disorders have shifted dramatically over time. In this chapter, you will see that some historical approaches for treatment of this group of people have been alarming at best, and abusive in the worst cases.

Historical Context

As we look to the past, it was probably Leo Kanner's 1957 book *Child Psychiatry* that brought the development of services for children in America to the forefront. In ancient times, a common belief was that those with emotional or behavioral disorders were possessed by the devil. During some periods, such as in ancient Egypt, treatment was enlightened and humane (Deutsch, 1949). Yet, the unknown mystery surrounding mental illness often fostered negative assumptions about its causes and, unfortunately, resulted in horrible treatment. Some societies believed that these disorders were contagious. In an effort to protect others from "catching" emotional or behavioral disorders, affected people were removed from the community. Treatments in the Middle Ages and later reflected such beliefs and commonly included imprisonment, placement in poorhouses, beatings, chainings, straitjacketing, and other cruel actions. In 1547, the first institution for people with mental disorders, St. Mary of Bethlehem, was established. In time, people referred to the institution as Bedlam, a term that now means a place of noise and uproar. People placed in the institution were chained, beaten, and starved—the conditions were intolerable. In fact, a popular form of entertainment in London was to take the family for an outing to view the "lunatics" at Bedlam.

myeducationlab) After reading this chapter, complete the Self-Assessment for Chapter 7 on MyEducationLab to gauge your initial understanding of chapter content.

By the 18th century, conditions began to improve for people with emotional or behavioral disorders. Philippe Pinel, a French psychiatrist, in 1792 ordered humanitarian reform. He called for better treatment for mental patients at Salpêtrière, a Paris asylum for the "insane," demanding that the patients be unchained (Brigham, 1847). During the 1800s in the United States, major reform in the identification and treatment of people with emotional or behavioral disorders began to occur with the guidance of several key supporters. Benjamin Rush, the father of American psychiatry and a signer of the Declaration of Independence, proposed more humane methods of caring for these children with emotional or behavioral disorders. Dorothea Dix influenced the founding of state institutions for people with mental disorders. By 1844, many states had institutions for people with mental disorders, and the Association of Medical Superintendents of American Institutions for the Insane (now the American Psychiatric Association) was founded. Unfortunately, although the initial visions for the early institutions were positive and hopeful, over time institutions became more custodial.

Before the late 1800s and the onset of public school for children with emotional or behavioral disorders, most children with these types of problems received no services at all. At the end of that century, compulsory education laws gave way to educational services for these youngsters. However, most students with emotional or behavioral disorders attended ungraded classes along with other students who found the general education setting to be too difficult. The early public school classes provided a range of services to these students such as mental health care, similar to today's wraparound services. Thus, a "safety net" of school, community, and social services existed to assist children and their families (Duckworth et al., 2001).

During the 1960s and 1970s, researchers, scholars, and educators created new ways to teach students with emotional or behavioral disorders. In 1962, Norris Haring and Lakin Phillips published *Educating Emotionally Disturbed Children*, a book that documented their experimental work in the Arlington, Virginia, public schools. Their approach emphasized the importance of behavioral principles, a structured environment, and interactions between the child's home and school environments. Eli Bower developed a definition of behavioral disorders that served as the foundation for the current federal and state definitions of emotional disturbance (Bower & Lambert, 1962). In the 1960s, Nicholas Hobbs introduced Project Re-Ed. This landmark effort demonstrated the effectiveness of an ecological approach that included a child's home and community environments. Based on this approach, children attended residential schools for short periods of time to acquire and become fluent in new skill sets. Then, the children returned to restructured community and family environments, now altered to support the child's newly acquired skills. Frank Hewett's Santa Monica Project developed the engineered classroom. This approach illustrated the positive outcomes of a highly structured classroom environment grounded in behavior management principles.

In 1964, a classic study about the effects of teacher attention on a preschooler's social interactions with his peers during playtime was published (Allen et al., 1964). This study, which emphasized applied behavioral analytic tools, sparked a new interest in the importance of how the environment can influence people's actions. Montrose Wolf, Don Baer, and Todd Risley are credited with bringing applied behavior analytic techniques to support children in classroom settings, with the application of token economies in classroom settings nationwide. Montrose Wolf is also credited with developing the Teaching-Family Model, which began at the University of Kansas and was later extended to a well-known program at Boys Town in Nebraska. These pioneering efforts have been replicated across the nation, in school-based and residential settings. They have also evolved and been further developed into the validated practices advocated through IDEA '04 and the professional literature. These practices provide options for improving outcomes for students with and at risk for emotional or behavioral disorders within and beyond the school setting.

Challenges That Emotional or Behavioral Disorders Present

Students with emotional or behavioral disorders are among some of the most difficult to teach given that they struggle not only behaviorally but also socially and academically. Although a challenging task, it is essential that administrators and educators develop systems and structures to (a) prevent the development of new cases of emotional or behavioral disorders as well as (b) respond more effectively to students with existing problems (Lane, 2007), given that these students struggle both within and beyond the school setting. Be sure to read Spotlighting Suzanne Storey. Learn how this vice principal helped develop a very successful positive behavior support program at her middle school, and think about how schools can set up structures to make a difference for so many. To learn more about positive behavior supports, visit http://www.pbis.org/main.htm.

When compared to general education students and students in other disability categories, students with emotional or behavioral disorders experience the least success. Their challenging behavior and limited social skills often demand teachers' attention, interfere with instruction, lead to strained social relationships, and negatively impact the learning environment for all students. Their academic problems are also clear in that they have significant problems in reading, writing, and mathematics as compared to their general education peers (Greenbaum et al., 1996; Landrum, Tankersley, & Kauffman, 2003; Mattison, Hopper, & Glassberg, 2002; Reid et al., 2004; Trout et al., 2003; Wagner & Davis, 2006). They also have greater academic deficits than students with other disabilities (Zigmond, 2006). At best, these academic difficulties appear to either remain stable (Anderson, Kutash, & Duchnowski, 2001; Mattison et al., 2002; Reid et al., 2004) or, at worst, deteriorate over time (Nelson et al., 2004). Students with emotional or behavioral disorders are more often retained in grade and have higher school dropout rates than any other disability category (Wagner & Davis, 2006).

Spotlighting *Suzanne Storey:* A Day in the Life

Suzanne Storey is a middle school vice principal.

My name is Suzanne Storey, and I am a vice principal in Middle Tennessee. I have been grateful for the opportunity to work with my staff to make a difference in the lives of students attending a progressive, public elementary school. My faculty was looking for something to grow the school's expectations that would foster an environment that encouraged academic, social, and behavioral growth for each individual student. The initial positive behavioral support (PBS) team made up of teachers, parents, students, school counselors, and administrators took the school needs and information to develop an impressive PBS program. As part of the primary intervention plan, the faculty and staff communicate their schoolwide expectations through a daily pledge, colorful posters that appear in all key settings, and engaging monthly lesson plans that include technology with the use of PowerPoint presentations.

Any adult—including administrators, teachers, staff, bus drivers, custodians, cafeteria workers, substitutes, and parent volunteers—who sees a student meeting these expectations may give that student a PBS ticket along with behavior-specific praise ("Nice job of walking in the hall without talking!") to reinforce the desired behaviors. Students turn these PBS tickets into colorful boxes located in their homeroom classes. Teachers use these tickets to select students for various jobs and privileges. Each morning, administration draws students' names from all the tickets turned in during each week to receive a range of reinforcers, including homework passes, classwide rewards, and tangible items. In addition, the PBS team hosts PBS assemblies that include a variety of fun activities as skits and cheerleading events to honor students who have received PBS tickets during the quarter. I have worked with the PBS team and the parent-teacher organization to coordinate the logistics of the PBS program.

Schoolwide data indicate that this program is associated with some impressive improvements, including decreases in office discipline referrals and improved attendance. Furthermore, the PBS team has been successful in analyzing their schoolwide data collected as part of regular school practices to identify students who require more intensive assistance, in the form of secondary and tertiary supports. It is clear that the PBS team, administration, faculty, staff, and parents are all committed to supporting *all* students within this impressive three-tiered model of prevention.

Unfortunately, once these students leave the school setting, things do not improve. Students with emotional or behavioral disorders have high rates of unemployment and underemployment, negative employment experiences, negative personal relationships, and a high need for mental health services (Bullis & Yovanoff, 2006; Walker, Ramsey, & Gresham, 2004; Zigmond, 2006). As a whole, children and youth with emotional or behavioral disorders pose tremendous costs to families and society (Kauffman, 2005; Quinn & Poirier, 2004), with the most extreme consequences illustrated in school shootings that have occurred in our nation (Lane, 2007).

In short, life within and beyond school is challenging for students with emotional or behavioral disorders (Walker et al., 2004). In fact, as shown in the film *The Aviator* and discussed in On the Screen, mental illness often begins in childhood and accelerates through adulthood. Because these students struggle in so many areas—behaviorally, socially, and academically—and because things don't get better for them once they leave the school setting, we must learn better methods of serving them effectively and early in their educational careers (Lee, Sugai, & Horner, 1999). We need to figure out how to make a difference.

Emotional or Behavioral Disorders Defined

Emotional or behavioral disorders (EBD) are difficult to define, with some thinking that people are identified as having emotional or behavioral disorders when adults in authority say so (Hallahan, Kauffman, & Pullen, 2009). The troubles with definitions stem, in part, from the fact that the education, mental health, and research

On the Screen: *The Aviator's Tailspin*

Howard Hughes was almost bigger than life. At age 18, he inherited the family business and used his vast wealth to pioneer the development of commercial aviation and also to fund his passion for making movies. He was an engineering and business genius who designed bombers and spy planes for the U.S. military during World War II; he also led the development of the commercial airline business as CEO of TWA, which flew worldwide. What probably made Hughes most well known, however, was being a flamboyant movie mogul who made epic films and lived the lifestyle of the Hollywood "rich and famous."

In 2004, the acclaimed Hollywood director Martin Scorsese brought to the screen the conflict between Hughes's naturally flashy, public personality and the mental illness that caused Hughes to withdraw from life. Scorsese and Leonardo DiCaprio, who played the part of Hughes, reveal the spiraling tragedy of mental illness and how it often begins in childhood, accelerates, and eventually consumes its victims. Although the condition can be controlled through medication today, Howard Hughes's life was ravaged by obsessive compulsive disorder (OCD), which ultimately resulted in self-imposed isolation and overwhelming fright of infection and human contact. Through *The Aviator*, we can better understand the challenges that emotional or behavioral disorders present to those affected.

—By Steven Smith

communities often use different terms when referring to similar types of behaviors. Definitions of this disability, including the one used in IDEA '04, are based on the one developed by Eli Bower (1960, 1982). Let's first look at the federal definition. IDEA '04 uses the term ***emotional disturbance*** to describe students with **emotional or behavioral disorders**. Not all students with emotional or behavioral disorders will necessarily require special education services. The special education category is reserved for those students whose behavior problems are so extreme that they adversely influence their educational performance (see Table 7.1).

Previous versions of IDEA used the term *serious emotional disturbance* to describe this disability area, but *serious* was dropped in 1999 when the U.S. Department of Education developed the regulations for the 1997 version of IDEA. Although the government changed the name of this special education category by removing the "serious" component, it did not change the substance of the definition. The government explained the reason for changing the name of the disability category as follows: "[It] is intended to have no substantive or legal significance. It is intended strictly to eliminate the pejorative connotation of the term 'serious'" (U.S. Department of Education, 1999, p. 12542). In addition, some implied parts of the federal definition are important to understand. For example, although only one characteristic listed in the IDEA '04 definition need be present for the student to qualify for special education, whatever the characteristics, the child's educational performance must be adversely affected. Because most people experience some mild maladjustment for short periods

emotional disturbance The term used in IDEA '04 for emotional or behavioral disorders

emotional or behavioral disorders A disability characterized by behavioral or emotional responses very different from all norms and referent groups with adverse effects on educational performance

Because of the many consequences of emotional or behavioral disorders, it is important for everyone—teachers, mental health services, and community agencies—to invest in helping these students to be more successful. Resources available in communities can help children and youth stay out of trouble and succeed at school (Sinclair et al., 1998; Tobin & Sugai, 1999). Although many community-based programs are in place to support these youngsters, we take a look here at one such program that is making a difference.

The Chicago Youth Centers (CYC) is a large independent youth service center that provides a range of programs to over 11,000 youngsters every year (CYC, 2008). CYC was founded in 1956 with the goal of serving some of Chicago's most challenging neighborhoods by offering a range of after-school programs in academics, athletics, arts, and counseling. The CYC program offers six content areas—nature and environment, math and science; health, social, and physical development; academic support and enhancement; the arts; career exploration, business and community outreach; and leadership development. It also works with many local schools to offer after-school programs in some of the poorest inner-city areas of Chicago. One of CYC's programs, Girl Power, helps young girls by focusing on promoting education and prevention of teenage pregnancy and drug use. This program offers much success, with thousands of former participants having gone on to college and become civic and business leaders. Even more, many of these successful youth have returned to volunteer at CYC. Yet, we need even more programs such as CYC to serve the many children and youth with emotional or behavioral disorders. To learn more about CYC and how to get involved, visit its Web site at **www.chicagoyouthcenters.org**.

over the course of our lives, the definition also requires that the child exhibit the characteristic for a long time, to a marked degree, or significant level of intensity.

The IDEA '04 term and definition have been criticized by many professionals (Kauffman & Landrum, 2009). To them, using only the word *emotional* excludes students whose disability is only behavioral. The exclusion of students who are "socially maladjusted" contributes to this misunderstanding because the term is not actually defined in IDEA '04, although many educators interpret the term *social maladjustment* as referring to students with **conduct disorders** or those youth who have been adjudicated for rule violations (APA, 2003; see Table 7.1). Also the reference to "educational performance" has been narrowly interpreted to mean only academic performance and does not take into consideration other types of performance such as behavioral or social performance, life skills, or vocational skills.

conduct disorders A psychiatric term describing externalizing, acting-out behaviors

Responding to these criticisms, a coalition of 17 organizations, which calls itself the National Mental Health and Special Education Coalition, drafted another definition (see Table 7.1) and continues to lobby federal and state governments to adopt it (Forness & Knitzer, 1992). However, some people feel that it is unlikely that this more inclusive definition will be accepted due to concerns about it identifying too many children (Kauffman, personal communication, July 14, 2002). Yet, it is useful to see this disability from another perspective—one that acknowledges a complete view in terms of both the key features and how it can exist with other types of disabilities.

Emotional or behavioral disorders can be divided into three groups that are characterized by

- externalizing behaviors,
- internalizing behaviors, or
- low-incidence disorders.

externalizing behaviors Behaviors directed toward others (e.g., aggressive behavior)

Some emotional or behavioral disorders manifest themselves outwardly, in an undercontrolled way. **Externalizing behaviors** constitute an acting-out style that

Table 7.1 • Definitions Related to Emotional or Behavioral Disorders

Source	Definition
Federal government	**Emotional Disturbance:** The term means a condition exhibiting one or more of the following characteristics over a long period of time and to a marked degree that adversely affects a child's educational performance: • An inability to learn that cannot be explained by intellectual, sensory, or health factors. • An inability to build or maintain satisfactory interpersonal relationships with peers and teachers. • Inappropriate types of behavior or feelings under normal circumstances. • A general pervasive mood of unhappiness or depression. • A tendency to develop physical symptoms related to fears associated with personal or school problems. Emotional disturbance includes schizophrenia. The term does not apply to children who are socially maladjusted, unless it is determined that they have an emotional disturbance. *U.S. Department of Education* (2006, p. 1262)
National Mental Health and Special Education Coalition	**Emotional or Behavioral Definition:** The term *emotional or behavioral disorder* means a disability characterized by behavioral or emotional responses in school so different from appropriate age, cultural, or ethnic norms that they adversely affect educational performance. Educational performance includes academic, social, vocational, and personal skills. Such a disability: • is more than a temporary, expected response to stressful events in the environment; • is consistently exhibited in two different settings, at least one of which is school-related; and • is unresponsive to direct intervention in general education, or the child's condition is such that general education interventions would be insufficient. Emotional or behavioral disorders can coexist with other disabilities. This category may include children or youths with schizophrenic disorders, affective disorders, anxiety disorder, or other sustained disorders of conduct or adjustment when they adversely affect educational performance in accordance with [the opening part of the definition]. *Forness and Knitzer* (1992, p. 13)
DSM-IV-TR	*Oppositional Defiant Disorder* a recurrent pattern of negativistic, defiant, disobedient, and hostile behavior toward authority figures . . . and is characterized by the frequent occurrence of at least four of the following behaviors: losing temper (Criterion A1), arguing with adults (Criterion A2), actively defying or refusing to comply with the requests or rules of adults (Criterion A3), deliberately doing things that will annoy other people (Criterion A4), blaming others for his or her mistakes or misbehavior (Criterion A5), being touchy or easily annoyed by others (Criterion A6), being angry and resentful (Criterion A7), or being spiteful or vindictive (Criterion A8). *APA* (2003, p. 100)
DSM-IV-TR	*Conduct Disorder* a repetitive and persistent pattern of behavior in which the basic rights of others or major age-appropriate societal norms or rules are violated, as manifested by the presence of three (or more) of the following criteria in the past 12 months, with at least one criterion present in the past 6 months: Aggression to people and animals—often bullies, threatens, or intimidates others (Criterion A1), often initiates physical fights (Criterion A2), has used a weapon that can cause serious physical harm to others (e.g., a bat, brick, broken bottle, knife, gun) (Criterion A3), has been physically cruel to people (Criterion A4), has been physically cruel to animals (Criterion A5), has stolen while confronting a victim (e.g., mugging, purse snatching, extortion, armed robbery) (Criterion A6), has forced someone into sexual activity (Criterion A7); Destruction of property—has deliberately engaged in fire setting with the intent of causing serious damage (Criterion A8), has deliberately destroyed others' property (other than by fire setting) (Criterion A9); Deceitfulness or theft—has broken into someone else's house, buildings, or car (Criterion A10), often lies to obtain goods or favors or to avoid obligations (i.e., "cons" others) (Criterion A11), has stolen items of nontrivial value without confronting a victim (e.g., shoplifting, but without breaking and entering, forgery) (Criterion 12); Serious violations of rules—often stays out at night despite parental prohibitions, beginning before age 13 years (Criterion 13), has run away from home overnight at least twice while living in parental or parental surrogate home (or once without returning for a lengthy period) (Criterion, 14), or is often truant from school, beginning before age 13 years (Criterion 15). *APA* (2003, pp. 93–94)

Sources: From 34 *CFR* Parts 300 and 303, *Assistance to States for the Education of Children with Disabilities and the Early Intervention Program for Infants and Toddlers with Disabilities; Final Regulations* (p. 1262), U.S. Department of Education, 2006, *Federal Register,* Washington, DC; S. R. Forness and J. Knitzer, 1992, "A New Proposed Definition and Terminology to Replace 'Serious Emotional Disturbance' in IDEA" (p. 13), *School Psychology Review, 21.* Copyright 1992 by the National Association of School Psychologists, Bethesda, MD. Reprinted by permission of the publisher. www.nasponline.org <http://www.nasponline.org/>; and *Diagnostic and Statistical Manual of Mental Disorders* (4th ed., Text Revision) (pp. 93–94, 100), by the American Psychiatric Association (APA), 2003, Arlington, VA: APA. Reprinted with permission.

Table 7.2 • Examples of Externalizing and Internalizing Behavior Problems

Externalizing Behaviors	Internalizing Behaviors
Violates basic rights of others	Exhibits painful shyness
Violates societal norms or rules	Is teased by peers
Has tantrums	Is neglected by peers
Causes property loss or damage	Is depressed
Is hostile	Is anorexic
Argues	Is bulimic
Is defiant	Is socially withdrawn
Is physically aggressive	Tends to be suicidal
Ignores teachers' reprimands	Has unfounded fears and phobias
Steals	Verbalizes feelings of low self-esteem
Damages others' property	Has excessive worries
Demonstrates obsessive/compulsive behaviors	Panics
Causes or threatens physical harm to people or animals	Exhibits self-destructive behavior
Uses lewd or obscene gestures	Entertains ideas of suicide
Is hyperactive	

internalizing behaviors Behaviors directed inward (e.g., withdrawn, anxious, depressed)

could be described as aggressive, impulsive, coercive, and noncompliant. Other disorders are more accurately described as "inward" or overcontrolled tendencies. **Internalizing behaviors** are typical of an inhibited style that could be described as withdrawn, lonely, depressed, and anxious (Gresham et al., 1999). Students who exhibit externalizing and internalizing behaviors are the two main groups of students with emotional or behavioral disorders, but they do not account for all of the conditions that result in placement in this special education category. The fourth edition of the *Diagnostic and Statistical Manual* (DSM-IV-TR) published by the American Psychiatric Association (APA, 2003) also describes disorders usually first diagnosed in children. However, not all of the disorders presented in the DSM-IV-TR necessarily qualify a student for special education services by the federal government (tic disorders, mood disorder, and conduct disorders). Table 7.2 defines and explains some of the common externalizing and internalizing behaviors.

Remember that behaviors that disturb others and interrupt instruction (e.g., externalizing behaviors) are identified more often and earlier than behaviors that do not capture teacher attention (e.g., internalizing behaviors). Teachers must be alert to internalizing behaviors, which are equally serious but are not always identified, leaving children without appropriate supports (Lane, 2003). Also, of course, emotional or behavioral disorders can coexist with other disabilities. Let's look at each of these types in turn.

Externalizing Behaviors

When we think about emotional or behavioral disorders, we probably first think of behaviors that are "out of control"—aggressive behaviors expressed outwardly, usually toward other persons. Some typical examples are noncompliance, hyperactivity, coercion, and aggression. Young children who have serious challenging behaviors that persist over time are the most likely to be referred for psychiatric services (Maag, 2000). Three common problems associated with externalizing behavior are hyperactivity, aggression, and delinquency. Hyperactivity was discussed in Chapter 6 because it is a common characteristic of ADHD. Remember that ADHD and emotional or behavioral disorders often occur in combination (Lynam, 1996). So it shouldn't be surprising to find that hyperactivity is a common problem among these children as well.

Aggression may show up in different ways; it may be turned toward objects, toward the self, or toward others. The DSM-IV-TR does not directly define aggression, but it does include elements of aggression in two of the disorders it describes: conduct disorders and oppositional defiant disorder (see again Table 7.1). Aggressive behavior is troublesome, especially when it is observed in very young children. Not only is the aggressive behavior concerning in itself, but also because it often indicates problems in the future such as violence, delinquency, and school dropout. A pattern of early aggressive acts beginning with annoying and bullying, followed by physical fighting, is a clear pathway to violence in late adolescence, especially for boys (Talbott & Thiede, 1999).

Some 30% to 50% of youth in correctional facilities are individuals with disabilities (IDEA Practices, 2002). In this group, learning disabilities and emotional or behavioral disorders are about equally represented (45% and 42%, respectively). Delinquency, or juvenile delinquency, is defined by the criminal justice system rather than by the medical or educational communities. Delinquency is defined by illegal acts committed by juveniles, which could include crimes such as theft or assault. While some children who are delinquent also have emotional or behavioral disorders, many do not. Similarly, not all children with emotional or behavioral disorders are also delinquent. Yet, it is important to know that many of these children and youth are at risk for being involved with the criminal justice system (Bullis & Yavnoff, 2006).

Internalizing Behaviors

Internalizing behaviors are typically expressed by being socially withdrawn. Examples of internalizing behaviors include

- anorexia or bulimia,
- depression, and
- anxiety.

Serious eating disorders that usually occur during students' teenage years are **anorexia** and **bulimia** (Manley, Rickson, & Standeven, 2000). These disorders occur because of individuals' (typically girls') preoccupation with weight and body image, their quest for thinness, and their fear of becoming overweight. A number of causes have been offered to explain these problems, such as the media's projection of extreme thinness as the image of beauty and health, competition among peers, a quest for perfectionism, personal insecurity, and strife within the family. Yet, regardless of the cause, teachers can help by noticing these preoccupations early and providing those in need with assistance from the school-site counselor, nurse, or prereferral intervention team.

It is often difficult to recognize depression in children. Among the components of **depression** are guilt, self-blame, feelings of rejection, lethargy, low self-esteem, and negative self-image. These depressive symptoms in children tend to vary according to the child's age (Morris, Shah, & Morris, 2002). For example, depression in preschoolers tends to show up as anger, problems with sleep and feeding as well as separation anxiety (Carlson & Kashani, 1988). In 6- to 8-year-olds, they tend to have trouble in school, be accident-prone, and seek attention (Edelsonh et al., 1992). Nine- to 12-year-olds tend to exhibit lethargy, report low self-esteem, engage in self-destructive behavior, and even report suicidal ideation (Kaslow & Rehm, 1998).

These symptoms of depression are often overlooked or may be interpreted as meaning that a totally different problem exists. Because children's behavior when

anorexia Intense fear of gaining weight, disturbed body image, chronic absence or refusal of appetite for food, causing severe weight loss (25% of body weight)

bulimia Chronically causing oneself to vomit or otherwise remove food to limit weight gain

depression A state of despair and dejected mood

they are depressed often appears so different from the depressed behavior of adults, teachers and parents may have trouble recognizing childhood depression. For example, a severely depressed child might attempt to harm himself by running into a busy street or hurling himself off a ledge. Adults might think the child is being reckless, rather than depressed. Also, because children often do not have the verbal skills, personal insight, or experience to recognize and label feelings of depression, they often cannot explain how they are feeling.

Finally, **anxiety disorders** may show up as extreme anxiety when being separated from family, friends, or a familiar environment; as excessive shrinking from contact with strangers; or as unfocused, excessive worry and fear. Like depression, anxiety disorders are difficult to recognize in children. Because withdrawn children engage in very low levels of positive interactions with their peers, peer rating scales may help educators identify these disorders given that many adults are not aware of how children interact with one another outside the classroom. As mentioned previously, children with internalizing behavior problems are often overlooked by teachers, making it difficult to support these youngsters. For those who do receive intervention support, medications such as antidepressants and antianxiety agents may be a component of a more comprehensive intervention plan. If medication does become a part of the intervention plan, it is important for teachers and parents to work collaboratively to make sure that medication is delivered as prescribed, particularly if medication is to be taken during the school day.

Low-Incidence Disorders

Some disorders occur very infrequently in school-age children but are quite serious when they do occur. For example, **schizophrenia**, sometimes considered a form of psychosis or a type of pervasive developmental disability (APA, 2003), rarely occurs in children even though about 1% of the general population over the age of 18 has been diagnosed as having schizophrenia. When childhood schizophrenia does occur, it can have devastating effects on a family and places great demands on service systems. It usually involves bizarre delusions (e.g., believing one's thoughts are controlled by the police), hallucinations (e.g., voices telling one what to think), "loosening" of associations (disconnected thoughts), and incoherence. Schizophrenia is most prevalent between the ages of 15 and 45. Experts indicate that the earlier the onset, the more severe the disturbance in adulthood (Newcomer, 1993). Children with schizophrenia have serious difficulties, requiring IEPs that involve the collaboration of members from the multidisciplinary team.

Excluded Behavior Problems

Two groups of children—the **socially maladjusted** and those with conduct disorders—are not eligible for special education services under the label of emotional disturbance in the IDEA '04 definition (unless they have another qualifying condition as well). Although social maladjustment is widely discussed, particularly when politicians and educators talk about discipline and violence in schools, IDEA '04 does not call it out as a special education category or as a subcategory of emotional or behavioral disorders (see Table 7.3 for recommended programs to prevent bullying). In the DSM-IV-TR, the APA (2003) defines conduct disorders as "a repetitive and persistent pattern of behavior in which the basic rights of others or major age-appropriate societal norms or rules are violated" (p. 93; again see Table 7.1). Section 504 and ADA do not have exclusions for social maladjustment, so the educational system is required to make accommodations for students with social maladjustment or conduct problems even though they do not qualify for special education services (Zirkel, 1999).

The law is clear that social maladjustment and conduct disorders are not subsets of emotional or behavioral disorders, but some argue that social maladjustment and conduct disorders are actually similar behavior patterns (Forness & Kavale, 2001; Forness & Knitzer, 1992). But how to help such students, in practice, is much

---

anxiety disorders Conditions causing painful uneasiness, emotional tension, or emotional confusion

schizophrenia A rare disorder in children that includes bizarre delusions and dissociation with reality

socially maladjusted A term applied to students who do not act within society's norms but are not considered students with emotional or behavioral disorders

Table 7.3 • Recommended Programs to Prevent Bullying

Bullying Prevention Program

- *Description:* This empirically validated program is considered to be the "gold standard" of programs designed to reduce and prevent bullying in schools. The program focuses on restructuring the school environment both to decrease the opportunities to engage in bullying and to reduce the negative social consequences of bullying.
- *Age groups:* Elementary, middle school, and junior high students
- *Contact information:*
  Center for the Study and Prevention of Violence Institute of Behavioral Science
  University of Colorado at Boulder
  Box 442
  Boulder, CO 80309–0442
  Fax: (303) 443–3297

Steps to Respect

- *Description:* This program was designed by the Committee for Children and is based on social learning principles. Steps to Respect is intended to reduce bullying and to develop prosocial relationships with peers within the context of a school-based program.
- *Age groups:* Elementary students
- *Contact information:*
  Committee for Children
  568 First Avenue South, Suite 600
  Seattle, WA 98104-2804
  Fax: (206) 438-6765

Bully-Proofing Your School

- *Description:* This program is a highly used, research-validated program that involves three domains: (a) increasing awareness of bullying problems, (b) providing explicit instruction in how to protect yourself, and (c) developing a positive school climate.
- *Age groups:* Elementary and middle school students
- *Contact information:*
  Sopris West Educational Services
  4093 Specialty Place
  Longmont, CO 80504-5400
  Fax: (888) 819–7767

Source: Adapted from Walker, Ramsey, and Gresham (2004, pp. 272–274).

less clear (Costenbader & Buntaine, 1999). Why is there so much confusion about the educational needs of children who are socially maladjusted or who have conduct disorders? Some explanations related to definitional issues and others to what people think is best for the students involved (Kauffman, 1999; Kauffman & Landrum, 2009). Here are five reasons:

- There is not a clear definition of social maladjustment.
- It is very difficult—if not impossible—to distinguish students with externalizing emotional or behavioral disorders from students with conduct disorders.
- A more inclusive definition may increase special education enrollment posing additional challenges for school in terms of resources (e.g., money, personnel) and behavioral support.
- Because the needs of students with conduct disorders may be best met by specialists prepared to deal with their problems, they should be supported within the special education structure, even if technically they do not qualify as students with disabilities.
- Many people believe these students are just choosing to misbehave and do not have disabilities.

Characteristics

Students with emotional or behavioral disorders often show some common social, behavioral, and academic characteristics. By being aware of these characteristics, educators can identify and support these students more effectively. Table 7.4 lists typical signs and characteristics that these children often exhibit.

Social Skills

Typically, these students are less socially skilled than their peers. Many students with emotional or behavioral disorders have antisocial behaviors such as limited interpersonal skills, verbal and physical aggression, and coercive tendencies that make it difficult for them to get along with both peers and adults (Walker et al., 1992). Social skills influence the way people perform academically in school, in their personal relationships, in their work relationships, and in the community.

Table 7.4 • Possible Signs or Characteristics of Emotional or Behavioral Disorders

Social	Behavioral	Academic
Rejected by peers	Exhibits verbal and physical aggression	Performs below peers on key academic skills
Interprets neutral cues as hostile	Exhibits anxiety, depression, and withdrawal	Shows low levels of academic engagement
Isolated socially	Exhibits hyperactivity, impulsivity, and distractibility	Acts out to escape work that is too difficult

myeducationlab Go to the Activities and Applications section in Chapter 7 of MyEducationLab, and complete Activity 1. As you watch the video and answer the accompanying questions, consider how the teacher incorporates her social skills curriculum into her teaching.

Being socially competent can mean a number of things: the way you exercise self-control when you have conflicts, the way you cooperate with others, and the way you assert yourself when you need to make your needs known (Elliott & Gresham, 1991; Gresham, 2002). In short, we use social skills to interact with others and perform most daily tasks. Because students with emotional or behavioral disorders have skills deficits (*can't do* problems), performance deficits (*won't do* problems), and fluency problems (*can't do very well* problems) in the area of social skills, they present problems with social skills to themselves, their families, their peers, and their teachers (Gresham, 2002; Gresham et al., 1999; Lane, Kalberg, & Menzies, 2008).

These students' behavior patterns not only can cause problems for the individual students but can hurt others as well. For example, some students with externalizing problems are prone to what Hill Walker, Frank Gresham, and their colleagues call "behavioral earthquakes"—behaviors that occur rarely but have severe consequences when they do occur (e.g., setting fires, being cruel to others, abusing animals, and assaulting adults; Walker & Severson, 1992). Students with externalizing behavioral disorders exhibit at least some of the following behaviors in excess:

- Tantrums
- Aggression
- Noncompliance
- Coercive behaviors
- Poor academic performance

In this regard, teachers can make a real difference through the instructional procedures they select. By using effective teaching procedures and actively engaging students with emotional or behavioral disorders in learning, teachers can set the stage for improved classroom behaviors as well as improved academic performance. This can be done by providing engaging lessons designed for students' individual skill level so that all learners, including those with externalizing and internalizing behaviors, are able and motivated to participate in the lessons.

Explicit instruction in social skills can help improve students' overall social competence, meaning that others will judge them to be socially skilled (Bullis, Walker, & Sprague, 2001). Effective social skills training programs provide instruction in students' individual deficits using an explicit instruction paradigm (e.g., tell, show, do, practice), rather than teaching a more global or "canned" curriculum (e.g., Lane et al., 2003; Miller, Lane, & Wehby, 2005). In this approach, skills that are not in the students' behavioral repertoire—"can't do" problems (skill deficits) rather than "won't do" problems (performance deficits) are taught (Gresham, 2002). Key components of effective programs make the difference. For example, instruction in social skills is initiated as early as possible. Teachers and parents are trained in the use of positive discipline techniques. The instruction is embedded within the general education curriculum, providing students with numerous opportunities to practice their newly acquired skills. This is done to promote generalization and maintenance of the desired social skills. Peers learn to help and

When the rules of the game are taught, clearly understood, and followed, important social skills needed in life are also learned.

provide support for each other. The outcomes of such a program can be outstanding, but it must begin early (Frey, Hirschstein, & Guzzo, 2000; Hawkins et al., 1999). Individuals who participated in social skills training programs as first graders were, at age 18,

- 20% less likely to commit violent crimes,
- 38% less likely to drink heavily, and
- 35% less likely to become pregnant or contribute to a pregnancy.

Academic Performance

"School failure is the common link between delinquency and disability" (U.S. Department of Education, 2001, p. II-3). As we discussed earlier, students with emotional or behavioral disorders typically do not perform well academically (Lane, 2004). They could be referred to as underachievers, and they lack basic skills in all academic areas (e.g., reading, writing, and math). Of course, the more severe the disability, the greater overall performance is affected, and the greater the likelihood of the child becoming delinquent and having recurring problems with the law (Archwamety & Katsiyannis, 2000). Clearly, personal struggles affect one's ability to attend to school tasks and learning in general. Failure at academic tasks compounds the difficulties these children face, not only at school but also in life beyond the school setting. Their frustration with the educational system (and its frustration with them) results in these students having the highest dropout rates of all students (National Center for Educational Statistics [NCES], 2005; Wagner & Davis, 2006). And, outcomes for students with emotional or behavioral disorders do not improve when they are out of school. They still struggle in their interpersonal relationships, have trouble in getting and maintaining employment, and access mental health services at a high rate (Bullis & Yavonoff, 2006; Walker et al., 2004). Therefore, teachers and parents need to recognize the importance of improving their academic skills, particularly in the areas of reading, writing, and mathematics so that these students can have the skill sets necessary to participate more fully in school (Lane, Harris, et al., 2008; Lane et al., 2001; Lane, Wehby, et al., 2002). If students are more engaged academically, this leaves less opportunity to be disruptive or avoid academic tasks in other ways (e.g., complaints about feeling sick [somatic complaints]). Instruction should be delivered in a systematic and predictable manner. See Tips for Effective Instruction to learn some guidelines for giving instructions or commands to students.

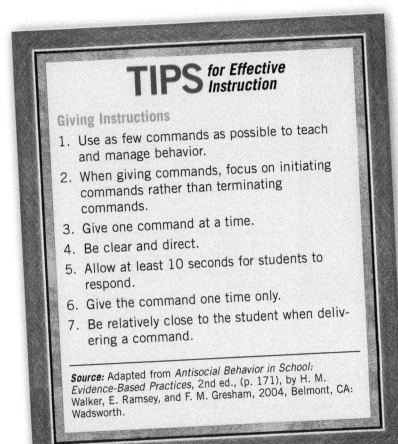

Delinquency

Clearly, students served through the emotional or behavioral disorders category have a greater probability than others of running into trouble with the law and winding up in the juvenile justice system (Walker & Sprague, 2000). Once they are in the criminal justice system, they are less likely to receive services and supports specified in their IEPs (National Center on Education, Delinquency and Juvenile Justice [NCJJ], 2002). For more information about youth with and without disabilities and the juvenile justice system, go to www.edjj.org, the Web site of the National Center on Education, Disability, and Juvenile Justice (EDJJ). Furthermore, the paths of those with emotional or behavioral disorders leading to long-term negative outcomes are now taking shape (Walker & Sprague 1999). Look at Figure 7.1, which highlights some of the major markers or signals for quick and early intervention in an effort to alter predictable patterns of negative results.

In recent years, students' behaviors at school have become increasingly caustic, hostile, and even violent (Bender, Shubert, & McLaughlin, 2001; Maag, 2001). Although there have been some declines in juvenile violence in recent years, the prevalence of violent crimes continues to be highly disturbing. For example, 28 out of every 1,000 students are victims of crime, and 6% of all victims of aggressive acts are hurt on school grounds (DeVoe et al., 2003). It should come as no surprise that high school students who completed a national survey in 2003 reported that the fear of school-related crime prompted 5 out of 100 students to miss school at least once (Snyder & Sickmund, 2006). These are just some of the statistics that illustrate what a frightening place school can be for many students (Lane et al., 2008).

Yet, it is also important to recognize that despite all the media attention and parents' perceptions that schools are out of control, school violence is actually on the decline, and schools are the safest place where children can spend their days (Child Defense Fund [CDF], 2004). School shootings such as those that occurred at Columbine High School in Colorado; Red Lake, Minnesota; and Hillsborough, North Carolina raise serious concerns, particularly given the extreme consequences of these violent acts (Kauffman & Landrum, 2009; see Information Please Database, 2007, for additional information on school violence). But, it is the increase in more frequent and small acts of defiance that also has educators worried. Verbal and physical aggression is on the increase. Some scholars and social observers have speculated about why this is so (Begley, 1999; Bender, Shubert, & McLaughlin, 2001):

- Aggression, violence, and alienation observed in schools simply mirror their presence in society at large.
- Individuals who see high rates of violence become desensitized, devaluing life.
- Fewer hospital and center school placements are available, limiting supports for these students.
- General education teachers are not trained to deal with violence and aggression.

Figure 7.1 • The Path to Long-Term Negative Outcomes for At-Risk Children and Youth

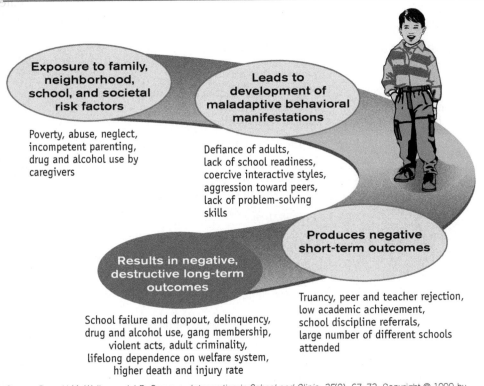

Exposure to family, neighborhood, school, and societal risk factors

Poverty, abuse, neglect, incompetent parenting, drug and alcohol use by caregivers

Leads to development of maladaptive behavioral manifestations

Defiance of adults, lack of school readiness, coercive interactive styles, aggression toward peers, lack of problem-solving skills

Produces negative short-term outcomes

Truancy, peer and teacher rejection, low academic achievement, school discipline referrals, large number of different schools attended

Results in negative, destructive long-term outcomes

School failure and dropout, delinquency, drug and alcohol use, gang membership, violent acts, adult criminality, lifelong dependence on welfare system, higher death and injury rate

As Americans puzzle about the "whys" of school violence and struggle with the fear associated with these horrific occurrences, educators and researchers must focus their efforts on (a) identifying predictors and (b) designing effective prevention efforts. Violence is comparatively rare, but the prospect of even a single case demands that schools be prepared. Fortunately, several researchers are turning their attention to the problem and are providing teachers and administrators with information about how to prevent school violence and what actions to take if it does occur (Bender & McLaughlin, 1997; CDF, 2001, 2004; Myles & Simpson, 1998). For suggestions on preventing school violence, as well as what to do if a crisis occurs, see Accommodating for Inclusive Environments.

Prevalence

About 1% of all school-age children are identified as having this disability and are receiving special education services under the label of emotional disturbance (Office of Special Education Programs [OSEP], 2008). However, some believe that the actual prevalence should be approximately 3% to 6% of all students (Kauffman & Landrum, 2009).

You may wonder why there is a large discrepancy between those currently receiving services and those who may have emotional or behavioral disorders. Two major reasons may explain why it is difficult to estimate accurately the prevalence of emotional or behavioral disorders. First, the definition remains unclear and rather subjective. Second, because the label is viewed as stigmatizing, many educators and school districts are reluctant to identify many children.

Gender and race are important factors in prevalence, with clear differences showing up in the identification of this exceptionality. Males are far more likely than females to be identified as having an emotional disturbance. The reason for this

Accommodating for Inclusive Environments
Being Prepared for School Violence

Develop Schoolwide Positive Behavior Support Programs to

- establish common rules and expectations for all students in all school settings (e.g., classroom, hallways, cafeterias, etc.),
- teach these rules and expectations to all students,
- reinforce students who follow the rules and meet these expectations, and
- provide more intensive levels of support (secondary and tertiary interventions) to meet the behavioral, social, and academic needs of students who are not responding to the schoolwide (primary) intervention efforts.

Be Alert to

- whispers and talk of potential confrontation,
- unattended book bags and backpacks,
- students with a history of violence, and
- closed classroom doors.

Make Plans for

- teacher buddy systems,
- responding to the sounds of gunshots,
- hostage crises, and
- all-clear signals.

Practice for a Crisis by Knowing

- where students should go during an incident,
- whom to notify, and
- roles for every staff member.

Train and Inform All School Staff Members About

- general methods used to resolve conflict,
- standard procedures to follow, and
- the contents of every behavioral intervention plan.

Be Prepared to

- develop trust and positive relationships with all students,
- consistently apply behavioral techniques and consequences,
- dress appropriately (comfortable shoes, loose clothing), and
- put valuables and fragile items out of reach.

Apply These Principles If a Crisis Occurs

- Remain calm and in control.
- Keep tone of voice steady and firm.
- Seek assistance.
- Ignore accusations.

Prepare for Emergencies

- Obtain a copy of your school's emergency plans.
- Review emergency procedures.

gender difference is not clear, but it is probably linked to boys' higher propensity to be troublesome and violate school rules, coupled with girls' tendency toward less disruptive, internalizing behaviors that are less likely to result in referral. Whereas Asian American and Hispanic students tend to be underrepresented in this special education category, African Americans are overrepresented (OSEP, 2008). In fact, African American students are almost twice as likely to be identified as having emotional or behavioral disorders than would be expected from their actual percentage in the general population. Take a look at Considering Culture to see how parents and teachers may have conflicting viewpoints about how to best help students with emotional or behavioral problems as well as how to address these differing perspectives.

Causes and Prevention

As is true of most disabilities, it is difficult—if not impossible—to determine the specific causes of emotional or behavioral disorders. However, relationships between some causal factors and this disability are becoming more clear. For example, children who experience physical abuse tend to have a higher probability of being identified with emotional or behavioral disorders (Cauce et al., 2000).

Considering Culture: *Nearly at an Impasse!*

Donalene Lewis and her son's teacher, Melinda, begin at an impasse! Jamal is a fifth grader in Melinda's class, and Melinda thinks he should be referred for special education testing because of his behavior in the classroom. Jamal is not paying attention in class, frequently disrupts his classmates, and is prone to inappropriate and abusive verbal outbursts. Melinda feels that he has behavioral disorders and she wants help managing his behavior. Melinda knows that Jamal's mother is struggling to support her family and that she works several part-time jobs to keep their apartment and provide basic needs. Recently, Melinda asked Mrs. Lewis to meet with her, and during their conference, Melinda raised the possibility that Jamal might need some extra services. Donalene hit the roof! She recounted her struggle raising Jamal—his prematurity and long stay in the hospital, his repeated subsequent hospitalizations, and her tireless attempts to get him the medical care that he needed. She emphatically stated, "And now he is at Drew Elementary School with other kids in his neighborhood. He's doing fine in school and he likes playing basketball on the playground. There's no way he's going to be put in special education just because that's what they do with Black kids! Now I know we can't talk about everything wrong with society. But why is it always the Black kids that are diagnosed? Jamal is just a little more rambunctious than others, and the school should help him to get along. That's what a school is supposed to do."

Melinda feels herself begin to get defensive and even angry that she should have to cope with this. She finds herself just wanting to get Jamal out of the classroom! But she also remembers how great Jamal is at science projects; he is always eager and creative. And it is obvious how much this mother cares about her youngster and wants what is best for him. Melinda invites Mrs. Lewis to review Jamal's schoolwork. She points out the areas in which he is falling behind, but she also points out all the strengths Jamal shows, particularly in science. She invites Mrs. Lewis to visit the classroom and observe how the other children react when Jamal has an outburst and how marginalized he is becoming; his classmates are avoiding him during free time and many don't want to be partnered with him for group projects. She has noticed Jamal walking with some older kids after school—kids who often get into trouble in the neighborhood. Melinda asks Mrs. Lewis to review this information, visit the class, and then meet with her again in several weeks to discuss the observations they both have made.

Questions to Consider

1. Can you understand Mrs. Lewis's perspective? Can you understand why she feels that Jamal will be better served by not being labeled and isolated?

2. Did you know that children of color are over-represented in the population of children in special education? Why do you think that is the case?

3. As a teacher, what can you do to bridge this communication divide and get Jamal the help that he may need, while acknowledging and honoring Mrs. Lewis's concerns?

—By Eleanor Lynch, San Diego State University and Marci Hanson, San Francisco State University

---

Also, there appears to be a link between the factors related to poverty and emotional or behavioral disorders (CDF, 2004; Hosp & Reschly, 2002). Finally, for some children, a biological explanation will emerge (Forness & Kavale, 2001).

Causes

The reasons that such problems arise in a particular child are usually difficult to identify precisely, and it is quite likely that a disability is the result of several factors that tend to co-occur (Walker & Sprague, 2000). Let's take a look at three general areas that can contribute to emotional or behavioral disorders: biology, home and community, and school.

Biology   Just as for many other disabilities, more and more biological and genetic causes for emotional or behavioral disorders are being identified (Forness & Kavale, 2001). For example, research suggests a relationship between prenatal drug exposure and childhood emotional or behavioral disorders: 53% of drug-exposed participants in Head Start preschool programs are identified as having these disabilities as early as kindergarten (Sinclair, 1998). Furthermore, mood disorders, depression, and schizophrenia may have a genetic foundation (APA, 2003). The reason that it is important to know if biological reasons contribute to emotional or behavioral disorders is because this information can be used to inform intervention efforts. For example, knowing that depression has a biological cause allows for the development and use of medications prescribed to target this condition (Forness & Kavale, 2001). Antidepressants are now an important component in many treatment programs for depression (Pappadopulos & Jensen, 2001). As researchers continue to find biological causes, more medical and behavioral treatments will become available.

Home and Community   As you may know, culture and environment provided a context for all behavior (Maag, 2000). Everyone plays a range of roles—as a member of an immediate family, an extended family, or a community network (neighborhood, church, clubs). All of these environments and the interactions that take place in these environments shape how people grow and develop, whether positively or negatively. Although a single negative experience does not necessarily lead to the development of emotional problems, it is possible that multiple risk factors such as poverty, abuse, neglect, parental stress, inconsistent expectations and rules, confusion, and turmoil over long periods of time can contribute to the development of such problems. Some factors that can collectively contribute to the development of emotional or behavioral problems are poverty and certain parenting styles (CDF, 2004; Hosp & Reschly, 2002; Reid & Patterson, 1991). Some examples of parenting behaviors that can be problematic are poor supervision, punitive and inconsistent discipline styles, low rates of positive interactions, and high rates of negative interactions (Reid & Patterson, 1991). Furthermore, children whose parents are violent and have arrest records also tend to become violent and to find themselves in trouble with the law (Hallahan, Kauffman, & Pullen, 2009; Rudo et al., 1998). Another link with poverty is clear: Students whose family incomes are in the bottom 20% of American families are five times more likely to drop out of school than their peers whose family incomes are in the top 20% of American families (NCES, 2001).

School   Teachers and schools can also play a large role in how students develop, academically and behaviorally (Tolan, Gorman-Smith, & Henry, 2001). Teachers' expectations influence the types of questions they ask students, the feedback they offer, and the number and nature of their teacher–student interactions. What educators do makes a difference—for either better or worse. For example, a teacher who is unskilled in managing the classroom or is not well equipped to manage individual student differences may unintentionally create an environment wherein frustration or withdrawal is a common response. However, teachers skilled at managing classroom behavior can provide instruction that meets students' academic and behavioral needs consistently. When effective teaching and behavior management methods are in place, students' academic, behavioral, and social outcomes improve (Bryant, Smith, & Bryant, 2008; Walker et al., 2004). Good teachers are able to analyze their relationships with their students and the learning environment. In short, strong teachers can identify preventive approaches to keep problems from occurring as well as use data-based approaches to respond to existing problems. Here are some key components of safe and effective schools (Walker et al., 2004; Walker & Sprague, 2000):

- Consistency of rules, expectations, and consequences in all key settings
- Positive school climate

- Schoolwide strategies for resolving conflict
- High level of supervision in all school settings
- Cultural sensitivity
- Strong feelings of identification and involvement on the part of students
- High levels of parent and community involvement
- Well-utilized space and lack of overcrowding

Prevention

One of the first steps in preventing the development of emotional or behavioral disorders is determining which specific behaviors (e.g., aggression) can predict later problems. Remember, behaviors indicative of risk at one stage of development may not be the same behaviors indicative of risk at another stage of development. Why might this be so? Standards for normal or typical behavior change as children grow up and move across the developmental continuum. When children behave quite differently from what is expected for their age group, it may become a cause for concern. For example, the behavior of an 8-year-old who suddenly begins to wet the bed, clings to his mother, and stops talking creates great concern. Even though almost identical behavior would be totally acceptable for a toddler for a short period of time, an 8-year-old who acts in this way is perceived as having a problem. Many other behaviors may indicate concern at one age, but not another (e.g., tantrums, smearing feces).

When students are engaged in learning, their behavior reflects their engagement.

The fact that behavior inappropriate for an individual's age draws attention and can play a role in the individual's being identified as having an emotional or behavioral disorder makes some experts worry about subjectivity in the identification process. Fortunately, systematic screening tools are designed for use across the K–12 continuum to detect students with emotional or behavioral disorders. The *Systematic Screening for Behavior Disorders* (Walker & Severson, 1992) can be used at the elementary level to look for students with externalizing or internalizing behavior problems. The *Student Risk Screening Scale* (Drummond, 1994) was originally designed for use at the elementary level but recently has been used in middle and high schools (Lane, Kalberg, & Edwards, 2008; Lane, Robertson, & Graham-Bailey, 2007). Finally, the *Strengths and Difficulties Questionnaire* (SDQ; Goodman, 1997) is available for use for ages 3 to 17. Two benefits of using systematic screening tools to look for students with emotional or behavioral disorders are that it (a) removes some of the subjectivity and (b) reduces the burden placed on teachers to identify students who may need additional support.

Some concerns about this category of special education focus on the disproportionate number of African American males receiving special education services under the label of emotional disturbance (Townsend, 2000; OSEP, 2008). While African American boys are overrepresented, other groups, such as Asian Americans and girls, are underrepresented in this category. The possible explanations for this disproportionate representation include a lack of reliable methods for identifying these children—especially students with internalizing behaviors. Current knowledge can guide educators' actions until more accurate assessment procedures are available:

- Systematic screening tools should be implemented across the K–12 continuum.
- Evaluation measures should come from at least two different settings.
- Performance in both academics and social skills should be considered.
- Information should come from a range of people in the child's life.
- Many methods to assess students' behavior should be used (behavior rating scales, ecological assessments, interviews, standardized tests, social work evaluations, psychiatric analyses, functional assessments).

Overcoming Challenges

Preventing the development of new cases of emotional or behavioral disorders and supporting existing cases can be accomplished in many different ways, but the implementation of three different approaches could cause a substantial reduction in the prevalence of this disability:

- Medical management
- Reducing overrepresentation
- School-based interventions

Medical management can help reduce the number of students with emotional or behavioral disorders in two ways: by preventing the condition or by eliminating or ameliorating the symptoms as soon as the condition is evident. For example, consider the case of fetal alcohol syndrome. First, the behavioral effects of fetal alcohol syndrome can be prevented if women do not drink when pregnant. Second, intervention efforts can be implemented to support those with the condition. In some cases the condition can be treated through medication. Considerable controversy exists about the use of prescription drugs to reduce hyperactivity and the disruption that the condition causes (Zametkin & Earnst, 1999). Because American children are being prescribed and taking drugs such as Ritalin and other stimulants at a rate some five times higher than children elsewhere in the world, many educators have been calling for a greater use of classroom management interventions and interventions based on the reason that problem behaviors occur (functional assessment-based interventions) to reduce both inappropriate behavior and avoid overreliance on medication (Pancheri & Prater, 1999; Umbreit, Lane, & Dejud, 2004). Some experts who have studied this issue believe that medication is effective (Forness & Kavale, 2001). However, they have also concluded that some medication is even more powerful when used in combination with behavior management techniques. In the same study, Steve Forness and Ken Kavale found that the majority of children with school behavior problems have treatable psychiatric disorders, such as mood disorders, anxiety disorders, or schizophrenia. Antidepressants are effective in some of these cases.

For many years, the overrepresentation of African American boys in special education has concerned policymakers, educators, and parents (National Alliance of Black School Educators [NABSE] & ILIAD Project, 2002). More so than any other disability group, these youngsters are clearly overrepresented in the emotional disturbance category of IDEA '04 (OSEP, 2008). Although the number of youths held in the juvenile justice system is small—less than 1% of all youths—more than half of them—58%—are diverse (CDF, 2004).

Furthermore, African American students are three times more likely to be suspended from school (Townsend, 2000). Being suspended is part of a vicious cycle that compounds students' problems at school. Namely, some students are suspended for not performing well behaviorally at school. Yet, by being suspended they cannot participate in the academic learning opportunities at school. They also miss the opportunity to learn and demonstrate the desired behavior patterns to facilitate academic success. This situation then leads to lower academic achievement and higher probability of future misbehavior, particularly if being out of school is more reinforcing than being in school. Collectively, these factors may contribute to special education referrals. It is important that educators become more culturally sensitive and help students understand rules of conduct and what is considered appropriate behavior at school as well as in the community (Cartledge, Kea, & Ida, 2000; Sugai & Horner, 2002).

In recent years, school-based interventions have focused on building three-tiered models of **positive behavior support** (PBS) containing primary (schoolwide), secondary (more focused, often small groups), and tertiary (highly focused, individualized) levels of support. This three-tiered model of support is comparable to the RTI

positive behavior support A three-tiered model of support with progressively more intensive levels of intervention

model discussed in Chapters 1 and 5 in that the model is designed to meet all students' needs by providing progressively more intensive levels of support for students identified as needing more assistance as determined by analyzing existing data. In the PBS model, the primary prevention program involves establishing schoolwide expectations for all key areas. Expectations are clear, concise, and simple (e.g., follow directions, be responsible, be safe, be prepared), with detailed illustrations of how these behaviors look in different settings. Then, students are given opportunities to practice and receive reinforcement for meeting these expectations (Lewis & Sugai, 1999; Sugai & Horner, 2002). Systematic reviews of primary prevention programs at the elementary (Lane, Kalberg, & Edwards, 2008), middle, and high school (Lane et al., 2006) levels suggest that such programs are associated with decreases in office referrals and suspensions. Several studies have also reported improved hallway and recess behavior and some have even found improvements in students' social interactions and academic outcomes. One important premise of such programs is preventing problem behaviors by taking an instructional approach to behavior (Horner et al., 2001; Lane, Kalberg, & Menzies, in press). For those who do not respond to these primary prevention efforts, more focused intervention (e.g., secondary and tertiary levels) is provided (Lane, Wehby, et al., 2003). Tertiary levels of prevention are reserved for students with the most intensive needs. One type of tertiary support are function-based interventions in which a **functional behavioral assessment** is conducted to determine the cause of the behavior and then teach the students more reliable, efficient ways of getting their needs met (Umbreit et al., 2007). Some educators add a mentorship element, where successful secondary students with emotional or behavioral disorders help elementary students understand classroom expectations and how to act appropriately (Burrell et al., 2001).

Early intervention can shape patterns of behavior to prevent students from going on to have long-term problems that impact not only themselves but society as well (Bullis et al., 2001; Feil, Walker, & Severson, 1995; Strain & Timm, 1998; Walker & Sprague, 2000). Very young children who exhibit antisocial behavior, set fires, are cruel to animals, and are highly aggressive are most at risk for having serious externalizing behavioral disorders. Fortunately, these students can be identified early on with the use of the systematic screening tools that we described earlier. Students who are identified during the preschool years can participate in structured and intensive preschool programs with a goal of receiving the early intervention necessary to prevent the development of emotional or behavioral problems and reduce the need for disciplinary actions in the school setting (see What IDEA '04 Says About Discipline and Students with Disabilities).

Unfortunately, despite the growing number of systematic screening tools available for use and the knowledge that has been generated about how to prevent the development of emotional or behavioral disorders, oftentimes these tools and supports are not put in place. In a provocative commentary, Jim Kauffman (1999) noted that despite discussions about the importance of prevention efforts, actions in the last decade of the 20th century did not keep pace for a number of possible reasons. Possibly due to fear of misidentifying children or concerns about having to support students who are identified, public systems tend to provide intervention services too

---

What IDEA '04 Says About . . .

Discipline and Students with Disabilities

- Students who violate student conduct code will be individually considered for changes in placement, with consideration given to unique circumstances.
- Conduct code violations can result in removal to Interim Alternative Educational Settings (IAES), another setting, or suspension for up to 10 school days to the extent that such alternatives are applied to students without disabilities (SWD).
- Students removed from current placements continue to receive educational services in order to progress toward IEP goals.
- Within 10 school days of a change-of-placement decision, IEP team must determine whether the behavior was the result of either (a) the disability or (b) poor implementation of the IEP.
- If either of these applies (manifestation determination), the team must (a) conduct a behavioral assessment, (b) implement a behavioral intervention, and (c) return the child to the original placement.
- When behavioral intervention plans are already in existence, the team will review and modify them as necessary.
- Regardless of manifestation determination, students may be removed to IAES for up to 45 school days for violations involving weapons, drugs, or infliction of serious bodily injury.

functional behavioral assessments A process in which interviews, observations, and environmental manipulations are conducted to determine "why" certain behaviors occur

myeducationlab Go to the Activities and Applications section in Chapter 7 of MyEducationLab, and complete Activity 2. As you watch the video and answer the accompanying questions, consider how the PBS program has changed the behavior of students at an elementary school.

TIPS for Classroom Management

GETTING STUDENTS INVOLVED

1. Provide students with a high rate of opportunities to respond.
2. Incorporate choice that allows students a chance to choose which tasks to complete first.
3. Have students complete a series of quick tasks that they are likely to complete without a struggle (high-probability tasks) before asking them to do tasks that they may not prefer as much (low-probability tasks).
4. Maintain close proximity to students as your presence will help keep them engaged and help them control their behaviors.
5. Provide instructional tasks that are neither too easy nor too difficult, but are within their instructional level.
6. Provide high rates of positive feedback and behavior-specific praise for correct responding.

late, when the chance of success is reduced. To be more effective, intervention must begin early and include practices that are evidenced based, meaning that sufficient research supports the use and effectiveness of such practices (Gersten et al., 2005; Horner et al., 2005). Clearly, for most children, particularly those at low risk, classroom interventions can be successful. However, Kauffman (1999) estimates that some 5% to 10% of students in general education may require intensive, intrusive, individualized help. But the way the education system is set up essentially "prevents prevention." Here is how Kauffman thinks it should work:

- Reinforce desirable behavior.
- Use reductive techniques to decrease undesirable behavior.
- Provide direct instruction for both social and academic skills.
- Correct the environmental conditions that foster deviant behavior.
- Provide students with clear expectations.
- Standardize responses to children across the entire school setting.
- Monitor students' behavior closely.

In addition to Kauffman's recommendations, other practices can prevent inappropriate behavior and help students acquire more desirable behaviors. Functional behavioral assessments can help teachers determine what events set the stage for the undesirable behavior to occur and those conditions (e.g., positive or negative reinforcement in the areas of attention, tasks/activities, or sensory input) that encourage the problem behavior to continue (Umbreit et al., 2007). Many teachers use a less complicated system that employs the antecedent, behavior, and consequence events to target behavior for specific interventions. Tips for Classroom Management offers guidelines for other approaches to classroom management that focus on getting students involved, leaving them limited time to be off task or engage in problem behavior (Davis et al., 1992; Shores, Gunter, & Jack, 1993; Stichter et al., 2006; Sutherland, Alder, & Gunter, 2003).

What teachers do in school and classroom settings can make a real difference in reducing and preventing behavior problems for both those at risk for emotional or behavioral disorders and those already identified (Kamps et al., 1999). Here's what works:

- *Behavior management.* Include a point system for appropriate behavior and task completion, wherein good behavior is charted and students earn rewards.
- *Systematic intervention plans.* Use a hierarchy of tactics, depending on students' behavior.
- *Home–school communication.* Include notes to the home and home-based reward systems.
- *Peer involvement.* Have classmates reinforce each other for meeting expectations.
- *Classroom structure.* Employ guided practice and well-organized transitions from activity to activity.
- *Supervised free periods.* Have adults monitor unstructured parts of the school day (recess, hall changes, lunch).
- *Consistent standards.* Be sure all school staff members use the same standards for acceptable behavior and hold high expectations for academic performance.

Assessment

A range of assessment tools and procedures are needed to identify and better serve students with emotional or behavioral disorders (Walker et al., 2004). Specifically, we need reliable, valid, precise, and cost-effective instruments that will allow educators to

- screen large numbers of students;
- determine which students have, or are at risk for, emotional or behavioral disorders;
- inform placement decisions;
- monitor student progress;
- provide necessary and sufficient intervention and instruction; and
- document the effectiveness of various intervention efforts.

In each case, the purpose of the assessment is to generate information that will contribute to the best possible decisions for the student (Witt et al., 1988).

Early Identification: Screening

The main reason for using screening tools such as the *Systematic Screening for Behavior Disorders* (Walker & Severson, 1992), *Student Risk Screening Scale* (Drummond, 1994), and the *Strengths and Difficulties Questionnaire* (Goodman, 1997) is to identify students who show "soft signs" that are associated with emotional or behavioral disorders. What are soft signs? As you'll recall, not all students with emotional or behavioral disorders

have acting-out problems. Some students have internalizing behavioral disorders, which means that they are often painfully shy, anxious, or depressed. These students may struggle in their interactions with peers and teachers. Still other students have externalizing behavioral disorders, which means they exhibit verbal and physical aggression and noncompliance, which pose significant challenges to their teachers by defying their authority and interfering with instruction. Given this wide range of students with emotional or behavioral disorders, it is important to use screening tools that are able to detect different types of behavioral concerns, such as the *Systematic Screening for Behavioral Disorders*.

Behavior in the classroom is directly related to classroom events, and data about the events that come before, during, and after an inappropriate or disruptive behavior can lead to solutions and application of the most effective interventions possible.

By using screenings across the K–12 grade span, it is possible to identify and support students of all ages. The goal of screening is to catch students early and provide the support necessary to prevent the development of more serious problems that may require special education services as well as other supports (Lane, 2004). Yet many schools do not use systematic screening. Why? Just as Kauffman (1999) suggested, some educators may be concerned about having to provide extra supports to students who are identified during the screening process. Limited resources complicate the implementation of early screening. However, in the long run, it may be less costly to identify and support these students early on in their educational careers rather than intervening later when the behavior problems have become more extreme. Other educators may be concerned that students identified via screening might eventually go on to require special education services under the IDEA '04 label of *emotional disturbance*. Some view this label as "stigmatizing" and believe it has implications regarding how these students can be disciplined at school (Kauffman, 1999). These are just some of the reasons that screening instruments, despite the low cost, are available but are not always used.

Prereferral: Early Intervention

General education teachers use their knowledge and skills to support students with and at risk for emotional or behavioral problems to the maximum extent possible. For example, teachers often

- develop group-based classroom management plans to support good behavior;
- collaborate with parents to help these students develop the skills necessary to be successful in the classroom;
- modify assignments to ensure that the task demands are within their skills set; and
- provide individualized behavior supports to help them meet the multiple academic, social, and behavioral expectations of the classroom setting.

Yet, when behavioral excesses and deficits become so extreme that they interfere with teacher's ability to instruct all students or when the students' academic performance is far below grade level, the teacher may refer the student to the prereferral intervention team (Lane, Mahdavi, & Borthwick-Duffy, 2003).

The prereferral intervention is a general education process in which professionals work together with parents to design interventions for use in the general education classroom. The goal of the prereferral intervention process is to help students perform more successfully in the general education setting and reduce the number of inappropriate referrals to special education. The interventions generated by the team of professionals are put into place by the classroom team with the necessary supports. It is recommended that data be collected to

- ensure that people agree with the intervention goals, procedures, and outcomes;
- be sure the intervention is put in place as designed—with treatment integrity;
- monitor student progress; and
- determine when to fade or modify the plan.

If the interventions proposed by the prereferral intervention team embody these recommendations (Lane & Beebe-Frankenberger, 2004) but do not produce the intended objectives, the next step is to make a referral to determine if the student qualifies for special education services under IDEA '04.

Identification

If interventions generated by the prereferral team do not meet the specified objectives, teachers may seek parent permission to begin a more formal process of assessing the student to determine whether he or she qualifies for special education services. This process involves a range of assessments, among them measures of cognitive ability, achievement in various skill areas, social competence, and behavioral performance. These tools and procedures include student-administered tests, behavior rating scales, and direct observations, all of which are only conducted with written permission from the parent or guardian.

The multidisciplinary team is responsible for interpreting assessment results. If the team determines that special education services as specified in IDEA '04 are warranted, and if the parent agrees, the student receives those services specified on the IEP. As we discussed in Chapter 2, students who qualify for special education services are not necessarily placed in self-contained or segregated classrooms because the provision of least restrictive environment (LRE) must be met.

Evaluation: Testing Accommodations

Once a student is identified as needing special education services, her or his performance is evaluated in a variety of ways. First, the goals and objectives specified in the IEP, which include social, behavioral, and academic areas, are evaluated via direct measures of performance in the curriculum and their behavior observed at school. For example, people other than the classroom teacher can measure aggressive acts or noncompliance by a using direct observation techniques (e.g., tally marks for the number of occurrences or a stop watch to measure the length or duration of occurrence). Oral reading fluency (e.g., correct words read per minute) and writing skills (e.g., number of story elements contained in a writing prompt) may be assessed using curriculum-based probes designed for a given grade level, like those described in more detail in Chapter 5. It is important that each objective be monitored frequently, with assessment tools that are feasible to administer, reliable, and sensitive enough to detect change.

Second, students take the same state- and districtwide achievement tests as general education students and students who are receiving special education services under other high-incidence disability categories. Depending on the nature of the student's disability, it is possible that modifications such as additional time may be specified in the IEP and provided during instruction and testing situations. These assessment results provide information on present levels of functioning and how the student is progressing. Again, it is important that all assessments be reliable, valid, and feasible in a school setting (Walker et al., 2004).

Early Intervention

As you may recall, students with emotional or behavioral disorders often experience negative outcomes at school, as well as when they leave the school system. One potential explanation for these dismal outcomes stems, in part, from an educational system that struggles to identify and support these children and youth in a manner that recognizes their multiple needs. Given that behavior and academic problems are most easily fixed when they are identified at a young age, early intervention is very important (Kazdin, 1987; Lane, 2004). Severe disabilities, such as a psychosis, sometimes manifest themselves during the early developmental period, but some types of emotional or behavioral disorders can be challenging to identify in young children. For example, some internalizing behavior problems are not typically identified until children are of school age. However, as we discussed earlier in this chapter, extreme externalizing behaviors are often obvious by age 3. Although many preschoolers behave well and learn social rules quickly, some do not (Little, 2002). Indeed, 15% of preschoolers engage daily in three or more acts of overt aggressive behavior (e.g., hitting and kicking, pushing), and 10% exhibit daily episodes of serious antisocial behavior (e.g., calling names, playing mean tricks). Early intervention is important, because it allows teachers and parents to identify and support children who display soft signs of emotional or behavioral problems when such behaviors are more easily changed.

Benefits

There are many benefits to early identification and support of young children with emotional or behavioral disorders (Bullis et al., 2001; Feil et al., 1995; Walker & Sprague, 1999, 2000). First, problem behaviors seen in preschoolers tend to be very

myeducationlab Go to the Activities and Applications section in Chapter 7 of MyEducationLab, and complete Activity 3. As you watch the video and answer the accompanying questions, consider ways in which very young children might be displaying "soft signs" of future emotional or behavioral problems.

stable over time. In other words, they do not go away as children get older. Without necessary supports, they may even worsen. Behavior problems often seem to follow a path. Here's a common sequence:

1. A child progresses from noncompliance at home, to temper tantrums, and then to the teacher reporting problems relating to interacting with others.
2. Prior behavior problems begin to predict present and future learning problems.
3. Delinquent and criminal tendencies emerge.
4. Early intervening with child and family can break the predictable and negative sequence.

While children with early onset of antisocial behavior (e.g., aggression) are only 3% to 5% of all children and youth, they account for 50% of all crimes committed. We can all make a difference in the lives of these individuals and their families by advocating for early identification and intervention.

Review again Figure 7.1. That figure illustrates the path that leads to long-term negative outcomes for too many of these students. Fortunately, quick, direct, and intensive early intervention can alter this path and lead to positive outcomes instead.

Early intervention can address problems early on, before they grow more serious or become firmly entrenched patterns. This can help avoid the need for more intensive interventions later in the child's life and reduce stress of the persons involved with the child (e.g., parents, siblings, teachers, and peers). In a developing strand of longitudinal research, Phil Strain, Matt Timm, and their colleagues are demonstrating the power of early intervention (Strain et al., 1982; Strain & Timm, 1998, 1999, 2001). They have followed up 40 individuals, now in their late twenties and early thirties, who participated in the Regional Intervention Project (RIP), a behavioral intervention program for preschool-age children at risk for emotional or behavioral disorders. Their results are impressive and demonstrate the power of early intervention during the preschool years. Their outcomes are unlike what would be expected of young children displaying serious aggressive and antisocial behaviors. Can you believe that two of their subjects are enrolled in doctoral programs, three have earned master's degrees, three have received bachelor's degrees, five others are enrolled in college, and three are high school graduates? Only three are high school dropouts. Compare these results with those typically seen for students with emotional or behavioral disorders who have a 55% high school dropout rate! Other studies of early intervention have also shown the power of such programs. For example, the one developed by Hill Walker and colleagues, First Steps to Success, shows that early intervention programs can make a difference (Walker et al., 1998). This is particularly true when the programs have the following components:

- Parent involvement
- Teaching, through examples, about the relationship between behavior and its consequences
- Instruction on appropriate behaviors for different settings (setting demands)
- Showing how to make and keep friendships

Signals of Risk

The relationships among emotional or behavioral disorders, serious juvenile problems, and poor adult outcomes are clear. Signals of later problems in young boys and girls include the following five characteristics (Day & Hunt, 1996; Miller-Johnson et al., 1999; Strain & Timm, 1998; Walker et al., 2004).

- Problem behaviors are identifiable by age 3 and often stable by age 8.
- Overt (e.g., bullying) and covert (e.g., stealing) antisocial activities are becoming behavior patterns.
- Problems happen across settings (at home, at school, and in the community).
- The child is both overactive and inattentive.
- Extreme aggression is frequent.

Of these five characteristics of young children prone to later problems, the single-best predictor is aggression. For example, sixth graders referred for special services because of both violent and nonviolent inappropriate social behaviors are likely to present chronic discipline problems during their remaining school years and also to drop out of school (Tobin & Sugai, 1999). Some students who exhibit these five characteristics are apt to experience other negative outcomes: substance abuse, teen pregnancy, sexually transmitted diseases, problems with personal relationships, chronic unemployment, problems in their employment, and psychiatric disorders (depression and personality disorders; Wagner & Davis, 2006). Long-term follow-up studies have established the effectiveness of early intervention for these individuals, so it is essential that these extra supports be implemented as early as possible—ideally during the preschool years (Strain & Timm, 1998). Many preschoolers need direct intervention to learn early that aggressive and antisocial behaviors are not acceptable and instead learn more prosocial ways of getting their needs known.

Teaching Students with Emotional or Behavioral Disorders

Although many people think that all students with emotional or behavioral disorders receive their education in self-contained settings, they actually can receive their education in a variety of settings such as general classrooms, resource rooms, separate special education classrooms, special schools, the juvenile justice system, institutions, and hospitals. Also, they live in a variety of settings: family homes, community-based residential group homes, halfway houses, and with foster families. Despite the movement toward inclusive programming for students receiving special education services, the placement rates of students with emotional or behavioral disorders has changed little over the past 5 years, with many more students with emotional or behavioral disorders placed in highly restrictive settings than their peers with other disabilities (OSEP, 2008).

Regardless as to where they are educated, teaching students with emotional or behavioral disorders is challenging for many reasons. One key challenge is providing an educational program that meets their behavioral, social, and academic needs. Historically, educational programs for these students have focused mainly on their behavioral and social needs. Only in the last 20 or so years have researchers and educators focused on academic interventions to address their limited academic skills (Lane, 2004; Mooney, Denny, & Gunter, 2003). One goal in educating these students is to make sure that they receive a balanced educational program that addresses their skill and performance deficits in social, behavioral, and academic areas. Gone are the days when educational programs focused almost exclusively on "just behavior." We are now learning more about how to teach these students important skill-sets such as reading, written expression (Lane, Harris, et al., 2008), and mathematics (Lane, Harris, et al., 2008; Trout et al., 2003). Some studies conducted with students at risk for emotional and behavioral disorders have found that improving their academic skills is associated with improved behaviors as well (Lane et al., 2001).

Obviously, emotional or behavioral disorders can have substantial effects on the life of the individual, whether child or adult. Therefore, early detection and intervention are very important. Once students with behavioral or emotional problems are identified and receive appropriate services, they generally have an opportunity to improve their academic skills, enhance their personal relations, enjoy more satisfying interactions with other people, and experience more positive outcomes after they leave school. Yet, without intervention, academic deficits (as well as social and behavior problems) have been known to remain the same or even worsen over time, even with the support of special education services (Greenbaum et al., 1996; Lane et al., 2005; Mattison et al., 2002; Nelson et al., 2004). This disability also affects their relationships with family members, adults,

myeducationlab Go to the Building Teaching Skills and Dispositions section in Chapter 7 of MyEducationLab, and complete the activities provided in the two IRIS Modules:

"Addressing Disruptive and Noncompliant Behaviors (Part 1): Understanding the Acting-Out Cycle." The first in a two-part series, this module discusses problem behavior in terms of the stages of the acting-out cycle and suggests ways to respond to students in the cycle's different phases.

"Addressing Disruptive and Noncompliant Behaviors (Part 2): Behavioral Interventions." The second in a two-part series, this module describes interventions that can increase initial compliance to teacher requests as well as interventions that can be implemented to decrease disruptive and noncompliant behaviors.

their peers, and their teachers—who have the highest turnover rates in the field of education (U.S. Department of Education, 2001).

Access to the General Education Curriculum

In recent years, we have identified validated methods (Babyak, Koorland, & Mathes, 2000; Cocharan et al., 1993; Dawson, Venn, & Gunter, 2000; Falk & Wehby, 2001; Scott & Shearer-Lingo, 2002) and curricula (e.g., *Phonological Awareness Training for Reading*; Lane, 1999; Lane et al., 2001; Lane, Wehby, et al., 2002) to improve the reading skills of students with or at risk for emotional or behavioral disorders. Some of these validated methods include

- peer tutoring,
- story mapping,
- modeling, and
- repeated readings.

Less attention has been devoted to teaching writing and math skills as compared to reading. However, personalized instruction has resulted in improved spelling for these students (McLaughlin, 1992), and more recently, evidence supports the effectiveness of self-regulation strategies, like those described in Chapter 6, to improve these students' abilities to write both stories and persuasive prompts (Lane, Harris, et al. 2008). Tutoring and explicit instruction have also been proved to boost performance in basic math skills (Franca et al., 1990; Harper et al., 1995; Nelson, Johnson, & Marchand-Martella, 1996). Study strategies, such as mnemonics and other learning strategies, like those described in Chapter 5, have helped these students learn important academic skills. Although it is encouraging to find specific instructional techniques that promote basic skills in reading, writing, and math skills, there are few validated practices to guide us on how best to teach students with emotional or behavioral disorders more complex, higher-level skills.

Instructional Accommodations

Hill Walker and his colleagues offer the following guidelines for implementing evidenced-based interventions with these students (Walker et al., 2004):

- Get ready to teach and support these students by establishing a positive relationship grounded in trust, safety, and predictability.
- Use proactive approaches to clarify expectations and rules for academic and social performance.
- Teach relevant skills (e.g., hand raising and waiting to be called on by the teacher) that are likely to produce even better results than the undesirable behaviors (e.g., talking out or yelling).
- Use systematic screening tools to look for students who might be at risk for emotional or behavioral problems as early as possible so that early intervention can begin.
- Teach empathy, social skills, and problem-solving strategies as part of the regular school program.
- Realize that even basic academic demands could be frustrating or aversive to these youngsters.

Many students with emotional or behavioral disorders come from families characterized by a high degree of stress and/or chaos. Often school is seen as an aversive, unpredictable place by these students because they did not come to school prepared with many of the requisite skills they need to be successful in the school setting. Beginning with a proactive, positive plan that explicitly teaches expected behaviors in all settings (e.g., classroom, playground, hallways, lunchtime) basically levels the playing field for these students. If they do not respond to these primary intervention efforts, more intensive intervention must be implemented.

Data-Based Practices: Functional Assessment-Based Interventions

When IDEA was reauthorized in 1997, behavioral intervention plans became a requirement. Most students with emotional or behavioral disorders, especially those with externalizing behavior problems, have a behavioral intervention plan as part of their IEP. These are highly individualized plans based on the reasons why problem behaviors occur with a goal of decreasing undesirable behaviors and increasing more desirable behaviors that allow students to get their needs met in a more appropriate way. Let's take a look at the current requirements in What IDEA '04 Says About Functional Behavioral Assessments.

Functional assessment-based interventions are interventions designed based on the reasons *why* problem behaviors occur (Umbreit et al., 2007). Basically, the process works like this: The teacher and/or parent identify a specific behavior (target behavior) that they want to change such as disruptive behavior. After a clear operational definition of the behavior is written, the next goal is to collect some information to figure out why the behavior occurs. In other words, why is the child so disruptive? The process for determining the motive for the target behavior is referred to as functional behavioral assessment. In brief, descriptive (e.g., interviews, direct observations of behavior, rating scales) and experimental (e.g., functional analysis) procedures are used to identify

- the antecedent conditions (things that come before the behavior) that set the stage for the target behavior (e.g., disruption) to occur and
- the consequences (things that occur after the target behavior happens) that keep the target behavior going.

These pieces of information are used to generate a hypothesis statement regarding the function of the target behavior such as "Steven's disruption appears to allow him to (a) gain teacher attention and (b) escape too difficult tasks." In general, all behaviors occur to either obtain (positive reinforcement) or avoid (negative reinforcement) one of three things (Umbreit et al. 2007):

- attention,
- activities or tasks, or
- tangible or sensory conditions.

It is possible to test the hypothesis statement by systematically manipulating environmental conditions (e.g., teacher attention or task difficulty) to confirm the consequences that maintain the target behavior.

The next step is to design an intervention based on the *function* of the target behavior, or *why* the target behavior occurs. As part of the intervention, the student is taught a new replacement behavior (e.g., compliance) that gives the student a new more reliable, efficient way of meeting his or her needs (e.g., getting teacher attention and escaping a too difficult task). These interventions include three parts:

- adjusting to the antecedent conditions that prompt the target (problem) behavior,
- increasing the rate of reinforcement (e.g., praise, teacher attention) for the more desirable replacement behavior, and
- removing reinforcement for the target behavior (placing the target behavior on extinction, meaning that it doesn't work any more!)

Functional assessment procedures were first designed in clinical settings to help support students with developmental disabilities (Iwata, et al., 1982). However, since that time functional assessment-based interventions have been used to change

What IDEA '04 Says About . . .

Functional Behavioral Assessments

Students who violate the student conduct code may receive a functional behavioral assessment and behavioral intervention services and modifications (including a behavioral intervention plan), if appropriate.

In cases of manifestation determination, the IEP team must

- either conduct a functional behavioral assessment and implement a behavioral intervention plan or,
- for students with a current behavioral intervention plan in place, review previous functional behavioral assessments and modify the existing plan, if necessary.

A Closer Look at Data-Based Practices

Functional Assessment-Based Interventions

John Umbreit and colleagues (2007) designed a systematic approach to conducting functional assessment-based interventions that has been widely tested with students with behavioral challenges. Using this approach, information from all the functional assessment tools (interviews, ratings scales, and direct observations) are placed into a Function Matrix to determine the hypothesized function(s) (see Figure A). The Function Matrix is a six-celled grid used to examine whether or not the student is doing a specific behavior to either get (positive reinforcement) or avoid (negative reinforcement) something. Specifically, the Function Matrix is used to determine if the behavior occurs to get or avoid attention, tangibles/activities, or sensory stimulation. After reviewing the data in the Function Matrix, the teacher and behavior specialist can develop a hypothesis statement about why the behavior is occurring. This hypothesis can be tested by conducting a functional analysis to confirm (or deny) the hypothesis.

Figure A • The Function Matrix

	Positive Reinforcement (Access Something)	**Negative Reinforcement (Avoid Something)**
Attention		
Tangibles/ Activities		
Sensory		

Next, they developed a Function-Based Intervention Decision Model to guide intervention planning (see Figure B). This model contains two questions: (a) Is the replacement skill in the child's repertoire? and (b) Does the classroom environment represent effective practices? Answers to these two questions will help focus the intervention on one of three following interventions:

Figure B • Function-Based Intervention Decision Model

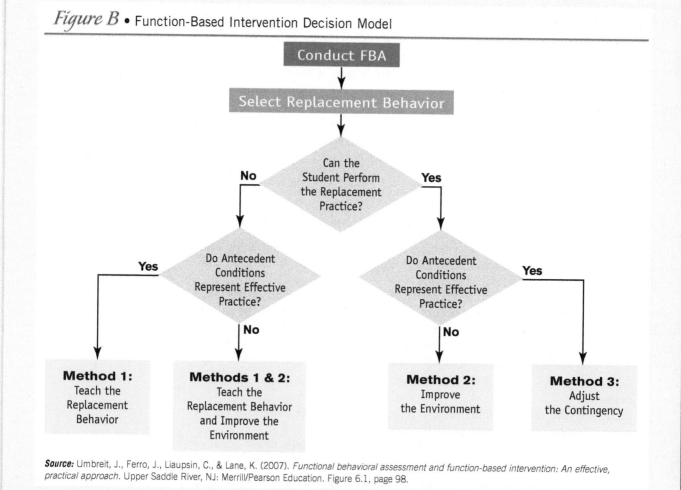

Source: Umbreit, J., Ferro, J., Liaupsin, C., & Lane, K. (2007). *Functional behavioral assessment and function-based intervention: An effective, practical approach.* Upper Saddle River, NJ: Merrill/Pearson Education. Figure 6.1, page 98.

Method 1: Teach the replacement behavior. This method is used when the replacement behavior is not in the student's repertoire. This method involves explicitly teaching the student the desired replacement behavior(s) (e.g., social skills or organizational skills).

Method 2: Improve the environment. This method is used when the student knows how to do the replacement behavior; however, the antecedent conditions that set the stage for the target behavior may not offer the most effective conditions for learning to occur. This method involves (a) removing or adjusting existing unpleasant events and (b) providing a situation that prompts the desired replacement behavior. Examples include designing or rearranging the physical classroom to meet the academic and behavioral task demands and giving students high rates of opportunities to respond.

Method 3: Adjust the contingencies. This method is used when the students can do the behavior and the classroom includes effective practices. This intervention focuses on modifying the rate of reinforcement so that the students get lower rates of reinforcement for doing the target behavior and higher rates of reinforcement when they use the replacement behavior.

Each method includes three components: teaching or adjusting antecedents; reinforcing the occurrence of the replacement behavior; and withholding reinforcement (extinction) of the target behavior. Once the intervention method is selected, the details of the plan are put in place to link the function of the target behavior to the appropriate intervention. Next, the intervention is put in place and

data are collected to see what people think about the plan (social validity), how well the plan is put in place (treatment integrity), and how the students' behavior changes (target and replacement behavior)

Steps to Follow

1. Collect functional assessment information and analyze it using the Function Matrix.
2. Complete the Function-Based Intervention Decision Model to guide intervention planning by answering the two questions:
   - Is the replacement skill in the child's repertoire?
   - Does the classroom environment represent effective practices?
3. Select the appropriate intervention method.
   - Method 1: Teach the replacement behavior.
   - Method 2: Improve the environment.
   - Method 3: Adjust the contingencies.
4. Design the details of the plan, making sure that the plan fits within the teachers' instructional style
5. Put the plan in place, and monitor social validity, treatment integrity, and student performance

myeducationlab Go to the Building Teaching Skills and Dispositions section in Chapter 7 of MyEducationLab, and complete the activities provided in the IRIS Module, Functional Behavior Assessment, and answer the accompanying questions.

a number of behaviors (e.g., on task, aggression, compliance) in a range of educational settings (e.g., general education classes, self-contained classrooms, self-contained schools; Lane, Kalberg, & Shepcaro, 2007). This type of intervention has been particularly effective for students with

- attention deficit hyperactivity disorders and behavioral concerns (Ervin et al., 1998),
- emotional or behavioral problems (Kern et al., 1994; Kern et al., 2001), and
- students at risk for emotional and behavioral disorders (Umbreit et al., 2004).

However, we want to call your attention to one important caution: Functional assessments may not be appropriate for high-impact behaviors that rarely occur (Nichols, 2000). This can be a real problem, because many low-frequency infractions (e.g., hitting a teacher, setting a fire, bringing a gun to school) are the most dangerous and serious.

Why did behavioral intervention plans become adopted as part of IDEA '04? The law reflects concerns of Congress and the public about violence, discipline, and special education students. In the earlier versions of IDEA, students with disabilities could not be expelled if their disruptive behavior was caused by the disability. Students with emotional or behavioral disorders were typically protected by what was called the "stay put provision." Under that provision, educational services could not be stopped, and these students could not be expelled from school. The 1997 version of IDEA changed that protection. Students with disabilities who violate school rules, particularly in the areas of weapons violence and drugs, are subject to disciplinary actions just like their peers without disabilities. But there are limits, and the end result is that students with disabilities who are violent or "out of control" have behavioral intervention plans. These plans seek to eliminate undesirable behaviors and replace them with appropriate ones. The behavioral intervention plan designed based on results of the functional assessment process becomes part of the student's IEP. Review A Closer Look at Data-Based Practice: Functional Assessment-Based Interventions on the preceding pages for information on one standardized approach to conducting functional assessment-based interventions (Umbreit et al., 2007).

Some of the benefits of using functional assessment-based interventions are that they are a respectful process that incorporates teaching students more desirable behaviors that still meet their needs. Some of the behavioral strategies involved in the intervention plans include these:

- *Curricular adjustments:* Increase or decrease tasks to make sure they are within the students' instructional range (Umbreit et al., 2004).
- *Behavior-specific praise:* Be clear about expected behavior (Maag, 2001; Sutherland, Wehby, & Yoder, 2001).
- *Reinforcement systems:* Use token economies or point systems where good behavior is traded in for privileges or prizes (Cruz & Cullinan, 2001).

Furthermore, functional assessment-based interventions typically do not include punishment. Punishment is technically defined as the introduction of a consequence (e.g., raising your voice) that reduces the rate or strength of the target behavior occurring in the future. Punishment has many different forms (Maag, 2001). It has been administered in the form of fines, restitutional activities (e.g., cleaning the classroom for defacing a wall), suspension, and even corporal punishment. Unlike positive approaches to manage classroom behaviors, punishment tends to produce an immediate result. However, the effects are often short-term, and the unwanted behavior may return soon—and often with a vengeance (Axelrod & Hall, 1999)!

Taken to its highest level, punishment is very serious and negative. Many states still allow the application of corporal punishment (paddling, spanking, rapping hands), with parent permission. However, punishment is *not* a recommended practice. All educators should be aware of the potentially devastating effects that corporal punishment can have on children. But despite all its negative effects and the lack of research to support its use, corporal punishment persists (Lohrmann-O'Rourke & Zirkel, 1998). Those most vulnerable to its application are students with disabilities, students from poverty, and culturally and linguistically diverse boys (Townsend, 2000).

Many people mistakenly believe that punishment must involve physical hitting, screaming, or embarrassment for the child, which means that many different tactics—including corporal punishment—fall within this category. But not all punishment is counterproductive. Some teachers find that certain forms of punishment can be an important part of an effective teaching plan to change unwanted behaviors. For example, mild reprimands, temporary withdrawal of attention, and the loss of certain privileges are all punishing tactics (they are intended to reduce the frequency of the target behavior) but do not necessarily have the negative long-term effects of corporal punishment (Bryant et al., 2008). Corporal punishment should be avoided in school settings, because it

- only temporarily halts undesired behaviors,
- does not teach new skills or knowledge,
- causes teachers to become engaged in power struggles with students,
- leads to an unhealthy and negative interaction with students,
- is initiated and dictated by the student, and
- models a negative style of interaction with others.

Remember, too, that any form of punishment should always be accompanied by teaching a new behavior. All classrooms must be safe and orderly environments where students can feel secure as they attempt the difficult tasks of learning and where they can trust the educators charged with this important responsibility. Fortunately, many schools are embracing more proactive, systemwide approaches to supporting behaviors that do not involve the use of punishment (Horner & Sugai, 2002; Lane, 2007).

 **myeducationlab** Go to the Activities and Applications section in Chapter 7 of MyEducationLab, and complete Activity 4. As you watch the video and answer the accompanying questions, notice how the MotivAider is used to facilitate independent seatwork for a student with behavior problems related to his ADHD.

Technology

Here, we'd like to introduce you to the MotivAider®. A MotivAider is a relatively simple, inexpensive electronic device that can be used to monitor behavior. It looks like a pager and clips on a waistband or belt. You can set MotivAider to vibrate at a given interval. This vibration serves as a prompt or reminder to do something.

In the classroom setting the MotivAider can be used by teachers as part of a functional assessment-based plan to remind them to look up and provide one or more students who are engaged with behavior-specific praise. Teachers can use this technology to collect information on how students are performing. (Are the students academically engaged when the vibration occurs?) The MotivAider also can be used by students as part of a self-monitoring plan in which they use the MotivAider to prompt them to ask the question "Am I doing the assigned work?" If so, the student records yes on the self-monitoring sheet. As you can see, this is a simple yet effective device that can be incorporated into intervention and assessment plans for a range of students, including those with emotional or behavioral disorders (see Lane, Weisenbach, et al., 2006, for an illustration). You might want to look at this Web site for additional information about this technology: http://www.motiv-aider.com/.

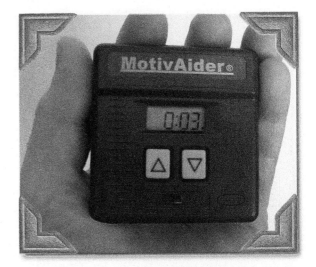

Simple devices that remind the student of important tasks that need to be completed can help keep the routine flowing and classroom life under control.

Transition

Often, students with disabilities face significant challenges when they leave the school setting and transition from school to life. This is particularly true for students with emotional or behavioral disorders (Wagner & Davis, 2006; Wehmeyer et al., 2000). As we mentioned earlier in this chapter, students with emotional or behavioral disorders often have extremely negative outcomes after leaving high school. These students often experience worse outcomes than typically developing students as well as other students with high-incidence disabilities (Wagner & Davis, 2006). Some of these outcomes include

- unemployment and underemployment,
- high rates of divorce,
- frequent need to access mental health services,
- continued difficulties in interpersonal relationships, and
- contact with the justice system.

How might these dismal outcomes be changed? Treatment and intervention are part of the answer. Students in the criminal justice system do not receive services, supports, or the delivery of intensive IEPs (NCJJ, 2002). Also, their transition back to their communities and home schools is problematic (Griller-Clark, 2001). That is, these students do not receive support services (e.g., preplacement planning and counseling), their IEPs frequently include no detailed transition plan, and these students' educational records often are not even transferred to their receiving schools. Clearly, such lack of attention to transitions is not helpful. To learn more about students with disabilities and the justice system, visit the Web site of the EDJJ at www.edjj.org.

Students with emotional or behavioral disorders who receive counseling experience some improved outcomes (Hunter, 2001; Schoenwald & Hoagwood, 2001). Social skills training (Gresham, 2002), instruction in **self-determination** (review again the data-based practices section found in Chapter 8), and stable home environments also contribute to better outcomes as adults (McConaughy & Wadsworth, 2000; Test et al., 2000; Wehmeyer et al., 2000).

self-determination A set of behaviors that include making decisions, choosing preferences, and practicing self-advocacy

"HEY, MOM! WHEN DO I GET A TIME-OUT FROM MY TIME-OUT?"

Source: DENNIS THE MENACE © NORTH AMERICA SYNDICATE

Collaboration

Clearly students with emotional or behavioral disorders struggle in school—academically, socially, and behaviorally. One compounding problem for students with emotional or behavioral disorders is school failure, and school failure compounds other problems these individuals face. As we have noted, educational and lifelong outcomes can be improved. Yet, improvement requires the concerted efforts of many partners—school, community, and social services—to assist both families and children (Eber et al., 2002). This is especially true when the goal is to provide educational services to these students in inclusive settings.

As you learned in Chapters 1 and 2, a uniform definition of the term *inclusion* or agreement about how it should be implemented is elusive. Since the original passage of IDEA in 1975, debate and controversy have surrounded issues about how to determine the "right" balance between LRE and FAPE. Many teachers find that including students in general education settings who present challenging, and often disruptive behavior, to be a daunting task. Proof of this fact lies in the exceptionally low rate of participation in general education by students with emotional or behavioral disorders, which is some of the lowest of all students with disabilities (OSEP, 2008). General educators may be concerned about providing services in inclusive settings for several reasons:

- Feeling ill equipped to manage the aggressive, noncompliant behaviors characteristic of these students (Gaetano, 2006)
- Concerns about managing their mental health needs in the general education setting (Cheney & Barringer, 1995)
- Questions about the actual benefits—academically and socially—of receiving services in general education settings (Kauffman & Landrum, 2009)
- Challenges associated with providing explicit instruction in social skills in the general education setting (Walker & Sprague, 1999, 2000)

It may be that inclusion is not desirable in some cases and not possible in others. Students detained by the criminal justice system, for example, are unable to participate in inclusive classes. During the time of their incarceration, it is especially important that their educational needs not be neglected. Students have a right to receive appropriate and individualized special education even if they are in correctional settings, including halfway houses and prisons. Unfortunately, students in these settings often do not receive the intensive education, in either social or academic skills, they need.

As we consider collaboration efforts to better serve students with emotional or behavioral disorders, we would like you to think about two things. First, let's think about the importance of collaborating with mental health workers. Second, let's consider how the PBS model can support collaborative and inclusive experiences for students with emotional or behavioral disorders.

Collaborating with Related Service Providers: Working with Mental Health Providers

Accessing America's mental health care system can be a daunting experience even for the most capable and most affluent individuals. For those who have limited resources or who distrust the social services system, the barriers can be so great that needed services are not sought or received, even when they are required as part of a student's IEP (CDF, 2004). These barriers may include lack of transportation, child care for other children, information about what services are available and where they can be received, and emotional support. In January 2001, the Surgeon General's National Action Agenda for Children's Mental Health stressed the importance of coordinating services across many agencies to ensure that children in need of mental health services receive them (Hoagwood, 2001b). Advocating for **wraparound services** reflects recognition of the importance of supporting children and families in trouble and the knowledge that comprehensive early intervention can prevent a bleak future. Therefore, it is imperative that educators, mental health professionals, and parents collaborate to provide coordinated support to meet with academic and mental health needs of students with emotional or behavioral disorders. Remember, the terminology used by the educational and mental health systems are not always aligned, making communication challenging at times. Nonetheless, it is a challenge that must be addressed.

Collaborative Practices: The Potential Role of the PBS Team

Although PBS team members are not considered by IDEA '04 as related service providers, they have the potential to promote positive, inclusive, collaborative practices that benefit students with emotional or behavioral disorders or who are at risk for developing the disability. For example, PBS teams can use the school-wide screening data (e.g., *Systematic Screening for Behavior Disorders, Student Risk Screening Scale,* or *Strengths and Difficulties Questionnaire*) collected as part of regular school practices to look for students with or at risk for emotional or behavioral disorders. This can be done across the K–12 grade span, with PBS selecting and implementing validated screening tools deemed most appropriate and reasonable by their faculty members (Lane, Kalberg, & Menzies, 2008).

The PBS team can look at the information gleaned from these screening tools as well as other academic screening procedures (e.g., curriculum-based assessments such as *Dynamic Indicators for Basic Early Literacy Skills* [Kaminski & Good, 1996] and AIMS WEB™) collected as part of RTI models, discussed in Chapters 1 and 5, to determine which students have behavioral and academic needs that are not being met by regular school practices (Lane, Kalberg, & Menzies, 2008). Then the PBS team can provide these students with targeted, secondary prevention supports such as social skills groups, anger management groups, homework clubs, and check-in/check-out programs to prevent them from developing further problems. This information can also be used to identify students who require even more individualized, intensive interventions such as functional assessment-based interventions or mental health services. In short, the PBS team can help implement multitiered models of prevention, early intervening services, and support that can (a) avoid the development of new cases of emotional or behavioral disorders and (b) respond more effectively to the needs of students with emotional or behavioral disorders (Lane, 2007). The federal government supports a center that focuses on these techniques. To learn more about PBS, visit www.pbis.org.

Turning around the dismal outcomes experienced by many individuals with emotional or behavioral disorders can be achieved, but it takes sustained efforts and supports from professionals across the school years.

wraparound services A service delivery model in which needs are met through collaboration of many agencies and systems (education, mental health, social services, community)

Partnerships with Families and Communities

Parenting a child with emotional or behavioral disorders can be a challenging task at times. Often, parents report that they feel blame about their children's problems, and they make significant financial sacrifices to secure services for their children (Ahearn, 1995). Increasingly, though, teachers are paying more attention to both the contributions and the needs of family members. Furthermore, teachers are listening and responding to parents' concerns. Let's look at two issues that often arise in the family lives of these children: negotiating the mental health care system and foster home placement.

Parents' Role in Supporting Mental Health Services

As we mentioned previously, parent involvement is critical in achieving child mental health and positive outcomes. Parents attending school events, volunteering to help in their child's classroom, and providing follow-up to behavioral intervention programs initiated at school are all necessary to the development of good child mental health. Engaging families, particularly those from diverse cultures, takes considerable effort and skill (Cartledge et al., 2000). Communication is one key to developing the trust and respect necessary to make families want to become actively involved at school. Also, children whose families are involved with the school system have greater academic success.

For some children, however, parental efforts alone are not sufficient. Mental health care services make a difference in the lives of these students and their families. Unfortunately, the mental health needs, particularly of students with emotional or behavioral disorders who live in poverty, are not addressed because of fragmented services and gaps in treatment (CDF, 2004). Educators can assist parents in getting the professional help they need if families are connected to schools. As you have learned throughout this text, parent–school partnerships emerge when educators are culturally competent, respect family members, increase communication, and keep their promises.

Foster Care

The U.S. Department of Health and Human Services estimates that some 588,000 children are in the foster care system in this nation (Adoption and Foster Care Analysis and Reporting System, 2002). While this number represents a 5% reduction from the previous year (between 2000 and 2001), the impact on society and these children is still concerning as social service agencies are reluctant to take children from their families and place them in an alternative home environment.

The number of children living in foster care is alarming, but even more so is the percentage of children in the foster care system with emotional or behavioral disorders (Armsden et al., 2000). Estimates range from 35% to 60%, a percentage almost five times higher than in the general student population. Not surprisingly, a number of these youngsters have internalizing problems such anxiety, depression, and social withdrawal. Of course, the relationship between placement and these problems is not entirely clear—meaning that it is not known whether these emotional or behavioral problems are one reason for the children's placement in foster homes or whether the placements and histories of disrupted attachments contribute to these problems.

The plight of these children is exacerbated by poor continuity of services. For example, some 20,000 young people "age out" of foster care programs each year on their 18th birthdays (Ama & Caplan, 2001). Many of them are still in high school, trying to graduate with a high school diploma. However, because few transition programs are available, they end up homeless, facing one more serious challenge in their young lives.

What can be done to improve these individuals' situations? Educators can create positive, predictable school environments that provide (Sugai & Horner, 2002)

- clear expectations taught to all students,
- opportunities to practice the expectations,
- reinforcement for meeting the expectations, and
- extra supports for students who do not respond to schoolwide efforts.

It also is important to ensure that these children have access to the mental health services they need to resolve their concerns about family life (Hoagwood, 2001a) and to meet the related services requirement specified in the IEP.

Summary

Defining emotional or behavioral disorders reflects, in part, societal standards for behavior and expectations about the development of children. Many behaviors that our society labels as disordered in a particular individual might be acceptable if that person were a different age, lived in a different society, came from a different culture, or exhibited the behaviors under different circumstances. Yet, some behaviors are considered disturbed regardless of surrounding circumstances. Early screening and evidenced-based interventions implemented with the context of multitiered models of prevention with children with emotional or behavioral disorders are beneficial to meeting the many needs of these youngsters within a variety of educational settings.

 **myeducationlab** Now go to MyEducationLab at www.myeducationlab.com and take the Self-Assessment to gauge your initial comprehension of chapter content. Once you have taken the Self-Assessment, use your individualized Study Plan for Chapter 7 to enhance your understanding of the concepts discussed in the chapter.

Answering the Chapter Objectives

1. How does an unclear definition influence how we identify and support students with emotional or behavioral disorders?

   * Makes it difficult to coordinate services with mental health providers
   * Makes it difficult to determine eligibility

2. What are the academic and social characteristics of these students?

   * Poor social skills
   * Acquisition and performance deficits in academic and social areas
   * Poor academic performance that doesn't improve over time

3. What are the main causes of emotional or behavioral disorders?

   * Biology
   * Home and community
   * School

4. What are the critical strategies needed to improve learning outcomes for these students?

   * Implement screening instruments.
   * Use validated practices.
   * Provide early intervention.
   * Provide sound instruction that meets their academic and behavioral needs.
   * Provide multitiered models of prevention to support their complex needs.

5. What strategies improve postsecondary outcomes for these students?

   * Deliver prevention and intervention strategies during the preschool years.
   * Provide engaging instruction to keep students in school.
   * Address their academic, social, and behavioral needs.
   * Work collaboratively with families, foster care, and mental health services.

Council for Exceptional Children ADDRESSING THE PROFESSIONAL STANDARDS

Council for Exceptional Children (CEC) knowledge standards addressed in this chapter: BD1K3, BD1K1, BD2K3, BD2K1, BC8S2, BC4S1, BD4K3, BD10K4, BD10K2

Appendix A: CEC Knowledge and Skill Standards Common Core has a full listing of the standards listed here.

Appendix B: CEC Knowledge and Skill Common Core Standards and Associated Subcategories are broken down by chapter.

CHAPTER 8

Intellectual Disabilities or Mental Retardation

Chapter Objectives

After studying this chapter, you will be able to

1. Justify discontinuing the use of the term *mental retardation*.

2. Discuss the key components of the 2002 AAIDD (AAMR) definition of intellectual disabilities and explain the levels of severity and outcomes of people with this disability.

3. Explain the four levels of supports and how they make a difference in the lives of people with intellectual disabilities.

4. Describe two ways in which causes of disabilities can be organized, and list three major known causes of intellectual disabilities.

5. Describe self-determination and how that data-based approach makes a difference in the results of individuals with intellectual disabilities.

Gottfried Mind, sometimes called the "Raphael of Cats," depicted cats almost exclusively and was known to have an obsession with the focus of his work and life. When Mind was not painting or drawing cats, he was carving them out of chestnuts. His modest apartment was filled with cats and kittens, and when he worked, cats were in his lap and on his shoulders. Mind (1768–1814) was born and lived all his life in Bern, Switzerland. He was known all over Europe, and his work was popular with cat lovers. Most of his work remains in private collections today and is rarely seen in public. He is probably one of the few artistic masters of the 18th and 19th centuries with documented intellectual disabilities. He had cretinism and died of a stroke at age 46.

A Cat in a Cage, Gottfried Mind/The Bridgeman Art Library/Getty Images.

myeducationlab After reading this chapter, complete the Self-Assessment for Chapter 8 on MyEducationLab to gauge your initial understanding of chapter content.

intellectual disabilities, mental retardation, or cognitive disabilities Impaired intellectual functioning, limited adapted behavior, need for supports, and initial occurrence before age 18

In 2007, the oldest professional organization concerned with individuals with disabilities changed the term we use to refer to individuals with cognitive disabilities from *mental retardation* to *intellectual and developmental disabilities*. Over the years, many different terms have been used. Each—*imbecile, moron, idiot, retardate*—initially was neutral, but in turn they took on negative connotations, even becoming harmful and mean-spirited slurs used to insult others (Turnbull et al., 2002). Why might this be so? Rud and Ann Turnbull and Steve Warren of Kansas University, Steve Eidelman and Paul Marchand of The Arc (a parent organization), and many others are confident that the reason for terms becoming negative is because of the stigma that society associates with disabilities in general and with cognitive disabilities in particular. So, in 2007 what was then called the American Association for Mental Retardation (AAMR) changed its name to the American Association for Intellectual and Developmental Disabilities (AAIDD). The organization also asked the nation to abandon the term *mental retardation,* which had been used for 50 years (Prabhala, 2007). In 2007, the name of some of AAIDD's publications also were changed to reflect the now-preferred term, *intellectual and developmental disabilities* (Taylor, 2007). Sadly, the group did so believing that this new term would follow the path of previous terms and also take on negative connotations. As Steve Eidelman, executive director of The Arc (now of the University of Delaware), reminds us, simply changing a name does not change the systemic reasons for bias. "Changing the term (*mental retardation*) will make many people happy. That happiness will quickly fade when the new term is used as a pejorative" (Turnbull, et al., 2002 p. 1).

Although AAMR is now AAIDD and a new term for **cognitive disabilities** has been adopted, IDEA '04 still uses **mental retardation**. Also, many people adopting the new term are using, as we are in this text, just **intellectual disabilities** to describe the disability that results in impaired cognitive abilities and the need for assistance or supports to achieve independence and participation in the community. Differences in abilities experienced by people with intellectual disabilities, and the way society reacts to those differences can create obstacles or opportunities for these individuals and their families. People with this disability, and those who teach them and provide them with supports, often must make very special efforts to learn all the skills needed in adult life. Although many may require considerable special assistance and supports from teachers and others, it is always important to remember that individuals with intellectual disabilities are people first. They are members of families, they have relationships with friends and neighbors, and they have personalities shaped by their innate characteristics as well as by their life experiences. These students go to school, plan for the future, hope for a good job, wonder whom they will marry, and anticipate adulthood.

Where We've Been . . . What's on the Horizon?

Intellectual disabilities, regardless of terms used to describe the condition, have always been a part of human history. Systematic efforts in education and treatment did not begin until the late 1700s when farmers from the countryside of southern France brought a young boy they found in the woods to a doctor in Paris. On that landmark day in 1798, when Jean-Marc-Gaspard Itard started working with Victor, "the wild boy of Averyon," special education began (Itard, 1806/1962). To learn more about this remarkable story and the origins of special education, see this chapter's On the Screen and also consider seeing the film.

Historical Context

By the mid–19th century, residential institutions had appeared throughout Europe and Great Britain. In 1848, Samuel Gridley Howe, the first director of the Perkins Institute for the Blind in Boston, expanded the center to include individuals with intellectual and developmental disabilities. Later it became a separate institution, the Walter E. Fernald State School. Ironically, Howe clearly predicted the hazards of

On the Screen: *In the Beginning*

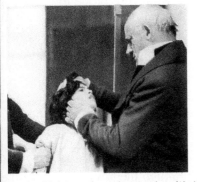

The film *L' Enfant Sauvage* (The Wild Child) tells the true story of the beginnings of special education. The film also gives us insight about life in France during the early 1800s, a period of enlightenment and keen, emotional discussions about the differences between humans and animals. The discovery and treatment of the Wild Child sparked considerable debate at that time about these issues.

Made by the world-renowned director François Truffaut, the film opens with a boy, possibly 12 years old, living much like an animal, unsupervised in the woods of France, who is discovered by local farmers. His hair and fingernails have grown long. He does not walk but, rather, hunches over and uses all four limbs to move quickly through the trees. He has a tremendous ability to climb. He does not speak, so the people who found him believe he is deaf and mute. Not knowing what to do with the child, they take him to a facility for deaf/mute children. The other children begin to pick on and ostracize the boy because his behavior is not like the others'. Dr. Jean Itard, who is played by Truffaut, takes a special interest in the boy and his case. He discovers that boy, whom he names Victor, is capable of hearing; however, since the boy had lived in the woods most of his life, he only associates sounds with danger. Itard moves Victor to his home in the country where he attempts to socialize the boy and teach him language. Victor begins to show signs of emotion and empathy, key human characteristics to the French, when his caretaker and the estate's housekeeper is crying over the death of her husband.

Though he made exceptional progress, Victor never attained a complete transformation from the wild child of the woods of France to a man of Parisian society. At the end, Itard concluded that his instructional efforts were unsuccessful and that he was a failure. Itard was unaware that his efforts and remarkable teaching techniques would make a difference in the lives of children with disabilities for centuries to come.

—By Steve Smith

residential institutions: Isolating people with disabilities both geographically and socially from mainstream society leads not only to separation but also to fear, mistrust, and abuse. Despite warnings to keep their numbers down and their size small, institutions spread across America. By 1917, all but four states had institutions for people with intellectual disabilities, and many of them were large.

This rise in the number and size of these institutions was based on unjustified fear of these people and their supposed negative effect on society (Brown & Radford, 2007; Winzer, 1993). In 1877, Richard Dugdale, a member of the New York Prison Association, made up a story about the Jukes family to illustrate that people with cognitive disabilities were a danger to society. Dugdale believed that it was a hereditary condition and that people with intellectual disabilities were the source of the crime, poverty, and other social ills plaguing the country at that time. The logic worked this way: The Jukes (and families like them) were, because of high rates of reproduction, the source of poverty, immorality, crime, and more "feeblemindedness." They were a menace to society, and good people should be protected from them. Members of such families therefore should be cast away and put in institutions. Because cognitive disabilities are hereditary and thought to be a cause of a decline in the overall American intellect, calls went out for a massive sterilization effort: These people should not be allowed to have more offspring (Smith & Lazaroff, 2006). Dugdale was not the only propagator of such theories, referred to as **eugenics**. In 1912, Henry Goddard released the story of Deborah Kallikak, who came from a family of "feebleminded" people who were prone to becoming criminals. Goddard maintained that because intellectual disabilities were passed on by heredity, nothing could be done to correct the situation. Goddard's conclusion, like Dugdale's, was that such people should be removed from society and their population controlled (Gelf, 1995; Smith & Lazaroff, 2005). Such negative attitudes contributed to the terrible conditions that prevailed in institutions for people with intellectual disabilities—conditions that were hidden from the public until 1965 when Burton Blatt published the horrific photographic essay "*Christmas in Purgatory*."

During the 1960s and 1970s, researchers developed and refined new systems of instruction. Behavioral approaches that included token economies, positive reinforcement, direct or explicit instruction, and task analysis (breaking tasks down into small, teachable units) proved highly effective, and through them, students with intellectual disabilities learned skills they had never mastered with instructional procedures used previously (Ayllon & Azrin, 1964, 1968; Birnbrauer et al., 1965). Jim Lent and his colleagues at the Mimosa Cottage Project in Parsons, Kansas, demonstrated that children with intellectual disabilities could learn many complex tasks and skills used in daily life and on the job (Lent & McLean, 1976). Procedures developed at this research center have become the foundation of most special education programs.

Benjt Nirje in Sweden, also in the 1960s, inspired a new philosophy—a new movement—called normalization, which took hold worldwide (Nirje, 1969). **Normalization** is the concept that people with intellectual disabilities should have available to them "patterns of life and conditions of everyday living which are as close as possible to the regular circumstances and ways of life of society" (Nirje, 1976, p. 67). At about the same time, Bob Perske formulated the concept of **dignity of risk**, which is a practice based on the premise that people with intellectual disabilities should experience life's challenges and adventures but not be overprotected (Perske, 1972). Wolf Wolfensberger used the principle of normalization to call for the closing of all U.S. institutions for people with intellectual disabilities (Wolfensberger, 1972).

Television exposés, court actions, and eventually the rise of the advocacy movement subsequently led to widespread deinstitutionalization. But toward the beginning of the effort to improve living conditions for people with intellectual disabilities, it took investigative reporting to shock the American public into insisting that the care and treatment of people living at state residential schools and institutions be improved. In 1972, one such daring reporter, Geraldo Rivera (see the photo), launched his career by using a stolen key to enter Willowbrook State School on Staten Island in New York. He showed the world the brutal and terrible conditions in which residents were forced to live at the time. The conditions were not isolated to Willowbrook; they were commonplace. Today, besides living with a family member, most people with intellectual disabilities (some 400,000) live in the community with supports, and few live in large institutions, locked away from public scrutiny (Lakin, Braddock, & Smith, 2004a).

Challenges That Intellectual Disabilities Present

People with cognitive disabilities face multiple challenges. The disability they have makes learning more difficult than it is for typical learners, and tasks that seem easy and natural to most people of the same age can be almost overwhelming. However, their challenges are compounded because they also face considerable bias and prejudice resulting from the stigma associated with the condition.

As you learned in the opening paragraphs of this chapter, bias is not relegated to the past; it is part of many of these individual's daily lives. You've already learned about the stories of the Jukes and the Kallikaks; the horrific situations in segregated, large institutions like Willowbrook; and how labels, or the ways people are classified and the terms used, send messages laden with prejudice. In the

---

eugenics A worldwide movement of over 100 years ago that sought to protect society from false threats of people who are different

normalization Making available ordinary patterns of life and conditions of everyday living

dignity of risk The principle that taking ordinary risks and chances is part of the human experience

1960s and 1970s, the classification system used divided people with intellectual disabilities into two basic groups based only on IQ scores: educable mental retardation (EMR)—the category for those with IQ scores from 50 to 80—and trainable mental retardation (TMR)—the category for those with IQ scores between 25 and 50. The message seemed to be that some of these individuals could only be "trained" and not truly educated. The insults are obvious.

It is important for all of us to recognize that negatively laden terms can be personally hurtful to the individuals involved. Labels, name-calling, and stigma are frequently experienced by people with intellectual disabilities, whether at school or in the community (Finlay & Lyons, 2005). Karen Loven, of Oakdale, Minnesota, has developmental disabilities and reminds us that words do matter. She says, "People have been calling me names no matter where I go. I have a disability. I'm not retarded. You can't even walk down the street without people calling you names" (Associated Press, 2005). Clearly, we can each make a real difference in the acceptance of all individuals by not condoning—let alone making—negative assumptions and statements. In Karen's home state, Minnesota, members of the legislature, like members of AAIDD, understand the importance of language and what individuals with disabilities are called. These legislators proposed a bill to erase terms like *feebleminded, mental retardation, handicapped,* and *idiot* from all existing and future state statutes.

Robert Perske reminds us that assaults against people with intellectual disabilities are not over (Perske, 2006). In 1971, a movie called *Who Should Survive* showed how a Down syndrome infant was allowed to die because a simple surgery was withheld, leaving the 15-day-old baby to die of starvation. He also tells us about how in 1982 another baby with Down syndrome did not receive necessary minor surgery to correct the connection between his esophagus and stomach. He, too, was allowed to starve to death, but that time public outcries resulted in laws that now protect newborns in such situations. Such outrages, however, are not relegated to the past. In February 2008, after a time when the Iraqi government and American soldiers thought the bombings in Baghdad might be coming to an end, the popular pet market where children love to come see colorful birds was bombed. Some 65 people were killed and another 150 wounded in a brutal blast (Farrell & Al-Husaini, 2008). The terrible turn this time, however, is that the terrorists used two women with intellectual disabilities as their "suicide" bombers. Whether subtle or blatant, Perske reminds us that we must always be alert to possible injustices and transgressions of social justice and individuals with disabilities.

Television news commentator Geraldo Rivera launched his career in the early 1970s when he exposed the terrible conditions that people with intellectual disabilities endured at Willowbrook State School in New York.

Making a Difference

Best Buddies

Across America, the dream of families and of their sons, daughters, brothers, and sisters with intellectual disabilities is to be a part of everyday communities. Unfortunately, successful integration in schools, workplaces, and mainstream society remains elusive for many. Sufficient opportunities for socialization and job coaching are not available for people with intellectual disabilities to become independent and to be fully included in their communities. The necessary supports are not yet in place for an inclusive America to be a reality.

Probably because of his family's long history of advocacy and volunteerism on behalf of people with intellectual disabilities, Anthony Shriver (shown at

left)—nephew of John, Robert, and Ted Kennedy, son of Eunice Shriver, and brother of Maria Shriver—saw a need to create opportunities for people to reach out to other people. Shriver also understood that students without disabilities, from middle school through college, needed a vehicle to create friendships and supports for others faced with cognitive challenges. As a response, in 1989 while at Georgetown University, he initiated the first chapter of **Best Buddies** and encouraged his college friends to work with him to expand the program.

Today, Best Buddies comprises six divisions that involve over 350,000 participants every year. All 50 states have chapters, and programs are active on six continents. The middle school, high school, and college divisions match students with peers with intellectual disabilities to foster one-on-one friendships structured around social activities. College students and those with intellectual disabilities both profit from the Best Buddies program, reporting mutually beneficial friendships and participation in community activities (Hardman & Clark, 2006). Through the citizens' division, people from corporate and civic communities are paired with individuals with intellectual disabilities so they can share time together; the jobs' division is a supported employment program. One exciting program, e-Buddies, creates e-mail friendships.

To become a Best Buddies volunteer, to establish a campus chapter, or to learn more about any of the six divisions, go to **www.bestbuddies.org**.

Best Buddies A program that pairs college students with people with intellectual disabilities to build relationships, friendships, and opportunities for supports

Intellectual Disabilities or Mental Retardation Defined

Two different definitions are used in the United States today. Most states follow IDEA '04, the federal definition, which still uses the term *mental retardation* (Müller & Markowitz, 2004). However, many professionals prefer the one adopted in 2002 by AAMR, the organization now calling itself AAIDD, because it is more detailed and allows for a clearer understanding of the supports the individual needs at school, at home, and in the community. Both basic definitions are shown in Table 8.1. Although not specifically called out, the practice when using the IDEA '04 definition is that the disability occurs or is identified during or before an individual's school years. While some are questioning the importance of the age criterion, the AAIDD definition specifies that the disability must occur before the individual's 18th birthday (Simpson, 2007).

Table 8.1 • Definitions of Mental Retardation or Intellectual Disabilities

Source	Definition
Federal government	Mental retardation means significant subaverage general intellectual functioning, existing concurrently with deficits in adaptive behavior and manifested during the developmental period, that adversely affects a child's educational performance.
American Association of Mental Retardation	Mental retardation is a disability characterized by significant limitations both in intellectual functioning and in adaptive behavior as expressed in conceptual, social, and practical adaptive skills. This disability originates before age 18.

Sources: Information taken from 34 *CFR* Parts 300 and 303, Assistance to States for the Education of Children with Disabilities and the Early Intervention Program for Infants and Toddlers with Disabilities; Final Regulations (p. 1263), U.S. Department of Education, 2006, *Federal Register*, Washington, DC, and *Definition of Mental Retardation* (p. 1), by R. Luckasson, S. Borthwick-Duffy, W. H. E. Buntinx, D. L. Coulter, E. M. Craig, A. Reeve, R. L. Schalock, M. E. Snell, D. M. Spitalnik, S. Spreat, and M. J. Tassé, 2002, Washington, DC: American Association on Mental Retardation (AAMR).

Accompanying the AAIDD definition* (the tenth definition this professional organization has developed and supported since 1921), and expanding on how it should be applied, are five assumptions:

1. Limitations in present functioning must be considered within the context of community environments typical of the individual's age peers and culture.
2. Valid assessment considers cultural and linguistic diversity as well as differences in communication and in sensory, motor, and behavioral factors.
3. Within an individual, limitations often coexist with strengths.
4. An important purpose of describing limitations is to develop a profile of needed supports.
5. With appropriate personalized supports over a sustained period, the life functioning of the person with mental retardation generally will improve. (Luckasson et al., 2002, p. 1)

Both the current AAIDD definition and its predecessor, which was in effect between 1992 and 2002, have a positive orientation. They address the interplay among capabilities of individuals; environments in which they live, learn, and work; and how well each person functions with various levels of support. The 2002 definition includes a cautious use of IQ scores and focuses more on the needs of each individual to be as independent as possible. Before then, definitions used a deficit perspective and described only the limitations of the individual. Definitions following the deficit perspective used expressions such as "significantly subaverage general intellectual functioning," "deficits in adaptive behavior," and "deficits in intellectual functioning." Today, intellectual disabilities is conceptualized in terms of the adaptive behavior each individual possesses and the intensity of supports (intermittent, limited, extensive, or pervasive) needed for the individual to function in the community as independently as possible (Luckasson et al., 1992, 2002; Polloway, 1997).

The condition of intellectual disabilities is described and defined by AAIDD in terms of three major components:

- Intellectual functioning
- Adaptive behavior
- Systems of supports

Across each of these components, the disability varies along a continuum. Most of these individuals face mild cognitive challenges, have adequate adaptive behavior to live and work independently in the community, and usually require few supports. Some of these individuals, however, require considerable supports. Let's examine each of the AAIDD components in turn.

Intellectual Functioning

In its explanation of the 2002 definition, AAIDD stresses that individuals with intellectual and developmental disabilities have **intellectual functioning** "significantly below average," or below levels attained by 97% of the general population. In other words, all of these individuals face major challenges in this area; their cognitive performance is hampered by the disability.

Level of intellectual functioning may be determined by clinical judgment or by a score on a standardized test of intelligence. In our discussion of the deficit perspective of disabilities found in Chapter 1, we discussed the normal or bell-shaped curve and the idea that those individuals who score in the middle of that distribution are considered "average," and those who score at least two standard deviations below the mean for the test are considered to be significantly "below average." People with intellectual disabilities are not typical learners; they do score at least two standard deviations below the mean on tests of intelligence, and they need extra help to learn all that is necessary to be as independent as possible in the community as adults.

Although in its previous definition AAIDD attempted to avoid reference to IQ scores and standardized tests, it proved too hard to implement without specific

---

* The term *mental retardation* is found in this definition because the definition predates the change of the term to *intellectual and developmental disabilities*.

myeducationlab Go to the Activities and Applications section in Chapter 8 of MyEducationLab, and complete Activity 1. As you watch the video and answer the accompanying questions, look for characteristics of the different levels of intellectual disability, and consider the educational implications for a child with intellectual disabilities.

intellectual functioning Cognitive abilities

criterion. So, the 2002 definition uses IQ scores to partially explain intellectual disabilities by using a cutoff score of about 70. This definition also codes intellectual abilities to express levels of severity in the following ways:

- *Mild intellectual disabilities:* IQ range of 50 to 69
  - *Outcomes:* Has learning difficulties, is able to work, can maintain good social relationships, contributes to society
- *Moderate intellectual disabilities:* IQ range of 35 to 49
  - *Outcomes:* Exhibits marked developmental delays during childhood, has some degree of independence in self-care, possesses adequate communication and academic skills, requires varying degrees of support to live and work in the community
- *Severe intellectual disabilities:* IQ range of 20 to 34
  - *Outcomes:* Has continuous need for supports
- *Profound intellectual disabilities:* IQ under 20
  - *Outcomes:* Demonstrates severe limitations in self-care, continence, communication, and mobility; requires continuous and intensive supports

Adaptive Behavior

adaptive behavior Performance of everyday life skills expected of adults

Adaptive behavior is what everyone uses to function in daily life. People with cognitive problems, as well as many people without disabilities, have difficulty because they do not have the skills needed in different situations or because they do not know what skill is needed in a particular situation. Regardless, lacking proficiency in the execution of a wide variety of adaptive skills can impair one's abilities to function independently. What, then, are these "conceptual, social, and practical skills"? Practical skills include such activities of daily life as eating, dressing, toileting, mobility, preparing meals, using the telephone, managing money, taking medication, and housekeeping. Social skills might include using social conventions, like using the words "Please" and "Thank you" and knowing how to terminate a conversation. Take a look at Figure 8.1 for more examples of these three major areas of adaptive skills.

Figure 8.1 • Adaptive Skill Areas

Systems of Supports

Everyone needs and uses **systems of supports**: the networks of friends, family members, and coworkers, along with social service and governmental agencies that help us manage daily life. We ask our friends for advice. We form study teams before a difficult test. We expect help from city services when there is a crime or a fire. We join together for a neighborhood crime watch to help each other be safe. And we share the excitement and joys of accomplishments with family, friends, and colleagues. For all of us, life is a network of supports. Some of us need more supports than others, and some of us need more supports at certain times of our lives than at other times.

Figure 8.2 is a diagram of the four levels of intensity for different types of supports that people often need. It shows areas where supports can be provided and how that support might be delivered. Remember, supports can be offered at any one of four levels of intensity:

- Intermittent
- Limited
- Extensive
- Pervasive

Some people with intellectual disabilities require supports in every area, others might need supports for only one area, and the level of support can vary from one area to another.

systems of supports A network of supports everyone develops to function optimally in life

Characteristics

Although every person is an individual and stereotypes can be unfair and inaccurate when applied to individual people, it is helpful to understand some characteristics that educators frequently encounter when working with students with intellectual disabilities. The three defining characteristics are

- problems with cognition,
- problems with adaptive behavior, and
- a need for supports to sustain independence.

Remember, every individual has unique strengths and abilities, but it is also important to know the characteristics often caused by specific syndromes or conditions. For example, most individuals with fragile X syndrome have difficulties with social communications, in understanding nonverbal behaviors, in using expressive language, and in being engaged in academic learning (Philofsky et al., 2004; Roberts et al., 2007). They avoid eye contact, turn away from face-to-face contacts during conversations, and have stylized and ritualistic greetings. However, despite all these general characteristics, it is important to remember, as Geri Nicholas discovered and shares with us in this chapter's Spotlighting feature, that every individual with intellectual disabilities is unique, presenting different needs and abilities.

Cognition

The most defining characteristic of intellectual disabilities is impaired cognitive ability. Because one criterion for identification is a score on a test of intelligence that falls below 70, individuals with intellectual disabilities are below those of 97% of their peers in cognitive abilities (review again the normal curve shown in Figure 1.1). Impaired cognition makes simple tasks difficult to learn. It can interfere with communicative competence, because the content of messages are harder to deliver or comprehend. It influences how well one can remember and how flexible one is in the application of knowledge and skills already learned. Ultimately, the degree of cognitive impairment determines the types of curriculum content these individuals are taught: academic, life skills, or both.

Figure 8.2 • Systems of Supports

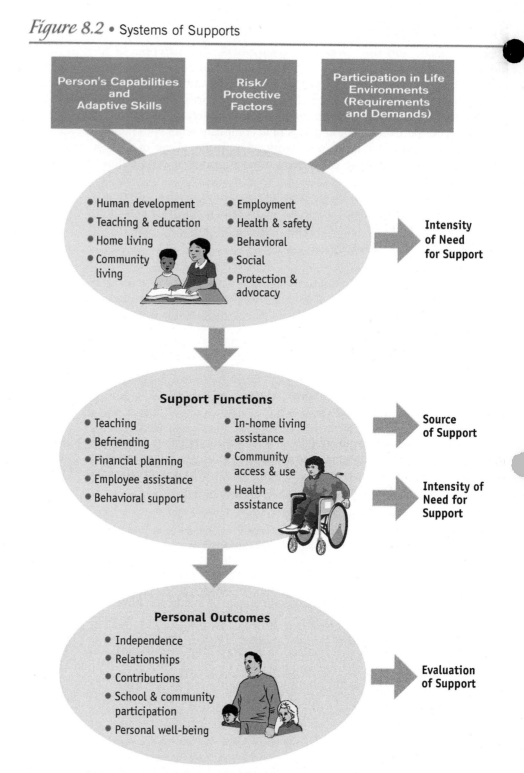

Source: *Mental Retardation: Definition, Classification, and Systems of Supports, by AAMR.* Copyright 2002 by American Association on Intellectual and Developmental Disabilities. Reproduced with permission of American Association on Intellectual and Developmental Disabilities in the formats Textbook and Other book via Copyright Clearance Center.

Learning new skills, storing and retrieving information (memory), and transferring knowledge to either new situations or slightly different skills are challenges for individuals with intellectual disabilities. Memory—especially short-term memory—is often impaired. The student may also have trouble with long-term memory, finding it hard to remember events or the proper sequence of events, particularly when

Spotlighting *Geri A. Nicholas:* A Day in the Life

Geri A. Nicholas, M. A. in counseling psychology and a school counselor, has extensive experience working with children and adolescents with all disabilities.

When I was a teacher in a northern California high school, I was asked to teach social communications to a group of approximately 14 students with severe disabilities, including students with cognitive disabilities. Many could not speak, and all had difficulties with social communication. I had decided early on that I would not read any of the students' charts because I didn't want to know each student's specific disability label. I started the class with everyone sitting in a circle and began with talking about feelings, showing a visual picture and word for each feeling. During each class, the students were asked to check in and explain how they felt for the day. If they could not speak, they could use the card to express how they felt. All students were encouraged to share any story along with their feelings. It took a few times before they got the idea, and I had to continually stress that they must listen and not interrupt.

We worked on role playing about how to say hello, how to shake hands, and how to make friends, stressing personal space and the importance of respecting one another. As the class continued and the students were able to listen and follow directions, they began to visit different parts of the school. My goal was to help them feel safe in their environment. Our high school has a large campus with many areas that most of them had never visited. Their comfort zone was their classroom, just

outside their classroom, and the field for physical education. Eventually they visited the office and were introduced to the administration, the health aide, the secretaries, the treasurer, the librarians, and other staff. They also observed performances in the drama and music departments. They participated in many different art projects such as sidewalk chalk and finger-painting. We had parties and celebrated not only holidays but any small accomplishment. Compliments and listening skills were role-modeled.

It was amazing to watch the changes that occurred. Mario, who had been barely verbal, started sharing bits of the news. Parker, who had always barked and annoyed others, stopped barking so much and could be quieted by a friend when asked politely to stop. Evelia, who hadn't been coming to school often, started showing up more—and with a smile. She learned to share and could be seen skipping. Joseph, who the previous semester had been seen curled in a ball sitting alone against the fence, said to me, "I love school." Trisha, who had been diagnosed as having intellectual disabilities, was misdiagnosed. All of the students were smiling more; and each student was put into at least one mainstream class—some, two or three. They learned to listen and, more important, to be kind to one another. Many would start the day giving me a hug or telling me I looked pretty. The transformation that occurred was miraculous, especially the change in myself. I felt joy that I had not experienced before. I will always hold my experience with this particular class as one of the most memorable and important to my growth as a person. I am forever grateful.

---

the events are not clearly identified as important. Even when something is remembered, it may be remembered incorrectly, inefficiently, too slowly, or not in adequate detail. Teachers can assist students in developing memory strategies and help them compensate for their lack of abilities in this area in many ways. For example, the student can learn to create picture notebooks that lay out the sequence of steps in a task that needs to be performed, the elements of a job that need to be done, or a checklist of things to do before leaving the house.

One characteristic of intellectual disabilities is a reduced ability to acquire knowledge through **incidental learning**—that is, to acquire learning as an unplanned result of their ordinary daily experiences. For some, it seems that explicit instruction is required for almost every task to be learned. Teachers must plan for the generalization (transfer) of learning so that newly learned skills are applied in a variety of settings (school, home, neighborhood), are performed with and for different people, and are expanded to similar but different contexts. Tips for Effective Instruction offers some ideas on how to help children generalize their learning of new skills and knowledge.

incidental learning
Understanding and mastering knowledge and skills through observation and without instruction

Adaptive Behavior

Review Figure 8.2 again, and think about each skill and its importance to independent functioning in the community. Adaptive behavior is not a problem area only for

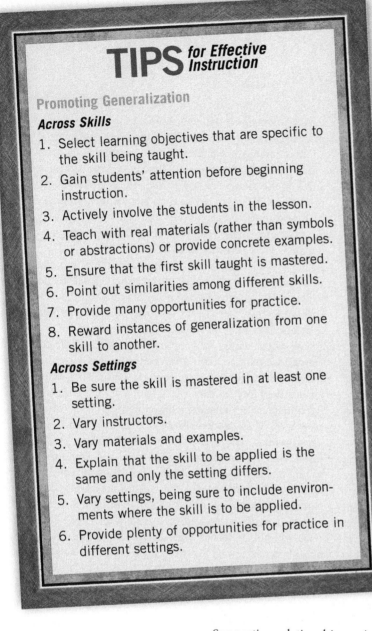

TIPS for Effective Instruction

Promoting Generalization

Across Skills

1. Select learning objectives that are specific to the skill being taught.
2. Gain students' attention before beginning instruction.
3. Actively involve the students in the lesson.
4. Teach with real materials (rather than symbols or abstractions) or provide concrete examples.
5. Ensure that the first skill taught is mastered.
6. Point out similarities among different skills.
7. Provide many opportunities for practice.
8. Reward instances of generalization from one skill to another.

Across Settings

1. Be sure the skill is mastered in at least one setting.
2. Vary instructors.
3. Vary materials and examples.
4. Explain that the skill to be applied is the same and only the setting differs.
5. Vary settings, being sure to include environments where the skill is to be applied.
6. Provide plenty of opportunities for practice in different settings.

people with intellectual disabilities. Think about some people you know who are very smart, get great grades in school, but cannot manage daily life. These individuals probably have difficulties with some adaptive skills. Now think about people you know who are highly successful on the job but have no social skills. Or think of those who have great personal hygiene and grooming skills but are unable to balance their personal budgets. All of these people have problems in at least one adaptive skill area. Adaptive skills are not behaviors that people, regardless of ability or disability, always master without instruction. Many IEP goals for adaptive behaviors stress independence. However, Craig Kennedy (2001) wisely cautions that this direction may be somewhat misguided: "Simply put, people with severe disabilities have to depend on other people" (p. 123). He suggests that goals should be thought of in terms of interdependence, where at least two peers work together, providing each other with assistance and support.

Need for Supports

In recent years, need for support has become the focus of how services for individuals with intellectual disabilities are designed (Harries et al., 2005). Such an approach is more positive and constructive than thinking only about the nature of the disability. Four sources of supports can be made available to people with intellectual disabilities:

- Natural supports
- Nonpaid supports
- Generic supports
- Specialized supports

natural supports Supports that occur as a natural result of family and community living

nonpaid supports Ordinary assistance given by friends and neighbors

generic supports Public benefits to which everyone has access

specialized supports Disability-specific benefits to help people with disabilities participate in the community

Supportive relationships exist among people in almost every setting and in almost every aspect of life. People help each other in simple and complex day-to-day tasks. **Natural supports** are the individual's own resources, family, friends, and neighbors. Natural supports can also come from coworkers on the job or peers at school (Drew & Hardman, 2007; Kennedy & Horn, 2004). Remember the Making a Difference feature in this chapter. Best Buddies was designed to create more natural supports for individuals with intellectual disabilities by connecting them with college students. With more and more of such programs available, supports needed for a greater community presence for more individuals with intellectual disabilities will become a reality.

Nonpaid supports are ordinary neighborhood and community supports. Examples of these kinds of supports include clubs, recreational leagues and groups, and private organizations. Everyone has access to **generic supports**, which are such services as public transportation and states' human services systems. **Specialized supports** are disability-specific, such as human services delivered to families of children with disabilities, special education, special early intervention services, and vocational rehabilitation services. The amount of support needed can vary for each individual and can change over time. Think of support as a fluid concept that is responsive by providing only as much assistance as needed, when it is necessary.

Prevalence

The U.S. Department of Education's Office of Special Education Programs (OSEP) reports that less than 1% of all students are identified and served through its mental retardation category (OSEP, 2008). (Remember, IDEA '04 still uses the term *mental retardation* and not *intellectual disabilities*.) A prevalence rate of less than 1% is far less than one would expect when considering that 3% of IQ scores fall below the cutoff scores for intellectual disabilities. Why would the identification rate be one-third of the predicted rate? Here are three reasons:

- The stigma associated with this disability makes many professionals reluctant to use this category for special education eligibility.
- Other special education categories, such as multiple-severe disabilities and autism spectrum disorders, also include some students with low scores on tests of intelligence, so not all students with cognitive disabilities are identified as having intellectual disabilities as their primary problem.
- Concern about students of color being overrepresented in this special education category leads educators and parents to use another special education category, such as learning disabilities, to get students needed services and supports.

As we discussed in Chapter 3, it is important to continually be alert to signs of overrepresentation and disproportionate identification of diverse students as needing special education services, particularly through the federal mental retardation category. Although concerns have been voiced for many years, students of color, particularly African American and Native American students, are overrepresented in this category (OSEP, 2008). Although African American students represent some 12% of the student population, they represent 33% of students identified as having mental retardation (National Center for Education Statistics [NCES], 2007). Native Americans represent a very small percentage of the national school population, some 0.08%, and 1.28% of those identified as having mental retardation. Could these over-predicted identification rates reflect a relationship between poverty and disabilities? Possibly so. But why, then, are Hispanics not overrepresented as well? Latinos/Latinas represent 14% of the general student population and 14% of those served through IDEA's mental retardation category.

OSEP does not report prevalence data for individual conditions that are associated with any disability. However, some statistics are available from other government agencies. For example, the Centers for Disease Control and Prevention (CDC) estimate that Fetal Alcohol Spectrum Disorders, which include fetal alcohol syndrome (FAS) and fetal alcohol effects (FAE), occur anywhere between 0.02 and 1.5 of 1,000 live births, with the rates varying in different regions of the country (CDC, 2006). Alaska has the highest rates of these disorders, particularly among Alaska Natives who have a rate three times higher than the national prevalence rate (Müller, 2007). This fact could explain, in part, the overrepresentation of Native American students in this special education category. In all cases, the condition can be prevented if pregnant women do not drink alcohol. The experts at CDC believe that some 310,000 U.S. children between the ages of 1 and 5 have lead poisoning, another preventable reason for intellectual disabilities and other problems (CDC, 2007a). Fragile X syndrome, the most common inherited cause of intellectual disorders, affects 1 in 4,000 males and 1 in 6,000 females (Fragile X Research Foundation, 2008).

Causes and Prevention

In several cases, possibly as many as one-third, the cause or reason for intellectual disabilities is unknown (The Arc, 2005). However, with improvement of medical technology, more and more specific causes, many of them genetic, are being identified. The link between the identification of specific causes of a disability and the development and implementation of preventive measures is clear. When a cause is identified, ways to prevent debilitating effects have often followed soon after. But it takes action for solutions actually to prevent or reduce the impact of the condition.

It is important to recognize that some students may be receiving services through the federal special education category of mental retardation but may be misidentified because of bias and discrimination about diverse students and students who are poor. We discussed issues about the overrepresentation of some groups of diverse learners in Chapter 3 and also in the section about prevalence you just read. It is also important to understand and remember that the ravages of poverty and its risk factors, such as limited access to health care, disrupted lives, and fewer early intervention opportunities, can and do lead to intellectual disabilities (CDF, 2004; National Research Council, 2002). Many also believe there is a connection between child abuse and neglect and intellectual disabilities (CDF, 2004). Despite concerns about overrepresentation, students who need and qualify for the sustained supports and services of special education should not be denied them.

Causes

Many different systems for organizing the causes of disabilities can be applied. Sometimes they are divided into three groups, organized by time of onset—that is, by when the event or cause first occurred:

- *Prenatal:* causes that occur before birth
- *Perinatal:* causes that occur during the birth process
- *Postnatal:* causes that happen after birth or during childhood

prenatal Before birth

Examples of **prenatal** causes include genetics or heredity, toxins taken by the pregnant mother, disease, and neural tube defects. Genetic causes include conditions such as fragile X syndrome and Down syndrome, as well as phenylketonuria (PKU). Prenatal toxins include alcohol, tobacco, and drug exposure resulting from the behavior of the mother during pregnancy. **Perinatal** causes include birth injuries. Some of these situations might be due to oxygen deprivation (anoxia or asphyxia), umbilical cord accidents, obstetrical trauma, or head trauma. **Postnatal** causes are often due to the environment. Toxins like lead poisoning, child abuse and neglect, and accidents are examples of causes that occur during childhood and can result in lifelong disabilities.

perinatal During birth

postnatal After birth

Another way to group causes of intellectual disabilities is less confusing because this system categorizes causes by specific reason:

- Genetic or hereditary
- Toxins
- Child abuse and neglect

Let's use this system to learn about some specific causes of intellectual disabilities, grouped together by these three reasons.

fragile X syndrome The most common inherited reason for intellectual disabilities

Genetic Causes Today, more and more genetic causes of intellectual disabilities are being identified. One well-known example is **fragile X syndrome**, which is inherited and caused by a mutation on the X chromosome. Identified in 1991, it is now recognized as the most commonly known inherited cause of intellectual disabilities, affecting about 1 in 4,000 males and 1 in 8,000 females (Fragile X Research Foundation, 2008; Taylor, Richards, & Brady, 2005). Cognitive problems in those affected can be severe. It is believed that some 86% of fragile X–affected males have intellectual disabilities, while 6% have autism.

Down syndrome A chromosomal disorder with identifiable physical characteristics resulting in delays in physical and intellectual development

Another example of a genetic cause for intellectual disabilities is due to a chromosomal abnormality. **Down syndrome**, named after the English doctor who first described an individual with the condition in 1866, is a chromosomal disorder wherein the individual has too few or too many chromosomes. The nucleus of each human cell normally contains 23 pairs of chromosomes for a total of 46 chromosomes. In the most common type of Down syndrome, trisomy 21, the 21st set of chromosomes contains three chromosomes rather than the normal pair. Certain identifiable physical characteristics, such as an extra flap of skin over the innermost corner of the eye (an epicanthic fold), are usually present in cases of Down syndrome. The degree of cognitive problems varies, depending in part on how soon the disability is identified, the adequacy of the supporting medical care, and the timing of the early intervention. The great majority of people with Down syndrome have a high incidence of medical problems (National Down Syndrome Society [NDSS], 2008). For example, about half have congenital heart problems, and these individuals have a 15 to 20 times greater risk of developing leukemia.

Some genetic causes of disabilities are not so definite but rather result from interplay between genes and the environment. **Phenylketonuria (PKU)**, also hereditary, occurs when a person is unable to metabolize phenylalanine, which builds up in the body to toxic levels that damage the brain. If untreated, PKU eventually causes intellectual disabilities. Changes in diet (eliminating certain foods that contain this amino acid, such as milk) can control PKU, although cognitive problems can be seen in both treated and untreated individuals. Because of the devastating effects of PKU, it is critical that the diet of these individuals be strictly controlled. Here, then, is a condition rooted in genetics, but it is an environmental factor (a protein in milk) that becomes toxic to the individuals affected and causes the disability. And prompt diagnosis, parental vigilance, and alert teachers are crucial to minimizing the intellectual disabilities. Now we highlight some toxins that do not have a hereditary link.

phenylketonuria (PKU) An inherited condition that results in intellectual disabilities from a buildup of toxins from foods containing amino acids (like milk)

Toxins Poisons that lurk in the environment, **toxins**, are both prenatal and postnatal causes of intellectual disabilities, as well as of other disabilities. Clearly, exposures to toxins harm children and are a real source of disabilities. Here are two reasons why toxins deserve special attention:

toxins Poisonous substances that can cause immediate or long-term harm

- Toxic exposures are preventable.
- Toxins abound in our environment.

Recently, Americans were reminded to always be on guard about dangers lurking in the environment. Just when the public thought that the dangers of **lead poisoning** were diminishing and children were protected from its consequences, alarms were sounded. Why would we think children were safe? Two sources of lead poisoning are exhaust fumes from leaded gasoline and lead-based paint, neither of which is manufactured in the United States any longer. Unfortunately, the environment is not free from lead poisoning. Lead from gasoline emissions remains in the soil and lead-based paint is still on the walls of older apartments and houses. Children can get lead poisoning in many ways: by playing in contaminated dirt, breathing lead directly from a paint source, eating paint chips, or touching old paint and then putting their fingers in their mouths. It is estimated that possibly 25% of households still have deteriorating lead paint not out of the reach of young children (National Safety Council, 2004; Painter, 2007). The national outcry in 2007, however, did not come from worry about these two sources of lead poisoning. It came from the knowledge that toys made in other countries for American companies were found to have high levels of lead in their decorative paint or in their plastic composition (CDC, 2007b, 2007c; Lipman, 2007). It is important to remember that lead can be removed from the environment and everyone can be safe from this cause of disability.

lead poisoning A preventable cause of intellectual disabilities cause by the toxin lead in the environment

Alcohol, another toxin, is a major cause of disabilities. **Fetal alcohol spectrum disorders**, which includes **fetal alcohol syndrome (FAS)** and **fetal alcohol effects (FAE)**, are strongly linked to intellectual disabilities and result from a mother's drinking alcohol during pregnancy. Experts believe that FAS is *the* leading

fetal alcohol spectrum disorders, including fetal alcohol syndrome (FAS) and fetal alcohol effects (FAE) Congenital conditions caused by the mother's drinking alcohol during pregnancy resulting in reduced intellectual functioning, behavior problems, and sometimes physical differences

preventable cause of cognitive problems (CDC, 2006). FAS cost U.S. taxpayers $5.4 billion in 2003 alone, and the costs in quality of life to the individuals affected and their families are immeasurable (U.S. Senate Appropriations Committee, 2004). The characteristics of these disorders are challenging, for they include learning problems, language impairments, difficulties generalizing learning from one situation or task to another; and these disorders also present behavioral issues such as hyperactivity, inattention, low self-esteem, aggression, and impulsivity (Duquette et al., 2006). For these reasons, many of the states with high rates of FAS/FAE are investing in education and other public information activities in hopes of preventing and thereby reducing the rate of these devastating conditions (Müller, 2007).

In a unique and comprehensive study, conducted some years ago by Ann Streissguth and her colleagues, the tragic effects of mothers drinking alcohol on their unborn babies became obvious (Bennington & Thomson, 2006). The average IQ of people with FAS is 79, very close to the cutoff score for intellectual disabilities. This means that almost half of those with FAS qualify for special education services because of cognitive problems. The group's average adaptive behavior score is 61, indicating a strong need for supports. These data explain why some 58% of individuals with FAS have intellectual disabilities and why some 94% require supplemental assistance at school. Unfortunately, most of these people are not free of other problems in the areas of attention, verbal learning, and self-control (CDC, 2007a).

Prevention

Many cases of intellectual disabilities can be prevented by directly addressing the cause. We just discussed two causes of intellectual disabilities that are totally preventable: lead poisoning and FAS/FAE. Lead paint was banned in the United States in 1978, but most older homes still have coats of the toxic material, which can be removed, preventing many cases of disabilities (CDC, 2007c). All toys should be tested for lead in the plastic they are made of and in the paint used to decorate them (Associated Press, 2007).

According to The Arc (2005), a parent organization, many cases of intellectual disabilities are prevented today that could not be some 30 years ago. For example, each year 9,000 cases of intellectual disabilities are prevented via the measles and Hib vaccines, 1,250 cases via newborn screening for PKU and congenital hypothyroidism, and 1,000 cases via the anti-Rh immune globulin. Even more cases are preventable. Most of the strategies listed on Table 8.2 are simple and obvious, but the effects can be significant. For example, in the case of child abuse, teachers now have a legal (and, many believe, a moral) responsibility to report suspected cases so that further damage to the child might be avoided.

Education, medical technology, and access to health care are at the heart of many preventive measures. For example, public education programs can also help pregnant women understand the importance of staying healthy and avoiding alcohol. Other strategies involve testing the expectant mother and analyzing the family's genetic risk factors. Some medical tests help couples considering whether to have children of their own or whether gene therapy might be effective. Many couples with a high probability of having a child with a genetic reason for a disability decide to adopt their family. When medical tests reveal genetic problems of the fetus, couples make decisions accordingly. It is estimated that as many as 80% to 90% of pregnancies are terminated upon the news of the future birth of a Down syndrome baby (Harmon, 2007). Some prevention procedures screen infants and halt the devastating effects of certain conditions either through treatment or early intervention. Also, children are protected from disease through vaccinations and from injury through safety measures. Creating positive, nurturing, and rich home and school environments improve the results of children. Note that not all of these strategies are biological or medical. It is important to look at all aspects of the child and the environment.

The importance of immunization programs to protect children and their mothers from disease cannot be overemphasized (The Arc, 2005; CDF, 2004, 2007). The inci-

Table 8.2 • Prevention of Intellectual Disabilities

For Pregnant Women	For Children	For Society
Obtain early prenatal medical care.	Guarantee universal infant screening.	Eliminate the risks of child poverty.
Seek genetic counseling.	Ensure proper nutrition.	Make early intervention programs universally available.
Maintain good health.	Place household chemicals out of reach.	Provide parent education and support.
Avoid alcohol, drugs, and tobacco.	Use automobile seatbelts, safety seats, and cycle helmets.	Protect children from abuse and neglect.
Obtain good nutrition.	Provide immunizations.	Remove environmental toxins.
Prevent premature births.	Prevent or treat infections.	Provide family planning services.
Take precautions against injuries and accidents.	Have quick and easy access to health care.	Provide public education about prevention techniques.
Prevent or immediately treat infections.	Prevent lead poisoning.	Have universal access to health care.
Avoid sexually transmitted diseases.	Guarantee proper medical care for all children.	Vaccinate all children.
	Provide early intervention programs.	
	Eliminate child abuse and neglect.	

dence of disabilities, including intellectual disabilities, has been greatly reduced by immunization against viruses such as rubella, meningitis, and measles. However, immunization is still not provided universally in part because one in nine families in the United States does not have health insurance (CDF, 2007). But, the problem of not being protected from disease is not always lack of health insurance. Some families do not have access to immunizations because a health care facility is unavailable or too far from home, or because the immunizations are still too expensive even with help from insurance. Other families ignore or are uninformed about the risks of skipping vaccinations. Some avoid immunizations, believing the risk of getting the disease from the vaccination itself is greater than the risk of being unprotected. As a result, easily preventable cases of intellectual disabilities due to infection still occur.

Besides vaccines, other measures prevent disabilities. Here are a few more examples. The prenatal period is so important to the future of each individual. Pregnant mothers need to stay healthy, take proper vitamins, and eat well. There are good examples of why this is essential. Folic acid and vitamin B, found in citrus fruits and dark, leafy vegetables (or taking vitamin supplements), reduces the incidence of **neural tube defects**, such as spina bifida, a condition where the back is not closed along the spinal column, and anencephaly, being born without a brain (March of Dimes, 2006). The March of Dimes, along with government agencies, are confident that up to 70% of neural tube defects can be prevented by women taking the right amounts of folic acid and vitamin B before and during pregnancy. Think of the difference yet to be made if all potential moms ate well and planned ahead!

neural tube defects Another name for spinal cord disorders, which always involve the spinal column and usually the spinal cord

Overcoming Challenges

In each chapter of this text, you learn about different ways that challenges presented by disabilities can be overcome. In this chapter, we feature a story about a remarkable individual. Robert Guthrie was a scientist who applied his knowledge and observation skills to unravel the mystery of PKU. By studying his own son and his niece, both of whom had PKU, he was able to figure out an inexpensive, early

Maria Shriver, author of *What's Wrong with Timmy?* as well as sister of Anthony Shriver, who founded Best Buddies, and niece of President John F. Kennedy, follows in her family's footsteps by showing us all how we can make a difference in the lives of people with disabilities through our own actions.

screening method to detect PKU in infants, before the condition's devastating effects could ravage a young child. Earlier in this chapter you learned that PKU is a genetic reason for intellectual disabilities, but it is actually drinking milk that causes severe intellectual disabilities. Infant screening can detect the problem. Here's how it works: In a procedure Guthrie developed in 1957, a few drops of the newborn's blood are taken from the heel to determine whether the infant has the inherited genetic disorder that prevents metabolizing phenylalanine, a naturally occurring amino acid found in milk. This test, which costs a few cents, makes it possible to change any affected baby's diet before the disastrous effects of PKU can begin to mount. In the past, PKU was responsible for 1% of all severe cases of intellectual disabilities, nearly all of which are now identified and the severity of the problem substantially reduced (PKU.org, 2007).

Assessment

You learned earlier in this chapter that identifying individuals with intellectual disabilities includes assessments of three components: adaptive behavior, intellectual functioning, and need for supports. These assessments are used to identify the individuals, guide the development of their instructional programs, and determine the interventions and the intensity of services required.

The use of standardized tests of intelligence has been criticized for years in the courts, among professionals, and by parents. You learned in Chapters 1 and 3 that the use of IQ tests with culturally and linguistically diverse students has led to lawsuits, which motivated some states to ban their use when diverse students are being identified as having a disability. Despite the problems they are subject to, IQ tests continue to be used (except in states like California where the courts have banned their use), probably because they are relatively simple to administer and provide a definitive answer—a score for people to use (AAMR, 2002). Innovative methods, such as response to intervention that use frequent progress monitoring, curriculum-based measurements (CBM), and other direct measures of student performance (portfolios) to identify students eligible for special education, are being promoted (U.S. Department of Education, 2006). But for now, IQ tests remain a common means of assessing intellectual functioning.

Here is something important to know about and consider. Although the concept of "mental age" is outdated and misleading, some professionals mistakenly still use the idea to explain what an individual's intellectual functioning might mean. It should not be used for it misrepresents individuals' abilities and potential. Here's how the notion of mental age (MA) works. It is used in an attempt to relate intelligence, developmental level, and age. Mental age is explained as the chronological age (CA) of typical learners whose average IQ test performance is equivalent to that of the individual with intellectual disabilities. For example, a man who is age 35 with an IQ score of 57 might be said to have a mental age of 9 years, 5 months. The idea is that the 35-year-old is like a 9-year-old, but such comparisons are imprecise and inaccurate, because adults have the physical attributes, interests, and experiences of their adult peers without disabilities, and the abilities across children of the same age are not consistent, either. Describing adults in terms of the MA of children ignores or underestimates many important characteristics. At the same time, the MA comparison can overestimate certain intellectual skills, such as the use of logic and foresight in solving problems of adults who face cognitive problems. Because of such inaccuracies, it is best not to use MA to refer to a person's abilities.

Early Identification

Many students with intellectual disabilities, particularly those who face moderate to severe problems, come to school already identified as having disabilities. Such individuals tend to face challenges during their school years and in their adult lives (Keogh, Bernheimer, & Guthrie, 2004). For those with biological reasons for their intellectual disabilities, families and doctors recognize the problem early in life, sometimes during infancy or while they are toddlers. Children identified with disabilities early in life receive special early intervention programs specified in their IFSPs (see Chapter 2 for a review). Other children with cognitive problems are identified during the preschool years because they are not developing speech, language, or motor skills at the same rate as their classmates without disabilities. In such cases, it is often the alert preschool teacher who initiates the referral process by working with professionals in the local child find office.

Prereferral

Individuals who are not identified with cognitive disabilities until their school years typically have mild problems with adaptive behavior and find learning the academic skills taught in kindergarten, first grade, and second grade challenging. Such difficulties signal their disability. Typically, their learning patterns indicate an overall delay, making it impossible for them to stay on a par with their classmates without disabilities across all skill areas. Thus, whereas a student with learning disabilities may have challenges with one academic skill area, such as reading, the student with intellectual disabilities has problems keeping up in all areas.

The prereferral step in the school identification process for special education services can be particularly important to diverse students who are being considered. First, it is important to get special services to those who need them. Second, it is equally important not to make a mistake and assign students to the federal mental retardation category for special education if they do not have cognitive disabilities. Thus, teachers need all the information they can gather about students' classroom performance, must use data-based instructional practices for every skill area of concern, and must monitor students' performance to determine under what conditions they learn the best. The team conducting the evaluation for the purpose of identification will then have the information they need to determine which diagnostic tests they should employ for the next step in the IEP process (again, see Chapter 2 for a review).

Identification

Assessment of individuals' adaptive behavior remains a hallmark of the identification of intellectual disabilities. Since 1959, professionals have agreed that IQ scores alone are not enough to qualify individuals for services, to predict their outcomes, or to assist in the development of appropriate educational programs (Kennedy & Horn, 2004). Adaptive behavior must also be considered (look again at Figure 8.1). Measures of adaptive skill areas are used to determine whether the individual actually performs the everyday skills expected of an individual of that age in a typical environment.

Assessment of adaptive skills is typically done through interviews and observation. Because parents and teachers are the source of information and may be biased in their assessments, some practitioners express concern about the accuracy of these evaluation methods. The tendency to overestimate an individual's skills or to assess them inaccurately against a nonspecified age-relevant standard is great. Nevertheless, researchers are becoming more confident about using assessments of adaptive skills and need for supports (Thompson et al., 2004). They believe that indicators of adaptive skills provide a more accurate picture of individuals' strengths and needs for support than scores on tests of intelligence. Today, more standardized assessment instruments are available to help assess adaptive behavior. For example, Assessment of Adaptive Areas (AAA) is a test that enables the examiner to convert scores to age equivalents across adaptive skill areas. This highly useful instrument brings more objectivity to the determination of individuals' abilities, helps professionals determine what supports are needed, and allows for better communication with families about these important areas. The Supports Intensity Scale (SIS), developed by AAIDD in 2004, measures the intensities of supports that each person needs to participate fully in community life. SIS helps make these determinations by conducting at least two interviews, which could include the person with the disability, a parent or sibling, or a staff member who has worked with the individual. The test is now being adopted throughout the United States and also in Italy, Australia, and many other countries worldwide (Harries et al., 2005; Leoni, 2007).

Evaluation: Alternate Assessments

Students with intellectual disabilities have one of the lowest rates of participation in general education programs when compared to other students with disabilities. Only about 16% of these students spend more than 80% of their school day learning alongside of their peers without disabilities, and some 30% participate between 40% and 79% of the school day accessing the general education curriculum (OSEP, 2008). Many students with intellectual disabilities participate in an alternate curriculum; many of them are part of the small group of learners whose progress is monitored differently.

In Chapter 2, you learned about three groups of learners with disabilities and how schools' accountability systems align with the curriculum in which they are participating. Most students with disabilities take standard state- and districtwide assessments to monitor their academic progress; however, they do so with accommodations so their disability does not mask their growth. The second group of students—some 2% of all schoolchildren—participate in the general education curriculum but have reduced achievement standards, so their progress is measured with assessments that have been modified and reflect reasonable benchmarks for grade-level content (Morrier, 2007). Many of these students have mild to moderate intellectual disabilities. This second group is receiving considerable attention as professionals are working hard to develop guidelines for ways to assess skills that are linked to grade level content (Browder et al., 2007).

Students with more severe intellectual disabilities are members of the third group, which IDEA '04 and the No Child Left Behind Act (NCLB) excuse from the required annual state- and districtwide assessments (U.S. Department of Education, 2006, 2007). These students, some 1% of all students, have their progress evaluated through **alternate assessments**—evaluations of yearly progress through alternate means (e.g., portfolios). These students' IEP goals do not reflect the complete general education curriculum. They are not working toward a regular high school diploma but, rather, are participating in a functional or life skills curriculum, and their IEPs clearly identify both the alternate curriculum and the means for alternate assessments. Different systems are used to document their progress toward achieving their IEP goals (National Center for Educational Outcomes [NCEO], 2007). Many states use portfolios, direct measures of a skill or specific instructional targets (e.g., benchmarks of con-

alternate assessments Means of measuring the progress of students who do not participate in the general education curriculum

sumer mathematics, curriculum-based measurements of sight word vocabulary), and checklists. When appropriate, assessments may include standardized tests that measure gains in academic areas, like reading or written language.

Early Intervention

Early identification and intervention are important to children with intellectual disabilities and their families. Early intervention can reduce the severity of cognitive disabilities or may even prevent them (Guralnick, 1998; U.S. Department of Education, 2001). Preschool experiences provide the foundation for the development of important skills useful later in school and in life, and they occur at a time when the family is beginning its long involvement in the education of their child with a disability.

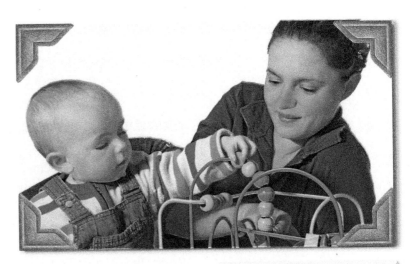

Early intervention often works best when the child is engaged in the therapy. Here a baby with motor development delays is stimulated to develop muscle coordination and movement by "playing" with a bead maze.

The power of early intervention is remarkable, and early childhood education programs are essential for young children with disabilities and young children who are at risk for developmental delay or school failure. The data prove this point indisputably. A well-controlled and randomized study followed up two groups of low-income African American 3- and 4-year-olds at age 40 (Schweinhart, 2005). One group attended preschool, and the other did not. Those who received preschool experiences outperformed those who did not on all measures: IQ scores, high school graduation, income, home and car ownership, and citizenship. The study also showed that return to taxpayers was great: Every tax dollar spent on the preschool experience provided an economic return of $17 from education savings, taxes on earnings, welfare savings, and savings of some of the costs that crime inflicts on society. And, of course, these calculations do not fully reflect the human benefits. The longitudinal effects of high-quality preschool experiences show how early intervention makes real differences in the lives of people—all people.

It is quite probable that inclusive education is more of a reality at preschools across the nation than at elementary, middle, and high schools. The preschool curriculum lends itself to inclusive practices, and worries about achieving high scores on state and district achievement tests are not a concern with this age group. Findings from the long-standing program at the University of North Carolina–Chapel Hill clearly show benefits found in many high-quality inclusive preschools (Division for Early Childhood [DEC], 2007; Manuel & Little, 2002):

- Children with and those without disabilities play together.
- Children with disabilities show higher rates of social interactions.
- Typically developing children have no negative consequences.
- Typically developing children show a greater appreciation and respect for individual differences.

However, not all preschool programs achieve equally. What are some of the features of effective preschool settings? Here is a list of some of their key features:

- Full-day program
- Accredited standing
- Well-prepared teachers
- No more than about a third of the preschoolers has disabilities
- Positive interactions with children
- Family partnerships
- Multidisciplinary team approach (including SLPs, special educators, PTs, behavior analysts)
- Fun

Policymakers, parents, and educators recognize the importance of comprehensive and sustained services for these children while they are toddlers and preschoolers. They also understand that students participating in early intervention programs are very diverse in their types of disabilities and in the severity of their disabilities.

Teaching Students with Intellectual Disabilities

The majority of students with intellectual disabilities have mild cognitive problems. Increasingly, these students are included in general education classes. Their learning goals are often similar or identical to those of their peers without disabilities. Often teachers adapt their techniques, adjust the curriculum, and provide accommodations. They modify worksheets, provide more detailed instructions about how assignments are to be completed, include students in setting goals, and have students participate in the evaluation of their own work. Some students cannot fully access the general education curriculum. They participate, but with reduced achievement standards (Morrier, 2007; U.S. Department of Education, 2007). Some techniques, such as specific instructions and positive feedback, help avoid behavior problems and maintain students' interest in class activities. Some examples are found in Tips for Classroom Management.

Access to the General Education Curriculum

As we mentioned earlier, many students with intellectual disabilities do not access the general education curriculum and attend general education classes along with their neighborhood friends. In fact, only some 16% of them are included in general education classes for over 80% of the school day (OSEP, 2008). An additional 30% of these students spend close to half of their time learning alongside their peers without disabilities. These participation rates decrease as students move to their high school years and begin to learn the skills needed as adults to live and work independently in the community. From these data it is clear: Most students with intellectual disabilities do not fully access the general education curriculum. Clearly, there is room for improvement in participation rates.

Instructional Accommodations

For many students with intellectual disabilities who do access the general education curriculum, accommodations (e.g., extended time to complete assignments, note takers to help them write down important points from lectures) are not sufficient. For some assignments, they may need only accommodations; but for some content in the general education curriculum, they need further help. They require more adjustments, or **modifications**, where assignments or tests are reduced or altered. Students may be allowed to master fewer objectives or to provide only specific parts of answers, or they may be given alternative assignments (e.g., photo essays instead of written reports). Accommodating for Inclusive Environments provides some ways to ensure students' learning through modifications in the content contained in the general education curriculum.

modifications Adjustments to assignments or tests, reducing the requirements

Data-Based Practices: Self-Determination

People with intellectual disabilities typically have fewer opportunities to develop skills needed for independence naturally. They are allowed fewer choices than other groups of people with disabilities or their peers without disabilities (Wehmeyer, 2007). Every day, people make choices for themselves. They decide for them where to sit, where to eat, what to eat, how long to stay, where to go, which movie or show to see, and with whom to interact. Particularly those who were allowed to make few choices while they were growing up, the need or even the opportunity to make decisions is unfamiliar. Other people make even the simplest

TIPS for Classroom Management
GUIDING STUDENTS THROUGH INSTRUCTION AND FEEDBACK

Instruction

1. Ensure that students understand classroom rules and expectations.
2. Use simple instructions and directions about expected classroom behaviors.
3. Actively involve the students in the lesson.
4. Prompt students about how they are supposed to behave during each type of lesson.
5. Explain the consequences of misbehaving or disturbing the lesson.

Feedback

1. Use simple, clear, and direct feedback regarding the exact behaviors required.
2. Remind students about how they are supposed to behave during each type of lesson.
3. Praise students during the lesson for meeting the classroom expectations.
4. Deliver consequences for misbehaving or disturbing the lesson.
5. Reward students for meeting expectations over an entire period.

decisions for them. Many individuals with intellectual disabilities are not permitted the time necessary to actually develop an understanding of their own preferences, likes, and dislikes (Eisenman, 2007a, 2007b). Possibly as a result of excessive use of adult-directed (by teachers, parents, and family members) reward systems, some individuals do not develop a strong internal motivation that can serve as the drive necessary to work hard to achieve a personal goal. Teachers can make a difference in these outcomes.

As in other chapters, in this section we focus on one instructional approach. Of course, many effective strategies are available and selecting one was difficult. However, we decided to highlight an important skill needed for success at school, in life, and in the community (Rusch, 2008). Whether participating in a curriculum that focuses on skills needed for daily living or in the general education curriculum, many students with disabilities need explicit instruction and guided practice so they can be more independent (Shogren et al., 2007). The goal is for these individuals to become self-determined, and for those who achieve this goal, the benefits are many. Those with higher levels of **self-determination** are more likely to graduate from high school, hold jobs after high school, and experience success in adult life (Eisenman, 2007a; Hughes, Washington, & Brown, 2008). Therefore, we decided to highlight in this chapter's Closer Look At Data-Based Practices ways to include self-determination in the instructional routine. Think about how you could expand on the teaching suggestions described in this feature. Also, think about more ways to integrate self-determination into all aspects of the school day.

Students learning self-determination skills often study how to make choices, advocate for oneself, set goals, solve problems, have autonomy, and evaluate their own

self-determination Making decisions, choosing preferences, and exercising self-advocacy needed for independent living

Accommodating for Inclusive Environments
Steps for Success in a Modified General Education Curriculum

Specify the Instructional Objectives

- List the objectives in observable terms such that they will communicate to others.
- Focus the objectives on what is directly the instructional target.
- Plan how the objectives will be evaluated to ensure continued student progress.

Sequence Skills

- Be sure prerequisite skills are mastered first.
- Sequence easy skills before more difficult ones.
- Plan to teach confusing concepts separately.

Match Instructional Tactic with Topic or Skill to Be Taught

- Select a tactic that has been proven through rigorous research.

- Monitor its effectiveness continuously.
- Change tactic when it is no longer effective.

Provide Many Opportunities for Practice

- Have students apply their learning in different settings.
- Have students apply their learning with slightly different or expanded tasks or skills.

Be Certain That the Skill Is Truly Mastered

- Have the student demonstrate mastery when performing the skill independently.
- Have the student demonstrate mastery in a variety of settings.

performance (Eisenman, 2007a; Wehmeyer, 2006, 2007). Students can spend considerable time and effort learning and practicing the components of self-determination. Fortunately, opportunities to teach self-determination skills abound, and instruction does not have to take time from other content areas. Rather, what is really needed is a change in orientation, in how instruction is delivered and what is integrated into the teaching routine (Holverstott, 2005). Think about how to promote elements of self-determination, rather than setting aside time to create new instructional activities for this purpose. Here are two ideas: Although not a frequent event, the development of a student's IEP provides wonderful opportunities to discuss needs for supports, types of supports and services, and interests (Jones, 2006). The second idea is to use a simple checklist, like the one shown in A Closer Look at Data-Based Practices, to ensure a balance of self-determination elements are integrated into instruction (Martin, Woods, & Sylvester, 2008). Self-determination topics must be part of the curriculum, particularly for high school students, for it is now clear that these are adaptive skills, highly related to success in all aspects of adult life (Hughes et al., 2008).

Technology

Many of us spend increasing portions of our day on the computer, where papers are prepared, budgets maintained, information sought, and friends kept close. People now correspond via e-mail at a relatively high rate, and until recently students with intellectual disabilities were often excluded from this exchange. But thanks to a Best Buddies program called **e-Buddies**, e-mail is now an important part of school and daily life for students with intellectual disabilities (e-Buddies, 2005; Hardman & Clark, 2006). This program helps students with intellectual disabilities connect with each other across the nation and across the

e-Buddies A program that creates e-mail friendships between people with and without intellectual disabilities

A Closer Look at Data-Based Practices

Self-Determination

An individual who is empowered is a person who is able to make decisions about life. The person is able to make informed choices about where to live, how to live, where to work, what to eat, and which leisure-time activities to pursue. Making such choices requires some complex abilities, such as knowing what activities and results are preferred, understanding the consequences of decisions, solving problems, advocating for oneself, and evaluating the results. Gaining these skills does not come naturally to most of us, but in particular individuals with intellectual disabilities often require explicit instruction and practice in real-life settings to become independent adults. Teachers can help students gain the required skills by making and using a checklist to ensure that a balance of self-determination activities are integrated into daily instructional opportunities.

Steps to Follow

1. Help students understand themselves, their abilities, and preferences.

   a. Provide students with ways for self-discovery (interest inventories, functional assessments, discussion groups).

   b. Share with individual students their previous and current IEPs, including goals, objectives, and descriptions of instructional needs.

   c. Have students participate in the development of goals and objectives for the upcoming IEP meeting.

   d. Help students understand the implications of their disability as well as personal strengths (internet searches, fact sheets, self-reflections).

2. Have students learn what supports and services should be available to them and participate in the decision process for the selection, implementation, and evaluation of services and supports.

   a. Have each student suggest the special education and related services, supports, and accommodations they need while participating in their annual IEP meeting.

   b. Have students set benchmarks for academic improvement, select accommodations they need, monitor their progress, and reward themselves when goals are achieved.

3. Teach students to make effective choices.

   a. Help students assess their own knowledge and skills and determine what they want to learn about a topic.

   b. Require students to analyze choice options and evaluate choices made.

   c. Ask students to articulate personal goals and self-monitor their attainment.

Self-Determination Checklist

- ✔ Chose activity
- ✔ Planned engagement
  - __ Observe ✔ Do
- ✔ Done in community
- ✔ Evaluated Performance
  - ✔ Liked __ Disliked
  - ✔ Good job __ Needs improvement
- ✔ Used experience for next choice

world! It also facilitates the development of friendships between people with and people without disabilities. This program helps students with intellectual disabilities become motivated to use computers and systems of communication; a challenge for many individuals who face cognitive challenges (Zubai-Ruggieri, 2007). The benefits of being able to use computers and the Internet are obvious to most of us, but can be particularly helpful to those with intellectual disabilities. Relating to the goals of self-determination, those who use the Internet report a sense of empowerment and liberation by being able to purchase things online, communicating with others whether with voice activation or videoconferencing technology. Explicit instruction about how to use a computer, assistance in buying one, help with setting up the computer's devices (e.g., hooking up cameras, activating microphones), and using accessible software could well become an important part of this century's functional curricula. The result can be better access to and participation in the community.

Learning that is facilitated and supported by technology engages us all.

functional curriculum Teaching skills needed for daily living

PEARSON
myeducationlab Go to the Activities and Applications section in Chapter 8 of MyEducationLab, and complete Activity 2. As you watch the video and answer the accompanying questions, compare functional versus academic curricula, and justify a functional curriculum for some students with disabilities.

quality of life A subjective and individual-specific concept reflecting social relationships, personal satisfaction, employment, choice, leisure, independence, and community presence

Transition

For all of us, success after school is related to how well prepared we are for adulthood. Transition education does make a difference: Graduates of special education programs are more likely to be employed and to have higher earnings, particularly if they had received vocational education, paid work experience, strong parental involvement, and interagency collaboration during their high school years (Kohler & Field, 2003; Rusch, 2008). Congress understood the importance of ensuring that some students with disabilities be allowed to spend their instructional time not accessing the general education curriculum but, rather, working on the development of life skills that improve results. The accompanying box, What IDEA '04 Says About Transition and Functional Skills, points out the importance of spending time during the transition years mastering these important skills.

The skills needed to be successful adults are many and complex. For many students with moderate to severe intellectual disabilities, mastering these skills requires both explicit instruction and time for practice beyond what is typically available in the general education setting. Together when skills needed to succeed in daily life are the focus of instruction, they form what is called a **functional curriculum**, a curriculum that focuses on skills used in daily life before and after graduation (Rusch, 2008). What is a functional curriculum? It includes topics that address adaptive behavior: skills needed to hold a job; live in the community; have friends, and travel independently from home, to work, or to a recreational activity. Here's an example. Researchers have found that adults with intellectual disabilities do not use cell phones (Bryen, Carey, & Friedman, 2007). Despite the high use by the general public, cell phones are not accessible to these individuals. In a functional curriculum, students should be taught what kind to purchase, how much cost they can afford, and how to use the phone's features. In a functional curriculum, students' reading, writing, and mathematics instruction often focuses on practical skills. Here are a few examples:

n Reading survival words
  - *Street signs: Walk, Don't Walk, Stop*
  - *Safety words: Danger, Poison, Keep Out*
n Writing
  - *Receiving information:* taking phone messages, writing directions to get to a restaurant, taking notes on how to do a job
  - *Delivering information:* leaving notes for someone else, providing instructions
n Mathematics
  - *Daily life:* telling time, using money
  - *Measurement:* cooking measures, woodworking

One overarching goal of special education and transition programs is for individuals with disabilities to achieve to their maximum potential and have happy, productive lives. **Quality of life** is a person's satisfaction with life, which includes a sense of contentment that results in part from feelings of dignity, value, worth, and respect (Wolfensberger, 2002). An assessment of quality of life helps determine how well the individual's needs and desires are being met and reflects outcomes such as empowerment, self-determination, independence, social belonging, community presence, and life satisfaction (Schalock, Gardner, & Bradley, 2007). Quality of life is a complex and elusive concept. Judgments about quality of life must be made by each individual, for what one person perceives as good may not be perceived as good by another. In other words, no single standard can be applied to all people (Edgerton, 1996). It is hard to get uniform indicators to evaluate quality of life, but some general areas are worth considering:

- Employment
- Friendships
- Independence

Let's look briefly at each of these three areas in turn for they can help us better understand the enormity of the knowledge and skills individuals with disabilities need to master during the precious, last few years of school.

Employment

Young adults who live and work in the community express greater satisfaction with their lives than those who do not (Kraemer, McIntyre, & Blacher, 2003; Schalock et al., 2007). People with intellectual disabilities who work in the community have higher satisfaction scores than those who work in sheltered workshops, who work in day/activity centers, or who do not work. These findings are important because they inform educators about many of the goals that should be included in the transition statements of students' IEPs (see Chapter 2 for a review). As we are reminded in this chapter's Considering Culture, educators must also always keep the individual's culture in mind when making important decisions, such as possible vocational opportunities, that impact the person and his or her family.

Jobs are important because they give us an opportunity to earn money, to form friendships, to engage in the social activities of the community, and to develop a sense of self-satisfaction about making a contribution. Achieving success on the job, however, can be challenging for many people with intellectual disabilities. A traditional means of helping these individuals after the high school years and in the workplace is through vocational rehabilitation services, which are provided by every state. **Vocational rehabilitation** is a government service that provides training, counseling, and job placement services; vocational rehabilitation has been effective with clients who avail themselves of these services and who have mild intellectual disabilities (Moore, Harley, & Gamble, 2004). Those with moderate to severe intellectual disabilities often need more assistance to gain paid work in the community. **Supported employment** is funded by governmental agencies and assists individuals who could not otherwise hold a competitive job by helping them locate a job, learn the skills needed to be successful in that position, and keep the job. Supported employment began over 20 years ago, has evolved over the years, and pays off daily. This system has proved that people with disabilities, who previously were considered unable to work in the community, can be productive workers (Parent et al., 2008).

Through supported employment, a job developer finds or even designs work that an individual with intellectual disabilities or other severe disabilities can accomplish. A **job coach** might work alongside the individual, helping her or him to learn all parts of the job. Coworkers are trained to assist their coworkers with disabilities as they work alongside them (Parent et al., 2008). In addition to work experience, another benefit of supported employment programs is the development of friendships that exist at work and after hours—something important to everyone (Chadsey & Beyer, 2001). And, in return, social networks have a positive influence on employment (Eisenman, 2007b).

What IDEA '04 Says About. . .

Transition and Functional Skills

The transition process should focus on improving a student's achievement to facilitate development of skills necessary to function in postschool activities that include

- postsecondary education;
- vocational education;
- integrated employment (including supported employment);
- continuing and adult education, adult services;
- independent living; and
- community participation.

In addition to instruction and related services provided for younger students, the individually determined process may include

- community experiences,
- employment objectives,
- other postschool adult living objectives,
- acquisition of daily living skills, and
- functional vocational evaluation.

myeducationlab Go to the Activities and Applications section in Chapter 8 of MyEducationLab, and complete Activity 3. As you watch the video and answer the accompanying questions, think about what experiences prepare students with Down syndrome for adult life, and why gainful employment is important for students with disabilities.

vocational rehabilitation A government service that provides training, career counseling, and job placement

supported employment A government program to help individuals with disabilities be successful in competitive employment situations

job coach A transition specialist who teaches vocational skills in the community and in actual job settings

Considering Culture *Finding the Right Vocational Opportunity*

Martin has taught the "Transition to Work" class for students with intellectual disabilities at Jefferson High School for 7 years. He has won awards from the local Chamber of Commerce and the Arc for his skill in finding "real-world" placements that often become full-time jobs for his students when they complete school. This year he has encountered a situation that is new to him. After he worked diligently to get a training placement in a popular coffee shop for Amira Abdullah, a 16-year-old with intellectual disabilities, her parents have refused to allow her to participate. In a meeting with Amira and her parents, her father said, "Amira may not work at this place. We would not allow any of our girls to serve the public or be unsupervised in such a setting. It is immodest and asking for trouble and embarrassment. To imagine Amira, with her special problems, in such a situation does not make sense."

Martin knew that Mr. Abdullah's background and faith caused him to hold very traditional views of women, but he also knew the value of vocational skills for Amira. As the meeting continued, he talked with Mr. and Mrs. Abdullah about all the things that Amira would learn: money management, self-fulfillment, and personal independence. Mr. Abdullah listened politely and then explained that all of those things would be handled within the family—that there was no need for outsiders to teach such things. At this point Amira said quietly, "Papa, my friends are going to work. I want to work, too." Mr. Abdullah seemed surprised, but his wife smiled slightly as she looked fondly at Amira. Martin was also surprised to hear Amira speak out, and it gave him an idea. He knew that Mr. Abdullah had a very successful business, so he wondered aloud if it would be possible to respect Mr. Abdullah's concerns *and* honor Amira's request. He asked Mr. Abdullah to think about creating a training opportunity within his business where Amira could continue to learn under family supervision with the help of a job coach. They talked about possibilities, and then Mr. Abdullah asked if they could meet with Martin again the next week.

When they met again, Mr. Abdullah said that the whole family had talked and that Amira's brothers and sisters had been very persuasive. They had all had small jobs in the business and thought that Amira should, too. Mrs. Abdullah said that Amira knows everyone in the building and everyone knows her. Perhaps she could deliver the mail and be a courier within the building. She said that she thought Amira would do well but that they did not know how to teach her the job and its responsibilities. Martin happily stepped in, complimenting them on the idea and assuring them that he and a job coach would teach Amira how to do the job. Within a few months, Amira was going to work, earning her own money, and feeling very proud that, like her friends, she had a job.

Questions to Consider

1. If you had been in Martin's position, what do you think your first reaction to Mr. Abdullah's concerns might have been?

2. Sometimes teachers become frustrated with students' parents because they think the parents are being overprotective. Did you ever feel that your parents were overprotective? In what circumstance? Do you think their behavior was based on cultural or religious traditions and beliefs or on concern for your well-being?

3. What are examples of cultural or religious values that may affect individuals with disabilities differently than those without disabilities?

—By Eleanor Lynch, San Diego State University, and Marci Hanson, San Francisco State University

Friendships

Concerns about friendships and people with intellectual disabilities are not new (Janney & Snell, 2006; Snell & Brown, 2008). One goal promoted by inclusive education is to increase the social interaction skills and expand the friendships of students with disabilities. Programs, like the one you read about in the Making a Difference feature of this chapter, encourage friendships of those with and without disabilities. Unfortunately, some recent information indicates that such friendships, those where individuals without disabilities are encouraged to make friends with people with intellectual disabilities, are not long lasting (Matheson, Olsen, & Weisner, 2007). Some reasons for this disappointing finding are based in the nature of friendships and the development of companionships themselves: common interests, trust, reciprocal relationships, and shared values. Long-term, more lasting friendships do develop among individuals with intellectual disabilities. In fact, these relationships seem to be more stable and positive than friendships between them and high school students without disabilities.

Key factors that help individuals with intellectual disabilities make friends are proximity and similarity. In other words, being neighbors, attending the same community centers, and being classmates allow for people to become familiar with each other naturally. Then friendships develop that are built on similar interests such as wanting to see the same movie, go to the mall together, or share a meal. Clearly, educators need to address social skills and help their students learn how to make friends. This is important because friendships contribute to later participation in community programs and less likelihood of having feelings of loneliness and isolation when adults (Fish et al., 2007; Stancliff et al., 2007).

Independent Living

Historically, individuals with intellectual disabilities, even some whose IQ scores fall into the mild range, have found themselves confined to residential institutions. During the last half of the 20th century, the deinstitutionalization movement sought to close all institutions and bring all people with intellectual disabilities to community settings. Today, more people with cognitive disabilities are living in the community away from large institutions and outside their family homes. This progress has been relatively recent. Since 1993 and 2003, 30% more of these individuals lived in community placements, and more than twice as many lived in small residential arrangements with anywhere from one to six people living in a household (Lakin, Braddock, & Smith, 2004b). Despite these improvements, the rate of reducing the size and number of large, congregate institutions for persons with intellectual disabilities has slowed. Bringing about a further increase in community living for people with high needs for support involves considerable effort, person-centered planning, and individualized instruction (Agran & Wehmeyer, 2008; Holburn et al., 2004).

Because living independently in the community is related to being satisfied with life, it is a most important goal (Schalock et al., 2007). For many, community living has positively replaced less satisfactory experiences with residential institutional life. However, merely living in a community setting, such as a group home or some other supportive housing arrangement, does not guarantee life satisfaction (Perry & Felce, 2005). Social support from staff, peers, and community members can be a critical variable for success (Hughes, Washington, & Brown, 2008). Also, we now know that the number of people living in the setting makes a difference in the members' quality of life. When advocating for those students in transition programs who will need intensive supports to live in the community when adults, teachers should know that the optimal number appears to be around six (Emerson et al., 2001). Evidently, people come to develop natural supports and friendships with each other when there are neither too few nor too many to develop supportive networks.

myeducationlab Go to the Building Teaching Skills and Dispositions section in Chapter 8 of MyEducationLab and complete the activities in the IRIS Module, "School Counselors: Facilitating Transitions for Students with Disabilities from High School to Post-School Settings." This module provides information for counselors and other education professionals to assist high school students with disabilities in the transition from the school environment to a postschool setting.

Collaboration

As you just learned, the transition years of school are most important for individuals with intellectual disabilities. It is during this time that the foundation for an excellent quality of life—comprised of employment, independent living, and friendships—is laid.

The skills to learn are many, and it is here where members of multidisciplinary teams truly make a difference in the lives and results of individuals with disabilities. The special education teacher not only provides explicit instruction and coordinates the talents of others. The special education teacher often has another important role: advocate. Concerns abound about the delivery of related services and students with moderate to severe intellectual disabilities. Some parents believe that their children are not receiving the related services they deserve (Sauer, 2007). In some cases, the services are not available; in others, less direct or intensive services are offered, such as an SLP consulting with a general education teacher instead of providing direct therapy. Because of the importance of multidisciplinary teams working together to develop the skills individuals need as adults to succeed, special education teachers often find themselves in the important position of advocating that their students receive all the related services they need. Let's think again about community presence and participation, which contribute to quality-of-life outcomes for individuals with intellectual disabilities.

Collaboration with Related Services Providers: Therapeutic Recreation Specialists

Those with greater presence and participation in the community have fewer feelings of loneliness and tend to have more friends and natural supports. Those individuals often are the ones who engage in recreational activities during their leisure time. Developing the skills and habits so an individual seeks out a bowling league, a pickup basketball game, hiking club, or a gym when an adult typically begins during the school years. For typical learners, these skills and interests are often developed on the playground and the school's athletic fields. For individuals with disabilities, they are often developed through special education and its related services.

Adapted physical education (PE) is not a related service; it is listed in IDEA '04 as a special education service (U.S. Department of Education, 2006). These teachers know what levels of exercise are safe. They help develop muscles and strength through exercise, but perhaps what is most important is that they teach and encourage students to engage in recreational activities. Adaptive PE teachers help students learn and enjoy individual and team sports (National Consortium for Physical Education and Recreation for Individuals with Disabilities [NCPERID], n.d.). Learning how to play recreational sports during the school years leads to participating in community recreational activities as an adult. It is through these activities that people stay healthy, do not experience loneliness, and make friends with a common interest. Adapted PE teachers seek the assistance from many different professions as they plan and deliver services to students with intellectual disabilities. They may work with both physical therapists and occupations therapists to be sure that the activities planned for individuals are appropriate. They also may work with another related service provider, **recreational therapists**. Many of these professionals work in the community or with older adults who might also need assisted-living services. In school settings, recreational therapists teach students how to throw a ball, swing a racquet, play board games, or seek out community resources and recreational activities. They also help students take the recreational skills they learn at school and apply them in the community by playing the sport, joining a league, or finding others who enjoy the same leisure-time activities (National Council for Therapeutic Recreation Certification [NCTRC], 2008).

myeducationlab Go to the Activities and Applications section in Chapter 8 of MyEducationLab, and complete Activity 4. As you watch the video and answer the accompanying questions, take note of how paraprofessionals structure learning tasks for their students.

adapted physical education (PE) A special education direct service, not a related service, that teaches physical education, recreational skills, and sports to individuals with disabilities

recreational therapy A related service that helps students learn to access community and recreational programs

Collaborative Practices: Developing Extracurricular Involvement

Successful integration of people with intellectual disabilities at school and in society requires considerable teamwork and effort. As you should now be aware, school for these individuals is not just about learning academic subjects. Recreation, leisure, and extracurricular involvement for these youngsters rarely happens without considerable teamwork from teachers and from related service providers. However, the importance of such involvement cannot be underemphasized for they increase the likelihood of developing friends, achieving community integration, having postschool success, and improving the overall quality of life (Kleinert, Miracle, & Sheppard-Jones, 2007).

One of the first steps in developing extracurricular involvement is to identify activities in which students can participate. Developing such a list can require a team of people working together. Parents, teachers, directors of community programs, and volunteers might work together to find the right array of available choices from which students can choose. The next step is to arrange transportation; and, in part for insurance purposes, be sure that arrangements are coordinated through the school's principal and administration. Sometimes, the district can arrange transportation for activities that are off campus. Of course, not all activities need to be in the community; some opportunities are at school (Kleinert et al., 2007). School clubs, sports teams, band, or choir all are opportunities for involvement. But, in all cases, it is important for teachers to communicate, check progress, provide supports, and arrange for accommodations when necessary. The skills learned through such opportunities are skills learned for life.

Partnerships with Families and Communities

It is estimated that over a half a million adults with intellectual disabilities are over the age of 60, and, like the rest of the U.S. population, they are living longer, healthier lives. So, expectations are that their numbers are expected to triple in the next 25 years (Hodapp, Glidden, & Kaiser, 2005). The majority of them do not live in institutions but rather in the community, either with their parents or under their careful watch. In the last 30 years, more and more individuals with intellectual disabilities grow up at home, attend neighborhood schools, and live their adult lives in the community. During this time, researchers who studied families focused on mothers, but not as much on siblings or dads (Stoneman, 2005). However, as parents of children with disabilities grow older, it is brothers and sisters—**siblings**—who assume supervision and care responsibilities. Adult siblings often maintain regular and personal contacts with their brothers or sisters with disabilities and stand ready to assume the role of caregiver (Hannah & Midlarksy, 1999, 2005). Many—36% in one study—even intend to reside with their sibling when their parents' health or age prevents their continuing to care for their son or daughter with disabilities. However, little large-scale research has been conducted to reveal important information about siblings of individuals with intellectual disabilities—the kinds of supports they give and the kinds of supports they themselves need.

siblings Brothers and sisters

Individuals with disabilities are as unique as their siblings and their families. Researchers acknowledge that coming to a better understanding of these relationships will be challenging, for there are many factors to consider (Hodapp et al., 2005). For example, the gender of the sibling may make a difference in these caretaking relationships. Do sisters feel a stronger responsibility for their brother or sister with a disability than their brothers? Does the size of the family change the relationships? Do older siblings respond differently than younger ones? As the family ages, do roles and obligations change? How does culture interplay with families' coping skills when it comes to disability? And, of course, how much can we generalize from one individual situation to another?

Although research about siblings of individuals with disabilities is limited, some important findings can help educators as they work both with the student with intellectual disabilities and his or her family. At one time popular belief was that having a family member with a disability was not necessarily a "good thing" for the typically developing siblings, but that belief does not hold true (Stoneman, 2005). Although disabilities can contribute to family stress, many families with a member who has a disability get along as typical families do (Dykens, 2005). Educators, as they work with such families, should not make a terrible mistake of assuming that these families are in crisis. These brothers and sisters are like brothers and sisters of families that do not have a member with a disability. However, research has shown that they do spend a lot of time with their sibling with a disability. So, educators can be a tremendous help to these school-age brothers and sisters by teaching them to

- select appropriate play activities,
- create play accommodations,
- apply techniques that sustain interactions,
- manage disruptive behaviors,
- avoid arguing and fighting, and
- decide when to seek assistance.

Elise McMillan, a mom of a child with Down syndrome, so simply, yet eloquently, points out many mother's desires for more supports from educators and wishes for all other families with a member with a disability:

> More information for families and siblings, more advice, and more support would all make the journey easier to navigate. Hopefully, most siblings would get to the same point as did our son, Jim: "When you ask me who in the world has had the biggest impact on my life, the answer is my brother, Will. From him, I have learned patience, and also what is really important. (McMillan, 2005, p. 351)

Summary

People with intellectual disabilities (formerly called mental retardation and sometimes referred to as cognitive disabilities) have significantly impaired intellectual functioning and problems with adaptive skills. They require a variety of supports that may vary in intensity and duration. Some individuals require all four types of supports—natural, nonpaid, generic, specialized—at an intense level across their lifetimes to achieve community presence, be independent, and attain a high quality of life. Other individuals require few supports to take their rightful places in society. Intellectual disabilities emerge during the developmental period, between birth and age 18.

Answering the Chapter Objectives

1. Why, after 50 years of using the term *mental retardation*, would there be a call to change its name to *intellectual and developmental disabilities?*

- To interrupt the negative association with the term *mental retardation*
- To reduce the bias and discrimination experienced by individuals with intellectual disabilities

2. What are the key components of the 2002 AAIDD definition, and how are levels of severity and outcomes categorized?

- Key components
  - *Intellectual functioning:* difficulties learning and remembering

- *Adaptive behavior:* problems with skills needed in daily life
- *Systems of supports:* networks of friends, family members, coworkers, social service and governmental agencies
- Level of severity and outcomes
  - *Mild intellectual disabilities:* IQ range of 50 to 69
    Outcomes: Has learning difficulties, is able to work, can maintain good social relationships, contributes to society
  - *Moderate mental retardation:* IQ range of 35 to 49
    Outcomes: Exhibits marked developmental delays during childhood, has some degree of independence in self-care, possesses adequate communica-

tion and academic skills, requires varying degrees of support to live and work in the community
- *Severe intellectual disabilities:* IQ range of 20 to 34
  Outcomes: Has continuous need for supports
- *Profound intellectual disabilities:* IQ under 20
  Outcomes: Demonstrates severe limitations in self-care, continence, communication, and mobility; requires continuous and intensive supports

3. What are the four levels of supports, and how do they make a difference in the lives of people with intellectual disabilities?

Systems of supports help individuals achieve community presence, attain quality of life, live independently, and hold competitive jobs.

- *Natural supports:* the individual's own resources, family, friends, neighbors, coworkers, classmates
- *Nonpaid supports:* clubs, recreational leagues, private organizations
- *Generic public supports:* transportation, state's human services
- *Specialized supports:* special education, early intervention preschools, transition and vocational rehabilitation services

4. What are two ways to organize causes of disabilities, and what are the major known reasons for intellectual disabilities?

- Causes can be grouped two ways:
  - *Time of onset:* prenatal, perinatal, or postnatal
  - *Reason:* heredity, environment, and/or society
- Major types or reasons
  - *Genes and heredity:* fragile X syndrome, Down syndrome, phenylketonuria (PKU)
  - *Environment:* toxins, child abuse and neglect, discrimination and bias
  - *Conditions:* disease, low birthweight

5. Why does teaching self-determination make a difference in the outcomes of students?

Self-determination teaches
- how to make choices and decisions;
- self-advocacy; and
- skills necessary for adult life, independent living, work, and community presence

myeducationlab Now go to MyEducationLab at www.myeducationlab.com and take the Self-Assessment to gauge your initial comprehension of chapter content. Once you have taken the Self-Assessment, use your individualized Study Plan for Chapter 8 to enhance your understanding of the concepts discussed in the chapter.

Council for Exceptional Children **ADDRESSING THE PROFESSIONAL STANDARDS**

Council for Exceptional Children (CEC) knowledge standards addressed in this chapter:

MR1K4, MR1K1, MR2K3, MR2K1, MR8S1, MR4K1, MR7S3, MR10S1

Appendix A: CEC Knowledge and Skill Standards Common Core has a full listing of the standards listed here.

Appendix B: CEC Knowledge and Skill Common Core Standards and Associated Subcategories are broken down by chapter.

CHAPTER 9

Physical or Health Disabilities

Imagine a World . . .

where the promise of the future and joy of the present have no restraints . . .

Chapter Objectives

After studying this chapter, you will be able to

1. Explain how physical disabilities and health disabilities are organized.

2. Discuss the steps teachers should take to assist a student who is having a seizure.

3. Describe accommodations to the learning environment that help students with physical disabilities.

4. Describe accommodations and assistance that help students with health disabilities.

5. Explain how barriers that students with physical disabilities experience can be reduced and how the students can be better prepared for increased community presence and participation.

 *Andrew Wyeth*—a member of the artistic dynasty whose family members included N. C. Wyeth, his father, and Henriette Wyeth Hurd, his sister and the wife of Peter Hurd—was home schooled because of his frail health. He began painting at a very young age, under the tutelage of his famous father, who illustrated for the *Saturday Evening Post* and was a very successful artist of his day. Andrew Wyeth painted *Christina's World*, shown here, in 1948. Christina had physical disabilities, and this famous painting is meant to depict her yearning for her home.

Many students who face a physical challenge or have a special health care need do not have a physical or health disability that requires special education. Remember, as we discussed in Chapter 1, special education services are reserved for those students whose educational performance is hampered by an impairment or condition. Such is very much the situation for students with physical or health problems. Most students with these problems do not experience educational difficulties. Some of them receive special accommodations, some as simple as receiving extra help from peers or teachers to ensure when they are absent they receive homework and understand in-class assignments. It is a small group of these students who have disabilities that make their educational needs so great that they do require special education services, even home-bound or hospital services, for some period of their school careers.

Physical and health disabilities are both very diverse disabilities. They are diverse not in the sense of cultural and linguistic differences or diversity but because they include a wide range of conditions. The reasons for disabilities caused by different health and physical conditions vary; the resulting needs also can differ greatly. Here are a few examples of the wide range of conditions that present challenges, even disabilities, to students, their families, and their teachers:

- Asthma, a chronic health condition, is the leading cause of school absenteeism (Asthma and Allergy Foundation of America [AAFA], 2007). It is on the rise and affects over 6.2 million children (National Institute of Environmental Health Sciences [NIEHS], 2007).
- Juvenile diabetes makes it harder for students to learn and also results in serious, lifelong health care issues. Because of the growing numbers of children who are overweight, it now affects almost 2 out of every 1,000 students (Getch, Bhukhanwala, & Newharth-Pritchyell, 2007).
- Sickle cell anemia, an inherited condition, affects a startling 8% of African Americans (National Human Genome Research Institute, [NHGRI], 2007). Some children with this condition experience serious health problems that require extensive accommodations and sometimes even sustained special services.
- Juvenile arthritis affects about 1 out of every 1,000 children and ranges in severity from limiting mobility and the ability to participate in school activities to requiring few accommodations (Arthritis Foundation, 2007).

Unfortunately, whether these individuals require special education services or not, they too often share unnecessary discrimination and challenges because of society's attitudes and bias. In this way, students with physical and health disabilities have much in common with their classmates who come from culturally or linguistically diverse backgrounds. Youth, beauty, and physical fitness are obsessions of modern American society. Through singers, dancers, and actors, the entertainment industry projects ideals of beauty not within the reach of most adolescents. The advertising industry urges us to purchase certain styles of clothes, special cosmetics and hair products, new exercise equipment, and even cars to make ourselves more attractive. Have you noticed messages about physical perfection in television shows, commercials, music videos, and movies? Have you or your friends assigned popularity ratings to others (such as ranking them on a scale of 1 to 10) on the basis of physical appearance? Sometimes, American society equates physical perfection with virtue or goodness, imperfection and deformities with evil (Longmore, 2003). Think, for example, of the deformed Darth Vader, always dressed in black in the Star Wars films. This symbolism has been repeated in many books and movies, including *The Hunchback of Notre Dame* (see Chapter 1), *Dark Crystal, The Lion King,* and *The Wizard of Oz.* However, evidence exists that attitudes may be changing. Certainly the charming, animated characters with disabilities in the film *Finding Nemo* present an honest yet positive view of the challenges that individuals with physical disabilities often face (see On the Screen in this chapter).

Students with **physical disabilities** are those individuals who face physical challenges because their bodies are impaired and those impairments are so significant that

physical disabilities Conditions related to a physical deformity or impairment of the skeletal system and associated motor function; physical impairments; orthopedic impairments

On the Screen: *Important Messages from Strange Places*

Sometimes messages embedded in movies are more important than a film's entertainment value. The ability of film creators to instruct, send important messages, and change attitudes became obvious with the widely popular animated movie, *Finding Nemo.* This award-winning movie has helped millions of young people understand that everyone is different and that disabilities do not have to be a barrier to independence. Many young children with disabilities, particularly those with physical disabilities, have embraced *Nemo* as "their story."

Nemo, a clown fish, has a malformed fin and wants to show his dad that he is capable of doing many things on his own. After Nemo's mother dies, Marlin, Nemo's father, becomes overprotective. Marlin's worst fears are realized when Nemo is playing at the edge of the Great Barrier Reef and is taken by a diver. Marlin does everything he can to get his son back, including even braving the open sea. Through his adventures he meets Dory, a blue tang with short-term memory loss. Marlin gains the support of many fish and animals—a school of fish, sea turtles, and a pelican—that help him bring his son home. Marlin becomes a hero, and Nemo is an inspiration to many people, even though he is just a fish. *Finding Nemo*, made by Pixar and Disney Studios, is one of the most profitable films ever made. It won the Oscar in 2003 for the best animated feature film and was nominated for four other Oscars.

—By Steven Smith

they impact their educational performance. Students with **health disabilities** or **special health care needs** are those individuals whose health situations are precarious and therefore whose ability to learn is compromised. Unfortunately, prejudices found in society frequently are reflected in schools as well. These students—whose appearance is unusual because of deformities or muscle problems, or whose very walking ability, to say nothing of their athletic prowess, is challenged by wheelchairs or braces—often suffer prejudice in school. All of us can participate in eliminating discrimination and harsh circumstances, but educators are in a very special position because they can create appropriate and supportive learning environments.

health disabilities or special health care needs Chronic or acute health problems resulting in limited strength, vitality, or alertness; other health impairments

Where We've Been ... What's on the Horizon?

The situation for individuals with physical and health disabilities is very different today. Although much work still must be accomplished, great improvements in attitudes, accommodations, educational practices, and interventions have improved the lives of these individuals and their families. Not long ago, students with physical and health disabilities were isolated and educated in separate schools, and people with these challenges found it almost impossible to participate in daily life because of barriers everywhere (curbs, stairs, doors too heavy to open, and a lack of accessible recreational opportunities). They were also shunned because they looked different or were thought of as sick and even dangerous to be around. Today, life in general and at school is more accessible and accepting. Also, advances in both medical and assistive technology have dramatically improved the ability of people with these disabilities to participate more fully in daily life.

Historical Context

The history of physical and health disabilities is as old as the history of the human race. For example, evidence of treatment for spinal cord injuries goes back to prehistoric times, the earliest documented treatment being the application of meat and honey to the neck (Maddox, 1987). Beginning with Hippocrates (400 B.C.), treatment for neck and back deformities included traction and even stretching a person's body on a rack. Even though it was usually not successful, spinal surgery was performed as long ago as A.D. 600. Imagine conducting such surgery so long ago, particularly since it was not until the mid-1800s that anesthesia became available and sterile techniques were used. Some conditions were understood to be diseases, but many misunderstandings about the origin and the proper treatment of physical and health conditions prevailed. For example, Hippocrates knew that epilepsy originated in the brain but thought that sitting in the sun too long was the cause (Scheerenberger, 1983). Some in ancient Greece believed that disabling conditions were caused because the gods were displeased with an individual or the person's parents (Braddock & Parish, 2002). Fascination with differences seems to be part of human nature. A member of the English parliament, William Hay, himself a person with a disability, eloquently documented this obsession several hundred years ago in an essay he wrote about his own feelings and others' reactions to his different physical appearance (Deutsch, 2005). Possibly, what may be normal human reaction to differences contributes to the bias that must be overcome so individuals with disabilities are treated fairly.

As you learned in Chapter 1, when we reviewed the history of legislation and advocacy for people with disabilities, people with disabilities became civil rights activists demanding changes in access to everyday life. In particular, people with physical and health disabilities, like Ed Roberts (who appears in the accompanying photo), led the way by orchestrating wheelchair sit-ins and demonstrations (Shaw, 1995; Stone, 1995). Such actions from members of the disability community prompted the passage of Section 504 of the Rehabilitation Act (prohibiting discrimination) in 1973 and later, in 1990, the creation of the Americans with Disabilities Act (ADA) (requiring removal of barriers in the physical environment).

Ed Roberts, founder of the World Institute on Disabilities and a leader in the civil rights movement for people with disabilities, was an aggressive advocate for people with disabilities. His legacy is the community participation people with disabilities expect today.

Perspectives on the best ways to educate students with physical and health disabilities have changed across the years. Although today the vast majority of these students attend their neighborhood schools, such was not always the case. Developed with the best ideas and intentions about innovative practices, the first U.S. educational residential school dedicated entirely to students with physical disabilities was established in Boston in 1893. It was called the Industrial School for Crippled and Deformed Children (Eberle, 1922). Around the 1900s, the first public school classes in the United States for "crippled children" were established in Chicago (La Vor, 1976). Separate schools were the most common service delivery option for almost a century. Today, we often view separate schools as negative, as segregating one group of students from another. Then, the intention was to provide the best treatment possible by centralizing services, often in separate schools, so expensive equipment (e.g., therapeutic swimming pools) and highly specialized professionals could be made available to these students at one place. Although such centers allowed for treatment, education, and facilities not feasible when these youngsters attend schools spread across a wide geographic region, the result was isolation and segregation.

Advances in medicine have eliminated some diseases and conditions and reduced the impact of others. For a look at "then versus now," compare this introductory text's topics with those found in one published in 1948, *Helping Handicapped Children in School* (Dolch, 1948). That text included separate chapters titled "Crippled Children" and "Health Handicaps." The chapter on "crippled children" focused primarily on heart trouble caused by rheumatic fever, measles, scarlet fever, and diphtheria. These diseases, once common, are now rare. The chapter on "health handicaps" included a section about infected and decayed teeth.

Challenges That Physical and Health Disabilities Present

While life has improved for people with physical and health disabilities since the initial passage of ADA in 1990, much work remains to be accomplished to both change attitudes and remove all physical barriers that impede individuals' access to the activities of daily life. Fortunately, the public now understands that everyone profits, people with and without disabilities, from the removal of physical barriers—such as doors too heavy to open, school entrances too steep to negotiate, and unsuitable bathrooms (Kudlick & Longmore, 2006). Even though not all problems are resolved, important changes signal a better future of access and inclusion in mainstream society. Here are a few examples:

- Accessible trails for outdoor adventures in the national park system
- Rental cars with special adaptations necessary for drivers with disabilities
- Specially equipped taxi cabs that allow people who use wheelchairs the freedom to conduct business or visit museums and places of interest
- Cruise ships that offer passengers health services, such as dialysis for kidney patients
- Special skiing, boating, sailing, and camping programs designed for children and youth with physical and health disabilities
- Specially designed household appliances that make life easier for people with limited mobility and strength
- Bionic limbs to replace those that are missing or damaged

Making a Difference
The Hole in the Wall Camps

For many children, attending camp is a high point of their year. They look forward to the outdoor experience where they can meet new friends and participate in activities such as canoeing, telling stories and roasting marshmallows by a fire in the evening, hiking in the woods, swimming in a lake, and learning more about themselves. For children with chronic or life-threatening illnesses, going to summer camp was an impossible dream, because typical camps did not provide the medical attention they needed and because they felt too different from campers without special health care needs. Until 1988, no camps met the needs of these youngsters or their families.

In 1986, Paul Newman had a vision to make camping experiences available to children with chronic medical problems any time of the year and provide their families with a much-needed respite from constantly caring for their sick children. The first Hole in the Wall Camp opened in Connecticut. Revolving around a Wild West

theme, it provides campers with a week-long experience where all their medical needs can be met free of cost to the campers and their families.

Staffed by hundreds of volunteers—including doctors, nurses, and camp counselors—more Hole in the Wall Camps followed in New York (Double H Ranch), Florida (Camp Boggie Creek), North Carolina (Victory Junction Gang), and California (Painted Turtle Camp). Camps have also been created in Ireland, France, Africa, and the Middle East. Almost 100,000 seriously ill children from 34 states and 27 countries have participated in these state-of-the-art programs.

To learn more about all of the Hole in the Wall Camps, to see videos of campers enjoying the facilities, to hear the late Paul Newman describe his joy about making a difference, and to learn how you might become involved, visit **www.holeinthewallcamps.org**.

Physical and Health Disabilities Defined

orthopedic impairments The term used in IDEA '04 for physical disabilities resulting in special health care needs

other health impairments The term used in IDEA '04 for health disabilities; special health care needs

The federal government considers physical disabilities and health disabilities as separate special education categories. IDEA '04 uses the term *orthopedic impairments* to refer to conditions that in this text we call physical disabilities. Students with physical disabilities have problems with the structure or the functioning of their bodies. The federal government, through IDEA '04, uses the term *other health impairments* to describe, collectively, conditions and diseases that create special health care needs or health disabilities for students. The IDEA '04 definitions for these disabilities are found in Table 9.1. These two special education categories are not as separate or discrete as their definitions make them seem. For example, some conditions typically grouped under physical disabilities or orthopedic impairments also result in long-term health problems and visa versa. One student with cerebral palsy may face physical challenges and need considerable assistance from a physical therapist (PT) to learn how to control movement for speech and walking, and yet have no special health care needs (Owens, Metz, & Haas, 2007). Another student also with cerebral palsy may have physical limitations, seizures,

Table 9.1 • Definitions of Physical and Health Disabilities

Source	Physical Disabilities (Orthopedic Impairments)
Federal government	Orthopedic impairment means a severe orthopedic impairment that adversely affects a child's educational performance. The term includes impairments caused by a congenital anomaly, impairments caused by disease (e.g., poliomyelitis, bone tuberculosis, etc.), and impairments from other causes (e.g., cerebral palsy, amputations, and fractures or burns that cause contractures).
	Health Disabilities (Other Health Impairments)
Federal government	Other health impairment means having limited strength, vitality, or alertness, including a heightened alertness to environmental stimuli, that results in limited alertness with respect to the educational environment, that— **1.** Is due to chronic or acute health problems such as asthma, attention deficit disorder or attention deficit hyperactivity disorder, diabetes, epilepsy, a heart condition, hemophilia, lead poisoning, leukemia, nephritis, rheumatic fever, and sickle cell anemia; and **2.** Adversely affects a child's educational performance.

Source: From 34 *CFR* Parts 300 and 301, Assistance to States for the Education of Children with Disabilities and Preschool Grants for Children with Disabilities; Final Rule (pp. 1263–1264), U.S. Department of Education, August 14, 2006, *Federal Register*, Washington, DC.

and serious health care issues (Pelligrino, 2007). However, possibly more than is true of any other group, many students with physical or health problems require accommodations to participate in general education environments but do not require special education services. IDEA '04, as explained in What IDEA '04 Says About Eligibility and Educational Significance, makes it clear that not all students with physical or health conditions have disabilities that qualify them for special education services.

Physical Disabilities

The diagram shown in Figure 9.1 shows the conditions that comprise the two major groups of physical disabilities:

- Neuromotor impairments
- Muscular/skeletal conditions

Neuromotor impairments are conditions caused by damage to the central nervous system (the brain and the spinal cord). The resulting neurological impairment limits muscular control and movement. **Muscular/skeletal conditions** are impairments that affect the limbs or muscles. Individuals with these conditions usually have trouble controlling their movements, but the cause is not neurological. Some need to use special devices and technology even to do simple tasks—such as walking, eating, or writing—that most of us take for granted. And, because physical disabilities are often so obvious, it is easy to overlook the associated difficulties many of these individuals have with social skills and self-esteem (Best, Heller, & Bigge, 2005; Coster & Haltiwanger, 2004).

Explanations for many conditions that lead to a physical disability are found in Table 9.2. We attempted to order these conditions by prevalence; however, that is impossible to do so precisely. We do not know how many students are affected by various physical and health conditions. One reason is that no national registry exists for individual conditions and another is that many children are affected by more than

neuromotor impairments
Conditions involving the nerves, muscles, and motor functioning

muscular/skeletal conditions
Conditions affecting muscles or bones and resulting in limited functioning

Figure 9.1 • Conditions That Can Result in the Two Different Types of Physical Disabilities

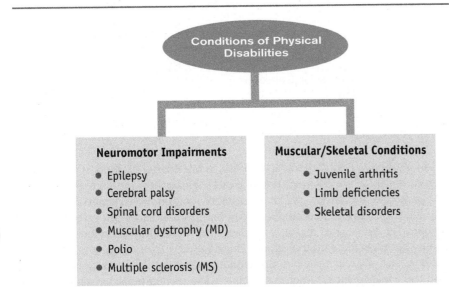

Table 9.2 • Types of Physical Conditions

Condition*	Description
Neuromotor Impairments	
Seizure disorders	*Epilepsy,* the most common type of neuromotor impairment in children, is a condition of recurrent convulsions or seizures caused by abnormal brain electrical activity. It is treated with medication, which in most cases controls and eventually corrects the impairment.
Cerebral palsy (CP)	*Cerebral palsy* is an incurable and nonprogressive condition caused by brain injury that sometimes limits the individual's ability to control muscle groups or motor functioning in specific areas of the body or, infrequently, the entire body. It may be associated with multiple disabilities. Physical therapy offers benefits.
Spinal cord disorders	*Spina bifida,* a neural tube birth defect, is the improper closure of the protective tissue surrounding the spinal cord. It results in limited neurological control of those organs and muscles that are below the level of the lesion. Most spinal cord problems result in health care needs that include good skin care, management of bladder and bowel care, and physical therapy.
	Spinal cord injuries, typically the result of injuries from accidents or abuse, can cause severe motor impairments and even paralysis. Increasing numbers of children suffer traumatic head or spinal cord injuries resulting in permanent disabilities.
Muscular dystrophy (MD)	*Muscular dystrophy,* an exceptionally rare, incurable, and progressive disease, weakens and then destroys the affected individual's muscles. Health care needs center on lung function support, prevention of pneumonia, and physical therapy.
Polio	*Polio,* caused by a viral infection and almost totally prevented in children immunized in the United States, attacks the spinal cord and can result in paralysis and motor disabilities. Health care needs parallel those for spinal cord disorders.
Multiple sclerosis (MS)	*Multiple sclerosis,* a chronic disease typically not occurring in children, causes the myelin covering the nerve fibers of the brain and spinal cord to deteriorate, impeding the transmission of electrical signals from the brain to other parts of the body. Health care needs parallel those for MD.
Muscular/Skeletal Conditions	
Juvenile arthritis	*Juvenile arthritis* is a treatable disease caused by an autoimmune process resulting in swelling, immobility, and pain in joints. About 1 in 1,000 children are affected. For all muscular/skeletal conditions, health care needs can include medication to suppress the process, physical therapy to maintain joint and muscle functioning, medical monitoring, counseling (when needed), and application of universal design principles.
Limb deficiencies	*Skeletal problems* in which the individual's limb(s) is shortened, absent, or malformed. They may occur from congenital conditions or from injuries.
Skeletal disorders	*Dwarfism,* a condition caused by abnormal development of long bones, may result in varying degrees of motor disabilities. Treatment may include human growth hormone to improve height.
	Osteogenesis imperfecta, sometimes known as brittle bone disease, is a condition in which normal calcification of the bones does not occur, leading to breakage and abnormal healing of bones with accompanying loss of height.
	Scoliosis, a curvature of the spine that occurs in children during puberty and may, in severe form, limit mobility.

*Conditions are ordered by overall estimated prevalence during childhood.

one condition (Epilepsy Foundation, 2007a). So, while many students with cerebral palsy also have epilepsy, we do not have an exact idea about how many students are involved or how the frequency of the conditions should be counted or double-counted. We have, however, attempted to order our discussions by prevalence as best as possible because we believe that it is important for educators to understand which conditions they are most likely to experience during their education careers. For example, it is unlikely that any teacher will work with a student with polio because it is now prevented in the United States. Other conditions, such as multiple sclerosis, are found in adults but seldom seen in children; and some, such as muscular dystrophy and spina bifida, have extremely low prevalence rates. Throughout this chapter, we focus on those conditions, such as epilepsy, cerebral palsy, and sickle cell anemia, that are more prevalent and that teachers have a greater likelihood of meeting in the classroom.

When responsible educators encounter diseases and conditions they know little about, they seek out all the information they need to provide an appropriate education to students involved. Educators also understand that these disabilities range in severity from mild to severe. And, in many cases, they are only one of multiple conditions an individual must face (Batshaw, Pelligrino, & Roizen, 2007). For example, epilepsy is frequently found in children with intellectual disabilities. But remember never to make the terrible error of associating health or physical disabilities with a cognitive disability. They do not always go hand in hand. Now, let's focus on some specific physical disabilities.

Neuromotor Impairments   The first neuromotor impairment we discuss may be the most common, but students might not know a classmate has the condition because it is so well controlled and often cured by medication. **Epilepsy,** also called **seizure disorders** or convulsive disorders, is a condition where the individual has recurrent seizures resulting from sudden, excessive, spontaneous, and abnormal discharge of neurons in the brain. Seizures can be accompanied by changes in the person's motor or sensory functioning and also can result in loss of consciousness (Epilepsy Foundation, 2007a). For some 70% of those affected, medication ends the occurrence of seizures. When epilepsy coexists with other conditions, such as intellectual disabilities or cerebral palsy, the rate of successful treatment through medication is much lower than 70%, the rate it is for individuals who only have epilepsy.

Another neuromotor impairment encountered in schools is cerebral palsy. **Cerebral palsy (CP)** is not a disease but, rather, a nonprogressive and noninfectious condition that affects body movement and muscle coordination (United Cerebral Palsy [UCP] Education Foundation, 2007). It is often a result of brain damage due to insufficient oxygen getting to the brain before or during the birth process, but it can be acquired during early childhood as well. *Acquired cerebral palsy* occurs after birth but during early childhood and is usually caused by brain damage resulting from accidents, brain infections, stroke, or child abuse. Regrettably, it cannot be cured (at least today).

Muscular/Skeletal Conditions   One of the muscular/skeletal conditions most commonly seen in children is limb deficiencies. **Limb deficiencies** can be the result of a missing or nonfunctioning arm or leg and can be either acquired or congenital. Regardless of when the impairment occurred, the result is a major impediment to normal physical activity and functioning. Although the root of the disability is physical, many individuals with a limb deficiency have difficulty adjusting to their situation. The attitudes of teachers and classmates, and of course the support given by family members, can be major contributors to their psychological health. **Robotics**—the science and technology that develop computer-controlled mechanical devices, including artificial arms and legs—now provides much assistance to those with missing limbs. Because of the tragic cases of so many soldiers returning from war with missing limbs, robotics and the technology required to create **prosthetics** that work like natural limbs are improving dramatically. A future-looking example of prosthetic limbs is the arm used by Claudia Mitchell and shown in Figure 9.2. The scientists at the Rehabilitation Institute of Chicago refer affectionately to Claudia as their $4 million woman, and she is testing out what is a prototype of future artificial arms that have great mobility, hands that rotate, and fingers that can pick up small objects. What is even more remarkable, the parts move when her brain tells them to (Davis, 2006). Such freedom of movement was thought to be impossible only a few years ago (except, of course, by screenwriters who created film characters like RoboCop or the new bionic woman on TV).

A relatively common muscular/skeletal condition affecting joints and the function of muscles is **juvenile arthritis**. Some 300,000 students have juvenile arthritis (Arthritis Foundation, 2007). Just over one-fourth of students with juvenile arthritis qualify for

epilepsy or seizure disorders A tendency to experience recurrent seizures resulting in convulsions; caused by abnormal discharges of neurons in the brain

cerebral palsy (CP) A neuromotor impairment; a nonprogressive disease resulting in motor difficulties associated with communication problems and mobility problems

limb deficiencies Missing or nonfunctioning arms or legs resulting in mobility problems

robotics The science of using technology to create high-tech devices that perform motor skills

prosthetics Artificial arms or legs

juvenile arthritis A chronic and painful muscular condition seen in children

Figure 9.2 • The $4 Million Bionic Woman

myeducationlab Go to the Activities and Applications section in Chapter 9 of MyEducationLab, and complete Activity 1. As you watch the video, consider the challenges faced by students with limb deficiencies and how they might be met with the help of new technologies and effective instruction.

special education services; most of the others receive accommodations through Section 504. Although there are many different forms of this disease, it is typically chronic and painful. Juvenile arthritis usually develops in early childhood and can cause many absences from school. These children often need help keeping up with their classmates because they miss so much class instruction. Teachers must understand that their ability to move may be inconsistent (better at different times of the day) and that sitting for extended periods of time can cause them to become stiff and to experience considerable pain. These children need to be allowed to move around a lot. Those who have a high rate of absences probably need tutoring and extra help to keep up with their peers (Arthritis Foundation, 2007). Some promising medical treatments can reduce the amount of disability from the disease. However, such medications can have side effects that alter some aspect of personality and physical appearance.

Health Disabilities

Remember, as you learned in Chapters 1 and 6, IDEA '04 includes the condition of attention deficit hyperactivity disorder (ADHD) in the "other health impairments" category. ADHD is *not* a separate disability category for special education. Because most people do not think of ADHD as a health condition and because the characteristics of ADHD are very different from those of the conditions more traditionally considered as a health disability, we address ADHD in a separate chapter in this text (see Chapter 6 again).

The two types traditionally considered as comprising health disabilities are

- chronic illnesses and
- infectious diseases.

Study Table 9.3. It includes definitions of illnesses and diseases seen in children that are organized by type and illustrated in Figure 9.3. Of course, some general principles apply to all children who are sick, whatever the cause. All children have episodes of illness during childhood, but most of these are of short duration and not very serious. For a small number, however, their illnesses are chronic, lasting for years or even a lifetime. Students with chronic illnesses often do not feel well enough to consistently focus their attention on instruction or may not be at school when important content is presented.

For many years the term *medically fragile* was used to describe all children with special health care needs, but it is now more selectively applied. **Medically fragile** is a status; it is not assigned to any specific condition but, rather, reflects the individual's health situation. Students can move in and out of fragile status. It is important to understand that because of medical technology, a greater number of medically fragile children now survive health crises. In the past, many of these youngsters would not have lived long enough to go to school. Others would have been too sick to attend their neighborhood schools and would have received most of their schooling

medically fragile A term used to describe the status of individuals with health disabilities

Table 9.3 • Types of Health Conditions

Condition*	Description
Chronic Illnesses	
Asthma	*Asthma,* a condition caused by narrowing of airways accompanied by inflammatory changes in the lining of the airways, may result in severe difficulty in breathing with chronic coughing. Health care needs include reducing allergens in the environment, providing appropriate medications, and at times limiting strenuous activities.
Diabetes	*Diabetes* is the loss of the ability of the pancreas to produce enough insulin, resulting in problems with sugar metabolism. Health care needs include the monitoring of blood sugar levels, providing appropriate diet and exercise regimens, and having a knowledgeable response for insulin reactions.
Cystic fibrosis	*Cystic fibrosis* is a genetic birth defect that results in chronic lung infections and digestive difficulties. Health care interventions include aggressive care of lung infections and function and replacement of required enzymes for aiding digestion. Students may require special accommodations for their medical needs across the school day.
Congenital heart defects	*Congenital heart conditions* can result in high rates of school absences for specialized health care. Most have had surgical intervention and medical monitoring by specialists. Health care needs include taking medications during the school day.
Tuberculosis (TB)	*Tuberculosis,* a disease caused by bacterial infection, rarely causes severe disease in children older than infancy. Most often the bacteria remain sequestered and harmless until late adulthood or when the body's immune system fails. The rates of infection are on the rise in many parts of the United States.
Childhood cancer	*Cancer,* the abnormal growth of cells, can affect any organ. The most common types of cancer in children are leukemia and lymphomas. For all types of cancer, children may feel too ill to profit from classroom instruction when going through treatment.
	Leukemia causes an abnormal increase in the white blood cells, which are important in the body's defenses against infection. It often results in anemia and enlargement of the lymph glands, spleen, and liver.
	Lymphomas are malignant and cause enlargement of the lymph nodes.
Blood disorders	*Sickle cell anemia,* a hereditary disorder, causes a distortion in the red blood cells that restricts their passage through the blood vessels. The rate of this inherited condition is especially high among African Americans; affected students need activity limited during a sickling crisis.
	Hemophilia, a genetic condition typically linked with males, is characterized by poor blood clotting, which can result in massive bleeding from cuts and internal hemorrhaging from bruises.
Infectious Diseases	
STORCH	*STORCH* is the acronym for a group of congenital infections that have the potential of causing severe, multiple impairments. It stands for syphilis, toxoplasmosis, other, rubella, cytomegalovirus, and herpes.
HIV and AIDS	*Human immunodeficiency virus* (HIV), a potentially fatal viral infection, in children results from an infected mother transmitting the virus to her newborn child or from transfusion with blood or blood products carrying the virus; in adolescents, from risky behaviors. The HIV virus then causes *acquired immunodeficiency syndrome* (AIDS). Health care needs include confidential care, careful monitoring of general health, specialists to care for potentially overwhelming lung infections, medications that slow or cure infections, counseling, and health education.
Hepatitis B	*Hepatitis B,* a viral disease, is infectious and causes inflammation of the liver. It is characterized by jaundice and fever. Cases of this dangerous virus are on the increase, particularly in those who share needles. A vaccine to prevent the disease and its impact is routinely available.

*Conditions are ordered by estimated overall prevalence during childhood.

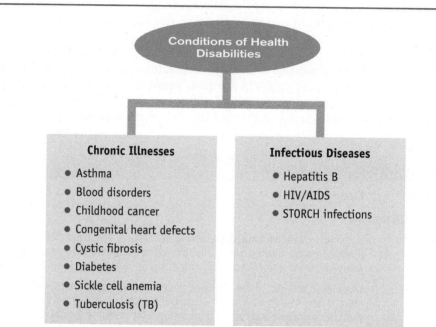

through services delivered to a hospital or to their home. Even though many are now well enough to attend school, they require ongoing medical management. For most, it is necessary for teachers to be familiar with procedures that must be followed if an emergency occurs. The "if, thens" must be carefully outlined and planned in collaboration with doctors and the medical profession (Sobo & Kurtin, 2007). Although the contingencies for the worst-case scenarios must be arranged, in most cases the accommodations required for these students are not terribly dramatic. (However, not having backup power for a student's ventilator could have disastrous results.)

Chronic Illnesses

The authors of IDEA '04 clarified that few students with health conditions actually need special education services (see again What IDEA '04 Says About Eligibility and Educational Significance). Many of these students, however, do need special accommodations so that their illnesses do not hinder their learning.

The most common chronic illness among children is **asthma**, a pulmonary disease causing labored breathing that is sometimes accompanied by shortness of breath, wheezing, and a cough. It is the leading cause of school absences and hospitalizations of children (AAFA, 2007; NIEHS, 2007). Many factors (e.g., chalk dust, dirt in the environment, dust mites, and pollen) can trigger an asthma attack, as can physical activity or exertion. Many students who have asthma are unable to participate in sports or even in physical education activities.

Another health condition of great concern to parents, educators, and the medical community is **juvenile diabetes**. One of the two types of diabetes that occurs among children is preventable, and it is the type that is on the rise because of the increased number of American children and youth who are overweight (Getch et al., 2007; National Diabetes Information Clearinghouse, 2007). Teachers of students with diabetes must be alert for many characteristics of this disease directly influence a student's ability to learn. Particularly when blood sugar levels are out of balance, some of these students experience blurred vision, confusion, inattention, headache, or fatigue. Diabetes is a life-threatening and debilitating disease. Educators can help by monitoring the exercise and diet of all their students.

asthma The most common, chronic health condition resulting in difficulty breathing

juvenile diabetes An inability of the body to produce insulin

Infectious Diseases

In part because they are so frightening and in part because they are so dangerous, infectious diseases catch our attention. However, in many instances, occurrence is rare, and the public reaction to those who contract the disease is irrational. Here's an example. The **human immunodeficiency virus (HIV)** is a very serious disease and a potentially fatal viral infection that is transmitted primarily through the exchange of bodily fluids in unprotected sex or by contaminated needles. Before blood-screening procedures were instituted, the virus was also transmitted in blood transfusions. HIV is the virus responsible for **acquired immunodeficiency syndrome (AIDS)**, a deadly disease that destroys the immune system and can be communicated to an unborn child by an infected mother. From the beginning of the epidemic through 2002, a total of 9,300 American children were infected with HIV/AIDS (National Institute of Allergy and Infectious Disease, 2004). In 2005, the Centers for Disease Control (CDC) reported a total number of 68 cases for U.S. children under the age of 13 (CDC, 2007a). Few teachers will meet a student with HIV/AIDS.

Hepatitis B is an infectious disease like HIV/AIDS that is also rare among children. It, too, is passed on to unborn children by an infected mother or transmitted by unprotected sex, shared needles, and other risky behavior. A vaccine can now protect infants and children from this disease (National Center for HIV/AIDS, Viral Hepatitis, STD, and TB Prevention, 2007). For many years, parents and educators were concerned about HIV/AIDS and hepatitis B and whether noninfected children could catch the disease from a classmate. It is now clear that this is highly unlikely. With proper precautions (the use of gloves when bandaging a child's cut finger and normal sanitary procedures such as frequently washing your hands), everyone at school is safe and will not catch such diseases.

> **human immunodeficiency virus (HIV)** A microorganism that infects the immune system, impairing the body's ability to fight infections
>
> **acquired immunodeficiency syndrome (AIDS)** A usually fatal medical syndrome caused by infection from the human immunodeficiency virus (HIV)

Characteristics

The characteristics of students with physical and health disabilities are as unique to the individuals as the conditions that created their special needs. For example, some students with physical disabilities require substantial alterations to the physical environment, so that learning is accessible to them, but are quite similar to their typical classmates in many learning characteristics. For others, their health situation is so consuming that everything else becomes secondary, but at another point in time need only a few special accommodations. The lives of family members change dramatically when a child becomes chronically ill. Lizzy tells us about a day in her life in the accompanying box. It is important for educators to understand the stress and concerns that families like theirs bring to school at different points across a child's illness.

The education professionals who make a real difference in the academic lives of these students are first and foremost responsive to the individual learning needs they bring to school. Thus, instead of making generalizations about these students, here we will discuss three of the more common, though still low-incidence, conditions seen at schools. We will look more closely, then, at

- epilepsy,
- cerebral palsy, and
- sickle cell anemia.

Epilepsy

Seizures may involve the entire brain (**generalized seizures**) or only a portion of the brain (**partial seizures**). The frequency of seizures may vary from a single isolated incident to hundreds in a day. Some individuals actually anticipate their seizures because they experience a **preictal stage**, or an **aura**, and have heightened sensory signals of an impending seizure, such as a peculiar smell, taste, vision, sound, or action. Others might experience a change in their behavior. Knowing

> **generalized seizures** Seizures involving the entire brain
>
> **partial seizures** Seizures involving only part of the brain
>
> **preictal stage or aura** Warning of an imminent seizure in the form of heightened sensory awareness

Spotlighting *Lizzy*: A Day in the Life

Sarah Elizabeth Solomon, or Lizzy, is a high school student with spastic quadriplegic cerebral palsy. Her mother expands on Lizzy's story in Chapter 14's Spotlighting feature.

Hi! My name is Sara Elizabeth Solomon, but everyone calls me Lizzy. I am in the tenth grade at Hillsboro High School in Nashville, Tennessee. I am not really sure there is a typical day in my life. They are all busy and full of school, work, and, of course, play.

I have spastic quadriplegic cerebral palsy, which makes doing some of the routine things in life a little more difficult. Having cerebral palsy makes it hard to move my muscles; therefore, it takes me twice as long or sometimes even longer to do the things I need to do (e.g., dressing, doing homework). In the morning, I start my day with getting dressed. Recently, my mom went out of town and left my 17-year-old sister Skye in charge. I was worried that my sister would oversleep and we would not have enough time to get dressed and ready for school. So I got up at 2 o'clock in the morning and was completely dressed by 7 when we had to leave. That morning I used my dressing stick and my reacher as aids to get myself dressed. My dressing stick helps me with getting my shoes and socks on and off. My reacher helps me pick up things when I drop them or get them when they are out of my arm's reach. My persistence and determination keep me going! Even though it took me 5 hours to get dressed, I was proud of myself.

I have a service dog named Cary, and he is very helpful to me throughout my day. He can pick up things for me, turn on and off lights, open and close doors, untie my shoes, and take my socks off. He is a big help at home and out in the commu-

nity. He carries things for me if we go shopping. Not only is he a big help, but he is a constant friend and companion.

Because of my physical needs and the demands of my schedule, I have an assistant at school, Mrs. Worthy. Mrs. Worthy helps me with things like toileting and getting to and from class. I take mostly honors classes and some AP classes, so I have a very busy schedule and LOTS of homework. I leave my classes a few minutes early so I have time to get from class to class without getting run over by the other students. Really, they are probably more worried that I will run over them, as I'm a pretty fast walker!

After I get home from school, I usually spend 3 to 4 hours on homework. It probably takes me twice as long on homework because of my motor skills. Once I am done with homework, I take a bath or a shower. If it is a night when I don't have too much homework, I spend more time trying to get undressed and shower. I can almost shower independently, but it does take me a while. Otherwise, my mom helps me take a bath and get ready for bed.

Aside from my schoolwork, I am busy with other extracurricular activities, both in and out of school. My favorite thing to do is go to my Young Life Christian group. We do lots of fun things together like swimming, playing games, having dances, and making photo albums. I am active in Girl Scouts and am a member of the school's marching band. Several days a week I practice my piano, and I have a piano lesson every Sunday. Much of my time is spent on the business I started 4 years ago. My business, Lizzy Lines, is a note card business, and my cards represent kids with disabilities doing everyday things that kids like to do or be involved with. When I have free time, I love to play on the computer and watch *So You Think You Can Dance* or *American Idol*!

---

about an aura pattern is helpful, because it enables the person to assume a safe position or warn the teacher and companions before a seizure begins.

The Epilepsy Foundation (2007b) identifies four main types of seizures:

- Absence seizures
- Simple partial seizures
- Complex partial (psychomotor) seizures
- Generalized tonic-clonic seizures

Some seizures are difficult for the individual involved and others to recognize. For example, **absence seizures** or **petit mal seizures** are characterized by short lapses in consciousness. Because absence seizures are not dramatic, a teacher might wrongly assume that the child is merely daydreaming or not paying attention. **Simple partial seizures**, which cause people affected to think that their environments are distorted and strange and that inexplicable events and feelings have occurred, can also be difficult to identify. With these seizures, teachers might incorrectly believe that the student is acting out or exhibiting bizarre behavior patterns. **Complex partial seizures** (also called psychomotor or focal seizures) are short in duration, and the individual returns to normal activities quickly. Sometimes, teach-

absence seizures or petit mal seizures Seizures characterized by a short lapse in consciousness; petit mal seizures

simple partial seizures Seizures that cause people affected to think their environments are distorted or strange

complex partial seizures A type of epilepsy causing a lapse in consciousness

ers interpret the child's behavior during this type of seizure as misbehavior or clown-ing. This situation can be confusing to the child, who is unaware of the episode. **Generalized tonic-clonic seizures** (formerly referred to as grand mal seizures) are the most serious type of seizure and result in convulsions and loss of consciousness. The dramatic behaviors exhibited during a tonic-clonic seizure may at first be fright-ening to the teacher and to other students in the class. The student may fall to the floor and experience a stiff (tonic) phase, in which the muscles become rigid, fol-lowed by a clonic phase, in which the individual's arms and legs jerk. Tips for Class-room Management describes how to manage each type of seizure at school.

generalized tonic-clonic seizures Grand mal seizures; the most serious type of epilepsy, resulting in convulsions and loss of con-sciousness

TIPS for Classroom Management

MANAGING SEIZURES AT SCHOOL

1. *Absence seizure:* Momentary loss of awareness, sometimes accompa-nied by blinking or movements of the face or arms; may be frequent; fully aware after an episode
   - Be sure key parts of the lesson are not missed.

2. *Simple partial seizure:* Consciousness not lost; unable to control body movements; experiences feelings, visions, sounds, and smells that are not real
   - Comfort and reassure if the child is frightened

3. *Complex partial seizure:* Consciousness clouded, unresponsive to instructions, inappropriate and undirected behaviors, sleepwalking appearance, of short duration (a minute or two); prolonged confusion after an episode, no recall of seizure
   - Gently guide child back to seat.
   - Speak softly.
   - Ensure child's safety.
   - Ignore uncontrollable behaviors.
   - Ensure full consciousness before changing locations.
   - Help child sort out confusions.

4. *Generalized tonic-clonic seizure:* Body stiffens and jerks; may fall, lose consciousness, lose bladder control, have erratic breathing; lasts several minutes; can be confused, weary, or belligerent afterward
   - Remain calm.
   - Reassure classmates.
   - Ease child to floor.
   - Clear area.
   - Rest head on a pillow.
   - Turn on side.
   - Do not put anything in child's mouth.
   - Do not restrain.
   - Let rest after jerking ceases.
   - Reengage in class participation.

Source: Adapted from *Understanding Epilepsy: First Aid* by the Epilepsy Foundation (2007c). Available from www.epilepsyfoundation.org/about/firstaid.

Cerebral Palsy

The severity of the condition depends on the precise location of brain damage, the degree of brain damage, and the extent of involvement of the central nervous system (Pelegrino, 2007). Individuals with cerebral palsy whose motor functioning is affected show these characteristics alone or in combination: jerky movements, spasms, involuntary movements, and lack of muscle tone. Often, individuals with cerebral palsy have multiple disabilities, probably resulting from the same damage to the brain that caused the cerebral palsy. For example, many individuals who have severe difficulties in motor functioning also have trouble mastering oral speech. These individuals have speech impairments and physical disabilities. Although some degree of intellectual disabilities is present in about half of the children with cerebral palsy, others, like Christy Brown (whose life story was featured in the movie, *My Left Foot*—see On the Screen in Chapter 4) and Lizzy (see Spotlighting in Chapters 9 and 14), are intellectually gifted. It is a tragic mistake to assume that cerebral palsy and intellectual disabilities always occur in combination. Figure 9.4 illustrates four ways in which areas of the body can be affected by cerebral palsy: monoplegia, paraplegia, hemiplegia, and quadriplegia.

Another way in which cerebral palsy is classified is in terms of how the individual's movement is affected:

- **Spastic cerebral palsy**: Movements are very stiff.
- **Athetoid cerebral palsy**: Involuntary movements are purposeless or uncontrolled, and purposeful movements are contorted.
- **Ataxia cerebral palsy**: Movements such as walking are disrupted by impairments of balance and depth perception.

Many individuals with cerebral palsy have impaired mobility and poor muscle development. Even if they can walk, their efforts may require such exertion and be so inefficient that they need canes, crutches, or a wheelchair to get around. Students with cerebral palsy may also need braces to help support the affected limbs and make them more functional or to prevent contractures that would eventually lead to bone deformities and further mobility limitations. Proper positioning of the body also must be considered. Many children need wedges, pillows, and individually designed chairs and worktables so that they can be comfortable; breathe easier; avoid injuries, contractures, and deformities; and participate in group activities.

spastic cerebral palsy
Characterized by uncontrolled tightening or pulling of muscles

athetoid cerebral palsy
Characterized by purposeless and uncontrolled involuntary movements

ataxia cerebral palsy
Characterized by movement disrupted by impaired balance and depth perception

Figure 9.4 • Areas of the Body Affected by Cerebral Palsy

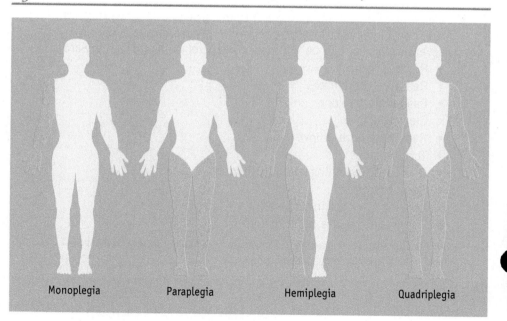

| Monoplegia | Paraplegia | Hemiplegia | Quadriplegia |

Sickle Cell Anemia

Some diseases strike one group of students more than another. For example, **sickle cell anemia** is a hereditary, life-threatening blood disorder, and 95% of all cases occur among African Americans (NHGRI, 2007). This condition causes the red blood cells to become rigid and take on a crescent, or sickle, shape. During what is called a "sickling crisis," this rigidity and the crescent shape of the cells do not allow blood to flow through the vessels, depriving some tissues of oxygen and resulting in extreme pain, swollen joints, high fever, and even strokes. Tips for Effective Instruction provides important information about appropriate responses to characteristics of sickle cell anemia and how best to help students who have special health care needs because of this condition (Emory University School of Medicine, 2005).

Prevalence

Determining the exact prevalence of the physical and health conditions affecting children and youth that result in disabilities is difficult, if not impossible. Here are a few reasons:

- No national registries of students by specific conditions
- Conditions' coexistence and the likelihood of double-counting students
- Not all conditions result in the need for special education services

The federal government does, however, report the number and percentage of students who receive special education services through one of its 14 special education categories. Remember, the number of students with physical and health disabilities is relatively low (see Figure 1.2 again in Chapter 1 for a review of the prevalence rates among students in each special education category). These two special education categories are typically considered low-incidence disabilities. In the 2006–2007 school year, the physical disabilities category included some 0.11% of all students. In that same school year, including students identified as needing special education services because of ADHD, 1.16% of all students were served through the federal government's "other health impairments" category (Office of Special Education Programs [OSEP], 2008).

Why is the health disabilities category so large in comparison to physical disabilities? Why is it one of the fastest-growing disability areas? The reasons all come to students with ADHD being included and counted in the health disabilities category. Health disabilities is the biggest low-incidence category and has grown at an amazing rate since 1997 when ADHD was first included here. From the 1991–1992

TIPS for Effective Instruction

Teaching Students with Sickle Cell Anemia

1. Emotional stress or strenuous exercise can trigger a sickling crisis. Monitor the student carefully.

2. Work closely with the student and family. Develop plans for peers to bring assignments home and explain them when the student has to be absent.

3. Frequent hospitalizations are common. Provide students with makeup work so they can stay current with assignments when hospitalized or absent from school.

4. Pain episodes are prevented by drinking more water. Let the student keep a water bottle at hand and allow for frequent bathroom breaks.

5. Pain episodes are prevented by avoiding extreme temperatures. Do not let the student either get overheated or be exposed to excessive cold.

6. Anemia causes people to tire easily. Encourage rest periods, and let the individual quietly step out of sports and recreational activities.

7. Sickle cell anemia places the individual at risk for other infections. Keep safe and sterile classroom and school environments.

8. Be alert for instances of fever, headache, chest pain, abdominal pain, numbness, or weakness. If you observe one of these symptoms, call a doctor or the school nurse.

9. Children are sensitive. Avoid calling undue attention to the child.

Source: Adapted from the Georgia Comprehensive Sickle Cell Center, www.SCinfo/teacher.htm, the Sickle Cell Foundation of Georgia, Emory University School of Medicine, Department of Pediatrics, Morehouse School of Medicine, http://www.scinfo.org/teacher.htm.Can

sickle cell anemia A hereditary blood disorder that inhibits blood flow; African Americans are most at risk for this health condition

to the 2000–2001 school year, the health impairments category increased by almost 400%. It increased again, by almost 300%, between 2000–2001 and 2006–2007, making an overall percentage increase of 1,167 over this 15-year period (U.S. Department of Education, 2002; OSEP, 2008). Remember, this dramatic increase is not because the number of students with ADHD has grown or because the number of health disabilities has spiked but, rather, because of a shift in the reporting of students to this category.

While the overall prevalence of these two disabilities is low, the number of different diseases and conditions results in a variety of accommodations. Also, the impact of these individuals' health or physical situation, varies greatly. This list merely highlights the diversity of conditions that exist among schoolchildren:

- Asthma is the most common chronic illness among children, probably affecting almost 10% of schoolchildren (AAFA, 2007).
- Diabetes among individuals under the age of 20 is estimated to be about 0.22% (National Diabetes Information Clearinghouse, 2007).
- Epilepsy affects less than 1% of all students in the United States, and most cases are controlled by medication (Epilepsy Foundation, 2007a).
- About 0.03% of all children have cerebral palsy, and some of them do not require special education services (CDC, 2007b).
- Although the severity of the condition varies, some 8% of all Black children have sickle cell disease (NHGRI, 2007). Since Black students comprise some 14% of all schoolchildren, the overall percentage is most likely a little higher than 0.01% of all students.
- Cystic fibrosis is a hereditary and progressive disease and is most common among White students, but it only affects a very small percentage of children, 1 in 2000 (Best et al., 2005).

Causes and Prevention

There are almost as many different causes, preventions, and treatments as there are different illnesses, diseases, and conditions that result in disabilities. (Review again Tables 9.2 and 9.3 for summaries of the different physical and health conditions that result in disabilities in children.) When confronted with a specific condition, responsible teachers learn as much as they can about it so individual students' programs reflect the impact of the disability, their own and their family's priorities, and those skills that are needed to achieve independent living as an adult. Table 9.4 highlights some causes and prevention techniques for many physical and health conditions and disabilities.

Causes

The known reasons for physical and health disabilities are as follows:

- Infections and allergies
- Heredity
- Accidents and injuries
- Multiple factors

Infections from diseases such as hepatitis B, HIV/AIDS, congenital cytomegalovirus (CMV), and STORCH can result in lifelong special health care needs. As you have learned, asthma is most often the result of an allergic reaction to certain substances (allergens) found in the environment. A variety of substances can trigger reactions, and they vary with the individual. For some people, it may be foods; for others, plants, environmental pollutants, chemicals, cigarette smoke, dust mites, cockroaches, pets, or viruses (AAFA, 2007).

We have known for hundreds of years that heredity or genetic profiles are the cause of many disabilities. However, as medical research improves, more and more

Table 9.4 • Causes and Prevention of Physical and Health Disabilities

Physical Disabilities		Health Disabilities	
Causes	**Prevention**	**Causes**	**Prevention**
Motor vehicle accidents	Child restraints	Infections and disease	Access to health care Frequent hand washing
	Safety belts		
	Auto air bags		Use of disposable gloves
	Motorcycle helmets		
	Following driving rules		Vaccinations Good hygiene
Water and diving accidents	Diving safety	Asthma	Removal of allergens
	Swimming safety		
Gunshot wounds	Gun control	Poisoning/toxins	Safe storage
	Weapons training		First aid
	Ammunition locked away		Call Poison Control Center
Sports injuries	Protective equipment	Premature birth	Prenatal care
	Headgear		Access to health care
	Conditioning/training		
Child abuse	Family support services	HIV infection	Abstinence or safe sex
	Alert teachers		Avoidance of drugs
	Parent training		Use of gloves around blood

disabilities that were thought to have an "unknown" reason are now being understood to have a genetic link. Here are a few examples of conditions that have a genetic cause:

- Sickle cell anemia is the most common inherited blood disorder in the United States (NHGRI, 2007).
- Hemophilia, a bleeding disorder that affects 400 newborns each year, is carried by the mother and passed on to the son (National Heart Lung and Blood Institute, 2007).
- Muscular dystrophy, also an X-linked recessive disorder, is a relatively rare neuromotor disease (with an incidence of about 2 in every 10,000 people) and results in progressive inability to walk and use muscles (National Institute of Neurological Disorders and Stroke, 2007).

Quite possibly, disabilities caused by injuries are the most preventable. Whether from accidents or child abuse, injuries can lead to cerebral palsy, seizure disorders, spinal cord injuries, brain damage, and even death. For example, spinal cord injury in young children, which is often caused by automobile accidents, can also result from child abuse. In older children, the most common causes of spinal cord injury are car accidents, falls and jumps, gunshot wounds, and diving accidents. These cases underscore the importance of safety equipment (e.g., seat belts, helmets, protective gear) and caution.

"IT'S EITHER A BOO-BOO OR AN OWWIE, BUT THE DOCTORS NEED TO RUN SOME MORE TESTS BEFORE THEY DECIDE."

© Guy & Rodd/Distributed by Universal Uclick via CartoonStock.com

Source: Guy and Rodd/www.CartoonStock.com.

Some conditions, like cerebral palsy, can result from many different causes. For example, in congenital cerebral palsy, a developing infant may have been deprived of enough oxygen when something went wrong during birth. Cerebral palsy may also be the result of premature birth, very low birthweight, blood type (Rh) incompatibility, a pregnant mother's infection, or attacks on the fetus or newborn by dangerous microorganisms (CDC, 2007b). *Acquired cerebral palsy* can be caused by vehicle accidents, brain infections such as meningitis, poisoning through toxins such as lead (ingested in paint chips from walls), serious falls, or injuries from child abuse.

Prevention

It is important to remember that many disabilities occur through no one's fault and cannot be avoided. For most conditions that cannot be prevented, the effects often can be lessened through treatment. Look again at Table 9.4 to see how some disabilities can be prevented by simple actions, increased access to health care, and smart hygiene. Ensuring that the classroom is clean, toys are washed, and sick children are referred to the school nurse or the parents can minimize the spread of disease.

Access to health care is a key ingredient to the prevention of many disabilities and is a means to reduce the impact of those that cannot be avoided (Children's Defense Fund [CDF], 2005). Prenatal care can ensure access to intensive medical care for the mother and infant if problems occur; provide diagnosis and treatment for diseases in the mother that can damage the developing infant; and help prevent exposure of the fetus to infections, viruses, drugs, alcohol, and other toxins. The cost of providing prenatal care to all pregnant women would reduce the overall costs of health care as well as the personal and financial costs of disabilities that could have been avoided. Also, vaccinations (immunizations) safeguard children from infectious diseases and avoid millions of dollars in health care costs and the complication of millions of lives by disabilities. Vaccines have almost eradicated some diseases in the United States and have thus reduced the rate of disabilities caused by such diseases. Remarkably, however, only 78% of America's children are protected, mostly because their families are living in poverty or they do not have health insurance (CDF, 2005).

Overcoming Challenges

Remember that some conditions, even when the cause is known, can't be prevented. Also, treatment doesn't guarantee a cure, but the impact of the condition, its severity, or the frequency of its occurrence might be reduced. Here are a few examples.

Medical advances have helped many individuals who would otherwise have faced overwhelming challenges. For example, although surgery is not a complete cure for all spinal column (neural tube) defects, its use in infants born with these conditions (to repair their backs and prevent infections such as meningitis) generally avoids intellectual disabilities. Some children with spina bifida have hydrocephaly, a buildup of excess fluid in the brain. For them, a shunt surgically implanted to drain excess spinal fluid from the brain reduces the degree of or eliminates associated intellectual disabilities. On the horizon are more medical advances. While today bone marrow transplants are the only cure for sickle cell anemia, cord blood stem cell transplants and gene therapy hold future promises of either eliminating the condition or reducing its impact substantially (NHGRI, 2007).

Prevention and treatment are not just in the hands of those in the medical profession. Although teachers can't cure diseases, they can and do make a real difference in reducing the frequency of episodes of some illnesses by carefully considering the classroom environments they foster. As you have learned, asthma is often triggered by exposure to specific allergens, many of which can be eliminated. This reduces the chance of asthma attacks and cuts down on the resulting illnesses and absences from school (AAFA, 2007; NIEHS, 2007). Teachers also play a very special role by helping these individuals find activities that reduce unsafe physical exertion. For all students with health disabilities, consultation with the student, the parents, the school nurse, and perhaps the student's physician leads to the development of plans that reduce the probability of health-related episodes or can be put into action when a crisis occurs.

Advances in assistive devices or equipment—wheelchairs, prosthetic devices, computers—help individuals with physical and health disabilities overcome some challenges. Such technology improves access and participation at school, in the community, and in all aspects of daily life. For example, special wheelchairs have been designed for marathon races, basketball, and skiing. Some chairs have electronic switches to enable persons with only partial head or neck control or finger or foot control to move about independently. Prosthetic devices, like the arm shown in Figure 9.2, provide freedom of movement never thought possible only a few years ago. Computer technology also helps those who face challenges from restricted movement. For example, computers can be operated by voice, the gaze of an eye, a mouthstick, a sip-and-puff breath stick, a single finger, a toe, a headstick, or some other creative method suitable to an individual's abilities. Special keyboards, like the ones discussed in the Technology section of this chapter, are available for people with limited dexterity or hand strength. Finally, unlike students with physical disabilities who use equipment and special devices to gain fuller participation in daily life, **technology-dependent students** use medical equipment—such as ventilators that help them breathe—to survive.

technology-dependent students Individuals who probably could not survive without high-tech devices (such as ventilators)

Assessment

Astute educators carefully monitor and evaluate the physical and health status of their students with special physical or health care needs. Such needs are often inconsistent, requiring frequent changes in accommodations and considerations. Some situations are directly related to medications and treatment, and others are a function of the disease, illness, or condition. For example, children who receive cancer treatment go through periods of feeling too sick to profit from much of the instructional day. Sometimes these periods may last only several hours, and at other times they may result in frequent or long-term absences. The right courses of action must be individually determined and uniquely responsive.

Early Identification

Family doctors or pediatricians typically diagnose physical and health disabilities. Some conditions are identified at birth or soon afterward because symptoms or risk variables for the conditions either are immediately apparent or are discovered through **universal screening**—testing of all newborns—mandated by the state in which the infant lives. In Chapter 8 about intellectual disabilities, you learned that PKU is now identified through universal screening of newborns, preventing severe mental retardation through early identification and treatment. The medical profession increasingly has the ability to identify more conditions early. For example, sickle cell anemia can now be identified through newborn screenings (Emory University School of Medicine, 2005). Early identification also happens through alert preschool teachers, the services of states' child find offices (see Chapter 2), and the bringing together of a multidisciplinary array of professionals (e.g., physical therapists [PTs], occupational therapists [OTs], and school nurses).

universal screening Testing of everyone, particularly newborns, to determine existence or risk of disability

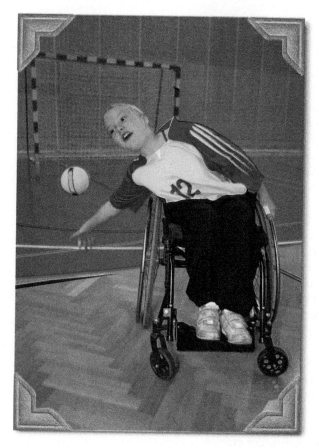

Playing sports is now everyone's opportunity.

Prereferral

Because most students with physical and health disabilities are identified outside the educational community, prereferral is not a typical option. However, as individual IEPs are developed or reevaluated, teachers collaborating with health professionals, PTs, OTs, and the family provide valuable information that contributes to the development of effective education programs for these students. The prereferral and IEP process can help determine what accommodations and services students require so they can meet their educational goals.

Identification

Although teachers rarely participate in the initial diagnosis of disease or physical conditions, they are in a unique position to help these students and their families. Because students spend a considerable portion of their day at school, educators are often the first to notice a change in the physical or health status of their students. In some cases, they are quickly able to determine whether the intensity of an accommodation needs to be altered. One student may now be able to work more independently, while another needs additional supports. In other cases, alert teachers notify parents of changes in students' physical or health status so that referrals to health care professionals can be made without loss of precious time.

Evaluation: Testing Accommodations

As you have learned through What NCLB and IDEA '04 Say About High-Stakes Testing in Chapter 2, test taking is an important area in which teachers should make adjustments for students with disabilities. Such accommodations or modifications should be individually determined and should reflect the specific problems the student faces (U.S. Department of Education, 2006). Assessment and evaluation should reflect what the student knows and should not present an inaccurate picture of the student's abilities by focusing more on the disability than on what the student has learned. The risk is that without accommodations, the test will merely measure the degree of physical difficulty experienced by the individual, rather than her or his actual intellectual or academic abilities. (Imagine trying to take a timed test while your body goes through uncontrollable jerky movements.)

What accommodations do teachers usually select for students with disabilities? Findings are consistent. Teachers most often use the following accommodations in testing situations (Hall, 2007; Thompson et al., 2005):

- *Scheduling accommodations:* providing extra time to take the test
- *Setting accommodations:* allowing the student to take the test in a distraction-free setting or in another place
- *Accommodations regarding directions:* reading the directions to the student, simplifying the direction statements
- *Accommodations for struggling readers:* reading the items to the student

Testing accommodations are usually offered as a group or set of adjustments, not provided one at a time (Crawford, 2007). In other words, several accommodations are delivered together, whether or not each individual one is needed. This is not the best practice. Because of the unique needs of each student with disabilities, it is important that teachers select accommodations on an individual basis. One rule of thumb is to use, in testing situations, the same accommodations that the student has used effectively during instruction.

Early Intervention

Whether disabilities are physical or health related, early intervention programs provide a strong foundation for the child and family. To ensure the success of children's intervention programs, the early intervention team must support parents' efforts and reinforce their enthusiasm. Motor development and positioning and the development of communication skills are often target areas for young children with physical and health disabilities.

For some children, particularly those with physical disabilities, early intervention programs focus primarily on motor development (Best et al., 2005). For example, children born with cerebral palsy may have reflex patterns that interfere with the typical motor development that sets the stage for maximum independence, including body schema, body awareness, purposeful motor use, and mobility. Proper positioning and handling, as well as lifting and assisting with movement, often require skill and knowledge about the condition and its individual effects on the young child. So before teachers or parents begin working with the infant, toddler, or preschooler, they must be trained and supervised to be sure that they do not put the child at risk for injury. Enlisting multidisciplinary team members such as the OT, PT, and school nurse can ensure the development of an effective program delivered by the right people. The student's program usually includes a regimen of special exercises to develop motor skills. The purpose may be to strengthen weak muscle groups through the use of weights or to adapt to and use artificial limbs or orthopedic devices. Once teachers and family members know how to assist the child with the exercises, they should not hesitate and should encourage the youngster to move, play, and interact with the environment.

Because this is a time of tremendous physical and sensorimotor growth, normal motor patterns must be established as early as possible. For those children who already have abnormal motor patterns, repeating those patterns should not be encouraged. The child should always, both at school and at home, be positioned properly so that alignment, muscle tone, and stability are correct during all activities. Specific equipment, such as foam rubber wedges, Velcro straps, and comfortable mats are used to properly position children with physical disabilities. Although some of this equipment is costly, other items can be made rather inexpensively. Parents and teachers need to keep in touch with therapists to be certain that they are working properly with their children. Teachers must also remember that children should not remain in the same position for too long. They should be repositioned every 20 minutes or so.

Communication is difficult for some of these young children (Owens et al., 2007). Parents and professionals should acknowledge and reinforce every attempt at communication. Although determining how a child with severe disabilities is attempting to communicate can be difficult, an observant person can learn a great deal about the child's communication abilities, even when others believe that the child cannot communicate at all. A good observer will be able to answer questions like these: In what specific ways does the child react to sounds? How does the child respond to certain smells? Does the child have different facial movements when different people enter the room? Does the child gaze at certain objects more than others? How is anger expressed to the family? Through careful observation and experience, parents, teachers, and family members can recognize meaningful communication even when others believe there is none. Parents and professionals should also remember that communication is a two-way street. Children learn to communicate with others by being communicated with. Talk to the child, express feelings with face and body, play games together, and encourage the child to listen to tapes and the radio.

Teaching Students with Physical and Health Disabilities

Recall that each student with physical and health disabilities has individualized needs, even those whose diagnoses seem to be the same. Although many of their special needs seem similar to those of students with other types of disabilities, each student has a unique combination of challenges that must be addressed. As with many students with disabilities, many of these students need flexible schedules, more time to learn academic tasks, and extra assistance. However, one area of particular concern to students with physical disabilities is having a learning environment free from physical barriers that inhibit their movement and their interactions with the curriculum and with classmates. Students with health disabilities may require different approaches, each reflecting their health status and each flexibly applied across short periods of time. We begin our discussion with more general ideas about how to help these students better access the general education curriculum. Then we continue the conversation about their education with suggestions on how to enhance the physical environment.

Access to the General Education Curriculum

About half of students with physical and health disabilities spend a substantial portion of their day learning the general education curriculum alongside classmates without disabilities. Many are on the path to a standard diploma. Even so, there is room for considerable improvement. Across the nation, the following percentages of these students spend at least 79% of their day in the general education program (OSEP, 2008):

- 47% of students with physical disabilities, and
- 55% of students with health disabilities.

Many school students with physical and health disabilities dream of graduating from high school and going on to college. One important key to attaining that goal is being able to access the general education curriculum and receive the accommodations necessary to master the skills and knowledge necessary to pursue and complete postsecondary education with success. It might surprise you to learn that although the general education participation rates for students with physical and health disabilities is not the highest of all groups of disabilities, their rates of attending colleges and universities are some of the highest (National Center for Education Statistics [NCES], 2006). Critical to helping students fully access the general education curriculum, achieve to the highest levels possible, and transition to postsecondary educational opportunities are teachers who plan activities that are relevant to students, help all students learn and work together, and instruct how to use strategies that help them approach difficult content. For students who are distracted because of their health situations or have frequent absences, arming them with strategies that help them be more efficient learners may well be the key to improving their success and graduation rates.

myeducationlab) Go to the Activities and Applications section in Chapter 9 of MyEducationLab, and complete Activity 2. As you watch the video and answer the accompanying questions, consider accommodations a teacher can make for a student with physical disabilities.

Instructional Accommodations

Adjustments to the learning environment are often easy to make but still critical to success. Sometimes, simple schedule flexibility is all that is needed. At other times, extending due dates so that the student with a health condition has more time to complete complex assignments is sufficient. However, if students become too sick or fragile to attend school, more complicated measures may be necessary to help them keep up and be on track when they return. Here are just a few ideas that have been successful (Best et al., 2005; Betz & Nehring, 2007):

- Ensure that the district provides a home or hospital teacher for long periods of illness.
- Use Internet videoconferencing or telephone hookups so that important lessons aren't missed and that class participation can happen away from school.
- Videotape special activities or class sessions.
- Have classmates take turns acting as a note taker or a neighborhood peer tutor after school.
- Incorporate features of distance learning into instruction and assignments so that students who must be absent can engage in learning away from school.

Accommodating for Inclusive Environments
Removing Barriers to Learning

Modify the Classroom's Physical Environment
- Apply features of universal design.
- Improve classroom traffic patterns.
- Provide safe and secure space to store AT devices.
- Remove hazards.
- Create flexible seating arrangements.

Incorporate Technology into Instruction
- Utilize distance education technology.
- Set up I-chat or videoconferencing.
- Record important lectures.
- Arrange for e-textbooks for all subjects.
- Create listserve for class communications and homework.

Allow High-Tech Assistive Technology Devices
- Substitute word processing for handwriting.
- Have student(s) use adapted computer keyboards.
- Allow voice options (tape recordings, voice-to-text).

Make Accommodations for Learning
- Provide extended time.
- Give abbreviated assignments.
- Offer flexible due dates.

- Assign note takers.
- Support neighborhood classmates as peer tutors.

Provide Accommodations for Testing
- Allow the use of instructional accommodations in testing.
- Provide scheduling accommodations.
- Provide setting accommodations.
- Read or simplify directions.
- Read items to student.

Allow Low-Tech Assistive Technology Devices
- Provide special or adapted pencils.
- Provide book holders.
- Use page turners.

myeducationlab Go to the Activities and Applications section in Chapter 9 of MyEducationLab, and complete Activity 3. As you watch the video and answer the accompanying questions, think about the importance of high expectations and positive teacher attitudes in an inclusive school for students with physical disabilities and special health care needs.

Students with physical disabilities may need other kinds of accommodations. Teachers often look for complex answers when only simple solutions are required. Here are a few easy ways to create accommodations for students who cannot write as fast and efficiently as others (Best et al., 2005; Betz & Nehring, 2007):

- Allow students extra time to complete written assignments.
- Let students use computers for their written work so they can increase their speed and produce pleasing documents.
- Have a classmate make an extra copy of lecture notes by using carbon paper or photocopying them.
- Have students tape-record instead of write their assignments.

These simple adjustments send a threefold, important message: All students have a fair chance, everyone is important, and expectations are high. Accommodating for Inclusive Environments provides some more tips about adapting instructional settings.

Data-Based Practices: Universal Design

You learned about the ADA law in Chapter 1. Possibly more than for any other group, that law has helped individuals with physical disabilities because it insists that buildings and other parts of our physical environment have fewer obstacles that present challenges to freedom of movement and independence. Although principles of universal design have been incorporated into architectural thought since ADA was passed in 1990, the spirit of the law and concepts of universal design are not always evident in the community or at school. Take for example, a fancy New York restaurant that provides an elevator for its patrons who use wheelchairs that opens to an area where cleaning equipment is stored (Bruni, 2007). The restaurant provided access, as is required by ADA, but sends a clear message about how it values some of its customers. Comparable situations exist everywhere, even at schools.

While older buildings are exempt from the law and still others do not have to meet code until they are scheduled for remodeling, new and remodeled schools must meet the ADA law's special architectural and building codes, but they should also embrace the spirit of universal design. Even if the law were met to the fullest, subtle—and not so subtle—barriers will still exist in every classroom and in every school. In other words, the concept of "barrier-free" is far from being achieved, providing wonderful learning opportunities for everyone. Some barriers are beyond what teachers and classmates can resolve, but many can be reduced or eliminated. As demonstrated in this chapter's Closer Look at Data-Based Practices, problem-solving activities can help the entire class think about important issues and also result in an improved physical environment for students who face challenges to their inclusion, freedom of movement, and independence because of physical disabilities.

The benefits of a unit about how the physical environment impacts learning and life can be great. Class members become sensitive to the physical environment and to how it can create unnecessary barriers to learning and social interaction. They must consider many complex aspects of space and design. As the entire class works to create a better learning environment, everyone's learning styles and needs must be considered. Several factors need to be thought about when redesigning physical space. Many students with severe physical impairments require bulky language boards, computers for communication that require access to electrical outlets, or specially fitted chairs and desks. Students with physical problems may require special worktables and perhaps extra space for maneuvering bulky equipment such as crutches or wheelchairs. These issues may present challenges not only during instruction and small-group work activities but also for storage and security. Math skills are applied as classroom floor plans are developed and considered. The exercise necessitates and the result is often the creation of the spirit of belonging and being part of the school community.

Technology

In this section of each chapter, we focus on a piece of software or an assistive technology (AT) device that assists students with disabilities to participate more fully at school. As you learned in Chapter 2, AT includes a wide array of devices and tools that enable individuals to interact with others, benefit from school, and participate in mainstream society (Poel, 2007). The adaptations that technology provides for individuals with special physical and health considerations include **high-tech devices**, such as computers that control the environment, ventilators, or hardware and software allowing for voice output. **Low-tech devices** assist persons with simple adjustments, such as holders to keep books at the correct level to see print on a page, objects that help turn pages of books, or rubber bands wrapped around pencils to make them easier to hold.

Many students with motor problems, like those with certain kinds of cerebral palsy, have difficulties using a standard computer keyboard because their fingers slip over to another key. One type of AT device is particularly helpful in such situations. It is a special keyboard that allows for more efficient use of a computer and with less frustration (Brundige, 2007). The keyboard can be customized in many different ways for various purposes, from creating a written assignment to taking a test. For writing a paper, the keys may be set farther apart, and an overlay can protect them, making it harder to press an unwanted key. When taking a test, the answer choices can easily become part of the keyboard so the student

high-tech devices Complex assistive technology devices that use computers or computer chips

low-tech devices Simple assistive technology devices such as communication boards, homemade cushions, or a classroom railing

A Closer Look at Data-Based Practices

Universal Design

Universal design principles should be applied to every classroom and all aspects of every school facility to ensure students with physical challenges are welcomed and included. Ensuring that the inclusive concepts of these important principles are part of the school culture provides many opportunities for problem solving and challenge-based learning experiences. Class members can work together to evaluate the functionality of their learning environment and to decide how best to use space that embodies the spirit of universal design. Through drawings and models, they can generate visual design alternatives to the way their environment is currently structured. This activity can create a more exciting and useful learning environment for every class member and can be particularly helpful to students who face physical challenges.

Steps to Follow

1. Conduct an assessment of the school's physical environment.
   a. Determine where barriers exist in every location (e.g., bathrooms, lunchroom, playgrounds, gym, library).
   b. Consider issues such as height of bathroom sinks, mirrors, towel dispensers, door handles, doormats, rugs, and door thresholds.
   c. Create two lists of modifications: those that are structural where improvement must be advocated for and those that can be resolved by teachers and students.
2. Conduct an assessment of the classroom.
   a. Evaluate the room's arrangement (e.g., furniture arrangement, storage space) to be sure that space and design do not restrict access to learning.
   b. Collect data by using simple frequency counts to study the traffic patterns in the classroom.

3. Take action.
   a. In the classroom, reorganize desks, tables, work areas, storage space, and learning centers.
   b. For resolution of physical barriers that teachers and students cannot resolve, develop and act on an advocacy plan.

Example

Shown here is an example of a classroom floor plan reflecting universal design principles. This plan, developed by a middle school class, allows students who use wheelchairs access to work, equipment storage, and movement patterns.

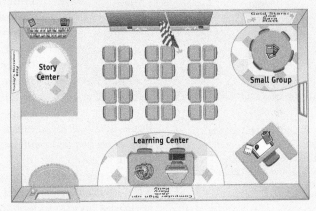

 Go to the Activities and Applications section in Chapter 9 of MyEducationLab and complete Activity 4, in the IRIS Module: Effective Room Arrangements. Consider what makes certain room arrangements effective for students at various grade levels and of different abilities.

with physical disabilities can take an end-of-unit test along with the rest of the class. Specially designed keyboards, like the ones shown in the accompanying photo, simply plug into the computer's USB port.

Transition

Being a college graduate is the dream of most high school students, including those with physical and heath disabilities. In fact, their participation rates in postsecondary education are among some of the highest of students with disabilities. The National Center for Education Statistics (NCES, 2006) reports that some 11% of all college students indicate that they have a disability. About one-fourth of those students have a physical disability, and 17% reported a health disability. This participation rate has improved over the years, in part because college campuses are more accessible and because more students with disabilities receive necessary accommodations. Although students who pursue an alternate path to high school graduation do attend college, the more traditional way is to earn a standard high school diploma. Inter-

Some assistive technology devices, like this special computer keyboard, help students show their academic abilities.

estingly, almost half of the states do not report graduation rates for their students with disabilities (Hall, 2007). We believe states' accountability requirements should be higher because without a high school diploma, the chance of attending college is small, and a college degree is the ticket to a high-paying job (NCES, 2007). In fact, the difference in annual average annual income levels between those having a high school diploma and those having a bachelor's degree was almost $10,000 in 2005.

Whether a college graduate or not, independent living is the goal for most adults with physical and health disabilities. The "independent living movement"—people helping themselves to live on their own—has had great influence on the lives of people with disabilities. Increasingly, these adults take control of their lives and their jobs, establish friendships, do not live with their parents, have families of their own, and exert political power. Legislation such as ADA has had a tremendous impact on the ability of adults with disabilities to pursue their rights and end discrimination, but they must be prepared to take their places in mainstream society. High school transition programs can be very helpful in this regard, by teaching students how to be responsible for planning their own lives, advocate for themselves, locate the resources they need, and take active roles in their medical management (Betz & Nehring, 2007). For some students whose health care or physical issues are so great, the later high school years is a time when these individuals are preparing to leave home and live in an adult care facility where they can receive the intensive supports they need but still participate as independently and fully as possible in daily life (Betz & Telfair, 2007).

Independence is important to all people but is of vital concern to many people with physical and health disabilities. Earlier in this chapter, you learned about improved access, independence, and participation for many aspects of life: housing, school, work, travel, and leisure activities. Opportunities have been expanded through removal of barriers, specialized activities, and assistive technology. One more service is helping many individuals with physical and health disabilities gain even more independence. When we think of **service** or **assistance animals**—animals individually trained to benefit a person with a disability—we usually think of a guide dog for people with visual disabilities. But more and more animals, particularly dogs and Capuchin monkeys, are assisting people with physical limitations to live independently and participate in society more fully (Canine Companions for Independence, 2007; Delta Society, 2007). Amazingly, service monkeys can help in many ways, from opening the refrigerator door to get a bottle of water, to turning the pages of a book (see photo). All service animals are highly trained; they are not pets. Certain important rules should guide our interactions with the working team of dog and person (handler) with a disability:

- Speak to the person first and do not distract the dog.
- Ask and receive permission before touching a service dog.
- Do not offer the animal food.
- Don't be offended if the handler doesn't want to talk about him- or herself or about the animal.

service or assistance animals
Animals (dogs, monkeys, guide dogs) trained to serve the individual needs of people with disabilities

Collaboration

Almost half of students with physical or health disabilities spend over 80% of every school day in general education classes (OSEP, 2008). Thus, it is likely that general education teachers, as well as special education professionals, will work closely with these students' multidisciplinary teams as everyone collaborates to implement each student's

IEPs. Also, perhaps more than other groups of students with disabilities, many students with physical and health disabilities are served by the full range of special education services, as well as several different professions that can be represented on multidisciplinary teams of related service providers. Many of these professionals, such as rehabilitation engineers, have unique contributions to make to the education of students with physical disabilities. It might be only for these students that such expertise is needed. For example, rehabilitation engineers working in tandem with assistive technologists might devise mobility systems and special seating arrangements for a student with a very unique physical need. Together, they might create equipment that attaches other devices (e.g., communication devices) to wheelchairs, and then a physical therapist might help the student learn how to use the right muscles to make everything work. However, for most students with physical and health disabilities, the multidisciplinary team called together is not this complex, but it still needs coordination.

Highly trained service animals, like this monkey, help people with disabilities enjoy greater independence by doing tasks like turning the pages of a book.

Collaborating with Related Services Providers: School Nurses, PTs, and OTs

As we mentioned, students with physical and health disabilities are very diverse in the types and complexity of conditions they have. Each multidisciplinary team is established to meet the unique needs of each individual student and, therefore, is composed of different professions that have particular expertise to address the special health care or physical needs presented by so many different conditions. So, it is important not to associate a particular set of related services with either physical disabilities or health disabilities. Of course, it is natural and typically correct to think of school nurses being especially helpful in meeting the needs of students with health disabilities and their families. Remember, a **school nurse** is a related service provider described in IDEA '04 as a professional who helps students receive an appropriate education. What is very important is that all educators seek the help of the family and of students' multidisciplinary teams who can assist in designing the best instructional environment possible.

For students with physical disabilities, a common set of professionals come together to help students overcome the challenges they face controlling their muscles and moving freely whether walking or writing a paper. In addition to school nurses, physical therapists and occupational therapists play unique roles in the assessment of the needs of students with physical and health disabilities and in the implementation of their IEPs. For example, **physical therapists (PTs)** evaluate the quality of the students' movement and later teach them how to compensate for and change inefficient motor patterns. **Occupational therapists (OTs)** work closely with PTs to assess and later work with upper-body movement, fine-motor skills, and daily living activities. Together, PTs and OTs analyze the student's physical characteristics and determine what assistive devices will benefit the individual (Best et al., 2005).

Collaborative Practices: School Nurse as Case Manager

More and more students with complex health care needs attend general education classes at their neighborhood schools (OSEP, 2008). Meeting the needs of individual students with special health care needs can now require specialists to travel great distances and work at more schools to meet these needs, making communication and scheduling more complicated. In addition to an IEP, some of these students also have an individualized health care plan that carefully spells out specific accommodations and modifications needed by the student. The coordination and scheduling of these services and personnel can become complicated. Also, while some of these students require few accommodations to succeed and access the gen-

school nurse A professional who assists with or delivers medical services at school, coordinates health services, designs accommodations for students with special health care needs, and provides a special education–related service

physical therapist (PT) A professional who treats physical disabilities through many nonmedical means and works to improve motor skills; a special education–related service provider

occupational therapist (OT) A professional who directs activities that help improve muscular control and develop self-help skills and provides a special education–related service

eral education curriculum, at some points in some of these students' educational careers, they are too sick to attend their neighborhood school. These students might require instruction delivered to their homes or even to hospital settings.

Regardless of the situation, it is critical that the student's educational program and access to the general education curriculum be disrupted as little as possible and that the student and the family are supported as much as possible during times of a health crisis. So a new role for school nurses, **case manager**, is emerging (National Association of School Nurses [NASN], 2007). This job is very important not only to the student with the disabilities and that student's family, but to every educator and related service provider working with the target individual. Case management duties often include the following:

- Community liaison, in particular with the student's medical team
- Health and illness interpretation and translation to school personnel
- Coordinator of related service providers
- Coordinator of special education services across settings
- Facilitator of communication assisting with transition from one setting to another
- Advocate (IRIS Center, 2007)

In addition to coordinating services of related services providers, school nurses serving as case managers provide great benefits to students and their families as students with health disabilities move through different special education arrangements. For example, a very small percentage—less than 0.81% of students with health disabilities, or fewer than 5,000 students annually—has such chronic illnesses that they require that their education be delivered to their homes or to a hospital setting (OSEP, 2008). But, for those students the seamless coordination of special education services is critical. When these students are well enough and transition back to their neighborhood schools, they usually do so on a part-time basis, gradually increasing their time at school. Often, the process is not facilitated, and communication is less than adequate. This new role for the school nurse can be critical to educational success, improved communication, and reducing the stress of everyone working with the student with a health disability.

myeducationlab Go to the Building Teaching Skills and Dispositions section in Chapter 9 of MyEducationLab, and complete the activities in the IRIS Module, "Working with Your School Nurse: What General Education Teachers Should Do to Promote Educational Success for Students with Health Needs." This module is designed for school personnel who may be collaborating with the school nurse during IEP meetings or during other occasions involving the health problems of students with disabilities.

Partnerships with Families and Communities

Having a child with a chronic or life-threatening health problem can be an overwhelming situation. The child's care can become all-consuming (Sobo & Kurtin, 2007). Families of children with severe physical limitations often find themselves facing one challenge after another. In some cases, the home must be reconfigured, remodeled, or modified to meet the physical or health needs of the child (Homer & Cooley, 2007). Another challenge facing families of individuals with special health care needs is sorting out how to manage and negotiate the "medical maze" or, as some might say, identifying resources available in the medical–health care community. At times families are seeking information about conditions and appropriate health care responses for their children. At other times they are trying to locate health or community services to assist them with the care of their child who has either a health or a physical disability. One common theme heard over and over again is how overwhelming life becomes when a child is sick. Today, families frequently turn to the Internet for information, which they discover is "sometimes . . . like being hit by a tidal wave" (Smith, 2005, p. 1). So families often turn to schools and teachers for help.

One place to begin the search for information is the National Dissemination Center for Children with Disabilities, which is just called NICHCY. OSEP, a division of the U.S. Department of Education, funds this clearinghouse (www.nichcy.org) designed to help those looking for resources and information about students with disabilities.

Providing useful information to family members might be time-consuming and is sometimes not directly linked to instruction, but it can be part of building important bonds with parents and extended family members. For many educators, such

Considering Culture: *Culture Clash*

Semira is 12 years old and has significant physical problems. She travels by wheelchair and has no functional use of her arms and legs. As a result, she must be assisted in all of her daily living activities and must be repositioned frequently throughout the day. To escape violence in their home country of Somalia, Semira's parents left for the United States soon after she was born. With help from family members who sponsored them, Semira and her parents have begun to acclimate to the differences in culture. They do, however, hold traditional beliefs and follow traditional practices. It is their adherence to these traditional ways that has resulted in today's meeting with Semira's teacher, Mrs. Jackson.

Semira's parents have been keeping her at home since the beginning of the semester, and her teacher does not understand why. Semira is not hospitalized, nor is she sick. Mrs. Jackson's concern had been increasing, so she called Semira's home to ask whether she could come talk with them and visit Semira. When Mrs. Jackson arrived at the house, she was greeted warmly by Semira's father and mother, who immediately served tea and cakes. Semira was in her wheelchair smiling and happy to see Mrs. Jackson. After greetings and general conversation Mrs. Jackson said, "I hope that Semira will be returning to school soon. We all miss her." Semira's father seemed reluctant to speak but finally said, "We think that we will keep Semira at home and provide her education at home."

Mrs. Jackson was surprised and asked why they had made that decision. Semira's father said that now that Semira is becoming a young lady, school may not be right for her. Mrs. Jackson countered by saying that being with her peers is especially important now that she is becoming a teenager. The conversation continued, and finally Semira's father said, "Since the new term, there have been men at school—the new assistant in your classroom and the physical education teacher. We know that they lift Semira in and out of her wheelchair and that they hold her during some of the class activities. In our culture, men and women do not touch like this. It is not appropriate for these men to have such close contact with our daughter."

Mrs. Jackson realized that this family's cultural beliefs were very different from hers and different from the school culture. She asked Semira's father whether Semira could return to school if different arrangements were made for lifting and positioning her. He agreed that as long as a woman did these tasks modestly, such considerations were acceptable to the family. Mrs. Jackson agreed to make other arrangements, and within a week a plan acceptable to all was in place.

Questions to Consider

1. Gender roles are often linked to cultural beliefs. Can you give examples of any gender differences that are important in the culture(s) you include in your identity?

2. How do you think you would respond if a family's cultural beliefs and practices supported highly traditional gender roles?

3. What do you think the teacher's role should be when a family's cultural beliefs and practices collide with the school's culture?

—By Eleanor Lynch, San Diego State University, and Marci Hanson, San Francisco State University.

tasks come naturally, as part of their "helping" orientation. Of course, there are many other important ways in which educators need to partner with families and be sensitive to their concerns. Such sensitivity does not always come spontaneously but, rather, requires careful thought. The story in Considering Culture makes the point that educators have many issues to consider—some of them not initially obvious—when providing an appropriate education for students with disabilities.

It seems like all children enjoy stuffed animals; particularly ones they can relate to. Sarah Bear, promoted by Heather Mills, former wife of Beatle star Paul McCartney and who lost a leg in a motorcycle accident, is a great toy for young children with limb disabilities.

The Sarah Bear, a therapeutic friend who encourages us to celebrate our differences, was inspired by triathlete and motivational speaker Sarah Reinertsen, and was invented by Brian Lorenz. Sarah Bear is available at www.glabeebers.com and a portion of the proceeds benefits the Challenged Athletes Foundation.

Summary

Physical and health disabilities can present unique challenges to students and their families, classmates, and teachers. These students require considerable flexibility, accommodations, and adjustments to both their learning and their physical environments. These two special education categories, particularly if one separates ADHD from the overall prevalence of health disabilities, represent low-incidence disabilities that contain many rare diseases and conditions. Even when ADHD is included, these two special education categories together represent only about 2% of all students. Most of these students access the general education curriculum and graduate from high school, but their graduation rates certainly need improvement. As advances in technology and opportunities for community presence expand, one important challenge facing educators is helping their students be well prepared to take advantage of an ever-changing world.

Answering the Chapter Objectives

1. How are physical and health disabilities classified and organized?

- Physical disabilities
  - *Neuromotor impairments:* seizure disorders, cerebral palsy, spinal cord disorders, polio, muscular dystrophy (MD), multiple sclerosis (MS)
  - *Muscular/skeletal conditions:* juvenile arthritis, limb deficiencies, skeletal disorders

- Health disabilities
  - *Chronic illnesses:* asthma, diabetes, cystic fibrosis, sickle cell anemia, epilepsy, congenital heart defects, tuberculosis (TB), childhood cancer, blood disorders
  - *Infectious diseases:* HIV/AIDS, STORCH infections, hepatitis B

2. What are some steps teachers should take when a child is having a seizure?

- Seek medical assistance.
- Create a safe place free from hazards.
- Loosen clothing, particularly around the neck.
- Protect the head from injury.
- Turn the person sideways to ensure free passage of air.
- For seizures lasting longer than 5 minutes, call for an ambulance.
- Upon return of consciousness, keep the individual calm and offer further assistance.

3. What accommodations to the learning environment help students with physical disabilities?

- *Modify the physical environment:* apply principles of universal design; widen aisles; remove hazards; change seating arrangements; create accessible workstations; provide storage for AT devices.
- *Alter student response demands:* (as appropriate) speak instead of write; use word processing instead of writing; have a classmate take notes.
- *Adapt materials and equipment:* allow use of special writing tools; voice-activated computers, or adapted computer keyboards.

4. What accommodations and assistance can help students with health disabilities?

- *Modify instruction:* allow more time to complete assignments; abbreviate assignments; allow for a flexible schedule for completion.

- *Arrange for extra assistance:* tutors (peers, parents, volunteers); video lectures; use distance delivery systems; set up I-chat or videoconferencing; assign a peer tutor.
- *Adapt materials:* use handouts with lectures; assign books with e-versions; allow voice options.
- *Seek support from related services:* school nurse as case manager for home–school collaboration.

5. How might the barriers that people with physical disabilities face be reduced? And in what ways can students be better prepared for increased community presence and participation?

Barriers include
- coping with inaccessible environments, where their impaired mobility hinders their participation in mainstream society;
- dealing with bias, rejection, and discrimination;
- difficulties living independently;
- difficulties finding jobs;
- social rejection by people without disabilities.

Individuals require
- accessible physical and learning environments;
- acceptance and understanding;
- goals that foster independence;
- accommodations for their individual learning, physical, and health needs;
- special teaching, scheduling, counseling, therapies, equipment, and technology.

myeducationlab) Now go to MyEducationLab at www.myeducationlab.com, and take the Self-Assessment to gauge your initial comprehension of chapter content. Once you have taken the Self-Assessment, use your individualized Study Plan for Chapter 9 to enhance your understanding of the concepts discussed in the chapter.

Council for Exceptional Children ADDRESSING THE PROFESSIONAL STANDARDS

Council for Exceptional Children (CEC) knowledge standards addressed in this chapter:

PH1K2, PH1K1, PH2K2, PH2K3, PH8S3, PH5K1, PH10S6, PH10K3, PH10S5

Appendix A: CEC Knowledge and Skill Standards Common Core has a full listing of the standards listed here.

Appendix B: CEC Knowledge and Skill Common Core Standards and Associated Subcategories are broken down by chapter.

CHAPTER 10

Deaf and Hard of Hearing

Chapter Objectives

After studying this chapter, you will be able to

1. List and explain the major causes of hearing loss.

2. Discuss why universal hearing screening of newborns is so important to the outcomes of deaf children.

3. Discuss the concept of Deaf culture, list examples or signs of Deaf culture, and describe its importance to the Deaf.

4. Explain variables that must be considered when planning instruction for students with hearing problems.

5. List the major types of assistive technology specifically designed for people with hearing problems, and provide examples for each.

Dorothy Brett was born of a noble British family. Although her childhood was quite sheltered, as a young adult and a student at the Slade Art College in London, she became exposed to other young artists and liberal thinkers of the day. Her associations with the Bloomsbury Group (two of its more famous members were writer and publisher Virginia Woolf and economist John Maynard Keynes) broadened her horizons. In 1924, Brett followed D. H. Lawrence—a famous English novelist, poet, and artist of the time—to New Mexico to be part of a utopian colony. Lawrence returned to England, but Brett remained in America and became part of an artists' colony, often referred to as the Taos Artists. Brett was "partially deaf" almost her entire life. In a self-portrait she completed in 1924 and the photo included here, she displays the hearing aid of the day, an *ear trumpet*. Brett named hers Toby (Hignett, 1983).

Dorothy Brett, Spring. *Private Collection, New Mexico, Courtesy Owings-Dewey Fine Art, Santa Fe, New Mexico.*

myeducationlab After reading this chapter, complete the Self-Assessment for Chapter 10 on MyEducationLab to gauge your initial understanding of chapter content.

deaf Profound hearing loss

hard of hearing Hearing losses that impair understanding of sounds and communication

Life today for people with hearing loss is very different than it was only a generation ago. Technology and medical advances have made a great difference and many improvements are on the horizon. Now, many cases of significant hearing loss can be prevented or corrected, so fewer children require special services than ever before. Children who do require specialized services, however, often need considerable assistance from technology, their teachers, and their families.

The vast majority of us take the process of hearing for granted; we don't think about how remarkable and effortless it is to be able to turn sounds into meaning. The content or associations of sound affect us in different ways. We are warmed by the sound of an old friend's voice, startled by a loud clap of thunder, fascinated by the sound of the wind rushing through trees, lulled by the ocean, excited by the roar of a crowd, consumed by the music of a rock group, and inspired by the uplifting sounds of a symphony. One important way in which most of us learn about the thoughts, ideas, and feelings of others is by listening to people tell us about their experiences. Through this exchange we expand our knowledge, share ideas, express emotions, and function in typical workplaces and social settings. People who are **deaf**—those with profound hearing loss who cannot understand sounds with or without hearing aids—and people who are **hard of hearing**—those with hearing losses that impair their understanding of sounds, including communication—profit from listening devices and other hearing technologies that enable them to comprehend oral speech and communications.

Where We've Been . . . What's on the Horizon?

We know through the writings of Aristotle, Plato, and the emperor Justinian that ancient Greeks and early Romans discussed issues concerning people who were deaf. Over the history of Western civilization, attitudes have varied. Some societies protected such people; others ridiculed and persecuted them and even put them to death (Branson & Miller, 2002). As you will learn, many people with profound hearing loss consider themselves members of a minority group with its own culture and heritage, while others think of deafness and hard of hearing as a disability to overcome.

Historical Context

The history of the deaf—their educational opportunities, treatment by society, and the development of their culture—is fascinating. Throughout time, this group of individuals has been surrounded by controversy as they have sought fair treatment and social justice.

Documents dating back to the 1500s mention physicians in Europe who worked with people who were deaf. Pedro Ponce de Leon (1520–1584), a Spanish monk believed to have been the first teacher of deaf students, had remarkable success teaching his students to read, write, and speak. William Holder and John Wallis, who lived during the 1600s, are credited with instituting educational programs in England for deaf individuals. Like the Spanish before them, they advocated using writing and manual communication to teach speech. By the 1700s, schools for the deaf had been established in England, Scotland, France, and Germany.

Thomas Hopkins Gallaudet, a young divinity student, went to study in England and France so he could start the first special school for the deaf in the United States. At that time, the French at the school begun by l'Epée were experimenting with methods of manual communication, mainly sign language. Gallaudet was greatly influenced by the effectiveness of these methods, and he brought Laurent Clerc, a deaf Frenchman and the person now thought of as the father of Deaf culture in America, to the United States to start an era for the education of the deaf (Van Cleve, 2007). Together, in 1817, Clerc and Gallaudet began the first American school for deaf students in Hartford, Connecticut. This is the residential school attended by many of the Deaf children of Martha's Vineyard, about whom you learned in Chapter 1.

Thomas Hart Benton often spent his summers on Martha's Vineyard where some of his neighbors were the Deaf residents of the island. Two of them appear in this painting.

Thomas Hart Benton, *"The Lord is my Shepherd"*, tempura on canvas. Collection of the Whitney Museum of American Art, New York. Art (c) T.H. Benton and R.P. Benton Testamentary Trusts/UMB Bank Trustee/Licensed by VAGA, New York, NY

As you learned in Chapter 1, the story of the English settlers of Martha's Vineyard is important in the history of America, and it set the foundation of Deaf culture in the United States. In the 17th century, these pioneers settled on the island off the coast of Connecticut and Massachusetts. In those days, island living was restrictive. The settlers were free to marry whomever they wanted to, and the prevalence of deafness was exceptionally high. The recessive gene for deafness they carried from Kent, England, affected everyone living on Martha's Vineyard in some way. In one community on the island, 25% of the citizens were deaf. Almost everyone living on the island had a deaf family member, and everyone on the island was bilingual. Hearing and deaf people learned the sign language their ancestors developed and brought with them from England. They developed oral and sign language skills simultaneously early in life. Many of the Vineyard Deaf were highly successful, active in all aspects of society and their church (Groce, 1985). Many of them became wealthy businesspeople, in part because they had the benefits of education that most other people of the day did not. Throughout the 1800s, life was much the same for these founders of Deaf culture in the United States.

While the deaf on Martha's Vineyard were flourishing, others were impressed by the results of oral approaches being used in Europe. And thus began the highly contentious debates about the benefits of oral communication versus manual communication or sign language. Some even refer to this period of time as the "Hundred Years' War" (Drasgow, 1998). The battles were initiated and fueled through the debates of Edward Gallaudet, Thomas Gallaudet's son, and Alexander Graham Bell (Adams, 1929; Alby, 1962). Each of these men had a deaf mother and a highly successful father. Bell invented the telephone and the audiometer and worked on the phonograph. Gallaudet was the president of the nation's college for the deaf and was a renowned legal scholar. These two men clashed. Bell believed that residential schools and the use of sign language fostered segregation. He also felt that communities of deaf people would lead to more deaf people marrying each other and that the result would eventually be a deaf variety of the human race (Greenwald, 2007). Therefore, he proposed legislation to prohibit two deaf adults from marrying, eliminate residential schools, ban the use of manual communication, and prevent people who were deaf from becoming teachers. Gallaudet strongly opposed Bell's positions, and he won support from Congress for the manual approach and for separate center schools.

An important historical marker for people who are hard of hearing is the development of wearable, electronic hearing aids in the 1950s. "Hearing aids" did exist before, but they could only make sounds a little louder. One version, the hearing trumpet, was used by Dorothy Brett, the artist whose work and picture are shown at the beginning of this chapter. Advances in batteries developed during World War II and transistors developed during the 1950s allowed hearing aids to be small and easy to use. Today's versions use microchips to tailor sound amplification to the needs of the individual. This technology allows many hard of hearing children to require few, if any, special education services.

Unlike people with other disabilities, many people with profound hearing loss consider themselves not people with disabilities but, rather, people who are members of a minority group. They consider themselves "Deaf" (notice the capital *D*). They are members of the Deaf community and are united by **Deaf culture**, a culture rich in heritage and traditions. In the United States their primary language is **American Sign Language (ASL)**—a language that uses manual communication signs, has all of the elements (grammar, syntax, idioms) of other languages, and is not parallel to English in either structure or word order. ASL is not a mere translation of oral speech or of the English language (as is Signed English); it is a fully developed language. Many high schools and colleges and universities allow ASL as an option to meet a foreign language requirement.

Since the late 1980s, Deaf pride has also united the Deaf community quite publicly. In 1988, Gallaudet University's Board of Trustees appointed a hearing president who did not know ASL. Protests from Deaf Gallaudet students and the Deaf community erupted, and the crisis was dubbed the "Deaf President Now Movement" (Gannon, 1989). The campus was closed, and the students marched on Washington, DC. The result was that I. King Jordan became the first Deaf college president of Gallaudet University and the first Deaf college president in the nation. When Jordan retired in 2006, the movement rose again. This time the board of trustees appointed a deaf president who was born deaf but did not learn ASL until she was in her twenties. Questions arose about whether she was "deaf enough" (Mendoza, 2006). The trustees withdrew their appointment. Robert Davilla, former assistant secretary of education for the Office of Special Education and Rehabilitation Services and former provost at Gallaudet, was appointed president. He met the community's criteria: deaf from birth, attended a residential school for the deaf, proficient in ASL, and speaks and signs both Spanish and English.

Challenges That Hearing Loss Presents

Most of us communicate with others through a process of telling and listening. This process is one important way in which we learn about the world we live in, subjects at school, and others' perspectives on issues and concerns. Those who cannot hear or speak oral language have a more restricted ability to communicate—a difference that shapes the way these students are taught, the content of their curricula, and the related services they require for an appropriate education.

Issues are very different across groups of students with hearing loss. For example, students with moderate to mild hearing loss profit from hearing aids and may not even qualify for special education services. Unfortunately, these students' special needs are often overlooked because the assumption is that their assistive devices fully compensate for their disability (Harrington, 2003). A second group of these learners use oral language as their means of communication and learning. A third group uses sign language often, a practice that separates them from the hearing community. The use of ASL, the language and manual communication system of the Deaf community, has become the focal point of the controversy. Some argue that all young children with profound hearing loss should learn ASL as their native language and that English become their second language. However, hearing parents are often concerned that their children will become isolated from them and their family members if they learn ASL as their primary language; one reason for the rise in the number of cochlear implants among infants.

Deaf culture Structures of social relationships, language (ASL), dance, theater, literature, and other cultural activities that bind the Deaf community

American Sign Language (ASL) The language of Deaf Americans that uses manual communication; a signal of Deaf culture

Making a Difference:
Gallaudet University and I. King Jordan

Again and again we are reminded how personal connections can change the lives of those involved and affect the lives of many others. The connection between Thomas Hopkins Gallaudet and Dr. Mason Cogswell, the father of a daughter who was deaf, is an example of one that impacted generations (Van Cleve, 2007). Gallaudet and Cogswell were neighbors in Hartford, Connecticut. Because there was no school for his daughter, Alice Cogswell, the medical doctor sought the help of Gallaudet, an itinerant preacher. In 1816, Dr. Cogswell sent Gallaudet to Europe to study methods for the "proper" education of deaf individuals. Gallaudet returned to the United States with Laurent Clerc, a French educator of the deaf who used manual communication systems. Together in Hartford, they began the first American school for the deaf. In 1864, Gallaudet's son, Edward, carried on and established in Washington, DC, what is now called Gallaudet University alongside Kendall Green Elementary School, which was begun in 1856 (Laurent Clerc National Deaf Education Center, 2005). What these pioneers began has evolved into a movement, a culture, and the Deaf community.

King Jordan and Gallaudet U.

It is a very special man, I. King Jordan, who brought Gallaudet and Deaf culture to national standing when he assumed the presidency of the only liberal arts university in the world that provides specially designed programs to deaf and hard of hearing college students. In 1988, the campus was in turmoil, students were on strike and marching on the nation's capitol, and protests were vehement about the appointment of a hearing president who did not know ASL and could not communicate with many students, faculty, alumni, or the Deaf community. Jordan became the first deaf president since the university's founding in 1864, and a remarkable president he was until his retirement in 2006. He brought positive attention to the school, is a role model for many Deaf people, was a successful fundraiser, and is credited with successful efforts that resulted in the construction of two large research centers. On March 28, 2006, the U.S. Senate passed a resolution of thanks to Dr. Jordan for his remarkable career, his advocacy, and his leadership not only to the Deaf community but also to the nation.

Deafness and Hard of Hearing Defined

Although the federal government in IDEA '04 describes two groups of students with hearing loss—those who are deaf and those who are hard of hearing—it considers them as belonging to one special education category, which it calls "hearing impairments." The government's definitions for deafness and for hearing impairments are provided in Table 10.1, along with the definitions for students with hearing loss used by a federally sponsored information resource center.

Hearing loss results when the hearing mechanism is damaged or obstructed in such a way that sounds cannot be perceived or understood. The damage can occur either before or after birth. To better understand impaired hearing, it is helpful to know how the process of hearing works when the hearing mechanism is functioning properly. We will discuss that briefly and then study three factors that affect problems associated with hearing loss:

- Degree of loss
- Age when the loss occurs
- Type of hearing loss

Table 10.1 • Definitions of Deaf and Hard of Hearing

Source	Definition of Deafness
Federal government	Deafness means a hearing impairment that is so severe that the child is impaired in processing linguistic information through hearing, with or without amplification, that adversely affects a child's educational performance. *U.S. Department of Education (2006, p. 1261)*
	Definition of Hard of Hearing (Hearing Impairment)
Federal government	Hearing impairment means an impairment in hearing, whether permanent or fluctuating, that adversely affects a child's educational performance but that is not included under the definition of deafness *U.S. Department of Education (2006, p. 1262)*
Federally funded Technical Assistance Clearinghouse	A person who is hard of hearing perceives some sound and has sufficient hearing to use auditory-based methods of communication, sometimes with visual supplements. Some people who are severely hard of hearing use oral-aural communication, which combines speech, speech-reading, use of personal hearing aids (including the newer cochlear implant technology), and other augmentative devices. *HEATH Resource Center (American Council on Education) (2005, p. 2)*

Sources: From 34 *CFR* Parts 300 and 303, *Assistance to States for the Education of Children with Disabilities and the Early Intervention Program for Infants and Toddlers with Disabilities; Final Regulations* (pp. 1261, 1262), U.S. Department of Education, 2006, *Federal Register*, Washington, DC; and *Students Who Are Deaf or Hard of Hearing in Postsecondary Education* (p. 2), 2005, HEATH Resource Center (American Council on Education), Washington, DC.

The Process of Hearing

Hearing is a "distance sense" that developed to alert us to dangers in the environment, but it also connects us with others. The way it works is truly amazing. Sound waves pass through the air, water, or some other medium. They cause the eardrum to vibrate. These vibrations are carried to the inner ear, where they pass through receptor cells that send impulses to the brain. The brain translates these impulses into meaningful sound. Refer to Figure 10.1, a diagram of the ear, to trace the process of normal hearing as sound moves from the outer ear, through the middle ear, and then to the inner ear and finally is translated into electrochemical signals and transmitted to the brain via the auditory (eighth cranial) nerve.

In general, here is how it works. A person speaks, and the sound waves that make up the words pass, or propagate, through the air or some other medium. The **pinna** (sometimes called the auricle) is the outer structure that we commonly call the ear. Sound waves are caught by the pinna and funneled down the auditory canal to the middle ear. The middle ear is an air-filled chamber that contains the **tympanic membrane** or **eardrum**. The middle ear also contains the **Eustachian tube**, which equalizes the pressure on the two sides of the eardrum. Sound waves cause the eardrum to vibrate, and those vibrations cause the hammer (malleus) and anvil (incus) to move and the stirrup (stapes) to oscillate. These three tiny bones together are called the **ossicles**. The eardrum converts pressure variations to mechanical vibrations, which are then transmitted to the fluid contained in the compartments of the inner ear: the cochlea and the semicircular canals (which help us keep our balance).

The **cochlea** is a hollow, spiral-shaped bone that actually contains the organs of hearing (see Figure 10.1, Cross Section of the Cochlea). The mechanical vibrations caused by variations in the pressure that the stirrup exerts on the fluid are transmitted to the basilar membrane of the cochlea. This membrane supports the **hair cells**, which respond to different frequencies of sound. Each hair cell has about a hundred tiny, rigid spines, or cilia, at its top. When these hair cells move, they displace the fluid that surrounds them and produce electrochemical signals,

pinna The outer structure of the ear

tympanic membrane or eardrum Vibrates with the presence of sound waves and stimulates the ossicles of the middle ear

Eustachian tube Equalizes pressure on both sides of the eardrum

ossicles Three tiny bones (hammer or malleus, anvil or incus, stirrup or stapes) in the middle ear that pass information to the cochlea

cochlea Contains the organs of hearing

hair cells Part of the cochlea that responds to different frequencies of sound and produces electrochemical signals sent on to the brain

Figure 10.1 • The Structure of the Human Ear

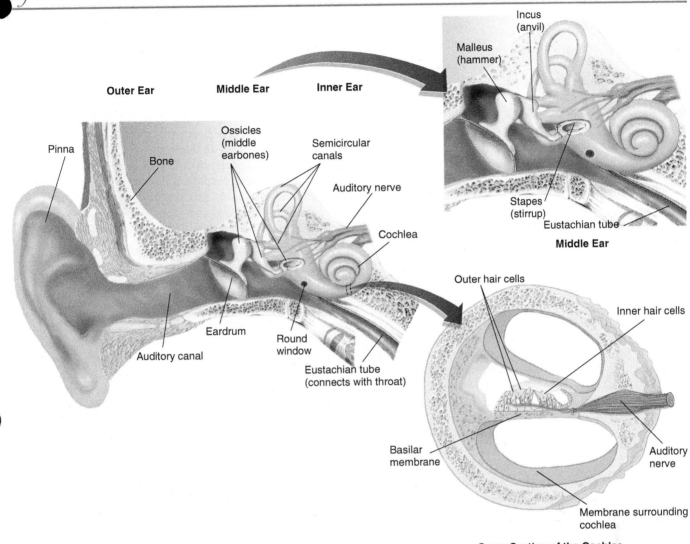

Cross Section of the Cochlea

Source: From N. R. Carlson, *Physiology of Behavior*, 8th ed. Published by Allyn and Bacon. © 1998 by Pearson Education. Adapted by permission of the publisher.

which are sent through nerve cells along the **auditory nerve** (the eighth cranial nerve) to the brain, where the signals are perceived as tones. When these hair cells vibrate, they also create very low-level sounds called **otoacoustic emissions (OAEs)**. The ability to recognize OAEs with special computer equipment makes it possible to diagnose deafness in newborns and then implement critical early intervention services (National Center for Hearing Assessment and Management [NCHAM], 2008). For more information about universal hearing screenings and assessments, go to www.infanthearing.org.

Obstructions or damage anywhere along this path (from the outer ear, through the middle ear, to the inner ear) can result in hearing loss. The type of loss and how it is treated vary depending on its severity and on where the problem occurs. The impact is also affected by the individual's age at the time of the damage. In summary, the three parts of the hearing mechanism are

- *outer ear:* the pinna and auditory canal;
- *middle ear:* the eardrum, Eustachian tube, and ossicles (hammer, anvil, and stirrup); and
- *inner ear:* the cochlea, its membranes and hair cells, and the semicircular canals.

auditory nerve The eighth cranial nerve; carries messages from the hearing mechanisms to the brain

otoacoustic emissions (OAEs) The low level of sound produced when the hair cells inside the inner ear vibrate

Types of Hearing Loss

There are two general types of hearing loss:

- Conductive hearing loss
- Sensorineural hearing loss

conductive hearing loss Hearing impairment due to damage or obstruction to the outer or middle ear that obstructs transfer of sound to the inner ear

Blockage or damage to the outer or middle ear that prevents sound waves from traveling (being conducted) to the inner ear is called a **conductive hearing loss**. Generally, someone with a conductive hearing loss has a mild to moderate hearing disability. Some conductive hearing losses are temporary; in fact, we have all probably experienced a conductive hearing loss at some point in our lives. For example, you may have experienced a temporary loss of hearing as a consequence of a change in air pressure when flying in an airplane or riding in a car in the mountains.

Children often experience head colds and ear infections that result in a temporary loss of conductive hearing. Therefore, it is likely that on any given day, 20% of elementary school students have a mild conductive hearing loss, and some 80% of all children experience such hearing problems at some time between kindergarten and fifth grade (Gordon-Langbein & Metzinger, 2000). If the hearing loss was caused by a head cold, the hearing difficulties disappear once the ear infection clears up. Many conductive hearing losses that would otherwise *not* be considered temporary can usually be corrected with hearing aids or through surgery or other medical techniques.

sensorineural hearing loss Hearing impairment due to damage to the inner ear or the auditory nerve

When damage to the inner ear, its hair cells, or the auditory nerve causes the problem, it is referred to as a **sensorineural hearing loss**. Some people refer to this type of hearing loss as nerve deafness. The greater the damage to the hair cells, the more severe the hearing loss (National Institute on Deafness and Other Communication Disorders [NIDCD], 2007c). Sensorineural hearing losses are much more difficult to correct than conductive hearing losses, and they are less common in children. Individuals affected by a sensorineural loss are able to hear different frequencies at different intensity levels; their hearing losses are not flat or even. Teachers of students with sensorineural losses need to understand that hearing aids can have mixed results.

Degree of Hearing Loss

Hearing loss is often categorized as follows (MacKenzie, 2007):

- *Mild hearing loss (21–40 decibels [dB]):* Only speech that is soft or is produced at a distance is difficult to hear or understand.
- *Moderate hearing loss (41–55 dB):* Typical conversational speech is hard to follow.
- *Moderately severe hearing loss (56–70 dB):* Only loud speech can be heard.
- *Severe hearing loss (71–90 dB):* Even loud speech is hard to understand.
- *Profound hearing loss (91 dB +):* Considered deaf, the individual must use assistive listening devices to understand information presented orally.

residual hearing The amount of functional hearing a person has

Classifying hearing loss in these terms is difficult and does not always accurately represent the individual's ability to hear or the type of accommodations needed. Why might this be so? The answer rests partly in the amount and type of **residual hearing**—how much functional hearing—the person has. If the amount of loss is considerable and is predominantly in the sound ranges of speech, using oral communication will be more difficult than if the loss occurs outside the speech bands (more details about this are provided in the Assessment section of this chapter). If the loss is conductive, the pattern is "flat"—that is, there is about the same amount of loss across the frequencies of different speech sounds; but if the loss is sensorineural, the ability to understand sounds (to hear) is uneven. Regardless, it is important to know that with a mild loss, the individual can still hear nearly all speech sounds and can hear most conversations (MacKenzie, 2007). At the other end of the continuum, most people with profound hearing loss have hearing abilities that provide them with little useful hearing even if they use hearing aids.

Individuals with hearing loss are also grouped by their functional hearing abilities. Here's how to think about a functional organizational system: People who are hard of hearing can process information from sound, usually with the help of a hearing aid. Nearly all people who are deaf perceive some sound, but they cannot use hearing as their primary way to gain information.

Age of Onset

As you have learned, the type and degree of hearing loss are important factors in the impact of hearing losses, but possibly most important is the age when the hearing loss occurs. As with most other disabilities, hearing loss can be congenital—occurring at or before birth—or acquired (adventitious)—occurring after birth. But, with hearing losses the more important consideration is whether the hearing loss occurred before or after the individual developed oral language. Individuals who are **prelingually deaf** become deaf before they learn to speak and understand language. They are born deaf, are identified late, or lose their hearing as infants. Their inability to hear language seriously affects their abilities to communicate with others and to learn academic subjects taught later in school. It is estimated that deafness in some 70% of prelingually deaf children is genetics (Nance & Dodson, 2007). Although the number is small, some 18% of prelingually deaf children have at least one deaf parent (Gallaudet Research Institute [GRI], 2006). Children in this group typically learn to communicate during the normal developmental period. However, instead of learning oral communication skills, many learn through a combination of manual communication (sign language) and oral language (Gleason & Ratner, 2009). Individuals who experience profound hearing loss after they have learned to speak and understand language are often referred to as being **postlingually deaf**. Many are able to retain their abilities to use speech and to communicate with others orally. And, more and more of these individuals are profiting from cochlear implants (Royer, 2008).

prelingually deaf Having lost the ability to hear before developing language

postlingually deaf Having lost the ability to hear after developing language; acquired or adventitious deafness

Characteristics

It's hard to generalize about students with hearing loss. They are all individuals with different learning styles and abilities, but they do share one characteristic: Their ability to hear is limited. As we have noted, the severity of the hearing loss and the age at which the loss occurred determine how well a person will be able to interact with others orally. IDEA '04 stresses the importance of the communication needs and style of students with hearing loss; those important points are summarized in What IDEA '04 Says About Considering the Communication Needs of Students with Hearing Loss. Another factor is whether the individual has coexisting disabilities. Some 40% of students with hearing impairments have additional disabilities (Vernon, 2007). For example, trauma before or at birth often results in more than one disability. However, students whose deafness is inherited tend not to have multiple disabilities. The needs of students who are deaf differ from the needs of those who are hard of hearing. Also, among those who are deaf, two distinct groups exist: those who are Deaf and those who are deaf. Accordingly, we will discuss the characteristics of members of these two groups separately.

Students Who Are Members of the Deaf Community

In America, Deaf persons are members of the Deaf community, use ASL as their primary language, and typically do not use oral language as their means of communication. In other countries, Deaf communities exist but they use their own sign language as their means of communication. For example, in Britain they use BSL, in Greece GSL, and so on. Deaf communities around the world report a sense of empowerment, belonging, and optimism (Davey, 2005; Nikolaraizi & Makri, 2004/2005). Furthermore, diverse members of the Deaf community often share determination and a positive outlook; this underscores the truly multicultural nature of deafness from a minority group perspective (Anderson & Miller, 2004/2005). As we consider Deaf people, their culture, and their language, think about how being a member of the Deaf community affects the lives of these individuals.

Deaf Culture   Members of the Deaf community consider the Deaf a minority group much like ethnic and racial minorities in this country (Branson & Miller, 2002; Zazove et al., 2004). To them, deafness is not a disability but, rather, one aspect of their lives that binds them together as a minority group rich in culture, history, language, and the arts. The language of the American Deaf community is ASL, which is used in all aspects of their culture. For example, plays are written in ASL and performed by Deaf theater groups around the world. ASL is also the language of a folk literature that has developed over the years. This community unites in many ways by coming together socially and for the purpose of advocacy, such as when they began the Deaf President Now Movement in 1988 and to denounce the appointment of the successor to I. King Jordan in 2006.

For many Deaf people, being **Deaf of Deaf** (being born Deaf of Deaf parents) or even being a **CODA** (child of a Deaf adult) is a source of considerable pride (Soloman, 1994). Although these individuals clearly represent a minority within a minority, life can be substantially easier for them. They learn sign language as their native language, which they develop naturally just as hearing babies develop oral language (Gleason & Ratner, 2009). For these individuals, their deafness is a language difference, not a disability. Like those who were members of the Deaf communities that thrived on Martha's Vineyard during the 1800s, they themselves are part of the Deaf community (Van Cleve, 2007). Some Deaf people do not want to live in the hearing world. In fact, to the delight of many and the criticism of others, some Deaf families are even looking to re-create the separateness of the "old days" on Martha's Vineyard by creating a city just for them, with all of the accommodations and comforts universally available (Szalay, 2005).

Deaf of Deaf Members of the Deaf community who are prelingually deaf and have at least one parent who is Deaf

CODA A child of a Deaf adult who may or may not be Deaf

ASL: Deaf Language   ASL or American Sign Language is the fifth-most commonly studied foreign language on college campuses across the country (Davey, 2005). It is a complete and complex language and is not a translation of the English. Not to be confused with ASL, **signed English** is a manual communication translation of English. ASL has its own rules for grammar, punctuation, and sentence order. Also, as we have noted, ASL is not a universal language. For example, British Sign Language (BSL) is very different from ASL, which is the language of the Deaf community and the focal point for Deaf culture in the United States. To most people who are Deaf, it is a second language. Only about 5% of Deaf individuals are born of Deaf parents and learn ASL as their native language. The vast majority of others are assimilated into the culture later in life, often at residential schools for the Deaf.

signed English Translation of English into a form of manual communication

Students with Profound Hearing Loss

The second group of deaf individuals have profound hearing loss, but they are not members of the Deaf community, do not use ASL as their native language, and use oral communication when others are talking and express themselves orally. Instructionally, these two groups are very different from each other. What about the majority of the prelingually deaf? Some 83% of deaf children have two hearing parents (GRI, 2006). The effort to develop language, either oral or manual, is considerable. But, the earlier the diagnosis, the better the outcomes for speech, language, and academic achievement (Herer, Knightly, & Steinberg, 2007; White, 2007).

Academic Achievement   A long-term concern about deaf and hard of hearing students is their low academic achievement, particularly in the area of reading (Dillon & Pisoni, 2006; Moores, 2001). The attainment of good reading skills is important to hard of hearing and deaf individuals, so they can (Cuculick & Kelly, 2003)

- profit from captions for television and film,
- use the Internet and communicate through e-mail,
- do well in high school and college, and
- obtain and succeed at higher-paying jobs when in the workforce.

Achievement data across many years consistently show that these students graduate from high school with an average reading level at about the fourth grade, leaving them unable to read most newspapers, which are written at least at the fifth-grade level (Dillon & Pisoni, 2006; Luft, 2008; Moores, 2001). Although they represent less than 10% of deaf children, the academic achievement of those born of at least one Deaf parent, who learn ASL as their native language, typically do *not* have academic problems (GRI, 2006). Also, early results indicate that many students with cochlear implants also have achievement levels far surpassing deaf and hard of hearing students of some 20 years ago (Dillon & Pisoni, 2006; Herer et. al., 2007). Of course, it is very recent that infants and young children have received cochlear implants, so it is really too early to make sweeping generalizations. In addition, academic achievement levels are higher because educators now focus their instruction on reading and other academic areas instead of primarily teaching language-related skills.

Speech Abilities   Being able to hear is related to the ability to speak intelligibly. Although there are some remarkable exceptions, as a general rule of thumb, as the degree of hearing loss increases, the intelligibility of speech decreases, even after years of therapy (Gleason & Ratner, 2009; Svirsky et al., 2002). When investigators compared two groups of children between the ages of 5 and 10—those with profound hearing loss and those with mild to severe hearing loss—the evidence was unmistakable. The speech of those with profound losses was not intelligible. For those with mild to severe losses, the speech of 82% was intelligible (Yoshinaga-Itano & Sedey, 2000).

However, because of universal infant hearing screenings, more infants and toddlers are receiving early intervention services than ever before (White, 2006). Early identification allows for infants, only a few months old, to be fitted with hearing aids and for parents to make decisions about cochlear implants when their child is still an infant (Warner-Czyz, Davis, & Morrison, 2005). Infants who receive early intervention have much better results than those who do not (White, 2007). However, it is important to understand that attaining high levels of intelligible speech does not come automatically to members of either group.

Students Who Are Hard of Hearing

Students who are hard of hearing have milder losses than their peers who are deaf. Typically, they have conductive hearing losses, which are more easily helped with a hearing aid. Unfortunately, however, these students are easily overlooked or their disability minimized. It is important for educators to understand that students who are hard of hearing find it more difficult than their classmates without disabilities to learn vocabulary, grammar, word order, and language (National Dissemination Center for Children with Disabilities [NICHCY], 2004). Even a mild hearing loss in one ear can cause a student to struggle academically (Haller & Montgomery, 2004; Tharpe, 2004). One reason may be the extra effort it takes to listen carefully to the teacher, take notes, and process what is being presented. Another reason is that we often don't realize that a little difference in hearing ability makes a big difference in what is understood. For example, in a noisy classroom, even a loss of 16 dB (just within the range of what is considered normal hearing) results in missing up to 10% of what a teacher says a mere 3 feet away from the student with the hearing loss (Harrington,

TIPS for Classroom Management

MAKING ADJUSTMENTS FOR EASE OF HEARING AND SEEING SPEAKERS

- Place the student as close to the speaker as possible.
- Instead of a blackboard, use an overhead projector or a computer with a projection system so the speaker can face the class when talking. (Be sure there is no glare obstructing the projection.)
- Reduce background noise as much as possible.
- Do not stand with direct light behind you.
- For class discussions, make certain the student knows who is about to speak, and ensure that he or she is able to see each individual who is talking.
- For class discussions, arrange students' chairs in a circle so the student can see everyone's face.

2003). Without amplification, those with losses of 35 to 40 dB—clearly in the range of a mild loss—may miss 50% of what the teacher or classmates say during discussions! Clearly, these students should be supported with many visuals, such as pictures, graphs, charts, and written notes about the topic of discussion, as well as with special seating arrangements so they can see everyone who is taking turns speaking. Tips for Classroom Management provides some suggestions about helping students who are hard of hearing to profit more from the general education curriculum.

Prevalence

Hearing loss is the most common birth defect in America today, but it is still a low-incidence disability among children (Alexander Graham Bell Association, 2008). However, its prevalence is greatest among older Americans because hearing loss is associated with age. Estimates are that almost half of people over the age of 70 have hearing losses (Nance & Dodson, 2007).

Substantially less than 1% (0.14%) of all students receive special education services through the federal hearing impairments category (Office of Special Education Programs [OSEP], 2008). However, these data do not reflect the actual number of students with hearing loss. The reasons relate to how different states report their students with disabilities and how they actually define the problem. While some students only have a hearing loss, it is often combined with other conditions or disabilities. Remember, the federal government only reports students by their primary disability. For example, some 75% of individuals with Down syndrome have a hearing impairment, typically a conductive hearing loss (Schauer, 2005). However, these students are usually reported as having intellectual disabilities through the federal mental retardation category. Most students with a hearing loss and another disability are usually reported in the multiple disabilities category, and not in the federal hearing impairments category. Also, the government's counts do not include students with hearing loss who do not need special education services because hearing aids allow them to hear well enough to participate in typical classroom activities without additional assistance. Considering these factors, the number of students who are deaf and hard of hearing is underestimated.

Causes and Prevention

It is not a surprise to learn that hearing loss can result from illness, injury, or heredity. Teachers should understand the causes of hearing loss, because the type and reason for the loss can have a bearing on the accommodations used for effective instruction. Of course, understanding the cause also helps design preventive measures.

Causes

While the cause of hearing loss in many children is not known, more and more genetic reasons are being identified. Some 70% of infants born with congenital deafness have a genetic cause for their hearing problems (Nance & Dodson, 2007). Sometimes deafness in infants is caused by disease or infection, such as congenital cytomegalovirus (CMV) infection. Affecting about 2% of all newborns, in rare cases CMV, a herpes virus, can cause mild to profound sensorineural hearing losses and other disabilities as well. The four most common *known* causes for children's deafness and hearing problems, in order of prevalence, are as follows:

1. *Heredity and genetics.* The most common known causes of deafness and profound hearing loss in children, documented as being responsible for more than 150 different types of deafness, have a hereditary origin. Genetic reasons for deafness are often congenital and result in sensorineural hearing problems. Most children whose deafness is inherited are less likely to have multiple disabilities.

2. *Meningitis.* The second-most common known cause of childhood deafness is a disease that affects the central nervous system (specifically the meninges, the coverings of the brain and spinal cord, and their circulating fluid). Most cases that involve a hearing loss are bacterial infections rather than the more lethal viral meningitis. This disease is the most common cause of students' postnatal deafness. It is a major cause of acquired profound sensorineural hearing losses that are not present at birth. These hearing losses may occur after the individual has developed some speech and language.

3. *Otitis media.* Infections of the middle ear result in an accumulation of fluid behind the eardrum that interrupt the process of hearing. The condition can be corrected and treated with antibiotics and other medical procedures. For many years, it was thought to be a major cause of language impairment for infants and toddlers who experienced chronic and persistent infections because their hearing of good language models was interrupted. Newer information does not support this claim (Herer, et. al., 2007). However, chronic and untreated otitis media can damage the eardrum and cause a permanent mild to moderate, conductive hearing loss (Centers for Disease Control [CDC], 2007). Typically these individuals fall into the hard of hearing group, have conductive hearing losses, and profit from the use of hearing aids.

4. *Noise.* **Noise-induced hearing loss (NIHL)** is the reason for hearing loss in over 22 million teenagers and adults (NIDCD, 2007c). Perhaps what is most shocking about NIHL is the level of noise, sustained over a period of time, that can cause serious hearing problems, even deafness. It occurs slowly, across years of exposure, without any pain or awareness. Figure 10.2 shows the decibel levels of common sounds. While the one-time sound of an explosion can result in deafness, exposure to noise of 75 dB for sustained periods of time can also damage the ear's hair cells (see Figure 10.1 again). Traffic noise is typically at 85 dB. The greater the damage to the hair cells, the greater the hearing loss.

noise-induced hearing loss (NIHL) A major cause of sensorineural hearing loss due to damage to the hair cells from sustained noise in the environment

Prevention

Because NIHL is not well understood by the public and is 100% preventable, we want to raise your attention to the dangers of excessive noise in the environment. Teachers can make a difference and protect their students by raising their awareness about the dangers of noise and helping them know the noise or decibel levels produced by

Figure 10.2 • Decibel Levels of Noise in American Environments

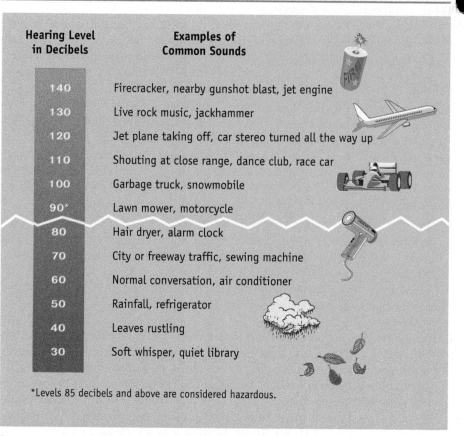

Hearing Level in Decibels	Examples of Common Sounds
140	Firecracker, nearby gunshot blast, jet engine
130	Live rock music, jackhammer
120	Jet plane taking off, car stereo turned all the way up
110	Shouting at close range, dance club, race car
100	Garbage truck, snowmobile
90*	Lawn mower, motorcycle
80	Hair dryer, alarm clock
70	City or freeway traffic, sewing machine
60	Normal conversation, air conditioner
50	Rainfall, refrigerator
40	Leaves rustling
30	Soft whisper, quiet library

*Levels 85 decibels and above are considered hazardous.

Source: U.S. Congress Select Committee on Children, Youth, and Families.

events in the environment. Students should know that the sound levels of a rock concert often reach 125 dB. Sound from an iPod or MP3 player is proving to be a major source of NIHL. Young males are more likely to acquire NIHL because they frequently engage in activities such as mowing the lawn, firing a gun, riding a motorcycle, and fixing a car engine.

As with NIHL, many other cases of childhood hearing loss are preventable. For example, maternal rubella (German measles) was once a major cause of deafness in newborns; in 1972, it was responsible for almost 11% of known causes of deafness, but by 1998, immunizations caused that rate to drop to 1%. Vaccines are available to prevent meningitis, but no national immunization program protects all children from its ravages.

Overcoming Challenges: Hearing Aids and Cochlear Implants

Technology and assistive devices can be credited with much of the improved access to mainstream society experienced by people with disabilities. Improvements in technology that help people hear sounds are advancing at a rapid pace. Also, more and more assistive devices are now available that help people compensate for significant hearing losses. Such assistive technologies—telecommunication devices, computerized speech-to-text translations, and alerting devices—are discussed later in this chapter in the Technology section.

assistive listening devices (ALDs) Equipment (e.g., hearing aids, audio loops, FM transmission devices) that helps improve use of residual hearing

Most deaf and hard of hearing students come to school using some sort of assistive listening device. **Assistive listening devices** help people with hearing losses by increasing the amplification of sounds in the environment, including others' speech. Hearing aids and cochlear implants both help people hear sounds, but they are very different from each other in the ways they work (NIDCD, 2007a, 2007b).

Hearing aids amplify sounds, so the damaged ear can detect the sound and then process it for meaning. Cochlear implants bypass the portion of the ear that is damaged and directly stimulate the auditory nerve. Teachers need to understand these assistive listening devices and what to expect from them, so we talk about each in the following sections. The federal government also discusses both devices in its regulations of IDEA '04. What IDEA '04 Says About Hearing Aids and Cochlear Implants gives some specific information about these federal guidelines.

Hearing Aids Most conductive losses can be corrected with medicine or surgery. So, students who use **hearing aids** typically have sensorineural hearing losses. Hearing aids amplify sound so that the person can hear more easily. These assistive listening devices generally have three basic parts (NIDCD, 2007b):

- *Microphone:* receives sound waves and converts them to electric signals
- *Amplifier:* increases the power of the signals
- *Speaker:* sends sounds to the ear

Advances in hearing aid technology have changed the lives of people with hearing losses. Compare today's hearing aids with the hearing trumpet used by Dorothy Brett, the artist whose work is shown at the beginning of this chapter. Today's hearing aids allow deaf and hard of hearing people to participate in family conversations, discussions at school, and all aspects of daily life. There are two different types of hearing aids:

- Analog
- Digital

Analog hearing aids make all sounds—background noise as well as speech sounds—louder, but digital aids are able to adjust loudness to individual's hearing profiles. First introduced in 1987, **digital hearing aids** automatically adjust volume by amplifying sounds only to the degree necessary to compensate for the loss at each frequency of sound (Rickets, 2008). The first versions were not very popular because of their size and weight, but today's versions have many advantages over the earlier versions of hearing aids, including having directional microphones, background noise and feedback reduction, and speech enhancement. Both types come in four different styles:

- Behind the ear (BTE)
- In the ear (ITE)
- In the canal (ITC)
- Completely in the canal (CIC)

Teachers should recognize that most children and teenagers do not select BTEs because of their obvious appearance. Because of peer pressure, they select a type of hearing aid that is less effective but is hidden in the ear. Teachers also need to know that hearing aids are very expensive. Although the most expensive device is not always "the best," a good hearing aid often comes at great expense to families (Ross, 2008). Many insurance companies do not cover hearing aids, and if they do, the copayment responsibilities are substantial. IDEA '04 can help families with the costs of hearing aids for infants, toddlers, and schoolchildren; however, the aids remain the property of the government, and often the approved hearing aid is analog instead of digital (Hager, 2007). So, teachers can make a difference by helping to protect the aid from damage, teaching students responsibility, and implementing strategies so the aid is not lost.

What IDEA '04 Says About . . .

Hearing Aids and Cochlear Implants

Through its assistive technology and related services provisions, IDEA '04 specifically addresses the use of hearing aids, while indirectly addressing cochlear implants. For example, districts must ensure that

- assistive technology devices and/or services are made available to a child with a hearing disability, and
- hearing aids worn in school by children with hearing impairments are functioning properly.

Furthermore,

- the term *assistive technology device* does not include a surgically implanted medical device or its replacement;
- the term *related services* does not include a surgically implanted medical device, nor does it include optimization of functioning, maintenance, or replacement of the device.

---

hearing aids Assistive listening devices that intensify sound

analog hearing aids Assistive listening devices that amplify all sounds uniformly, including background noise and speech sounds regardless of individuals' hearing profiles

digital hearing aids Assistive listening devices that amplify sound according to individuals' hearing profiles

**SIGN? WHAT SIGN? SPEAK UP, MY HEARING AID
ISN'T WORKING!**

cochlear implant A microprocessor, surgically placed in the hearing mechanism, that replaces the cochlea so people with sensorineural hearing loss can perceive sounds

Cochlear Implants Cochlear implants are surgically implanted and help those with sensorineural hearing losses. These devices have four important parts (NIDCD, 2007a):

- *Microphone;* picks up sounds from the environment
- *Speech processor:* selects and organizes sounds from the microphone
- *Transmitter/receiver/stimulator:* receives signals from processor and converts them to electric impulses
- *Electrode array:* collects impulses and sends to regions of the auditory nerve

Figure 10.3 shows a typical cochlear implant, which converts acoustic information to electrical signals that stimulate the individual's remaining auditory nerve fibers.

Because data indicate that speech and oral language outcomes are better when young individuals with profound deafness receive implants as infants, more and more children now receive **cochlear implants** before their first birthday (Dettman et al., 2007). Typically, children receive one implant, but recently more and more are receiving bilateral cochlear implants because it is believed that sound localization is better with two implants (Bohnert et al., 2006).

Cochlear implants were first used with adults, and then a few years later, in 1990, children over the age of 2 became eligible. The government estimates that some 23,000 adults and 15,500 children have these implants (NIDCD, 2007a). For adults who had speech before their hearing became impaired, cochlear implants allow them to hear and understand sounds once again. For them, the turnaround from silence to communicating with others, even talking to friends on the telephone when there is no possibility of using visual cues about what is being said, is almost miraculous (Royer, 2008). However, for children who never had functional hearing, and therefore did not develop meaning for sounds in the environment, cochlear

Figure 10.3 • Cochlear Implant

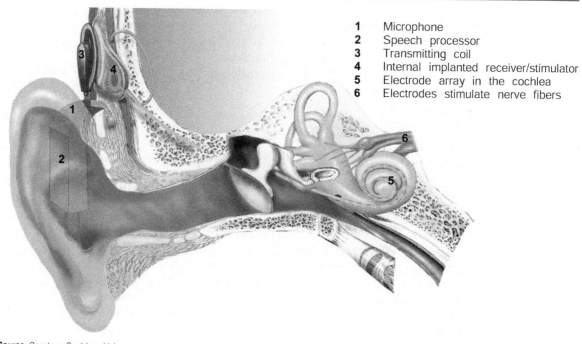

1	Microphone
2	Speech processor
3	Transmitting coil
4	Internal implanted receiver/stimulator
5	Electrode array in the cochlea
6	Electrodes stimulate nerve fibers

Source: Courtesy Cochlear Ltd.

implants are not the same "cure" for hearing loss or deafness (Med-El Corporation, 2008). These individuals face considerable challenges developing speech, which is neither guaranteed nor an easy developmental process. Researchers are now learning that many individuals who received cochlear implants during early childhood rely on both sign language and oral speech to communicate with others (Moores, 2008). Teachers need to understand that students with cochlear implants may have speech that is difficult to understand and that they will be receiving intensive speech and language therapy in addition to their study of the general education curriculum. Teachers also need to be alert to changes in these students' abilities to hear in the classroom and on the playground because children's bodies change and the implants often need adjustments (Med-El Corporation, 2008).

Outcomes of cochlear implants for children do not always meet families' expectations (Zaidman-Zaot & Most, 2005). Some believe that the implants will resolve the hearing loss entirely. Such is not typically the case with prelingually deaf children. What parents need to understand is that the rehabilitation process is often long and arduous, particularly if the child has multiple disabilities. Even for students without additional disabilities, it takes years of intensive speech and language therapy to develop correct use of vowels and consonant sounds (Warner-Czyz et al., 2005). Of course, the group is small and still very young, but the speech, language, and academic achievement results of children who received cochlear implants before their first birthday are encouraging (Herer et al., 2007; Ripper, 2008).

Assessment

As you have learned, sound is caused by perception of the vibration of molecules propagated through some medium such as air, water, or wires. Two qualities of sound are measured in the assessment process: frequency and intensity. The **frequency of sound** is the number of vibrations per second. High frequencies are perceived through our ears as high pitch or tone; low frequencies are perceived as low pitch or deep sounds. **Hertz (Hz)** is the unit in which frequency is measured. The normal ear hears sounds that range from approximately 20 Hz to 20,000 Hz; speech sounds fall about in the middle of the human hearing range (between 250 Hz and 4,000 Hz). Those of you who have some knowledge of music might find Sheila Lowenbraun's (1995) explanation of hertz helpful. The frequency of middle C on the piano is approximately 250 Hz. The next vertical line on the audiogram, 500 Hz, is approximately one octave above middle C; 1,000 is two octaves above middle C; and so on. (See the scale in Figure 10.4 on page 349.) Humans cannot perceive some sounds, whatever their hearing abilities. For example, some dog whistles use high frequencies that are beyond humans' hearing range.

The second sound quality assessed is **sound intensity**, or loudness. **Decibels (dB)** are the units employed to measure the intensity of sounds. Softer, quieter sounds have lower decibel measurements; louder sounds have higher decibel numbers. A decibel level of 125 or greater is painful to the average person. Decibel levels ranging from 0 to 120 are used to test how well an individual can hear different frequencies; a child with normal hearing should be able to perceive sounds at 0 dB. The scale used to assess hearing has been adjusted so that 0 indicates no loss and numbers greater than 0 indicate the degree or amount of loss. Small numbers indicate mild losses; large numbers indicate moderate to severe or profound losses.

Early Identification: Universal Newborn Hearing Screening

Only a few years ago it was common that young children who were born with profound hearing loss were not identified until they were 2 to 3 years of age or not even until they came to school for kindergarten (Commission on the Education of the Deaf, 1988). Today, some 95% of these youngsters are identified at birth (White, 2007). This opportunity for early intervention, including early use of hearing aids,

frequency of sound The number of vibrations per second of molecules through some medium, like air, water, or wires, causing sound

hertz (Hz) The unit of measure for sound frequency

sound intensity Loudness

decibel (dB) The unit of measure for intensity of sound

is the result of **universal newborn hearing screening** being implemented across the nation (NCHAM, 2008). Early detection is cost-effective, reliable, and produces positive results. It has long been known that those identified before they are 6 months old experience half the delays of those identified after they are 18 months old (Yoshinaga-Itano & Apuzzo, 1998).

Prereferral: Hearing Screenings

As described in Chapter 2, the prereferral stage in the special education identification process is important to ensure that students with disabilities are identified correctly and quickly. Students with mild to moderate hearing losses are frequently overlooked and are often incorrectly thought to have an attention or learning problem. Some states and school districts screen all of their students for both hearing and vision problems, but not all do. Regardless, teachers should be attentive and should refer questionable students to an SLP for an initial assessment. If a student needs further diagnosis by an **audiologist**—a specialist in the assessment of hearing abilities—a multidisciplinary team will be put into place. But it is important to remember that many students with mild hearing losses go unnoticed and that the educational (and social) results can be tragic. With quick action, students whose hearing problems can be at least partially solved by the use of a hearing aid can profit from classroom instruction. Those students whose wait for services was long because their hearing loss was not identified early can still profit from the services of SLPs and from therapy for language development. Thus, even high school teachers should be attentive to possible hearing problems among their students.

Identification: Auditory Assessments

Earlier we reviewed how infants' hearing is assessed. Different methods are used for babies and adults. For children and adults, audiologists use **pure sounds**—sound waves of specific frequencies—at various combinations of hertz and decibels and also at various bands of pitch and loudness. These assessments are conducted in soundproof rooms so that distractions such as those found in classrooms are eliminated. They also use special equipment, such as an **audiometer**, an instrument that produces sounds at precise frequencies and intensities. The results of these audiology assessments are plotted on an **audiogram**, which is a grid or graph. Along the top of the graph are hertz levels; the vertical lines represent different levels of sound frequency, in hertz. Each ear is tested separately. A hearing threshold is determined by noting when the person first perceives the softest sound at each frequency level. Sometimes a hearing threshold is reported only for the better ear, and sometimes an average of an individual's scores at three different frequencies (500, 1,000, 2,000 Hz) is used. Any score falling below the 0-dB line on an audiogram represents some degree of hearing loss, because the audiometer is set to indicate that a person has no hearing loss at 0 dB for various hertz levels.

Most children's hearing is assessed by the **air conduction audiometry method**, which uses pure-tone sounds generated by an audiometer. Earphones are placed over the child's ears, and the child raises his or her hand when hearing a sound. Such testing is usually done by a pediatrician at a well-child checkup or by a school nurse. When a hearing loss is suspected, audiologists use an additional procedure to determine whether the loss was due to damage in the outer, middle, or inner ear. The **bone conduction audiometry method** uses a vibrator placed on the forehead so that sound can bypass the outer and middle ear and go directly to the inner ear. When the bone conduction thresholds are normal (near 0 dB) and the air conduction thresholds are abnormal, the hearing loss is conductive. Now let's review the audiograms of two children, Travis and Heather. Because Travis and Heather were suspected of having hearing losses, the audiologist used both the air conduction and the bone conduction methods.

Travis's audiogram, shown in Figure 10.4, indicates that he has a conductive hearing loss. The loss, of about 40 dB, is in the mild range with the amplification of hear-

Figure 10.4 • Travis's Audiogram Showing a Conductive Hearing Loss

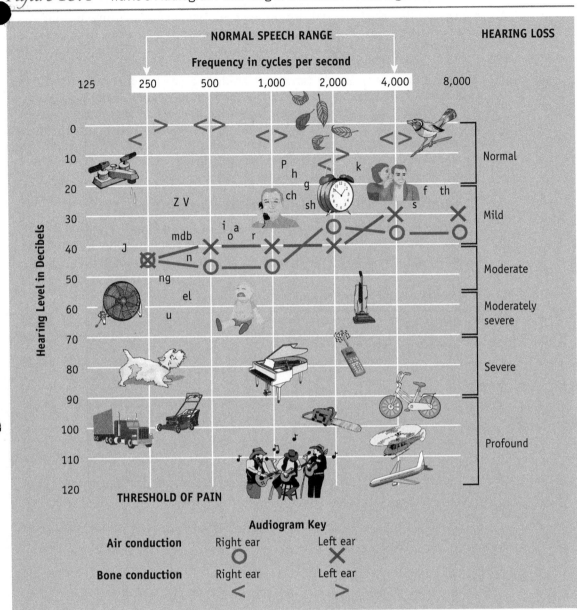

Source: Adapted from *Hearing in Children* (5th ed., p. 18) by J. L. Northern and M. P. Downs, 2002, Baltimore: Lippincott, Williams and Wilkins. Adapted with permission.

ing aids. Note how flat the profile is for Travis's air conduction test. However, the bone conduction test reveals that when the middle ear is bypassed, his hearing is much closer to 0 dB. Travis's hearing loss either is temporary or can be corrected through surgery or other medical treatment. Note also that different codes are used for Travis's right and left ears: O for the right ear and X for the left ear. Remember that each ear is tested independently. Travis's hearing threshold for each ear is marked on his audiogram. Most children with normal hearing have auditory thresholds (the points when they first perceive sound) at approximately 0 dB; Travis's thresholds are considerably below 0. Travis's hearing abilities are plotted on an audiogram form designed by Northern and Downs (2002). This form graphically shows where various speech and other sounds occur and helps us visualize how sounds at different frequencies come together to convey meaning. If the individual's hearing threshold falls below the picture, then that person cannot perceive the sound pictured. Without a hearing aid, Travis, for example, can perceive only a few sounds (/ng/, /el/, and /u/).

Heather has a sensorineural hearing loss, as indicated in her audiogram, which is shown in Figure 10.5. A sensorineural hearing loss is caused by a defect in or damage to the inner ear and can be more serious than conductive hearing losses. Heather has a 30-dB loss. Note the similarity between her scores from the air conduction and bone conduction tests. Heather's hearing was also tested with her hearing aids on. Note that with the use of aids, Heather's hearing loss is no longer so serious; it is now at a mild functional level. The shaded area on this audiogram (sometimes called the speech banana because of its shape) marks the area where speech sounds fall. Because Heather's hearing abilities lie above this area on her audiogram (see the top of the audiogram), the audiologist knows that Heather can hear the speech sounds at the sound intensities measured during the hearing assessment. Along the side of the graph are intensity levels measured in decibels, so horizontal lines represent different levels of loudness.

Evaluation: State- and Districtwide Assessments

Like other students with disabilities, the vast majority of those with hearing loss participate in the annual assessment required by NCLB. Students who are hard of hearing join their classmates without disabilities in these evaluations, but they use the

Figure 10.5 • Heather's Audiogram Showing a Sensorineural Hearing Loss

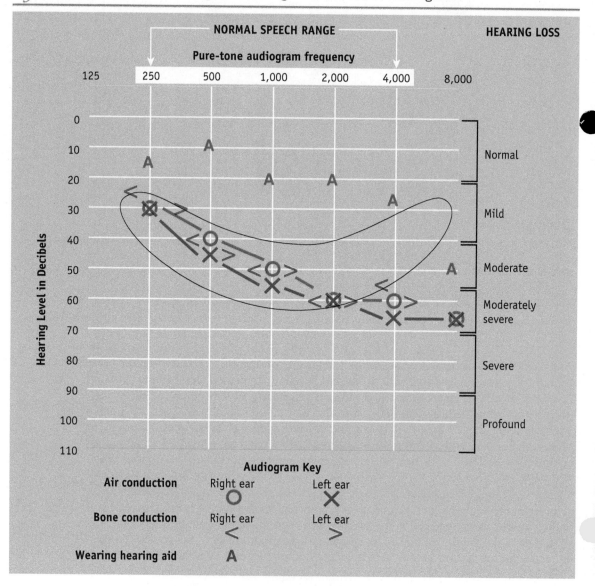

accommodations that are specified in their IEPs and are used during instruction. Some testing accommodations for both deaf and hard of hearing students might include written directions that augment the oral directions given by the teacher about how to take the test, directions delivered in sign by an interpreter, or instructions given individually. Also, many of these students are eligible to receive modified or alternate assessments (see again Chapters 1 and 2 for reviews).

Early Intervention

Early intervention positively affects the lifelong outcomes of deaf and hard of hearing children (Nittrouer & Burton, 2003; Marschark, 2001). With more and more states adopting universal hearing screening for infants, early intervention is becoming more commonplace (Hager, 2007). Although there is still room for improvement in the goal of identifying and providing services to all infants with hearing loss, more have IFSPs and receive family-centered early intervention services for children from birth to 2 years of age, and the results are astonishing (Vernon, 2007). So, while preschool makes a difference, even earlier intervention makes an even bigger difference in the achievement, speech, and language abilities of these youngsters (White, 2006).

Why are early identification and the resulting intervention services so important? Here are a few reasons:

- Early identification allows children to be fitted with hearing aids as soon as possible, which can be as early as 4 weeks old, or to be scheduled for cochlear implants during infancy, before their first birthday.
- Early intervention, before the age of 6 months, pays off in better reading achievement and speech abilities in later years.
- Preschool programs allow students with hearing losses to develop language at the right developmental periods of their lives.
- Early intervention programs help families better understand and meet the very special needs of their family members.

Evidence connecting language development and academic achievement for deaf students is mounting. You just learned that deaf and hard of hearing students have significantly low academic achievement, but these old data may well not hold true for today's preschoolers who receive the benefits of early identification and ensuing early intervention services (Marschark, 2001; Nittrouer & Burton, 2003; White 2006, 2007). Deaf children of Deaf parents learn sign language during their infancy as their native language. They "babble" with their hands at about the same time that hearing infants make babbling sounds. They produce two-word utterances at about the same time as their peers who do not have hearing losses. These Deaf youngsters learn English as a second language. By the time they reach school age, most of them are reading at two grade levels above deaf children of hearing parents (Marschark, 1993).

As we mentioned, family-centered early intervention programs out-perform preschools (Vernon, 2007). What is key to such success is communication between professionals and families. Professionals must be sensitive to families' experiences and cultures. The story told in this chapter's Considering Culture illustrates the importance of forming partnerships with families on the basis of respect and understanding.

Teaching Students with Hearing Loss

A full array of educational services should be available to every deaf or hard of hearing student. Multidisciplinary services typically provided are delivered by an array of professionals: audiologists, SLPs, interpreters, and teachers of the deaf. For those with multiple disabilities, they also usually include services provided by OTs and PTs. The education these students receive reflects many different instructional methods, accommodations, and adjustments to the classroom routine. Clearly, each student's needs are unique, as is the education they receive.

Children learn and practice many skills through imaginary play. Dolls, like this signing Barbie®, that reflect one's culture and language can send important messages about approval to children.

Access to the General Education Curriculum: Deafness and LRE

IDEA has always mandated that all students with disabilities receive a free appropriate education (FAPE) in the least restrictive environment (LRE). What is the least restrictive environment for deaf children? IDEA '04 makes some specific statements about addressing the communication needs of students with hearing loss. For a reminder, read again What IDEA '04 Says About Considering the Communication Needs of Students with Hearing Loss on page 340. It is necessary to weigh these issues carefully when determining what constitutes an appropriate education and what environment is the least restrictive for these students. Many parents and members of the Deaf community believe that the general education classroom is *not* the least restrictive setting for deaf children, particularly for those who use sign language when they are adolescents.

> The general education classroom with an interpreter can be a restrictive environment if the student cannot communicate with peers and with staff in the school. The residential school settings where students live in dorms and attend school with peers who are deaf and hard of hearing have a 24-hour communication environment. That educational environment might be the least restrictive environment—one that does not restrict the student as he or she communicates with peers and staff and participates in extracurricular activities without communication barriers. (Fielder, 2001, p. 58*)

This interpretation of LRE is very different from the position held by many advocates and parents of students with intellectual disabilities (see again Chapter 8). Deaf advocates believe that Deaf students need to learn Deaf culture, become proficient in ASL, and form a critical mass to feel included, not isolated or rejected because too few others use or understand their method of communication (Steffan, 2004). Of course, isolation does not have to be the outcome of general education, such is particularly true for those who use oral communication. Indications are that those who receive cochlear implants early do not experience feelings of loneliness

---

Teaching Exceptional Children by Fielder, B.C. Copyright 2001 by Council for Exceptional Children (VA). Reproduced with permission of Council for Exceptional Children (VA) in the formats Textbook and Other book via Copyright Clearance Center.

Considering Culture: *"Why Don't They Understand How Important It Is?"*

Darlene, a preschool teacher, was at her wits' end! She requested a meeting with her school's consulting teacher for students who are deaf and with an audiologist. She wanted some suggestions about how to help little Ani Fiatoa better. Ani is a bouncy, smiling 3½-year-old who is enrolled in the Lively Oaks Elementary School's preschool program. The Fiatoa family moved to the city two years ago from the South Pacific, where Ani was born. At 18 months of age, Ani was diagnosed with a severe hearing loss, and she now uses hearing aids in both ears. Ani's parents are warm and loving and seem to like Ani's placement in a regular community preschool, where she is learning to socialize with children without hearing loss. She also is learning sign language from Ms. Peek, the itinerant teacher who is a specialist in deaf education. The Fiatoa family attends meetings when requested and *seem* to endorse the program's strategies. However, Darlene was frustrated. It is difficult for her to get Ani to make eye contact—an essential skill for communicating, particularly with sign language. On numerous occasions, Darlene has explained to Ani's family members that eye contact is crucial. She also has encouraged them to take sign language classes. They don't seem concerned. Darlene even observed that Ani rarely makes eye contact with her parents.

Darlene described these issues to a friend who had worked in the South Pacific. The friend explained that it is disrespectful in some cultures for children to make eye contact with elders. This was an "aha" experience for Darlene! Perhaps the Fiatoas weren't merely disregarding her suggestions but rather had trouble integrating these teaching strategies into the ways their family members communicated. Darlene read more about the childrearing practices and customs of the South Pacific and then consulted with Ms. Peek to identify strategies that would be respectful of the family's preferred communication patterns and also support Ani's use of sign language. One idea was to make a videotape of Ani and her teacher signing. Darlene could then talk with the Fiatoas, show the tapes, and ask whether they would be comfortable using more eye contact to help Ani learn sign language. This strategy worked like a charm.

Questions to Consider

1. What are some strategies and resources that you can use to learn more about the customs and preferences of the many cultural groups in the United States? Check out the references listed in this text, search the Internet, and read novels that describe the practices and customs of various groups.

2. Can you identify community resources to contact when you meet a family from a cultural group with which you are not familiar? Ideally, these resources would be individuals who are bicultural and are well acquainted with the practices of the given cultural group as well as with those of the mainstream culture. (They are often referred to as cultural guides in the literature.)

—By Eleanor Lynch, San Diego State University, and Marci Hanson, San Francisco State University

any greater than their hearing classmates (Schorr, 2006). For those students, being educated alongside hearing students often leads to better speech and language skills and improved academic achievement (Ripper, 2008).

While many in the Deaf community advocate strongly for residential schools as the placement option for students with profound hearing loss, more and more students, both deaf and hard of hearing, attend typical public schools and general education classes. Only some 13% of these students attend separate schools, some residential (OSEP, 2008). More of these students, like the main character in this chapter's On the Screen feature, attend their local public school with their neighborhood friends.

On the Screen: *Caught in a Cover-up*

Set on Scotland's coast, *Dear Frankie* tells the charming story of a 9-year-old deaf boy, his single mom, and a fictitious sea-faring father. Frankie looks forward to letters from his father, actually written by his mother. Frankie writes letters to his "dad" about all his exciting adventures and his life at home in Scotland. However, the story twists when one day a ship comes to port that has the same name that Frankie's mother picked for the ship of his "pen pal" dad. To avoid being revealed, his mother hires a stranger to pretend to be Frankie's dad. Then, complicating matters further, Frankie's biological father wants to reconnect with his son.

This engaging film visits many themes, including loneliness, vulnerability, resilience, and relationships. It provides a rare and touching glimpse of the family life of a fully included student who is deaf, has friends, functions well academically, and is basically a happy child. The film shows the struggles of a single mother with a child with a disability. It also suggests the great lengths to which family members often go to create happiness in the lives of their children.

—By Steven Smith

Interpreting what LRE means is possibly more controversial for students who are deaf than for any other group of students. Multidisciplinary teams of professionals, possibly the student, and the student's parents should come together to decide what is the LRE for each individual student by answering the following questions:

- How severe is the student's hearing loss?
- Is the student able to use speech?
- Can appropriate educational services be made available locally?
- Are the necessary support services available?

Table 10.2 helps us understand the many different issues that must be considered when determining what the LRE should be for individual students with hearing loss. Remember also that LRE decisions may be different for elementary-age students than they are for high school students who might not have opportunities for friendships or participation in extracurricular activities, sports, or even class discussions when they are the only deaf student at a school.

Instructional Accommodations

Because of advances in medical and hearing aid technology, many students with mild to moderate hearing losses do not require special education services. Of those who do qualify for special education services, some 54% have moderate-severe to profound hearing losses (GRI, 2006). Some 86% of deaf and hard of hearing students who qualify for special education services attend general education classes for over 40% of the school day (OSEP, 2008). So, general and special education teachers have important roles to play in the education of these students.

Table 10.2 • LRE and Placement Considerations

	Type of Hearing Loss	
	Hard of Hearing	**Deaf**
Severity of loss	Youngsters with mild to moderate hearing loss can remain in the general education curriculum with consultative or supportive services from various experts such as SLPs and audiologists.	Students with severe to profound hearing loss require intensive instruction in communication skills and need assistance from an array of related services.
Potential for using residual hearing	Most of these students profit from hearing aids, thereby allowing them to benefit, with some adaptations, from typical oral methods of instruction.	Most deaf students have little useful residual hearing and require considerable accommodations to benefit from oral instructions.
Academic achievement	The academic achievement levels of deaf and hard of hearing students tend to be lower than levels of their hearing peers. Students with less hearing loss and no multiple disabilities are usually close to grade level but might need some additional academic instruction.	The academic achievement levels of deaf students are considerably below those of their hearing peers. These students need considerable instruction in basic language and communication skills, as well as intensive academic remediation.
Communicative needs	Many of these students go undetected for a long time. If the loss occurred before or during the youngsters' development of language, it is likely that they will require SLP services as well as academic assistance.	Total communication is the most commonly used approach with deaf youngsters, but the help of educational assistants is necessary, and in many rural regions this expertise is not available.
Preferred mode of communication	Most of these students should be expected to become proficient using oral language.	Most students who are postlingually deaf learn (or retain) their use of oral language. Intelligible speech and lipreading are typically unattainable goals for most prelingually deaf children, so for them manual communication is preferred.
Placement preference	The vast majority of these students attend their neighborhood schools with their hearing peers.	Many deaf students also attend their neighborhood schools. However, a significant number of them prefer center schools where their classmates share their deafness and their mode of communication.

Teachers can help students with hearing problems gain better access to the general education curriculum and participate in class activities by modifying the delivery of instruction (Nussbaum, 2005). The lists included in Accommodating for Inclusive Environments remind us that even small adjustments can make a big difference in how well students with hearing loss are able to access the curriculum and participate in learning activities with their classmates (Yarnell & Schery, 2003). Most hard of hearing students require only these simple adjustments, as long as an array of supplemental services, supports, accommodations, and assistance are available when needed. Some students with hearing loss require more supports. For them, just sitting closer to the teacher is not enough. For those with multiple disabilities, teachers must address all of the student's learning needs, not just those related to hearing abilities. Technology, discussed later in this chapter, is often an important part of providing both appropriate and meaningful instruction to these students and should be considered along with other accommodations because together they can make a positive difference for these learners.

Data-Based Practices: Communication Systems and Scaffolding

In this section, we discuss two different and important aspects of instructional programs that make a difference for deaf and hard of hearing students: how instruction is delivered and scaffolding instruction to support students' learning. Although they do not select the system a student uses, special education and general educa-

Accommodating for Inclusive Environments
Adjusting Classroom Routines

Teacher's Communications

- Articulate clearly, but do not talk louder unless you have an unusually soft voice.
- Address the student directly.
- Use the student's name first, before asking a question.
- Do not exaggerate your lip movements.
- Do not chew gum or cover your mouth when talking.
- Do not turn your back to the class when speaking.
- Avoid moving around the classroom while speaking.
- Speak somewhat more slowly.
- Repeat information by paraphrasing.

Additional Teacher Assistance

- Alert student to shifts in content and topics of instruction.
- Use handouts to support important information from lectures, guest speakers, field trips, and instructional media.
- Post key terms (information, vocabulary).
- Restate other students' questions if they cannot be clearly heard or seen by the student who is deaf or hard of hearing.
- Spend time talking with the student with hearing loss to become familiar with each other's speech.

- Bend down to be at the student's eye level when talking to small groups or working individually with the student.
- Reduce classroom's background noise as much as possible.
- Remind the student to check the batteries for technology and assistive listening devices daily.

Assistance from Classmates

- Ask classmates to rotate as note takers.
- Set up a buddy system: one classmate per class, unit, or topic.

Collaboration with Others

- Seek advice and information about the student's hearing status from parents and family.
- Keep a file about important settings for either hearing aids or implants.
- Become aware and informed about the proper use of the student's technology, and know how to troubleshoot.
- If the student has an educational interpreter, create times for planning and systems for partnering.
- Consult with a certified teacher of the deaf.

---

tion teachers should understand the different communication options available for deaf students. The data-based practice we feature in this chapter is easy for teachers to implement, and it is effective! Remember that each individual's needs differ from the next, but, more importantly, those of deaf students are very different from those of hard of hearing students.

Communication Systems   Most students with hearing loss have considerable residual hearing, use hearing aids, speak, and do not use any form of manual communication (GRI, 2006). Students with severe and profound hearing loss use different forms of communication. It is beyond the scope of an introductory text to provide details about five different means of delivering or conveying instruction to those with severe to profound hearing losses. However, some knowledge is important because different communication systems affect how instruction is delivered and accommodations that need to be made. Here are the five communication systems typically used to deliver instruction to students who are deaf:

oral-only approach A method of instruction for students with hearing loss, using only oral communication

- *Oral-only.* Used with most students with cochlear implants, the **oral-only approach** teaches and uses speech exclusively and encourages students to use as much of their residual hearing as possible. The system relies on speechreading (lipreading) and oral speech. In the strictest systems, children are not allowed to use any form of manual communication such as finger spelling or signing. Emerging evidence indicates that this approach produces better speech and academic achievement for many students (Ripper, 2008).

- *Total communication.* Oral speech and manual communication (signing) are combined in the **total communication approach**. Total communication allows the child to communicate through whatever mode is easiest and most effective. Most students who are deaf, including many with cochlear implants, use this method (GRI, 2006; Moores, 2008). When students are taught through a total communication approach, typically oral speech and **finger spelling**—where each letter of the alphabet is assigned a sign—are used, not ASL. Signed English uses finger spelling exclusively to translate English: Words are spelled out, but the rules of grammar and language are the same as for English speech. Finger spelling is often used along with ASL when no sign exists for a word or name.

- *Cued speech.* When hand signals are used to help deaf people read lips, it is called **cued speech**. These cues help the individual determine whether the word spoken was *pan* or *bat*, which look alike to the person reading lips (Gleason & Ratner, 2009). Cued speech is popular with hearing parents because it is easy to learn and follows the format and structure of the English language (which ASL does not).

- *American Sign Language (ASL).* Although you have heard a lot about ASL, the language of the Deaf, it is important to put it into perspective: only about 10% of teachers of the deaf use ASL in their school classes (Moores, 2008).

- *Bilingual-bicultural.* The **bilingual-bicultural (bi-bi) approach** is modeled after bilingual education to teach English as a second language (Gleason & Ratner, 2009). It is the newest method for teaching Deaf students. In this system, ASL is used as the child's first language and written English as the second language.

Scaffolding As you learned in the Characteristics section of this chapter, the academic achievement levels of many deaf and hard of hearing students are disappointing. Of course, there are exceptions. For example, as a group, those who are Deaf of Deaf and learn ASL as infants as their primary, native language tend not to experience low academic achievement (Evans, 2004). In this chapter, you have also learned about emerging information about some individuals who receive cochlear implants before the age of 1; they, too, are showing signs of good academic growth (Ripper, 2008). And, of course, many without multiple disabilities who benefit from hearing aids and develop good language skills, whether they use manual or oral systems, during early childhood learn well alongside hearing students. However, for many of these students, learning to read and write at grade level is a challenge, and they need additional assistance to master the content of the general education curriculum (Dillon & Pisoni, 2006). With well over half of all deaf and hard of hearing students now attending general education classes for the vast majority of the school day, teachers should differentiate instruction and provide instructional supports to ensure all students learn and profit from content instruction. For these reasons, we selected **scaffolding** for the data-based practice to highlight in this chapter's A Closer Look at Data-Based Practice. It is effective across the grades, from elementary to high school, and content areas. Although not designed specifically for deaf and hard of hearing students, it can have dramatic benefits because it helps tailor instruction and provide supports that reflect each student's individual learning needs.

Scaffolding adds supports and assistance to instruction for those who need them (IRIS Center, 2008; Reid & Lienemann, 2006). It is particularly useful when teaching new skills that include several steps. One important feature of scaffolding is that help is given only as long as necessary and is gradually removed, so the learning becomes independent. Scaffolding can be used to teach academic content, core skills, or steps in different learning strategies (like ones described in

total communication approach A method of instruction for students with hearing loss that employs any and all methods of communication (oral speech, manual communication, ASL, gestures)

finger spelling A manual communication system that uses the English alphabet

cued speech Hand signals for "difficult to see" speech sounds; assists with speechreading

bilingual-bicultural (bi-bi) approach A method of instruction for students who are deaf, combining practices of ESL and bilingual education; uses ASL as the native language and teaches reading and writing in English as a second language

scaffolding Differentiating instruction by providing assistance and supports by modeling and practice of multistepped skill or content areas and gradually removing the supports until accurate, independent performance is achieved

myeducationlab) Go to the Activities and Applications section in Chapter 10 of MyEducationLab, and complete Activity 1. As you watch the video and answer the accompanying questions, think about ways in which technology can facilitate the success of students with hearing loss in general education settings.

FM (frequency-modulated) transmission devices Assistive listening devices that provide oral transmissions directly from the teacher to students with hearing loss

audio loop A listening device that directs sound from the source directly to the listener's ear through a specially designed hearing aid

telecommunication devices Devices that provide oral information in alternative formats (e.g., captions for TV or movies)

captions Subtitles that print words spoken in film or video

open captions Subtitles or tickers that are part of the screen-image for everyone to see

closed captions Subtitles available only to those who select the option

rear window captioning (RWC) Closed captioning used in movie theaters that projects printed words on the back of the seat in front of the moviegoer

text telephone (TTY) A device that allows people to make and receive telephone calls by typing information instead of speaking; formerly called the telecommunication device for the deaf (TDD)

telecommunications relay service (TRS) A telephone system where an operator at a relay center converts a print-telephone message to a voice-telephone message; required by federal law

Chapter 5, "Learning Disabilities"). Learn more about scaffolding by interacting with the IRIS Center's module about scaffolding: http://iris.peabody.vanderbilt.edu/sca/chalcycle.htm.

Technology

People with hearing loss, as a group, are some of the most "technologically-dependent" among individuals with disabilities. They benefit from the growing number of technology devices and gadgets designed for everyone. They also benefit from the many assistive technology devices designed specifically for them. Because teachers need to plan for, use, or facilitate students' use of such equipment in the classroom, we introduce some of them to you now.

Assistive Listening Devices Assistive listening devices can help individuals hear sounds through amplification and by reducing background noise. In the Overcoming Challenges: Hearing Aids and Cochlear Implants section of this chapter, we talked about two assistive listening devices: hearing aids and cochlear implants. A third type of assistive listening device helps reduce background noise, which is a major problem in many classrooms, lecture halls, theaters, auditoriums, recreational centers, cafeterias, and other large rooms. **FM (frequency-modulated) transmission devices** have many advantages. They allow freedom of movement for both teacher and students. The teacher speaks into a small microphone either clipped to a shirt or worn lavaliere style (as a pendant on a chain). Students receive sound through a small receiver connected directly to their hearing aids. Background noise is reduced, and teachers are free to move around the classroom without worrying about always needing to have their faces in full view of all their students. **Audio loops** can amplify sound and reduce background noise in large rooms such as school auditoriums. They are often found in concert halls and theaters. These inexpensive devices route sound from its source directly to the listener's ear through a specially equipped hearing aid or earphone via a wire connection or use of radio waves.

Telecommunication Devices Assistive **telecommunication devices** improve access to and enjoyment of cinema and television through sight. Although the public resisted the use of **captions,** printed words that appear at the bottom of a TV screen, when the idea was first introduced, **open captions** help us all learn about the news at busy airports or know scores of sporting events when enjoying games at noisy restaurants. The first captioned television show, *The French Chef with Julia Child,* aired in 1972. In the 1980s, **closed captions** gave viewers a choice whether to see captions on the TV screen or not. Since 1993, all television sets made are equipped with an internal, microsized decoder that allows captions to be placed anywhere on the screen. Teachers should know that captions are an option whenever educational television programs are being shown at school. All that needs to happen is for the device to be activated. A third type of captioning is not universally available. **Rear window captioning (RWC)** allows people with profound hearing losses to see first-run movies at their local theaters with friends and family and not have to wait until they are available in captioned DVDs. Such systems typically project captions from a message board on the theater's rear wall onto a clear plastic screen that attaches to the moviegoer's seat.

An assistive device that has been very important to those who cannot use a typical telephone is the **text telephone (TTY)**, formerly referred to as the telecommunication device for the deaf (TDD). The TTY prints out the voice message, converting speech to text. One major limitation is that TTYs are required at both the sending and the receiving ends. So, the Federal Communications Commission now requires all states to have a **telecommunications relay service (TRS)**, which allows a TTY user to "talk" to a person who uses a standard phone. An operator at a relay center places the call on a voice line and reads the typed message from the TTY to the non-TTY user. The relay service enables deaf individuals to use the phone, via an 800 phone number, for everything from calling a doctor to ordering

A Closer Look at Data-Based Practices

Scaffolding

Scaffolding instruction can provide additional supports and assistance to students struggling to learn new skills or content. It often provides just the extra help needed so students can succeed. Because so many deaf and hard of hearing students are low achievers and so many more are attending general education classes, scaffolding instruction could provide the assistance necessary to help them learn and improve achievement.

Steps to Follow

1. Determine the type of assistance required—content scaffolding (gradually increases content difficulty), task scaffolding (increasingly withdraws supports), or material scaffolding (uses written prompts or cues).

2. Model or demonstrate the steps to follow to execute the task, strategy, or assignment correctly. Repeat the demonstration until the student understands how to perform each step and can explain why each step is important and necessary.

3. Arrange for individual or group practice opportunities.

4. Continue to model parts of the skill that remain difficult, allowing the student to complete the elements of the assignment that have been mastered (e.g., the student sounds out words where the phonics skill is mastered; the teacher helps with those words where the phonics is not yet known).

5. Coach until the task can be performed accurately (e.g., the learning strategy for editing paragraphs written for a social studies assignment is used accurately several times in a row).

6. Ensure that the student can do the assignment independently.

7. Assign similar tasks where the student works without assistance from classmates or the teacher.

Example of a Learning Tool Mastered by Scaffolding Instruction

The figure illustrates an example of a way to help students take notes by separating the main ideas from details. Although this approach is relatively simple, certainly making complicated history and science content easier to study, many students need help through the application of scaffolding techniques to master the technique.

History Notes About the Civil War

Main Ideas	Details	Key Words	Notes
Reasons for conflict	Economics		Industry in North Agriculture in South; needed free labor
	Social justice	Civil rights	Southern crop cotton
		Slavery	No machines for picking
		Plantation	African American slaves

 myeducationlab Go to the Building Teaching Skills and Dispositions section in Chapter 10 of MyEducationLab, and complete the activities in the IRIS Module, "Providing Instructional Supports: Facilitating Mastery of New Skills." This module explores the importance of scaffolding and modeling for students as they learn new skills and strategies.

---

a pizza. TTYs and TRS systems may become unnecessary in years to come. Although advances are forthcoming, wireless phones and other wireless technology are not yet universally useful to those who use hearing aids (Kelley, 2006). However, today's wireless phones that provide text messaging and e-mail options may soon replace the need for TTYs and TRS services and are yet another example of how today's technology can benefit everyone.

Speech-to-Text Translations An important feature of many computers and of various types of software is that oral speech is instantly translated into printed words. Obviously, the benefits for individuals with hearing loss are great. Speech-to-text translations allow students to profit from lectures, particularly those in auditoriums where taking notes, reading lips, or even watching the hands of an educational interpreter can be a daunting task. **Real-time captioning (RTC)** allows students to read

real-time captioning (RTC) Practically instantaneous translations of speech into print; an accommodation for deaf students attending lectures

what is being said as a lecture or speech is being delivered (National Technical Institute for the Deaf [NTID], 2008). A system developed by NTID and Rochester Institute of Technology (RIT), C-Print®, can translate up to 300 words a minute and is the fastest translation system currently available. C-Print uses a laptop computer, a specially developed word abbreviation software program, and a computer visual display. The trained C-Print captionist listens to the lecture and types codes that represent words into the computer; the transcription is instantly shown on a monitor or on the individual's laptop. Many students, not just those with hearing loss, benefit from RTC because missed words are instantly seen on the screen and a printout of the lecture is available immediately.

Real-time captioning (RTC) allows everyone to read those parts of lectures they missed because they couldn't hear the teacher (or maybe because they were not paying attention and thinking about what to wear to Saturday night's party).

alerting devices Assistive devices for people who are deaf to make them aware of events in their environment through a means other than sound (e.g., flashing lights, vibrators)

Alerting Devices Individuals with profound hearing losses often rely on signals, other than the typical sounds hearing people use, to catch their attention. Teachers should know about such devices, for deaf students often bring **alerting devices** to class, or the school might provide them for security or safety. Many items like alarm clocks that vibrate the bed or light systems that signal a doorbell, crying baby, or telephone are used at home and use alerting technology. An alerting device found at school uses a flashing light to signal a fire alarm or recess bell. Some of these systems are wireless, allowing great flexibility in their placement.

Transition

The purpose of school-to-work transition programs for students who are deaf or hard of hearing is to improve adult outcomes of these individuals. Obtaining equitable employment, being able to get and hold a job commensurate with one's abilities, earning a fair wage, and being satisfied with the job are important. College graduation can be essential to finding a well-paying and satisfying job. But, as we have noted, many students who have hearing loss also have difficulties with reading: As a group, their average reading achievement levels are at the elementary school level (Luft, 2008). Students with higher reading achievement levels are more likely to graduate from high school, attend college, and graduate.

College options have increased for deaf and hard of hearing students over the years. Several decades ago, deaf students had few postsecondary options, and those existed primarily because of funding from the federal government. The original programs—all still in operation today—provided different types of education. Typically, deaf students could not attend a local college close to home. Now Gallaudet University serves both undergraduate and graduate students and is the nation's only liberal arts university primarily for deaf students. The National Technical Institute for the Deaf (NTID) at the Rochester Institute of Technology in New York offers technical and vocational degrees. Four other federally funded postsecondary schools (Seattle Community College, California State University–Northridge, St. Paul Technical College, and the University of Tennessee Consortium) provide 2-year and 4-year degrees. These original programs are now just part of the large number of postsecondary schools that welcome deaf and hard of hearing students.

IDEA '04 does not have authority over colleges and universities; however, many of the accommodations that students received during their elementary and high school careers are now available to them at 2- and 4-year institutions of higher education (HEATH, 2005). Most colleges and universities provide an array of accommodations: note takers, interpreting services, speech-to-text translations of lectures, and assistive listening devices in classrooms. Such readily available supports allow students with hearing loss to choose from many different schools. To help them,

Gallaudet University publishes a directory, *College and Career Programs for Deaf Students,* that not only catalogs accredited programs but also describes accommodations provided (Hochgesang et al., 2007).

Collaboration

Collaboration with many different professional is at the core of educational programs for students with hearing loss. Multidisciplinary teams comprise a diverse range of expertise and professionals. It is commonplace that these students receive special services from audiologists who assess their hearing abilities and from SLPs who provide therapy to improve speech and language skills—a significant problem area for most of these students. Deaf students also receive instruction from special educators who have unique certification in deaf education. So, the team that comes together to work with students with hearing loss are highly specialized and often work with these students throughout their school years.

Collaboration with Related Services Providers: Educational Interpreters

One essential service needed by many deaf students enrolled in general education programs is assistance with the translation of spoken English. **Educational interpreters** are related service providers who convert spoken messages into the student's preferred communication system, which may be a signed system such as ASL or signed English. For many teachers, working with the assistance of an interpreter is a novel experience that might occur only once in their teaching career. For the teacher inexperienced in working with students who use sign language, there is much to learn, plan for, and coordinate (Williams & Finnegan, 2003). And for many interpreters, working with students in school settings is also a unique experience (Linehan, 2000). A close working relationship is required between this related service provider and the teacher, where the interpreter needs to learn academic content and the teacher needs to learn how to work with a translator.

educational interpreters Related service providers for deaf students; they translate or convert spoken messages to the deaf person's preferred mode of manual communication

Collaborative Practices: Respecting Roles

The teacher and the interpreter must coordinate efforts to ensure they understand each other's roles. In Spotlighting Christy Neria, you will see the insight that interpreters often have about human relations, selflessly helping others participate in classrooms and in society. The delicate balance of roles and responsibilities in classrooms can be hard to achieve. Classrooms are busy, crowded places; and hearing loss complicates instruction, communication, and class discussions. Table 10.3

Table 10.3 • Roles and Responsibilities of Educational Interpreters, Teachers, and Students Who Are Deaf

The Interpreter	The Teacher	The Deaf Student
Holds long conversations with the student after class	Introduces the interpreter to the class	Makes certain the interpreter uses preferred mode of communication
Asks for clarification when the teacher speaks too fast or was not heard	Talks to the student, not to the interpreter	Notifies the interpreter when there is going to be a change in schedules or when that person will not be needed
Considers teaching hearing students some basic signs	Adjusts pace of speech to allow for the translation	Is clear about whether the interpreter should speak for the student
Only interprets; does not tutor or provide assistance with assignments	Arranges for peers to take notes for their peer who is deaf	Determines desired role with peers
Maintains confidentiality of personal and private information	Seeks assistance of interpreter when working with others (e.g., SLPs)	Meets with the interpreter on a regular basis to provide feedback, resolve problems, and evaluate progress

Spotlighting *Christy Neria:* A Day in the Life

Christy Neria is an interpreter for deaf and hard of hearing students.

The bell rang as I headed off to my second interpreting assignment of the day, seventh-grade English class. The only student I interpreted for during this period was named Sally, a girl who was hard of hearing and was recently learning to sign. Realizing her developing skills, I was aware of the need to code switch, to interpret using lip movement and a more Conceptually Accurate Signed English (CASE) approach to assure comprehension of the message being delivered. In my mind, my job was to deliver the message and be the communication facilitator—nothing more, nothing less.

On this particular day, my eyes were awakened to the starting realization that perhaps I should be more than a communication automaton. I learned that being an educational interpreter may require me to deliver more than merely an exchange of words between the student and classroom participants. That morning, I began interpreting as my hands worked in a synchronous motion to the message being conveyed. Suddenly, Sally's eyes filled with tears as she got up out of her seat and dashed out the door. My hands froze. I was bewildered with what to do. All eyes in the classroom were on me, which was another forbidden act. I was taught that the role of an interpreter is to be almost invisible, more of a voice than an entity. Nonetheless, the classroom instructor encouraged me to follow Sally to find out what was wrong.

I found her just outside the quad area where she sat listlessly with tears trailing down her cheeks. My instinct to comfort her set in as I put my arm around her and asked her what was wrong. With trembling hands and damp eyes, she explained her distress as she revealed to me her insecurities, hurt, and sadness about being hard of hearing and feeling out of place in both the deaf and hearing worlds. Just learning sign, she felt inadequate to participate with other culturally deaf students while not feeling able to communicate effectively with hearing students, either. We talked for a while, and for a moment I forgot my "interpreter" role. She appeared to feel better after our conversation, and for the weeks to come she began to confide in me when she needed to. Subsequently, she grew as a student and a signer while her identity was beginning to take shape as a young lady.

This experience made me realize the need to step outside my "traditional" role at times. Regardless of what the educational interpreting courses state, being an interpreter is more than just facilitating and translating a language; it also involves developing partnerships and trust with the students you work with. Supporting Sally during her moment of confusion and heartache was truly an enlightening moment for me.

myeducationlab Go to the Activities and Application section in Chapter 10 of MyEducationLab, and complete Activity 2. As you watch the video and answer the accompanying questions, consider how students with hearing loss benefit from the assistance of an aide in inclusive classrooms.

shows the roles and responsibilities of the classroom teacher, the educational interpreter, and the student. Everyone has important issues to consider when students with profound hearing losses and their educational interpreters learn and work together in inclusive educational settings.

As responsibilities and duties are defined, it should become clear that the teacher has the primary responsibility and the interpreter plays a supporting role (Antia & Kreimeyer, 2001). In other words, the teacher delivers instruction and remediation (when necessary), and the interpreter facilitates communication. Because the interpreter may not be an expert in the content of the curriculum, the teacher should give the interpreter copies of lesson plans, lists of key terms, and textbooks to ensure clear and accurate translation of the teacher's lectures and instructions. The teacher and interpreter also work together on a number of issues, many of which are minor but quite important. For example, the interpreter should sit in a glare-free, well-lit location that has a solid-color background and does not block anyone's view of the blackboard or of the teacher.

Teachers and interpreters also need to agree on and understand each other's roles—how much extra help the teacher provides the student and how much extra help the interpreter offers. Tips for Effective Instruction provides some useful ideas for developing partnerships with these professionals.

Partnerships with Families and Communities

Although language, social and emotional development, and technology are important to the overall development of deaf and hard of hearing children, possibly the most important factor in these children's lives is acceptance and inclusion by their families. Some parents and other family members (grandparents, siblings, extended family members) adjust quickly to the demands presented by a child with hearing loss. This is particularly true for children whose parents are deaf. To Deaf parents, the birth of a Deaf child is typically cause for great celebration—and also a great relief (Blade, 1994). These parents know ASL, use it as their native language, and teach it to their infant through the normal developmental process. However, the birth of a deaf child to hearing families can be frightening, even devastating. Such is common among Latinos. Reinforced by their cultural beliefs, some family members feel shame and guilt with the birth of a child with a hearing disability (Polanco & Guillermo, 2007), while other family members pity or feel sorry for the child with a hearing loss.

Today, particularly with the Internet making information almost immediately available, parents have more assistance than ever before. Both private (e.g., the Alexander Graham Bell Association for the Deaf and Hard of Hearing: www.shhh.org) and public organizations (e.g., National Center for Deafness and Other Communication Disorders of the National Institutes of Health: www.nidcd.nih.gov) provide information briefs and resource pages that are helpful to parents. Because infants with hearing loss are identified earlier, more children and their parents receive early intervention services available through IDEA and often coordinated by social service agencies. When those services are brought to the infant's or toddler's home through a family-centered approach, the outcomes are remarkable (Vernon, 2007).

TIPS for Effective Instruction

Working with Educational Interpreters

Planning and Organization

- Interpreters and teachers set up standard meeting times.
- They have established clear roles for working together during instruction.
- All meetings regarding the student are scheduled when the student's interpreter can attend.
- Storage and working space are designated for the interpreter.
- Lesson plans and supporting materials are shared days before the instructional activity.
- Teachers and interpreters have time to meet before the instructional activity to clarify vocabulary and content.

Classroom Organization and Management

- The interpreter and the student are able to see the teacher and each other.
- Placement for the interpreter is not distracting to the student's classmates.
- Glare and other visual obstructions are eliminated.

Courtesy and Social Conventions

- Everyone talks directly to the student.
- Eye contact is with the student, not with the interpreter (even when the interpreter is speaking and translating manual communication for the student).
- The interpreter is not an academic tutor or classroom manager who resolves disruption.
- Invite the interpreter to teach the class some sign language or share Deaf literature.

Summary

Hearing, like vision, is a "distance sense" that provides us with information from outside our bodies. When hearing is limited, it affects the individual in significant ways, limiting communication, access to orally presented information, and independent living. Advances in assistive and medical technology (e.g., universal screening, hearing aids, cochlear implants, speech-to-text translations) have changed the lives of people with hearing problems. These advances provide them with devices that both help compensate for challenges in hearing sounds in the environment and in communicating with others, and also actually improve acuity and sound perception. More than any other group of people with disabilities, the Deaf make up a community united by a rich culture and a unique communication system. Deafness and hard of hearing is a low-incidence disability for children, affecting far less than 1% (i.e., 0.14%) of all students.

Answering the Chapter Objectives

1. What are the major causes of hearing loss? Provide an explanation for each cause.

   - The majority of causes for hearing loss are unknown. There are four major known causes of hearing loss.
     - *Hereditary conditions:* most common cause of prelingual deafness; can be both congenital and sensorineural
     - *Meningitis:* a disease that affects the central nervous system; the most common cause of acquired deafness in children; results in a sensorineural hearing loss; vaccines are available to protect people from this disease, but universal protection is not available.
     - *Otitis media:* middle ear infections; chronic, untreated otitis media interrupts normal language development and can result in permanent conductive hearing loss.
     - *Noise:* totally preventable cause of hearing loss that is gradual in onset and the result of loud sounds in the environment

2. What is universal hearing screening of newborns, and why is it important?

   - Universal screening allows for the identification of hearing loss at birth, reducing the (previous) average age of identification from 2½ to 3 years of age to 3 to 4 months.
   - Early identification allows for services to children and their families to begin immediately and sets the stage for better language and cognitive development.
   - Early identification leads to early use of hearing aids, often as early as 4 months of age, and earlier decisions about the benefits of cochlear implants to the individual child.

3. What is Deaf culture? Give some examples or signs of Deaf culture, and describe its importance to the Deaf.

   - Deaf culture is
     - beliefs, customs, practices, and social behavior of the Deaf community;
     - reflected in art, music, theater, literature, and related intellectual activities.
   - Signs of Deaf Culture are
     - American Sign Language (ASL) binding the Deaf community and
     - advocacy and political action.
   - Its significance is that
     - culture removes the association of deafness with disability and reinterprets deafness as a characteristic of a (historically misunderstood) minority group, and
     - ASL is a bona fide language at the heart of a proud heritage and traditions.

4. What variables need to be considered when planning instruction for students with hearing problems?

   - *Amount of loss:* the deaf or hard of hearing
   - *Age of onset:* prelingually deaf or postlingually (after the age of 2) deaf
   - *Type of loss:* conductive or sensorineural
   - *Speech intelligibility:* how well and comfortable the individual is with oral speech
   - *Communication mode:* oral speech or manual communication
   - *Assistive technology:* devices used, requirements of the equipment

5. What are the major types and examples of assistive technology specifically designed for people with hearing problems?

- *Assistive listening devices:* both digital and analog hearing aids (BTE, ITE, ITC, CIC), cochlear implants, FM transmission devices
- *Telecommunication devices:* captioning, text telephone (TTY), telecommunications relay service
- *Speech-to-text translations:* computerized speech recognition, real-time captioning, C-Print
- *Alerting devices:* special signaling devices for alarms, doorbells, telephone rings

myeducationlab⁾ Now go to MyEducationLab at www.myeducationlab.com, and take the Self-Assessment to gauge your initial comprehension of chapter content. Once you have taken the Self-Assessment, use your individualized Study Plan for Chapter 10 to enhance your understanding of the concepts discussed in the chapter.

Council for Exceptional Children — ADDRESSING THE PROFESSIONAL STANDARDS

Council for Exceptional Children (CEC) knowledge standards addressed in this chapter: DH1K4, DH1K1, DH1K3, DH2K2, DH8K2, DH4K3, DH7K1, DH10S1, DH10S2

Appendix A: CEC Knowledge and Skill Standards Common Core has a full listing of the standards listed here.

Appendix B: CEC Knowledge and Skill Common Core Standards and Associated Subcategories are broken down by chapter.

CHAPTER 11

Low Vision and Blindness

Naomi Chowdhuri Tyler and
Deborah Deutsch Smith

Imagine a World . . .

where everyone achieves to their fullest potential . . .

Chapter Objectives

After studying this chapter, you will be able to

1. Divide visual disabilities into two functional subgroups.

2. Discuss ways to accommodate the general education setting for students with visual disabilities.

3. Explain why orientation and mobility targets must be an intensive part of the curriculum for many students with visual disabilities.

4. Describe types of assistive technology that benefit people with visual disabilities at school, in the workplace, and in independent living.

5. Discuss issues surrounding braille and reading literacy.

Michael Naranjo is a world-renowned sculptor whom you will meet in this chapter's *Spotlighting* feature. He lost his vision in the Vietnam War when he was a very young man, and he honed his skills as an artist after his injuries. His work is part of important collections around the word, including the Vatican, the White House, and the Albuquerque Art Museum Sculpture Garden. He and his wife Laurie are very generous, contributing their time and expertise to Very Special Arts, a community program for young artists with disabilities. They also establish Tactile Art Exhibits at museums and botanical gardens across the country.

myeducationlab After reading this chapter, complete the Self-Assessment for Chapter 11 on MyEducationLab to gauge your initial understanding of chapter content.

distance senses Senses—both hearing and vision—used to gain information; developed to guard against danger

visual disabilities Impairments in vision that, even with correction, affect educational performance, access to the community, and independence

We seldom give much thought to the process of seeing, even though most of us use it automatically. We stop to reflect on the beauty of a particular sunset, a flower in bloom, or the landscape after a snowstorm. Most of us use vision at work, when we use the Internet, write memos, look up telephone numbers, or direct people to various offices. We use vision for recreation when we see a movie, watch television, or read a book. We also use vision for self-defense; we look in all directions before crossing a street or when driving through a four-way stop. We use our sense of sight all of our waking hours, yet rarely do we think about vision and how it functions. Unlike touch and taste, vision and hearing are **distance senses**, senses that provide us with information outside our bodies. These senses developed to alert us to the presence of helpful as well as dangerous elements in the environment.

Clearly, those of us with unimpaired vision profit from this sense. In contrast, people with **visual disabilities** have limited use of their sight. But, with systematic instruction, advances in technology, and elimination of barriers associated with stereotypes and discrimination, most can lead fully integrated and independent lives.

Where We've Been . . . What's On the Horizon?

Records from ancient Egypt confirm that people with visual disabilities were accepted in some societies of the ancient world. Homer, the Greek poet who in the eighth century B.C. composed the *Odyssey* and the *Iliad*, was blind. The ancient Greeks held Homer and his work in the highest regard, considering him a source of wisdom and a model of heroic conduct. Despite evidence of the acceptance of some individuals who were blind, there is no record of a systematic attempt to educate them or integrate them into society until the 18th century. And, even with efforts to develop educational programs, the bias and discrimination experienced by people who are blind continue today. A recently produced film about the life of Ray Charles documents how attitudes and opportunities can change even across one lifetime (read this chapter's On the Screen: *Ray,* the Power of Music, for more information). Before thinking more about today, let's trace the development of educational services for students with visual disabilities.

Historical Context

In 1784, Valentin Haüy opened the first school for the blind. At this Parisian school, the Institution for Blind Youth, he conceived a system of raised letters on the printed page. The French Revolution in 1789 ended Haüy's work on this innovative reading system, but by the early 1800s, another Frenchman had developed a tactile system for reading and writing. Louis Braille, who was blind, designed an embossed six-dot cell system, the forerunner of the reading and writing method used today.

In 1821, Samuel Gridley Howe opened the first center school for students who were blind in the United States, the New England Asylum for the Blind (now the Perkins School for the Blind). Around 1832, the New York Institute for the Blind and the Pennsylvania Institution for the Instruction of the Blind were founded. These 19th-century schools were private boarding schools, usually attended by children from wealthy families.

The first day classes for students with visual disabilities began in Scotland in 1872. The Scottish Education Act required students who were blind to be educated with their sighted classmates and to attend schools in their local communities. Note that our mainstreaming and inclusion movements were not new concepts: Their roots are deep in the history of education of students with disabilities. In the United States, the first concentrated attempts to integrate students who are blind into local public schools were made in Chicago. In 1900, Frank Hall, the superintendent for the Illinois School for the Blind, convinced people to allow

On the Screen: *Ray, the Power of Music*

Through Jamie Foxx's 2004 Oscar-award winning performance, the life of the talented singer and musician Ray Charles comes to the screen. The film *Ray* provides a sometimes raw but always candid look at America during the 20th century. Beyond offering fine acting performances and remarkable music, the film teaches lessons of American history. What we see and hear through this film is not just the great talent of a remarkable and self-taught musician who could change his unique style to evolve with the times. We also learn how attitudes evolve across a lifetime. This film not only reveals the truth about growing up poor and Black in the rural South but also shows us what life was like at residential schools for the blind. In addition, it reveals struggles many individuals face—and overcome—to reach their potential. Ray Charles fought prejudice on two levels: race and disability. *Ray* shows in vivid terms how bias and discrimination can consume individuals, threatening to destroy their talents and deprive us of their gifts. This film is as much about disability as it is about race, genius, the music business, and life's excesses.

—By Steven Smith

students who were blind to attend local schools in a region of Chicago near where they lived. These students attended general education classes but also had a special education teacher who taught braille and helped them participate in the general education curriculum. The concept of access to the general education curriculum was being fostered even then! Hall also developed a mechanical writer—a small, portable machine for taking notes and completing other written tasks in braille—the precursor to the sophisticated technology available today.

Edward Allen taught the first class for the partially sighted in 1913 in Boston; later that year, Robert Irwin started a class in Cleveland. These programs were modeled after classes in England in which schoolwork was almost exclusively oral. Reading and writing tasks were kept to a minimum, thought to preserve what limited sight a person had, and students attending these classes participated in general education as much as possible. This method was popular for almost 50 years (from about 1915 to 1965), until Natalie Barraga's research on visual efficiency appeared in 1964 (Barraga, 1964; Barraga & Collins, 1979). She proved that vision can become more limited when it is not used.

In addition to reading and writing difficulties, freedom of movement is a challenge for those with limited or no sight. Between 1918 and 1925, guide dogs were trained to help French and German veterans of World War I and were were introduced in the United States in 1928 (Tuttle & Ferrell, 1995). The more popular method to assist mobility is the long cane, developed around 1860. Richard Hoover, after whom the Hoover cane is named, is credited with developing a mobility and orientation system in 1944. Before this time, there was no systematic method for teaching individuals how to move freely in their environments.

Second-grade teacher Angela Wolf, who is blind, successfully instructs her students in all academic subjects.

retinopathy of prematurity (ROP) A cause of visual disabilities from prematurity where excess oxygen used to help the infant breathe but damages the retina

visual efficiency How well a person can use sight

During the 1950s, premature infants were supplied with extra oxygen needed for them to survive; ironically, this resulted in **retinopathy of prematurity (ROP)**, a condition that causes visual disabilities ranging from mild visual loss to blindness. During the 1960s, the rubella (German measles) epidemic left many children with multiple disabilities, often including visual disabilities. The dramatic increase in students with visual disabilities strained the capacity of residential schools, which before World War II had served 85% of all students with visual disabilities (Sacks & Rosen, 1994). At the same time, parents began to call for their children to attend their local public schools. Today, the majority of students with visual disabilities lives at home and attends local public schools. Only 4% of students with visual disabilities (about 1,100 students) attend residential schools (Office of Special Education Programs [OSEP], 2008).

Advances in technology have significantly influenced the lives of individuals with visual disabilities. Over the past 30 years, improvements in computer capabilities have allowed for efficient and inexpensive print enlargements and immediate translation of print to braille. The first print-to-voice translator, the Kurzweil Reader, was developed in the 1970s. Although crude and expensive when compared to today's versions of optical scanners and everyday computers that translate print to voice, they did provide immediate access to printed text not available before. This machine was the breakthrough technology that allows individuals who are blind immediate access to all printed information, yet it only hinted at the remarkable innovations now developed and still to come.

What might be on the horizon? Clearly, we can only imagine and dream of future inventions that will make the world more accessible to people with visual disabilities. One thing is clear: If the technology is designed for the mass market and everyone can benefit from it, the costs will go down and the availability will increase (Fruchterman, 2003). Here's an example: Over a century ago the radio brought news and entertainment to people wherever they were. While providing service to all, the radio benefited people who could not read the size of print used in newspapers or could not enjoy movies shown in local theaters. The next such breakthrough might well be cell phone technology (Fruchterman, 2003). Present cell phones can download software, provide access to the Internet, store music, and help us plan our day. Greater demand will cause costs to decrease. With the addition of voice recognition and braille device hookups, people with visual disabilities then will have greater access to the world.

Challenges That Visual Loss Presents

People with visual disabilities vary widely in their visual abilities. **Visual efficiency**—how well a person can use sight—is an interesting factor because it is not perfectly associated with the ability to see; people with the same visual acuity or the same amount of peripheral vision may differ in their visual efficiency or their abilities to use their sight. Visual efficiency influences how individuals learn best (through visual, tactile, or auditory channels) and what accommodations students profit from the most. For example, a student's visual efficiency could affect how the classroom needs to be organized, where the child should sit, whether additional equipment (assistive technology, braillers) is required, and whether adapted materials (texts with enlarged print) are necessary.

Because of advances in technology, the passage of the ADA law, and changing attitudes, more people who are blind or have low vision are assuming their places in the mainstream of society. Opportunities are increasing. Angela Wolf (see photo) recently completed the teacher education program at the University of Texas and earned an elementary general education teaching certificate. An activist, busy professional, and wife of a musician, Angela applies outstanding teaching skills to help her students progress in reading and the rest of their academic subjects. Most amazingly, her second graders don't take advantage of the fact that Angela is blind; rather, they assume more responsibility for their behavior and don't let classmates abuse the situation. Here's what one of her students has to say: "She can teach without seeing, and that's really hard to do. Especially when kids aren't always good. She's special and very smart and knows all of our voices, even from the other side of the room" (Randall, 2005). Angela is not alone in illustrating that expectations for people with disabilities are often based on perceptions rather than on reality (Runyan & Jenkins, 2001).

Making a Difference
Bookshare.org

Benetech

Jim Fruchterman

For most of us, the use and availability of books is something we take for granted. Students in public schools assume they will receive their textbooks at the beginning of the school year. Anyone who has a library card has thousands of books available to peruse at their leisure. In contrast, access to books is not as simple for people with visual disabilities—in fact, it can prove to be quite complicated and frustrating. Students with visual disabilities, their teachers, or parents, must make specific requests for accessible versions of their texts (e.g., books on tape, braille). Often, this request must go through a state-level contact person, who in turn forwards the request to an authorized provider, who then produces the textbook in specialized formats (National Instructional Materials Accessibility Standard [NIMAS], 2006). It is quite common for the student to finally receive the book, in the format requested, after weeks or even months have passed, often at great expense to the district or state. When Ryan Strunk, a blind high school student, requested a braille version of his geometry book, the production of the 40-volume text ended up costing more than $17,000! (Strunk, 2004).

Bookshare.org provides a welcome solution to the problems of accessible reading materials. It is a project of Benetech, a nonprofit company whose goal is to apply technology to solve some of the world's problems—specifically those surrounding literacy, the environment, and human rights. Founded by engineer and rocket scientist Jim Fruchterman and funded in part by OSEP, Bookshare.org has created a digital library of over 39,000 books, and it adds new books at the rate of 700 to 800 new titles per month. It gathers an army of employees and volunteers who digitally scan books. Bookshare.org develops collaborative partnerships with book and newspaper publishing companies (e.g., Scholastic and HarperCollins), which in turn provide free copies of accessible books. The electronic files are then deposited into a digital library, which can be accessed by Bookshare members. Because the type of print disability may vary, the files can be accessed by programs that translate text to speech, transfer text to braille, provide large-print versions, or allow for dual-mode access (i.e., the words on the screen are highlighted while the user listens to the audio). The programs used to access the files can also be downloaded to a personal computer, free of charge. And, in a move that is certainly appreciated by users who constantly deal with the high price of disability-specific technological devices, Bookshare's staff continually work to expand the hardware options available for downloading. For example, not every schoolchild has access to a computer at home; yet, many have MP3 players or cell phones, which will soon be able to access the Bookshare.org files as well.

Bookshare.org members must show proof of a print disability, which can include visual impairments (low vision and blindness), reading/learning disabilities (typically students whose IEPs include text accommodations), and physical disabilities (who have difficulty holding a book or turning pages). Adult members pay a $25 initial setup fee and a $50 annual membership, which then provides them with access to thousands of titles. Thanks to funding from OSEP, students with print disabilities in the United States are entitled to free membership in Bookshare.org—a free library card of their own. A school can also register for a single membership and access the materials for all of its students with print disabilities without cost.

Bookshare.org aims for a 7-day turnaround time for specific K–12 textbook requests. Popular titles such as *New York Times* best sellers, Caldecott and Newbery Award winners, and Young Reader's Choice books are available for immediate download. The end result of this immense collaborative effort is a system that finally allows individuals with print disabilities to access the same reading materials, at the same time, as their sighted classmates, peers, and colleagues. As one enthusiastic Bookshare member wrote, "To everyone at Bookshare.org I send my heartfelt thanks. Thank you for believing in our dreams and making so much possible!"

For more about Jim Fruchterman, Benetech, and Bookshare.org, go to **http://www.benetech.org**.

Low Vision and Blindness Defined

The federal government in IDEA '04 includes blindness as part of its visual impairments category and does not define low vision or blindness separately. As you will notice when you review Table 11.1, the government uses the term *visual impairment* for what we call visual disabilities and *partial sight* for what we refer to as low

Table 11.1 • Definitions of Low Vision and Blindness

Source	Definition of Visual Disabilities
Federal government	Visual impairment including blindness means an impairment in vision that, even with correction, adversely affects a child's educational performance. The term includes both partial sight and blindness. **U.S. Department of Education (2006, p. 1265)**
	Definitions of Low Vision
Education professionals	A level of vision which, with standard correction, hinders an individual in the planning and/or execution of a task, but which permits enhancement of the functional vision through the use of optical or nonoptical devices, environmental modifications and/or techniques. **Corn (1989, p. 28)**
United Nations and Centers for Disease Control	Visual acuity between 20/70 and 20/400, with the best possible correction, or a visual field of 20 degrees or less **Centers for Disease Control (2005, p. 1)**
	Definition of Blindness
United Nations and Centers for Disease Control	Visual acuity worse than 20/400, with the best possible correction, or a visual field of 10 degrees or less **Centers for Disease Control (2005, p. 1)**
	Definition of Legally Blind
Nonprofit Organization	Central visual acuity of 20/200 or less in the better eye, with best correction, or a diameter of visual field that does not subtend an angle greater than 20 degrees at its widest point **American Foundation for the Blind (2005, p. 1)**

Sources: From 34 *CFR* Parts 300 and 303, Assistance to States for the Education of Children with Disabilities and the Early Intervention Program for Infants and Toddlers with Disabilities; Final Regulations (p. 1265), U.S. Department of Education, 2006. *Federal Register*, Washington, DC; Vision Impairment by Centers for Disease Control (CDC), National Center on Birth Defects and Developmental Disabilities, 2005, p. 1; "Instruction in the use of vision for children and adults with low vision: A proposed program model." by A. Corn, 1989, *RE:view, 21*, p. 28; "Key Definitions of Statistical Terms, Statistics and sources for professionals. American Foundation for the Blind (AFB), 2008a.

vision. The government has an additional term and definition for individuals who have severe visual loss. Although discussed later in this section, the criteria for *legal blindness* are found on Table 11.1 as well.

Visual loss results when the body's mechanism for vision is damaged or obstructed in such a way that objects in the environment cannot be perceived or understood. To better understand impaired vision, it is helpful to know how the process of vision works when these mechanisms are functioning properly. Then, as we did for hearing, we'll study three important factors that impact problems these individuals face:

- Degree of loss
- Age when the loss occurs
- Type of loss

So, before learning about different ways vision can be impaired at different points in a person's life, let's turn our attention to how the visual process works.

The Process of Vision

When people see normally, four elements must be present and operating:

- Light
- Something that reflects light
- An eye processing the reflected image into electrical impulses
- A brain receiving and giving meaning to these impulses

As you read the next paragraph, use the picture of the eye in Figure 11.1 to trace how the normal visual process works.

Light rays enter the front of the eye through the cornea. The **cornea** is transparent and curved. The **iris**, the colored part of the eye, expands and contracts in response to the intensity of light it receives. The **pupil** is the opening in the center of the iris. Light rays pass through the pupil to the **lens**, which is behind the iris. The lens brings an object seen into focus by changing its thickness. The process of adjust-

cornea The transparent, curved part of the front of the eye

iris The colored part of the eye

pupil The hole in the center of the iris that expands and contracts, admitting light to the eye

lens The part of the eye, located behind the iris, that brings objects seen into focus

Figure 11.1 • The Structure of the Human Eye

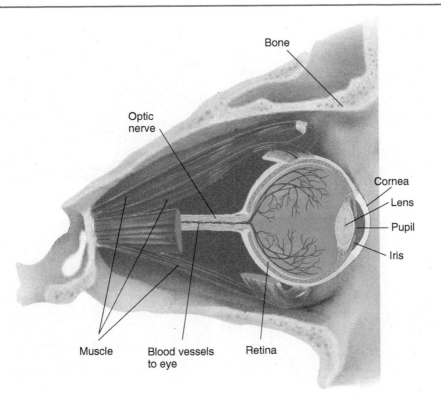

Bone
Optic nerve
Cornea
Lens
Pupil
Iris
Muscle
Blood vessels to eye
Retina

accommodation The focusing process of the lens of the eye

retina The inside lining of the eye

visual efficiency How well someone sees

visual acuity Sharpness of response to visual, auditory, or tactile stimuli

peripheral vision The outer area of a person's visual field

tunnel vision or restricted central vision Severe limitation in peripheral vision; limitations in the width of the visual field

residual vision The amount and degree of vision a person has functional use of, despite a visual disability

ment by the lens to bring things that are close and those that are far away into focus is called **accommodation**. The lens focuses light rays onto the **retina**, the inside lining at the back of the eye. It is made up of photosensitive cells that react to light rays and send messages along the optic nerve to the visual center of the brain.

Types of Visual Loss

As we have noted, how well people can use their sight is called **visual efficiency**. Visual efficiency is influenced by many factors, including the person's acuity and peripheral vision, environmental conditions, and psychological variables. **Visual acuity** is how well a person can see at various distances. **Peripheral vision** is the width of a person's field of vision, or the ability to perceive objects outside the direct line of vision. This aspect of vision helps people move freely through their environment. It helps them see large objects and movement. Severe limitation in peripheral vision is sometimes called **tunnel vision** or **restricted central vision**. Some people with visual disabilities have little functional use of sight, but most have substantial use of their vision, particularly with correction (glasses or contact lenses).

Most people do not realize that the vast majority of people with visual disabilities use vision as their primary method of learning. For many, their **residual vision**, which is the amount of vision they have left, can be further developed.

Normal acuity

Impaired acuity

Normal visual field

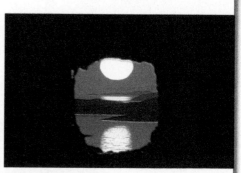

Impaired peripheral fields

Impaired lower visual field

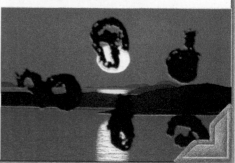

"Blind spots" in the visual field

Having an impaired visual field is different from having decreased visual acuity, yet both may occur simultaneously. The visual field is the area one can see when looking straight ahead, typically 160 to 180 degrees wide. When a person's visual field is reduced to 20 degrees or less, he or she is considered legally blind.

Credit: Courtesy of the IRIS Center for Training Enhancements, Peabody College, Vanderbilt University.

The vision of some is static, remaining the same from day to day, whereas others find that their ability to see varies by the day, time of day, or setting (Levin, 1996). For some, higher or lower levels of illumination affect how well they can see, but for others, lighting level makes little difference. For others, distance and contrast significantly affect how well they can process information presented through the visual channel. Some are color-blind; others are not. For most, optical aids such as glasses have a positive effect.

The eye is a very complicated mechanism. Damage to any part of the eye can result in serious limitations in one's abilities to see and process information through the visual channel. Table 11.2 lists conditions that affect various parts of the eye by using an organizational system originally suggested by Tuttle and Ferrell (1995). These conditions can result in blindness or severe visual disabilities. Advances in medical technology can reduce the severity of many disorders and can fix others completely, but not all can be corrected at the present time.

Table 11.2 • Types of Visual Loss

Type	Definition
Conditions of the Eye	
Myopia	Nearsightedness; condition allows focus on objects close but not at a distance.
Hyperopia	Farsightedness; condition allows focus on objects at a distance but not close.
Astigmatism	An eye disorder that produces images on the retina that are not equally in focus.
Amblyopia	Also known as "lazy eye," reduced vision in one eye due to inadequate use during early childhood.
Modify strabismus	Improper alignment of the eyes, which can cause one or both eyes to turn in (crossed), out, up, or down.
Conditions of the Eye Muscles	
Strabismus	Improper alignment of the two eyes causes two images to be received by the brain, with the possible result of one eye becoming nonfunctional.
Nystagmus	Rapid, involuntary movements of the eye interfere with bringing objects into focus.
Conditions of the Cornea, Iris, and Lens	
Glaucoma	Fluid in the eye is restricted, causing pressure to build up and damage the retina.
Aniridia	Undeveloped iris, due to lack of pigment (albinism), results in extreme sensitivity to light.
Cataract (opacity of the crystalline lens)	A cloudy film covers the lens of the eye.
Conditions of the Retina	
Diabetic retinopathy	Changes in the eye's blood vessels are caused by diabetes.
Macular degeneration	Damage to a small area near the center of the retina results in restricted central vision and difficulties in reading and writing.
Retinopathy of prematurity (ROP)	Excess oxygen to infants causes retinal damage; was called retrolental fibroplasia.
Retinal detachment	Detachment of the retina interrupts transmission of visual information to the brain.
Retinitis pigmentosa	Genetic eye disease leads progressively to blindness; night blindness is the first symptom.
Retinoblastoma	A tumor that impairs vision.
Condition of the Optic Nerve	
Atrophy	Reduced function of the optic nerve

Degree of Visual Loss

Professionals divide visual disabilities into two subgroups: low vision and blindness. Individuals with **low vision** use sight to learn, but their visual disabilities interfere with daily functioning. **Blindness** means that the person uses touch and hearing to learn and does not have functional use of sight. Parents and professionals use functional definitions to assign individuals to one of these two subgroups. Remember, this classification system is based on how well people can use their sight, even if its use is severely limited.

The term *low vision* was coined in the 1950s (Mogk & Goodrich, 2004), but Anne Corn developed the definition commonly used today some 30 years ago. That definition is found in Table 11.1. According to the functional definition, students with low vision use their sight for many school activities, including reading. In contrast, students who are blind do not have functional use of their vision and may perceive only shadows or some movement. These youngsters must be educated through tactile and other sensory channels and are considered functionally blind. Blindness can occur at any age, but its impact varies with age.

Legally blind is the federal government's term for individuals who are eligible to receive special tax benefits and materials, and is yet another way to categorize people with visual problems. (The definition and criteria to qualify for benefits through this category is also found in Table 11.1.) The designation of legal blindness is used despite a long-term movement toward functional definitions of visual disabilities and the fact that many people who meet the qualifications for this classification use print to read and gain information.

Age of Onset

Similar to the classifications for deaf and hard of hearing students that you learned about in the previous chapter, individuals with visual disabilities can be classified by the age of onset (when the disability occurred):

- **Congenitally blind** (existing at birth or during infancy)
- **Adventitiously blind** (occurring after the age of 2)

This distinction is important because people who lose their sight after age 2 remember what some objects look like. The later the disability occurs, the more they remember. Visual memory is an important factor in learning, for it can influence one's development of concepts and other aspects important to learning.

Characteristics

Because the needs of students who are blind differ from those who have low vision, we have separated discussions about their common characteristics into these two general groups. Remember that, as with all other individuals with disabilities, no consistent set of characteristics fits every student. Teachers must adjust their approach to working with a student based on his or her individual characteristics and needs with the demands of each situation.

Students with Low Vision

Students with low vision read print and typically access the general education curriculum alongside their peers without disabilities. Most students with low vision *do* require accommodations and some extra assistance from classmates and teachers.

Reading Standard Print   The vast majority of students with low vision learn to read and write, watch television, and use their vision to function in society. The majority have sufficient functional vision to read the standard print (12-point font) used in elementary and high school textbooks and to move in their environments

---

low vision The degree of visual loss; vision is still useful for learning or the execution of a task

blindness The degree of visual loss; not having a functional use of sight

legally blind A category of blindness used to qualify for federal and state benefits

congenital blindness Blindness present at birth or occurring during early infancy

adventitious blindness Blindness acquired after the age of 2

independently (Wilkinson & Trantham, 2004). They can read the same printed books as their classmates, but will do so at a much slower rate (Gompel, van Bon, & Schreuder, 2004). As such, they will likely need more time to complete reading assignments. These students may hold the books closer to their eyes than their peers to adjust for varying type and print style (Wilkinson & Trantham, 2004). Many of these students, however, cannot read smaller print like that in newspapers. Fortunately, most newspapers are now available online where the print size can be adjusted by changing the standard viewing options available on all computers.

Reading Enlarged Print **Enlarged print** offers the option of having the print on the page larger than what is typical. Enlarged print versions of reading materials have been available for many years. Many standard publications (e.g., dictionaries, thesauruses, and atlases as well as Book-of-the-Month Club titles and *Reader's Digest*) are available in enlarged type.

Many students with low vision use their sight to read, but they need specially adapted or enlarged-text versions of the books used in their classes. One complaint has been the excessive length of time it often takes to get large-print accommodations (Frank, 2000). Fortunately, this barrier is easily overcome today, thanks to the availability of copiers, scanners, and computers that readily adjust the size of what is printed. Also, as you learned in the section on universal design for learning (UDL) in Chapters 1 and 2, IDEA '04 mandates that publishers provide electronic versions of adopted textbooks. Bookshare.org (read again this chapter's Making a Difference feature) helps all who need e-versions of texts so they can overcome their print disabilities. The fact that each individual with a print disability is now able to select the modification option (e.g., print size, format) that is best for them, and is able to do so quickly, is clear evidence that printed information is much more accessible than it was only a few years ago.

Students with low vision who use enlarged print, and their teachers, often need assistance in determining how much text needs to be adjusted. Determining the amount of increase is a complicated process that calculates the individual's speed or rate of reading text passages across a range of print sizes (Bailey et al., 2003; Lueck et al., 2003). **Teachers of students with visual impairments (TVIs)** are valuable resources; general and special educators should consult with these educators when varying the print size for either instruction or assessments. You will learn more about TVIs later in this chapter's Collaboration section.

Another group of students with low vision cannot profit from print whether it be standard size or enlarged. These individuals have good central vision but a limited visual field. For them, enlargements may be a hindrance. However, audio versions of books, **personal readers** (people who read text to them), or computer-generated print-to-voice systems (described later in the Overcoming Challenges section) may be good alternatives.

Students Who Are Blind

Students who are blind differ greatly from students with low vision (HEATH Resource Center, 2001). Many of these individuals do not read print but, rather, have printed materials translated into nonprint formats: recorded, print-to-speech, or braille. They typically use aids to move around independently. For some, learning how to socialize and interact easily with others does not come naturally. Let's first turn our attention to a special reading system developed for people who cannot see print.

Reading Braille Some people who are blind use a tactile system for reading and writing. **Braille** is a coded system of dots embossed on paper so that individuals can feel a page of text. In part because of the availability of print-to-voice options, the number of people who use braille is declining. Therefore, concerns about the reading abilities of students with visual disabilities came to the attention of Congress. So, Congress addressed the issue of braille instruction in IDEA '04. Read

enlarged print Adjusted size of print so individuals with low vision can read

teachers of students with visual impairments (TVIs) Specially trained and certified teachers who provide direct or consultative special education services related to the effects of vision loss

personal readers People who read for others

myeducationlab Go to the Activities and Applications section in Chapter 11 of MyEducationLab, and complete Activity 1. As you watch the video and answer the accompanying questions, consider how a visual disability impacts a student's educational progress, as well as accommodations teachers can make.

braille A system of reading and writing that uses dot codes that are embossed on paper; tactile reading; created in 1824 by Louis Braille as a precursor to the method used today

What IDEA '04 Says About . . .

Braille and Its Use

The IEP Team for each student with a visual disability must consider special factors about each child's method of reading:

- All IEPs for children with visual disabilities must address the issue of braille instruction and the use of braille in classroom settings.

- Evaluate the child's reading and writing skills, educational needs, and future need for instruction in braille or use of braille.

- Provide instruction in braille and allow the child to use braille, if that method is deemed appropriate for that student.

- The decision whether to use braille with any student cannot be based on factors such as the availability of alternative reading methods or the availability of braille instruction.

- Once the decision is made, services and materials must be delivered without undue delay.

What IDEA '04 Says About Braille and Its Use to learn the law's requirements on this topic.

It is important for teachers to understand that new technology allowing greater access to print may well reduce the popularity of braille even more. Here are a few reasons why:

- Reading with braille can be cumbersome and slow.
- Becoming even minimally proficient using braille method takes extensive training and practice.
- Braille also uses different codes for different types of reading, such as math and music, which makes it even more difficult for students with cognitive impairments to master the system completely.
- Few teachers know how to use or teach braille.

One barrier faced by those who use braille is now overcome. As we have discussed, braille versions of texts used in the general education classroom are now readily available and cost is no longer an issue. Because of the inclusion of braille in IDEA '04, concerns about the literacy rates of this group of learners, and improved availability of braille versions of texts, more experts are thinking about braille instruction and the goal of braille literacy for students who are blind (Wormsley, 2004). Table 11.3 shows the 12 components of instruction leading to braille literacy, as identified by Koenig and Holbrook (2000), and provides some applications of these instructional targets.

orientation The mental map people use to move through environments; a topic of instruction for students who are blind

Orientation and Mobility Students with very low visual efficiency need special orientation and mobility training to increase their ability to move around independently. **Orientation** is the mental map people have about their surroundings (Hill, 1986). Most of us use landmarks and other cues to get from one place to another. Think about how you get from your house to a friend's home or from one class to another on campus. What cues or landmarks do you use? These cues or landmarks make up our mental maps and our orientation to our environments. Students with visual disabilities must learn mental landmarks and need to know their schools well. They need to know emergency evacuation procedures, exit paths from the school buildings, and ways to safely move through their environment both during normal school hours and in times of stress (Cox & Dykes, 2001). **Mobility** is the ability to travel safely and efficiently from one place to another. **Orientation and mobility (O&M) instructors** are the professionals responsible for teaching these skills.

mobility The ability to travel safely and efficiently from one place to another; a topic of instruction for students who are blind

orientation and mobility (O&M) instructors Professionals who teach students who are blind to move freely through their environments and travel safely from place to place independently

According to the American Foundation for the Blind's (AFB) most recent data, 109,000 blind adults use the long cane; the majority are younger adults (AFB, 2008b). Most cane users are under the age of 65, probably because learning how to be independently mobile by using a long cane is difficult, and proficient use requires many years of instruction and practice. Here's how it works. While a person is walking, the cane is tapped on the ground and makes a sound. It helps the user know when a hallway ends, when stairs begin and end, and when doors are reached. A long cane does not always help the individual avoid obstacles found in modern society. For example, protruding and overhanging objects are undetectable with the traditional long canes. But there is a new answer to avoid such dangerous situations (Eye of the Pacific, 2008). The Laser-Cane® now allows for safer travel through offices, busy streets, and shopping malls. This device resembles a long cane but adds a device that emits three invisible beams. When a beam is not returned to the device (such as when it doesn't bounce back from a sidewalk), a sound alerts the user that he or she is approach-

Table 11.3 • Braille Literacy Skill Areas

1. **Emergent Braille Literacy**
   Listen to adults read; develop hand-finger skills; observe proficient braille reading.

2. **Pre-braille—Early Formal Literacy**
   Learn hand-finger skills, tactile discrimination, and hand movement; expand conceptual knowledge and vocabulary; develop early reading skills; become motivated.

3. **Beginning Braille Literacy**
   Learn braille decoding and word analysis skills; learn braille writing; build fluency; apply literacy skills throughout day.

4. **Begin Dual Media (print and braille)**
   Learn print and braille reading concurrently; learn print and braille writing concurrently; develop vocabulary, comprehension, and reading for specific purposes; engage in leisure reading.

5. **Intermediate Braille Literacy**
   Use reading as a tool for learning; continue fluency building; incorporate technology into reading experiences.

6. **Advanced Braille Literacy**
   Learn computer braille and foreign language braille; continue using and developing braille for math and science, continue inclusion of technology; balance literacy tools (braille and recorded material).

7. **Braille Literacy for Those with Print Literacy**
   Learn tactile perception, hand movements, and letter or symbol recognition in braille; begin learning contractions; learn braille writing skills; apply literacy skills daily.

8. **Listening, Aural-Reading and Live-Reader Skills**
   Develop auditory skills (e.g., auditory awareness, sound localization); acquire information by listening; learn how to use recorded textbooks; direct activities of live readers.

9. **Technology Skills**
   Gain access to printed information through technology; take notes by using braille: use speech-synthesizing devices; use the Internet to gather information.

10. **Keyboarding and Word-Processing**
    Master touch typing; use word processing software, along with all editing features; apply keyboarding and word processing in daily applications.

11. **Slate-and-Stylus Skills**
    Master a variety of slate and stylus equipment; become proficient in their use; apply these skills in practical situations.

12. **Signature-Writing Skills**
    Learn how to write a signature for legal purposes; practice with many different writing tools (e.g., pens, pencils); understand about when and why signatures are necessary; apply skill appropriately.

Sources: *Journal of Visual Impairment & Blindness* by A. J. Loenig and M. C. Holbrook. Copyright 2000 by American Foundation for the Blind (AFB). Reproduced with permission of American Foundation for the Blind (AFB) in the formats Textbook and Other book via Copyright Clearance Center.

ing a step down. A vibrator signals that there is an obstruction ahead. By using global positioning technology (the technology that provides automobile drivers with maps and directions), the cane creates standard routes (from home to work and back), announces points of interest in the surrounding area (including ATM machines), and also provides map cards with the name of the streets to help people be more independent and mobile.

Learning to use a long cane is part of the school curriculum for these students. Orientation and mobility instruction is part of every school day.

Not all people who need assistance with mobility use long canes; some use guide dogs. The number of guide dog users is relatively small. Of the 1.3 million legally blind people in America, only about 7,000 use guide dogs (less than 4%) to help them move about independently (AFB, 2008b).

Even when using a long cane or a guide dog, there are times, such as when crossing a busy street or entering an unfamiliar building, that assistance from sighted people is helpful. In such a situation, the sighted person must be sensitive to several issues:

- Be sure the person wants help.
- Ask the individual to be sure he or she wants assistance.
- If the answer is yes, guide the individual by offering your arm, holding it in a relaxed position.
- The individual usually will gently grasp your arm at or above your elbow and will walk slightly behind or to your side. (Never push or pull as you walk.)
- Enjoy a conversation, and walk with ease.

As you can tell, learning to be independently mobile can be a daunting task for many individuals who are blind. Building enough confidence to tackle a city street takes years of practice. Yet, some learning experiences can be fun. Sports and recreation programs and activities not only contribute to better orientation and mobility skills but also help students become engaged and active. Special sports programs are available to individuals who are blind or have low vision. Special skiing, hiking, baseball, bowling, bicycling, and horseback riding are very popular. However, some people with visual disabilities choose not to participate in special programs but, rather, compete with sighted athletes and excel. In 2000, Marla Runyan became the first legally blind track athlete to compete in the Olympics. When she runs, Marla has enough sight to make out the bright white lines on the track and detect the other runners around her. Her peripheral vision is intact, so she can run independently without supports or an assistant. Another outstanding blind athlete is Erik Weihenmayer (2001), who chose climbing as his passion. While few sighted individuals have ever scaled Mount Everest, Erik accomplished that feat as part of his quest to scale the Seven Summits—the highest mountains on each continent. Approximately 100 climbers have ever achieved that status, and Erik is the only one who is blind.

It is not necessary to climb mountains or run marathons to enjoy outside activities. Those with visual disabilities do not need to be super athletes to participate in athletic events. Here's one example: Teams of teenagers with visual disabilities, along with guides, took a 4-day, 139-mile bicycling trip from Nashville to the home of Helen Keller via the Natchez Trace (Associated Press, 2002; Duzak, 2002). In addition to learning the joy of the freedom of mobility and movement, students who participate in sports and recreational opportunities learn important social skills that benefit them at school and later in life (Shapiro et al., 2005).

Social Skills For all of us, the process of learning social skills begins in infancy and continues to develop throughout childhood. The infant learns to make eye contact, smile, and respond to facial expressions and gestures of others. For those whose vision is restricted, the process of developing social skills and learning how to interact appropriately with others usually does not happen automatically, and early intervention is important. Direct, or explicit, instruction in these skills must begin with family members and continue during the preschool and throughout the school years (Miller & Menacher, 2007). Children must learn to interact with playmates during preschool, and with teachers and peers during the school years. Children should learn important social skills, such as how to join and participate in play activities, resolve conflicts, attract and direct attention of peers, and maintain friendships. Whereas sighted children learn these skills through typical interactions, many of those with visual disabilities need explicit instruction to develop these skills.

Consider how sight contributes to social interactions. Most of us adjust our behavior in response to nonverbal cues from others, which often guide our social

Friends and family can be instrumental in helping a blind person experience activities, such as bike riding, that might not be possible without assistance.

interactions. Next time you are interacting with friends, consider how nonverbal cues (facial expressions, a shrug of the shoulders) affect the meaning of a message. Now think about how the literal message (without the nonverbal cues) of the interaction would be understood by someone who could not use sight during the interaction. The result of receiving incomplete communication messages can have a serious impact on the individual.

Students with visual disabilities may exhibit social behaviors that many consider unacceptable, which in turn draw negative feedback from peers (Eaton & Wall, 1999). In general, students with visual disabilities tend to be less assertive than their sighted peers, which may disturb the necessary balance and equilibrium in social exchanges (Buhrow, Hartshorne, & Bradley-Johnson, 1998). Many lack play skills, ask too many irrelevant questions, and engage in inappropriate acts of affection (Rettig, 1994). Inappropriate or immature social behaviors can inhibit a child's ability to interact positively with others, to be included in small social groups, and to make friends (MacCuspie, 1992). Teachers, families, and peers can make a positive difference by helping these students develop social competence (Jindal-Snape, 2005). Fortunately for busy teachers, research shows that the application of self-management strategies (read again A Closer Look at Data-Based Practices in Chapter 6) and help from classmates can make a real difference. Peers can be taught to model appropriate social skills, to prompt their classmate when these skills should be applied, and to provide feedback. Teachers can also help students understand explicit and implicit rules of games and social interactions. Meanwhile, parents can organize small play groups at home and give direct feedback to their child about his or her interpersonal interactions (Celeste, 2007).

Many individuals who are blind develop inappropriate behaviors, such as rocking or inappropriate hand movements (McHugh & Lieberman, 2003; Miller & Menacker, 2007). It is important for teachers to understand such behaviors. Here's what we now know:

- Stereotypic rocking is associated with blindness, particularly in cases of congenital blindness (e.g., ROP).
- These mannerisms are more often seen in individuals who, as infants, spent long periods hospitalized.
- Stereotypic rocking does not destroy property nor result in injury to others.
- The behavior is often annoying to others and interferes with typical socializations.
- Although the behavior is often persistent, it can be modified, reduced, and eliminated.

Prevalence

According to the AFB, approximately 1.3 million Americans are legally blind, and there are some 10 million with low vision or blindness (AFB, 2008c). However, the vast majority of these people are over the age of 65. Worldwide, only 4% of all blind people are children (Hatton, 2001). Visual disabilities are clearly associated with increasing age. The proportion of children with visual disabilities is much smaller than the proportion of people with this disability in the general population. Advances in medicine have had two major effects on the incidence of visual loss: (1) The incidence of visual disabilities has increased with the increasing number of older Americans, and (2) the incidence of visual disabilities in children has greatly decreased (Mogk & Goodrich, 2004). Among preschoolers, 1 in 20 has a visual problem that could result in permanent loss if not treated properly (Prevent Blindness America [PBA], 2005c). Approximately 1 in 4 school-age children has impaired vision; the majority are correctable using eyeglasses or contacts. Most do not need special education services because their vision problems can be corrected to the point where their educational performance is not negatively affected. About 6 of every 10,000 students (about 0.06%) have visual disabilities and receive special services (National Center For Educational Services [NCES], 2008; OSEP, 2008). Nationally, only 25,369 students between the ages of 6 and 17 are receiving special education because of low vision or blindness. The vast majority are students with low vision. However, many children with visual disabilities are not counted in this special education category. Nearly two-thirds of children with visual disabilities have more than one disability (Centers for Disease Control [CDC], 2005). If the visual disability is combined with a hearing impairment, the child will most likely be included in the deaf-blind special education category (see Chapter 13); if the child has a vision impairment and moderate or severe intellectual disabilities, the likelihood is for that child to be included in the multiple disabilities category (also see Chapter 13 for more information about multiple-severe disabilities).

Causes and Prevention

Medical technology is helping to identify more specific causes of disabilities, information that may then lead to either cures or preventive measures. For example, two causes of visual disabilities were reduced dramatically during the last part of the 20th century: retinopathy of prematurity (ROP) and rubella. Today, precautions are being taken to prevent many cases of ROP in low-birthweight babies; if it is not prevented, it often can be corrected with eye surgery. Today, a vaccine protects everyone from rubella, a cause of congenital visual disabilities and of multiple disabilities.

Causes

Although medical advances have reduced the prevalence of visual disabilities in children, medical technology can cause increases in this disability as well. Today more infants survive premature birth and very low birthweights of less than 2 pounds. The most common causes of blindness among children are complications caused by premature births (PBA, 2005c). Heredity also contributes to a large number of vision problems. And, accidents, household injuries, and sports activities cause eye damage to thousands of children each year.

The most common eye problems in children are myopia (nearsightedness), strabismus (crossed eyes), and amblyopia ("lazy eye") (PBA, 2005c). Amblyopia is often caused by a misalignment of the eyes, or one eye's ability to focus better than the other's. As with strabismus, this misalignment usually results from the inability of the eye muscles to work together. Glasses, surgery, and eye exercises are all successful treatment options for these conditions. Prevention, however, is preferable to treatment in cases where the vision problem can be avoided.

Prevention

Researchers are working to identify genes that cause some forms of blindness. The gene that causes retinitis pigmentosa has now been located and isolated, and there is hope of a cure in the near future. Other medical advances—such as laser treatment, surgery, and corneal implants—also help reduce the incidence of visual disabilities among children or lessen their severity. According to Prevent Blindness America (2005b), nearly 90% of all eye injuries and 50% of blindness cases can be prevented. Putting sharp objects (even pencils) out of the reach of children, being certain that toys are safe, and getting help as soon as possible when injuries do happen can make all the difference. Early treatment can avoid a lifetime of visual problems. Table 11.4 provides a list of measures that can prevent vision injuries in children.

For those visual disabilities that cannot be avoided, their impact can be lessened through early and consistent treatment. Unfortunately, not all U.S. children have early access to health care. Considering the long-term costs to society and to these individuals, the problem of access to health care must be addressed.

Overcoming Challenges: Technology

The telephone and the phonograph are examples of technological advances that were created for the general population but that have great benefits for people with visual disabilities because they offer inexpensive access to both entertainment and information. Large-print books, digital versions of novels, audio books, and computers are also examples of items developed for the general population that have increased access to print for people with visual disabilities. Now everyone has greater access to printed information through electronic books and laptop computers that allow the reader to increase the size of print or to switch from print to voice easily.

These exciting technological advances open up a new world for people with visual disabilities. Clearly, these advances facilitate their participation and give them independence in all aspects of modern society. However, three major barriers inhibit their access: cost, complexity, and information. With the average costs of assistive devices ranging from $1,000 to $10,000 and the vast number of options available, careful selection of the right equipment is important. However, as we

---

Table 11.4 • Preventing Vision Loss

Home Eye Safety	Sports Eye Safety
Pad or cushion sharp corners, such as those on furniture edges.	Wear proper safety goggles, especially for basketball and sports that use racquets.
Install locks on cabinets and drawers in kitchens and bathrooms	Make sure that baseball batting helmets have face shields.
Store sharp personal items (cosmetics or toiletries), utensils, and desk supplies out of children's reach.	Use U.S. Amateur Hockey Association–approved helmets and face shields when playing hockey.
Do not purchase toys with sharp points, shafts, spikes, or dangerous edges.	Be aware that regular glasses do not provide enough protection.
Avoid toys that fire projectiles.	
Keep BB guns locked safely away from children.	
Use proper restraints (car seats, boosters, seat belts) in cars.	
Implement extreme precautions when using fireworks.	

Sources: Prevent Blindness America (2005b). Eye Safety at Home. Retrieved July 28, 2008 from http://www.preventblindness.org/safety/homesafe.html; and Prevent Blindness America (2005c). Sports Eye Safety. Retrieved July 28, 2008 from http://www.preventblindness.org/safety/sportspage1.html.

Devices such as this one, a CCTV, allow for instantly enlarged print and can be adjusted to the exact visual needs of the user.

visual input devices Assistive technology to help people with visual disabilities with their vision

closed-circuit television (CCTV) An assistive visual input technology; uses a television to increase the size of objects or print

audio input devices Assistive technology to help people with visual disabilities by changing what would be seen into information that is heard

audiodescriptions An assistive audio input technology; presents visual information on screen or stage via oral narrations

myeducationlab Go to the Activities and Applications section in Chapter 11 of MyEducationLab, and complete Activity 2. As you watch the video and answer the accompanying questions, consider the possibilities afforded by assistive devices to students with visual disabilities.

mentioned earlier, when equipment is developed for the mass market (cell phones are a good example), people with disabilities also benefit because the devices are both accessible and afford able (Fruchterman, 2003). Assistive devices can be grouped into three categories:

- Visual input devices
- Audio input devices
- Tactile input devices

Visual input devices **Visual input devices** are equipment or technologies that help people with visual loss access visual information in the environment. Many of these devices are used to enlarge print, so it is easier for a person with visual loss to see and read. For example, **closed-circuit television (CCTV)** technology allows video magnifiers to enlarge the print found in printed texts and books (American Association of Retired Persons [AARP], 2006; Lighthouse International, 2005). By means of a small television camera with a zoom lens and a sliding reading stand on which the printed materials are placed, greatly enlarged printed material (up to 60 times the original size) can be viewed on a television monitor. Another version, the Magni-Cam, has a TV camera embedded in something that looks like a computer mouse that can roll over printed pages. Such equipment provides immediate access to all types of printed materials, such as magazines and food and prescription-drug labels.

Other equipment can increase print size. Most standard copy machines can also adjust print size. Personal computers can produce large-print displays on the computers' screens, allowing persons with low vision to adjust the size and style of print to match their own visual efficiencies, and making the Internet a wonderful source of information. In addition, printers allow the user to select different font sizes for hard-copy printout. These features enable teachers to prepare different versions of handouts—one for students with visual disabilities and one for sighted classmates.

Audio input devices **Audio input devices** are equipment or technologies that enable people to hear what otherwise would be read or seen (e.g., talking ATMs). Bank of America has the largest network of talking ATMs, making accessible banking a reality for people who are blind (Bank of America, 2008). Talking books are not new and have been available through the Library of Congress since 1934. The American Printing House for the Blind (APHB) provides compressed-speech (eliminating natural pauses and accelerating speech) versions recorded on tape and CDs; these can be ordered from regional resource and materials centers. Today, audio books are available at most bookstores. Developed for the general public, audio versions of many classics and current best-sellers allow people with visual disabilities greater access to books and print materials. And, as you learned in the Making a Difference feature earlier, digitally scanned books, newspapers, and other print materials are now available in a variety of formats (e.g., braille, audio), thanks to the efforts of Bookshare.org.

Another technique allows people with limited vision to enjoy plays, movies, television, and home videos. **Audiodescriptions** are narrations that describe the nonverbal cues and visual information that sighted audiences see on the screen or stage. This system, initially developed for television, uses the added sound track available in stereo televisions to describe aspects (costumes, scenes, sets, body language) important to a fuller understanding of the story. A similar system has been devised for theaters; it uses an earphone and a tiny FM receiver. The explanations occur in the pauses or otherwise silent parts of the film or play. This accommodation is not so common in movie theaters, because many cinema owners are unwilling to shoulder the financial expenses necessary to equip a theater, even though systems allowing for both captions for deaf moviegoers and audiodescriptions for blind patrons are now available (McMahon, 2000). TV shows that have audiodescription are becoming more common, because the second audio track that is necessary to play the descriptions is now included on most TV sets (Media Access Group, 2008).

Tactile input devices **Tactile input devices** are equipment or technologies that allow people to use touch to gain information. For example, a well-known tactile system is braille, which allows people to read by feeling letters that have been translated into patterns of dots raised or embossed on a flat surface such as paper. People who use braille as their preferred reading method find the Perkins Brailler to be a compact and portable machine that embosses special paper with the braille code. The Perkins Brailler is inexpensive but less efficient than electronic versions that use microprocessors to store and retrieve information. For example, Braille 'n Speak® functions

as an organizer, note taker, calendar, and talking clock. The new braille PDA uses wireless technology to give its users access to the Internet, a planner, speech output, and phone service (APHB, 2008). While the price has decreased in recent years, it still costs nearly $1,140.

Personal computers with special printers transform print into braille. When a specially designed braille printer is attached to a microcomputer, standard text can be translated into braille, allowing a teacher who does not know how to use braille to produce braille copies of handouts, tests, and other class materials. Some new printers even produce braille and print on the same page.

Only a few years ago, diagrams and illustrations were omitted from braille versions because of the inability of technology to produce them easily. Today a new system, Tactile Access to Education for Visually Impaired Students (TAEVIS), uses a special type of paper, backed with plastic and coated with a heat-sensitive chemical, to produce raised versions of diagrams.

One major limitation of braille texts is that they are so much larger than standard texts. For instance, the seventh book in the Harry Potter series, *Harry Potter and the Deathly Hallows,* is 759 pages in length, which is a large book for any child (or even an adult) to handle. However, the braille version of the book was 1,072 pages, and a whopping 11 volumes (Royal National Institute for the Blind, 2008). (Note: In a first-ever publishing feat, the braille and audio versions of the book were released at the same time as the print version, enabling readers with visual disabilities to have access to the exciting series climax at the same time as their friends). A **refreshable braille display** is a small device that hooks up to

A small braille PDA that fits in the palm of the hand and syncs with computers uses Bluetooth technology to "talk" with cell phones and the Internet. It includes a personal organizer and even produces speech output.

tactile input devices Assistive technology that allows people to use touch to gain information

refreshable braille display Allows for short sections of braille text to be downloaded to a computer

Refreshable braille displays help braille users avoid carrying heavy, multi-volume books, while increasing their access to print materials available via computer.

a computer. Text from the computer is downloaded to the display, which raises and lowers a series of plastic pins, to provide short braille passages. Once the user has read all the characters on the display, they can press a key to refresh the display and load the next sentence or passage. Not surprisingly, the display is expensive, ranging in price from $5,500 to $11,000 (AFB, 2008a). As the technology improves, the costs are anticipated to decrease, and the products described here will continue to improve access to the world of print for individuals with visual disabilities.

Assessment

Professionals and parents use assessment information to decide whether a student should learn to read using print or braille, or if the student needs a curriculum that includes orientation and mobility training. These assessments also are used to specify the level and type of education placements the child will receive, accommodations to be provided, and which related services must be specified in the student's IEP. Such decisions determine what types of special education services a student receives, but they also have lifelong implications.

Early Identification

photoscreening A system used to test visual acuity for those who cannot participate in the evaluation either because of age or ability

Early identification of visual loss is very important not only to reduce its impact on learning, but also to prevent the problem from worsening (PBA, 2005a). For students who are very young or have multiple disabilities, other testing options are available. For example, **photoscreening** is the system for testing acuity when the individual cannot actively or reliably participate in visual assessments. Photoscreening uses a special camera to take a picture of the individual's eyes that is then examined to look for signs of vision problems.

Snellen chart A chart used to test visual acuity, developed in 1862

Prereferral: Vision Screenings

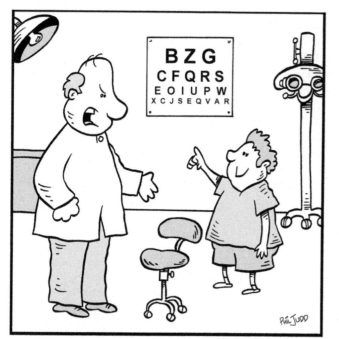

"No you can't take a copy home to prepare for your eye exam next week!"

Source: www.CartoonStock.com

Most states require that all students have a visual screening test. Trained volunteers often conduct initial screenings and then refer students who may have a vision problem for further testing. Student's visual acuity is often tested in the school nurse's office or by a pediatrician using the Snellen chart. The **Snellen chart**, originally developed by a Dutch ophthalmologist in 1862, comes in two versions and is used to screen visual acuity. One test uses the letter *E* placed in various positions in different sizes; the other uses alphabet letters in different sizes. When screening large numbers of people, a more efficient adaptation of the Snellen chart projects the *E* on a television monitor placed 10 to 20 feet away from the viewer. The viewer matches a key on a computer with the direction or placement of the *E* on the screen, and the computer analyzes the data.

Schoolwide visual screenings can help identify students with visual disabilities and get them needed services early. Alert teachers and parents, familiar with the possible signs of a visual problem (see Table 11.5 for a list), can help identify such students even sooner and ultimately reduce the impact of the disability. A school nurse, pediatrician, or ophthalmologist should check students who exhibit one or more of these characteristics. Although not required, each child's screening should

Table 11.5 • Possible Signs of Vision Problems

Appearance of the Eyes	**Problems with Schoolwork**	**Behavior and Movement**
Eyes • water excessively; • are red or continually inflamed; • appear crusty; • seem dull, wrinkled, or cloudy; • are swollen; • look gray or white (one or both pupils); • are not aligned.	The student has difficulty • reading small print; • identifying details in pictures; • discriminating letters; • with close work.	The student • appears clumsy; • bumps or trips over objects; • can't catch a ball, button clothes, or tie shoes; • covers an eye while reading; • tilts head; • holds object close to an eye to view it; • complains of dizziness after working on an assignment.

include teachers' observations about classroom behaviors and performance. For example, teachers should indicate whether a particular child complains about scratchy or itchy eyes or headaches, rubs the eyes excessively, or has difficulty discriminating letters or symbols when completing classroom assignments. Such information is especially helpful when recommendations are made about placement and the types of special assistance a child should receive.

Identification: Visual Assessments

Two types of eye specialists provide diagnosis and treatment: ophthalmologists (medical doctors who specialize in eye disorders) and optometrists. **Ophthalmologists** are doctors who conduct physical examinations of the eye, prescribe corrective lenses and medicines, prescribe drugs, and perform surgery. **Optometrists** are professionals who measure vision, prescribe corrective lenses, and also make functional recommendations. An **optician** is a specialist who fills the ophthalmologist's or optometrist's prescription for glasses or corrective lenses.

Although parents and professionals are advocating for the use of functional definitions of visual disabilities, many states still use measures of acuity to qualify youngsters for special education services. Normal visual acuity is measured by how accurately a person can see an object or image 20 feet away. Normal vision is thus said to be 20/20. A person whose vision is measured at 20/40 can see at 20 feet what people who do not need visual correction (glasses or contact lenses) can see at 40 feet away. **Field of vision**—how wide an area that can be seen—is measured in degrees. Normal field of vision is about 160 to 170 degrees horizontally (CDC, 2005). In Table 11.1, we noted that people whose visual field is restricted to no more than 20 degrees are classified as legally blind. Although states and school districts vary in the criteria they use to determine eligibility for special services, people with visual acuity measuring 20/70 to 20/200 in the better eye, with correction, are typically considered to have low vision (AFB, 2008b). Acuity below 20/200 classifies an individual as legally blind.

Assessing functional vision can be complicated and imprecise. Information must be gathered from multiple sources. Diagnosticians, parents, general educators, teachers of students who are blind or have low vision, school nurses, and eye specialists can all provide important information. Children with visual disabilities are another source of information, but you may be surprised to learn that they are often very unreliable. Many parents report that their blind children, possibly motivated by the desire to please a doctor or a diagnostician, may report and simulate a different level of blindness than they actually possess (Erin & Corn, 1994). For example, some children falsely indicate that they can see things: a car coming, the moon at

ophthalmologist A medical doctor who specializes in eye disorders

optometrist A professional who measures vision and can prescribe corrective lenses (eyeglasses or contact lenses)

optician A person who fills either the ophthalmologist's or optometrist's prescriptions for glasses or corrective lenses

field of vision The width of the area a person can see; measured in degrees

night, or the color of an object. Decisions about visual status must be made from accurate information, but surprisingly, collecting such information can prove to be quite challenging.

Evaluation: Testing Accommodations

Students with visual disabilities often require accommodations during instruction. Those accommodations must also be available to them during weekly quizzes or annual state- or districtwide tests. Students who cannot access print may need help during testing situations. Personal readers are people—teachers, paraprofessionals—who read the directions and test items to the student. Computerized adapted testing, which can provide magnified text or translation to refreshable braille displays, is becoming more widely adopted, although it may require higher technical skills for test proctors (Kamei-Hannan, 2008). Students who can read print usually do so at a much slower rate than their peers without visual loss (Gompel et al., 2004). These students need extra time to take tests so their achievement is not masked by not having time to read the questions. Also slow reading gives them an extra disadvantage when answering multiple-choice questions (Evans & Douglas, 2008; Kamei-Hannen, 2008). As such, they usually qualify for extended time on tests. Teachers must work together to determine the fair amount of time needed to complete tests.

Early Intervention

The preschool years provide the foundation for lifelong learning and independence. During this time, the foundations are laid for social skills, academic success, and independence. Yet, children with visual disabilities may have problems in these areas. Recall that those who are congenitally blind (born blind) and those who became blind at a very early age (adventitiously blind) have little or no memory of how the world looks. They do not see their mother's smile or the toys in their cribs. These infants are not stimulated like sighted infants and so they have limited opportunities for learning. A good preschool program can give young children with visual disabilities the right start so that the disadvantages this disability can cause are minimized. The teacher of a preschooler with visual disabilities should coordinate a multidisciplinary team of specialists, including an ophthalmologist, occupational therapist, physical therapist, O&M instructor, and social worker.

Play

Researchers are learning that play is a very important part of human development (McGaha & Farran, 2001). Through play, young children learn to socialize, interact with others, and cooperate. Young children also learn about their environment, develop motor skills, and often enhance their language skills via discovery and exploration, which are encouraged through play activities. Because of their disability, blind and low vision children play very differently from others and are also delayed about 2 years behind their sighted peers in the development of play skills (Hughes, Dote-Kwan, & Dolendo, 1998).

Characteristics of play for children with visual disabilities include: engaging in high rates of solitary play, not playing spontaneously, seeking play with adults rather than other children, not taking conversational turns, and selecting toys that are concrete, familiar items (McGaha & Farran, 2001; Tröster & Brambring, 1992, 1994). These behaviors may be inadvertently reinforced by parents, whose expectations for children's physical activity levels decrease in proportion to the level of vision loss (Stuart, Lieberman, & Han, 2006). As children become accustomed to solitary play, their need for social engagement may decrease (Shapiro et al., 2008). Delayed play development might well contribute to later difficulties in social

TIPS for Classroom Management

PROMOTING POSITIVE SOCIAL INTERACTIONS

For the student with low vision or blindness

- Provide instruction and practice in everyday social conventions (turning toward or facing someone who is speaking).
- Prompt and reinforce students when they display appropriate body language.
- Teach appropriate methods for initiating conversations and activities with others.
- Teach and monitor appropriate eating etiquette (e.g., chewing with your mouth closed), and explain why improper manners might irritate peers.
- Provide instruction on nonverbal cues, such as tone of voice, to interpret another person's emotional state or reaction.

For classroom peers

- Explain the nature of the student's visual impairment (if the student is comfortable with this).
- Provide examples of what the student can and cannot see (e.g., "Shaquan can tell that a shadow approaching is a person, but he can't identify which person it is").
- Coach them to call the student's name when they want his attention, rather than simply starting a conversation (in which the student may not realize he is expected to be a part).
- Encourage them to identify themselves to the student when initiating contact.
- Explain why a student might engage in a certain behavior that they find annoying (e.g., holding onto a peer's clothing when going out to recess) and positive ways to communicate how they would prefer the student to behave.

interactions. Sighted children often find it difficult to adjust their play to the ability levels of blind children, who prefer noisy play activities to abstract or symbolic ones (Tröster & Brambring, 1994). Quick and sometimes unpredictable movements can disorient children with visual disabilities, and a lack of understanding about characteristics of students with visual disabilities can cause frustrations among peers (Celeste, 2007). Some experts are convinced that simply providing inclusive opportunities does not ensure interactions and play among sighted preschoolers and those who are blind; adult intervention may be necessary to ensure continued positive interactions between children (Eaton & Wall, 1999; Hughes et al., 1998; McGaha & Farran, 2001). Tips for Classroom Management provides detailed examples of how teachers can improve the positive social interactions in their classrooms.

Independence

Orientation and mobility are major curriculum targets for many students with visual disabilities. Because instruction in this area needs to begin as early as possible, parents and professionals are encouraging the introduction of the long cane to children between the ages of 2 and 6 (Pogrund, Fazzi, & Schreier, 1993). Although some O&M instructors believe that young children should begin learning how to use a long cane with the adult size that they will use later in life (which would be extra long for their present size), research findings indicate that children are better off learning how to use a mobility cane that is cut to their size (Clarke, Sainato, & Ward, 1994). Sometimes called the kiddy cane or the Connecticut precane, this homemade version of the long cane is tailored to the size of the user, even a preschooler. It is made of rigid, white PVC pipe and is cut at midchest height. It has a red stripe at the bottom and tape across the top for a grip. Because the home is the most natural setting for infants' and toddlers' educational programs, most programs for blind infants include home-based instruction with considerable parent involvement. One of the most important lessons parents can learn is to encourage later independence. To this end, they must allow their infants and toddlers to explore the environment, even if they get the same bumps and bruises as young children without visual loss.

Teaching Students with Visual Loss

The educational needs of students with low vision differ from those who are blind. Students with low vision might require some extra tutorial assistance to learn the same number of phonetic rules as their classmates or additional time to read their history assignment. Teachers can help these students in many ways. They can make adjustments in the way they lecture and present information to students. You have already learned about orientation and mobility as an additional curriculum target, but students with visual loss require extra topics of instruction. For example, they might need to learn independent life skills so that they can manage an apartment, pay their bills, shop for food, cook their meals, and hold competitive jobs without assistance from others. Clearly, the curriculum for many students with visual loss is packed. The crucial factor is that the educational and developmental goals, and the instruction designed to meet those goals, reflect the specific needs of each student (Spungin, 2002).

Access to the General Education Curriculum: Literacy

Today, a large percentage (about 57%) of students with visual disabilities spend over 80% of their school day in general education classrooms. Nearly 88% of low vision and blind students receive their education at a neighborhood school, possibly with support from a resource specialist or itinerant teacher (OSEP, 2008). These students participate in the general education curriculum with their sighted classmates and, if they do not also have coexisting disabilities, perform well academically. This is reflected by the fact that these students have the highest graduation rates of all high school students with disabilities. Many use aids (e.g., glasses or technology that enlarges type) to help them enhance their vision for accessing information from printed material, whether it be in textbooks or on the chalkboard. Others, even those with low vision, use their tactile senses and some employ braille as their reading method. Some members of both groups rely on auditory means to gain information and use neither print nor braille. One of the singular characteristics of this group of learners is the variety of ways in which they access information. In all cases, professionals agree that literacy should be a goal for each student with a visual disability and that direct instruction of print or braille is the best way to help them become fully literate (Corn & Koenig, 2002; Wormsley, 2004).

Many individuals who are blind are not proficient readers, regardless of the reading method they use. Research studies show contradictory findings about the phonological awareness of braille readers (Monson & Bowen, 2008). Initial results of a

myeducationlab Go to the Building Teaching Skills and Dispositions section in Chapter 11 of MyEducationLab, and complete the activities in the IRIS Module, "Instructional Accommodations: Making the Learning Environment Accessible for Students with Visual Disabilities." This module highlights tips for modifying lessons and ways to make lessons accessible for students with visual disabilities.

recent study suggest that only half of elementary students with visual disabilities read on grade level (Barclay et al., 2007; Swenson, 2008). One obvious reason for these students' reading difficulties is their visual disabilities. Another reason is that many of these individuals have coexisting disabilities, such as learning disabilities or developmental disorders. Students with low vision who also have coexisting disabilities often benefit from learning strategies developed for students with learning disabilities (read again A Closer Look at Data-Based Practices in Chapter 5) that emphasize comprehension by skimming passages to look for the main ideas. Although some teachers might conclude that braille instruction is not appropriate for these learners, many vision experts do not agree (Dote-Kwan et al., 2001; Wormsley, 2004). They think that instructional methods need to be adjusted. They suggest additional instructional strategies, also borrowed from the field of learning disabilities, be used so these students can master reading, whether the method used to access information be print or braille. Students learning braille, like many students without visual loss, need instruction in phonemic awareness, phonics, and sight words.

Literacy is a goal for all Americans and an expectation for all high school graduates, and braille literacy is a goal being advocated by experts for those students who find print, even enlarged print, inaccessible (Swenson, 2008; Wormsley, 2004). Education professionals suggest that all students be exposed to a literacy-rich school environment, and the same is true for students learning braille. So, how does the concept of a braille-rich environment apply? The notion is that just as sighted learners are exposed to print—whether they can actually read the words yet—students learning braille should be exposed to braille everywhere in their environments as well. How can teachers help create a braille-rich environment for these students? They can seek the assistance of the vision teacher and help label the learner's immediate environment in braille: signs in the hallways, names on lockers, personal belongings, on and off light switches, bathroom doors, class schedules, and notices on bulletin boards. Ultimately, all teachers have an important role in promoting literacy for students with visual disabilities, and braille-rich environments can be fun and inclusive for all (Farrenkopf, 2008; Holbrook, 2008).

Instructional Accommodations

Most students with visual disabilities require accommodations and assistive devices (beyond eye glasses) to access the general education curriculum and succeed at school. One important rule applies: Each individual has different needs, so different responses to those needs are necessary. In other words, there is no single answer to the question "What accommodations benefit students with visual disabilities?" Accommodating for Inclusive Environments includes more suggestions about how to modify the learning environment so classrooms are safe and maximal learning can occur.

Some other minor adjustments in teaching style help all students gain more from the learning environment. One such modification is the careful use of language. For example, many of us, when speaking, use words that substitute for other words, rather than terms that concretely name their referents; we say *it*, *this*, and *there* without naming the things or locations we are discussing. For example, an adult might say, "Go get it. It's over there," instead of saying, "Please get the large book at the end of my desk." Clearly, concrete and specific instruction is more helpful to a blind student.

Several common classroom situations typically rely on visual observations to convey knowledge. Teachers frequently use classroom demonstrations, movies, videos, or projected slides and pictures to provide students with content knowledge. With a few minor adjustments (see Tips for Effective Instruction), these instructional practices can be just as beneficial for students with visual impairments as for their sighted peers.

A commonly used accommodation for all students with disabilities is extended time. Many students with visual disabilities do require more time to complete assignments because it takes them more time to read. In these cases, teachers often set a later due date for homework or major projects, but they also insist that this

myeducationlab Go to the Building Teaching Skills and Dispositions section in Chapter 11 of MyEducationLab and complete the activities in the IRIS Module, "Serving Students with Visual Impairments: The Importance of Collaboration." This module underscores the importance of the general education teacher's collaborating with professionals and other individuals knowledgeable about the needs of students with visual disabilities.

Accommodating for Inclusive Environments
Modifying the Physical Environment

Make the Classroom Safe

- Open or close doors fully (a half-open door can be a dangerous obstacle).
- Teach all students to push empty chairs under their desks.
- Familiarize students with potential problem areas such as low obstacles (trash cans), protruding objects (pencil sharpeners), and changes in floor elevation (steps).
- Secure rugs or mats firmly to the floor.

Arrange the Furniture Carefully

- Eliminate clutter, including electrical cords, from the room, particularly in aisles and movement paths.
- Keep frequently used furniture and materials in consistent places.
- Place coat cubbies or stands near classroom entrance; position other storage areas to be easily accessible.
- Provide larger desks and storage areas to accommodate technology devices.

Consider Lighting Needs

- Use window shades with adjustable blinds to allow for increase or reduction of light.
- Seat the student where glare is minimized.

- Use glare-resistant computer screens.
- Use floor or desk lamps to provide additional lighting if necessary.
- Avoid placing equipment in front of windows.

Use Contrasting Colors

- Cover the student's desk with brightly colored paper to help him or her locate it easily.
- Attach high-contrast, colorful shapes to drawers, cupboards, and other frequently used materials.
- Use dark letters on pale backgrounds for bulletin boards.

Source: IRIS Center (2006a).

myeducationlab Go to the Building Teaching Skills and Dispositions section in Chapter 11 of MyEducationLab and complete the activities in the IRIS Module, "Accommodations to the Physical Environment: Setting Up a Classroom for Students with Visual Disabilities." The resources in this module offer helpful tips on setting up the physical aspects of your classroom and will introduce types of equipment used by students with visual disabilities.

---

extended deadline be met. Other teachers reduce or change the requirement somewhat and allow students to make an oral report instead of a written one, or assign a 10-page paper instead of a 20-page report. Another common accommodation is the use of a computer for both in-class assignments and homework. Regardless of these accommodations, teachers should not lower their expectations for students with visual disabilities.

Data-Based Practices

As mentioned earlier, students with low vision or blindness usually require extra instruction in areas such as orientation, mobility, and assistive devices (Miller & Menacker, 2007). These areas are considered part of their **expanded core curriculum**. As you read this chapter's Closer Look at Data-Based Practices, think about how specialized many of these skills are, and how much of a difference they make in the lives of students with visual loss.

We introduced the concept of universal design for learning (UDL) in Chapters 1 and 2, but because of its great benefit to students with visual disabilities we are reminding you about it here. UDL extends the principles of universal design that are outlined in the ADA law. As you learned in Chapters 1 and 9, universal design creates accommodations to the physical environment so that buildings, parking lots, and

expanded core curriculum
Includes skills such as orientation and mobility, braille reading, independent living skills, and use of assistive technology in addition to the general education

communities are more accessible to people with disabilities. We learned that when universally designed environments become commonplace, everyone benefits! In Chapters 1 and 2, we cited the example of curb cuts and in both chapters provided photos to show you how they were instituted to help people who use wheelchairs but have come to be appreciated by anyone looking for an easier way to negotiate a curb. Captioned television is another example. Originally developed to enable people who are deaf to access information and entertainment shown (and heard) on television, it is now used by everyone—people exercising in the gym, those learning English as a second language, and fans watching a sporting event at a crowded restaurant.

UDL applies expressly to classroom settings. The premise is that the learning environment—not the student—is the barrier (Hitchcock et al., 2002). Although all students, including those with disabilities, can benefit from a learning environment that provides multiple ways to access information, students with visual disabilities definitely find that flexible means of interacting with instruction meets many of the instructional challenges they face. When text can be displayed and accessed in multiple ways, students can select the means that best suits their learning preferences. UDL uses technology to allow individuals to adjust the size of print to meet their visual requirements, to translate print into speech, or convert print to braille. It also exploits the advances of technology to hyperlink to dictionaries so that students who need assistance with vocabulary can become independent learners and find explanations of unknown words or unfamiliar concepts. Graphics or animation can support the content by providing visual illustrations of the information being learned. Thus, universal screening frees both students and teachers from the chores of finding or developing accommodations. Think of the opportunities on the horizon when not only our physical environments but also our learning environments are universally accessible.

Raised-relief globes, such as these, allow students to tactilely explore the Earth's geographical features.

A Closer Look at Data-Based Practices

Expanded Core Curriculum

Students with visual disabilities typically have additional instructional needs, related to their inability to make observations or modify their actions based on what they see. The expanded core curriculum addresses these needs and covers the following skills (Hatlen, 1996; IRIS Center, 2006a):

- Compensatory or functional, including options for accessing information (braille, large print, audio)
- Orientation and mobility
- Social
- Independent living (self-care, food preparation, money management)
- Recreation and leisure
- Vocational and career
- Assistive technology
- Visual efficiency (the effective use of existing vision)

Roles and Responsibilities

The expanded core curriculum addresses a set of very specialized skills. Therefore, experts in visual disabilities—such as the TVI or O&M instructor—are typically the professionals who provide the instruction in these areas. Specific time must be allocated for instruction in these critical skills, which often means that students are pulled out of the general education class at various times during the week. All of the professionals who are responsible for the student's education must work collaboratively to schedule instructional time and arrange opportunities to make up missed work.

Technology

In the Overcoming Challenges section of this chapter, you learned about many assistive devices developed specifically for people with visual loss. You learned how visual input devices using CCTV technology that help enlarge the size of print. You learned about audio input devices that provide information through the auditory channel instead of the visual channel: audiodescriptions, audio versions of books, and speech-to-text translations. We discussed tactile input devices such as equipment that helps create braille versions of text. And, you learned about the digital library available through Bookshare.org, which allows students multiple options for accessing print. Many of the devices discussed earlier can be considered high-tech devices. In this section, we introduce two commonplace low-tech devices that can be of great assistance to students with low vision.

Students with visual disabilities frequently need to access print or pictures at their desk spontaneously, such as for a magazine, handout, or a note from a friend. In many instances, it is not practical to use a CCTV or to order digital files. Small, handheld magnifiers come in handy in near-vision situations. The user passes the magnifier over the text or image, and the lens enlarges the image. Magnifiers come in a variety of sizes and magnification levels. Some come with built-in stands, which are helpful for students with poor motor control; others come with a small light attached. In contrast, handheld telescopes come in handy for far-vision activities, such as reading off of a chalkboard, projection screen, or even reading street signs. As with magnifiers, telescopes come in a variety of sizes and magnification levels.

A TVI or other vision specialist should work with the student in order to provide him or her with the most appropriate device. A variety of factors must be considered. For example, some telescopes with large magnification levels subsequently allow for only a limited range of sight; a student may not be able to read an entire line of text on a board at once but instead may need to physically turn her head (and her hand holding the telescope) from one side to the other as she reads. A similar situation can occur with magnifiers, and a student may need practice tracking

Many types of magnifiers enlarge text or different images. These are used to help the individual see things up close, like the words in a book or items on a written test.

from the end of one line back to the beginning of the next without getting lost. While the devices can help learners access the material, teachers need to be aware that they will do so more slowly and will thus require extra time on assignments or activities.

Transition

Some young adults with visual disabilities have a difficult time adjusting to independence and the world of work. Many of these individuals do not possess literacy skills necessary to be successful in the community or on the job. Many do not possess other skills (e.g., social, vocational, self-advocacy) needed to be competitive in the workplace. When such deficiencies are coupled with bias and discrimination, the result is underemployment and a group of individuals not achieving to their capabilities. With education specifically directed toward literacy, career education, and job training, this situation can be corrected.

Telescopes are enlargers that help students see details that are at a distance, such as information written on a blackboard.

Postsecondary Options

As you have learned, more and more students with disabilities are attending college. In fact, some 16% of first-year students with disabilities attending 4-year colleges report having visual disabilities (Henderson, 2001). Graduating from college has a significant bearing on a person's career and earning power, but less than half of those with visual disabilities who enter college graduate. Their reasons for leaving college are usually based not on the academic demands but rather on the difficulties of living independently. Fortunately, the skills needed for successful college life can be taught either before or during the college years.

One exemplary program, the University of Evansville's summer precollege program, teaches students who are blind the mobility, orientation, academic, and life skills needed for college life (Evansville Association for the Blind, 2005). At this 40-year-old program, students learn how to negotiate a college campus, do their laundry, live in a dormitory, and take notes during lectures. For students who have participated in the program, college is a less frightening and more successful experience. General tips about college are helpful and increase chances for graduation. Here are some suggestions for students with visual disabilities (HEATH, 2001):

- Begin the search for a college program early.
- Interview the campus coordinators of services for students with disabilities as well as current students with visual disabilities.
- Register for classes as early as possible to order e-textbooks and adapt other course materials.
- Contact readers, locate assistive devices, and arrange for accommodations.
- Meet with faculty individually to explain which accommodations are effective, advise them of your unique learning needs, and explain assistive devices that you will bring to class.
- Stay in close communication with faculty.

Regardless of the approach, it is clear that students who are blind or have low vision can improve their chances for success in college and in later life by participating in programs specifically designed to develop skills needed for independence and employment.

Transition to Work

Students who are blind or have low vision have one of the highest high school graduation rates of all students with disabilities. They also attend college at a rate close to that of their peers without disabilities. Yet, despite their high educational levels, adults with visual disabilities have a harder time finding and retaining employment; adults with low vision experience more success than their blind peers (Shaw, Gold, & Wolffe, 2007). Although adults with visual disabilities hold jobs at every level (e.g., artists, scientists, engineers, teachers, business administrators), as a group they tend to be under-employed or unemployed at rates far beyond expectations (Oddo & Sitlington, 2002). Only about half of adults with visual disabilities between the ages of 22 and 50 are working (AFB, 2008c). So, more formal education is not the only answer to better jobs and higher salaries for these individuals (Capella-McDonnall, 2005).

Why do so many individuals who are blind have difficulty finding good jobs? Alexander Shaw and his colleagues (2007) found that the top challenges experienced by young adults in their study were restricted resources (e.g., unable to access employment information), attitudes of employers, and personal reasons (disorganization). They also found that employers were often uninformed about working with people with visual disabilities, which could create reluctance to hire these individuals. For example, an employer may worry that they would have to purchase expensive assistive technology to accommodate the person's needs, not realizing that programs exist to cover these costs.

Students with visual disabilities also lack job opportunities and work experience during their teen years, which could impact future employment. During high school, many sighted classmates hold part-time jobs. These teenagers learn about finding and keeping jobs and also about salaries, wages, and benefits. For students who are blind, however, their high school years are focused on educational tasks, and they often spend their summers learning important skills (e.g., orientation and mobility) that they need for independence. Unfortunately, not having practical work experience can later put them at a disadvantage in the job market. Some experts (Kirchner & Smith, 2005; Nagle, 2001; Oddo & Sitlington, 2002) suggest the following:

- Community employment during high school
- Internships in real work settings during high school
- College graduation
- Education of potential employers about the skills and abilities of workers with visual disabilities
- Informing employers about how the costs of special equipment can be paid by state, federal, and private programs

Bias, discrimination, and lack of opportunities all affect long-term outcomes for adults with visual disabilities. However, an individual's ability to counteract these negative influences through their own actions should not be discounted. Michael Naranjo, the renowned artist (whose work is shown at the opening of this chapter and found in museums around the world), has a perspective about disability that may surprise you, but also may be a contributing factor in his grand success. He shares his views in this chapter's Spotlighting.

Access to the Community

Many adults with visual disabilities express frustration about their limited access to recreational, leisure, and cultural activities. Even so, more cultural events are accessible than ever before. For example, the New York Philharmonic, the Chamber Music Society, and the Great Performances at Lincoln Center provide music programs in different formats—standard print, enlarged print, and braille. The ADA law has helped expand community opportunities. Tactile exhibits are becoming commonplace at museums and sculpture gardens. Michael Naranjo, the artist mentioned earlier, has had many people explore his work in tactile exhibits, like the one that ran for 6 months (between October of 2008 and April of 2009) at the Grounds for Sculpture in Hamilton, New Jersey. And even children's theater performances are now offering "freeze frames" so young people can feel the costumes and sets of plays (Ansariyah-Grace, 2000). Although guide dogs were not allowed in zoos only a few years ago, they now join their companions visiting most sections of these parks. There is, nevertheless, considerable room for improvement. Possibly, greater public exposure will make a difference.

Spotlighting *Michael Naranjo:* A Day in the Life

Michael Naranjo, a blind artist, is shown here "seeing" Michelangelo's famous sculpture "David" with his hands. Scaffolding around the statue was erected especially for his benefit.

Michael Naranjo is an accomplished and world-renowned artist who has no functional use of his vision; his work is featured on the opening page of this chapter.

The last thing that I remember seeing was a Vietcong through the end of the sights on my rifle. And he was looking for some more of my friends, my fellow soldiers to shoot at. He suddenly turned his head toward me, and we were 20 yards apart. He looked at me, and I could see his eyes. I just remember seeing his eyes. Our eyes met; our eyes locked. And in 2 seconds, we knew what was going to happen. I put the sights of my rifle right at him, and I shot. The moment after shooting, my friend who was right behind me said something. And so I ducked, and a grenade rolled into my hand. I let go of my rifle, and I pulled my hand back away from this grenade, and it exploded, and I was suspended. And I was blind.

I was raised in Santa Clara Pueblo, which is on the Rio Grande River and is about 30 miles north of Santa Fe, New Mexico. My mother was a potter, and even as a child I was interested in art, helping her mix white and brown clay from the hillsides. In college, after seeing a film about Michelangelo's *David* and *Pieta*, I knew I wanted to be a sculptor. I still have those early pieces that I made when I could see. In 1967, I was drafted into the army and was sent to Vietnam. After I was wounded, I was sent to different hospitals and finally to a school for people who were blind.

At the workshop at that school, the instructor gave me laces and two strips of leather with holes punched along the side. I was told, "We make wallets here. When you learn how to make wallets, you'll learn to weave a rug." I refused. After many conversations between my instructor and the director, they finally met my request for a block of wood and a carving tool. I wanted to make something myself. I was very happy. For the next month I carved a fish jumping out of the water. I don't think anyone looked at the piece or would have known what it was, but *I* knew. When I do workshops with children, they always ask me whether what they are creating is "right" or "wrong." I tell them, "No one can tell you that it's wrong if that's how you feel about it."

Today I am a busy artist. My work is in galleries and museums. I have fun. It's not like work at all. I don't know if I would have been a better sculptor if I could see. My work might be somewhat different or the same. I don't know, but one thing is for sure: I don't think that I am disabled. I don't have a disability. I don't have time to have a disability because I am working too much, too hard, and I'm having too much fun doing what I'm doing. And I haven't got time in my life to think/feel disability, to think blind.

Collaboration

Collaborative services from experts in the field of visual disabilities should be available to all students who have low vision or who are blind. Many different professionals may need to work together to provide an appropriate education for these students, who may require an extensive array of services. For example, the district's teachers of students with visual impairments (TVIs), as well as professionals providing outreach services from a center school (e.g., state's school for the blind), can help general educators structure both the physical and the academic environment to ensure the success of inclusive efforts (De Mario & Caruso, 2001). TVIs—who are considered special education teachers by IDEA '04—help determine how to access printed materials and provide important information about accommodations needed during instruction and assessments. O&M instructors—who are considered related service providers by IDEA '04—help students improve freedom of movement in the classroom, at home, and in the community. Let's think about how these experts contribute to these students' very special education.

Collaborating with Related Service Providers: TVIs and O&M Instructors

As noted earlier, a TVI is a special educator who specializes in visual disabilities and serves as a resource to other educators, parents, and students. A TVI has knowledge in both instruction and assessment, and has knowledge of other agencies that provide supports for students with visual disabilities. He or she may work directly with the student and may also provide consultative services and support to the general education teacher and other professionals at the child's school. Specifically, the TVI can

- provide instruction in disability-specific skills, such as braille;
- reinforce concepts from the core academic subjects;
- teach components of the expanded core curriculum;
- conduct assessments to determine a student's abilities, needs, and necessary accommodations;
- work with appropriate organizations and agencies to access instructional materials (e.g., braille, books on tape);
- create materials to support academic success (e.g., braille labels for classroom items, print copies of a student's braille work or braille versions of classroom handouts) (IRIS Center, 2007).

An O&M instructor is a related service provider who teaches the skills necessary for Students to independently navigate their classroom, school, home, and community. Students studying orientation skills learn to identify where they are, determine where they want to go, and come up with a plan to arrive at their destination. O&M instructors teach students to use auditory cues and landmarks to help them with orientation. Mobility skills, as you learned earlier, allow students to travel from one location to another. When working with students with visual disabilities, an O&M instructor may

- evaluate a student's functional vision to determine its use in O&M activities;
- assess the student's O&M skills as well as their progress in the expanded core curriculum;
- provide instruction in various low-vision and mobility devices;
- help students orient themselves in various environments;
- teach students specific routes from one location to another;
- consult with family members and relevant school professionals on issues such as environmental design, reinforcing learned O&M skills, and services and equipment;
- provide information on additional resources, such as recreational opportunities or guide dog facilities (IRIS Center, 2007).

Collaborative Practices: A Team of Professionals

Remember that a large proportion of students with visual disabilities spend the majority of their school day in the general education classroom. While a large number of specially trained professionals may work with the student over the course of a week, the primary responsibility for a student's academic instruction still rests with the general education teacher. The TVI and the O&M instructor can provide support to the general education teacher through ongoing consultation and collaboration. During consultation, a vision specialist may explain how to implement specific learning strategies and instructional accommodations, how to work a particular device, or make suggestions to support O&M activities during the course of the regular school day. Through collaboration, the general education teacher and the vision specialist work together when planning, implementing, or evaluating a specific component of the child's educational program. The key to making consultative and collaborative practices work is to develop effective communication techniques. Professionals need to communicate regularly on topics such as changes to the daily schedule (e.g., assemblies or field trips), appropriate times to pull the student from class for work on the expanded core curriculum, length of time each person will work with the student, planning time availability, and other relevant issues.

Considering Culture: *A "Special" Child*

Reynaldo Reynoso is four years old, is blind, and has just entered a regular preschool. Things aren't going well. Although Reynaldo has many abilities and skills he learned during his years in early intervention programs with an orientation and mobility specialist, he doesn't use those skills. He clings to the teacher. Whenever he is asked to do something he doesn't want to do, he has kicking and screaming tantrums.

Ms. Stein, his teacher, is very experienced with preschoolers with and without special needs and is very good at welcoming children into her class, supporting their development, and setting appropriate limits. Puzzled by Reynaldo's behavior, she called his mother and set up a meeting with her. At the meeting Ms. Stein began by describing some of Reynaldo's positive qualities and discussing the goals of the preschool program. She then asked Mrs. Reynoso how she thought Reynaldo was doing.

Mrs. Reynoso spoke glowingly about Reynaldo, commented that he "has a mind of his own," and mentioned no concerns.

Ms. Stein continued, "I do have some concerns about Reynaldo's behavior. He doesn't like to do anything independently. He relies too much on the classroom assistant or me. He wants one of us to be with him all of the time. When we move away from him or expect him to do something that we know he can do for himself, he clings to us, cries, and kicks."

Mrs. Reynoso said, "We don't worry about Reynaldo's behavior. To us, he is a gift from God, a *milagro* [miracle]. We want to be sure that he has everything he wants. Our family is very lucky to have been chosen for this special gift."

Ms. Stein wasn't sure what to say, but she knew that Reynaldo couldn't continue to behave in this way in her classroom. And she was worried about this behavior continuing when he was older and went to elementary school. She described some of his behavior more specifically, commenting on the disruption that it caused in the classroom and emphasizing the problem it presented to Reynaldo.

Mrs. Reynoso became concerned and asked what they could do to help. Ms. Stein discussed behavior management techniques that work well with preschoolers and said she would use them at school as well. She also offered to help Mrs. Reynoso implement the techniques at home. Finally, she inquired whether Mrs. Reynoso would like to meet other mothers of children with visual disabilities who share her Caribbean background. Mrs. Reynoso was eager to meet another mother, and the meeting ended with a plan in place.

Questions to Consider

1. How well do you think Ms. Stein handled this situation? What else do you think she could have done and said?

2. Mrs. Reynoso considered Reynaldo to be a milagro, a gift from God. What are some other cultural beliefs associated with individuals with disabilities?

—By Eleanor Lynch, San Diego State University, and Marci Hanson, San Francisco State University

Partnerships with Families and Communities

Family members play very special roles as they help their children grow up. Their responsiveness in complying with children's requests, repeating or rephrasing their communications, facilitating turn taking, and giving directions and instructions contributes considerably to positive development in expressive and receptive language (Pérez-Pereira & Conti-Ramsden, 2000). As with all children, the relationships among family, school, and culture affect those with visual disabilities in many ways. Sometimes, one set of beliefs clashes with another set of beliefs, and it is important for teachers and parents to talk about them frankly. As you read this chapter's Considering Culture on page 399, you will understand the importance of developing partnerships with families, the trust that must be nurtured for partnerships to be effective, and the benefits that the efforts yield.

To understand their visual differences, students need to gain knowledge about their visual status, the cause of their vision problem, and the likelihood that it might improve or worsen. Many of the children have great confusion about their disabilities, which is apparent by the questions they ask about their blindness. In an old, but unique study, parents were asked to list questions that their children had asked about their vision (Erin & Corn, 1994). Among the frequently asked questions were the following: When would they be able to see? Would they be able to see when they got older? Why did God make them blind? Why could they not see some certain things (such as rainbows)? How do their eyes look? Would anything help them see better? Are they special? Why are they different? What is it like to see? Why did they fail the vision test?

Families have many responsibilities. They must help their children develop skills across a range of areas: communication, independent living, mobility, sensory development, fine- and gross-motor skills, cognition, and social skills. And parents want more help from schools to learn how to teach these skills more effectively to their children (Milian, 2001). In this regard, teachers can make an important difference to parents—sometimes with an action as simple as being a good listener and providing support.

Summary

For most of us, the primary way we learn is through vision. We observe the actions of others and imitate their behaviors. We are often shown how to do a task when we learn a new skill. We gain information by watching television or reading. In contrast, people with visual disabilities have a restricted ability to use their sight, which can affect how they function as independent adults. The category of visual disabilities is one of the smallest in special education, but the incidence of visual disabilities increases with age. Although these students have been successfully included in general education for many years, they do not find integration the norm when they are adults. Many have not found competitive employment and are not included in the mainstream of American society. Stereotypes and lack of current information impede their participation. Improvement in this area is essential and will require the concerted efforts of adults with this disability, their families, and their advocates. With changed attitudes, this group will participate more fully in society and take their places alongside sighted people.

Answering the Chapter Objectives

1. How can the category of visual disabilities be divided into two functional subgroups?

   Several options are possible:
   - Group students on the basis of the severity of the disability or the amount of their functional use of sight: low vision and blind.
   - Group students by age of onset: congenitally blind (at birth or during infancy) and adventitiously blind (after the age of 2).
   - Identify those with visual disabilities and those who are "legally blind," which qualifies people for special tax benefits and materials.

   More than half of children with visual disabilities have an additional disability, often placing them in the multiple disabilities category.

2. What are some ways in which the learning environment can be modified to accommodate students with visual disabilities?

Teachers can help by
- using commonsense teaching strategies such as advance organizers, oral summaries, printed information, and handouts of lectures;
- positioning low-vision students where they can benefit most from each instructional activity (e.g., close to the chalkboard, away from the glare of a window);
- eliminating dangerous obstacles and hazards;
- providing consistent organization, expectations, and consequences in the physical and instructional environments.

3. Why must orientation and mobility be long-term curriculum targets for many low-vision students and most blind students, and what specific skills must be included?

- Good orientation and mobility skills are needed for independent living, maintaining a household, personal care, transportation to and from work, mobility within the workplace, and sports and recreation.
- Orientation and mobility skills are complex and difficult to master, taking years of instruction and practice.
- Challenges in the physical environment include escalators, elevators, public transportation, orientation to new places, and use of maps.

4. What advances in assistive technology can assist people with visual disabilities at school, in the workplace, and in independent living?

- *Visual aids:* enlarged print displays, large-print newspapers, closed circuit television (CCTV) enlargements
- *Audio aids:* talking books, talking watches and clocks, audiodescriptions
- *Tactile aids:* labels for household appliances, tactile maps, braille books, computerized text-to-braille software
- *Digital files:* electronic versions of print materials that can be transformed into a variety of formats, including audio, large print, braille, and bimodal (speech combined with print) options

5. What are the issues surrounding braille literacy and individuals who are blind?

For those who do not read print, braille is their access to the print world and their means of achieving literacy. However, braille literacy has been declining because
- braille instruction is not uniformly or consistently available,
- not enough teachers are proficient in braille, and
- cognitive disabilities may make it difficult to learn.

The unique needs and abilities of each individual should be matched to reading style, and appropriate instruction should be delivered.

myeducationlab Now go to MyEducationLab at www.myeducationlab.com and take the Self-Assessment to gauge your initial comprehension of chapter content. Once you have taken the Self-Assessment, use your individualized Study Plan for Chapter 11 to enhance your understanding of the concepts discussed in the chapter.

 Council for Exceptional Children **ADDRESSING THE PROFESSIONAL STANDARDS**

Council for Exceptional Children (CEC) knowledge standards addressed in this chapter:

VI1K2, VI1K3, VI2K5, VI2K1, VI8K2, VI4K8, VI10K1, VI10K2, VI10S1

Appendix A: CEC Knowledge and Skill Standards Common Core has a full listing of the standards listed here.

Appendix B: CEC Knowledge and Skill Common Core Standards and Associated Subcategories are broken down by chapter.

CHAPTER 12

Autism Spectrum Disorders

Matt Tincani

Imagine a World . . .

where every family gathering is a celebration . . .

Chapter Objectives

After studying this chapter, you will be able to

1. Understand the relationship among autism, Asperger syndrome, and PDD-NOS as autism spectrum disorders (ASD).

2. Identify core characteristics of individuals within the autism spectrum.

3. List the causes of ASD.

4. Describe how environments can be structured so that individuals with ASD maximally benefit from instruction.

5. Identify data-based instructional strategies for students with ASD.

Stephen Wiltshire is an English artist with autism. His unique talents and abilities have caught the attention of the public and the artistic communities worldwide. From the time when he was a very young child, Wiltshire was able to reproduce, down to the most amazing details, practically anything he saw. His panoramas of London, viewed from the top of the Eye (a large Ferris wheel), are precise. And, what is most amazing, he executes his drawings from memory, sometimes days after he has seen what will be the focus of his artwork. He now has his own gallery in London and he travels around the world, including Dubai, drawing more amazing scenes providing us a glimpse of life as he sees it. Wiltshire's ink sketch of San Francisco's Chinatown was, as many of his works are, drawn from memory. It is perfect down to the very details of the Chinese street signs, which he cannot read or write with meaning.

Autism spectrum disorders (ASD) have been the subject of much recent attention. Newspapers, magazines, and television news shows feature almost daily stories about the "autism epidemic." One reason for concern is that ASD can produce substantial impairments in social and intellectual functioning. Another reason for alarm is that the number of reported ASD cases has increased substantially in recent years. The Centers for Disease Control and Prevention (CDC) now report that as many as 1 in 150 children in the United States have an ASD (Rice, 2007). Nonetheless, continual advancements in screening, diagnosis, and intervention offer hope to individuals with this group of disorders.

ASD is a broad term that includes three conditions characterized by limitations in three areas of development: communication, social interaction, and repetitive behaviors or interests. Autism is one of the specific diagnoses included within ASD. In addition to autism, Asperger syndrome and pervasive developmental disorder—not otherwise specified (PDD-NOS) also are conditions included in the group of disabilities called ASD.

Where We've Been . . . What's on the Horizon?

Autism was first identified in the last century. Considerable confusion has surrounded this condition and its causes since it was first recognized. Until fairly recently autism was narrowly defined, restricting its diagnosis to only those individuals with severe disabilities. Today, it is understood that like most other disabilities, autism can range from mild to severe problems. Also, present-day experts consider autism as one of a spectrum of similar disorders. So, to better understand today's conceptualization of ASD, let's see how this field emerged and the direction of its development.

Historical Context

Although ASD has always been part of the human condition, its discrete identification is relatively recent. ASD was first identified by Johns Hopkins psychiatrist Leo Kanner, who in 1943 published his landmark paper "Autistic Disturbances of Affective Contact." Kanner described 11 children who displayed "extreme autistic aloneness" and failed to communicate or to form normal social relationships with those around them. Kanner borrowed the term *autism* from Eugene Bluer, a Swiss psychiatrist who coined the term in 1911. Bluer used the term *autism* to describe patients with schizophrenia who actively withdrew into their own world. Almost simultaneously, but independently of Kanner, Viennese psychiatrist Hans Asperger (1944/1991) described a similar condition that would later be named Asperger syndrome. At the time that Kanner's and Asperger's works were published and throughout much of the 20th century, psychiatry offered little hope for the treatment of individuals with ASD. Encouraged by the work of Bruno Bettelheim, ASD was falsely viewed as being caused by bad parenting, including "refrigerator mothers." The effects of the psychoanalytic view of ASD were devastating. Parents blamed one another for the disorder, and treatment efforts were focused on ineffective psychoanalysis methods and institutional placements.

Beginning in the 1960s, the conceptualization and treatment of ASD changed dramatically. First, researchers began to investigate the epidemiological basis for ASD. No evidence was found to support the psychoanalytic theory that autism was the result of bad parenting (Wing, 1989). Instead, experts began to believe that ASD resulted from neurobiological problems with a genetic basis. Second, a number of researchers, most notably Ivar Lovaas, demonstrated that behaviorally based teaching techniques could produce measurable improvements in language and intellectual functioning of children with ASD. Third, parents organized themselves and advocated for themselves and their children. Bernard Rimland spearheaded this advocacy movement. He was a psychologist who dedicated his career to studying ASD after his son was diagnosed with the condition. Rimland helped collect and organize the information known about ASD, but he also joined with other parents to form a parent advocacy group called the National Society for Autistic Children, now called the Autism Society of America (www.autism-society.org). Finally, thanks to the work of Uta Firth (1991) and others, Asperger syndrome has become increasingly recognized as a distinct condition within the ASD spectrum.

Challenges That Autism Spectrum Disorders Present

We have come a long way since the mid–20th century in our understanding of ASD. Today, children with these disorders are educated within inclusive school settings more than ever before, and researchers have developed a body of data-based teaching strategies for students on the spectrum (Simpson et al., 2005). Still, ASD presents serious challenges, challenges that tend to persist throughout the individual's life span.

Temple Grandin is a prominent spokesperson for people with ASD. Grandin is a successful college professor and world-renowned animal husbandry expert. She also has autism. By speaking openly about her experiences as a person with autism, she provides insight into the lives of people on the spectrum and the unique challenges they face. In her 1996 book, *Thinking in Pictures and Other Reports of My Life with Autism,* she writes, "I think in pictures. Words are like a second language to me. I translate both spoken and written words into full-color movies, complete with sound, which run like a VCR tape in my head. When somebody speaks to me, his words are instantly translated into pictures" (p. 19). She also writes of her struggles with autism, including her difficulties in learning to express her emotions:

> Some people believe that people with autism do not have emotions. I definitely do have them, but they are more like the emotions of a child than of an adult. My childhood temper tantrums were not really expressions of emotion so much as circuit overloads. . . . When I get angry, it is like an afternoon thunderstorm; the anger is intense, but once I get over it, the emotion quickly dissipates. . . . I still have difficulty understanding and having a relationship with people whose primary motivation in life is governed by complex emotions, as my actions are guided by intellect. (pp. 87–90)

Grandin's writings illustrate how people with ASD struggle to understand their worlds as they relate to others. Despite living with autism her entire life, Grandin has developed into a successful, independent adult. We will learn more about how the specific impairments of ASD challenge individuals, families, and educators later in this chapter.

Fortunately, ASD is very much in the public spotlight and gaining the recognition it deserves from public officials who provide the funds to better understand and more appropriately educate individuals with ASD. Many advocates now work on behalf of people with ASD to raise awareness and support for ASD research. Bob and Suzanne Wright, described in the Making a Difference Feature, are two prominent advocates who are making a difference in the lives of people with ASD.

Making a Difference
Bob and Suzanne Wright

Bob and Suzanne Wright are not typical grandparents. They are the founders of Autism Speaks, a leading national organization dedicated to autism. Bob, who retired as vice chairman of General Electric and chairman and CEO of NBC Universal in May 2006, and his wife Suzanne first learned about autism when their grandson Christian was diagnosed with autism in 2004.

Bob and Suzanne were desperate to help their grandson, and they were ready to use all of their resources to get treatment for Christian. They were shocked to find out that very few options were available. Like most families dealing with this devastating disorder, finding quality treatment supported by science was very difficult. "We discovered, to our surprise, just how scarce the resources are for parents dealing with autism, and how thin the knowledge is. We had so many questions,

and instead of answers, we found a bewildering array of theories and guesses" (Wright, 2005). They were also surprised to find out that quality treatment was very expensive. "I could not believe how devastating it can be for some other families. They have to take second and third mortgages to cover the care and schooling. . . . We have to do something" (Arango, 2007).

On February 25, 2006, Bob and Suzanne founded Autism Speaks with intentions of raising money for research to find the causes, identify effective treatments, and find a cure for autism. Today Autism Speaks also strives to increase awareness about how autism affects individuals, families, and society. Through donors and fund-raising events, Autism Speaks has generated tens of millions of dollars for research. Bob and Suzanne have increased awareness of autism by doing interviews on major television shows, on radio programs, and in magazine and newspaper articles. With heightened awareness of autism by the public and intense advocacy by Autism Speaks, President George W. Bush signed the Combating Autism Act in December 2006. The Combating Autism Act authorizes hundreds of millions of dollars for autism research, prevention, and treatment through 2011.

Autism Speaks is growing rapidly. Several prominent autism organizations have merged with Autism Speaks in order to achieve greater goals. Without Autism Speaks, it is unlikely that awareness and funding would have obtained its current status. Thanks to Bob and Suzanne Wright, groundbreaking research, treatment, and supports are becoming more available. To learn more about Autism Speaks, visit **www.autismspeaks.org**.

Autism Spectrum Disorders (ASD) Defined

An important way that we learn more about ASD is through research. The basic science of ASD is rapidly emerging, with new findings being announced weekly about how brain development and genetics interact to produce ASD. Although researchers are far from totally understanding the causes for ASD, this information may tell us much about what ASD truly is and how it develops. Perhaps these findings will lead to very early identification and the possible amelioration of ASD's most devastating biological and behavioral effects.

At the same time, rapid strides are being made in the development of educational supports for children, youth, and adults with ASD. Increasingly, individuals with ASD are being educated in inclusive settings, learning from the same curriculum as other children and developing lasting friendships with them. This is an exciting time to be involved in the education of students with ASD. More than ever before, there is increased optimism about our ability to understand ASD and more effectively educate individuals with these disabilities.

ASD is a diverse set of three syndromes:

- Autism
- Asperger syndrome
- Pervasive developmental disorder—not otherwise specified (PDD-NOS)

Each of the three types of ASD has specific diagnostic criteria. So, one way to think of ASD is as an umbrella of disorders—one of which is autism with the others sharing a range of traits with it. Figure 12.1 illustrates ASD in this way. These conditions share similar behavioral characteristics in the areas of (a) social interaction, (b) verbal or nonverbal communication, and (c) repetitive behaviors or interests. Unusual responses to sensory stimuli are also often present. The key word in the term ASD is *spectrum*, which implies similar characteristics but great variance in the actual behavioral patterns exhibited. Accordingly, even persons within the *same* category on the spectrum—autism, Asperger syndrome, or PDD-NOS—have very different and diverse sets of characteristics. Thus, ASD is a truly heterogeneous set of

Figure 12.1 • Autism Spectrum Disorders (ASD) Umbrella

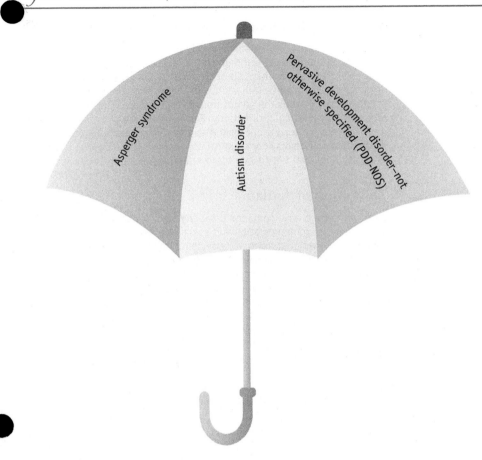

conditions. Table 12.1 shows the IDEA '04 definition of autism and the National Institute of Mental Health (NIMH) definition of ASD. Individual definitions and descriptions of each of the ASD conditions are found in their respective sections.

Professionals are just beginning to understand ASD, so different views of each condition, their symptoms, and severity are still developing. To some, the ASD umbrella represents distinctly different types of autism. Others, however, suggest that types of autism may be formed across diagnostic categories and may instead be based on level of intellectual functioning, age of onset, or number or severity of symptoms (Tanguay, Robertson, & Derrick, 1998).

Only a few years ago, experts included five conditions in the ASD umbrella. However, current thinking only includes the three we discuss next. Although two conditions—Rett syndrome and childhood disintegrative disorder (CDD)—are still described in the 2003 edition of DSM-IV-TR, they are not currently considered part of the spectrum. However, for a basic understanding of conditions often associated with ASD, it is helpful to know about these two conditions.

Discovered more than 40 years ago by Andreas Rett, an Austrian physician, **Rett syndrome** is a genetic condition. The signs of the syndrome appear early in life, but only after a period of seemingly normal development that then stops and begins to reverse (Percy, 2001). Unlike many genetic conditions, Rett syndrome only occurs in girls. Behaviorally, it is characterized by a progressive expression of repeated, stereotypic hand wringing; lack of muscle control; along with communication and social deficits. Sometimes initially misdiagnosed as autism, Rett syndrome has different characteristics. Autism is not usually characterized by hand wringing and a progressive loss of motor skills. Children with Rett syndrome tend to have better social skills when compared to children with autism. And, while about half of the individuals with autism have mental retardation or intellectual disabilities, most children

Rett syndrome A pervasive developmental disorder with a known genetic cause that occurs only in girls

Table 12.1 • Definitions of Autism Spectrum Disorders and Autism

Source	Definition of Autism Spectrum Disorders (ASD)
National Institute of Mental Health (NIMH)	All children with ASD demonstrate deficits in 1) social interaction, 2) verbal and nonverbal communication, and 3) repetitive behaviors or interests. In addition, they will often have unusual responses to sensory experiences, such as certain sounds or the way objects look. Each of these symptoms runs the gamut from mild to severe. They will present in each individual child differently. For instance, a child may have little trouble learning to read but exhibit extremely poor social interaction. Each child will display communication, social, and behavioral patterns that are individual but fit into the overall diagnosis of ASD.

Strock (2007, p. 2) |

	Definition of Autism
Office of Special Education Programs (OSEP), federal government	*Autism* means a developmental disability significantly affecting verbal and nonverbal communication and social interaction, generally evident before age three, that adversely affects a child's educational performance. Other characteristics often associated with autism are engagement in repetitive activities and stereotyped movements, resistance to environmental change or change in daily routines, and unusual responses to sensory experiences. **(i)** Autism does not apply if a child's educational performance is adversely affected primarily because the child has an emotional disturbance, as defined in paragraph (c)(4) of this section. **(ii)** A child who manifests the characteristics of autism after age three could be identified as having autism if the criteria in paragraph (c)(1)(i) of this section are satisfied.

U.S. Department of Education (2006, pp. 1260–1261) |

Sources: From *Autism spectrum disorders* by M. Strock (2007, p. 4); and 34 *CFR* Parts 300 and 301, Assistance to States for the Education of Children with Disabilities and the Early Intervention Program for Infants and Toddlers with Disabilities; Final Regulations (pp. 1260–1261), U.S. Department of Education, 2006, *Federal Register*, Washington, DC.

---

childhood disintegrative disorder (CDD) A pervasive developmental disorder; the individual has typical development until about the age of 5 or 6

with Rett syndrome do. It develops progressively and results in cognitive disabilities typically more severe than are observed in people with autism.

A far rarer disorder than autism is **childhood disintegrative disorder (CDD)**. The most distinguishing aspect of CDD is that these children develop as their peers without disabilities do until they are 5 or 6 years old, at which time a developmental regression begins. In particular, these children lose already acquired language and social skills. Eventually, their behaviors are similar to the behavior patterns of children with autism; however, their long-term outcomes are far worse because the regression continues to deepen. Of the disorders related to ASD, CDD is the least understood.

As scientists' understanding of the neurobiology and genetics of ASD develops, the underlying differences in the brains of people with various types of ASD may reveal an organizational scheme consistent with or completely different from our current behavioral definitions. As it stands now, no consensus exists among experts about what dimensions should be used to develop subtypes of ASD. Now, to gain a better understanding of the similarities and differences among them, let's examine each of the three conditions currently considered as part of the spectrum.

Autism

autism One of the autistic spectrum disorders (ASD); ranges from low to high functioning

Technically, the term *autism* refers to a specific diagnosis within the ASD cluster, much like the words *sports car* identify a specific type of motor vehicle that has similarities and differences with other automobiles. The term *autism* is often used in place of the term *ASD* to refer to all of the disorders included under the ASD umbrella, but this is technically inaccurate. Instead, *autism* should be used as one specific type of disorder within the ASD umbrella of disorders.

The IDEA '04 definition is found in Table 12.1, and the one developed by the American Psychiatric Association (APA) in its *Diagnostic and Statistical Manual of Mental Disorders* is found on Table 12.2 (APA, 2003). Note that the IDEA '04 definition of autism is a general description and lacks the specificity needed to fully appreciate the different ways in which ASD can be expressed. Now compare the IDEA '04 definition to the DSM-IV-TR definition. According to that description, all children with autism have impairments in communication, impairments in social skills, and restricted range of interests.

People with autism have difficulty communicating. Approximately 50% of persons with autism do not talk (Wetherby & Prizant, 2005). Often labeled as nonverbal, these individuals may express their needs through gestures, such as pointing, or they use augmentative or alternative communication (AAC) systems, such as the Picture Exchange Communication System (PECS; see A Closer Look at Data-Based Practices later in this chapter). For children with autism who can talk, their speech patterns are often characterized by **echolalia**—or repetition of words they have previously heard—limited vocabulary, poor intonation, and pronoun reversal (e.g., child says "*You* want a drink" rather than "*I* want a drink"). Children with autism also have trouble with the pragmatics of speech. (Read again Chapter 4 for a review of pragmatics and language impairments.) For example, they may have difficulties starting conversations, ending conversations, making eye contact, or taking turns speaking.

echolalia Repeating words, sounds, or sound patterns with no communicative intent, meaning, or understanding; a speech pattern that may occur immediately or even days later

Table 12.2 • DSM-IV Diagnostic Criteria for Autism

A. A total of six (or more) items from (1), (2), and (3), with at least two from (1) and one each from (2) and (3):

1. Qualitative impairment in social interaction, as manifested by at least two of the following:

a. Marked impairment in the use of multiple nonverbal behaviors such as eye-to-eye gaze, facial expression, body postures, and gestures to regulate social interaction

b. Failure to develop peer relationships appropriate to developmental level

c. A lack of spontaneous seeking to share enjoyment, interests, or achievements with other people (e.g., by a lack of showing, bringing, or pointing out objects of interest)

d. Lack of social or emotional reciprocity

2. Qualitative impairments in communication as manifested by at least one of the following:

a. Delay in, or total lack of, the development of spoken language (not accompanied by an attempt to compensate through alternate modes of communication such as gesture or mime)

b. In individuals with adequate speech, marked impairment in the ability to initiate or sustain a conversation with others

c. Stereotyped and repetitive use of language or idiosyncratic language

d. Lack of varied, spontaneous make-believe play or social imitative play appropriate to developmental level

3. Restricted repetitive and stereotyped patterns of behavior, interests, and activities as manifested by at least one of the following:

a. Encompassing preoccupation with one or more stereotyped and restricted patterns of interest that is abnormal either in intensity or focus

b. Apparently inflexible adherence to specific, nonfunctional routines or rituals

c. Stereotyped and repetitive motor mannerisms (e.g., hand or finger flapping or twisting, or complex whole-body movements)

d. Persistent preoccupation with parts of objects

B. Delays or abnormal functioning in at least one of the following areas, with onset prior to age 3 years: (1) social interaction, (2) language as used in social communication, or (3) symbolic or imaginative play

C. The disturbance is not better accounted for by Rett's disorder or childhood disintegrative disorder.

Source: From *Diagnostic and Statistical Manual of Mental Disorders* (4th ed., Text Revision, p. 75), by the American Psychiatric Association (APA), 2003, Arlington, VA: APA. Reprinted with permission.

Children with autism are often excluded from social interactions with peers.

stereotypies Nonproductive behaviors (e.g., twirling, flapping hands, rocking) that an individual repeats at a high rate; commonly observed in youngsters with autism spectrum disorders; also called stereotypic behaviors

autistic savant An individual who displays many behaviors associated with autism yet also possesses discrete abilities and unusual talents

Social impairments are another area of concern for children with autism. This often means that they do not spontaneously initiate social interactions with others, and may seem to live in their own worlds. As a result, children with autism often have fewer friendships with peers than other children. Instead, they may prefer to spend a significant amount of their time alone. Children with autism also frequently have difficulties understanding the meaning of social situations, adding to their difficulties in forming social relationships.

People with autism typically have repetitive patterns of behavior, referred to as **stereotypies** (sometimes called stereotypic behaviors), or they might have unusual or very focused interests (Lewis & Bodfish, 1998). For example, a child with autism may be interested only in spinning the wheel of a toy car or only in wiggling the string of a pull toy. In addition, some children may have rigid or set patterns of behavior. For example, one child might line toys up in a specific way and follow the same routine every day. If these patterns of behavior are violated, a tantrum might result to protest the disruption. Another child may repeat the same movement, such as waving a hand in front of his or her eyes, over and over again.

It is important to remember that about 75% of people with autism have intellectual disabilities (Sturmey & Sevin, 1994). (Remember, IDEA '04 uses the term *mental retardation;* see Chapter 8 for a review.) Thus, 25% of people with autism have average or above-average intelligence. It is also important to know, however, that intellectual disabilities are not part of the autism diagnosis. This wide range of cognitive ability has resulted in people using terms such as *low-functioning autism* and *high-functioning autism.* Low-functioning autism refers to children with autism and intellectual disabilities who are often nonverbal, whereas *high-functioning autism* usually refers to children with minimal or no intellectual disabilities and who are verbal. Although these terms provide a general description of children's intellectual functioning, they have less value in helping educators design appropriate individualized educational programs for children with autism.

Are there subtypes of autism? As our discussion illustrates, the skills children diagnosed with autism exhibit vary greatly. Some experts think that different levels of intellectual functioning, variety in the age of onset, and number and severity of symptoms suggest subtypes of autism (Tidmarsh & Volkmar, 2003). That is, "autism" may not be one single thing but, rather, a tight clustering of highly related disorders that manifest themselves in multiple but often similar ways. This idea, along with classifications of differential responses to interventions, may lead to the identification of different subtypes of autism (Gillum & Camarata, 2004). For example, some children with autism and communication problems respond well to interventions using spoken language, but others respond better to visually oriented interventions.

Regardless, one potential subtype of autism, **autistic savants**, is far more interesting to the general public than to researchers. The number of people who are autistic savants is very small, less than 1% of individuals diagnosed with autism, but the public is fascinated by the paradox of this group's abilities (Begley & Springen, 1996). Some, like the character Raymond in the film *Rain Man,* described in this chapter's On the Screen, can instantly count the number of wooden matches that have fallen on the floor, remember the dates of important events, or recall the numbers of all of the winning lottery tickets for the past year. Others have outstanding musical or artistic abilities. Even in light of these talents, these individuals are unable to initiate or maintain conversations and often have other severe disabilities. For example, 9-year-old Alex Mont can solve complicated mathematics problems,

On the Screen: *Rain Man*

Charlie Babbit receives word that his wealthy father has died and that the majority of the estate is bequeathed to an autistic brother, of whom he was unaware. Charlie kidnaps his brother from the institution where he had been living for over 30 years, in an effort to get custody of Raymond so he can gain access to the inheritance. However, Charlie grows to care for Raymond and comes to realize that Raymond's disability is too overwhelming, requiring professional care.

This classic film explores a rare form of autism, wherein the person is extremely gifted (autistic savant) in mathematics but is extremely low functioning in adaptive skills. Although Raymond is more verbal than most people with autism, many scenes depict the "disconnectedness" they often exhibit. Furthermore, the film demonstrates Raymond's dependence on familiarity and sameness and on an environment providing comfort, routine, and safety. This film won Oscars in the categories of Best Director, Best Original Screenplay, and Best Picture, and Dustin Hoffman's performance as Raymond earned him the Best Actor award.
—By Steven Smith

even calculus, but has difficulties comprehending social cues. Alex also could not distinguish a horse from a cow until after he finished kindergarten. While these splinter skills are fascinating to the observer, they are rarely functional for the individual with autism.

Asperger Syndrome

First described by Dr. Hans Asperger, **Asperger syndrome** is a collection of behavioral characteristics that are associated with problems developing adequate social skills and with restricted or unusual interests. Table 12.3 provides the DSM-IV-TR description of this type of ASD. Although the communication of people with Asperger syndrome may be peculiar, this characteristic is not due to a delay in language development. In fact, children with Asperger syndrome develop speech and language on a par with children without disabilities. Other aspects of communication, however, are problematic. Some children with Asperger syndrome understand language very literally, which can make it difficult for them to form flexible conceptual categories, understand jokes, or interpret the behavior of others (e.g., gestures). For these individuals, the social use of language can be a particular challenge, as can be the ability to comprehend other people's feelings or emotions (Safran, 2001).

Unlike individuals with autism, the majority with Asperger syndrome have normal intelligence, and they should not be confused with those individuals with high-functioning autism. Children with autism are diagnosed when a language delay becomes apparent, whereas children with Asperger syndrome develop language normally. The distinction between autism and Asperger syndrome, however, may turn out to be only a matter of semantics. Presently, controversy exists about whether

Asperger syndrome One of the autism spectrum disorders (ASD) where cognition is usually in the average or above-average range

Table 12.3 • DSM-IV-TR Diagnostic Criteria for Asperger Syndrome

A. Qualitative impairment in social interaction, as manifested by at least two of the following:

1. Marked impairments in the use of multiple nonverbal behaviors such as eye-to-eye gaze, facial expression, body postures, and gestures to regulate social interaction
2. Failure to develop peer relationships appropriate to developmental level
3. A lack of spontaneous seeking to share enjoyment, interests, or achievements with other people (e.g., by a lack of showing, bringing, or pointing out objects of interest to other people)
4. Lack of social or emotional reciprocity

B. Restricted repetitive and stereotyped patterns of behavior, interests, and activities, as manifested by at least one of the following:

1. Encompassing preoccupation with one or more stereotyped and restricted patterns of interest that is abnormal either in intensity or focus
2. Apparently inflexible adherence to specific, nonfunctional routines or rituals
3. Stereotyped and repetitive motor mannerisms (e.g., hand or finger flapping or twisting, or complex whole-body movements)
4. Persistent preoccupation with parts of objects

C. The disturbance causes clinically significant impairment in social, occupational, or other important areas of functioning.

D. There is no clinically significant general delay in language (e.g., single words used by age 2 years, communicative phrases used by age 3 years).

E. There is no clinically significant delay in cognitive development or in the development of age-appropriate self-help skills, adaptive behavior (other than in social interaction), and curiosity about the environment in childhood.

F. Criteria are not met for another specific pervasive development disorder or schizophrenia.

Source: From *Diagnostic and Statistical Manual of Mental Disorders* (4th ed., Text Revision, p. 84), by the American Psychiatric Association (APA), 2003, Arlington, VA: APA. Reprinted with permission.

there are any meaningful differences in the behaviors or performance of people with high-functioning autism and Asperger syndrome. It will take years of additional research before scientists fully resolve this issue. Besides typical intelligence, children with Asperger syndrome have other unique characteristics, which can include the following (Smith Myles & Simpson, 2002):

- Social stiffness and awkwardness
- Tendency to focus on a favorite conversational topic
- Inflexibility with routines
- Difficulty understanding nonverbal cues
- Limited awareness of others' feelings
- Concrete and literal thinking
- Good comprehension of factual material
- Obsessive interests
- Poor organizational skills
- Emotional vulnerability and stress
- Sensory problems
- Clumsiness
- Low self-esteem and depression

Pervasive Developmental Disorder—Not Otherwise Specified (PDD-NOS)

PDD-NOS is the third disorder included within the ASD umbrella. Problems in the areas of communication, social skills, and unusual behaviors, including a restricted range of interests, are the three common characteristics of ASD. Each type of ASD is different in how these behavioral profiles are expressed. Almost every, but not all, individuals with ASD exhibit all three areas of concern to some extent. However, when they do not, or when problems in all three areas are mild, a different diagnosis is made. In these cases, the disorder is identified as **pervasive developmental disorder—not otherwise specified (PDD-NOS)**. (Although the DSM-IV-TR describes PDD-NOS, it does not provide a table of its common characteristics.) The PDD part of the diagnosis signifies characteristics very similar to those of autism and Asperger syndrome, but the characteristics are not as clearly expressed. The NOS part refers to other specified disorders or syndromes. Although they share characteristics, PDD-NOS is currently considered as distinct from the other types of ASD (Walker et al., 2004).

Characteristics

Despite the heterogeneity of ASD, some general statements can be made about characteristics that people with these disorders share (see Table 12.4 for many of these specific characteristics). ASD is a lifelong disability, and no specific physical characteristics are associated with the condition. Although identified during early childhood, ASD is present very early in development. Although ASD results in unique profiles of symptoms across individuals and conditions, it typically affects three important areas that help define the condition (Barnhill, 2001):

- Communication
- Social interactions
- Restricted range of interests or behavioral repertoires

pervasive developmental disorder—not otherwise specified (PDD-NOS) One of the autistic spectrum disorders (ASD) in which not all three ASD characteristics (problems in communication, social interaction, and repetitive or manneristic behaviors) are present or they are mild

myeducationlab Go to the Activities and Applications section in Chapter 12 of MyEducationLab for, and complete Activity 1, an IRIS Information Brief: "Autism and Pervasive Developmental Disorders."

Table 12.4 • Characteristics of Autism

Impairment in Reciprocal Social Interactions

- Normal attachments to parents, family members, or caregivers do not develop.
- Friendships with peers fail to develop.
- Cooperative or peer play is rarely observed.
- Emotions, such as affection and empathy, are rarely displayed.
- Nonverbal signals of social intent (smiling, gestures, physical contact) tend not to be used.
- Eye contact is not initiated or maintained.
- Imaginative play is seldom observed.
- The lack of social-communicative gestures and utterances is apparent during the first few months of life.
- Preferred interaction style could be characterized as "extreme isolation."
- Understanding of others' beliefs, emotions, or motivations is greatly impaired.
- Joint attention deficits (not being able to cooperate or share interest with others in the same event or activity) impair normal social reciprocation.

Poor Communication Abilities

- Functional language is not acquired fully or mastered.
- Content of language is usually unrelated to immediate environmental events.
- Utterances are stereotypic and repetitive.
- Gestures, facial expressions, and nonverbal cues are poorly understood.
- Conversations are not maintained.
- Spontaneous conversations are rarely initiated.
- Speech can be meaningless, repetitive, and echolalic.
- Many fail to use the words *I* and *yes* and have problems with pronouns in general.
- Both expressive and receptive language are extremely literal.
- Verbal turn-taking, choosing a topic, and contributing properly to a conversation are rare.

Insistence on Sameness

- Marked distress is typically experienced over trivial or minor changes in the environment.
- Aspects of daily routine can become ritualized.
- Obsessive and compulsive behavior is frequently displayed.

- The need to complete self-imposed, required actions is intense.
- Stereotypic behaviors (rocking, hand-flapping) are repeated in cycles difficult to stop.

Unusual Behavior Patterns

- Hypersensitive and/or inconsistent behaviors are the response to visual, tactile, or auditory stimulation.
- Aggression to others is common, particularly when compliance is requested.
- Self-injurious or outwardly aggressive behavior (hitting, biting, kicking, head-banging) is common and frequent.
- Extreme social fears are manifested toward strangers, crowds, unusual situations, and new environments.
- Loud sounds (barking dogs, street noises) can result in startle or fearful reactions.
- Severe sleep problems occur with frequency.
- Noncompliant behavior to requests from others results in disruption to the individual and others (tantrums).
- Self-stimulation (twirling objects, rocking) consumes a considerable amount of time and energy.
- The ability to pretend is lacking.

Spotlighting *Belinda Pandey:* A Day in the Life

Belinda Pandey is the mother of two children with autism. Here, she shares a story about her older boy with ASD.

Today I was whining on the phone to Mom about how hard it is to parent a child with autism. I related Justin's total meltdown at the store today and how embarrassing and frustrating it was. I went on to complain about the stress and the expense of trying to get the services that Justin needs, the sleepless nights, being bitten and scratched, and the endless poop cleanup. I bemoaned the fact that he is just going to get bigger and stronger and less manageable. There were a few "why me's," and "I did not sign up for this" was said at least once.

Mom listened quietly until I was finished ranting. Then she said, "I know it's hard to be you. Think how hard it is to be him." I felt so ashamed. She's absolutely right. Since getting Justin's diagnosis I have been treating him like he is a

problem to be solved. I have been focusing on how his autism is disrupting our lives and trying to "fix" him. I have been dragging him from therapy to therapy, changing his food, and plying him with supplements. I have lost sight of the fact that he is a sweet little boy who is doing the best he can given the circumstances.

I haven't tried to understand how he sees the world; it must be so terrifying and confusing for him. He has no way to know what is coming up next or how to prepare for it. He has no way to tell us that something is painful or scary. He has no way to ask for comfort or help. It's so easy to take it personally when he tantrums or lashes out; but, it's not personal—it's the only way he has to communicate. Instead of focusing on how "bad" he is being, I need to focus on what he is trying to say and help him learn a more appropriate way to say it.

Above all I need to remember that he's just a little kid, and he's doing the best he can.

---

self-injury Self-inflicted injuries (head banging, eye poking)

aggression Hostile and attacking behavior, which can include verbal communication, directed toward self, others, or the physical environment

In addition to these three defining characteristics of ASD and those described in the DSM-IV-TR diagnostic criteria (review those definitions found in Tables 12.2 and 12.3), individuals with ASD may be unusually sensitive to sensory input, such as loud noises or soft touches (Talay-Ongan & Wood, 2000). Some individuals with ASD have serious problems with their behavior. They might turn these tendencies inward and hurt themselves, inflicting **self-injury**, or they might turn such behavior outward and hurt others through what is called **aggression**. Others with ASD have trouble developing the abilities necessary to understand other people's perspectives or to predict others' behavior—both important skills for successful communication (Baron-Cohen, 2001). In the Spotlighting feature you learn more from Belinda Pandey, a parent of two children with ASD.

A Strength-Based Perspective

Reflecting on the characteristics described in this chapter, it is easy to understand how children with ASD have difficulties succeeding in school. Even so, students can make substantial educational progress with the right interventions. Just like the rest of us, people with ASD are unique and have a variety of strengths and abilities. For example, although children with Asperger syndrome tend to focus their conversations on a particular topic of interest, they also tend to become experts on that topic, or **special interest area**. By engaging a student in his or her special interest area, teachers can encourage conversations, reduce anxiety, and increase academic motivation (Winter-Messiers et al., 2007). Therefore, it is useful for teachers to understand children with ASD in terms of their strengths and abilities, as well as their problem areas. With this in mind, let's proceed to a discussion of how many students have ASD.

special interest area A topic of interest that can be used to encourage conversations, reduce anxiety, and increase academic motivation

Prevalence

Prevalence is the number of cases of a condition within a population at a particular point in time. The prevalence of ASD has been the subject of much recent controversy and debate. In 2007, CDC reported that the prevalence of ASD was about

1 in 150 children in the United States (Rice et al., 2007). This figure reflects data from national studies, which found that the prevalence rates of ASD were 10 times higher than those reported in the 1980s and 1990s (Yeargin-Allsopp et al., 2003). Experts agree that ASD is being diagnosed more frequently; however, a consensus does not yet exist about why this is happening. Some feel that factors such as broadening diagnostic criteria and increased public awareness account for the relatively rapid increase in reported cases (Fombonne, 2003). Others suggest that environmental factors, including ingredients in vaccines, have contributed to a real increase in ASD. Although there is no scientific evidence to support the role of vaccines in increasing rates of ASD (Schechter & Grether, 2008), debate about why the ASD prevalence has risen will likely continue. For more information about the CDC's Autism and Developmental Disabilities Monitoring (ADDM) Network, visit www.cdc.gov/ncbddd/autism/addm.htm.

Despite the national concern about rising cases of ASD, this disability remains very low incidence (Office of Special Education Programs [OSEP], 2008). Since 1990, when autism became a separate special education category, states have reported to the federal government the number and percentage of students with ASD identified and served in the public schools. Only 0.34% of all students ages 6 through 21 provided with special education services are identified through the IDEA '04 autism category. Although students with ASD account for a relatively small portion of all students with disabilities served under IDEA '04, current trends suggest that numbers of students served within this category will continue to rise.

Causes and Prevention

Much recent research has focused on identifying the causes of ASD. In the future, scientists hope to use this information to facilitate early identification of ASD in infants and toddlers, or to prevent the development of ASD altogether. Unfortunately, research to date has not yielded specific reasons why children develop these disorders, and scientists are still years away from completely understanding the contributing factors. Nonetheless, some general conclusions about the causes of ASD can be drawn.

Causes

As we learned earlier in the chapter, ASD is not caused by bad parenting. Rather, most experts agree that ASD is a neurobiological disorder that has a genetic basis. Scientists have studied the patterns of ASD within families, finding that children who have an identical twin, fraternal twin, or sibling with ASD are more likely to have ASD themselves (Newschaffer, Falb, & Gurney, 2005). Although it is clear that genetics figure strongly in why children develop these disorders, it is not yet understood which genes place an individual at risk. The genetic pattern for inheritance of ASD is complex and will require many additional studies for scientists to fully understand. To complicate matters, significant numbers of children experience loss of skills before the signs of ASD fully develop (Rogers, 2004). Developmental regression has led some experts to speculate that a combination of biological and environmental factors could trigger the onset of ASD, but little scientific evidence currently supports this view.

Current research is beginning to show linkages between behavioral characteristics, developmental trajectories, neurobiology, and genetics as they relate to ASD, but many myths about the cause of ASD remain on the Internet and in the popular media. Some causes suggested in recent years have included environmental toxins, gastrointestinal anomalies, vitamin deficiencies, and vaccines. Such speculation about possible causes of ASD creates dangerous situations. For example, some parents believe that the measles/mumps/rubella (MMR) vaccine causes ASD. Although strong evidence indicates that no such link exists (Schechter & Grether, 2008), some parents are withholding MMR vaccines from their children because they are concerned that the

Figure 12.2 • Healing Thresholds Web Site

Educational professionals and parents alike use the Internet to learn more about ASD. Healing Thresholds is a Web site that provides concise information about ASD therapies, research, and news developments. The site is especially helpful because it presents scientifically based information in a way that is easy to understand. Healing Thresholds features include

- information about popular therapies, such as applied behavior analysis, including the research support for each;
- layperson summaries of peer-reviewed ASD research;
- briefs on ASD-related developments in the news; and
- a virtual community center where members can share ideas and experiences about ASD.

To learn more, visit Healing Thresholds at http://autism.healingthresholds.com.

vaccine may cause their child to develop ASD. The unfortunate result of this practice will be an increase in cases of measles, mumps, and rubella among children who do not receive the vaccine (Cowley, Brownell, & Footes, 2000).

Parents and professionals often use the Internet to learn more about ASD. While thousands of Web sites provide information about these disorders, much of this information is inaccurate or out-of-date. One site, however—www.healingthresholds.com—contains accurate, concise, and current information about ASD research and interventions (see Figure 12.2).

Prevention

Unfortunately, because there is so much to learn about the causes of ASD, prevention is not currently a realistic goal. Perhaps in the future, as researchers learn more about why ASD occurs, steps can be taken to prevent children from being born with or later developing characteristics associated with ASD. Until then, educational interventions are our primary basis for improving symptoms associated with ASD.

Overcoming Challenges

Just as there is rampant lay speculation about possible causes of ASD, there is also an ongoing stream of "cures" (Seroussi, 2000). The Internet and popular press are littered with stories of children being "cured" using vitamins, special diets, or newly discovered medical drugs, often based on a single case history. Parents and professionals who support these alternative treatments may believe in them and think these treatments help remediate a child's symptoms, but no scientific evidence validates these claims. Until ASD is well understood and consistently effective treatments are developed, the causes and treatments for ASD will remain the subject of considerable speculation, conjecture, and controversy.

However, it is important to remember that ASD is a significant, lifelong disability. Long-term outcomes, even for those with average intelligence, in the areas of independent living, employment, and life satisfaction are inconsistent (Sperry, 2001). Most people with ASD require comprehensive services and supports across the life span. In general, the more severe the form of ASD, the greater the supports needed by the individual. Effective services and supports require high levels of coordination and consistency. Unfortunately, because services offered by social service agencies, health care providers, and mental health systems are often fragmented, these goals are difficult to achieve.

From early in life, the skill deficits of children with ASD affect their learning, as well as their development of social relationships. They do not participate in turn-taking exchanges. This lack of reciprocal social interaction adversely affects the acquisition and use of preverbal communication (e.g., gestures), as well as the eventual acquisition of speech and language skills (Stone & Yoder, 2001). Most cultural mores are passed from generation to generation via implicit teaching that involves social interactions and observational learning. Both of these means of learning represent problem areas for children with ASD. Most instruction at school is socially mediated and language based, again problem areas for students with ASD. Thus, the social and communication problems faced by children with ASD create a cascade of obstacles to learning and development (Carpenter, Pennington, & Rogers, 2002). In this way, ASD pervasively affects the person's entire developmental trajectory.

myeducationlab Go to the Activities and Applications section in Chapter 12 of MyEducationLab, and complete Activity 2 to learn more about social skills instruction for a child with autism and her typically developing peers in a resource room.

Assessment

Experts are focusing more attention on early screening and identification of ASD than ever before. One important reason is that ASD is often not diagnosed until two or more years after the initial signs appear (Filipek et al., 2000). If diagnosis is delayed, then intervention is delayed. Several major medical organizations, including the American Academy of Pediatrics, have developed recommendations for the screening and diagnosis of ASD in young children (Johnson & Myers, 2007; See Figure Figure 12.3). Importantly, these guidelines create a role for pediatricians to assist in the identification of ASD through early screenings. Educationally, early diagnosis is critical because it can lead to earlier intervention and better educational outcomes. For more information about the American Academy of Pediatrics guidelines for screening and evaluation of children with ASD, visit www.aap.org/healthtopics/autism.cfm.

As we have learned, ASD is a complex, lifelong disorder. There are many differences in how ASD develops among children; therefore, assessment is not a straightforward procedure. Rather, diagnosing ASD involves careful evaluation of the individual's history and unique behavioral characteristics. Three general considerations inform the ASD assessment process (Ozonoff, Goodin-Jones, & Solomon, 2005):

- Maintain a developmental perspective.
- Include information from multiple sources and contexts.
- Conduct multidisciplinary assessments.

Figure 12.3 • Early Signs of ASD

Early signs of ASD in children less than 24 months old may include

- a family history, including siblings that are diagnosed with ASD;
- poor eye contact;
- poor response to other's voices;
- poor attempts at interactive play;
- more interest in looking at objects than people;
- delayed pointing to request or share;
- decreased to-and-fro babbling and jargoning;
- lack of warm, joyful, reciprocating expressions.

Source: Information from Johnson and Meyers, (2007).

The first of these considerations, maintain a developmental perspective, means that clinicians must carefully evaluate the child's acquisition of developmental milestones to assess which deficits are occurring. For example, one child with ASD may be quite verbal but have significant impairments in social interaction, while another may lack verbal skills altogether but respond to others' directions. A developmental perspective provides a complete picture of the individual child's strengths and weaknesses. The second consideration, include information from multiple sources and contexts, suggests that information from multiple settings and situations increases the accuracy of assessment. So, the assessment team should consider the child's skills across multiple settings (e.g., home vs. school), including familiar and unfamiliar situations. The third consideration, conduct multidisciplinary assessments, means that involving professionals from different disciplines (e.g., psychology, speech language pathology, special education) provides a more complete picture of the child's skills. Multidisciplinary assessment also facilitates the development of comprehensive intervention programs to teach skills (see Chapter 2 for more on multidisciplinary assessment).

Until recently, children with ASD were not diagnosed until the age of 5, but in part because of new assessment tools, now it is possible to diagnose children as young as the age of 2 (Bryson, Rogers, & Fombonne, 2003). For example, the *Autism Diagnostic Observation Scale* (ADOS) and the *Screening Test for Autism in Two Year Olds* (STAT), along with developmental assessments and parent reports, can help identify very young children with ASD. Because many typically developing children are just beginning to develop spoken language at the age of 2, and because the diagnostic features of ASD include language delay, both the ADOS and the STAT include measures examining other skills, such as children's ability to imitate motor movements. Apparently, children with ASD also have early deficits in motor imitation skills that can be used for diagnosis before deficits in language become apparent.

Researchers are still developing instruments that can accurately diagnose ASD in children younger than the age of 2 (Bryson et al., 2003). In fact, efforts are underway to develop methods to detect ASD even before a child's first birthday. Around 9 months of age, children without disabilities begin to engage in what psychologists describe as joint attention. **Joint attention** involves two people such as a child and a parent. It occurs when first one person looks at an object, then looks at the other person, and finally when the two people simultaneously look at the object. That is, they together (or jointly) look at (or attend) to the same object. Researchers believe that joint attention is important in the development of both language and social skills (Mundy & Neal, 2001). While children with ASD do participate in joint attention episodes, their pattern and type of participation are different from those of children without disabilities (Shienkopf et al., 2000). Why is this information important? Potentially, it can help us understand more about the development of social and language skills as well as the core characteristics of ASD. Such information might also lead to earlier identification of children with ASD.

Trained psychologists who have experience in diagnosing children with ASD are required to administer most assessment instruments used to identify ASD. One screening tool that does not require training is the *Checklist for Autism in Toddlers* (CHAT). It was developed to help physicians spot early warning signs. Another measure, the *Childhood Autism Rating Scale* (CARS; Schopler et al., 1980), is widely used to confirm a diagnosis and also to monitor the child's growth over time. CARS also describes the severity of problems that a child with ASD demonstrates.

Early Intervention

While children can be diagnosed with ASD before the age of 3, empirical evidence demonstrating which practices and programs are best for these very young children is still emerging. In other words, the ability to diagnose children with ASD has outpaced the validation of effective interventions. A few practices developed for older

joint attention The ability to mutually interact or to share interest in events or objects

children with ASD and other developmental disabilities have also proven to be effective with toddlers with ASD. For example, Schertz and Odom (2007) used a parent-mediated approach to increase joint attention in two-year-old children with ASD. Similarly, the *Walden Program* is effective with preschoolers with ASD and has been adapted to serve even younger children. Others, like the *Inclusive Program for Very Young Children with Autism*, are being developed from collective information about child development, the nature of ASD, and existing interventions that have been validated with 2-year-olds with ASD (Garfinkle & Kaiser, 2004).

Many parents turn to homeopathic remedies, including high doses of vitamins and special diets, as alternative therapies for both younger and older children with ASD. Most experts view homeopathic treatments skeptically because little scientific evidence supports their effectiveness in improving skills (Smith, McAdam, & Napolitano, 2007). It is important to weigh the unlikely benefits of alternative remedies against the costs and potentially undesirable effects of these treatments. For example, a special diet that restricts certain ingredients may constrain a child's already limited food choices and elicit challenging behaviors when preferred foods are not available.

Some children may be prescribed psychotropic medications to reduce the behavioral excesses of ASD, including stereotypies and aggression. Although evidence supports the effectiveness of psychotropic medications in suppressing undesirable behaviors in some children, response is inconsistent and medications are unlikely to help children learn new skills (Harris, LaRue, & Weiss, 2007). Prescription medications may also produce significant side effects. For these reasons, psychotropic medications should be used sparingly, particularly with children younger than 5 years old, and only when other strategies to reduce problem behavior have been exhausted (Bryson et al., 2003).

In contrast, educational programs for 3- to 5-year old children are some of the most developed and best studied, but much is still to be learned (Handleman & Harris, 2000). For example, no one program is consistently effective, so universal recommendations about educational programming cannot be made. Also, no guidelines can suggest whether one type of program would be better than another for a particular child. Finally, few studies have measured the effectiveness of a treatment program using randomized, control group experiments, and no studies have compared the effectiveness of one program against that of another.

Although no programs have been completely validated, research has identified some key features of effective programs that make a difference in the lives of these preschoolers. These key features are apparent even across programs that differ in philosophy, theoretical background, intensity of services, and timing of instruction with peers (Dawson & Osterling, 1997; Harris & Handleman, 1994; Levy, Kim, & Olive, 2006). Key elements of successful programs include

- highly supportive teaching environments,
- low staff-to-student ratios,
- plans for generalization,
- interventions to promote language and communication,
- predictable and routine schedules,
- behavioral approaches to address challenging behaviors,
- supports to facilitate program transitions, and
- parent involvement and support.

These programs also include some common targets for instruction. For example, students with ASD profit from instruction that is clear, specific, and concrete. More important content that teachers should include in their curriculum for these preschoolers is found in Tips for Effective Instruction.

Even though most effective programs for young children with ASD share some features, significant differences exist across programs. (Some disagreements among the advocates of different programs have been so intense that they have had to be resolved in the courts!) Two particular programs are popular in the education of preschoolers with ASD: the *Treatment and Education of Autistic*

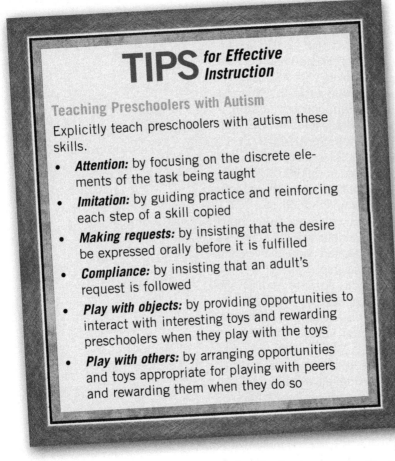

TIPS *for Effective Instruction*

Teaching Preschoolers with Autism

Explicitly teach preschoolers with autism these skills.

- **Attention:** by focusing on the discrete elements of the task being taught
- **Imitation:** by guiding practice and reinforcing each step of a skill copied
- **Making requests:** by insisting that the desire be expressed orally before it is fulfilled
- **Compliance:** by insisting that an adult's request is followed
- **Play with objects:** by providing opportunities to interact with interesting toys and rewarding preschoolers when they play with the toys
- **Play with others:** by arranging opportunities and toys appropriate for playing with peers and rewarding them when they do so

and *Communication-Handicapped Children* (TEACCH) and the *Young Autism Program* (YAP). Let's look at some highlights of these programs.

TEACCH

One program often used with students with autism was developed at the University of North Carolina at Chapel Hill. TEACCH is an intervention program that emphasizes the use of structured teaching (Lord & Schopler, 1994). **Structured teaching** involves adapting materials and environments to help children make sense of the world. Once new skills are acquired, children are taught to perform them more and more independently. The program relies on "start-to-finish boxes" as well as visual supports and schedules in teaching. The underlying philosophy of the program is that children with ASD are missing skills that they can compensate for through visual supports and other forms of structure, but they cannot learn. TEACCH is an individualized program that supports families through collaboration and training. In this program, parents become cotherapists. Although TEACCH has not been evaluated with rigorous research studies, preliminary evidence suggests it is beneficial for students with ASD (Smith et al., 2007).

The Young Autism Program (YAP)

YAP, one well-known program, grew out of the work of Ivar Lovaas at UCLA (Lovaas, 1987). Sometimes it is simply referred to as "the Lovaas program" or, incorrectly, as "ABA" (which stands for applied behavior analysis[1]). YAP is an intensive (up to 40 hours per week) program that uses the principles of **behavior analysis** (e.g., positive reinforcement, extinction, and shaping) that have been developed by behavior analysts over the last five decades, beginning with the work of Dr. Charles B. Ferster at the Indiana University Medical Center (Ferster & DeMeyer, 1961). YAP incorporates **discrete trial teaching**, a highly structured technique involving teacher-directed activities, repetition of skills through practice, and careful application of rewards. The goal of YAP is to teach the child, one skill at a time, all the skills the child needs to participate independently in all facets of daily living. While there is considerably more research to support YAP in comparison to TEACCH, YAP has been evaluated primarily in home-based rather than school-based settings (Sallows & Graupner, 2005).

Comprehensive Approaches

Neither TEACCH nor YAP by itself is likely to address the unique educational needs of every child with ASD. Therefore, comprehensive approaches that incorporate an array of research-supported techniques, including those found in TEACCH and YAP, maxi-

structured teaching A feature of the instructional program, TEACHH, developed for students with autism where visual aids (start-to-finish boxes) are used to help students comprehend their environments

behavior analysis Research methodology using single-case designs; derived from the work of B. F. Skinner; paradigms describing human behavior in terms of events that stimulate or cause a behavior's occurrence, maintains behavior, and increases its likelihood

discrete trial teaching A highly structured technique using teacher-directed activities, repetition of skills through practice, and use of rewards

---

[1] Laypersons often refer to the UCLA program as "ABA therapy." This is incorrect. ABA stands for applied behavior analysis (Baer, Wolf, & Risley, 1968). ABA is the science of behavior first developed in the laboratory by experimental psychologists such as B. F. Skinner and then applied to educational and other settings. YAP and other programs for children with ASD use ABA techniques, but ABA is not synonymous with any one treatment program but is the basis of most effective treatments for ASD.

mize the educational potential of each child. One example of a comprehensive approach is the *Pyramid Approach to Education in Autism* (Bondy & Sultzer-Azaroff, 2002). Developed at the Delaware Autistic Program, a statewide public school program for students with ASD (Bondy, 1996), the Pyramid Approach uses a broad spectrum of data-based techniques to support skill acquisition across domains. These techniques include visual supports and discrete trial teaching, in addition to incidental teaching strategies, delayed prompting, reward systems, activity schedules, and other behavioral strategies known to be effective for children with ASD (Matson et al., 1996). In tandem with effective practices, the Pyramid Approach adopts a functional perspective on selection of instructional goals and emphasizes the importance of community integration. Importantly, the Pyramid Approach is specifically designed to be implemented in public school settings with students of a variety of ages and functioning levels.

Teaching Students with ASD

Many of the principles that are effective in working with younger children with ASD also work well when incorporated into educational programs for older children, adolescents, and young adults with ASD (Kennedy & Horn, 2004). In particular, consistent structure, support of functional communication, instruction on social skills, and a functional and positive approach are important for school-age children with ASD (Scott, Clark, & Brady, 2000). Educators must collaborate to develop appropriate and individualized instructional plans. Here are some questions that educators may consider when planning students' educational programs (Bondy & Sulzer-Azaroff, 2002):

myeducationlab Go to the Activities and Applications section in Chapter 12 of MyEducationLab, and complete Activity 3 to learn more about academic instruction in reading and language for children with autism in a resource room.

- What are the long-term goals of the student's education (e.g., getting a job, living independently)?
- What skills will the student need in future environments?
- What skills do typically-developing children perform?
- What are the student's strengths and weaknesses?
- What pivotal behaviors should the student learn?
- What skills will the student need in school, including inclusive settings?
- What skills will the student need in the home and community?

Four areas in particular have come to the forefront in recent years about how to effectively educate school-age learners with ASD. These include accessing the general education curriculum, making instructional accommodations, using data-based practices, and using technology.

Accessing the General Education Curriculum

A major barrier to the academic and social inclusion of students with ASD is lack of access to the general education curriculum. Traditionally, students with ASD have been taught a separate curriculum, often one that was age inappropriate and non-functional. For example, in previous decades it was common to see teenagers with ASD being taught, as a primary instructional objective, to sort different-colored chips into bins. Such a curriculum was not academically challenging, nor did it facilitate the development of social skills for interacting with others. However, in the past two decades, educators have shifted their focus to ensure what students with ASD learn is aligned with what students without disabilities learn (e.g., science, history, mathematics, English/language arts). This content alignment encourages students with and without ASD to access similar general education material. It also provides a basis for common learning and social experiences (Ryndak & Alper, 2003).

Instructional Accommodations

Access to the general educational curriculum and inclusive environments helps maximize the educational potential of each student with ASD. Because there is such a large ability range for students with ASD, the general education curriculum must be adjusted to each student's strengths and needs. For example, students with ASD are unlikely to fully benefit from the social aspects of general education unless the teacher implements specific classroom modifications and supports to promote social interactions (Laushey & Heflin, 2000). Instructional accommodations allow educators to tailor the general education curriculum to the needs of students with ASD, while minimally changing the learning environment for other students. Here are a few general principles:

- Events should be made predictable.
- Expectations need to be carefully explained.
- A positive learning environment must be fostered.

By making accommodations, like those listed in Accommodating for Inclusive Environments, students with ASD are more easily and meaningfully included in general education classrooms.

Data-Based Practices

Along with access to the general education curriculum and instructional accommodations, most programs for students with ASD include explicit strategies to reduce distracting behaviors that interfere with learning and successful interactions. Challenging behaviors that hinder students' academic progress and social skills can range from stereotypies, such as hand flapping and excessive rocking, to more serious behaviors like aggression, self-injury, and property destruction. In the past, some educators relied on punishment to reduce problem behaviors. Three significant problems with punishment are that it (Cooper, Heron, & Heward, 2007)

positive behavior support A three-tiered model of support offering progressively more intensive levels of intervention

functional behavioral assessment A process in which interviews, observations, and environmental manipulations are conducted to determine why certain behaviors occur

- produces only temporary reductions in negative behaviors;
- does not teach any new skills; and
- leads to negative side effects, including the child withdrawing from and avoiding the educational environment.

Today, educators adopt a more positive and functional approach to reducing challenging behavior called **positive behavior support** (see Chapter 7 for a detailed description of positive behavior support). One critical aspect of positive behavior support involves assessing which events in the environment trigger and maintain problem behaviors. This process is called **functional behavioral assessment** (again, see Chapter 7). For example, through functional behavioral assessment the educational team may discover that a student's disruptive hand flapping is more frequent when difficult assignments are presented and that hand flapping results in escape from demanding tasks. With this information, the team can design strategies to reduce the challenging behavior based on its functions. One strategy, **functional communication training**, involves teaching the student a more appropriate response that is functionally equivalent to the problem behavior (Durand & Merges, 2001). In the current example, the team could teach the student to request a break rather than flapping his or her hands to temporarily escape from the task. For more information about a proactive approach to classroom management based on positive behavior support, read this chapter's Tips for Classroom Management.

functional communication training A strategy to reduce problem behaviors by teaching functionally equivalent alternatives

Strategies like functional communication training are most effective when used in combination with proactive systems that teach children to manage their own behaviors. Visual supports include a variety of techniques that help students with ASD to understand routines, transition independently from one lesson to the next, and acquire new skills. **Activity schedules** are specific visual support strategies that enable students to achieve higher levels of independence (Stromer et al., 2006). Activity schedules can range from simple written or pictorial directions

activity schedules Written or pictorial directions to help perform skills and routines

TIPS for Classroom Management

POSITIVE BEHAVIOR SUPPORT

Modify the classroom environment to minimize challenging behavior.

1. Carefully identify the inappropriate behavior(s) in observable terms.
   - For example: *Raymond flaps his hands in front of his face.*

2. Analyze events that trigger the problem behavior(s) and change them.
   - For example: *Raymond engages in this behavior when he has nothing to do, is bored, or the work is too hard for him. He continues with flapping his hands until he is reminded to work on his assignment or is given work to do that he can accomplish.*

3. Determine events that trigger the problem behavior and change them.

4. Determine substitute behaviors to develop.
   - For example: *Independent seatwork, reading silently, computing math problems are substitute behaviors, Mrs. Norega, his teacher has selected as alternate behaviors to Raymond's hand flapping.*

5. Teach and reward alternate behaviors.
   - For example: *Mrs. Norega carefully matches assignments with Raymond's skills and has alternative work available. She also prompts Raymond with these words: "Raymond, time to go back to work." And, for completing assignments, he earns a colored pencil (at the moment one of his favorite things to collect).*

6. Work with everyone to be sure that there is consistency across all settings, such as home and school.
   - For example: *Mrs. Norega implements her program for teaching Raymond functionally equivalent behaviors and gathers data to evaluate its effectiveness. Using the data from her successful program, she shows other teachers who work with Raymond and his parents how to implement it as well.*

Social Stories™ Short stories that describe a specific activity and the behavioral expectations associated with that activity

augmentative and alternative communication (AAC) Assistive technology that helps individuals communicate, including devices that actually produce speech

picture exchange communication system (PECS). A technique where pictures are used to communicate, for individuals with autism who are nonverbal

placed in a student's notebook to interactive computer-based programs that include video clips with models of appropriate behavior. Depending on the type and purpose, activity schedules can be carried with the student or placed on the wall of the classroom, as seen in the photos.

Difficulty with social interactions is a defining characteristic of ASD. Social situations are often puzzling for students on the spectrum who have difficulty understanding the rules and norms of appropriate behavior. Therefore, it is often necessary for educators to explicitly teach social skills. **Social Stories™** is a popular strategy for helping students with ASD learn how to cope and interact in various situations (Gray & Garand, 1993). A Social Story is a short story written for an individual that describes a specific activity and the behavioral expectations associated with that activity. For example, a Social Story about lining up in the classroom might describe the instruction given by the teacher, what the students do and why, and how the target individual should respond. Other common social situations addressed by Social Stories could include sharing, turn taking, greeting, and coping with teasing. While the research on Social Stories is still emerging, preliminary studies have found them to be effective in improving social and behavioral skills of students with ASD (Sansosti, Powell-Smith, & Kincaid, 2004).

There are many strategies available for teaching communication to students with ASD. Because approximately 50% of persons with ASD do not talk, **augmentative and alternative communication (AAC)** devices provide another means to promote functional interactions (Cafiero, 2005). AAC devices range from high-tech computer tools with touch screens that enable users to generate sophisticated messages, to low-tech systems that help individuals articulate their basic wants and needs. Some team members may express concerns that AAC systems hinder students' speech by teaching them to rely on devices for communication. To the contrary, no scientific evidence suggests that AAC devices hinder speech. In fact, AAC systems may actually promote speech for some users with ASD (Tincani, 2004; Tincani, Crozier, & Alazetta, 2006).

Of the low-tech AAC strategies available, one that capitalizes on the visual strengths of students with ASD is the **picture exchange communication system (PECS)** (Charlop-Christie et al., 2002; Frost & Bondy, 2002; Schwartz, Garfinkle, & Bauer, 1998; Schwartz et al., 2001). PECS is a carefully sequenced approach for teaching people with ASD to communicate by exchanging pictures. Read this chapter's A Closer Look at Data-Based Practices to learn how PECS helps students with ASD become functional communicators by helping them express their desires and needs to others.

Technology

Students with ASD do not usually need high-tech supports to be successful in school. Rather, a variety of both low-tech and high-tech devices are available to support the development of communication, social interactions, and academic skills. Some examples of technology-based supports for students with ASD include (Tincani & Boutot, 2005)

- low-tech AAC systems, such as PECS;
- high-tech AAC devices, including voice output communication aides (VOCAs);
- interactive programs to support reading and writing skills; and
- multimedia programs to promote social and self-management skills.

While less research has been done on technology-based learning systems compared to other interventions for ASD, some promising practices are emerging. One example of a multimedia intervention, **video modeling,** involves the child viewing a model performing a desired behavior to teach social, communication, play, or functional skills (Bellini & Akullian, 2007). The student can view peers, siblings, or adults engaging in desired behaviors, or, as with video self-modeling, the child can view him- or herself performing specific skills. Video modeling capitalizes on the visual strengths of learners with ASD and helps teach targeted skills by providing clear examples. High-tech interventions like video modeling are becoming more popular as video recording equipment and software programs become less expensive and more available. Still, the potential benefits of high-tech interventions must be weighed against the costs, training, and other resources necessary to implement these tools.

video modeling A multimedia intervention in which the student imitates a model performing desired behaviors

myeducationlab Go to the Building Teaching Skills section in Chapter 12 of MyEducationLab, and complete the activities. As you watch the videos and answer the accompanying questions, compare how different types of multimedia and instructional software can enhance instruction for students who have autism.

Transition

Transitions are common in life. Some of those transitions are made with excitement and others with fear or trepidation. For some of us, a move to a new city is filled with joy, and the thrill of what is waiting around the next corner is uplifting. For others, transitioning to a new town is fraught with worry. Each of us is different, and each situation is different. The same is true for individuals with ASD. In particular, successful transitions at two different times—moving from early intervention programs and leaving the shelter of school and on to adult services—make real differences in the lives of these individuals and their families. Let's take a look at each of these points of time in turn.

Transition to Preschool

Myriad rules, regulations, and funding mechanisms guide how infants, toddlers, and preschoolers with disabilities, including ASD, receive early intervention services. Most early-identified infants and toddlers with disabilities—until their third birthday—receive early intervention services through Part C of the IDEA law. Part C services typically are designed to serve the family, as well as the child with the disability. Often, these services are brought to the family's home, incorporating parents and siblings, rather than just professionals, as agents of intervention. Part B services are designed for preschoolers and students up through their high school years (for some up to the age of 21). Services are delivered at schools: preschools, elementary schools, middle schools, and high schools. Some families find the transition from one type of service to another too great, and asked the federal government for other options. For this reason, the Federal government responded by providing alternatives. These are described in What IDEA '04 Says About Options for Children Ages 3 to 5.

What IDEA '04 Says About . . .

Options for Children Ages 3 to 5

Federal funds to support the preschool education of students with disabilities who are beyond age three are allocated through Part B of IDEA. Part C of the law outlines the requirements for early intervention services for infants and toddlers.

Parents of children eligible for preschool services provided through Part B may choose to continue early intervention services under Part C. This continuation of Part C early intervention services:

- must have an educational component that
  - promotes school readiness and
  - incorporates preliteracy, language, and numeracy skills;
- may continue until the child is eligible to enter kindergarten;
- must be developed and implemented jointly through the state and local school systems;
- must be approved by the parents through informed written consent.

A Closer Look at Data-Based Practices:

The Picture Exchange Communication System

Interacting with others and exchanging information can be challenging for many individuals with ASD. Yet, it is very important to develop functional communication skills, skills that allow each of us to express our wants and needs. Many children with ASD must be taught functional communication, abilities that children without disabilities develop naturally, through explicit instruction. One technique that has proven successful is called the Picture Exchange Communication System (PECS) developed by Andy Bondy and Lori Frost. PECS is a system for teaching functional communication to students with language difficulties, including students with ASD. Although PECS is often used with non-verbal individuals, PECS may also help persons who have limited speech to better communicate their wants and needs. PECS is unique because it is the only augmentative and alternative communication (AAC) system that teaches students to initiate communication from the beginning. In PECS, students are taught to communicate by exchanging picture symbols.

Steps to Follow

1. Conduct a reinforcer assessment
   a. Determine what a student wants through observation, interview of others and presenting a variety of items to the student.

2. Prepare materials.
   a. The picture symbols can come from a variety of sources, including photographs, magazines, the Internet, commercially available collections of picture cards, and computer programs specifically designed to generate picture symbols.
   b. A PECS exchange board is created (see illustration in this box).

3. Phase 1: Teach students how to communicate.
   a. Two trainers are used in this phase. One picture symbol is presented at a time.
   b. When the student reaches toward a desired item, one trainer assists the student to pick up a picture symbol and to exchange it with a partner to request that item. Verbal instructions (e.g., "What do you want?") are avoided to help the student to become more independent.
   c. Once students learn to initiate communication, PECS focuses on increasing students' spontaneity, expanding their vocabulary, and helping them to engage in more complex conversations.
   d. Students become motivated to communicate through the use of highly preferred items identified through a reinforcer assessment.

Source: Picture used with permission from Pyramid Educational Products. Pyramid reserves all rights to the picture.

4. Phase 2: Foster student's independence and persistence.
   a. Students are taught to travel an increasing distance to get a picture symbol from a communication book, and to travel an increasing distance to exchange a picture with a partner.
   b. The second trainer who is providing physical prompts gradually fades out to promote independence. Verbal instructions are avoided.
   c. By teaching the students how to travel, students learn how to gain the attention of others in a way that is functional.
   d. Students are taught to carry their communication books.
   e. The trainers create many opportunities for communication to occur throughout the day.

5. Phase 3: Teach students to discriminate preferences from an expanding array of picture symbols.
   a. Students learn to discriminate between a picture symbol for a highly preferred item (e.g., candy) and a non-preferred item (e.g., sock), paying attention to the symbols in order to communicate the right message.
   b. Students learn to discriminate among a variety of preferred items (e.g., spin toy and ball).
   c. The number of picture symbols in the communication book is gradually increased to expand vocabulary.

6. Phase 4: Introduce sentence structure.
   a. Students are taught to construct a sentence (i.e., "I want [item].") to request something through a technique called backward chaining.

7. Expanding sentence structure
   a. Students learn to request items by their attributes (e.g., "I want blue candy.").

8. Phase 5: Respond to questions.
   a. Individuals learn to answer the question, "What do you want?"

9. Phase 6: Comment on the environment.
   a. Students learn to answer a comment question, (e.g. "what do you see?").
   b. Some students learn to comment spontaneously by assembling sentences, such as "I see (item)" or "I hear (sound)."

Example of a PECS Sentence Strip

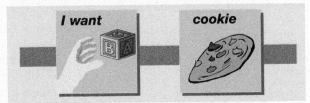

Source: Adapted from the *Picture Exchange Communication System* training manual by L. Frost and A. Bondy 2002, Newark, DE: Pyramid Educational Products, Inc.

 myeducationlab Go to the Activities and Applications section in Chapter 12 of MyEducationLab, and complete Activity 5 to learn more about inclusive practices.

Transition to Services for Adults

An important part of educational programming for students with ASD is the successful transition from supports provided at school to adult focused supports (Wehman, 2000). Just like the rest of us, people with ASD want to live independently and have meaningful, sustaining employment. Although many persons with ASD have talents and skills that make them employable, their difficulty with social interactions and their need for routine often results in a need to receive **supported employment**. For adults with ASD, supported employment can address several major areas of assistance (Muller et al., 2003). Some examples of these are

- mastering the job application process,
- adapting to new routines,
- communicating in the workplace, and
- navigating social interactions with employers and coworkers.

In addition, like other adults, people with ASD often want opportunities to continue their education after high school, but for these individuals, additional supports may be required to insure ongoing success (Getzel & Wehman, 2004). In general, the difficulties faced by people with ASD are similar to those faced by others with disabilities. Transition components of IEPs (see Chapter 2 for a review) are necessary and important, but issues such as living and working independently require ongoing support for people with ASD and their families. Transition outcomes, such as living and working in the community, become the focus of educational programming in high school and on through adulthood.

For people with ASD, life as an adult can be a challenging and rewarding part of life, as it is for all of us. However, people with ASD may need additional supports to succeed. Many of these individuals, like Jessy Park, are happy, successful adults, particularly when they are able to focus on their interests, preferences, and opportunities to continue to grow as individuals (Park, 2001). Jessy is an artist whose work is receiving national attention, but she is unable to live independently or interact with people comfortably enough to live and participate in the community without additional help from others. With these supports, she does well; without them, she often struggles to succeed. Anthony Crudale, another recognized artist with ASD, is a college graduate and a marathon runner (Raia, 2001). Although he drives a car and has a college degree,

myeducationlab Go to the Activities and Applications section in Chapter 12 of MyEducationLab, and complete Activity 4. As you watch the video and answer the accompanying questions, notice the interactions between the pre-school children who have autism and their typically developing peers in this inclusive classroom.

supported employment A strategy used in job training in which the student is placed in a paying job and receives significant assistance and support and the employer is helped with the compensation

at age 24 he requires assistance to live independently and work. His mother worries that people do not understand ASD and that Anthony's inability to maintain eye contact with other people, his short verbal responses, and his inability to carry on conversations make others uncomfortable. She believes that he, and others with ASD, are excellent employees because of characteristics like focusing on specific tasks, attention to detail, and the need to complete jobs, but that others in society need to understand the unique characteristics of people with ASD. These observations highlight the fact that for people with ASD to be successful as adults, they require understanding and support from others in their community.

Collaboration

peer supports An instructional strategy that facilitates social interaction and access to the general education curriculum

Students with ASD must have access to the least restrictive environment (LRE), which in school contexts often means general education settings and peers without disabilities (Ryndak & Alper, 2003). Sometimes, this access is hard to achieve and maintain. Using techniques such as adapting or modifying the school curriculum and using **peer supports** can help teachers encourage behaviors that will allow students to remain engaged in instruction provided in the general education classroom (Kennedy & Horn, 2004). One peer supports strategy involves pairing the child with ASD and a peer buddy who does not have a disability (Laushey & Heflin, 2000). In dyads, the peer buddy can facilitate communicative responses and social interactions that would otherwise not occur.

Such interventions, along with adjustments and accommodations, become part of the package necessary to ensure LRE and a free appropriate public education (FAPE) to students who are challenging to teach. Interdisciplinary teams of professionals, including general and special educators and related services professionals such as behavior analysts, need to work together to identify the specific accommodations needed for each student. It is imperative that students with ASD experience typical and supported interactions with peers without disabilities. Such inclusion provides these students with appropriate role models, where they can observe how others behave and interact with each other. Some programs, such as *Learning Experiences: An Alternative Program for Preschoolers and Parents (LEAP),* integrate children with autism into inclusive settings at the outset of treatment (Hoyson, Jamieson, & Strain, 1984; Strain & Hoyson, 2000). With older students, the focus is on inclusive education and skill building in the LRE. However, it is important to remember that the following elements must be present:

- Sufficient structure
- Supports for functional communication
- Use of behavior analysis techniques
- Supports for social interactions

Collaborating with Support Personnel: Behavior Analysts

behavior analyst A support professional with expertise in applying principles of behavior to develop interventions for students with ASD and other disabilities

Board Certified Behavior Analyst™ (BCBA) A behavior analyst who has fulfilled national certification requirements, including coursework and fieldwork, has passed a competency exam, and holds at least a master's degree in a related field (e.g., education, psychology)

task analysis Breaking down problems and tasks into smaller, sequenced components

As we are discovering, children with ASD need to learn many different things, including communication and socialization, as well as adaptive daily living and functional skills. Teaching techniques based in the science of behavior analysis are effective in helping people with ASD acquire new skills and maintain existing ones (Rosenwasser & Axelrod, 2002). **Behavior analysts** are support personnel with expertise in applying behavioral principles to teach specific learning objectives. Increasingly, school systems are employing **Board Certified Behavior Analysts™ (BCBAs)**, nationally certified professionals who have fulfilled coursework and supervised experience requirements to demonstrate their expertise in applying behavioral techniques (Shook, 2005). For example, a special education teacher who wants to teach a child with ASD to initiate social interactions could work with a BCBA to **task analyze** social skills, develop appropriate prompting and error correction procedures, and implement data collection systems.

Collaborative Practices: Minimizing Conflict

It is critical for educators to acknowledge that developing a student's educational program is a team-based process (see Chapter 2 for a review of the IEP process). Therefore, disagreements can occur as the team selects a student's educational goals and interventions. Conflicts are more likely when team members have strong yet opposing feelings about which programs and strategies are most effective. For example, it is common for parents of children with ASD to advocate for a program primarily based on applied behavior analysis, like the YAP, while professional team members support a more eclectic approach (Etscheidt, 2003). Here are five steps for team members to follow in order to minimize conflicts during the teaming process (Tincani, 2007*):

1. Establish an evidence base for potential interventions.
2. Solicit input and evaluate the compatibility of potential interventions with team members' values.
3. Assess the capacity of team members to support interventions.
4. Assess the compatibility of the interventions with schoolwide programs and administrative supports.
5. Implement and evaluate the selected interventions.

Partnerships with Families and Communities

Having a child with ASD is a challenge, even for the most confident parents (Powell, Hecimovic, & Christensen, 1992). Many parents blame themselves for not being able to solve their children's problems. Others, like the parent discussed in this chapter's Considering Culture, may have difficulty coming to terms with their child's ASD. Clearly, the challenges the entire family faces when a family member has ASD can seem overwhelming. Having a brother or sister with ASD can also be challenging, leaving the sibling many times without understanding what to do when an inappropriate behavior occurs in public or when friends ask about their sibling. Children with ASD often lack independent play and leisure skills, which means that parents must spend more time providing direct care to their children. One result is that parents have less time to take care of other important activities of daily living, such as self-care and household chores.

Perhaps more frustrating are the struggles that families have in forming normal relationships with their children with ASD. Some parents report difficulties connecting with or relating to their child. This experience is common with children who do not like physical affection such as hugs or who are socially avoidant. Parents who believe they are in part responsible for their children's successful education often find it very frustrating when learning is not achieved or is achieved very slowly.

Nevertheless, ASD is not readily apparent to others—these children do not typically have physical features indicating a disability. Although this may seem fortunate, many families find it a source of concern. For example, one mother was worried that on shopping trips, strangers would say "Hi" to her child. The mother worried that her child would ignore the stranger's greeting and the stranger would assume that she was a bad mother because her child was rude. To prevent this from happening, the mother used signs with her child, even though the child did not understand them. The mother thought that her use of signs would cue others that her child had a disability. Another mother kept a letter from her son's pediatrician in

Kelly, who has autism, is the younger sister of Katani, one of the Beacon Street Girls, a popular series of books of the same name. Both autism and dyslexia are presented in these books.

Considering Culture: *Coming to Terms*

Jin and Mei are the parents of a 3-year-old boy named Shen. Jin and Mei migrated to the United States 2 years before Shen was born. They were very active in their community before Shen's birth, attending church regularly and volunteering at a local charity. Shen is the only child in the family, has just turned 3 years old, and spends 8 hours of his day attending a preschool program while both of his parents work. Mei began to feel concerned about Shen's development when he was about a year old. Shen wasn't walking yet, didn't babble, and was most content when left alone in his crib. When Mei shared these concerns with her husband, Jin convinced her that everything was fine and that she need not worry. Shen's pediatrician agreed, so Mei stopped sharing her concerns with others.

As Shen grew older, he began to engage in long and intense tantrums several times a day. Shen would scream, cry, and throw objects for reasons his parents could not understand. Jin thought this was normal for a 2-year-old child. Soon the disruptive tantrums prevented Jin and Mei from attending church. They were embarrassed that their son could not behave like the other young children in church. While Mei sensed that something was different with their child, Jin always explained that Shen "was just being a boy" and that he would be fine once he got

a little older. Again, Shen's pediatrician tried to allay Mei's fears. The doctor told Mei that boys tend to develop slower than girls. "Let's just wait another 6 months and see how things go," he said.

Carla, Shen's preschool teacher, had a nephew with autism and knew about the importance of early intervention. She recognized several characteristics that resembled autism, immediately spoke with her supervisor, and after a few weeks she approached Jin about her concerns. Carla was surprised at the defensive reaction Jin had. Jin accused her of picking on his son, stated that the other kids were causing his son to get upset at school, and threatened to stop bringing Shen to school. Carla felt embarrassed about the whole incident but still wanted to help Shen and his family.

Questions to Consider

1. What could Carla have done before approaching Jin about Shen's apparent disability?

2. Knowing that early intervention is the key to better outcomes, if you were Carla how could you approach the family again in order to get Shen the services he could benefit from?

—By Jason Travers

---

her purse, describing her son's ASD diagnosis. Her son was nonverbal but screamed when in noisy situations or when unpredictable changes occurred. This screaming had happened several times in public, resulting in the police being called on more than one occasion. This mother was afraid of being arrested for child abuse.

The behaviors that define the ASD umbrella make being a parent challenging. Many programs recognize these difficulties and provide supports for families. Some programs offer support groups and information on how to access community services such as respite care. Other programs help parents develop skills they need to raise their child more effectively. For example, the TEACCH program in North Carolina offers an 8-week course for parents. These teaching sessions provide information about the nature of ASD, as well as presenting techniques whereby parents can "co-treat" their child with ASD. Regardless of the model, support from professionals, support from other parents of children with ASD, access to information, and access to high-quality comprehensive services are paramount.

Summary

As a group, autism, Asperger syndrome, and PDD-NOS comprise the autism spectrum disorders (ASD). Although most experts no longer consider them to be ASD, Rett syndrome and CDD are also pervasive developmental disorders and are described in the DSM-IV-TR. ASD is a complex set of conditions, which present common problems in the areas of: communication, social interaction, and repetitive behaviors/interests. Early intervention is important, but while current diagnostic approaches allow for identification of ASD in children as young as 2 years of age, the diagnosis is not often made until 5 years of age. Data-based practices for individuals with autism exist and rely largely on behavior analysis approaches, but other effective strategies, such as TEACCH, also have been developed. Effective approaches for individuals with ASD, regardless of the person's age, all share certain features, including sufficient structure, supports for functional communication, use of behavior analysis techniques, and supports for social interactions. ASD is a lifelong disorder, and most persons require support into adulthood. If such supports are provided, people with ASD can lead fulfilling and successful lives as adults.

Answering the Chapter Objectives

1. What is the relation between autism and other autism spectrum disorders (ASD)?

   - Autism is one of three types of conditions included under the umbrella of ASD.
   - The three ASD conditions are autism, Asperger syndrome, and PDD-NOS.
   - Rett syndrome and CCD are related syndromes considered to be pervasive developmental disorders.

2. What core characteristics identify individuals within the autism spectrum?

   - Problems with communication
   - Limited social interaction
   - Repetitive behaviors or unusual interests

3. What is known about the causes of autism spectrum disorders?

   - ASD has a neurobiological basis that effects brain development and probably has some genetic basis.

   - The degree to which brain development, genes, and the environment interact has yet to be determined.

4. How can learning environments be structured so that individuals with autism spectrum disorders will maximally benefit from instruction?

   - Provide sufficient structure
   - Support functional communication
   - Use behavior analysis techniques
   - Support social interactions

5. What are data-based instructional strategies for students with ASD?

   - Positive behavior support
   - Functional communication training
   - Visual supports and activity schedules
   - Social stories
   - AAC systems such as PECS.

myeducationlab Now go to MyEducationLab at www.myeducationlab.com and take the Self-Assessment to gauge your initial comprehension of chapter content. Once you have taken the Self-Assessment, use your individualized Study Plan for Chapter 12 to enhance your understanding of the concepts discussed in the chapter.

Council for Exceptional Children   ADDRESSING THE PROFESSIONAL STANDARDS

Council for Exceptional Children (CEC) knowledge standards addressed in this chapter.

IC1K2, IC1K1, IC2K4, IC2K3, IC8K1, IC4S3, IC4K4, IC10K2, IC10K1

Appendix A: CEC Knowledge and Skill Standards Common Core has a full listing of the standards listed here.

Appendix B: CEC Knowledge and Skill Common Core Standards and Associated Subcategories are broken down by chapter.

CHAPTER 13

Very Low-Incidence Disabilities

Imagine a World . . .

where everyone automatically receives the support they need for full and happy lives . . .

Chapter Objectives

After studying this chapter, you will be able to

1. Explain the major characteristics of students with multiple-severe disabilities.

2. Describe the impact of deaf-blindness.

3. Discuss how cases of traumatic brain injury (TBI) can be prevented.

4. Explain alternate assessments and what they mean for students with low-incidence disabilities.

5. Provide a rationale for the community to be some students' LRE and the curriculum they access is functional.

Jenny McKenzie is an inspirational and award-winning artist. She has achieved these accomplishments although she is deaf-blind. McKenzie contracted viral encephalitis before her fourth birthday, and the result was a progressive and severe loss of vision and hearing. By the time she was 13, she could no longer see the blackboard or hear her teacher, even with glasses and hearing aids to help her. The disease also caused her challenges when using her hands, so she developed her own unique style of holding a brush, working an a flat surface as she creates each new wonderful piece of art.

myeducationlab After reading this chapter, complete the Self-Assessment for Chapter 13 on MyEducationLab to gauge your initial understanding of chapter content.

very low-incidence disabilities Disabilities whose prevalence and incidence are very low

deaf-blindness A dual disability involving both vision and hearing problems

multiple-severe disabilities Exceptionally challenging disabilities where more than one condition influences learning, independence, and the range of intensive and pervasive supports the individual and the family require; developmental disabilities

traumatic brain injury (TBI) Head injury, causing reduced cognitive functioning, limited attention, and impulsivity

This chapter is organized somewhat differently from the other chapters in this text. Instead of learning about one special education category or disability that includes different conditions, information about three distinct special education categories is presented here. Like the other special education categories, these, too, can include many conditions and various ways the disability affects individuals. And, like other disability categories, they represent individuals with very diverse learning profiles and needs for supports and accommodations. These three are **very low-incidence disabilities**, and most often they are severe in nature, requiring substantial and intensive accommodations, modifications, supports, instruction, and special education services.

In previous chapters, you have already learned about many elements that are the same for each of these three disabilities. For example, in Chapter 10, you learned how hearing loss affects individuals; and in Chapter 11, you discovered how visual loss affects learning and instruction. In this chapter, you learn about individuals who have *both* visual and hearing problems—those with **deaf-blindness**. Students with **multiple-severe disabilities** have some combination of disabilities that you have learned about in early chapters. In many cases, those with multiple-severe disabilities have intellectual disabilities, which we discussed in Chapter 8, along with another disability, such as a physical or health disability (Chapter 9). Students with **traumatic brain injury (TBI)** often present characteristics similar to students with learning disabilities (Chapter 5) or those with health disabilities.

Although each very low-incidence disability has a separate definition (see Table 13.1), they do share many things. For example, those affected must overcome many challenges to gain independence, meaningful employment, and community presence. Typically, in order for these goals to be attained, intensive and pervasive supports from a wide range of individuals and systems must be in place. So, in this chapter we combine some discussions that are presented separately in other chapters.

Where We've Been . . . What's on the Horizon?

Confusion has surrounded people with low-incidence disabilities since the beginning of time. Their proper place in society has often been denied them, and questions of how best to educate them so they can achieve their potential and participate fully in the community continue to be raised. These individuals' disabilities present major challenges to themselves, their families, the schools, and society. However, we now know—from the evidence of their participation in schools and in the community—that education makes a real difference in their results and lifts our expectations for what they can and do achieve.

Historical Context

Lessons about the remarkable achievements and community participation of people with low-incidence and severe disabilities began long ago. Yet despite success stories, society denied many of them opportunities to develop and flourish. Here's an example of an individual who surprised everyone and proves that the determination of teachers and the individuals themselves can overcome what seems insurmountable.

Probably the most famous person with deaf-blindness is Helen Keller. She was a woman of many accomplishments, but none of her achievements, which included graduating from Radcliffe with honors in 1904, would have been possible without the efforts of her teacher, Anne Sullivan (Holcomb & Wood, 1989). Sullivan's "family tree" is interesting and noteworthy. Samuel Gridley Howe was the founder of the Perkins School for the Blind. Located in Boston, it was the first

Table 13.1 • Definitions of Very Low-Incidence Disabilities

Source	
	### Definition of Severe Disabilities
Technical Assistance Center	People with severe disabilities are those who traditionally have been labeled as having severe to profound mental retardation. These people require ongoing, extensive support in more than one major life activity in order to participate in integrated community settings and enjoy the quality of life available to people with fewer or no disabilities. They frequently have additional disabilities, including movement difficulties, sensory losses, and behavior problems. ***NICHCY (2004, p. 1)***
	### Definition of Multiple Disabilities
Federal government	Concomitant impairments (such as mental retardation-blindness, mental retardation-orthopedic impairment, etc.), the combination of which causes such severe educational needs that they cannot be accommodated in special education programs solely for one of the impairments. Multiple disabilities does not include deaf-blindness. ***U.S. Department of Education (2006, p. 1263)***
	### Definitions of Deaf-blindness
Federal government	Deaf-blindness means concomitant hearing and visual impairments, the combination of which causes such severe communication and other developmental and learning needs that the persons cannot be appropriately educated in special education programs solely for children and youth with deafness or children with blindness. ***U.S. Department of Education (2006, p. 1261)***
Technical Assistance Center	Although the term deaf-blind implies a complete absence of hearing and sight, in reality, it refers to children with varying degrees of vision and hearing losses. The type and severity differ from child to child. The key feature of deaf-blindness is that the combination of losses limits access to auditory and visual information. ***National Consortium on Deaf-Blindness (2007, p. 1)***
	### Definition of Traumatic Brain Injury
Federal government	Traumatic brain injury means an acquired injury to the brain caused by an external physical force, resulting in total or partial functional disability or psychosocial impairment, or both, that adversely affects a child's educational performance. Traumatic brain injury applies to open or closed head injuries resulting in impairments in one or more areas, such as cognition; language; memory; attention; reasoning; abstract thinking; judgment; problem solving; sensory, perceptual, and motor abilities; psychosocial behavior; physical functions; information processing; and speech. The term does not apply to brain injuries that are congenital or degenerative, or to brain injuries induced by birth trauma. ***U.S. Department of Education (2006, p. 1265)***

Sources: From 34 *CFR* Parts 300 and 301, Assistance to States for the Education of Children with Disabilities and Preschool Grants for Children with Disabilities; Final Rule (pp. 1261, 1263, 1265), U.S. Department of Education, August 14, 2006, *Federal Register,* Washington, DC; NICHCY (2004, p. 1); National Consortium on Deaf-Blindness (2007, p. 1).

school in the United States for students who are blind. One of Howe's pupils was Laura Dewey Bridgman, herself a person with deaf-blindness, who talked to other people by tapping letters and using a manual alphabet. She used braille for reading. Bridgman became a teacher, and one of her students, Anne Sullivan, was a girl with low vision. When Sullivan grew up, she learned of a 6-year-old girl with deaf-blindness living in Alabama. Sullivan visited young Helen Keller and brought her a gift, a doll that had been given to her by Laura Bridgman. Sullivan became Helen Keller's teacher and lifelong companion. Of her disabilities, Keller said, "Blindness separates a person from things, but deafness separates him from people" (Miles, 2005, p. 6). Clearly, the case of Helen Keller is unique and remarkable. Although it is unrealistic to expect the outcomes for all individuals with low-incidence disabilities to be like hers, Keller's story serves to remind us of the importance of not making assumptions about an individual's potential based on the disability they have, hard work, intensive instruction, and meaningful supports.

This photo of Helen Keller was taken in 1888 but was just found in 2007. The photo is the only one showing her holding the famous doll that Anne Sullivan, her teacher, gave her. Certainly this famous teacher-and-pupil pair proved to the world that people with multiple and severe disabilities can achieve beyond most people's expectations.

In Chapter 1, you learned that Congress first passed IDEA in 1975 because many students with disabilities were excluded from school and had no opportunity to benefit from a special education complete with the related services they needed. In those days, the students most often excluded, denied a free public education, or had a limited access to the general education curriculum were those children and youth with severe and very low-incidence disabilities. They were the ones that caught the attention of Congress. Today, although many receive special education services outside the general education class for a large portion of the school day, these students do receive FAPE in what their IEP Teams consider the most LRE possible. Many, during their high school years, use the community as their classrooms, learning in natural and real-life settings—yet another interpretation of LRE. Regardless of what their instructional programs comprise, they participate in one of several accountability options.

In the not-so-distant past, living arrangements for adults with low-incidence disabilities were segregated, many times away from cities and towns. They spent their lives in large residential institutions with little or no access to the community or chance to have a community presence. Today, most children with severe disabilities grow up at home with their brothers and sisters, and as adults they live in the community in apartments or group homes. In addition, thanks to successful transition programs, they find competitive employment in the community as well.

Challenges That Low-Incidence Disabilities Present

Having more than one major disability presents unique challenges to the individual and the family. The combined effects of two disabilities create a pattern of problems different from those presented by one disability alone (NICHCY, 2004). For example, deaf children who also have intellectual disabilities or students who have both vision and hearing problems need teachers who are spe-

cialists in more than one area. They also need teachers who understand the special problems that this unique combination of disabilities raises.

When disabilities come in combinations, the impact is significant in so many ways. Besides the seriousness of the disability itself, unfounded assumptions about these individuals' abilities and potential can limit their educational opportunities, the expectations held for them, and ultimately their outcomes. In fact, many individuals with severe disabilities are still relegated to nursing homes and institutions, receive only minimal services, and are afforded no education. Clearly, prophecies of poor outcomes are self-fulfilling under such conditions! But when people are not limited by attitudes and perceptions, a world of possibilities opens up.

Take, for example, the story of Rick Hoyt, born with cerebral palsy and multiple-severe disabilities (see www.teamhoyt.com for a photo album and more details about this inspirational story). Doctors told Rick's parents after his birth that there was little hope for his development or of his ever being able to communicate, but the Hoyts refused to believe them. When Rick was 10 years old, Tufts University engineers designed a special communication system for him. Rick uses head movements to select letters and words, and a computer "speaks" for him, allowing him to share his wit, humor, and conversations with others. He also lives in his own apartment. Today, "Team Hoyt"—the father-and-son team that competes in many marathons, including the 2008 Boston Marathon—inspire us all not to be restricted by assumptions but, rather, to seek to break all barriers.

Making a Difference
Sprout and Anthony Di Salvo

The joy and fun of getting out for a weekend adventure, taking a drive in the country, or traveling with friends to Mexico or Disney World are something we all look forward to. Unfortunately, most people with very low-incidence disabilities have few opportunities to experience such pleasures. In 1979, Anthony Di Salvo founded the Sprout Organization of New York City to provide a range of organized trips to people who have need for intensive supports. Some 30 years ago such an idea—taking people with very challenging needs on holidays without their family members—was unheard of and even unthinkable. Since Sprout's beginning, however, it has continued to expand its

services. Today, Sprout serves over 1,800 people a year, providing vacations and recreational opportunities that are age-appropriate. The Sprout programs serve as

Anthony Di Salvo

models for others. Although not nearly enough exist, more travel programs are available today, across the country, for people with severe disabilities because of the example set by Sprout.

Filling any important need for people with disabilities can be all-consuming. Some might suggest that arranging and delivering many exciting traveling opportunities is sufficient. But not to Anthony Di Salvo! He didn't stop with the development of a vacation program. He continued to see needs, and he continues to put his creativity to the test. As you have learned in Chapter 1, people with disabilities have been marginalized in film and television. Few actors with disabilities are able to find work, and few filmmakers with disabilities are employed in the entertainment industry. The idea behind the Sprout Film Festival, initiated in 2003 and now held each year at the Metropolitan Museum of Art's educational center, was to reinforce accurate portrayals of people with disabilities, break down stereotypes, and show that people with disabilities can be serious filmmakers. The 3-day event showcases outstanding films made by and with people with disabilities and culminates in a grand awards celebration. What an exciting opportunity for so many who have had little chance to show off their skills and talents! To see folks having a great time traveling, making their own movies, or participating at annual Sprout Film Festivals, visit **www.gosprout.org.**

Multiple-Severe Disabilities

While IDEA '04 does not call out multiple-severe disabilities as a separate special education category, the U.S. Department of Education (2006) does so in its regulations of IDEA '04. Review again the different definitions for multiple-severe disabilities that are presented in Table 13.1. Regardless of the term or definition used to describe this disability, it is important that IEPs for students with multiple-severe disabilities include goals and objectives that aim at developing skills that promote independence and community presence by working with each person's unique learning needs (Kennedy & Horn, 2004; Snell & Brown, 2006).

Characteristics of Multiple-Severe Disabilities

Individuals with multiple-severe disabilities display a wide range of skills and abilities, as well as a wide range of problem areas where they need intensive instruction. According to NICHCY (2004), this group of individuals shares some common characteristics:

- Problems transferring or generalizing learning from one situation to another, one setting to another, and one skill to another
- Limited communication abilities
- Difficulties with memory
- Need for supports for many of life's major activities (domestic, leisure, community participation, vocational)
- Need for services from many different related service providers

These characteristics are not consistent across every individual. For some, supports are needed in only one life activity; but for many of these individuals, supports are needed for access and participation in mainstream society (NICHCY, 2004). For example, an individual with a cognitive disability might need supports to pay bills and manage a budget. If that individual also has a moderate hearing loss, she or he might need an assistant to facilitate communication at the doctor's office but might function at work with only natural supports from coworkers.

Students with multiple disabilities definitely benefit from one-on-one instruction; however, additional value often occurs when these students participate in carefully constructed groups (Snell & Brown, 2006). During group work, students learn from each other. They observe appropriate behavior and see how others respond in discussions. For many, it is also more motivating to learn alongside classmates rather than doing so independently, in isolation, or working only with adults. However, teachers have many things to consider when implementing groups where students' abilities are mixed, which is the case in inclusive general education settings. Tips for Classroom Management provides some useful guidelines for group instruction.

Prevalence

Relatively speaking, few students have multiple-severe disabilities. Only 0.20%, or 132,846 of all American students ages 6 to 21, are included in the federal special education category of multiple disabilities (Office of Special Education Programs [OSEP], 2008a). Depending on how states include individuals in one category or another, fewer or more students can be considered as having this disability. For example, some states do not include in this category students with learning disabilities who also have a hearing problem, but other states do (Müller & Markowitz, 2004). Some states include in the mental retardation (intellectual disabilities) category students who also have a mild visual disability, but some states report these students to the federal government in the multiple disabilities category. So, precise numbers about the national prevalence of this disability cannot be provided.

Causes and Prevention

Many factors can cause disabilities. As you have learned throughout this academic term, heredity, problems during pregnancy, problems at birth, and incidents after birth can all lead to a lifelong set of challenges—sometimes even to multiple-severe disabilities. Because of advances in medical technology, many children born with multiple-severe disabilities now have long life expectancies (McDonnell, Hardman, & McDonnell, 2003). Although reasons for the majority of birth defects are unknown, many could have been prevented with pre-pregnancy visits to the doctor

TIPS for Classroom Management
GUIDELINES FOR GROUP INSTRUCTION

1. Teach same concept at multiple levels using modified materials.
2. Allow for different ways to answer or participate.
3. Give everyone a short turn.
4. Praise students who listen and watch others during their turns.
5. Include everyone in demonstrations.
6. Keep waiting time to a minimum by keeping group size and teacher talking to a minimum.
7. Encourage cooperation.
8. Discourage competition.

Source: Adapted with permission from M. E. Snell and F. Brown (2006), *Instruction of Students with Severe Disabilities* (6th ed.), p. 131. Upper Saddle River, NJ: Merrill/Pearson.

Enjoying a ride on a merry-go-round takes some confidence and experience for children who are deaf-blind, but what joy these old fashioned rides can bring!

to determine potential risk factors (e.g., hereditary possibilities, health and lifestyle issues) and to ensure good prenatal health care during pregnancy (March of Dimes, 2006, 2008). Universal access to health care and raised public awareness of prevention strategies help reduce the number of children and families affected (Children's Defense Fund [CDF], 2006).

Deaf-Blindness

Deaf-blindness has one of the lowest incidence rates of all disabilities, yet it is one of the most diverse in terms of learning profiles (Müller, 2006). When you hear the word *deaf-blindness,* you probably think of people who have no vision and no hearing abilities. Although this is true for some individuals with deaf-blindness, the vast majority has some residual hearing and/or vision. In fact, according to the National Deaf-Blind Census, more of them have some functional use of their vision than have some hearing (National Consortium on Deaf-Blindness [NCDB], 2008a). Regardless, the world for children with deaf-blindness can be exceptionally restricted. When hearing and vision both fall into the ranges of severe or profound losses, the immediate world may well end at one's fingertips (Miles, 2005).

Special funding for students with deaf-blindness began in 1969, well before the initial passage of IDEA. This national funding was a response to a rubella epidemic that swept the nation, resulting in dramatic increases in the numbers of babies with disabilities, particularly blindness, deafness, and deaf-blindness. Table 13.1 provides the IDEA '04 definition as well as the more functional definition that some believe leads to a more accurate identification of those involved, as well as the provision of appropriate services for these students (Brown & Bates, 2005).

Characteristics of Deaf-Blindness

Almost half of students with deaf-blindness have enough residual vision to allow them to read enlarged print, see sign language, move about in their environment, and recognize friends and family (Miles, 2005). Some have sufficient hearing to understand some speech sounds or hear loud noises; some can develop speech themselves. But others have such limited vision and hearing that they profit little from either sense. In addition to their visual and hearing losses, the majority of these individuals have other disabilities, such as intellectual disabilities, that further complicate their education. Most individuals with deaf-blindness need considerable supports for their worlds to be safe and accessible; these students' educational programs need to be carefully thought through and must be uniquely designed to ensure that each of these children meets his or her potential.

Deaf-blindness should never be minimized; it is serious and has significant effects on all those involved: the individuals, their families, and their teachers. It definitely affects these students' education, which is often so individualized and intensive that it does not occur in the general education setting. According to NCDB, only 9% of these students (some 503 nationally) attend general education classes for most of their school day—18% when resource rooms are included. Some 82% attend separate classes, specialized centers, or hospital schools (NCDB, 2007b).

The degree and amount of vision and hearing loss are not uniform, and the combination of these losses affects each individual differently. Increasingly, over the last 20 years, more and more individuals included in the National Deaf-Blind Census have more than one additional coexisting disability (Killoran, 2007). In fact, it is estimated that over 90% of these individuals have multiple disabilities (NCDB, 2007a). Table 13.2 shows the complexity of disabilities included in the national census.

Table 13.2 • Combinations of Disabilities Among Students with Deaf-Blindness

Vision Loss	Hearing Loss	Additional Disabilities
17% totally blind or light perception only	39% severe to profound hearing loss	66% cognitive disabilities
24% legally blind	13% moderate hearing loss	57% physical disability
21% low vision	14% mild hearing loss	38% complex health care needs
17% cortical vision impairment	6% central auditory processing disorder	9% behavioral challenges
21% other	28% other	30% other

Source: Information from Killoran (2007).

The combination of hearing and visual loss often presents three important characteristics that teachers and family members must consider:

- Feelings of isolation
- Problems with communication
- Problems with mobility

Feelings of isolation are a particular problem for many individuals with deaf-blindness. The world of these individuals is restricted, but this is an area that educators can and must address. Tips for Effective Instruction provides some suggestions about including students with severe disabilities and reducing their feelings of isolation, through everyone becoming more "disability-sensitive."

Possibly the greatest challenge facing individuals with deaf-blindness is learning to communicate (NCDB, 2008b). Some never learn to talk. Children with this condition are dependent on others to make language accessible to them and help them join the many adults with this disability who have achieved some level of independence. For many of these individuals, the way they approach their world is through touch (Miles, 2005). Thus, various forms of manual communication (e.g., sign language, body language, gestures) can be their primary means to express their needs and also to learn and grow. Some of these students learn a different kind of sign language to communicate with others. **Hand over hand** is a tactile form of sign language where the signs are conveyed through touch. In this system, fingers placed in the other person's palm form the means of interaction.

hand over hand Sign language for individuals with deaf-blindness where signs are conveyed through touch

Like all blind students, those with deaf-blindness face challenges relating to independent mobility. Their movement is often restricted and can even put them in dangerous situations. The components of purposeful movement—becoming aware of one's environment, changing locations, seeking protection from danger, deciding when to move—are instructional targets for many of these students. Clearly, for the 90% who have additional disabilities that are combined with vision and hearing problems, overcoming feelings of loneliness and isolation, learning to communicate, and achieving independence require very individualized educational programs.

Prevalence

Two different databases are used to record the number of students with deaf-blindness (Müller, 2006). One is maintained by the national technical assistance center funded by the federal government to provide support to the states to help them provide high-quality services to these students. It is referred to as the National Deaf-Blind Census. The other database is maintained by OSEP, the division of the U.S. Department of Education that is charged with the responsibility of implementing IDEA. The Census includes students who have vision and hearing losses and also other disabilities. The OSEP database includes students with a combination of hearing and vision losses only. According to the Census, some 7,985 students—ages 6 to 21—are identified as having deaf-blindness and receive special education services (NCDB, 2008a). However, for that same year, the federal government reports that only 1,413 students were included

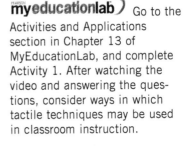

myeducationlab Go to the Activities and Applications section in Chapter 13 of MyEducationLab, and complete Activity 1. After watching the video and answering the questions, consider ways in which tactile techniques may be used in classroom instruction.

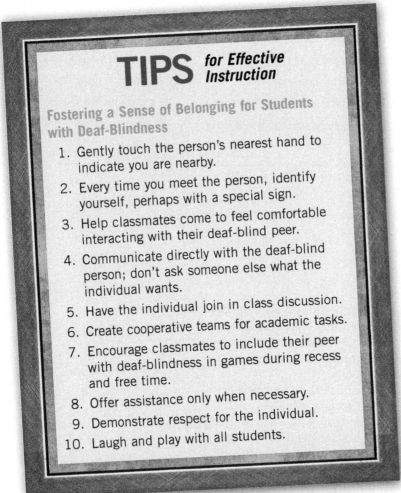

TIPS for Effective Instruction

Fostering a Sense of Belonging for Students with Deaf-Blindness

1. Gently touch the person's nearest hand to indicate you are nearby.
2. Every time you meet the person, identify yourself, perhaps with a special sign.
3. Help classmates come to feel comfortable interacting with their deaf-blind peer.
4. Communicate directly with the deaf-blind person; don't ask someone else what the individual wants.
5. Have the individual join in class discussion.
6. Create cooperative teams for academic tasks.
7. Encourage classmates to include their peer with deaf-blindness in games during recess and free time.
8. Offer assistance only when necessary.
9. Demonstrate respect for the individual.
10. Laugh and play with all students.

in this category across the entire nation—a number so small that it represents 0.00% of all U.S. students (OSEP, 2008a).

The reason for the vastly different prevalence indicators between the nation's deaf-blind technical assistance center and the numbers reported by the states to the federal government rests with reporting criterion. The federal government insists that states report students' disabilities in only one area, and many deaf-blind students are reported in the multiple disabilities category because they have so many additional problems. Where a student is counted is probably not so important. What is important is for these students to receive the very specialized services they need that address issues of communication, mobility, isolation, and ultimately independence.

Causes and Prevention

Although most causes of deaf-blindness are unknown, prematurity and heredity are the most common reasons (NCDB, 2007c). The role of heredity is becoming more clearly understood. In 1994, only 18 different hereditary syndromes had been associated with this disability (Heller & Kennedy, 1994). Today, more than 50 genetic causes of deaf-blindness have been identified (NCDB, 2007c).

Usher syndrome is a genetic cause of deaf-blindness, a cause thought to account for some 50% of all cases of deaf-blindness (Keats & Lentz, 2008). With all three types of Usher syndrome, the individuals have congenital deafness and progressive blindness, along with intellectual disabilities. So, they are born deaf and then lose their ability to see across their lifetime. In addition, many individuals with Usher syndrome have problems with walking, balance, and other motor activities. This recessive, X-linked genetic syndrome is rare, affecting 4.4 out of every 100,000 people. However, its prevalence varies by locale. For example, in Louisiana some 15% to 20% percent of students with deaf-blindness have Usher syndrome, and 30% of all deaf individuals in three parishes (counties) have the syndrome (Melancon, 2000). By comparison, nationally only 3% of students with deaf-blindness have Usher syndrome. Why the concentration of Usher syndrome in Louisiana? Remember the story of the Deaf on Martha's Vineyard who came to America from Kent, England, carrying a gene for congenital deafness? The Cajuns have a similar story. When they came to Louisiana from Nova Scotia, they brought with them the gene responsible for the Usher syndrome. Because Cajun communities are small and tight-knit, the prevalence is higher in this part of the United States. This knowledge makes it possible to prevent some cases.

Traumatic Brain Injury

About one million children annually experience a head injury, and more than 30,000 of those injuries result in lifelong disabilities (NICHCY, 2006). Prior to the 1960s, most children whose brains were seriously damaged died soon after the trauma. Changes in emergency treatment, imaging technology, and surgical and pharmaceutical treatments now routinely save children's lives. Some 95% survive today (Michaud et al., 2007).

After the medical emergencies are over, however, it often takes intensive special education services and accommodations for the problems resulting from the accident to be resolved. The IDEA '04 definition for TBI was introduced in 1990 when TBI became a separate special education category. Before then, TBI was included in the "other health impairments" category, even though many of these students received services alongside peers with learning disabilities. The federal government's definition is shown in Table 13.1 at the beginning of this chapter. Educators need to know that TBI *is not*

- a condition present at birth or
- caused by a stroke, brain tumor, or other internally caused brain damage.

However, it is also important for educators to understand that TBI *is*

- due to a concussion or head injury, possibly from an accident or child abuse,
- not always apparent or visible, and
- may or may not result in loss of consciousness

Characteristics of TBI

Unlike the other very low-incidence disabilities discussed in this chapter, TBI ranges in severity from mild to severe (National Institute of Neurological Disorders and Stroke [NINDS], 2007). Brain injury often results in these symptoms: dizziness, headache, selective attention problems, irritability, anxiety, blurred vision, insomnia, fatigue, motor difficulties, language problems, behavior problems, or cognitive and memory problems (NICHCY, 2006). These problems can last for a very short time or for years. In many cases the effects eventually disappear, but some cases of TBI result in lifelong problems. Youngsters with moderate to severe injuries often experience dramatic changes in their cognitive, language, motor, sensory, and behavioral performances (Michaud et al., 2007). Some of these students are typical learners one day but then, after their injury, have significant disabilities. In these cases, it is also common for the individual to experience depression or withdrawal. Some common characteristics of students with TBI are shown in Table 13.3.

Many students with TBI have similar learning characteristics as their classmates with learning disabilities. They often exhibit memory deficits, attention problems, language impairments, and reduced academic performance. Many benefit from instructional procedures proved effective with students with learning disabilities: direct or explicit instruction, learning strategies, structured school days, and organized classes where expectations are clearly specified (see again Chapter 5 for ideas about effective instructional methods). Others, because of their head injuries, experience seizures and receive many of the same accommodations as students with epilepsy. And, for

Table 13.3 • Frequent Characteristics of TBI

Physical	Cognitive	Social/Emotional	Educational
Headaches	Short-term memory problems	Mood swings	Difficulty with multistep tasks
Fatigue	Long-term memory problems	Anxiety	Requires consistent schedule and routine
Muscle contractions	Attention deficits	Depression	Needs distractions reduced
Imbalance	Disorganization	Restlessness	Requires shortened assignments
Paralysis	Nonsequential thinking	Lack of motivation	Must have lots of opportunities for practice of new skills

Source: Information from NICHCY (2006, pp. 3–6).

those whose health has become compromised, many experience similar situations as their classmates with physical disabilities or health impairments who have to negotiate the medical system along with schooling (Michaud et al., 2007).

Students with TBI and their families face great emotional turmoil after the injury. They must adjust to changes in ability, performance, and behavior (NICHCY, 2006). As is so tragically shown in the movie featured in this chapter's On the Screen, the characteristics can be almost insurmountable, even with attempts to compensate for them. Even those with mild cases of TBI must cope with sudden changes in performance; what came easily before can now be filled with frustration and confusion. Attempting tasks once easy to perform may lead to repeated failure. Many youngsters with TBI tend to have uneven abilities, a fact that is confusing to the individuals and to their teachers. These students also often experience reduced stamina, seizures, headaches, hearing loss, and vision problems (Michaud et al., 2007). Because many of these students tire easily, some receive home instruction, often for a year, before returning to school part-time. Many of these youngsters have difficulty adjusting to and accepting their newly acquired disability, which can result in behavior problems and reduced self-esteem. Alert teachers can make a difference in the lives of these students by helping them focus their attention, understand the accommodations and supports they require for success, and develop new organizational skills.

Prevalence

According to the federal government, 23,864 students, ages 6 through 21, receive special education services because of TBI (OSEP, 2008a). These students represent a percentage of all students so small that it registers at 0.04%. Remember, many

On the Screen: *One Thoughtless Night Leads to Many*

The 2007 film *The Lookout* shows the ongoing tragedy of traumatic brain injury. The bright future of four adolescents was dimmed by an accident on a dark road. The road was darker than it should have been because Chris, an admired high school hockey player, had turned off the car's lights so the two couples could see fireflies. Their car slammed into a piece of farm equipment left on the side of the road, and in an instant lives were changed forever. Two of his friends died, one young girl lost a leg, and Chris's TBI affects his memory and thinking skills the rest of his life. Although brutal and violent at times, the movie shows the devastation of brain injury, the frustration of memory loss, and how people affected fight to compensate by taking notes and relying on friends, in Chris's case, a roommate who is blind.

—By Steve Smith

students with TBI require special education services for some time after their injury, but they may not need sustained supports. So, data reflecting participation in general education programs may be misleading. Regardless, it is important to know that almost two-thirds of these students learn alongside classmates without disabilities, some with support from resource programs, for most of the school day (OSEP, 2008a). This pattern of access to the general education curriculum is different from students with the other low-incidence disabilities discussed in this chapter, who typically need intensive, sustained, and individualized programs usually provided outside the general education classroom.

Causes and Prevention

Half of all cases of TBI are caused by "transportation accidents," such as car accidents, motorcycle accidents, and bicycle accidents. Some 20% are due to violence, such as injury from firearms or child abuse. A very small percentage is due to sports injuries (NINDS, 2007). TBI injuries typically occur among older children, particularly teenage boys, who are careless in the street; do not take safety precautions while bicycling, skiing, or skateboarding; engage in high-risk behaviors such as driving too fast or mixing alcohol or drugs with driving; and participate in contact sports. Less straightforward to address is the sad fact that for many young children, a very common cause of TBI is child abuse, including *shaken baby syndrome* where an infant is shaken so hard that it causes brain injury (The Arc, 2004).

Tragic cases of TBI can be prevented when everyone uses safety gear all of the time.

Many cases of TBI can be prevented or the injuries minimized. For example, wearing helmets when bicycling or skateboarding, not driving a car or motorcycle when using intoxicating substances, and avoiding high-risk behaviors can prevent tragic accidents. Immediate medical attention is also important to ensure that damage is kept in check through surgery and other medical technologies (NINDS, 2007). Access to health care is critical; however, many times children try to hide their injuries from parents and teachers because they are embarrassed that they broke rules or behaved irresponsibly, and other times the serious nature of the injury is not understood. Quick action can be critical to long-term outcomes (Michaud et al., 2007; NINDS, 2007).

Educational Considerations for Students with Low-Incidence Disabilities

Now let's turn our attention to education's response to these very low-incidence disabilities. Remember, although these disabilities represent separate special education categories served through IDEA '04, many of these students have complex coexisting conditions that result in the need for exceptional, unique, and highly individualized educational responses. Thus, although there is no single answer to how best to educate these students, we combined discussions in the remainder of this chapter around issues of these students' assessment, evaluation, education, and transition experiences. We conclude with several examples of how educators can collaborate, work with families, and develop community partnerships.

Assessment

The path toward identification as having a disability is often different for those with low-incidence disabilities than for those with high-incidence disabilities. Because of universal infant screenings, better medical technology, and more informed pediatricians, more and more instances of disabilities are identified when these individuals are infants or toddlers. Because their delays in development become obvious when they do not walk or talk on time, toddlers are identified so they can receive important intervention services during early childhood. Thus, unless the onset of the disability occurs later—as with students who incur a head injury sometime after birth—most individuals with low-incidence disabilities are identified before they reach kindergarten or first grade.

As with all students, individuals with low-incidence disabilities participate in schools' accountability systems. Many take state- and districtwide assessments with accommodations or modifications (see Chapter 2 for a review), but more than any other other group, these students have the effectiveness of their educational programs tested through alternate means. Let's first think about early identification.

Early Identification Because of improved identification procedures, many infants are identified and receive critical early intervention services in their first few years of life. The number of children, birth through age 2, and their families receiving special services increased from 128,000 in 1988 to 304,510 in 2006 (U.S. Department of Education, 2000; OSEP, 2008b). The reasons for these early and increased participation rates are the quick response of the medical and social services communities and the widespread awareness of well-documented signals for long-term serious **developmental disabilities**.

developmental disabilities Severe disabilities including intellectual disabilities

More than with other groups of students with disabilities, those with multiple disabilities, including deaf-blindness, have individualized family service plans (IFSPs), and many receive services in their homes and then in specialized preschools. These families receive services to assist them as they learn how to interact in special ways with their baby with severe disabilities. It is these families that benefit from the services of many different professionals so that secondary disabilities and problems can be prevented or reduced in severity (McDonnell et al., 2003).

Prereferral We have noted that most students with severe disabilities are identified long before their school years. However, for many students with TBI, this is not the case. And medical professionals are often slow to determine which of these youngsters have long-term problems. Even when accidents are serious, injury to the brain may go unnoticed at first. Too often, families bring their children home from the hospital not knowing that long after the broken bones are mended, the head injury could result in long-term disabilities (NINDS, 2007). Most families are unaware of the signs associated with TBI, and medical staff at the hospital may not have informed parents that their children might have long-term cognitive effects from their injuries. Sometimes it is educators who must confirm families' worst (and often unspoken) fears: "The bicycle accident several weeks ago caused more than a broken leg; it may have also caused brain injury. You better take Justin to the doctor again." So, often school personnel actually play a critical role in bringing important services to students with TBI as quickly as possible.

Surprisingly, alert teachers are often the first to suspect that injuries may go far beyond broken bones or obvious bruises. They see many different characteristics that signal possible brain injury. Many of those were listed in Table 13.3. However, before teachers actually suggest to families that their son or daughter may have additional problems, they should take responsible actions. They may seek advice from the district's school nurse. They might consult with the principal and other school officials. And most important, they need to document the student's classroom performance. Using progress monitoring (see Chapter 5 again for a review), they compare academic and social behaviors before and after the incident that might have resulted in brain injury. Teachers sensitive to changes in their students' performance make a genuine long-term difference because they not only bring problems more quickly to the attention of those who can help but also provide evidence that saves valuable time during the diagnostic process.

Identification The ways in which students with multiple and coexisting disabilities are identified are as unique as the individuals themselves. Many of them are identified at birth. Doctors and hospitals' nursing staffs know well the signs that alert them to disabilities in newborns and the signals of the risk of disabilities. Also, universal infant screening procedures bring babies with hearing and vision problems to the attention of service providers during the critical months after birth. And for those not identified with disabilities during the first 6 weeks of life, alert pediatricians often identify infants and toddlers who are not developing in typical ways. It is a very rare case for a student with multiple-severe disabilities to be first diagnosed with problems during the elementary school years. The main exceptions, of course, are those individuals with major injuries from a car accident whose age of onset is after their entrance to kindergarten.

The situation for students with TBI is different, but the ways in which individuals with TBI are identified will probably surprise you. As you might expect, medical professionals typically identify children with TBI. However, as we have just discussed, children and youth with TBI too often are not identified immediately after their injuries. This happens because many of these youngsters show no visible signs (cuts, bruises) of brain injury (NICHCY, 2004). The impact of what has sometimes been called the silent epidemic may go misunderstood for months. How can this be? Think about Ryan, who was not wearing a helmet, despite his mother's warnings, and fell while skateboarding. Because he did not want to tell his mother that he was not wearing his helmet, he also did not tell her about the accident. Instead, he told his mom that he was tired and went off to his room to take a nap. So, here it can be the educational system that makes a difference by beginning with prereferral procedures, identifying students with problems, and introducing intervention services of a multidisciplinary team as early as possible.

Evaluation: Alternate Assessments—The "1% Kids" Remember, IDEA '04 and the No Child Left Behind Act require all students—those with and without disabilities—be included in the national accountability system. As you learned in Chapter 2, most students with disabilities participate in standard state- or districtwide assessments, using a variety of accommodations (e.g., braille, extra time) and modifications (e.g., altered tests to reflect abbreviated learning objectives), and these adjustments must be called out in the student's IEP (Soukup et al., 2007). The U.S. Department of Education (2006) allows other assessment options for a limited number of students with disabilities.

For students not participating fully in the general education curriculum, the government allows each state to use **alternate assessments**—another form of testing and evaluation of learning gains. Such students are given these alternate assessments on **alternate achievement standards**. These standards might reflect achievement expectations of those participating in the general education curriculum but with fewer objectives or different expectations. Such assessments must reflect the general education curriculum (e.g., reading, math, science). Alternatate assessments are also used to document progress of those participating in alternatate curricula. Therefore, their tests reflect academic skills and possibly also functional skills that are targets of instruction and specified on the student's IEP (Browder et al., 2004).

How many students may participate in alternate assessments? The government allows states to get credit for proficient scores from alternate assessments in their overall reporting, as long as the number included "does not exceed 1.0 percent of all students in the grades assessed (about 9 percent of students with disabilities)" (Briggs, 2005, p. 28). What IDEA '04 Says About Alternate Assessments and the "1% Kids" provides more information about alternative assessments and who is eligible to use them.

Most students with disabilities participate in state- and districtwide assessments by using accommodations (Soukup et al., 2007). Great variability exists across states and districts about what accommodations can be made available (National Center on Educational Outcomes [NCEO], 2007; Thurlow, 2007). Adjustments to students'

alternate assessments A means of measuring the progress of students who do not participate in the general education curriculum

alternate achievement standards Fewer objectives or different expectations for achievement when participating in the general education curriculum

Alternate Assessments and the "1% Kids"

Students with disabilities are to be included in general state- and districtwide assessments, with appropriate accommodations and modifications as necessary. Some students with disabilities who cannot participate in regular assessments may take alternate assessments. States are permitted to assess up to 1% of students against alternate achievement standards with alternate assessments.

IDEA stipulates that these alternate assessments must

- be aligned with the state's challenging academic content and student achievement standards, and
- measure student achievement against any alternate academic achievement standards that the state has developed.

If an IEP Team determines that a student should take an alternate assessment, the IEP must include

- a statement of why the child cannot participate in the regular assessment,
- an explanation of why the selected alternate assessment is appropriate for the student, and
- a description of benchmarks, or short-term objectives, that are aligned with alternate achievement standards.

performance evaluations or testing routines might include breaks, a test scheduled at a different time, or extended time. Accommodations might reflect changes in the materials used for the test, such as enlarged-print or braille versions of the test. The presentation of the test's items may vary from that used for students without disabilities; for example, someone may read the questions to the student. Also, students may provide their answers by using a different format than everyone else; for example, they may not have to use the machine-scored answer sheet.

Although they must reflect grade-level achievement standards, alternate assessments are different from accommodations (Briggs, 2005). Designed for students who can't participate in the standard grade-level assessment, they might differ in these ways:

- *Format:* portfolios or different versions of achievement tests
- *Narrower range of topics or fewer objectives:* different set of expectations
- *Less complex questions:* stated more simply

Students who fall into and slightly above the 1% group also have expressed concerns about participating in these assessments, even alternate versions (Bowie, 2007; Williams, 2007). They indicate that such testing is extremely stressful to them, too difficult, and a waste of their time. Clearly, only time will tell whether these standards and assessment requirements will remain or be modified as educators better understand the implications of applying them.

Early Intervention

The benefits of high-quality education for all of us cannot be overestimated. For students with low-incidence disabilities, high-quality early intervention and preschool education can determine critical outcomes: the number and intensity of supports they will need as adults, their attainment of independence, their level of community presence, and their quality of life (Rafferty, Piscitelli, & Boettcher, 2003). Sometimes, families with great resources—either financial or personal—decide that they need only minimal support from early intervention teams. You will learn of one such example in this chapter's Considering Culture. Parents and extended family members are often at the heart of early intervention services, making a difference in the lives of their children. This is true whether they take advantage of publicly available services or not. What is important is that infants and toddlers with extensive needs because of their disabilities receive extra help learning, growing, and getting prepared for life and their school years.

More infants and toddlers with disabilities are receiving early intervention services through IDEA (OSEP, 2008b). It is important for professionals, families, and policymakers to agree about what to expect from these programs, so that they can be evaluated. After considerable work by a broad range of stakeholders, five outcomes for families participating in services supported through IDEA '04 have been agreed on (Bailey et al., 2008). Families should

- understand their child's strengths, abilities, and special needs
- know their rights and advocate effectively for their children
- help their child develop and learn
- have support systems
- access desired services, programs, and activities in their community. (p. 4)

Considering Culture: *The Family as the Mainstream*

Pablo is 10 months old. He has significant disabilities that have interfered with his cognitive, motor, and physical development. When he was 5 months old, he and his family began participating in an early intervention program that included home visits, group interaction, and special services from therapists. Recently, his mother has canceled the majority of home visits and has not participated in the group program with Pablo. The program staff is concerned, and the service coordinator telephoned Mrs. Alvarado to talk with her about these changes.

In their conversation, Mrs. Alvarado said that she, her husband, and their parents had talked about the program and decided that it was no longer necessary. She said, "We know that Pablo will never be like other children, and we don't think that school is important for him. We have a large family. They all love Pablo and will always take care of him." The service coordinator listened and then talked about how important it was for Pablo to have the services that the program provided. She talked about the importance of his being with other children and the importance of other families for Mrs. Alvarado. Mrs. Alvarado was polite but firm. She said that their lives were full of medical appointments for Pablo, soccer for the older children, church, and family gatherings.

The service coordinator was stunned. She couldn't imagine that anyone would refuse services. Soon after she finished talking with Mrs. Alvarado, she called Carmelita, Pablo's home visitor. When she described the conversation, Carmelita was not surprised. She said, "The Alvarado family is large and very close. They have raised many children, and Pablo's mother is probably right. They don't need any more appointments than they already have. He is not the only child in the family, and they are very caring parents who will ask for help if they need it." She said that she would call Mrs. Alvarado to tell her how much she had enjoyed working with Pablo and meeting the family.

When Carmelita called Mrs. Alvarado, she explained that she would miss Pablo and the rest of the family but that she understood how the needs of the entire family had to come first. She then asked Mrs. Alvarado if she could stay in touch by phone "just to check in on Pablito." Mrs. Alvarado was happy not to lose touch, and Carmelita continues to provide telephone support and keep the lines of communication open between the program and the Alvarado family.

Questions to Consider

1. Although IDEA '04 mandates that states and U.S. territories provide early intervention programs and services for infants and toddlers with disabilities (ages birth to three), parents have the right to refuse services. Why do you think that this right is part of the law?

2. How do you think you would feel if a parent said that your services were not needed?

—By Eleanor Lynch, San Diego State University, and Marci Hanson, San Francisco State University

---

Where programs for infants and toddlers are often delivered to the family at their home, those for preschoolers (between the ages of 3 and 5) with severe disabilities are most often in organized programs. Many of these classes are fully inclusive where preschoolers with and without disabilities learn and grow together (McWilliams, Wolery, & Odom, 2001). The benefits of inclusive early intervention programs are great in terms of motor development, language skills, social interaction abilities, and academics. In these programs, students with and without disabilities learn from each other. Students without disabilities who are developing along typical patterns provide role models for language, social behavior, and motor skills. Their peers with disabilities have long-term benefits from such preschool experiences.

Teaching Students with Low-Incidence Disabilities

Students with very low-incidence disabilities present unique sets of complex profiles to their families and their teachers. Despite being assigned to a category, each student should be considered a unique member of a diverse group of learners, all of whom exhibit different learning styles and characteristics. Accordingly, instructional programs must be designed on an individual basis to meet each student's needs. However, despite their diversity, these children often share many common goals and desired outcomes.

Access to the General Education Curriculum Many students with very low-incidence disabilities do not have access to the general education curriculum as their primary objective. Although these students may participate in general education classes, which many of them do for some period during the school day, they may well be striving to meet other curriculum targets, such as independent living. Of this group, students with TBI have the highest participation rate in general education (OSEP, 2008a). Of those between the ages of 6 and 21, about 42% attend general education classes for more than 79% of the school day. Students with deaf-blindness, however, have a much lower participation rate. Some 21% of them learn alongside students without disabilities for more than 79% percent of the school day. However, the general education participation rate, at 13%, is even lower for students with multiple disabilities.

Some important reasons explain these relatively low participation rates. They access the general education curriculum less for many reasons:

- They require more intensive, individualized instruction.
- Their IEP goals focus on achieving adult independence and community presence.
- They participate in a functional curriculum that includes direct instruction on targets such as daily living, vocational skills, and self-determination.

The instruction they receive is also different from the instruction delivered by general educators. For example, these students have structured class schedules, use of concrete examples, controlled teacher language, reduction or elimination of distractions, instruction in varied natural settings, and rigorously applied behavioral tactics. Multidisciplinary team members evaluate each student's progress continually to balance the drawbacks and benefits of every educational option available. They must also work together to see that the necessary accommodations and modifications are in place when students do access the general education curriculum to ensure successful outcomes in general education settings.

Instructional Accommodations As you have learned throughout this text, each student with a disability requires different forms of assistance, accommodations, or modifications to the instructional program to achieve maximally. Such is very much the case with students who have very low-incidence disabilities.

Some simple adjustments to and modifications in the classroom routine can make such a difference, allowing students with disabilities access to the general education curriculum. For example, a student with TBI who spends only half a day at school benefits greatly when the classroom schedule is adjusted so instruction on important academic tasks happens during the morning. Careful thought about the order of presentation can also make a difference: which subjects to schedule first, what instruction to provide before recess and after recess, and so forth. Homework assignments can be abbreviated to accommodate for reduced stamina.

Many students with multiple disabilities have problems that affect balance, coordination, and the ability to carry books and class materials. A student with cerebral palsy, who uses a wheelchair or walker and also a speech synthesizer, often finds that getting from classroom to classroom is an overwhelming event. For this student, an extra set of textbooks assigned for home use and a special storage space in each class so books do not need to be carted from room to room can make learning alongside classmates without disabilities possible.

Most students with deaf-blindness require more intensive supports to participate in the general education curriculum and classroom successfully. Some of them receive assistance from paraprofessionals who provide extra instructional assistance. Most often, paraprofessionals support the classroom teacher with all the students with disabilities in the class. However, in cases of the most challenging disabilities, a paraprofessional may be assigned full-time to only one student.

Data-Based Practices   The unique learning needs of students with very low-incidence disabilities made it difficult for us to decide which instructional practice to feature in this chapter. For example, students with TBI often find that organizing strategies, such as graphic organizers and **story maps** you learned about in Chapters 4 and 5, help them focus, visualize information, and put structure to their learning efforts. For students who have difficulties controlling their behavior, functional behavioral assessments, which you learned about in Chapter 7, help teachers figure out what features of the environment contribute to the initiation and maintenance of inappropriate behavior. For those with low vision, the curriculum must include orientation and mobility skills, which you learned about in Chapter 11. So, we decided here to discuss the high school extension of a **functional curriculum**, instruction in natural settings. For more information about functional curriculum and the needs of students with multiple and severe disabilities, go to the Web site of the National Secondary Transition Technical Assistance Center, www.nsttac.org.

Remember, a functional curriculum includes instructional areas that have a direct relationship to a person's daily needs, and it is not appropriate for every student with low-incidence disabilities (Alwell & Cobb, 2006; Westling & Fox, 2004). The IEP Team decides whether a particular student should access a functional curriculum rather than focusing solely on the general education curriculum. If the team determines that the development of academic skills such as mathematics, reading, and social studies will not be achieved at a level of usefulness in daily life, then a functional curriculum is introduced. The student and teachers concentrate on learning functional words such as those found on menus and traffic signs or those that indicate warnings or danger. Other important skills, not addressed in the general education curriculum—transportation skills, money and purchasing skills, leisure skills, personal care—become a focus of instruction to ensure that the individual can gain as much independence as possible.

Before the age of 14, most vocational and life skills instruction occurs at school: in the classroom, in the cafeteria, in the school building, and on the school grounds (Snell & Brown, 2006). However, after the age of 14, the labor laws allow students to work in the community. It is at this point that instruction for the functional curriculum often moves away from the school. Many students with complex and compounding disabilities need to practice skills learned in one setting across many different ones to generalize learning. Important skills needed in daily life must be taught in natural or real settings to become useful. For students with such needs, **community-based instruction (CBI)** is a proven practice that improves these individuals' inclusion in daily life and competitive employment when they are adults (Alwell & Cobb, 2006). Some experts believe that many students with multiple-severe disabilities spend as much as 90% of their school day learning in community settings (NICHCY, 2001). For this reason, we highlighted some important components of CBI in this chapter's A Closer Look at Data-Based Practices.

Technology   The increased availability of technology and understanding about how technology can help compensate for complex disabilities is a major reason why the federal government is making a considerable investment in technology for students with disabilities (National Center for Technology Innovation, 2008). Another important reason for this investment is that people with disabilities use technology. According to the U.S. Census Bureau (2007), some 36% of people

story maps Simple diagrams used to organize and recall important elements and features of stories

functional curriculum Instruction in natural settings relating to life and vocational skills.

community-based instruction (CBI) A strategy of teaching functional skills in the environments in which they occur

A Closer Look at Data-Based Practices

Community Based Instruction (CBI)

Not all high school students with disabilities access the general education curriculum all of the time. An appropriate education for some often reflects a functional curriculum that includes vocational training, instruction in transportation-related skills, and other topics important for daily living, independence, and community presence as an adult. For students under age 14, education and training in these important skills can be simulations, which can occur in the classroom or other places at school. Once students are older and the labor laws allow, it is important that learning happens in real-life settings, in situations that reflect the student's interests and preferences and that are feasible and designed for success. Instruction is systematic and delivered by special education personnel, job coaches, or teachers. Learning and experiences occur as the student commutes, using public transportation, from school to work and then at job sites in the community, with real bosses and coworkers.

Steps to Follow

1. Conduct an assessment of the student's preferences and interests.
   - Determine the student's job preferences and interests.
   - Involve the student in determination of the type of job and employment site.
   - Practice at school before placing at a job site or pairing with an employee.
2. Establish community-based training sites.
   - Develop a list of work site opportunities (e.g., range of businesses, different work opportunities, size of businesses).
   - Identify and analyze job appropriateness (e.g., interest, age appropriateness, skill requirements), and match with the student.

- Be sure the site is welcoming; interview the boss and coworkers.
- Select job sites that are feasible in terms of distance and transportation from school and home.
- Establish open communication pathways between the school and work site.
- Develop job site evaluation criteria.
3. Ensure that the student knows the implicit and explicit rules of the work site and has the skills to meet expectations.
   - The student uses transportation to travel from school, arrive at work on time, and independently return home.
   - The student dresses appropriately, takes breaks properly, and executes the work tasks correctly.
   - The student seeks help when necessary, works well with a mentor or job coach, interacts appropriately with coworkers, and finds natural supports in the workplace.

Example of a Transportation Map

The visual developed by a high school student serves as directions to get from school to work to home using public transportation.

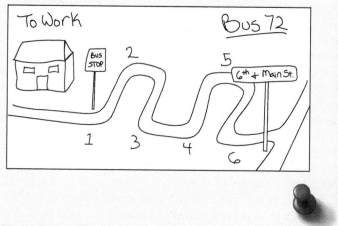

---

with severe disabilities use a computer, and 29% of them access the Internet. Clearly, technology helps these individuals

- communicate more effectively,
- increase their levels of independence,
- control their environments,
- have greater mobility, and
- gain access to information.

augumentative and alternative communication devices (AAC) Other methods for communicating, such as communication boards, communication books, sign language, and computerized voices

Technology has opened up avenues of communication for many students who are unable to communicate with others through oral speech (Byrant & Bryant, 2003). We introduced the idea of **augmentative and alternative** communication devices (AAC) in Chapter 4 and feature it again here because AAC allows for communication and participation not otherwise possible for many individuals with multiple-severe disabilities (Kangas & Lloyd, 2006; Noonan & Siegel, 2003). Also, AAC is a documented proven practice, supported by rigorous research. AAC has many benefits providing individuals who could not otherwise communicate a means of "talking" and communicating (Alwell & Cobb, 2007).

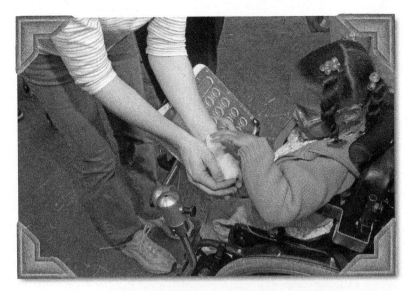

AAC supplements or replaces spoken communication. Whether in the form of simple devices, such as communication boards, or complicated speech synthesizers that actually speak for the individual, AAC technology enables individuals to make their needs known, express their feelings, and interact with others (Alwell & Cobb, 2007; McCormick & Wegner, 2003). Like so many others, Rick Hoyt—whom you met earlier in this chapter—would be unable to exchange his thoughts with others if it were not for the AAC system he uses to talk through a computer. Simpler, low-tech systems have words and/or pictures placed on a flat surface or in books. The student uses such illustrated communication boards by pointing to the appropriate symbols or pictures. Symbols can be customized to the individual; the words or symbols on the board reflect the specific features of the environments in which he or she operates.

AAC devices, like this communication device, let individuals with disabilities participate in everyday conversations, talk with their teachers, and be part of class discussions.

Transition

Unlike their peers without disabilities and many of their peers with high-incidence disabilities, most students with very low-incidence disabilities have a transition component of their IEPs (see Chapter 2 again for a review). Also, many of these students continue to receive services through IDEA '04 through age 21. During the high school years, some access the general education curriculum and graduate with a standard high school diploma, but those with the most complex disabilities focus on the transition to adulthood and prepare for successful independent living and a real community presence.

Remember not to make assumptions about individuals with disabilities. Students with multiple-severe disabilities, those who are deaf-blind, and those with TBI do go to college. It is a grave error to assume that they don't or can't! Think again about Helen Keller, who graduated from Radcliffe, now part of Harvard, at the turn of the last century. Consider Stephen Hawking, whose scientific theories are challenging for most of us. Also, reflect on what the world would be like without their contributions. Today, almost every college campus offers services for students with disabilities. The resources they provide (e.g., tutors, classes in study skills, interpreters, access to online texts), allow more and more students with complex learning needs to succeed in postsecondary education. So, it is important that high school counselors and teachers direct their students to the widest possibilities and greatest choices for options after high school (Kochhar-Bryant, Shaw, & Izzo, 2007).

Many students with low-incidence disabilities, however, have an overarching transitional goal that guides their last years of schooling: achieving a presence in their community by living as independently as possible. This goal often precludes postsecondary education and requires carefully orchestrated instruction and guided experiences in the community, which can take many years of hard work by the individual with the disability, family members, and teams of professionals

(Alwell & Cobb, 2006; Kochhar-Bryant, Shaw, & Izzo, 2007). Transition plans are individually determined but often reflect (Brown, 2007)

- employment,
- community participation,
- recreation and leisure,
- continuing education or services from state agencies,
- independent living,
- self-determination, and
- quality of life.

Many experiences that prepare individuals with complex disabilities to take their places in the community begin early in their school years (Kocchar-Bryant et al., 2007). For example, students during their elementary and middle school years should be introduced to sports and recreational activities both at school and in the community (Kleinert, Miracle, & Sheppard-Jones, 2007). When in high school, they should participate in school sports and extracurricular activities. Such early introduction to leisure and recreation helps adults with low-incidence disabilities know how to make friends and participate in social activities after work. They take advantage of opportunities like sharing time with friends, vacationing, gathering at a local pub, attending a Super Bowl party, or having dinner at a restaurant. Of course, having increased opportunities for travel and recreation programs for adults with disabilities, like the ones developed by Sprout (read the Making a Difference feature of this chapter again), need to be available in every community across the nation.

Make no assumptions about what people can accomplish! College graduation is a personal goal for many, but some don't have a chance to even attend college because someone important had the wrong perceptions about disabilities.

Two more features of transition programs make a difference in the outcomes of individuals with low-incidence disabilities and should always be considered and embraced:

- Personal choice
- Opportunities for nonsegregated work and living

Everyone performs better in situations where she or he has the skills necessary to succeed—but also when the tasks are of interest. For these reasons, educators are realizing the importance of the individual's preferences and interests in making effective plans for living arrangements and employment opportunities (Lohrmann-O'Rourke & Gomez, 2001; Stuart & Smith, 2002). The importance of promoting individual choice and self-determination (read again A Closer Look at Data-Based Practices in Chapter 8) as a precursor to community-based instruction is widely acknowledged among experts in this field (Brown et al., 2007; Holburn & Vietze, 2002). What is now being called "person-centered planning" is just that! It involves the individual with disabilities and the family in decisions about services needed, jobs to be supported, living arrangements, and related preferences. Unfortunately, only some 40% of adults with low-incidence disabilities have input about their living arrangements or daily activities (Brown, 2007).

Evidence documents that competitive work is an achievable goal for almost all individuals with disabilities, including those with the most complex disabilities (Greenfield, 2008). While it may be that job coaches, natural supports from trained coworkers, and additional training from social services are necessary, real jobs in nonsegregated settings instead of sheltered workshops are an important choice. However, one study found that only 9% of these adults found supported employment or other community work (Brown, 2007). Certainly, everyone must work toward improving this percentage!

Normalization and community presence means being able to share time with friends in public places, just like everyone else.

Collaboration

Compounding their problems, many individuals with low-incidence disabilities face other challenges. Many of them experience health problems (e.g., seizure disorders, heart disease) or physical problems (e.g., cerebral palsy, vision or hearing problems) and face communication challenges. Consequently, they and their families interface with many professionals from many disciplines—all with different styles of interaction, terms and jargon, and approaches. Multiple modes of interactions can complicate an already difficult situation. But, when multidisciplinary teams of related service providers (e.g., physical therapists, assistive technology specialists, speech/language pathologists) are brought together and their expertise is orchestrated to meet the needs of each student, the outcomes are amazing.

Multidisciplinary teams that serve students with very low-incidence disabilities are composed of a wide range of professionals. Expertise is needed in so many areas that it is impossible for one or even two teachers to provide an appropriate education for these students. Clearly, collaboration among many different teachers (general educators, special education teachers, paraprofessionals, orientation and mobility instructors, teachers of students with visual disabilities, teachers of the deaf), as well as multidisciplinary team members representing many different related services (assistive technology specialists, SLPs, OTs, PTs), is commonplace for these students and their families.

Collaborating with Educational Specialists: Interveners

As the needs of students with low-incidence disabilities become better understood, new roles and services are being defined. Here are a few examples. Students who are deaf-blind often need help to access information and have meaningful linkages to the environment (Olson, 2004). Many students who are deaf receive assistance from sign language interpreters, but students who are deaf-blind require somewhat different services. An **intervener** is a paraprofessional who works under the supervision of a teacher (Carnes & Barnard, 2003; Sommer & Walt, 2006). These paraprofessionals are trained not only to translate but also to use sign language, which in some cases may use the tactile hand-over-hand techniques. Unlike sign language interpreters, interveners provide instruction and facilitate all aspects of learning for the student with deaf-blindness (D'Luna, 2006). As you learn in this chapter's Spotlighting, interveners serve many important aspects of these students' life at school.

intervener A paraprofessional who serves many roles including sign language interpreter and teacher

Spotlighting *Christopher:* A Day in the Life

This story is written by Ann Bielert, an intervener working with students with deaf-blindness
I have been an intervener for 17 years. I have worked with several children ranging in age from 6 to 22 years old. Each student was unique in their world of deaf-blindness. Each one taught me to go beyond what I had learned in books and workshops throughout the years. These very special students have been my best teachers.

Last year, I had the opportunity to meet a 10-year-old boy named Christopher (shown riding a carousel on p. 440). He is a strong, healthy young man. He is also deaf-blind. His family had worked very hard to provide the best program for him at school. The summer of 2007, they had their first taste of quality intervention with Christopher, and they were unwilling to give up what they knew worked—a well-trained intervener.

This family's determination is what brought me to Christopher. My work with Christopher began in the fall of 2007. I knew from my years as an intervener that trust and bonding with a deaf-blind student was crucial. This was my first concern. He had to know that I valued him as an individual. I wanted him to know that I was there as that bridge for him to learn what was going on in a world that he had not seen or heard.

Christopher loves to go places. He likes physical activities such as swinging, swimming, scooter boards, and rough play with his dad. I found that he learns best by doing real-life activities.

To communicate, Christopher uses object symbols. At the begining of this story, he had very limited signing skills and often was not willing to let me sign into his hands. I thought he might enjoy a trip to the food court in the mall. That morning we loaded his calendar box with his symbols for this outing: his wallet, the seat belt strap (bus ride), a token (for the carousel), and an empty juice box. Part of the time, Christopher allowed me to sign into his hands.

The school bus picked us up at 10:00 A.M. They dropped us off at the doors going into the food court. We walked over to McDonald's. I signed "apple juice" to him. Christopher gave the employee his empty juice box to let her know he wanted juice. She gave him a full juice box, and Christopher paid for it. We then trailed down to the pizza place, a short distance. I signed "pizza," and Christopher reached out for it. He paid his money, and we sat down.

After he finished eating, it was time for the carousel. I gave him the token symbol and signed "play, horse." He stood up. We walked to the token machine. I helped Christopher put a dollar in the machine to get one token to ride. He gave the token to the attendant and rode one time. I knew he wasn't finished riding by his tight grip on the pole. I gave him another dollar and signed "more, play, horse." He understood that I understood him. We were not "finished." He could ride more. He got off the horse and got another token. He rode again.

The next week we went again to the mall. When we got to the token machine, I helped him get out $2 and signed "play, horse, one, two, and then finished." He smiled and counted "one, two." He gave the attendant his two tokens.

When he finished the first ride, I signed "one ride, finished." After the second ride, I signed "second ride, finished." He understood and nicely got off the horse. Robbie Blaha says to take one thing or activity and just keep adding on and decorating it, like a Christmas tree.

I thought Christopher would enjoy riding a real horse. A few months later, he started horseback riding lessons. His mom, dad, and big sister, Kaylina came to the stables. We all were apprehensive because of his fear of animals.

Christopher was helped onto the horse by his dad. As soon as the horse began walking, we all saw a huge smile on Christopher's face. Christopher eagerly put his hands on top of mine for me to sign. This was a huge opportunity to introduce new signs and vocabulary.

Collaborative Practices: The Role of Interveners

Interveners intercede and work between a child and the environment, helping the child gain access to information that others gain via vision and hearing (Sommer & Walt, 2006). Interveners do more than just translating; they typically work on an individual basis with a student who is deaf-blind. Part of this professional's role is to facilitate inclusive efforts, so here is one more member of the collaborative team working with general educators to provide FAPE in the LRE. Accommodating for Inclusive Environments lists some of the major activities that interveners perform to make participation in the general education classroom and access to the general education curriculum possible for students who are deaf-blind.

Accommodating for Inclusive Environments
The Role of the Intervener

Interveners facilitate participation of students who are deaf-blind in the general education classroom by the following:

1. Facilitating the access of environmental information usually gained through vision and hearing, but which is unavailable or incomplete to the individual who is deaf-blind

   The intervener can
   - present information in ways that match the unique capabilities of the individual with deaf-blindness, so that he or she can detect and interpret it;
   - facilitate opportunities for direct learning and the development of concepts that others learn incidentally.

2. Facilitating the development and use of receptive and expressive communication skills

   The intervener can
   - provide a consistently responsive environment to the individual's reactions and communicative behaviors;

- act as a bridge to facilitate communication with others.

3. Developing and maintaining a trusting, interactive relationship, which can promote social and emotional well-being

   The intervener can
   - increase and strengthen the individual's positive interaction with others;
   - facilitate opportunities for the individual to have control through choice making, problem solving, and decision making.

Source: Adapted from *The Intervener in Early Intervention and Educational Settings for Children and Youth with Disabilities,* by L. Alsop, R. Blaha, & E. Kloos, 2000. Briefing Paper. Monmouth, OR: National Technical Assistance Consortium for Children and Young Adults Who Are Deaf-Blind. Adapted with permission.

Interveners also help teachers by creating learning environments. They help design classrooms that are uncluttered both visually and physically (D'Luna, 2006). They ensure that pictures on the bulletin board are of high contrast, allowing images to be clearly seen. They are cautious that the student is seated so glare from windows is minimized, assistive technology devices provide ultimate help, and the classroom is cleared for ease of movement and mobility.

Partnerships with Families and Communities

One key to improving community participation for adults with low-incidence disabilities is developing partnerships with community agencies and businesses. As a reminder, it is important for CBI to be successful so that a wide range of choices for job placements is available, so the interests, abilities, and needs of participating students can be met (Brown, 2007). For this to occur requires the support from the entire community and many businesses. Partnerships with local community groups such as Rotary and Kiwanis, churches, and volunteer groups can help develop work sites for students. They can also help identify individuals who might serve as coaches and other natural supports for students while participating in CBI and after graduation as they seek their places in the community.

The concept of supports was stressed throughout the 2002 definition of intellectual disabilities discussed in detail in Chapter 8. The idea is to help individuals with significant needs for sustained assistance and their families become independent and function in the community (Luckasson et al., 2002). The focus is on the type and amount of supports that individuals need to remain in the community, living, working, and playing alongside people without disabilities. The family

myeducationlab Go to the Building Teaching Skills and Dispositions section in Chapter 13 of MyEducationLab, and complete the activity, IRIS Module, "Collaborating with Families." Designed to help teachers build positive relationships with families, this module highlights the diversity of families and addresses the factors that school personnel should understand about working with the families of children with disabilities.

is one obvious source of natural support for all individuals with disabilities, particularly those with low-incidence disabilities (Van Haren & Fielder, 2008). In some cases, support requires more than commitment; it requires a wealth of personal resources and an effective system of supports that assist and sustain families.

Community agencies help adults with disabilities attain services and programs to achieve success and independence in the community. For this reason, representatives should be involved in the development of transition components of these students' IEPs (Kochhar-Bryant et al., 2007). And, it is strongly encouraged that interagency agreements be established so the transition from school to adult life includes supports that are needed for successful community presence. The goals are many and include living in homes, apartments, and neighborhoods like everyone else, instead of living in an institution far from their home communities.

Families are important natural supports; however, individuals with disabilities reach the age of majority, like everyone else, and can make decisions that may or may not be in agreement with family members' (U.S. Department of Education, 2006). Every effort should be made to include parents and families as full members of the individual's multidisciplinary team. However, it is important for professionals to understand that a family member with low-incidence disabilities may stretch resources and capabilities of many families. The daily physical care and round-the-clock assistance that some individuals require, along with financial and logistic difficulties, can be overwhelming. Professionals and social service agencies can make a difference by providing the safety net that families need and also help individuals with disabilities meet their personal goals.

Summary

Although the size of the disability group is of little importance to the individuals or the families affected, these three special education categories all comprise very few students. Together, multiple-severe disabilities, deaf-blindness, and traumatic brain injury account for less than 1% of all schoolchildren. But these disabilities are often severe, affecting overall performance significantly and requiring considerable resources and intensive individualized instruction. Many of these individuals also have additional problems in cognition, language, speech, and/or motor skills. Many have intellectual disabilities. Individuals with low-incidence disabilities have complex learning needs that require the collaborative input of many experts from comprehensive multidisciplinary teams.

Answering the Chapter Objectives

1. What are the major characteristics of children with multiple-severe disabilities?

- Difficulties with generalization (situations, settings, and skills)
- Limited communication abilities
- Poor memory
- Need for ongoing and intensive supports for many major life activities (domestic, leisure, community participation, vocational)
- Presence of at least two disabilities whose combination results in complex educational needs

2. How would you describe the impact of deaf-blindness on those affected?

People with deaf-blindness

- live in very restricted environments,
- have problems with communication and mobility, and
- require special adaptations and instruction for both vision and hearing deficits.

Many people with deaf-blindness

- develop speech and can learn to read print;
- need support from others to make their environments safe and accessible;

- often experience significant feelings of isolation; and
- have additional disabilities, such as intellectual disabilities, speech or language impairments, physical disabilities, and health problems.

3. How can many cases of TBI be prevented?

- *Common causes:* domestic accidents, motorcycle accidents, car accidents, pedestrian and bicycle accidents, assaults, sports injuries, and child abuse
- *Prevention measures:* wearing protective gear (seat belts, helmets) and avoiding drugs and alcohol when operating a vehicle

4. What are alternate assessments, and what do these assessments entail?

Alternate assessments

- are a form of evaluation used to assess annually the progress of those students with the most severe disabilities;
- reflect both certain goals of the general education curriculum and additional instructional targets, such as those included in functional curricula; and
- include accommodations as specified on students' IEPs.

Only a limited number of students in each state may participate in alternative assessments—1% of all students, which is estimated to be about 9% of all students with disabilities. Various forms of assessments are allowed:

- Different forms of standardized tests
- Items that reflect a narrower range of topics or fewer objectives
- Portfolios

Debate surrounds the "1% cap." Many educators and parents believe that more students should be allowed to take alternate assessments and that for some students, performance measures should not be mandated to include general education curriculum topics.

5. Why do some students access a functional curriculum using the community as LRE? Indicate the key components of community-based instruction.

Community-based instruction (CBI) using a functional curriculum is a proven, validated practice.

- Functional curriculum includes mastery of
  - functional sight words (survival words, items on menus, words in recipes),
  - transportation skills,
  - money use,
  - leisure skills and recreation, and
  - personal care.

Community-based instruction has these key components:

- Delivers instruction in real-life or natural settings
- Is age-appropriate
- Leads to competitive employment
- Involves transition experts, job coaches, and coworkers
- Partners schools and businesses

myeducationlab Now go to MyEducationLab at www.myeducationlab.com and take the Self-Assessment to gauge your initial comprehension of chapter content. Once you have taken the Self-Assessment, use your individualized Study Plan for Chapter 13 to enhance your understanding of the concepts discussed in the chapter.

Council for Exceptional Children ADDRESSING THE PROFESSIONAL STANDARDS

Council for Exceptional Children (CEC) knowledge standards addressed in this chapter:

IC1K5, IC1K1, IC2K3, IC2K1, IC8K3, IC4S2, IC7K1, IC10S4, IC10S5

Appendix A: CEC Knowledge and Skill Standards Common Core has a full listing of the standards listed here.

Appendix B: CEC Knowledge and Skill Common Core Standards and Associated Subcategories are broken down by chapter.

CHAPTER 14

Giftedness and Talents

Imagine a World . . .

*where anyone and everyone
can make a difference . . .*

Chapter Objectives

*After studying this chapter, you will be
able to*

1. Explain the renewed interest in gifted
   education.

2. List common characteristics of giftedness, observed regardless of the definition applied.

3. Discuss reasons for the underrepresentation of some subgroups of gifted
   learners, and explain why educators are
   concerned.

4. Describe different acceleration options
   available.

5. Provide examples of two major gifted
   education approaches used in inclusive
   settings.

Leonardo da Vinci lived and worked in Italy during the late 1400s, a period when traditions were challenged and intellectual giftedness and creativity were treasured and fostered. Leonardo lived during the Renaissance, a time that signaled the end of the Middle Ages and a rise in intellectual freedom. During this time, the arts (painting, sculpture, and architecture), literature, and science challenged what were thought to be "truth." Leonardo was truly a "Renaissance man" who achieved greatness in many areas. He is probably best known for his painting the *Mona Lisa*, which is now exhibited in the Louvre in Paris, but art was only one aspect of his genius. Leonardo sketched many inventions (e.g., pulleys, weights, cannons, water wheels, canal locks) that were centuries ahead of his time. Fascinated with flight, he systematically studied birds to create ways humans could also fly. These sketches are of his versions of a helicopter and a parachute. He maintained that if the ratio were correct—12 ells (1 ell is equal to 45 inches) across and 12 ells deep—that man could throw himself off a cliff without injury.

myeducationlab After reading this chapter, complete the Self-Assessment for Chapter 14 on MyEducationLab to gauge your initial understanding of chapter content.

gifted or talented Terms describing individuals with high levels of intelligence, creativity, outstanding abilities, and capacity for high performance

Since the beginning of this century, concerns about the competitiveness of America in the world markets and the achievement of America's students has become the focus of Congress, education professionals, and the public (Henfield, Morre, & Wood, 2008). The passage of the *No Child Left Behind Act* (NCLB) in 2001 was a clear signal that policymakers believed that the nation was facing a crisis, and calls went out to "close the achievement gap" and to improve the academic performance of struggling students. Accountability systems were put into place. Throughout this academic term, you have learned about state- and districtwide assessments, high-stakes testing, and many measures and instructional methods (e.g., response to intervention) that seek to focus teachers' and administrators' attention in particular on urban schools and low-achieving students. Evidence now suggests that those measures are successful: The achievement gap has narrowed! Scores of the lowest-performing students have improved (Loveless, 2008).

Since accountability systems have been enacted, the achievement gap has narrowed, in part because not all groups of students' scores have risen. While lower-achieving students have gained substantially and show signs of continued improvement, higher-achieving students' test scores have improved only a very little (Finn & Petrilli, 2008). Many reasons could explain this disparity in growth in achievement, but perhaps the most important reason centers on which students are the focus of instruction. Because of the incentives, and disincentives, associated with state and national accountability systems, teachers and principals report they feel pressured to focus on struggling learners rather than on already high-achieving students (Farkas & Duffett, 2008).

A shift in direction may well be on the horizon. Concerns about the nation's global competitiveness may well change attitudes about educational opportunities, accountability systems, and funding for special programs for the brightest and most talented of America's students. **Gifted or talented** students have high potential to succeed at school and later in life as leaders who make unique contributions to society. Why, then, have their academic achievement and development of talents not received comparable attention?

Where We've Been . . . What's on the Horizon?

Unfortunately, opportunities—particularly from the educational system—are inconsistent for the most able of America's students. The risk is that the gifts of many with high potential are lost to themselves and to the rest of us. The protections of a unique and appropriate education guaranteed to students with disabilities are not available to gifted or talented students. IDEA '04 does not include students considered gifted or talented, nor has any previous version of this law done so. The time may well be now to put into place national guarantees and increased funding so gifted and talented students receive an appropriate education that helps each of these individuals reach their potential (Finn & Petrilli, 2008). Because of concerns about the nation's reduced competitiveness in the global economy, calls are now being voiced for more attention to be paid to gifted and talented students (Siegle, 2008a, 2008b). To advocate successfully for these students, it is important to understand the history of gifted education.

Historical Context

Periods of brilliance have waxed and waned across time. When special attention is given to a particular skill, the result is a remarkable outcome or result. Effort and special education or training make a difference in developing talent.

Historians and anthropologists have documented evidence of special attention given to individuals' outstanding abilities. They have long recognized distinct periods of history where unique abilities and extraordinary achievement occurred. For example, as early as 3000 B.C., the Egyptians sent the best students (along with royalty) to court schools or assigned mentors to work with them in intensive internships to develop their special talents (Hunsaker, 1995). The Indus civilization that flourished in northern India between 2400 and 1800 B.C. demonstrated advanced concepts of city planning and architecture. Indus cities were built on a regular grid with major streets running north and south. A drainage system served an entire city, and each home had a bathroom and toilet connected to a sewer system. During the time of the ancient Greeks, athletic prowess and excellence in the fine arts reached peak levels that are obvious in the legacies of their civilization: their philosophical writings, dramas, architecture, and sculpture. In ancient China, literary works, architecture, music, and art far surpassed the standards of other cultures. During the second century B.C., the Chinese wrote books, at first using silk for paper, on topics such as astronomy, medicine, and pharmacology. Confucius, a Chinese philosopher who lived around 500 B.C., proposed special education for gifted children, and by A.D. 618, gifted and talented children were brought to the Chinese imperial court for a special education. Between A.D. 300 and 750, the Teotihuacán culture in Mexico developed a sophisticated craft industry that produced figurines, pottery, and tools for export throughout the region. In West African cultures, specialized education was provided to children on the basis of the children's status, recognized characteristics, or cleverness.

In Western cultures, interest in people's innate and superior abilities was stimulated by the work of Charles Darwin and Sir Francis Galton in the mid-1800s. Darwin is most famous for his theories about natural selection and the evolution of species. Before his time, no one had studied, on a broad scale, individual differences among people or issues related to intelligence and heredity (Clark, 2008). Most chroniclers of gifted education in the United States stress the importance of the intelligence test in drawing attention to students with great potential and outstanding abilities (Esping & Plucker, 2008). Alfred Binet developed the first one in 1905 (Binet & Simon, 1905). Although it was not originally developed to identify gifted students, this test nonetheless marked the beginning, in the United States, of interest in such individuals. Some programs for the gifted were established as early as 1866, but real development and growth in educational services for these individuals did not come until the 1920s. Leta Hollingworth, one of the early pioneers in the field of education of the gifted, who joined the faculty at Teachers

Leta Hollingworth provided the foundation for many of the methods used today in education of the gifted.

College, Columbia University, in 1916, taught the first course and wrote the first textbook in this area. One of Hollingworth's major contributions to the field was her theories that giftedness is affected by *both* heredity and environment, a concept widely held today (Clark, 2008). Both Hollingworth and her contemporary, Lewis Terman, were interested in individuals who were extraordinarily gifted, studying children and adults with IQ scores as high as 180. In 1925, Terman began a classic, long-term follow-up study, but that work did not give rise to widespread programs of gifted education. Special programs for gifted and talented students have not been consistently available in America, which is true even today.

Across time, Americans have demonstrated a wavering commitment to gifted and talented students. Reasons for the lack of universal enthusiasm for gifted education reflect the nation's foundational ideas about equity and social justice—a fact we should all understand. During the 18th century, many leaders of the country leaned toward the view that education was best for the elite. Thomas Jefferson, however, argued against elitism, believing that the purpose of education was to foster democracy. During the 19th century, egalitarianism—the notion that no one should get special treatment—became popular. The egalitarian position was extreme, holding that no individual could be considered better than anyone else, regardless of innate abilities, status, or education. John Gardner (1984) believed that the concept of equal opportunity derived from the egalitarian attitude that special education for gifted children is undemocratic, elitist, unnecessary, and wasteful.

However, when security, national pride, or position in the global economy is perceived to be at stake, cries go out calling for a national investment in gifted and talented individuals. Here's an important example. In 1957, Russia launched the first space satellite, named *Sputnik*. This launch was viewed as a risk to national security and a blow to national pride, and the United States vowed to catch up and surpass the competition. Hence, federal funding was appropriated to establish programs; develop ways to identify students with high academic achievement, particularly in math and science; and conduct research to find effective methods for providing excellent educational experiences. Gifted students were seen as a great national resource—the people who would make the United States the leader once again. Such attention paid off! America won the "race for space" and developed other remarkable innovations in science and technology.

Attitudes soon changed. The 1960s saw rise to the civil rights movement, and gifted education was seen as elitist and separate. So, when IDEA was passed in 1975 and guaranteed students with disabilities special and unique educational services, gifted and talented students were not included in these guarantees.

Challenges Giftedness and Talents Present

Perhaps one of the biggest challenges facing gifted and talented students is overcoming the assumption that they do not need special attention or unique educational programs to reach their full potential and develop their talents. Although in 1988 Congress passed a national law, the Jacob K. Javits Gifted and Talented Students Education Act, it does not include guarantees or full protections like IDEA '04 does for students with disabilities. No national mandate requiring states to provide special programs or services to gifted and talented students exists. Also, this federal law is terribly underfunded and in many years has faced the risk of being eliminated. In 2005, the U.S. House of Representatives voted for zero funding for gifted education programs, although the U.S. Senate reinstated some of the funds in that year's appropriations budget (National Association for Gifted Children [NAGC], 2005). The fiscal year (FY) 2009 budget proposed by the president of the United States included no funding for gifted education. In FY 2009, Congress did appropriate funding for the Jacob K. Javits Gifted and Talented Students Education Act, but with no increase in funding over the previous year. Also, that funding level was one of the smallest totals in the overall education budget. Here's a comparison of

Figure 14.1 • A Comparison of Gifted Education Policies Across the States

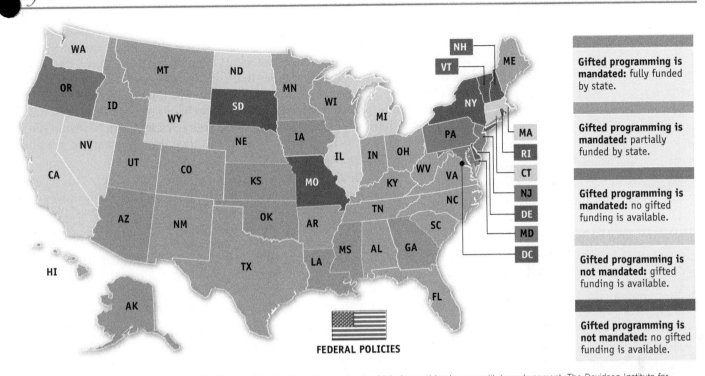

FEDERAL POLICIES

Gifted programming is mandated: fully funded by state.

Gifted programming is mandated: partially funded by state.

Gifted programming is mandated: no gifted funding is available.

Gifted programming is not mandated: gifted funding is available.

Gifted programming is not mandated: no gifted funding is available.

Source: Reprinted with the permission of the Davidson Institute for Talent Development, which does not imply or constitute endorsement. The Davidson Institute for Talent Development is a 501(c)3 nonprofit operating foundation founded in 1999 to support profoundly intelligent young people. For more information on the Davidson Institute, please visit www.DavidsonGifted.org.

note: The Early Reading First program was funded at almost $113 million, while the Javits program was funded at $7.5 million (Washington Partners, 2008).

Because there is no national mandate, every state has a different policy about gifted education. Figure 14.1 compares services offered across the states. Notice that what is available and how those services are supported differ greatly from state to state (Davidson Institute for Talent Development, 2008). Here's another snapshot from NAGC (2008). In 2005:

- Eight states did not allocate any funds for gifted education.
- Fourteen states budgeted less than $500,000.
- Only 28 states had a mandate to provide gifted education; in 8 of those states, full funding is provided by the state.

As you have read, negative attitudes about gifted education are deeply rooted in America's concept of equity and also stem from myths about gifted and talented students. Assumptions seem to be that these individuals will thrive without special programs—that they can make it on their own. Quite sadly, this is simply untrue: Gifted individuals often do not reach their potential because their educational programs did not meet their needs (Benbow & Stanley, 1996).

Giftedness and Talents Defined

What does it mean to be considered gifted or talented? Let's start answering this question by coming to an understanding of how the concepts giftedness and talents have been defined and have evolved. Definitions are important because they reflect beliefs about who qualifies and what services they should receive. Across time, the definitions of giftedness have ranged from a narrow view based exclusively on cognition, reasoning, and the score a person receives on a test of intelligence, to a multidimensional view of intelligence, aptitudes, abilities, creativity, and talents.

David Dinkins

African American boys who live in challenging circumstances are particularly at risk for not achieving to their potential. They often do not have role models or mentors who can show them that success at school is the path toward success in life. These Black boys do not know Black men who have successful careers in business, industry, science, or technology. They and their families do not have associations with community leaders. Such youth often believe that college is not in their future, and they do not grasp the possibility of their becoming leaders themselves.

In 1963, David Dinkins (a former mayor of New York City), Dr. William Hayling, Jackie Robinson (the famed baseball player), and other business and industry leaders decided to take action. They were concerned about the poor quality of life and the dismal outcomes of too many Black boys in New York City. These men formed the concept of what became 100 Black Men of America, Inc., and is now an international organization. Their idea was that if they could channel resources into youth development, providing young African American males with mentors who would also serve as role models, they might be able to make a real difference both for the community and for these individuals.

The original idea has since become a thriving, active international organization of 103 chapters comprising over 10,000 Black men: corporate executives, physicians, attorneys, entrepreneurs, entertainers, elected officials, professional athletes, educators, and other professionals. Each of these men volunteers his time and resources to mentor Black boys, helping them succeed in school, go on to college, and pursue productive careers. For more about this organization, its members, and how to join them in making a difference in the lives of so many children and youth, visit the Web site **www.100blackmen.org**.

In 1869, Galton proposed his theory that genius was attributable solely to heredity and that eminence was due only to two factors: (1) an internal motivation to excel and (2) intellect. Both of these factors were thought to be genetically determined. As early as 1925, Lewis Terman studied individuals with exceptionally high cognitive aptitude; individuals with IQ scores of over 140 (Manning & Besnoy, 2008). Terman's definition reflects a narrow view of giftedness in which high intelligence is closely associated with high academic achievement. In addition to tying giftedness to a score on an IQ test, Terman also believed intelligence to be a fixed characteristic—one that people are born with and one that does not increase or decrease across time.

Today's professional educators are much less confident than Terman was in the results of standardized tests. They now recognize that such tests can be inherently biased against individuals who are not from the dominant American culture or who have not received a strong and traditional educational foundation. They also understand that intelligence, like any other trait, is influenced by both genetics and environment and is not a fixed characteristic of the individual or is signaled only by a high score on an intelligence test. Perhaps Mary Frasier, founder and former director of the Torrance Center for Creative Studies, explained giftedness and talent in the simplest and most straightforward way: "I define giftedness as the potential to excel at the upper end of any talent continuum" (Frasier as cited in Grantham, 2002, p. 50).

Definitions of giftedness are used to identify students and make them eligible for special programs. Table 14.1 provides definitions commonly used to describe students who are considered gifted or talented. One view of giftedness gained national prominence in 1978 with the adoption of what came to be referred to as the "Marland definition," named after Sidney Marland, the U.S. Commissioner of

Table 14.1 • Definitions of Giftedness and Talents

Source	Definitions of Giftedness and Talent Development
U.S. Department of Education (The Marland Definition)	[T]he term "gifted and talented children" means children and, whenever applicable, youth, who are identified at the preschool, elementary, or secondary level as possessing demonstrated or potential abilities that give evidence of high performance capability in areas such as intellectual, creative, specific academic or leadership ability or in the performing and visual arts and who by reason thereof require services to activities not ordinarily provided by the school. Gifted and talented will encompass a minimum of 3 to 5 percent of the school population. *Marland (1972, pp 10–11)*
Federal Government, NCLB	Students, children, or youth who give evidence of high achievement capability in areas such as intellectual, creative, artistic, or leadership capacity, or in specific academic fields, and who need services or activities not ordinarily provided by the school in order to fully develop those capabilities *Elementary and Secondary Education Act, PL 107-110, Title IX, Part A, Definition 22, 2002*

Sources: Marland (1972); No Child Left Behind, Elementary and Secondary Education Act (2002).

Education in 1972. With the passage of the Jacob K. Javits Gifted and Talented Students Education Act of 1988 (PL 100-297), a broader perspective about the concept of education of the gifted and talent development emerged, and that basic definition was retained in the NCLB law. These two definitions are the basis for the current states' definition and the federal definition.

Many educators embrace the idea about giftedness that was proposed in 1983 by Howard Gardner, in a book entitled *Frames of Mind* and further developed across the years (Gardner, 1983, 1993; see also Esping & Plucker, 2008). This concept explains a broader view of giftedness and talents than those that tie intelligence to a score on a test of intelligence, which is really linked to academic achievement. The theory of multiple intelligence supports the idea that there are many dimensions of intelligence and a person may excel in one or more areas, but not necessarily all of them. Gardner first proposed seven dimensions of intelligence—eight dimensions are now included—and a ninth intelligence area, existential intelligence, is being considered for inclusion (Gardner, 1983, 1993; Smith, 2008). A summary of the eight multiple intelligences is presented in Table 14.2.

Table 14.2 • Gardner's Eight Multiple Intelligences

Intelligence	Explanation	Adult Outcomes
1. Linguistic	The ability to think in words and use language in complex ways	Lawyer, poet, public speaker, writer
2. Logical-mathematical	The ability to calculate, quantify, and hypothesize and to recognize patterns	Engineer, mathematician, scientist
3. Spatial	The capacity to think three-dimensionally	Architect, artist, pilot, surgeon
4. Body-kinesthetic	The ability to use the body and hands skillfully	Choreographer, rock climber, skilled artisan
5. Musical	Sensitivity to rhythm, pitch, melody, and tone	Acoustic engineer, composer, musician
6. Interpersonal	The ability to understand and act productively on others' actions and motivations	Actor, political leader, salesperson, teacher, therapist
7. Intrapersonal	The ability to understand one's own feelings and capabilities	Autobiographer, sensitive individual, good decision maker
8. Naturalist	The ingenuity to observe patterns, create classifications, and develop and understand systems	Archeologist, farmer, hunter, landscape architect

Source: From Mindy Kornhaber, et al. *Multiple Intelligences: Best Ideas from Research and Practice*, 1e. Published by Allyn and Bacon, Boston, MA. Copyright © 2004 by Pearson Education. Adapted by permission of the publisher.

Characteristics

As with any group of people, it is unfair to generalize group characteristics to individual members. On the other hand, it is easier to understand a group when some commonly observed features are described. Consensus among experts suggests some characteristics that gifted people share (Clark, 2008; Davis & Rimm, 2004; Reis & Housand, 2008). These are listed in Table 14.3. Compare these characteristics with those found embedded in Gardner's multiple intelligences, and you should see why no single characteristic describes giftedness. However, many believe that five areas of focus can be used to consider giftedness and talents among individuals (Reis & Housand, 2008, p. 66):

- Intellectual ability
- Specific academic aptitude
- Creative or productive thinking
- Leadership ability
- Visual and performing arts

Although gifted and talented students make up a heterogeneous group, some special characteristics make some of these students more vulnerable and cause challenges that can impede possibilities of achieving to their potential. In particular, let's turn our attention to three subgroups of gifted and talented students who deserve some very special attention and for whom educators can make a difference in their lives:

- Females
- Diverse students
- Students with disabilities

Females

Since the 1920s, when gifted individuals as a group came to the attention of educators, differences between males' and females' academic achievement and outcomes have been noted. Bias, stereotypes, and resulting reduced opportunities may be at the root of such differences. For example, although many of his research associates were women who went on to highly productive academic careers, Lewis Terman included very few women in his study of gifted individuals (Rogers, 1999). During the same time period, Leta Hollingworth argued that the prevailing notion that women were intellectually inferior to men was incorrect; rather, women did not have equal opportunities to excel and realize their potential. Gender differences, particularly girls' poor achievement in math, science, and computer sciences, still concern many experts today (Clark, 2008). However, it is important to recognize that more girls than boys participate in programs for gifted and talented students: 6.3% of boys participate in programs for gifted and talented students, while 7.0% of girls do (National Center for Educational Statistics [NCES], 2007).

Although some educators are concerned about gifted girls' overall performance, we decided to highlight these students' reluctance in the areas of science and math. The reason for concern rests in data of women, their college choices, advanced degrees obtained, and careers (Halpern et al., 2007). Here are the facts: Women earn 45% of doctoral degrees, but less than one-third of these advanced degrees are in chemistry, computer sciences, math, physics, and engineering; almost half of all women are in the workforce, but only 26% have careers in science or engineering. What might be reasons for such outcomes? As with researchers many years ago, those conducting related research today believe that gender differences are due to girls' lower self-esteem and lack of confidence (Halpern et al., 2007; Preckel et al., 2008; Silverman, 2005). They also stress that bias both at school and, later, in the workplace is probably a culprit. Society's expectations for people and the roles they assume are crucial factors in the achievement levels and career choices of both genders.

myeducationlab Go to the Activities and Applications section in Chapter 14 of MyEducationLab, and complete Activity 1. As you watch the video and complete the accompanying questions, reflect on your perceptions what makes someone "gifted" and note some of the intellectual skills that are common to gifted students.

Table 14.3 • Common Characteristics of Gifted Students

Intellectual/Academic	Social/Emotional
Reasons abstractly	Criticizes self
Conceptualizes and synthesizes	Empathizes
Manages and processes information quickly and meaningfully	Plays with older friends
Solves problems	Persists
Learns quickly	Is intense
Shows intellectual curiosity	Exhibits individualism
Has wide interests	Has strength of character
Dislikes drill and routine	Demonstrates leadership abilities
May show unevenness	Is concerned about ethical issues
Generalizes learning	Takes risks
Remembers great amounts of material	Is independent and autonomous
Displays high level of verbal ability	Is highly sensitive to others and self
Prefers learning in a quiet environment	Has mature sense of humor
Adapts to new learning situations	Is nonconforming
Applies varied reasoning and thinking skills	Uses different modes of expression
Uses nonstandard pools of information	Experiences great stress from failure
Is highly motivated by academic tasks	
Focuses and concentrates on topic or idea for long periods of time	

While gifted girls in the United States tend not to elect coursework or choose careers in science and math, gifted girls in Britain, for example, respond to unique offerings and special programs. For example, once single-sex programs for girls became available, and when that curriculum incorporated more concrete and real-life examples, girls' performance levels soared (Freeman, 2003). Experts suggest that teachers can make a real difference by providing girls with role models, giving them feedback and encouragement, and also incorporating highly interesting activities into the instructional program (Halpern, et al., 2007).

Culturally and Linguistically Diverse Students

You learned in Chapter 3 that culturally and linguistically diverse students face many challenges. Three related issues are of great concern to education professionals and makers of national policy about diverse students (Clemons, 2008; NCES, 2007). These students

- are overrepresented in disability categories,
- are underrepresented in gifted education programs, and
- drop out of school at a high rate.

While NCLB and accountability systems, such as high-stakes testing and a focus on annual yearly progress, have centered on low-achieving students, particularly those who attend urban schools, as we discussed in the opening sections of this chapter, new concerns are being voiced about their high-achieving classmates (Finn & Petrilli, 2008). Diverse students, particularly those who are poor and attend urban

This kindergartener already demonstrates advanced reading and conceptual abilities. Teachers must continually challenge and support such children so that they do not become bored, and their superior abilities stifled.

schools, are of particular concern (Farkas & Duffet, 2008). Here are a few reasons for this concern: Urban schools have

- fewer instructional resources,
- more uncertified teachers,
- less experienced teachers,
- fewer honors classes, and
- larger class sizes and bigger campuses.

Let's consider a few of these issues and think of solutions that aim to increase diverse students' opportunities to achieve to their potential.

Of this there is no question: African American, Native American, and Hispanic students participate in special programs for gifted and talented students at rates substantially below what their percentages in the general school population would predict (NCES, 2007). According to NCES, while 6.7% of all American students are identified as gifted and talented, only 3.5% of Black students, 4.3% of Hispanic students, and 5.2% of Native American students qualify for special programs in their states. The picture for Asian Americans is very different; almost 12% of them are identified as gifted and talented students (NCES, 2007). Of importance in this regard is the great variation among groups of students included in the federal Asian/Pacific Islander category. Particular groups of these students are more likely to live in poverty (e.g., Samoans, Hmong), and they are less likely to be identified or receive benefits of special programs for gifted or talented students (Paik & Walberg, 2007).

Poor students too often attend poor schools. Although many federal programs focus on low-achieving, urban schools, the focus is on those students who struggle (Finn & Petrilli, 2008). The mantra "close the achievement gap" has become a self-fulfilling prophecy. Since 2000, students with the lowest achievement levels are improving considerably; but, as we noted at the opening of this chapter, those with the highest achievement levels are not (Loveless, 2008). National accountability systems have produced increases in the academic performance of low-achieving students, particularly those from diverse backgrounds. However, comparable increases in performance have not been noted for high-achieving students, including those who attend urban schools. Although teachers believe firmly in equity, those working at urban schools acknowledge that the system is not doing all it can to improve the achievement of their brightest high achievers (Farkas & Duffet, 2008). The lack of basic course offerings hinders the advancement of students. For example, many urban schools do not offer sufficient number of algebra or geometry courses. They have few enriched, honors, or accelerated programs. These reduced opportunities are reflected in students' outcomes. Why might this sad situation be so? Mary Frasier believed that "people in their heart of hearts really think that when kids are poor they cannot possibly perform at the level of kids who are advantaged" (Frasier as cited in Grantham, 2002, p. 50).

Educators must also understand that many diverse students, particularly African Americans, do not want to participate in gifted education programs (Ford & Whiting, 2007; Henfield et al., 2008). These students do not want to feel different or to be called out as exceptional. And, in many instances, they do not feel welcomed by teachers of gifted education. Sometimes, as you will learn in this chapter's Considering Culture, it is not diverse children, but their families who do not support their children's participation in gifted education programs. Clearly, educators must convince both students and parents from diverse backgrounds of the benefits of special programs for gifted and talented students.

What solutions can the educational system offer diverse high-achieving students and their families? Some ideas are daring, unspeakable only a few years

Considering Culture: *Standing Out or Fitting In*

Rhonda has been playing the piano since she was 3 years old and composing music since she was 5. Now in second grade, she is showing remarkable ability in math. Her teacher, Ms. Clark, is eager to refer her to a program for students who are gifted and talented where she thinks Rhonda's special abilities will be fostered. Ms. Clark has developed a portfolio of Rhonda's work to share with her parents. Ms. Clark plans to show it to them at the meeting where she'll request permission for a formal assessment.

Ms. Clark began the meeting by showing Rhonda's parents her work and pointing out how advanced she was compared to others her age. She then requested their permission to allow an assessment, which is required for Rhonda to qualify for programs and services for the gifted and talented. Rhonda's father responded, speaking quietly and deliberately. "Like all of our children, Rhonda is special. She has been blessed with gifts that others do not have, but all children bring gifts to the family and to the tribe. We are pleased that she is doing so well."

The response was not what Ms. Clark expected, and she wasn't certain whether Rhonda's parents had agreed to the assessment or not, so she asked again. "So, do we have your permission for the assessment?"

Rhonda's father paused and then said, "Being with her cousins in the class is important. It would not be good for her to be moved. To be better than others or call attention to one's personal ability and achievement is not the tribal way. We care for one another, not for one *above* another."

Ms. Clark was not prepared for this response. Her first thought was to argue for the assessment and the programs and services available for students who are gifted and talented, but she paused before she spoke. In that moment of reflection, she realized that the tribe's values were an integral part of Rhonda's life, that Rhonda was happy in her class, and that she was involved in many challenging activities in school, at home, and within the tribe that fostered her talent and ability. Perhaps special services weren't the answer for Rhonda. Instead of arguing. Ms. Clark said. "Thank you for describing your values to me. There are many ways to encourage Rhonda's abilities without isolating her from her classmates, her family, and the values that are important to you. I will continue to support Rhonda's musical and mathematical abilities without violating your wishes."

Questions to Consider

1. What values were Rhonda's parents expressing in their refusal to have her assessed and placed in programs designed specifically for students who are gifted and talented?

2. If you had been in Ms. Clark's position, what do you think you would have said to Rhonda's parents?

—By Eleanor Lynch, San Diego State University, and Marci Hanson, San Francisco State University

ago, and even illegal (Finn & Petrilli, 2008). The vast majority of teachers believe that students, particularly for high school mathematics, should be homogeneously grouped (Farkas & Duffet, 2008). This notion quietly suggests "tracking," a concept outlawed many years ago because policymakers believed that tracking denied equal opportunities to all students. Other ideas focus on providing incentives to schools that show an increase in achievement among gifted and high-achieving students, developing more magnet and special schools that aim at developing specific talents (e.g., special schools for the arts, math and science development) and accelerated opportunities. Attention must be paid to improving academic performance and fostering talents, but also it must seek to reduce dropout rates among these students. How might these goals be accomplished? Some experts believe that the curriculum must become more challenging and motivating, instruction needs to be more engaging and exciting, teachers must be specially trained, and extracurricular activities should support what is being learned in the classroom (Naglieri & Ford, 2005; Roberts, 2008). Others are confident that parent and community partnerships are critical for success and improved outcomes (Briggs, Reis, & Sullivan, 2008). Of this educators are confident: When it all goes right, students flourish.

Students with Disabilities

When you think of people with disabilities who are also gifted and have developed outstanding talents, you might think of people like Stephen Hawking, Ludwig van Beethoven, Thomas Edison, Helen Keller, Franklin D. Roosevelt, Stevie Wonder, Ray Charles, Itzhak Perlman, and others. Despite their disabilities, their genius and major contributions to their respective fields have brought them considerable recognition. Remember that regardless of disability, anyone can have exceptional abilities, talents, or creativity. Never make an assumption about an individual from a casual meeting. In Chapter 9, you met Lizzy; in this chapter's Spotlighting feature, her mom, Amy Solomon-Harris, tells you more about raising a gifted child with physical disabilities.

During the 1970s, June Maker drew the profession's attention to the needs of a particular subgroup of learners: gifted students with learning disabilities. In 1977, she first published the results of her research, shedding light on this previously ignored group of learners and stressing the importance of providing them with a truly unique educational experience (Maker, 1977, 1986). This group of learners has come to be referred to as **twice-exceptional students**.

twice-exceptional students
Gifted students with disabilities

Twice-exceptional students face considerable bias. If the gifted student has learning disabilities, which characteristic should the teacher address? If the student has ADHD, are the behavioral issues a reflection of the disability, or is the student bored with the academic content and not being challenged? Most educators, however, do not believe that such a group could exist or do not understand how to address these students' educational needs (Manning & Besnoy, 2008). It has long been known that special education services that address both the student's giftedness and special needs make a real difference in the lives of these students (Nielsen & Mortorff-Albert, 1990).

Clearly, gifted students with learning disabilities are at great disadvantage because of the importance of reading and writing in the general education curriculum (Cooper, Ness, & Smith, 2004). For them, explicit instruction to instill the fundamentals of reading (review again Chapter 5) is critical, so advanced content that is presented in complicated texts is not overwhelming. Also, gifted students with reading disabilities benefit from technology like their peers who only have learning disabilities do. For them, listening to text instead of reading it can allow them to access an advanced general education curriculum. So, they profit from the National Instructional Materials Accessibility Standard (NIMAS) provisions of IDEA '04 that you learned about in Chapters 1 and 11. It is certainly difficult to demonstrate potential for academic excellence when accessing the curriculum in traditional ways does not come easily. But there are many ways to make a difference in these students' educational experiences (Nielsen, 2002; Nielsen & Higgins, 2005). Tips for Effective Instruction on p. 474 provides some simple guidelines to follow. When all goes well, individual success can be stunning. Certainly Charles Schwab's story, told in Chapter 5's Making a Difference, attests to this fact. Gifted individuals with learning disabilities have and do overcome these challenges.

Spotlighting *Amy Harris-Solomon: A Day in the Life*

Amy Harris-Solomon is the mother of Lizzy, a gifted child with physical disabilities resulting from cerebral palsy. Lizzy's story is featured in the Spotlighting box in Chapter 9.

My daughter, Lizzy, has just finished her freshman year in our local high school. Her course load included Spanish Honors, English Honors, Biology Honors, AP World History, Algebra, and Band. She is on the International Baccalaureate track at her school and will formally enter that degree program in her junior year. In addition to her schoolwork, Lizzy is an accomplished pianist and is active in many organizations such as Young Life and Girl Scouts. She has owned and operated her own business, Lizzy's Lines, for the past several years and has won first and second place in a national young entrepreneurship business plan competition 2 years in a row. On the walls in her room are accolades from the Council for Exceptional Children, Mayor's Office, Tennessee House of Representatives, Black Enterprise, and the president of the United States. Alongside these are articles about Lizzy in our local newspaper, national publications, and her personal favorite article about her business featured in *The National Examiner*. Lizzy is an exceptional youth in many ways. She is a bright, capable gifted young female who also happens to have spastic quadriplegic cerebral palsy.

There are many challenges associated with Lizzy's having a physical disability and being gifted. Probably the biggest challenge is the misconception society in general has regarding people who have physical disabilities. People sometimes assume that a person who uses a wheelchair has cognitive delays as well. While this assumption appears more prevalent in the community (e.g., a server asks me what Lizzy wants to eat), it does occur in educational settings, and especially with general education teachers.

Lizzy's first year in high school has been successful overall. As is the case at the beginning of nearly every school year and transition, it takes a little while for the teachers to really understand Lizzy's needs and abilities. They seem to start the year a bit nervous and unsure of what to expect. As a parent, I try not to get overinvolved at the very beginning of the year and let these things work themselves out. Thankfully, with Lizzy's perseverance and determination, she seems to rise to the occasion, and before long, teachers are placing appropriate expectations on Lizzy and her schoolwork. It seems that once the teachers get to know Lizzy and develop a comfort level with her disabilities, they really begin to recognize her strengths, talents, and abilities.

It is only possible for Lizzy to achieve success if her needs are appropriately identified and the educational environment and staff are supportive of the needs. These needs may change based on the demands of individual classes, teachers, or grade-level requirements. High school has brought new challenges. One has been that Lizzy must advocate for herself and be an active member of the team in identifying appropriate accommodations to meet the demands of her accelerated classes. I am learning that the hardest part of love truly is letting go and trusting that Lizzy will be capable of advocating for herself to get the right amount of support and encouragement. It seems in high school that her voice is the most important voice to be heard.

Along with being her own advocate comes the responsibility of taking on some of the ownership of being her own case manager. An example of this is making sure all her teachers are familiar with and understand the allowable accommodations on her IEP. We have discovered that there are many things that Lizzy has to do in her advanced program that typically are not part of an IEP, such as having a reader on an Advanced Placement World History district assessment. We have recognized the importance of learning the guidelines well in advance and making sure that the appropriate supports are in place for Lizzy. Other team members do their part as well and are available to help, but the initiative and the follow-through for much of the communication and coordination of the services starts with us.

Lizzy fully expects to attend college and has already begun her search. She wants to study business. Sometimes I wish there was more time to simply enjoy high school life; however, with all the changes in systems and services in college, it will take much time and attention on our parts for this transition to be successful. It seems you always have to have one eye on the future!

Prevalence

Remember, education of gifted or talented students is neither mandated nor funded by IDEA '04, so states do not include prevalence information about their gifted and talented students in reports to the federal government along with data about students with disabilities. States do report data about their gifted and

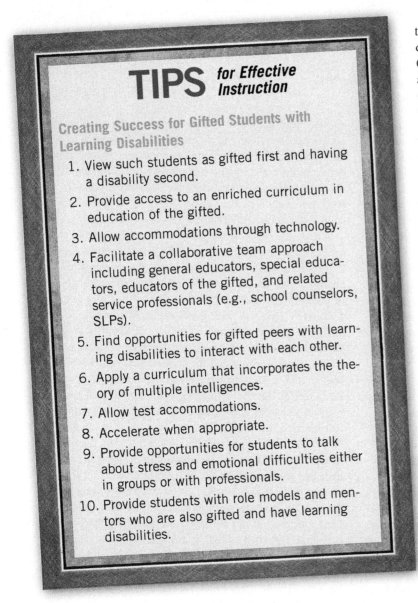

TIPS for Effective Instruction

Creating Success for Gifted Students with Learning Disabilities

1. View such students as gifted first and having a disability second.
2. Provide access to an enriched curriculum in education of the gifted.
3. Allow accommodations through technology.
4. Facilitate a collaborative team approach including general educators, special educators, educators of the gifted, and related service professionals (e.g., school counselors, SLPs).
5. Find opportunities for gifted peers with learning disabilities to interact with each other.
6. Apply a curriculum that incorporates the theory of multiple intelligences.
7. Allow test accommodations.
8. Accelerate when appropriate.
9. Provide opportunities for students to talk about stress and emotional difficulties either in groups or with professionals.
10. Provide students with role models and mentors who are also gifted and have learning disabilities.

talented students to the U.S. Department of Education's National Center for Educational Statistics (NCES). The data reported by that agency are surprising. Across the nation, 6.7% of all students are identified as gifted and talented (NCES, 2007). This percentage is much higher than what you should expect from earlier discussions about the lack of special programs available to gifted and talented students. Remember, many states identify students but do not mandate special programs. So, gifted education might be offered at some schools but not others. You might also be surprised by the higher percentage of gifted students than you would expect when applying traditional models of giftedness. Let's take a few moments to consider how the way we think about giftedness and the resulting numbers of individuals identified are related.

Because IQ is implied or called out in almost every definition of giftedness, it is helpful to review the idea of a normal curve and the distribution of test scores it represents. We introduced this concept in Chapter 1, when we discussed how characteristics might be thought of as forming a distribution with the average, the most number of scores, in the middle. Look at Figure 14.2— it shows how individuals' scores on tests of intelligence come together to form a normal curve. As you read more about the prevalence of gifted students, use this illustration to provide a perspective about criterion used and the resulting number of students who qualify. If 6% of all children were identified as gifted and talented, then the IQ cutoff would be a score of 124; of course, some children with lower scores on such tests might be included because they are exceptionally artistic, creative, or musical.

In the Where We've Been and Definitions sections of this chapter, we discussed Terman's ideas about giftedness. To him, only those who score in the highest 1% on an intelligence test would be considered gifted, and only 1 in every 100 children would qualify for special services or a special education for gifted students. Look at the top end or right side of Figure 14.2. There, you will see that about 1% translates to three standard deviations above the mean and an IQ score cutoff of 145. If an IQ of 130 were used as the minimum score needed to qualify for a special education for gifted students, then all students who scored at least two standard deviations above the mean would qualify, and such calculations would include slightly more than 2% of all students.

Considerable variation occurs across the nation in regard to the percentage of students who are considered gifted and talented. While the national average is 6.7%, 3% of all students in Connecticut are identified as gifted and talented, but almost 14% of all students in Maryland have been so identified (NCES, 2007). Most likely, it is not the case that children in Maryland are smarter and more talented than those who live in Connecticut. Rather, the criterion for qualifying for gifted education is different from state to state. Without national guidelines, such inconsistencies will

Figure 14.2 • IQ Scores Distributed Along a Normal Curve

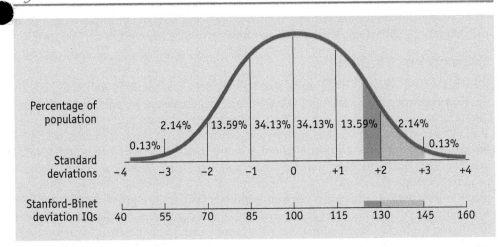

continue, leaving many students without the educational opportunities they deserve and require.

Causes and Prevention

Throughout this book we have talked about important ways to prevent disabilities. Knowing more about the causes of a disability enables researchers to pinpoint reasons for that disability's occurrence and then provide guidance about how to prevent at least some of the conditions that contribute to it. In the case of giftedness, of course, our hope is not to prevent it from occurring but, rather, to foster talents whenever we can.

Causes

Both environment and heredity play important roles in the development of the intellect. On the one hand, the strong genetic link to superior intelligence has long been recognized (Silverman, 2005). The IQ scores of highly gifted children—those above 160—are like their parents' and grandparents' scores. Also, environmental factors correlate with both increased and diminished giftedness. Remember from your studies about disabilities that IQ is not a fixed characteristic in people. Early intervention programs have brought about demonstrable improvement in these scores, and these enhancements persist across time (Schweinhart, 2005). Attitudes, motivation, expectations, and values expressed in different cultures, societies, socioeconomic levels, and families influence the development of talent (Ford & Whiting, 2007). In other words, education does make a difference in the results of gifted and talented students.

Prevention

One important goal for everyone interested in gifted and talented youngsters is to prevent as many situations as possible that negatively affect talent development. Attitudes and opinions expressed by family, friends, TV, and print media (including textbooks) influence behavior and teach role expectations (Reis, 2003). As we have discussed, the lack of programs that foster academic excellence and creativity are ways to prevent excellence.

Experts in talent development believe that the educational system inhibits creativity (Clark, 2008). They believe that the suppression of creativity begins early, during the preschool and early elementary school years. Teachers tend to favor highly intelligent students who do well academically, but they do not encourage divergent, independent, or imaginative behavior. For example, many educators tend to promote realism instead of imagination. Dolls actually "talk," expressing needs like real children. Computerized toys teach children the correct answers to arithmetic problems and the correct way to spell words. The qualities that educators value seem to be getting along with others, working toward a goal, and adapting for the common good. Many of these qualities are not compatible with being creative or expressing individual differences (Kirschenbaum, 1998). If creativity is not fostered, it can be lost.

Overcoming Challenges

Educators must come to understand that they may inadvertently be inhibiting creativity. However, managing divergent thinking can be a challenge to teachers who are trying to meet the needs of children with a wide range of abilities and interests. Accountability systems (e.g., high-stakes testing) focus instruction on content standards and can create the pressure on educators for the entire class to attain a standard level of achievement. Such pressure can be overwhelming. Many teachers feel that just to progress through the curriculum at the required pace leaves little time for topics not listed in their state's curriculum content standards (Farkas & Duffett, 2008). One negative outcome of such accountability systems is that content not included on the tests is stripped from class instructional time. In other words, activities that focus on thinking skills, art, music, and creativity are eliminated from classroom instruction, sometimes without much thought about the consequences. Fostering creativity and divergent thinking isn't just putting the fun back in school; it is talent development as well.

Assessment

Assessment is the gatekeeper to gifted education. The methods used reflect our beliefs about what giftedness and talents are, how many students should be included, and the types of programs that should be available. If the nation is only interested in providing gifted education to a few academically talented students, then only those with exceptionally high scores on IQ and achievement tests would be declared eligible. If the educational system seeks to be more inclusive, then multiple methods of identifying students are put into place (Johnsen, 2008). Of course, assessment and identification is only one side of the equation. Excellent programs that develop talent must be in place. But, before thinking about educational options, let's consider ways that identify every gifted and talented student.

Early Identification

Gifted children express their uniqueness almost from birth. Surely you've noticed that rare, precocious toddler shopping with his mom! These infants and toddlers master developmental milestones early (Clark, 2008; Farmer, 1996). They are walking independently well before they are 1 year old; they are talking in complete sentences before they are 2. It is common to see these babies turning pages in books by the time they are 6 months old and reading books before they come to school. Highly gifted youngsters are obvious to family members—and to practically everyone they meet. Table 14.4 provides the age when typically developing children are able to do specific tasks and also indicates the age when gifted children are able to perform that task. A quick comparison of when these developmental markers are acquired shows the dramatic head start that keeps gifted preschoolers ahead of their age-mates across the early childhood period, and across their lifetimes if necessary supports from families and schools are provided during their school years (Karnes & Stephens, 2008). These developmental markers are one way that pediatricians and day care providers help recognize these children early in their lives.

Prereferral

For students who were not identified as gifted during their preschool years, teachers begin the identification process. They usually make the initial referral. Identification of talent should begin early, so an appropriate education can be developed and delivered as soon as possible (Johnsen, 2008). Early identification is particularly important to those from diverse backgrounds, who are at risk of not being identified

Table 14.4 • Comparison of Developmental Milestones: Typical and Gifted Children

Development Milestones

	Typical Development	30% Advanced
Gross motor		
Rolls over	3 months	2.1 months
Sits alone	7	4.9
Stands alone well	11	7.7
Walks alone	12.5	8.8
Walks up stairs	18	12.6
Turns pages of book	18	12.6
Runs well	24	16.8
Jumps with both feet	30	21.0
Rides tricycle using pedals	36	25.2
Throws ball	48	33.6
Skips with alternate feet	60	42.0
Fine motor		
Plays with rattle	3	2.1
Holds object between finger and thumb	9	6.3
Scribbles spontaneously	13	9.1
Draws person with two body parts	48	33.6
Draws recognizable person with body	60	42.0
Draws person with neck, hands, and clothes	72	50.4
Language development		
Vocalizes two different sounds	2.3	1.6
Says first word	7.9	5.5
Responds to name	9	6.3
Babbles with intonation	12	8.4
Vocabulary of 4–6 words	15	10.5
Names an object	17.8	12.5
Vocabulary of 20 words	21	14.7
Combines several words spontaneously	21	14.7
Uses simple sentences	24	16.8
Uses personal pronouns	24	16.8

Source: Reprinted by permission of the Publisher. From Eleanor G. Hall & Nancy Skinner, *Somewhere to Turn: Strategies for Parents of Gifted and Talented Children,* New York: Teachers College Press, © 1980 by Teachers College, Columbia University. All rights reserved.

or of having educational opportunities that both nurture and address any skill areas that might be weak (Bernal, 2003; Johnsen, 2008). At the prereferral stage, teachers should think broadly about which students should be sent on for formal identification. Educators should think about which students show signs of outstanding skills in these areas: verbal and nonverbal reasoning, leadership, academics, art, creative writing or poetry, and oral language (e.g., storytelling, humor).

Christopher Paolini is clearly a prodigy. At the age of 15, he wrote his first novel, *Eragon,* a story of a magical dragon and a young boy living in medieval times. The book was wildly successful. That first book is now part of a series, referred to as the Inheritance Cycle. The third book in the series, *Brisingr,* was released September 19, 2008. The movie version of *Eragon* was released over the 2006 winter holiday.

Identification

Finding individuals whose intellectual abilities fall within or close to the top 1% of all students is not as difficult as finding those students who have outstanding abilities and potential but are in the top 3% to 5% of all students. Experts are confident that standardized tests reveal the most precocious and highly intelligent students (Lubinski et al., 2006). After conducting longitudinal research over many, many decades, these experts are confident that 13-year-olds who score higher than 60% of all individuals taking the SAT should receive special attention. Their data indicate that those who score in the top 1% excel in art, history, literature, languages, drama, and other related fields (Benbow & Lubinksi, 2007). These extraordinary individuals clearly should be identified early and their talent fostered and developed to its fullest.

Most educators, however, are not confident in the use of standardized tests to make important educational decisions about most individuals. Regardless, IQ tests are still the most common means of identifying gifted students and are typically included in every assessment (Ford & Whiting, 2007). Rather than overrelying on IQ scores, experts recommend that multiple assessments be used to identify gifted students (Johnsen, 2008; Clark, 2008). Such multiple assessments might include

- achievement tests with no upper limits or ceilings;
- peer, teacher, and parent checklists;
- parent, teacher, peer, and community nominations;
- portfolios of student's work;
- data and notes from behavioral observations;
- tests of verbal and nonverbal problem solving; and
- indications of leadership.

Remember our discussions about the history of gifted education and how there have been periods of genius across history. Recall that these periods saw different abilities valued and developed. Such investments would yield similar results today, and ideas about who should be included define the identification process. For example, if you are looking for students who have outstanding fine motor skills, you might look for students with the neatest handwriting. Or, if you are searching for individuals who might become the best engineers, you might devise a system to identify the preschoolers most adept at creating buildings and bridges with inter-

locking blocks. If, however, you are looking for students whose school administrators believe should be included in special programs for students who are gifted, you are likely to create identification procedures to find the "bright achievers." This is exactly what some experts believe: The schools have defined those who are gifted as high achievers and academically able (Gagné, 2004). The way to find such students is to use IQ tests, achievement tests, and grades.

Evaluation

Underachievement is of great concern to most experts in the area of gifted education (Clemons, 2008; Hébert, 2006). Efforts to halt the cycle of underachievement must begin early. In this regard, the annual accountability efforts outlined in NCLB are most helpful. When gifted students' scores on state- and districtwide achievement tests are below what is expected, quick action should be taken. Teachers should seek to boost motivation and self-esteem. They should also bring additional educational services to the student. Concerted efforts to help such students truly make a difference, avoiding disengagement and the eventuality of leaving school early.

Early Intervention

Recognizing giftedness in young children is important because talents need to be fostered and developed early in these youngsters' lives. Early identification may lead to early entrance into preschool or the selection of an enriched or special preschool for gifted young children, and it also signals to parents that their child may need unique educational opportunities across the school years (Rimm, 2008). Not responding to these preschoolers' unique educational needs early can lead to diminished accomplishments during later school years; this unfortunate situation is too often observed in students who live in poverty (Johnsen, 2008). Look again at Table 14.4, and study the developmental differences between gifted infants and toddlers and their typically developing peers.

While gifted preschoolers achieve developmental benchmarks ahead of typical developing children, educators and parents need to understand that skills do not develop evenly (Cukierkorn et al., 2007). A common pattern is for gifted preschoolers to have an amazing vocabulary and ability to engage in remarkable conversations, but their motor skills have not yet developed at the same accelerated rate. This situation can be misunderstood by untrained teachers and by parents, and to the children it is often exceptionally frustrating. It is common for young gifted children to come to preschool already reading books, but it is not uncommon for them to be unable to hold a pencil well enough to write a story. Therefore, it is very important for preschool teachers to provide a curriculum that is flexible and individualized (Cukierkorn et al., 2007). These preschoolers are usually able to handle complex and

Signs of giftedness appear early in life.

abstract language relationships earlier than most. Their language skills not only develop more rapidly than those of their peers who are not gifted, but they also develop differently, with their language reflecting their superior mental capacity very early (Hoh, 2005). They can come to understand metaphors (such as "Presidents are heads of state" and "Time flies") long before their classmates. Typical peers do not understand such abilities, and teachers must ensure that the gifted preschooler is not ridiculed or inhibited by peers.

Educational programs in which gifted preschoolers participate must be challenging so these young children's motivation to learn is not stifled. Gifted individuals, whether preschoolers or students, should not be assigned lessons on content that they have already mastered—one problem for those included in general education classes where instruction is not differentiated (Cukierkorn et al., 2007). Time after time, stories are told about children who come to kindergarten already reading but, instead of being allowed to continue developing their reading skills, are forced to engage in readiness activities with classmates. For these students, instructional time might better be spent on enrichment activities, such as classifying and organizing information or thinking critically and creatively.

Teaching Gifted and Talented Students

A variety of educational services, varying by locale and in philosophy and orientation, are offered to gifted and talented students. As we discussed earlier in this chapter, special services are inconsistently available; not every state has special programs, nor does every school district in states that do offer special programs. However, policymakers and experts in gifted education are calling out for a national guarantee to each gifted and talented student that an appropriate and challenging education be accessible and available (Finn & Petrilli, 2008; Siegle, 2008a, 2008b). Clearly, no consensus exists about what type of program is best for individual students, and as for their peers with disabilities, there should be no single option or answer (Tomlinson & Hockett, 2008). One conclusion is that an array of programs, even including separate programming for students by ability or interests rather than age, must be part of the answer to what comprises an appropriate education for these students (Farkas & Duffett, 2008).

When gifted education is delivered, it is done so through a variety of placement options: general education classrooms, resource rooms or pullout programs, self-contained classes, magnet schools, and other types of special schools. Regardless of the placement option used, these key features should be part of these programs:

- Problem-based learning
- Abstract thinking
- Reasoning activities
- Creative problem solving
- Content mastery
- Breadth and depth of topic
- Independent study
- Talent development

Access to the General Education Curriculum: Acceleration

The case for students with disabilities being able to access the general education to the greatest extent their abilities allow has been well made by professionals, policymakers, and parents. However, for students who are gifted and talented, the argument has not been clearly articulated or understood until recently. Today's consensus among professionals is that gifted students must access the curriculum *at their own level* (Bernal, 2003; Jeffrey, 2008). They must be intellectually and academically challenged, which cannot be accomplished without additional instruction or opportunities: They need opportunities beyond what is available to typical learners participating in general education classes. A simple answer to these challenges is available: acceleration.

Acceleration is an option that allows students to move through the curriculum more rapidly than their peers who learn in more typical ways (NAGC, 2004). Because acceleration is effective, popular with many gifted and talented learners, and not expensive; it is popular with many school district administrators (Hertberg-Davis &

acceleration Moving students through a curriculum or years of schooling in a shorter period of time than usual

Callahan, 2008; Lubinski & Benbow, 1995). Acceleration can take many different forms (Tomlinson & Hockett, 2008). Many different acceleration options are used across the country. Here are a few examples:

- Grade skipping
- Advanced placement courses
- Ability groups such as honors sections.

One form of acceleration, more common in elementary schools, is **grade skipping**. This approach has students advance to a grade ahead of their classmates of the same age. Grade skipping often occurs at or during kindergarten, when a child's giftedness is apparent because he or she can already read books, write stories, or solve mathematics problems. Grade skipping is common again toward the end of high school. In what is often called *early entrance programs*, high school juniors or seniors skip their remaining years and begin their college studies (Noble, Childers, & Vaughn, 2008). Because of the renewed interest in these programs, we discuss them in more detail in the Transition section of this chapter.

In high school, the most common form of acceleration available to gifted students is **advanced placement (AP)** courses (Hertberg-Davis & Callahan, 2008). Although not developed for gifted students, it provides an option for more challenging learning to students who are high achievers in specific areas of study. AP courses enable students, while in high school, to take classes for which they earn college credit. Advanced placement allows students to study course content in more depth. A side benefit is that they do not have to take these courses over again in college. AP courses sets students on a clear path to college. Unfortunately, diverse, urban, gifted, and high-achieving students do not participate in AP courses at the same rates as their peers who are more advantaged and live in the suburbs (Ford & Whiting, 2007). There are three primary reasons for this sad situation:

- Advanced placement is less readily available to students who attend urban schools (Tornatzky, Pachon, & Torres, 2003).
- Many students of color, particularly African Americans, decide not to participate in AP courses often because of peer pressure (Henfield et al., 2008).
- Teachers of AP classes have not had any special preparation to know how to work effectively with diverse or gifted students (Roberts, 2008).

To increase the participation rates of gifted students in AP courses will require substantial effort from educators, families, and school leaders (Hertberg-Davis & Callahan, 2008). AP courses need to be universally available. Teachers of AP courses will need to learn how to better meet the needs of gifted students, particularly those who are culturally diverse. Students need to better understand why these courses are beneficial to them now and in the future. And, students must not respond to teasing from peers who do not qualify for such programs.

Policymakers are promoting yet another form of acceleration, **ability grouping** (Finn & Petrilli, 2008). This approach has students of comparable abilities working together in courses or activities in which they excel. **Honors sections** are one example of ability grouping. Advanced ability groups are easily arranged in middle school and high school, where students attend different sections of classes or where honor sections are available. However, as we discussed earlier in this chapter, these arrangements are not common because education professionals fear that they smack of tracking, a practice that is illegal and seems elitist.

The benefits of acceleration are great (NAGC, 2004). It adjusts the pace of instruction, provides an appropriate challenge, avoids boredom from repetitious instruction, and reduces the time required to master curricular content. The following benefits are also cited (Colangleo, Assouline, & Gross, 2004):

- Students can complete the traditional general education curriculum in a shorter period of time and may be able to finish high school several years early.
- Academic material can be completed more quickly, allowing students to study related topics in more depth.

myeducationlab Go to the Building Teaching Skills and Dispositions section in Chapter 14 of MyEducationLab, and complete the activity in the IRIS Module, "Content Standards: Connecting to Standards-Based Curriculum to Instructional Planning." Teachers are required to implement the adopted content standards even if their students surpass them! This module serves as a basic guide for the process.

grade skipping A form of acceleration; advances students to a grade ahead of their age peers

advanced placement (AP) courses High school courses that carry college credit

ability grouping Placing students with comparable achievement and skill levels in the same classes or courses

honors sections Advanced classes for any student who shows high achievement in specific subject areas

- Research efficacy validates this approach.
- Some students develop better self-concepts and more positive attitudes about course content and school.
- Gifted students are not segregated from more typical learners, because although they are not placed with students of the same age, they are participating in general education programs.
- The approach is cost-effective for schools and families: special teachers do not have to be hired or special sections do not have to be offered, saving schools from expending precious resources; and college can be completed in a shorter time, saving families a portion of college tuition costs.

Instructional Accommodations

Many educators feel that acceleration does not lend itself well to the elementary school. Also, for some students, grade skipping is inappropriate because they are not socially ready to join older peers for their studies. These justifications are used to support other options, such as

- differentiated instruction and
- enrichment.

differentiated curriculum
Instruction above and beyond the general education curriculum and content.

Differentiating Instruction   Today, most gifted elementary students are included in general education classes. As you learned in Chapter 2, differentiated instruction is used with students with disabilities to provide them supports and additional assistance as they access the general education curriculum. For gifted learners, however, the concept is used to extend and expand learning of the basic curriculum and content standards. Through a **differentiated curriculum**, they receive different learning experiences that are above and beyond those provided to typical learners through the general education curriculum (Callahan, 2008; Van Tassel-Baska & Stambaugh, 2006). A differentiated curriculum can be achieved in many different ways: by modifying the standard curriculum's content, the learning environment, or the instruction provided (Tomlinson & Hockett, 2008). Tips for Classroom Management provides examples of ways to extend content found in the general education curriculum to create a differentiated curriculum for gifted learners.

enrichment Adding topics or skills to the traditional curriculum or presenting a particular topic in more depth

Enrichment   Another means of meeting the educational needs of both high achievers and gifted elementary students is called **enrichment**. Broadly speaking, this approach adds topics, broadens the content being presented, or provides more depth to the general education curriculum (Tomlinson & Hockett, 2008). Students can work independently on special assignments, possibly preparing more in-depth reports on the time period being presented in the social studies text. A group of students might spend time each week working together gathering additional information from the Internet about a scientific topic; this chapter's Accommodating for Inclusive Environments provides some ideas about resources available on the Web that can be used to enrich and enhance instruction. Groups of students, possibly coming together as clubs, also provide a means for enrichment. Meeting once a week, students can share interests and extend their learning possibly through a transdisciplinary approach where they each focus on a different aspect of the topic. For example, they could explore environmental studies from many perspectives: economic, scientific, political, and historical. Here's another example. The annual FIRST Robotics Competition provides the opportunity for high school club members to apply their science and math talents, come together to build a robot, and test its agility and innovative elements against other teams' robots. Such activities help students extend their learning and have a lot of fun in the process.

How can general education teachers find time in the busy school day to enrich students' curriculum? This question is a concern of many. To allow for enrichment activities takes time from the already packed instructional day. **Curriculum compacting** recaptures instructional time by reducing (or even eliminating) coverage of topics that gifted students either have already mastered or will master in a fraction

curriculum compacting Saving instructional time for enrichment activities

TIPS for Classroom Management

DIFFERENTIATING THE CURRICULUM FOR GIFTED STUDENTS

General Education Assignment	Differentiated Assignment
Discuss plot, setting, and characters in the novel *The Pearl* by John Steinbeck.	Compare and contrast the plot, setting, characters, motivation, theme, and climax of *The Pearl* with *Of Mice and Men,* two novels by John Steinbeck. How would you characterize the author's style?
Charles invested $10,000 in stock in January. When he sold it in December, the price was up 10 percent from his purchase price. What was his profit on this stock?	Which would you rather choose? a. Eighty percent profit in year 1, and 50 percent loss in year 2 b. Five percent profit in year 1, and 5 percent profit in year 2. Explain your reasoning in writing, and share your thinking with the class.
Pretend you are a newscaster studying World War II. Select one of the following to complete, based on your role: a. Write a news report that outlines a significant event in the war. b. Re-create a significant event and describe how that event was critical to the outcome of the war. c. Design a flyer based on a significant event.	Using a medium of your choice (song, dance, poster, PowerPoint presentation, flowchart, etc.), illustrate the cause-and-effect relationships among the precipitating events of World War II.

Source: From Van Tassel-Baska, Joyce & Tamra Stambaugh *Comprehensive Curriculum for Gifted Learners* 3e. Published by Allyn and Bacon, Boston, MA. Copyright © 2006 by Pearson Education. Adapted by permission of the publisher.

of the time that their peers need. Saved time can then be reallocated to enrichment activities such as mentoring, independent study, internships, and/or advanced study (Tomlinson & Hockett, 2008).

One popular and long-standing enrichment model is worth knowing about because it seeks to address the learning needs not just of the top 3% to 5% of students, but rather allow some 15% to 20% to participate in advanced activities (Renzulli, 1999, 2004; Renzulli & Reis, 2007). The **enrichment triad/revolving-door model** seeks to modify the entire educational system by including all students with high potential for creative production. The result is that a larger pool of culturally and linguistically diverse students receive opportunities to be challenged. How does the program work? Students revolve into and out of different levels of their program, which includes three types of skills categories. Here are a few examples of each type:

enrichment triad/revolving-door model An inclusive model for gifted education where 15% to 20% of a school's students participate in activities to develop thinking skills, problem solving, and creativity

- *Type 1*: Enrichment activities expose the entire class of general education students to new and exciting topics of study carried out through a variety of instructional approaches (speakers, field trips, demonstrations, videotapes and films, and interest centers).

Accommodating for Inclusive Environments

Enriching Instruction Through the Internet

Area of Interest	Topic	Provider	Web Site
Math and science	Math challenges	Dr. Math	http://mathforum.org
	Geology, biology, chemistry, physics, and more	Lee Summit, Missouri School District	http://its.leesummit.k12.mo.us/science.htm
	Space exploration	Jet Propulsion Labs, NSA	http://www.jpl.nasa.gov
	Weather	National Oceanic and Atmospheric Association	http://oceanservice.noaa.gov/kids/
	Environmental education	EnviroLink Network	http://envirolink.org/
	Astronomy	University of Washington	http://www.astro.washington.edu
Social studies	American government	FirstGov for Kids	http://www.kids.gov/
	American history	Library of Congress	http://www.loc.gov/families
	Art history	Getty	http://www.getty.edu/art
		Smithsonian	http://www.smithsonianeducation.org/students/index.html
Research skills	How to conduct Internet research	Big 6 Associates	http://www.big6.com/kids
Connecting	World issues	UNICEF	http://www.unicef.org/voy/

- *Type 2*: Activities encourage all students to develop their cognitive and affective abilities through their own expressive skills (writing a play, doing a pen-and-ink sketch, using equipment).
- *Type 3*: Opportunities to apply advanced investigative and creative skills are given to students who are motivated, and those who show great interest are provided with specialized instruction and activities to explore particular topics, issues, or ideas.

Data-Based Practices

Enrichment and programs that differentiate instruction provide ways to challenge gifted and talented students who are accessing the curriculum alongside their general education classmates. Busy teachers often find that creating additional activities for gifted students is difficult, but the Center for Gifted Education at the University of Arkansas is helping by providing blueprints that help teachers incorporate biographies into the curriculum (Robinson, 2006). These blueprints are guides that provide structure and a format when supplementing history units with published biographies of people from that time period. This chapter's Closer Look at Data-Based Practices provides the steps to follow when creating guides for students to use before they read the biography, questions to answer while they are reading the biography, and follow-up activities for them to complete to integrate their learning to the history unit that is being taught. As you have learned, keeping the interest of gifted learners is a chal-

A Closer Look at Data-Based Practices

Enriching and Differentiating Through Biographies

Biographies are a favorite choice of reading material and are of high interest to many adults as well as young gifted readers. Biographies can be used to enrich and differentiate the general education curriculum, particularly complementing a history unit. They teach life's lessons, are interdisciplinary, can provide historical details and perspectives, are multidimensional, and are often of high interest. Ann Robinson's format for using biographies, *Blueprints for Biographies*, guides teachers and students through the use of three clusters of questions to guide discussions or serve as a reading guide.

Steps to Follow

1. Pick a biography.
   - The book should be engaging.
   - The book should be factually accurate.
   - It should be sensitive to multicultural concerns.
   - It should be identified as a biography and not historical fiction.
2. Develop questions.
   - For use before the book is read:
     - Focus student attention.
     - Build student interest.
     - Check for prior knowledge of vocabulary and concepts.
   - For use while the book is being read:
     - Analyze components of the biography.
     - Help make inferences.
     - Record reactions to the story.
   - For use to extend learning:
     - Make personal connections to the person in the biography.
     - Relate to modern-day personalities.
3. Create extension activities:
   - Write a paper.
   - Prepare an analysis from a particular perspective.
   - Write a review of literature.
   - Execute a portrait study (e.g., painting, photography, engraving).

Example of a Portrait Study

This photograph of FDR was used to illustrate a biography of President Roosevelt.

Source: Adapted from *Blueprints for Biography: Differentiating the Curriculum for Talented Readers* by Ann Robinson (2006 Fall), Compass Points, pp. 7–8. Copyright 2006 NAGC. Reprinted with permission of the National Association for Gifted Children. No further reprints or redistribution is permitted without the consent of NAGC.

lenge that must be overcome, particularly when these students are included in general education classes. Not only enriching instruction through the use of supplemental books but also guiding students' thinking can have multiple benefits. Students can approach the history unit from multiple perspectives, glean the emotions of the time, and might have insights about how the past relates to the present. Of course, one hope is that these students will be more engaged in the learning process and develop a passion for investigating historical facts and evaluating different points of view.

Another data-based practice relating to gifted and talented students that we want to mention reflects growing interest in administrative arrangements or types of educational programs made available to these students and their families. Even though, as you have learned, some believe that separate programs for these students are unfair and inequitable, there is now a growing consensus that gifted students require more intensive instruction (Finn & Petrilli, 2008; Siegle, 2008a, 2008b). Suggestions include more opportunities for acceleration, magnet schools, advanced placement courses blocked strictly for gifted students, and even separate schools or classes. Such

Clubs like this high school robotics team bring gifted students together to work and learn together and apply their knowledge in innovative ways. During regional and national competitions, teams have to maneuver their robots in ways that can stretch the imagination of what's possible.

special schools are not a new idea, and some, like Juilliard School, have developed musical prodigies' abilities to remarkable levels. This school had an important role in the life of the central character in this chapter's On the Screen, providing him with learning opportunities he could not otherwise have experienced.

Some gifted students attend special classes, and even special schools are once again growing in popularity with parents and students. Support for separate programs may be due to their unique and comprehensive elements: acceleration, enrichment, counseling, parent involvement, supplemental programs for those with special learning needs, behavior management, and developing specific talents. Some students receive the majority of their instruction in a special class, possibly at their neighborhood school, where they are educated in a homogeneous environment in which all the other students have comparable abilities. While some advantaged youngsters receive their education at exclusive private schools, a few students nationwide have access to special public schools designed exclusively for gifted students. For example, recently the state of Nevada opened a new school for highly gifted students, the Davidson Academy of Nevada (Green, 2006). There, students from the ages of 9 to 16 have their own individualized learning plan and are able to work at their own pace. Other options are magnet schools, which often emphasize a theme, specializing in the performing arts, math, or science, and are available to students who pass qualifying exams or auditions. With renewed interest in gifted education, more program offerings will be available. Some will seek to better enrich and differentiate instruction provided in the general education setting, others will provide a variety of forms of acceleration, and yet others will include a range of administrative arrangements. All of these seek to provide a more responsive education to gifted and talented learners.

Technology

Technology can be a tool, an inspiration, and a means to independent learning for all students. For students bored by instruction paced too slowly for them or on topics they have already mastered, technology can enable them to study advanced topics more in depth. As we have mentioned (see again this chapter's Accommodating feature), resources available from the Internet can allow students to work on accelerated or enriched topics while their general education classmates work on their own assignments. For example, students learning about other planets and solar systems can experience traveling through space by visiting the Web site of NASA's Jet Propulsion Laboratory (JPL): www.jpl.nasa.gov. They can take a virtual tour of the wonderful art in the collection at the Louvre in Paris (in English if they enter through Google). Virtual tours

On the Screen: *A Modern Fairy Tale*

The film *August Rush*, though somewhat unrealistic, shows the power and nature of a talent, how it must be fostered and developed, and the importance of family. This fairy tale of a movie is an example of a gifted child who, with instruction and education, was able to achieve his dreams of coming together with his family.

Evan's mother, a concert cellist, is tricked by her father into thinking her baby died in childbirth, but instead he takes the infant to an orphanage. Instead of continuing her musical career, she abandons her talent and does not perform again. At 11, Evan leaves the orphanage and makes his way to New York, convinced that he will find his parents and be reunited. He meets a younger child, who shows Evan how to play a guitar. Never having played before, Evan does so in an unorthodox manner, but with a masterful ease. This quickly grabs the attention of a local hustler who uses children to earn money. Evan escapes the hustler's abuse, finds shelter in a church, plays the organ, and is identified by the minister as a musical prodigy. The minister takes the boy to Juilliard School, where his talents impress, and he is admitted and begins developing his gifts.

Evan creates dramatic musical pieces, hoping to attract the attention of his parents. In a final concert to be held in Central Park for hundreds if not thousands of people, Evan believes finally the music can go out into the world and reunite him with his parents. Through far-fetched incidents, his parents end up at the park at the same time. The film demonstrates the importance of family, the power of talent, but the need for its development.   —By Steve Smith

---

of many other museums bring art and natural history to students' computers. Students can participate in important conversations about current events and issues with others worldwide. For example, UNICEF "assembles" students around the world to discuss important topics like global warming and hunger.

Advances in **distance education technology**, often used in college courses, can have great benefits for gifted students, as well. It can be used to compensate for the lack of programs and resources often the case at poor, urban schools (Olszewski-Kubilus & Lee, 2008). Although not typically designed for use by high school students, distance education does provide access to advanced courses and challenging content that are otherwise not available. It also can be used to facilitate differentiated and enriched instruction, particularly for those who live in rural and remote areas (Manning & Besnoy, 2008). For example, one student can work on a tutorial in chemistry or physics while a classmate is learning how to program the computer to develop an environmental monitoring and control system. Distance education can increase options for acceleration opportunities for those who do not have advanced courses available at their local schools (Tomlinson & Hockett, 2008). Students can take online courses for credit from anywhere in the nation. Distance education often has drawbacks for younger students that educators can address (Olszewski-Kubilus & Lee, 2008). Instead of working in isolation, students can work in pairs or teams as they master course content. They also can participate in online discussions with classmates, some of whom they may never meet in person.

Some distance education offerings are designed for and used exclusively by students participating in gifted education. For example, Stanford University's Educational

distance education technology
Telecommunications technology used to deliver instruction to many different sites

Distance education technology and online courses provide many benefits to gifted students who could not otherwise participate in advanced courses or acceleration opportunities. Students living in rural areas can take a short course to enrich their study of high school literature, or those attending urban schools that do not offer AP courses can take a college course for credit online.

Program for Gifted Youth (EPGY) is one of many university programs that offer special online courses for high school students who want to study specific content in more depth. Johns Hopkins' Center for Talented Youth offers multimedia courses in math and science, some of which are designed for elementary students. Duke University's Talent Identification Program (Duke TIP) has coursework in a variety of subjects (e.g., social psychology, history of the ancient world, anatomy and physiology) that includes online discussions to support its distance learning opportunities.

Experts have some cautions about use of distance education technology with gifted and talented students (Olszewski-Kubilus & Lee, 2008). Here are a few: Students' completion rates are disappointing, with rates well below 80%; students' interests must be matched with the course offerings; and students must have independent study skills to be successful. Of course, the benefits of distance delivery options for gifted students outweigh these concerns; and with careful selection and assignment, they can provide the missing ingredient for many students.

Transition

Despite common beliefs, longitudinal studies have clearly shown that gifted children do not necessarily grow up to be highly successful, accomplished adults without help from the educational system and their families (Benbow & Stanley, 1996; Oden, 1968; Terman, 1925; Terman & Oden, 1959). Surprisingly, many gifted and talented students drop out of high school because they are bored with the curriculum and not challenged by the instruction (Clemons, 2008). We just talked about some ways, such as AP courses and honors programs, that help engage gifted high school students. Other options are available, such as magnet schools that focus on particular talents and interests. Early entrance to college has not been widely available in recent years. Renowned programs, like the one offered for years at the University of Chicago, have closed. However, there is a renewed interest in early entrance programs because of their popularity with gifted students and their families. Early college entrance can be considered yet one more type of acceleration program. Let's look at what one university offers gifted adolescents.

The University of Washington in Seattle provides two early entrance options to very gifted students (Noble et al., 2008). The Early Entrance Program supports students younger than age 15 as they learn and study in college courses, and the Academy for Young scholars is designed for students who come to the university after grade 10. Students select this option because of dissatisfaction with their middle and high school programs, not feeling challenged, and having a passion for learning. These students' parents are pleased with their children's programs at the university but, of course, express concerns about issues like supervision, advising, and social life. However, with a supportive program like the ones designed at the University of Washington, early entrance for almost all of these students is viewed as successful and rewarding.

Collaboration

One key to successfully enriching instruction and differentiating the curriculum is collaboration. Many gifted students attend general education classes entirely, while others who participate in programs using a form of acceleration also spend most of their school day with their general education classmates. Gifted education teachers are an important resource to general education teachers. Working closely together, they can ensure that an appropriate education is provided to gifted students. The National Association for Gifted Children (NACG) stresses in its position statement "Collaboration Between Gifted and General Education Programs" that collaboration is not a replacement of gifted education options but rather is part of a continuum of services that should be available to meet the unique learning needs of gifted students (NACG, 1998).

Collaborating with Specialists: Gifted Education Teachers

The specialist in education of the gifted helps general education teachers differentiate instruction, deliver enrichment activities, and ensure that gifted students remain challenged in their schoolwork. For example, general education teachers often need assistance when they schedule a commonly applied technique that groups gifted students with their general education classmates. Many resources go untapped. Teachers are overcommitted. Many feel that all of their time and energy must be spent on improving the academic achievement of the most struggling students (Farkas & Duffett, 2008). Help in differentiating instruction for the gifted student often rests with the specialist in gifted education and with the district's curriculum team (VanTassel-Baska & Wood, 2008). Together, these experts can help in adapting the existing curriculum, develop activities to enrich the core content, and arrange for guest speakers or field trips.

Collaborative Practices: Creating a Responsive Education

Successful collaboration efforts do not happen by accident (Friend & Bursuck, 2006; Robinson, 1999). It takes considerable effort and planning. Teachers working together must

- have open and ongoing communication,
- define the educational problems that individual students or groups of students are facing,
- research the problem and identify approaches that might be effective,
- identify backup or alternative solutions,
- pool resources,
- develop a plan of action,
- decide on a meeting schedule and keep it, and
- determine how to evaluate the solution's effectiveness (agree on criteria or level of student performance needed to retain the intervention).

These tasks seem self-evident, but they are not easily accomplished, particularly when teachers are working in isolation. Collaboration and partnerships among general education teachers, teachers of gifted education, district-level curriculum experts, and community members make a real difference when seeking ways to enrich and enhance instruction.

Partnerships with Families and Communities

As you have learned in every chapter of this text, partnerships among educators, families, and communities are critical to students' success. Most certainly, such partnerships make a difference in the lives of gifted and talented students (Briggs et al., 2008). Let's look at how each of these often underutilized resources can be better captured.

Families

Providing a rich home environment is one of the most important things that all families do, for their children who are gifted and talented and for those who are not. However, parents of gifted and talented youngsters often need help from professionals who understand the unique challenges most gifted and talented youngsters and their families face.

One problem faced by many gifted and talented students is underachievement (Clemons, 2008). Major reasons for this situation rest with motivation, being bored and not challenged, and lack of study and organizational skills. In this regard, parents and families have important roles to play. Parental involvement is instrumental in improving attitudes about school and improved self-perception. They can help their children stay focused, even when school assignments are not challenging by adding enrichment activities to homework. For example, they can work with their children to find additional information from the Web that extends and broadens learning (Rimm, 2008). They can provide field trips to local museums and science exhibits, concerts, or plays that tie to what is being learned at school.

Parents and families must set high expectations but not create undue pressure to overachieve (Rimm, 2008). Stressing perfection often inhibits risk taking, an important feature of problem solving and creativity. Consensus among experts is that gifted children must learn that failure is part of life. Competitive praise sometimes leads to unhealthy competition, which in turn can result in poor social adjustment, bragging with typical peers, and rejection. Also, support and encouragement to not drop out of school and to participate in AP courses, enrichment activities, and gifted education makes a difference in lives of children, even when peer pressure suggests alternative paths. Clearly, families have important jobs and often need the help of professional educators who are experts in gifted education.

Finally, parents and families also need to guide gifted children in making appropriate choices and in holding realistic expectations for themselves and others. These children seem to be more mature than others of their age, but appearances can be deceiving (Clark, 2008). One result of the combination of these characteristics can be stress unlike that experienced by their peers (Nichols & Baum, 2000). And remember that these children, just like others of their age, are not capable of making complex decisions or setting their own goals and directions. Families make a difference by maintaining open lines of communication through family meetings, talking with their children about values and how to balance life's events, and helping them determine what is important and what is not.

Communities

Gifted and talented students need role models and experiences that provide an anchor to their learning at school. **Mentorships** pair students who have special interests with adults who have expertise in those areas or (like the volunteers of the 100 Black Men of America described in this chapter's Making a Difference feature) pair students with highly successful adults who serve as role models and provide guidance to talented youngsters. Mentorships need to be carefully arranged by teachers, but the effects are often amazing. They have both an immediate and a long-term impact on the students' retention in programs for education of the gifted, as well as positively influencing college and career paths (Corwin, 2001; Grantham, 2004). The powerful relationship that often develops between a gifted youngster and his or her mentor can reverse stubborn patterns of underachievement (Hébert & Olenchak, 2000). **Internships**, another example of community experience, are working assignments that enable gifted high school students who have expressed interest in a particular career to gain experience with that profession.

Establishing mentorships and internship experiences requires partnerships with communities. Such opportunities allow for career exploration, the development of role models, and true enrichment. However, they are not always easy to arrange (Clark, 2008). They must be aligned with students' interests, placements must carefully match mentors and students, and logistics of travel and time from school are all challenges to overcome. Local business and community clubs can be most helpful in this regard. The community holds an untapped wealth of resources, which, if carefully orchestrated, make real differences in the lives and outcomes of those with great potential that needs to be fostered and developed.

mentorship A program in which a student is paired with an adult in order to learn to apply knowledge in real-life situations

internship A working assignment that enables a student to gain experience with a profession

Summary

Gifted students do not have a disability that presents obstacles to their learning and participating in society. However, they can be handicapped by our social and educational systems, which can present barriers to their achieving their full potential. Gifted individuals possess unique intellectual abilities that can be developed into talents. Subgroups of learners who are gifted and talented—females, twice-exceptional, and diverse—need extra special attention from education professionals so that they meet their potential. One challenge facing educators is to develop and put in place a consistent array of educational options that will facilitate each individual's development.

Answering the Chapter Objectives

1. Why is there a renewed interest in gifted education?

   * The nation perceives its standing in the global economy as being threatened.
   * The "achievement gap" has narrowed at the expense of high-achieving and gifted and talented students.

2. Regardless of the definition applied, what descriptors can be used for gifted and talented individuals?

   * Demonstrate high intellectual abilities
   * Score well on tests of intelligence
   * Learn more quickly than peers
   * Apply complex thinking skills
   * Achieve significantly higher than their classmates academically
   * Tend to become leaders
   * Are sensitive
   * Are successful

3. Why are educators concerned about issues related to underrepresentation of some subgroups of gifted learners?

   * Diverse students do not have equal access to honors or to special programs for gifted students.

   * Fewer African American, Hispanic, and Native American children receive educational services for gifted students than would be expected from their percentage in the general student population.
   * The identification process is biased and favors students from, and talents encouraged in, the dominant culture.

4. What are some examples of acceleration options?

   * Advanced placement
   * Honors sections
   * Ability grouping
   * Early college entrance

5. What are two approaches to gifted education used in general education settings?

   * *Differentiated instruction and curriculum:* provide assignments that extend general education content, integrate the Internet, provide supports for twice-exceptional learners
   * *Enrichment:* interdisciplinary instruction, mentorships, internships, enrichment triad/revolving-door model, curriculum compacting

myeducationlab Now go to MyEducationLab at www.myeducationlab.com, and take the Self-Assessment to gauge your initial comprehension of chapter content. Once you have taken the Self-Assessment, use your individualized Study Plan for Chapter 14 to enhance your understanding of the concepts discussed in the chapter.

Council for Exceptional Children — ADDRESSING THE PROFESSIONAL STANDARDS

Council for Exceptional Children (CEC) knowledge standards addressed in this chapter: GT1K2, GT1K5, GT2K5, GT2K9, GT8K4, GT4S3, GT5S5, GT10S6, GT10K2

Appendix A: CEC Knowledge and Skill Standards Common Core has a full listing of the standards listed here.

Appendix B: CEC Knowledge and Skill Common Core Standards and Associated Subcategories are broken down by chapter.

Appendix A
CEC Knowledge and Skill Standards Common Core

Special Education Standard #1: Foundations

KNOWLEDGE:

CC1K1 Models, theories, and philosophies that form the basis for special education practice.

CC1K2 Laws, policies, and ethical principles regarding behavior management planning and implementation.

CC1K3 Relationship of special education to the organization and function of educational agencies.

CC1K4 Rights and responsibilities of students, parents, teachers, and other professionals, and schools related to exceptional learning needs.

CC1K5 Issues in definition and identification of individuals with exceptional learning needs, including those from culturally and linguistically diverse backgrounds.

CC1K6 Issues, assurances and due process rights related to assessment, eligibility, and placement within a continuum of services.

CC1K7 Family systems and the role of families in the educational process.

CC1K8 Historical points of view and contribution of culturally diverse groups.

CC1K9 Impact of the dominant culture on shaping schools and the individuals who study and work in them.

CC1K10 Potential impact of differences in values, languages, and customs that can exist between the home and school.

SKILL:

CC1S1 Articulate personal philosophy of special education.

Special Education Standard #2: Development and Characteristics of Learners

KNOWLEDGE:

CC2K1 Typical and atypical human growth and development.

CC2K2 Educational implications of characteristics of various exceptionalities.

CC2K3 Characteristics and effects of the cultural and environmental milieu of the individual with exceptional learning needs and the family.

CC2K4 Family systems and the role of families in supporting development.

CC2K5 Similarities and differences of individuals with and without exceptional learning needs.

CC2K6 Similarities and differences among individuals with exceptional learning needs.

CC2K7 Effects of various medications on individuals with exceptional learning needs.

Special Education Standard #3: Individual Learning Differences

KNOWLEDGE:

CC3K1 Effects an exceptional condition(s) can have on an individual's life.

CC3K2 Impact of learners' academic and social abilities, attitudes, interests, and values on instruction and career development.

CC3K3 Variations in beliefs, traditions, and values across and within cultures and their effects on relationships among individuals with exceptional learning needs, family, and schooling.

CC3K4 Cultural perspectives influencing the relationships among families, schools and communities as related to instruction.

CC3K5 Differing ways of learning of individuals with exceptional learning needs including those from culturally diverse backgrounds and strategies for addressing these differences.

Special Education Standard #4: Instructional Strategies

SKILL:

CC4S1 Use strategies to facilitate integration into various settings.

CC4S2 Teach individuals to use self-assessment, problem solving, and other cognitive strategies to meet their needs. (Replaces CC4.S12)

CC4S3 Select, adapt, and use instructional strategies and materials according to characteristics of the individual with exceptional learning needs.

CC4S4   Use strategies to facilitate maintenance and generalization of skills across learning environments.

CC4S5   Use procedures to increase the individual's self-awareness, self-management, self-control, self-reliance, and self-esteem.

CC4S6   Use strategies that promote successful transitions for individuals with exceptional learning needs.

Special Education Standard #5: Learning Environments and Social Interactions

KNOWLEDGE:

CC5K1   Demands of learning environments.

CC5K2   Basic classroom management theories and strategies for individuals with exceptional learning needs.

CC5K3   Effective management of teaching and learning.

CC5K4   Teacher attitudes and behaviors that influence behavior of individuals with exceptional learning needs.

CC5K5   Social skills needed for educational and other environments.

CC5K6   Strategies for crisis prevention and intervention.

CC5K7   Strategies for preparing individuals to live harmoniously and productively in a culturally diverse world.

CC5K8   Ways to create learning environments that allow individuals to retain and appreciate their own and each other's respective language and cultural heritage.

CC5K9   Ways specific cultures are negatively stereotyped.

CC5K10   Strategies used by diverse populations to cope with a legacy of former and continuing racism

SKILL:

CC5S1   Create a safe, equitable, positive, and supportive learning environment in which diversities are valued.

CC5S2   Identify realistic expectations for personal and social behavior in various settings.

CC5S3   Identify supports needed for integration into various program placements.

CC5S4   Design learning environments that encourage active participation in individual and group activities.

CC5S5   Modify the learning environment to manage behaviors.

CC5S6   Use performance data and information from all stakeholders to make or suggest modifications in learning environments.

CC5S7   Establish and maintain rapport with individuals with and without exceptional learning needs.

CC5S8   Teach self-advocacy.

CC5S9   Create an environment that encourages self-advocacy and increased independence.

CC5S10   Use effective and varied behavior management strategies.

CC5S11   Use the least intensive behavior management strategy consistent with the needs of the individual with exceptional learning needs.

CC5S12   Design and manage daily routines.

CC5S13   Organize, develop, and sustain learning environments that support positive intracultural and intercultural experiences.

CC5S14   Mediate controversial intercultural issues among students within the learning environment in ways that enhance any culture, group, or person.

CC5S15   Structure, direct, and support the activities of paraeducators, volunteers, and tutors.

CC5S16   Use universal precautions.

Special Education Standard #6: Communication

KNOWLEDGE:

CC6K1   Effects of cultural and linguistic differences on growth and development.

CC6K2   Characteristics of one's own culture and use of language and the ways in which these can differ from other cultures and uses of languages.

CC6K3   Ways of behaving and communicating among cultures that can lead to misinterpretation and misunderstanding.

CC6K4   Augmentative and assistive communication strategies.

SKILLS:

CC6S1   Use strategies to support and enhance communication skills of individuals with exceptional learning needs.

CC6S2   Use communication strategies and resources to facilitate understanding of subject matter for students whose primary language is not the dominant language.

Special Education Standard #7: Instructional Planning

KNOWLEDGE:

CC7K1   Theories and research that form the basis of curriculum development and instructional practice.

CC7K2   Scope and sequences of general and special curricula.

CC7K3   National, state or provincial, and local curricula standards.

CC7K4   Technology for planning and managing the teaching and learning environment.

CC7K5   Roles and responsibilities of the paraeducator related to instruction, intervention, and direct service.

SKILLS:

CC7S1   Identify and prioritize areas of the general curriculum and accommodations for individuals with exceptional learning needs.

CC7S2   Develop and implement comprehensive, longitudinal individualized programs in collaboration with team members.

CC7S3   Involve the individual and family in setting instructional goals and monitoring progress.

CC7S4   Use functional assessments to develop intervention plans.

CC7S5   Use task analysis.

CC7S6   Sequence, implement, and evaluate individualized learning objectives.

CC7S7   Integrate affective, social, and life skills with academic curricula.

CC7S8   Develop and select instructional content, resources, and strategies that respond to cultural, linguistic, and gender differences.

CC7S9   Incorporate and implement instructional and assistive technology into the educational program.

CC7S10   Prepare lesson plans.

CC7S11   Prepare and organize materials to implement daily lesson plans.

CC7S12   Use instructional time effectively.

CC7S13   Make responsive adjustments to instruction based on continual observations.

CC7S14   Prepare individuals to exhibit self-enhancing behavior in response to societal attitudes and actions.

Special Education Standard #8: Assessment

KNOWLEDGE:

CC8K1   Basic terminology used in assessment.

CC8K2   Legal provisions and ethical principles regarding assessment of individuals.

CC8K3   Screening, pre-referral, referral, and classification procedures.

CC8K4   Use and limitations of assessment instruments.

CC8K5   National, state or provincial, and local accommodations and modifications.

SKILLS:

CC8S1   Gather relevant background information.

CC8S2   Administer nonbiased formal and informal assessments.

CC8S3   Use technology to conduct assessments.

CC8S4   Develop or modify individualized assessment strategies.

CC8S5   Interpret information from formal and informal assessments.

CC8S6   Use assessment information in making eligibility, program, and placement decisions for individuals with exceptional learning needs, including those from culturally and/or linguistically diverse backgrounds.

CC8S7   Report assessment results to all stakeholders using effective communication skills.

CC8S8   Evaluate instruction and monitor progress of individuals with exceptional learning needs.

CC8S9   Create and maintain records.

Special Education Standard #9: Professional and Ethical Practice

KNOWLEDGE:

CC9K1   Personal cultural biases and differences that affect one's teaching.

CC9K2   Importance of the teacher serving as a model for individuals with exceptional learning needs.

CC9K3   Continuum of lifelong professional development.

CC9K4   Methods to remain current regarding research-validated practice.

SKILLS:

CC9S1   Practice within the CEC Code of Ethics and other standards of the profession.

CC9S2   Uphold high standards of competence and integrity and exercise sound judgment in the practice of the professional.

CC9S3   Act ethically in advocating for appropriate services.

CC9S4   Conduct professional activities in compliance with applicable laws and policies.

CC9S5   Demonstrate commitment to developing the highest education and quality-of-life potential of individuals with exceptional learning needs.

CC9S6   Demonstrate sensitivity for the culture, language, religion, gender, disability, socio-economic status, and sexual orientation of individuals.

CC9S7   Practice within one's skill limit and obtain assistance as needed.

CC9S8   Use verbal, nonverbal, and written language effectively.

CC9S9   Conduct self-evaluation of instruction.

CC9S10   Access information on exceptionalities.

CC9S11   Reflect on one's practice to improve instruction and guide professional growth.

CC9S12   Engage in professional activities that benefit individuals with exceptional learning needs, their families, and one's colleagues.

Special Education Standard #10: Collaboration

KNOWLEDGE:

CC10K1   Models and strategies of consultation and collaboration.

CC10K2   Roles of individuals with exceptional learning needs, families, and school and community personnel in planning of an individualized program.

CC10K3   Concerns of families of individuals with exceptional learning needs and strategies to help address these concerns.

CC10K4   Culturally responsive factors that promote effective communication and collaboration with individuals with exceptional learning needs, families, school personnel, and community members.

SKILLS:

CC10S1   Maintain confidential communication about individuals with exceptional learning needs.

CC10S2   Collaborate with families and others in assessment of individuals with exceptional learning needs.

CC10S3   Foster respectful and beneficial relationships between families and professionals.

CC10S4   Assist individuals with exceptional learning needs and their families in becoming active participants in the educational team.

CC10S5   Plan and conduct collaborative conferences with individuals with exceptional learning needs and their families.

CC10S6   Collaborate with school personnel and community members in integrating individuals with exceptional learning needs into various settings.

CC10S7   Use group problem solving skills to develop, implement and evaluate collaborative activities.

CC10S8   Model techniques and coach others in the use of instructional methods and accommodations.

CC10S9   Communicate with school personnel about the characteristics and needs of individuals with exceptional learning needs.

CC10S10   Communicate effectively with families of individuals with exceptional learning needs from diverse backgrounds.

CC10S11   Observe, evaluate and provide feedback to paraeducators.

Source: From CEC Knowledge and Skill Base for All Beginning Special Education Teachers. Copyright 2005

Appendix B

CEC Knowledge and Skill Standards Common Core and Associated Subcategories

CHAPTER 1

CC1K8: Historical points of view and contribution of culturally diverse groups.

CC1K5: Issues in definition and identification of individuals with exceptional learning needs, including those from culturally and linguistically diverse backgrounds.

CC10S6: Collaborate with school personnel and community members in integrating individuals with exceptional learning needs into various settings.

CC1K1: Models, theories, and philosophies that form the basis for special education practice.

CC1K4: Rights and responsibilities of students, parents, teachers, and other professionals, and schools related to exceptional learning needs.

CC1K2: Laws, policies, and ethical principles regarding behavior management planning and implementation.

CC7S1: Identify and prioritize areas of the general curriculum and accommodations for individuals with exceptional learning needs.

CHAPTER 2

GC4K1: Sources of specialized materials, curricula, and resources for individuals with disabilities.

GC1K5: Continuum of placement and services available for individuals with disabilities.

GC8K2: Laws and policies regarding referral and placement procedures for individuals with disabilities.

GC8K3: Types and importance of information concerning individuals with disabilities available from families and public agencies.

GC8S3: Select, adapt and modify assessments to accommodate the unique abilities and needs of individuals with disabilities.

CHAPTER 3

CC5K9: Ways specific cultures are negatively stereotyped.

CC1K5: Issues in definition and identification of individuals with exceptional learning needs, including those from culturally and linguistically diverse backgrounds.

CC6K2: Characteristics of one's own culture and use of language and the ways in which these can differ from other cultures and uses of languages.

CC2K3: Characteristics and effects of the cultural and environmental milieu of the individual with exceptional learning needs and the family.

CC8S2: Administer nonbiased formal and informal assessments.

CC3K5: Differing ways of learning of individuals with exceptional learning needs including those from culturally diverse backgrounds and strategies for addressing these differences.

CC5S1: Create a safe, equitable, positive, and supportive learning environment in which diversities are valued.

CC10K4: Culturally responsive factors that promote effective communication and collaboration with individuals with exceptional learning needs, families, school personnel, and community members.

CC10S10: Communicate effectively with families of individuals with exceptional learning needs from diverse backgrounds.

CHAPTER 4

CC1K8: Historical points of view and contribution of culturally diverse groups.

CC1K5: Issues in definition and identification of individuals with exceptional learning needs, including those from culturally and linguistically diverse backgrounds.

CC6K2: Characteristics of one's own culture and use of language and the ways in which these can differ from other cultures and uses of languages.

CC6K1: Effects of cultural and linguistic differences on growth and development.

CC8K4: Use and limitations of assessment instruments.

CC6K4: Augmentative and assistive communication strategies.

CC7S14: Prepare individuals to exhibit self-enhancing behavior in response to societal attitudes and actions.

CC10S9: Communicate with school personnel about the characteristics and needs of individuals with exceptional learning needs.

CC10K3: Concerns of families of individuals with exceptional learning needs and strategies to help address these concerns.

CHAPTER 5

LD1K1: Historical foundations, classical studies, and major contributors in the field of learning disabilities.

LD1K5: Current definitions and issues related to the identification of individuals with learning disabilities.

LD2K3: Psychological, social, and emotional characteristics of individuals with learning disabilities.

LD2K1: Etiologies of learning disabilities.

LD8S1: Choose and administer assessment instruments appropriate to the individual with learning disabilities.

LD4S9: Implement systematic instruction in teaching reading comprehension and monitoring strategies.

LD5S1: Plan instruction for independent functional life skills relevant to the community, personal living, sexuality, and employment.

LD10K1: Co-planning and co-teaching methods to strengthen content acquisition of individuals with learning disabilities.

LD10K2: Services, networks, and organizations that provide support across the life span for individuals with learning disabilities.

CHAPTER 6

GC1K3: Historical foundations, classic studies, major contributors, major legislation, and current issues related to knowledge and practice.

GC1K1: Definitions and issues related to the identification of individuals with disabilities.

GC2K4: Psychological and social-emotional characteristics of individuals with disabilities.

GC2K1: Etiology and diagnosis related to various theoretical approaches.

GC8S1: Implement procedures for assessing and reporting both appropriate and problematic social behaviors of individuals with disabilities.

GC4S3: Teach learning strategies and study skills to acquire academic content.

GC7K2: Model career, vocational, and transition programs for individuals with disabilities.

GC10S2: Select, plan, and coordinate activities of related services personnel to maximize direct instruction for individuals with disabilities.

GC10K1: Parent education programs and behavior management guides that address severe behavior problems and facilitation communication for individuals with disabilities.

CHAPTER 7

BD1K3: Foundations and issues related to knowledge and practice in emotional/behavioral disorders.

BD1K1: Educational terminology and definitions of individuals with emotional/behavioral disorders.

BD2K3: Social characteristics of individuals with emotional/behavioral disorders.

BD2K1: Etiology and diagnosis related to various theoretical approaches in the field of emotional/behavioral disorders.

BD8S2: Assess appropriate and problematic social behaviors of individuals with emotional/behavioral disorders.

BD4S1: Use strategies from multiple theoretical approaches for individuals with emotional/behavioral disorders.

BD4K3: Resources and techniques used to transition individuals with emotional/behavioral disorders into and out of school and post-school environments.

BD10K4: Role of professional groups and referral agencies in identifying, assessing, and providing services to individuals with emotional/behavioral disorders.

BD10K2: Parent education programs and behavior management guides that address severe behavioral problems and facilitate communication for individuals with emotional/behavioral disorders.

CHAPTER 8

MR1K4: Historical foundations and classic studies of mental retardation/developmental disabilities.

MR1K1: Definitions and issues related to the identification of individuals with mental retardation/developmental disabilities.

MR2K3: Psychological, social/emotional, and motor characteristics of individuals with mental retardation/developmental disabilities.

MR2K1: Causes and theories of intellectual disabilities and implications for prevention.

MR8S1: Select, adapt and use instructional assessment tools and methods to accommodate the abilities and needs of individuals with mental retardation and developmental disabilities.

MR4K1: Specialized materials for individuals with mental retardation/developmental disabilities.

MR7S3: Plan instruction for independent functional life skills relevant to the community, personal living, sexuality, and employment.

MR10S1: Collaborate with team members to plan transition to adulthood that encourages full community participation.

CHAPTER 9

PH1K2: Historical foundations, related to knowledge and practices in physical and health disabilities.

PH1K1: Issues and educational definitions of individuals with physical and health disabilities.

PH2K2: Etiology and characteristics of physical and health disabilities across the life span.

PH2K3: Secondary health care issues that accompany specific physical and health disabilities.

PH8S3: Use results of specialized evaluations to make instructional decisions for individuals with physical and health disabilities.

PH5K1: Adaptations of educational environments necessary to accommodate individuals with physical and health disabilities.

PH10S6: Participate in transdisciplinary teams to provide integrated care and transition services.

PH10K3: Roles and responsibilities of school and community-based medical and related services personnel.

PH10S5: Collaborate with families of and service providers to individuals who are chronically or terminally ill.

CHAPTER 10

DH1K4: Issues and trends in the field of education of individuals who are deaf or hard of hearing.

DH1K1: Educational definitions, identification criteria, labeling issues, and incidence and prevalence figures for individuals who are deaf or hard of hearing.

DH1K3: Etiologies of hearing loss that can result in additional sensory, motor, and/or learning differences.

DH2K2: Impact of the onset of hearing loss, age of identification, and provision of services on the development of the individual who is deaf or hard of hearing.

DH8K2: Specialized procedures for evaluation, eligibility, placement, and program planning for individuals who are deaf or hard of hearing.

DH4K3: Instructional strategies for teaching individuals who are deaf or hard of hearing.

DH7K1: Model programs, including career/vocational and transition, for individuals who are deaf or hard of hearing.

DH10S1: Coordinate support personnel to meet the diverse communication needs of the individual who is deaf or hard of hearing and the primary caregivers.

DH10S2: Provide families with knowledge, skills, and support to make choices regarding communication modes/philosophies and educational options across the lifespan.

CHAPTER 11

VI1K2: Historical foundations of education of individuals with visual impairments.

VI1K3: Educational definitions, identification criteria, labeling issues, and incidence and prevalence figures for individuals with visual impairments.

VI2K5: Psychosocial aspects of visual impairment.

VI2K1: Development of the human visual system.

VI8K2: Ethical considerations, laws, and policies for assessment of individuals with visual impairments.

VI4K8: Strategies for teaching basic concepts to individuals with visual impairments.

VI10K1: Strategies for assisting families and other team members in planning appropriate transitions for individuals with visual impairments.

VI10K2: Services, networks, publications for and organizations of individuals with visual impairments.

VI10S1: Help families and other team members understand the impact of a visual impairment on learning and experience.

CHAPTER 12

IC1K2: Historical foundations, classic studies, major contributors, major legislation, and current issues related to knowledge and practice.

IC1K1: Definitions and issues related to the identification of individuals with disabilities.

IC2K4: Psychological and social-emotional characteristics of individuals with disabilities.

IC2K3: Etiologies and medical aspects of conditions affecting individuals with disabilities.

IC8K1: Specialized terminology used in the assessment of individuals with disabilities.

IC4S3: Use a variety of nonaversive techniques to control targeted behavior and maintain attention of individuals with disabilities.

IC4K4: Resources, and techniques used to transition individuals with disabilities into and out of school and post-school environments.

IC10K2: Collaborative and/or consultative role of the special education teacher in the reintegration of individuals with disabilities.

IC10K1: Parent education programs and behavior management guides that address severe behavior problems and facilitation communication for individuals with disabilities.

CHAPTER 13

IC1K5: Laws and policies related to provision of specialized health care in educational settings.

IC1K1: Definitions and issues related to the identification of individuals with disabilities.

IC2K3: Etiologies and medical aspects of conditions affecting individuals with disabilities.

IC2K1: Etiology and diagnosis related to various theoretical approaches

IC8K3: Types and importance of information concerning individuals with disabilities available from families and public agencies.

IC4S2: Use appropriate adaptations and assistive technology for all individuals with disabilities.

IC7K1: Model career, vocational, and transition programs for individuals with disabilities.

IC10S4: Collaborate with team members to plan transition to adulthood that encourages full community participation.

IC10S5: Collaborate with families of and service providers to individuals who are chronically or terminally ill.

CHAPTER 14

GT1K2: Models, theories, and philosophies that form the basis for gifted education.

GT1K5: Issues in definition and identification of individuals with gifts and talents, including those from culturally and linguistically diverse backgrounds.

GT2K5: Characteristics and effects of the cultural and environmental milieu of the child and the family.

GT2K9: Effects of families on the development of individuals with gifts and talents.

GT8K4: Screening, pre-referral, referral, and identification procedures for individuals with gifts and talents.

GT4S3: Teach individuals to use self-assessment, problem solving and other cognitive strategies to meet their needs.

GT5S5: Create an environment that encourages self-advocacy and increased independence.

GT10S6: Communicate with school personnel about the characteristics and needs of individuals with gifts and talents.

GT10K2: Concerns of families of individuals with gifts and talents and strategies to help address these concerns.

Source: From CEC Knowledge and Skill Base for All Beginning Special Education Teachers. Copyright 2005

Glossary

ability grouping Placing students with comparable achievement and skill levels in the same classes or courses

absence seizures or petit mal seizures Seizures characterized by a short lapse in consciousness; petit mal seizures

acceleration Moving students through a curriculum or years of schooling in a shorter period of time than usual

accommodation The focusing process of the lens of the eye

accommodations Supports to compensate for disabilities; adjustments to assignments or tests

acquired immunodeficiency syndrome (AIDS) A usually fatal medical syndrome caused by infection from the human immunodeficiency virus (HIV)

activity schedules Written or pictorial directions to help perform skills and routines

adapted physical education (PE) A special education direct service, not a related service, that teaches physical education, recreational skills, and sports to individuals with disabilities

adaptive behavior Performance of everyday life skills expected of adults

advance organizers A tactic that previews lectures and provides organizing structures to acquaint students with the content, its organization, and importance before the lesson

advanced placement (AP) courses High school courses that carry college credit

adventitious blindness Blindness acquired after the age of 2

aggression Hostile and attacking behavior, which can include verbal communication, directed toward self, others, or the physical environment

air conduction audiometry method A method to test hearing that uses pure-tone sounds generated by an audiometer

alerting devices Assistive devices for people who are deaf to make them aware of events in their environment through a means other than sound (e.g., flashing lights, vibrators)

alternate assessments Means of measuring the progress of students who do not participate in the general education curriculum

alternate achievement standards Fewer objectives or different expectations for achievement when participating in the general education curriculum

alternative and augmentative communication (AAC) Assistive technology that helps individuals communicate, including devices that actually produce speech

American Sign Language (ASL) The language of Deaf Americans that uses manual communication; a signal of Deaf culture

Americans with Disabilities Act (ADA) Antidiscrimination legislation guaranteeing basic civil rights to people with disabilities

analog hearing aids Assistive listening devices that amplify all sounds uniformly, including background noise and speech sounds regardless of individuals' hearing profiles

anorexia Intense fear of gaining weight, disturbed body image, chronic absence or refusal of appetite for food, causing severe weight loss (25% of body weight)

anxiety disorders Conditions causing painful uneasiness, emotional tension, or emotional confusion

array of services Constellation of special education services, personnel, and educational placements

articulation disorder Abnormal production of speech sounds

Asperger syndrome One of the autism spectrum disorders (ASD) where cognition is usually in the average or above average range

assistive listening devices (ALDs) Equipment (e.g., hearing aids, audio loops, FM transmission devices) that helps improve use of residual hearing

assistive technology (AT) Equipment (devices) or services to help compensate for an individual's disabilities

Assistive Technology Act (ATA) Law that facilitates increased accessibility through technology

asthma The most common, chronic health condition resulting in difficulty breathing

ataxia cerebral palsy Characterized by movement disrupted by impaired balance and depth perception

athetoid cerebral palsy Characterized by purposeless and uncontrolled involuntary movements

attention deficit hyperactivity disorder A condition of hyperactivity, impulsivity, inattention; included in other health impairments

attributions Explanations individuals give themselves for their successes or failures

audio input devices Assistive technology to help people with visual disabilities by changing what would be seen into information that is heard

audio loop A listening device that directs sound from the source directly to the listener's ear through a specially designed hearing aid

audiodescriptions An assistive audio input technology; presents visual information on screen or stage via oral narrations

audiogram A grid or graph used to display a person's hearing abilities

audiologist A related service provider who diagnoses hearing losses and auditory problems

audiometer An instrument audiologists use to measure hearing

auditory nerve The eighth cranial nerve; carries messages from the hearing mechanisms to the brain

augmentative and alternative communication devices (AAC) Other methods for communicating, such as communication boards, communication books, sign language, and computerized voices; assistive technology that helps individuals communicate, including devices that actually produce speech

authentic assessments Performance measures that use work generated by the student

autism One of the autistic spectrum disorders (ASD); ranges from low to high functioning

autism spectrum disorders (ASD) A group of disorders with similar characteristics including difficulties with communication, social interaction, and manneristic behaviors

autistic savant An individual who displays many behaviors associated with autism yet also possesses discrete abilities and unusual talents

automatic speech recognition (ASR) Technology that converts speech to text almost instantaneously

behavior analysis Research methodology using single-case designs; derived from the work of B. F. Skinner; paradigms describing human behavior in terms of events that stimulate or cause a behavior's occurrence, maintains behavior, and increases its likelihood

behavior analyst A support professional with expertise in applying principles of behavior to develop interventions for students with ASD and other disabilities

behavioral intervention plan Includes a functional assessment and procedures to prevent and intervene for behavioral infractions

Best Buddies A program that pairs college students with people with intellectual disabilities to build relationships, friendships, and opportunities for supports

bilingual education Teaching in and seeking mastery of students' native language and English

bilingual paraprofessionals Classroom assistants fluent in at least two languages

bilingual-bicultural (bi-bi) approach A method of instruction for students who are deaf, combining practices of ESL and bilingual education; Uses ASL as the native language and teaches reading and writing in English as a second language

blindness The degree of visual loss; not having a functional use of sight

Board Certified Behavior Analyst™ (BCBA) A behavior analyst who has fulfilled national certification requirements, including coursework and fieldwork, has passed a competency exam, and holds at least a master's degree in a related field (e.g., education, psychology)

bone conduction audiometry method A method to test for conductive hearing loss that uses a vibrator placed on a person's forehead so sound bypasses the outer and middle ear and goes directly to the inner ear

braille A system of reading and writing that uses dot codes that are embossed on paper; tactile reading; created in 1824 by Louis Braille as a precursor to the method used today

bulimia Chronically causing oneself to vomit or otherwise remove food to limit weight gain

captions Subtitles that print words spoken in film or video

case manager A professional who coordinates related services for individual students

cerebral palsy (CP) A neuromotor impairment; a nonprogressive disease resulting in motor difficulties associated with communication problems and mobility problems

child find A requirement of IDEA '04 to help refer and identify children and youth with disabilities

childhood disintegrative disorder (CDD) A pervasive developmental disorder; the individual has typical development until about the age of 5 or 6

civil rights Rights that all citizens of a society are supposed to have to ensure social justice

classifying A thinking skill; the ability to categorize items or grouping concepts by their common characteristics

classroom English English skills required to access the general education curriculum and profit from instruction

cleft lip A congenital condition where the upper lip is not formed or connected correctly to allow for correct articulation of sounds, resulting in a speech impairment

cleft palate An opening in the roof of the mouth causing too much air to pass through the nasal cavity, resulting in a speech impairment

closed captions Subtitles available only to those who select the option

closed-circuit television (CCTV) An assistive visual input technology; uses a television to increase the size of objects or print

cochlea Contains the organs of hearing

cochlear implant Microprocessor, surgically placed in the hearing mechanism, that replaces the cochlea so people with sensorineural hearing loss can perceive sounds

CODA A child of a Deaf adult who may or may not be Deaf

code switching Using two languages in the same conversation; a sign of developing dual language proficiency

collaboration Professionals working in partnerships to provide educational

services; school personnel with different expertise working in partnerships

communication Transfer of knowledge, ideas, opinions, and feelings

communication boards Low-tech assistive technology devices that display pictures or words that the individual can point to in order to communicate

communication disorders Disorders in speech, language, or hearing that impair communications

communication signals A variety of nonverbal cues that announce some immediate event, person, action, or emotion

communication symbols Voice, letters of the alphabet, or gestures used to send communication messages

communicative competence Proficiency in all aspects of communication in social and learning situations

community-based instruction (CBI) A strategy of teaching functional and vocational skills in the environments in which they occur

comorbidity coexisting disabilities

complex partial seizures A type of epilepsy causing a lapse in consciousness

composition index A tool for measuring disproportionate representation in which the percentage of students from a particular racial group receiving special education services is compared with their percentage in the overall school population

computerized language translators Computers that provide translations of written text from one language to another

conduct disorders A psychiatric term describing externalizing, acting-out behaviors

conductive hearing loss Hearing impairment due to damage or obstruction to the outer or middle ear that obstructs transfer of sound to the inner ear

congenital blindness Blindness present at birth or occurring during early infancy

consulting teacher Special education teachers serving as a resource to general education teachers

content An aspect of language that governs the intent and meaning of the message delivered in a communication

content enhancement strategies Methods to help students organize and remember important concepts

contextualized instruction Embeds students' cultures, interests, and backgrounds into instruction

continuum of services Describes each level of special education services as being more restrictive and coming in a lock-stepped sequence

conversational English Being able to use English in general communications but not necessarily for academic learning

cooperative learning Small groups of students working together to learn the same material

cornea The transparent, curved part of the front of the eye

co-teaching General and special education teachers team teaching

cross-cultural dissonance When the home and school cultures are in conflict

cued speech Hand signals for "difficult to see" speech sounds; assists with speech reading

cultural pluralism The concept that all cultural groups are valued components of the society with each group's language and traditions maintained

culturally competent Knowing and understanding the cultural standards from diverse communities

culturally diverse Being from a cultural group that is not Euro-centric or of mainstream America

culturally responsive Curriculum that includes multiple perspectives

curriculum-based measurement (CBM) Evaluating students' performance by collecting data frequently and directly on academic tasks

curriculum compacting Saving instructional time for enrichment activities

Deaf Profound hearing loss

Deaf culture Structures of social relationships, language (ASL), dance, theater, literature, and other cultural activities that bind the Deaf community

Deaf of Deaf Members of the Deaf community who are prelingually deaf and have at least one parent who is Deaf

deaf-blindness A dual disability involving both vision and hearing problems

decibel (dB) The unit of measure for intensity of sound

demographics Characteristics of a human population

depression A state of despair and dejected mood

developmental disabilities Severe disabilities including intellectual disabilities

dialects Words and pronunciation from a geographical region or ethnic group, different from those of standard language

differentiated curriculum The flexible application of curriculum targets to ensure content mastery, in-depth learning, and exploration of additional issues and themes; instruction above and beyond the general education curriculum and content

differentiating instruction Adjusting instruction to meet the needs and learning styles of individuals or groups of learners; providing an individualized array of instructional interventions

digital divide Unequal availability of technology due to socioeconomic status

digital hearing aids Assistive listening devices that amplify sound according to individuals' hearing profiles

dignity of risk The principle that taking ordinary risks and chances is part of the human experience

disability Result of conditions or impairments

discrepancy formulas Calculations used to determine the gap between achievement and intelligence (potential); used to identify students with learning disabilities

discrete trial teaching A highly structured technique using teacher-directed activities, repetition of skills through practice, and use of rewards

disproportionate representation Unequal proportion of group membership; over- or underrepresentation

distance education technology Telecommunications technology used to deliver instruction to many different sites

distance senses Senses—both hearing and vision—used to gain information; developed to guard against danger

Down syndrome A chromosomal disorder with identifiable physical characteristics resulting in delays in physical and intellectual development

dual discrepancy A condition where both rate of learning and performance are below that of classmates

due process hearing Noncourt proceeding before an impartial hearing officer used if parents and school personnel disagree on a special education issue

dynamic assessment Assessment process used by SLPs to determine potential effectiveness of different language interventions

dysfluencies Hesitations or repetitions of sounds or words that interrupt a person's flow of speech—stuttering, for example; a speech disorder

early intervening Providing explicit and intensive instruction to all struggling students to prevent compounding learning problems

Ebonics A learned and rule-governed dialect of nonstandard English, spoken by some African Americans

e-books Electronic versions of textbooks allowing for the application of universal design for learning

e-Buddies A program that creates e-mail friendships between people with and without intellectual disabilities

echolalia Repeating words, sounds, or sound patterns with no communicative intent, meaning, or understanding; a speech pattern that may occur immediately or even days later

Education for All Handicapped Children Act (EHA) or Public Law 94-142; Individuals with Disabilities Education Act (IDEA) Originally passed in 1975 to guarantee a free appropriate public education for all students with disabilities; the special education law

educational interpreters Related service providers for deaf students who translate or convert spoken messages to the deaf person's preferred mode of manual communication

emotional disturbance The term used in IDEA '04 for emotional or behavioral disorders

emotional or behavioral disorders A disability characterized by behavioral or emotional responses very different from all norms and referent groups with adverse effects on educational performance

English as a second language (ESL) Instructing students in English until English proficiency is achieved; does not provide support in the student's native or primary language

English language learners (ELLs), English learners (ELs) or limited English proficient (LEP) Students learning English as their second language

enlarged print Adjusted size of print so individuals with low vision can read

enrichment Adding topics or skills to the traditional curriculum or presenting a particular topic in more depth

enrichment triad/revolving-door model An inclusive model for gifted education where 15% to 20% of a school's students participate in activities to develop thinking skills, problem solving, and creativity

epilepsy or seizure disorders A tendency to experience recurrent seizures resulting in convulsions; caused by abnormal discharges of neurons in the brain

eugenics A worldwide movement of over 100 years ago that sought to protect society from false threats of people who are different

Eustachian tube Equalizes pressure on both sides of the eardrum

evidence- or data-based practices Thoroughly researched, validated, proven effective through evidence or years of clinical practice

executive functions Higher-order cognitive functions that influence the ability to plan, self-regulate, and engage in goal-directed behavior

expanded core curriculum Includes skills such as orientation and mobility, braille reading, independent living skills, and use of assistive technology in addition to the general education

explicit instruction Directly instructing on the topic of concern

expressive language The ability to convey thoughts, feelings, or information

externalizing behaviors Behaviors directed towards others (e.g., aggressive behavior)

fetal alcohol spectrum disorders, including **fetal alcohol syndrome (FAS)** and **fetal alcohol effects (FAE)** Congenital conditions caused by the mother's drinking alcohol during pregnancy resulting in reduced intellectual functioning, behavior problems, and sometimes physical differences

fidelity Instruction or intervention is implemented effectively and is consistent with the methods outlined by the program's instructions

field of vision The width of the area a person can see; measured in degrees

finger spelling A manual communication system that uses the English alphabet

FM (frequency-modulated) transmission devices Assistive listening devices that provide oral transmissions directly from the teacher to students with hearing loss

form The rule system of language; includes phonology, morphology, and syntax

fragile X syndrome The most common inherited reason for intellectual disabilities

free appropriate public education (FAPE) Ensures that students with disabilities receive necessary education and services without cost to the family

frequency of sound The number of vibrations per second of molecules through some medium like air, water, or wires, causing sound

functional behavioral assessments (FBA) A process in which interviews, observations, and environmental manipulations are conducted to determine why certain behaviors occur; behavioral evaluations to determine the exact nature of problem behaviors

functional communication training A strategy to reduce problem behaviors by teaching functionally equivalent alternatives

functional curriculum Teaching skills needed for daily living; instruction in natural settings relating to life and vocational skills

generalize To transfer learning from particular instances to other environments, people, times, or events

generalized seizures Seizures involving the entire brain

generalized tonic-clonic seizures Grand mal seizures; the most serious type of epilepsy, resulting in convulsions and loss of consciousness

generic supports Public benefits to which everyone has access

gifted or talented Terms describing individuals with high levels of intelligence, creativity, outstanding abilities, and capacity for high performance

goal setting Determining desired behavior and its criterion

grade skipping A form of acceleration; advances students to a grade ahead of their age peers

graphic organizers Visual aids used to assist students organize, understand, and remember academic content

hair cells Part of the cochlea that responds to different frequencies of sound and produces electrochemical signals sent on to the brain

hand over hand Sign language for individuals with deaf-blindness where signs are conveyed through touch

handicaps Challenges and barriers imposed by others

hard of hearing Hearing losses that impair understanding of sounds and communication

health disabilities or special health care needs Chronic or acute health problems resulting in limited strength, vitality, or alertness; other health impairments

hearing aids Assistive listening devices that intensify sound

hertz (Hz) The unit of measure for sound frequency

heterogeneity Variation among members in a group

high-incidence disabilities Special education categories with the most students

high-stakes testing State- and districtwide assessments to ensure all students' progress in the curriculum

high-tech devices Complex assistive technology devices that use computers or computer chips

homeless Not having a permanent home

honors sections Advanced classes for any student who shows high achievement in specific subject areas

human immunodeficiency virus (HIV) A microorganism that infects the immune system, impairing the body's ability to fight infections

hyperactivity Impaired ability to sit or concentrate for long periods of time

IEP Teams Multidisciplinary teams that guide individualized special education services for each student with a disability

impulsivity Impaired ability to control one's own behavior

inattention Inability to pay attention or focus

incidental learning Understanding and mastering knowledge and skills through observation and without instruction

individualized education program (IEP) Management tool to identify and organize needed services

individualized family service plan (IFSP) Identifies and organizes services and resources for infants and toddlers (birth to 3) and their families

intellectual disabilities, mental retardation, or cognitive disabilities Impaired intellectual functioning, limited adapted behavior, need for supports, and initial occurrence before age 18

intellectual functioning Cognitive abilities

interim alternative educational setting (IAES) Special education placement to ensure progress toward IEP goals, assigned when a serious behavioral infraction requires removal from current placement

internalizing behaviors Behaviors directed inward (e.g., withdrawn, anxious, depressed)

internship A working assignment that enables a student to gain experience with a profession

intervener A paraprofessional who serves many roles including sign language interpreter and teacher

IQ/achievement discrepancy The old criterion required for learning disabilities identification; 2-year difference between potential or expected performance (based on a score on a test of intelligence [IQ]) and a score from an achievement test

iris The colored part of the eye

itinerant Working in different locations

job coach A transition specialist who teaches vocational skills in the community and in actual job settings

joint attention The ability to mutually interact or to share interest in events or objects

juvenile arthritis A chronic and painful muscular condition seen in children

juvenile diabetes An inability of the body to produce insulin

language Rule-based method used for communication

language delays Slowed development of language skills; may or may not result in language impairments

language differences Emerging second language acquisition or nonstandard English

language disorder Difficulty or inability to master the various systems of rules in language, which then interferes with communication

language-sensitive environments Classrooms that encourage, foster, and support language development

lead poisoning A preventable reason of intellectual disabilities caused by the toxin lead in the environment

learned helplessness Usually a result of repeated failure or excessive control by others; individuals become less willing to attempt tasks or understand their actions result in success

learning disability (LD) A disability of unexpected underachievement typically involving reading that is resistant to treatment

least restrictive environment (LRE) Educational placement with the most inclusion and integration with typical learners as possible and appropriate

legally blind A category of blindness used to qualify for federal and state benefits

lens The part of the eye, located behind the iris, that brings objects seen into focus

letter fluency Quickly reading and naming letters of the alphabet

limb deficiencies Missing or nonfunctioning arms or legs resulting in mobility problems

linguistically diverse Having a home or native language other than English

loudness An aspect of voice, referring to the intensity of the sound produced while speaking

low-incidence disabilities Prevalence and incidence are very low; special education categories with few students

low vision The degree of visual loss; vision is still useful for learning or the execution of a task

low-tech devices Simple assistive technology devices such as communication boards, homemade cushions, or a classroom railing

manifestation determination Determines whether a student's disciplinary problems are due to the disability

mastery measurement A system of progress monitoring; evaluates learning of discrete skills frequently, often daily

mathematics/learning disabilities A condition where a student's learning disability is most significant in areas of mathematics

medically fragile A term used to describe the status of individuals with health disabilities

melting pot The concept of a homogenized United States in which cultural traditions and home languages are abandoned for the new American culture

mentorship A program in which a student is paired with an adult in order to learn to apply knowledge in real-life situations

mnemonics A learning strategy that promotes remembering information by associating the first letters of items in a list with a word, sentence, or picture (e.g., HOMES for the Great Lakes)

mobility The ability to travel safely and efficiently from one place to another; a topic of instruction for students who are blind

modifications Adjustments to assignments or tests, reducing the requirements

modified achievement standards Goals and benchmarks from the general education curriculum but modified by reducing the number of objectives or their complexity

morphology Rules that govern the structure and form of words and comprise the basic meaning of words

motivation Need to succeed, drive not to fail

multicultural education Incorporates the cultures of all students into instruction

multidisciplinary teams Individually determined groups of professionals with different expertise

multiple intelligences Multidimensional approach to intelligence; allowing

those exceptional in any one of eight areas to be identified as gifted

multiple-severe disabilities Exceptionally challenging disabilities where more than one condition influences learning, independence, and the range of intensive and pervasive supports the individual and the family require; developmental disabilities

multitiered approaches Approaches that provide levels of more and more intensive services to prevent or intervene early

multitiered instruction Differentiating instruction for behavior, social skills, or academic areas to intervene early, prevent disabilities, and support struggling learners with and without disabilities

muscular/skeletal conditions Conditions affecting muscles or bones and resulting in limited functioning

mutual accommodation Acceptance and use of students' language and culture within the classroom, while also teaching them the expectations and culture of the school

National Instructional Materials Accessibility Standard (NIMAS) Assists states in providing accessible or e-versions of textbooks to students with disabilities; called out in IDEA '04

nativism A strong opposition to immigration, which is seen as a threat to maintaining a country's dominant culture

natural supports Supports that occur as a natural result of family and community living

neural tube defects Another name for spinal cord disorders, which always involve the spinal column and usually the spinal cord

neuromotor impairments Conditions involving the nerves, muscles, and motor functioning

No Child Left Behind Act (NCLB) Reauthorization of the Elementary and Secondary Education Act mandating higher standards for both students and teachers, including an accountability system

noise-induced hearing loss A major cause of sensorineural hearing loss due to damage to the hair cells from sustained noise in the environment

noncategorical or cross-categorical special education Special education services delivered by students' needs, not by their identified disability

nondiscriminatory testing Assessment that accounts for cultural and linguistic diversity

nonpaid supports Ordinary assistance given by friends and neighbors

normal or bell-shaped curve Theoretical construct of the typical distribution of human traits such as intelligence

normalization Making available ordinary

patterns of life and conditions of everyday living

obturator A device that creates a closure between the oral and nasal cavities when the soft palate is missing or damaged; helps compensate for a cleft palate

occupational therapist (OT) A professional who directs activities that help improve muscular control and develop self-help skills and provides a special education–related service

open captions Subtitles or tickers that are part of the screen image for everyone to see

ophthalmologist A medical doctor who specializes in eye disorders

optician A person who fills either the ophthalmologist's or optometrist's prescriptions for glasses or corrective lenses

optometrist A professional who measures vision and can prescribe corrective lenses (eyeglasses or contact lenses)

oral-only approach A method of instruction for students with hearing loss, using only oral communication

orientation The mental map people use to move through environments; a topic of instruction for students who are blind

orientation and mobility (O&M) instructors Professionals who teach students who are blind to move freely through their environments and travel safely from place to place independently

orthopedic impairments The term used in IDEA '04 for physical disabilities resulting in special health care needs

ossicles Three tiny bones (hammer or malleus, anvil or incus, stirrup or stapes) in the middle ear that pass information to the cochlea

other health impairments The term used in IDEA '04 for health disabilities; special health care needs

otitis media Middle ear infection that can interrupt normal language development

otoacoustic emissions (OAEs) The low level of sound produced when the hair cells inside the inner ear vibrate

overrepresentation Too many students from a diverse group participating in a special education category, beyond the level expected from their proportion of students

partial seizures Seizures involving only part of the brain

peer supports An instructional strategy that facilitates social interaction and access to the general education curriculum

peer tutoring Classmates helping each other

Peer-Assisted Learning Strategies (PALS) A validated method in which students coach each other to improve academic learning; peer tutoring for reading and mathematics

people first language Appropriate way to refer to most groups of people with disabilities

perinatal During birth

peripheral vision The outer area of a person's visual field

personal data assistants (PDAs) Devices that allow the user to send text-messages, use e-mail, and access the web via wireless telephone systems

personal readers People who read for others

pervasive developmental disorder—not otherwise specified (PDD-NOS) One of the autistic spectrum disorders (ASD) in which not all three ASD characteristics (problems in communication, social interaction, and repetitive or manneristic behaviors) are present or they are mild

phenylketonuria (PKU) An inherited condition that results in intellectual disabilities from a buildup of toxins from foods containing amino acids (like milk)

phonics The sounds represented by letters and letter groups

phonological awareness Understanding, identifying, and applying sound–symbol relationships (letter sounds, rhyming); identifying, separating, or manipulating sound units of spoken language

phonology The rules within a language used to govern the combination of speech sounds to form words and sentences

photoscreening A system used to test visual acuity for those who cannot participate in the evaluation either because of age or ability

physical disabilities Conditions related to a physical deformity or impairment of the skeletal system and associated motor function; physical impairments; orthopedic impairments

physical therapist (PT) A professional who treats physical disabilities through many nonmedical means and works to improve motor skills; a special education–related service provider

picture exchange communication system (PECS) A technique where pictures are used to communicate; for individuals with autism who are nonverbal

pinna Outer structure of the ear

pitch An aspect of voice; its perceived high or low sound quality

portfolio assessment Authentic assessments where students select their work for evaluation

positive behavior support A three-tiered model of support offering progressively more intensive levels of intervention

postlingually deaf Having lost the ability to hear after developing language; acquired or adventitious deafness

postnatal After birth

postsecondary education Educational opportunities beyond high school; 2-year or 4-year colleges and univer-sities

pragmatics The appropriate use of language in social contexts

preictal or aura stage Warning of an imminent seizure in the form of heightened sensory awareness

prelingually deaf Having lost the ability to hear before developing language

prenatal Before birth

prereferral First step in the IEP process that begins to determine a student's eligibility for special education services

prevalence Total number of cases at a given time

process/product debate The argument about whether perceptual training or direct (explicit) instruction is more effective to teach reading

progress monitoring Assessing student's learning through direct and frequent assessments directly on the target of concern; systematically and frequently assessing students' improvement directly on the skills being taught

prosthetics Artificial arms or legs

pull-in programming Special education or related services delivered exclusively in the general education classroom

pull-out programs Providing special services outside the general education classroom

pupil The hole in the center of the iris that expands and contracts, admitting light to the eye

pure sounds Pure-tone sound waves; used across specific frequencies to test an individual's hearing ability

quality of life A subjective and individual-specific concept reflecting social relationships, personal satisfaction, employment, choice, leisure, independence, and community presence

reading/learning disabilities A condition where a student's learning disability is most significant in reading

real-time captioning (RTC) Practically instantaneous translations of speech into print; an accommodation for deaf students attending lectures

rear window captioning (RWC) Closed captioning used in movie theaters that projects printed words on the back of the seat in front of the moviegoer

receptive language Understanding information that is received, either through seeing, hearing, or touching

recreational therapy A related service that helps students learn to access community and recreational programs

refreshable braille display Allows for short sections of braille text to be downloaded to a computer

Rehabilitation Act of 1973, Section 504 First law to outline the basic civil rights of people with disabilities

related services Special education services from a wide range of disciplines and professions

residual hearing The amount of functional hearing a person has

residual vision The amount and degree of vision a person has functional use of, despite a visual disability

resistant to treatment A defining characteristic of learning disabilities; when validated methods typically applied in general education settings are not effective to cause sufficient learning

resonating system Oral and nasal cavities where speech sounds are formed

respiratory system The system of organs whose primary function is to take in oxygen and expel gases

response to intervention (RTI) A multitiered prereferral method of increasingly intensive interventions; used to identify "nonresponders" or students with learning disabilities

retention Repeating a school year or delaying entrance into kindergarten or first grade

retina The inside lining of the eye

retinopathy of prematurity (ROP) A cause of visual disabilities from prematurity where excess oxygen used to help the infant breathe, but damages the retina

Rett syndrome A pervasive developmental disorder with a known genetic cause that occurs only in girls

risk index A tool for measuring disproportionate representation, representing the percentage of students from a particular racial group who receive special education services

risk ratio A tool for measuring disproportionate representation where the risk index for one group is divided by the risk index for another group. A risk ratio of 1.0 indicates proportionate representation. Risk ratios above or below 1.0 represent over- and under-representation respectively

robotics The science of using technology to create high-tech devices that perform motor skills

scaffolding Differentiating instruction by providing assistance and supports by modeling and practice of multistepped skill or content areas and gradually removing the supports until accurate, independent performance is achieved

schizophrenia A rare disorder in children that includes bizarre delusions and dissociation with reality

school nurse A professional who assists with or delivers medical services at school, coordinates health services, designs accommodations for students with special health care needs, and provides a special education–related service

self-advocacy Expressing one's rights and needs

self-determination Making decisions, choosing preferences, and exercising self-advocacy needed for independent living

self-injury Self-inflicted injuries (head banging, eye poking)

self-instruction or self-talk Self-induced statements to assist in self-regulation

self-management or self-regulation strategies Includes many techniques, used individually or in combinations by the individual, to modify behavior or academic performance

self-monitoring Keeping a record (data) of one's own performance

self-reinforcement Awarding self-selected reinforcers or rewards to oneself contingent on achieving criterion

semantics The system within a language that governs content, intent, and meanings of spoken and written language

sensorineural hearing loss Hearing impairment due to damage to the inner ear or the auditory nerve

service or assistance animals Animals (dogs, monkeys, guide dogs) trained to serve the individual needs of people with disabilities

service manager Case manager or coordinator who oversees the implementation and evaluation of IFSPs

sheltered English instruction Restating concepts and instructions, using visuals and concrete examples, to provide language support to ELLs

siblings Brothers and sisters

sickle cell anemia A hereditary blood disorder that inhibits blood flow; African Americans are most at risk for this health condition

signed English Translation of English into a form of manual communication

simple partial seizures Seizures that cause people affected to think their environments are distorted or strange

Snellen chart A chart used to test visual acuity, developed in 1862

social competence Being able to understand and respond appropriately in social situations

socially maladjusted A term applied to students who do not act within society's norms but are not considered students with emotional or behavioral disorders

Social Stories™ Short stories that describe a specific activity and the behavioral expectations associated with that activity

sound intensity Loudness

spastic cerebral palsy Characterized by uncontrolled tightening or pulling of muscles

special education categories System used in IDEA '04 to classify disabilities for students

special education services Individualized education and services for students with disabilities and sometimes includes gifted and talented students

special interest area A topic of interest that can be used to encourage conversations, reduce anxiety, and increase academic motivation

specialized supports Disability-specific benefits to help people with disabilities participate in the community

speech Vocal production of language

speech impairments Abnormal speech that is unintelligible, is unpleasant, or interferes with communication

speech mechanisms Includes the various parts of the body—tongue, lips, teeth, mandible, and palate—required for oral speech

speech synthesizers Assistive technology devices that create voice

speech/language pathologist (SLP) The professional who diagnoses and treats speech or language impairments; a related services provider

statement of transitional services Component of IEPs for students older than age 16 to assist students moving to adulthood

stay-put provision Prohibits students with disabilities from being expelled because of behavior associated with their disabilities

stereotypies Nonproductive behaviors (e.g., twirling, flapping hands, rocking) that an individual repeats at a high rate; commonly observed in youngsters with autism spectrum disorders; also called stereotypic behaviors

story maps Simple diagrams used to organize and recall important elements and features of stories

Strategic Instruction Model™ (SIM) Instructional methods to help students read, comprehend, and study better by helping them organize and collect information strategically; a supplemental high school curriculum designed for students with learning disabilities; developed at the University of Kansas Center for Research on Learning (CRL)

structured teaching A feature of the instructional program, TEACHH, developed for students with autism where visual aids (start-to-finish boxes) are used to help students comprehend their environments

stuttering The lack of fluency in an individual's speech pattern, often characterized by hesitations or repetitions of sounds or words

supported employment A strategy used in job training in which the student is placed in a paying job and receives significant assistance and support, and the employer is helped with the compensation

syntax Rules that govern word endings and order of words in phrases and sentences

systems of supports A network of supports everyone develops to function optimally in life

tactile input devices Assistive technology that allows people to use touch to gain information

task analysis Breaking down problems and tasks into smaller, sequenced components

teachers of students with visual impairments (TVIs) Specially trained and certified teachers who provide direct or consultative special education services related to the effects of vision loss

technology-dependent students Individuals who probably could not survive without high-tech devices (such as ventilators)

telecommunication devices Devices that provide oral information in alternative formats (e.g., captions for TV or movies)

telecommunications relay service (TRS) A telephone system where an operator at a relay center converts a print-telephone message to a voice-telephone message; required by federal law

text telephone (TTY) A device that allows people to make and receive telephone calls by typing information instead of speaking; formerly called the telecommunication device for the deaf (TDD)

total communication approach A method of instruction for students with hearing loss that employs any and all methods of communication (oral speech, manual communication, ASL, gestures)

toxins Poisonous substances that can cause immediate or long-term harm

traumatic brain injury (TBI) Head injury causing reduced cognitive functioning, limited attention, and impulsivity

tunnel vision or restricted central vision Severe limitation in peripheral vision; limitations in the width of the visual field

twice-exceptional students Gifted students with disabilities

tympanic membrane or eardrum Vibrates with the presence of sound waves and stimulates the ossicles of the middle ear

typical learners Students and individuals without disabilities

underrepresentation Insufficient presence of individuals from a diverse group in a special education category; smaller numbers than would be predicted by their proportion of students

unexpected underachievement A defining characteristic of learning disabilities; when poor school performance cannot be explained by other abilities or potential

universal design Barrier-free architectural and building designs that meet the needs of everyone, including people with physical challenges

universal design for learning (UDL) Increases access to the curriculum and instruction for all students

universal newborn hearing screening
Testing of all newborns for hearing loss

universal screening Testing of everyone, particularly newborns, to determine existence or risk of disability; testing all students to identify those in need of assistance or more intensive instruction

very low-incidence disabilities Disabilities whose prevalence and incidence are very low

vibrating system The orderly function of the larynx and vocal folds to vibrate and produce sounds and pitch

video modeling A multimedia intervention in which the student imitates a model performing desired behaviors

visual acuity Sharpness of response to visual, auditory, or tactile stimuli

visual disabilities Impairments in vision that, even with correction, affect educational performance, access to the community, and independence

visual efficiency How well a person can use sight

visual input devices Assistive technology to help people with visual disabilities use their sight

vocational rehabilitation A government service that provides training, career counseling, and job placement

voice carryover (VCO) A TTY allowing both voice and text

voice problem Abnormal spoken language production, characterized by unusual pitch, loudness, or quality of sounds

wraparound services A service delivery model in which needs are met through collaboration of many agencies and systems (education, mental health, social services, community)

References

CHAPTER 1

Americans with Disabilities Act of 1990. PL No. 101-336, 104 Stat. 327.

Artiles, A. J., & Bal, A. (2008). The next generation of disproportionality research: Toward a comparative model in the study of equity in ability differences. *Journal of Special Education, 42,* 4–14.

Assistive Technology Act of 2004. PL No. 108-364.

Bacon, E., Banks, J., Yong, K., & Jackson, F. R. (2007). Perceptions of African American and European American teachers on the education of African American boys. *Multiple Voices, 10,* 160–172.

Ballard, J., Ramirez, B. A., & Weintraub, F. J. (1982). *Special education in America: Its legal and governmental foundations.* Reston, VA: Council for Exceptional Children.

Bengeny, J. C., & Martens, B. K. (2007). Inclusionary education in Italy: A literature review and call for more empirical research. *Remedial and Special Education, 28,* 80–94.

Branson, J., & Miller, D. (2002). *Damned for their difference: The cultural construction of deaf people as disabled.* Washington, DC: Gallaudet University Press.

Browder, D. M., & Cooper-Duffy, K. (2003). Evidence-based practices for students with severe disabilities and the requirement for accountability in "No Child Left Behind." *Journal of Special Education, 37,* 157–163.

Brown v. Board of Education, 347 U.S. 483 (1954).

Bryant, D. P., Smith, D. D., & Bryant B. (2008). *Teaching students with special needs in inclusive settings.* Boston: Allyn & Bacon.

Burdette, P. (2007). Diploma options for students with disabilities: Synthesis of the NCEO document. *In Forum.* Arlington, VA: National Association of Directors of Special Education.

Burlington School Committee v. Department of Education, 471 U.S. 359 (1985).

California Teachers Association. (2007, February). Response to intervention: Quick deployment of resources can rescue struggling students. *California Educator,* pp. 6–21.

Carter v. Florence County School District 4, 950 F. 2d 156 (1991).

Cedar Rapids School District v. Garret F., 106 F.3rd 822 (8th Cir. 1997), cert. gr. 118 S. Ct. 1793 (1998), aff'd, 119 S. Ct. 992 (1999).

Center for Applied Special Technology. (2006). *Universal design.* Retrieved December 16, 2006, from www.cast.org.

Center on Positive Behavioral Interventions and Supports. (2007). Retrieved April 25, 2008, from http://www.pbis.org/schoolwide.htm.

Chamberlain, L. (2007, January 7). Design for everyone, disabled or not. *New York Times,* Real Estate.

Chambers, J. G., Parrish, R. B., & Harr, J. J. (2004). *What are we spending on special education services in the United States, 1999–2000? 2004 Update.* Washington, DC: Special Education Expenditure Project, American Institutes for Research.

Cook, B. G., Cameron, D. L., & Tankersley M. (2007). Inclusive teachers' attitudinal rations of their students with disabilities. *Journal of Special Education, 40,* 230–238.

Darling-Hammond, L. (2005, April). *Correlation between teachers and student achievement.* Presentation at the American Education Research Association. Montreal.

Darling-Hammond, L. (2006a). Constructing 21st-century teacher education. *Journal of Teacher Education, 57,* 300–314.

Darling-Hammond, L. (2006b, November). *Developing a profession of teaching.* Presentation to CalTEACH Annual Faculty Professional Conference, San Jose.

Deshler, D. D. (2003, May/June). A time for modern-day pioneers. *LDA Newsbriefs, 38,* 3–9, 24.

Deutsch, H. (2005). The body's moments: Visible disability, the essay and the limits of sympathy. *Prose Studies, 27,* 11–26.

DiPaola, M. F., & Walther-Thomas, C. (2003). *Principals and special education: The critical role of school leaders.* Gainesville, FL: Center on Personnel Studies in Special Education.

Division for Learning Disabilities. (2007). *Thinking about response to intervention and learning disabilities: A teacher's guide.* Arlington, VA: Council for Exceptional Children.

Doe v. Withers, 20 IDELR 422 (1993).

Easter Seals. (2008). *Resources: Writing about disability.* Retrieved November 23, 2007, from www.easterseals.com/site/PageServer?pagename=ntl_writedisability

Education for All Handicapped Children Act (EHA) PL No. 94-142.

Education for All Handicapped Children Act (EHA) (reauthorized). PL No. 99-457.

Elementary and Secondary Education Act. PL No. 107-110.

Erevelles, N. (1996). Disability and the dialects of difference. *Disability & Society, 11,* 519–537.

Fairbanks, S., Sugai, G., Guardino, D., & Lathrop, M. (2007). Response to intervention: Examining classroom behavior support in second grade. *Exceptional Children, 73,* 288–310.

Florian, L. (2007). Reimagining special education. In L. Florian (Ed.), *The Sage handbook of special education* (pp. 7–20). Thousand Oaks, CA: Sage.

Florian, L., Hollenweger, J., Simeonsson, R. J., Wedell, K., Riddell, S., Terzi, L., & Holland, A. (2007). Cross-cultural perspectives on the classification of children with disabilities: Part 1. Issues in the classification of children with disabilities. *Journal of Special Education, 40,* 36–45.

Friend, M., & Bursuck, W. D. (2006). *Including students with special needs: A practical guide for classroom teachers* (4th ed.). Boston: Allyn & Bacon.

Fuchs, D., & Deshler, D. D. (2007). What we need to know about responsiveness to intervention (and shouldn't be afraid to ask). *Learning Disabilities Research and Practice, 22,* 129–136.

Fuchs, D., Fuchs, L. S., & Vaughn, S. R. (Eds.). (2008). *Responsiveness to intervention.* Newark, DE: International Reading Association.

Fuchs, D., & Young, C. L. (2006). On the irrelevance of intelligence in predicting responsiveness to reading instruction. *Exceptional Children, 73,* 8–30.

Futernick, K. (2007). *A possible dream: Retaining California teachers so all students learn.* Sacramento: CSU Center for Teacher Quality.

Gehrke, R. S., & Murri, N. (2007). Beginning special educators' intent to stay in special education: Why they like it here. *Teacher Education and Special Education, 22,* 179–190.

Gersten, R., Fuchs, L. S., Compton, D., Coyne, M., Greenwood, C., & Innocenti, M. S. (2005). Quality indicators of group experimental and quasi-experimental research in special education. *Exceptional Children, 71,* 149–164.

Groce, N. E. (1985). *Everyone here spoke sign language: Hereditary deafness on Martha's Vineyard*. Cambridge, MA: Harvard University Press.

Grossman, H. (1998). *Ending discrimination in special education*. Springfield, IL: Thomas.

Hammond, H., & Ingalls, L. (2003). Teachers' attitudes toward inclusion: Survey results from elementary school teachers in three southwestern rural school districts. *Rural Special Education Quarterly, 22*, 22–30.

Harbort, G., Gunter, P. L., Hull, K., Brown, Q., Venn, M. L., Wiley, L. P., & Wiley E. W. (2007). Behaviors of teachers in co-taught classes in a secondary school. *Teacher Education and Special Education, 30*, 13–23.

Harry, B. (2007). The disproportionate placement of ethnic minorities in special education. In L. Florian (Ed.), *The Sage handbook of special education* (pp. 67–84). Thousand Oaks, CA: Sage.

Harry, B., Arnaiz, P., Klingner, J., & Sturges, K. (2008). Schooling and the construction of identity among minority students in Spain and the United States. *Journal of Special Education, 42*, 15–26.

Harry, B., & Klingner, J. (2007). *Why are so many minority students in special education?* New York: Teachers College Press.

Hitchcock, C., & Stahl, S. (2003). Assistive technology, universal design, universal design for learning: Improved learning opportunities. *Journal of Special Educational Technology, 18*, 45–52.

Honig v. Doe, 484 U.S. 305, 108 S. Ct. 592 (1988).

Horner, R. H., Carr, E. C., Halle, J., McGee, G., Odom, S., & Wolery, M. (2005). The use of single-subject research to identify evidence-based practice in special education, *Exceptional Children, 71*, 165–179.

Individuals with Disabilities Education Act. PL No. 101-476.

Individuals with Disabilities Education Act. PL No. 105-17, 111 Stat. 37.

Individuals with Disabilities Education Improvement Act of 2004. PL No. 108-446.

Institute of Medicine. (2007). *The future of disability in America*. Washington, DC: National Academies Press.

IRIS Center. (2008). *Accessing the general education curriculum: Inclusion considerations for students with disabilities*. Nashville: IRIS Center, Vanderbilt University http://iris.peobody.vanderbilt.edu

Irving Independent School District v. Tatro, 468 U.S. 833 (1984).

Kauffman, J. M. (1997). Caricature, science, and exceptionality. *Remedial and Special Education, 18*, 130–132. Newark, NJ: Harwood.

Kauffman, J. M., & Hallahan, D. P. (2005). *Special education: What it is and why we need it*. Boston: Allyn & Bacon.

Lane, K. L. (2007). Identifying and supporting students at risk for emotional and behavioral disorders within multi-level models: Data driven approaches to conducting secondary interventions with an academic emphasis. *Education and Treatment of Children, 30*, 135–164.

Leafstedt, J. M., Richards, C., LaMonte, M., & Cassidy, D. (2007). Perspectives on co-teaching: Views from high school students with learning disabilities. *Learning Disabilities, 14*, 177–185.

Longmore, P. (2002). *San Francisco State University: Institute on disability*. Retrieved June 21, 2002, from http://online.sfsu.edu/~longmore/

Longmore, P. (2003). *Why I burned my book and other essays on disability*. Philadelphia: Temple University Press.

Lynch. E. W., & Hanson, M. J. (2004). *Developing cross-cultural competence: A guide for working with children and their families* (3rd ed.). Baltimore: Brookes.

Mills v. Board of Education of the District of Columbia, 348 F. Supp. 866 (1972).

Müller, E., & Markowitz, J. (2004). *Disability categories: State terminology, definitions and eligibility criteria*. Washington, DC: Project Forum, National Association of State Directors of Special Education.

National Center for Education Statistics. (2006). What proportion of students enrolled in postsecondary education have a disability? *Fast Facts*. Retrieved April 27, 2008, from http://nces.ed.gov/fastfacts/display.asp?id=60

National Center for Learning Disabilities. (2004). *No Child Left Behind and students with learning disabilities: Ensuring full participation and equal accountability*. Retrieved September 14, 2004, from www.ld.org/advocacy

No Child Left Behind Act of 2001. PL 107-110.

Nussbaum, M. C. (2006). *Frontiers of justice: Disability, nationality, species membership*. Cambridge, MA: Belknap Press of Harvard University Press.

Obiakor, F., & Utley, C.A. (2007). Let your work speak: Challenge to multicultural general and special education. *Multiple Voices, 10*, v–vii.

Office of Special Education Programs. (2006). *IDEA regulations: National Instructional Materials Accessibility Standard (NIMAS)*. Retrieved December 16, 2006, from http://IDEA.ed.gov

Office of Special Education Programs. (2008). *Students served under IDEA, Part B*: Fall 2006. Retrieved from www.ideadata.org

Pennsylvania Association for Retarded Children v. Commonwealth of Pennsylvania, 343 F. Supp. 279 (E. D. Pa., 1972).

Peters, J. W. (2007, October 14). Who is fit to vote? A vote will decide. *New York Times*.

Peters, J., & Bill, P. (2004, Summer). Assistive technology, universal design affect the future of children. *Pacesetter, 27*, 20–21.

Prabhala, A. (2007, February 20). *Mental retardation is no more: New name is intellectual and developmental disabilities*. Retrieved March 20, 2007, from www.aamr.org

Prater, M. A. (2003). Learning disabilities in children's and adolescent literature: How are characters portrayed? *Learning Disability Quarterly, 26*, 47–62.

Rehabilitation Act of 1973, Section 504, 19 U.S.C. Section 794.

Rice, N., Drame, E., Owens, L., & Ferattura, E. M. (2007). Co-instructing at the secondary level: Strategies for success. *Teaching Exceptional Children, 39*, 12–18.

Riddell, S. (2007). A sociology of special education. In L. Florian (Ed.), *The Sage handbook of special education* (pp. 34–45). Thousand Oaks, CA: Sage.

Rodríguez, M. A., Gentilucci, J., & Sims, P. G. (2005, November 11). *Preparing principals to support special educators: Interactive modules that enhance course content*. Paper presented at the Annual Meeting of the University Council for Educational Administration, Nashville, TN.

Roos, P. (1970). Trends and issues in special education for the mentally retarded. *Education and Training of the Mentally Retarded, 5*, 51–61.

Rowley v. Hendrick Hudson School District, 458 U.S. 176 (1982).

Safran, S. P. (1998). The first century of disability portrayal in film: An analysis of the literature. *Journal of Special Education, 31*, 467–479.

Safran, S. P. (2000). Using movies to teach students about disabilities. *Teaching Exceptional Children, 32*, 44–47.

Sandomierski, T., Kincaid, D., & Algozzine, B. (2008). Response to intervention and positive behavior support: Brothers from different mothers or sisters with different misters? *Positive Behavioral Interventions and Supports Newsletter, 4*. Retrieved April 24, 2008, from www.pbis.org/news/New/Newsletters/Newsletter4-2.aspz

Schaffer v. Weast, 546 U.S. 49 (2005).

Schettler, R., Stein, J., Reich, F., Valenti, M., & Wallinga, D. (2000). *In harm's way: Toxic threats to child development*. Cambridge, MA: Greater Boston Physicians for Social Responsibility. (www.igc.org/psr)

Science Daily. (2008, April 4). Rise in autism is related to changes in diagnosis, new study suggests. *Science News*. Retrieved April 11, 2008, from www.sciencedaily.com/releases/2008/04/080408112107.htm

Scruggs, T. E., Mastropieri, M. A., & McDuffie, K. A. (2007). Co-teaching in inclusive classrooms: A metasynthesis of qualitative research. *Exceptional Children, 73*, 392–416.

Severson, H. H., Walker, H. M., Hope-Doolittle, J., Kratochwill, T. R., & Gresham, F. M. (2007). Proactive, early screening to detect behaviorally at-risk students: Issues, approaches, emerging innovations, and professional practices. *Journal of School Psychology, 45*, 193–223.

Siperstein, G. N., Parker R. C., Bardon, J. N., & Widaman, K. F. (2007). A national study of youth attitudes toward the inclusion of students with intellectual diabilities. *Exceptional Children, 73*, 435–455.

Smith, J. D., & Lazaroff, K. (2006). "Uncle Sam needs you" or does he? Intellectual disabilities and lessons from the "Great Wars." *Mental Retardation, 44*, 433–437.

Smith v. Robinson, 468 U.S. 992 (1984).

Sopko, K. M. (2008). State support of education-related assistive technology. *In Forum*. Alexandria, VA: National Association of State Directors of Special Education.

Steinmetz, E. (2006). *Americans with disabilities: 2002 household economic studies*. Washington, DC: U.S. Census Bureau.

Timothy W. v. Rochester, New Hampshire, School District, 875 F. 2d 945 (1989).

Torgeson, J. K. (1996). Thoughts about intervention research in learning disabilities. *Learning Disabilities, 7*, 55–58.

United Nations General Assembly. (2007). *Convention on the rights of persons with disabilities.* Retrieved January 10, 2007, from www.un.org/eas/socdev/enable/rights/convtexte.htm

U.S. Department of Education. (1995). *Seventeenth annual report to Congress on the implementation of the Individuals with Disabilities Education Act.* Washington, DC: U.S. Government Printing Office.

U.S. Department of Education. (2006, August 14). 34 *CFR* Parts 300 and 301, Assistance to States for the Education of Children with Disabilities and Preschool Grants for Children with Disabilities: Final rule. *Federal Register,* Washington, DC.

Van Cleve, J. V. (Ed.). (2007). *The deaf history reader.* Washington, DC: Gallaudet University Press.

West, J. (1994). *Federal implementation of the Americans with Disabilities Act, 1991–1994.* New York: Milbank Memorial Fund.

Winzer, M. A. (2007). Confronting difference: An excursion through the history of special education. In L. Florian (Ed.), *The Sage handbook of special education* (pp. 21–33). Thousand Oaks, CA: Sage.

Zobrest v. Catalina Foothills School District, 963 F. 2d 190 (1993).

CHAPTER 2

Barnhill, G. P. (2005). Functional behavior assessment in schools. *Intervention in School and Clinic, 40,* 131–143.

Bigby, L. M. (2004). Medical and health related services: More than treating boo-boos and ouchies. *Intervention in School and Clinic, 39,* 233–235.

Borthwick-Duffy, S. A., Palmer, D. S., & Lane, K. L. (1996). One size doesn't fit all: Full inclusion and individual differences. *Journal of Behavioral Education, 6,* 311–329.

Bowie, L. (2007, October 22). Special ed is drawn into exam debate. *Baltimore Sun.* Retrieved October 22, 2007, from www.baltimoresun.com

Bradley, R., Danielson, L., & Hallahan, D. P. (Eds.). (2002). *Identification of learning disabilities: Research to practice.* Mahwah, NJ: Erlbaum.

Brown, M. R., Paulsen, K., & Higgins, K. (2003). Remove environmental barriers to student learning. *Intervention in School and Clinic, 39,* 109–112.

Brown-Chidsey, R. (2007). No more "waiting to fail." *Educational Leadership, 65,* 40–46.

Bryant, D. P., & Bryant, B. R. (2003). *Assistive technology for people with disabilities.* Boston: Allyn & Bacon.

Bryant, D. P., Smith, D. D., & Bryant, B. R. (2008). *Teaching students with special needs in inclusive classrooms.* Boston: Allyn & Bacon.

Buehler, V. (2004, July/August). Easy as 1-2-3 IEPs. *Volta Voices, 11,* 20–23.

Burdette, P. (2007). *Response to intervention as it relates to early intervening services: Recommendations.* Alexandria, VA: National Association of State Directors of Special Education, Project Forum.

Capizzi, A. M., & Fuchs, L. S. (2005). Effects of curriculum-based measurement with and without diagnostic feedback on teacher planning. *Remedial and Special Education, 26,* 159–174.

Center for Applied Special Technology. (2007). *Summary of 2007 national summit on universal design for learning working groups.* Wakefield, MA: Author.

Compton, D. L., Fuchs, D., Fuchs, L. S., & Bryant, J. D. (2006). Selecting at-risk readers in first grade for early intervention: A two-year longitudinal study of decision rules and procedures. *Journal of Educational Psychology, 98,* 394–409.

Cook, B. G., Cameron, D. L., & Tankersley, M. (2007). Inclusive teachers' attitudinal ratings of their students with disabilities. *Journal of Special Education, 40,* 230–238.

Cox, M. L., Herner, J. G., Demczyk, M. J., & Nieberding, J. J. (2006). Provision of testing accommodations for students with disabilities on statewide assessments: Statistical links with participation and discipline rates. *Remedial and Special Education, 27,* 346–354.

Crawford, L. (2007). *State testing accommodations: A look at their value and validity.* New York: National Center for Learning Disabilities.

Curran, C. M., & Harris, M. B. (1996). *Uses and purposes of portfolio assessment for general and special educators.* Albuquerque: University of New Mexico Press.

Darling-Hammond, L. (2005, April). *Correlation between teachers and student achievement.* Presentation at the American Education Research Association. Montreal.

Darling-Hammond, L. (2006a). Constructing 21st-century teacher education. *Journal of Teacher Education, 57,* 300–314.

Darling-Hammond, L. (2006b, November). *Developing a profession of teaching.* Presentation to CalTEACH Annual Faculty Professional Conference, San Jose.

Demchak, M. A., & Greenfield, R. G. (2003). *Transition portfolios for students with disabilities: How to help students, teachers, and families handle new settings.* Thousand Oaks, CA: Corwin Press.

Dworetzky, B. (2004). Effective practices for involving families of children with disabilities in schools. *Newsline: The Federation of Children with Special Needs, 24,* 1, 12.

Earles-Vollrath, T. L. (2004). Mitchell Yell: IDEA 1997 and related services. *Intervention in School and Clinic, 39,* 236–239.

Elementary and Secondary Education Act. PL No. 107-110.

Etzel-Wise, D., & Mears, B. (2004). Adapted physical education and therapeutic recreation in schools. *Intervention in School and Clinic, 39,* 223–232.

Fisher, D., Frey, N., & Thousand, J. (2003). What do special educators need to know and be prepared to do for inclusive schooling to work? *Teacher Education and Special Education, 26,* 42–50.

Foegen, A., Jiban, C., & Deno, S. (2007). Progress monitoring measures in mathematics: A review of the literature. *Journal of Special Education, 41,* 121–139.

Friend, M. & Cook, L. (2007). *Interactions: Collaboration skills for school professionals* (5th ed.). Boston: Allyn & Bacon.

Fuchs, L. S., Fuchs, D., Compton, D. L., Bryant, J. D., Hamlett, C. L., & Seethaler, P. M. (2007). Mathematics screening and progress monitoring at first grade:

Implications for responsiveness to intervention. *Exceptional Children, 73,* 311–330.

Fuchs, L. S., Fuchs, D., Hosp, M., & Jenkins, J. R. (2001). Oral reading fluency as an indicator of reading competence: A theoretical, empirical, and historical analysis. *Scientific Studies of Reading, 5,* 239–256.

Fuchs, L. S., Fuchs, D., & Powell, S. (2004). *Using CBM for progress monitoring.* Washington, DC: American Institutes for Research.

Futernick, K. (2007). *A possible dream: Retaining California teachers so all students learn.* Sacramento: CSU Center for Teacher Quality.

Haager, D., & Klingner, J. K. (2005). *Differentiating instruction in inclusive classrooms: The special educator's guide.* Boston: Allyn & Bacon.

Hall, D. (2007). *Graduation matters: Improving accountability for high school graduation.* Washington, DC: Education Trust.

Hammond, H., & Ingalls, L. (2003). Teachers' attitudes toward inclusion: Survey results from elementary school teachers in three southwestern rural school districts. *Rural Special Education Quarterly, 22,* 22–30.

Hébert, T. (2001, June). Man to man: Building channels of communication between fathers and their talented sons. *Parenting for High Potential,* pp. 18–22.

Holbrook, M. D. (2007). *Standards-based individualized education program examples.* Arlington, VA: National Association of State Directors of Special Education, Project Forum.

Hong, B. S. S., Ivy W. F., Gonzalez, H. R., & Ehrensberger, W. (2007). Preparing students for postsecondary education. *Teaching Exceptional Children, 40,* 32–38.

Hoover, J. J., & Patton, J. R. (2004). Differentiating standards-based education for students with diverse needs. *Remedial and Special Education, 25,* 74–78.

Hughes, M. T., Valle-Riestra, D. M. & Arguelles, M. E. (2002). Experiences of Latino families with their child's special education program. *Multicultural Perspectives, 4,* 11–17.

Hyatt, K. (2007). The new IDEA: Changes, concerns, and questions. *Intervention in School and Clinic, 42,* 131–136.

Individuals with Disabilities Education Improvement Act of 2004. PL No. 108-446. 118 Stat. 2647.

IRIS Center. (2007). *RTI: Considerations for school leaders.* Nashville: Vanderbilt University. (STAR Legacy Module available from http://iris.peabody.vanderbilt.edu)

Ketterlin-Geller, L. R., Yovanoff, P., & Tindal, G. (2007). Developing a new paradigm for conducting research on accommodations in mathematics testing. *Exceptional Children, 73,* 331–347.

King-Sears, M. E., & Evmenova, A. S. (2007). Premises, principles, and processes for integrating TECHnology into instruction. *Teaching Exceptional Children, 40,* 6–14.

Konrad, M., & Trela, K. (2007). Go 4 it . . . now: Extending writing strategies to support all students. *Teaching Exceptional Children, 39,* 42–51.

Kravetz, J. (2005, January 7). Under new IDEA, districts no longer required to provide, maintain implants. *The Special Educator, 20,* 1, 6.

Küpper, L. (2007, July). The top 10 basics of special education (Module 1). *Building the legacy: IDEA 2004 training curriculum.* Washington, DC: National Dissemination Center for Children with Disabilities. Available at www.nichcy.org/training/contents.asp

Layton, C. A., & Lock, R. H. (2007). Use authentic assessment techniques to fulfill the promise of No Child Left Behind. *Interventions, 27, 169–173.*

Lovitt, T. C., & Cushing, S. S. (1994). High school students rate the IEPs: Low opinions and lack of ownership. *Intervention in School and Clinic, 30,* 34–37.

Madaus, J. W., & Shaw, S. F. (2006). The impact of the IDEA 2004 on transition to college for students with learning disabilities. *Learning Disabilities Practice, 21,* 273–281.

Magiera, K., Smith, C., Zigmond, N., & Gebauer, K. (2005). Benefits of co-teaching in secondary mathematics classes. *Teaching Exceptional Children, 37,* 20–24.

Marino, M. T., Marino, E. C., & Shaw, S. F. (2006). Making informed assistive technology decisions for students with high incidence disabilities. *Teaching Exceptional Children, 38,* 18–25.

McMaster, K. L., & Espin, C. (2007). Technical features of curriculum-based measurement in writing: A literature review. *Journal of Special Education, 41,* 68–84.

McMaster, K. L., Fuchs, D., Fuchs, L. S., & Compton, D. L. (2005). Responding to nonresponders: An experimental field trial of identification and intervention methods. *Exceptional Children, 71,* 445–463.

Morrier, M. J. (2007). *Summary of U.S. Department of Education Conference Call on NCLB 2% regulations.* Washington, DC: Higher Education Consortium for Special Education, Memo.

Müller, E., & Burdette, P. (2007). *The national instructional materials accessibility standard (NIMAS): Current state implementation.* Arlington, VA: National Association for State Directors of Special Education, Project Forum.

National Association of School Nurses. (2006). *Individuals with Disabilities Education Act (IDEA): Management of children in the least restrictive environment: Issue Brief.* Retrieved January 8, 2008, from www.nasn.org

National Association of State Directors of Special Education. (2007). *Reauthorization of the Elementary and Secondary Education Act (ESEA): NASDSE reauthorization priorities.* Alexandria, VA: author.

National Center for Educational Outcomes. (2007). *Online accommodations bibliography.* Retrieved December 22, 2007, from www:cehd.umn.edu/NCEO)AccomStudies.htm#keywords

National Center for Educational Statistics. (2002). *Condition of education: 2002.* Washington, DC: U.S. Department of Education.

National Center for Educational Statistics. (2007a). *Fast facts: Drop out rates of high school students.* Retrieved January 3, 2008, from www.nces.ed.gov

National Center for Educational Statistics. (2007b). *Fast facts: What proportion of students enrolled in postsecondary education have a disability?* Retrieved January 3, 2007, from www.nces.ed.gov

Neal, J., Bigby, L. M., & Nicholson, R. (2004). Occupational therapy, physical therapy, and orientation and mobility services in public schools. *Intervention in School and Clinic, 39,* 218–222.

Neubert, D. A. (2003). The role of assessment in the transition to adult life process for students with disabilities. *Exceptionality, 11,* 63–75.

NIMAS Development and Technical Assistance Center. (2007). *NIMAS in IDEA 2004.* Wakefield, MA: CAST.

No Child Left Behind Act of 2001. PL 107-110.

Obiakor, F. W., & Ford, B. A., (2002). Educational reform and accountability: Implications for African Americans with exceptionalities. *Multiple Voices, 5,* 83–93.

Office of Special Education Programs. (2007). *Students served under IDEA, Part B: Fall 2006.* Retrieved December 30, 2007, from www.ideadata.org

Praisner, C. L. (2003). Attitudes of elementary principals toward the inclusion of students with disabilities. *Exceptional Children, 69,* 135–145.

Rehabilitation Act of 1973. Section 504, 19 U.S.C. Section 794.

Ritchey, K. D. (2006). Learning to write: Progress-monitoring tools for beginning and at-risk writers. *Teaching Exceptional Children, 39,* 22–26.

Ryan, A. L., Halsey, H. N., & Matthews, W. J. (2003). Using functional assessment to promote desirable student behavior in schools. *Teaching Exceptional Children, 35,* 8–15.

Safer, N., & Fleischman, S. (2005). Research matters: How student progress monitoring improves instruction. *Educational Leadership, 62,* 81–83.

Samuels, C. A. (2007, October 31). "Universal design" concept pushed for education. *Education Week,* p. 1.

Sataline, S. (2005, January 30). A matter of principal. *Boston Globe Magazine.*

Serfass, C., & Peterson, R. L. (2007). A guide to computer-managed IEP record systems. *Teaching Exceptional Children, 40,* 16–21.

Smith, R., Salend, S., & Ryan, S. (2001). Closing or opening the special education curtain. *Teaching Exceptional Children, 33,* 18–23.

Sopko, K. M. (2003). *The IEP: A synthesis of current literature since 1997.* Washington, DC: National Association of State Directors of Special Education (NASDSE), Project Forum.

Soukup, J. H., Wehmeyer, M. L., Bashinski, S. M., & Bovaird, J. A. (2007). Classroom variables and access to the general education curriculum. *Exceptional Children, 74,* 101–120.

Stecker, P. M., Fuchs, L. S., & Fuchs, D. (2005). Using curriculum-based measurement to improve student achievement: Review of research. *Psychology in the Schools, 42,* 795–819.

Test, D. W., Mason, C., Hughes, C., Konrad, M., Neale, M., & Wood, W. M. (2004). Student involvement in individualized education program meetings. *Exceptional Children, 70,* 391–412.

Thompson, S., Lazarus, S., Clapper, A., & Thurlow, M. (2004). *Essential knowledge and skills needed by teachers to support the achievement of students with disabilities.*

EPRRI Issue Brief Five. College Park, MD: Institute for the Study of Exceptional Children and Youth, Educational Policy Reform Research Institute.

Thurlow, M. L. (2007). *Research impact on the state accommodation policies for students with disabilities.* Paper presented as part of a research symposium entitled "Research Influences Decisions for Assessing English Language Learners and Students with Disabilities" at the American Educational Research Association, Chicago.

Tornatzky, L. G., Pachon, H. P., & Torres, C. (2003). *Closing achievement gaps: improving educational outcomes for Hispanic children.* Los Angeles: Center for Latino Educational Excellence, Tomás Rivera Policy Institute, University of Southern California.

U.S. Department of Education. (2002). *The twenty-fourth annual report to Congress on the implementation of IDEA.* Washington, DC: U.S. Government Printing Office.

U. S. Department of Education. (2006, August 14). 34 *CFR* Parts 300 and 301, Assistance to States for the Education of Children with Disabilities and Preschool Grants for Children with Disabilities: Final rule (pp. 1263–1264). *Federal Register,* Washington, DC.

U.S. Department of Education. (2007a). *Measuring the achievement of students with disabilities: What families and schools need to know about modified academic achievement standards.* Washington, DC: Author.

U.S. Department of Education. (2007b, January). *Q and A: Questions and answers on individualized education programs (IEPs), evaluations and reevaluations.* Retrieved December 13, 2007, from http://idea.ed.gov

Wagner, M., Newman, L., Cameto, R., Levine, P., & Garza, N. (2006). *An overview of findings from Wave 2 of the National Longitudinal Transition Study-2 (NLTS2).* (NCSER 2006-3004). Menlo Park, CA: SRI International.

Whitbread, K. (2004). Access to the general education curriculum for All students. *The inclusion notebook: Problem solving in the classroom and community.* Farmington, CT: A. J. Pappanikou Center for Developmental Disabilities, University of Connecticut.

Williams, J. (2007, November 8). Calif. exit exam boosts dropout numbers. *Associated Press.* Retrieved November 8, 2007, from http://ap.google.com

Williams IV, J. J. (2007, March 21). Cheating can tempt test givers. *Baltimore Sun.* Retrieved March 26, 2007, from www.baltimoresun.com

Wood, W. M., Karvonen, M., Test, D. W., Browder, D., & Algozzine, B. (2004). Promoting student self-determination skills in IEP planning. *Teaching Exceptional Children, 36,* 8–16.

Zarate, M. E. (2007). *Understanding Latino parental involvement in education: Perceptions, expectations, and recommendations.* Los Angeles: University of Southern California, Tomás Rivera Policy Institute.

Zenisky, A. L., & Sireci, S. G. (2007). *A summary of the research on the effects of test accommodations: 2005–2006* (Technical Report 47). Minneapolis: University of Minnesota, National Center on Educational Outcomes.

CHAPTER 3

Antunez, B., (2001, July). *What legal obligations do schools have to English language learners?* ASK NCELA No. 23. Washington, DC: National Clearinghouse for English Language Acquisition and Language Instruction Educational Programs, George Washington University.

Antunez, B., & Zelasko, N. (2001, August). *What program models exist to serve English language learners?* ASK NCELA No. 22. Washington, DC: National Clearinghouse for English Language Acquisition and Language Instruction Educational Programs, George Washington University.

Artiles, A. J. (2003). Special education's changing identity: Paradoxes and dilemmas in views of culture and space. *Harvard Educational Review, 73,* 164–202.

Artiles, A. J., & Bal, A. (2008). The next generation of disproportionality research: Toward a comparative model in the study of equity in ability differences. *Journal of Special Education, 42,* 4–14.

Artiles, A. J., Harry, B., Reschly, D. J., & Chinn, P. C. (2002). Over-identification of students of color in special education: A critical overview. *Multicultural Perspectives, 4,*3–10.

Baca, L. M., & Cervantes, H. T. (Eds.). (2004). *The bilingual special education interface* (4th ed.). Upper Saddle River, NJ: Merrill/Pearson Education.

Banks, J. A. (2006). *Cultural diversity and education: Foundations, curriculum, and teaching* (5th ed.). Boston: Pearson Education.

Banks, S. (2004). Voices of tribal parents and caregivers of children with special needs. *Multiple Voices, 7,* 33-47.

Bernal, E. M. (2000). Three ways to achieve a more equitable representation of culturally and linguistically different students in GT programs. *Roeper Review, 24,* 82–88.

Bondy, E., Ross, D. D., Gallingane, C., & Hambacher, E. (2007). Creating environments of success and resilience: Culturally responsive classroom management and more. *Urban Education, 42,* 326–348.

Brice, A., & Rosa-Lugo, L. I. (2000). Code switching: A bridge or barrier between two languages? *Multiple Voices, 4,* 1–9.

Brown v. Board of Education, 347 U.S. 483 (1954).

Brown, M. R., Higgins, J., Pierce, R., Hong, E., & Thoma, C. (2003). Secondary students' perceptions of school life with regard to alienation: The effects of disability, gender, and race. *Learning Disability Quarterly, 26,* 227–238.

Bryant, D. P., Smith, D. S., & Bryant, B. R. (2008). *Teaching students with special needs in inclusive classrooms.* Boston: Pearson Education.

Calhoon, M. B., Al Otaiba, S., Greenberg, D., King, A., & Avalos A. (2006). Improving reading skills in predominantly Hispanic Title I first-grade classrooms: The promise of peer-assisted learning strategies. *Learning Disabilities Research & Practice, 21,* 261–272.

Cartledge, G., & Kourea, L. (2008). Culturally responsive classrooms for culturally diverse students with and at risk for disabilities. *Exceptional Children, 74,* 351–371.

Cartledge, G., & Loe, S. A. (2001). Cultural diversity and social skill instruction. *Exceptionality, 9,* 33–46.

Castellano, J. A., & Díaz, E. I. (Eds.). (2002). *Reaching new horizons: Gifted and talented education for culturally and linguistically diverse students.* Boston: Allyn & Bacon.

Cheng, L. L. (1996). Beyond bilingualism: A quest for communication competence. *Topics in Language Disorders, 16,* 9–21.

Cheng, L. L. (1999). Moving beyond accent: Social and cultural realities of living with many tongues. *Topics in Language Disorders, 19,* 1–10.

Cheng, L. L., & Chang, J. (1995). Asian/Pacific Islander students in need of effective services. In L. L. Cheng (Ed.), *Integrating language and learning for inclusion: An Asian-Pacific focus* (pp. 3–59). San Diego, CA: Singular Publishing Group.

Chicago Public Schools. (2008) CPS at a glance. Retrieved April 27, 2008, from http://www.cps.k12.il.us/AtAGlance.html

Children's Defense Fund. (2006). *The state of America's children: 2006.*Washington, DC: Author.

Coutinho, M. J., & Oswald, D. P. (2006). *Disproportionate representation of culturally and linguistically diverse students in special education: Measuring the problem.* Denver: NCCRESt.

Cuccaro, K. (1996, April 3). Teacher observations key in bilingual assessment. *Special Education Report, 22,* 1, 3.

Cummins, J. (1984). *Bilingualism and special education: Issues in assessment and pedagogy.* San Diego, CA: College-Hill.

D'Anguilli, A., Siegel, L.S., & Maggi, S. (2004). Literacy instruction, SES, and word-reading achievement in English-language learners and children with English as a first language: A longitudinal study. *Learning Disabilities Research & Practice, 19,*202–213.

Davis, C., Brown, B., Bantz, J., & Manno, C. (2002). African American parents' involvement in their children's special education programs. *Multiple Voices, 5,*13–27.

de Valenzuela, J. S., Copeland, S. R., & Qi, C. H. (2006). Examining educational equity: Revisiting the disproportionate representation of minority students in special education. *Exceptional Children, 72,* 425–441.

Diana v. State Board of Education, No. C-70-37 Rfp (N.D. Calif. 1970).

Diaz, Y., Knight, L. A., & Chronis-Tuscano, A. (Winter, 2008). Adaptation and implementation of behavioral parent training for Latino families: Cultural considerations and treatment acceptability. *Report on Emotional and Behavioral Disorders in Youth, 8,* 2–8.

Donovan, M. Z., & Cross, C. T. (Eds.) (2002). *Minority students in special education and gifted education.* Committee on Minority Representation in Special Education. Washington, DC: National Academy Press.

Dresser, N. (1996). *Multicultural manners: New rules of etiquette for a changing society.* New York: Wiley.

Dyson, A., & Gallannaugh, F. (2008). Disproportionality in special needs education in England. *Journal of Exceptional Children, 42,* 36–46.

Fletcher, T. V., Bos, C. S., & Johnson, L. M. (1999). Accommodating English language learners with language and learning dis-

abilities in bilingual education classrooms. *Learning Disabilities Research & Practice, 14,* 80–91.

Ford, D. Y., Grantham, T. C., & Whiting, G. W. (2008). Culturally and linguistically diverse students in gifted education: Recruitment and retention issues. *Exceptional Children, 74, 289–306.*

Ford, D. Y., Howard, R. C., Harris III, J. J., & Tyson, C. A. (2000). Creating culturally responsive classrooms for gifted African American students. *Journal for the Education of the Gifted, 23,* 397–427.

Fry, R. (2005). *The high schools Hispanics attend: Size and other key characteristics.* Washington, DC: Pew Hispanic Center.

Fuchs, D., Fuchs, L. S., Al Otaiba, S., Thompson, A., Yen, L., McMaster, K. M., Svenson, E., & Yang, N. J. (2001). K-PALS: Helping kindergarteners with reading readiness: Teachers and researchers in partnerships. *Teaching Exceptional Children, 33,* 76–80.

Fuchs, D., Fuchs, L. S., Mathes, P. G., & Simmons, D. C. (1997). Peer-Assisted Learning Strategies: Making classrooms more responsive to diversity. *American Educational Research Journal, 34,* 174–206.

Furger, R. (2004, November). High school's new face. *Edutopia Magazine.* Retrieved December 27, 2004, from www.edutopia.org

Garcia, E. E. (2001). *Hispanic education in the United States.* Lanham, Rowman & Littlefield.

Gardner, H. (1983). *Frames of mind: The theory of multiple intelligences.* New York: Basic Books.

Garrett, M. T., Bellon-Harn, M. L., Torres-Rivera, E., Garrett, J. T., & Roberts, L. C. (2003). Open hands, open hearts: Working with Native youth in the schools. *Intervention in School and Clinic, 38,*225–235.

Gay, G., & Kirkland, K. (2003). Developing cultural critical consciousness and self-reflection in preservice teacher education. *Theory into Practice, 42,* 181–187.

Gersten, R., & Baker, S. (2000). *Topical summary: Practices for English language learners.* Eugene, OR: National Institute for Urban School Improvement.

Gollnick, D. M., & Chinn, P. C. (2006). *Multicultural education in a pluralistic society* (7th ed.). Upper Saddle River, NJ: Merrill/Pearson Education.

Good, T. L., & Nichols, S. L. (2001). Expectancy effects in the classroom: A special focus on improving the reading performance of minority students in first-grade classrooms. *Educational Psychologist, 36,* 113–126.

Goode, T. (2002, August). *Cultural competence.* Presentation to the National Council on Disability, Cultural Diversity Committee, Washington, DC.

Grupp, L. L. (2004). Felipe's story: In response to the National Research Council report. *Multiple Voices, 7,* 1–15.

Harry, B. (2002). Trends and issues in serving culturally diverse families of children with disabilities. *Journal of Special Education, 36,* 131–138.

Harry, B. (2007). The disproportionate placement of ethnic minorities in special education. In L. Florian (Ed.), *The SAGE Handbook of special education.* Thousand Oaks, CA: Sage.

Harry, B. (2008). Collaboration with culturally and linguistically diverse families: Ideal versus reality. *Exceptional Children, 74,* 372–388.

Harry, B., & Klingner, J. (2006). *Why are so many minority students in special education? Understanding race and disability in schools.* New York: Teachers College Press.

Harry, B., Arnaiz, P., Klingner, J., & Sturges, K. (2008). Schooling and the construction of identity among minority students in Spain and the United States. *The Journal of Exceptional Children, 42,* 15–25.

Haynes, J. (2005). *Using the Internet for content based instruction.* Retrieved January 5, 2005, from http://www.everythingesl.net/inservices/internet_resources.php

Hébert, T. P., & Beardsley, T. M. (2001). Jermaine: A critical case study of a gifted Black child living in rural poverty. *Gifted Child Quarterly, 45,* 85–103.

Henning-Stout, M. (1996). "¿Que podemos hacer?": Roles for school psychologists with Mexican and Latino migrant children and families. *School Psychology Review, 25,* 152–164.

Holman, L. J. (1997). Working effectively with Hispanic immigrant families. *Phi Delta Kappan, 78,*647–649.

Hosp, J. L. & Reschly, D. J. (2002). Predictors of restrictiveness of placement for African-American and Caucasian students. *Exceptional Children, 68,* 225–238.

Hosp, J. L. & Reschly, D. J. (2003). Referral rates for intervention or assessment: A meta-analysis of racial differences. *Journal of Special Education, 37,* 67–80.

Hughes, M. T., Valle-Riestra, D. M., & Arguelles, M. E. (2002). Experiences of Latino families with their child's special education program. *Multicultural Perspectives, 4,* 11–17.

Individuals with Disabilities Education Improvement Act of 2004. PL No. 108-466.

Ingersoll, R. (2001). *Teacher turnover, teacher shortages, and the organization of schools.* Seattle: University of Washington, Center for the Study of Teaching and Policy.

Jairrels, V., Brazil, N., & Patton, J. R. (1999). Incorporating popular literature into the curriculum for diverse learners. *Intervention in School and Clinic, 34,* 303–306.

Joseph, L. M., & Ford, D. Y. (2006). Nondiscriminatory assessment: Considerations for gifted education. *Gifted Child Quarterly, 50,* 42–51.

Kalyanpur, M. (2008). The paradox of majority underrepresentation in special education in India. *Journal of Exceptional Children, 42,* 55–64.

Kea, C. D., & Utley, C. A. (1998). To teach me is to know me. *Journal of Special Education, 32,* 44–47.

Kishi, G. (2004). Pihana Na Mamo:. *Students of Hawaiian Ancestry.* Honolulu: Native Hawaiian Special Education Project, Hawaii Department of Education.

Kornhaber, M., Fierros, E., & Veenema. S. (2004). *Multiple intelligences: Best ideas from research and practice.* Boston: Allyn & Bacon.

Kozol, J. (1991). *Savage inequalities: Children in America's schools.* New York: Crown.

Kozol, J. (1995). *Amazing grace: The lives of children and the conscience of a nation.* New York: Crown.

Kozlesksi, E. B., Sobel, D., & Taylor, S. V. (2003). Embracing and building culturally responsive practices. *Multiple Voices, 6,* 73–87.

Kraft, S. G. (2001, February). HHS: Full early childhood inclusion maximizes kids' potential. *Early Childhood Report, 12,* 7.

Krause, M. (1992). Testimony to the Select Senate Committee on Indian Affairs on S. 2044, *Native American Languages Act of 1991,* to assist Native Americans in assuring the survival and continuing vitality of their languages (pp. 16–18). Washington, DC: United State Senate.

Ladson-Billings, G. (2001). Crossing over to Canaan: The journey of new teachers in diverse classrooms. San Francisco: Jossey-Bass.

Larry P. v. Riles, Civil Action No. C-70-37 (N.D. Calif. 1971).

Lau v. Nichols, 414 U.S. 563 (1974).

Lee, V. E., & Burkam, D. T. (2002). *Inequality at the starting gate.* Washington, DC: Economic Policy Institute.

Linan-Thompson, S., Vaughn, S., Prater, K., & Cirino, P. T. (2006). The response to intervention of English Language Learners at risk for reading problems. *Journal of Learning Disabilities, 39,* 390–398.

Lynch, E. W., & Hanson, M. J. (2004). *Developing cross-cultural competence: A guide for working with young children and their families* (3rd ed.). Baltimore: Brookes.

Maker, C. J., Nielson, A. B., & Rogers, J. A. (1994). Giftedness, diversity and problem solving. *Teaching Exceptional Children, 27,* 4–18.

Malveaux, J. (2002, December). Quality pre-school education pays off, long-term study says. *Early Childhood Report, 13,*1,4.

Markowitz, J. (Ed.). (1999). *Education of children with disabilities who are homeless.* Proceedings of Project FORUM convened April 5–7, 1999. Alexandria, VA: National Association of State Directors of Special Education.

McLaughlin, M. J., Pullin, D., & Artiles, A. J. (2001, November). Challenges for transformation of special education in the 21st century: Rethinking culture in school reform. *Journal of Special Education Leadership, 14,* 51–62.

Metropolitan Nashville Public Schools. (2008). *2007–2008 facts.* Retrieved April 28, 2008, from http://www.mnps.org/AssetFactory.aspx?did=15321

Milian, M. (1999). Schools and family involvement: Attitudes among Latinos who have children with visual impairments. *Journal of Visual Impairment & Blindness, 93,* 277–290.

Montgomery, W. (2001, March/April). Creating culturally responsive, inclusive classrooms. *Teaching Exceptional Children 33,* 4–9.

Müller, E., & Markowitz, J. (2004 March). *English language learning with disabilities: Synthesis brief.* Arlington, VA: National Association of State Directors of Special Education, Project Forum.

National Alliance of Black School Educators & ILIAD Project. (2002). *Addressing overrepresentation of African American students in special education.* Arlington, VA: Council for Exceptional Children, and Washington, DC: National Alliance of Black School Educators.

National Center for Culturally Responsive Educational Systems. (2006).

Disproportionate representation of culturally and linguistically diverse students in special education: Measuring the problem. Denver, CO: Author.

National Center for Educational Outcomes. (2005a). *Accommodations for LEP students/English Language Learners.* Retrieved January 3, 2005, from http://education.umn.edu/NCEO/LEP/Accommmodations/Accom_lep.htm

National Center for Educational Outcomes. (2005b). *Accountability for LEP students/English Language Learners.* Retrieved January 3, 2005, from http://education.umn.edu/NCEO/LEP/Accountability/Account_lep.htm

National Center for Educational Statistics (2003). Bilingual education/ Limited English proficient students. *Fast Facts.* Retrieved March 14, 2008, from http://nces.ed.gob/fastfacts/display.asp?id=96

National Center for Educational Statistics (2007a). Dropout rates in the United States: 2005. Retrieved April 27, 2008, from http://nces.ed.gov/pubs2007/2007059.pdf

National Center for Educational Statistics (2007b). *Status and trends in the education of racial and ethnic minorities.* Retrieved March 14, 2008, from http://nces.ed.gov/pubs2007/minoritytrends/#2

National Clearinghouse for English Language Acquisition and Language Instruction Educational Programs. (2003). *Descriptive study of services to LEP students and LEP students with disabilities.* Special Topic Report #1: Native Languages of LEP Students. Washington, DC: Author.

National Clearinghouse for English Language Acquisition and Language Instruction Educational Programs. (2008). *The growing numbers of limited English proficient students: 1995/96 to 2005/2006.* Author: Washington, DC. Retrieved March 28, 2008, from http://www.ncela.gwu.edu/policy/states/reports/statedata/2005LEP/GrowingLEP_0506.pdf

National Reading Panel. (2000). *Teaching children to read: An evidence-based assessment of the scientific research literature on reading and its implications for reading instruction* (NIH Pub. No. 00-4754). Washington, DC: National Institute of Child Health and Human Development.

Neal, L. I., McCray, A. D., Webb-Johnson, G., & Bridgest, S. T. (2003). The effects of African American movement styles on teachers' perceptions and reactions. *Journal of Special Education, 37,* 49–57.

Nieto, S., & Bode, P. (2008). *Affirming diversity: The sociopolitical context of multicultural education* (5th ed.). White Plains, NY: Longman.

Obiakor, F. E. (1994). *The eight-step multicultural approach: Learning and teaching with a smile.* Dubuque, IA: Kendall/Hunt.

Office of Special Education Programs. (2008). *Students served under IDEA, Part B: Fall 2006.* Retrieved March 14, 2008, from www.ideadata.org

Ochoa, S. H., Robles-Pina, R., Garcia, S. B., & Breunig, N. (1999). School psychologists' perspectives on referrals of language minority students. *Multiple Voices, 3,* 1–14.

Ortiz, A. A. (1997). Learning disabilities occurring concomitantly with linguistic differences. *Journal of Learning Disabilities, 30,* 321–332.

Ortiz, A. A., Wilkinson, C. Y., Robertson-Courtney, P., & Kushner, M. I. (2006). Considerations in implementing intervention assistance teams to support English Language Learners. *Remedial and Special Education, 27,* 53–63.

Ortiz, A. A., & Yates, J. R. (2001). A framework for serving English language learners with disabilities. *Journal of Special Education, 14,* 72–80.

Parette, H. P., & Petch-Hogan, B. (2000, November/December). Approaching families: Facilitating culturally/linguistically diverse family involvement. *Teaching Exceptional Children, 33,* 4–10.

Patton, J. M., & Baytops, J. L. (1995). Identifying and transforming the potential of young gifted African Americans: A clarion call for action. In B. A. Ford, F. E. Obiakor, & J. M. Patton (Eds.), *Effective education of African American exceptional learners: New perspectives* (pp. 27–68). Austin, TX: Pro-Ed.

Pew Hispanic Center. (2002, January). *Educational attainment: Better than meets the eye, but large challenges remain.* Washington, DC: Author.

Pew Hispanic Center. (2008). *Statistical portrait of Hispanics in the United States, 2006.* Washington, DC: Author.

Phyler v. Doe, 102 S. Ct. 2382 (1982).

Potter, D. (2002, January 24–30). An extraordinary young man. *Lakota Journal, Health,* pp. C-1, C-4.

Reid, R., Casat, C. D., Norton, H. J., Anastopoulos, A. D., & Temple, E. P. (2001). Using behavior rating scales for ADHD across ethnic groups: The IOWA Conners. *Journal of Emotional and Behavioral Disorders, 9,* 210–218.

Reschly, D. J. (2002). Minority overrepresentation: The silent contributor to LD prevalence and diagnostic confusion. In R. Bradley, L. Danielson, & D. P. Hallahan (Eds.), *Identification of learning disabilities: Research to practice* (pp. 361–368). Mahwah, NJ: Erlbaum.

Rogers-Dulan, J. (1998). Religious connectedness among urban African American families who have a child with disabilities. *Mental Retardation, 36,* 91–103.

Rossell, C. (2004/2005). Teaching English through English. *Educational Leadership, 62,* 32–36.

Rothstein, R. (2004, May 19). Social class leaves its imprint. *Education Week,* pp. 40–41.

Rueda, R., Lim, H. J., & Velasco, A. (2008). Cultural accommodations in the classroom: An instructional perspective. *Multiple Voices, 10,* 61–72.

Ruiz, N. (1995). The social construction of ability and disability: I. Profile types of Latino children identified as language learning disabled. *Journal of Learning Disabilities, 29,* 491–502.

Sadowsky, M. (2006, July/August). The school readiness gap. *Harvard Education Letter.* Cambridge, MA. Retrieved April 27, 2008, from http://www.edletter.org/past/issues/2006-ja/readinessgap.shtml

Saenz, L. M., Fuchs, L. S., & Fuchs, D. (2005). Peer-Assisted Learning Strategies for English language learners with learning disabilities. *Exceptional Children, 71*(3), 231–247.

Salend, S. J., & Salinas, A. (2003). Language differences or learning difficulties: The work of the multidisciplinary team. *Teaching Exceptional Children, 35,* 35-43.

Santos, R., Fowler, S., Corso, R., & Bruns, D. (2000). Acceptance, acknowledgement, and adaptability: Selecting culturally and linguistically appropriate early childhood materials. *Teaching Exceptional Children, 32,* 14–22.

Schettler, R., Stein, J., Reich, F., Valenti, M., & Wallinga, D. (2000). In harm's way: toxic threats to child development. Cambridge, MA: Greater Boston Physicians for Social Responsibility (www.igc.org/psr).

Seymour, H. N., Abdulkarim, L., & Johnson, V. (1999). The Ebonics controversy: An educational and clinical dilemma. *Topics in Language Disorders, 19,* 66–77.

Shapiro, J., Monzo, L. D., Rueda, R., Gomez, J. A., & Blacher, J. (2004). Alienated advocacy: Perspectives of Latina mothers of young adults with developmental disabilities on service systems. *Mental Retardation, 42,* 37–54.

Short, D., & Echevarria, J. (2004/2005). Teacher skills to support English language learners. *Educational Leadership, 62,* 9–13.

Sileo, R. W., & Prater, M. A. (1998). Preparing professionals for partnerships with parents of students with disabilities: Textbook considerations regarding cultural diversity. *Exceptional Children, 64,* 513–528.

Skiba, R. J., Poloni-Staudinger, L., Simmons, A. B., Feggins-Azziz, L. R., & Chung, C. (2005). Unproven links: Can poverty explain ethnic disproportionality in special education? *Journal of Special Education, 39*(3), 130–144.

Skiba, R. J., Simmons, A. B., Ritter, S., Gibb, A. C., Rausch, M. K., Cuadrado, J., & Chung, C. (2008). Achieving equity in special education: History, status, and current challenges. *Exceptional Children, 74*(3), 264–288.

Slater, R. B. (2004). The persisting racial gap in college student graduation rates. *Journal of Blacks in Higher Education, 45,* 77–85.

Stiefel, L., Schwartz, A. E., & Conger, D. (2003). *Language proficiency and home languages of students in New York City elementary and middle schools.* New York: New York University, Taub Urban Research Center.

Suro, R. (2002). *Counting the "Other Hispanics": How many Colombians, Dominicans, Ecuadorians, Guatemalans and Salvadorans are there in the United States?* Washington, DC: Pew Hispanic Center.

Suro, R., & Singer, A. (2002, July). Latino growth in metropolitan American: Changing patterns, new locations. *Survey Series: Census 2000.* Washington, DC: Brookings Institution.

Taylor, O. L. (1997). *Testimony of Orlando L. Taylor on the subject of "Ebonics" to the United States Senate Committee on Appropriations Subcommittee on Labor, Health and Human Services and Education.* Washington, DC: United States Senate.

Thurston, L. P., & Navarrete, L. A. (2003). Rural, poverty-level mothers: A comparative study of those with and without children who have special needs. *Rural Special Education Quarterly, 22,* 15–23.

Thorp, E. K. (1997). Increasing opportunities for partnership with culturally and linguistically diverse families. *Intervention in School and Clinic, 32,* 261–269.

Thurlow, M. L. & Liu, K. K. (2001, November). Can "all" really mean students with disabilities who have limited English proficiency? *Journal of Special Education, 14,* 63–71.

Tiedt, P. L., & Tiedt, I. M. (2005). *Multicultural teaching: A handbook of activities, information, and resources* (7th ed.). Boston: Allyn & Bacon.

Tomás Rivera Policy Institute. (2005). *Challenges in improving Latino college enrollment: Opportunities for systemic change.* University of Southern California: Author.

Tornatzky, L. G., Pachon, H. P., & Torres, C. (2003). *Closing achievement gaps: Improving educational outcomes for Hispanic children.* Los Angeles: Center for Latino Educational Excellence, Tomás Rivera Policy Institute, University of Southern California.

Tyler, N. T., Lopez-Reyna, N., & Yzquierdo, Z. (2004). The relationship between cultural diversity and the special education workforce. *Journal of Special Education, 38,* 22–38.

U. S. Department of Education. (2002). *Twenty-fourth annual report to Congress on the implementation of the Individuals with Disabilities Education Act.* Washington, DC: U.S. Government Printing Office.

U.S. Department of Education. (2006, August 14). 34 CFR Parts 300 and 301, Assistance to States for the Education of Children with Disabilities and Preschool Grants for Children with Disabilities: Final rule. *Federal Register,* Washington, DC.

Van Kuren, L. (2003). Exceptional and homeless. *Today, 9,* 1–2, 7, 13.

Voltz, D. (2005). Cultural influences on behavior. *Who's in charge? Developing a comprehensive behavior management system. STAR Legacy Module.* Nashville, TN: IRIS Center for Faculty Enhancement, Peabody Vanderbilt University (http://iris.peabody.vanderbilt.edu).

Vraniak, D. (1998, Summer). Developing systems of support with American Indian families of youth with disabilities. *Health Issues for Children & Youth & Their Families, 6,* 9–10.

Waldfogel, J. (2006). *What children need.* Cambridge, MA: Harvard University Press.

Weinstein, C. S., Tomlinson-Clarke, S., & Curran, M. (2004). Toward a conception of culturally responsive classroom management. *Journal of Teacher Education, 55,* 25–38.

Werning, R., Loser, J. M., & Urban, M. (2008). Cultural and social diversity: An analysis of minority groups in German schools. *Journal of Exceptional Children, 42,* 47–54.

Yates, J. R., Hill, J. L., & Hill, E. G. (2002, February). "A vision for change" but for who? A "personal" response to the National Research Council report. *DDEL News, 11,* 4–5.

Yzquierdo, Z. (2005). *Distinctions between language differences and language disorders.* Nashville, TN: Peabody College of Vanderbilt University, Department of Special Education.

Yzquierdo, Z., & Blalock, G. (2004). Language-appropriate assessments for determining eligibility of English language learners for special education services. *Assessment for Effective Intervention, 29*, 17–30.

Zelasko, N., & Antunez, B. (2000). *If your child learns in two languages*. Washington, DC: National Clearinghouse for Bilingual Education, George Washington University.

CHAPTER 4

American Speech-Hearing-Language Association Ad Hoc Committee on Service Delivery in the Schools. (1993). Definitions of communication disorders and variations. *ASHA, 5*(Suppl. 10), pp. 40–41.

American Speech-Hearing-Language Association. (2002). *ASHA 2002 desk reference* (Vol. 3). Rockville, MD: Author.

American Speech-Hearing-Language Association. (2008a). The ASHA leader online: Facts about cleft lip and palate. Retrieved June 24, 2008, from www.asha.org

American Speech-Hearing-Language Association. (2008b). Membership profile: Highlights and trends, ASHA counts for 2007. Retrieved June 11, 2008, from www.asha.org

Anderson, N. B., & Shames, G. H. (2006). *Human communication disorders: An introduction* (7th ed.). Boston: Allyn & Bacon.

Baca, L. M., & Cervantes, H. T. (Eds.). (2004). *The bilingual special education interface* (4th ed.). Upper Saddle River, NJ: Merrill/Pearson Education.

Bakken, J. P., & Whedon, C. K. (2002). Teaching text structure to improve reading comprehension. *Intervention in School and Clinic, 37*, 229–233.

Bauman-Waengler, J. (2008). *Articulatory and phonological impairments: A clinical focus* (3rd ed.). Boston: Pearson Education.

Bernthal, J. E., & Bankson, N. W. (2004). *Articulation and phonological disorders* (5th ed.). Boston: Allyn & Bacon.

Blackorby, J., Wagner, M., Cadwallader, T., Cameto, R., Levine, P., & Marder, C., with Giacaione, P. (2002). *Behind the label: The functional implications of disability*. Menlo Park, CA: SEELS Project, SRI International.

Blank, M., Rose, S. A., & Berlin, L. J. (1978). *The language of learning: The preschool years*. New York: Grune & Stratton.

Boulineau, T., Fore III, C., Hagan-Burke, S., & Burke, M. D. (2004). Use of story-mapping to increase the story-grammar text comprehension of elementary students with learning disabilities. *Learning Disability Quarterly, 27*, 105–121.

Bremer, C. D., Vaughn, S., Clapper, A. T., & Kim, J. (2002). Collaborative strategic reading (CSR): Improving secondary students' reading comprehension skills. *Improving Secondary Education and Transition Services Through Research, 1*, 1–7.

Children's Defense Fund. (2005). *The state of America's children: 2005*. Washington, DC: Author.

Cleminshaw, H., DePompei, R., Crais, E. R., Blosser, J., Gillette, Y., & Hooper, C. R. (1996). Working with families. *ASHA, 38*, 34–45.

Compton, D. L. (2002). The relationship between phonological processing, orthographic processing, and lexical development in reading-disabled children. *Journal of Special Education, 35*, 201–210.

Conture, E. G. (2001). *Stuttering: Its nature, diagnosis, and treatment*. Boston: Allyn & Bacon.

Culatta, B., & Wiig, E. H. (2006). Language disabilities in school-age children and youth. In N. B. Anderson and G. H. Shames (Eds.), *Human communication disorders: An introduction* (7th ed, pp. 352–358). Boston: Allyn & Bacon.

Dockrell, J. E., Lindsay, G., Connelly, V., & Mackie, C. (2007). Constraints in the production of written text in children with specific language impairments. *Exceptional Children, 73*(2), 147–164.

Ely, R. (2005). Language and literacy in the schools. In J. B. Gleason (Ed.), *The development of language* (6th ed.). Boston: Allyn & Bacon.

Falk-Ross, F. C. (2002). *Classroom-based language and literacy intervention: A programs and case studies approach*. Boston: Allyn & Bacon.

Fletcher, J. M., Lyon, G. R., Barnes, M., Stuebing, K. K., Francis, D. J., Olson, R. K., Shaywitz, S. E., & Shaywitz, B. A. (2002). Classifications of learning disabilities: An evidence-based evaluation. In R. Bradley, L. Danielson, & D. P. Hallahan (Eds.), *Identification of learning disabilities: Research to practice* (pp. 185–250). Mahwah, NJ: Erlbaum.

Fuchs, D., & Fuchs, L. S. (2005). *Response to intervention (RTI): Preventing and identifying LD*. Videoconference presentation to the New York City School System, Vanderbilt University, Nashville, TN.

Gleason, J. B. (2009). The development of language: An overview and a preview. In J. B. Gleason & N. B. Ratner (Eds.), *The development of language* (7th ed.). Boston: Pearson Education.

Gregory, J. H., Campbell, J. H., Gregory, C. B., & Hill, D. G. (2003). *Stuttering therapy: Rationale and procedures*. Boston: Allyn & Bacon.

Hall, B. J., Oyer, J. J., & Haas, W. H. (2001). *Speech, language, and hearing disorders: A guide for the teacher* (3rd ed.). Boston: Allyn & Bacon.

Harwood, L., Warren, S. F., & Yoder, P. (2002). The importance of responsivity in developing contingent exchanges with beginning communicators. In J. Reichle, D. R. Beukelman, & J. C. Light (Eds.), *Exemplary practices for beginning communicators: Implications for ACC* (pp. 59–96). Baltimore, MD: Brookes.

Horton, S. V., Lovitt, T. C., & Bergerud, D. (1990). The effectiveness of graphic organizers for three classifications of secondary students in content area classes. *Journal of Learning Disabilities, 23*, 12–22, 29.

Inspiration Software. (1998–2005). Inspiration®. Portland, OR: Author.

Inspiration Software. (2000–2005). Kidspiration®. Portland, OR: Author.

Ives, B., & Hoy, C. (2003). Graphic organizers applied to higher-level secondary mathematics. *Learning Disabilities Practice, 18*, 36–51.

Jenkins, J. R., & O'Connor, R. E. (2002) Early identification and intervention for young children with reading/learning disabilities.

In R. Bradley, L. Danielson, & D. P. Hallahan (Eds.), *Identification of learning disabilities: Research to practice* (pp. 99–149). Mahwah, NJ: Erlbaum.

Justice, L. M. (2004). Creating language-rich preschool classroom environments. *Teaching Exceptional Children, 37*, 36–44.

Kangas, K. A., & Lloyd, L. L. (2006). Augmentative and alternative communication. In G. H. Shames and N. B. Anderson (Eds.), *Human communication disorders: An introduction* (7th ed., pp. 436–470). Boston: Allyn & Bacon.

Klingner, J. K., Vaughn, S., Hughes, M. T., Schumm, J. S., & Elbaum, B. (1998a). Outcomes for students with and without learning disabilities in inclusive classrooms, *Learning Disabilities Research & Practice, 13*, 153–161.

Klingner, J. K., Vaughn, S., & Schumm, J. S. (1998b). Collaborative strategic reading during social studies in heterogeneous fourth-grade classrooms. *Elementary School Journal, 99*, 3–22.

Lombardo, L. A. (1999). Children score higher on tests when child care meets standards. *Early Childhood Reports, 10*, 4.

Longmore, P. K. (2003). *Why I burned my book and other essays on disability*. Philadelphia: Temple University Press.

Lyon, G. R, Fletcher, J. M., Shaywitz, S. E., Shaywitz, B. A., Torgesen, J. K., Wood, F. B., Schulte, A., & Olson, R. (2001). Rethinking learning disabilities. In C. E. Finn, A. J. Rotherham, & C. R. Hokansan (Eds.), *Rethinking special education for a new century* (pp. 259–288). Washington DC: Thomas B. Fordham Foundation and the Progressive Policy Institute.

Maugh II, T. H. (1995, August 11). Study finds folic acid cuts risk of cleft palate. *Los Angeles Times*, p. A20.

McCormick, L. (2003). Language intervention and support. In L. McCormick, D. R. Loeb, & R. L. Schiefelbusch (Eds.), *Supporting children with communication difficulties in inclusive settings: School-based language intervention*. Boston: Allyn & Bacon.

Melzi, G., & Ely, R. (2009). Language and literacy in the school years. In J. B. Gleason & N. B. Ratner, (Eds.), *The development of language* (7th ed.). Boston: Pearson Education.

Menn, L., & Stoel-Gammon, C. (2009). Phonological development: Learning sounds and sound patterns. In J. B. Gleason & N. B. Ratner (Eds.), *The development of language* (7th ed.). Boston: Pearson Education.

Moore, G. P., & Kester, D. (1953). Historical notes on speech correction in the preassociation era. *Journal of Speech and Hearing Disorders, 18*, 48–53.

Norris, J. A., & Hoffman, P. R. (2002). Phonemic awareness: A complex developmental process. *Topics in Language Disorders, 22*, 1–34.

Office of Special Education Programs. (2008). *Students served under IDEA, Part B: Fall 2006*. Retrieved March 14, 2008, from www.ideadata.org

Olswang, L. B., Coggins, T. E., & Timler, G. R. (2001). Outcome measures for school-age children with social communication problems. *Topics in Language Disorders, 21*, 50–73.

Ortiz, A. A., Wilkinson, C. Y., Robertson-Courtney, P., & Kushner, M. I. (2006). Considerations in implementing intervention assistance teams to support English Language Learners. *Remedial and Special Education, 27*(1), 53–63.

Owens, Jr., R. E. (2006). Development of communication, language, and speech. In N. B. Anderson & G. H. Shames (Eds.), *Human communication disorders: An introduction* (7th ed., pp. 25–58). Boston: Allyn & Bacon.

Owens, Jr., R. E., Metz, D. E., & Haas, A. (2006). *Introduction to communication disorders: A life span perspective* (3rd ed.). Boston: Allyn & Bacon.

Pan, B. A. (2005). Semantic development: Learning the meanings of words. In J. B. Gleason (Ed.), *The development of language* (6th ed.). Boston: Allyn & Bacon.

Payne, K. T., & Taylor, O. L. (2006). Multicultural influences on human communication. In N. B. Anderson & G. H. Shames (Eds.), *Human communication disorders: An introduction* (7th ed., pp. 93–125). Boston: Allyn & Bacon.

Plante, E., & Beeson, P., M. (2008). *Communication and communication disorders: A clinical introduction* (3rd ed.). Boston: Pearson Education.

Ramig, P. R., & Shames, G. H. (2006). Stuttering and other disorders of fluency. In N. B. Anderson & G. H. Shames (Eds.), *Human communication disorders: An introduction* (7th ed., pp. 183–221). Boston: Allyn & Bacon.

Ratner, N. B. (2009). Atypical language development. In J. B. Gleason & N. B. Ratner, (Eds.), *The development of language* (7th ed.). Boston: Pearson Education.

Roberts, J. E., & Zeisel, S. A. (2002). *Ear infections and language development.* Washington, DC: U.S. Department of Education and American Speech-Language-Hearing Association.

Robinson, N. B. (2003). Families: The first communication partners. In L. McCormick, D. R. Loeb, & R. L. Schiefelbusch (Eds.), *Supporting children with communication difficulties in inclusive settings: School-based language intervention.* Boston: Allyn & Bacon.

Rock, M. L. (2004). Graphic organizers: Tools to build behavioral literacy and foster emotional competency. *Intervention in School and Clinic, 40,* 10–18.

Salend, S. J. (2005). *Creating inclusive classrooms: Effective and reflective practices for all students* (5th ed.). Upper Saddle River, NJ: Merrill/Pearson Education.

Salend, S. J., & Salinas, A. (2003). Language differences or learning difficulties: The work of the multidisciplinary team. *Teaching Exceptional Children, 35,* 35–43.

Sander, E. K. (1972). When are speech sounds learned? *Journal of Speech and Hearing Disorders, 37,* 62.

Small, L. H. (2005). *Fundamentals of phonetics: A practical guide for students* (2nd ed.). Boston: Allyn & Bacon.

Sunderland, L. C. (2004). Speech, language, and audiology services in public schools. *Intervention in School and Clinic, 39,* 209–217.

U.S. National Park Service. (2008). A Trail of Tears Reading 3: "Every Cherokee man, woman, and child must be in motion . . .". Retrieved July 1, 2008, from http://www.nps.gov/history/nr/twhp/wwwlps/lessons/118trail/118facts3.htm

Utley, C. A., & Obiakor, F. (Eds.). (2001). *Special education, multicultural education, and school reform: Components of quality education for learners with mild disabilities.* Springfield, IL: Thomas.

Van Riper, C., & Erickson, R. L. (1996). *Speech correction: An introduction to speech pathology and audiology* (9th ed.). Boston: Allyn & Bacon.

Vaughn, S., Bos, C. S., & Schumm, J. S. (2007). Teaching exceptional, diverse, and at-risk students in the general education classroom (4th ed). Boston: Pearson Education.

Vaughn, S., Klingner, J. K., & Bryant, D. (2001). Collaborative strategic reading as a means to enhance peer-mediated instruction for reading comprehension and content-area learning. *Remedial and Special Education, 22,* 66–74.

Vaughn, S., & Linan-Thompson, S. (2004). *Research-based methods of reading instruction: Grades K–3.* Alexandria, VA: Association for Supervision and Curriculum Development.

Wagner, M., Newman, L., Cameto, R., Garza, N., & Levin, P. (2005). *After high school: A first look at the postschool experiences of youth with disabilities.* A report from the National Longitudinal Transition Study-2 (NLTS2). Menlo Park, CA: SRI International.

Wetherby, A. M. (2002). Communication disorders in infants, toddlers, and preschool children. In G. H. Shames & N. B. Anderson (Eds.), *Human communication disorders: An introduction* (6th ed., pp. 186–217). Boston: Allyn & Bacon.

CHAPTER 5

Ahearn, E. M. (2003). *Specific learning disability: Current approaches to identification and proposals for change.* Washington, DC: National Association of State Directors of Special Education Project Forum.

Bender, W. (2008). *Learning disabilities: Characteristics, identification, and teaching strategies* (6th ed.). Boston: Allyn & Bacon.

Bishop, A. G. (2003). Prediction of first-grade reading achievement: A comparison of fall and winter kindergarten screenings. *Learning Disability Quarterly, 26,* 189–200.

Boone, R., & Higgins, K. (2007). The role of instructional design in assistive technology research and development. *Reading Research Quarterly, 42* (1), 135–140.

Bradley, R., Danielson, L., & Hallahan, D. P. (Eds.). (2002). *Identification of learning disabilities: Research to practice.* Mahwah, NJ: Erlbaum.

Brinckerhoff, L. C. (2005, March 8). Teens with LD and/or AD/HD: Shopping for college options. *Monthly Message.* www.SchwabLearning.org

Bryan, T. (1974). Peer popularity of learning disabled children. *Journal of Learning Disabilities, 7,* 621–625.

Bryan, T., Burstein, K., & Ergul, C. (2004). The social-emotional side of learning disabilities: A science-based presentation of the state of the art. *Learning Disability Quarterly, 27,* 45–51.

Bryant, B. R., Bryant, D. P., Kethley, C., Kim, S. A., Pool, C., & Seo, Y.-U. (2008). Prevention mathematics difficulties in the primary grades: The critical features of instruction in textbooks as part of the equation. *Learning Disabilities Quarterly, 31,* 21–36.

Bryant, D. P., & Bryant, B. R. (2003). *Assistive technology for people with disabilities.* Boston: Allyn & Bacon.

Bryant, D. P., & Bryant, B. R. (2008). Introduction to the special series: Mathematics and learning disabilities. *Learning Disabilities Quarterly, 31,* 3–8.

Bryant, D. P., Smith, D. D., & Bryant, B. R. (2008). *Teaching students with special needs in inclusive classrooms.* Boston: Allyn & Bacon.

Bui, Y., N., Schumaker, J. B., & Deshler, D. D. (2006). The effects of a strategic writing program for students with and without learning disabilities in inclusive fifth-grade classes. *Learning Disabilities Research and Practice, 21,* 244–260.

Bursuck, W. D., Smith, T., Munk, D., Damer, M., Mehlig, L., & Perry, J. (2004). Evaluating the impact of a prevention-based model of reading on children who are at risk. *Remedial and Special Education, 25,* 303–313.

Caffrey, E., & Fuchs, D. (2007). Differences in performance between students with learning disabilities and mild mental retardation: Implications for categorical instruction. *Learning Disabilities Research and Practice, 22,* 119–128.

Carlson, C. L., Booth, J. E., Shin, M., & Canu, W. H. (2002). Parent-, teacher-, and self-rated motivational styles in ADHD subtypes. *Journal of Learning Disabilities, 35,* 103–113.

Chambers, J. G., Shkolinik, J., & Pérez, M. (2003). *Total expenditures for students with disabilities, 1999–2000: Spending variation by disability.* Report 5. Washington, DC: American Institutes for Research, Special Education Expenditure Project.

Chard, D. J., Baker, S. K., Clarke, B., Jungjohann, K., Davis, K., & Smolkowski, K. (2008). Preventing early mathematics difficulties: The feasibility of a rigorous kindergarten mathematics curriculum. *Learning Disabilities Quarterly, 31,* 11–20.

Children's Defense Fund. (2007). *Annual report: 2006.* Washington, DC: Author.

Compton, D. (2002). The relationships among phonological processing, orthographic processing, and lexical development in children with reading disabilities. *Journal of Special Education, 35,* 201–210.

Coyne, M. D., Zipoli, R. P., & Ruby, M. F. (2006). Beginning reading instruction for students at risk for reading disabilities: What, how and when. *Intervention in School and Clinic, 41,* 161–168.

Davidson, H. P. (1934). A study of reversals in young children. *Journal of Genetic Psychology, 45,* 452–465.

Davidson, H. P. (1935). A study of the confusing letters B, D, P, and Q. *Journal of Genetic Psychology, 46,* 458–468.

Deno, S., & Mirkin, P. (1974, Spring). Data-based instruction: A system for improving learning and preventing reading failure. *Manitoba Journal of Educational Research*, p. 1.

Denton, C. A., Vaughn, S., & Fletcher, J. M. (2003). Bringing research-based practice in reading intervention to scale. *Learning Disabilities Research and Practice, 18*, 201–211.

Deshler, D. (2005, January). A closer look: Closing the performance gap. *StrateNotes, 13*, 1–5.

Deshler, D., & Roth, J. (2002, April). Strategic research: A summary of learning strategies and related research. *StrateNotes, 10*, 1–5.

Dion, E., Morgan, P. L., Fuchs, D., & Fuchs, L. S. (2004). The promise and limitations of reading instruction in the mainstream: The need for a multilevel approach. *Exceptionality, 12*, 163–173.

Dollarhide, C. T., & Saginak, K. A. (2008). *Comprehensive school counseling programs: K–12 delivery systems in action.* Boston: Allyn & Bacon.

Eaton, M., & Lovitt, T. C. (1972). Achievement tests vs. direct and daily measurement. In G. Semb (Ed.), *Behavior analysis and education: 1972.* Lawrence: University of Kansas, Project Follow Through.

Ehri, L. C., Nunes, S. R., Willows, D. M., Schuster, B. V., Yaghoub, Z. Z., & Shanahan, T. (2001). Phonic awareness instruction helps children learn to read: Evidence from the national reading panel's meta-analysis. *Reading Research Quarterly, 36*, 250–287.

Elksnin, L. K., & Elksnin, N. (2004). The social-emotional side of learning disabilities. *Learning Disability Quarterly, 27*, 3–8.

Elksnin, L. K., Bryant, D. P., Gartland, D., King-Sears, M., Rosenberg, M. S., Scanlon, D., Stronider, R., & Wilson, R. (2001). LD summit: Important issues for the field of learning disabilities. *Learning Disability Quarterly, 24*, 297–305.

Elliott, S. N., Malecki, C. K., & Demaray, M. K. (2001). New directions in social skills assessment and intervention for elementary and middle school students. *Exceptionality, 9*, 19–32.

Finn, Jr., C. E., Rotherham, A. J., & Hokanson Jr., C. R. (Eds.). (2001). Conclusions and principles for reform. In C. E. Finn Jr., A. J. Rotherham, & C. R. Hokanson Jr. (Eds.), *Rethinking special education for a new century* (pp. 259–288). Washington, DC: Thomas B. Fordham Foundation and the Progressive Policy Institute.

Fletcher, J. M., Lyon, G. R., Barnes, M., Stuebing, K. K., Francis, D. J., Olson, R. K., et al. (2002). Classifications of learning disabilities: An evidence-based evaluation. In R. Bradley, L. Danielson, & D. P. Hallahan (Eds.), *Identification of learning disabilities: Research to practice* (pp. 185–250). Mahwah, NJ: Erlbaum.

Foegen, A., Jiban, C., & Deno, S. (2007). Progress monitoring in mathematics. *Journal of Special Education, 41*, 121–139.

Frey, N. (2005). Retention, social promotion, and academic redshirting: What do we know and need to know? *Remedial and Special Education, 26*, 332–346.

Frostig, M. (1978). Five questions regarding my past and future and the past, present, and future of learning disabilities. *Journal of Learning Disabilities, 11*, 9–12.

Fuchs, D., & Deshler, D. D. (2007). What we need to know about responsiveness to intervention (and shouldn't be afraid to ask). *Learning Disabilities Research and Practice, 22*, 129–136.

Fuchs, D., & Fuchs, L. S. (2005, April 20). *Response to Intervention (RTI): Preventing and identifying LD.* Presentation via videoconferencing for the New York City Schools, Vanderbilt University, Nashville, TN.

Fuchs, D., Fuchs, L. S., & Compton, D. L. (2004). Identifying reading disabilities by responsiveness-to-instruction: Specifying measures and criteria. *Learning Disability Quarterly, 27*, 216–229.

Fuchs, D., Fuchs, L. S., Mathes, P. G., Lipsey, M. W., & Roberts, P. H. (2002). Is "learning disabilities" just a fancy term for low achievement? A meta-analysis of reading differences between low achievers with and without the label. In R. Bradley, L. Danielson, & D. P. Hallahan (Eds.), *Identification of learning disabilities: Research to practice* (pp. 747–762). Mahwah, NJ: Erlbaum.

Fuchs, D., Fuchs, L. S., & Vaughn, S. R. (Eds.). (2008). *Responsiveness to intervention.* Newark, DE: International Reading Association.

Fuchs, D., & Young, C. L. (2006). On the irrelevance of intelligence in predicting responsiveness to reading instruction. *Exceptional Children, 73*, 8–30.

Fuchs, L. (2003). Assessing intervention responsiveness: Conceptual and technical issues. *Learning Disabilities Research and Practice, 18*, 172–186.

Fuchs, L., Fuchs, D., Compton, D. L., Bryant, J. D., Hamlett, C. L., & Seethaler, P. M. (2007). Mathematics screening and progress monitoring at first grade: Implications for responsiveness to intervention. *Exceptional Children, 73*, 311–330.

Fuchs, L., Fuchs, D., & Hollenbeck, K. N. (2007). Extending responsiveness to intervention to mathematics at first and third grades. *Learning Disabilities Research and Practice, 22*, 13–24.

Gartland, D., & Strosnider, R. (2007). The documentation disconnect for students with learning disabilities: Improving access to postsecondary disability services: A report from the National Joint Committee on Learning Disabilities. *Learning Disability Quarterly, 30*, 265–274.

Gerber, M. M. (2007). Globalization, human capital, and learning disabilities. *Learning Disabilities Research and Practice, 22*, 216–217.

Greatschools.org. (2008). *Kids quiz Charles Schwab about the personal side of learning disabilities.* Retrieved February 22, 2008, from www.schwablearning.org/articles .aspx?r=775

Gresham, F. M., Sugai, G., & Horner, R. H. (2001). Interpreting outcomes of social skills training for students with high-incidence disabilities. *Exceptional Children, 67*, 331–344.

Hallahan, D. P., Lloyd, J. W., Kauffman, J. M., Weiss, M. P., & Martinez, E. A. (2005). *Learning disabilities: Foundations, characteristics, and effective teaching* (3rd ed.). Boston: Allyn & Bacon.

Hammill, D. D. (1990). On defining learning disabilities: An emerging consensus. *Journal of Learning Disabilities, 23*, 74–84.

Hammill, D. D. (2004). What we know about the correlates of reading. *Exceptional Children, 70*, 453–468.

Hammill, D., & Larsen, S. (1974). The effectiveness of psycholinguistic abilities. *Exceptional Children, 41*, 5–14.

Haring, N. G. (1978). *The fourth R: Research in the classroom.* Upper Saddle River, NJ: Merrill/Pearson Education.

Harris, K. R., Graham, S., Mason, L., & Friedlander, B. (2008). *Every child can write: Educators' guide to powerful writing strategies.* Baltimore, MD: Brookes.

Hasselbring, T. S., & Bausch, M. E. (2005/2006). Assistive technologies for reading. *Educational Leadership, 63*, 72–75.

Hollenbeck, A. F. (2007). From IDEA to implementation: A discussion of foundational and future responsiveness-to-intervention research. *Learning Disabilities Research & Practice, 22*, 137–146.

Hong, B. S. S., Ivy, F. W., Gonzalez, H. R., & Ehrensberger, W. (2007). Preparing students for postsecondary education. *Teaching Exceptional Children, 40*, 32–88.

IRIS Center. (2008a). Classroom assessment: An introduction to monitoring academic achievement in the classroom. *On-line IRIS STAR Legacy Module.* Nashville, TN: IRIS Center for Training Enhancements, Vanderbilt University (http://iris.peabody .vanderbilt.edu).

IRIS Center. (2008b). Guiding the School Counselor: An overview of roles and responsibilities. *On-line IRIS STAR Legacy Module.* Nashville, TN: IRIS Center for Training Enhancements, Vanderbilt University (http:// iris.peabody.vanderbilt.edu).

IRIS Center. (2008c). Response to intervention (RTI): Overview. *On-line IRIS STAR Legacy Module.* Nashville, TN: IRIS Center for Training Enhancements, Vanderbilt University (http://iris.peabody.vanderbilt .edu).

Isaacson, S. (2004). Instruction that helps students meet state standards in writing. *Exceptionality, 12*, 39–54.

Ives, B. (2007). Graphic organizers applied to secondary algebra instruction for students with learning disorders. *Learning Disabilities Research and Practice, 22*, 110–118.

Jenkins, J. R., & O'Connor, R. E. (2002). Early identification and intervention for young children with reading/learning disabilities. In R. Bradley, L. Danielson, & D. P. Hallahan (Eds.), *Identification of learning disabilities: Research to practice* (pp. 99–149). Mahwah, NJ: Erlbaum.

Johnson, D. R., Mellard, D. F., & Lancaster, P. (2007). Helping young adults with learning disabilities plan and prepare for employment. *Teaching Exceptional Children, 39*, 26–32.

Jones, D. (2003, November 10). Charles Schwab didn't let dyslexia stop him. *USA Today*, p. B5.

Kamps, D., Abbott, M., Greenwood, C., Arrreaga-Mayer, C., Wills, H., Longstaff, J., Culpepper, M., & Walton, C. (2007). Use of evidence-based, small-group reading instruction for English language learners in elementary grades: Secondary-tier intervention. *Learning Disability Quarterly, 30,* 153–168.

ato, M. M., Nulty, B. N., Olszewski, B. T., Doolittle, J., & Flannery, K. B., (2007). Helping students with disabilities transition to college. *Teaching Exceptional Children, 39,* 18–23.

Kavale, K. A., & Forness, S. R. (1996). Social skill deficits and learning disabilities: A meta-analysis. *Journal of Learning Disabilities, 29,* 226–237.

Kavale, K. A., & Mostert, M. P. (2004). Social skills interventions for individuals with learning disabilities. *Learning Disability Quarterly, 27,* 31–43.

Keogh, B. K. (1974). Optometric vision training programs for children with learning disabilities: Review of issues and research. *Journal of Learning Disabilities, 7,* 36–48.

Kirk, S. A. (1977). Specific learning disabilities. *Journal of Clinical Child Psychology, 6,* 23–26.

Kirk, S. A., McCarthy, J. J., & Kirk, W. D. (1968). *Illinois test of psycholinguistic abilities* (ITPA). Urbana: University of Illinois Press.

Kovaleski, J. F., & Prasse, D. P. (2008). Response to instruction in the identification of learning disabilities: A guide for school teams. *Helping Children at Home and School II: Handouts for Families and Educators,* National Association of School Psychologists. Retrieved April 5, 2008, from www.nasp.org

Kuhne, M., & Wiener, J. (2000). Stability of social status of children with and without learning disabilities. *Learning Disability Quarterly, 23,* 64–75.

Kunsch, C. A., Jitendra, A. K., & Sood, S. (2007). The effects of peer-mediated instruction in mathematics for students with learning problems: A research synthesis. *Learning Disabilities Research and Practice, 22,* 1–12.

Lane, K. L., Wehby, J. H., & Cooley, C. (2006). Teacher expectations of students' classroom behavior across the grade span: Which social skills are necessary for success? *Exceptional Children, 72,* 153–167.

Le Mare, L., & de la Ronde, M. (2000). Links among social status, service delivery mode, and service delivery preference in LD, low-achieving, and normally achieving elementary-aged children. *Learning Disability Quarterly, 23,* 52–62.

Lerner, J. (1993). *Learning disabilities: Theories, diagnosis, and teaching strategies* (6th ed.). Boston: Houghton Mifflin.

Lienemann, T. O., Graham, S., Leader-Janssen, B., & Reid, R. (2006). Improving the writing performance of struggling writers in second grade. *Journal of Special Education, 40,* 66–78.

Lindsley, O. (1990). Precision teaching: By teachers for children. *Teaching Exceptional Children, 22,* 32–37.

Lissner, L. S. (2005). *Choosing a college.* Washington, DC: Advocacy Institute. Retrieved May 10, 2005, from www.advocacyinstitute.org

Lloyd, J. W., Keller, C., & Hung, L.-Y. (2007). International understanding of learning disabilities. *Learning Disabilities Research and Practice, 22,* 159–160.

Lovitt, T. C. (2007). *Promoting school success* (3rd ed.). Austin, TX: Pro-Ed.

Lovitt, T. C., & Hansen, C. (1978). The use of contingent skipping and frilling to improve oral reading and comprehension. *Journal of Learning Disabilities, 9,* 481–487.

Lyon, G. R., Fletcher, J. M., Shaywitz, S. E., Shaywitz, B. A., Torgesen, J. K., Wood, F. B., Schulte, A., & Olson, R. (2001). Rethinking learning disabilities. In C. E. Finn, Jr., A. J. Rotherham, & C. R. Hokanson Jr. (Eds.), *Rethinking special education for a new century* (pp. 259–288). Washington, DC: Thomas B. Fordham Foundation and the Progressive Policy Institute.

Macheck, G., R., & Nelson, J. M. (2007). How should reading disabilities be operationalized? A survey of practicing school psychologists. *Learning disabilities Research & Practice, 22,* 147–157.

Madaus, J. W. (2005). Navigating the college transition maze: A guide for students with learning disabilities. *Teaching Exceptional Children, 37,* 32–37.

Madaus, J. W. (2006). Employment outcomes of university graduates with learning disabilities. *Learning Disabilities Quarterly, 29,* 19–31.

Madaus, J. W., & Shaw, S. F. (2006). The impact of the IDEA 2004 on transition to college for students with learning disabilities. *Learning Disabilities Research and Practice, 21,* 273–281.

Mazzocco, M., M., M., & Thompson, R. E. (2008). Kindergarten predictors of math learning disability. *Learning Disabilities Research and Practice, 20,* 142–155.

McBride, A., Scatton, L., & Coley, R. J. (2007). Students with learning disabilities transitioning from high school to college: Highlights from the Achievement Gap Symposium. *Policy Notes: News from the ETS Policy Information Center, 15,* 1–16.

McMaster, K., & Espin, C. (2007). Technical features of curriculum-based measurement in writing: A literature review. *Journal of Special Education, 41,* 68–84.

McNamara, B. E. (2007). *Learning disabilities: Bridging the gap between research and classroom practice.* Upper Saddle River, NJ: Merrill/Pearson.

McNamara, K., & Hollinger, C. (2003). Intervention-based assessment: Evaluation rates and eligibility findings. *Exceptional Children, 69,* 181–193.

Menzies, H. M., Mahdavi, J. N., & Lewis, J. L. (2008). Early intervention: From research to practice. *Remedial and Special Education, 29,* 67–77.

Mooney, J., & Cole, D. (2000). *Learning outside the lines.* New York: Simon & Schuster.

Morgan, P. L., & Sideridis, G. D. (2006). Contrasting the effectiveness of fluency interventions for students with or at risk for learning disabilities: A multilevel random coefficient modeling meta-analysis. *Learning Disabilities Research and Practice, 21,* 191–210.

Müller, E., & Markowitz, J. (2004). *Disability categories: State terminology, definitions & eligibility criteria.* Alexandria, VA: National Association of State Directors of Special Education, Project Forum.

National Center for Educational Statistics. (2003). *Digest of education statistics tables and figures: 2003.* Washington, DC: U.S. Department of Education. Retrieved May 10, 2005, from http://nces.ed.gov/programs/digest/d03

National Institutes of Health, National Institute of Neurological Disorders and Stroke. (2007). *What are learning disabilities?* NINDS Learning Disabilities Information Retrieved February 23, 2008, from www.ninds.nih.gov.

Nelson, J. R., Benner, G. J., & Gonzalez, J. (2003). Learner characteristics that influence the treatment effectiveness of early literacy interventions: A meta-analytic review. *Learning Disabilities Research and Practice, 18,* 255–267.

Nowicki, E. A. (2003). A meta-analysis of the social competence of children with learning disabilities compared to classmates of low and average to high achievement. *Learning Disability Quarterly, 26,* 171–188.

Office of Special Education Programs. (2005). *Number of children served under IDEA, by disability and age group (6–21), 1994 through 2003 (2003).* Data Table AA9. Retrieved from www.ideadata.org

Office of Special Education Programs. (2008). *Students served under IDEA, Part B: Fall 2006.* Retrieved March 20, 2008, from www.ideadata.org

Ofiesh, N. S., Hughes, C., & Scott, S. S. (2004). Extended test time and postsecondary students with learning disabilities: A model for decision making. *Learning Disabilities Research and Practice, 19,* 57–70.

Olswang, L. B., Coggins, T. E., & Timler, G. R. (2001). Outcome measures for school-age children with social communication problems. *Topics in Language Disorders, 21,* 50–73.

Okolo, C., M., Englert, C. S., Bouck, E. C., & Heugtsche, A. M. (2007). Web-based history learning environments: Helping all students learn and like history. *Intervention in School and Clinic, 43,* 3–11.

Pearl, R. (1982). LD children's attributions for success and failure: A replication with a labeled LD sample. *Learning Disabilities Quarterly, 5,* 173–176.

Pullen, P. C., & Justice, L. M. (2003). Enhancing phonological awareness, print awareness, and oral language skills in preschool children. *Intervention in School and Clinic, 39,* 87–98.

Reid, R., & Lienemann, T. O. (2006). *Strategy instruction for students with learning disabilities.* In K. R. Harris & S. Graham (Series Eds.), *What works for special-needs learners.* New York: Guilford Press.

Reschly, D. J. (2002). Minority overrepresentation: The silent contributor to LD prevalence and diagnostic confusion. In R. Bradley, L. Danielson, & D. P. Hallahan, (Eds.), *Identification of learning disabilities: Research to practice* (pp. 361–368). Mahwah, NJ: Erlbaum.

Rovet, J. (2004). Turner syndrome: Genetic and hormonal factors contributing to a specific disability profile. *Learning Disabilities Research and Practice, 19,* 133–145.

Santangelo, T., Harris, K. R., & Graham, D. (2008). Using self-regulated strategy development to support students who have "Trubol giting thangs into werds." *Remedial and Special Education, 29,* 78–89.

Schumaker, J. B., & Deshler, D. D. (2003). Can students with LD become competent writers? *Learning Disability Quarterly, 26*, 129–141.

Shaw, S. (2005). College opportunities for students with learning disabilities. *Projects*. Washington, DC: Advocacy Institute. Retrieved May 10, 2005, from www .advocacyinstitute.org

Shaw, S. (2007). Services for students with learning disabilities: It's the program, not the place. *New Times for DLD, 25*, 1–2.

Sideridis, G. D. (2007). International approaches to learning disabilities: More alike or more different? *Learning Disabilities Research and Practice, 22*, 210–215.

Simmons, D. C., Kame'enui, E. J., Harn, B., Coyne, M. D., Stoolmiller, M., Santoro, L. E., Smith, S. B., Beck, C. T., & Kaufman, N. K. (2007). Attributes of effective and efficient Kindergarten reading intervention: An examination of instructional time and design specificity. *Journal of Learning Disabilities, 40*, 331–347.

Skylar, A., Higgins, K., & Boone, R. (2007). Strategies for adapting WebQuests for students with learning disabilities. *Intervention in School and Clinic, 42*, 20–28.

Speece, D. L., Case, L. P., & Molloy, D. E. (2003). Responsiveness to general education instruction as the first gate to learning disabilities identification. *Learning Disabilities Research and Practice, 18*, 147–156.

Speece, D. L., Mills, C., Ritchey, K. D., & Hillman, E. (2003). Initial evidence that letter fluency tasks are valid indicators of early reading skill. *Journal of Special Education, 36*, 223–233.

Swanson, H. L., & Deshler, D. D. (2003). Instructing adolescents with learning disabilities: Converting a meta-analysis to practice. *Journal of Learning Disabilities, 36* (2), 124–135.

Switzky, H. N., & Schultz, G. F. (1988). Intrinsic motivation and learning performance: Implications for individual educational programming for learners with mild handicaps. *Remedial and Special Education, 9*, 7–14.

Teglasi, H., Cohn, A., & Meshbesher, N. (2004). Temperament and learning disability. *Learning Disability Quarterly, 27*, 9–20.

Therrien, W. J., & Kubina, R. M. (2006). Developing reading fluency with repeated reading. *Intervention in School and Clinic, 41*, 156–160.

Torgesen, J. K. (2002). Empirical and theoretical support for direct diagnosis of learning disabilities by assessment of intrinsic processing weaknesses. In R. Bradley, L. Danielson, & D. P. Hallahan (Eds.), *Identification of learning disabilities: Research to practice* (pp. 565–652). Mahwah, NJ: Erlbaum.

Torgesen, J. K., & Wagner, R. K. (1998). Alternative diagnostic approaches for specific developmental reading disabilities. *Learning Disabilities Research & Practice, 13*, 220–232.

Troia, G. (Ed.). (2008). *Writing instruction and assessment for struggling writers: From theory to evidence-based practices*. New York: Guilford.

Troia, G. A., & Graham, S. (Eds.). (2004). Students who are exceptional and writing disabilities: Prevention, practice, intervention, and assessment. *Exceptionality, 12*, 1–66.

U.S. Department of Education. (1995). *The seventeenth annual report to Congress on the implementation of IDEA*. Washington, DC: U.S. Government Printing Office.

U.S. Department of Education. (2002). *Twenty-fourth annual report to Congress on the implementation of the Individuals with Disabilities Education Act*. Washington, DC: U.S. Government Printing Office.

U.S. Department of Education. (2006, August 14). 34 *CFR* Parts 300 and 301, Assistance to States for the Education of Children with Disabilities and Preschool Grants for Children with Disabilities: Final rule. Federal Register.

Vaughn, S., Elbaum, B., & Boardman, A. G. (2001). The social function of students with learning disabilities: Implications for inclusion. *Exceptionality, 9*, 47–65.

Vaughn, S., & Fuchs, L.S. (2003). Redefining learning disabilities as inadequate response to instruction: The promise and potential problems. *Learning Disabilities Research and Practice, 18*, 137–146.

Vaughn, S., & Linan-Thompson, S. (2004). *Research-based methods of reading instruction: Grades K–3*. Alexandria, VA: Association for Supervision and Curriculum Development.

Wallace, T., Espin, C. A., McMaster, K., Deno, S. L., & Foegen, A. (2007). CBM progress monitoring within a standards-based system: Introduction to the special series. *Journal of Special Education, 41*, 66–68.

Ward, M. J. (2007). *The picture of college freshmen in greater focus: An analysis of selected characteristics by types of disabilities*. HEATH Resource Center, On-line Clearinghouse of Postsecondary Education for Individuals with Disabilities. Retrieved November 18, 2007, from www.heath.gwu.edu/node/293

Warger, C. (2008). *Five homework strategies for teaching students with disabilities*. ERIC/OSEP Digest. Retrieved April 11, 2008, from http//:findarticles.com

Wayman, M. M., Wallace, T., Wiley H. I., Tichá, R., & Espin, C. A. (2007). Literature synthesis on curriculum-based measurement in reading. *Journal of Special Education, 41*, 85–120.

Welsch, R. G. (2007). Using experimental analysis to determining interventions for reading fluency and recalls of students with learning disabilities. *Learning Disability Quarterly, 30*, 115–129.

Wiederholt, J. L. (1974). Historical perspectives on the education of the learning disabled. In L. Mann & D. Sabatino (Eds.), *The second review of special education* (pp. 103–152). Philadelphia: Journal of Special Education Press.

Wiener, J. (2004). Do peer relationships foster behavioral adjustment in children with learning disabilities? *Learning Disability Quarterly, 27*, 21–30.

CHAPTER 6

American Academy of Pediatrics. (2005). *ADHD—Treatment with medication*. Medical Library. Retrieved March 18, 2005, from www.medem.com

American Psychiatric Association. (2000). *Diagnostic and statistical manual of mental disorders* (4th ed., Text Revision). Washington, DC: Author.

Austin, V. L. (2003). Pharmacological interventions for students with ADD. *Intervention in School and Clinic, 38*, 289–296.

Barkley, R. A. (2002). Consensus statement on ADHD. *European Child and Adolescent Psychiatry, 11*, 96–98.

Barkley, R. A. (2005). Taking charge of ADHD: The complete, authoritative guide for parents. New York: Guilford Press.

Barkley, R. A. (2006). *Attention-deficit hyperactivity disorder: A handbook for diagnosis and treatment* (3rd ed.). New York: Guilford Press.

Barkley, R. A., & Edwards, G. (2007). Diagnostic interview, behavior rating scales, and the medical examination. In R. A. Barkley (Ed.) *Attention-deficit hyperactivity disorder* (3rd ed., pp. 337–368). New York: Guilford Press.

Bernstein, J. H., & Waber, D. P. (2007). Executive capacities from a developmental perspective. In L. Meltzer, (Ed.), *Executive function in education* (pp. 39–54). New York: Guilford Press.

Biederman, J., Mick, E., & Garaone, S. V. (2000). Age-dependent decline of symptoms of attention deficit hyperactivity disorder: Impact of remission definition and symptom type. *American Journal of Psychiatry, 157*, 816–818.

Bonafina, M. A., Newcorn, J. H., McKay, K. E., Koda, V. H., & Halperin, J. M. (2000). ADHD and reading disabilities: A cluster analytic approach for distinguishing subgroups. *Journal of Learning Disabilities, 33*, 297–307.

Bryan, T. (1997). Assessing the personal and social status of students with learning disabilities. *Learning Disabilities Research and Practice, 12*, 63–76.

Carbone, E. (2001). Arranging the classroom with an eye (and ear) to students with ADHD. *Teaching Exceptional Children, 34*, 72–81.

Carlson, C. L., Booth, J. E., Shin, M., & Canu, W. H. (2002). Parent-, teacher-, and self-rated motivational styles in ADHD subtypes. *Journal of Learning Disabilities, 35*, 103–113.

Children and Adults with Attention-Deficit/Hyperactivity Disorder. (2007, November). *CHADD statement: Research on AD/HD Treatment misrepresented in media*. Retrieved January 21, 2008, from www.chadd.org

Children and Adults with Attention-Deficit/Hyperactivity Disorder. (2008). *The disorder named AD/HD*. CHADD Fact Sheet #1. Retrieved January 21, 2008, from www.chadd.org

Connor, D. F. (2007). Stimulants. In R. A. Barkley, (Ed.), *Attention-deficit hyperactivity disorder*, (3rd ed., pp. 608–647). New York: Guilford Press.

Daly, P. M., & Ranalli, P. (2003). Using countoons to teach self-monitoring skills. *Teaching Exceptional Children, 35*, 30–35.

Denckla, M. B. (2007). Executive function: Binding together the definitions of attention-deficit/hyperactivity disorder and learning disabilities. In L. Meltzer, (Ed.), *Executive function in education* (pp. 5–18). New York, NY: Guilford Press.

Dietz, S., & Montague, M. (2006). Attention deficit hyperactivity disorder comorbid with emotional and behavioral disorders and learning disabilities in adolescents. *Exceptionality, 14*, 19–33.

Dillon, R. F., & Osborne, S.S. (2006). Intelligence and behavior among individuals identified with attention deficit disorders. *Exceptionality, 14*, 3–18.

Duhaney, L. M. G. (2003). A practical approach to managing the behaviors of students with ADD. *Intervention in School and Clinic, 38*, 267–279.

DuPaul, G. J., Barkley, R. A., & Connor, D. E. (1998). Stimulants. In R. A. Barkley (Ed.), *Attention-deficit hyperactivity disorder* (pp. 510–551), New York: Guilford Press.

DuPaul, G. J., Ervin, R. A., Hook, C. L., & McGoey, K. E. (1998). Peer tutoring for children with attention deficit hyperactivity disorder: Effects on classroom behavior and academic performance. *Journal of Applied Behavior Analysis, 31*, 579–592.

DuPaul, G. E., Schaughency, E. A., Weyandt, L. L., Tripp, G., Kiesner, J., Ota, K., & Stanish, H. (2001). Self-report of ADHD symptoms in university students: Cross-gender and cross-national prevalence. *Journal of Learning Disabilities, 34*(4), 370–379.

DuPaul, G. J., & Stoner, G. (2003). *ADHD in the schools: Assessment and intervention strategies* (2nd ed.). New York: Guilford Press.

Elliott, S. N., & Marquart, A. M. (2004). Extended time as a testing accommodation: Its effects and perceived consequences. *Exceptional Children, 70*(3), 349–367.

Forness, S. R., & Kavale, K. A. (2001). Are school professionals missing their best chance to help troubled kids? *Emotional & Behavioral Disorders, 1*, 80–83.

Fowler, M. (2002). *Attention-deficit/ hyperactivity disorder.* Washington, DC: National Dissemination Center for Children with Disabilities. Retrieved August 26, 2004, from www.nichcy.org

Fowler, M. (2004). *Attention-deficit/ hyperactivity disorder: Briefing paper* (3rd ed.). Washington, DC: National Dissemination Center for Children with Disabilities.

Fuchs, D., & Fuchs, L. S. (1998). Researchers and teachers working together to adapt instruction for diverse learnings. *Learning Disabilities Research & Practice, 13*, 126–137.

Gantos, J. (1998). *Joey Pigza swallowed the key.* New York: Farrar, Straus & Giroux.

Gay, G. (2002). Preparing for culturally responsive teaching. *Journal of Teacher Education, 53*, 106–116.

Gephart, H. R. (2003). Attention-deficit/ hyperactivity disorder: Diagnosis and treatment through adulthood. *Primary Psychiatry, 10*, 27–28.

Getzel, E. E., McManus, S., & Briel, L.W. (2004). An effective model for college students with learning disabilities and attention deficit hyperactivity disorders. *National Center on Secondary Education and Transition (NCET): Research to Practice Brief, 3*, 1–5.

Gotsch, T. (2002, March 13). Medication issue could emerge in IDEA debate. *Special Education Report, 28*, 1–2.

Graham, S., Harris, K. R., & Olinghouse, N. (2007). Addressing executive function problems in writing: An example from the self-regulated strategy development model. In L. Meltzer, (Ed.), *Executive function in education* (pp. 216–236). New York: Guilford Press.

Hallowell, E. M., & Ratey, J. J. (2005). *Delivered from distraction: Getting the most out of life with attention deficit disorder.* New York: Random House.

Harris, K. R., Friedlander, B. D., Saddler, B., Frizzelle, R., & Graham, S. (2005). Self-monitoring of attention versus self-monitoring of academic performance: Effects among students with ADHD in general education classroom. *The Journal of Special Education, 39*(3), 145–156.

Hoffman, B., Hartley, K., & Boone, R. (2005). Reaching accessibility: Guidelines for creating and refining digital learning materials. *Intervention in School and Clinic, 40*, 171–176.

Hoffmann, H. (1999). *Struwwelpeter: Fearful stories and vile pictures to instruct good little folks.* Venice, CA: Feral House.

Honos-Webb, L. (2005). *The gift of ADHD: How to transform your child's problems into strengths.* Oakland, CA: New Harbinger.

Individuals with Disabilities Education Act. PL No. 105-17, 111 Stat. 37.

Individuals with Disabilities Education Improvement Act of 2004. PL No. 108-446. 118 Stat. 2647.

Jensen, P. S. (2000). ADHD: Advances in understanding its causes, and best treatments. *Emotional and Behavioral Disorders in Youth, 1*, 9–10, 19.

Kaplan, B. J., Crawford, S. G., Dewey, D. M., & Fisher, G. C. (2000). The I.Q.s of children with ADHD are normally distributed. *Journal of Learning Disabilities, 33*, 425–432.

Kendall, J., Hatton, D., Beckett, A., & Leo, M. (2003). Children's accounts of attention-deficit/hyperactivity disorder. *Advances in Nursing Science, 26*, 114–130.

Kessler, R. C., Adler, L., Ames, M., & Barkley, R. (2005). The prevalence and effects of adult attention deficit/hyperactivity disorder on work performance in a nationally representative sample of workers. *Journal of Occupational and Environmental Medicine, 47*, 565.

Lucangeli, D., & Cabrele, S., (2006). Mathematical difficulties and ADHD. *Exceptionality, 14*, 53–62.

Mathur, S., & Smith, R. M. (2003). Collaborate with families of children with ADD. *Intervention in School and Clinic, 38*, 311–315.

Mayes, S. D., Calhoun, S. L., & Crowell, E. W. (2000). Learning disabilities and ADHD: Overlapping spectrum disorders. *Journal of Learning Disabilities, 33*, 417–424.

Meltzer, L. (2007). Executive function: Theoretical and conceptual frameworks. In L. Meltzer, (Ed.), *Executive function in education* (pp. 1–3). New York: Guilford Press.

Meltzer, L., & Krishnan, K. (2007). Executive function difficulties and learning disabilities: Understandings and misunderstandings. In L. Meltzer, (Ed.), *Executive function in education* (pp. 77–105). New York: Guilford Press.

Merrell, K. W., & Boelter, E. (2001). An investigation of relationships between social behavior and ADHD in children and youth: Construct validity of the home and community social behavior scales. *Journal of Emotional and Behavioral Disorders, 9,* 260–269.

Miranda, A., Jarque, S., & Tàrraga, R. (2006). Interventions in school settings for students with ADHD. *Exceptionality, 14*, 35–52.

Montague, M., & Dietz, S. (2006). Preface: Attention deficit hyperactivity disorder. *Exceptionality, 14*, 1–2.

Moran, S., & Gardner, H. (2007). "Hill, Skill, and Will": Executive function from a multiple-intelligences perspective. In L. Meltzer, (Ed.), *Executive function in education* (pp. 19–38). New York: Guilford Press.

Müller, E., & Markowitz, J. (2004). *Disability categories: State terminology, definitions and eligibility criteria.* Alexandria, VA: National Association of State Directors of Special Education, Project Forum.

National Association of School Nurses. (2005). *Controlled substances in the school setting.* Retrieved February 21, 2008, from www .nasn.org.

National Association of School Nurses. (2006). *School health nursing services role in health care.* Retrieved February 21, 2008, from www.nasn.org.

National Center for Educational Statistics. (2007). *Fast facts: What proportion of students enrolled in postsecondary education have a disability?* Retrieved February 21, 2008, from www.nces.ed.gov.

National Institute of Mental Health. (2006). *Attention Deficit Hyperactivity Disorder.* Bethesda, MD: National Institutes of Health. Retrieved January 21, 2008, from www.nimh.nih.gov.

National Institutes of Health Consensus Development Conference Statement. (2000). Diagnosis and treatment of attention-deficit/hyperactivity disorder (ADHD). *Journal of the American Academy of Child and Adolescent Psychiatry, 39*, 182–193.

Office of Special Education Programs. (2003). *Identifying and treating attention deficit hyperactivity disorder: A resource for school and home.* Washington, DC: U.S. Department of Education, Office of Special Education and Rehabilitative Services.

Olmeda, R. E., Thomas, A. R., & Davis, C. P. (2003). An analysis of sociocultural factors in social skills training studies with students with attention deficit/hyperactivity disorder. *Multiple Voices, 6*, 58–72.

Pappadopulos, E., & Jensen, P. S. (2001, Spring). What school professionals, counselors, and parents need to know about medication for emotional and behavioral disorders in kids. *Emotional & Behavioral Disorders in Youth*, 35–37.

Pierce, K. (2003). Attention-deficit/hyperactivity disorder and comorbidity. *Primary Psychiatry, 10*, 69–70, 75–75.

Powell, S., & Nelson, B. (1997). Effects of choosing academic assignments on a student with attention deficit hyperactivity disorder. *Journal of Applied Behavior Analysis, 30*, 181–183.

Rehabilitation Act of 1973. Section 504, 19 U.S.C. Section 794.

Reid, R., & Lienemen, T. O. (2006). *Strategy instruction for children with learning disabilities: What it is and how to do it.* New York: Guilford Press.

Reid, R., Trout, A. L., & Schartz, M. (2005). Self-regulation interventions for children with attention deficit/hyperactivity disorder. *Exceptional Children, 71*(4), 361–377.

Salend, S. J., Duhaney, D., Anderson, D. J., & Gottschalk, C. (2004). Using the Internet to improve homework communication and completion. *Teaching Exceptional Children, 36,* 64–73.

Salend, S. J., Elhoweris, H., & van Garderen, D. (2003). Educational interventions for students with ADD. *Intervention in School and Clinic, 38,* 280–288.

Salend, S. J., & Rohena, E. (2003). Students with attention deficit disorders: An overview. *Intervention in School and Clinic, 38,* 259–266.

Schnoes, C., Reid, R., Wagner, M., & Marder, C. (2006). ADHD among students receiving special education services: A national survey. *Exceptional Children, 72,* 483–496.

Shaw, G., & Giambra, L. (1993). Task unrelated thoughts of college students diagnosed as hyperactive in childhood. *Developmental Neuropsychology, 9,* 17–30.

Still, G. F. (1902). Some abnormal psychical conditions in children. *The Lancet, 1,* 1008–1012, 1077–1082, 1163–1168.

Strauss, A. A., & Lehtinen, L. (1947). *Psychology and education of the brain-injured child.* New York: Grune & Stratton.

U.S. Department of Education. (2002). *The twenty-fourth annual report to Congress on the implementation of IDEA.* Washington, DC: U.S. Government Printing Office.

U.S. Department of Education. (2006, August 14). 34 *CFR* Parts 300 and 301, Assistance to States for the Education of Children with Disabilitie and Preschool Grants for Children with Disabilities. *Final rule. Federal Register,* Washington, DC.

Van Kuren, L. (2003, November–December). Technology: The great equalizer. *CEC Today, 10,* 1, 5–6, 15.

Volpe, R. J., DuPaul, G. J., Loney, J., & Salisbury, H. (1999). Alternative selection criteria for identifying children with ADHD: Observed behavior and self-reported internalizing symptoms. *Journal of Emotional and Behavioral Disorders, 7,* 103–109.

Ward, J., & Guyer, K. E. (2000). Medical management of ADHD. In B. P. Guyer (Ed.), *ADHD: Achieving success in school and life* (pp. 38–54). Boston: Allyn & Bacon.

Weyandt, L. L. (2007). *An ADHD primer* (2nd ed.). Mahwah, NJ: Erlbaum.

Weyandt, L. L., Iwaszuk, W., Fulton, K., Ollerton, M., Beatty, N., Fouts, H., Schepman, S., & Greenlaw, C. (2003). The internal restlessness scale: Performance of college students with and without ADHD. *Journal of Learning Disabilities, 36,* 382–389.

Willcutt, E. G., & Pennington, B. F. (2000). Comorbidity of reading disability and attention-deficit/hyperactivity disorder: Differences by gender and subtype. *Journal of Learning Disabilities, 33,* 179–191.

CHAPTER 7

Adoption and Foster Care Analysis and Reporting System. (2002). *Child welfare statistics.* Retrieved from www.acf.dhhs.gov/programs/cb/dis/afcars/scstats.html.

Ahearn, E. (Ed.). (1995, February). Summary of the 16th annual report to Congress on

special education. *Liaison Bulletin,* pp. 1–3. Alexandria VA: National Association of School Departments of Special Education.

Allen, K. M., Hart, B. M., Buell, J. S., Harris, F. R., & Wolf, M. M. (1964). Effects of social reinforcement on isolated behavior of a nursery school child. *Child Development, 35,* 511–518.

Ama, S., & Caplan, E. H. (2001). The human face of foster care in America. *Focal Point, 15,* 25–26.

American Psychiatric Association. (2003). *Diagnostic and statistical manual of mental disorders* (4th ed., Text Revision) (DSM-IV-TR). Washington, DC: Author.

Anderson, J. A., Kutash, K., & Duchnowski, A. J. (2001). A comparison of the academic progress of students with EBD and students with LD. *Journal of Emotional and Behavioral Disorders, 9,* 106–115.

Archwamety, T., & Katsiyannis, A. (2000). Academic remediation, parole violations, and recidivism rates among delinquent youth. *Remedial and Special Education, 21,* 161–170.

Armsden, G., Pecora, P. J., Payne, V. H., & Szatkiewicz, J. P. (2000). Children placed in long-term foster care: An intake profile using the child behavior checklist/4–18. *Journal of Emotional and Behavioral Disorders, 8,* 49–64.

Axelrod, S., & Hall, R. V. (1999). *Behavior modification: Basic principles.* Austin, TX: Pro-Ed.

Babyak, A. E., Koorland, M., & Mathes, P. G. (2000). The effects of story mapping instruction on the reading comprehension of students with behavioral disorders. *Behavioral Disorders, 25,* 239–258.

Babyak, A. E., Luze, G. J., & Kamps, D. M. (2000). The good student game: Behavior management for diverse classrooms. *Intervention in School and Clinic, 35,* 216–223.

Begley, S. (1999, May 3). Why the young kill. *Newsweek,* pp. 32–35.

Bender, W. N., & McLaughlin, P. J. (1997). Weapons violence in schools: Strategies for teachers confronting violence and hostage situations. *Intervention in School and Clinic, 32,* 211–216.

Bender, W. N., Shubert, T. H., & McLaughlin, P. J. (2001). Invisible kids: Preventing school violence by identifying kids in trouble. *Intervention in School and Clinic, 37,* 105–111.

Bower, E. M. (1960). *Early identification of emotionally disturbed children in school* (Rev. ed.). Springfield, IL: Thomas.

Bower, E. M. (1982). Defining emotional disturbance: Public policy and research. *Psychology in the Schools, 19,* 55–60.

Bower, E. M., & Lambert, N. M. (1962). *A process for in-school screening of children with emotional handicaps.* Princeton, NJ: Educational Testing Service.

Brigham, A. (1847). The moral treatment of insanity. *American Journal of Insanity, 4,* 1–15.

Bryant, D. P., Smith, D. D., & Bryant, B. (2008). *Teaching students with special needs in inclusive classrooms.* Boston: Allyn & Bacon.

Bullis, M., Walker, H. M., & Sprague, J. R. (2001). A promise unfulfilled: Social skills

training with at-risk and antisocial children and youth. *Exceptionality, 9,* 67–90.

Bullis, M., & Yovanoff, P. (2006). Twenty-four months after high school: Paths taken by youth diagnosed with severe emotional and behavioral disorders. *Journal of Emotional and Behavioral Disorders, 14,* 99–107.

Burrell, B., Wood, S. J., Pikes, T., & Holliday, C. (2001). Student mentors and protégés learning together. *Teaching Exceptional Children, 33,* 24–29.

Carlson, G. A., & Kashani, J. H. (1988). Phenomenology of major depression from childhood through adulthood: Analysis of three studies. *American Journal of Psychiatry, 145,* 1222–1225.

Cartledge, G., Kea, C. D., & Ida, D. J. (2000). Anticipating differences, celebrating strengths: Providing culturally competent services for students with serious emotional disturbance. *Teaching Exceptional Children, 32,* 30–37.

Cauce, A., Paradise, M., Ginzler, J., Embry, L., Morgan, C. J., Lohr, Y., & Theofelis, J. (2000). The characteristics and mental health of homeless adolescents: Age and gender differences. *Journal of Emotional and Behavioral Disorders, 8,* 230–239.

Cheney, D., & Barringer, C. (1995). Teacher competence, student diversity, and staff training for the inclusion of middle school students with emotional and behavioral disorders. *Journal of Emotional and Behavioral Disorders, 3,* 174–182.

Chicago Youth Centers. (2008). Success stories! Retrieved March 9, 2008, from http://www.chicagoyouthcenters.org/programs/index.html

Children's Defense Fund. (2001). *The state of America's children: 2001.* Washington, DC: Author.

Children's Defense Fund. (2004). *The state of America's children: 2004.* Washington, DC: Author.

Cochran, L., Feng, H., Cartledge, G., & Hamilton, S. (1993). The effects of cross-age tutoring on the academic achievement, social behaviors, and self-perceptions of low-achieving African-American males with behavioral disorders. *Behavioral Disorders, 18,* 292–302.

Costenbader, V., & Buntaine, R. (1999). Diagnostic discrimination between social maladjustment and emotional disturbance. *Journal of Emotional and Behavioral Disorders, 7,* 2–10.

Cruz, L., & Cullinan, D. (2001). Awarding points, using levels to help children improve behavior. *Teaching Exceptional Children, 33,* 16–23.

Davis, C. A., Brady, M. P., Williams, R. E., & Hamilton, R. (1992). Effects of high-probability requests on the acquisition and generalization of responses to requests in young children and behavior disorders. *Journal of Applied Behavior Analysis, 25,* 905–916.

Dawson, L., Venn, M. L., & Gunter, P. L. (2000). The effects of teacher versus computer reading models. *Behavioral Disorders, 25,* 105–113.

Day, D. M., & Hunt, A. C. (1996). A multivariate assessment of a risk model for juvenile delinquency with an "under 12 offender" sample. *Journal of Emotional and Behavioral Disorders, 4,* 66–72.

Deutsch, A. (1949). *The mentally ill in America: A history of their care and treatment from colonial times* (2nd ed.). New York: Columbia University Press.

DeVoe, J. F., Peter, K., Kaufman, P., Ruddy, S. A., Miller, A. K., Plany, M., Snyder, T. D., & Rand, M. R. (2003). *Indicators of school crime and safety: 2003*. Washington, DC: National Center for Educational Statistics, U.S. Departments of Education and Justice.

Drummond, T. (1994). *The Student Risk Screening Scale (SRSS)*. Grants Pass, OR: Josephine County Mental Health Program.

Duckworth, S., Smith-Rex, S., Okey, S., Brookshire, M., Rawlinson, D., Rawlinson, R., Castillo, S., & Little, J. (2001). Wraparound services for young schoolchildren with emotional and behavioral disorders. *Teaching Exceptional Children, 33,* 54–60.

Eber, L., Smith, C. R., Sugai, G., & Scott, T. M. (2002). Wraparound and positive behavioral supports in the schools. *Journal of Emotional and Behavioral Disorders, 10,* 171–180.

Edelsohn, G., Ialongo, N., Werthamer-Larsson, L., Crockett, I., & Kellam, S. (1992). Self-reported depressive symptoms in first-grade children: Developmentally transient phenomena. *Journal of the American Academy of Child and Adolescent Psychiatry, 31,* 282–290.

Elliott, S., & Gresham, F. M. (1991). *Social skills intervention guide*. Circle Pines, MN: American Guidance Service.

Ervin, R. A., DuPaul, G. J., Kern, L., & Friman, P. C. (1998). Classroom based functional and adjunctive assessments: Proactive approaches to intervention selection for adolescents with attention deficit hyperactivity disorder. *Journal of Applied Behavior Analysis, 31,* 65–78.

Falk, K. B., & Wehby, J. H. (2001). The effects of peer-assisted learning strategies on the beginning reading skills of young children with emotional or behavioral disorders. *Behavioral Disorders, 26,* 344–359.

Feil, E. G., Walker, H. M., & Severson, H. H. (1995). The early screening project for young children with behavior problems. *Journal of Emotional and Behavioral Disorders, 3,* 194–202.

Forness, S. R., & Kavale, K. A. (2001). Are school professionals missing their best chance to help troubled kids? *Emotional and Behavioral Disorders, 1,* 80–83.

Forness, S. R., & Knitzer, J. (1992). A new proposed definition and terminology to replace "serious emotional disturbance" in IDEA. *School Psychology Review, 21,* 12–20.

Franca, V. M., Kerr, M. M., Reitz, A. L., & Lambert, D. (1990). Peer tutoring among behaviorally disordered students: Academic and social benefits to tutor and tutee. *Education and Treatment of Children, 3,* 109–128.

Frey, K. S., Hirschstein, M. K., & Guzzo, B. A. (2000). Second step: Preventing aggression by promoting social competence. *Journal of Emotional and Behavioral Disorders, 8,* 102–112.

Gaetano, C. (2006, August 31). General ed. teachers face special ed. realities. *Sentinel*, East Brunswick, NJ. Retrieved from ebs.gmnews.com/news/2006/0831/Schools/043.htm

Gersten, R., Fuchs, L. S., Compton, D., Coyne, M., Greenwood, C., & Innocenti, M. S. (2005). Quality indicators for group experimental and quasi-experimental research in special education. *Exceptional Children, 71,* 149–164.

Goodman R (1997) The Strengths and Difficulties Questionnaire: A research note. *Journal of Child Psychology and Psychiatry, 38,* 581–586.

Greenbaum, P. E., Dedrick, R. F., Friedman, R. M., Kutash, K., Brown, E. C., Lardierh, S. P. (1996). National Adolescent and Child Treatment Study (NACTS): Outcomes for children with serious emotional and behavioral disturbance. *Journal of Emotional and Behavioral Disorders, 4,* 130–146.

Gresham, F. M. (2002). Social skills assessment and instruction for students with emotional and behavioral disorders. In K. L. Lane, F. M. Gresham, & T. E. O'Shaughnessy (Eds.), *Interventions for children with or at risk for emotional and behavioral disorders* (pp. 242–258). Boston: Allyn & Bacon.

Gresham, F. M., Lane, K. L., MacMillan, D. L., & Bocian, K. M. (1999). Social and academic profiles of externalizing and internalizing groups: Risk factors for emotional and behavioral disorders. *Behavioral Disorders, 24,* 231–245.

Griller-Clark, H. (2001). Transition services for youth in the juvenile justice system. *Focal Point, 15,* 23–25.

Hallahan, D. P., Kauffman, J. M., & Pullen, P. (2009). *Exceptional children: Introduction to special education* (11th ed.). Boston: Allyn & Bacon.

Harper, G. F., Mallette, B., Meheady, L., Bentley, A. E., & Moore, J. (1995). Retention and treatment failure in classwide peer tutoring: Implications for further research. *Journal of Behavioral Education, 5,* 399–414.

Hawkins, J. D., Catalano, R. F., Kosterman, R., Abbott, R., & Hill, K. G. (1999). Preventing adolescent health-risk behaviors by strengthening protection during childhood. *Archives of Pediatrics & Adolescent Medicine, 1153,* 226–234.

Hoagwood, K. (2001a). Evidence-based practice in children's mental health services: What do we know? Why aren't we putting it to use? *Emotional and Behavioral Disorders in Youth, 1,* 84–87, 90.

Hoagwood, K. (2001b). Surgeon general's conference on children's mental health sets out a national action agenda. *Emotional and Behavioral Disorders in Youth, 1,* 40–44.

Horner, R. H., Carr, E. G., Halle, J., McGee, G., Odom, S., & Wolery, M. (2005). The use of single-subject research to identify evidence-based practice in special education. *Exceptional Children, 71,* 165–179.

Horner, R., & Sugai, G. (2002). *School-wide positive behavior support: Implementers' blueprint and self-assessment*. Eugene: University of Oregon, OSEP Center on Positive Behavior Support.

Horner, R. H., Sugai, G., Lewis-Palmer, T., & Todd, A. W. (2001). Teaching school-wide behavioral expectations. *Emotional and Behavioral Expectations, 1,* 77–79, 93–95.

Hosp, J. L., & Reschly, D. J. (2002). Predictors of restrictiveness of placement for African-American and Caucasian students. *Exceptional Children, 68,* 225–238.

Hunter, L. (2001). The value of school-based mental health programs. *Emotional and Behavioral Disorders in Youth, 1,* 27–28, 46.

IDEA Practices. (2002). Youth with disabilities in the juvenile justice system. Retrieved July 17, 2002, from www.ideapractices.org

Individuals with Disabilities Education Improvement Act of 2004, 20 U.S.C. 1400 *et seq.* (2004) (reauthorization of Individuals with Disabilities Act 1990).

Information Please Database. (2007). A time line of recent worldwide school shootings. Retrieved February 13, 2008, from http://www.infoplease.com/ipa/A0777958.html

Iwata, B. A., Dorsey, M. E., Slifer, K. J., Bauman, K. E., & Richman, G. S. (1982). Toward a functional analysis of self-injury. *Analysis and Intervention in Developmental Disabilities, 2,* 3–20.

Kaminski, R. A., & Good III, R. H. (1996). Toward a technology for assessing basic early literacy skills. *School Psychology Review, 25,* 215–227.

Kamps, D., Kravits, T., Stolze, J., & Swaggart, B. (1999). Prevention strategies for at-risk students and students with EBD in urban elementary schools. *Journal of Emotional and Behavioral Disorders, 7,* 178–188.

Kanner, L. (1957). *Child psychiatry*. Springfield, IL: Thomas.

Kaslow, N. J., & Rehm, L. P. (1998). Childhood depression. In R. J. Morris & T. R. Kratochwill (Eds.), *The practice of child therapy* (3rd ed., pp. 48–90). Boston: Allyn & Bacon.

Kauffman, J. M. (1999). How we prevent the prevention of emotional and behavioral disorders. *Exceptional Children, 65,* 448–468.

Kauffman, J. M., & Landrum, T. J. (2009). *Characteristics of behavioral disorders of children and youth* (9th ed.). Upper Saddle River, NJ: Merrill/Pearson Education.

Kazdin, A. (1987). Treatment of antisocial behavior in children: Current status and future directions. *Psychological Bulletin, 102,* 187–203.

Kern, L., Childs, K., Dunlap, G., Clarke, S., & Falk, G. (1994). Using assessment-based curricular intervention to improve the classroom behavior of a student with emotional and behavioral challenges. *Journal of Applied Behavior Analysis, 27,* 7–19.

Kern, L., Delaney, B., Clarke, S., Dunlap, G., & Childs, K. (2001). Improving the classroom behavior of students with emotional and behavioral disorders using individualized curricular modifications. *Journal of Emotional and Behavioral Disorders, 9,* 239–247.

Landrum, T., J., Tankersley, M., & Kauffman, J. M. (2003). What is special about special education for students with emotional or behavioral disorders? *Journal of Special Education, 37,* 148–156.

Lane, K. L. (1999). Young students at risk for antisocial behavior: The utility of academic and social skills interventions. *Journal of Emotional and Behavioral Disorders, 7,* 211–223.

Lane, K. L. (2003). Identifying young students at risk for antisocial behavior: The utility of "teachers as tests." *Behavioral Disorders, 28,* 360–389.

Lane, K. L. (2004). Academic instruction and tutoring interventions for students with emotional/behavioral disorders: 1990 to present. In R. B. Rutherford, M. M. Quinn, & S. R. Mathur (Eds.), *Handbook of research in emotional and behavioral disorders* (pp. 462–486). New York: Guilford Press.

Lane, K. L. (2007). Identifying and supporting students at risk for emotional and behavioral disorders within multi-level models: Data driven approaches to conducting secondary interventions with an academic emphasis. *Education and Treatment of Children, 30,* 135–164.

Lane, K. L., & Beebe-Frankenberger, M. E. (2004). *School-based interventions: The tools you need to succeed.* Boston: Allyn & Bacon.

Lane, K. L., Gresham, F. M., & O'Shaughnessy, T. (2002). Identifying, assessing and intervening with children with or at-risk for behavior disorders: A look to the future. In K. L. Lane, F. M. Gresham, & T. E. O'Shaughnessy (Eds.), *Interventions for children with or at risk for emotional and behavioral disorders* (pp. 317–326). Boston: Allyn & Bacon.

Lane, K. L., Harris, K., Graham, S., Weisenbach, J., Brindle, M., & Morphy, P. (2008). The effects of self-regulated strategy development on the writing performance of second grade students with behavioral and writing difficulties. *Journal of Special Education, 41,* 234–253.

Lane, K. L., Kalberg, J. R., & Edwards, C. (2008). An examination of school-wide interventions with primary level efforts conducted in elementary schools: Implications for school psychologists. In D. H. Molina (Ed.), *School psychology: 21st century issues and challenges.* (pp. 253–278). New York: Nova Science.

Lane, K. L., Kalberg, J. R., & Menzies, H. M. (in press). *A step-by-step approach to developing comprehensive school-wide intervention programs to prevent and manage antisocial behavior.* Guilford Press.

Lane, K. L., Kalberg, J. R., & Shepcaro, J. C. (in press). *An examination of quality indicators of function-based interventions for students with emotional or behavioral disorders attending middle and high schools.* Unpublished manuscript.

Lane, K. L., Mahdavi, J. N., & Borthwick-Duffy, S. A. (2003). Teacher perceptions of the prereferral intervention process: A call for assistance with school-based interventions. *Preventing School Failure, 47,* 148–155.

Lane, K. L., O'Shaughnessy, T. E., Lambros, K. M., Gresham, F. M., & Beebe-Frankenberger, M. E. (2001). The efficacy of phonological awareness training with first-grade students who have behavioral problems and reading difficulties. *Journal of Emotional and Behavioral Disorders, 9,* 219–231.

Lane, K. L., Robertson, E. J., & Graham-Bailey, M. A. L. (2006). An examination of school-wide interventions with primary level efforts conducted in secondary schools: Methodological considerations. In T. E. Scruggs & M.A. Mastropieri (Eds.), *Applications of research methodology: Advances in learning and behavioral disabilities* (Vol. 19). Oxford: Elsevier.

Lane, K. L., Wehby, J. H., Little, M. A., & Cooley, C. (2005). Students educated in self-contained classes and self-contained schools: Part II—How do they progress over time? *Behavioral Disorders, 30,* 363–374.

Lane, K. L., Wehby, J., Menzies, H. M., Doukas, G. L., Munton, S. M., & Gregg, R. M. (2003). Social skills instruction for students at risk for antisocial behavior: The effects of small-group instruction. *Behavioral Disorders, 28,* 229–248.

Lane, K. L., Wehby, J. H., Menzies, H. M., Gregg, R. M., Doukas, G. L., & Munton, S. M. (2002). Early literacy instruction for first-grade students at-risk for antisocial behavior. *Education and Treatment of Children, 25,* 438–458.

Lane, K. L., Weisenbach, J. L., Little, M. A., Phillips, A., & Wehby, J. (2006). Illustrations of function-based interventions implemented by general education teachers: Building capacity at the school site. *Education and Treatment of Children, 29,* 549–671.

Lee, Y. Y., Sugai, G., & Horner, R. H. (1999). Using an instructional intervention to reduce problem and off-task behaviors. *Journal of Positive Behavior Interventions, 1,* 195–204.

Lewis, T. J., & Sugai, G. (1999). Effective behavior support: A systems approach to proactive schoolwide management. *Exceptional Children, 31,* 1–24.

Little, L. (2002, Winter). In preschool classrooms: Linking research to practice. *Early Developments,* pp. 7–9.

Lohrmann-O'Rourke, S., & Zirkel, P. A. (1998). The case law on aversive interventions for students with disabilities. *Exceptional Children, 65,* 101–123.

Lynam, D. R. (1996). Early identification of chronic offenders: Who is the fledgling psychopath? *Psychological Bulletin, 120,* 209–234.

Maag, J. W. (2000). Managing resistance. *Intervention in Schools and Clinics, 35,* 131–140.

Maag, J. W. (2001). Rewarded by punishment: Reflections on the disuse of positive reinforcement in schools. *Exceptional Children, 67,* 173–186.

Manley, R. S., Rickson, H., & Standeven, B. (2000). Children and adolescents with eating disorders: Strategies for teachers and school counselors. *Intervention in School and Clinic, 35,* 228–231.

Mattison, R. E., Hooper, S. R., & Glassberg, L. A. (2002). Three-year course of learning disorders in special education students classified as behavioral disorder. *Journal of the American Academy of Child & Adolescent Psychiatry, 41,* 1454–1461.

McConaughy, S. H., & Wadsworth, M. E. (2000). Life history reports of young adults previously referred for mental health services. *Journal of Emotional and Behavioral Disorders, 8,* 202–215.

McLaughlin, T. F. (1992). Effects of written feedback in reading on behaviorally disordered students. *Journal of Educational Research, 85,* 312–315.

Miller, M. J., Lane, K. L., & Wehby, J. (2005). Social skills instruction for students with high incidence disabilities: An effective, efficient approach for addressing acquisition deficits. *Preventing School Failure, 49,* 27–40.

Miller-Johnson, S., Coie, J. E., Maumary-Gremaud, A., Lockman, J., & Terry, R. (1999). Relationship between childhood peer rejection and aggression and adolescent delinquency severity and type among African-American youth. *Journal of Emotional and Behavioral Disorders, 7,* 137–146.

Mooney, P., Denny, R. K., & Gunter, P. L. (2004). The impact of NCLB and the reauthorization of IDEA on academic instruction of students with emotional or behavioral disorders. *Behavioral Disorders, 14,* 203–221.

Morris, R. J., Shah, K., & Morris, Y. P. (2002). In K. L. Lane, F. M. Gresham, & T. E. O'Shaughnessy (Eds.), *Interventions for children with or at risk for emotional and behavioral disorders* (pp. 223–241). Boston: Allyn & Bacon.

Myles, B. S., & Simpson, R. L. (1998). Aggression and violence by school-age children and youth: Understanding the aggression cycle and prevention/intervention strategies. *Intervention in School and Clinic, 33,* 259–264.

National Alliance of Black School Educators & ILIAD Project. (2002). *Addressing overrepresentation of African American students in special education.* Arlington, VA: Council for Exceptional Children, and Washington, DC: National Alliance of Black School Educators.

National Center on Education, Disability, and Juvenile Justice. (2002). Monograph series on education, disability, and juvenile justice. Retrieved July 13, 2002, from www .edjj.org/monographs/index.html.

National Center for Educational Statistics. (2001). Quick tables and figures. www .nces.ed.gov/quicktables.

National Center for Educational Statistics. (2005). Quick tables and figures. www .nces.ed.gov/quicktables.

Nelson, J. R., Benner, G. J., Lane, K., & Smith, B. W. (2004). An investigation of the academic achievement of K–12 students with emotional and behavioral disorders in public school settings. *Exceptional Children, 71,* 59–73.

Nelson, J. R., Johnson, A., & Marchand-Martella, N. (1996). Effects of direct instruction, cooperative learning, and independent learning practices on the classroom behavior of students with behavioral disorders: A comparative analysis. *Journal of Emotional and Behavioral Disorders, 4,* 53–62.

Newcomer, P. L. (1993). *Understanding and teaching emotionally disturbed children and adolescents* (2nd ed.). Austin, TX: Pro-Ed.

Nichols, P. (2000). Role of cognition and affect in a functional behavioral analysis. *Exceptional Children, 66,* 393–402.

Office of Special Education Programs. (2008). *Students served under IDEA, Part B: Fall 2006.* Retrieved March 25, 2008, from www.ideadata.org.

Pancheri, C., & Prater, M. A. (1999). What teachers and parents should know about Ritalin. *Teaching Exceptional Children, 31,* 20–26.

Pappadopulos, E., & Jensen, P. S. (2001). What school professionals, counselors, and parents need to know about medication for emotional and behavioral disorders in kids. *Emotional and Behavioral Disorders in Youth, 1,* 35–37.

Powell, R. (2002). Beauford Delaney the Color Yellow. Atlanta: High Museum of Art.

Quinn, S. R., & Poirier, J. M. (2004). Linking prevention research with policy: Examining the costs of the failure to prevent emotional and behavioral disorders. In R. B. Rutherford Jr., M. M. Quinn, & S. R. Mathur (Eds.), *Handbook of research in emotional and behavioral disorders* (pp. 78–97). New York: Guilford.

Reid, J. B., & Patterson, G. R. (1991). Early prevention and intervention with conduct problems: A social interactional model for the integration of research and practice. In G. Stoner, M. R. Shinn, & H. M. Walker (Eds.), *Interventions for achievement and behavior problems* (pp. 715–740). Silver Spring, MD: National Association of School Principals.

Reid, R., Gonzalez, J. E., Nordness, A. T., Trout, A., & Epstein, M. H. (2004). A meta-analysis of the academic status of students with emotional/behavioral disturbance. *Journal of Special Education, 38,* 130–143.

Rudo, Z. H., Powell, D. S., & Dunlap, G. (1998). The effects of violence in the home on children's emotional, behavioral, and social functioning: A review of the literature. *Journal of Emotional and Behavioral Disorders, 6,* 94–113.

Schoenwald, S. K., & Hoagwood, K. (2001). Effectiveness and dissemination in research: Their mutual roles in improving mental health services for children and adolescents. *Emotional and Behavioral Disorders in Youth, 2,* 3–4, 18–20.

Scott, T. M., & Shearer-Lingo, A. (2002). The effects of reading fluency instruction on the academic and behavioral success of middle school students in a self-contained EBD classroom. *Preventing School Failure, 46,* 167–173.

Shores, R. E., Gunter, P. L., & Jack, S. L. (1993). Classroom management strategies: Are they setting events for coercion? *Behavioral Disorders, 18,* 92–102.

Sinclair, E. (1998). Head Start children at risk: Relationship of prenatal drug exposure to identification of special needs and subsequent special education kindergarten placement. *Behavioral Disorders, 23,* 125–133.

Sinclair, M. F., Christenson, S. L., Evelo, D. L., & Hurley, C. M. (1998). Dropout prevention for youth with disabilities: Efficacy of a sustained school engagement procedure. *Exceptional Children, 65,* 7–21.

Snyder, H. N., & Sickmund, M. (2006). *Juvenile offenders and victims: 2006 National Report.* Washington, DC: U.S. Department of Justice, Office of Justice Programs, Office of Juvenile Justice and Delinquency Prevention.

Stichter, J. P., Lewis, T. J., Richter, M., Johnson, N. W., & Bradley, L. (2006). Assessing antecedent variables: The effects of instructional variables on student outcomes through in-service and peer coaching professional development models. *Education and Treatment of Children, 29,* 665–692.

Strain, P. S., Steele, P., Ellis, R., & Timm, M. (1982). Long-term effects of oppositional child treatment with mothers as therapists and therapist trainers. Journal of *Applied Behavior Analysis, 15,* 163–169.

Strain, P. S., & Timm, M. A. (1998). *The early childhood intervention study.* Unpublished manuscript, Regional Intervention Project, Nashville, TN.

Strain, P. S., & Timm, M. A. (1999). *Preliminary results from the early childhood intervention study.* Unpublished manuscript, Regional Intervention Project, Nashville, TN.

Strain, P. S., & Timm, M. A. (2001). Remediation and prevention of aggression: An evaluation of the Regional Intervention Project over a quarter of a century. *Behavioral Disorders, 26,* 297–313.

Sugai, G., & Horner, R. (2002). The evolution of discipline practices: school-wide positive behavior supports. *Child and Family Behavior Therapy, 24,* 23–50.

Sutherland, K. S., Adler, N., & Gunter, P. L. (2003). The effect of varying rates of opportunities to respond to academic requests on the classroom behavior of students with EBD. *Journal of Emotional and Behavioral Disorders, 11,* 239–248.

Sutherland, K. S., Wehby, J. H., & Yoder, P. J. (2001). An examination of the relation between teacher praise and students' with emotional/behavioral disorders opportunities to respond to academic requests. *Journal of Emotional and Behavioral Disorders, 10,* 5–14.

Talbott, E., & Thiede, K. (1999). Pathways to antisocial behavior among adolescent girls. *Journal of Emotional and Behavioral Disorders, 7,* 31–39.

Test, D. W., Karvonen, M., Wood, W. M., Browder, D., & Algozzine, B. (2000). Choosing a self-determination curriculum. *Teaching Exceptional Children, 33,* 48–54.

Tobin, T. J., & Sugai, G. M. (1999). Using sixth-grade school records to predict school violence, chronic discipline problems, and high school outcomes. *Journal of Emotional and Behavioral Disorders, 7,* 40–53.

Tolan, P., Gorman-Smith, D., & Henry, D. (2001). New study to focus on efficacy of "whole school" prevention approaches. *Emotional and Behavioral Disorders in Youth, 2,* 22–23.

Townsend, B. L. (2000). The disproportionate discipline of African American learners: Reducing school suspensions and expulsions. *Exceptional Children, 66,* 381–391.

Trout, A. L., Nordness, P. D., Pierce, C. D., & Epstein, M. H. (2003). Research on the academic status of children with emotional and behavioral disorders: A review of the literature from 1961 to 2000. *Journal of Emotional and Behavioral Disorders, 11,* 198–210.

Umbreit, J., Ferro, J., Liaupsin, C., & Lane, K. (2007). *Functional behavioral assessment and function-based intervention: An effective, practical approach.* Upper Saddle River, NJ: Pearson Education.

Umbreit, J., Lane, K. L., & Dejud, C. (2004). Improving classroom behavior by modifying task difficulty: The effects of increasing the difficulty of too-easy tasks. *Journal of Positive Behavior Interventions, 6,* 13–20.

U.S. Department of Education. (1999). Assistance to states for the education of children with disabilities program and the early intervention program for infants and toddlers with disabilities; proposed regulations. *Federal Register, 34, CFR* Parts 300, 301, and 304.

U.S. Department of Education. (2001). *The twenty-third annual report to Congress on the implementation of IDEA.* Washington, DC: U.S. Government Printing Office.

U.S. Department of Education. (2006, August 14). 34 *CFR* Parts 300 and 301, *Assistance to States for the Education of Children with Disabilities and Preschool Grants for Children with Disabilities: Final rule. Federal Register,* Washington, DC.

Wagner, M., & Davis, (2006). How are we preparing students with emotional disturbances for the transition to young adulthood? Findings from the National Longitudinal Transition Study-2. *Journal of Emotional and Behavioral Disorders, 14,* 86–98.

Walker, H. M., Irvin, I. K., Noell, J., & Singer, G. H. S. (1992). A construct score approach to the assessment of social competence: Rationale, technological considerations, and anticipated outcomes. *Behavior Modification, 16,* 448–474.

Walker, H. M., Kavanagh, K., Stiller, B., Golly, A., Severson, H. H., & Feil, E. G. (1998). First step to success: An early intervention approach for preventing school antisocial behavior. *Journal of Emotional and Behavioral Disorders, 6,* 66–80.

Walker, H. M., Ramsey, E., & Gresham, F. M. (2004). *Antisocial behavior in school: Evidence-based practices* (2nd ed.). Belmont, CA: Wadsworth.

Walker, H. M., & Severson, H. H. (1992). *Systematic screening for behavior disorders (SSBD): User's guide and technical manual.* Longmont, CO: Sopris West.

Walker, H. M., & Sprague, J. (1999). The path to school failure, delinquency, and violence: Causal factors and potential solutions. *Intervention in School and Clinic, 35,* 67–73.

Walker, H. M., & Sprague, J. R. (2000). Intervention strategies for diverting at-risk children and youth from destructive outcomes. *Emotional and Behavioral Disorders in Youth, 1,* 5–8.

Wehmeyer, M. L., Palmer, S. B., Agran, M., Mithaug, D. E., & Martin, J. E. (2000). Promoting causal agency: Self-determined learning model of instruction. *Exceptional Children, 66,* 439–453.

Witt, J. C., Elliott, S. N., Gresham, F. M., & Kramer, J. J. (1988). *Assessment of special children: Tests and the problem-solving process.* Glenview, IL: Scott, Foresman.

Zametkin, A. J., & Earnst, M. (1999). Problems in the management of attention-deficit-hyperactivity disorder. *New England Journal of Medicine, 340,* 40–46.

Zigmond, N. (2006). Twenty-four months after high school: Paths taken by youth diagnosed with severe emotional and behavioral disorders. *Journal of Emotional and Behavioral Disorders, 14,* 99–107.

Zirkel, P. (1999). How to determine eligibility of students with problem behaviors. *The Special Educator, 17,* 7–8.

CHAPTER 8

Agran, M., & Wehmeyer, M. (2008). Person-centered career planning. In F. Rusch (Ed.), *Beyond high school: Preparing adolescents for tomorrow's challenges* (2nd ed., pp. 55–77). Upper Saddle River, NJ: Merrill/Pearson Education.

Amiel-Tison, C., Allen, M.C., Lebrun, F., & Rogowski, J. (2002). Macropremies: Underpriviledged newborns. *Mental Retardation and Developmental Disabilities Research Reviews, 8,* 281–292.

Arc, The. (2005 May). Causes and prevention of mental retardation. *Frequently Asked Questions.* Retrieved June 17, 2005, from www.thearc.org

Associated Press. (2007, September 20). Citing toy recalls, safety agency asks Congress for support. *New York Times,* Business.

Ayllon, T., & Azrin, N. H. (1964). Reinforcement and instructions with mental patients. *Journal of Experimental Analysis of Behavior, 7,* 327–331.

Ayllon, R., & Azrin, N. H. (1968). Reinforcer sampling: A technique for increasing the behavior of mental patients. *Journal of Applied Behavior Analysis, 1,* 13–20.

Bennington, L. K., & Thomson, G. (2006). Fetal alcohol syndrome. *Healthline.* Retrieved January 27, 2008, from www.healthline.com/galecontent/fetal-alcohol-syndrome-2

Birnbrauer, J. S., Wolf, M. M., Kidder, J. D., & Tague, C. E. (1965). Classroom behavior of retarded pupils with token reinforcement. *Journal of Experimental Child Psychology, 2,* 219–235.

Blatt, B. (1965). *Christmas in purgatory: A photographic essay on mental retardation.* Syracuse, NY: Human Policy Press.

Browder, D.M., Wakeman, S. Y., Flowers, C., Rickelman, R. J., Pugalee, D., Karvonen, M. (2007). Creating access to the general curriculum with links to grade-level content for students with significant cognitive disabilities: An explication of the concept. *Journal of Special Education, 32*(3), 130–153.

Brown, I., & Radford, J. P. (2007). Historical overview of intellectual and developmental disabilities. In I. Brown & M. Percy (Eds.), *A comprehensive guide to intellectual and developmental disabilities.* Baltimore, MD: Brookes.

Bryen, D. N., Carey, A., & Friedman, M. (2007). Cell phone use by adults with intellectual disabilities. *Intellectual and Developmental Disabilities, 45,* 1–9.

Centers for Disease Control and Prevention. (2006). *Fetal alcohol spectrum disorders.* Retrieved January 26, 2008, from www.cdc.gov/ncbddd/fas/fasask.htm#chracter.

Centers for Disease Control and Prevention. (2007a). *General lead information: Questions and answers.* Retrieved January 26, 2008, from www.cdc.gov/nceh/lead/faq/about.htm on.

Centers for Disease Control and Prevention. (2007b). *Tips to prevent lead exposure.* Retrieved January 26, 2008, from www.cdc.gov/nceh/lead/faq/tips.htm.

Centers for Disease Control and Prevention. (2007c). *Toys and childhood lead exposure.* Retrieved January 26, 2008, from www.cdc.gov/nceh/lead/faq/toys.htm.

Chadsey, J., & Beyer, S. (2001). Social relationships in the workplace. *Mental Retardation and Developmental Disabilities Research Reviews, 7,* 128–133.

Children's Defense Fund. (2004). *The state of America's children: 2004.* Washington, DC: Author.

Children's Defense Fund. (2007). *Annual report: 2006.* Washington, DC: Author.

Division for Early Childhood of the Council for Exceptional Children. (2007). *Promoting positive outcomes for children with disabilities: Recommendations for curriculum, assessment, and program evaluation.* Missoula, MT: Author.

Drew, C., & Hardman, M. (2007). *Intellectual disabilities across the lifespan* (9th ed.). Upper Saddle River, NJ: Merrill/Pearson Education.

Duquette, C., Stodel, E., Fullarton, S., & Hagglund, J. (2006). Teaching students with developmental disabilities: Tips from teens and young adults with fetal alcohol spectrum disorder. *Teaching Exceptional Children, 39,* 28–31.

Dykens, E. M. (2005). Happiness, well-being, and character strengths: Outcomes for families and siblings of persons with mental retardation. *Mental Retardation, 43,* 360–364.

e-Buddies. (2005). Retrieved July 3, 2005, from http://www.ebuddies.org

Edgerton, R. B. (1996). A longitudinal-ethnographic research perspective on quality of life. In R. L. Schalock (Ed.), *Quality of life: Conceptualization and measurement* (pp. 83–90). Washington, DC: American Association on Mental Retardation.

Eisenman, L. T. (2007a). Self-determination interventions: Building a foundation for school completion. *Remedial and Special Education, 28,* 2–8.

Eisenman, L. T. (2007b). Social networks and careers of young adults with intellectual disabilities. *Intellectual and Developmental Disabilities, 45,* 199–208.

Elementary and Secondary Education Act. PL No. 107–110.

Emerson, E., Robertson, J., Gregory, N., Hatton, C., Kessissoglou, S., Hallam, A., Järbrink, K., Knapp, M., Netten, A., & Walsh, P. N. (2001). Quality and costs of supported living residences and group homes in the United Kingdom. *American Journal on Mental Retardation, 106,* 401–415.

Farrell, S., & Al-Husaini, M. (2008, February 2). Two bombings wreak carnage in Iraqi capital. *New York Times.*

Finlay, W. M. L., & Lyons, E. (2005). Rejecting the label: A social constructionist analysis. *Mental Retardation, 43,* 120–134.

Fish, T. R., Rabidoux, P., Ober, J., & Graff, V. L. W. (2007). Community literacy and friendship model for people with intellectual disabilities. *Mental Retardation, 44,* 443–446.

Fragile X Research Foundation. (2008). *About fragile X: Cause.* Retrieved January 26, 2008, from www.fraxa.org/aboutfx_cause.aspx.

Gelf, S. (1995). The beast in man: Degenerationism and mental retardation, 1900–1920. *Mental Retardation, 33,* 1–9.

Guralnick, M. J. (1998). Effectiveness of early intervention for vulnerable children: A developmental perspective. *American Journal on Mental Retardation, 102,* 319–345.

Hannah, M. E., & Midlarsky, E. (1999). Competence and adjustment of siblings of children with mental retardation. *American Journal on Mental Retardation, 104,* 22–37.

Hannah, M. E., & Midlarsky, E. (2005). Helping by siblings of children with mental retardation. *American Journal on Mental Retardation, 110,* 87–99.

Hardman, M. L., & Clark, C. (2006). Promoting friendship through best buddies: A national survey of college program participants. *Mental Retardation, 44,* 56–63.

Harmon, A. (2007, May 9). Prenatal test puts Down syndrome in hard focus. *New York Times.*

Harries, J., Guscia, R., Kirby, N., Nettelbeck, R., & Taplin, J. (2005). Support needs and adaptive behaviors. *American Journal on Mental Retardation, 110,* 393–404.

Hodapp, R. M., Glidden, L. M., & Kaiser, A. P. (2005). Siblings of persons with disabilities: Toward a research agenda. *Mental Retardation, 43,* 334–338.

Holburn, S., Jacobson, J. W., Schwartz, A. A., Flory, M. J., & Vietze, P. M. (2004). The Willowbrook futures project: A longitudinal analysis of person-centered planning. *American Journal on Mental Retardation, 109,* 63–76.

Holverstott, J. (2005). Promote self-determination in students. *Intervention in School and Clinic, 41,* 39–41.

Hughes, C., Washington, B. H., & Brown, G. L. (2008). Supporting students in the transition from school to adult life. In F. Rusch (Ed.), *Beyond high school: Preparing adolescents for tomorrow's challenges* (2nd ed. pp. 266–287). Upper Saddle River, NJ: Merrill/Pearson Education.

Individuals with Disabilities Education Improvement Act of 2004. PL No. 108–446. 118 Stat. 2647.

Itard, J. M. G. (1806/1962). *Wild boy of Aveyron.* G. Humphrey and M. Humphrey, Trans. Englewood Cliffs, NJ: Prentice Hall. (Originally published in Paris by Gouyon, 1801.)

Janney, R., & Snell, M. (2006). *Social relationships and peer support: A teacher's guide to inclusive practices* (2nd ed.). Baltimore, MD: Brookes.

Jones, M. (2006). Teaching self-determination: Empowered teachers, empowered students. *Teaching Exceptional Students, 39,* 12–17.

Kennedy, C. H. (2001). Social interaction interventions for youth with severe disabilities should emphasize interdependence. *Mental Retardation and Developmental Disabilities Research Review, 7,* 122–127.

Kennedy, C. H. & Horn, E. (2004). *Including students with severe disabilities.* Boston: Allyn & Bacon.

Keogh, B.K., Bernheimer, L.P., & Guthrie, D. (2004). Children with developmental delays twenty years later: Where are they? How are they? *American Journal of Mental Retardation, 109,* 219–230.

Kleinert, H. L., Miracle, S. A., & Sheppard-Jones, K. (2007). Including students with moderate and severe disabilities in extracurricular and community recreation activities: Steps to success. *Teaching Exceptional Children, 39,* 33–38.

Kohler, P. D., & Field, S. (2003). Transition-focused education: Foundation for the future. *Journal of Special Education, 37,* 174–183.

Kraemer, B. R., McIntyre, L. L., & Blacher, J. (2003). Quality of life for young adults with mental retardation during transition. *Mental Retardation, 41,* 250–262.

Lakin, K. C., Braddock, D., & Smith, G. (2004a). States' initial response to the president's New Freedom Initiative: Slowest rates of deinstitutionalization in 30 years. *Mental Retardation, 42,* 490–493.

Lakin, K. C., Braddock, D., & Smith, G. (2004b). Trends and milestones. *Mental Retardation, 42,* 490–493.

Lent, J. R., & McLean, B. M. (1976). The trainable retarded: The technology of teaching. In N. G. Haring & R. L. Schiefelbush (Eds.), *Teaching special children* (pp. 197–223). New York: McGraw-Hill.

Leoni, M. (2007). Best practices in quality of life and supported living prompt the adoption of SIS in Italy. *Supports Intensity Scale News.* Retrieved from www.siswebsite.org/page.ww?section=News&name=Press+Release+Detail&pressrelease.id=48

Lipman, E. (2007, September 19). More retailers found to have lead-tainted items. *New York Times,* Business.

Luckasson, R., Borthwick-Duffy, S., Buntinx, W. H. E., Coulter, D. L., Craig, E. M., Reeve, A., Schalock, R. L., Snell, M. E., Spitalnik, D. M., Spreat, S., & Tassé, M. J. (2002). *Definition of mental retardation.* Washington, DC: American Association on Mental Retardation.

Luckasson, R., Coulter, D. L., Polloway, E. A., Reis, S., Schalock, R. L., Snell, M. E., Spitalnik, D. M., & Stark, J. A. (1992). *Mental retardation: Definition, classification, and systems of supports.* Washington, DC: American Association on Mental Retardation.

Manuel, J., & Little, L. (2002). A model of inclusion. *Early Developments, 6,* 14–18.

March of Dimes. (2006). *Folic acid.* Retrieved January 27, 2008, from http://marchofdimes.org

Martin, J. E., Woods, L. L., & Sylvester, L. (2008). Building an employment vision: Culturally attuning vocational interests, skills, and limits. In F. R. Rusch (Ed.), *Beyond high school: Preparing adolescents for tomorrow's challenges* (2nd ed., pp. 78–109). Upper Saddle River, NJ: Merrill/Pearson Education.

Matheson, C., Olsen, R. J., & Weisner, T. (2007). A good friend is hard to find: Friendship among adolescents with disabilities. *American Journal on Mental Retardation, 112,* 319–329.

McMillan, E. (2005). A parent's perspective. *Mental Retardation, 43,* 351–353.

Moore, C. L., Harley, D. A., & Gamble, D. (2004). Ex-post-facto analysis of competitive employment outcomes for individuals with mental retardation: National perspective. *Mental Retardation, 42,* 253–262.

Morrier, M. J. (2007). *Summary of U.S. Department of Education conference call on NCLB 2% regulations.* Washington, DC: Higher Education Consortium for Special Education, Memo.

Müller, E. (2007, January). *Fetal alcohol spectrum disorder: Several state initiatives.* Alexandria, VA: National Association of State Directors of Special Education, Project Forum.

Müller, E. & Markowitz, J. (2004). *Disability categories: State terminology, definitions & eligibility criteria.* Alexandria, VA: National Association of State Directors of Special Education, Project Forum.

National Center on Educational Outcomes. (2007). Frequently asked questions: Alternate assessments for students with disabilities. *Special Topic Area.* Retrieved February 7, 2008, from http://education.unm. edu/nceo

National Center for Education Statistics. (2007). *Status and trends in the education of racial and ethnic minorities.* Table 1a. Retrieved January 27, 2008, from http://nces.ed.gov/pubs2007/minoritytrends/tables/table_1a.asp

National Consortium for Physical Education and Recreation for Individuals with Disabilities. (n.d.). *Physical education for children with disabilities: A guide for families and educators.* Retrieved February 10, 2008, from www.ncperid.org/index.htm.

National Council for Therapeutic Recreation Certification. (2008). *Recreation therapy.* Retrieved February 10, 2008, from http://nctrc.org/documents/NXCTRCProfileBroch_001.pdf.

National Down Syndrome Society. (2008). *Questions and answers about Down syndrome.* Retrieved January 26, 2008, from www.ndss.org.

National Research Council. (2002). *Minority students in special education and gifted education.* Committee on Minority Representation in Special Education, M. Suzanne Donovan and Christoper T. Cross, Eds. Washington, DC: National Academy Press.

National Safety Council. (2004 December 23). *Lead poisoning: What is it and who is affected?* Retrieved January 26, 2008, from www.nsc.org.

Nirje, B. (1969). The normalization principle and its human management implications. In R. Kugel & W. Wolfensberger (Eds.), *Changing patterns in residential services for the mentally retarded* (pp. 179–195). Washington, DC: President's Committee on Mental Retardation.

Nirje, B. (1976). The normalization principle. In R. B. Kugel & A. Shearer (Eds.), *Changing patterns in residential services for the mentally retarded* (Rev. ed., pp. 231–240). Washington, DC: President's Committee on Mental Retardation.

Office of Special Education Programs. (2008). *Students served under IDEA, Part B: Fall 2006.* Retrieved February 5, 2008, from www.ideadata.org.

Painter, K. (2007, March 26). Don't discount lead poisoning: Exposure affects older kids, causes behavioral problems. *USA Today,* p. 4D.

Parent, W., Gossage, D., Jones, M., Turner, P., Walker, C., & Feldman, R. (2008). Working with parents: Using strategies to promote planning and preparation, placement, and support. In F. Rusch (Ed.), *Beyond high school: Preparing adolescents for tomorrow's challenges* (2nd ed., pp. 110–134). Upper Saddle River, NJ: Merrill/Pearson Education.

Perry, J., & Felce, D. (2005). Factors associated with outcome in community group homes. *American Journal on Mental Retardation, 110,* 121–135.

Perske, R. (1972). The dignity of risk. In W. Wolfensberger (Ed.), *The principle of normalization in human services* (pp. 194–200). Toronto: National Institute on Mental Retardation.

Perske, R. (2006). Perspectives: The "big bang" theory and Down syndrome. *Mental Retardation, 44,* 430–432.

Philofsky, A., Hepburn, S. L., Hayes, A., Hagerman, R., & Rogers, S.J. (2004). Linguistic and cognitive functioning and autism symptoms in young children with fragile X syndrome. *American Journal on Mental Retardation, 109,* 208–218.

PKU.org. (2007). *The history of PKU.* Retrieved January 27, 2008, from www.pku.org

Polloway, E. A. (1997). Developmental principles of the Luckasson et al. (1992) AAMR definition of mental retardation: A retrospective. *Education and Training in Mental Retardation and Developmental Disabilities, 32,* 174–178.

Prabhalla, A. (2007, February 20). Mental retardation is no more—New name is intellectual and developmental disabilities. *aaiddnews.* Washington, DC: American Association on Intellectual and Developmental Disabilities.

Roberts, J. E., Hennon, E. A., Rice, J. R., Dear, D., Anderson, K., & Vandergrift, N. A. (2007). Expressive language during conversational speech in boys with fragile X syndrome. *American Journal on Mental Retardation, 112,* 1–17.

Rusch, F. R. (2008). *Beyond high school: Preparing adolescents for tomorrow's challenges* (2nd ed.). Upper Saddle River, NJ: Merrill/Pearson Education.

Sauer, J. S. (2007). No surprises, please: A mother's story of betrayal and the fragility of inclusion. *Intellectual and Developmental Disabilities, 45,* 273–277.

Schalock, R. L., Gardner, J. F., Bradley, V. J. (2007). *Quality of life: Applications for people with intellectual and developmental disabilities.* Washington, DC: American Association on Intellectual and Developmental Disabilities.

Schweinhart, L. J. (2005). *The High/Scope Perry Preschool study through age 40: Summary, conclusions, and frequently asked questions.* Ypsilanti, MI: High/Scope Educational Research Foundation. Retrieved June 17, 2005, from www.highscope.org

Shogren, K. A., Wehmeyer, M. L., Palmer, S. B., Soukup, J. H., Little, T. D., Garner, N., & Lawrence, M. (2007). Examining individual and ecological predictors of self-determination of students with disabilities. *Exceptional Children, 73,* 488–509.

Simpson, M. (2007). Developmental concept of idiocy. *Intellectual and Developmental Disabilities, 45,* 23–32.

Smith, J. D., & Lazaroff, K. (2006). "Uncle Sam needs you," or does he? Intellectual disabilities and lessons from the "Great Wars." *Mental Retardation, 44,* 433–437.

Snell, M. E., & Brown, F. (2008). *Instruction of students with severe disabilities* (6th ed.). Upper Saddle River, NJ: Merrill/Pearson Education.

Stancliff, R. J., Lakin, K. C., Doljanac, R., Byun, S.-Y, Taub, S., & Chiri, G. (2007). Loneliness and living arrangements. *Intellectual and Developmental Disabilities, 45,* 380–390.

Stoneman, Z. (2005). Siblings of children with disabilities: Research themes. *Mental Retardation, 43,* 339–350.

Taylor, S. J. (2007). The journal now and then: The editor's perspective. *Intellectual and Developmental Disabilities, 45,* 271–272.

Taylor, R. L., Richards, S.B., & Brady, M. P. (2005). *Mental retardation: Historical perspectives, current practices, and future directions.* Boston: Allyn & Bacon.

Thompson, J. R., Bryant, B., Campbell, E. M., Craig, E. M., Hughes, C., Rothholz, D., Schalock, R. L. Silverman, W., Tasse, M. J., & Wehmeyer, M. L. (2004). *Supports Intensity Scale: Users' manual.* Washington, DC: American Association on Mental Retardation.

Turnbull, R., Turnbull, A., Warren, S., Eidelman, S., & Marchand, P. (2002). Shakespeare redux, or *Romeo and Juliet* revisited: Embedding a terminology and name change in a new agenda for the field of mental retardation. *Mental Retardation, 40,* 65–70.

U.S. Department of Education. (2001). *Twenty-third annual report to Congress on the implementation of the Individuals with Disabilities Education Act.* Washington, DC: U.S. Government Printing Office.

U. S. Department of Education. (2006, August 14). 34 *CFR* Parts 300 and 301, Assistance to States for the Education of Children with Disabilities and Preschool Grants for Children with Disabilities; Final rule (pp. 1263–1264). *Federal Register,* Washington, DC.

U.S. Department of Education. (2007). *Measuring the achievement of students with disabilities: What families and schools need to know about modified academic achievement standards.* Washington, DC: Author.

U.S. Senate Appropriations Committee. (2004, September 15). *Senate Appropriations Committee report on the Labor/HHS/ Education bill.* Washington, DC: U.S. Senate.

Wehmeyer, M. L. (2006). *Life beyond the classroom: Transition strategies for young people with disabilities* (4th ed.). Baltimore MD: Brookes.

Wehmeyer, M. L. (2007). *Promoting self-determination in students with developmental disabilities.* New York: Guilford Press.

Winzer, M. A. (1993). *The history of special education: From isolation to integration.* Washington, DC: Gallaudet University Press.

Wolfensberger, W. (1972). *The principle of normalization in human services.* Toronto: National Institute on Mental Retardation.

Wolfensberger, W. (2002). Social role valorization and, or versus, "empowerment." *Mental Retardation, 40,* 252–258.

Zubai-Ruggieri, R. (2007). Making links, making connections: Internet resources for self-advocates and people with developmental disabilities. *Intellectual and Developmental Disabilities, 45,* 209–215.

CHAPTER 9

Americans with Disabilities Act of 1990, PL No. 101–336, 104 Stat. 327.

Arthritis Foundation. (2007). School success. Retrieved November 11, 2007, from www .arthritis.org/resources/school_success.asp

Asthma and Allergy Foundation of America. (2007). *Asthma Facts and Figures.* Retrieved October 30, 2007, from http:// www.aafa.org/display.cfm?id=8&sub=42

Batshaw, M.L., Pelligrino, L., & Roizen, N. J. (Eds.). (2007). *Children with disabilities* (6th ed.). Baltimore, MD: Brookes.

Best, S., Heller, K. W., & Bigge, J. L. (2005). *Teaching individuals with physical or multiple disabilities.* Upper Saddle River, NJ: Merrill/Pearson Education.

Betz, C. L. & Nehring, W. M. (Eds.). (2007). *Promoting health care transitions for adolescents with special health care needs and disabilities.* Baltimore, MD: Brookes.

Betz, C. L. & Telfair, J. (2007). Health care transitions: An introduction. In C. L. Betz & W. M. Nehring (Eds.), *Promoting health care transitions for adolescents with special health care needs and disabilities* (pp. 3–20). Baltimore, MD: Brookes.

Braddock, D., & Parish, S. (2002). An institutional history of disability. In D. Braddock (Ed.), *Disability at the dawn of the 21st century and the state of the states.* Washington, DC: American Association on Mental Retardation.

Brundige, A. F. (2007). Assessing reading, listening, and observational comprehension in students with physical disabilities. *Closing the Gap, 26,* 1, 9–11.

Bruni, F. (2007, September 12). When accessibility isn't hospitality. *New York Times,* Dining and Wine.

Canine Companions for Independence. (2007). *Canine Companions program.* Retrieved November 21, 2007, from http:// www.caninecompanions.org/nation/ our_program.html

Centers for Disease Control. (2007a, June). *CDC HIV/AIDS Facts: Revised 2005 HIV/AIDS surveillance report.* Retrieved November, 1, 2007, from http://www.cdc.gov/hiv

Centers for Disease Control. (2007b). *Developmental disabilities: Cerebral palsy.* Retrieved October 31, 2007, from http:// www.cdc.gov/ncbddd/dd/cp3.htm# common

Children's Defense Fund (2005). *The state of America's children: 2005.* Washington, DC: Author.

Coster, W. J., & Haltiwanger, J. T. (2004). Social-behavioral skills of elementary students with physical disabilities included in general education classrooms. *Remedial and Special Education, 25,* 95–103.

Crawford, L. (2007). *State testing accommodations: A look at their value and validity.* New York: National Center for Learning Disabilities.

Davis, R. (2006, September 16). Meet the $4 million woman: Bionic arm puts life firmly back in the amputee's grasp. *USA Today, LIFE,* p. 8D.

Delta Society. (2007). *Improving human health through service and therapy animals.* Retrieved November 18, 2007, from www.deltasociety.org

Deutsch, H., (2005). The body's moments: Visible disability, the essay and the limits of sympathy. *Prose Studies, 27,* 11–26.

Dolch, E. W. (1948). *Helping handicapped children in school.* Champaign, IL: Garrard.

Eberle, L. (1922). The maimed, the halt and the race. *Hospital Social Service, 6,* 59–63. Reprinted in R. H. Bremner (Ed.) (1970), *Children and youth in America: A documentary history. Vol. II, 1866–1932* (pp. 1026–1928). Cambridge, MA: Harvard University Press.

Emory University School of Medicine. (2005). *Sickle cell information for teachers, students, and employers.* Sickle Cell Information Center. Retrieved July 8, 2005, from www.scinfo.org

Epilepsy Foundation. (2007a). *Epilepsy and seizure statistics.* Retrieved November 1, 2007, from www.epilepsyfoundation.org/ about/statistics.cfm

Epilepsy Foundation. (2007b). *Seizure and symptoms.* Retrieved October 29, 2007, from www.epilepsyfoundation.org/types/ types/types.cfm

Epilepsy Foundation. (2007c). *Understanding epilepsy: First Aid.* Retrieved October 29, 2007, from www.epilepsyfoundation.org/ about/firstaid

Getch, Y., Bhukhanwala, F., & Neuharth-Pritchett, S. (2007). Strategies for helping children with diabetes in elementary and middle schools. *Teaching Exceptional Children, 39,* 46–51.

Hall, D. (2007). *Graduation matters: Improving accountability for high school graduation.* Washington, DC: Education Trust.

Homer, C. J., & Cooley, W. C. (2007). Creating a medical home for children with special health care needs. In C. L. Betz & W. M. Nehring (Eds.), *Promoting health care transitions for adolescents with special health care needs and disabilities* (pp. 135–148). Baltimore, MD: Brookes.

Individuals with Disabilities Education Improvement Act of 2004. PL No. 108–446. 118 Stat. 2647.

IRIS Center. (2007). *STAR Legacy module: School nurses: Roles and responsibilities in the school setting.* http://iris.peabody .vanderbilt.edu

Kudlick, C., & Longmore, P. (2006, November). Disability and the transformation of historians' public sphere. *Perspectives: Forum on Disability.* American Historical Association. Retrieved November 12, 2007, from http://www .historians.org/perspectives/issues/2006/ 0611/0611for2.cfm

La Vor, M. L. (1976). Federal legislation for exceptional persons: A history. In F. J. Weintraub, A. Abeson, J. Ballard, & M. L. La Vor (Eds.), *Public policy and the education of exceptional children* (pp. 96–111). Reston, VA: Council for Exceptional Children.

Longmore, P. (2003). *Why I burned my book and other essays on disability.* Philadelphia: Temple University Press.

Maddox, S. (Ed.). (1987). *Spinal network: The total resource for the wheelchair community.* Boulder, CO: Author.

National Association of School Nurses. (2007). *Issue brief: School nursing services role in health care.* Retrieved November 7, 2007, from www. nasn.org/Default.aspx?tabid=348

National Center for Education Statistics (NCES). (2006). *Fast facts: What percentage of students enrolled in postsecondary education have a disability?* Retrieved November 16, 2007, from http:// www.nces.ed.gov/fastfacts/display .asp?id=60

National Center for Education Statistics. (2007). *Fast facts: What is the average income for students graduating from postsecondary institutions compared with those graduating from high school?* Retrieved November 18, 2007, from http://www .nces.ed.gov/fastfacts/display.asp?id=77

National Center for HIV/AIDS, Viral Hepatitis, STD, and TB Prevention, Centers for Disease Control. (2007). *Viral hepatitis B: Fact sheet.* Retrieved November 11, 2007, from http://www.cdc.gov/NCIDOD/diseases/hepatitis/b/fact.htm

National Diabetes Information Clearinghouse. (2007). *National diabetes statistics.* Retrieved November 1, 2007, from http://diabetes.niddk.nih.gov/dm/pubs/ statistics

National Heart, Lung, and Blood Institute, National Institutes of Health. (2007). *What is hemophilia?* Retrieved November 14, 2007, from http://www.nhlbi.nih.gov/health/dci/Diseases/hemophilia/hemophilia_what.html

National Human Genome Research Institute, National Institutes of Health. (2007). *Learning about sickle cell disease.* Retrieved November 1, 2007, from http://www.genome.gov

National Institute of Allergy and Infectious Diseases. (2004). *HIV infections in infants and children.* Retrieved July 7, 2005, from www.niaid.nih.gov/factsheets/hivchildren.htm

National Institute of Environmental Health Sciences. (2007). *Asthma.* Retrieved November 2, 2007, from http://www.niehs.nih.gov/health/topics/conditions/asthma.index.cfm

National Institute of Neurological Disorders and Stroke. (2007). *Muscular dystrophy information page.* Retrieved November 14, 2007, from http://www.ninds.nih.gov/disorders/md/md.htm

Office of Special Education Programs. (2008). *Students served under IDEA, Part B: Fall 2006.* Retrieved August 23, 2008, from www.ideadata.org

Owens, R. E., Metz, D. E., & Haas, A. (2007). *Introduction to communication disorders: A life span perspective* (3rd ed.). Boston: Allyn & Bacon.

Pelligrino, L. (2007). Cerebral palsy. In M. L. Batshaw, L. Pelligrino, & N. J. Roizen (Eds.), *Children with disabilities* (6th ed., pp. 387–408). Baltimore, MD: Brookes.

Poel, E. W. (2007). Enhancing what students can do: Assistive technology devices can help students with special needs fully participate in the classroom. *Educational Leadership, 64* 64–66.

Rehabilitation Act of 1973. Section 504, 19 U.S.C. Section 794.

Scheerenberger, R. C. (1983). *A history of mental retardation.* Baltimore: Brookes.

Shaw, B. (1995, May/June). Ed Roberts: 1939–1995. *Disability Rag,* p. 25.

Smith, B. (2005). *NICHCY connections . . . to weighing information for what it's worth.* Retrieved July 11, 2005, from www.nichcy.org

Sobo, E. J., & Kurtin, P.S. (2007). *Optimizing care for young children with special health care needs.* Baltimore, MD: Brookes.

Stone, K. G. (1995, March 19). Disability rights pioneer inspired his community. *Albuquerque Journal,* p. C6.

Thompson, S. J., Morse, A. B., Sharpe, M., & Hall, S. (2005). *Accommodations manual: How to select, administer, and evaluate use of accommodations for instruction and assessment of students with disabilities* (2nd ed.). Washington, DC: Council of Chief State School Officers.

United Cerebral Palsy Research and Education Foundation. (2007). *Did you know?* Retrieved November 11, 2007, from http://www.ucpresearch.org

U.S. Department of Education. (2002). *Twenty-fourth annual report to Congress on the implementation of the Individuals with Disabilities Education Act.* Washington, DC: U.S. Government Printing Office.

U.S. Department of Education. (2006, August 14). 34 *CFR* Parts 300 and 301, Assistance to States for the Education of Children with Disabilities and Preschool Grants for Children with Disabilities: Final rule (pp. 1263–1264). *Federal Register,* Washington, DC.

CHAPTER 10

Adams, M. E. (1929). 1865–1935: A few memories of Alexander Graham Bell. *American Annals of the Deaf, 74,* 467–479.

Alby, J. F. (1962, Spring). The educational philosophy of Thomas Hopkins Gallaudet. *Buff and Blue,* 17–23.

Alexander Graham Bell Association. (2008). *Give every child a* sound *start.* Washington, DC: Author.

Anderson, G. B., & Miller, K. R. (2004/2005). Appreciating diversity through stories about the lives of Deaf people of color. *American Annals of the Deaf, 149,* 375–383.

Antia, S. D., & Kreimeyer, K. H. (1996). Social interaction and acceptance of deaf or hard-of-hearing children and their peers: A comparison of social-skills and familiarity-based interventions. *Volta Review, 98,* 157–180.

Blade, R. (1994, October 31). Sign language is beautiful, close-knit Deaf community says. *Albuquerque Tribune,* p. A5.

Bohnert, A., Spitzlei, V., Lippert, K. L., & Keilmann, A. (2006). Bilateral cochlear implantation in children. *Volta Review, 106,* 343–364.

Branson, J., & Miller, D. (2002). *Damned for their difference: The cultural construction of deaf people as disabled.* Washington, DC: Gallaudet University Press.

Centers for Disease Control. (2007). Fluid in the middle ear (otitis media with effusion). *Get smart: A Guide for Parents: Questions and Answers.* Retrieved May 21, 2008, from www.cdc.gov/drugresistance/community

Commission on the Education of the Deaf. (1988). *Toward equality: Education of the deaf.* Washington, DC: U.S. Government Printing Office.

Cuculick, J. A., & Kelly, R. R. (2003). Relating Deaf students' reading and language scores at college entry to their degree completion rates. *American Annals of the Deaf, 148,* 279–286.

Davey, M. (2005, March 21). As town for Deaf takes shape, debate on isolation re-emerges. *New York Times.*

Dettman, S. J., Leigh, J. R., Dowell, R. C., Pinder, D., & Briggs, R. J. S. (2007). The narrow window: Early cochlear implant use. *Volta Voices, 14,* 28–31.

Dillon, C. M., & Pisoni, D. B. (2006). Non word repetition and reading skills in children who are deaf and have cochlear implants. *Volta Review, 106,* 121–145.

Dragsow, E. (1998). American Sign Language as a pathway to linguistic competence. *Exceptional Children, 64,* 329–342.

Evans, C. J. (2004). Literacy development in deaf students: Case studies in bilingual teaching and learning. *American Annals of the Deaf, 149,* 17–27.

Fiedler, B. C. (2001). Considering placement and educational approaches for students who are deaf and hard of hearing. *Teaching Exceptional Children, 34,* 54–59.

Gallaudet Research Institute. (2006). *Regional and national summary report of data from the 2006–2007 annual survey of deaf and hard-of-hearing children and youth.* Washington, DC: Author.

Gannon, J. R. (1989). *The week the world heard Gallaudet.* Washington, DC: Gallaudet University Press.

Gleason, J. B., & Ratner, N. B. (2009). *The development of language* (7th ed.). Boston: Pearson/Allyn & Bacon.

Gordon-Langbein, A. L., & Metzinger, M. (2000). Technology in the classroom to maximize listening and learning. *Volta Voices, 7,* 10–13.

Greenwald, B. H. (2007). Taking stock: Alexander Graham Bell and eugenics, 1883–1922. In J. V. Van Cleve (Ed.), *The Deaf history reader.* Washington, DC: Gallaudet University Press.

Groce, N. E. (1985). *Everyone here spoke sign language: Hereditary deafness on Martha's Vineyard.* Cambridge, MA: Harvard University Press.

Hager R, M. (2007). Obtaining hearing aids for children. *Volta Voices, 14,* 20–24.

Haller, A. K., & Montgomery, J. K. (2004). Noise-induced hearing loss in children: What educators need to know. *Teaching Exceptional Children, 36,* 22–27.

Harrington, M. (2003). Hard of hearing students in the public schools: Should we be concerned? *Volta Voices, 11,* 18–22.

HEATH Resource Center (HEATH). (2005). *Students who are deaf or hard of hearing in postsecondary education.* Washington, DC: American Council on Education.

Herer, G. R., Knightly, C. A., & Steinberg, A. G. (2007). Hearing: Sounds and silences. In M. L. Batshaw, L. Pellegrino, & N. J. Roizen (Eds.), *Children with disabilities* (6th ed., pp. 157–184). Baltimore, MD: Brookes.

Hignett, S. (1983). *Brett from Bloomsbury to New Mexico: A biography.* New York: Franklin Watts.

Hochgesang, J. A., Dunning, L. M., Benaissa, S., DeCaro, J. J., & Karchmer, M. A. (2007). *College and career programs for deaf* (12th ed.). Washington, DC: Gallaudet University Press.

IRIS Center for Training Enhancements. (2008). *STAR Legacy Module: Providing instructional supports: Facilitating mastery of new skills.* Nashville, TN: Vanderbilt University. Retrieved from http://iris.peabody.vanderbilt.edu/sca/chalcycle.htm

Kelley, B. (2006, January/February). Steve Largent on wireless technology. *Hearing Loss,* pp. 10–13.

Laurent Clerc National Deaf Education Center. (2005). *The history of Kendall Demonstration Elementary School.* Retrieved July 25, 2005, from http://clerccenter.gallaudet.edu

Linehan, P. (2000). *Educational interpreters for students who are deaf and hard of hearing: Quick turn around.* Alexandria, VA: National Association for State Directors of Special Education, Project Forum.

Lowenbraun, S. (1995). Hearing impairment. In E. L. Meyen & T. M. Skrtic (Eds.), *Exceptional children and youth: An introduction* (4th ed., pp. 453–486). Denver, CO: Love.

Luft, P. (2008). Examining educators of the Deaf as "highly qualified" teachers: Roles and responsibilities under IDEA and NCLB. *American Annals of the Deaf, 152,* 429–440.

MacKenzie, D. J. (2007). Audiology and hearing loss. In R. E. Owens Jr., D. E. Metz, & A. Haas (Eds.), *Introduction to communication disorders: A life span perspective* (3rd ed., pp. 404–463). Boston: Allyn & Bacon.

Marschark, M. (1993). *Psychological development of deaf children.* New York: Oxford University Press.

Marschark, M. (2001). *Language development in children who are deaf: A research synthesis.* Alexandria, VA: Project Forum, National Association of State Directors of Special Education.

Med-El Corporation. (2008). The cochlear implant process. Part 2: Road to success. *Volta Voices, 15,* 18–21.

Mendoza, M. (2006, October 13). Protestors vow to keep university barricaded. *Los Angeles Times,* p. A19.

Moores, D. F. (2001). *Educating the deaf: Psychology, principles, and practices* (5th ed.). Boston: Houghton Mifflin.

Moores, D. F. (2008). Half of what we taught you is wrong: The problem is we don't know which half. *American Annals of the Deaf, 152,* 427–428.

Nance, W., & Dodson, K. (2007). Clinical and ethical implications of deafness research. *Volta Voices, 14,* 16–19.

National Center for Hearing Assessment and Management. (2008). *EHDI legislation.* Logan: Utah State University. Retrieved May 18, 2008, from www.infanthearing.org

National Dissemination Center for Children with Disabilities. (2004, January). *Deafness and hearing loss.* Fact Sheet 3. Washington, DC: Author.

National Institute on Deafness and Other Communication Disorders. (2007a). *Cochlear implants.* NIH Pub. No. 00-4798. Retrieved May 14, 2007, from www.nidcd.nih.gov

National Institute on Deafness and Other Communication Disorders. (2007b). *Hearing aids.* NIH Pub. No. 99-4344. Retrieved May 15, 2007, from www.nidcd.nih.gov

National Institute on Deafness and Other Communication Disorders. (2007c). *Noise-induced hearing loss.* NIH Pub. No. 97-4233. Retrieved May 14, 2007, from www.nidcd.nih.gov

National Technical Institute for the Deaf. (2008). *C-Print®: Speech-to-text system.* Rochester, NY: Author.

Nikolaraizi, M., & Makri, M. (2004/2005). Deaf and hearing individuals' beliefs about the capabilities of deaf people. *American Annals of the Deaf, 149,* 404–414.

Nittrouer, S., & Burton, L. R. (2003). The role of early language experience in the development of speech perception and language processing abilities in children with hearing loss. *Volta Review, 103,* 5–57.

Northern, J. L., & Downs, M. P. (2002). *Hearing in children* (5th ed.). Philadelphia: Lippincott, Williams & Wilkins.

Nussbaum, D. (2005). *In the classroom . . . Children with a cochlear implant.* Retrieved May 11, 2008, from http://clerccenter.gallaudet.edu

Office of Special Education Programs. (2008). *Students served under IDEA, Part B: Fall 2006.* Retrieved May 23, 2008, from www.ideadata.org.

Polanco, R., & Guillermo, I. (2007). Cultural attitudes toward hearing loss: An inside perspective. *Volta Voices, 14,* 32–35.

Reid, R., & Lienemann, T. O. (2006). Strategy instruction for students with learning disabilities. In K. R. Harris & S. Graham (Series Eds.), *What works for special-needs learners.* New York: Guilford Press.

Ricketts, T. A. (2008). Digital hearing aids: Current "state of the art." Retrieved May 13, 2008, from www.asha.org

Ripper, J. (2008). Research answers critical questions about pediatric hearing loss. *Volta Voices, 15,* 24–3.

Ross, M. (2008). Premium digital hearing aids. *Hearing Loss, 29,* 22–25.

Royer, M. (2008). Buried treasure. *Hearing Loss, 29,* 26–31.

Schauer, P. (2005). *Hearing impairment in Down syndrome.* Retrieved May 16, 2008, from www.kennedykrieger.org

Schorr, E. A. (2006). Early cochlear implant experience and emotional functioning during childhood: Loneliness in middle and late childhood. *Volta Review, 106,* 365–379.

Soloman, A. (1994, August 28). Defiantly deaf. *New York Times Magazine,* pp. 38–45, 64–68.

Steffan, R. C. (2004). Navigating the difficult waters of the No Child Left Behind Act of 2001: What it means for education of the Deaf. *American Annals of the Deaf, 149,* 46–50.

Svirsky, M. A., Chin, S. B., Miyamoto, R. T., Soan, R. B., & Caldwell, M. D. (2002). Speech intelligibility of profoundly deaf pediatric hearing aid users. *Volta Review, 102,* 175–198.

Szalay, J. (2005, March 26). Our town: A home for the Deaf. *New York Times.*

Tharpe, A. M. (2004, November 18). *Even minimal, undetected hearing loss hurts academic performance.* Paper presented at the American Speech-Language-Hearing Association National Convention, Pennsylvania Convention Center.

U.S. Department of Education. (2006, August 14). 34 *CFR* Parts 300 and 301, *Assistance to States for the Education of Children with Disabilities and Preschool Grants for Children with Disabilities; Final rule. Federal Register,* Washington, DC.

Van Cleve, J. V. (2007). *The Deaf reader.* Washington, DC: Gallaudet University Press.

Vernon, J. (2007). Preparing professionals for a changing landscape. *Volta Voices, 14,* 18–21.

Warner-Czyz, A. D., Davis, B. L., & Morrison, H. M. (2005). Production accuracy in young cochlear implant recipient. *Volta Review, 105,* 151–173.

White, K. R. (2006). Early intervention for children with permanent hearing loss: Finishing the EHDI revolution. *Volta Review, 106,* 237–258.

White, K. R. (2007). Closing the gaps for infants and young children with hearing loss. *Volta Voices, 14,* 30–33.

Williams, C. B., & Finnegan, M. (2003). From myth to reality: Sound information for teachers about students who are deaf. *Teaching Exceptional Children, 35,* 40–45.

Yarnell, B. J., & Schery, T. (2003 November). *Kids with cochlear implants: Supporting inclusive education.* Paper presented at the American Speech-Language-Hearing Association, Chicago.

Yoshinaga-Itano, C., & Sedey, A. (2000). Early speech development in children who are deaf or hard of hearing: Interrelationships with language and hearing. *Volta Review, 100,* 181–211.

Zaidman-Zait, A., & Most, T. (2005). Cochlear implants in children with hearing loss: Maternal expectations and impact on the family. *Volta Review, 105,* 129–150.

Zazove, P., Meador, H. E., Derry, H. A., Gorenflo, D. W., & Saunders, E. W. (2004). Deaf persons and computer use. *American Annals of the Deaf, 148,* 376–384.

CHAPTER 11

American Association of Retired Persons. (2006). *Gold violin: Thoughtfully designed products for seniors.* Retrieved July 31, 2008, from www.goldviolin.com

American Foundation for the Blind. (2002). *When you have a visually impaired student in your classroom: A guide for teachers.* New York: AFB Press.

American Foundation for the Blind. (2008a). *Refreshable Braille display.* Retrieved July 25, 2008, from www.afb.org

American Foundation for the Blind. (2008b). *Statistics and sources for professionals.* Retrieved July 11, 2008, from www.afb.org

American Printing House for the Blind. (2008). *APH Products: Braille 'n Speak® Scholar.* Retrieved July 31, 2008, from http://www.aph.org/products/scholar.html

Ansariyah-Grace, T. (2000, August 6). Touched by arts. *The Tennessean,* pp. 1F–2F.

Associated Press (2002, June 1). Blind bicyclists to ride the Trace to Keller's home. *The Tennessean,* p. B1.

Bank of America. (2008). Accessible banking: ATMs. Retrieved July 31, 2008, from http://www.bankofamerica.com/accessiblebanking/index.cfm?template=ab_atm&statecheck=CA

Bailey, I. L., Lueck, A. H., Greer, R.B., Tuan, K. M., Bailey, V. M., & Dornbusch, H. G. (2003). Understanding the relationships between print size and reading in low vision. *Journal of Low Vision and Blindness, 97,* 325–333.

Barclay, L., D'Andrea, F.M., Erin, J., Hannan, C., Holbrook, C., Sacks, S. & Wormsley, D. (2007, December). *ABC braille study: A five-year longitudinal study of literacy environments, skills, and experiences of children who are blind.* Paper presented at the Getting in Touch with Literacy Conference, St. Pete Beach, FL.

Barraga, N. C. (1964). *Increased visual behavior in low vision children.* New York: American Foundation for the Blind.

Barraga, N. C., & Collins, M. E. (1979). Development of efficiency in visual functioning: Rationale for a comprehensive program. *Journal of Visual Impairment and Blindness, 73,* 121–126.

Buhrow, M. M., Hartshorne, T. S., & Bradley-Johnson, S. (1998). Parents' and teachers' ratings of the social skills of elementary-age students who are blind. *Journal of Visual Impairment and Blindness, 92,* 503–511.

Cappella-McDonnall, M. (2005). Predictors of competitive employment for blind and visually impaired consumers of vocational rehabilitation services. *Journal of Visual Impairment and Blindness, 99,* 303–315.

Celeste, M. (2007). Social skills intervention for a child who is blind. *Journal of Visual Impairment & Blindness, 101,* 521–533.

Centers for Disease Control. (2005). *Vision impairment.* Atlanta: National Center on Birth Defects and Developmental Disabilities. Retrieved August 7, 2005, from www.cdc.gov/ncbddd/dd/ddvi.htm.

Clarke, K. L., Sainato, D. M., & Ward, M. E. (1994). Travel performance of preschoolers: The effects of mobility training with a long cane versus a precane. *Journal of Visual Impairment and Blindness, 88,* 19–30.

Corn, A. L. (1989). Instruction in the use of vision for children and adults with low vision: A proposed program model. *RE:view, 21,* 26–38.

Corn, A., & Koenig, A. J. (2002). Literacy for students with low vision: A framework for delivering instruction. *Journal of Visual Impairments and Blindness, 96,* 305–321.

Cox, P., & Dykes, M. (2001). Effective classroom adaptations for students with visual impairments. *Teaching Exceptional Children, 33,* 68–74.

De Mario, N., & Caruso, M. (2001). The expansion of outreach services for specialized schools for students with visual impairments. *Journal of Visual Impairment and Blindness, 95,* 488–491.

Dote-Kwan, J., Chen, D., & Hughes M. (2001). A national survey of service providers who work with young children with visual impairments. *Journal of Visual Impairment and Blindness, 95,* 325–337.

Duzak, W. (2002, June 3). Young cyclists who are blind ride the Trace. *The Tennessean,* p. 12B.

Eaton, S. B., & Wall, R. S. (1999). A survey of social skills instruction in preservice programs for visual disabilities. *RE:view, 31,* 40–45.

Erin, J. N., & Corn, A. L. (1994). A survey of children's first understanding of being visually impaired. *Journal of Visual Impairment and Blindness, 88,* 132–139.

Evans, S., & Douglas, G. (2008). E-learning and blindness: A comparative study of the quality of an e-learning experience. *Journal of Visual Impairment and Blindness, 102,* 77–88.

Evansville Association for the Blind. (2005). *Summer college program.* Retrieved July 25, 2008, from http://eab.evansville.edu/college.htm

Eye of the Pacific. (2008). *Electronic aids.* Retrieved July 31, 2008, from http://www.eyeofthepacific.org/electronic%20aids.htm

Farrenkopf, C. (2008). Reading instruction: Best practices and realities in Canada's largest school district. *Journal of Visual Impairment and Blindness, 102,* 200–203.

Frank, J. (2000). Requests by persons with visual impairment for large-print accommodation. *Journal of Visual Impairment and Blindness, 94,* 716–719.

Fruchterman, J. R. (2003). In the palm of your hand: a vision of the future of technology for people with visual impairments. *Journal of Visual Impairment and Blindness, 97,* 585–591.

Gompel, M., van Bon, W. H. J., & Schreuder, R. (2004). Reading by children with low vision. *Journal of Visual Impairment and Blindness, 98,* 77–89.

Hatlen, P. (1996). *The core curriculum for blind and visually impaired students, including those with multiple disabilities.* Retrieved July 31, 2008, from http://www.tsbvi.edu/agenda/corecurric.htm (National Agenda Web site hosted by Texas School for the Blind and Visually Impaired).

Hatton, D. (2001). Model registry of early childhood visual impairment: First-year results. *Journal of Visual Impairment and Blindness, 95,* 418–433.

HEATH Resource Center. (2001). *Students who are blind or visually impaired in post-secondary education.* Washington, DC: George Washington University. Retrieved August 7, 2005, from www.heath.gwu.edu

Henderson, C. (2001). *College freshmen with disabilities: A biennial statistical profile.* Washington, DC: HEATH Resource Center, American Council on Education.

Hill, E. W. (1986). Orientation and mobility. In G. R. Scholl (Ed.), *Foundations of education for blind and visually handicapped children and youth: Theory and practice* (pp. 315–340). New York: American Foundation for the Blind.

Hitchcock, C., Meyer, A., Rose, D., & Jackson, R. (2002). Providing new access to the general curriculum: Universal design for learning. *Teaching Exceptional Children, 35,* 8–17.

Holbrook, M. C. (2008). Teaching reading and writing to students with visual impairments: Who is responsible? *Journal of Visual Impairment and Blindness, 102,* 203–206.

Hughes, M., Dote-Kwan, J., & Dolendo, J. (1998). A close look at the cognitive play of preschoolers with visual impairments in the home. *Exceptional Children, 64,* 451–462.

IRIS Center. (2006a). *Accommodations to the physical environment: Setting up a classroom for students with visual disabilities.* Retrieved July 27, 2008, from http://iris.peabody.vanderbilt.edu/v03_focusplay/chalcycle.htm

IRIS Center. (2006b). *Instructional accommodations: Making the learning environment accessible to students with visual disabilities.* Retrieved July 27, 2008, from http://iris.peabody.vanderbilt.edu/v03_focusplay/chalcycle.htm

IRIS Center. (2007). *Serving students with visual impairments: The importance of collaboration.* Retrieved July 27, 2008, from http://iris.peabody.vanderbilt.edu/v03_focusplay/chalcycle.htm

Jindal-Snape, D. (2005). Use of feedback from sighted peers in promoting social interaction skills. *Journal of Visual Impairment and Blindness, 99,* 403–412.

Kamei-Hannan, C. (2008). Examining the accessibility of a computerized adapted test using assistive technology. *Journal of Visual Impairment and Blindness, 102*(5), 261–271.

Kirchner, C., & Smith, B. (2005). Transition to what? Education and employment outcomes for visually impaired youths after high school. *Journal of Visual Impairment and Blindness, 99,* 499–503.

Koenig, A., & Holbrook, M. (2000). Ensuring high-quality instruction for students in braille literacy programs. *Journal of Visual Impairment and Blindness, 94,* 677–694.

Levin, A. V. (1996). Common visual problems in classrooms. In R. H. A. Haslam & P. J. Valletutti (Eds.), *Medical problems in the classroom: The teacher's role in diagnosis and management* (pp. 161–180). Austin, TX: Pro-Ed.

Lighthouse International. (2005). *Lighthouse catalog.* New York: Lighthouse Store.

Lueck, A. H., Bailey, I. L., Greer, R. B., Tuan, K. M., Bailey, V. M., & Dornbusch, H. G. (2003). Exploring print-size requirements and reading for students with low vision. *Journal of Low Vision and Blindness, 97,* 335–355.

MacCuspie, P. A. (1992). The social acceptance and interaction of visually impaired children in integrated settings. In S. Z. Sacks, L. S. Kekelis, & R. J. Gaylord-Ross (Eds.), *The development of social skills by blind and visually impaired students* (pp. 83–102). New York: American Foundation for the Blind.

McGaha, C., & Farran, D. (2001). Interaction in an inclusive classroom: The effects of visual status and setting. *Journal of Visual Impairment and Blindness, 95,* 80–94.

McHugh, E., & Lieberman, L. (2003). The impact of developmental factors on stereotypic rocking of children with visual impairments. *Journal of Visual Impairment and Blindness, 97,* 453–474.

McMahon, P. (2000, February 4). Hearing-impaired wage fight in theaters. *USA Today,* p. 3A.

Media Access Group. (2008). *Descriptive video service.* Retrieved July 31, 2008, from http://main.wgbh.org/wgbh/access/

Milian, M. (2001). School's efforts to involve Latino families of students with visual impairments. *Journal of Visual Impairment and Blindness, 95,* 389–402.

Miller, M. M., & Menacker, S. J. (2007). Vision: Our window to the world. In M. L. Batshaw, L. Pellegrino, & N. J. Roizen (Eds.), *Children with disabilities* (pp. 137–156). Baltimore, MD: Brookes.

Mogk, L., & Goodrich, G. (2004). The history and future of low vision services in the United States. *Journal of Visual Impairment and Blindness, 98,* 585–600.

Monson, M. R., & Bowen, S. K. (2008). The development of phonological awareness by braille users: A review of the research. *Journal of Visual Impairment and Blindness, 102,* 210–220.

Nagle, K. (2001, December). Transition to employment and community life for youths with visual impairments: Current status and future directions. *Journal of Visual Impairment and Blindness, 95,* 725–738.

National Center for Educational Statistics. (2008). Enrollment trends. *Fast Facts.* Retrieved July 11, 2008, from http://nces.ed.gob/fastfacts/ display.asp?id=96

National Instructional Materials Accessibility Standard. (2006). *State director of special education suggested responsibilities regarding NIMAS and NIMAC.* Retrieved July 27, 2008, from http://nimas.cast.org/about/resources/sea_sped

Oddo, N. S., & Sitlington, P. L. (2002). What does the future hold? A follow-up study of graduates of a residential school program. *Journal of Visual Impairment and Blindness, 96,* 842–851.

Office of Special Education Programs. (2008). *Students served under IDEA, Part B: Fall 2006.* Retrieved July 11, 2008, from www.ideadata.org

Peréz-Pereira, M., & Conti-Ramsden, G. (2001). The use of directives in verbal interactions between blind children and their mothers. *Journal of Visual Impairment and Blindness, 95,* 133–149.

Pogrund, R. L., Fazzi, D. L., & Schreier, E. M. (1993). Development of a preschool "Kiddy Cane." *Journal of Visual Impairment and Blindness, 86,* 52–54.

Prevent Blindness America (2005a). *Children's vision screening.* Retrieved July 25, 2008, from www.preventblindness.org

Prevent Blindness America (2005b). *Eye safety at home.* Retrieved July 28, 2008, from http://preventblindness.org

Prevent Blindness America (2005c). *Quick facts: Children's eye problems.* Retrieved July 11, 2008, from www.preventblindness.org

Prevent Blindness America (2005d). *Sports eye safety.* Retrieved July 28, 2008, from http://preventblindness.org

Randall, K. (2005). *Uncommon vision: Blind student focuses on her goal to become elementary school teacher.* Austin: University of Texas, Office of Public Affairs, College of Education. Retrieved August 5, 2005, from http://www.utexas.edu/features/2005/wolf

Rettig, M. (1994). The play of young children with visual impairments: Characteristics and interventions. *Journal of Visual Impairment and Blindness, 88,* 410–420.

Royal National Institute for the Blind. (2008). Harry Potter and the Deathly Hallows *in braille, audio, and large print.* Retrieved July 25, 2008, from www.rnib.org

Runyan, M., & Jenkins, S. (2001). *No finish line: My life as I see it.* New York: Putnam's.

Sacks, S. Z., & Rosen, S. (1994). Visual impairment. In N. G. Haring, L. McCormick, & T. G. Haring (Eds.), *Exceptional children and youth* (6th ed., pp. 403–446). Upper Saddle River, NJ: Merrill/Pearson Education.

Shapiro, D. R., Moffett, A., Lieberman, L., & Dummer, G. M. (2005). *Journal of Visual Impairment and Blindness, 99,* 15–25.

Shapiro, D. R., Moffett, A., Lieberman, L., & Dummer, G. M. (2008). Domain-specific ratings of importance and global self-worth of children with visual impairments. *Journal of Visual Impairment and Blindness, 102,* 232–244.

Shaw, A., Gold, D., & Wolffe, K. (2008). Employment-related experiences of youths who are visually impaired: How are these youths faring? *Journal of Visual Impairment and Blindness, 101,* 7–21.

Spungin, S. (Ed.). (2002). *When you have a visually impaired student in your classroom: A guide for teachers.* New York: American Foundation for the Blind.

Strunk, R. (2004). Transitions—reflections of a blind student. *Future Reflections, 22.* Baltimore, MD: National Federation of the Blind.

Stuart, M. E., Lieberman, L. J., & Han, K. (2006). Parent–child beliefs about physical activity: An examination of families of children with visual impairments. *Journal of Visual Impairment and Blindness, 100,* 223–234.

Swenson, A. M. (2008). Reflections on teaching reading in Braille. *Journal of Visual Impairment and Blindness, 102,* 206–209.

Tröster, H., & Brambring, M. (1992). Early social-emotional development in blind infants. *Child: Care, Health and Development, 18,* 421–432.

Tröster, H., & Brambring, M. (1994). The play behavior and play materials of blind and sighted infants and preschoolers. *Journal of Visual Impairment and Blindness, 88,* 421–432.

Tuttle, D. W., & Ferrell, K. A. (1995). Visually impaired. In E. L. Meyen & T. M. Skrtic (Eds.), *Exceptional children and youth: An introduction* (4th ed., pp. 487–531). Denver: Love.

Weihenmayer, E. (2001). *Touch the top of the world.* New York: Dutton.

Wilkinson, M. E., & Trantham, C. S. (2004). Characteristics of children evaluated at a pediatric low vision clinic: 1981–2003. *Journal of Low Vision and Blindness, 98,* 693–702.

Wormsley, D. P. (2004). *Braille literacy: A functional approach.* New York: AFB Press.

CHAPTER 12

American Psychiatric Association. (2003). *Diagnostic and statistical manual of mental disorders* (4th ed. Text Revision). Washington, DC: Author.

Arango, T. (2007, March 5). Bob Wright's next move. *Fortune.* Retrieved February 2, 2008, from http://robots.cnnfn.com/magazines/fortune/fortune_archive/2007/03/05/8401263/index.htm

Asperger, H. (1944/1991). "Autistic psychopathy" in childhood (U. Frith, Trans. Annot.). In U. Frith (Ed.), *Autism and Asperger syndrome* (pp. 37–92). New York: Cambridge University Press.

Baer, D. M., Wolf, M. M., & Risley, T. R. (1968). Some current dimensions of applied behavior analysis. *Journal of Applied Behavior Analysis, 1,* 91–97.

Barnhill, G. P. (2001). What is Asperger syndrome? *Intervention in School and Clinic, 36,* 259–265.

Baron-Cohen, S. (2001). Theory of mind and autism: A review. In G. Lavaine Masters (Ed.), *International review of research in mental retardation.* New York: Academic Press.

Begley, S., & Springen, K. (1996, May 13). Life in a parallel world: A bold new approach to the mystery of autism. *Newsweek,* p. 70.

Bellini, S., & Akullian, J. (2007). A meta-analysis of video modeling and video self-modeling interventions for children and adolescents with autism spectrum disorders. *Exceptional Children, 73,* 264–287.

Bondy, A. (1996). What parents can expect from public school programs. In C. Maurice, G. Green, & S. C. Luce (Eds.), *Behavioral intervention for young children with autism* (pp. 323–330). Austin TX, Pro-Ed.

Bondy, A., & Sultzer-Azaroff, B. (2002). *The Pyramid approach to education in autism.* Newark, DE: Pyramid Educational Products.

Bryson, S. E., Rogers, S. J., & Fombonne, E. (2003). Autism spectrum disorders: Early detection, intervention, education, and psychopharmacological management. *Canadian Journal of Psychiatry, 48,* 506–516.

Cafiero, J. M. (2005). *Meaningful exchanges for people with* autism: *An introduction to augmentative and alternative communication.* Bethesda, MD: Woodbine House.

Carpenter, J., Peninngton, B. E., & Rogers, S. T. (2002). Interrelations among social-cognitive skills in young children with autism. *Journal of Autism and Developmental Disorders, 32,* 91–106.

Charlop-Christy, M. H., Carpenter, M., Le, L., LeBlanc, L. A., & Kellet, K. (2002). Using the picture exchange communication system (PECS) with children with autism: Assessment of PECS acquisition, speech, social-communicative behavior, and problem behavior. *Journal of Applied Behavior Analysis, 35,* 213–231.

Cooper, J. O., Heron, T. E., & Heward, W. L. (2007). *Applied behavior analysis* (2nd ed.). Upper Saddle River, NJ: Merrill/Pearson Education.

Cowley, G., Brownell, G., & Footes, D. (2000, July 31). Parents wonder: Is it safe to vaccinate? *Newsweek,* p. 52.

Dawson, G., & Osterling, J. (1997). Early intervention in autism. In M. J. Guralnick, (Ed.), *The effectiveness of early intervention.* Baltimore: Brookes.

Durand, V. M., & Merges, E. (2001). Functional communication training: A contemporary behavior analytic intervention for problem behavior. *Focus on Autism and Other Developmental Disabilities, 16,* 110–119.

Etscheidt, S. (2003). An analysis of legal hearings and cases related to individualized education programs for children with autism. *Research and Practice for Persons with Severe Disabilities, 28,* 51–69.

Ferster, C. B., & DeMyer, M. K. (1961). The development of performances in autistic children in an automatically controlled environment. *Journal of Chronic Diseases, 13,* 312–345.

Fombonne, E. (2003). The prevalence of autism. *Journal of the American Medical Association, 289,* 87–89.

Frith, U. (1991). *Autism and Asperger syndrome.* Cambridge: Cambridge University Press.

Frost, L., & Bondy, A. (2002). *The Picture Exchange Communication System training manual* (2nd ed.). Newark, DE: Pyramid Educational Products.

Garfinkle, A., & Kaiser, A. P. (2004). Communication. In C. H. Kennedy & E. Horn (Eds.), *Including students with severe disabilities.* Boston: Allyn & Bacon.

Getzel, M., & Wehman, P. (2004). *Going to college: Expanding opportunities for people with disabilities.* Baltimore, MD: Brookes.

Gillum, H., & Camarata, S. (2004). Importance of treatment efficacy research on language comprehension in MR/DD research. *Mental Retardation and Developmental Disabilities Research Reviews, 10,* 201–207.

Grandin, T. (1996). *Thinking in pictures and other reports of my life with autism.* New York: Vintage Books.

Gray, C. A., & Garand, J. D. (1993). Social stories: Improving responses of students with autism with accurate social information. *Focus on Autistic Behavior, 8,* 1–10.

Handleman, J. S., & Harris, S. L. (2000). *Preschool education programs for children with autism.* Autism, TX: Pro-Ed.

Harris, S. L., & Handleman, J. S. (1994). *Preschool education programs for children with autism.* Austin, TX: Pro-Ed.

Harris, S. L., LaRue, R. H., & Weiss, M. J. (2007). Programmatic Issues: In P. Sturmey and A. Fitzer (Eds.), *Autism spectrum disorders: Applied behavior analysis, evidence, and practice* (pp. 232–264). Austin, TX: Pro-Ed.

Hoyson, M., Jamieson, B., & Strain, P. (1984). Individualized group instruction of normally developing and autistic-like children: The LEAP curriculum model. *Journal of the Division of Early Childhood, 1,* 151–171.

Johnson, C. P., & Myers, S. M. (2007). Identification and evaluation of children with autism spectrum disorders. *Pediatrics, 120,* 1183–215.

Kanner, L. (1943). Autistic disturbances of affective contact. *Nervous Child, 2,* 217–250.

Kennedy, C. H., & Horn, E. (2004). *Including students with severe disabilities.* Boston: Allyn & Bacon.

Laushey, K. M., & Heflin, L. J. (2000). Enhancing social skills of kindergarten children with autism through the training of multiple peers as tutors. *Journal of Autism and Developmental Disorders, 30,* 183–193.

Levy, S., Kim, A. H., & Olive, M. L. (2006). Interventions for young children with autism: A synthesis of the literature. *Focus on Autism and Other Developmental Disabilities, 21,* 55–62.

Lewis, M. H., & Bodfish, J. W. (1998). Repetitive behavior disorders in autism. *Mental Retardation and Developmental Disabilities Research Reviews, 4,* 80–89.

Lord, C., & Schopler, E. (1994). TEACCH services for preschool children. In S. Harris & J. Handleman (Eds.), *Preschool education programs for children with autism.* Austin, TX: Pro-Ed.

Lovaas, O. I. (1987). Behavioral treatment and normal educational and intellectual functioning in young autistic children. *Journal of Consulting and Clinical Psychology, 55,* 3–9.

Lovaas, O. I. (1993). The development of a treatment-research project for developmentally disabled and autistic children. *Journal of Applied Behavior Analysis, 26,* 617–630.

Matson, J., Benavidez, D., Compton, L., & Paclawskyj, T. (1996). Behavioral treatment of autistic persons: A review of research from 1980 to the present. *Research in Development Disabilities, 17,* 433–465.

Muller, E., Schulerb, A., Burton, B. A., & Yates, G. B. (2003). Meeting the vocational support needs of individuals with Asperger syndrome and other autism spectrum disabilities. *Journal of Vocational Rehabilitation, 18,* 163–175.

Mundy, P., & Neal, A. R. (2001). Neural plasticity, joint attention, and transactional social-orienting model of autism. In L. M. Glidden (Ed.), *International review of research in mental retardation: Autism* (Vol. 23, pp. 139–168). San Diego: Academic Press.

Newschaffer, C. J., Falb, M. D., & Gurney, J. G. (2005). National autism prevalence trends from United States special education data. *Pediatrics, 115,* 277–282.

Office of Special Education Programs. (2008). *Students served under IDEA, Part B: Fall 2006.* Retrieved February 5, 2008, from www.ideadata.org

Osterling, J., & Dawson, G. (1994). Early recognition of children with autism: A study of first birthday home videotapes. *Journal of Autism and Developmental Disorders, 24,* 247–257.

Ozonoff, S., Goodlin-Jones B. L., & Solomon, M. (2005). Evidence-based assessment of autism spectrum disorders in children and adolescents. *Journal of Clinical Child and Adolescent Psychology, 34,* 523–540.

Park, C. C. (2001). *Exiting Nirvana: My daughter's life with autism.* Boston: Little, Brown.

Percy, A. K. (2001). Rett syndrome: Clinical correlates of the newly discovered gene. *Brain Development, 23,* Suppl. 1: S202–S205.

Powell, T. H., Hecimovic, A., & L. Christensen. (1992). Meeting the unique needs of families. In D. E. Befkell (Ed.), *Autism: Identification, education and treatment.* Hillsdale, NJ: Erlbaum.

Raia, J. (2001, June 18). Autism doesn't slow this marathoner. *Los Angeles Times,* p. D7.

Rice, C. (2007). Prevalence of autism spectrum disorders—Autism and Developmental Disabilities Monitoring Network, six sites, United States, 2000. *Morbidity and Mortality Weekly Report, 56,* 1–11.

Rogers, S. J. (2004). Developmental regression in autism spectrum disorders. *Mental Retardation and Developmental Disabilities Research Reviews, 10,* 139–143.

Rosenwasser, B. & Axelrod, S. (2002). More contributions of applied behavior analysis to the education of people with autism. *Behavior Modification, 26,* 3–8.

Ryndak, D., & Alper, S. (2003). *Curriculum and instruction for students with significant disabilities in inclusive settings* (2nd ed.). Boston: Allyn & Bacon.

Safran, S. P. (2001). Asperger syndrome: The Emerging challenge to special education. *Exceptional Children, 67,* 151–160.

Sallows, G. O., & Graupner, T. D. (2005). Intensive behavioral treatment for children with autism: Four-year outcome and predictors. *American Journal on Mental Retardation, 110,* 417–438.

Sansosti, F. J., Powell-Smith, K. A., & Kincaid, D. (2004). A research synthesis of social story intervention for children with autism spectrum disorders. *Focus on Autism and Other Developmental Disabilities, 19,* 194–204.

Schechter R., & Grether, J. K. (2008). Continuing increases in autism reported to California's developmental services system: Mercury in retrograde. *Archives of General Psychiatry, 65,* 19–24.

Schertz, H. H., & Odom, S. L. (2007). Promoting joint attention in toddlers with autism: A parent-mediated developmental

model. *Journal of Autism and Developmental Disorders, 37,* 1562–1575.

Schopler, E., Reicheler, J., DeVeillis, R. F., & Daly, K. (1980). Toward objective classification of childhood autism: Childhood Autism Rating Scale (CARS). *Journal of Autism and Developmental Disorders, 10,* 91–103.

Schwartz, I. S., Boulware, G. L., McBride, B. J., & Sandall, S. R. (2001). Functional assessment strategies for young children with autism. *Focus on Autism and Other Developmental Disabilities, 16,* 222–227.

Schwartz, I. S., Garfinkle, A. N., & Bauer, J. (1998). The Picture Exchange Communication System: Communicative outcomes for young children with disabilities. *Topics in Early Childhood Special Education, 18,* 144–159.

Scott, J., Clark, C., & Brady, M. (2000). *Students with autism: Characteristics and instructional programming.* San Diego: Singular.

Seroussi, K. (2000). *Unraveling the mysteries of autism and pervasive developmental disorder: A mother's story of research and recovery.* New York: Simon & Schuster.

Shienkopf, S. J., Mundy, P., Oller, D. K., & Steffens, M. (2000). Vocal atypicality of preverbal autistic children. *Journal of Autism and Developmental Disorders, 30,* 345–354.

Shook, G. L. (2005). An examination of the integrity and future of the Behavior Analyst Certification Board credentials. *Behavior Modification, 29,* 562–574.

Simpson, R., deBoer-Ott, S., Griswold, D., Myles, B., Byrd, S., Ganz, J., et al. (2005). *Autism spectrum disorders: Interventions and treatments for children and youth.* Thousand Oaks, CA: Corwin Press.

Smith, T. S., McAdam, D., & Napolitano, D. (2007). Autism and applied behavior analysis. In P. Sturmey & A. Fitzer (Eds.), *Autism spectrum disorders: Applied behavior analysis, evidence, and practice* (pp. 1–29). Austin, TX: Pro-Ed.

Smith Myles, B., & Simpson R. L. (2002). Asperger syndrome: An overview of characteristics. *Focus on Autism and other Developmental Disabilities, 17,* 132–137.

Sperry, V. W. (2001). *Fragile success: Ten autistic children, childhood to adulthood.* Baltimore MD, Brookes.

Stone, W. L., & Yoder, P. J. (2001). Predicting spoken language level in children with autism spectrum disorders. *Autism, 5,* 341–361.

Strain, P. S., & Hoyson, M. (2000). The need for longitudinal, intensive social skill intervention: LEAP follow-up outcomes for children with autism. *Topics in Early Childhood Special Education, 20,* 116–122.

Stromer, R., Kimball, J. W., Kinney, E. M., & Taylor, B. A. (2006). Activity schedules, computer technology, and teaching children with autism spectrum disorders. *Focus on Autism and Other Developmental Disabilities, 21,* 14–24.

Sturmey, P., & Sevin, J. A. (1994). Defining and assessing autism. In J. L. Matson (Ed.), *Autism in children and adults: Etiology, assessment, and intervention* (pp. 13–36). Pacific Grove, CA: Brooks/Cole.

Talay-Ongan, A., & Wood, K. (2000). Unusual sensory sensitivities in autism: A possible crossroads. *International Journal of*

Disability, Development and Education, 47, 201–212.

Tanguay, P. E., Robertson, J., & Derrick, A. (1998). A dimensional classification of autism spectrum disorder by social communication domains. *Journal of the American Academy of Child and Adolescent Psychiatry, 37*, 271–277.

Tidmarsh, L., & Volkmar, F. R. (2003). Diagnosis and epidemiology of autism spectrum disorders. *Canadian Journal of Psychiatry, 48*, 517–525.

Tincani, M. (2004). Comparing the picture exchange communication system and sign language training for children with autism. *Focus on Autism and Other Developmental Disabilities, 19*, 152–163.

Tincani, M. (2007). Beyond consumer advocacy: Autism spectrum disorders, effective instruction, and public schools. *Intervention in School and Clinic, 43*, 47–51.

Tincani, M., & Boutot, E. A. (2005). Autism and technology: Current practices and future directions. In D. L. Edyburn, K. Higgins, & R. Boone, (Eds.), *The handbook of special education technology research and practice* (pp. 413–421). Whitefish Bay, WI: Knowledge by Design.

Tincani, M., Crozier, S., & Alazetta, L. (2006). The Picture Exchange Communication System: Effects on manding and speech development for school-aged children with autism. *Education and Training in Developmental Disabilities, 41*, 177–184.

U.S. Department of Education. (2006). Assistance to states for the education of children with disabilities program and the early intervention program for infants and toddlers with disabilities; Final rule. *Federal Register, 34.* CRF Parts 300 and 301.

Walker, D. R., Thompson, A., Zwaigenbaum, L., Goldberg, J., Bryson, S. E., et al. (2004). Specifying PDD-NOS: A comparison of PDD-NOS, Asperger syndrome, and autism. *Journal of the American Academy of Child and Adolescent Psychiatry, 43*, 172–180.

Wehman, P. (2000). *Life beyond the classroom: Transition strategies for young people with disabilities* (3rd ed.). Baltimore MD: Brookes.

Wetherby, A. M., & Prizant, B. M. (2005). Enhancing language and communication development in autism spectrum disorders: Assessment and intervention guidelines. In D. Zager (Ed.), *Autism spectrum disorders: Identification, education, and treatment* (3rd ed., pp. 327–365). Mahwah, NJ: Erlbaum.

Wing, L. (1989). Autistic adults. In C. Gillberg (Ed.), *Diagnosis and treatment of autism* (pp. 419–432). New York: Plenum Press.

Winter-Messiers, M. A., Herr, C. M., Wood, C. E., Brooks, A. P., Gates, M. A., et al. (2007). How far can Brian ride the Daylight 4449 Express? A strength-based model of Asperger syndrome based on special interest areas. *Focus on Autism and Other Developmental Disabilities, 22*, 67–79.

Wright, B. (2005). *Bob Wright: "I want my grandson back."* Retrieved February 2, 2008, from http://www.msnbc.msn.com/id/7024923/

Yeargin-Allsopp, M., Rice, C., Karapurkar, T., Doernberg, N., Boyle, C., & Murphy, C. (2003). Prevalence of autism in a US metropolitan area. *Journal of the American Medical Association, 289*, 49–55.

CHAPTER 13

Alsop, L., Blaha, R., & Kloos, E. (2000). *The intervener in early intervention and educational settings for children and youth with deafblindness.* NTAC Briefing Paper. Retrieved June 18, 2008, from http://tr.wou.edu/ntac/documents/spotlight/intervener.pdf

Alwell, M., & Cobb, B. (2006). *Teaching functional skills to youth with disabilities: Executive summary.* National Secondary Transition Technical Assistance Center. Retrieved June 6, 2008, from www.nsttac.org

Alwell, M., & Cobb, B. (2007). *Teaching social/communicative interventions to youth with disabilities: Executive summary.* National Secondary Transition Technical Assistance Center. (Retrieved on June 6, 2008, from www.nsttac.org

Arc, The. (2004). *Shaken baby syndrome.* Retrieved June 12, 2008, from www.thearc.org

Bailey, D. B., Hebbeler, K., Olmsted, M., Raspa, M., & Bruder, M. (2008). *Measuring families outcomes: Considerations for large-scale data collection in early intervention.* Retrieved June 4, 2008, from www.fpg.unc.edu/~eco/papers.cfm

Bowie, L. (2007, October 22). Special ed is drawn into exam debate. *Baltimore Sun.* Retrieved October 22, 2007, from www.baltimoresun.com

Briggs, K. (2005). *Alternate achievement standards for students with the most significant cognitive disabilities: Non-regulatory guidance.* Washington, DC: U.S. Department of Education.

Browder, D., Flowers, C., Ahlgrim-Delzell, L., Karvonen, M., Spooner, F., & Algozzine, R. (2004). The alignment of alternate assessment content with academic and functional curricula. *Journal of Special Education, 37,* 211–223.

Brown, D., & Bates, E. (2005). A personal view of changes in the deaf-blind population, philosophy, and needs. *Deaf-Blind Perspectives, 12,* 1–5.

Brown, I. (2007). Transition from school to life. In I. Brown & M. Percy (Eds.), *A comprehensive guide to intellectual and developmental disabilities* (pp. 511–526). Baltimore, MD: Brookes.

Brown, I., Galambos, D., Poston, D. J., & Turnbull, A. P. (2007). Person-centered and family-centered support. In I. Brown & M. Percy (Eds.), *A comprehensive guide to intellectual and developmental disabilities* (pp. 351–363). Baltimore MD: Brookes.

Bryant, D. P., & Bryant, B. R. (2003). *Assistive technology for people with disabilities.* Boston: Allyn & Bacon.

Carnes, S., & Barnard, S. (2003). Oregon deaf-blind project intervener training program. *Deaf-Blind Perspectives, 10,* 1–3.

Children's Defense Fund. (2006). *The state of America's children: 2006,* Washington, DC: Author.

D'Luna, D. (2006). The intervener: Big idea, substantial results, *reSources, California Deaf-Blind Services, 12,* 1–5.

Greenfield, R. (2008). Customized employment: A strategy for developing inclusive employment opportunities. *Deaf-Blind Perspectives, 15,* 1–7.

Heller, K. W., & Kennedy, C. (1994). *Etiologies and characteristics of deaf-blindness.* Monmouth, OR: Teaching Research Publications.

Holburn, S., & Vietze, P.M. (2002). *Person-centered planning.* Baltimore MD: Brookes.

Holcomb, M., & Wood, S. (1989). *Deaf woman: A parade through the decades.* Berkeley, CA: DawnSignPress.

Kangas, K.A., & Lloyd, L. L. (2006). Augmentative and alternative communication. In N. B. Anderson & G. H. Shames (Eds.), *Human communication disorders: An introduction* (7th ed., pp. 436–470). Boston: Allyn & Bacon.

Keats, B. J., & Lentz, J. (2008). Usher syndrome Type 1. *Gene reviews, NCBI Bookshelf.* Retrieved June 10, 2008, from www.ncbi.nim.nih.gov/bookshelf/br.fcgi?book=gene&part=usher1

Kennedy, C. H., & Horn, E. (2004). *Including students with severe disabilities.* Boston: Allyn & Bacon.

Killoran, J. (2007). *The national deaf-blind child count: 1998–2005 in review.* Monmouth, OR, and Sands Point, NY: National Technical Assistance Consortium for Children and Young Adults Who Are Deaf-Blind.

Kleinert, H.L., Miracle, S., & Sheppard-Jones, K. (2007). Including students with moderate and severe intellectual disabilities in school extracurricular and community recreational activities. *Intellectual and Developmental Disabilities, 45,* 46–55.

Kochhar-Bryant, C. A., Shaw, S., & Izzo, M. (2007). *What every teacher should know about transition and IDEA 2004.* Boston: Allyn & Bacon.

Lohrmann-O'Rourke, S., & Gomez, O. (2001). Integrating preference assessment within the transition process to create meaningful school-to-life outcomes. *Exceptionality, 9,* 157–174.

Luckasson, R., Borthwick-Duffy, S., Buntinx, W. H. E., Coulter, D. L., Craig, E. M., Reeve, A., Schalock, R. L., Snell, M. E., Spitalnik, D. M., Spreat, S., & Tassé, M. J. (2002), *Definition of mental retardation.* Washington, DC: American Association on Mental Retardation.

March of Dimes. (2006). *Quick references and fact sheets: Birth defects,* Retrieved June 15, 2008, from www.marchofdimes.com/professionals/14332_1206.asp

March of Dimes. (2008). *Pregnancy & Newborn Health Education Center.* Available from www.marchofdimes.com

McCormick, L., & Wegner, J. (2003). Supporting augmentative communication. In L. McCormick, D. F. Loeb, & R. L. Shiefelbusch (Eds.), *Supporting children with communication difficulties in inclusive settings: School-based language intervention* (pp. 435–460). Boston: Allyn & Bacon.

McDonnell, J. J., Hardman, M. L., & McDonnell, A. P. (2003). *Introduction to persons with moderate and severe disabilities: Educational and social issues* (2nd ed.). Boston: Allyn & Bacon.

McWilliams, R. A., Wolery, M., & Odom, S. L. (2001). Instructional perspectives in inclusive preschool classrooms. In M. J. Guralnick (Ed.), *Early childhood inclusion: Focus on change* (pp. 503–530). Baltimore: Brookes.

Melancon, F. (2000). A group for students with Usher syndrome in South Louisiana. *Deaf-Blind Perspectives, 8*, 1–3.

Michaud, L. J., Duhaime, A.-C., Wade, S. L., Rabin, J., P., Jones, D. O. & Lazar, M. F. (2007). Traumatic brain injury. In M. L. Batshaw, L. Pellegrino, & N. J. Roizen (Eds.), *Children with disabilities* (6th ed.). Baltimore: Brookes.

Miles, B. (2005, January), *Overview on deaf-blindness*. Retrieved August 29, 2005, from www.dblink.org/lib/overview.htm.

Müller, E. (2006). Deaf-blind child counts: Issues and challenges. *In Forum: Brief Policy Analysis*. Alexandria, VA: National Association of State Directors of Special Education, Project Forum.

Müller, E., & Markowitz, J. (2004). *Disability categories: State terminology, definitions and eligibility criteria*. Alexandria, VA: National Association of State Directors of Special Education, Project Forum.

National Center for Technology Innovation. (2008). *About NCTI*. Retrieved June 14, 2008, from www.nationaltechcenter.org

National Consortium on Deaf-Blindness. (2007a, November). *Children who are deaf-blind: Practice perspectives—Highlighting information on deaf-blindness*. http://nationaldb.org/documents/products/population.pdf

National Consortium on Deaf-Blindness. (2007b). *The 2006 National Child Count of Children and Youth Who Are Deaf-Blind*. http://nationaldb.org/documents/products/Childcountview0607Final.pdf

National Consortium on Deaf-Blindness. (2007c). *Primary etiologies of deaf-blindness—Frequency*. Retrieved June 10, 2008, from www.nationaldb.org/ISSelectedTopics.php?topicID=990topicCatID=24.

National Consortium on Deaf-Blindness. (2008a). *National child count*. Retrieved June 6, 2008, from www.nationaldb.org/TACHIldCount.php

National Consortium on Deaf-Blindness. (2008b). *Communication interactions: It takes two*. Retrieved June 10, 2008, from www.nationaldb. org/NCDBProducts .php?prodID-31

National Center for Educational Outcomes. (2007). *Online accommodations bibliography*. Retrieved December 22, 2007, from www.cehd.umn.edu/NCEO)/AccomStudies .htm#keywords

National Institute of Neurological Disorders and Stroke. (2007). *Traumatic brain injury: Hope through research*. Washington, DC: National Institutes of Health. Retrieved June 12, 2008, from www.ninds.nih.gov/disorders/tbi/tbi.htm

National Information Center for Children and Youth with Disabilities. (2001) *Severe and/or multiple disabilities*. Washington, DC: Author.

National Dissemination Center for Children with Disabilities. (2004). *Severe and/or multiple disabilities*. Fact Sheet 10. Washington, DC: Author. Retrieved August 30, 2005, www.nichcy.org

National Dissemination Center for Children with Disabilities. (2006). *Traumatic brain injury*. Fact Sheet 18. Washington, DC: Author. Retrieved May 29, 2008, www.nichcy.org

Noonan, M. J., & Siegel, E. B. (2003). Special needs of students with severe disabilities or autism. In L. McCormick, D. F. Loeb, & R. L. Shiefelbusch (Eds.), *Supporting children with communication difficulties in inclusive settings: School-based language intervention* (pp. 409–434). Boston: Allyn & Bacon.

Office of Special Education Programs (2008a). *Children served under IDEA, Part B: Fall 2006*. Retrieved from www.ideadata.org

Office of Special Education Programs. (2008b). *Children served under IDEA, Part: Fall 2006*. Retrieved from www. ideadata.org

Olson, J. (2004). Intervenor training. *Deaf-Blind Perspectives, 12*, 1–5.

Rafferty, Y., Piscitelli, V., & Boettcher, C. (2003). The impact of inclusion on language development and social competence among preschoolers with disabilities. *Exceptional Children, 69*, 467–479.

Snell, M. E., & Brown, F. (2006). *Instruction of students with severe disabilities* (6th ed.). Upper Saddle River, NJ: Merrill/Pearson Education.

Sommer, N., & Walt D. (2006). *Interveners and support service providers: The concepts, philosophies and use of these services*. Retrieved June 17, 2008, from www.wou .edu/education/sped/srocc/training_conference01_interveners.htm (Western Region Outreach Center and Consortia).

Soukup, J. H., Wehmeyer, M. L., Bashinski, S. M., & Bovaird, J. A. (2007). Classroom variables and access to the general education curriculum. *Exceptional Children, 74*, 101–120.

Stuart, C. H., & Smith, S. W. (2002). Transition planning for students with severe disabilities: Policy implications for the classroom. *Intervention in School and Clinic, 37*, 234–236.

Thurlow, M. L. (2007). *Research impact on the state accommodation policies for students with disabilities*. Paper presented as part of a research symposium entitled "Research Influences Decisions for Assessing English Language Learners and Students with Disabilities" at the American Educational Research Association, Chicago.

U.S. Census Bureau. (2007). *Facts for features: Americans with Disabilities Act: July 26*. Retrieved June 6, 2008, from www.census .gov/Press-Release/www/realses/archives/facts_for_special_editions/010102.html

U.S. Department of Education. (2000). Characteristics of children and families entering early intervention. In *Twenty-second annual report to Congress on the implementation of the individuals with Disabilities Education Act* (pp. IV–1 through IV–13) Washington, DC: U.S. Government Printing Office.

U.S. Department of Education. (2006, August 14). *34 CFR Parts 300 and 301, Assistance to States for the Education of Children with Disabilities and Preschool Grants for Children with disabilities; Final rule*. *Federal Register*, Washington, DC.

Van Haren, B., & Fielder, C. R. (2008). Support and empower families of children with disabilities. *Intervention in School and Clinic, 43*, 231–235.

Westling, D. L., & Fox, E. (2004). *Teaching students with severe disabilities* (3rd ed.).

Upper Saddle River, NJ: Merrill/Pearson Education.

Williams, J. (2007, November 8). *Calif. exit exam boosts dropout numbers*. Retrieved November 8, 2007, from http://ap.google .com

CHAPTER 14

Benbow, C. P., & Lubinski, D. (2007). *Future career path of gifted youth can be predicted by age 13*. Nashville, TN: Vanderbilt News.

Benbow, C. P., & Stanley, J. C. (1996). Inequity in equity: How "equity" can lead to inequity for high-potential students. *Psychology, Public Policy, and Law, 2*, 249–292.

Bernal, E. M. (2003). To no longer educate the gifted: Programming for gifted students beyond the era of inclusionism. *Gifted Child Quarterly, 47*, 183–191.

Binet, A., & Simon, T. (1905). Méthodes nouvelles pour le diagnostic du niveau intellectual des anormaux. *L'Année psychologique, 11*,191–336.

Briggs, C. J., Reis, S. M., & Sullivan, E. E. (2008). A national view of promising programs and practices for culturally, linguistically, and ethnically diverse gifted and talented students. *Gifted Child Quarterly, 52*, 131–145.

Callahan, C. M. (2008). Assessing and improving services provided to gifted students: A plan for program evaluation. In F. A. Karnes & K. R. Stephens (Eds.), *Achieving excellence: Educating the gifted and talented* (pp. 230–245). Columbus, OH: Merrill/Pearson Education.

Clark, B. (2008). *Growing up gifted: Developing the potential of children at home and school* (7th ed). Upper Saddle River, NJ: Merrill/Pearson Education.

Clemens, T. L. (2008). *Underachieving gifted students: A social cognitive model*. Storrs: National Research Center on the Gifted and Talented, University of Connecticut.

Colangelo, N., Assouline, S., & Gross, M. (2004). *A nation deceived: How schools hold back America's brightest students (Vol. 1)*. Iowa City: University of Iowa Press.

Cooper, E. E., Ness, M., & Smith, M. (2004). A case study of a child with dyslexia and spatial-temporal gifts. *Gifted Child Quarterly, 48*, 83–94.

Corwin, M. (2001). *And still we rise: The trials and triumphs of twelve gifted inner-city students*. New York: HarperCollins.

Cukierkorn, J. R., Karnes, F. A., Manning, S. J., Houston, H., & Besnoy, K. (2007). Serving the preschool gifted child: Programming and resources. *Roeper Review, 29*, 271–276.

Davidson Institute for Talent Development. (2008). *Gifted education policies*. Retrieved June 21, 2008, from www.gt-cybersource .org/StatePolicy.aspxZVaviD=6_1.

Davis, G. A., & Rimm, S. B. (2004). *Education of the gifted and talented* (6th ed.). Boston: Allyn & Bacon.

Esping, A., & Plucker, J. A. (2008). Theories of intelligence. In F. A. Karnes & K. R. Stephens (Eds.), *Achieving excellence: Educating the gifted and talented* (pp. 36–48). Upper Saddle River, NJ: Merrill/Pearson Education.

Farkas, S., & Duffett, A. (2008). Results from a national teacher survey. In Thomas B.

Fordham Institute (Ed.), *High-achieving students in the era of NCLB*. Washington, DC: Thomas B. Fordham Institute.

Farmer, D. (1996). Parenting gifted preschoolers. *Austega.com*. Retrieved July 6, 2008, from www.gt-cybersource.org/Record .aspx?rid=11252 (Davidson Institute for Talent Development.)

Finn Jr., C. E., & Petrilli, M. J. (2008). Foreword. In Thomas B. Fordham Institute (Ed.), *High-achieving students in the era of NCLB*. Washington, DC: Thomas B. Fordham Institute.

Ford, D. Y., & Whiting, G. W. (2007). A mind is a terrible thing to erase: Black students' underrepresentation in gifted education. *Multiple Voices, 10*, 28–44.

Freeman, J. (2003). Gender difference in gifted achievement in Britain and the U.S. *Gifted Child Quarterly, 47*, 202–211.

Friend, M., & Bursuck, W. D. (2006). *Including students with special needs: A practical guide for classroom teachers* (4th ed.). Boston: Allyn & Bacon.

Gagné, F. (2004). An imperative, but, alas, improbable consensus. *Roeper Review, 27*, 12–14.

Gardner, H. (1983). *Frames of mind: Theory of multiple intelligences*. New York: Basic Books

Gardner, H. (1993). *Multiple intelligences: The theory in practice*. New York: Basic Books.

Gardner, J. W. (1984). *Excellence: Can we be equal and excellent too?* (Rev. ed.). New York: Norton.

Grantham, T. C. (2002). Underrepresentation in gifted education: How did we get here and what needs to change? *Roeper Review, 24*, 50–51.

Grantham, T. C. (2004). Multicultural mentoring to increase Black male representation in gifted programs. *Gifted Child Quarterly, 48*, 232–245.

Green, N. (2006, Spring). New school for profoundly gifted learners opens this fall in Nevada. *Compass Points*, pp. 1, 7.

Halpern, D. H., Aronson, J., Reimer, N., Sipkins, S., Star, J. R., & Wentzel, K. (2007). *Encouraging young girls in math and science: IES practice guide*. Washington, DC: U.S. Department of Education, Institute for Educational Sciences, National Center for Educational Research.

Hébert, T. P. (2006). Gifted university males in a Greek fraternity: Creating a culture of achievement. *Gifted Child Quarterly, 50*, 26–41.

Hébert, T. P., & Olenchak, F. R. (2000). Mentors for gifted underachieving males: Developing potential and realizing promises. *Gifted Child Quarterly, 44*, 196–207.

Henfield, M. S., Moore III, J. L., & Wood, C. (2008). Inside and outside gifted education programming: Hidden challenges for African American students. *Exceptional Children, 74*, 433–453.

Hertberg-Davis, H., & Callahan, C. M. (2008). A narrow escape: Gifted students' perceptions of advanced placement and international baccalaureate programs. *Gifted Child Quarterly, 52*, 199–216.

Hoh, P. S. (2005). The linguistic advantage of the intellectually gifted child: An empirical study of spontaneous speech. *Roeper Review, 27*, 178–185.

Hunsaker, S. L. (1995). The gifted metaphor from the perspective of traditional civilizations. *Journal for the Education of the Gifted, 18*, 255–268.

Individuals with Disabilities Education Improvement Act of 2004. PL No. 108–446.

Jacob K. Javits Gifted and Talented Students Education Act of 1988. PL 100–297.

Jeffrey, T. (2008 Spring). Differentiating content using a conceptual lens. *Compass Points*, pp. THP 8–9.

Johnsen, S. K. (2008). Identifying gifted and talented learners. In F. A. Karnes & K. R. Stephens (Eds.), *Achieving excellence: Educating the gifted and talented* (pp. 135–153). Upper Saddle River, NJ: Merrill/Pearson Education.

Karnes, F. A., & Stephens. K. R. (Eds.). (2008). *Achieving excellence: Educating the gifted and talented*. Upper Saddle River, NJ: Merrill/Pearson Education.

Kirschenbaum, R. J. (1998). The creativity classification systems: An assessment theory. *Roeper Review, 21*, 20–26.

Kornhaber, M., Fierros, E., & Veenema, S. (2004). *Multiple intelligences: Best ideas from research to practice*. Boston: Allyn & Bacon.

Loveless, R. (2008). An analysis of NAEP data. In Thomas B. Fordham Institute, *High-achieving students in the era of NCLB*. Washington, DC: Thomas B. Fordham Institute.

Lubinski, D., & Benbow, C. P. (1995). Optimal development of talent: Respond educationally to individual differences in personality. *Educational Forum, 59*, 381–392.

Lubinski, D., Benbow, C. P., Webb, R. M., & Bleske-Rechek, A. (2006). Tracking exceptional human capital over two decades. *Psychological Science, 17*, 194–199.

Maker, C. J. (1977). *Providing programs for the gifted handicapped*. Reston, VA: Council for Exceptional Children.

Maker, C. J. (1986). Education of the gifted: Significant trends. In R. J. Morris & B. Blatt (Eds.), *Special education: Research and trends* (pp. 190–221). New York: Pergamon.

Manning, S., & Bosnoy, K. D. (2008). Special populations. In F. A. Karnes & K. R. Stephens (Eds.), *Achieving excellence: Educating the gifted and talented* (pp. 116–134). Upper Saddle River, NJ: Merrill/Pearson Education.

Marland, S. P, Jr. (1972). *Education of the gifted and talented. Vol. 1. Report to Congress of the United States by the U.S. Commissioner of Education*. Washington, DC: U.S. Government Printing Office.

Naglieri, J. A., & Ford, D. Y. (2005). Increasing minority children's participation in gifted classes using the NNAT: A response to Lohman. *Gifted Child Quarterly, 49*, 29–36.

National Association for Gifted Children (1998). *Position paper: Collaboration between gifted and general education programs*. Retrieved July 9, 2008, from www.nagc.org/index.aspx?id=462

National Association for Gifted Children. (2004). *Position paper: Acceleration*. Retrieved September 8, 2005, from www .nagc.org/policy/pp_acceleration.html

National Association for Gifted Children. (2005). *Funding for the Javits program in fiscal year 2006*. Retrieved September 6,

2005, from www.nagc.org/policy/javits/ javits_funding_FY2006.html

National Association for Gifted Children. (2008). *The big picture: Gifted education in the U.S.* Retrieved June 21, 2008, from www.nagc.org/index.aspx?id=532.

National Center for Education Statistics. (2007). *Digest of education statistics: 2007 tables and figures*. Retrieved June 21, 2008, from http://nces.ed.gov/programs/digest/ d07/tables/dt07_o51.asp

Nichols, H. J., & Baum, S. (2000, December). High achievers: Keys to helping youngsters with stress reduction. *Parenting for High Potential*, pp. 9–12.

Nielsen, M. E. (2002). Gifted students with learning disabilities: Recommendations for identification and programming. *Exceptionality, 10*, 93–111.

Nielsen, E., & Mortorff-Albert, S. (1990). The effects of special education programming on the self-concept and school attitude of learning disabled/gifted elementary students. *Roeper Review, 12*, 29–36.

Nielsen, M. E., & Higgins, L. D. (2005). The eye of the storm: Services and programs for twice-exceptional learners. *Teaching Exceptional Children, 38*, 8–15.

Noble, K. D., Childers, S. A., & Vaughan, R. C. (2008). A place to be celebrated and understood: The impact of early university entrance programs from parents' points of view. *Gifted Child Quarterly, 52*, 256–268.

No Child Left Behind Act of 2001. PL 107–110.

Oden, M. H. (1968). The fulfillment of promise: 40-year follow-up of the Terman gifted group. *Genetic Psychology Monographs, 77*, 3–93.

Olszewski-Kubilus, P., & Lee, S.-Y. (2008). Specialized programs serving the gifted. In F. A. Karnes & K. R. Stephens (Eds.), *Achieving excellence: Educating the gifted and talented* (pp. 192–209). Columbus, OH: Merrill/Pearson Education.

Paik, S. J., & Walberg, H. J. (Eds.). (2007). *Narrowing the achievement gap: Strategies for educating Latino, black, and Asian students*. New York: Springer.

Preckel, F., Goetz, T., Pekrun, R., & Kleine, M. (2008). Gender differences in gifted and average-ability students: Comparing girls' and boys' achievement, self-concept, interest, and motivation in mathematics. *Gifted Child Quarterly, 52*, 146–159.

Reis, S. (2003). Gifted girls, twenty-five years later: Hopes realized and new challenges found. *Roeper Review, 25*, 154–157.

Reis, S., & Housand, A. M. (2008). Characteristics of gifted and talented learners: Similarities and differences across domains. In F. A. Karnes & K. R. Stephens (Eds.), *Achieving excellence: Educating the gifted and talented* (pp. 62–81). Upper Saddle River, NJ: Merrill/Pearson Education.

Renzulli, J. S. (1999, October). A rising tide lifts all ships: Developing the gifts and talents of all students. *Phi Delta Kappan, 80*, 104–111.

Renzulli, J. S. (2004). The myth: The gifted constitute 3–5% of the population. In J. S. Renzulli (Ed.), *Identification of students for gifted and talented programs*. Thousand Oaks, CA: Corwin Press and the National Association for Gifted Children.

Renzulli, J. S., & Reis, S. M. (2007). *Enriching curriculum for all students.* Thousand Oaks, CA: Sage.

Rimm, S. (2008). Parenting gifted children. In F. A. Karnes & K. R. Stephens (Eds.), *Achieving excellence: Educating the gifted and talented* (pp. 262–277). Upper Saddle River, NJ: Merrill/Pearson Education.

Roberts, J. L. (2008). Teachers of the gifted and talented. In F. A. Karnes & K. R. Stephens (Eds.), *Achieving excellence: Educating the gifted and talented* (pp. 246–261). Columbus, OH: Merrill/Pearson Education.

Robinson, A. (2006, Spring). Blueprints for biography: Differentiating the curriculum for talented readers. *Compass Points,* pp. 7–8.

Robinson, S. M. (1999). Meeting the needs of students who are gifted and have learning disabilities. *Intervention in School and Clinic, 34,* 195–204.

Rogers, K. B. (1999). The lifelong productivity of the female researchers in Terman's genetic studies of genius longitudinal study. *Gifted Child Quarterly, 43,* 150–169.

Schweinhart, L. J. (2005). *The High/Scope Perry Preschool study through age 40: Summary, conclusions, and frequently asked questions.* Ypsilanti, MI: High/Scope Educational Research Foundation. Retrieved June 17, 2005, from www.highscope.org

Siegle, D. (2008a, Spring). Message from the NAGC President. *Compass Points,* 1, 6.

Siegle, D. (2008b). The time is now to stand up for gifted education: 2007 NAGC presidential address. *Gifted Child Quarterly, 52,* 111–113.

Silverman, L. (2005). *What we have learned about gifted children.* Denver: Gifted Development Center. Retrieved August 8, 2005, from www.gifteddevelopment.com

Smith, M. K. (2008). Howard Gardner, multiple intelligences and education. *The encyclopaedia of informal education.* Retrieved July 5, 2008, from www.infed.org.

Terman, L. (1925). *Genetic studies of genius* (Vol. 1). Stanford, CA: Stanford University Press.

Terman, L. M., & Oden, M. H. (1959). *The gifted group at midlife.* Stanford, CA: Stanford University Press.

Tomlinson, C. A., & Hockett, J. A. (2008). Instructional strategies and programming models for gifted learners. In F. A. Karnes & K. R. Stephens (Eds.), *Achieving excellence: Educating the gifted and talented* (pp. 154–169). Upper Saddle River, NJ: Merrill/Pearson Education.

Tornatzky, L. G., Pachon, H. P., & Torres, C. (2003). *Closing achievement gaps: Improving educational outcomes for Hispanic children.* Los Angeles: Center for Latino Educational Excellence, Tomás Rivera Policy Institute, University of Southern California.

VanTassel-Baska, J., & Stambaugh, T. (2006). *Comprehensive curriculum for gifted learners* (3rd ed.). Boston: Allyn & Bacon.

VanTassel-Baska, J., & Wood, S. (2008). Curriculum development in gifted education: A challenge to provide optimal learning experiences. In F. A. Karnes & K. R. Stephens (Eds.), *Achieving excellence: Educating the gifted and talented* (pp. 209–229). Upper Saddle River, NJ: Merrill/Pearson Education.

Washington Partners. (2008, June). *Funding table for selected FY 2009 education programs.* Washington, DC: Author.

Name Index

AAMR, 280
Abdulkarim, L., 80
Adams, M. E., 333
Adler, N., 246
Adoption and Foster Care
    Analysis and Reporting
    System, 260
Agran, M., 291
Ahearn, E., 259
Ahearn, E. M., 174
Akullian, J., 425
Alazetta, L., 424
Alby, J. F., 333
Alexander Graham Bell
    Association, 342
Algozzine, B., 28
Al-Husaini, M., 267
Allen, K. M., 227
Alper, S., 421, 428
Alsop, L., 457
Alwell, M., 451, 453, 454
Ama, S., 260
American Academy of Pedi-
    atrics (AAP), 209, 212
American Association of
    Retired Persons (AARP), 384
American Association on Intel-
    lectual Developmental Dis-
    abilities (AADD), 272
American Foundation for the
    Blind (AFB), 372, 378, 380,
    381, 386, 387, 392, 396
American Printing House for
    the Blind, 386
American Psychiatric Associa-
    tion (APA), 200, 201, 203,
    230, 231, 232, 234, 242,
    409, 412
American Speech-Hearing-
    Language Association
    (ASHA), 116, 117, 123, 130,
    135, 136, 138, 140, 149, 150
Anderson, G. B., 339
Anderson, J. A., 227
Anderson, N. B., 128, 133
Ansariyah-Grace, T., 396
Antia, S. D., 362
Antunez, B., 103, 104, 105
APHB, 385

Apuzzo, 348
Arango, T., 406
The Arc, 275, 278, 445
Archwamety, T., 237
Arguelles, M. E., 54, 111
Armsden, G., 260
Arthritis Foundation, 298, 305,
    306
Artiles, A. J., 5, 6, 81, 87, 100,
    101, 102
Associated Press, 267, 278, 380
Assouline, S., 481
Asthma and Allergy Founda-
    tion of America (AAFA),
    298, 308, 314, 317
Austin, V. L., 208, 209, 212
Axelrod, S., 256, 428
Ayllon, R., 266
Ayllon, T., 266
Azrin, N. H., 266

Babyak, A. E., 252
Baca, L. M., 77, 96, 99, 103,
    106, 130
Bacon, E., 5
Baer, D. M., 420
Bailey, D. B., 448
Bailey, I. L., 379
Baker, S., 106
Bakken, J. P., 138
Bal, A., 5, 6, 87, 101
Ballard, J., 15
Bank of America, 384
Banks, J. A., 74, 101
Banks, S., 111
Bankson, N. W., 123, 124
Barclay, L., 391
Barkley, R. A., 196, 197, 198,
    200, 202, 206, 208, 209,
    211, 220
Barnard, S., 455
Barnhill, G. P., 64, 413
Baron-Cohen, S., 414
Barraga, N. C., 369
Barringer, C., 258
Bates, E., 440
Batshaw, M.L., 305
Bauer, J., 424
Baum, S., 490

Bauman-Waengler, J., 147
Bausch, M. E., 182
Baytops, J. L., 99
Beardsley, T. M., 98
Beebe-Frankenberger, M. E.,
    248
Beeson, P. M., 123, 124, 131,
    132, 136, 138
Begeny, J. C., 24
Begley, S., 238, 410
Bellini, S., 425
Benbow, C. P., 465, 478, 481,
    488
Bender, W. N., 156, 161, 168,
    238, 239
Benner, G. J., 176
Bennington, L. K., 278
Bergerud, D., 148
Berlin, L. J., 142
Bernal, E. M., 89, 477, 480
Bernheimer, L. P., 281
Bernstein, J. H., 208
Bernthal, J. E., 123, 124
Besnoy, K. D., 466, 472, 487
Best, S., 303, 314, 319, 320,
    321, 325
Betz, C. L., 320, 321, 324
Beyer, S., 289
Bhukhanwala, F., 298
Biederman, J., 203
Bigby, L. M., 44, 45
Bigge, J. L., 303
Bill, P., 28
Binet, A., 463
Birnbrauer, J. S., 266
Bishop, A. G., 170, 177
Blacher, J., 289
Blackorby, J., 135
Blade, R., 363
Blaha, R., 457
Blalock, G., 97, 99
Blank, M., 142
Boardman, A. G., 165
Bode, P., 84
Bodfish, J. W., 410
Boelter, E., 203, 204, 212
Boettcher, C., 448
Bohnert, A., 346
Bonafina, M. A., 202

Bondy, A., 421, 424, 426, 427
Bondy, E., 84, 85
Boone, R., 182, 184
Borthwick-Duffy, S. A., 248
Bos, C. S., 81, 148
Boulineau, T., 148
Boutot, E. A., 425
Bowen, S. K., 390
Bower, E. M., 227, 229
Bowie, L., 65, 448
Braddock, D., 266, 291, 300
Bradley, L., 288
Bradley, R., 68, 156, 173
Bradley-Johnson, S., 381
Brady, M. P., 276, 421
Brambring, M., 388, 389
Branson, J., 5, 332, 340
Brazil, N., 103
Bremer, C. D., 145
Brice, A., 80
Briel, L. W., 219
Briggs, C. J., 472, 489
Briggs, K., 447, 448
Brigham, A., 226
Brinckerhoff, L. C., 190
Browder, D. M., 18, 282, 447
Brown, D., 440
Brown, F., 291, 438, 439, 451
Brown, G. L., 285, 291
Brown, I., 454, 457
Brown, M. R., 54, 95, 110, 112
Brown-Chidsey, R., 47, 53
Brownell, G., 416
Brundige, A. F., 322
Bruni, F., 322
Bryan, T., 165, 166, 167, 197
Bryant, B. R., 27, 37, 38, 43,
    83, 145, 162, 164, 175, 182,
    184, 242, 256, 452
Bryant, D. P., 27, 37, 38, 43,
    83, 145, 162, 164, 175, 182,
    184, 242, 256, 452
Bryen, D. N., 288
Bryson, S. E., 418, 419
Buehler, V., 54
Buhrow, M. M., 381
Bui, Y. N., 181
Bullis, M., 228, 233, 236, 237,
    245, 249

Morris, Y. P., 233
Morrison, H. M., 341
Mortorff-Albert, S., 472
Mostert, M. P., 165
Müller, E., 19, 36, 106, 159, 212, 268, 275, 278, 427, 439, 440, 441
Mundy, P., 418
Murri, N., 4, 10
Myers, S. M., 417
Myles, B. S., 239

Nagle, K., 396
Naglieri, J. A., 472
Nance, W., 339, 342, 343
Napolitano, D., 419
National Alliance of Black School Educators (NABSE), 97, 244
National Association for Gifted Children (NAGC), 464, 465, 480, 481, 489
National Association of School Nurses (NASN), 45, 220, 326
National Association of State Directors of Special Education (NASDSE), 66
National Center for Culturally Responsive Educational Systems (NCCRES), 87
National Center for Educational Outcomes (NCEO), 65, 99, 100, 282, 447
National Center for Education Statistics (NCES), 23, 42, 62, 63, 86, 95, 186, 219, 237, 242, 275, 320, 323, 324, 382, 468, 469, 470, 474
National Center for Hearing Assessment and Management (NCHAM), 337, 348
National Center for HIV/AIDS, Viral Hepatitis, STD, and TB Prevention, 309
National Center for Learning Disabilities, 18
National Center for Technology Innovation, 451
National Center on Education, Delinquency and Juvenile Justice (NCJJ), 238, 257
National Clearinghouse for English Language Acquisition and Language Instruction Educational Programs (NCELA), 76, 86, 87
National Consortium for Physical Education and Recreation for Individuals with Disabilities (NCPERID), 292
National Consortium on Deaf-Blindness (NCDB), 435, 440, 441, 442
National Council for Therapeutic Recreation Certification (NCTRC), 292
National Diabetes Information Clearinghouse, 208, 314

National Down Syndrome Society (NDSS), 277
National Heart Lung and Blood Institute, 315
National Human Genome Research Institute (NHGRI), 298, 313, 314, 315, 316
National Information Center for Children with Disabilities (NICHCY), 341, 435, 436, 438, 442, 443, 444, 447, 451
National Institute of Allergy and Infectious Diseases, 309
National Institute of Environmental Health Sciences (NIEHS), 298, 308, 317
National Institute of Mental Health (NIMH), 206, 208, 209, 211
National Institute of Neurological Disorders and Stroke (NINDS), 159, 315, 443, 445, 446
National Institute on Deafness and Other Communication Disorders (NIDCD), 343, 344, 345, 346, 338
National Institutes of Health (NIH), 156, 159
National Instructional Materials Accessibility Standard (NIMAS), 371
National Reading Panel, 95
National Research Council, 276
National Safety Council, 277
National Technical Institute for the Deaf (NTID), 360
Navarrete, L. A., 94
Neal, A. R., 418
Neal, J., 44
Neal, L. I., 83
Nehring, W. M., 320, 321, 324
Nelson, B., 215
Nelson, J. M., 174
Nelson, J. R., 176, 227, 251, 252
Ness, M., 472
Neubert, D. A., 63
Newcomer, P. L., 234
Newschaffer, C. J., 415
NICHCY (National Information Center for Children with Disabilities), 341, 435, 436, 438, 442, 443, 444, 447, 451
Nichols, H. J., 490
Nichols, P., 255
Nichols, S. L., 92
Nicholson, R., 44
Nielsen, E., 472
Nielsen, M. E., 472
Nielson, A. B., 98
Nieto, S., 84
NIH Consensus Development Conference Statement, 210
Nikolaraizi, M., 339
NIMAS Development and Technical Assistance Center, 36

Nirje, B., 266
Nittrouer, S., 351
Noble, K. D., 481, 488
Noonan, M. J., 453
Norris, J. A., 126
Northern, J. L., 349
Norwicki, 167
Nussbaum, D., 355
Nussbaum, M., 5

Obiakor, F., 5, 137
Obiakor, F. E., 81
Obiakor, F. W., 39
Ochoa, S. H., 97
O'Connor, R. E., 126, 133, 142, 161, 176
Oddo, N. S., 396
Oden, M. H., 488
Odom, S. L., 419, 449
Office of Special Education (OSEP), 19, 21, 23, 28, 42, 43, 62, 87, 88, 89, 109, 134, 135, 149, 151, 159, 160, 167, 187, 208, 210, 212, 213, 221, 239, 240, 243, 244, 251, 258, 275, 282, 284, 313, 314, 320, 324, 325, 326, 342, 353, 354, 370, 382, 390, 415, 439, 442, 444, 445, 446, 448, 450
Ofiesh, N. S., 186
Okolo, C. M., 184
Olenchak, F. R., 490
Olinghouse, N., 161, 216
Olive, M. L., 419
Olmeda, R. E., 197
Olsen, R. J., 291
Olson, J., 455
Olswang, L. B., 127, 132, 166
Olszewski-Kubilus, P., 487, 488
Ortiz, A. A., 97, 99, 130
Osborne, S. S., 208
OSEP (Office of Special Education), 19, 21, 23, 28, 42, 43, 62, 87, 88, 89, 109, 134, 135, 149, 151, 159, 160, 167, 187, 208, 210, 212, 213, 221, 239, 240, 243, 244, 251, 258, 275, 282, 284, 313, 314, 320, 324, 325, 326, 342, 353, 354, 370, 382, 390, 415, 439, 442, 444, 445, 446, 448, 450
Osterling, J., 419
Oswald, D. P., 87
Owens, R. E., Jr., 131, 136, 149, 302, 319
Oyer, J. J., 123
Ozonoff, S., 417

Pachon, H. P., 54, 481
Paik, S. J., 470
Painter, K., 277
Pan, B. A., 143
Pancheri, C., 244
Pappadopulos, E., 210, 242
Parent, W., 289
Parette, H. P., 112

Parish, S., 300
Park, C. C., 427
Parrish, R. B., 19
Patterson, G. R., 242
Patton, J. R., 37, 99, 103
Paulsen, K., 54
Payne, K. T., 130
Pearl, R., 163
Pelligrino, L., 303, 305, 312
Peninngton, B. E., 417
Pennington, B. F., 202
Percy, A. K., 407
Pérez, M., 167
Peréz-Pereira, M., 399
Perry, J., 291
Perske, R., 266, 267
Petch-Hogan, B., 112
Peters, J., 28
Peters, J. W., 4
Peterson, R. L., 58
Petrilli, M. J., 462, 469, 470, 471, 480, 481, 485
Pew Hispanic Center, 87, 94
Philofsky, A., 271
Pierce, K., 200, 202
Piscitelli, V., 448
Pisoni, D. B., 341, 357
PKU.org, 280
Plante, E., 123, 124, 131, 132, 136, 138
Plucker, J. A., 463, 467
Poel, E. W., 322
Pogrund, R. L., 390
Poirier, J. M., 228
Polanco, R., 363
Polloway, E. A., 269
Potter, D., 78
Powell, R., 7
Powell, S., 68, 215
Powell, T. H., 429
Powell-Smith, K. A., 424
Prabhalla, A., 11, 264
Praisner, C. L., 54
Prasse, D. P., 162
Prater, M. A., 8, 103, 244
Preckel, F., 468
Prevent Blindness America (PBA), 382, 383, 386
Prizant, B. M., 409
Pullen, P. C., 176, 228, 242
Pullin, D., 100

Quinn, S. R., 228

Radford, J. P., 265
Rafferty, Y., 448
Raia, J., 427
Ramig, P. R., 117, 128
Ramirez, B. A., 15
Ramsey, E., 228, 235
Ranalli, P., 216
Randall, K., 371
Ratey, J. J., 205
Ratner, N. B., 124, 132, 136, 138, 141, 144, 339, 340, 341, 357
Rausch, M. K., 89
Rehm, L. P., 233

Subject Index

Mathematics core skills, 175
Mathematics/learning disabilities, 162
McKenzie, Jenny, 433
MD (muscular dystrophy), 303, 304, 315
Medically fragile individuals, 307, 308
Medication
    ADHD and, 196, 197, 209–210, 212,
        219–220
    anxiety disorders and, 234
    EBD and, 244
    OCD and, 229
    seizure disorders and, 304, 305
Melting pot concept, 75
Meningitis, 343
Mental age, 280–281
Mental health providers, 258–259
Mental health services, 260
Mental retardation. *See* Intellectual
        disabilities
Mentorships, 490
Mind, Gottfried, 263
Minorities. *See* Culturally and linguistically
        diverse (CLD) students
Mnemonics, 181, 182
Moby Dick (film), 9
Modifications, instructional, 37, 284
Modified achievement standards, 66–67,
        68
Morphology and words, 126
Moss, P. Buckley, 155
MotivAider, 257
Motivation, learning disabilities and, 163
MS (multiple sclerosis), 303, 304
Multicultural education, 101–103
Multidisciplinary teams, 19
Multiple intelligences, 98, 467, 467
Multiple sclerosis (MS), 303, 304
Multiple-severe disabilities
    causes and prevention, 439–440
    characteristics of, 438–439
    definitions of, 434, 435
    prevalence of, 439
Multitiered approaches, prereferral
        process and, 47
Multitiered instruction, 28–29
Muscular dystrophy (MD), 303, 304 315
Muscular/skeletal conditions, 303, 304,
        305–306
Mutual accommodation of language and
        culture, 84
My Left Foot (film), 8, 117–118, 312

Naranjo, Michael, 367, 397
National Instructional Materials Access
        Center, 36
National Instructional Materials Accessibil-
        ity Standard (NIMAS), 28, 472
Nativism, 75
Natural supports, 274
NCLB. *See* No Child Left Behind Act
        (NCLB)
Neria, Christy, 362
Neural tube defects, 279
Neuromotor impairments, 303, 304, 305
Newman, Paul, 301–302
Nicholas, Geri A., 273
NIHL (noise-induced hearing loss),
        343–344

NIMAS (National Instructional Materials
        Accessibility Standard), 28, 472
No Child Left Behind Act (NCLB)
    alternate assessments and, 282
    data-based practices and, 24–25, 157
    gifted and talented students and, 467,
        469, 481
    on highly qualified teachers, 45, 46, 47
    on high-stakes testing, 65, 66, 99
    on modified achievement standards, 66,
        68
    provisions, 18
Noise-induced hearing loss (NIHL),
        343–344
Noncategorical special education, 43–44
Nondiscriminatory testing, 97–99
Nonpaid supports, 274
Nonstrategic approaches to learning, 164
Normal curve, 6
Normalization, 16, 266

OAEs (otoacoustic emissions), 337
Obturator, 147
Ocampo, Alaine, 149–150
Occupational therapists (OTs), 325
Of Mice and Men (film), 9
O&M. *See* Orientation and mobility
        (O&M)
"1kids," 447–448
100 Black Men of America, 466
Open captions, 358
Operation Smile, 119
Ophthalmologists, 387
Oppositional defiant disorder, 231
Opticians, 387
Optometrists, 387
Oral-only approach, 356–357
Orientation and mobility (O&M)
    blind students and, 378–380, 390
    O&M instructors, 378, 397–399
Orthopedic impairments, 302
Ossicles, 336, 337
Other health impairments, 203, 302
Otitis media, 137, 343
Otoacoustic emissions (OAEs), 337
OTs (occupational therapists), 325
Overrepresentation, 50, 75, 87, 89, 244,
        275

PALS (Peer-Assisted Learning Strategies),
        106, 107
Pandey, Belinda, 414
Paolini, Christopher, 478
PBIS (positive behavior intervention sup-
        ports), 104, 106
PBS. *See* Positive behavior support
        (PBS)
PDD-NOS (pervasive developmental dis-
        order-not otherwise specified),
        404, 406–407, 412–413
PECS (picture exchange communication
        system), 424, 426–427
Peer-Assisted Learning Strategies (PALS),
        106, 107
Peer-mediated instruction, 104, 106
Peer supports, 428
Peer tutoring, 106, 107
People first language, 11

Perceptions, treatment of people with
        disabilities and, 7–10
Performance gaps, 177, 178
Peripheral vision, 374
Personal readers, 377
Pervasive developmental disorder-not
        otherwise specified (PDD-NOS),
        404, 406–407, 412–413
Peter Pan (film), 9
Phelps, Michael, 206
Phenylketonuria (PKU), 277, 278,
        279–280, 317
Phonics, 176, 179
Phonology and phonological awareness,
        126, 142, 176, 179
Photoscreening, 386
Phyler v. Doe (1982), 75
Physical or health disabilities
    assessment, 317–318
    causes and prevention, 314–317
    challenges of, 301–302, 316–317
    characteristics of, 309–313
    collaboration with school nurses,
        324–326
    definitions of, 302–309
    described, 298, 299
    diversity of, 298–299
    early intervention, 319
    family and community partnerships,
        326–328
    health disabilities, 306–308
    historical context, 299–301
    physical disabilities, 303–306
    prevalence of, 313–314
    professional standards on, 329
    teaching and, 319–324
Physical therapists (PTs), 325
Picture exchange communication system
        (PECS), 424, 426–427
Pinna, 336, 337
Pitch of voice, 124
PKU (phenylketonuria), 277, 278,
        279–280, 317
Play, visual disabilities and, 388–389
Polio, 303, 304
Portfolio assessment, 68
Positive behavior intervention supports
        (PBIS), 104, 106
Positive behavior support (PBS)
    ASD and, 422
    classroom management and, 423
    EBD and, 244–245, 259
    multitiered instruction and, 28–29
    school violence preparedness, 240
    success of PBS teams, 228
Postlingually deaf, 339
Postsecondary education
    CLD students and, 108–109
    deafness and hearing impairments and,
        360–361
    transition to, 185–187, 188
    visual disabilities and, 395–397
Poverty, 92–93
Pragmatics, language and, 127, 142, 145
Preictal stage, seizures and, 309–310
Prelingually deaf, 339
Prenatal, perinatal, and postnatal causes
        of intellectual disabilities, 276

Prereferral
  ADHD and, 211
  CLD students and, 96–97
  EBD and, 248
  gifted and talented students, 476–478
  hearing screenings, 348
  IEP process and, 47–49
  intellectual disabilities and, 281
  learning disabilities and, 170–173
  physical or health disabilities and, 318
  speech or language impairments and, 138
  TBI and, 446
  vision screenings, 386–387
Prevalence of disabilities, 19, 21
  ADHD, 206–207
  ASD, 414–415
  CLD students, 84–90
  deaf-blindness, 441–442
  EBD, 239–240, 241, 243, 244
  gifted and talented students, 473–475
  hearing impairments, 342
  intellectual disabilities, 275
  learning disabilities, 167–168
  multiple-severe disabilities, 439
  physical or health disabilities, 313–314
  speech or language impairments, 134–135
  traumatic brain injury, 444–445
  visual disabilities, 381–382
Prevention of disabilities
  ADHD, 208–210
  ASD, 415–416
  deaf-blindness, 442
  deafness and hearing impairments, 343–344
  diverse students and, 93–94
  EBD, 240–247
  intellectual disabilities and, 278–279
  learning disabilities, 168–169
  multiple-severe disabilities, 439–440
  physical or health disabilities, 314–317
  speech or language impairments, 135–138
  traumatic brain injury, 445
  visual disabilities, 382–383
Prevention of hearing loss, 343–344
Process/product debate, 157
Professional standards
  on ADHD, 223
  on ASD, 431
  on CLD students, 113
  on deafness and hearing impairments, 365
  on disabilities, 31
  on emotional or behavioral disorders, 261
  on gifted and talented students, 491
  on IEPs, 71
  on intellectual disabilities, 295
  on learning disabilities, 193
  on physical or health disabilities, 329
  on speech or language impairments, 153
  on very-low incidence disabilities, 459
  on visual disabilities, 401
Profound hearing loss, 340–341
Program revision, IEP process and, 64–69

Progress monitoring
  assessments and, 67–69
  CLD students and, 104, 106
  IEP process and, 64–69
  special education and, 25–26
  speech or language impairments and, 140–141
Project Eye-to-Eye, 199
Project Opportunity, 188
Prosthetics, 305, 317
PTs (physical therapists), 325
Pull-in programming, 40
Pull-out programs, 43
Pupil, 373
Pure sounds, 348

Quality of life, intellectual disabilities and, 288–289

Race, EBD and, 239–240, 241, 243, 244
Rain Man (film), 410, 411
Ramirez, Martin, 73
Ray (film), 8, 369
Reading
  academic performance and language disorders, 133
  braille, 377–378, 379
  core skills, 176, 179
  early reading instruction, 176–177
  enlarged print, 377
  fluency and proficiency, 157–158, 179
  reading/learning disabilities, 161–162
  standard print, 376–377
Real-time captioning, 359–360
Rear window captioning (RWC), 358
Receptive language, 132, 145
Recreational therapy, 292
Referral, IEP process and, 49
Refreshable braille display, 385–386
Rehabilitation Act of 1973, Section 504, 14–15, 300
Related services, 19, 44–45
Related services providers. See
  Educational interpreters; Mental health providers; School counselors; Speech/language pathologists (SLPs); Therapeutic Recreation Specialists
Residual hearing, 338
Residual vision, 374
Resistant to treatment, 141, 162
Resonating system, 122
Respiratory system, 121–122
Response to intervention (RTI)
  CBM and, 171–172, 173, 182, 183
  CLD students and, 104, 106
  learning disabilities and, 170–174
  multitiered instruction and, 28–29
Restricted central vision, 374
Retention of students, 175
Retina, 373, 374
Retinopathy of prematurity (ROP), 370, 382
Rett syndrome, 407–408
Risk index, 88–89
Risk ratios, 88–89
Risk signals, 250–251
Roberts, Ed, 300

Robotics, 305
ROP (retinopathy of prematurity), 370, 382
RTI. See Response to intervention (RTI)
Rubella, 382

Scaffolding, students with hearing impairments and, 357–358, 359
Schizophrenia, 234
School counselors, 187–189
School environment, EBD and, 242–243
School nurses
  ADHD prereferral and, 211
  collaboration with, 219–220, 324–326
Schwab, Charles, 158–159
Seguin, Edouard, 21
Seizure disorders, 303, 304–305, 309–311
Seizure types, 309, 310–311
Self-advocacy, 56
Self-determination
  data-based practices, 284–286, 287
  EBD and, 257
  student IEP involvement and, 56
Self-injury, 414
Self-management strategies, 216–217
Semantics, 127
Sensorineural hearing loss, 338
Service animals, 324
Service delivery options, 41, 42–43
Service managers, IFSPs and, 56
Services. See Special education services; Transition services
Setting and grouping options, special education services, 41–44
Sheltered English instruction, 104
Shine (film), 8
Siblings, 293–294, 429
Sickle cell anemia, 298, 307, 308, 313, 314, 315
Signed English, 340, 357
SIM (Strategic Instruction Model), 181
Skeletal disorders, 303, 304, 305
SLPs. See Speech/language pathologists (SLPs)
Snellen chart, 386
Social competence
  language disorders and, 132–133
  learning disabilities and, 166
Social justice, 4–5
Socially maladjusted students, 234–235
Social skills and behavior
  ADHD and, 204–205
  ASD and, 410
  blind students and, 380–381
  EBD and, 235–237
  learning disabilities and, 165–167
Social Stories, 424
Sociological perspective on disabilities, 7
Software, speech or language impairments and, 148, 149
Solomon, Lizzy, 118, 119, 310, 472, 473
Sound frequency and intensity, 347
Southern Poverty Law Center (SPLC), 76–77
Special education
  accessibility of, 23–24
  categories, 19
  collaboration and co-teaching, 26–27